Adobe®
Creative Suite® 4
Bible

Adobe® Creative Suite® 4 Bible

Ted Padova

Kelly L. Murdock

WILEY

Wiley Publishing, Inc.

Adobe® Creative Suite® 4 Bible

Published by
Wiley Publishing, Inc.
10475 Crosspoint Boulevard
Indianapolis, IN 46256
www.wiley.com

Copyright © 2009 by Wiley Publishing, Inc., Indianapolis, Indiana

Published simultaneously in Canada

ISBN: 978-0-470-34518-4

Manufactured in the United States of America

10 9 8 7 6 5 4 3 2 1

For general information on our other products and services or to obtain technical support, please contact our Customer Care Department within the U.S. at (800) 762-2974, outside the U.S. at (317) 572-3993 or fax (317) 572-4002.

Library of Congress Control Number: 2008941623

Trademarks: Wiley, the Wiley logo, and related trade dress are trademarks or registered trademarks of John Wiley & Sons, Inc. and/or its affiliates, in the United States and other countries, and may not be used without written permission. Adobe and Creative Suite are trademarks or registered trademarks of Adobe Systems Incorporated. All other trademarks are the property of their respective owners. Wiley Publishing, Inc., is not associated with any product or vendor mentioned in this book.

Wiley also publishes its books in a variety of electronic formats. Some content that appears in print may not be available in electronic books.

From Ted Padova:

For Arnie

From Kelly Murdock:

There are superheroes a plenty, and although they're fun to see,
they don't come in handy for the tasks that really bother me.

I'm not too often in peril from disasters and the like

So I'd rather see a some superheroes for when minor disasters
strike

Such as Plumberman, who can fix a leak at 4:00 in the morning,

Or The Amazing Advisor who can see spot trouble and offer
early warning.

SuperErrand Guy who can fly the kids to school so they're
always on time,

and retrieve the kitten from the tree so I don't have to climb.

Someone like MasterTech who can make the copier work,

and can configure the network without a single smirk.

SuperClean who always remembers to put the garbage out

and get the kids to do their chores without a single shout.

Someone like Mechanicman, who can fix the car and sink,

and unclog the drain before it starts to stink.

Or Superchef, who can fix a romantic dinner for two

and even does the dishes when he's through.

On second thought, I don't need all this help with my life,

I have a superhero around already, and I call her my wife.

To Angie, thanks for all you do, 2008.

About the Authors

Ted Padova is the author of more than two dozen computer books, including *Adobe Acrobat PDF Bible*, versions 4, 5, 6, 7, 8, and 9; *PDF Forms Using Acrobat and LiveCycle Designer Bible; Color Management for Digital Photographers Only; Color Management for Digital Photographers For Dummies; Photoshop Elements 6 For Dummies; PowerPoint 2007 Just the Steps For Dummies; Illustrator Illuminated;* and *Adobe Reader 7 Revealed.*

Ted has been involved in PostScript imaging for more than a decade and started a computer service bureau in 1990 in Ventura, California. He retired as CEO and managing partner of The Image Source Digital Imaging and Photo Finishing Centers of Thousand Oaks and Ventura, California, in 2004 and now spends his time writing and speaking nationally and internationally on digital imaging, Adobe Acrobat, and PDF.

Kelly Murdock has been authoring computer books for several years and still gets immense enjoyment from the completed work. His book credits include various Web, graphics, and multimedia titles, including seven editions of *3ds Max Bible.* Other major accomplishments include *Master VISUALLY HTML and XHTML, Maya Revealed* (two editions), *Poser Revealed* (two editions), *Edgeloop Character Modeling, JavaScript Visual Blueprint, Adobe Atmosphere Bible, 3D Game Animation For Dummies,* and coauthoring duties on two editions of the *Illustrator Bible* (versions 9 and 10).

With a background in engineering and computer graphics, Kelly has had many opportunities to flex his design muscles from Web site creation and design to freelance 3D design projects. He currently heads a design company called Logical Paradox Design with his brother Chris.

Credits

Senior Acquisitions Editor
Stephanie McComb

Project Editor
Martin V. Minner

Technical Editor
Colin Fleming

Copy Editor
Gwenette Gaddis Goshert

Editorial Manager
Robyn Siesky

Business Manager
Amy Knies

Senior Marketing Manager
Sandy Smith

Vice President and Executive Group Publisher
Richard Swadley

Vice President and Executive Publisher
Barry Pruett

Project Coordinator
Erin Smith

Graphics and Production Specialists
Jennifer Mayberry
Christin Swinford
Ronald Terry

Quality Control Technician
Melissa Bronnenberg

Proofreading
Broccoli Information Mgt.

Indexing
Slivoskey Indexing Services

Contents

Contents

Contents

Contents

Contents

Contents

Contents

Part V: Using Creative Suite and Microsoft Office   599

Chapter 19: Importing Microsoft Word Documents 601

Contents

Contents

Part VIII: Deploying Documents   1039

Contents

Acknowledgments

The authors would like to thank Colin Fleming, who did a great job as technical editor. His insights and comprehensive knowledge of the software have proved extremely helpful in creating this work. Thanks also to Stephanie McComb, Marty Minner, Gwenette Gaddis Goshert, and the many other editors at Wiley who are always a pleasure to work with. Additionally, we would like to thank the many individuals at Adobe Systems, far too numerous to mention, who have worked passionately on a terrific suite of programs to bring all of us the most advanced software applications developed to date for the creative professional.

From Ted Padova:

I'd like to thank my coauthor Kelly Murdock for his hard work and dedication to this project. This is the fourth edition Kelly and I have worked on together, and it's continually a pleasure to work with him. Without Kelly, I'd be lost when it comes to 3D imagery, Adobe Flash, and Adobe Dreamweaver. Kelly's coverage of these areas is a special bonus for this book in addition to so many other areas he worked on.

I'd also like to thak some of the people who are continually helpful in working with the Adobe User Group in Davao City, Philippines. There are many. Some very generous assistance has been provided by Chris Cubos, Blogie Robillo, and MiGs™.

From Kelly Murdock:

Along with the thanks to an excellent group of editors at Wiley, I'd like to express my thanks to Ted for allowing me to be, once again, a part of this project. Usually it is tough to work with a coauthor, but Ted is awesome to work with and shares his talents and experience openly.

Introduction

Welcome to the *Adobe Creative Suite 4 Bible*—your comprehensive guide to working with the complete suite of Adobe's Design Suite Premium imaging programs. In this book, we make an effort to help you understand the design and productivity features available from all the Creative Suite 4 (CS4) programs and how the documents you create from the individual applications work together to help you publish content for print, Web hosting, and CD-ROM replication.

Much has changed from the Creative Suite 3 programs to the newest incarnation of the Creative Suite. We're beginning to see the full integration of the former Macromedia programs working seamlessly with the Adobe Creative Suite programs that were originally created by Adobe Systems. You'll find Adobe Flash being a huge participant when adding content to all your designs and layouts prepared for screen viewing.

With the introduction of Adobe Acrobat 9, you'll find the new Acrobat.com service a great new upgrade feature. When you want to hold a conference, show off your designs, share documents, engage in shared reviews, aggregate form data, and more, Acrobat.com is your online library for communicating and reviewing your design concepts with your clients.

So why would we spend time covering subjects that are individually treated in other Wiley Bible publications? That's a good question, and the answer should be clear to you before you walk out of your local bookstore with this sizeable volume. It's true that there is a Wiley Bible covering each of the individual programs mentioned in this book. These other works are comprehensive and teach you about almost every tool and feature related to the specific programs.

This book is much different from the other Bibles. Our primary focus is to cover workflow solutions for independent designers and members of design teams working in agencies, publication houses, and any firm related to publishing for screen, print, or Web. Therefore, we don't go into minute detail on each program, and often we point you to one of the other fine Wiley publications to amplify your learning.

We assume you have some experience in at least one of the programs covered in this book. You may be a designer who works religiously with Adobe Photoshop, QuarkXPress, or a non-Adobe program. Or you may work with Adobe Illustrator and Adobe Photoshop, but know little about page-layout programs. You need to know essential methods for integrating application documents among the CS4 programs. Perhaps you don't need to know every aspect of Adobe InDesign, but you want to create sophisticated layouts using many outstanding type features and want to know how to import images in your designs, prepare interactive documents, or import Adobe Flash files.

If you're switching from another program or you want to add one of the CS4 applications to your design toolbox, this book helps you understand the relationships among programs and how to seamlessly integrate files among the most sophisticated suite of software applications ever developed for creative professionals.

As we said, the focus is on workflow solutions. In this book, you learn how to set up the CS4 applications for workflow environments, step through the creative workflow process, and get to productivity without having to master every feature in a program. The tools and tasks related to office workers and business professionals have been left out. Rather, the emphasis is on complete coverage of tools and workflows to help creative professionals get up to speed fast.

How to Read This Book

The *Adobe Creative Suite 4 Bible* is made up of 40 chapters in nine parts. Unlike other comprehensive computer publications that target beginning users, this volume assumes you have some basic knowledge of at least one imaging program like Photoshop, an illustration program, or a layout program. We further assume you know something about user interfaces common to imaging programs that use palettes, menus, and tools. And we make the assumption that you know some aspects of the professional printing market for commercial prepress and printing.

Because you have some knowledge of computer programs similar to those found in the Creative Suite, you can jump in anywhere and learn about any feature set. In most chapters, we include a discussion concerning the integration of the CS4 programs. Therefore, a chapter dealing with text includes text handling not only in InDesign, but also in Illustrator, Photoshop, Dreamweaver, and Acrobat. Rather than think of the programs you want to learn about, search more for the techniques and features you want to learn.

To give you a broad idea of how the programs work together, we recommend you look over Chapter 2, where we provide steps you can replicate to produce a design piece using the CS3 programs. Chapter 3 helps you understand the interoperability of the CS4 programs.

Apart from Chapter 2 and the specific features you want to learn, keep in mind that this book, like other Wiley Bible publications, is a reference work. Keep it handy as you work in the CS4 applications, and refer to the index and contents when you need help working on a task or trying to further understand one of the programs.

Icons

What would a Bible be without icons? The use of icons throughout the book offers you an at-a-glance hint of what content is being addressed. You can jump to the text adjacent to these symbols to help you get a little more information, warn you of a potential problem, or amplify the concept being addressed in the text. In this book, you'll find the following icons:

CAUTION A caution icon alerts you to a potential problem in using one of the CS applications, any tools or menus, or any issues related to exchanging files between programs. Pay close attention to these caution messages to avoid some problems.

NOTE A note icon signifies a message that may add more clarity or help you deal with a feature more effectively.

TIP Tips help you find shortcuts to produce results or work through a series of steps to complete a task. Some tips provide you with information that may not be documented in the Help files accompanying each of the CS programs.

CROSS-REF Walking you through steps and techniques in a linear fashion is almost impossible for a suite of programs. The applications have so many interrelated features that covering all aspects of a single feature in one part of a book just doesn't work. Therefore, some common features for commands, tools, actions, or tasks may be spread out and discussed in different chapters. When the information is divided among different parts of the book, you'll find a Cross-Ref icon that refers you to another part of the book covering related information.

The Book's Contents

To simplify your journey through the Creative Suite applications, the book is broken up into nine separate parts. The 40 chapters address features common to creative production workflows. These parts are covered in the following sections.

Part I: Getting Started with Workflow Solutions

To begin, we offer some basic information related to the Creative Suite Premium Edition. We give you a tour of the programs in the form of steps to produce design pieces and teach you how these applications work together to help you publish your content. You learn how to set up the work environments in all the programs and understand the different user interfaces both common and unique to each program.

Part II: Getting Started with Design Workflows

Design workflow is a broad term and may mean different things to different people. This part clarifies the meaning of workflow solutions as they apply to creative professionals and the CS applications, as well as introduces you to tools for versioning documents and creating consistent color across the CS programs.

Part III: Working with Objects and Images

You have basically three elements used to communicate messages in artwork. Images, objects, and type constitute the content of your products. In this part, we focus on objects you might create in Illustrator, InDesign, and Photoshop, as well as images that are edited in Photoshop and imported into other CS4 programs.

Part IV: Working with Type

Setting type and working with type as text and objects are standard design practices everyone uses. With many features for setting type in the CS4 applications, this part offers you a glimpse into how you can use the programs to implement these impressive features.

Part V: Using Creative Suite and Microsoft Office

Whether Microsoft Office is part of your design toolbox or you acquire files from clients who provide you with Office documents, it's hard to talk about layout and design without introducing Office files. This part covers working with files that originate in Office programs and end up in one or more of the CS4 applications.

Part VI: Integrating Creative Suite Documents

The CS4 applications offer you tools to create artwork. Bringing together the documents created in each of the individual programs into single files and portfolios is what you'll find in the chapters in Part VI.

Part VII: Preparing Documents for Deployment

Among other things, you'll want to know what options you have for securing your files, optimizing files for efficient distribution, and sources available to your for sharing files. This part covers many issues related to preparing files for deployment.

Part VIII: Deploying Documents

After you prepare files for deployment, it's time to exchange, review, and share files. With many new options for sharing, you'll want to carefully look over the Web conferencing and sharing opportunities available with Acrobat.com that we cover in this part.

Part IX: Printing and Digital Prepress

Printing files is still a major function of every creative professional's workflow. This part covers printing to composite printers and preparing files for commercial printing.

Staying Connected

About every five minutes, new products and new upgrades are distributed. If you purchase a software product, you can often find an updated revision not too long after release. Manufacturers are relying more and more on Internet distribution and less on postal delivery. You should plan on making routine visits to Adobe's Web site as well as the Web sites of manufacturers of third-party products. Anyone who has a Web site will offer a product revision for downloading or offer you details on acquiring the update.

Internet connection

With newer releases of computer software, it's essential that you have an Internet connection. The CS4 programs routinely prompt you to check for updates over the Internet. To optimize your performance with all the programs, you should run the software on a computer that has an Internet connection.

Contact Adobe Systems

Adobe Systems maintains a comprehensive Web site where you can find information on product upgrades, conferences and seminars, aftermarket books, help and technical support, as well as tips and techniques. Visit Adobe's Web site at `www.adobe.com` for the latest news related to all the CS4 applications. Be certain to look over Chapter 6 where you can find easy access to Adobe's Web pages carrying tips and techniques from within Adobe Bridge.

Registration

Regardless of whether you purchase the Creative Suite or individual applications, Adobe Systems has made it possible to register the product. You can register on the Web or mail a registration form to Adobe. You'll find great advantages in being a registered user. First, update information will be sent to you, so you'll know when a product revision occurs. Second, information can be distributed to help you achieve the most out of using all the Creative Suite programs. By all means, complete the registration. It will be to your benefit.

Contacting Us

If, after reviewing this publication, you feel some important information was overlooked or you have any questions concerning the Creative Suite programs, you can contact us and let us know your views, opinions, hoorahs, complaints, or provide information that might get included in the next revision. If it's good enough, you might even get a credit line in the acknowledgments. By all means, send a note. E-mail inquiries can be sent to:

Ted at `ted@west.net`

Kelly at `kmurdock@sfcn.org`

If you happen to have some problems with any of the CS programs, keep in mind, we did not engineer the programs. Inquiries for technical support should be directed to the software manufacturer(s) of any products you use. This is one more good reason to complete your registration form.

Part I

Getting Started with Workflow Solutions

This part begins with an overview of the Adobe Creative Suite 4 applications. In Chapter 2 we cover a workflow where you can use most of the programs in the Creative Suite to demonstrate how they interact. In Chapter 3 we cover the many similarities and differences among the Creative Suite applications.

Chapter 1

Introducing the Creative Suite

IN THIS CHAPTER

Understanding why Adobe developed the Creative Suite

Knowing the Creative Suite applications

Working with OpenType fonts

The Adobe Creative Suite 4 Design Premium package is composed of several programs designed to work together to accomplish all your publishing needs for output to print, screen viewing, and Web hosting. Instead of marketing the individual program components of the Creative Suite, Adobe Systems has spent much of its marketing effort targeting the entire Creative Suite to design professionals.

This chapter offers a description of the Creative Suite programs and gives you an idea of how they work together. In this chapter, you learn about the purpose of each program and the relationship each program has with other members of the Creative Suite team. In addition, you receive a brief summary of new features contained in the latest releases of the individual programs.

Why Creative Suite?

Each program in the Creative Suite version 4 is an upgrade from the CS3 applications, and each is available for upgrades individually. So why is Adobe Systems spending so much marketing effort informing users about the benefits of the Creative Suite? And why talk about the Creative Suite as a single entity when users are likely to upgrade the individual software programs in their design studios? These may be the first questions on your mind as you see the advertising for Adobe imaging product upgrades.

The answer is that Creative Suite is a single design solution where the whole is greater than its parts. For years, Adobe Systems built several different applications like Adobe Illustrator and Adobe InDesign with similar core technologies like PDF. These programs evolved with common elements so that you, the creative professional, could easily exchange files among Adobe programs.

Rather than rely on a single program to perform tasks such as illustration, layout, and printing, Adobe offers you several applications, each a tool designed for a specific purpose to help you become more efficient in your creative process. These tools seamlessly integrate into the greater toolbox called Adobe Creative Suite. After working in individual programs, you can collect the creative elements together using Adobe Bridge and Adobe InDesign CS4 as the tool to perform layout assembly. You can then travel to output by exporting files to PDF documents in Adobe Acrobat, or you can host parts of your layout on a Web site using Adobe Dreamweaver CS4.

NOTE   Adobe Bridge is a separate executable application introduced in the Creative Suite version 2. Adobe Bridge is included when you purchase any of the CS4 standalone products but is not available for purchase as a separate product. For more information on Adobe Bridge, see the section "Adobe Bridge" later in this chapter.

As standalone programs, Adobe Creative Suite 4 offers many new marvelous tools with enhanced features to create, design, and express your ideas. Collectively, these tools build upon the integration and interoperability introduced in the first version of the Creative Suite.

Native file support

The strongest argument for using Adobe Photoshop CS4, Adobe Illustrator CS4, Adobe InDesign CS4, and Adobe Flash CS4 together is that native file formats are easily transported among the various CS4 programs. You no longer need to decide about saving Photoshop files as TIFF, EPS, GIF, PNG, or JPEG. Rather, you can import a native Photoshop PSD or Illustrator AI file into Adobe InDesign CS4 complete with layers and transparency. You also can import native Illustrator and Photoshop files directly in Adobe Flash CS4 and Fireworks CS4. The native file format import feature alone can save space on your hard drive, because you need to save only a single file. Additionally, you save time in importing the correct file because only a single file is saved from the host application and used in your page layout. You also can directly open native Illustrator CS4 files in any Adobe Acrobat viewer, and you can open PDF documents in Illustrator and import them into InDesign.

CROSS-REF   For information on importing native file formats across programs, see Part III.

Consistent user interface

Programs that creative professionals use today are sophisticated and complicated. One of the major problems facing many designers is the large learning curve necessary to become productive in a computer program. When you use programs from several different software manufacturers, your learning curve increases. Application-software companies develop software according to standards each company sets forth in the design of the user interface. One company may make extensive use of context-sensitive menus, while another company may avoid them. One company may use palettes and panes liberally, while another company relies on menu commands and dialog boxes. Add to these differences the extended use of keyboard shortcuts; program differences require you to spend lots of time learning shortcuts. Additionally, the key sequence in one program may invoke a different command than the same key sequence in another program, and that can cause you lots of confusion.

In workflow environments, consistency is crucial. Time is money, and the time required to train your staff cuts into your productivity and your profits. When tools are developed by a single software manufacturer, the result is a more consistent design of the user interface and the keyboard shortcuts that access menus, tools, and commands. Adobe has taken the user interface design one step further by offering customizable keyboard shortcuts and custom workspaces in all CS4 programs.

Having a consistent look and feel in the user interface enables you to develop an intuitive sense for how to use a particular program to create a design project. The more you learn about a manufacturer's products, the faster you can become productive. In some cases, you can jump into a new program, poke around, and understand many features without reading exhaustive manuals and books.

CROSS-REF For information on customizing workspaces and keyboard shortcuts, see Chapter 3.

Versioning tools

How many times have you created a tight comp and had a client tell you that he or she likes another version of the layout? You may create duotone images in Photoshop, offer a proof print to your client, and hear that he wants another spot color in the Photoshop images. You offer a second proof, and the client says the first proof print is really the one that best fits his or her campaign. You're back at your design studio scrambling through your hard drive looking for the first versions, locating the files, and importing or relinking them back into the layout.

The Creative Suite lets you easily revisit earlier versions of illustrations, photo images, and layouts. Along with the standalone programs in the Creative Suite, you also receive Version Cue, a marvelous utility that permits you to save multiple versions of a design in the same file. You decide what version to promote to the current look, and the linked file in your InDesign CS4 document dynamically updates. In workflow environments, nothing more easily tracks the current version of a design and quickly gets you to final output with the correct version.

CROSS-REF For more information on installing and using Version Cue and working with versions and alternates, see Chapter 7.

Consistent color management

Have you ever created an illustration, dropped it into a layout program, and seen a completely different color rendered in the layout? How about scanned images appearing with one color in Adobe Photoshop and different color values in the layout program? With the Adobe Creative Suite, you can access the same color engine and color-management policies among the design programs and Adobe Acrobat. In Creative Suite 4, you can manage color across all the print-oriented programs including Photoshop, Illustrator, InDesign, and Acrobat using Adobe Bridge. You assign color profiles in Photoshop, Illustrator, or InDesign, and these applications all can conform to the same color management settings.

NOTE There is no support for color management or policies in Flash CS4, Dreamweaver CS4, Fireworks CS4, or Device Central CS4.

CROSS-REF For more information on managing color across the Creative Suite programs, see Chapter 5. For more information on using Adobe Bridge, see Chapter 6.

Dynamic object and image editing

Ever have last-minute changes that you need to make before the last FedEx pickup of the day? A layout is complete, but you must quickly change an illustration or a photo image. In programs like Adobe InDesign CS4, a double-click of the mouse button or the selection of a menu command launches the editing program that created the object or image and opens the file in a document window. You make your edits and save the file, and the edited version is dynamically updated. This kind of quick editing saves a number of steps and streamlines your workflow.

CROSS-REF For more information on dynamic object and image editing, see Chapter 24.

Visual file exchanges

Let's face it; creative people are more visual and often work best in situations where they can first see a document before importing it into another program. More than ever before, Adobe has created a visually friendly workplace for you. You can easily drag and drop objects and images between document windows from one program to another, drag files from the desktop to open document windows, and copy and paste objects and images between documents.

NOTE With Adobe Bridge, you can see all your files with thumbnail previews and drag and drop files into different application documents. You also can drag and drop Microsoft Word and Excel files into Adobe InDesign CS4 directly from the Bridge window.

CROSS-REF For more information on importing and exchanging documents among programs, see Part III. For information on using Adobe Bridge, see Chapter 6.

Support for PDF

With InDesign CS4 as the central core of your Creative Suite programs for design purposes, PDF is the central file format for file exchanges and printing. All the Adobe CS4 programs, except for Flash and Dreamweaver, support PDF imports and exports, and these CS4 applications use the same Adobe PDF settings. In Creative Suite 4, PDF exports and imports are easier. InDesign CS4, as well as Photoshop CS4 and Illustrator CS4, supports exports to PDF/X format, which is a reliable document format used for commercial printing. Photoshop CS4 supports the creation of PDF slide shows; Illustrator CS4 and InDesign CS4 support PDF creation with Adobe PDF layers. InDesign CS4 now supports importing layered PDF documents and toggling layered views directly from within InDesign. You also can apply the same layer views to layered Photoshop and Illustrator CS4 documents. InDesign CS4 also supports multipage PDF file imports. Additionally, you can import media such as movie clips and sound files in InDesign CS4 and export them to PDF. Because PDF is the reliable standard for onscreen document viewing and output to professional printing devices, the CS4 programs take advantage of core PDF architecture. Finally, Fireworks CS4 can also author PDF. This allows a Web site to be shared and commented upon using standard Acrobat tools and techniques.

CROSS-REF For more information on PDF/X and commercial printing, see Chapter 40. For more information on PDFs and multimedia, see Chapter 29.

Understanding the Creative Suite

The Adobe Creative Suite 4 comes in two design-oriented versions:

- **Adobe Creative Suite 4 Design Standard:** This includes Adobe Photoshop CS4, Adobe Illustrator CS4, Adobe InDesign CS4, and Adobe Acrobat 9 Pro.
- **Adobe Creative Suite 4 Design Premium:** This includes the same programs with the addition of Adobe Flash CS4 Professional, Fireworks CS4, and Adobe Dreamweaver CS4. Also, Adobe Photoshop CS4 is replaced with Adobe Photoshop CS4 Extended.

Both design suites also include the common additional features of Adobe Bridge CS4, Adobe Version Cue CS4, and Device Central CS4.

Adobe also has Creative Suite versions for Web and video professionals. For Web professionals, the suite options include:

- **Adobe Creative Suite 4 Web Standard:** This includes Adobe Dreamweaver CS4, Adobe Flash CS4 Professional, Adobe Fireworks CS4, and Adobe Contribute CS4.
- **Adobe Creative Suite 4 Web Premium:** This includes the same programs with the addition of several of the design packages including Adobe Photoshop CS4 Extended, Adobe Illustrator CS4, Soundbooth CS4, and Adobe Acrobat 9 Professional.

Both Web design suites also include the common additional features of Adobe Bridge CS4, Adobe Version Cue CS4, and Device Central CS4.

For video professionals, the available suite includes:

- **Adobe Creative Suite 4 Production Premium:** This includes Adobe After Effects CS4 Professional, Adobe Premiere Pro CS4, Adobe Soundbooth CS4, and Adobe Encore CS4, along with the other design packages.

The Adobe Creative Suite 4 Master Collection includes just about everything, except the kitchen sink.

We cover all the programs found in the Design Premium version throughout this book, but although we get a little into Web development, we don't cover the video products at all. In addition to the programs, you also get a large set of OpenType faces with the Creative Suite editions.

Each of the programs is an upgrade from previous CS3 versions of the software along with the new version of Adobe Bridge, and Adobe Systems intends to upgrade the products in tandem for future versions. Therefore, you can be confident that the next upgrade of a program like Photoshop CS4 will appear along with upgrades to Illustrator CS4, InDesign CS4, and Dreamweaver CS4.

Adobe Bridge

Adobe Bridge, shown in Figure 1.1, is an updated executable application introduced in the Creative Suite version 2. With Adobe Bridge, you can view document thumbnail previews for all Adobe applications as well as many non-Adobe applications.

 **CROSS-REF**   **For information on using Adobe Bridge, see Chapter 6.**

FIGURE 1.1

The Adobe Bridge is the central navigation tool for all CS4 applications.

You can use Adobe Bridge, which is your central navigation tool, to manage document assets and attributes. For example, using Adobe Bridge, you can assign common color management settings to all the print-oriented CS4 applications, as well as add metadata to all your documents and run keyword searches on that metadata. These features are available with Adobe Bridge:

- **Bridge Home:** Adobe Bridge contains Bridge Home when used with the Creative Suite. The Bridge Home is the dashboard of the Creative Suite where you can view news feeds for each of the individual CS4 products, view your most recent activities, read about tips and techniques for using Adobe software, and much more.

- **Camera Raw:** You can open and edit camera raw images from Adobe Bridge and save them in Photoshop CS4-compatible file formats. (Note that opening camera raw images in Adobe Bridge requires you to have Photoshop CS4 installed on your computer.) You can edit camera raw settings in Adobe Bridge before opening files in Adobe Photoshop CS4.

- **Color Management:** Using Adobe Bridge, you can synchronize color management settings across the print-oriented applications to ensure consistent color in all your CS4 application documents. You can import and export color settings for sharing among service providers and workgroups.

- **File Browsing:** As a file browser, Adobe Bridge is similar to the File Browser contained in earlier versions of Adobe Photoshop. Using Adobe Bridge as a file browser enables you to view thumbnail images of all Adobe application files and many other files created in other authoring programs. You can view page thumbnails from InDesign and Acrobat PDF documents. You also can view hidden files that your operating system uses on your computer. You can organize, sort files, create new folders, and move and delete files. You can edit metadata, rotate images, and run batch commands and automation scripts.

- **Launching Adobe Bridge:** You can launch Adobe Bridge as a separate executable program. You also can launch Bridge directly from within Adobe Photoshop CS4, Adobe Illustrator CS4, Adobe InDesign CS4, Adobe Flash CS4 Professional, Fireworks CS4, and Adobe Dreamweaver CS4.

 Adobe Bridge CS4 includes an preference option to Start Bridge at Login that makes Bridge available when you start your computer.

- **Version Cue:** In addition to launching all the CS4 applications from within Adobe Bridge, you also can access Adobe Version Cue CS4. You can create versions of documents, create alternates, apply document security, organize files into Version Cue private and shared project folders, and perform many other Version Cue-related tasks.

Adobe Photoshop CS4

If you're a creative professional, chances are good that you're no stranger to Adobe Photoshop. Adobe's flagship image-editing program is now in version 11 with the CS4 upgrade. As a stand-alone product, Photoshop has some very nice additions to an already feature-rich program. New enhancements to Photoshop add tools and options specific to interests by graphic designers, photographers, and Web designers. Adobe Photoshop CS4 offers you more integration with the other

CS applications and some unique new editing tools. This version of Photoshop adds more polish to the program and enhancements that are likely to become favorites for creative professionals.

These items are among some of the more impressive additions to the program you'll find:

CROSS-REF For information related to new 3D features in Adobe Photoshop, see Chapter 14.

■ **3D Object support:** The new 3D features in Photoshop CS4 Extended let you load, view, rotate, and change the rendering method of 3D objects. Figure 1.2 shows the default soda can primitive.

FIGURE 1.2

The 3D features let you work with 3D objects.

■ **3D Paint Mode:** Once a 3D object is loaded, you can use the 3D Paint Mode to paint directly on the surface of the object, as shown in Figure 1.3. This is a huge timesaver for creating texture maps on 3D objects.

■ **3D Rotate and Orbit Tools:** Within the Tools palette are two new tools for rotating and orbiting about 3D objects. These tools are non-modal and don't require a confirmation dialog box before continuing.

FIGURE 1.3

3D Paint Mode lets you paint directly on the surface of 3D objects.

NOTE   **The 3D features are available only in Photoshop CS4 Extended.**

■ **Adjustment and Mask panels:** The new Adjustment and Mask panels let you apply subtle tonal changes to images in a non-destructive manner.

Adobe Illustrator CS4

Tried and true Adobe Illustrator is the premier illustration program for designers and artists. The advantages for using illustration programs together with other applications in the Creative Suite are significantly in favor of Adobe Illustrator.

New impressive tools have been added to Illustrator as well as some polish on editing features.

CROSS-REF   **For more information on using Adobe Illustrator CS4 and some of its new features, see Part III.**

You'll also find these new features in Illustrator CS4:

- **Blob Brush tool:** Illustrator's new Blob Brush tool lets you paint pressure-sensitive paths that blend with one another to create a single object, as shown in Figure 1.4. The Blob brush detects color and only combines paths of like colors.

FIGURE 1.4

The Blobby Brush tool lets you paint with random effects.

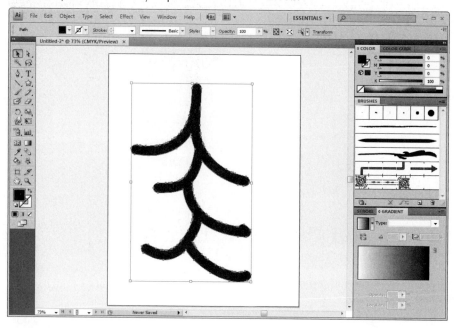

- **Appearance panel:** The Appearance panel has been overhauled allowing more immediate editing of objects including apply stroke, fill, and effects. A Visibility icon for each appearance attribute makes it easy to turn attributes on and off.

- **Multiple Artboards:** Illustrator now lets you work with multiple artboards.

Adobe InDesign CS4

InDesign is the central hub of your creative workflow. This is where you bring together the images and objects that you create in Adobe Photoshop CS4 and Adobe Illustrator CS4. You can import type created in a word-processing program, import from Adobe's InCopy, or set type in the InDesign Story Editor or in other ways. With InDesign's free-form ease of page layout, you can lay out a design for publication. You can then export the InDesign document as a PDF file suited for print, Web hosting, electronic file exchanges, or CD/DVD-ROM replication. If you want to include your design as an HTML file for Web hosting, you can export the document for Dreamweaver CS4. As you can see, InDesign's role among the Creative Suite programs is the anchor where files are imported to assemble a design and ultimately export for final output.

Among the more significant new additions are these gems:

- **Export Options:** The new export options allow InDesign documents to be moved to other formats. These options include a cleaner method for getting documents online using the XFL export feature. Another option exports to SWF for use in Flash.
- **Rotated Spread Views:** Spread views can be rotated 90 degrees.
- **Smart Guides:** These guides make it easier to align and orient objects in InDesign.
- **Preflight panel:** The new Preflight panel, shown in Figure 1.5, makes it easy to prepare documents for printing and exporting.

FIGURE 1.5

InDesign's new Preflight panel checks for errors.

Adobe Flash CS4 Professional

Flash works with vectors much like Illustrator, but unlike Illustrator, Flash is key at creating animated and interactive elements that are common on the Web.

It is great to see the inclusion of Flash into Creative Suite bringing with it the ability to add motion graphics to Web and online projects. Many of Flash's tools work in a similar manner to Illustrator's, and much work has been done to make the two products work well together. Files in Illustrator can be moved to Flash and back without losing any work.

Although the entire package is new to Creative Suite, Flash CS4 Professional also includes a number of new features, including the following:

■ **New Animation features:** Flash CS4 includes a new approach for animating objects that makes it easier to work with. The new features include a set of motion presets. The new IK feature makes animating objects under the control of master bone objects possible.

■ **3D and Procedural Modeling:** Flash includes support for 3D objects and a new procedural modeling ability.

CROSS-REF For more information on using the new features in Flash CS4 Professional, look at Chapter 23.

Adobe Dreamweaver CS4

Adobe Dreamweaver CS4 is a Web-authoring and site-management program. It has been tightly integrated with the CS4 applications and works well with them.

CROSS-REF For more information on using the new features in Dreamweaver CS4, see Chapter 27.

These are some of the new feature highlights:

■ **Live View:** Dreamweaver CS4 includes a new mode for viewing Web pages. Live View offers the ability to run scripts and preview content immediately within Dreamweaver.

■ **Compatible Interface:** The Dreamweaver CS4 interface has been overhauled and made to look like the other Adobe products, as shown in Figure 1.6.

■ **Subversion support:** Version control support using Subversion is now included in Dreamweaver CS4.

CROSS-REF In Chapter 27 of this book, we offer you a starting point for using Dreamweaver to create a Web site. In other chapters, we cover the integration of Dreamweaver with the other CS4 programs. However, our treatment of Dreamweaver is light, and you'll need to acquire some other guides and publications in order to become proficient in using the program.

FIGURE 1.6

Adobe Dreamweaver CS4 uses the same palettes and interface design as the other CS applications.

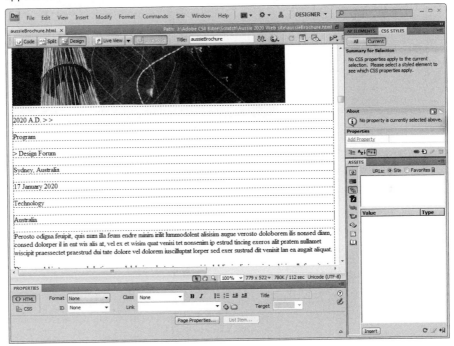

Adobe Fireworks CS4

Adobe Fireworks CS4 is an excellent package for creating, processing, and optimizing graphics for the Web. It is also very helpful in creating user interfaces.

 **Fireworks is a new addition to Creative Suite CS4. Our coverage of Fireworks is limited.**

Adobe Acrobat Professional 9

Whereas Adobe InDesign CS4 is the hub of your creative satellite, PDF is at the center of the file-format universe. All the print-oriented CS4 programs export and import PDF documents, and the expansion for PDF support is found in the new product upgrades. For design workflows, Adobe

Acrobat Professional in version 9 offers you many tools to facilitate collaboration with colleagues, clients, and prepress technicians. You can do these things:

- Set up e-mail–based reviews for markup and approval of design concepts and proofs
- Enable PDF documents with special usage rights so users of the free Adobe Reader program can participate in comment and review sessions
- Export comments and corrections directly to Microsoft Word text documents (on Windows XP with Office XP only)
- PDF Portfolios
- Prepare files for digital prepress and printing including the ability to convert composite black to K-only output
- Authenticate and secure documents
- Develop media shows and slide presentations for kiosks, meetings, and presentations
- Review sessions and forms hosted by Acrobat.com
- Organize your design environment and catalog design campaigns embedding native files in PDFs for an organized storage system
- Search for content contained on CDs, DVDs, network servers, and Web sites

All in all, Acrobat 9 Pro has a significant place in your design workflow.

Acrobat 9 Pro was released several months earlier than the other CS4 programs and is not on the same development cycle as the other CS4 programs. Part of the reason for the early release of Acrobat was the necessity to develop the PDF specifications used by all the other CS4 programs.

Adobe Acrobat is unlike the other CS4 programs in that the application is designed to serve many different office professionals. Acrobat might be used by engineers, legal professionals, business office workers, government workers, school districts, and just about anyone in any industry working on a computer today. Therefore, there are a number of tools that you, as a creative professional, may not use in Acrobat just because those tools may not serve your needs.

Adobe Drive and Version Cue

You'll find the new enhancements to Version Cue another step toward complete integration of the Adobe CS4 applications. Together with Adobe Bridge, this release of the Creative Suite helps you easily manage documents and revisions. Adobe Version Cue is now in version CS4 like the other CS applications. Adobe Drive provides a way to connect to external servers and share files.

Device Central CS4

Another helpful component installed as part of the suite is Device Central CS4. This application is a lifesaver if you need to configure your pages to be displayed on mobile devices such as next-generation phones. Device Central includes a broad collection of mobile devices that are emulated so you can view exactly how your pages will look on various devices.

OpenType fonts

In addition to the programs contained in the Creative Suite, you also can find a large set of installed OpenType fonts after completing your CS4 applications installation. OpenType fonts are based on font technology developed by Adobe Systems and Microsoft. OpenType fonts offer you new type-handling features among many of the CS4 applications. You should convert your type library to OpenType fonts as soon as possible. You'll derive these benefits from using OpenType fonts:

- **Cross-platform support:** OpenType fonts are completely cross-platform. You can copy the same font to either Mac OS or Windows. Obviously, licensing restrictions do apply, so be certain to check these restrictions before installing fonts on multiple computers.

- **Reliability:** If you experience font problems when you print, be certain to first reevaluate your font sets. Off-brand fonts, especially many TrueType fonts, can create embedding problems. Furthermore, some quality fonts carry licensing restrictions that prevent font embedding. If you create PDF files with font embedding, be certain to review the licensing restrictions on your fonts and check whether font embedding is prohibited. Many quality fonts offer you complete embedding permissions that help prevent problems when it comes time to print your creations. Good-quality fonts that permit font embedding include those found in the Adobe type library of OpenType fonts.

- **More glyphs:** A *glyph* is an individual font character. TrueType fonts and all earlier PostScript fonts contain a maximum 256 glyphs. The new OpenType fonts can contain more than 65,000 glyphs. These additional characters offer you many special characters, precisely proportioned fractions, and foreign-language character alternatives. A portion of a glyph set for an OpenType font installed with the Creative Suite is shown in Figure 1.7.

- **Multi-language support:** All the OpenType Pro fonts contain characters needed for multiple-language typesetting.

NOTE OpenType fonts are available in Pro and Standard families. The OpenType Pro families provide a certain type of characters, but OpenType Standard families use the OpenType technology and don't have a broad set of glyphs.

- **Easier font management:** OpenType fonts contain only a single file for font viewing onscreen and fonts used for printing. Unlike PostScript fonts containing separate files for screen views and each face in a font set contained in a separate file, OpenType fonts are built in a single file, thereby providing you more ease in keeping track of fonts, installing them, and locating them.

FIGURE 1.7

OpenType fonts offer you more than 65,000 characters.

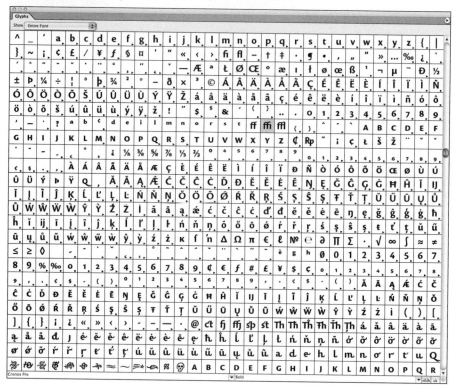

Several CS4 applications support a Glyphs palette where you can view an entire font in a scrollable window. You can insert a character at the insertion point by double-clicking a glyph in the palette. You no longer need to open a utility to view all characters in a given font set when you use programs like Adobe InDesign CS4 and Adobe Illustrator CS4.

Summary

- The Creative Suite is a collection of applications offering professional designers complete integration for print, Web design, and screen viewing.

- Programs from a single software vendor provide consistent user interfaces and similar menu and tool functions, which reduce learning curves for new hires.

- Adobe Bridge is a central navigation tool offering features for viewing, editing, and managing Adobe CS4 application documents and non-Adobe files.

Chapter 2

Taking a Tour of the Creative Suite

The best way to understand the possibilities that the various Creative Suite applications offer is to walk through an example workflow that takes a project through each of the various applications. This tour starts out with Acrobat, where you can create a PDF file of an initial sketch that you can e-mail to all members of the creative team for review. The reviewers' feedback return is in the form of comments compiled within a single PDF file. This cycle continues until all members of the creative team approve the design.

With an approved design, you can use Photoshop and Illustrator to create and edit images and objects for the project. You can then import all this content into InDesign, where you lay them out with text. The final layout is then exported back to Acrobat, where you can print it or repurpose it for use on the Web using Dreamweaver and Flash.

Starting with a Sketch in Acrobat

When a project first starts, you typically want to get input from several individuals on the creative team before the design is approved. Calling a meeting where all members of the creative team meet to discuss the design would accomplish the goal, but Acrobat makes another solution possible.

Using Acrobat, you can scan a rough design sketch into Acrobat where it is converted to a PDF file. Then you can e-mail this PDF file to members of the creative team. Each member of the team makes his comments into the PDF file and e-mails the document back to its owner. All the comments are then compiled into a single PDF document that provides feedback. This cycle can then be iterated until all involved approve the design.

CROSS-REF You can find complete coverage on e-mail review sessions in Chapter 36.

Scanning a sketch into Acrobat

Projects always start with an idea, but to share these ideas with others, you usually sketch them out roughly. You may then scan these rough sketches into a digital format where you can more easily distribute them. Using a scanner or a digital camera, you can directly import sketches or scan images into Acrobat.

STEPS: Scanning a Sketch into Acrobat

1. **Initiate a scan in Acrobat.** Within Acrobat, choose File ➪ Create PDF ➪ From Scanner ➪ Black and White. This command opens the Acrobat Scan dialog box, shown in Figure 2.1. You also can disable the Make Searchable and Add Metadata options, and click Ok.

FIGURE 2.1

The Acrobat Scan dialog box

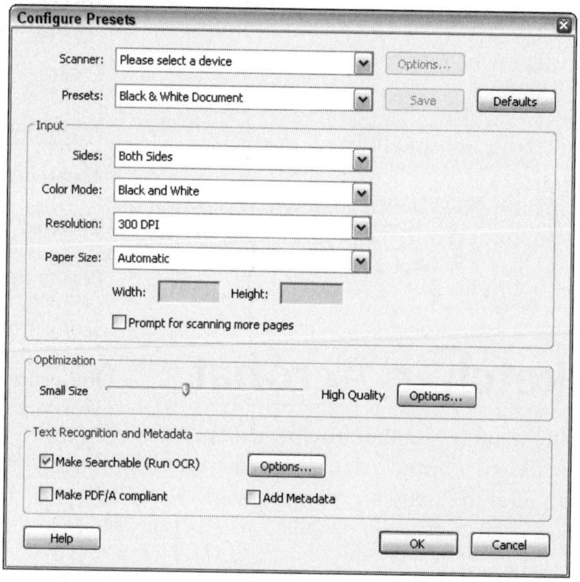

2. **Set the scanner preferences.** After you click Scan, a dialog box for your scanner appears. Select the options appropriate for your sketched image, and click Preview to check the scanning options. If you're comfortable with the preview, click Scan.

3. **Save the PDF file.** After the scanned file is loaded into Acrobat, as shown in Figure 2.2, you need to save the file before you redistribute it. To save the scanned image, choose File ⇨ Save As. This command opens a file dialog box where you can name the file and specify a folder where you want to save the file.

FIGURE 2.2

A scanned image in Acrobat

Submitting a sketch for e-mail review

With a sketch scanned into Acrobat, you can send the PDF file out for review using e-mail or using a browser. These steps walk you through an e-mail review cycle. In actual projects, this review cycle may be repeated many times as needed.

STEPS: Submitting a Sketch for E-mail Review

1. **Send a PDF file for e-mail review.** To send the selected PDF file out for e-mail review, choose Comments ⇨ Attach for Email Review. The Attach for Email Review wizard starts, and the first page of the wizard opens, as shown in Figure 2.3. Here, you specify the PDF file to send out for review. The default file is the current open file. You can edit your current profile and e-mail address at a future time using the Identity panel of the Preferences dialog box (Acrobat/Edit ⇨ Preferences).

FIGURE 2.3

The Attach for Email Review wizard dialog box

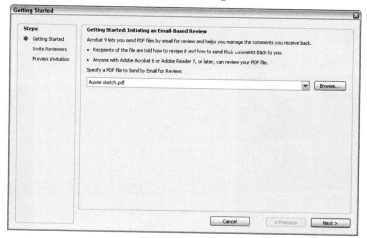

2. **Specify the reviewers' e-mail addresses.** The next step in the Attach for Email Review wizard, lets you enter the e-mail addresses of the individuals you want to review the attached PDF document. Clicking the Address Book button opens a contact manager where you can enter lists of individuals.

3. **Extending a review invitation.** The final step of the Attach for Email Review wizard automatically composes the e-mail subject and message body text for you, as shown in Figure 2.4, but you can edit the e-mail text as desired. When the e-mail addresses and message are completed, click Send Invitation. Acrobat delivers the e-mail message to your system's default e-mail application. If your e-mail system is set to automatically send out e-mails, the e-mail is sent automatically. But if not, you need to send out the e-mails manually.

FIGURE 2.4

The third step lets you compose the e-mail that is sent to the reviewers.

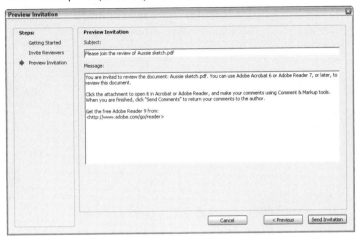

Adding comments to the PDF

When a reviewer receives an e-mail requesting feedback, he can double-click the attached file to open it in Acrobat. Within Acrobat, the Commenting toolbar may be used to add notes and comments to the sketch.

STEPS: Adding Comments to an E-mail PDF File

1. **Open an e-mail that you have received and want to review.** Using your system e-mail client, the review request is sent out with the PDF file attached.

> **NOTE** E-mail reviews can mix comments from Macintosh and Window platforms without any issues.

2. **Open the attached PDF in Acrobat.** If you double-click the attached PDF file, it opens within Acrobat. Comments are added to the document using the Commenting toolbar, which opens automatically when a review-enabled PDF is opened. The Commenting toolbar also may be accessed by choosing Tools ➪ Commenting ➪ Show Commenting Toolbar.

3. **Add review comments to the PDF.** Click the Note Tool button in the Commenting toolbar. Click in the document where you want the note to be positioned. A note text area appears where you can type your message. Figure 2.5 shows the sketch document with some review comments added.

FIGURE 2.5

A sketch with comments attached

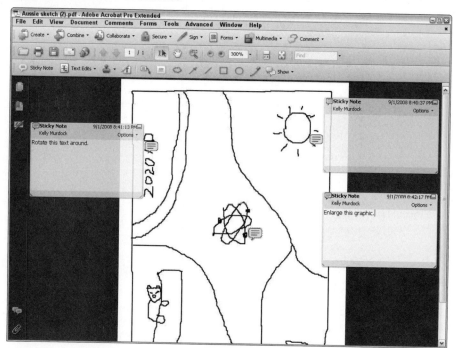

4. **Return comments.** After you've finished making comments, choose Comments ⇨ Send for Shared Review or click the Send Comments button in the Commenting toolbar. The PDF with its comments is sent back to the original sender.

Collecting review comments

When the reviewed documents are returned to the original sender, the comments are merged into the original document. These comments may then be summarized and printed.

STEPS: Collecting Review Comments

1. **Merge comments with the original document.** When a review PDF file is returned, it also can be double-clicked within the e-mail message to open it within Acrobat. Acrobat recognizes the document as one that was sent out for review and incorporates the comments into the original document. When this happens, a message dialog box appears.

2. **View and print a list of comments.** After a reviewed document is merged into the original PDF file, you open the list of comments by clicking the Comments tab to the left. All comments in the PDF file appear at the bottom of the document, as shown in Figure 2.6.

FIGURE 2.6

The Comments tab opens comments on the document.

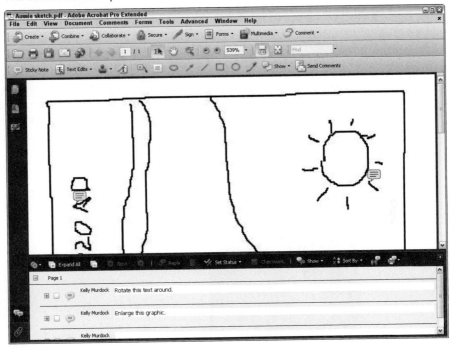

3. **Sort comments.** The buttons along the top of the comments list let you set the status of comments and sort them by type, page, author, date, color, or check mark status.

4. **Print comments.** To print the comments, click the Print button at the top of the Comments list or choose File ➪ Print with Comments Summary.

Editing Images in Photoshop

When you have a good idea of the content that needs to be in the final document, you can use Photoshop to edit and prepare the images to be included. These edits can include altering the image properties to adjust the image levels, color balance, brightness, and contrast. Another common way to edit images is to crop the image to the relevant portion. For images that aren't rectangular, you may need to extract a portion of an image. For images that appear on top of other page elements, you'll want to add transparency. All these tasks may be completed in Photoshop.

CROSS-REF Many Photoshop editing features are covered in Chapter 10.

Adjusting image properties

After all the images for the project have been identified, Photoshop's image adjustment features may be used to change the image levels or its brightness and contrast. Adequate contrast is essential for objects that are to be combined with text.

STEPS: Adjusting Image Levels and Contrast

1. **Open an image in Photoshop.** Within Photoshop, choose File ➪ Open and select an image to load. Because these images are to be used within a brochure, the levels and contrast need to be adjusted in order for the text that comes on top of the images to be legible. Figure 2.7 shows the original image.

FIGURE 2.7

This figure shows the original image before any adjustments.

---

2. **Auto-adjust the image levels.** With the image selected, open the Adjustments panel with Window ➪ Adjustments. Within the Adjustments panel, select the Levels button. The Levels settings appear, as shown in Figure 2.8. This panel shows the Shadows, Midtones, and Highlights of the image. To auto-correct the balance of these levels, click Auto. The levels are evenly spaced, and the image is adjusted.

3. **Adjust the brightness and contrast.** To change the brightness and contrast of the image, click the Return button in the Adjustments panel and then choose the Brightness/Contrast button. This opens settings with sliders for the Brightness and Contrast values. Set the Brightness value to −35 and the Contrast value to −30. A preview of the settings is shown on the image. This provides ample contrast for the image. Figure 2.9 shows the resulting image.

FIGURE 2.8

The Levels settings in the Adjustments panel

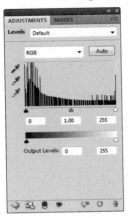

FIGURE 2.9

The image has sufficient contrast.

4. **Save the image.** Choose File ➪ Save to save the image with its changes.

Cropping images

Although the levels and the contrast of the image look good, the image contains some background items that distract from the main image. These unwanted details are easily removed using Photoshop's Crop tool.

STEPS: Cropping an Image

1. **Open an image in Photoshop.** Within Photoshop, choose File ➪ Open and select an image that you want to crop.

2. **Use the Crop tool.** Click the Crop tool in the toolbar, and drag within the interior of the image. This places a marquee with handles on each edge and corner. Click and drag the handles to precisely position the cropping marquee, as shown in Figure 2.10. Double-click within the cropping marquee to complete the crop.

FIGURE 2.10

The marquee shows where the image is to be cropped.

3. **Save the image.** Choose File ➪ Save to save the image with its changes.

Editing images

Photoshop includes many different tools for editing an existing image, but some of the most useful are the Clone and Healing Brushes. With these brushes, you can remove unwanted details and generally clean up an otherwise unusable image. In the following steps, the unwanted detail is the reflection off the glass of the cabinet in which the statue sits.

STEPS: Using the Spot Healing Tool

1. **Open an image in Photoshop.** Within Photoshop, choose File ➪ Open and select an image that you want to fix.

2. **Select the Spot Healing tool from the Toolbox.** With the Spot Healing tool selected, drag over the areas that you want to fix. In the example, you drag over portions of the sky where some unwanted dots exist. The Spot Healing brush uses surrounding pixels to color over the spots. Figure 2.11 shows the image after the spots have been removed.

FIGURE 2.11

You can use the Spot Healing Brush to remove problems from the image.

3. **Save the image.** Choose File ⇨ Save to save the image with its changes.

Creating Illustrator Objects

Images included in a design are best edited in Photoshop, but your design also might call for vector-based objects such as logos, maps, and shapes. These objects are easiest to create in Illustrator. For this example, we trace images into objects using the Live Trace feature and create some background objects.

CROSS-REF Many Illustrator and Photoshop editing features are covered in Chapter 10 and Chapter 11.

Using Live Trace

Illustrated elements can add much to a design, and Illustrator's new Live Trace feature makes tracing bitmap images into objects easy. You can define and reuse the Live Trace presets to create unique looks such as cartoons, rough sketches, and technical illustrations.

STEPS: Tracing Bitmap Images with Live Trace

1. **Open a raster image in Illustrator.** Within Illustrator, create a new file with the File ➪ New menu and choose File ➪ Place and place an image that you want to trace.

TIP An alternative to creating and placing a file in Illustrator is to locate an image in Adobe Bridge and with the image selected, choose the File ➪ Place ➪ In Illustrator menu. This automatically creates a new file in Illustrator and places the selected file in it.

2. **Create a Live Trace object.** With the bitmap image selected, click the Live Trace button in the Options bar. This applies the default Live Trace preset. From the Options bar, choose the Color 6 preset. Figure 2.12 shows the results of applying Live Trace to the bitmap image.

FIGURE 2.12

Live Trace converts bitmap images into objects.

3. **Save the image.** Choose File ➪ Save to save the image with its changes.

Creating and filling objects

Illustrator's Toolbox includes many tools for creating objects. These objects may be freehand lines drawn with the Pen, Pencil, or Paintbrush tools; straight lines; text; or various shapes, including rectangles, ellipses, polygons, stars, arcs, spirals, and grids.

After you create an object by dragging it in the art board, you can select a fill color or define the width and color of its outline, called a *stroke*.

STEPS: Creating a Background Object

1. **Open Illustrator.** Within Illustrator, choose File ⇨ New and create a new image.

2. **Create an object profile curve.** Click the Pen tool in the Toolbox. Then click and drag in the art board to create a profile curve. Select the Direct Selection tool, align the top and bottom points and drag the tangent handles to make the profile curve smooth, as shown in Figure 2.13. The profile curve should have the first and last points aligned horizontally.

FIGURE 2.13

The profile curve defines the shape of the object.

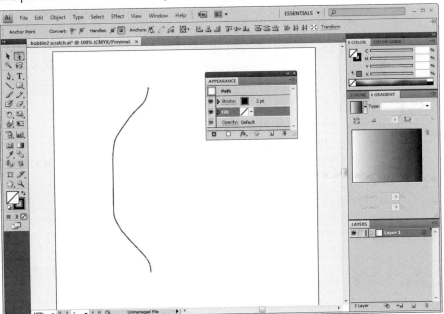

3. **Add fill and stroke colors.** Open the Appearance panel with the Window⇨Appearance menu. Click the Fill box and select the light blue swatch in the Swatches palette to color this object light blue. Then click the Stroke box in the Toolbox; then select the None color to remove the stroke color.

4. **Reflect the object.** Select the Object⇨Transform⇨Reflect menu command to open the Reflect dialog box. Select the Vertical option, and click the Copy button. Then click OK.

5. **Align the two halves.** Select the View⇨Smart Guides option to enable the guides to automatically align the halves. With the Selection tool, select and move one of the halves until the midlines are aligned to each other, as shown in Figure 2.14.

FIGURE 2.14

Two filled objects are aligned to match their first and last points.

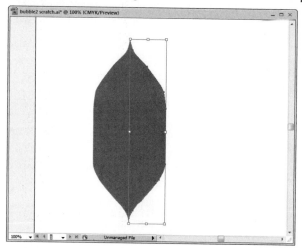

6. **Join the paths.** With the Direct Selection tool, select the two bottom points and choose the Connect Selected End Points on the Options bar. Select the Corner option in the dialog box that appears. Then repeat the same command for the top two points. This makes the object fill span the entire interior space.

7. **Add a gradient mesh.** Click the Mesh tool, and select a point on the top half of the object where the light is shining and change its color to a lighter blue. Figure 2.15 shows the final bubble ready to be used as part of the background.

8. **Save the file.** Choose File⇨Save to save the file.

FIGURE 2.15

A gradient mesh adds some depth to the object.

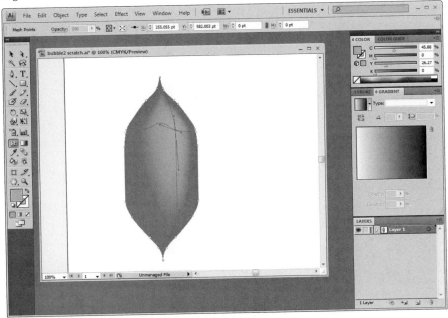

Using effects

One common way to distort objects in Illustrator is with effects. Effects are applied to objects in memory, allowing you to edit, remove or turn them on and off anytime using the Appearance palette. A large variety of effects are available in the Effect menu.

CROSS-REF Applying Illustrator effects is covered in Chapter 25.

STEPS: Extruding an Object

1. **Open Illustrator and select a file.** Within Illustrator, choose File ➪ Open and select a file that you want to apply an effect to.

2. **Create the objects.** Before you can apply an effect to separate objects, you need to create the objects. For this example, a simple atom is created using overlapping ellipses and a circle in the center.

3. **Extrude the object.** With the objects selected, choose Effect ➪ 3D ➪ Extrude and Bevel. The 3D Extrude and Bevel dialog box opens. Select the Off-Axis Front option from the Position drop-down list, and set the Extrude Depth to 20 pt. Then click OK. An extrude effect is applied to the atom, as shown in Figure 2.16.

FIGURE 2.16

You can use the 3D extrude effect to give objects a sense of depth.

4. **Save the file.** Choose File ⇨ Save to save the file.

Using Adobe Bridge

The best tool to access the volumes of content available in a project is Adobe Bridge. You open Adobe Bridge using the Go To Bridge icon in the upper-left corner of most of the CS4 applications.

CROSS-REF   Adobe Bridge is covered in more detail in Chapter 6.

After you create a new project, you can easily add files to the project. Simply drag and drop the files from their current location into the Project folder in Adobe Bridge.

STEPS: Accessing Files using Adobe Bridge

1. **Open Adobe Bridge.** From within Illustrator, click the Go to Bridge button in the upper-left corner of the interface. This opens the Adobe Bridge interface.

2. **Locate the project folder.** Within Adobe Bridge, locate the folder that holds all the edited content from the pane on the left. Thumbnails for all files within the folder display within Adobe Bridge, as shown in Figure 2.17.

FIGURE 2.17

Adobe Bridge displays thumbnails for all files in the project file.

3. **Open a file to work with.** Select a file within the project file, and right-click the file thumbnail. A pop-up menu appears. Select the Open With option. The submenu lists all the various CS4 applications. You also can drag thumbnails directly to the different CS4 applications.

 **TIP** If you double-click a file, then it will be opened automatically in its default editor.

Creating a Layout in InDesign

After you create all the content for the project using Photoshop and Illustrator, you can use InDesign to lay out the project in preparation for printing. Each object within InDesign is contained within a frame. These frames are easily moved and resized.

Images and objects placed within frames in a layout aren't embedded within the layout but instead are only links to the actual image and object files. This allows the representative images to be updated quickly. When the layout is exported or printed, InDesign looks at content referenced as links and loads the actual linked files into the exported or printed document.

CROSS-REF Creating layouts and using master pages are covered in Chapter 36.

Setting layout properties

Before the content is placed on the pages, creating a document lets you create all the pages and spreads contained in the project. You also can specify the number of pages as well as the page dimensions, margins, and columns.

STEPS: Creating an InDesign Layout

1. **Create a new InDesign document.** Within InDesign, choose File ➪ New ➪ Document. In the New Document dialog box, shown in Figure 2.18, set the number of pages to 6 and enable the Facing Pages option. Set the Width to 7 inches and the Height to 10 inches, and click the Portrait Orientation button. Then set all the margins to 0.5 inches and the columns to 1, with a gutter of 0.

FIGURE 2.18

The New Document dialog box

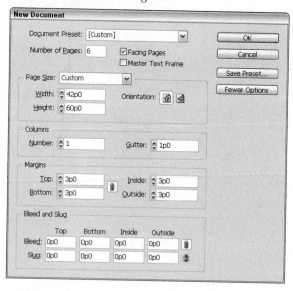

2. **Set the bleed and slug dimensions.** While still in the New Document dialog box, click More Options to reveal the fields for setting the bleed and slug dimensions. Set the Top Bleed value to 0.125 inches, and click the Make All Settings the Same button to the right of the Bleed fields. Then set the Bottom Slug value to 0.75 inches, and click OK.

3. **View the layout pages.** To see the layout pages, open the Pages palette by choosing Window ➪ Pages. The Pages palette is shown in Figure 2.19.

FIGURE 2.19

The Pages palette lets you view and select pages in a layout.

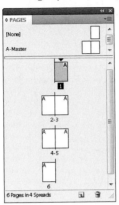

4. **Save the file.** Choose File ⇨ Save to save the layout.

Importing content into InDesign

With a layout created, you can begin to import content into the InDesign layout by choosing File ⇨ Place. Imported objects appear within frames that allow them to be moved easily about the layout.

Another easy way to import content is to select multiple files in the Adobe Bridge interface and simply drag them into InDesign.

STEPS: Importing Content into InDesign

1. **Place images from Photoshop.** Choose File ⇨ Place. The Place dialog box, shown in Figure 2.20, looks like the Open file dialog box, except it lets you select a much large number of file types. Select the image file to place in the layout, and click Open. The image is automatically loaded into the frame at its default size using the proportional placing feature.

2. **Place objects from Illustrator.** You also can use the File ⇨ Place menu command to place objects created in Illustrator. For Illustrator objects, enable the Show Import Options check box in the Place dialog box. This causes the Place PDF dialog box, shown in Figure 2.21, to appear. In the Crop To drop-down list, select the Bounding Box option; enable the Transparent Background check box. Then click OK. The object to be placed appears on the cursor. Click in the upper-left section of the image to place the object.

3. **Resize the placed object.** The placed object appears within a frame. By dragging the handles, you can resize the frame, but the placed object's size doesn't change until you choose Object ⇨ Fitting ⇨ Fit Content to Frame Proportionally. If you use the Scale tool, you can size the frame and content together.

4. **Save the file.** Choose File ⇨ Save to save the layout.

FIGURE 2.20

The Place dialog box opens a variety of file formats.

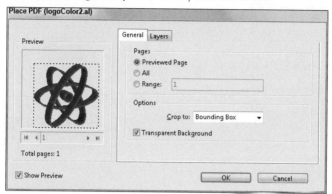

FIGURE 2.21

The Place PDF dialog box defines how objects are cropped.

Creating Master pages in InDesign

Using Master pages, you can place objects such as page numbers that appear on every page of the document. Master pages are created and accessed using the Pages palette.

STEPS: Using Master Pages

1. **Create a new Master spread.** Master pages are defined using the Pages panel. Using the panel menu (which can be accessed by clicking on the small icon in the upper-right corner of the palette), select the New Master palette menu command. In the New Master dialog box, shown in Figure 2.22, type a prefix and a name for the master. Then type **2** as the number of pages, and click OK. The Master appears in the top of the Pages palette.

FIGURE 2.22

The New Master dialog box

2. **Apply the Master to pages.** With the new Master spread selected in the Pages palette, select the Apply Master to Pages palette menu command. In the Apply Master dialog box that appears, type the page numbers to which you want to apply the Master spread. The Pages palette is updated with the Prefix for the Master spread, as shown in Figure 2.23.

FIGURE 2.23

Master pages are displayed at the top of the Pages palette.

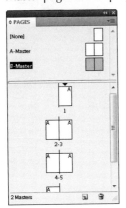

3. **Add page numbers to the Master spread.** Switch to the new master page by selecting it in the Pages palette. Select the Type tool, and drag within the Master pages where you want the page numbers to appear. With the text cursor blinking in the text object, choose Type ➪ Insert Special Character ➪ Markers ➪ Current Page Number. The Prefix for the Master spread is listed in the text object. However, when you view a page that uses the Master page, the correct page number displays.

4. **Save the file.** Choose File ➪ Save to save the layout.

Threading text

You can make text flow continuously from one text frame to another. This process is called threading text. You accomplish it by clicking the small plus icon in the lower-right corner of the text frame and then click another text frame. This small plus icon in the lower right of the text frame is contained within the out port and the similar icon on the upper left of the second text frame is called the in port. The out port turns red when some overflowing text exists in the text frame.

STEPS: Threading Text Across Multiple Text Frames

1. **Create a text frame.** Text frames hold text. To create a text frame, click the Type tool and drag in the layout where you want the frames to be located, as shown in Figure 2.24.

The Type tool creates a text frame.

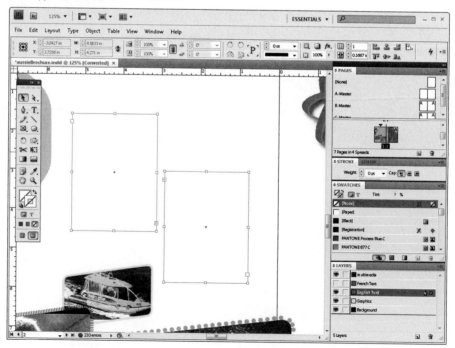

2. **Add text to the text frame.** With the text cursor blinking in the text frame, type the text into the first text frame. (Or you can select the text that you want to paste from another application like a Word Processor and copy it to the Clipboard. Then, within InDesign, choose Edit ➪ Paste.) The text appears, as shown in Figure 2.25, using the font and size specified in the Type menu. Notice how all the text doesn't fit in the first text frame so the out port is colored red.

FIGURE 2.25

You can add text to a text frame by copying and pasting.

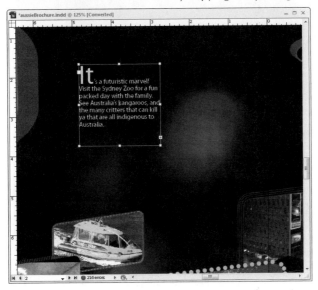

3. **Click the red out port for the first text frame.** Then click the second text frame, and the text spills over into the second text frame. Click the out port for the second text frame, and link it to the third text frame until all five text frames are linked, as shown in Figure 2.26.

4. **Save the file.** Choose File ➪ Save to save the layout.

FIGURE 2.26

Text runs from text frame to text frame naturally when frames are threaded.

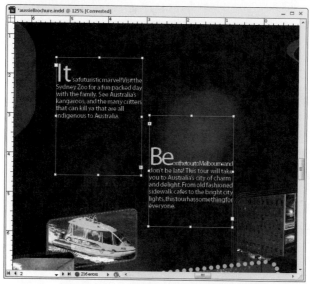

Preparing a Layout for Print

When the document layout is complete, InDesign includes some useful features that are helpful as you prepare the document to be printed such as previewing separations and exporting the document as a PDF file.

 **See Part IX for more on printing using the Creative Suite applications.**

Previewing separations

When InDesign documents are printed, they are split into four different passes called separations, one for each color representing Cyan, Magenta, Yellow, and Black (CMYK). These separations are then combined or *overlaid* to create the finished print. Often, previewing a document's separations prior to printing can help identify potential problems, allowing you to fix these problems before a costly print run. Separations for the current document may be viewed using the Separations Preview palette.

STEPS: Previewing Separations

1. **Open the Separations Preview palette.** To open the Separations Preview palette, shown in Figure 2.27, choose Window ➪ Output ➪ Separations Preview. Select the Separations option in the View field to see a list of the separations.

FIGURE 2.27

The Separations Preview lists a document's separations.

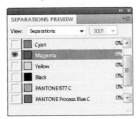

2. **View a separation.** To see a separation in the layout, click the separation's name and all separations except for the one you click are hidden, and the document is updated to show only the selected separation, as shown in Figure 2.28.

FIGURE 2.28

The Visibility icons let you select which separations are displayed in the layout.

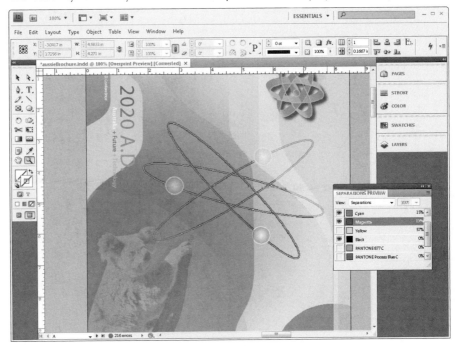

Exporting to PDF for printing

When exporting the layout to PDF, InDesign includes several export presets that you can use to configure the document for a specific destination. One of these presets is for print.

STEPS: Exporting to PDF

1. **Export to PDF using the Print preset.** Choose File ➪ Adobe PDF Presets ➪ High Quality Print. This opens a file dialog box where you can name the file to be exported. After you click Save, the Export Adobe PDF dialog box, shown in Figure 2.29, opens.

FIGURE 2.29

The Export Adobe PDF dialog box

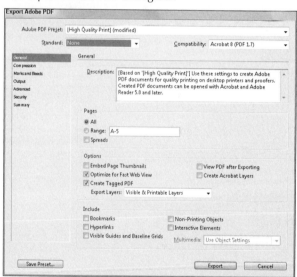

2. **Open the PDF within Acrobat.** In the General panel of the Export Adobe PDF dialog box, enable the View PDF after Exporting option to have the document open in Acrobat after it's exported. Then click Export.

Soft-Proofing in Adobe Acrobat

After a print file is exported to the PDF format, you can use Acrobat to soft-proof the print before it is sent to the print house. Acrobat 9 Pro includes some powerful print tools that can detect potential print errors before they occur. These print production tools are located in the Advanced ➪ Print Production menu.

Checking color in Acrobat

You use the Output Preview tool to check the colors within the current PDF document. Selecting this menu option opens the Output Preview dialog box, shown in Figure 2.30. This dialog box offers options to preview the color Separations and any Color Warnings caused by Overprinting and Rich Black.

FIGURE 2.30

The Output Preview dialog box lets you preview color separations and Color Warnings.

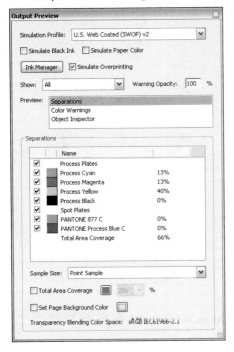

The Convert Colors tool is used to convert RGB, CMYK, and Grayscale color definitions to the target color space. It also lets you embed the color profile within the PDF document.

Flattening transparency

The Advanced ➪ Print Production ➪ Flattener Preview menu opens a Flattener Preview window, as shown in Figure 2.31, where you can quickly get a view of the transparent objects in the PDF file. You also can set the resolution for objects that get rasterized and view with updates the effect on the document objects.

FIGURE 2.31

The Flattener Preview dialog box lets you preview the effect of flattening transparent objects.

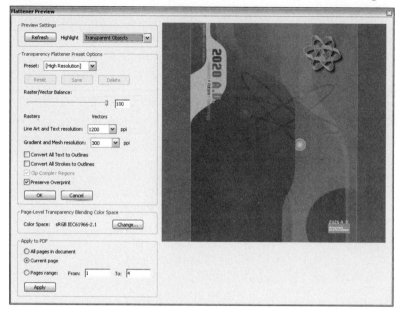

Creating a PDF/X file

Adobe is a contributor and supporter of several ISO defined standards for high-resolution print formats. The most aggressive format is the PDF/X format. In order for a document to meet this standard, it must pass a rigorous battery of tests. You can check a document for PDF/X compliance using the Preflight tool, which is accessed using the Advanced ➪ Print Production ➪ Preflight menu command. This command opens the Preflight dialog box, shown in Figure 2.32.

FIGURE 2.32

The Preflight dialog box is used to check the current document for PDF/X compatibility.

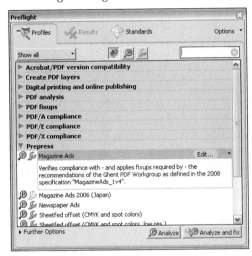

The Preflight dialog box lists the potential errors being checked. Clicking Execute tests the document and displays all noncompliant errors in the Results tab.

STEPS: Checking a PDF Document for Errors

1. **Open Adobe Acrobat.** Locate the exported InDesign PDF print document, and open it within Acrobat.

2. **View the Output Preview.** Choose Advanced ➪ Print Production ➪ Output Preview. This opens the Output Preview dialog box. In the Output Preview dialog box, enable the Show Overprinting option to view all overprinting in the current document, as shown in Figure 2.33. Close the Output Preview dialog box.

FIGURE 2.33

You can view Overprinting using the Output Preview tool.

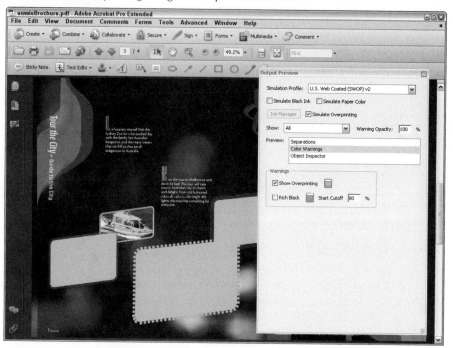

3. **Check the transparency flattening.** Choose Advanced ➪ Print Production ➪ Flattener Preview. This opens the Flattener Preview window. Drop the Raster/Vector Balance slider to 75, click Refresh, and select the Transparent Objects option from the top drop-down list. If the highlighted objects look fine, as shown in Figure 2.34, click Apply.

FIGURE 2.34

The Flattener Preview dialog box lets you see which objects are to be flattened.

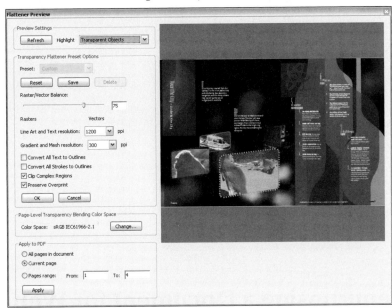

4.   Check the document against the PDF/X format. Choose Advanced ➪ Print Production ➪ Preflight to open the Preflight dialog box. Choose the profile you want to use such as PDF/X-1a (SWOP) and click Analyze and Fix to perform the error checking. The Results tab opens to display the errors with this file, as shown in Figure 2.35.

FIGURE 2.35

FIGURE 2.35

The Preflight dialog box checks for errors not compliant with the PDF/X format.

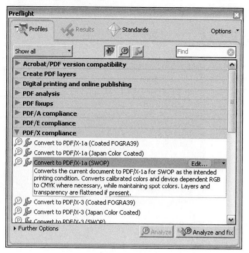

Repurposing a Document for Web Hosting

Completed print projects may be repurposed easily and used on the pages of a Web site. By doing this, you won't have to re-create designs specific to the Web. But Web pages require that the elements be optimized to reduce their file sizes.

Creative Suite 4 offers several ways to repurpose designs for delivery on the Web. Acrobat files may be posted online and viewed using an Acrobat Reader plug-in, but before posting existing PDF files, Acrobat's PDF Optimizer feature may be used to reduce the size of the PDF file.

In addition to PDF files, InDesign includes a feature that exports all content elements included in a layout into XHTML documents that can be opened within Dreamweaver where the elements may be reused in a Web page.

InDesign also can export designs to the Flash SWF file format or to the XFL format that can be imported within Flash.

Using PDF Optimizer

The PDF Optimizer interface in Acrobat includes many settings to downsample images, unembed fonts, and provide several cleanup options.

 **The PDF Optimizer is covered in Chapter 34.**

STEPS: Using the PDF Optimizer

1. **Open the PDF Optimizer.** With the file that you want to optimize open in Acrobat, choose Advanced ➪ PDF Optimizer. The PDF Optimizer interface, shown in Figure 2.36, includes multiple panes.

FIGURE 2.36

The PDF Optimizer interface

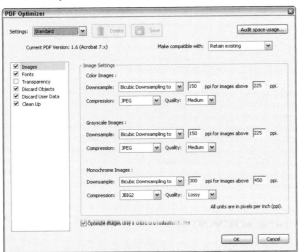

2. **Audit space usage.** Before changing any of the options, click Audit Space Usage at the top of the dialog box. Acrobat computes the size of all the various objects found in the PDF file and reports them in a Space Audit dialog box, shown in Figure 2.37.

51

3. **Configure image downsampling.** In the Images panel, select the Bicubic Downsampling option of 72 pixels/inch for all images above 72 pixels/inch. Then enable JPEG Compression with a Medium quality setting.

4. **Specify cleanup options.** Select the Clean Up panel, shown in Figure 2.38, and enable all the Remove and Discard options, making sure the Optimize the PDF for Fast Web View check box is enabled. Then click OK. In the file dialog box that opens, give the file a name and click OK.

FIGURE 2.37

The Audit Space Usage dialog box

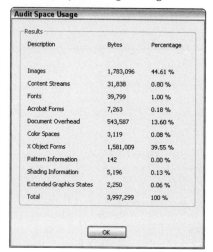

Exporting to Dreamweaver

InDesign documents may be exported and saved for use in Dreamweaver. This can make all images and objects in the design be downsampled and compressed and moved into a folder where Dreamweaver can reference them. How the images are optimized is customizable.

CROSS-REF   **More details on exporting content to Dreamweaver are covered in Chapter 26.**

The Clean Up panel of the PDF Optimizer dialog box

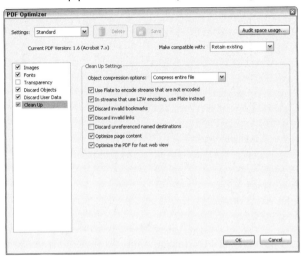

STEPS: Exporting an InDesign Layout for Dreamweaver and SWF

1. **Open an InDesign document.** Choose File ➪ Open, and locate the file that you want to export to XHTML.

2. **Select the Export command.** Choose File ➪ Export for Dreamweaver. This command opens a file dialog box where you can name the folder where the exported layout is placed.

3. **Set the Export options.** After a folder is selected, the XHTML Export Options dialog box, shown in Figure 2.39, appears. Using this dialog box, you can specify the look of the bullet and number lists and whether the entire document is exported or just the selection.

FIGURE 2.39

The XHTML Export Options dialog box

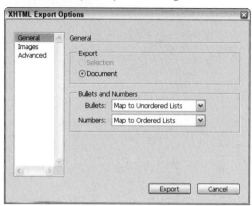

4. **Set the Image options.** Click the Images option in the left list to open the Images settings panel, shown in Figure 2.40. In this panel, you can specify how the layout's images get converted to the GIF or JPEG formats.

FIGURE 2.40

The Images settings in the XHTML Export Options dialog box

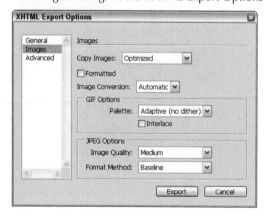

5. **View the exported file in Dreamweaver.** After you click the Export button, all the elements used in the layout are copied to the designated HTML file and all the converted images are copied to a subfolder. If you open the exported file in Dreamweaver, you can see the various images, text, and chart elements, as shown in Figure 2.41.

6. **Export to SWF.** To export to the SWF format, select the File ⇨ Export menu. In the file dialog box, select the SWF file format in the Save as Type drop-down list. The Export SWF dialog box, shown in Figure 2.42 appears. After selecting the settings, click Ok.

FIGURE 2.41

After the exported InDesign file is opened in Dreamweaver, you can check how effective the export was.

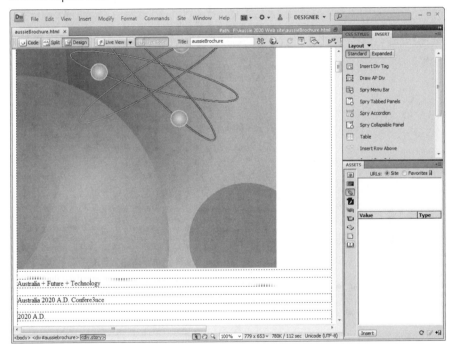

7. **View the exported SWF file in a Web browser**. Once the design is exported to the SWF file, you can open the HTML file to see the resulting file in a Web browser, as shown in Figure 2.43.

FIGURE 2.42

The Export SWF dialog box includes settings for scaling the pages.

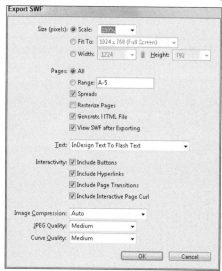

Enhancing Web pages with Flash

To add visual impact to your exported Web pages, you can use Flash to add movies and interactive elements. Flash can produce SWF files that are placed on a Web page. These SWF files require the Flash player be installed in the Web browser to view the Flash elements, but adding the Flash player is a simple installation and a common element for most browsers.

 Flash is an extensive product and coverage of Flash within this book is limited, but you can find the basics of using Flash in Chapter 23.

After the exported SWF file is opened in a Web browser, you can check how effective the export was.

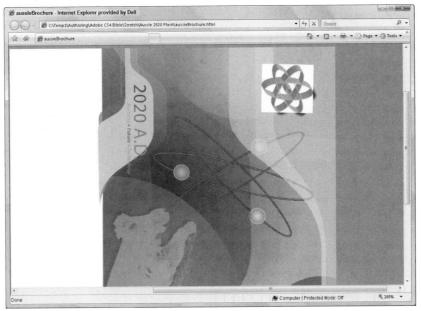

STEPS: Adding an animated item to a Web page

1. **Open Flash and load content.** With Flash open, choose File ➪ Import ➪ Import to Stage to load the kangaroo logo. All the pieces of the AI file are loaded into Flash. An Import settings dialog box lets you decide which items to import.

2. **Move the logo to its initial location.** With the Selection tool, drag the logo to its initial position.

3. **Create a motion tween.** Right-click the kangaroo logo and select the Create Motion Tween option. A dialog box appears asking if you want to convert this item to a symbol. Click Ok to continue. Flash creates the necessary keys and the motion tween.

4. **Position the logo's end location.** Drag the logo with the Selection tool to its ending location. Drag the red frame marker to see the logo move between these two positions.

5. **Enable onion skinning.** Click the Onion Skin button at the bottom of the Timeline panel to see the intermediate positions of the logo, as shown in Figure 2.44.

6. **Publish the resulting animation.** When the final animation looks fine, save the file as an FLA file so you can work on it again in the future. Then select File ➪ Publish Settings to open the Publish Settings dialog box. In the Formats tab, enable the Flash and HTML check boxes. In the HTML tab, disable the Loop option and click the Publish button. The files are saved to the hard drive where the HTML file can be loaded into a Web browser to see the resulting animation.

FIGURE 2.44

The animation controls in Flash are set using the Timeline palette.

Summary

- Sketched ideas may be scanned directly into Acrobat and saved as PDF files.

- PDF files may be submitted to reviewers by using e-mail. Reviewers can use Acrobat to enter comments into the PDF file, and those comments are returned to the original sender.

- Photoshop is useful for editing images including adjusting image properties, cropping, extracting, and editing images.

- Illustrator objects also are useful for enhancing a design. Using Illustrator's features such as Live Trace, fills, strokes, effects, and 3-D extruding, many interesting objects may be created.

- Adobe Bridge provides direct access to project assets including thumbnails.

- Content from multiple sources may be compiled and laid out in InDesign in preparation for printing and exporting.

- InDesign's Master pages let you place common elements that appear on multiple pages.

- Acrobat's print production tools are useful for soft-proofing documents.

- Using the PDF Optimizer found in Acrobat, complex PDF files may be significantly reduced in size.

- InDesign files may be exported for use in Dreamweaver making it possible to repurpose layouts for use on the Web.

- Flash is used to add animated and interactive elements to Web pages.

Chapter 3

Understanding User Interfaces

Working with several programs developed by a single software manufacturer has great advantages: The programs support a common user interface, and access to tools, menus, panels, and preferences is handled similarly among the programs. Even if you've never used a particular program in the Creative Suite, you can explore a program that's new to you with an intuitive sense of knowing how to perform one function or another based on your experiences with other CS4 applications. The common user interface, knowing where to look for tools and commands to execute actions, and familiarity with the methods help shorten your learning curve.

Each of the Creative Suite programs obviously has unique features, but many aspects are exactly the same from one program to the next. In some cases, you can customize a program to suit your individual needs or a standard implemented for your workgroup. In this chapter, we cover tools, menus, commands, and customizing options to bring the programs close together.

IN THIS CHAPTER

Understanding tools

Working with panels and workspaces

Identifying common user-interface features

Using keyboard shortcuts

Accessing Tools

Certainly, anyone who opens one of the Creative Suite 4 applications is aware of how to use tools nested in the Tools panels. Illustrator, Photoshop, InDesign, Fireworks, and Flash have many tools in common. Dreamweaver and Acrobat have fewer tools in common with these three programs, and Adobe Bridge has its own set of unique tools.

Figures 3.1, 3.2, 3.3, 3.4 and 3.5 show the Toolboxes from Illustrator, Photoshop, InDesign, Flash, and Fireworks respectively. Notice that the keyboard shortcuts used to access the tools are common in most cases among the programs (for example, the shortcut you use to select the Pen tool in Photoshop is the same shortcut you use to select the Pen tool in InDesign). The character in parentheses is used to select a tool in the Toolbox.

TIP The small set of arrows at the top-left corner of the Toolbox is used to toggle the Toolbox between single-width and double-width size.

FIGURE 3.1

Adobe Illustrator Toolbox

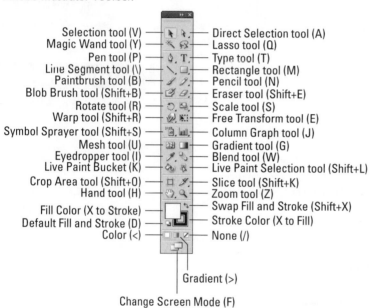

Selection tool (V) — Direct Selection tool (A)
Magic Wand tool (Y) — Lasso tool (Q)
Pen tool (P) — Type tool (T)
Line Segment tool (\) — Rectangle tool (M)
Paintbrush tool (B) — Pencil tool (N)
Blob Brush tool (Shift+B) — Eraser tool (Shift+E)
Rotate tool (R) — Scale tool (S)
Warp tool (Shift+R) — Free Transform tool (E)
Symbol Sprayer tool (Shift+S) — Column Graph tool (J)
Mesh tool (U) — Gradient tool (G)
Eyedropper tool (I) — Blend tool (W)
Live Paint Bucket (K) — Live Paint Selection tool (Shift+L)
Crop Area tool (Shift+O) — Slice tool (Shift+K)
Hand tool (H) — Zoom tool (Z)
Fill Color (X to Stroke) — Swap Fill and Stroke (Shift+X)
Default Fill and Stroke (D) — Stroke Color (X to Fill)
Color (<) — None (/)

Gradient (>)
Change Screen Mode (F)

FIGURE 3.2

Adobe Photoshop Toolbox

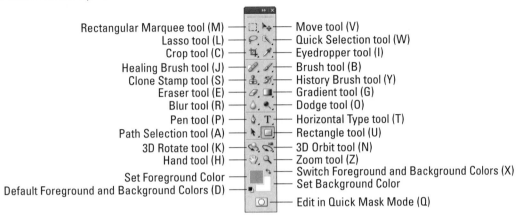

Rectangular Marquee tool (M) — Move tool (V)
Lasso tool (L) — Quick Selection tool (W)
Crop tool (C) — Eyedropper tool (I)
Healing Brush tool (J) — Brush tool (B)
Clone Stamp tool (S) — History Brush tool (Y)
Eraser tool (E) — Gradient tool (G)
Blur tool (R) — Dodge tool (O)
Pen tool (P) — Horizontal Type tool (T)
Path Selection tool (A) — Rectangle tool (U)
3D Rotate tool (K) — 3D Orbit tool (N)
Hand tool (H) — Zoom tool (Z)
Set Foreground Color — Switch Foreground and Background Colors (X)
Set Background Color
Default Foreground and Background Colors (D) —
Edit in Quick Mask Mode (Q)

FIGURE 3.3

Adobe InDesign Toolbox

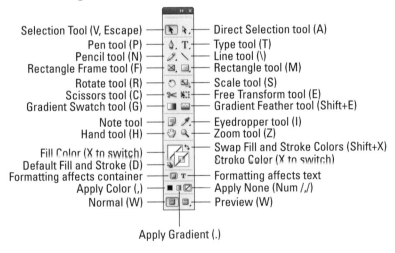

Selection Tool (V, Escape) — Direct Selection tool (A)
Pen tool (P) — Type tool (T)
Pencil tool (N) — Line tool (\)
Rectangle Frame tool (F) — Rectangle tool (M)
Rotate tool (R) — Scale tool (S)
Scissors tool (C) — Free Transform tool (E)
Gradient Swatch tool (G) — Gradient Feather tool (Shift+E)
Note tool — Eyedropper tool (I)
Hand tool (H) — Zoom tool (Z)
Fill Color (X to switch) — Swap Fill and Stroke Colors (Shift+X)
Default Fill and Stroke (D) — Stroke Color (X to switch)
Formatting affects container — Formatting affects text
Apply Color (,) — Apply None (Num /,/)
Normal (W) — Preview (W)
Apply Gradient (.)

FIGURE 3.4

Adobe Flash Toolbox

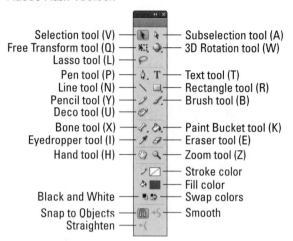

Selection tool (V) — Subselection tool (A)
Free Transform tool (Q) — 3D Rotation tool (W)
Lasso tool (L)
Pen tool (P) — Text tool (T)
Line tool (N) — Rectangle tool (R)
Pencil tool (Y) — Brush tool (B)
Deco tool (U)
Bone tool (X) — Paint Bucket tool (K)
Eyedropper tool (I) — Eraser tool (E)
Hand tool (H) — Zoom tool (Z)
— Stroke color
— Fill color
Black and White — Swap colors
Snap to Objects — Smooth
Straighten

FIGURE 3.5

Adobe Fireworks Toolbox

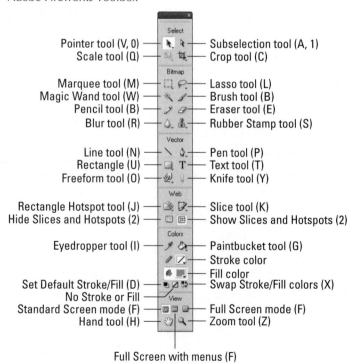

Pointer tool (V, 0) — Subselection tool (A, 1)
Scale tool (Q) — Crop tool (C)
Marquee tool (M) — Lasso tool (L)
Magic Wand tool (W) — Brush tool (B)
Pencil tool (B) — Eraser tool (E)
Blur tool (R) — Rubber Stamp tool (S)
Line tool (N) — Pen tool (P)
Rectangle (U) — Text tool (T)
Freeform tool (O) — Knife tool (Y)
Rectangle Hotspot tool (J) — Slice tool (K)
Hide Slices and Hotspots (2) — Show Slices and Hotspots (2)
Eyedropper tool (I) — Paintbucket tool (G)
— Stroke color
— Fill color
Set Default Stroke/Fill (D) — Swap Stroke/Fill colors (X)
No Stroke or Fill
Standard Screen mode (F) — Full Screen mode (F)
Hand tool (H) — Zoom tool (Z)
Full Screen with menus (F)

Although the interface for Dreamweaver matches most of the style of the other Adobe applications, it doesn't have a Toolbox.

Common tools for Illustrator, InDesign, Photoshop, and Flash

The tools common to Illustrator, Photoshop, InDesign, and Flash include the following:

- **Selection tool (V):** Notice that the Move tool in Photoshop behaves like the Selection tool used in the other programs. The Move tool in Photoshop uses the same keyboard shortcut (V). Additionally, Photoshop has a Path Selection tool used for selecting vector objects. The Path Selection tool works similarly to the Selection tools in Illustrator and InDesign. In InDesign, you use the Selection tool to move objects and to crop object and type frames.

- **Direct Selection tool (A):** The Direct Selection tool is used to reshape objects. In Photoshop, you access the Direct Selection tool by clicking the Selection tool and holding down the mouse button. A pop-up toolbar opens from which you can select the Direct Selection tool. In Flash, this is called the Subselection tool.

   When you click an object with the Direct Selection tool, the anchor points are shown deselected. Clicking a single anchor point or a path segment moves just that point or segment, thereby reshaping the object. In all programs, you reshape paths using the Direct Selection tool. In InDesign, you also use the Direct Selection tool to move objects around a placeholder frame, select the content to clear it from the frame, or manipulate elements of a group without ungrouping.

- **Pen tool (P):** The familiar Pen tool that originated in Adobe Illustrator is found in Photoshop and InDesign alike. The Pen tool is used to draw freeform paths in all the programs.

NOTE Because Flash and Fireworks have existing users, it has a couple of tools that didn't initially correspond to the keyboard shortcuts in the other Adobe product, so some tools, such as the Pen tool, have several shortcuts that do the same thing.

- **Type tool (T):** As the name implies, the Type tool is used for typing text. In each program, you find additional options for the Type tool (except in Flash) by holding down the mouse button on the Type tool and selecting other type tools from the pop-up toolbars.

- **Line/Line Segment tool (\ in Illustrator and InDesign; U in Photoshop; N in Flash):** Drawing straight lines is handled with the Line tool (Photoshop, InDesign, and Flash) or Line Segment tool (Illustrator). In Photoshop, you access the Line tool by clicking the Rectangle tool and opening the pop-up toolbar, or by pressing Shift+U several times until the Line tool appears in the Toolbox.

- **Rectangle tool (M in Illustrator and InDesign; U in Photoshop; R or O in Flash):** The Rectangle tool appears at the top level in the Toolbox. In each program, click and hold down the mouse button to open a pop-up toolbar where you can select other tools like the Ellipse tool, Polygon tools, and other special vector-shape tools. In Photoshop, the objects you draw with these tools remain vector shapes until they are *rasterized* (the process of converting vector objects to raster images). In InDesign, the tools are used for artwork where you apply fills and strokes; however, the shapes can take the same form as the Frame tools and act as containers for text and placed graphics.

CROSS-REF For more information on rasterizing objects, see Part 3.

- **Pencil tool (N in Illustrator and InDesign; B in Photoshop; Y in Flash):** Use the Pencil tool for freeform drawing, much like you would use a pencil for an analog drawing.

- **Eyedropper tool (I):** The Eyedropper tool is used most often for color sampling in all three programs. In Adobe Bridge, you use this tool to work in the Camera Raw settings dialog box. In InDesign, the use broadens to sample certain styles such as type formatting.

- **Gradient tool (G):** Use the Gradient tool for drawing linear and radial gradients applied to shapes and selections.

- **Hand tool (H):** The Hand tool is used to move a document page around the monitor window.

- **Zoom tool (Z):** Click with the Zoom tool to zoom in on a document page. Press the Option/Alt key with the Zoom tool selected, and click to zoom out of the document page.

- **Fill/Stroke or Foreground/Background Color (D, X):** Press D to return colors to default values. Press X to switch between Foreground/Background and Stroke/Fill. In Illustrator, InDesign, and Flash, the tools are used for assigning strokes and fills to objects. In Photoshop, the colors are used for foreground and background colors. A change of color from the Colors panel, the color wheel, or the Swatches panel is reflected in the tools in the Toolbox.

NOTE The D and X shortcuts don't work this way in Flash.

Common tools for Illustrator and InDesign

Tools that are common to InDesign and Illustrator but that don't appear in the Photoshop Toolbox include the following:

- **Rotate tool (R):** Rotate objects by selecting and dragging or by supplying numeric values in a dialog box.

- **Scale tool (S):** Scale objects by selecting and dragging or by supplying numeric values in a dialog box.

- **Shear tool (O in InDesign; no equivalent in Illustrator):** Shear objects by dragging with the tool or entering numeric values in a dialog box. In Illustrator, the tool is accessed by holding down the mouse on the Scale tool and selecting the Shear tool from the pop-up toolbar.

- **Free Transform tool (E):** Transform objects (scaling, rotating, distorting) by clicking and dragging a selected object. Flash also has a Free Transform tool.

- **Scissors tool (C):** Use the Scissors tool to cut a path drawn with the geometric tools or the Pen tool.

Common tools for Illustrator, Photoshop, and Flash

Tools common to Illustrator and Photoshop but not found in InDesign include the following:

- **Lasso tool (L in Photoshop and Flash; Q in Illustrator):** Use the Lasso tool to select pixels in Photoshop and objects in Illustrator. The Lasso tool also is found in Flash.

- **Magic Wand tool (W):** In Photoshop, use this tool to select colors of common color values within a user-specified tolerance range. In Illustrator, use it to select objects of common color values.

- **Slice tool (K):** Use the Slice tool for slicing images/objects for Web hosting.

In addition to tools common to the programs, each application has a few unique tools. Photoshop has various tools for changing brightness values along with a Note tool (also found in Acrobat), cloning tools, and the History Brush tool. The Blend tool, Mesh tool, Graph tools, Warp tools, and Symbol Sprayer tools are unique to Illustrator. In InDesign, you find a Button tool similar to the Button Form Field tool in Acrobat. Flash has an Ink Bottle tool and InDesign has a Notes tool.

Adobe Bridge tools

Adobe Bridge has a few tools located in the Bridge window. Most actions you perform in Bridge are handled with menu commands. As an application, you don't edit documents using tools. The edits made from within Bridge are generally applied to an entire document or to initiating an edit that ultimately takes place in one of the other CS programs.

 **For a detailed description of Bridge tools, see Chapter 6.**

Acrobat tools

Because the tools in Acrobat are so different from the tools in Illustrator, InDesign, and Photoshop, it makes more sense to list them apart from the other programs. Acrobat is a program that serves many different business professionals, and some of the tools you find in Acrobat may not be used in your work as a creative professional. The more common tools used in Acrobat by creative professionals include:

- **Comment & Markup tools:** Shown in Figure 3.6, the Comment & Markup tools are used for adding comments to PDF files and participating in review sessions.

FIGURE 3.6

Comment & Markup tools

■ **Print Production tools:** Commercial printers use the Print Production tools, shown in Figure 3.7, to preview, prepare, and print PDF documents that are intended to print on commercial printing devices.

FIGURE 3.7

Print Production tools

CROSS-REF For information on using the Commenting & Drawing Markups tools, see Chapter 36. For information on using the Print Production tools, see Chapter 40.

Tools in Acrobat appear in separate toolbars. Unlike the other CS programs, the default position for the toolbars is horizontal across the top of the Acrobat window. Individual toolbars are docked in the Toolbar Well. You can open toolbars and dock them in the Toolbar Well, or remove them from the Toolbar Well and place them anywhere in the Acrobat window as floating toolbars. Access toolbars by choosing View ⇨ Toolbars and choosing the toolbar you want to see, or by opening a context menu on the Toolbar Well and selecting a toolbar to open as a floating toolbar. After a toolbar is opened in the Acrobat window, the toolbar can be docked in the Toolbar Well by dragging it to the Toolbar Well or selecting Dock All Toolbars from a context menu.

Dreamweaver tools

Dreamweaver CS4 doesn't have a standard Toolbox. Instead, positioned along the top edge of the window is a set of tabs. These tabs run horizontally along the top of the toolbar, and the available tools change depending on which tab is selected. What looks like a Toolbox in Dreamweaver CS4 is actually called the Insert panel, shown in Figure 3.8. Because much of the page building in Dreamweaver is done via drag and drop, you don't use all the tools in the same manner as tools you find in the other CS4 programs.

FIGURE 3.8

Click the Common tools group in the top-left corner of the Toolbox, and the tools change in the lower half of the Toolbox to tools used in laying out a Web page.

CROSS-REF For information on using tools in Dreamweaver, see Chapter 33.

Fireworks tools

Most of the Fireworks tools work exactly the same as their Illustrator counterparts. The Toolbar is segmented into different groups of tools, each identified by a label. Fireworks lets you work with vector and bitmap tools side-by-side.

Accessing Tool Options

In Illustrator and InDesign, you have some option choices for certain tools that are controlled in accompanying dialog boxes. Not all tools have associated dialog boxes, so you need to either poke around or become familiar with tools offering these extended option choices. In Illustrator or InDesign, double-click the mouse button on tools in the Toolbox, and you'll see a dialog box similar to the one shown in Figure 3.9 for tools supporting further options in dialog boxes.

Double-clicking one of the Symbol tools in the Illustrator Toolbox opens the Symbolism Tools Options dialog box.

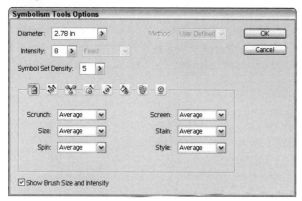

Illustrator tool options

Most often, double-clicking a tool opens an options dialog box typically not accessible other than by double-clicking a given tool. In some cases, double-clicking a tool opens a panel, a dialog box accessible through other commands, or a preference setting. Here's what happens when you double-click tools in Illustrator:

- **Selection tools:** You need to have an object selected in the document window in order to open a dialog box when clicking either the Selection tool or the Direct Selection tool. When an object is selected and you double-click either tool, the Move dialog box shown in Figure 3.10 appears. You have options for moving objects and patterns at fixed distances. Like all dialog boxes that have a Preview check box, check the box and the view is rendered dynamically as you work in the dialog box.

- **Segment tools:** A dialog box respective to the selected tool opens where you can make choices about options. You also can access the same dialog box by selecting a tool and clicking the document page. The Segment tools include the Line Segment tool, the Arc Segment tool, the Spiral tool, the Rectangular Grid tool, and the Polar Grid tool. As shown in Figures 3.11 and 3.12, double-clicking different tools opens dialog boxes respective to the tool options.

FIGURE 3.10

Double-click on an object using the Selection tool or the Direct Selection tool to open the Move dialog box.

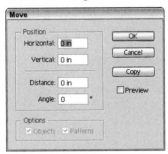

FIGURE 3.11

Double-click the Line Segment tool, and options associated with line segments are available in the Line Segment Tool Options dialog box.

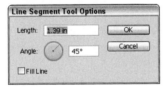

FIGURE 3.12

Double-click another Segment tool, and options respective to that tool appear in another dialog box. In this example, the Polar Grid tool was double-clicked.

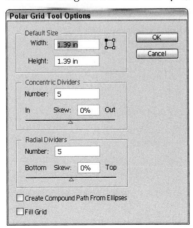

- **Shape tools:** The only tool in this group that opens a dialog box when you double-click the tool is the Flare tool. The Flare Tool Options dialog box is shown in Figure 3.13.

FIGURE 3.13

Double-click the Flare tool to open a dialog box.

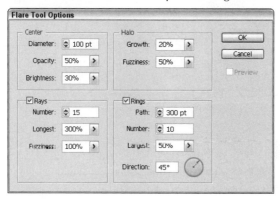

- **Paintbrush tool:** Doubling-click the tool opens the Paintbrush Tool Preferences dialog box, shown in Figure 3.14.

FIGURE 3.14

Double-click the Paintbrush tool, and the Paintbrush Tool Preferences dialog box opens.

- **Pencil tool/Smooth tool:** Although the toolbar for the Pencil tool contains three tools (Pencil, Smooth, and Erase), only the Pencil tool and the Smooth tool use a dialog box where you can make options choices. Double-click either tool, and a dialog box opens specific to the options for the selected tool. Figure 3.15 shows options choices for the Pencil tool.

FIGURE 3.15

Double-click the Pencil tool, and the Pencil Tool Preferences dialog box appears.

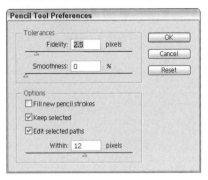

- **Blob Brush tool:** The Blob Brush Tool Options dialog box, shown in Figure 3.16, includes settings for controlling the Fidelity and the Smoothness of the paths drawn with this tool. It also includes settings for controlling the size, angle, and roundness of the brush.

FIGURE 3.16

Double-click the Blob Brush tool, and its options dialog box appears.

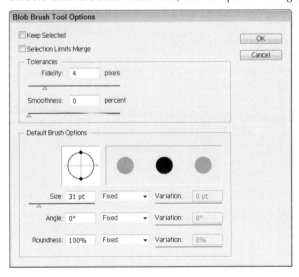

■ **Eraser/Scissors/Knife tools:** The Eraser tool lets you remove portions of an object just as you would erase the pixels in Photoshop. Using the Eraser Tool Options dialog box, shown in Figure 3.17, you can set the Angle, Roundness, and Diameter of the eraser tool. The Scissors tool is used to cut a path at a specified point, and the Knife tool can cut through an entire object dividing it in two.

FIGURE 3.17

The Eraser Tool Options dialog box lets you change the shape of the eraser tool.

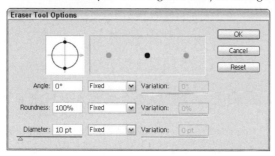

■ **Rotate/Reflect tools:** Double-clicking either tool opens a dialog box with options specific to the selected tool. In Figure 3.18, the Rotate dialog box appears when you click the Rotate tool.

FIGURE 3.18

Double-click the Rotate tool to open the Rotate dialog box.

■ **Scale/Shear/Reshape tools:** The Scale and Shear tools use dialog boxes for options settings. Note that double-clicking the Reshape tool does not open a dialog box; no options are available for this tool. Double-click either of the two other tools, and the options respective to that tool appear in a dialog box. Figure 3.19 shows the result of double-clicking the Scale tool.

Double-click either the Scale or Shear tool to open a dialog box where you can make options choices.

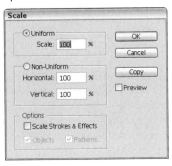

■ **Warp tools:** The Warp tools include the Warp tool, the Twirl tool, the Pucker tool, the Bloat tool, the Scallop tool, the Crystallize tool, and the Wrinkle tool. Selecting a different tool and double-clicking the selected tool opens a dialog box with options associated with that tool. In Figure 3.20, the Wrinkle tool options are shown.

Double-click the Wrinkle tool, and the Wrinkle Tool Options dialog box appears.

■ **Symbolism tools:** The Symbolism tools—Symbol Sprayer, Symbol Shifter, Symbol Scruncher, Symbol Sizer, Symbol Spinner, Symbol Stainer, Symbol Screener, and Symbol Styler—have one advantage over other tools with respect to selecting tools and adjusting attributes: As was shown earlier in Figure 3.8, you can select any of the eight Symbolism tools directly in the Symbolism Tool Options dialog box. Therefore, you don't need to leave the dialog box, select another tool, and then reopen the dialog box to make adjustments respective to the selected tool. Double-clicking any of the Symbolism tools offers you options for selecting different tools and making options choices for a selected tool.

■ **Graph tools:** The Graph tools include the Column Graph tool, the Stacked Column Graph tool, the Bar Graph tool, the Stacked Bar Graph tool, the Line Graph tool, the Area Graph tool, the Scatter Graph tool, the Pie Graph tool, and the Radar Graph tool. Double-clicking any tool in this group opens the Graph Type dialog box, shown in Figure 3.21. Like the Symbol tools, among the Graph tools options is the ability to select the tools in the Graph Type dialog box and make attribute changes for any one of the tools in the same dialog box. Double-click any tool, and you can make settings choices for the respective tool.

FIGURE 3.21

Double-click any one of the Graph tools, and you can change the options settings for that tool.

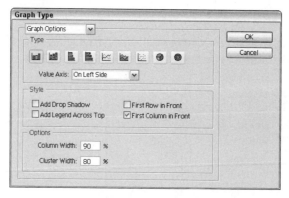

■ **Mesh tool:** The Mesh tool lets you create a gradient mesh that conforms to the shape of the selected object.

■ **Gradient tool:** The Gradient tool is used to create gradients using different stops, colors, and shapes.

■ **Eyedropper/Measure tools:** The Eyedropper tool is used to assess color values. When you double-click the tool, the Eyedropper Options dialog box opens, as shown in Figure 3.22. The second tool in the toolbar is the Measure tool used for measuring distances. If you double-click the Measure tool, the Preferences dialog box opens, which allows you to change Guide and Grid colors.

FIGURE 3.22

Double-click the Eyedropper tool to open the Eyedropper Options dialog box.

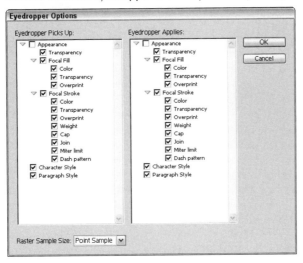

■ **Blend tool:** Double-click the Blend tool to open the Blend Options dialog box, shown in Figure 3.23. Notice that you also can open the same dialog box by clicking the Blend tool on one option and then pressing the Option/Alt key when clicking the second object to be included in the blend.

FIGURE 3.23

Double-click the Blend tool, and the Blend Options dialog box appears.

■ **Live Paint Bucket/Live Paint Selection tools:** The Paint Bucket tool has been replaced with the Live Paint Bucket tool. Additionally you find the Live Paint Selection tool. You use the Live Paint Bucket tool to apply a color, pattern, or gradient to a live paint group. You select multiple objects and click with the Live Paint Bucket tool to create a Live Paint Group. The Live Paint Selection tool can select edges of a Live Paint Group that can be painted with the Live Paint Bucket tool. It allows you to select zones to copy and paste as independent vector elements. Double-click either tool, and the same set of options appears for changing paint fills, paint strokes, and highlight colors, as shown in Figure 3.24.

FIGURE 3.24

Double-clicking the Live Paint Bucket tool brings up a set of options.

- **Artboard/Slice/Slice Selection tools:** The Artboard tool lets you set all the details for the artboard including its size and position. It is also used to create crop marks by accurately defining a crop area by dragging in the document. Double-clicking the Artboard tool opens the Artboard Options dialog box, shown in Figure 3.25. The Slice tool divides an image into several separate pieces that can be used on a Web page, and the Slice Selection tool lets you select the individual slices.

FIGURE 3.25

The Artboard Options dialog box lets you specify exact crop area dimensions.

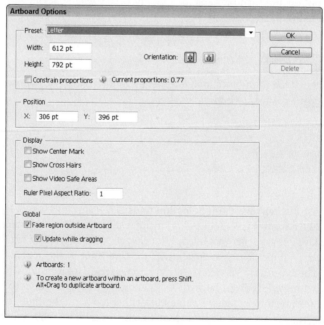

- **Hand tool:** Double-clicking the Hand tool sets the page view to a fit-in-window view. This view also is acquired in all CS applications by pressing ⌘/Ctrl+0 (zero). The Page tool provides a way to reposition the printable area. Double-click the Page tool to align the printable area with the artboard.

- **Zoom tool:** Double-click the Zoom tool to show the document window in an actual-size view (100 percent view).

- **Fill/Stroke tools:** Clicking the Fill or Stroke tool opens the system Color Picker, shown in Figure 3.26.

FIGURE 3.26

Double-click either the Fill or Stroke tool to open the Color Picker.

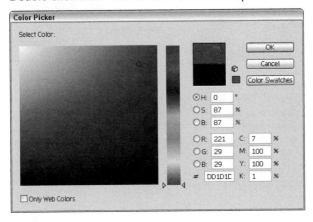

Photoshop tool options

In Photoshop, double-clicking tools produces an effect with the Hand tool and the Zoom tool only. Double-click the Hand tool, and you see the active document window zoomed to a Fit on Screen view. This view is similar to Fit Window view in other CS applications. Double-click the Zoom tool, and the window zooms to Actual Size view.

Remaining options for tools are addressed in Photoshop's Options bar. Click a tool, and the Options bar changes to reflect choices pertaining to the selected tool. In Figure 3.27, the Rectangular Marquee tool was selected.

FIGURE 3.27

When you click a tool in the Photoshop Toolbox, the Options bar changes options respective to the active tool.

InDesign tool options

InDesign is like a mixture of the UI (user interface) between Illustrator and Photoshop. In Illustrator, most tools have associated options dialog boxes accessed by double-clicking a tool in the Toolbox. Likewise, some of InDesign's tools also have similar options dialog boxes accessed the same way as in Illustrator. In Photoshop, tools don't have pop-up dialog boxes opened by double-clicking a tool; Photoshop uses an Options bar that changes options settings each time a different tool is accessed. Likewise, in InDesign, you have a Control panel where many options settings are made respective to the currently selected tool. Tools in InDesign that support dialog boxes for options settings include the following:

 **Accessing some dialog boxes when double-clicking a tool in the InDesign Toolbox requires you first to select an object in the document window.**

- **Selection/Direct Selection tools:** The same Move dialog box opens in InDesign as you find in Illustrator when double-clicking one of the Selection tools. Note that to open the Move dialog box, you select an object must be selected in the document window before you double-click either tool. Notice that the options for the Move dialog box are almost always the same in the various programs, but the items that can be moved do vary a little. In Illustrator, either Objects or Patterns are targeted for movement. In InDesign, the only option is to move the content of the selected object, as shown in Figure 3.28. If you use the Selection tool to select the object, the frame moves, and if you use the Direct Selection tool, the content of the frame moves.

FIGURE 3.28

InDesign's Move dialog box is almost identical to Adobe Illustrator's Move dialog box with the exception of the Options choices.

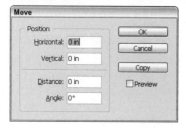

NOTE Within InDesign, if you use the move command with the frame selected, both the frame and the content move, but if you have only the content selected with the Direct Selection tool, the move command affects only the content.

■ **Pencil/Smooth tool:** The Pencil tool options are identical in Illustrator and InDesign. The Smooth tool options vary slightly between Illustrator and InDesign. InDesign supports an additional option for keeping objects selected, as shown in Figure 3.29.

FIGURE 3.29

InDesign's Pencil Tool Preferences dialog box offers similar options to those in Illustrator.

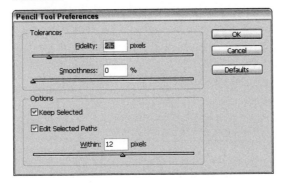

TIP Double-clicking the Line tool opens the Stroke panel.

■ **Polygon tool:** Double-click the Polygon tool to open the Polygon Settings dialog box, shown in Figure 3.30. A similar dialog box opens in Illustrator when you select the Polygon tool and click in the document window.

FIGURE 3.30

Double-click the Polygon tool to open the Polygon Settings dialog box.

■ **Eyedropper tool:** The Eyedropper tool in InDesign, as shown in Figure 3.31, can pick up colors and attributes.

FIGURE 3.31

Double-click the Eyedropper tool to open the Eyedropper Options dialog box.

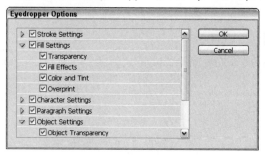

■ **Rotate tool:** The Rotate tool offers options settings in a dialog box similar to those found in Illustrator.

■ **Scale tool:** The Scale tool options are similar to those found in Illustrator.

■ **Shear tool:** Rounding out the last of the transformation tools, the Shear tool also has options choices similar to Illustrator.

TIP Within InDesign, double-click the Gradient tool to open the Gradient panel, double-click the Gradient Feather tool to open the Effects dialog box with the Gradient Feather settings displayed, and double-click the Measure tool to open the Info panel.

■ **Hand tool:** The same effect that you have in Illustrator takes place when you double-click the Hand tool in InDesign. A Fit Page view is the result of double-clicking the tool in the Toolbox.

■ **Zoom tool:** Likewise, double-clicking the Zoom tool is the same as in Illustrator, where an Actual Size view is displayed in the document window.

Flash tool options

The Flash tools work a little differently than the other CS4 apps. Within the Flash Toolbox, the bottom portion of the Toolbox (beneath the black/white, swap colors, and no color row of icons) is open to be filled with additional icons depending on the tool that is selected.

The Toolbox configuration shown in Figure 3.4 includes tools to Snap to Objects and Smooth and Straighten options. These icons are visible only when the Selection tool is enabled. However, when the Brush tool is selected, several different icons are displayed at the bottom of the Toolbox, as shown in Figure 3.32.

FIGURE 3.32

Several additional icons are displayed at the bottom of the Flash Toolbox when the Brush tool is selected.

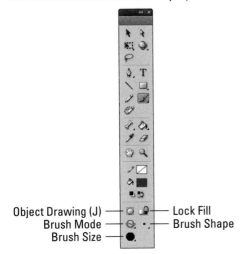

Object Drawing (J) —— Lock Fill
Brush Mode —— Brush Shape
Brush Size

Acrobat and Dreamweaver tool options

Acrobat, Fireworks, and Dreamweaver make use of extended tools. Neither program supports options settings in dialog boxes that open from double-clicking a tool. Options choices are contained in panels, preferences, and properties dialog boxes.

Using Panels and Workspaces

A common characteristic among all Adobe products is an extensive set of palettes. Palettes offer you options choices for various tool uses, menu commands, and extended features not available through the selection of a tool or menu command. For the most part, panels are accessed and used in all the CS programs similarly.

To open a panel, click the Window menu and select the panel you want to open. If a panel name appears with a check mark in the Window menu, the panel is already open. In Figure 3.33, you can see the Windows menu for Illustrator.

 Panels are typically listed alphabetically, but Flash, Fireworks, and Dreamweaver panels are divided into groups.

FIGURE 3.33

The Window menus for Illustrator

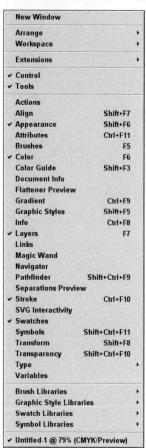

Acrobat also makes use of panels; however, accessing the panels is handled from a different menu. To open panels in Acrobat, choose View➪ Navigation Panels and choose the panel to open from the submenu, as shown in Figure 3.34.

FIGURE 3.34

Acrobat panels are accessed from a submenu by choosing View ⇨ Navigation Panels.

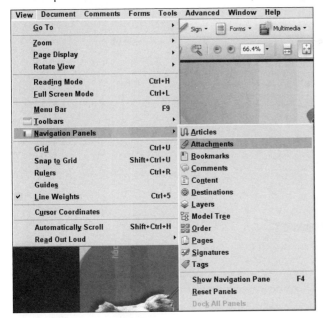

Managing panels

The extraordinary use of panels in all the CS applications requires you to spend a little time managing panels, showing only the panels you need for any given editing job. Opening all the panels at once in any program uses lots of screen space that you'll need to work on your documents. Fortunately, the programs have methods for docking panels in wells or beside the application window.

When a panel is docked to the edge of the window, a small double arrow appears in the upper-outside corner of the docked panel. Clicking this double arrow collapses the panels to a well located along the right edge of the interface (or to the left edge if that is where it was initially docked), as shown in Figure 3.35. Clicking again on the double arrows expands the panels out away from the edge to their full size.

FIGURE 3.35

Docked panels can be collapsed to the right edge.

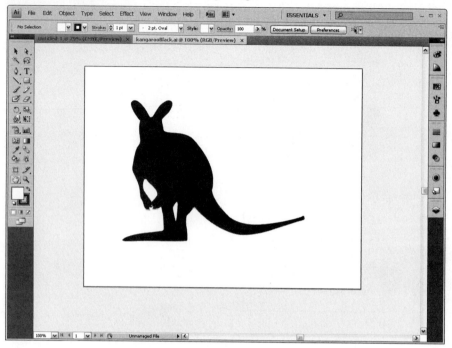

By dragging the gripper on the inside edge of the icon panel, you can change the width of the icon panels. This gives you control over how much space the docked panels take. In the General panel of the Preferences dialog box, the Auto-Collapse Icon Panels option causes any opened panels to be collapsed automatically as you begin to work.

Illustrator, Photoshop, InDesign, Fireworks, Dreamweaver, and Flash panels

Illustrator, Photoshop, InDesign, Fireworks, Dreamweaver, and Flash panels are all handled using the same methods, and the interface is fairly consistent between these applications. Panels are placed along the right side of the document window by default, as shown for Illustrator in Figure 3.36.

When you open a new panel by selecting the Window menu and then selecting a panel name that appears without a check mark, the panel opens in the application window. When opened, the panel may appear as a floating panel or in icon form. If it is grouped but not active, then the panel is opened. To move a panel in Illustrator, drag the panel by the title bar (the topmost horizontal bar running across the top of a panel) to any side of the application window. When you drag to the edge of the application window in any direction, the panel snaps into position. If you're dragging to the right side of the application window, the panel snaps to the right side but moves freely up and down.

FIGURE 3.36

Illustrator panels are positioned to any side of the application window.

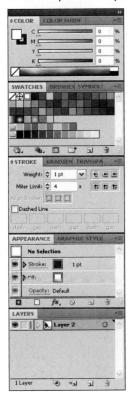

In each of these applications, by default, panels are docked along the right side of the application window, but they can be docked to either side of the screen. In the icon view method for managing panels, you can stack panels into several columns of icons, as shown for Photoshop in Figure 3.37.

FIGURE 3.37

Photoshop shows how several columns of icons can be lined up.

In Figure 3.38, InDesign panels are stashed on the right side of the screen.

FIGURE 3.38

Panels in InDesign are stashed to the right side of the application window.

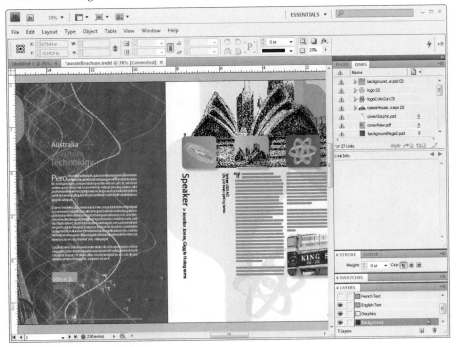

Acrobat panels

Acrobat uses a slightly different metaphor from the other CS applications. If you talk about panels in Acrobat, you also need to consider toolbars. Unlike the other CS programs, not all of Acrobat's tools are visible when you launch the program. Therefore, tools, as well as panels, need to be loaded in Acrobat for various editing tasks.

When you launch Acrobat, the default tool set appears at the top of the application window, as shown in Figure 3.39. These tool sets change as you load and hide individual toolbars. Individual tools are contained within toolbars that are docked in the Toolbar Well.

The default tools can be removed from the Toolbar Well at the top of the screen and hidden from view or used as a floating toolbar, or additional tools can be added to the Toolbar Well. To gain access to additional toolbars, choose View ⇨ Toolbars and select the toolbar you want to open from the submenu list. An easier method for accessing tools in Acrobat is to open a contextual menu. Ctrl-click (Mac) or right-click (Windows) on the Acrobat Toolbar Well to open a context menu.

FIGURE 3.39

A handful of tools appears docked in the Toolbar Well when you first launch Acrobat.

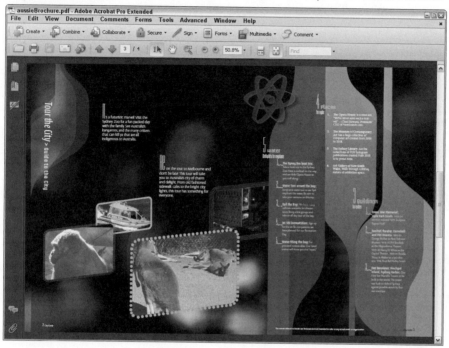

If you want to return the Toolbar Well view to defaults, open a context menu and select Reset Toolbars. Also, when toolbars appear as floating toolbars in the Document pane, you can easily dock the toolbars by selecting Dock All Toolbars from the same context menu.

NOTE   Acrobat's toolbars are undocked from the Toolbar Well by dragging the separator bar on the left side of the toolbar. Look for a vertical embossed line appearing to the left of some tools. Clicking and dragging on the separator bar is the only way to move toolbars around the Document pane.

In addition to toolbars, Acrobat also uses panels, as described for all the other CS applications. To open a panel, you need to access the Navigation Tabs submenu. When a panel is selected in the Navigation Tabs submenu, it opens as a free-floating panel, if it isn't already docked. Panels in Acrobat need to be docked in one specific place called the Navigation pane. Notice that panels in Acrobat are not docked on the left or right side of the application window, but rather within the Navigation pane that appears on the left side of the document window. To dock a panel in the Navigation pane, click any tab in the pane to expand the window. Click the tab in a floating panel, and drag it to the Navigation pane. The Comments & Attachments panels dock at a special place at the bottom of the Navigation pane.

TIP Panels also can be dropped in the Navigation pane without expanding the pane. Just drag a tab to the left of the vertical bar separating the tabs from the Document pane or on top of any tab in the closed pane.

Grouping panels

Panels can be nested in groups in all the CS applications. When using floating panels, you can group panels together; this give the appearance of a single panel with multiple tabs. Open any panel, and drag the tab from another open panel to the destination panel. When the cursor appears over the tab area in the target panel, release the mouse button and the target panel accepts the new addition. In Figure 3.40, you can see the Layers panel in InDesign being moved to a panel containing several tabs.

FIGURE 3.40

Panels are grouped together by dragging tabs from one panel to another.

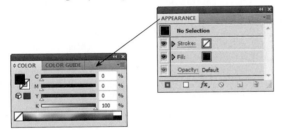

To ungroup a tab from a panel, click and drag the tab away from the panel. When you release the mouse button, the tab appears in its own panel.

Grouping panels also occurs at another level using the icon panels. To use the icon panels, drag a panel tab to a collapsed panel at one of the vertical edges of the application window. When the panel tab snaps into position, you can drag another panel tab to the grouped panel. Add as many tabs to a grouped panel as you like, but keep in mind they need to be grouped and ungrouped one panel at a time. In Figure 3.41, you can see several panels docked together in InDesign and another panel to be added to the group by dragging the tab to the grouped panels.

TIP Groups of panels can be iconized in a single move by holding down the Alt [Option] key when you drag a panel's tab to the side. This same trick works to drag an icon group away from the edge to turn it into a free-floating group of panels.

To add a panel to a group, click and drag the panel tab to the tab well in the docked panel group.

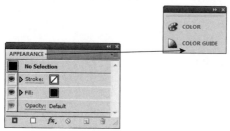

Panels also can be docked in a hierarchy in all CS programs except Acrobat. If you want panels in view without docking them on the sides of the application window, you can dock several panels together and move them around the application window as a grouped object. In any CS4 program except Acrobat, you can add a panel below another panel. Simply click a panel tab, and drag it to the base of the target panel. When the horizontal blue line appears at the base of the target panel, release the mouse button and drag one panel tab to the bottom of another panel, as shown in Figure 3.42. The left of this figure shows the panel as it is being docked, and the right shows the panels after being docked.

FIGURE 3.42

You can add a panel below another panel in any CS4 program, except Acrobat.

Be certain to drag a panel by the tab and move the cursor to the base of the target panel. When you see a horizontal blue line at the base of the target panel, release the mouse button and the panels are docked. When you drag the title bar on the top of the panel, both panels move together as a group. If you need to undock a panel, click the panel tab for the panel to be moved and drag it away from the group.

Saving workspaces

Panels offer you many options for addressing features and techniques available in the CS applications. They're essential program components, and you'll rarely edit without making use of options contained in at least one panel. Those panels you use most frequently are ones you'll want to keep open and have accessible every time you launch your program of choice.

Fortunately, all the CS4 applications remember the organization of your workspace each time you quit a program and relaunch it. If you rearrange panels and then quit the editing program, the next time you open the program, all the panel views are displayed according to the last view from that editing session.

In Acrobat, not only do all the panels in the Navigation pane keep their last position, but also all the toolbars keep their last position, exactly the same as the last Acrobat editing session. The same holds true for Illustrator, Photoshop, InDesign, Flash, Fireworks, and Dreamweaver with respect to panel positions. However, Illustrator, Photoshop, InDesign, Flash, Fireworks, and Dreamweaver have an additional benefit not found in Acrobat: options to save custom workspaces.

In workflow environments where computers may be shared, the ability to save workspaces is a true benefit. You can customize your work environment to suit your own personal choices for panel positions and save the panel views as your personal workspace. Notice that in Figure 3.43 the InDesign workspace includes several panels nested and docked along the right edge of the application window. To capture the position of the panels, choose Window ➪ Workspace ➪ Save Workspace. The Save Workspace dialog box opens, prompting you for a workspace name. Type a name for your workspace, and click Save. The new workspace is accessed in InDesign by choosing Window ➪ Workspace ➪ *workspace name* (where *workspace name* is the name you added). Each time you add a new workspace, the new workspace name is added to the Workspace submenu. Therefore, multiple users can save their own workspace preferences on the same computer.

Illustrator's, Photoshop's, Flash's and Dreamweaver's treatment in regard to saving workspaces is the same as you find with InDesign. The menu command is identical, and the same dialog box opens to prompt you for a workspace name.

Workspaces can also be selected from the application bar at the top of the interface. This provides a convenient way to quickly change between different workspaces.

The one thing to remember when adjusting workspaces is that all CS programs remember the last view you had before quitting the program. Therefore, if you save a workspace, then move panels out of their docked positions and rearrange them differently from the saved workspace, after quitting the program and relaunching it, the last view you created becomes the new default. To regain your workspace view, choose Window ➪ Workspace ➪ *workspace name* (where *workspace name* is the name you used when you saved the workspace). Some of the applications have a Reset Workspaces menu for resetting the workspace to its default.

FIGURE 3.43

To save a workspace in InDesign, first arrange your panels exactly as you want them to appear when you open the application.

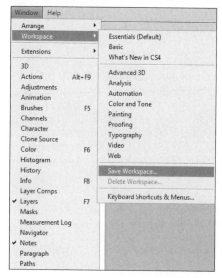

Some Common User-Interface Features

Tools, panels, and menus in the CS programs make for a common user interface where you can more easily discover new tools and editing techniques when learning a program. Some of the most advantageous of the common user-interface items in all CS programs include context menus and help documents.

Using context menus

If at any time you have difficulty finding a tool or menu command for a given task, first try to open a context menu. All CS applications use context menus, and the menu choices change according to the tool you select in the Toolbox or toolbar. Context menus are opened by right-clicking (Mac) or right-clicking (Windows). The context menu pops up at the cursor location, as shown in Adobe Bridge in Figure 3.44.

FIGURE 3.44

Ctrl-click (Mac) or right-click (Windows) to open a context menu.

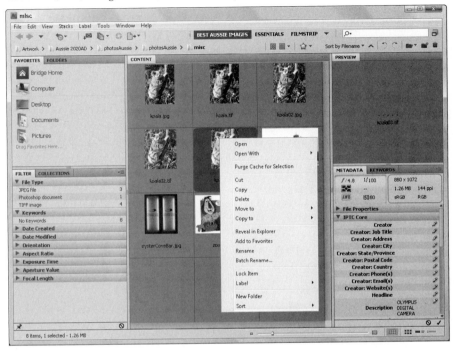

Context menus are not limited to document pages. You also can open context menus in some panels in Adobe Bridge, Photoshop, InDesign, Flash, Dreamweaver, and Acrobat. In Figure 3.45, you see a context menu opened in the Preview panel in Adobe Bridge.

TIP   As you work in the CS applications, try to get in the habit of opening a context menu when you want to edit an object, page, or function. The only way to determine whether a context menu offers a menu option is to poke around and try. As you become familiar with menu options, you'll begin to work much faster.

FIGURE 3.45

A context menu is opened in the Preview panel in Adobe Bridge.

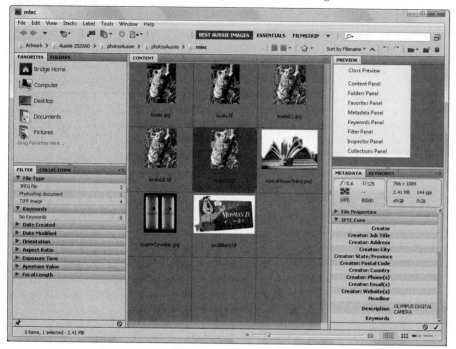

Getting help

You might think that with a purchase as substantial (both in terms of program features and the money you spent) as Creative Suite, you would get a hefty library of documentation. When you open the box for the CS installer DVDs, you quickly learn that accompanying documentation is not offered in printed form. Instead of providing printed user manuals, Adobe created several different types of help information files accessible as you work in the CS programs.

Help files

In terms of user guides and documentation, Adobe CS4 offers an elaborate form of help files that you access from the Help menu in all CS4 programs. While you're working in a program, and when you need to meet tight deadlines, the online help files should be a welcome addition to the CS4 features. In all programs but Acrobat, the help files are interconnected documents. In Acrobat, the help file is a document with a custom user interface.

From any CS4 program, open the Help menu and select *program name* Help (where *program name* is the name of the program you're currently using). For example, in Adobe InDesign, choose Help ➪ InDesign Help; in Photoshop, it's Help ➪ Photoshop Help; and so on.

After you access the Help command, the Adobe Help Viewer opens, as shown in Figure 3.46. Note that the *Help for* pull-down menu can take you to Help for a specific CS4 program. When you want help for Adobe Bridge, use the Help menu in the Bridge window.

Select Help for any Adobe CS program, including Bridge, and the Adobe Help Center opens.

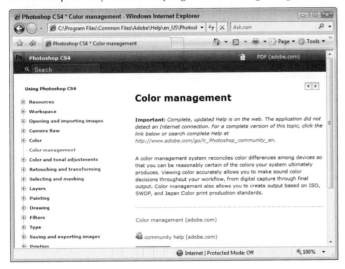

Online help

The Adobe online help offers you helpful tips and techniques posted online at the Adobe Web site. You can find many useful tips and techniques hosted as Web pages, video downloads, and PDF documents. There are descriptions for new program features, plug-ins and add-ons for different CS programs, upgrade information, and links to customer-support pages.

You can access online help and the latest news about the various CS4 applications in Bridge Home.

Because these help files are hosted online, you obviously need an Internet connection to access them. Be sure your Web browser is operational, and click the Online menu command in any CS program to open Web pages on the Adobe Web site.

TIP For access to tips and techniques using the CS programs, open Adobe Bridge and click Bridge Home in the Favorites pane. Scroll the different panes, and click Adobe Studio and Tutorials. Scroll the list in the next pane to the right, and click an item of interest. Your default Web browser opens and takes you to a related tip or technique hosted on the Adobe Web site. For more information on using the Bridge Center, see Chapter 6.

Updates

All the CS programs have the Help ⇨ Updates menu command. When you select Updates from the Help menu, the program from which the menu command was selected searches the Adobe Web site for update information. If an update exists, you're prompted to download it. Using the Updates menu command is an easy way to stay current with program upgrades and maintenance fixes. You should use this command frequently, because maintenance upgrades often repair bugs and programming errors in the applications. You can always expect an upgrade shortly after the release of each new program version.

Using Keyboard Shortcuts

Keyboard shortcuts are another item that could be listed as a common user-interface feature. We cover them here as a separate topic to elaborate a little bit more about the aspects of using keyboard shortcuts in the CS programs and of customizing shortcuts for your personal workflow.

If you want a comprehensive list of keyboard shortcuts, consult the program help files. Obviously, you don't want to spend lots of time memorizing the shortcuts, but you'll want to take advantage of using shortcuts common among the CS programs to perform identical tasks. One great advantage of using the CS programs is that, because the applications are developed by a single software manufacturer, the keyboard shortcuts from one program to the next are often the same. In some cases, however, you also find inconsistencies among the programs, or perhaps some features that could use keyboard shortcuts where they don't exist. Fortunately, several CS programs offer you an option to edit and redefine keyboard shortcuts.

There are some differences between the CS applications in handling custom keyboard shortcuts and in the features available in one program versus another. The following sections describe working with keyboard shortcuts and customizing them to suit your workflow according to each CS program.

Customizing keyboard shortcuts in Illustrator

Illustrator was the first of the CS programs developed by Adobe Systems, and it has a long tradition of assigned keyboard shortcuts to access tools and menu commands. As new programs have been developed, Adobe Systems has modified many keyboard shortcuts in Illustrator to match equivalent actions in other programs, such as in Photoshop. If you want to return to a familiar keyboard shortcut in Illustrator, you can customize the keyboard shortcut.

TIP If you work in a production environment and share your computer with others, it's a good idea to settle on agreed changes if they deviate from defaults used by other users. If you use your computer exclusively, you'll want to give a little thought to customizing keyboard shortcuts that are consistent between the CS programs. The more consistent you make your shortcuts, the less confusion you'll experience. Many workspaces can include both keyboard customization and menu customization. This can help with shared work environments.

To customize a keyboard shortcut, choose Edit ➪ Keyboard Shortcuts. The Keyboard Shortcuts dialog box opens, as shown in Figure 3.47. In this dialog box, you can add a new keyboard shortcut for a menu command or tool selection, or you can change existing keyboard shortcuts to other keystrokes you want to use.

FIGURE 3.47

Custom keyboard shortcuts are defined in the Keyboard Shortcuts dialog box.

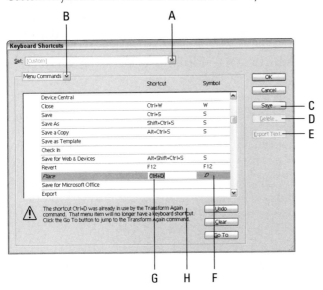

In the Keyboard Shortcuts dialog box, you have several options for creating a new shortcut or modifying an existing one. The options to understand in this dialog box include the following:

- **Set pull-down menu (A):** By default, the menu option is Illustrator Defaults. This menu choice remains listed in the pull-down menu so you can return to the Illustrator defaults at any time. When you assign a new keyboard shortcut or modify an existing one, the menu item changes to Custom. When you save your modified set, you're prompted to name the set. After saving, the name you use to identify your custom set is added to the pull-down menu.

- **Menu Commands/Tools (B):** Select from either Menu Commands or Tools to change shortcuts that invoke menu commands or select tools.

- **Save (C):** After changing the shortcuts to your personal liking, click Save to save your changes. The name you use for your set is added to the Set pull-down menu.

- **Delete (D):** The Delete button enables you to delete custom sets you add to the pull-down menu. To delete a set, first select the set to be deleted in the pull-down menu and then click Delete.

- **Export Text (E):** When you click Export Text, all your keyboard shortcuts are saved in a text file. You can use the text file to share with other workgroup members. For more information on custom keystrokes in workgroup environments, see the "Custom shortcuts for workgroups" sidebar in this chapter.

- **Shortcut edits (F):** To change a shortcut, first click in the Shortcuts column in the row for the item you want to change. For example, if you want to reassign the keystroke for accessing the Type tool, click the cursor in the Shortcut column where the Type row appears.

- **Symbol (G):** The keyboard shortcut to access a tool or invoke an action is defined in the Shortcut column. Adjacent to the Shortcut column is the Symbol column. The characters you add here appear in a menu list and/or tool tip. Notice that when you view the menus in all CS programs, you see the menu name and often the keys used for the shortcut to access the menu item.

- **Warning (H):** If you define a tool or a menu command with a key combination that is already used to select a tool or invoke a command, a warning is displayed at the bottom of the dialog box. If you don't want to interfere with an existing shortcut, click Undo. If you're overriding a preexisting shortcut, you can edit the shortcut used by another tool or menu command. Click Go To and you're taken to the item using the shortcut you overrode. Add a new shortcut if you so desire.

NOTE   Mac OS X does not permit assigning ⌘+Option modifiers.

Custom Shortcuts for Workgroups

If you make changes with keyboard shortcuts and want to share your custom set with other users, you can easily copy your custom keyboard set to other computers. When you save a custom set, the new definitions are saved to a file. This file is stored in the user logon Library/Preferences/Adobe Illustrator CS4 Settings folder (Mac) or the Documents and Settings\username\Application Data\Adobe\Adobe Illustrator CS4 Settings folder on Windows. To find the files on Windows, you need to turn on the ability to view hidden files and folders within the Tools ⇨ Folder Options ⇨ View ⇨ Advanced Settings ⇨ Files and Folders ⇨ Hidden Files and Folders ⇨ Show Hidden Files and Folders option. I know that's a mouthful, but that's where to find them and how to turn them on. Copy the .kys file from one computer to the same folder on the other computers, and the keyboard-shortcuts set is added to the Illustrator Set pull-down menu.

If you make changes to the keyboard shortcuts either in an isolated environment or when working as part of a group, it's handy to have a template or guide that you can refer to in order to refresh your memory on changes made to the shortcut keys. When you create a custom set and click Export Text, all features that can accept keyboard shortcuts are exported along with all those features assigned a keyboard shortcut. The file is a text file with the items and keyboard shortcuts listed with tabs and carriage returns. You can easily convert the text file to a table in InDesign.

 For more information on using the PDFMaker and converting Microsoft Word files to PDF, see Part V of this book.

Customizing keyboard shortcuts in Photoshop

Have you ever wondered why ⌘+I (Mac)/Ctrl+I (Windows) in Adobe Photoshop inverts an image, when a much more functional use of the shortcut might be to open the Image Size dialog box? Well, the good news for Photoshop users is that Photoshop CS4 supports creating custom menu and keyboard shortcuts just like Illustrator CS4. You can assign new keyboard shortcuts or remap existing keyboard shortcuts to menus and tools.

To change keyboard shortcuts, choose Edit ➪ Keyboard Shortcuts. The Keyboard Shortcuts and Menus dialog box opens, as shown in Figure 3.48.

FIGURE 3.48

The Photoshop Keyboard Shortcuts and Menus dialog box offers very similar options to those found in the Illustrator Keyboard Shortcuts dialog box.

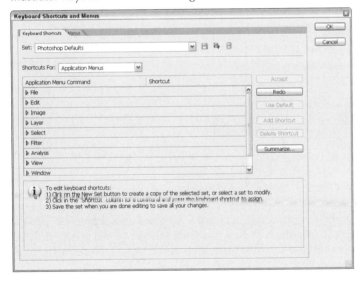

As you can see in Figure 3.48, the dialog box offers options very similar to the ones you find using the Illustrator Keyboard Shortcuts dialog box. The Set pull-down menu provides choices for using the default keyboard shortcuts or custom sets you create and save, much like those options discussed with Illustrator in the preceding section. From the Shortcuts For pull-down menu, you can choose to edit application menu commands, panel menus, or tools. When you select one of the categories from the Shortcuts For pull-down menu, the options change in the list below the pull-down menu. For Application Menus and Panel Menus, each menu is listed with a right-pointing arrow symbol adjacent to the menu name. Click the right-pointing arrow symbol, and the menu expands where each individual command is exposed. In Figure 3.49, you can see the Applications Menus selected from the Shortcuts For pull-down menu and the Layers panel expanded where all panel menu commands are listed. Notice that, by default, only three commands have shortcut-key equivalents.

Select the category you want from the Shortcuts For pull-down menu, and expand the menu or panel by clicking the symbol adjacent to a panel name.

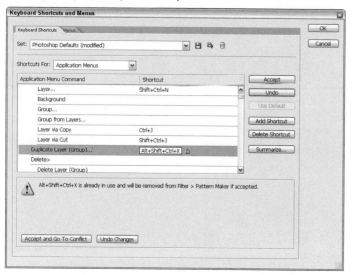

Most of the same options exist for creating, changing, and deleting keyboard shortcuts in Photoshop as you find in Illustrator. Photoshop enables you to export a list of all the assigned keyboard shortcuts; however, unlike the text-file export in Illustrator, Photoshop's export is in the form of an HTML file. Click Summarize in the Keyboard Shortcuts and Menus dialog box, and the Save dialog box opens, allowing you to navigate your hard drive and locate a folder destination for your file. After saving the file, you can view the list of shortcuts in your Web browser.

Customizing keyboard shortcuts in InDesign

Fortunately, the Keyboard Shortcuts dialog box for most of the CS applications that allow you to customize shortcuts is accessed with the same menu command. Select Edit ➪ Keyboard Shortcuts in InDesign, and the InDesign Keyboard Shortcuts dialog box opens. From a pull-down menu listed as Product Area, you see an extensive list of categories where keyboard shortcuts are assigned, as shown in Figure 3.50.

The Keyboard Shortcuts dialog box in InDesign contains an extensive set of categories from the Product Area pull-down menu.

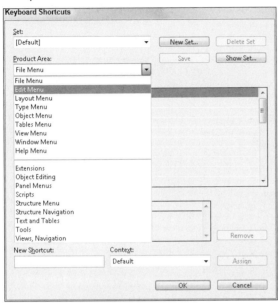

You select an option from the Product Area pull-down menu and click a command in the Commands list box. From this point, you have another option where you can narrow the assignment of the keyboard shortcut to one of five categories listed in the Context pull-down menu. For example, if you want to assign a keyboard shortcut to Fill with Placeholder text, you start by selecting Type Menu in the Product Area. In the Commands list, you select Fill with Placeholder Text. Then click in the New Shortcut field box, and press the keys to create the new shortcut. Then click OK and test the shortcut to see if it behaves as you expect. In Figure 3.51, you can see an example for assigning a keyboard shortcut to Fill with Placeholder Text.

You handle the basic options for creating new sets, saving a set, and selecting custom sets from the Set pull-down menu in a similar way to how you handle these operations in Illustrator and Photoshop. As an added benefit for users who are former QuarkXPress users, InDesign provides a QuarkXPress-equivalent set of shortcuts accessible from the Set pull-down menu. A PageMaker set also is available for users familiar with Adobe PageMaker shortcuts.

InDesign is also unique in that you can set keyboard shortcuts for specific situations by using the Context selector. This allows the same shortcut to be used for different commands depending on what you're doing.

FIGURE 3.51

The Keyboard Shortcuts dialog box shown with selections to assign a shortcut to Fill with Placeholder Text

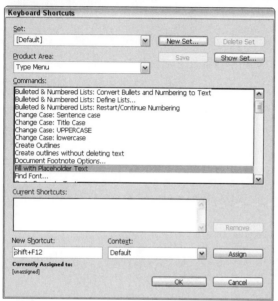

If you want to create a table describing the key shortcuts created for a custom set, click Show Set. Like Adobe Illustrator, the list of assigned keys and those commands where no assignment has been made are all listed in a text file. When you click Show Set, the list appears in your default text editor, as shown in Figure 3.52.

You can save the text file and open it in Microsoft Word or import the text in InDesign, where you can convert the text file to a table like the table conversion described when converting Illustrator text files. The text file for InDesign, unfortunately, is not as well formatted as the text file you have available in Illustrator. The InDesign text file doesn't convert to a table as cleanly as Illustrator's table conversion, so you may have to do a little editing to make a table guide for your workgroup.

FIGURE 3.52

Click Show Set in the Keyboard Shortcuts dialog box, and the list of keyboard shortcuts is listed in a text file.

Customizing keyboard shortcuts in Flash, Fireworks, and Dreamweaver

Keyboard shortcuts also can be assigned in Flash and Dreamweaver. Choose Edit (Dreamweaver) ➪ Keyboard Shortcuts to open the Keyboard Shortcuts dialog box for Dreamweaver, shown in Figure 3.53, and Flash ➪ Keyboard Shortcuts for Flash.

Dreamweaver supports a list of commands in a list box that is expanded by clicking a symbol adjacent to the menu name. On the Mac, a right-pointing arrow appears adjacent to the menu name; on Windows, the symbol is a plus sign. When expanded, the symbols change to a down-pointing arrow and a minus sign, respectively.

As you scroll down the list of commands in the list box, notice that the commands are nested in groups. Click the symbol adjacent to a menu command, and the list expands. In Figure 3.53, the Edit menu was expanded; then the Find command expanded to expand the nested group.

Dreamweaver also supports saving a text file or creating an HTML file for a list of commands you can use as a guide.

FIGURE 3.53

The Keyboard Shortcuts dialog box in Dreamweaver

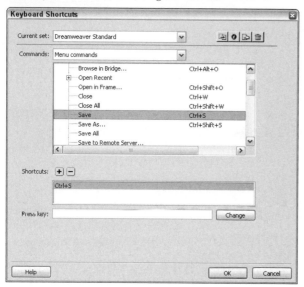

Working with keyboard shortcuts in Acrobat

Acrobat is the only program in the Creative Suite that doesn't support creation of custom keystrokes for shortcuts. However, while discussing keyboard shortcuts, there is one thing important to point out when working in Acrobat: By default, accessing tools with keystrokes is not enabled. Users of earlier versions of Acrobat soon find that pressing the H key and expecting to select the Hand tool doesn't produce a result when they first launch Acrobat. In order to use key modifiers to access tools, you need to change a preference setting.

Open the Preferences dialog box by choosing Acrobat ➪ Preferences (Mac) or Edit ➪ Preferences (Windows). The Preferences dialog box opens by default to show the General preferences. If General is not selected in the left pane, click General and the right pane changes to reflect the options available for the General preferences.

Be certain that the Use single-key accelerators to access tools check box is selected. If the check box is unchecked, pressing a key on your keyboard to access a tool won't work. By default, when you first load Acrobat, this check box is unchecked.

Unfortunately, you cannot change any keyboard shortcuts in Acrobat.

Summary

- Several CS programs have some common tools. The vast majority of common tools exist among Illustrator, Photoshop, and InDesign. The tools work similarly in the programs that use them. Accessing the tools using keystrokes also is common between the programs.

- Acrobat uses a variety of toolbars that can be opened and docked in the top-level Toolbar Well. Context menus help greatly in accessing tools in Acrobat.

- Some tool options are accessible in some CS programs by double-clicking a tool in the program's Toolbox. Corresponding dialog boxes open where attributes are assigned for a given tool.

- Illustrator, Photoshop, InDesign, Flash, and Dreamweaver offer options for saving workspaces. Workspaces involve arrangement of tools and panels and the overall look of a program's editing environment.

- All the CS programs have some common user-interface features. Among the more popular are context menus and access to help documents.

- All CS programs, with the exception of Acrobat, offer you options for customizing keyboard shortcuts.

Part II

Getting Started with Design Workflows

In this part we begin to talk about how the Creative Suite applications work together. We start by covering production workflows in Chapter 4 and then move on to color management in Chapter 5 where we talk about synchronizing color among the Creative Suite programs. In Chapter 6 we discuss using Adobe Bridge for managing files and continue in Chapter 7 where we talk about managing different versions of documents with Adobe Version Cue. In Chapter 8 we talk about managing PDF files with the Acrobat Organizer tool.

Chapter 4

Creating Production Workflows

T he Adobe Creative Suite is built around the concept of facilitating design production in workflow environments. Designers and production artists create workflows either as independent workers or as participants in workflow groups. A workflow helps you perform your work quickly and intelligently, often by streamlining redundant tasks. Workflows are designed to dramatically reduce the time you need to perform your work and reduce the time required to train new workers.

This chapter covers the initial development of production workflows as they relate to using the Adobe Creative Suite 4 Design Premium edition. With all the tools at hand, you'll gain an understanding of how to use the CS4 applications in workflows and how you can save time producing artwork.

Understanding Workflows

Workflows as they pertain to the Adobe Creative Suite can be divided into several groups. As a graphic designer, you may be primarily concerned with production workflows where artwork creations originate in programs like Adobe Illustrator CS4 and Adobe Photoshop CS4. Document assembly may be performed in Adobe InDesign CS4, and from InDesign CS4 you may export files to Adobe PDF or to Adobe Dreamweaver.

You may also be concerned with a color-management workflow to insure the color is consistent among all the applications you use to produce your artwork. This workflow might be a subset of your production workflow. The color-management workflow might extend beyond your office and continue to the print shop or service center. In this regard, you need to work together with service technicians working outside your environment.

CROSS-REF For information related to creating color-management workflows, see Chapter 5.

Yet another workflow that affects your final results when you prepare documents for print is the production center printing your jobs. Printers and service bureaus develop workflows to run their production lines from digital file to final output. The bridge between you and the service center might include color management and file preparation to meet the standards set forth by your vendors. If you design files for print, you need to understand that the production center is part of your workflow and there is a great benefit to working together with your vendors to ensure your workflow is efficient and your product is delivered on time.

CROSS-REF For more information on prepress and printing, see Chapter 40.

If you design files for Web hosting, you can include your Internet Service Provider (ISP) or your client's ISP in your workflow if your designs end up hosted on a site other than your own ISP. Working with ISP vendors is as important as working with print vendors. It is, therefore, equally important for you to include professionals at an ISP in your workflow.

CROSS-REF For more information on Web hosting and creating Web pages, see Chapter 27.

Regardless of whether you design files for print or for the Web, realize that you have two kinds of workflows with which you'll continually interact. Your internal workflow where you produce your artwork is something over which you have complete control. The workflows that extend to your print shop or ISP are something over which you don't have complete control, so you need to negotiate standards with the vendors to develop consistent reliable output.

In this chapter, we look at workflows you create in your office for design production and understanding workflow concepts as they apply to the Adobe Creative Suite. In several later chapters in this book, we address how to set up the CS4 programs to suit your production workflow.

Workflows for Independent Artists

If you're an independent designer working in a one-person shop, you have some advantages in that you can customize and work with the Creative Suite applications as you see fit. You don't need to concern yourself with setting up your environment to suit the needs of multiple users. The advantage is having it all your way; the disadvantage is you have to do everything yourself—acting as the creative director, artist, image editor, layout artist, Web designer, and office manager.

As someone who works with all the CS4 programs, you'll want to take a little time to plan your workflow and take more time to become productive in using all the CS4 applications. An example of a workflow for an independent graphic designer is illustrated in Figure 4.1.

FIGURE 4.1

An example of a production workflow for an independent designer

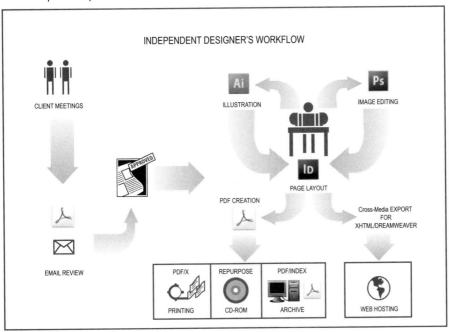

In the example workflow, you begin an assignment with a client meeting either personally or through e-mail or telephone calls. As you develop a concept and after interviewing your client, you prepare sketches or comps that are sent back to the client in an e-mail review using Adobe Acrobat Professional. If more than one person is part of a committee that ultimately approves your commission, each committee member receives your draft via e-mail for review. When the final comp is approved, you begin your work on the project.

NOTE When you prepare a PDF document for a review with your clients, be certain to enable the PDF with usage rights for Adobe Reader. The newest version of Acrobat takes care of this automatically. By enabling the PDF with rights, any member of a review team who doesn't use Acrobat Professional can use the free Adobe Reader program to participate in a review. For more information on enabling PDF documents, see Chapter 36.

You may start your project by creating a new folder in Adobe Bridge where all the assets for a client job are maintained. If you need illustrated art as well as photo images, you may spend some time in Adobe Illustrator CS4 and Adobe Photoshop CS4, where you create artwork. Document files are saved to the folder or subfolders you created with Adobe Bridge and the files are managed in the Bridge window. All layers are preserved in the documents, and you save your files in native formats.

If the copy is developed in a word processor foreign to you and not compatible with your text editors, you might ask your client to send you an RTF (Rich Text Format) file that you can place into Adobe InDesign CS4. You import the illustrations and images into Adobe InDesign, and fit the copy to the design.

You export the InDesign CS4 document as Adobe PDF and open the file in Adobe Acrobat Professional. You soft-proof the file to ensure that all colors will print as you expect and then repurpose the file for online delivery by reducing image resolution to create a smaller file. You may need to save this file as a copy with password security, which prevents your client from extracting data or printing the document. You enable the file with Adobe Reader usage rights and e-mail the enabled file to the client, who signs off on the design using a digital signature in the free Adobe Reader software. When you receive approval from your client, you e-mail or FTP the high-resolution PDF document to your printer.

> **CROSS-REF** For information on enabling PDFs with usage rights, see Chapters 30 and 36. For information on soft-proofing color, see Chapter 39. For information on repurposing files, see the section on document repurposing later in this chapter.

If Web design is part of your work, you return to Adobe InDesign CS4 and export the file for cross-media using the File ⇨ Export to Dreamweaver menu command for editing in Dreamweaver. You integrate the InDesign CS4 document in the Web site design and use repurposed PDFs designed for Web hosting and CD-ROM replication. If your Web design includes interactive elements, then you can use InDesign's Export to XFL feature to move your design to Adobe Flash.

> **CROSS-REF** The Export to XFL feature is discussed in more detail in Chapter 23.

If point-of-sale order forms are part of your commission, you create the form designs in InDesign CS4 or Adobe Illustrator CS4 and export/save to PDF. You use Acrobat Professional to add form fields and JavaScripts to create interactive forms. If you are a Windows user, you have the option for using Adobe Designer to create the PDF form. You return to Dreamweaver and add hyperlinks to the PDF forms and upload the forms via Dreamweaver to the client's Web site.

At the end of your job, you write all the files to a CD-ROM where PDFs contain attachments to quickly open the original application documents. You create a search index that you include on the CD to help you search PDF content. Metadata are supplied for files to permit searches and quick access to files. You collect your money and take a vacation, because you have an efficient workflow that saved you time.

As an independent designer, you benefit from knowing how to work effectively in the CS4 applications. You also derive extra benefits for keeping files reduced to a minimum by using only native file formats and using Version Cue if you need to create multiple versions or alternates of files. If you need to return to a project, having fewer files that are well documented throughout the design process helps you to easily revise content and create new designs for the same client. Because you add your files to a Version Cue project, you can use Adobe Bridge to return to the client's files and easily modify designs with alternates or new versions.

Modifying designs

You may think that the workflow described in the preceding section doesn't require all the CS4 programs to perform the same steps. It's true that if all there were to creating a design piece was following the same steps in a linear fashion, you could substitute the use of an illustration program and/or use another layout program. You would miss the exporting XHTML for Dreamweaver if you don't use InDesign CS4, but some layout programs do support exporting to HTML. What's not mentioned in the workflow is handling design modifications. Design modifications may occur during the design process where you need to nudge and move objects to create the look you want or when your client requests changes to objects, images, colors, type fonts, and so on.

The advantage of using the Creative Suite is more obvious when making changes to designs. As you change files, you can save different versions of the same file with Version Cue or you can use Version Cue to create alternates for files. If you need to change back to an earlier version, this tool alone will save you lots of time. If you need to move or nudge objects, having files imported from native formats opens up your freedom for moving design elements without affecting underlying objects.

CROSS-REF For information on using Version Cue and creating alternates, see Chapter 7.

Extending the workflow

Another advantage of using the Creative Suite is the easy portability of assets that can help you prepare files properly for vendors. When designing for print, you can acquire color profiles prepared by your vendor, designed for output on their devices.

CROSS-REF For information on creating color-management workflows, see Chapters 6 and 7.

In addition to color management, you want to check your files for potential errors. When documents are *preflighted*, your files are analyzed for potential printing problems. Both Adobe InDesign and Adobe Acrobat Professional contain sophisticated preflight tools using built-in and/or custom preflight profiles. You can acquire preflight profiles from your service provider to use in InDesign/ Adobe Acrobat Professional for checking files for proper printing. You can acquire preflight profiles from vendor Web sites or have them e-mailed directly to you.

CROSS-REF For understanding more about preflight and information on importing and exporting preflight profiles, see Chapter 40.

Workflows for Studios and Production Houses

If you work in a larger studio with coworkers participating in design projects, you need to be more concerned about the steps involved in your workflow and be consistent in all your tasks. Many studios that evolved with computer illustration and design often let employees determine which application software to use and which what methods for creating designs to employ. The unknowing creative directors, who at times were computer illiterate, paid little attention to which tools were used and only focused on the final artwork. Today, some firms spend lots of time updating documents from a variety of programs that their current staff no longer uses.

The first step in developing an efficient workflow is to begin with standards that all employees in a firm use. Deciding which application software to use, setting standards for file naming conventions, determining which archiving methods to use, and developing policies for updating documents are all preliminary steps that you should integrate in a workflow schema before engaging in production tasks. The time spent on management is insignificant when you compare it to the time it takes to train current employees and hire new ones.

As an example of a studio or production-center workflow, Figure 4.2 shows how creative production personnel participate in a design project. After a project is approved, artists working in Adobe Illustrator CS4 and image editors working in Adobe Photoshop CS4 save files to a server. Copy editors save files to the server for the page layout artists to acquire. The page layout artists retrieve files, complete the designs, and save the completed designs back to the server. All the files are viewed and managed in Adobe Bridge where all users can view the same collection; PDFs are exported from InDesign CS4 for print, Web hosting, CD-ROM replication, porting to handheld devices and tablets, and document archiving. Web designers retrieve exported InDesign files and edit them in Dreamweaver. PDFs are retrieved from the server for documents included on the Web site.

In this facility, it's easy to see how developing standards is critical for the workflow environment. When new employees are hired, they need to quickly fit into the workflow. Training new staff is a much easier task when following standards. If individual artists determine their own methods and use different programs to produce artwork, getting new employees up to speed is likely to take more time than you can afford.

An example of a production workflow for a studio or production center

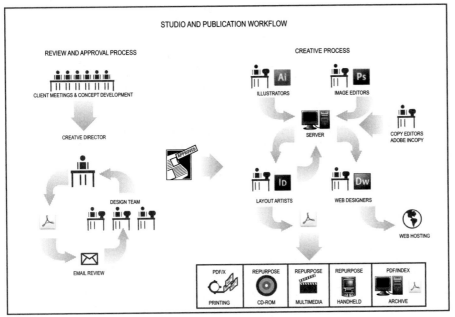

Document Repurposing

Document repurposing is taking a file suited for one output purpose and optimizing it for another output purpose. In regard to the Adobe Creative Suite, Acrobat is the application best suited for document repurposing.

If you design a piece for print in InDesign CS4, you have some options you can employ to repurpose a file. Because exporting to PDF is something you can do for printing, you can return to the InDesign file and export a second PDF document more suitable for Web hosting or screen displays. What goes on in InDesign CS4 is simply a matter of choosing the Adobe PDF settings most desirable for your output needs. To select the correct settings, follow these steps:

STEPS: Selecting the Correct Output Settings

1. **Choose File ⇨ Export in Adobe InDesign CS4.** The Export dialog box opens.
2. **From the Format pull-down menu, choose Adobe PDF.**

3. **Supply a name for the file in the Save As field, and click Save.** A second dialog box opens where you set the attributes for the PDF file.

4. **From the top-level Preset pull-down menu, choose the Adobe PDF setting you want to use.** Note that if you created presets either in InDesign CS4 or any other CS4 application, the preset appears in the Adobe PDF Preset pull-down menu. In Figure 4.3, a preset that was developed in Acrobat Distiller is selected from the menu list.

5. **Export to PDF.** Click Export to complete the file export to PDF.

FIGURE 4.3

PDF presets that you develop in any CS4 application appear in the Adobe PDF Preset menu when you export to PDF.

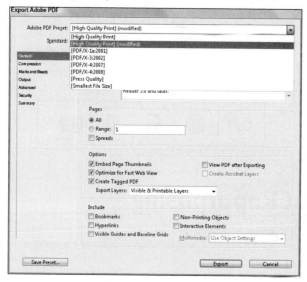

In InDesign CS4 and all the other CS4 applications, any preset developed in Acrobat Distiller or any other CS4 application is available to all CS4 applications including Adobe Acrobat Professional and Acrobat Distiller for the purpose of creating PDF files.

When you choose a setting that contains options for downsampling images, the resultant PDF document becomes a smaller file than when you create PDFs with settings where you apply no downsampling.

CROSS-REF To learn more about exporting to PDF from Adobe InDesign CS4, see Chapter 40.

Another method you have for repurposing PDF documents lies in Adobe Acrobat Professional. You can open a PDF in Acrobat and select the Advanced ⇨ PDF Optimizer menu command. The PDF Optimizer provides you with options for downsampling images as well as many other options for reducing file sizes. In addition to using the PDF Optimizer, you can also set up a Batch Sequence to optimize a collection of PDF files together using the same amounts of downsampling and applying other attribute choices.

CROSS-REF To learn more about PDF Optimizer and creating Batch Sequences, see Chapter 34.

Repurposing documents is one of the true benefits of an efficient workflow. If you relied on other methods to repurpose a document from print to Web hosting, you must open files in Adobe Photoshop CS4, downsample files, and save them as new files to disk. After downsampling the images, you must open your layout application and relink all the image links. Obviously, using PDF as your output format provides you with a much more efficient alternative when you need to repurpose documents.

NOTE Downsampling an image is the process of reducing file size by lowering the image's resolution (for example, taking a 300 ppi [pixels per inch] image and lowering the resolution to 72 ppi). You can downsample images in Adobe Photoshop and Adobe Acrobat, as well as use methods for downsampling from within Adobe Dreamweaver.

Setting Workflow Standards

Whether you're an independent designer or you own or manage an agency, there are some considerations you should think about when designing your workflow. Too often, individuals or managers become subordinates to vendors, contracting professionals, or production personnel instead of taking control of their environment and encouraging others to fit within their workflow schema.

Instead of having others dictate or impose standards on you, try to give some thought to the way you want to work and how you want others to fit into your workflow. The following sections offer some suggestions you may want to consider.

Set standards for the tools used in your workflow

When hiring employees or working with contract artists, ask people to use the same tools you use in your workflow. If you use all the programs in the Adobe Creative Suite, be certain to hire employees skilled in these tools and make it a necessary condition for all your contracting artists and professionals to use the same tools. The time to train people who fit in your workflow is dramatically reduced if they're skilled in using the same tools.

Use vendors who support the tools you use

We often hear design professionals complain, "My print shop or vendor doesn't like to print from InDesign" (or another product). Having your vendor dictate what tools you use to perform your work is like the tail wagging the dog. After all, who is paying money to whom? If your vendor doesn't support one of the tools you use, and you produce even a moderate amount of work, tell your vendor that if they don't support your selection of software, you'll be forced to use their competitor across the street. Try this on for size and see how many vendors turn you down.

Devote time to ongoing training

Creative professionals today are in a category similar to other professionals like medical workers, legal workers, psychologists, educators, and people in all kinds of professions that deal with government regulations. All these professions require continuing education units (CEU) to sustain licensure or maintain compliance with changing laws. As a design professional, you work in an ever-changing world of high technology. The world of the creative professional in some ways changes more rapidly today than that of almost any other occupation. New software upgrades are occurring every 18 months. This rapid change related to the tools you use requires you and your staff to engage in ongoing training and education.

To help you work more effectively in your workflow, try to set up training sessions that you can provide in-house or with your vendors. You might approach a vendor and ask them to sponsor an evening session to introduce a new product upgrade. You can find many Adobe professionals working in cities throughout the world who are willing and able to make visits to communities for speaking sessions without charging any fees. You can also ask local community colleges and universities to sponsor similar events and hold workshops and classes on products you use in your workflow. In large agencies, you can employ policies and provide time off for production artists to take classes and workshops benefiting your workflow.

Develop a paradigm for managing your projects

Sometimes locating files and making file edits takes more time than designing a new piece from scratch. To avoid time lost due to searching for files, converting old files to newer versions, and locating fonts and assets contained in design projects, try to spend some time managing your artwork in an effective manner. With the CS4 programs, you can use Adobe Bridge to organize all files located on hard drives and networked servers. For archived files as well as the files you manage in the Bridge, use Adobe Acrobat and create data sheets using form fields. You can use the form template to fill in new forms for each project as well as the source and location for the files. Try to complete a form for every project and supply all pertinent information on the data sheet related to personnel involved in the project and all related software used to create the project designs. Figure 4.4 illustrates a sample form created in Adobe Illustrator CS4 and opened in Adobe Acrobat where form fields were added.

FIGURE 4.4

A sample form created in Adobe Illustrator CS4 and opened in Adobe Acrobat where form fields were added

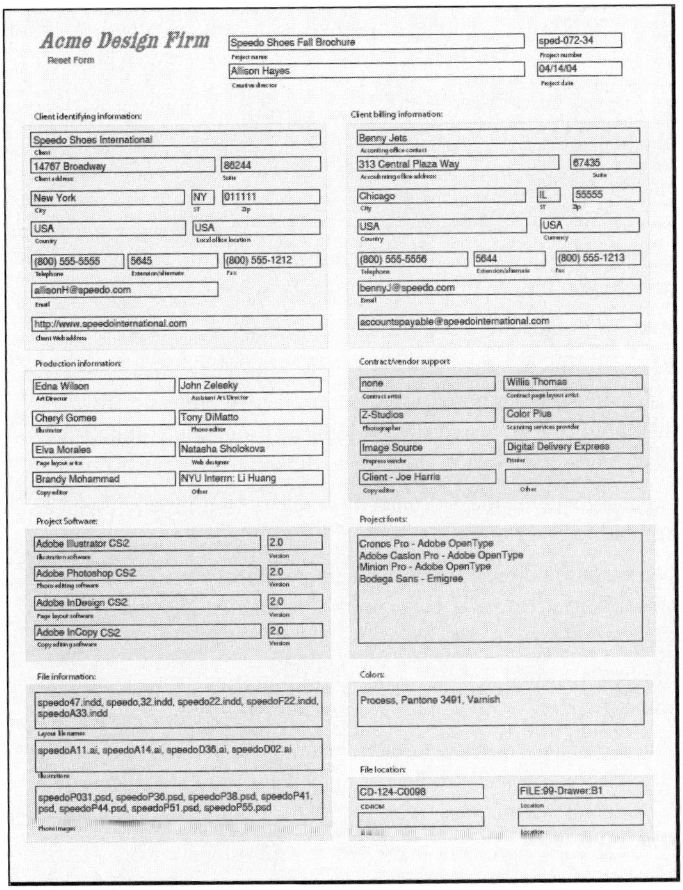

> **TIP** Files saved from Adobe Illustrator CS4 as native AI files with the Create PDF Compatible File option selected in the Illustrator Options dialog box can be opened directly in any Adobe Acrobat viewer including Adobe Reader.

As you can see in Figure 4.4, the agency personnel and contracting vendors are all listed by name. A separate document contains all the contact information for the contractors and vendors. The software and version numbers of the applications used in the project are listed, as well as design specifics such as fonts and colors. The fields in the lower-right corner describe the location of CD-ROMs and DVDs where the completed files are stored. You can store PDF forms like this on a network server and use Acrobat Search to search for them or you can create a collection where forms are searched using Adobe Bridge. In a matter of minutes, any employee in a company including new employees can locate the files for any given project.

You may find other helpful ideas that can assist you in managing your workflow and you may find other relevant information to add to data sheets. The most important issue at hand is realizing that a little time spent in managing and organizing your work always saves you more time when you need to rework files or produce new pieces for the same client.

Summary

- Efficient workflows help you work quickly and intelligently by reducing redundancy. Workflow standards can help you reduce time in training new workers.

- You have complete control over your internal workflow and what tools to use. Your workflow extends beyond your internal workflow and includes contractors and vendors.

- Adobe Creative Suite 4 is a complete workflow solution for creative professionals, whereby all document files are fully integrated throughout the programs. Applications help you update files, change design elements, and create different design versions.

- You use document repurposing when a file is designed for one output need and you're reworking the same file suited for a different output need.

- Independent design professionals and creative art department managers are advantaged when planning workflows and attracting others to conform to standards set by an individual or agency.

- When working with contract artists and vendors, you'll find it best to attract people who fit into your workflow rather than have others fit you into their workflow.

- Keeping accurate data sheets on client projects helps you save time in relocating files and provides quick access for revisiting projects from the same clients. You can manage your data sheets using Adobe Bridge or Acrobat Search.

- Continuing education is a necessary ingredient in a creative professional's work life. You can solicit help from vendors to support training sessions and utilize Adobe field specialists to help you stay abreast of new software upgrades.

Chapter 5

Creating Color Managed Workflows

IN THIS CHAPTER

Getting familiar with color profiles

Working with color in CS4 applications

Using profiles

Perhaps the greatest challenge to design professionals is getting color on printed output to look like the color displayed on computer monitors. Artists can easily overcome common design dilemmas such as working around font problems, learning functional aspects of applications software, avoiding pitfalls related to image handling, and a host of other nuisances that hinder progress. But when it comes to color matching, the problems are more complicated and the solutions are often misunderstood and obscure.

Fortunately, Adobe has been working for several years on creating a common color engine that can be shared among imaging applications. The result of Adobe's efforts is exemplified in the CS4 applications. All the CS4 programs share the same Adobe Color Engine (ACE) that takes you one step closer to reliable color-matching among application documents, your computer monitor, and the output devices you use. In addition, once you set up your color-viewing workspace and color profiles you can use Adobe Bridge to synchronize the same color settings among most of the CS4 applications. In this chapter, we cover some fundamental information related to color management among the Adobe CS4 applications.

Color management is a complex topic. An accurate description for identifying all the variables related to rendering reliable color is well beyond the scope of this chapter. For more sophisticated descriptions, look for books written specifically to help you understand and manage color on computers and output devices.

CROSS-REF For more information on managing color, see *Color Correction For Digital Photographers Only* (Padova/ Mason, Wiley Publishing) or *Color Management for Digital Photographers For Dummies* (Padova/Mason, Wiley Publishing).

Understanding Profiling

Color profiles provide the necessary information for the acquisition, display, and output of your images/documents. A color profile might be one you create through the use of calibration devices or ones you acquire from various equipment manufacturers. Color profiles interpret your images and documents in terms of display and output. Often, using a color profile can mean the difference between a printed image using the colors you expect on output and a rendered image with incorrect colors.

> **TIP** Color management is a complex issue. Fully comprehending the managing of color on computer systems and how color is reproduced on printing devices takes a lot of research and study. To learn more about color management, open Acrobat, click on the Search tool in the Acrobat toolbar, and type color management as your search criteria. Click on Search PDFs on the Internet in the Search pane, and the Yahoo.com search engine reports all PDF documents on the Internet where color management is found. You can download many PDF documents that offer you definitions of terms and thoroughly explain color management.

Profiles in workflows

The design of production pieces can make use of several different color profiles. You may have one profile developed for your scanner when acquiring an image through the scanning process. A calibrated profile converts the reflective artwork on your scanner platen to digital form, which captures and translates color the best it can, that is a close rendition of the print you scanned. When you open your scanned image in a program like Photoshop, you use a color workspace. The scanned image color space is converted to the monitor working space. This conversion is a temporary preview condition and does not change the data in your image. When you finish your editing session, you convert the workspace color to the output color using yet another profile for your output device. The converted color ideally translates the color space from what you see on your monitor to the color space of your printer; the color range you see on your monitor fits as close as possible to within the color space of your output device. Throughout the color-management workflow, you're converting color from one space to another using color profiles.

Calibrating color

Software applications provide you with basic tools for calibrating color. You have tools such as Adobe Gamma installed on Windows to calibrate your monitor for white balance, gamma, black point, and so on. On Mac OS X, the operating system provides you with tools to calibrate your monitor. On a more sophisticated level, you can purchase calibration systems that create monitor color profiles and output profiles for you printing devices. Using hardware devices for calibrating color is much more sophisticated than relying on the software tools that Adobe and Apple provide.

In some circumstances, you can use profiles that come with the installation of the CS4 applications. Profiles designed for four-color process printing on coated stock are generic and often do a reasonable job matching color from screen to press. As the lowest cost option, you can use simple software monitor-calibration tools and get fairly close to the kind of output you want on four-color process printing. However, if you're particular about color, and if your output varies to a range of devices including composite color printers, then you may want to invest in calibration equipment suited to create monitor and printer profiles for your workflow.

Color calibration systems can be purchased as low as $69 US, and the more sophisticated devices start at around $239 and go up to over $3,000 US. At the very least, a creative professional should look at those beginning a little over $200 US. This kind of investment goes a long way in helping you calibrate your color monitor and starts you off in a well-managed color workflow.

Acquiring profiles

If the thought of spending thousands of dollars to calibrate your system doesn't sit well with you, you have some alternatives. In large production centers, you can use a single calibration system to calibrate all the hardware in your environment. With this method, you need only a single calibration tool to create profiles for all the monitors and in-house output devices. Calibration tools are not like software, which you need to license for each user.

Independent graphic designers can solicit assistance from their service centers. Most print shops and service bureaus have calibration devices on hand. You can ask technicians to visit you to calibrate your monitor and provide you with the profiles they created for their equipment.

When you acquire profiles for output devices, you must install the profiles in the proper location on your hard drive. For Mac users, copy the profiles to `Hard Drive//Library/Application Support/Adobe/Color/Profiles/`. On Windows Vista and XP, copy acquired profiles or profiles you create as a result of your calibration system to `C:\Windows\System32\Spool\ Drivers\Color`. When you install profiles in these locations, the profiles are accessible from the applicable CS4 programs. In Figure 5.1, you can see a profile accessed in the Photoshop CS4 Print dialog box.

> **NOTE** Color management is available only within the print-oriented CS4 applications including Photoshop, Illustrator, InDesign, and Acrobat. The Web applications do not have these features.

FIGURE 5.1

When placed in the proper location on your hard drive, the profile is accessible from all the CS4 applications.

Profile embedding

You can embed color profiles in your images or documents. As a general rule, you should opt for profile embedding whenever possible. As a document prints, it assumes the profile of the printing device. When you embed a color profile in your documents, a color conversion takes place, translating the color within the embedded profile to the color within the output profile. In effect, this translation is a best effort to render all the color contained in your document with the closest matching color values in the output profile. If you elect not to embed a profile in your document, theoretically, the color workspace on the system outputting your file converts to the output profile. If there is great disparity between your monitor workspace and the service center's monitor workspace, the color conversion could result in color shifts.

Using online profile development resources

Discover a problem and someone is likely to provide a solution—for a fee, of course. If your problem is color profiling, then there are some online solution providers who can help by providing you a color profile to use both with in-house equipment and when using service centers. Some of the lowest cost centers such as Costco, Sam's Club, Office Depot, and others are providing photographic prints at incredibly low costs. Many of these mega-outlets can offer you photographic prints for less money than the cost of ink and paper for your desktop color printers. These stores use high-end photographic digital lab equipment like Fuji Frontier, Noritsu, Agfa D-Lab, Lightjet, Durst, and Chromira to name a few.

At $.19 a print or less, you wouldn't expect to see a high-end service technician editing your Photoshop files to get the color right, But what you can find is a service center that has developed color profiles for most professional photographic printing systems and services clients worldwide. You can acquire color profiles for a huge range of systems and paper stocks by logging on to www. drycreekphoto.com. On the Dry Creek Web site, you can download free color profiles custom developed for the most common equipment and paper stock.

If you need a custom profile developed for your own printing equipment or for equipment and stock not within its current library, you can commission Dry Creek Photo to develop a custom profile for you. As of this writing, custom profiles are created for $50 for a single profile with no updates and $99 for a printer/paper profile that includes up to 12 updates at no cost for one year.

In Photoshop, profiles are embedded at the time you save your Photoshop document. A little bit of code is added to the Photoshop file containing the profile data. For RGB images, the amount of data added to the original file is minimal. With CMYK images, the file sizes can grow as much as a few megabytes. Be aware that profile embedding is only available for certain file formats. Photoshop native files are supported, as are TIFF, EPS, JPEG, Large Document Format, Photoshop PDF, PICT (Mac), PICT Resource (Mac), and DCS (1 and 2) files. If the check box is grayed out in the Save or Save As dialog box, you need to change the file format to one of the supported formats.

Choose File ➪ Save As and check the box for Embed Color Profile: *Name of Profile to Be Embedded.* In Figure 5.2, you can see that a custom color profile is used.

In Illustrator, Photoshop, and InDesign, you assign profiles from a menu command. In these programs, choose Edit ➪ Assign Profile(s), and the Assign Profile(s) dialog box opens. In Figure 5.3, you can see that, in Illustrator, the choices are limited to three options. Choose Don't Color Manage This Document when you want color management turned off for the current file. Choose Working CMYK to assign the monitor working space. Choose Profile to select one of the installed color profiles used by your output devices.

FIGURE 5.2

Check the box to embed a profile for all image formats supporting color profile embedding.

FIGURE 5.3

The Assign Profile dialog box, where profile assignment is made

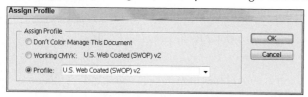

In InDesign, you have more options for assigning profiles, as well as a preview check box where you can preview the results of profile assignment. Use the same Edit ➪ Assign Profiles menu command, and the Assign Profiles dialog box, shown in Figure 5.4, opens.

FIGURE 5.4

InDesign's Assign Profiles dialog box

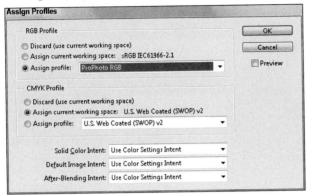

> **NOTE** There's a critical difference between InDesign and both Photoshop and Illustrator files. This difference is explicit in the InDesign Assign Profiles dialog box (hence the plural form of Profiles). Both PSD and AI files by nature can only have one color mode while an ID file must support both color modes simultaneously.

InDesign enables you to assign a working profile (RGB Profile) and an output Profile (CMYK Profile). In addition, you also can make choices for the rendering intent. Finally, check the Preview check box (which also is available in Photoshop), and the document pages behind the dialog box dynamically reflect the color profile you select in the Assign Profiles dialog box.

Profile mismatching

When you embed or assign a color profile to a document and your document is opened on a computer using another profile, there is a profile mismatch. When such mismatches occur, Illustrator, InDesign, and Photoshop all open dialog boxes to offer you some options on how to handle the mismatches. In Figure 5.5, you can see a file opening in Photoshop where a profile mismatch occurs.

The Embedded Profile Mismatch dialog box opens only when your color preferences are set to display profile mismatches. You can choose to convert color automatically in the Color Settings or open a dialog box where you can make decisions for converting color on an image-by-image basis.

The Photoshop Embedded Profile Mismatch dialog box

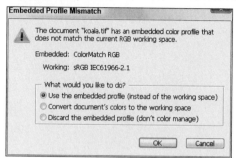

The options available in the Embedded Profile Mismatch dialog box include the following:

- **Use the embedded profile (instead of the working space):** Selecting this option leaves the image alone without converting color.

- **Convert document's colors to the working space:** This option assigns the current RGB workspace you've identified in your color settings. At the top of the dialog box, you can see the current RGB workspace (Working) listed. In Figure 5.5, the workspace is sRGB IEC61966-2.1.

- **Discard the embedded profile (don't color manage):** This option deletes the current embedded profile and does not convert color to the current workspace.

What to do when the Embedded Profile Mismatch dialog box opens confuses most people. As a general rule, the best option in a color-managed workflow is to convert color to calibrated systems. Therefore, when you know your RGB workspace is calibrated or you use the generic Adobe RGB (1998) profile, choose the Convert document's colors to the working space option. This choice converts the color embedded in the Photoshop image to the working space you use. In essence, all the color potentially assigned in the original image converts to the best representation that your current monitor space can assume.

In Illustrator, a similar dialog box used for color-profile assignment opens as a warning dialog box, informing you of the color mismatch. InDesign shows a warning dialog box that reports mismatches in both the embedded color policy and the color profile, as shown in Figure 5.6. The options choices are self-explanatory.

FIGURE 5.6

The InDesign Embedded Policy and Profile Mismatch dialog box

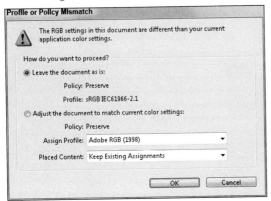

Color Management in the CS4 Applications

When you want to manage color among the CS4 applications, you can benefit greatly from Adobe's Common Color Architecture. The profile management and assignment is similar among all the Adobe CS4 programs, and when you understand how to manage color in one program, you can easily apply the same settings across all the programs. Each of the applications begins by addressing the color settings via menu commands.

With the CS4 applications, you need only set up the color settings in one program, then use the Bridge to synchronize color among the remaining programs. Typically, Photoshop is the tool you most often use for adjusting color settings, but because of the consistency among programs, you can use any one of the CS4 programs to adjust the settings. Color settings are identical in Photoshop, Illustrator, and InDesign. A few variances occur among these programs. To adjust color settings in the CS4 applications, choose Edit ⇨ Color Settings. Acrobat's color settings are adjusted in the Preferences dialog box.

CROSS-REF More on using Bridge to synchronize color settings is covered in Chapter 6.

Adjusting color settings

You can address Photoshop color settings by choosing Edit ⇨ Color Settings. The Color Settings dialog box shown in Figure 5.7 opens. Click More Options and the dialog box expands to offer additional settings. After you click More Options, it changes to Fewer Options. The options choices you have for managing color in any CS4 application include the following.

FIGURE 5.7

With the exceptions for Gray and Spot color handling in Photoshop, the Color Settings dialog box has the same appearance in Photoshop, Illustrator, and InDesign.

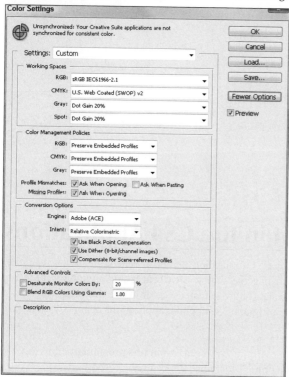

The first group is the Working Spaces where you select a color working space for your monitor. Ideally, you want your monitor color to be as close to the color produced on a printing device. The four adjustments to make for your working space include:

- **RGB:** The RGB space defines what you see on your computer monitor. This space is commonly referred to as your *working space*. Because you perform most of your image editing on RGB images, you work in this color space before eventually converting to CMYK color for commercial printing. In some cases, you may leave images in RGB mode or not convert them to CMYK if the output device is an RGB device. Certain large-format inkjet printers, photo printers such as Fuji Frontier, and film recorders are best imaged from RGB files. If you have a calibrated monitor, use the profile created by your calibration equipment. If you plan on designing files for commercial output to imagesetters, platesetters, or press, use the Adobe RGB (1998) profile if your monitor is not calibrated. If your output is designed for screen and Web viewing, use sRGB IEC61966-2.1 as your monitor space.

- **CMYK:** This profile is used for the output device—typically a CMYK printing device for composite printing and press. If you are designing artwork for press, use the U.S. Web Coated (SWOP) v2 for printing in the U.S. If printing outside the U.S., use the model common to the area where you print your files. For example, use the Japan Color 2001 Coated when printing on coated stock in Japan. The settings you choose in this pull-down menu affect your color conversion when you convert color in Photoshop. If you prepare CMYK files for direct output or importing in other applications via the Image ⇨ Mode ⇨ CMYK Color menu command, Photoshop characterizes the color according to the output profile.

- **Gray:** The pull-down menu choices affect grayscale images only in terms of dot gain and gamma adjustments. The actual result of making changes among the available settings affects the dot gain on press. In simple terms, you can target grayscale images to print darker or lighter. Decreasing the dot gain value leaves larger dots causing a darker image. You can also darken the image by increasing the gamma value. Increasing the dot gain creates smaller dots that spread out to become larger dots. The end result is dependent on the paper/ink combination that is being used.

- **Spot:** The choices here are similar to the choices available for Gray, because the spot color separations are printed like gray plates. Making adjustments to the dot gain also results in darker and lighter images.

The next section in the Color Settings dialog box is Color-management policies. The choices here affect the profile management and mismatching behavior. You can instruct Photoshop to react to profile mismatches or ignore them according to the settings made from the pull-down menus:

- **RGB:** You have three options from the pull-down menu. This first item deals with the RGB workspace. If your workspace is the one we suggested earlier in this section in "the RGB section—Adobe RGB (1998)—then a file saved with embedded profiles using any other profile from the RGB workspace is a mismatch. Accordingly, you can instruct Photoshop to turn off color management for working spaces by selecting Off, choose Preserve Embedded Profiles to not affect a color conversion, or select Convert to Working RGB where the saved profile is converted to the current RGB working profile. Turning off color management ignores all color profiling. Preserving Embedded Profiles keeps the color the same as assigned in the profile. Convert to Working RGB converts the color to the current RGB working space.

- **CMYK:** The same options are available from pull-down menus as those found in the RGB pull-down menus.

- **Gray:** The same options are available from the same kinds of pull-down menus.

- **Profile Mismatches: Ask When Opening:** When you select this check box, a dialog box prompts you when a mismatch occurs. For workflow environments, it's a good idea to check the box so you know when a color conversion is about to take place.

- **Profile Mismatches: Ask When Pasting:** If you copy data from one file and paste it into another file, you can copy an image with one embedded profile and paste the data into a document with another identified profile. Checking this box opens a dialog box alerting you to the color conversion.

- **Missing Profiles:** If you open legacy files or files that were not color-managed or have no profile assignment, you can instruct Photoshop to offer you an option for managing color in the opened files. A dialog box opens where you can assign profiles as the documents open in the Photoshop window.

- **Conversion Options:** You have choices for using the Adobe Color Engine (ACE) or color engines that your operating system supplies. For handling color among the CS4 applications and across platforms, use the Adobe Color Engine.

- **Intent:** There are four standard options related to color intent. *Intent* refers to what happens when color is converted, specifically in terms of white points and color equivalents. The options choices for intent include the following:

  - **Perceptual:** Perceptual preserves the overall color appearance through the process of changing colors in the source color space so they fit inside the destination color space. This option is a particularly good choice when you have a number of colors that reside outside the destination color space. The color equivalents are matched as close as possible.

  - **Saturation:** As the name implies, Saturation tries to preserve the most vivid colors from the source space to the destination space. You might select this option when you want to convert PowerPoint slides, Excel graphs and charts, and other documents where vivid colors are apparent.

  - **Relative Colormetric:** This option tries to closely match the white point in the destination space with the same whites in the source space. After converting white, the other colors are matched as closely as possible. If you're pondering which space to use between Perceptual and Relative, use this option, because the whites are more likely to be reproduced accurately.

  - **Absolute Colormetric:** This option is an effort to simulate the color including white point for one output device to a second device. If a white in the source document is a bluish white and the destination is a yellowish white, the conversion adds more cyan to simulate the cooler white, thus rendering a closer approximation of the original image.

- **Use Black Point Compensation:** As the intents take care of the whites in converting color from source images to destination images, the separate option for black point compensation takes care of black ink conversion. Without compensating for black when converting colors, you can end up with muddy non-rich blacks. As a matter of default, keep this check box checked.

- **Use Dither (8-bit/channel images):** 8-bit channel images are 24-bit color images (8-bits per channel for 3 channels). If color transitions are stepped or crude, you may need to smooth them out. This check box does just that. Keep the check box enabled for all color conversion.

■ **Compensate for Scene-referred Profiles:** If you're dealing with video, then the color profile you want to use is much different from that used for print media. This option converts the profile for use in AfterEffects or another video editing package.

■ **Desaturate Monitor Colors By:** By default, some bright colors tend to appear somewhat flat on your computer monitor when using the Adobe RGB workspace. To render the images more true to appearance and prevent any misleading representations, keep this check box enabled.

■ **Blend RGB Colors Using Gamma:** When colors are blended in Photoshop like image data appearing on one layer over another layer, the blending of the colors can show visible problems in shadows and on the edges of the layers. If you see visible problems like this, check this box.

After you make your settings adjustments, click Save. The Save dialog box opens and the proper folder on your hard drive are targeted for the saved file. Type a name for the color-management setting and click Save. This color-management setting is then recognized by all the other Design Suite CS4 applications and Adobe Bridge.

Synchronizing color settings

After adjusting settings in Photoshop, Illustrator, or InDesign, open the Bridge. Regardless of which program you use to make settings adjustments, choose File ⇨ Browse to open the Bridge window.

In Adobe Bridge, choose Edit ⇨ Creative Suite Color Settings. The Suite Color Settings dialog box shown in Figure 5.8 appears. At the top of the dialog box you can see if the color settings are synchronized. If they are not synchronized, select the color-management setting you saved after making the settings adjustments and click Apply. Settings are now identical in the applicable CS4 applications.

CROSS-REF   For more information on working with Adobe Bridge, see Chapter 6.

Swapping Color Settings

If you create a settings file and click Save, the file is accessible to all the CS4 applications and to other users when you provide them with the profile. You can post a color-management setting on your network server, e-mail the file, or copy it to a media disk. Other users in your workflow can copy the file to the folder on their computers where all other color settings are saved. See the section "Acquiring Profiles" for the precise location where profiles are saved on the Macintosh and Windows. Once added to the proper folder, other users need only open Adobe Bridge and synchronize the color as explained in the section "Synchronizing Settings."

FIGURE 5.8

Select the color-management setting you want to use and click Apply to synchronize settings across all Design Suite CS4 applications.

Printing with Profiles

All the information related to profiling and managing color is fine in a theoretical environment, but when it comes to the real world, you must implement all the work you do in setting up your environment and observe the results. Ideally, you would have a color-calibration device and calibrate your computer monitor and the output device for precise results.

When you use a color-calibration system, you calibrate your monitor and the output device and measure colors as they lay down on the substrate you use for your prints. You develop the profile for a given printer and a given paper. Once you develop the profiles, you edit your images according to the monitor working space so the color values on your monitor come within a predictable range on your output. In essence, the monitor and output device are in parity in terms of color.

To print an image from a program like Photoshop, you would follow these steps after calibrating your system.

STEPS: Printing Composite Color Using Calibrated Profiles

1. **Adjust the color settings.** Set up your color settings according to the calibrations you performed. Be certain to choose the monitor working space you used to calibrate your monitor.

2. **Print the Document.** With your document open in Photoshop, choose File ⇨ Print. A document preview is displayed in the Print dialog box.

3. **Target the print for color management.** From the Printer Profile pull-down menu select Color Management from the menu options. Refer to Figure 5.1 to see the Print dialog box.

4. **Select the color profile created for the printer and paper.** In the Profile pull-down menu, select the profile created for the paper.

5. **Select the Rendering Intent.** Select the intent from the menu options for Intent.

6. **Select print options for the target printer.** If you're printing to composite color devices, you have options for your printer via the print driver, as shown in Figure 5.9. Various color settings, paper types, speed for printing, and so on are options choices in the Print dialog box. Choose the options from the Print Settings (Mac) or Properties (Windows).

FIGURE 5.9

Set the print options from available settings defined by your print driver.

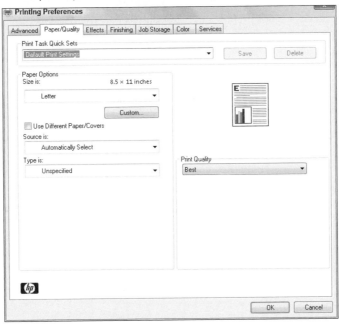

If you don't have a calibration system, you can run experiments using software tools to calibrate your monitor and test the output results. If you use this method, be ready to run tests many times before settling on a profile that works consistently for your printer.

CROSS-REF For more information on printing from Photoshop and the other CS4 applications, see Chapters 37 and 38.

Summary

- You can use color profiles to consistently reproduce color in your workflow among input devices, your viewing space, and your output equipment.

- Color calibration is optimum when using special tools to calibrate your computer monitor and output devices.

- You can acquire output profiles from service providers and install them on your computer.

- When profiles don't match, it's best to convert color to your calibrated workspace.

- The print-oriented Creative Suite applications use a common color engine developed by Adobe Systems.

- You apply color synchronization in Adobe Bridge.

- You can share color profiles and color settings that you developed in one CS4 application with other users in your workflow.

Chapter 6

Using Adobe Bridge

Adobe Bridge is the central hub for all CS4 apps. With the Adobe Bridge, you can organize all CS4 documents, version documents, learn tips and techniques on all the CS4 applications, and convert multiple camera raw images with different settings for saving and editing in Adobe Photoshop. You also can synchronize color management settings across the print oriented applications. In short, the Adobe Bridge is the center of the CS4 universe from where you control, manage, and maintain all your applications documents as well as enjoy some nifty features.

Getting Familiar with the Bridge Workspace

Adobe Bridge comes with both the Standard and Premium editions of the Creative Suite as well as with an individual copy of Photoshop CS4, Illustrator CS4, InDesign CS4, Flash CS4, or Dreamweaver CS4. Adobe Bridge is not included when you purchase a single copy of Acrobat Professional.

CROSS-REF Adobe Acrobat 9 Pro also includes the Organizer tool that works in some ways similar to the Bridge. Acrobat's Organizer is built into the program and used exclusively for managing PDF documents in Acrobat. For more information on Acrobat's Organizer, see Chapter 8.

To open the Bridge, follow these steps:

STEPS: Launch the Bridge

1. **Double-click the program icon.** Locate the Adobe Bridge program icon or the program alias, and double-click to launch the Bridge. Note that this method of launch is necessary when you work in Acrobat Professional or when you work without any other CS4 application open.

2. **Use a menu command in a CS4 program.** If you have Photoshop, Illustrator, InDesign, Acrobat, or Flash open, select File ⇨ Browse. In Dreamweaver, the command is File ⇨ Browse in Bridge. The Bridge opens in the foreground while the application from which the Bridge was launched remains open in the background. Using either method (Step 1 or Step 2) for launching the Bridge opens the Bridge window as shown in Figure 6.1.

   Within the Advanced panel in the Preferences dialog box, you can enable the Start Bridge at Login option to cause Bridge to open automatically when the computer starts.

FIGURE 6.1

You can launch the Bridge from the program icon or from any CS4 program including Adobe Acrobat.

Why Does Acrobat Have a Different Organization Tool?

Adobe Acrobat is the odd animal on the CS farm. Acrobat is developed and released before the other CS programs. If you permit us to speculate a moment, it is our belief that the development teams sometimes don't work in tandem when they upgrade the programs. Inasmuch as this release of the Creative Suite brings together more consistent interoperability between the programs than ever before, it has taken a complete development cycle before Acrobat has been endowed with Bridge accessibility.

A second reason for Acrobat's inclusion of an Organizer tool that is similar to Bridge is that Acrobat is the one program more often sold apart from other Adobe imaging and layout applications. Adobe implemented the Organizer in Acrobat to provide a file browser type utility for those users working with business programs who are not likely to purchase any of the CS programs.

TIP You also can launch Adobe Bridge by clicking the Bridge icon located at the left end of the Options bar in Photoshop, Illustrator, and InDesign. In Flash and Fireworks, you can access Bridge from the File ⇨ Browse in Bridge menu command. In Dreamweaver, the icon is located in the Insert panel, which is opened with the View ⇨ Toolbars ⇨ Standard menu.

CROSS-REF For information on editing metadata, see the section "Working with Metadata."

Using the Bridge interface

The Bridge has a standard interface similar to the other CS4 apps including several palettes and panels that are easy to move about the window. In the center of the Bridge interface is a large window that displays thumbnails for the current folder, as shown in Figure 6.2. This large window is also a panel that can be moved to any of the available columns.

The Content panel displays thumbnail images for all Adobe CS application documents. A description for each file is reported below the thumbnail image for filename (depending on the options that are enabled and the size of the thumbnails). The description information can include the creation date and time, image resolution, and dpi (dots per inch). The filenames are editable in the content area. Click a filename, and wait a moment for the I-beam cursor to appear.

FIGURE 6.2

Thumbnails are displayed for the current folder in the Content panel.

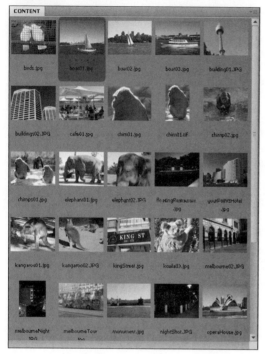

To the left of the main thumbnail display panel are the Favorites, Folders, Filter, and Collections panels, as shown in Figure 6.3.

The Bridge components contained in the left panel include the following:

> **A**   **Favorites/Folders:** Two tabs appear at the top of the left pane. The Favorites items include the items detailed in D through J below. When you click the Folders tab, you can navigate your hard drive and any connected and networked devices including external drives and memory sticks, by opening folders viewed in a hierarchy containing root and nested folders.

FIGURE 6.3

The left side of the Bridge offers many tools and options for working with Bridge tasks.

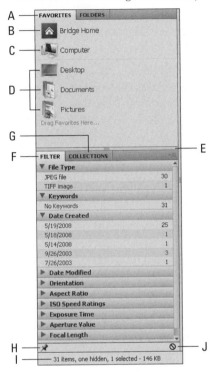

  B **Bridge Home:** Bridge Home is a Flash-based Web site with direct connections to Adobe news, training, and help for each of the CS4 applications. An Internet connection is required to access the Bridge Home content.

  C **Computer (My Computer):** Click the icon, and you navigate to the root location where your boot drive, external drives, CD drives, and network places are accessed.

 **The Version Cue option is also available if Version Cue is enabled. Using this option, you can start a new Version Cue project directly from within the Bridge.**

D **Desktop/Documents/Pictures:** These links (on the Macintosh) are designed to point to the standard file folders that hold documents and images. For Windows, you can customize similar folders in the Desktop, Documents, or Pictures folders.

E **Separator bar:** You can drag the separator bars to resize the panes.

F **Filter:** From the Filter panel, you have options to focus the files viewed in the Content area using several different criteria including Filename, Document Type, Date Created, File Size, Resolution, Dimensions, and so on.

G **Collections:** Collections are designed to contain sets of files that match a defined set of search parameters. There is also a Smart Collections feature that holds a dynamic search that constantly collects files that match the criteria of the smart collection.

H **Keep Filter when Browsing:** This option maintains the desired filter while browsing to another filter when enabled.

I **Status bar:** The text at the bottom of the panel displays details about the selected thumbnails.

J **Clear Filter:** This option removes the current filter setting and shows all files in the current folder.

The right side of the Bridge window, shown in Figure 6.4, includes a Preview panel for the current selection. You use it to view thumbnail images of all CS4 application documents and PDF files. The Preview panel can also be used to view several other media file types including .mov and .avi files. Non-Adobe documents that aren't recognized are shown in the window, but previews are not shown. The tools in these panels include:

A **Preview:** Click an image in the Content panel, and the selected document appears in the Preview pane. Note that previews for documents are provided for all CS application documents and for many different types of non-Adobe files including sound and multimedia files. The Preview pane can hold multiple selections allowing you to compare images side by side.

TIP **If you click the image in the Preview pane, the Loupe tool appears that lets you zoom in on a small section of the image.**

B **Document Title:** The filename is reported for the current selected file. You cannot edit the filename in the Preview pane.

C **Metadata:** Metadata is information that an authoring application automatically supplies. This information includes the creation and modification date as well as the custom data you can add to the file, such as copyright information or author name. The metadata are displayed for the current selected file in the content area.

D **Cancel:** Click Cancel if you edit metadata in a document and want to cancel all changes you made in the Metadata pane.

E **Apply:** Click the Apply check mark to apply an edit made in the Bridge to a file's metadata.

FIGURE 6.4

The panels to the right of the Content area contain tools for viewing image previews of the CS4 application documents.

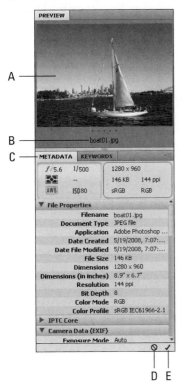

In the upper-left corner of the Bridge interface are several menu buttons, as shown in Figure 6.5. These buttons include the following:

The menu buttons feature some helpful menu shortcuts.

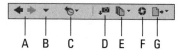

A   B   C   D   E   F G

A   Navigation arrows: As you view different folders, you can click the left arrow to view the previously viewed folder or the right arrow to trace your steps forward. Note that the right arrow becomes active only when you have first visited a previous folder by clicking the left arrow.

B   Go to Parent or Favorites: This button presents a drop-down list of all the parent folders for the current item. It also includes options for accessing the Favorites, Bridge Home, Desktop, Pictures, and Documents folders.

C   Reveal Recent Files: This button opens a folder of recently accessed folders. It also includes an option to Clear all Recent Files and Folders.

D   Get Photos from Camera: This button lets you access the Photo Downloader utility for obtaining digital photos from a docked camera.

E   Refine: The Refine button includes options for opening Review Mode, doing a Batch Rename, and viewing the File Info for the selected file.

F   Open in Camera Raw: This button opens the selected image in the Camera Raw processing dialog box.

G   Output: The Output button includes options for outputting the selected file to PDF or to the Web.

The upper-right corner of the Bridge interface contains several more menu buttons, as shown in Figure 6.6. These buttons include the following:

The right side of the interface includes some menu buttons.

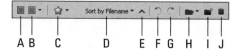

A B   C   D   E F G   H   I J

A **Prefer Embedded Images:** This button speeds the browsing of images by using any embedded previews instead of having to load and display the images.

B **Thumbnail Quality Settings:** This button includes options for the preview quality versus speed. Options include Prefer Embedded, High Quality on Demand, and Always High Quality. Another option lets you Generate 100% Previews.

C **Filter by Rating:** This button filters the thumbnails by the ratings applied to the various files. Other options let you show only rejected items, only unrated items, only labeled items, or only unlabeled items.

D **Sort Options:** This button offers a list of sorting options including by Filename, Type, Date Created, Date Modified, Size, Dimensions, Resolution, Color Profile, Label, and Rating. You also have a Manually option.

E **Ascending/Descending:** This button lets you toggle between ascending and descending order.

F **Rotate Left:** Select a thumbnail in the content area, and click the Rotate Left tool. The image is rotated left.

G **Rotate Right:** This button rotates the selected thumbnail right.

H **Open Recent Files:** Clicking this presents a list of recently opened files for the various CS4 applications. You also have a Clear Menu option.

I **Create New Folder:** As the icon implies, clicking it creates a new folder. If you have a folder open, the new folder is created within the current active folder.

J **Delete:** The familiar trash icon denotes deleting a file when you click it. First select an image in the content area, a range of images, or a folder, and then click the trash icon.

Finally, in the lower-right corner of the interface are several buttons and a slider for setting the view options and thumbnail sizes, as shown in Figure 6.7. These buttons include the following:

FIGURE 6.7

The thumbnail slider changes the size of the thumbnails.

A **Smallest Thumbnail Size:** This button zooms to the smallest thumbnail size.

B **Zoom Slider:** Move the slider to the left to zoom out of the thumbnail view and to the right to zoom in. Click the opposing icons to view the smallest and largest (M) sizes respectively.

C **Largest Thumbnail Size:** This button zooms to the largest thumbnail size.

D **Lock Thumbnail Grid:** This button creates a grid where each thumbnail has the same size. It also sizes the thumbnails within the Content panel to fit within the given space so you can page through thumbnails without seeing only part of a thumbnail.

E **View as Thumbnails:** This button makes all files visible as thumbnails.

F **View Contents as Details:** This button makes all files visible along with their details.

G **View Contents as List:** This button displays all files as a list similar to what you'd see in a Finder or Explorer view where all the file details are displayed within columns. You can sort the files by clicking on the column head.

Saving Bridge workspaces

When you practice a little using the Bridge to view files and mark documents with stars, you can easily understand simple methods for sorting and organizing all the content you use for a given project. When you create certain views such as navigating to a folder and sorting documents by stars and/or labels, you may want to return to the last view obtained in the Bridge. Fortunately, Adobe anticipated such needs and offers you a method of saving workspaces much like you save workspaces in other CS applications.

Workspaces are custom defined views that keep track of the position and placement of the various panels along with the different display options. Within the Window ➪ Workspace menu are options for managing workspaces including resetting, saving, and deleting the current workspace. You also can access several default workspaces including:

- **Essentials:** Displays all images using the standard default thumbnails and columns of panels to the left and right.

- **Filmstrip:** Displays all thumbnails along the bottom of the Content panel and the selected thumbnail in a large Preview panel above the horizontal thumbnails with the default panels to the left, as shown in Figure 6.8.

- **Metadata:** Displays a list of files with small thumbnails and file details sorted in columns, as shown in Figure 6.9.

- **Output:** Displays a large preview of the selected thumbnail along with a horizontal strip of thumbnails. The Output panel is displayed to the right.

- **Keywords:** Displays a list of larger thumbnails with all its file details to the right using the View Contents as Details option.

■ **Preview:** Displays a vertical column of thumbnails next to a large Preview panel on the right.

■ **Light Table:** Fills the entire window with the Content panel showing thumbnails.

■ **Folders:** Displays all thumbnails along with the Folders panel to the left.

The Filmstrip workspace displays a large version of the selected thumbnail.

FIGURE 6.9

The Metadata workspace displays all the file details in columns.

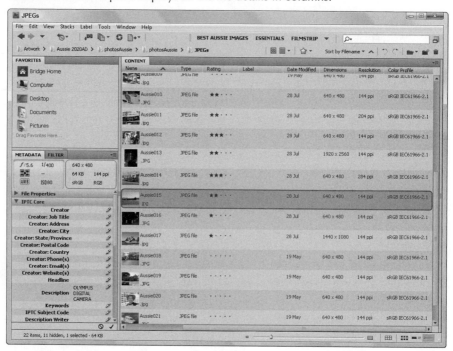

Any custom defined workspaces are displayed in the Options bar at the top of the interface for quick selection. You can reorder these links by dragging them to the left or right.

Managing panes

You can manage tabs in the Bridge much like you can with other CS applications to customize the workspace. In the Bridge, the tabs are always docked in the Bridge window, but you can move and mix them in the left or right panels. If you want to add more room for displaying thumbnails, drag all the tabs in the right column and drop them in the panes on the left. You can then toggle views among the Metadata, Keywords, and Preview tabs as shown in Figure 6.10.

CROSS-REF For information on adding and editing metadata, see the section "Working with Metadata," later in this chapter.

If you move your tabs around and you want to change the arrangement back to the original look, choose Window ➪ Workspace ➪ Reset Standard Workspace.

FIGURE 6.10

To provide more viewing room for thumbnails, drag the Preview, Metadata, and Keywords tabs to the right column of panes.

Managing windows

You can open multiple windows in the Bridge and work back and forth between windows much like when you work with multiple file folders on your desktop. To open another window, choose File ➪ New Window. The new window opens as an exact duplicate of the active window showing the same file location and window dimensions. You can then change folder locations and manage different tab views in different windows.

If you use the Window ➪ New Synchronized Window menu, then an identical view of the current window is displayed, but the new window is linked to the original window so that changes in one window are reflected in the synchronized window.

TIP   If you have a two-monitor configuration, then you can use a set of synchronized windows to show an expanded Preview pane on one monitor and the Content pane on the other monitor.

To close a window, click the close box in the upper-right corner or press ⌘/Ctrl+W.

Organizing Files and Folders

Just as you have many options for file organization on your computer desktop, the Bridge offers you many of the same options and more. When you work with the Creative Suite, you don't have to leave the Bridge to organize or edit any documents, and you can move and arrange files and folders all within the Bridge window.

Creating new folders

New folders are created in the Bridge window. At the top of the Bridge window, click the New Folder icon, and a new *untitled folder* is added to the folder in view. The text is highlighted when a new folder is added. Just type a name for your folder, and press the Return/Enter or Num Pad Enter key to register the name.

You can locate new folders by dragging them around the content area. The content area behaves similarly to a slide sorter where you can organize documents and folders according to personal preferences. Click and drag a folder or document around the content pane. When a vertical black separator bar appears, Bridge informs you that when you release the mouse button, the folder (or document) will be dropped to the right of the separator bar.

Adding files to folders

To create subfolders within folders and place files within folders, first add a new folder as described in the preceding section, "Creating new folders." Name your new folder. Select a group of files by Shift-clicking or ⌘/Ctrl-clicking. Drag the selected documents (and folders to nest the folders) to the new folder added in the Bridge. Release the mouse button, and all your files/folders are added to the subfolder.

You also can add files and folders to folders by dragging and dropping them from the desktop to the Bridge window. The Bridge is smart; when you drag a file from within an open folder in desktop view to the Bridge window and release the mouse button, Adobe Bridge drops the file in the respective folder. The Bridge view subsequently changes to the folder where the file is placed. In other words, your desktop view is completely mirrored in the Bridge window, and file locations are preserved when you drag them to and from the Bridge window.

Moving and copying files

You can easily drag and drop files between folders in the Bridge window to relocate them. The relocation of files in the Bridge window is mirrored on your desktop. If you drag a file from the Bridge window to your desktop or another folder, you likewise relocate the file on your desktop and the action is mirrored in the Bridge window.

If you have two hard drives or an external media device attached to your computer and you drag a file from the Bridge window to a secondary drive, the file is copied to the target drive. To move a file from a folder and ultimately from the Bridge window, press the ⌘/Ctrl key and click and drag from one media source to another. The file is copied to another drive and deleted from the source drive.

To copy a file from one folder to another folder on the same drive, press Option/Alt and drag and drop a file.

Navigating folders

When browsing your hard drive to find files, you'll want to view the Folders tab in the Bridge window. The Folders tab displays your computer hard drive and all drives attached and networked to your computer. Click a drive or folder to access files contained therein, or click the arrows adjacent to drives and folders to display nested folders.

You can easily return to last viewed folders by clicking on the Path Bar, as shown in Figure 6.11. Clicking the folder icon adjacent to the current folder moves you up one level, while clicking the left and right arrows helps navigate to previous and next views.

FIGURE 6.11

The Folders tab displays folders contained in the root drive and all attached media devices.

Path Bar

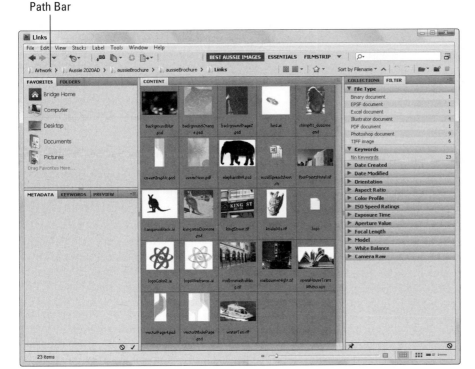

Rating and labeling files

You also can sort using one of five different ratings (identified as stars) that you can individually assign to files. Additionally, you can sort files by labels that also are individually user defined. When a document thumbnail is selected in the content area, five tiny stars appear below the thumbnail. Click a tiny star, and the icon becomes larger, as shown in Figure 6.12. In the figure, you can see several documents tagged with different stars and one image with the default rating.

FIGURE 6.12

Four files are rated. At the top left and right are one star, and at the bottom left and right three stars.

In addition to rating files with stars, you also can label files with color codes. Labeling files with colors is an easy way to mark a number of files imported from digital cameras, CDs, external media cartridges, or other sources used to copy files to your hard drive. As files are reviewed, you can mark them with one of five different colors. You can customize color names in the Preferences dialog box. Although you cannot change the colors, you can identify a color with a specific name. For example, you can use labels to identify files according to status in a workflow.

To change the color names, open the Preferences dialog box. On the Macintosh, choose Bridge ➪ Preferences. On Windows, choose Edit ➪ Preferences. Alternately, you can press ⌘/Ctrl+K. The Preferences dialog box opens. In the left panel, click Labels, and the right panel changes to show the Label options, as shown in Figure 6.13.

FIGURE 6.13

Open the Preferences dialog box, and click Labels to change label options.

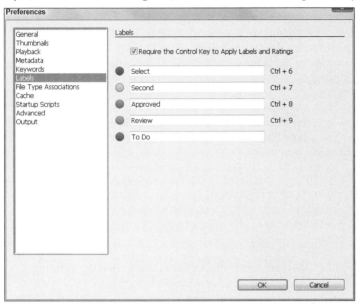

As shown in Figure 6.13, you can change the label name to a custom name by typing in the text box adjacent to any color. Changing labels should be something you do for your own personal file organization. If you change label names and share files with other users in your workgroup, the other users won't see the same label names.

NOTE XMP (eXtensible Metadata Platform) is an Adobe-specific set of data that provides information about a file and its use by Adobe applications. In order to store XMP data, a file must be XMP write capable. File types such as BMP (bitmap format), DCS (desktop color separation format), PICT (Macintosh Picture format), and Photoshop 6 PDF (Portable Document Format) are not XMP write capable.

After you label files, you can then sort and/or view them according to label, like sorting and viewing files according to stars. When you rate a file with a star rating and identify a document with a label, you can sort and/or view nested labels. For example, you can rate images with one, two, three, or four stars and label the same documents with different colors. You can then choose to display only red files with three or more stars, hence narrowing the number of displayed documents to those you specifically identify with a given identity.

You can view metadata you add in the Bridge when you work with the CS4 applications. If you label a Photoshop document in the Bridge with a label name, the name is visible when you open the file in Photoshop and select File ⇨ File Info. When the File Info dialog box opens, select Advanced in the left pane. In the right pane, you see a list of XMP and XML data. Click XMP Core

Properties, and open the nested list by clicking the right-pointing arrow. Scroll down the list, and you find xap:Label. The label name you supplied in the Bridge is identified with the same name you added in the Bridge.

Likewise, you can view metadata when you import photos in Adobe InDesign. In InDesign, don't use the File menu command. Rather, open the Info palette (Window ➪ Info). Select the Photoshop image in the layout, and from the palette flyout menu, select File Info. A dialog box opens with the same options as you find in Photoshop. Click Advanced, and view the XMP Core Data. The xap:Label displays the same label name.

NOTE The File ➪ File Info command shows information about the InDesign file instead of information about the placed PSD file, but if you select the placed item and use the Info panel, you can get info about the linked file.

Be aware that assigning a label color in the Bridge is just a means of visually identifying documents in the Bridge window. What's important is the label name. The name is written to the XMP data and thereby is visible to the other CS applications. When using labels in the Bridge, be certain to not use the color names if you want label names to be written to the XMP data. Descriptive names are more meaningful in your workgroup than color names.

You cannot write XMP data to certain file types mentioned earlier in this section on "Labeling files." Additionally, you cannot write XMP data to files that are locked, such as files you open from CD-ROMs. You may find that the label names for all these files are retained in the Bridge window, but don't be fooled. The labels are stored in the Bridge cache (a memory location on your hard drive). When the cache is cleared or the CD-ROM is viewed on a different machine, the label names for these files are not retained. The only label names retained are within the metadata for those file types supporting XMP write that aren't on a read-only storage device.

Deleting files

You can remove files and folders from your hard drive directly from within the Bridge window. To delete a file or folder, select the item(s) to delete and press the Delete/Backspace key or Del key. When you select one of these delete commands, a dialog box appears asking whether you'd like to Reject or Delete the file. Rejected files are given a sub-zero star rating and can be hidden using the View ➪ Show Rejected Files menu. If you use the Ctrl/⌘+Delete command, then the dialog box is skipped and the file is automatically deleted.

Likewise, you can select files/folders to delete and click the trash icon in the Bridge window. When you delete files using the Bridge, the files are moved to the trash can on your desktop. If you change your mind and want to retain files, move them out of the trash can in desktop view to the desired folder.

Using context menus

Like all the CS applications, the Bridge supports the use of context menus. Depending on the file type, menu options change. If you select any file type including non-Adobe application documents, and open a context menu on a file in the content area, the menu choices are as shown in Figure

6.14. You open context menus by right-clicking the mouse. On Macintosh with a one-button mouse, press the Ctrl key and click to open a context menu.

Select any file type and open a context menu.

Menu options for all files are slightly different depending on the type of file that is selected, but some of the common commands include the following:

- **Open:** Select a file, and choose open results in the same operation as double-clicking a file in the content or Preview pane. The default editing application opens the file.

- **Open With:** From the submenu, you have a list of programs from which to choose. You might have a PDF file that by default opens in Adobe Acrobat. If you want to open the file in Adobe Reader, use Open With and choose Adobe Reader from the menu options.

- **Test in Device Central:** This menu choice opens the file in a window that can emulate the display of the file on one of several different multimedia-enabled phones and PDAs.

- **Open in Camera Raw:** This menu choice opens the file into a Camera Raw window where you can alter the Camera Raw settings.

- **Cut, Copy,** and **Paste:** These commands let you cut, copy, and paste files between different folders.

- **Delete/Move to Trash:** This choice removes a file from a folder and deposits it in the trash can on the desktop. Choosing this menu command performs the same operation as selecting a file and clicking the trash icon in the Bridge window or pressing the Delete/ Backspace or Del keys.

- **Move to, Copy to:** These menu items let you move or copy the selected file to a selected folder from a menu.

- **Reveal in Explorer/Reveal in Finder:** This menu choice also is available under the File menu. If you want to find a file in a desktop view, select this menu command.

- **Add to Favorites:** You can add a file to your Favorite list. For more information about using Favorites, see the section "Adding Favorites" later in this chapter.

- **Rename/Batch Rename:** You can rename a single folder or file or a folder of files in a batch sequence. For more information on creating batch sequences, see the section "Batch processing with actions" later in this chapter.

- **Develop Settings:** This menu provides access to the Camera Raw settings for the selected file. You also have options for copying and pasting settings between files.

- **Generate High Quality Thumbnail:** This menu updates the current thumbnail to display it using high-quality settings.

- **Lock Item:** This locks the current file or folder so it cannot be moved or renamed. Locked items have a simple icon displayed in the upper-right corner.

- **File Info:** Select File Info, and the same dialog box you open in the CS programs opens in the Bridge. You can add metadata in the File Info dialog box.

- **Label:** From the submenu, you have choices the same as when using the label section in the Label menu. You cannot choose ratings from this submenu, but you can assign labels to selected documents.

- **New Folder:** This menu option creates a new folder in the current folder.

- **Sort:** This menu sorts the current contents passed on the selected sort option.

- **Start Meeting:** This option begins a new collaboration meeting with other users.

Working with stacks

If you have a group of images that are similar or that you want to group together, you can organize them by grouping them together into a stack. A stack is a group of images that are collected together to help make the folder structure simpler. Creating a stack of images doesn't delete or remove any individual items.

Creating a new stack

To create an image stack, just select several items and choose the Stacks ⇨ Group as Stack menu command. All the images are collected together into a stack, and the thumbnail for the stack changes to show that it is a stack, as shown in Figure 6.15. The number of items contained in the stack is displayed in the upper-left corner of the stack thumbnail, providing at a quick glance how many items are in the stack. If you select the Stack ⇨ Open Stack menu command, then all the individual items are displayed, but the individual items are still included in a bounding box to show that they are part of a stack. The Stack ⇨ Close Stack menu command is used to collapse a stack together again.

When a stack is closed, only the thumbnail for the item on top of the stack is displayed. If you click this thumbnail then only the single item is selected, and if you change the metadata you are only changing it for this one item. If you click the outline of the stack, then all the items in the stack are selected, and if you change the metadata for this selection, then it is changed for all the items in the stack.

 **TIP** You can quickly tell if one item or all items in the stack are selected by looking at the Preview pane. If the stack is selected, then multiple items are shown in the Preview pane.

NOTE Stacks can be labeled and rated just like individual files, but only the rating of the top file in the stack is displayed.

FIGURE 6.15

Image stacks combine several individual thumbnails together into a group.

Five image stack

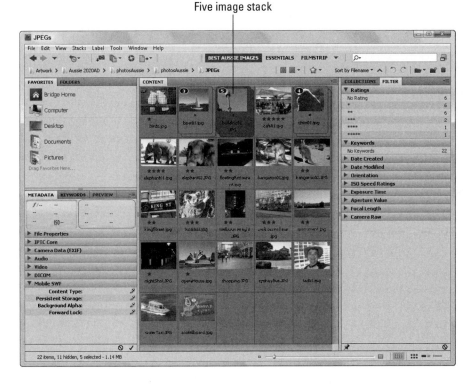

You can dissolve a stack using the Stacks ➪ Ungroup from the Stack menu. This returns all stacked items to their original thumbnails. You also can rotate the stack order when the stack is open using the Stacks ➪ Promote to Top of Stack or by dragging a file to the top of the stack. This makes the selected stack item appear as the visible thumbnail when the stack is closed.

New items can be added to an existing stack by dragging and dropping a file onto an existing stack. You also have options in the Stacks menu to Expand and Collapse all stacks.

Previewing a stack

When a stack includes ten or more images, you can cycle through the images using a Play button that appears when you move the mouse over the top of the stack. This displays each image in succession. Next to the Play button is a slider that you can drag to scrub through the images.

CAUTION If the Play button and slider don't appear when you move the mouse over the stack, then increase the size of the stack. The Play button and slider won't appear when the stack size is too small.

For the animated preview, you can set the Frame Rate at which the images are played back using the Stacks ➪ Frame Rate menu command.

TIP Stacks are very handy for previewing animation sequences that consist of multiple successive images.

Working with Collections

Collections in Bridge provide a way to save your search criteria so you don't need to reenter it anew every time. You can save searches as a Collection and easily retrieve files having met a given set of search criteria. This feature saves you much time when returning to search results.

NOTE Collections are found in Bridge and also in Acrobat and they both work fairly similar. Collections in Acrobat provide a way to have a single selectable item in the Organizer point to files in different locations.

CROSS-REF For information on using Acrobat's Organizer, see Chapter 8.

To create a new Collection, open the Find dialog box, shown in Figure 6.16. After defining a search and finding several folders the results are displayed in the Content panel. If you open the Collections panel and click the Save as Collection button, then a new collection icon is added to the Collection panel. This lets you create a new collection item that holds the designated search criteria.

FIGURE 6.16

Click Collections, and open a context menu in the content area to create a new Collections folder.

The Collections panel also supports Smart Collections. To create a Smart Collections, click the New Smart Collection button located at the bottom of the Collections panel. This opens the Find dialog box where you can define the custom search. The difference between a Smart Collection and a standard collection is that the Smart Collection continues to add files that meet the defined criteria to its set every time the Smart Collection is accessed.

Adding Favorites

You can add files and folders to the Favorites pane. Open a folder in the Bridge, and select a file or folder. From a context menu, select Add to Favorites. Likewise, you can select a file or folder and choose File ➪ Add to Favorites. Either command adds your file or folder to the list of Favorites and provides easy quick access to the files.

When you add files and folders to the Favorites pane, you are not copying files or moving them from one location to another. The Favorites are like document aliases or shortcuts and require very little storage space. When you delete a Favorite—either by selecting it and clicking the trash icon, using a key on your keyboard, or using a context menu—the Favorite is removed from the list, but your files remain in their original location.

CAUTION   Adding many files to the Favorites defeats part of the purpose for the Bridge—which is essentially to help you organize and manage your program documents. If you have a long list of Favorites and need to scroll the pane to find files, your organization becomes messy and unorganized. Be selective when you add files, and try to use folders where files for a current project are stored. Be certain to perform cleanup and remove files and folders routinely from the Favorites list after you complete projects or no longer use the files.

Batch renaming files

If you use a digital camera, you may want to take the cryptic names the camera uses to save your files and change them to more descriptive filenames. Bridge lets you add names and extensions to files in a snap. You can add names that give a better clue for what the contents of images are rather than names like P1010273 or CRW_6062.

To rename files using a batch command, follow these steps.

STEPS: Using Batch Rename

1. **Open a folder of files in the Bridge that you want to rename.** If you have digital camera files, use them for the following steps. If not, use any folder of photos. The original files won't be disturbed if you follow these steps.

2. **Select the files you want to rename.** Typically, you will rename an entire folder of files. When renaming all files in a folder, press ⌘/Ctrl+A to select all the images. If you want to select certain files for renaming, Shift-click or ⌘/Ctrl-click to select contiguous or non-contiguous groups.

TIP If you have files in different folders and you want to rename files from the different folders, first perform a search. You need some form of metadata common to all the files. Your search results are reported in a new Bridge window, even though the files are stored in different folders. Select all the files you want to rename, and save the results to either the source folder or a new folder. For more information on searching metadata, see the section "Searching in the Bridge" later in this chapter.

3. **Create a folder for the destination files.** You can choose to rewrite the existing filenames or write copies of the files to a different folder. The new folder will contain the renamed files. For these steps, use a second folder where the files are to be copied. You can create a new folder in the Bridge window where you view the files to rename.

4. **Select the Batch Rename command.** Open the Tools menu and select the command, or open a context menu on one of the selected images and choose Batch Rename. The Batch Rename dialog box opens, as shown in Figure 6.17.

5. **Choose a destination folder.** Select the radio button for Copy to other folder. This option copies the files to another folder while leaving the original images unedited. To specify the target folder for the copied images, click Browse. The Browse for Folder dialog box opens, and you can navigate to your hard drive and identify the target folder. Select the folder you want to use, and click Choose.

6. **Add a root name.** The default New Filename is the root name. The pull-down menu defaults to Text, and the name you want to use is typed in the text box on the right. If you stop here and process the batch, your filenames will appear as photo (1), photo (2), photo (3), where photo is used as the root name. Add a name to the text box, but don't click Rename yet.

FIGURE 6.17

Add a root name and a sequence number in the Batch Rename dialog box.

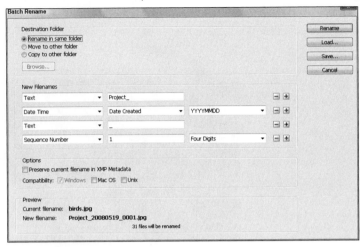

7. **Add a Sequence Number.** Rather than have your filenames appear as name+(1), and so on, you can add a sequence number so the name appears as photo001, photo002, photo003, and so on. To do so, you need to add another option in the New Filenames section of the Batch Process dialog box. Click the plus (+) symbol to the right of the text box, and the dialog box expands to reveal more options you can use for filenames. Open the second pull-down menu, and select Sequence Number from the menu commands. In the text box to the right of the menu choice, add "001" as shown in Figure 6.14. Note the example of the filename shown at the bottom of the dialog box under the *New filename* label.

TIP Depending on where you view files, such as desktop views, dialog boxes, applications windows, and so on, filenames do not always appear in dictionary order. A file labeled as *image9* may appear after *image89* in some windows or dialog boxes. To ensure proper reading order in all windows and dialog boxes, be certain to add leading zeros sufficient enough to accommodate the number of files you want to rename. For example, you can use a single leading zero and two digits for files numbered up to 99, two leading zeros and three digits to accommodate files numbered up to 999, and so on.

8. **Process the batch.** Select the check box to preserve the current filename in the XMP Metadata, and click Rename in the top-right corner. After the Bridge processes the files, open the target folder and view the results. In Figure 6.18, the files were changed to a root name of "Aussie"—where the files were shot—and a sequence number beginning with 001.

FIGURE 6.18

After running the Batch Rename command, the files are renamed and saved to the target folder.

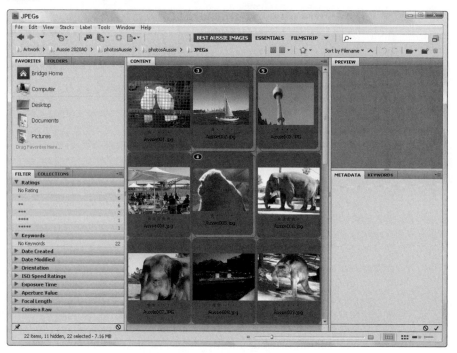

Working with Keywords and Metadata

Keywords and Metadata are data that can be used to describe your file. The information can be sorted, viewed in other applications, searched, and used to describe copyright information, identify files, and archive documents. With regards to user-supplied information, if you had to manually enter rows of field data in each and every file, metadata would be a useless tool. However, Adobe makes it much easier for you by providing a means for creating a template and using that template to apply common metadata to gigabytes of documents.

Using Keywords

Keywords are defined and stored in the Keywords panel and can be organized into categories called *sub-keywords*. To create a new keyword for the selected image, click the New Keyword button at the bottom of the Keywords palette. This adds a text field where you can type the new keyword. The new keyword is automatically added to the top of the current keyword set. You can also create new keyword sets using the New Keyword Set button at the bottom of the palette.

Keywords can be added to a new keyword set by dragging and dropping them into the new set. Dragging a keyword or a keyword set into the trash icon deletes it. Once a keyword is added to a file, you need to enable the check box to the left of the keyword to associate the keyword with the file. Once enabled, you can search for images by keyword.

At the bottom of the Keywords panel is a search bar where you can enter a specific term to search for. The icon lets you choose to search for keywords that contain, are equal to, or start with an entered value.

Metadata properties

The Bridge lets you see document metadata at a glance in the Metadata panel. The Bridge Metadata Preferences determine which fields are displayed in the panel. You caught a glimpse of the Metadata Preferences in the section "Labeling files" earlier in the chapter. Label data is metadata, but the edits you made for label names occur in a separate preference pane than the Metadata pane. You cannot add metadata in the preferences; the Metadata Preferences are used to display and hide the categories shown in the Metadata panel in the Bridge window. Therefore, your first task is to open the Preferences and select which fields you want to view and ultimately edit when you work in the Metadata panel.

Open the Preferences dialog box, and click Metadata in the left pane. Metadata are divided into several categories in the Bridge. Some of these categories are single items, and others contain a nested group of fields expandable when you click the right-pointing arrow to expand (and collapse) the category. The categories include the following:

- **File Properties:** This describes file attributes, and most often the data are imposed automatically when you create files. Items like file size, creation date, modification date, resolution, bit depth, dimensions, and so on are all part of the File Properties, and you cannot edit these items. Non-editable items do not provide field boxes for text entries in the Metadata pane in the Bridge.

- **IPTC (IIM, legacy):** These data are editable in the Metadata pane. You can add information here for things like copyright information, captions, document title, author, keywords, and location. By default, however, this set of data is hidden from view. You also can add the same information to the IPTC Core. IPTC Core is a newer specification, and you should use it for all the data you add to current documents. The IPTC (IIK legacy) data appears from legacy files created before October 2004.

- **IPTC Core:** Like IPTC (IIM, legacy), all the data here are editable. As a new specification developed by the International Press Telecommunications Council (IPTC) in October 2004, you should use it with all your current documents. The same field data are available in the IPTC Core fields where you find identifying information as described above with IPTC (IIM legacy).

- **Fonts:** Fonts are applicable only to Adobe InDesign and Illustrator files. All the fonts used in an InDesign document or in an Illustrator document are displayed below the font heading when you select a file. When any other file type is selected, the Fonts category disappears.

- **Plates:** Plates are applicable only to Adobe Illustrator files. The plates indicate any spot color plates that are specified for the file, such as CMYK.

- **Document Swatches:** Like Fonts, Swatches are visible only with Adobe InDesign and Illustrator files and likewise disappear when you select file types, other than InDesign or Illustrator documents. In Figure 6.19 you can see the metadata information for fonts and swatches when you select an InDesign file. Note that the remaining categories are collapsed in the Metadata pane.

FIGURE 6.19

Fonts and Swatches display when you select InDesign or Illustrator documents.

- **Camera Data (Exif):** This information is not editable. The data are derived from digital cameras and provide information related to the settings applied when the photograph was taken. Notice in Figure 6.20 that all the information displayed with a photo taken from a digital camera. Exchangeable image file (Exif) data are written when files are saved from digital cameras in RAW, DNG, and JPEG formats and also can be embedded in TIFF-formatted files.

FIGURE 6.20

Camera Data (Exif) are reported for photos taken with digital cameras.

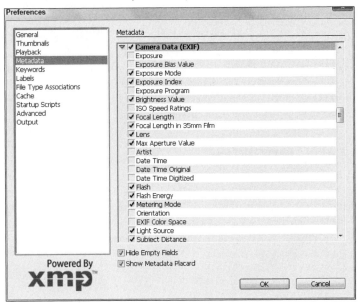

- **GPS:** Global Positioning System (GPS) data is useful for files containing a GPS system on the digital camera. If your camera does not have a GPS, then the data fields are left blank.

- **Camera Raw:** Camera Raw information describes the settings that Photoshop uses when you open a file and certain information about your camera and the settings used to shoot a photo.

- **Audio:** Any audio file data included in the file are described in these fields, including the Bit Rate, Channels, and Duration. You also can specify the Artist, Album, and Genre.

- **Video:** Any video segments included in the file are described here, including the Date Shot, Scene, Compressor used, and so on.

- **Edit History:** Edit History is like a log file that can keep track of editing history made in Adobe Photoshop.

- **Version Cue:** Version Cue information and comments are listed for Version Cue documents.

- **DICOM:** This data applies only to Photoshop CS3 Extended files and higher. It includes information for images saved using the Digital Imaging and Communications in Medicine (DICOM) format. This information can include the Patient's Name, ID, Date of Birth, Physician, and so on.

- **Mobile SWF:** This data holds information that enables images to be viewed on mobile devices and the options for displaying such images.

- **Viewing relevant data:** The many data fields available for metadata inclusion result in a long list. There are many different fields and categories you are likely not to use in any given editing session. Explore all the preference choices you have in the Metadata Preferences, and uncheck those items you never use or won't use for a collection of files. After disabling items you won't use, be certain to check the box for Hide Empty Fields. When you return to the Metadata pane in the Bridge window, only the fields that are checked are visible. This makes scrolling the list much easier, and you'll have an easier time when you need to add data to any given editable field. There is also an option to Show Metadata Placard that you can disable to hide the placard displayed at the top of the Metadata panel if you want more room to see the metadata.

Using XMP templates

If you want to edit a field, select a file and open the Metadata pane in the Bridge window and view the fields in the categories you have visible. On the right side of the pane, you can see a pencil icon for all the fields that are editable. If the icon is not present, you can't add data to the field. Click in a field, and the text box becomes active for any field marked with a pencil icon. In Figure 6.21, note the Creator: Emails(s) field is edited and the field boxes are outlined among the IPTC Core fields.

FIGURE 6.21

Look for fields containing a pencil icon, and click the field to make the text box active. Type the data you want to add to the document metadata.

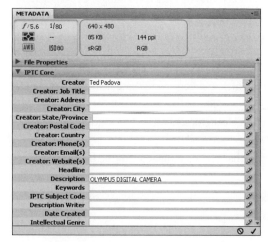

Obviously, if you have hundreds of files and many fields to edit, the process of manually typing data in fields is laborious, and you're not likely to add data to every image you take with a digital camera or use in a layout. Fortunately, you can supply common information to document metadata using templates.

Creating a template

You may be a photographer who shoots wedding, commercial, product, or other types of photography. If you perform a photo shoot and take the equivalent of several rolls or hundreds of digital photos, you are likely to use some common information in the metadata for your images on a given assignment. Typically you'll use your personal identifying information as well as information unique to the assignment such as location, client, project, and so on. All this information is common among the files and does not require you to add unique data for each file.

When you want to add common data to a group of images, you can easily create a metadata template and import the metadata into hundreds of photos with one click of the mouse. To see how a template is created, follow the steps detailed below.

STEPS: Creating a Metadata Template

1. **Select a Photoshop image in the Bridge.** You can use another CS application document, but for many artists the more common files you are likely to use more often are Photoshop documents. Select the Tools ➪ Create Metadata Template menu. This opens the Create Metadata Template dialog box.

NOTE You don't need to start with an image selected. With no file selected, you get a blank slate to work with. If the image already has some metadata defined, then you can use it as a template.

2. **Add data to the field boxes.** Several categories are listed in the Create Metadata Template dialog box, shown in Figure 6.22. Be certain to supply information that is common among all files. For example, for a given image, Author might be you or a professional photographer, and thus you would add the same common data to a large collection of files. Additionally you might have some descriptive information and keywords common among a group of files. However, the Document Title is typically a field that is unique among a group of images.

3. **Add IPTC information.** The fields where you find the most editable text boxes are contained in the IPTC section. Select IPTC Core, and add your personal contact information or the information of the photographer used for the photo shoot. Continue adding information relevant to your job in the IPTC Core category, and then move on to the other categories as appropriate.

4. **Name the template and save a Metadata Template.** Enter a name for the template in the top field and click the Save button. Note that you don't have an option to choose a destination folder. Metadata templates are automatically saved in a specific folder that the Bridge handles for you. The template is saved to the proper location and ready for use and can be selected from the Tools menu.

FIGURE 6.22

Add metadata for all common fields in the IPTC Core section.

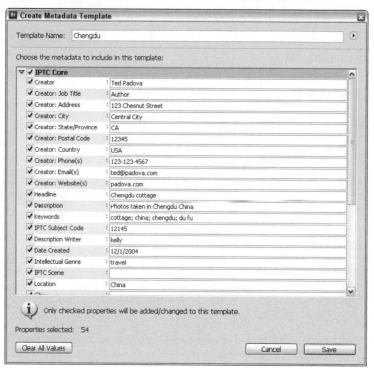

Appending and replacing data

After you create a Metadata template, it's time to add the template data to files. You have two choices. You can choose to replace data or append data. When you choose Replace Metadata, the existing properties are replaced with the template data. When you choose Append Metadata, the data from the template are added to fields only when non-existing data match the same fields. As a matter of rule, if you want the data to be identical in your files and the template data are current and correct, use the Replace Metadata command. To see how replacing (or appending) metadata is handled, follow these steps.

STEPS: Use a Metadata Template to Replace Data

1. **Select Files in the Bridge window.** You identify files to replace (or append) the template data by selecting them in the Bridge window. If you have a folder where you want all the files to be replaced with the template data, press ⌘/Ctrl+A to select all the files in the window. To select individual files in a folder, Shift-click or ⌘/Ctrl-click to make multiple selections.

TIP To select most files in a folder with several files unselected, select the fewer files first. Open the Edit menu, and select Invert Selection or press ⌘/Ctrl+Shift+I. The few files become deselected as the remaining files become selected.

2. **Open the Metadata palette menu.** Click the tiny right-pointing arrow in the top-right corner of the Metadata tab to open the flyout menu.

3. **Select the template to use to replace the data.** Select Replace Metadata from the menu options in the flyout menu, and select the template name you want to use in the sub-menu, as shown in Figure 6.23, or you can choose the Tools ⇨ Replace Metadata menu. If you have created only one template, you have only one choice in the submenu.

FIGURE 6.23

Select Replace (or Append) Metadata, and select a template name appearing in the sub-menu.

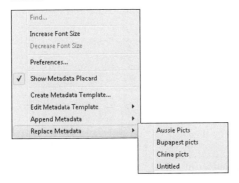

4. **Click OK in the warning dialog box.** An application alert dialog box opens asking you if you want to proceed. Click Yes in the dialog box.

5. **Pause to let the Bridge import the metadata.** In the lower-left corner of the Bridge window, you can see the status of the file updates. Be certain to wait until the Bridge completes its work. When finished, you can view the metadata on the selected files as shown in the example in Figure 6.24. If you divided a photo shoot into several folders, open each folder, select files, and use the Replace Metadata and your template to repeat updating the files.

FIGURE 6.24

Review the selected files, and you can see the metadata from the template added to the respective fields in each file.

▼ IPTC Core		
Creator	ted padova	
Creator: Job Title	Author	
Creator: Address		
Creator: City	Ventura	
Creator: State/Province	CA	
Creator: Postal Code	93003	
Creator: Country	USA	
Creator: Phone(s)		
Creator: Email(s)	ted@west.net	
Creator: Website(s)	http://www.west.net/~ted	
Headline		
Description	Photos taken in Chengdu China December 2004, January 2005	
Keywords	China; Chengdu	
IPTC Subject Code		
Description Writer		
Date Created		
Intellectual Genre		
IPTC Scene		
Location		
City	Chengdu	
State/Province	Sichuan Providence	
Country	China	
ISO Country Code	86	
Title		
Job Identifier	Adobe Creative Suite 2 Bible	
Instructions	use for Chengdu layout	
Provider	ted padova	
Source		
Copyright Notice	Downloaded files are free to distribute	
Rights Usage Terms	Public domain	

Deleting templates

Templates are stored as files on your hard drive. The Tools menu doesn't have a command for you to delete a template after you create one, but there is a command in the File Info dialog box that can delete Metadata templates. To find the folder where the template files are saved, select any file in the content area of the Bridge window. From a context menu, select File Info. Open the flyout menu in the top-right corner of the Bridge window, and select Show Templates, or you can just select the Create Metadata Template option and get the metadata templates folder. A folder opens on your desktop, and a subfolder titled *XMP* is selected. Double-click this folder to open it where two subfolders are contained therein. Open the folder labeled *Metadata Templates*. The template files are viewed inside the folder. Select any template you want to delete, and move it to the trash or you can use the Delete Metadata Template command in the palette menu of the File Info dialog box. The File Info dialog box dynamically updates to show a list of only the remaining templates in the Metadata Templates folder.

Searching in the Bridge

The Bridge provides you a powerful search engine where you can quickly search your hard drive, network server, and external media for files based on a large range of criteria. The exercises you performed earlier in this chapter for assigning labels to files (see the section "Labeling files") and adding metadata (see the section "Working with Metadata") become more meaningful when you use the labels and metadata information to search for documents. Not only the metadata such as filename, creation date, file size, and so on is searchable. You can search on all metadata you add to your documents.

You can narrow searches by adding multiple criteria and conditions as well as search on Boolean expressions. After you create a search in the Bridge, you can save your search results as a new Collection. Collections are saved in the Collections panel.

Searching documents

To search for files in the Bridge, you use the Find command. Open the Edit menu and select Find, and the Find dialog box opens, as shown in Figure 6.25. At first glance, the dialog box appears limited in providing you with many search options. Don't be fooled. You can dynamically expand the dialog box to provide you with an elaborate set of criteria and conditions.

FIGURE 6.25

Choose Edit ⇨ Find to open the Find dialog box.

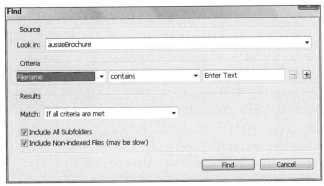

Before you perform a search, take a moment to look over all the options you have in the Find dialog box:

- **Look in:** The pull-down menu contains several categories, shown in Figure 6.26, from which you can select a location where you want to search for documents. The categories include:

- **Current Folder:** The current content area displays documents found in the current folder. You can change the current folder by clicking Browse to the right of the Look in pull-down menu. The Browse for Folder dialog box opens, and you can navigate to your hard drive and select a folder. Searching the current folder reports results found only in this folder.

FIGURE 6.26

Several categories appear in the Look in pull-down menu.

- **Recently Opened Folders:** The last several recently accessed folders are also listed below the current folder.

- **Favorites:** Favorites are grayed out unless you have identified documents or folders and added them to your Favorites. If you have several folders added to your Favorites, the search reports results from all folders that meet the search criteria. If you have, for example, five folders added to your Favorites and one file in each of the five different folders meet your search criteria, the five files display in a single Bridge window.

- **Hard Drive Roots:** The hard drive root along with any connected devices and networked drives may also be selected.

- **Criteria:** The criteria section of the Find dialog box is where you determine precisely what you want to search for. Several items are available to help narrow your search:

  - **Filename:** Filename is the default. Click Filename, and you find a list of metadata items to search as shown in Figure 6.27. All these items are self-explanatory. To use All Metadata at the bottom of the list, see the section "Searching metadata."

  - **Conditions:** The menu shown in Figure 6.28 shows the different conditions that need to be met to return results. Among the available options are: **contains** reports any text you type to the right of the Conditions menu. **does not contain** reports all data not containing the text you search. **is** means that the searched data must equal what you search for. **starts with** requires that you can type a character, several characters, a word, or several words, and the results are reported for data starting with what you add to the text box. **ends with** is the same as starts with, but results are reported for text matching the end of a data string. This item is frequently used for file extensions such as .jpg, .indd, .ai, and so on.

NOTE   The available conditions change depending on the criteria that you're searching for. For example, if you search for a specific rating, then the conditions are different, including 'greater than or equal to'.

FIGURE 6.27

Click Filename, and a pull-down menu displays the metadata items you can search.

FIGURE 6.28

Search conditions that must be met to return results

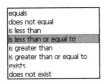

- ■ **Text box:** You type the items you want to search in this box. Text is typed for all items except Rating. When you select Rating, the text box changes to a pull-down menu where you can choose between one and five stars or No Rating. Some items require adhering to special formats. File size requires you to type numeric values to express the number of kilobytes, and dates require using date formats.

- ■ **Minus (-) and Plus (+):** Click the plus (+) symbol to add a new line of criteria. To see how additional criteria helps your search, see the section "Searching metadata." Click the minus (-) symbol to eliminate a row of criteria.

- **Match:** You have two options in the Match pull-down menu. Choosing **if any criteria are met** reports results for any text in a string matching the metadata or any text from two criteria. This option is similar to using Boolean OR. Choosing **if all criteria are met** requires all text in a string or all text in all criteria to match the metadata. This option is similar to using Boolean AND. For an example in using the Match items, see the section "Searching metadata."

- **Include All Subfolders:** When you search a folder from any of the Look in areas, you can search the root folder or the root folder and all subfolders. Select the check box when you want to search all the subfolders.

- **Include Non-indexed Files:** This item causes all files to be searched and not just those files that have been indexed. As it warns, this can take a while if enabled.

One special item to note when you use the Find dialog box is that any criteria you type in the text box is not case sensitive. Additionally, there is no switch to enable case sensitivity.

Searching metadata

After familiarizing yourself with the search options available to you in the Bridge, the best way to get up to speed is to start searching for files. A little practice here goes a long way in helping you master some of the power the Bridge provides you when searching for documents. To acquaint yourself with the search options, try to work through the following steps.

STEPS: Searching Metadata in Adobe Bridge

1. **Open a folder in the Bridge window.** When you perform a search using the Find command, you must have a Bridge window open. If no window is open, the Find command is grayed out.

2. **Chose Edit ⇨ Find.** The Find dialog box opens.

3. **Target a location to search.** Open the Look in pull-down menu to locate a recent folder. If the folder you want to search does not appear in the menu, click Browse and navigate your hard drive to locate a target folder to search. Note that you can choose a root folder with many subfolders and search all nested folders.

4. **Add the first line of criteria.** You can choose any one of the items in the first pull-down menu where you see the default name Filename. If you know that a filename contains a text string, use Filename. The second pull-down menu is a condition. If you know that a word or some characters are contained in a filename, use Contains, or select another option that more closely meets your requirements. Type the text string to search in the text box. From the Match pull-down menu, select if any criteria are met.

5. **Add a second line of criteria.** Click the plus (+) symbol to the right of the first row of criteria. A second row appears offering you the same options. In this line, select Filename again in the first pull-down menu. Select Contains, and type another text string in the text box. Make sure the same Match option is selected here as in Step 4. When you choose the same item to search and choose *if any criteria are met* from the Match pull-down menu, you are using Boolean OR to report your search results. In other words, you're asking Bridge to report the first text string OR the second text string to be contained in your search results. If you choose *if all criteria are met*, you are using Boolean AND where the results are reported only when the first text string AND the second text string are contained in the search results.

6. **Add a third line of criteria.** From the first pull-down menu, select All Metadata and likewise select *contains* in the second pull-down menu. In the text box, type one of the metadata items you added in a template when you performed steps earlier in this chapter in the section "Appending and replacing metadata." In this example, I'll use data supplied for author name. In the Match pull-down menu, change the option to the *if all criteria are met* option. The Find dialog box at this point should look like Figure 6.29.

FIGURE 6.29
_____

As you add additional rows of criteria to a search, the dialog box expands.

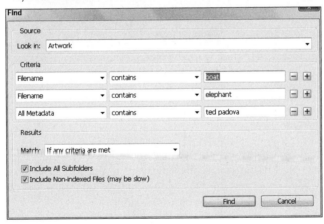

7. **Click Find in the top-right corner of the Find dialog box.** The results are reported in the existing Bridge window as shown in Figure 6.30.

FIGURE 6.30

Results are reported in the Content panel.

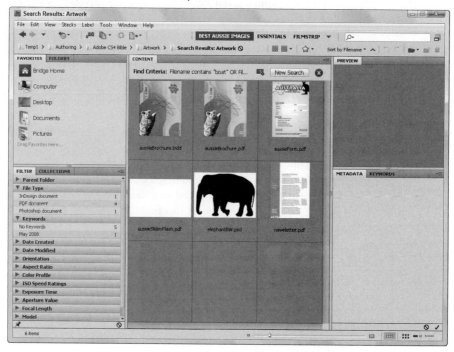

> **TIP** The criteria of your search are easily examined in the Bridge window after clicking Find. Look at the top of the Bridge window, and the criteria are reported in a line of text.

Take a moment to review what occurred in this example. If you duplicated the steps, here you are asking the Bridge to report results when a filename contains one text string AND a second text string AND the metadata contains a third text string. All conditions must be true for any results to be reported in a new Bridge window.

TIP If you have files scattered around your hard drive and not nested in a single folder, you can search an entire drive. The first step is to be certain you add some common identification to all files within a given work project. You can use a file-naming convention where all files in a given project have some common text in the filename, or add one item in the meta-data common to all files related to a given project—something like text added to a Description field. When you click Browse, select the drive where your files are contained. Additionally, set the criteria to search a string on a filename or All Metadata, and use the common identifier in the text box. When you click Find, all files from different folders are reported in a Bridge window. If you want to narrow the search to common file types, use another criteria item and search using a file extension.

CAUTION If you invoke a search on your hard drive, Bridge takes a long time to report your results—an extraordinarily long time on large hard drives. You cannot bail out of the search short of force quitting the program or shutting your computer down. If you perform such searches, be prepared to wait some time for the search to complete.

Opening Camera Raw Files

Camera raw is a format supported by many higher-end amateur and professional digital cameras. The camera raw file contains unprocessed data from the digital camera's image sensor. As such, you are working with a maximum amount of data, and you're not relying on the camera to process any image information. When you open a camera raw image, you have control over how you want the image interpreted, and thus you can make adjustments for lighting, brightness, sharpness, temperature, exposure, saturation, and more. Think of the camera raw format like a film negative, while JPEG and TIFF images are like photo prints. You can make prints from a negative and control exposure times for the prints, dodge, burn, and so on. If you make a print from a print, you're not working with all the data you had when the negative was made and therefore have much less control over lighting, exposure, contrast, and so on.

When you shoot several images containing similar content, lighting conditions, brightness values, and so on, you can make adjustments on one image for the proper processing and then use the Bridge to apply the same settings to similar images. The Bridge offers you several controls for making the camera raw processing more automated that can significantly speed up the process of opening the files.

Setting camera raw preferences

Camera raw has its own set of preferences apart from the Bridge preference settings. On the Macintosh, choose Bridge ➪ Camera Raw Preferences. On Windows, choose Edit ➪ Camera Raw Preferences to open the Camera Raw Preferences dialog box as shown in Figure 6.31.

FIGURE 6.31

The Camera Raw Preferences are contained in an individual dialog box apart from the other Bridge Preferences.

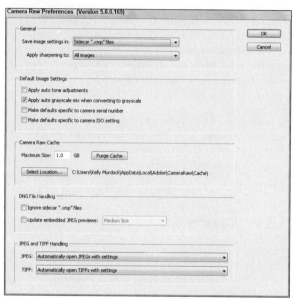

The Camera Raw Preferences offer a few options for working specifically with these file types, including these:

- **Save image settings in:** A pull-down menu offers two options for where Camera Raw settings are saved. This is an important adjustment when working with camera raw images, and you'll want to visit the preference options regularly to be certain you know where the settings are saved. The choices include:

  - **Sidecar XMP files:** This option is the best for collaborative workflow environments and for archiving images. The settings you apply to an image are saved in an XMP file in the same folder where the image resides. The filename uses the same base name as your image file with an .xmp extension. The XMP files can store IPTC metadata and other metadata associated with the file (see "Working with Metadata" earlier in this chapter). In Bridge, XMP sidecar files are hidden by default, but they are visible in the Macintosh Finder or Windows Explorer. When you copy, move, and delete camera raw images in the Bridge, the XMP sidecar files are moved along with their corresponding images. You can make the XMP sidecar files visible by choosing View ➪ Show Hidden Files in the Bridge. Be certain to copy these files when you store camera raw files on CDs and other kinds of external media.

  - **Camera Raw Database:** If you choose this option from the pull-down menu, the settings are stored in a Camera Raw database file on your local hard drive. The files are

stored in the user's Preferences folder located at Users/user name/Library/
Preferences (Macintosh) or the user's Application Data folder located at
Documents and Settings/user name/Application Data/Adobe/
CameraRaw (Windows). The filename where the preferences are stored is Adobe
Camera Raw Database. The database file is indexed by file content. Therefore, if you
move or rename camera raw files, the settings in the Camera Raw database stay connected with the images. It should be obvious that this method for saving settings is
less desirable for collaborative workflow environments as the settings are not available
to other users when retrieving files from offline media storage.

- **Apply sharpening to:** The Camera Raw plug-in can apply sharpening to camera raw images.
  If you want to use the plug-in to apply sharpening to the actual images, select All Images
  from the pull-down menu. If you select the Preview Images Only option from the pull-down
  menu, sharpening is applied only to the preview image leaving the camera raw file intact.

- **Apply auto tone adjustments:** This option causes all camera raw processed images to be
  adjusted automatically in tone using a default auto tone procedure.

- **Apply auto grayscale mix when converting to grayscale:** This option automatically
  does an auto grayscale mix anytime a camera raw file is converted to grayscale.

- **Make defaults specific to camera serial number:** When enabled, this option sets the
  defaults based on the camera's serial number. This keeps all settings consistent for any
  images downloaded from a specific camera.

- **Make defaults specific to camera ISO setting:** This option maintains the settings for all
  camera raw images that have a specific ISO setting. With this option, all camera raw
  images taken with the same ISO setting are consistent.

- **Camera Raw Cache:** When working with camera raw files, you have two cache files to
  deal with. The Bridge has its own cache where the processing of image thumbnails, previews, and metadata are stored. When files are saved to the cache, your computer speed
  increases so you can view items more quickly. The camera raw cache increases the speed
  of loading the Camera Raw dialog box and recalculating camera raw image previews after
  you make settings changes. This section of the Camera Raw Preferences dialog box handles the related camera raw cache:

  - **Maximum Size:** The default is 1GB. You can increase the cache size by editing the
    value in the text box. You can process about 200 images per gigabyte. If you are work-
    ing on significantly more images, open the preferences and increase the cache size.

  - **Purge Cache:** The cache occupies storage space on your hard drive. If you want to
    free up some room on your hard drive, click Purge Cache. Be aware that when you
    return to the Camera Raw dialog box, the time to view previews and settings takes
    longer as a new cache file is built.

  - **Select Location:** The default location where the cache file is saved appears in the dia-
    log box. This location is your boot drive. If you want to change the cache location,
    click Change Location and navigate to the folder where you want the cache saved. If
    you use secondary hard drives for scratch data, you can change the cache location to
    your data drive.

- **DNG File Handling:** These two options apply to DNG files. The first option causes the XMP file to be ignored. This is extra data that isn't needed in some cases. You also can define the size of the embedded JPEG preview thumbnails.

- **JPEG and TIFF Handling:** These options let you select to define how JPEG and TIFF images are opened. The options include Disable, Automatically Open with Settings, or Automatically Open All.

Using the Camera Raw plug-in

The Camera Raw dialog box appears in Bridge, Acrobat, and Photoshop because of a plug-in. Camera raw features are not hard coded in either program. Adobe created a plug-in to work with camera raw images because the plug-in requires some frequent updating. Camera manufacturers who support writing to the camera raw format all use a different flavor of camera raw. It's like Beta, VHS, and Super VHS, or cassette and 8-track. It's all tape, but the formats are different. As new cameras are made, newer camera raw formats are created. In order to regularly upgrade the camera raw features in Bridge and Photoshop, Adobe offers plug-in upgrades routinely so you can download and install them easily to keep your programs updated.

Adobe has been trying to get camera manufacturers to support the Adobe-developed format DNG (Digital Negative) so we can all experience consistency when saving and opening files from our digital cameras. Unfortunately, the battle does not look promising. After all, we're dealing with the hardheaded companies that battled over beta versus VHS and 8-track versus cassette. Granted, the battles of beta versus VHS were eventually won, but there were only two major players in those battles. With camera raw, the number of players is significantly greater, and the likelihood that every manufacturer will support DNG is unlikely. We wish Adobe luck in their efforts, but don't hold your breath.

When you open a camera raw image, it opens in the Camera Raw dialog box. You have two choices for where the Camera Raw dialog box appears. If you select an image and choose File ➪ Open, use a context menu and select Open, or use a keyboard shortcut and press ⌘/Ctrl+O, the Bridge switches to Photoshop and the Camera Raw plug-in is loaded from Photoshop. If you select an image and choose File ➪ Open in Camera Raw or use a context menu and select the same menu command, the Camera Raw plug-in is loaded from Bridge. The Camera Raw plug-in used by Photoshop and Bridge are the same one, they are just accessed from different applications.

You process the image regardless of where the Camera Raw dialog box appears, and when you finish making adjustments, you click Done or Open (Image). When you click Done, your settings are changed from the original default to adjustments made in the Camera Raw dialog box. You are returned to the Bridge window or to Photoshop, but the file does not open. If you click Open in the Camera Raw dialog box (or Open Image when multiple files are opened in the dialog box), the file opens in Photoshop regardless of which plug-in you use. Your original camera raw image remains unaffected when you open a file in Photoshop, and you can return to it to apply different settings to open again in Photoshop. If you apply settings without opening a file, you can return to defaults and the original image data are again available for making new settings adjustments.

 Adobe Bridge includes a preference setting in the General panel that controls whether a double-click opens the Camera Raw settings or not.

The Camera Raw dialog box can open and work with RAW, DNG, TIFF, and JPEG files. All adjustments made in the Camera Raw dialog box are non-destructive.

You also can process multiple images. In the Bridge, Shift-click to make a contiguous selection, or ⌘/Ctrl-click for a non-contiguous selection. From a context menu, select Open or press ⌘/Ctrl+O to open with Photoshop's Camera Raw plug-in, or select Open in Camera Raw from either the File menu or context menu to open using the Bridge plug-in. All files selected in the Bridge window open in the respective Camera Raw dialog box, where they appear listed in a Filmstrip along the left side of the dialog box.

When you open a camera raw photo in either Bridge or Photoshop, the Camera Raw plug-in opens the Camera Raw dialog box, shown in Figure 6.32. The Camera Raw dialog box has lots of options, so be certain to look over the descriptions of the following settings:

FIGURE 6.32

When you open a camera raw image in either Bridge or Photoshop, the Camera Raw plug-in opens the Camera Raw dialog box.

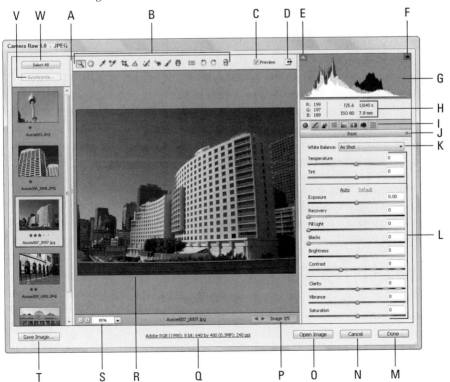

A **Separator bar:** Drag the separator bar to size the Filmstrip (I) and Preview (T). As the Filmstrip is sized up, the Preview is sized down and vice versa. Double-click the separator bar, and the Filmstrip hides from view offering more area to preview the image.

B **Tools:** Several tools appear at the top of the window:

- **Zoom tool (Z):** Click in the preview to zoom in. Press the Option/Alt key and click the Zoom tool to zoom out. Click and drag open a marquee to zoom into a defined area.

- **Hand tool (H):** Click and drag to move the document around the Preview area when zoomed in.

- **White Balance tool (I):** Click the White Balance tool in the image area to sample an area and set the white balance. If you click in an area that's too bright, a dialog box informs you that you cannot remap the white point to the sampled area.

- **Color Sampler tool (S):** Move the tool around the image area, and the RGB color values are reported in the RGB values (H). Click to plot a sampler point. Click again, and another point is sampled. You can plot as many as nine different color samples. Each sample's RGB values are reported below the tools area in the dialog box. When you click with the Color Sampler, a button appears. Click Clear Samples to delete all the sampled points.

- **Crop tool (C):** You can use the Crop tool to target an area you want to isolate to apply exposure controls. If you find the crop area to snap to proportions and you want to crop an image disproportionately, open a context menu (or the pull-down menu in the Crop tool icon) and select Normal from the menu commands. If you want fixed ratios, return to the context menu and select a fixed size that matches your needs. If you crop an area in the image preview and click done, you haven't changed the original raw image. Open the image again in the Camera Raw dialog box, and open a context menu using the Crop tool. Select Clear Crop from the menu commands.

- **Straighten tool (A):** This tool is used for straightening crooked images. For example, if a series of shots is taken on a tripod that's slightly crooked, you can fix all the images with a single swipe of the Straighten tool. It gives the user the same results as straightening in Photoshop, except the Straighten tool has these benefits: It doesn't require a two-step measurement *and* a rotation process as in Photoshop, it's a live adjustment that can be changed on the fly, it's stored in metadata and can be reverted or changed at any time without calculations, it combines rotation and cropping into one step, and it's much easier to apply to multiple images.

- **Retouch tool (B):** This tool lets you click and drag to locate and size an area to be retouched. Then a second equal-sized area can be moved about the image to define the sampled area used to retouch the first area. In the Options bar, you can set the size of the area and whether the type is Clone or Heal. The Heal option is feathered around the edges.

- **Red Eye Removal tool (E):** This tool lets you drag over an eye pupil to remove the redness without destroying the details of the area. In the Options bar, you can set the Pupil Size and how dark the area becomes.

- **Adjustment Brush tool (K):** This tool lets you drag over an area and apply one of many image adjustments as a brush. You can control the size, feather, flow, and density of the brush. Suppose you want to alter the brightness and saturation of a specific area of the image. This tool lets you easily control this by painting with the specific brightness and saturation settings. The adjustments that you have control over include Exposure, Brightness, Contrast, Saturation, Clarity, Sharpness, and Color.

- **Graduated Filter tool (G):** This tool lets you apply the same adjustment values available in the Adjustment Brush tool, except that you apply the adjustments as a gradient. By clicking this tool, you specify the initial gradient location and drag to set the end of the gradient. This is a great tool for adjusting horizons to create the perfect sunset.

- **Open Preference dialog (Ctrl+K):** This automatically opens the Camera Raw Preferences dialog box shown earlier.

- **Rotate image 90° counterclockwise (L):** This rotates the image left in a counterclockwise direction.

- **Rotate image 90° clockwise (R):** This rotates the image right in a clockwise direction.

- **Toggle mark for delete tool:** Select an image in the filmstrip, and click the trash icon. The file is marked for deletion. Files are not trashed in the Camera Raw dialog box until you first mark them and then click Done. Files are moved to the trash on your desktop. If you want to move them out of the trash and back to a folder, be certain to bring back both the CRW file and XMP file if saving your settings in sidecar files. This only works if more than one file is open.

C **Preview:** The Preview dynamically updates as you change settings. If you zoom in and out of the preview image and want to return to a fit page view, press ⌘/Ctrl+0 (zero). The keyboard shortcut is the same in all Adobe programs to fit in window or fit page. If the preview has a yellow exclamation point (!) icon over it, that indicates that the preview is being updated and is not accurate until the icon goes away.

D **Toggle Full Screen Mode:** Click this button to make the Camera Raw window fill the current screen resolution. Click a second time to return it to its previous size.

E **Shadows toggle:** When checked, the image shows clipped shadows as a colored highlights in red, green, blue or a combination of these colors, depending on the colors being clipped. Clipping indicates all areas where some color remapping will occur.

F **Highlights toggle:** Clipped highlights are shown in red, green, or blue.

G **Histogram:** The histogram displays the total range of the image data. As you make settings adjustments in the Camera Raw dialog box, the histogram dynamically updates to display a graph showing the data changes.

H **RGB values and Camera Metadata:** The values reported here are derived from the position of the current tool. As you move the tool around the Preview area, the color values change to report the values of the pixels beneath the tool. When you click in the Preview with the Color Sampler, the values for the plotted area are reported in the RGB values and duplicated below the tools. To the right of the RGB values are the Camera Metadata values.

I **Tabs:** The individual tabs change the default Basic pane to provide you with more editing options, including these:

- **Basic:** Basic is the default tab and the view you see in Figure 6.32. Use the sliders to adjust the image for proper white balance, temperature, and exposure settings. Additional controls adjust the clarity and vibrancy.

- **Tone Curve:** The curve settings in the Parametric panel offer settings for adjusting the highlights, lights, darks, and shadows. The Point panel controls are similar to those you find in Photoshop's Curves dialog box.

- **Detail:** Use this tab to adjust sharpening and noise reduction adjustments. If you hold down the Alt (Option) key while dragging these values, you see the isolated sharpening changes.

- **HSL/Grayscale:** Use this tab to control the Hue, Saturation, and Luminance values for the image and also to convert the image to grayscale.

- **Split Toning:** This tab includes sliders for the hue and saturation of the highlights and shadows. It also has a Balance control.

- **Lens Correction:** Lens corrections are made for Chromatic Aberration and Vignetting that you might find apparent in digital camera images. There is also a Post Crop Vignetting setting.

CROSS-REF For more control over correcting aberrations created from digital cameras, use the Lens Correction filter in Photoshop CS4, which is covered in Chapter 11.

- **Camera Calibration:** You may experience colorcasts and tint differences in shadows and non-neutral colors between the color profile used for your camera and the Camera Raw built-in profile. Use this tab to compensate for the differences.

- **Presets:** The Presets tab holds any defined groups of settings. At the bottom of this pane is a New Preset button that opens the dialog box, shown in Figure 6.33, where you can select the settings to include in the preset.

J **Flyout menu:** Click the right-pointing arrow to open the menu. Menu commands are available for saving and loading settings, exporting settings, deleting settings, setting new defaults, and opening the Camera Raw Preferences dialog box.

K **White Balance:** White balance sets the color balance of an image to reflect the lighting conditions under which the photo was taken. Here you'll find compensation for such items as sunlight, shade, flash, fluorescent, and tungsten lighting. You also have a Custom choice where the pull-down menu reflects custom if you change either the temperature or the tint.

L **Adjustment sliders:** The adjustment sliders affect the image brightness values. When one of the sliders is moved, the Preview image dynamically changes to reflect the new setting. You see a preview of each setting made with the adjustment sliders and can choose settings that best produce the image detail and color balance.

FIGURE 6.33

The New Preset dialog box lets you select which settings to save.

M **Done:** When you click Done, the settings you made apply to the image. The Camera Raw dialog box closes, but the file does not open in Photoshop.

N **Cancel:** Click Cancel to dismiss the dialog box without applying any settings. You also can press Esc to cancel out of the dialog box. Press Option/Alt, and the Cancel button changes to a Reset button. Click Reset, and all the settings made in your editing session are dismissed and return to the same appearance as when you opened the file(s) in the Camera Raw dialog box.

O **Open image:** Click Open Image to open the Preview image in Photoshop with the applied settings.

P **Image selection:** Use the left and right arrows to scroll images in the filmstrip up or down respectively. The readout to the right of the arrows displays the current image in the Preview window and the total number of images opened in the Camera Raw dialog box.

Q **Color Space/Bit Depth/Size /Resolution:** At the bottom of the preview pane is a link that lists the specified Color Space, the image's Bit Depth, its current Size, and Resolution. Clicking this link opens the Workflow Options dialog box, shown in Figure 6.34, where you can change any of these values. Select from four options for your color working space. The default is Adobe RGB (1998). If you are processing files for Web hosting, you may want to change the color space to sRGB IEC61966-1. Choose from 8-bit or 16-bit for a color depth value. If you have a camera that supports 16-bit images, leave them at 16-bit. High-bit images can be edited in Photoshop, and this format is preferred when adjusting Sharpening, Levels, Curves, or any other color or brightness controls. The current image resolution is reported in the text box. You can change image resolution by adding a new value in the text box. You can choose to view either pixels/inch or pixels/cm from the pull-down menu to the right of the Resolution text box. Using this option to change resolution when you have a number of files you want to process to the same resolution and size. From the pull-down menu, you can select different physical sizes for your image. Resizing the image by selecting a menu item does not affect image sampling.

NOTE   The Open in Photoshop as Smart Objects option in the Workflow Options dialog box gives you the flexibility to come back to Bridge and change the RAW processing setting for any placed images.

FIGURE 6.34

The Workflow Options dialog box lets you change the Color Space, Bit Depth, Size, and Resolution.

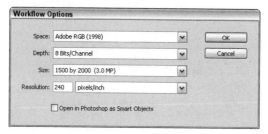

R   **Image Preview:** This displays the current image selected in the filmstrip. If only one image is open, the image appears in the Preview area. The preview image is targeted for the adjustments you make for all the other settings in the dialog box.

S   **Zoom settings:** In addition to using the Zoom tool, you can click the minus (-) symbol to zoom out or the plus (+) symbol to zoom in. From the pull-down menu, you can select fixed zoom sizes. Note that the text appearing between the symbols and the arrows used to open the pull-down menu is not an editable item. The readout is used for information only to show the zoom level in relation to actual size.

T   **Save image:** Click Save Image to save the settings applied to the image(s). If you want to return to defaults, open the image and select Camera Raw Defaults from the Settings (K) pull-down menu. The Save Options dialog box lets you save the image to the same location or to a different location. You also can rename the images by adding numerical suffixes.

U **Filmstrip:** The filmstrip shows a thumbnail preview for all files opened in the Camera Raw dialog box. You can click a thumbnail, and the image appears in the Preview area as well as the filmstrip. The file in the Preview area is the one targeted for editing. Note that if you open only one camera raw image at a time, the filmstrip becomes unavailable in the Camera Raw dialog box.

V **Synchronize:** When you open multiple files in the Camera Raw dialog box, you can apply settings to one image, then use Select All or individually select multiple images and synchronize the settings. When you select Synchronize, the Synchronize dialog box opens. You can use this dialog box to choose which settings to apply to the selected image. This dialog box offers the same options as the Paste Camera Raw Settings dialog box. See the section "Applying settings in Bridge" later in this chapter for more information.

W **Select All:** This selects all the images in the filmstrip. You can select all images and globally apply the same settings to the selected images. You also can Shift-click or ⌘/Ctrl-click in the filmstrip to select multiple images in a contiguous or non-contiguous group.

You can save any adjustments you make as settings or use them as new defaults. From the flyout menu adjacent to the Settings pull-down menu, you have a number of choices, as shown in Figure 6.35.

FIGURE 6.35

Open the flyout menu to save settings or create new defaults.

The default setting is Image Settings. You can change the settings by saving and loading settings, apply settings that you make as a new default, or you can select a defined preset. When you want to return to the image as it was taken, select Reset Camera Raw Defaults.

Applying settings in Bridge

In addition to options available in the flyout menu in the Camera Raw dialog box, you have similar menu commands when you choose Edit ⇨ Develop Settings ⇨ Camera Raw Defaults or when you open a context menu on a selected image. The submenu commands offer the following options:

- **Camera Raw Defaults:** This option is the same as selecting Reset Camera Raw Defaults in the flyout menu.

- **Previous Conversion:** If you convert an image and want to apply the same conversion setting, select an image or multiple images in the Bridge and choose Edit ⇨ Develop Settings ⇨ Previous Conversion.

- **Copy camera Raw Settings:** Assume that you made some conversion settings changes on an image and clicked Done in the Camera Raw dialog box. The settings are applied to your image. You can select the image, and choose Edit ⇨ Develop Settings ⇨ Copy Settings. The settings are now available for pasting into another image.

- **Paste Camera Raw Settings:** After copying settings, choose Edit ⇨ Develop Settings ⇨ Paste Settings. This option offers you discretionary selection for which settings to apply. Rather than paste all the settings changes into the selected image, the Paste Camera Raw Settings dialog box opens. This dialog box is identical to the New Presets dialog box (refer to Figure 6.41). As you can see in the dialog box, you can check the different settings you want to paste. Note that the options in this dialog box also are the same as when clicking Synchronize in the Camera Raw dialog box.

- **Clear Camera Raw Settings:** This command clears the settings that you applied to a camera raw file. Select a file in the Bridge, and choose Edit ⇨ Develop Settings ⇨ Clear Settings. The settings are dumped from the file, and the image returns to the defaults at the time it was shot. Note that clearing settings has nothing to do with the copy/paste features. If you clear settings, you can still paste settings on another image because the copied information was not disturbed when selecting Clear Camera Raw Settings.

- **Saved Presets:** Any saved presets are listed by name after the Clear command.

Saving camera raw files

If you make settings changes and click Open in the Camera Raw Settings dialog box, the file opens in Photoshop. From Photoshop, you can save files in a variety of formats. But Photoshop won't let you save back to camera raw. Photoshop does support a Photoshop Raw format, but it's not the same as camera raw. Camera raw saves uncompressed bits from a camera's CCD or CMOS. Photoshop Raw is a flexible file format designed for transferring images between applications and computer platforms.

If you want to adjust settings and save the adjusted images as a new file while preserving your settings and the camera raw format, click Save in the Camera Raw dialog box. When you click Save in the dialog box, the Save Options dialog box appears, as shown in Figure 6.36.

FIGURE 6.36

Click Save in the Camera Raw dialog box, and the Save Options dialog box opens.

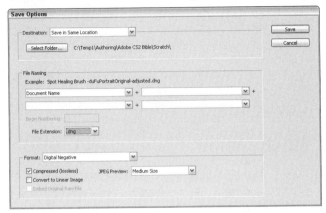

Attribute choices for your saved image from the Camera Raw Save Options include the following:

- **Destination:** Click Select Folder to navigate your hard drive and find a new location to save your file.

- **File Naming:** Supply a name for your file in the text box on the left and an extension on the right. If you have multiple files open in the Camera Raw dialog box, you can add additional names by clicking the plus (+) symbol to add more field boxes. You do not need to add or change extensions because the dialog box automatically supplies an extension in the File Extension pull-down menu when you change the format in the Format pull-down menu.

- **Format:** If you want to save back to raw format, you can choose the Adobe Digital Negative (DNG) format. The file is saved as a camera raw file. When you open the file, it opens in the Camera Raw dialog box. However, the file you save as DNG does not retain all the original raw information obtained from the file you first opened in the Camera Raw dialog box. The new settings prevail, and you can't return to original defaults. If you want to retain all data as the image was first taken with your camera, check the box at the bottom of the dialog box for Embed Original Raw File.

The remaining options in the Save Options dialog box for DNG files offer you choices for image compression, JPEG previews (only when DNG format is chosen), and Convert to Linear Image (stores the data in an interpolated format). Other formats for JPEG, TIFF, and Photoshop all have different attribute choices for their respective formats. These attribute choices are the same as you are familiar with when saving files from Photoshop.

Synchronizing Color Across the CS4 Programs

In Bridge, you can synchronize color across the CS4 applications that work with color policies including Photoshop, Illustrator, InDesign, and Acrobat. Bridge does not provide you options for creating color profiles or embedding profiles in application documents. Rather, you use Bridge to ensure that when you work with a given color space in Photoshop, you work with the same color space in InDesign and all other CS4 programs. Synchronizing color in Bridge ensures that a given monitor or printing profile in Photoshop or Illustrator is maintained when you import the images in InDesign. If you have one color setting in one program and a different color setting in another program, the Color Settings dialog box alerts you that your color settings are not synchronized.

CROSS-REF For information related to creating color profiles and working in color-managed workflows, see Chapter 5. This section presumes you have created a color profile, as detailed in Chapter 5.

To synchronize color across the CS4 applications in Bridge, follow these steps.

STEPS: Synchronizing Color in Adobe Bridge

1. **Launch Bridge.** Note that you do not need a Bridge window open in order to synchronize color.

2. **Open the Suite Color Settings.** Choose Edit ➪ Creative Suite Color Settings. The Suite Color Settings dialog box opens.

3. **Expand the list of color management settings.** By default, Bridge displays a short list of color management settings. Select the Show Expanded List of Color Settings Files check box, as shown in Figure 6.37.

4. **Select a color setting.** Color settings are created in other programs such as Adobe Photoshop or made available to you from service providers or other users in your workflow. If you have color settings installed properly on your computer, they are visible in the Suite Color Settings dialog box. Scroll the list of settings, and select the setting used in your workflow.

5. **Apply a color setting to synchronize color.** Click Apply after selecting the setting of your choice. Your color settings are now synchronized across the CS4 applications. If you open Photoshop, Illustrator, or InDesign, and choose Edit ➪ Color Settings, you'll find the same color settings applied to each application. In Acrobat, you need to choose Acrobat ➪ Preferences (Macintosh) or Edit ➪ Preferences (Windows), and click Color Management in the left pane. You should plan on double-checking Acrobat to be certain the color settings are applied.

FIGURE 6.37

Select the Show Expanded List of Color Settings Files check box to view all color settings accessible to the CS4 programs.

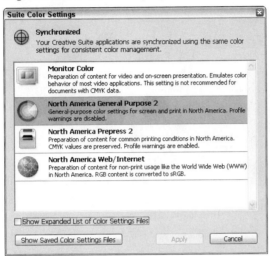

Synchronizing color settings is of particular benefit for creative professionals who work on design projects for both print and Web. When you begin a new project, be certain to visit the Bridge Suite Color Settings dialog box and synchronize your color. As you switch between print and Web designs, change your color settings accordingly. Bridge makes it easy for you to be certain you work in the same color space in each CS4 application.

 **For information on using color settings for print and Web, see Chapter 5.**

Using the Output Panel

You also can use Bridge to create a grid of thumbnails for printing or for a Web gallery using the Output panel. The easiest way to access the Output panel is to select the Output workspace from the Window ➪ Workspace ➪ Output menu, as shown in Figure 6.38.

At the top of the Output panel are options for creating a PDF file or a Web Gallery. For the PDF option, you can select one of several templates including 2x2 Cells, 4x5 Contact Sheets, and more. You also can specify overlay and watermarks.

The Web Gallery option includes templates along with fields where you can add textual information about the gallery images. Additional options upload the gallery directly to a server.

Both options include buttons for previewing the resulting pages.

FIGURE 6.38

The Output panel lets you create a grid of thumbnails.

Enabling Application Commands from the Bridge

Some of the automated features in several CS applications have been added as menu commands in the Bridge. You can execute actions and commands in the Bridge without leaving the window or opening any one of the other CS programs. Actually, the Bridge opens the applications for you when actions and internal program features are used. Photoshop, Illustrator, and InDesign are all supported with one or more features you are likely to use frequently.

Photoshop support

Among the automated features and commands integrated between the Bridge and the CS4 programs, Photoshop supports the most options. These options are located in the Tools ➪ Photoshop menu.

Batch processing with actions

The Photoshop Batch command is supported from within Bridge. When you choose Tools ➪ Photoshop ➪ Batch, Bridge opens Photoshop, and the Batch dialog box opens just like you see when executing a Batch from within Photoshop.

NOTE Before you run a Batch sequence in Photoshop, you should visit the Actions palette and load actions you use in your workflow. Photoshop CS4 defaults to a new set of actions that are used to change workspace appearances. Many of the familiar actions found in earlier versions of Photoshop are left out of the Default Actions set. If you need one of the actions formerly included in the default set, you need to load a saved actions file. See the section "Loading actions" nearby for more information.

After you explore some of the actions sets loaded by default, you may find these new default actions somewhat useless in your design work. The familiar actions you have used in earlier versions of Photoshop are installed with Photoshop CS4; you just need to load them to make them available in the Actions palette.

Loading actions

In the Actions palette, you can load action files, save action files, and replace action files. Loading actions appends a new action set to the palette. Replacing an action set removes the former actions and adds the new action set you load. If you haven't worked with loading actions in earlier versions of Photoshop, look over the following steps to see how action sets are loaded.

STEPS: Loading Actions

1. **Open the Actions palette.** By default, the Actions palette is visible when you launch Photoshop CS4. If the palette is not visible, choose Window ➪ Actions.

2. **Open the Load dialog box.** Click the palette menu icon of the Actions palette to open a palette menu. Scroll down the menu options, and select Load Actions and navigate to the appropriate folder. The Load dialog box opens as shown in Figure 6.39.

3. **Load an action set.** When you select Load Actions in the Actions palette menu, Photoshop opens the Photoshop Actions folder where all action sets are saved. Select one of the sets, and click Load. If you want to load actions that match the default actions in Photoshop CS1, select Sample Actions.atn and click Load. You can click to select a set and shift or ⌘/Ctrl-click to select multiple sets and load them all together. Look over the sets, and load those preconfigured actions you use in your workflow. As was the case in Photoshop CS1, you still have the opportunity to create custom actions. If you created custom actions in Photoshop CS1, you can navigate to your Photoshop CS1 folder and load custom action sets from the Photoshop Actions folder in the Photoshop CS1:Presets folder.

FIGURE 6.39

Select an action set to load in the Load dialog box.

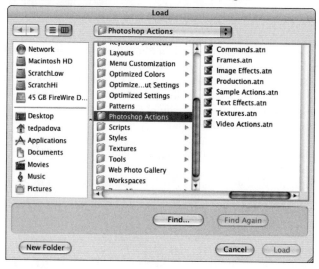

Running actions from the Bridge

If all you can do in the Bridge were run an action on a folder of files, there would be no benefit to running the action from Bridge or from Photoshop. However, the Bridge offers you one option that Photoshop doesn't. In Photoshop, you run actions on open files or on a folder of files. Photoshop does not offer you a discretionary selection of images you want to affect with an action. Bridge, on the other hand, lets you individually select files in the content area and apply actions to a selected group. If you use Bridge search and find files from different folders meeting your search criteria, the files are loaded in a new Bridge window. Subsequently, you can run an action on files from different folders—something you can't do in Photoshop's Batch dialog box.

When you have the files in view in a Bridge window, choose Tools ⇨ Photoshop ⇨ Batch. The Bridge immediately opens Photoshop (if not open) or switches to Photoshop and opens the Batch dialog box. You apply the same settings in the Batch dialog box for the action you want to use, where you want to save your files, and the naming conventions you want to use. When you click OK, the action steps are applied to the selected Bridge files.

Note that when you load action sets or create custom actions, all the actions are available in the Batch dialog box and can be run from Bridge or from within Photoshop.

Using Image Processor

Another cool feature in Photoshop CS4 is the Image Processor. You can select images in the Bridge and choose Tools ⇨ Photoshop ⇨ Image Processor to open Photoshop's Image Processor dialog box, as shown in Figure 6.40.

You can launch the new Image Processor in Photoshop CS4 from the Bridge.

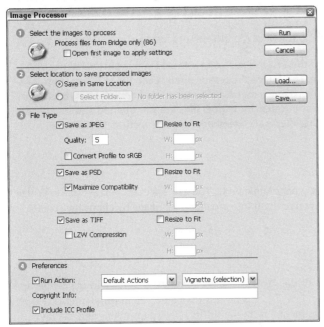

Using the Image Processor is like running several actions at once. Options include:

- **Select Files:** You can select files from the Bridge or from within Photoshop. When you select Bridge files, the number of files to process is reported in the Image Processor dialog box.

- **Select location to save processed images:** Essentially, you have the same option here as you do with actions. You can overwrite the processed images or save the processed files as copies to another folder.

- **File Type:** You can choose to save files as JPEG, Photoshop (PSD), or TIFF images. If you save files as JPEG, you have additional options for adjusting file compression (Quality text box), resizing images, and converting color profiles to sRGB. You might have used TIFF images in a layout that you want to print. You can repurpose the files for Web hosting when you use the JPEG option. You can size PSD files to fit, and you can flatten the images by checking Maximize Compatibility. Saving as TIFF also offers resizing, and you can use LZW compression.

- **Run Action:** You can add an action to the processing attributes. As one example, you might convert images to another format, resize them, and then add an action to convert images to grayscale.

- **Copyright Info:** You can add metadata for copyright information.
- **Include ICC Profile:** You can use the current color settings in Photoshop and embed an ICC profile.

When you finish setting attributes, click Run, and the files are processed.

NOTE   If all you want to do with the Image Processor is to add copyright metadata, don't use the Image Processor. The Image Processor opens each file in Photoshop, processes the image, and saves the results. Using a metadata template and adding copyright information in the Bridge works much faster because individual files are not opened and saved from Photoshop. For information on creating metadata templates, see the section "Creating a Template" earlier in this chapter.

Photomerge

Photomerge combines images to create a panoramic view. You can select the images in the Bridge of a scene shot at different angles and merge them into a panoramic image by choosing Tools ⇨ Photoshop ⇨ Photomerge.

Illustrator support

The Live Trace feature is supported in Bridge. You can select a Photoshop image in the Bridge and choose Tools ⇨ Illustrator ⇨ Live Trace. Live Trace is no less than amazing in producing vector art images from raster image files. When launched from the Bridge, Illustrator opens and the Live Trace dialog box appears where you can choose from an abundant number of attributes to create the vector art.

 For information on using Live Trace, see Chapter 9.

Viewing Slide Shows

A nice feature of the Bridge is viewing slide shows directly in Bridge. The slide show feature is not like creating a permanent slide show that you can when exporting to a PDF Presentation from Bridge or Photoshop. The slide show feature in Bridge is a temporary viewing option. You might have a collection of images you want to use in a design campaign and quickly preview the images you're contemplating using in your artwork. The slide show feature in Bridge displays all Photoshop, Illustrator, InDesign, Acrobat PDFs, and camera raw images. Dreamweaver pages are not supported with previews.

To view a slide show in Bridge, open a folder containing the images you want to preview. Choose View ⇨ Slide Show, or press ⌘/Ctrl+L. Note that the keyboard shortcut is the same as the one you view in Full Screen mode in Acrobat. The first image is opened in Adobe Bridge Slide Show.

You can access a quick help menu when viewing the slide show. Press H, and the help screen shown in Figure 6.41 appears. The help screen appears on top of the current slide in view.

Open a slide show in Bridge, and press H to view a help screen.

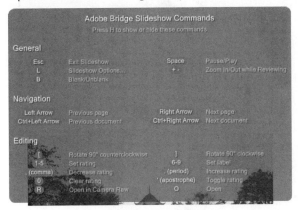

You can use various keyboard shortcuts to control slide show viewing. You can even make some edits to the files as you view them in Slide Show. Note that you can change labels and ratings while in Adobe Bridge Slide Show. Most of the keyboard shortcuts are self-explanatory when it comes to changing slides, opening a previous or next document, rotating images, pausing and playing, and so on.

When you click a slideshow image, the display mode changes. You can zoom in on the area where you click and clicking again zooms out. You can access the Slideshow Options by pressing the L key.

When you view images in Adobe Bridge Slide Show, just remember to use the H key and call upon help while viewing a show. If you want to compare documents, you can open multiple slide shows. Use the Bridge to open a folder, and press ⌘/Ctrl+L. Keep the slide show open, and select the Bridge window. Navigate to a new folder, and press ⌘/Ctrl+L again.

Using Review mode

The View menu includes a Review Mode feature. This mode places the current folder of images in a loop that you can quickly cycle through using the arrow keys, as shown in Figure 6.42. If you click on an image, you can zoom in on the image and examine it with the Loupe tool. If you drag the image downward, the image is dropped from the current set letting you limit the current collection.

If you right-click the image, you can rate, label, or apply specific commands to the image. After you exit Review Mode, all the remaining images are saved as a collection.

FIGURE 6.42

Review Mode lets you quickly flip through a set of images.

Using Compact mode

Compact mode resizes Bridge to be as small as it can become. Clicking the Expand button in the upper-right corner returns the window to its former size.

Summary

- The Bridge is a standalone executable application similar to the File Browser found in earlier versions of Photoshop. The Bridge is the center of the CS4 applications from which all document launching and organization can be accomplished.

- The Bridge supports saving workspaces. You can open multiple windows and work between Bridge windows for file management and organization.

- You can manage, resize, and group tabs in Bridge.

- You can mark files with ratings and labels and sort documents according to ratings and label identify.

- You can batch rename files in Bridge.

- You can edit document metadata in Bridge.

- Bridge supports the creation of XMP metadata templates. You can apply metadata from a template to folders of files.

- You can search files on metadata in folders, nested folders, and different folder locations.

- You can save searches as collections, and you can retrieve the results easily from the collections.

- You can open camera raw images using the Bridge Camera Raw plug-in. You can copy settings and paste settings into additional camera raw images in the Bridge window. You can return camera raw images to defaults in the Bridge window.

- You can synchronize color settings in the Bridge for the print-based CS applications.

- You can execute application automation commands in the Bridge for Photoshop and Illustrator.

- You can execute Photoshop's Batch commands from the Bridge.

- Images are viewed in a slide show format using the Slide Show feature.

Chapter 7

Using Version Cue

Version Cue is a file-versioning system that is tightly integrated into most of the CS4 version applications. Its key benefit is that it lets you set up projects for sharing over a network. All files within these projects are version-controlled, allowing members of the team to access the very latest versions of each file. The versioning features also ensure that team members don't accidentally save changes over the top of other changes.

Version Cue is accessed from within the File menu. Using the Adobe Version Cue CS4 Server utility, you can control all aspects of Version Cue from an administration interface. This interface lets you create and edit the access and authentication for users, create and define project properties, and lock files.

Setting Up the Version Cue Workspace

When CS4 is installed, Version Cue is also installed by default, but it is not enabled by default. Once the Version Cue server is started, it can be used.

NOTE Version Cue comes only as part of Creative Suite. If you purchased a license for only a single CS4 application, it won't include Version Cue, but the application can work with Version Cue if somebody else on your network has it installed.

Enabling Version Cue and setting preferences

Version Cue is installed by simply installing CS4. Version Cue preferences are set using the Adobe Version Cue CS4 Server dialog box. To access this dialog box, shown in Figure 7.1, double-click the Adobe Version Cue CS4 icon. This icon is found within the System Preferences (on the Mac) or in the Control Panel (in Windows). In the Adobe Version Cue CS4 Server dialog box, you can start or stop the Version Cue server. For Windows systems, you also have an option to Show Server Tray Icon, which makes the Version Cue CS4 icon visible in the system tray located in the lower-right corner of the interface. Mac users have an option to Show Version Cue CS4 Status in Menu Bar.

FIGURE 7.1

The Adobe Version Cue CS4 Server dialog box

The Server Visibility field lets you make the workspace shared or private. The two options are Visible to Others and Private.

You can use the next three preferences to optimize the workspace and to specify the type of files that you are versioning. You can set Workspace Size to Single User, Small (2–4 People), Medium (5–10 People), or Large (10+ People). By specifying the workspace size, Version Cue can make more connections available so users don't have to wait as long to gain access to the files. The Memory Usage field lets you specify the amount of memory on your local machine or on the network that is available for Version Cue to use. Increasing this value enables you to retrieve files very quickly but leaves less memory available for the other applications. You also can opt to turn Version Cue on when the computer starts.

Specifying workspace folders

When Version Cue is first enabled, two folders are created on your local system. The Version Cue folder is located in the Documents folder. This folder holds temporary working copies of the files that you're currently editing.

The other folders are located by default in a system folder separate from where the Creative Suite applications were installed. These folders, consisting of folders named Adobe Version Cue CS4\Server\data and Adobe Version Cue CS4\Server\backups, hold the information about the server setup and data backups of the server data and are referenced in the Locations panel of the Version Cue Preferences dialog box, shown in Figure 7.2.

CAUTION If you look at the files located in the data and backups folders, you won't be able to find any recognizable file formats. Do not manually move or edit any of these files; if you do, Version Cue won't work properly.

FIGURE 7.2

The Locations panel of the Version Cue Preferences dialog box lets you specify the location of data and backup folders.

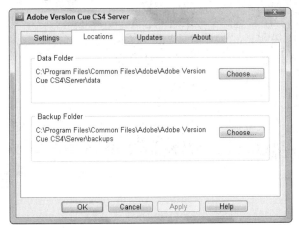

If you want to change the data and backups folder locations, you must turn Version Cue off and click Apply before the Choose button in the Locations panel becomes active. After the Choose button is active, you can click it to select a new directory.

Updating Version Cue

The Updates panel of the Version Cue Preferences dialog box, shown in Figure 7.3, includes a single button that lets you check for updates to the Version Cue. Your computer needs to be connected to the Internet in order for this button to work.

FIGURE 7.3

The Updates panel of the Version Cue Preferences dialog box checks the Adobe Web site for any Version Cue updates.

If any software updates are found, the Adobe Updater appears. The Adobe Updater lists any updates that are available. If you select the check box to the left of the update filename in the All Available Updates section, the size of the download and the time required to download the update are displayed at the bottom of the Updater. The Download Updates button also becomes active. Clicking this button begins the update process. If you select any of the updates listed, a description of the update is listed in the Description text field.

The Preferences button opens a dialog box, shown in Figure 7.4, where you set the Adobe Updater to automatically check for updates every month. You also can specify a directory to save the downloads.

Enabling Version Cue within a CS4 application

Although CS4 is enabled and turned on by default, each individual CS4 application can use its own preferences to turn off its ability to use Version Cue. The setting for enabling Version Cue for each separate CS4 app is found in the File Handling panel of the Preferences dialog box. For example, to enable or disable Version Cue for Photoshop, Illustrator, InCopy, InDesign, and Flash, open the Preferences dialog box (found in the application-name menu on the Mac or in the Edit menu in Windows) and select the File Handling panel (within Illustrator, the option is located in the File Handling & Clipboard panel). The option for enabling Version Cue for Acrobat 8 Professional is found in the General panel of the Preferences dialog box, which you can access by choosing Edit ➪ Preferences.

FIGURE 7.4

The Adobe Updater Preferences dialog box includes an option to automatically check for updates once a month.

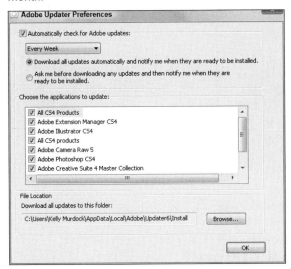

> **NOTE**   Version Cue is on by default in all listed applications, except for Flash. Also note that enabling Version Cue as an application's preference does not turn on the Version Cue server, but only sets the particular application to interact with Version Cue.

> **NOTE**   Version Cue also works with InCopy.

Within the File Handling panel of the Preferences dialog box, shown in Figure 7.5, is a Use Version Cue option. Enabling this option makes Version Cue available for that application.

> **NOTE**   Dreamweaver doesn't interact with Version Cue in anyway. Dreamweaver has support for Subversion, another popular file versioning system used in Web development.

Version Cue can also be enabled for all CS4 applications using the Startup Scripts panel in the Preferences dialog box in Adobe Bridge.

FIGURE 7.5

The File Handling panel of the Preferences dialog box for the various CS4 applications includes an Enable Version Cue option.

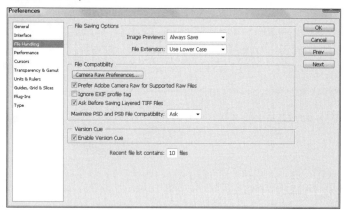

Working with Adobe Drive

When Version Cue is turned on and enabled for the working application, you need to create a Version Cue project where the project files are made accessible. You can then connect to the Version Cue project using Adobe Drive, shown in Figure 7.6.

FIGURE 7.6

Adobe Drive can be connected to Version Cue servers.

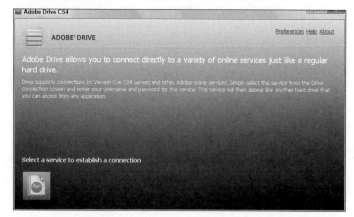

To create a connection to an established Version Cue server, click the Version Cue icon in the Adobe Drive dialog box. All available servers are displayed. Simply select the server you want to connect to and click the Connect button. If the server requires authentication, you're prompted to enter a Name and Password, as shown in Figure 7.7.

FIGURE 7.7

If the server requires authentication, you're prompted to log in.

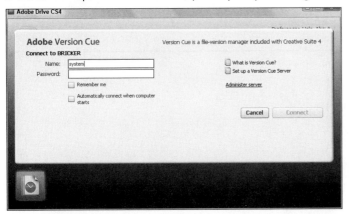

Once connected, the project appear as a drive in the Open and Save As dialog boxes within the various CS4 applications.

Accessing Version Cue Files

You must start the Version Cue server and create projects before they appear within Version Cue. Creating a new project is accomplished using the Version Cue Administrator utility. More on this utility is presented at the end of the chapter.

Opening Version Cue files

File contained within a Version Cue project are easily opened using the File ⇨ Open menu command. Simply point the file dialog box to the connected Adobe Drive and the established projects are displayed just like any other set of folders.

When a file is opened from a Version Cue project, the File ⇨ Check In menu option becomes available once some changes are made to the file. Using this option, you can save the current document to a Version Cue project. Version Cue keeps track of all the different versions of the saved files and lets you add a comment to describe the changes.

Saving Version Cue files

When you save Version Cue files by choosing File ➪ Save, the working copy updates, but the actual versioned copy isn't updated until you choose File ➪ Save As or File ➪ Check In.

When you're ready to save a new version of the edited file to the Version Cue repository, choose File ➪ Check In. This command opens a simple dialog box, shown in Figure 7.8, where you can quickly type a version comment and save the file. The version comment that you enter appears in the Version Cue file interface when you select the file.

Choosing File ➪ Check In lets you enter comments for the file.

Adding files to a Version Cue project

You can add single files, multiple files, or synchronize files to a Version Cue project, or you can drag and drop files into a Version Cue project using Adobe Bridge:

- **Single file:** Choose File ➪ Save As or File ➪ Check In to add single files to a Version Cue project.
- **Multiple files:** To add multiple files to a project, copy all the files into their correct folders of the working project file located in the connected Adobe Drive.

Deleting Version Cue files

To delete a Version Cue-managed file, you select the Version Cue file in the Adobe Drive folder and choose delete.

Accessing Version Cue files in Bridge

Although the connected Adobe Drive can be used to access Version Cue files, Adobe Bridge is often an easier way to access Version Cue files. Version Cue projects can be accessed immediately using the Adobe Drive folder.

Using the Version Cue CS4 Administration Utility

You can complete many Version Cue administrative tasks—including creating, deleting, backing up and editing projects, locking files, editing user access rights, and viewing logs and reports—using the Version Cue CS4 Administration Web pages.

You access this utility by clicking Server Administration in the Adobe Version Cue CS4 icon in the Control Panel or from the system tray in Windows or from the menu bar in Mac dialog box, or by selecting the Edit Properties menu command from the Project Tools pop-up menu and clicking Server Administration.

When you first access the Version Cue CS4 Administration Web pages, a login page appears, asking you to enter your username and password.

> **NOTE** All users on the system are given access to this utility, but only the user with the System Administrator username and password may set the rights of the other users.

The Version Cue CS4 Administration utility opens within a Web browser. After you create an account, you need to log in every time you access the utility using a login page.

After you've logged in, the home page of the utility appears, as shown in Figure 7.9. This home page includes four tabbed page links along the top—Home, Users/Groups, Projects, and Advanced. The home page also includes several common tasks that you may perform using this utility.

Adding and editing users

Clicking the Users/Groups link in the Version Cue CS4 Administration utility opens a page with several tasks. If you click the Manage User/Groups link, the page shown in Figure 7.10 appears. This page lists all the users and their information and allows you to create edit, edit, and delete users who have access to the workspace. Global permissions can also be set for the selected groups and users. Global permissions apply to all users and groups by default.

To add a new user, click New and a New User page opens where you can enter the information for a new user including his username, login, password, phone number, and e-mail address, as well as comments about that user. You also can specify the user's privileges as None, User, Project Creator, or System Administrator.

Clicking a user's name in the User page opens the Edit User page. The Edit User page is similar to the New User page. The Edit User page is where you can edit a user's information. This page also lets you specify the user's access to the various projects.

FIGURE 7.9

The Version Cue CS4 Administration utility home page includes links to several different utility pages and several basic tasks.

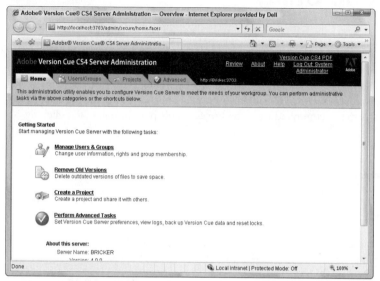

FIGURE 7.10

The Users/Groups page of the Version Cue Workspace Administration Utility

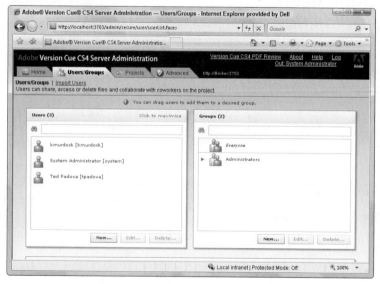

The Import Users button lets you import a list of users directly into the administration utility. Users can also be imported from an LDAP server using the LDAP Preferences link. LDAP attributes can also be mapped to Version Cue attributes. LDAP imported users are displayed using a different icon from users created manually.

Managing projects

The Projects page in the Version Cue CS4 Administration utility opens a page, shown in Figure 7.11, that lists all the available projects. From within this page, you can click New to create a new project. Using the buttons in the page, you also can duplicate, back up, export, and delete the selected projects.

FIGURE 7.11

The Projects page of the Version Cue Workspace Administration Utility lets you manage projects in the current workspace.

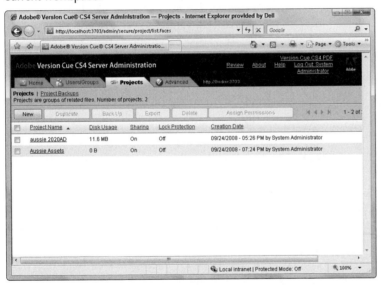

Creating and editing projects

Clicking New in the Projects page opens the New Project page, as shown in Figure 7.12. Here, you can select to create a blank project, import from a folder, import from an FTP server, or import from a WebDAV server. Each of these options walks you through the steps to create and define the properties for the project. Clicking Next moves to the next page.

FIGURE 7.12

The New Project page lets you create new projects using several different options.

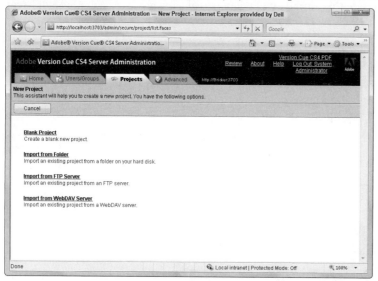

Clicking a project name in the Projects page opens an editing page that lists the properties for this project, its assigned users, and any project backups. The properties for each project that you may set include:

- **Share the Project with Others:** This option enables sharing this project with other users, so other users with rights to this project can view and access its files.

- **Enable Lock Protection:** Only one user can update the version of that file. Other users can open the file, but they're prevented from saving the file as a version of the original file. They may make changes and save the file with a different filename but not as a version of the original file.

CAUTION CS2 components and Acrobat 8 files work with Version Cue CS4, but you need to enable the Maximize Compatibility with CS2 Applications and Acrobat 8 option when the Version Cue folder is initially created.

Backing up projects

In the Projects pane, you can either click the project name link to edit the project info and create a backup, or you can use the check box to the left of the project name to select the project and use one of the buttons at the top of the Projects pane. If you click Back Up on the Projects page for a selected project, then a page, shown in Figure 7.13, appears. This is where you can verify the name that is used for the backup as well as which items are backed up. Clicking Save starts the backup process.

FIGURE 7.13

Clicking Back Up opens a page where you can select to back up the current project.

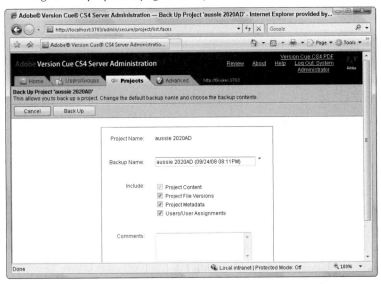

Back on the Projects page, the Backup List button (which is available only after you run a backup) opens a page that lists all the available backups. Selecting a backed up project from the list opens a page with a Restore button that you may use to restore the backed up project.

Using the Advanced features

Clicking the Advanced tab (located to the right of the Projects tab) opens a Web page with options to set Preferences, Import Version Cue CS2 Data workspaces, schedule maintenance, and set logs and reports. This page is shown in Figure 7.14 and offers the following options:

- **Setting Preferences:** The Preferences link opens a page of preferences including the Workspace Name, the Log Level and Log Size, an option to Compress the log file, and ports for the FTP and HTTP Proxies. The Security Preferences option includes settings for configuring SSL and the LDAP Preferences option is used to import LDAP users.

- **Import Version Cue CS3 Data:** The Import Version Cue 3.0 Data lets you quickly import all projects and user accounts saved with the previous version of CS.

- **Unlocking files:** The Advanced tab also includes an option to Reset Locks. You may find this invaluable for times when a critical file becomes permanently locked so no one can view it. Be aware that resetting the locks will kick all users out of their opened files.

- **Purging old files:** The Remove Old Files option gives you a page where you can delete all files older than a certain date, or you can specify that only a given number of versions are kept. This is a quick way to clean up a project to free some network disc space if needed.

- **Version Cue Backup:** This option gives you the ability to move the entire Version Cue server to another computer. The Administer Backups option lets you view and access the various project backups that you've made.

- **Restart Server:** If the server is having trouble and needs to be reinitialized, then the Restart Server option can be used to do this.

- **Viewing logs and reports:** The Workspace Log is a simple text file that keeps track of all system events. Every time a file is loaded and saved into a project, an entry is logged into the log file. Using this tool can help you find where a file is. It also can help troubleshoot any problems that appear. You can schedule reports to run regularly and to report any errors for a project. Regularly reading these generated reports will help keep your projects in tune and running smooth.

FIGURE 7.14

The Advanced tab includes links to several additional features.

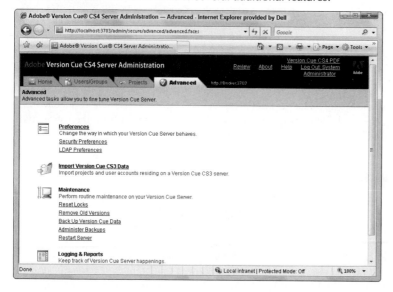

Summary

- You may access the Adobe Drive to connect to any established Version Cue projects.

- The Version Cue Server interface lets you control the server's availability.

- The Version Cue CS4 Administration utility may be accessed from the Version Cue Preferences dialog box. This browser-based tool is used to create and edit users and projects, back up and restore projects, and view project reports.

Chapter 8

Managing Adobe PDF Files

crobat has its own form of Bridge for viewing and organizing PDF documents. When Acrobat 7 Professional was developed, Adobe CS2 developers were still working on the Bridge. Because Acrobat 7 was released much earlier than the CS2 applications, inclusion for Bridge support was not possible in the earlier release. Things haven't changed in Acrobat 9 and the CS4 applications. The Acrobat Organizer is still the main document management tool used by Acrobat users. For Creative Suite users, most of the time you'll find yourself using the Bridge to organize and manage PDF documents as well as all the other CS4 documents.

The Organizer is like a junior cousin to the Bridge. Many Bridge tools and features are not included in the Organizer, but there are a few unique tools and features you can accomplish with the Organizer that you can't do with the Bridge. If PDF authoring is a major part of your workflow, perhaps you'll find working in the Organizer to be a better tool than using the Bridge. One obvious advantage is that when you work with Acrobat's Organizer you don't need to leave the program. When using the Bridge you need to toggle back and forth between the Bridge and Acrobat. It all depends on the kind of work you do and where you spend most of your time. If you are a casual user in Acrobat, then perhaps you might want to glance over the information contained in this chapter and note some of the unique features the Organizer has that the Bridge doesn't support.

> **NOTE** Working in Acrobat's Organizer also provides another benefit. Working in Organizer is much faster than working in the Bridge. During the initial release of Adobe Bridge, one disadvantage was that the Bridge runs slow, particularly when you view folders with many image files. In version CS4 of Adobe Bridge, the speed has greatly increased. However, the Bridge still remains a little slower than the Organizer.

IN THIS CHAPTER

Managing PDF files in the Organizer

Viewing PDF files and pages

CROSS-REF For information related to working with Adobe Bridge, see Chapter 6.

Using the Organizer Tool in Acrobat

To open the Organizer, choose File ➪ Organizer ➪ Open Organizer. You also can use the Shift+⌘(Ctrl)+1 shortcut. (In Windows, you can also choose File ➪ History ➪ Open Organizer.) When you select any of the options, the Organizer, shown in Figure 8.1, opens.

FIGURE 8.1

Click the Organizer tool or select Open Organizer from a menu command to open the Organizer window in Acrobat.

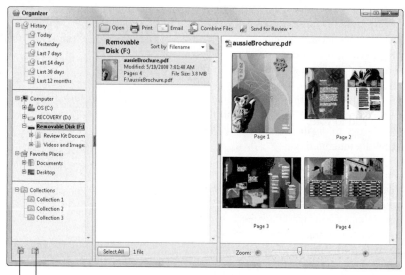

Create a New Collection

Add a Favorite Place

NOTE You can view PDF-only files in the Organizer. Unlike the Bridge where all files are viewed in the Content area, the Organizer supports only PDF documents.

The Organizer window contains three panes, a number of tools, and menu commands that you select from context menus. When you first open the Organizer, you find three panes in the Organizer window divided by two separator bars. On the left side of the window is the Categories pane, in the center is the Files pane, and on the right side is the Pages pane. You can adjust the size of the panes by clicking a separator bar and dragging it to the left or right. As one pane is sized down, the adjacent pane is sized up. You can adjust the size of the Organizer window by dragging the lower-right corner of the window.

Using the Categories pane

The Categories pane in the Organizer contains three types of categories. At the top of the pane is History, followed by My Computer (or your computer name), and at the bottom you find Collections:

■ **The History category**: Offers you the same choices for viewing history as you find in the File menu where you can see a list of recently opened files. As you click one of the History options, the files listed in the Files pane reflect the history period you choose. This is useful for opening PDF files that you accessed recently.

■ **The My Computer (your computer name) category**: Shows you a view of your hard drive and all servers and drives connected to your computer, similar to the Files tab in the Bridge. You can select a folder, and all PDFs within that folder are listed in the Files pane regardless of whether they appear in the view history. Below your accessible hard drives and servers you find Favorite Places. If you keep documents within folders you frequently access, right-click (Windows) or Control+click (Macintosh) to open a context menu over Favorite Places or click Add Favorite Place at the bottom of the Categories pane. The Browse For Folder dialog box, shown in Figure 8.2, opens (Windows), or the Select a folder to add to your favorite places dialog box opens on the Macintosh. Adding Favorites in this fashion is similar to adding Favorites in the Bridge.

FIGURE 8.2

Open a context menu on Favorite Places in the Open Files category, and a dialog box opens where you target a folder to add as a favorite place.

After you select a folder and click OK, the folder you selected appears at the bottom of the Favorite Places list.

■ **The Collections category:** Works similarly to Favorite Places, except that instead of adding folders to a list, you can select individual files and add them to a collection. You can add files to collections from different folders on your hard drive. By default, Acrobat offers you three collections: Collection 1, Collection 2, and Collection 3.

You manage collections through the use of a context menu. Open a context menu from any collection name in the Collections category, and the menu options appear as shown in Figure 8.3.

FIGURE 8.3

To manage collections, open a context menu on any collection name.

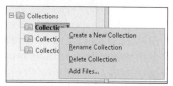

The menu selections should be self-explanatory. Select Create a New Collection to add another collection to the list. Select Rename Collection to rename a collection. Select Delete Collection to remove the collection. Note that when a collection is deleted, the files contained within that collection on your hard drive are not deleted. Click Add Files to add documents to your collection. After you add documents to a collection and click the collection name, all files added to the collection appear in the Files pane.

TIP After installing Acrobat, you may want to rename the default collection names to more descriptive names used in your workflow. Open a context menu on each collection name and select Rename Collection. The collection name is highlighted and ready for you to type a new name. One of the first collections you may want to create is one where you add Acrobat help documents such as the help guide, the Acrobat JavaScript Specification manual, the PDFMark Reference Manual, and so on.

Viewing PDF Files

The Files pane contains a list of all files derived from the choice you made in the Categories pane. For example, click a History category, and all files viewed within the selected history timeframe appear in a list sorted by metadata that you select from the Sort by pull-down menu.

CROSS-REF For information related to sorting metadata, see Chapter 6.

Beginning with the tools at the top of the pane, you find:

- **Open:** By default, the first file in the pane is selected. Click the Open tool to open the selected file. If no file is selected in the pane, the Open tool, as well as all other tools, are grayed out. A condition where you might not have a file selected is when you click a collection that contains no file in the collection folder or when you view a folder that contains no PDF documents. Otherwise, the first file, by default, is always selected when files are shown in the list.

- **Print:** Click a file in the list, and click the Print tool to print the file. When you click Print, the PDF document opens and the Print dialog box opens in the foreground. Make your print attribute choices in the Print dialog box, and click Print to print the file.

- **Email:** Select a file in the list and click the Email tool, and your default e-mail application opens with the selected file attached to a new e-mail message.

- **Combine Files:** Click this tool to open the Combine Files Wizard. In the Wizard, you can select PDF documents to combine into a single file or select a variety of different file formats that can be converted to a PDF. The tool works the same as selecting the File ⇨ Combine Files menu command in Acrobat.

NOTE Macintosh users are restricted to a limited number of file types that can be converted to PDF using the Combine Files Wizard. Windows users can convert all MS Office applications and a number of other file formats that aren't supported on the Mac using this menu command.

- **Send for Review:** Select a file in the list, and choose from the pull-down menu options to Attach for Email Review and Send for Shared Review.

CROSS-REF To learn more about the feature in Acrobat 9 for sending files for Shared Reviews, see Chapter 36.

Below the tools in the Files pane is a pull-down menu used for sorting files. You can sort files on metadata contained within the file. From the pull-down menu, shown in Figure 8.4, you have several choices for sorting files.

Sorting by Filename is the default and lists files in an alphabetical ascending order. The Title, Subject, Author, and Keywords items are part of the Document Properties Description that you supply at the time of PDF creation from some authoring programs or that you later add in Acrobat. Creator and Producer are part of the Document Description supplied by Acrobat and relate to the original authoring program and the application producing the PDF file. Number of Pages, File Size, and Modified Date are data that Acrobat adds to the Document Properties derived from the structure of the file. The Last Opened Date sorts the files according to the last time you viewed them in Acrobat with the most recent file listed first and in descending order.

FIGURE 8.4

Open the Sort by pull-down menu to sort files according to file metadata.

Ascending/descending sort order

CROSS-REF To learn more about Document Descriptions and Document Properties, see Chapter 34.

The icon to the right of the Sort by drop-down list lets you toggle between listing the files in ascending and descending order.

You can also manage files from a context menu opened on a file in the list. This menu has commands to perform the same tasks handled by the tools at the top of the pane. In Figure 8.5 you can see the top portion of the menu, duplicating the tools' functions, such as Open, Print, Email, Combine Files, Send for Review, and more.

FIGURE 8.5

Open a context menu on a file listed in the Files pane, and the menu options offer additional commands for managing files.

The Add to Collection menu item contains a submenu that lists all the collections in the Categories pane. As you add new collections to the Categories, they dynamically appear in the Add to Collection submenu. In Figure 8.6, note the submenu for adding files to existing collections.

The next menu item, Show in Explorer (Windows) or Show in Finder (Macintosh), takes you to Windows Explorer (Windows) or switches to Finder view (Macintosh) and opens the folder where the file is located. The Select All menu command selects all the files listed in the Files pane.

FIGURE 8.6

Clicking Add to a Collection opens a submenu that displays the existing collections by Collection name.

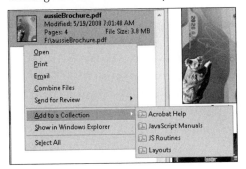

Using the Pages pane

By default, the Pages pane displays the first page in a PDF document of a file selected in the Files pane—something like the Preview in Adobe Bridge. One of the great features of the Organizer is that it shows multiple pages in the Pages pane for all files containing more than one page (refer to Figure 8.1). This feature is an advantage over the Bridge where only the cover pages are shown in the Content area and you need to manually scroll pages in the Preview pane to see additional pages in a document. When you select a multi-page document, all pages are displayed in thumbnail view in the Pages pane before you open the file. At the bottom of the pane is a zoom slider. Drag the slider left to display smaller thumbnails and to the right to make the thumbnail views larger. The minus and plus buttons display thumbnails smaller and larger, respectively, in zoom increments.

As you view multi-page documents in the Pages pane, you can double-click any page thumbnail to open the respective page in Acrobat. Select a page thumbnail and open a context menu, and a single menu command appears, enabling you to open that page.

Summary

- You use the Organizer tool in Acrobat to organize, sort, manage, and group PDF files. Tools in the Organizer provide options for creating PDF documents and initiating review sessions.

- PDF files are grouped in Collections where PDF documents are added using a single menu command.

- Sorting files on metadata in the Organizer is much more limited than sorting files in Adobe Bridge.

- You can view all pages in PDF files in the Organizer in the Pages pane.

Part III

Working with Objects and Images

Part III has to do with objects and images. In Chapters 9 and 10 we talk about creating objects and editing images. We discuss object and image styles, working with symbols, and using patterns. Chapter 11 covers acquiring and correcting images. In Chapter 12 we move on to object and image transformations and discuss rotating, skewing, scaling, and so on.

In Chapter 13 we cover the effects you can apply to objects and images in many CS4 applications. A special chapter devoted to 3D objects concludes this part.

Chapter 9

Creating, Selecting, and Editing Objects and Images

Creative Suite 4 documents have two groups of items: objects, which are editable and which include paths, shapes, type, and even multi-media elements, and images, which are pictures composed of an array of colored pixels. Although you have some crossover, you generally use Photoshop to work with images and Illustrator to work with objects. Most designs combine both of these items. Although all Creative Suite 4 applications use both objects and images and have similar tools, this chapter focuses mainly on Illustrator objects. Images in Photoshop are covered in the next chapter. The other CS4 applications of InDesign, Dreamweaver, Fireworks, and Acrobat have some of the same features for working with objects and images that are found in these two applications.

Several topics apply equally to both objects and images such as color, gradients, and transparency. Although these topics are covered in this chapter on objects, they apply equally to images covered in the next chapter.

This chapter covers lots of ground, including creating objects, the tools used to select them, and a sampling of the features used to edit them. The tools used to edit objects are as diverse as the tools and commands used to create and select them.

Creating Objects in Illustrator

The most common Illustrator objects are created using the various drawing tools. These tools are the second section of tools located in the Toolbox directly under the Selection tools, as shown in Figure 9.1. They consist of the Pen tool, the Type tool, the Line Segment tool, the Rectangle tool, the Paintbrush tool, and the Pencil tool. Each of these tools also has several additional flyout tools that you can use to create objects.

NOTE · The Illustrator Tools palette can toggle between a single vertical column and a double vertical column if you click the arrow icons in the upper-left corner. Photoshop
and InDesign also can toggle to a single horizontal orientation.

FIGURE 9.1

The Illustrator drawing tools

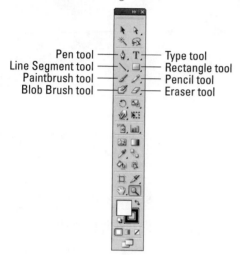

Pen tool ——— Type tool
Line Segment tool ——— Rectangle tool
Paintbrush tool ——— Pencil tool
Blob Brush tool ——— Eraser tool

Drawing in the workspace with any of these tools creates a line that Illustrator calls a *path*, which is
identified as an object. When you select an object, its path and the points that make up its path are
highlighted using the layer color. The various selection tools are covered later in this chapter.

In addition to the objects presented in this section, Illustrator includes some other tools that create
objects, such as the Symbol Sprayer and Graph tools.

Using the Pen tool

You use the Pen tool to draw several connected lines by simply clicking once where you want the
first anchor point and clicking again for each successive connected line.

But the power of the Pen tool isn't in creating straight lines. When you click with the Pen tool to
place an anchor point, you can drag to extend a direction line that lies tangent to the curve. At the
end of each direction line are direction points that may be moved to alter the curvature at the
point. Figure 9.2 shows a path created with the Pen tool.

TIP · If you hold down the Shift key while dragging to create a direction line, the direction line is constrained to 45-degree increments.

FIGURE 9.2

The Pen tool can include straight and curved segments.

Anchor point

Direction point

Direction line

You also can use the Pen tool to do the following:

- **End a path:** Hold down the ⌘/Ctrl key after clicking to create the last anchor point. You also can end a path by selecting another tool. If you press the ⌘/Ctrl key before clicking the last point, the Selection tool appears.

> **TIP** The Pen tool provides feedback when creating a new path, adding and deleting points, and closing a path using a small icon beneath and to the right of the tool's cursor.

- **Create a closed object:** Here, the first and last anchor points are the same. Position the last anchor point over the top of the first anchor point until a small circle appears as part of the cursor, and then click.

- **Add, delete, and convert anchor points on a line:** You can perform these tasks by using the Add or Delete Anchor Point tools, which are Pen tool flyout tools. Another flyout tool, the Convert Anchor Point tool, changes points without any direction lines to a smooth curve point. You simply click the point and drag out a direction line. This tool also changes smooth anchor points to corner points without a direction line when you click the anchor points. Holding down the Option/Alt key changes the cursor to the Convert Anchor Point tool.

- **Add or delete point on a path:** With the Pen tool selected, move the cursor over the top of the selected path. A small plus sign appears as part of the cursor when you're over the path; a small minus sign appears as part of the cursor when you're over a point that you may want to delete.

> **NOTE** The Pen, Add Anchor Point, Delete Anchor Point, and Convert Anchor Point tools are found in Illustrator, Photoshop, InDesign, Fireworks, and Flash.

Points created with the Pen tool can be selected with the Direct Selection or Lasso tools. If the point includes a direction line, the direction line and its points appear. When a direction line and its points are visible, you can drag them to alter the curvature around the point.

STEPS: Drawing with the Pen Tool

1. **Create a new Illustrator document.** Choose File ➪ New to create a new document.

2. **Enable a snapping grid.** Choose View ➪ Show Grid to make a grid appear. Then choose View ➪ Snap to Grid. This enables snapping so all points snap to the visible grid.

3. **Draw straight lines.** Click the Pen tool, and click several times to create an anchor point every time you click.

4. **Close the shape.** To close the shape, move the cursor until it's on top of the first anchor point and click. A small circle appears as part of the cursor when it's over the first anchor point. Figure 9.3 shows the simple shape made from straight lines using the Pen tool.

FIGURE 9.3

The Pen tool is used to create straight-line shapes.

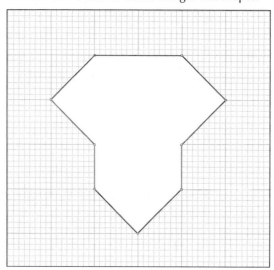

5. **Draw curved segments.** With the Pen tool still selected, click to create the same shape beneath the first one, but after clicking each point, drag to pull a direction line out from the point before you release the mouse button. This direction line defines the curvature of the corner. Continue to click around the shape until the shape is closed.

6. **Edit the path points.** Select the Direct Selection tool, drag over each anchor point, and compare it to the anchor point across from it. Drag the direction points to make them similar to their opposite corner to make the object symmetrical. Figure 9.4 shows the resulting shapes.

FIGURE 9.4

The Pen tool also is used to create curves.

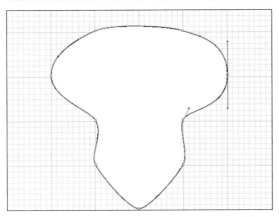

 Illustrator has a preference in the Selection & Anchor Display panel that highlights path points when you move the cursor over them. This helps make points easier to see.

Using the Type tool

You use the Type tool to create text objects. Clicking with the Type tool creates a Point type object, which you typically you use for a single line of text, such as a heading. You create an Area type object by clicking and dragging in the art board with the Type tool. All text that you type within a text area wraps to fit within the text object area.

CROSS-REF Type and all the Type tools are covered in detail in Part IV.

Text objects aren't limited to a rectangular area created by dragging with the Type tool. Using the flyout tools available under the Type tool, you can add text to a selected area or have text follow a path. You also have tools for creating text that runs vertically instead of horizontally.

NOTE Type objects you create with the Type tool are a unique type of object. You edit them using the Type tool; you can select them in a similar manner as other objects by dragging over them with the Selection tool.

Creating lines and shapes

You use the Line Segment tool to create simple straight lines by clicking and dragging on the art board. If you double-click with the Line Segment tool, a dialog box, shown in Figure 9.5, opens where you can specify the line's length and angle. Holding down the Shift key while dragging constrains the line to 45-degree increments; holding down the Option/Alt key while dragging extends the line in both directions from the clicked first point; and holding down the spacebar lets you move the line by dragging.

FIGURE 9.5

The Line Segment Tool Options dialog box

As flyouts under the Line Segment tool, Illustrator includes tools for creating arcs, spirals, rectangular grids, and polar grids. The Shift key constraints the Line Segment tool to straight horizontal, 45-degree, or vertical lines and the Alt [option] key extends the line outward from the point where you click at both ends.

 **TIP**   If you click the right edge of the tool flyout, you can tear off the flyout to access all the tools simultaneously.

The Rectangle tool creates rectangle objects by dragging in the art board. Clicking without dragging opens a simple dialog box where you can enter precise Width and Height values. Holding down the Shift key creates a perfect square when you drag; holding down the Option/Alt key while dragging creates the rectangle from the center outward; and holding down the spacebar lets you move and position the rectangle as you draw it out.

As flyout tools under the Rectangle tool, you can find the Rounded Rectangle, Ellipse, and Polygon tools. Dragging the Ellipse tool with the Shift key held down creates a perfect circle. Clicking with the Polygon tool opens a dialog box where you can specify a radius and the number of sides to include in the polygon. Illustrator also includes tools for creating pointed stars and flares as flyouts under the Rectangle tool. The Shift key constraints the Rectangle tool to perfect squares and the Alt [option] key creates a rectangle from the center outward where the center is the point where you first clicked.

Using the Paintbrush and Pencil tools

You can use both the Paintbrush and Pencil tools to draw freehand curves. The difference is that the Paintbrush tool applies art along a path. To draw with either the Paintbrush or Pencil tools, click and drag in the art board.

If you press the Option/Alt key and hold it down after starting a path, a small circle appears as part of the cursor, indicating that you're creating a closed path. When you release the mouse, regardless of where it's located, a line is drawn back to the first anchor point, creating a closed object.

If you double-click either tool in the Toolbox, a dialog box of preferences for the selected tool appears, such as the Paintbrush Tool Preferences dialog box, shown in Figure 9.6. In this dialog box, you can set Fidelity and Smoothness values as well as other options.

FIGURE 9.6

The Paintbrush Tool Preferences dialog box

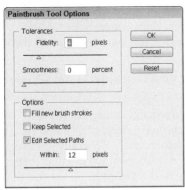

Paintbrush Tool Options

Tolerances
Fidelity: 4 pixels

Smoothness: 0 percent

OK
Cancel
Reset

Options
☐ Fill new brush strokes
☐ Keep Selected
☑ Edit Selected Paths
Within: 12 pixels

■ **Fidelity:** The Fidelity value determines how far the cursor can stray before a new anchor point is created. Increasing this value causes small changes in the path to be ignored. Figure 9.7 shows three curves drawn with the Paintbrush tool with different Fidelity settings. Notice how the curve with the lowest Fidelity value has the most anchor points.

FIGURE 9.7

Increasing Fidelity decreases the total number of anchor points.

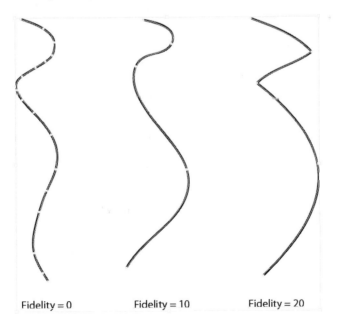

Fidelity = 0   Fidelity = 10   Fidelity = 20

- **Smoothness:** The Smoothness value ranges from 0 to 100 and sets the smoothness of the resulting path.

- **Fill New Brush Strokes option:** Only available for the Paintbrush tool, this option allows you to apply a fill to the path. If the path isn't closed, an imaginary line is drawn between the first and endpoints of the path, and the interior portion is colored with the fill color.

- **Keep Selected option:** This option causes the path to remain selected after you release the mouse button.

- **Edit Selected Paths option:** This option enables you to redraw portions of the path using the selected tool when the cursor is within the specified number of pixels. With this option, you can move the tool over the top of the selected path. If a small x displays as part of the cursor, a new path is created; if the small x disappears, you can drag over the path and replace that portion of the path with the new dragged path.

The flyout tools under the Pencil tool are the Smooth and Erase tools. You can drag the Smooth tool over the top of a selected path to reduce the number of anchor points and smooth the line. You can use the Erase tool to delete the path section that you drag over. You must select the path to use the Erase tool. Editing with these tools is covered later in the chapter.

 **TIP** You can temporarily enable the Smooth tool when you have the Paintbrush or Pencil tool selected by holding down the Option/Alt key.

Using the Blob Brush and Eraser tools

The Blob Brush tool (Shift+B) is a pressure sensitive tool that creates Beziér paths of like colors. This is a departure from standard Illustrator brush technology and when combined with the eraser allows great artistic expression of thin-thick line weights.

The Blob Brush tool lets you easily combine several paths of the same color into the same object. Figure 9.8 shows the branches of a tree that have been combined using the Blob Brush. The normal brush would keep each stroke as a separate path. Although the paths are combined, they remain independent from the trunk paths, which are a different color.

The Blob Brush Tool Options dialog box, shown in Figure 9.9, let you define the brush size and shape. You also can control the fidelity and smoothness of the overlapping paths. The Keep Selected option retains the selected object, which makes it easier to see how new paths are added to the selected path.

FIGURE 9.8

The Blob Brush tool combines several paths into a single object.

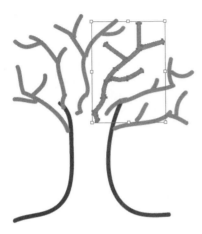

FIGURE 9.9

The Blob Brush Tool Options dialog box lets you define the characteristics of the Blob Brush tool.

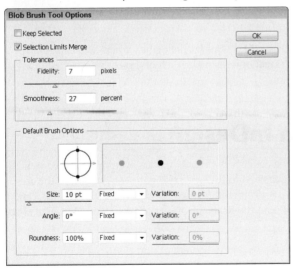

The Path Erase tool can erase portions of the selected path, but it is a detailed tool and has to be right on the path to work. The Eraser tool is much easier to work with and much more forgiving. It works on any objects whether selected or not.

When the Eraser tool is dragged over an open path it removes any portion of the path that is obscured, so it can quickly clean up any leftover path pieces. When the Eraser tool is used on a closed path, the tool changes the path as if the pixels underneath the tool were removed. Figure 9.10 shows an example of some closed paths that were altered with the Eraser tool. This provides a simple way to cut holes within a closed shape.

FIGURE 9.10

The Eraser tool can remove portions of a closed shape.

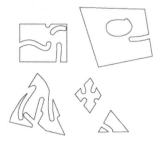

Double-clicking the Eraser tool opens the Eraser Tool Options dialog box where you can alter the tool's angle, roundness, and diameter. Additional options make each of these attributes fixed or random with a designated amount of variation.

Creating Objects in InDesign

InDesign, like Illustrator, relies heavily on the concept of objects. In fact, everything placed in an InDesign document is an object. Objects are created in InDesign using the tools found in the second section of the Toolbox, shown in Figure 9.11, including the Pen tool, the Type tool, the Pencil tool, the Line tool, the Rectangle Frame tool, and the Rectangle tool along with the additional tools available as flyouts.

All these tools include features that are similar to the Illustrator tools, but InDesign includes some additional object types created with the Frame and Shape tools. Frames offer a way to create an image placeholder, and the various shape tools are used to add a variety of shapes. The key difference between frames and shapes in InDesign is the initial state of the stroke and fills. The drawing tools, on the other hand, apply the current stroke and fill.

FIGURE 9.11

The InDesign drawing tools

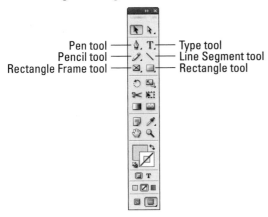

Pen tool — Type tool
Pencil tool — Line Segment tool
Rectangle Frame tool — Rectangle tool

CROSS-REF **Creating and using interactive buttons in InDesign is covered in Chapter 29.**

Creating Objects in Photoshop

Although Photoshop's forte is working with images, you also can use Photoshop to create *shapes*. The tools used to create objects in Photoshop are located in the third section of tools in the Toolbox, as shown in Figure 9.12. They include a Type tool, a Pen tool, and a Rectangle tool, along with several additional tools available as flyouts.

FIGURE 9.12

The Photoshop drawing tools

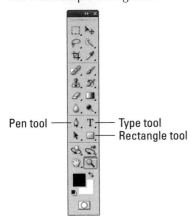

Pen tool — Type tool
Rectangle tool

When you select one of these drawing tools, the Options bar, shown in Figure 9.13, displays all the drawing tools. Selecting a drawing tool and clicking the drop-down options to the right of the Custom Shape Tool opens a pop-up menu of settings for the selected tool. These pop-up menus of settings let you enter precise Width and Height values for the shapes.

FIGURE 9.13

The Options bar displays all the different drawing tools.

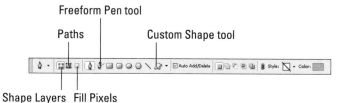

Freeform Pen tool

Paths   Custom Shape tool

Shape Layers   Fill Pixels

Photoshop also includes a Freeform Pen tool, as a flyout under the Pen tool that acts like Illustrator's Pencil tool. It lets you draw freehand paths. If you enable the Magnetic option in the Options bar, the Freeform Pen tool detects areas of contrast and snaps the line to follow a pixel image behind it.

 **If you're having trouble with the Pen tool, try enabling the Rubber Band option, which makes it easier to learn to use the Pen tool.**

Specifying custom shapes

The Photoshop object tools (referred to in Photoshop as drawing tools) also work just like their Illustrator counterparts. Among these tools is a unique tool called the Custom Shape tool, which is a flyout under the Rectangle tool and which is available in the Options bar at the top of the screen whenever any of the shape tools are active.

The Custom Shape tool lets you select a custom shape by right-clicking in the workspace after selecting the Custom Shape tool or through the drop-down menu on the Options bar, shown in Figure 9.14. You add the selected shape to the document by dragging with the tool. Add new shapes to the pop-up menu by choosing Edit ⇨ Define Custom Shape.

FIGURE 9.14

This pop-up palette lets you add Custom Shapes to the document.

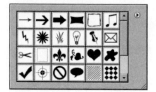

Photoshop custom shapes are similar to Illustrator's symbols, except that there are no update or replace features.

CROSS-REF Symbols are covered in the "Using Symbols, Graphic Styles, and Swatches," section later in this chapter.

Creating paths

If you select the Paths option in the Options bar, select a drawing tool, and then create a shape, Photoshop adds the shape to the Paths palette, shown in Figure 9.15. You can then use these paths to mask areas or define a clipping path. You also can convert them into a selection.

FIGURE 9.15

The Paths palette lets you store several paths.

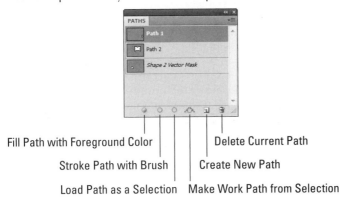

Fill Path with Foreground Color   Delete Current Path

Stroke Path with Brush   Create New Path

Load Path as a Selection   Make Work Path from Selection

You also can export paths to Illustrator by choosing File ➪ Export ➪ Paths to Illustrator or using the copy and paste commands.

CROSS-REF Using paths as clipping masks is covered in the "Creating a clipping mask in Illustrator" section later in this chapter.

Paths drawn on an image are temporary and appear with the name Work Path in the Paths palette. If you deselect the Work Path in the Paths palette and draw another path, then the new path replaces the first path. Because paths placed in the Paths palette are temporary, you can save them using the Save Path palette menu command. This opens a simple dialog box where you can name the saved path. The saved path then appears permanently in the Paths palette where it can be selected and reused.

Painting with shapes

All shapes drawn in Photoshop as objects are contained within special layers called *shape layers*. If a single shape layer includes multiple shapes, you can use the Pathfinder buttons to add, subtract, intersect, or exclude the overlapping areas.

CROSS-REF More on the Pathfinder commands is covered in the section "Using Pathfinder features."

If you select the Fill Pixels option in the Options bar when drawing a shape in Photoshop, the shape becomes rasterized and becomes part of the pixel layer. For these painted shapes, you can select a blending mode and an opacity. You also can rasterize existing shapes by choosing Layer ➪ Rasterize ➪ Shape.

Working with Smart Objects

Smart Objects are objects that know the application used to create them and by double-clicking on them or by selecting the Layer ➪ Smart Object ➪ Edit Contents menu you can open them within the source application for further editing. As the edits are made in the source application, the changes are propagated to the linked application, keeping all the content in synch.

Smart Objects are created in Photoshop using the Open As Smart Object menu command, but they also can be created by placing a file, pasting a file from Illustrator, or converting a Photoshop layer to a Smart Object. Smart Object layers are easy to identify in the Layers palette because they include a special icon in the lower-right corner of the thumbnail.

TIP One roundabout method for working with Smart Objects in Photoshop is to place a Photoshop image within the current document. This creates a Smart Object layer and lets you work with the image, such as transforming the image, in a nondestructive manner. If the original image needs to be edited, you can simply select the Layer ➪ Smart Objects ➪ Edit Contents menu and the image opens within Photoshop as a separate file. Any changes to the original file are updated in the other document when the original file is saved.

Creating and Editing Objects in Acrobat

All items in an Acrobat document are objects. Most of these objects are created from the original document when it's converted into a PDF file, but Acrobat 8 Professional also lets you create several objects that you can use to enhance the Acrobat document or to add review comments.

You select most Acrobat objects by choosing Tools ➪ Advanced Editing ➪ Select Object. When selected, the object highlights and you can move it by dragging it to a new location. If you right-click the object, a pop-up menu appears with commands to edit, align, center, distribute, and size the object. Most objects also include a pop-up menu option to access their Properties dialog box.

Adding document-enhancement objects

Objects used to enhance a PDF document—including the Article tool, the Movie tool, the Sound tool, the TouchUp Text and TouchUp Object tools, and several Form object tools—are located in the Tools ➪ Advanced Editing and the Tools ➪ Forms menus:

■ **Article tool:** Use this to add several threaded text areas to the document. To create an article object, drag to create each of the threaded text areas and press the Enter key to complete the article. After the article is completed, a Properties dialog box appears, where you can enter the title, subject, author, and keywords for the article.

■ **Video and Flash tools:** Use these to add movie or Flash files to an existing PDF document. After selecting either of these tools and dragging in the document, a dialog box opens where you can browse to the desired movie or sound file.

CROSS-REF The details of using movie and sound files within an Acrobat document are covered in Chapter 29.

■ **TouchUp Text tool:** Use this to edit an existing piece of text. Selecting the Text TouchUp tool and clicking in the document with the ⌘/Ctrl key held down opens a dialog box where you can select the font and mode for the new text.

■ **Form object tools:** The Tools ➪ Forms menu includes several form objects that you can easily add to an Acrobat document. After selecting a form object from the menu, you can drag with the mouse to specify the form object's size. These form object tools include a Button tool, a Check Box tool, a Combo Box tool, a List Box tool, a Radio Button tool, a Text Field tool, a Digital Signature tool, and a Barcode tool. When you create a form object, a Properties dialog box, shown in Figure 9.16, opens where you can specify all the settings for the form object. For example, the Button Properties dialog box includes four panels—General, Appearance, Options, and Actions—but other form objects include more panels.

FIGURE 9.16

A dialog box of properties helps define the object's appearance.

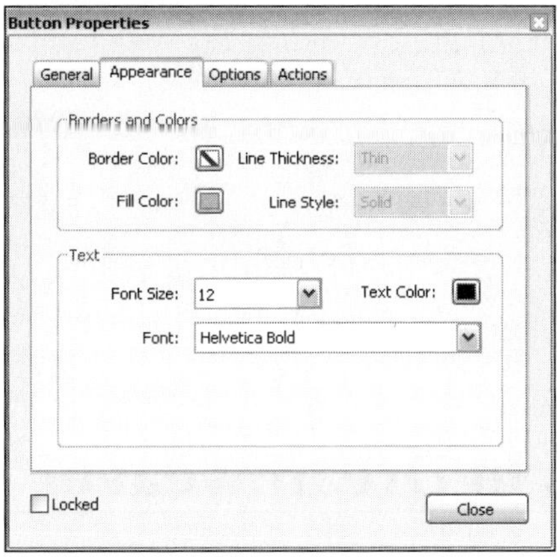

Adding commenting objects

All the commenting objects for reviewing a document are included in the Tools ⇨ Comment & Markup menu. The Comment & Markup menu includes the Sticky Note tool. Dragging with this tool in the document creates a Note object, which includes the name of the person making the comments, along with the date and time and a text area where the comments may be added.

The Comment & Markup menu also includes the Stamps submenu, which is used to add stamped image objects to the document. The Stamps submenu includes many different default stamps choices, including stamps that say Approved, Confidential, Void, and so on. Also included is a category of dynamic stamps that include the applier's name and date.

To add more attention to a comment, you may select to use one of the tools found in the bottom of the Comment & Markup menu. These tools include a collection of drawing tools, including tools for creating rectangles, ovals, arrows, lines, clouds, polygons, and polygon line objects.

The Comment & Markup menu also includes a Text Edits tool that creates highlighted text area objects, the Pencil tools, which lets you draw freehand objects, and the Pencil Eraser tool, which erases lines drawn with the Pencil tool. In addition, the Attach a File as a Comment menu command opens a dialog box where you can select a file to attach to the document. After you've selected the file, the File Attachment Properties dialog box, shown in Figure 9.17, appears; here, you can define how the attachment looks in the PDF document. The Record Audio Comment tool opens a Sound Recorder, where you can record a simple audio message or select a sound file to attach to the document.

FIGURE 9.17

The File Attachment Properties dialog box lets you choose the icon used to represent the attached file.

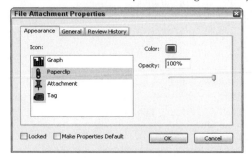

Creating Objects in Dreamweaver

Dreamweaver also uses objects extensively to lay out Web pages. All the objects that you can add to a Web page are available in different tabbed categories in the Insert panel. The various tabbed categories include Common, Layout, Forms, Data, Spry, Text, and Favorites. Selecting a category displays all the available objects as icon buttons. Figure 9.18 shows many of the objects in the Basic Objects category.

FIGURE 9.18

The Dreamweaver Insert bar includes dozens of objects in several different categories.

An object is added to a Web page by clicking its icon button to make the object's properties dialog box appear. After an object is created, you can access its properties in the Properties palette at the bottom of the interface. You also can add objects while using the Code view.

Painting Images

Unlike objects, which can be thought of as a group of items sitting on a shelf ready for you to place in a document, you create images by drawing them on a canvas or by loading an existing image file. All the CS4 applications also support images, but the first place to look is obviously Photoshop.

NOTE   **The process of creating objects within the CS4 applications is referred to as** *drawing,* **and the process of creating images is called** *painting.*

Painting images in Photoshop

The main tools used in Photoshop to paint images are the Paintbrush tool, the Pencil tool, and the Paint Bucket tool. All these tools apply the foreground color to the canvas.

Using the Paintbrush tool

The Paintbrush tool coupled with the Brushes palette offers unlimited flexibility and power in applying paint to the canvas. Selecting the Brush tool (B) in the Toolbox changes the cursor to match the shape of the selected brush. Dragging with this tool in the canvas paints a line using the properties set in the Brushes palette.

You may open the Brushes palette, shown in Figure 9.19, by choosing Window ⇨ Brushes (F5) or by clicking the Brushes tab on the right end of the Options bar. The Brushes palette includes many panels of properties that are opened by clicking the panel name listed to the left of the palette. Most of these panels include a check box that lets you enable or disable the properties contained in the panel. The panels are as follows:

FIGURE 9.19

The Brushes palette includes many preset brushes to start with.

Lock Options

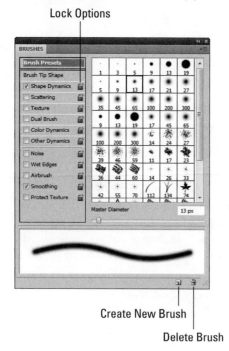

Create New Brush

Delete Brush

 The Brushes palette is active only when one of the painting tools is selected.

■ **Brush Presets:** This panel lets you choose a brush from a long list of presets. To select a preset brush, just click it and a preview of the selected brush appears at the bottom of the panel. You also can change the Master Diameter for the selected brush. In the Brush palette menu are several options for setting how the preset brushes are viewed, including Text Only, Small and Large Thumbnails, Small and Large Lists, and Stroke Thumbnail.

The Brush palette menu also includes a New Brush Preset option that is used to add a new preset to the Brush Preset panel. A set of brush presets may be saved to the local system using the Save Brushes palette menu command. The brush libraries are saved using an ABR file extension. Photoshop includes several brush libraries that may be loaded into the Brushes palette or selected from the bottom of the Brushes palette menu.

■ **Brush Tip Shape panel:** Shown in Figure 9.20, this panel displays thumbnails of the brush tips for the respective brush presets listed in the Brush Presets panel. The brush tip properties let you change the tip's diameter and orientation using controls to flip the brush tip and set its angle and roundness. You also can alter its Angle and Roundness values by dragging in the diagram pane to the right of the Angle and Roundness values. The Hardness value sets the diameter of the brush's hard center, where no softening takes place. The Spacing value determines the distance between successive brush marks in a stroke. Low Spacing values cause the brush tip to overlap into a continuous path.

FIGURE 9.20

The Brush Tip Shape panel of the Brushes panel

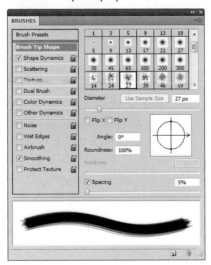

■ **Shape Dynamics and other panels:** This panel includes controls to add some randomness to the brush strokes, including the amount of jitter that is added. The Scattering panel is used to spread the brush tip over a given width with a specified density. The Texture panel lets you specify an underlying texture for the brush. The Dual Brush panel lets you select a secondary brush tip that is combined with the original brush tip to create a new unique pattern. The Color and Other Dynamics panels let you specify how the colors, transparency, and brightness change as the brush is painted.

The Noise, Wet Edges, Airbrush, Smoothing, and Protect Texture options don't open a panel of settings but may be enabled to change the characteristics of the selected brush.

When the Paintbrush tool is selected, the Options bar includes controls that let you select a tool preset or a brush tip. You also can select a blending mode to use and change the amount of opacity and flow that is applied to the brush.

As you paint with the Paintbrush tool, you can dynamically alter the brush size by dragging with the Ctrl and Alt (Option) keys held down. You also can change the brush's hardness value while painting by dragging with the Ctrl, Alt (Option), and Command keys held down.

STEPS: Painting with the Paintbrush Tool

1. **Open a Photoshop document.** With Photoshop open, choose File ➪ New to create a new document.

2. **Select a Brush.** Click the Paintbrush tool to select it. In the Options bar, click the Brushes tab to open the Brushes palette. Click the palette menu, and select the Special Effect Brushes command. A dialog box opens asking if you want to replace the brush sets. Click OK. The new brush set is displayed in the Brush Presets panel, as shown in Figure 9.21. In the Brush Presets panel of the Brushes palette, select the first brush preset, called the Azalea brush.

3. **Set the brush properties.** In the Swatches palette, select an orange color. This color becomes the new foreground color. Click the Color Dynamics panel in the Brushes palette, and drag the Hue Jitter over to 50%.

4. **Paint with a Preset brush.** Drag with the Paintbrush tool in the canvas. The Azalea brush paints a random assortment of colored flowers in the canvas, as shown in Figure 9.22.

FIGURE 9.21

The brushes in the Brush Presets panel

FIGURE 9.22

By altering the Hue Jitter in the Color Dynamics palette, the color of the flowers is changed as you paint with the brush.

Using the Pencil and Paint Bucket tool

The Pencil tool works just like the Paintbrush tool, except it produces a hard edge instead of a smooth, soft edge. The Pencil tool uses all the same controls found in the Brushes palette for specifying its shape and characteristics.

The Paint Bucket tool, located as a flyout under the Gradient tool, applies the selected foreground color or pattern to an area where all the contiguous pixels are the same or within the specified Tolerance. You can select the properties of the Paint Bucket tool in the Options bar when the Paint Bucket tool is selected. You also can select a blending mode and an opacity.

Working with images in the other CS4 applications

All the other CS4 applications can work with images, but these images are confined to an object or frame. This lets you transform the images within the work area and place them relative to the other objects, but Illustrator and InDesign don't include any tools that alter the pixels by painting. You can load images into Illustrator and InDesign using the File ➪ Place menu command. These loaded images appear within an object or frame.

You also can convert certain text and vector objects to their bitmap equivalents through a process called *rasterizing*. Raster images may be moved back to Photoshop using the Clipboard. When pasted into Photoshop, the images are contained within a frame that allows you to move the object, but when you select a different tool, a confirm dialog box asks if you want to place the object. Choosing to place the object permanently places it in the current image.

Illustrator also includes a Live Trace feature that works the opposite of rasterizing, allowing you to convert images into vectorized objects.

 Rasterizing objects eliminates their resolution independence. Scaling a rasterized object reveals all the individual pixels.

Rasterizing objects

You can rasterize Illustrator objects by choosing Object ➪ Rasterize. This opens the Rasterize dialog box, shown in Figure 9.23, where you can select a color model, a resolution, a background, an anti-aliasing option, and a clipping mask, as well as specify whether space is added to the object.

- **Color Model options:** Include RGB, CMYK, Grayscale, or Bitmap, depending on the color settings for the document.
- **Background options:** Define whether the object background is colored as white pixels or made transparent. Selecting the Transparent option causes an alpha channel to be saved with the document.

FIGURE 9.23

The Rasterize dialog box lets you specify a color model.

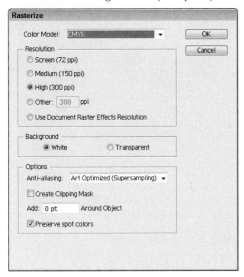

- **Anti-Aliasing options:** Include None, Art Optimized (which is used for graphics), and Type Optimized (which is used for text).
- **Create Clipping Mask:** Creates a clipping mask that hides all the background pixels. It isn't needed if the Transparent Background option is selected.
- **Add field:** Lets you specify a distance that is added to every edge of the rasterized object.

You can define all these settings for the document using the Document Raster Effects Settings dialog box, shown in Figure 9.24, which you open by choosing Effect ⇨ Document Raster Effects Settings. You use these settings for any effects that need to rasterize the object as the effect is being applied. The Document Raster Effects Settings dialog box also includes the Preserve Spot Colors where Possible option. This setting attempts to use spot colors where they can be used.

CROSS-REF More on using effects is covered in Chapter 13.

FIGURE 9.24

The Document Raster Effects Settings dialog box

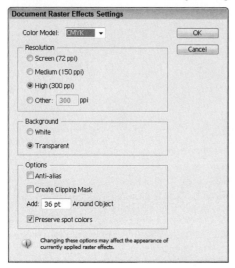

STEPS: Rasterizing Objects

1. **Create a new Illustrator document.** With Illustrator open, choose File ➪ New to create a new document. Select the RGB Color option in the New Document dialog box.

2. **Drag a symbol from the Symbols palette.** For a quick object that may be rasterized, drag a symbol from the Symbols palette onto the art board.

3. **Resize the object.** Because the object loses its resolution independence when it's rasterized, drag on the bounding-box handles of the symbol with the Shift key held down to maintain its aspect ratio until it is the size you want to use, as shown in Figure 9.25.

FIGURE 9.25

Sizing the object in Illustrator before rasterizing

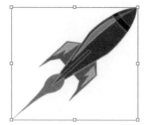

4. **Rasterize the symbol.** With the symbol selected, choose Object ⟹ Rasterize. The Rasterize dialog box appears. Select the RGB Color Mode, and change the Resolution depending on how the raster image intends to be used. Use Screen for images that are viewed on a computer monitor and High for raster images that are to be printed. Select Transparent as the Background, and select the Art Optimized Anti-Aliasing option. Then click OK. Figure 9.26 shows the rasterized symbol zoomed in so you can see the anti-aliasing.

FIGURE 9.26

The rasterized object appears the same as the object version, but if you were to scale the raster image, you would see the individual pixels.

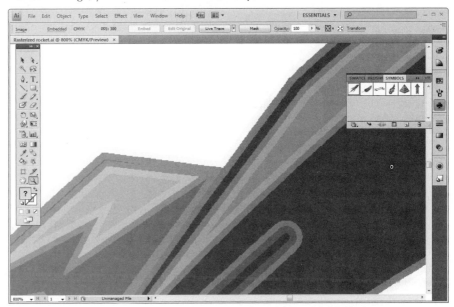

NOTE If you intend to use the image in Photoshop, then you can paste the object as a smart object. This preserves the vector data and rasterizes the image on the fly when copied to Photoshop.

Using Live Trace

Just as you can rasterize vector objects into pixel images, Illustrator also includes a feature that reverses the process. Illustrator's Live Trace takes raster images and traces them into editable objects. Figure 9.27 shows a simple sailboat image that has been traced into black and white objects.

FIGURE 9.27

Live Trace is used to convert raster images into vector objects.

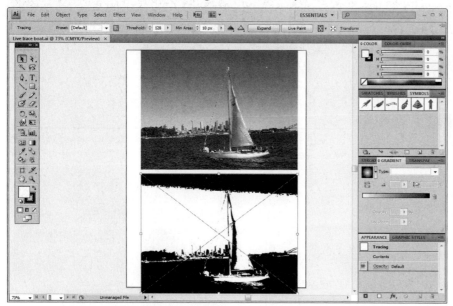

The Live Trace button appears in the Options bar anytime a raster graphic is selected in Illustrator. After a raster graphic is traced, the Options bar displays a drop-down list of Presets that you can select. The Options bar also includes a button to open the Tracing Options dialog box, shown in Figure 9.28. After tracing the image, the Options bar also includes a setting for controlling the Threshold and the Minimum Area. The Threshold value applies to the black and white tracing mode. All pixels in the trace area lighter than the Threshold value are converted to white, and all pixels darker are converted to black. The Minimum Area setting controls the size of the details considered during the trace pass. Details in pixel areas smaller than the Minimum Area value are ignored.

Live Trace also can be selected from the Object ⇨ Live Trace ⇨ Make menu, and the Tracing Options dialog box is accessed using the Object ⇨ Live Trace ⇨ Tracing Options menu. Each traced image includes the original raster image along with the traced result. Using the black and gray up arrow icons on the Options bar, you can set what is visible. Options for the raster image include No Image, Original Image, Adjusted Image, and Transparent Image. Options for the Vector traced image include No Tracing Result, Tracing Result, Outlines, and Outlines with Tracing.

FIGURE 9.28

The Tracing Options dialog box lets you define new tracing presets.

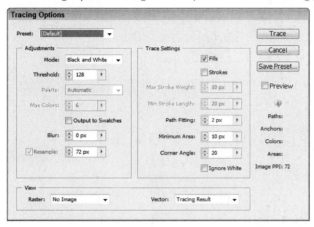

> **NOTE** The Live Trace options can be changed as long as the trace is not expanded or converted to a Live Paint object. A linked image can also be manipulated in Photoshop to alter the tone or contrast in order to influence the Live Trace outcome.

You can remove the existing tracing using the Object ➪ Live Trace ➪ Release menu command.

STEPS: Using Live Trace

1. **Open an Illustrator document.** With Illustrator open, choose File ➪ Open to open a document to trace that includes a raster image. Figure 9.29 shows the image before being traced.

2. **Select the bitmap image.** Choose the Selection tool, and click the raster image in the center of the artboard.

3. **Use Live Trace.** With the image selected, select the Object ➪ Live Trace ➪ Make command. This applies the default tracing preset, as shown in Figure 9.30.

FIGURE 9.29

This raster image is about to be traced.

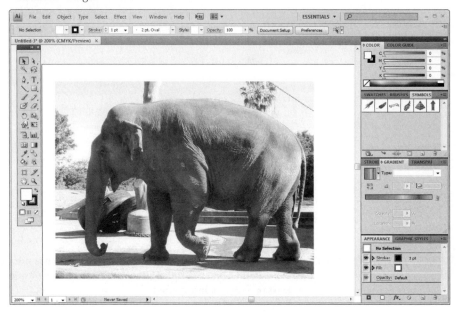

FIGURE 9.30

The default trace preset traces using black and white.

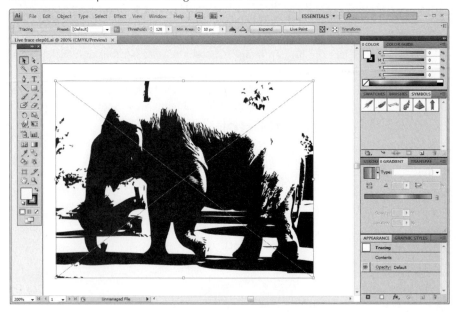

4. **Open the Tracing Options dialog box.** Select the Object ⇨ Live Trace ⇨ Tracing Options menu command. In the Tracing Options dialog box, choose the Color 16 option, then reduce the Blur value to 0, the Path Fitting value to 6 px, and the Minimum Area value to 2 px. Then click Trace.

5. **Expand the traced image.** With the traced image still selected, choose the Object ⇨ Live Trace ⇨ Expand menu command. This makes all the traced objects selectable. Figure 9.31 shows the final result.

FIGURE 9.31

The final traced image includes objects that can be selected and edited.

Selecting Objects

Before the properties of an object are displayed, you need to select the object that you want to change. Selecting an object is as easy as clicking it with the Selection tool. When selected, the object is surrounding with a bounding box. An object's bounding box may be used to transform the object.

NOTE Dreamweaver is the anomaly when it comes to selection. Because Dreamweaver doesn't have any selection tools, objects are selected in Design view by clicking them with the cursor.

 Transforming objects is covered in Chapter 12.

The core Selection tools—including the Selection and Direct Selection tools found in Illustrator, Photoshop, InDesign, Fireworks, and Flash—all work the same.

 Acrobat is also a little different in how it selects objects.

Using Illustrator and InDesign's Toolbox selection tools

Both the Illustrator and InDesign Toolboxes include several tools for selecting objects and parts of objects. These tools are located at the top of the Toolbox, as shown in Figure 9.32 for Illustrator include the Selection tool, Direct Selection tool, the Magic Wand tool, and the Lasso tool. InDesign includes the Selection and Direct Selection tools.

NOTE Illustrator and InDesign have a Group Selection tool that is used to select individual objects within a group and groups of objects.

FIGURE 9.32

The Illustrator selection tools

Selection tool —— Direct Selection tool
Magic Wand tool —— Lasso tool

- **Selection tool:** The simplest way to select objects is to click them with the Selection tool. You also can select multiple objects by dragging over them with the Selection tool (V). All objects that are at least partially included within the area that is dragged over are selected. You also may select multiple objects by holding down the Shift key while clicking each object.

TIP You can access the most recently used selection tool in Illustrator regardless of the current tool by holding down the ⌘/Ctrl key. This allows you to select an object quickly at any time. In InDesign, the ⌘/Ctrl key toggles to the Direct Selection tool if you're using the Pen tool and to the most recently used selection tool when one of the other tools is active. In Photoshop, the ⌘/Ctrl key accesses the Move tool when you're editing layers or working with pixels, but you get the Direct Selection tool when the Pen tool is active and you get the Selection tool when one of the other shape tools are active.

- **Direct Selection tool:** Use this to select individual points or segments on a path. When a path point is selected, it appears solid; unselected path points appear hollow. When the Direct Selection tool (A) is over the top of a line segment, a small line appears as part of the cursor; if the Direct Selection tool is over an anchor point, a small hollow square appears as part of the cursor and the selected anchor point appears larger to make it easier to select.

 If only a single path point is selected with the Direct Selection tool and the Scale tool is selected, then the scale only affects the direction handles on the selected point.

Using Illustrator's other selection tools

Illustrator's Group Selection tool (available as a flyout under the Direct Selection tool) may be used to select a single object that is part of a group. Clicking a grouped set of objects selects the object and the group it belongs to. Each successive click adds another group level.

Illustrator's Magic Wand tool (Y) is used to select all objects that have a similar fill color or pattern, but using the Magic Wand palette, shown in Figure 9.33, you can choose to have the Magic Wand tool select all objects with a similar fill color, stroke color, stroke weight, opacity, and blending mode. For each of these (except for blending mode), you can specify a Tolerance value. The Tolerance value determines how loose the selected attribute may be while still being selected.

FIGURE 9.33

The Magic Wand palette lets you select which attributes to select.

Illustrator's Lasso tool (Q) also may be used to select multiple path points on multiple objects. Every object that has a point encircled by the Lasso tool is selected. Holding down the Shift key lets you add to the current selection; holding down the Option/Alt key subtracts from the current selection.

 You cannot select objects that are locked or hidden. To unlock all objects, choose Object ➪ Unlock All (Alt+Ctrl+3 in Windows; Option+⌘+3 on the Mac). To show all hidden objects, choose Object ➪ Show All (Alt+Ctrl+3 in Windows; Option+⌘+3 on the Mac).

Selecting by Path Only

By default, you can select objects by clicking their fill, but this isn't your only option. If you have several overlapping objects, this option might lead to some frustration. The Selection & Anchor Display panel of the Preferences dialog box (opened with the Edit ➪ Preferences ➪ General menu command in Windows and with the Illustrator ➪ Preferences ➪ General menu command for Mac) includes an Object Selection by Path Only option. With this option enabled, objects are selected with the Selection tool only when you click or drag over their path and not their fill.

Using Photoshop's other selection tools

Although you use most of Photoshop's selection tools to make pixel selections, Photoshop also includes Selection and Direct Selection tools specifically for selecting objects. When you select a layer containing images in the Layers palette, you can use Photoshop's Marquee, Lasso, Magic Wand, or Quick Selection tools to select a pixel area. You move pixel selections using the Move tool, but the Move tool also is used to move objects when an object is selected.

When objects are created in Photoshop, each object resides on its own layer. Photoshop CS4 lets you select multiple layers by holding down the Shift key. Once multiple layers are selected, they can be moved and altered as needed.

Selecting objects with Illustrator's Layers palette

You can use the Layers palette to select all objects contained on a layer or individual objects within that layer. To the right of the layer name in the Layers palette is a circle button used to target objects. Clicking this target button for a given layer selects all objects on that layer. If you expand a layer, you can select the individual objects that make up the layer.

 Layers are covered in detail in Chapter 25.

Using Illustrator's Select menu

In addition to the Toolbox tools, there are many selection-menu commands available in the Select menu. Choose Select ➪ All (⌘/Ctrl+A) to select all objects in the scene. Choose Select ➪ Deselect (Shift+⌘/Ctrl+A) to deselect all objects in the document so that no objects are selected. Choose Select ➪ Reselect to select again all objects that were previously selected.

 Photoshop also includes a Select menu, but all these menu commands apply to the pixel selection tools, which are covered in Chapter 11.

Choosing Select ➪ Inverse selects all objects that weren't selected and deselects all objects currently selected.

Objects also can be selected using their stacking order. Choosing Select ➪ Next Object Above (Alt+Ctrl+] in Windows; Option+⌘+] on the Mac) selects the object immediately above the current object in the stacking order. Choosing Select ➪ Next Object Below (Alt+Ctrl+[in Windows; Option+⌘+[on the Mac) selects the object immediately below the current object in the stacking order. If the topmost or bottommost objects are selected when these commands are used, the current object remains selected.

 The First Object Above, Next Object Above, Next Object Below, and Last Object Below menu commands are found in InDesign's Object ➪ Select menu.

The Select ➪ Same menu includes several options for choosing all objects that have similar properties. The options include Appearance, Appearance Attribute, Blending Mode, Fill & Stroke, Fill Color, Opacity, Stroke Color, Stroke Weight, Graphic Style, Symbol Instance, and Link Block Series. These options also can be selected from the Options bar.

The Select ➪ Object menu includes several subobjects that you may select for the selected object. These options include All on Same Layers, Direction Handles, Brush Strokes, Clipping Masks, Stray Points, and Text Objects. Illustrator includes options to select Flash Dynamic Text and Flash Input Text object.

The Select ➪ Save Selection menu command lets you name and save the current selection of objects. The Save selections may be recalled at any time by selecting the selection name from the bottom of the Select menu. Choosing Select ➪ Edit Selection opens a dialog box where you can rename or delete a selection.

NOTE The Save Selection feature in Photoshop lets you save a selection as a mask in an alpha channel. These saved selections are stored in the Channels palette. When saving the selection to a channel, you can choose to combine the selection with other defined channels using the Replace, Add to, Subtract from, or Intersect with commands.

Selecting Pixels in Photoshop

Just as Illustrator and InDesign include several tools that select objects, Photoshop includes several tools that select specific pixels. The Selection tools are located at the top of Photoshop's Toolbox and include several Marquee tools, several Lasso tools, and the Quick Selection tool, as shown in Figure 9.34.

FIGURE 9.34

Photoshop's Toolbox includes several selection tools.

Rectangular Marquee tool

Move tool

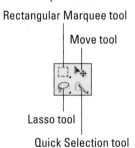

Lasso tool

Quick Selection tool

Using the Selection tools

When one of the Selection tools is selected, the Options bar displays four icon buttons that are used to create a new selection, add to the current selection, subtract from the current selection, and intersect with the current selection. These buttons let you continuously edit a selection until you have exactly what you want.

Holding down the Shift key while selecting an area adds to the current selection. Holding down the Option/Alt key subtracts from the current selection. Holding down the Shift+Option/Alt keys intersects the current selection.

The Options bar also lets you specify a feather amount and includes an option to enable anti-aliasing. Dragging with a selection tool in the canvas marks a selection with a blinking dashed line often called *marching ants*.

 **If a selection isn't visible, choose View ➪ Show ➪ Selection Edges.**

You can display only one selection on the canvas at a time, but you may save and load selections by choosing Select ➪ Save Selection and Select ➪ Load Selection.

Using the Marquee selection tools

The Marquee selection tools (M) included in Photoshop include the Rectangle Marquee tool, the Ellipse Marquee tool, the Single Row Marquee tool, and the Single Column Marquee tool. The difference among these tools is the shape of the selection they make.

In the Options bar, which appears directly under the menu at the top of the interface, shown in Figure 9.35, you can choose a selection Style as Normal, Fixed Aspect Ratio, and Fixed Size. If the Normal option is chosen, then a selection is made by clicking and dragging to specify the selection size. The Fixed Aspect Ratio option lets you specify Width and Height values. Dragging with this option produces a selection that maintains the specified aspect ratio. The Fixed Size option also lets you specify Width and Height values. Clicking and dragging with this option drags a selection of the specified dimensions in the image.

FIGURE 9.35

Selection tool options are displayed in the Options bar.

Holding down the Shift key while dragging with the Rectangle or Ellipse tools constrains the selection to a perfect square or circle. You also can hold down the Option/Alt key to drag from the center of the shape. Holding down the spacebar lets you move the current selection as you make it. When you release the spacebar, you can continue dragging to create the selection. The Single Row and Single Column Marquee tools let you click to select a single row or column of pixels.

At the right end of the Options bar is the Refine Edge button. Clicking this button opens the Refine Edge dialog box, shown in Figure 9.36. This dialog box lets you make adjustments to the selection using a set of simple sliders. The sliders let you change the Radius and Contrast of the selection edge and also the smoothness and feather amount. The Contract/Expand slider changes the size of the selection.

FIGURE 9.36

The Refine Edge dialog box lets you quickly change the selection edge attributes.

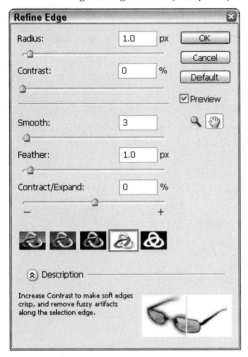

Using the Lasso selection tools

Photoshop actually includes three different Lasso tools (L):

- **Lasso tool:** You create a selection by drawing in the canvas. When you release the mouse, a straight line is drawn back to the point where you first clicked. If you hold down the Option/Alt key, you can click and drag to create straight lines. With the Option/Alt key held down, you also can press the Delete key to delete the last created straight line point or gradually delete the drawn path.

- **Polygonal Lasso tool:** This is the opposite of the Lasso tool. You create a selection by clicking at the endpoints of each successive straight line, but if you hold down the Option/Alt key, you can draw freehand. The Delete key also works to delete line segments. To close a selection created with the Polygonal Lasso tool, move the cursor near the starting point until a small circle appears as part of the cursor, and click or hold down the ⌘/Ctrl key and click, or simply double-click and a straight line is created from the cursor's position to the starting point.

- **Magnetic Lasso tool:** This automatically creates selection anchor points based on the contrast of the image below. To use this tool, set the Width, Edge Contrast, and Frequency values in the Options bar. The Width value specifies how far around the cursor the Magnetic Lasso tool looks for contrasting pixels. The Edge Contrast value sets the amount of contrast required for an edge to be selected. The Frequency value determines the number of anchor points used to define the selection area.

Click an image border that you want to trace with the Magnetic Lasso tool and drag along the image border. The tool places anchor points regularly along the path and connects them. If you click, you can manually place an anchor point as needed. The Delete key may be used to backtrack if needed, and holding down the Option/Alt key changes the Magnetic Lasso tool to the normal Lasso tool for dragging or the Polygonal Lasso tool for clicking. Double-click or drag back to the first point again to close the selection.

Using the Quick Selection and Magic Wand tools

The Quick Selection tool (W) lets you select like-colored sections using a brush. The Options bar offers controls for changing the brush's size and edge refinement. You also can add or subtract from the current selection. As you paint over the image, the Quick Selection tool automatically selects all the like-colored pixels within the section where you paint.

The Magic Wand tool is located as a flyout under the Quick Selection tool. It selects all areas with the same color or a color that is within the specified Tolerance value. The Tolerance value (found on the Options bar) can range between 0 and 255. Tolerance values of 0 require that the color values be exactly the same, and a Tolerance value of 255 is so forgiving that almost all colors are selected.

On the Options bar, the Contiguous option selects only those areas immediately connected to the selected color, but if the Contiguous option is deselected, all colors within the canvas that are within the Tolerance value are selected. The Use All Layers option makes selections from all layers but only from the selected layer if disabled.

STEPS: Building a Selection

1. **Open a Photoshop document.** With Photoshop open, choose File ➪ New to create a new document. Fill the entire image with a pattern by choosing Edit ➪ Fill. In the Fill dialog box that appears, select the Pattern option and choose one of the default patterns; then click OK.

2. **Choose an initial selection.** Click the Rectangle Marquee tool, and drag in the canvas to select a rectangular area.

3. **Subtract an interior section.** With the Rectangle Marquee tool still selected, click the Subtract from Selection button in the Options bar. Then drag over an interior section of the current selection. The interior section is removed from the selection.

4. **Use the Ellipse Marquee tool.** Click and hold the Rectangle Marquee tool to select the Ellipse Marquee tool from the flyout menu. Click the Add to Selection button in the

Options bar. Then select the Fixed Size Style with Width and Height values of 64 pixels. Click and drag the circular selection so it's positioned on top of each of the corners of the current selection.

5. **Save the selection.** With the selection completed, choose Select ⇨ Save Selection. In the Save Selection dialog box, give the selection a new name and click OK.

6. **Fill the selection.** Choose Edit ⇨ Fill; in the Fill dialog box, select to fill with the white color and click OK. The selection is now clearly visible, as shown in Figure 9.37.

FIGURE 9.37

Filling the selection with a color makes it easy to see.

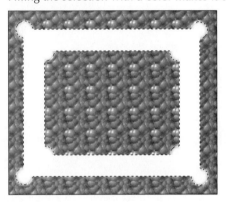

Using the Selection menu

In addition to the Selection tools, Photoshop also includes a Select menu that holds many commands that are helpful for selecting pixels. Choose Select ⇨ All (⌘/Ctrl+A) to select all canvas pixels; choose Select ⇨ Deselect (⌘/Ctrl+D) to eliminate any selections. Choose Select ⇨ Reselect (Shift+Ctrl+D in Windows; Shift+⌘+D on the Mac) to make the recent selection active again; choose Select ⇨ Inverse (Shift+Ctrl+I in Windows; Shift+⌘+I on the Mac) to deselect the current selection and select all pixels that weren't selected.

Selecting a color range

Choosing Select ⇨ Color Range opens a dialog box, shown in Figure 9.38, where you can select a range of colors in the image. With the dialog box open, the cursor changes to an eyedropper that you can use to click the preview pane in the Color Range dialog box or within the actual canvas. The Preview pane is set to show the selection or the image, or you can use the ⌘/Ctrl key to switch between these two.

NOTE If a selection exists in the canvas, opening Photoshop's Color Range dialog box displays the selected area only. If no selection exists, the entire image displays in the Color Range dialog box.

FIGURE 9.38

The Color Range dialog box

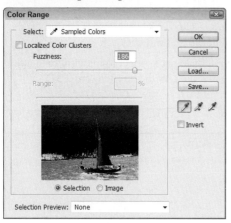

The Localized Color Clusters option causes areas similar in color to be taken into account. This provides a good way to separate foreground pixels from background colors like the sky. Increasing the Fuzziness value increases the color range included in the selection, much like the Tolerance value for the Magic Wand.

To add more colors to the selection, click the Add to Sample eyedropper; to remove colors, click the Subtract from Sample eyedropper. You also can select the Add to Sample eyedropper by holding down the Shift key and the Subtract from Sample eyedropper by holding down the Option/Alt key. The Invert option switches the colors used in the Preview pane.

The Select drop-down list at the top of the dialog box lets you select from several default colors, including reds, yellows, greens, cyans, blues, magentas, highlights, midtones, shadows, and out of gamut. The Out of Gamut selection in particular is useful as a color check prior to printing.

The Selection Preview options at the bottom of the dialog box project the selection back into the canvas using None, Grayscale, Black Matte, White Matte, or Quick Mask. Color Range selections may be saved using the AXT file extension and reloaded again.

Modifying a selection

The Select ⇨ Modify menu includes several commands that change the current selection. Each of these menu commands opens a simple dialog box, shown in Figure 9.39, where you can specify a pixel value. The Border menu command turns the selection into a border as wide as the specified Width value. The Smooth command eliminates any stray or jagged pixels by smoothing the entire selection. The Expand command increases the selection by the designated number of pixels. The Contract command reduces the selection by the designated number of pixels.

You can select a pixel value to expand the current selection.

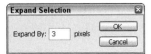

Choosing Select ➪ Grow increases the selection step-by-step by gradually selecting similar adjoining colors. Choosing Select ➪ Similar increases a selection by selecting all colors similar to the selected color through the entire image.

Transforming selections

Choosing Select ➪ Transform Selection adds a bounding box to the current selection that lets you move, rotate, scale, shear, and change the perspective of the selection using the same bounding box controls used on objects. After all the transformations are made using the bounding box, confirm the transformation by clicking on the Commit Transform button in the Options bar. If you select another tool before committing the transform, a confirmation dialog box appears letting you Apply, Cancel, or Not Apply all the transformations. The Cancel option removes the confirmation dialog box letting you transform the selection some more, but the Not Apply option returns the selection to its last transformation state.

Converting drawn paths into selections

Paths that are saved in the Paths palette may be turned into a selection using the Make Selection palette menu command. This opens the Make Selection dialog box where you can select a Feather Radius value and whether the selection is anti-aliased. You also can choose that the selection is a New Selection, added to the existing selection, subtracted from the existing selection, or intersected with the existing selection.

 **You also can Ctrl/⌘-click on the path to load it as a selection.**

Organizing Objects

Illustrator and InDesign both include several ways to organize objects. Chief among these is the Layers palette, which lets you place objects on separate layers. Other organization features are contained within the Object menu; these features help in grouping and preventing unwanted edits by locking and hiding objects.

CROSS-REF **The Object menu includes many other commands, such as commands to transform and arrange objects. These commands are covered in Chapter 12.**

Adding objects to layers

All of the print-oriented CS4 applications have layers accessed through a Layers palette. You create new layers by selecting the New Layer palette menu command or by clicking the New Layer icon button at the bottom of the palette. All new objects are added to the selected layer, and objects may be moved between layers.

NOTE   **Although Acrobat doesn't have a Layers palette, layers can exist in a PDF file created using one of the other CS4 applications and be viewed in Acrobat using the Layers interface.**

The first two columns of the Layers palette in Illustrator and InDesign let you hide or lock layers by clicking in the column boxes. Locked and hidden layers cannot be selected or edited.

CROSS-REF   **Turn to Chapter 25 for much more information on layers.**

Grouping objects

You may group together several selected objects by choosing Object ➪ Group (⌘/Ctrl+G). Groups also may be nested. When a single object that is part of a group is selected with the Selection tool, the entire group is selected, but individual objects that are part of a group may be selected using the Group Selection tool in Illustrator. Choose Object ➪ Ungroup (Shift+Ctrl+G in Windows; Shift+⌘+G on the Mac) to ungroup a grouped set of objects.

 **It is often easier to select individual members of a group with the Direct Selection tool than with the Group Selection tool.**

Hiding and locking objects

To prevent set objects from accidentally being selected or edited, you can lock and hide objects in Illustrator by choosing Object ➪ Lock and by choosing Objects ➪ Hide. Both of these menus let you lock (or hide) the current selection (⌘/Ctrl+2), all artwork above, or other layers. You cannot select objects you lock or hide. InDesign includes the menu commands Object ➪ Lock Position (⌘/Ctrl+L) and Object ➪ Unlock Position (Alt/Option+Ctrl/⌘+L).

Objects or layers that are locked have a small lock icon displayed in the second column of the Layers palette, as shown in Figure 9.40, and objects or layers that are hidden have no eye icon in the first column of the Layers palette. The Layers palette provides another way to quickly hide and lock objects by clicking the palette's columns.

NOTE   **You also can lock or hide layers in Photoshop using the Layers palette. Select the layer, and click the Lock Position or Lock All icons at the top of the Layers palette. When locked, a small lock icon appears to the right of the Layer name. You hide layers in Photoshop clicking the eye icon in the first column of the Layers palette.**

FIGURE 9.40

The Layers palette allows you to lock or hide layer objects.

Hidden layer

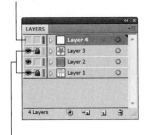

Locked layers

Filling and Stroking Objects

The two properties probably most common for objects are the object's fill and stroke. An object's *fill* is the color, gradient, or pattern that fills the interior portion of an object, and an object's *stroke* is the line or outline that makes up the object. Fills and strokes may be any color, or they may be set to no color. Fills also may be added with a gradient or a pattern.

 **Applying fill and stroke colors in Flash works differently than the other CS4 apps.**

 **InDesign can apply a gradient to a stroke, but the other applications cannot.**

Applying fill and stroke colors to objects in Illustrator and InDesign

Fill and stroke colors are applied to objects using the colors for each that are identified in the Fill and Stroke boxes located at the bottom of the Toolbox, as shown in Figure 9.41. The Fill box looks like a filled colored square; the Stroke box looks like a thick outlined square. The Fill box is active by default, but you can click the Stroke box to select it.

 **The X key toggles between the Fill and Stroke color swatches in the Toolbox.**

FIGURE 9.41

The Fill and Stroke boxes appear at the bottom of the Toolbox.

With either the Fill or Stroke box in the Toolbox active, you can change the box's color by selecting a new color from the Color or Swatches palette, or you can double-click the box to access a Color Picker dialog box.

The double-headed arrow that appears above and to the right of the Fill and Stroke boxes swaps the colors, so the Fill color becomes the Stroke color and vice versa. The small icon to the lower left of the Fill and Stroke boxes set the Fill and Stroke colors to their defaults, which are a white fill and a black stroke in Illustrator and Photoshop and no fill and a black stroke for InDesign.

 The keyboard shortcut to swap the Fill and Stroke colors is Shift+X; the keyboard shortcut for setting the fill and stroke colors to their defaults is D.

Below the Fill and Stroke boxes in the Toolbox are three simple icons, shown in Figure 9.42. These icons are used to set the active Fill or Stroke box to hold a Color (<), a Gradient (>), or None (/). When the None icon is clicked for either box, a red diagonal line appears in the box.

 Gradients may be applied only to a Fill, not to a Stroke, in Illustrator. If the Gradient button in Illustrator is clicked for a stroke, a gradient is added to the Fill box. InDesign can add gradients to strokes.

FIGURE 9.42

The icons under the Fill and Stroke boxes can fill the selected object with a color, a gradient, or neither.

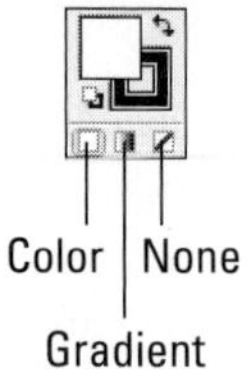

Color | None

Gradient

If the fill and stroke colors are changed without any objects selected, the default colors are applied to all new objects created from that point on.

The Color and the Swatches palette also includes Fill and Stroke boxes that match those in the Toolbox, as shown in Figure 9.43.

FIGURE 9.43

The Color palette also includes Fill and Stroke boxes.

One other place that may be used to change fill and stroke colors is the Appearance palette. Using the Appearance palette, shown in Figure 9.44, you can change the stacking order for fills and strokes. Attributes listed in the Appearance palette are applied to an object from front to back in the order that they appear in the Appearance palette.

FIGURE 9.44

The Appearance palette shows all an object's attributes.

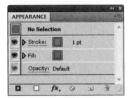

By dragging the fill above the stroke, the fill appears above the stroke, making any portion of the stroke that overlaps the fill hidden behind the fill.

Applying other stroke attributes

Although the only attribute that may be applied to a fill is a color, gradient, or pattern, strokes include several additional attributes. These attributes are applied using the Stroke palette, shown in Figure 9.45.

FIGURE 9.45

The Stroke palette includes additional stroke attributes.

The stroke weight defines how thick the stroke is. By default, half of the weight thickness appears on either side of the object path marked in the object's layer color when the object is selected. Stroke weights ranging from 0.25 points to 100 points may be selected from the pop-up menu to the right of the Weight field, or you may enter a custom weight value in the Weight field.

NOTE   **Entering a Weight value of 0 sets the stroke to None.**

Selecting the Show Options palette menu command causes several additional stroke attributes to appear at the bottom of the Stroke palette. These options are also visible when you access the stroke controls in the Options bar.

The row of icons that appears to the right of the Weight field lets you select from three different cap styles that are applied to the end of the stroke. The three options are Butt Cap, Round Cap, and Projecting Cap. Butt Cap squares the ends of a stroke, Round Cap applies half a circle to the stroke ends, and Projecting Cap applies a square end that is extended half a line width beyond the end of the stroke.

NOTE   **Selecting a cap style for a closed object with no dash such as a rectangle has no effect.**

Beneath the three cap style buttons are three Join options. These buttons define how the corners of an object appear and has an effect on dashed strokes, making them visible on closed objects. The Join options are Miter Join, Round Join, and Bevel Join. Miter Join draws the corners as sharp squares, Round Join rounds the corners, and Bevel Join replaces the corners with diagonal lines. The Miter Limit sets a limit for the corner point as a number times the weight when Miter Joins are automatically switched to Bevel Joins.

The Align Stroke options let you move a stroke so its thickness is centered on the objects boundary, so the stroke's thickness is inside the object, or so it is outside the object. Setting the Align Stroke option to Outside causes the stroke to be completely free of the fill color, but setting the alignment to Inside causes the stroke to conceal a portion of the fill color. Figure 9.46 shows each of these alignment options.

FIGURE 9.46

The Stroke palette includes options for specifying how the stroke is aligned.

Centered Stroke Alignment

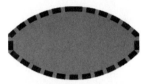

Inside Stroke Alignment

Outside Stroke Alignment

If the Dashed Line option is selected, you can enter the Dash and Gap values for three separate dashes, enabling you to create many unique dashed lines. Not all the Dash and Gap values need to be filled in. Whatever values are entered are repeated around the entire object.

Figure 9.47 shows several stroke samples of various weights, cap types, and dashed lines.

FIGURE 9.47

Altering the settings in the Stroke palette changes the attributes for the stroked path.

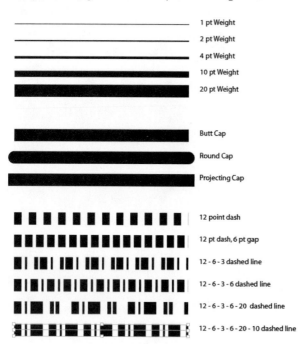

1 pt Weight

2 pt Weight

4 pt Weight

10 pt Weight

20 pt Weight

Butt Cap

Round Cap

Projecting Cap

12 point dash

12 pt dash, 6 pt gap

12 - 6 - 3 dashed line

12 - 6 - 3 - 6 dashed line

12 - 6 - 3 - 6 - 20 dashed line

12 - 6 - 3 - 6 - 20 - 10 dashed line

STEPS: Applying Fills and Strokes

1. **Create a new Illustrator document.** With Illustrator open, choose File ➪ New to create a new document. Choose Window ➪ Symbol Libraries ➪ Maps to open a palette of map symbols. Select and drag one of the symbols to the art board. The symbol is fairly small. Selecting a corner handle and dragging it away from the symbol while holding down the Shift key uniformly scales the symbol.

2. **Expand and ungroup the symbol.** With the symbol selected, choose Object ➪ Expand. In the Expand dialog box, select to expand both the Object and the Fill, and click OK. Next choose Object ➪ Ungroup three times to ungroup all the objects. The object now consists of three objects—a rounded black square, an airplane path, and the bounding path—as shown in Figure 9.48.

3. **Select and apply a fill.** Click the airplane path with the Selection tool. Notice that the Fill box is set to white and the Stroke box is set to None. With the Fill box selected, click a blue color in the Swatches palette.

You can select an object after expanding and ungrouping it.

4. **Select and apply a stroke.** Click the Stroke box at the bottom of the Toolbox to select it. Then choose a red color in the Swatches palette. In the Stroke palette, increase the Weight value to 10 pt and enable the Dashed Line option. Increase the stroke weight in the first dashed line field and 2 pt in the second field. The stroke is updated as you change the Stroke settings in the Stroke palette. The resulting fill and stroke are shown in Figure 9.49.

After applying a stroke and fill to the interior shape, the design is altered dramatically with a few simple changes.

5. **Copy the style to the Graphic Styles palette.** Choose Window ⇨ Appearance to open the Appearance palette. Drag the Appearance icon to the left of the Path title in the Appearance palette to the Graphic Styles palette, or just drag the object itself to the Graphic Styles palette. This copies the created style to the Graphic Styles palette where it's applied to other objects.

6. **Apply the copied style to the background object.** Select the background rounded square object, and drag the copied style from the Graphic Styles palette to the background object. This applies the same fill and stroke attributes to the square object, as shown in Figure 9.50.

FIGURE 9.50

Styles copied to the Graphic Styles palette may be easily applied to other objects.

Using Illustrator's Live Paint

If you create and fill a circle in Illustrator and overlap that circle with another circle object that also is filled and stroked, changing the color of the overlapped section becomes difficult. This is because the colors are inherited from each separate object. Illustrator's Live Paint feature overcomes these difficulties by splitting the overlapping objects into a series of edges and faces. You can fill each face independent of the other faces much like a simple coloring book.

Converting objects to Live Paint

You can convert selected objects to Live Paint objects by choosing the Object ⇨ Live Paint ⇨ Make menu command. Once converted, each independent path changes to an edge and each separate area converts to a face. This allows you to color each face independent of the others. Figure 9.51 shows two simple circle objects that are overlapped before and after they are converted to Live Paint objects.

CAUTION Live Paint objects have several limitations that you need to keep in mind. In particular, Live Paint objects can't use transparency, effects, symbols, blends, clipping masks, or pathfinder.

FIGURE 9.51

You can convert objects to Live Paint objects using the Object ⇨ Live Paint ⇨ Make menu command.

Before Live Paint

After Live Paint

You cannot convert some object types, such as type and brushes, to Live Paint objects directly, but if you first convert them to paths using the Type ⇨ Create Outlines or the Object ⇨ Expand menu commands, then you can perform the conversion to Live Paint with the Object ⇨ Live Paint ⇨ Make menu command.

CROSS-REF You also can convert bitmap images to Live Paint objects by first using the Live Trace feature. Simply select the bitmap image, and choose the Object ⇨ Live Trace ⇨ Convert to Live Paint menu command. Or, you can do this in one step, choose a raster image, use the Object ⇨ Live Trace ⇨ Make and the Convert to Live Trace command. An example of Live Trace is shown in Chapter 9.

Using the Live Paint tools

Once converted, you can fill faces using the Live Paint Bucket tool (shortcut, K) and select them with the Live Paint Selection tool (Shift+L). Moving the mouse over a face with either tool highlights the face boundaries in red. Double-clicking either tool opens a dialog box of options, as shown in Figure 9.52. With these options, you can select to apply only Paint Fills, only Paint Strokes, or both. You also can change the highlight color and width. And you can preview the swatch color as part of the cursor. You also can use the Live Paint Bucket and Live Paint Selection tools to convert the selected objects to Live Paint objects.

FIGURE 9.52

The Live Paint Bucket Options dialog box lets you choose to apply fills or strokes.

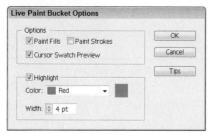

If you double-click a Live Paint face with the Live Paint Bucket tool, all contiguous faces are filled across an unstroked edge. A triple-click changes all faces with the same color to the current fill. Holding down the Shift key switches the current settings in the Live Paint Bucket Options dialog box. For example, if you select Paint Fills, the Shift key causes the Paint Strokes option to be selected.

Adding paths to a Live Paint object

If you want to add more paths to the existing objects to divide it into even more faces, simply double-click the face with the Selection tool where you want to add another path to isolate the face. Then draw the path using one of the drawing tools, and double-click the art board again with the Selection tool (not the Live Paint Selection tool, just the normal Selection tool). The new path is added to the Live Paint objects, and new faces are created. The new face won't be visible until you use the Live Paint Bucket to change the face attribute.

You also can add new paths to an existing Live Paint group using the Object ⇨ Live Paint ⇨ Make menu command or by dragging the path to the Live Paint group in the Layers palette. Figure 9.53 shows a simple line segment added to the existing overlapping circles. The new face is filled a different color.

FIGURE 9.53

You can add new paths to an existing Live Paint object.

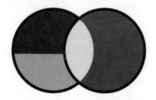

Editing Live Paint paths

Perhaps the coolest feature of a Live Paint object is that when you edit it, all the filled faces readjust to maintain their filled colors. Figure 9.54 shows the same two overlapping circles where the points have been selected and moved. Live Paint is smart enough to adjust the objects so that the faces remained filled.

FIGURE 9.54

Editing a Live Paint object readjusts the filled faces so they stay consistent.

Releasing and expanding a Live Paint group

If you need to apply a feature that Live Paint can't handle, such as transparency, you can dissolve the Live Paint group using the Object ➪ Live Paint ➪ Release menu command. This command converts the Live Paint group back into regular paths without any fills and with a 0.5 black stroke.

Expanding a Live Paint group maintains the current fills and strokes but separates each edge and face into a separate object. Figure 9.55 shows an expanded Live Paint group, which has had each edge and face moved using the Group Selection tool.

FIGURE 9.55

You can expand Live Paint groups into separate objects.

Managing fill gaps

If two paths don't exactly meet in the Live Paint group, a fill could spill over into the next face when you click with the Live Paint Bucket tool. To prevent this, you can manually edit all paths to eliminate existing gaps. To see any gaps in the current Live Paint group, choose View ➪ Show Live Paint Gaps. Gap Detection is enabled through the Gap Options dialog box, shown in Figure 9.56.

You can access the Gap Options dialog box using the Objects➪Live Paint➪Gap Options menu command. You can now set paint to stop at Small (3 pt), Medium (6 pt), or Large (12 pt) gaps or select the Custom option, and set your own gap size. You also can set the Gap Preview color and choose to automatically close all gaps in the Live Paint group with the Close Gaps with Paths button.

You can use the Gap Options dialog box to close any gaps in the current Live Paint group.

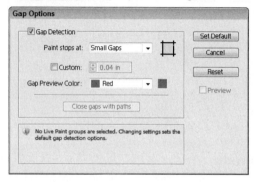

STEPS: Working with Live Paint

1. **Open an Illustrator document.** With Illustrator open, choose File➪Open to open a document that includes several overlapping objects such as the kite objects.

2. **Create a Live Paint group.** Select all the overlapping objects, and choose the Object➪Live Paint➪Make menu command. A new Live Paint Group layer is added to the Layers palette, and the entire group is selected and highlighted.

3. **Fill the Live Paint faces.** Select the Live Paint Bucket tool from the Toolbox, and change the fill color to blue. Then click the square backgrounds. Change the fill color to yellow, and click the elliptical portions of the kite. You can speed the coloring of each portion by double-clicking the area that needs to be filled. This automatically fills each face where a stroke doesn't exist. The resulting kite is shown in Figure 9.57.

FIGURE 9.57

You can easily fill this Live Paint group using the Live Paint Bucket tool.

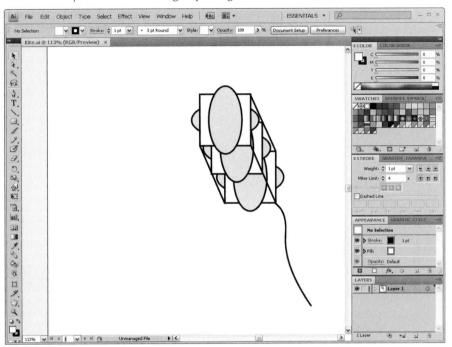

4. **Add a path to the Live Paint group.** Click and hold the Rectangle tool flyout until the Star tool is selected. Then drag in the art board to create a simple 5-pointed star object. Drag the star object with the Selection tool to the center of the top kite circle. Drag over the entire kite object, and choose the Object ➪ Live Paint ➪ Make menu command. Then change the fill color to red, and double click the star object to color it red, as shown in Figure 9.58.

FIGURE 9.58

New paths can be added to an existing Live Paint group.

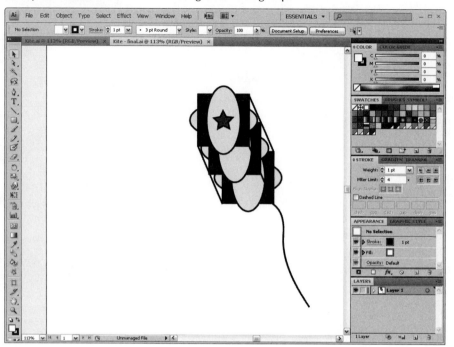

Filling and stroking a pixel selection

Although fills and strokes are mainly applied to objects, they also may be applied to a pixel selection in Photoshop using the Edit ⇨ Fill (Shift+F5) and Edit ⇨ Stroke menu commands. Both of these commands open a dialog box, shown in Figure 9.59, where you can select the color to use. The color options include Foreground Color, Background Color, Color (which opens a Color Picker), Pattern, History, Black, 50% Gray, and White. You also can select a blending mode, an opacity, and whether to preserve transparency.

 **If the Edit ⇨ Fill menu command is used with no selection, the entire canvas is filled with the selected color.**

The Stroke dialog box, shown in Figure 9.60, also includes options to specify the width and color of the stroke and whether to place the stroke inside, in the center, or outside of the selection.

FIGURE 9.59

The Fill dialog box lets you select the color or pattern.

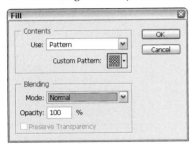

FIGURE 9.60

The Stroke dialog box lets you specify a width, a color, and whether the stroke appears inside, centered, or outside the selection.

Filling and stroking a Photoshop path

Paths in the Paths palette in Photoshop also may be filled and stroked using the Fill Path and Stroke Path palette menu commands. The Fill Path dialog box includes the same settings used to fill a selection along with a Feather Radius value and an Anti-aliased option.

The Stroke Path dialog box, on the other hand, includes a single option to select the Tool that is used to stroke the path, as shown in Figure 9.61. The options include all the various drawing and editing tools including Pencil, Brush, Eraser, Clone Stamp, Smudge, and so on.

FIGURE 9.61

The Stroke Path dialog box lets you select a tool to use to stroke the path.

Assigning Color

Color plays an important part in any design, and the color features found in the Creative Suite 4 applications are amazingly diverse. Whether your documents are designed for print, CD-ROM, or a Web site, colors are easily selected and manipulated. You add colors to objects using fills and strokes, and you paint images using an assortment of tools.

Learning the various color modes

Color is a major part of any design, and in the CS4 applications, you can access several different color models, including RGB, Web Safe RGB, CMYK, HSB, and Grayscale. Which color model you use depends on where you intend the artwork to end up. For example, the RGB color mode works well if you intend your design to be viewed on a computer monitor via a CD-ROM. However, if the design is going to be placed on a Web site, you'll want to consider using the Web Safe RGB color mode. For designs that are to be printed, the CMYK color mode is appropriate. The good news is that you can switch among these different color modes at any time using the Color palette menu.

 In Illustrator and InDesign, you can hold down the Shift key while clicking the color bar in the Color palette toggles through the different color modes.

 InDesign's color selector also can specify colors using the Lab color model.

RGB color mode

This color mode is used to display colors on a computer monitor. Inside a CRT computer monitor (or television) are thousands of tiny red, green, and blue electron streams that project beams of red, green, or blue light, one for each pixel. By changing the intensity of each gun, you can control the resulting color of each pixel. LCD screens use a different technique to produce the same colors by controlling the alignment of crystals. The RGB color mode produces colors by mixing together red, green, and blue. The amount of each color determines the final color. Figure 9.62 shows the Color palette with the RGB color mode selected.

NOTE The RGB color system is *additive,* meaning that the higher color values drive the color toward white. This is different from the *subtractive* color system used by the CMYK color mode, in which the higher color values drive the color toward black like mixing inks that act as filters to remove frequencies of light. The more of each color you have, the closer you get to black because you are removing light.

FIGURE 9.62

The Color palette for the RGB color mode includes separate sliders for Red, Green, and Blue values.

Within Photoshop, Illustrator, InDesign, and Flash, you can create colors by specifying the amount of each color to use. The values range from 0, which includes none of that color, to 255, which includes a full amount. A separate value is listed for red, green, and blue. By altering these color values, 16.7 million different colors are possible for an 8-bit image and high bit depths offer even more colors.

Common RGB Colors

One of the easiest ways to learn how to use the RGB color values is to examine the relationships between the various RGB values and their resulting colors. Consider the following table of colors and RGB values.

Color	R value	G value	B value
Bright red	255	0	0
Medium red	192	0	0
Dark red	128	0	0
Bright green	0	255	0
Bright blue	0	0	255
White	255	255	255
Black	0	0	0
Light gray	192	192	192
Medium gray	128	128	128
Dark gray	64	64	64
Yellow	255	255	0
Cyan	0	255	255
Magenta	255	0	255

For example, a color that includes a value of 255 for red, 0 for green, and 0 for blue would be pure red. Amounts of 255 of each color produces white, and amounts of 0 of each color produces black. Equal amounts of each of the three colors produces gray. Mixing red and green produces yellow, mixing green and blue produces cyan, and mixing red and blue produces magenta.

Web Safe color mode

The Web Safe color mode is a subset of the RGB color mode that includes a limited palette of colors displayed more consistently without dithering on a browser regardless of the system used to view the design. Figure 9.63 shows the Color palette with the Web Safe color mode selected. Notice how the color values are displayed as hexadecimal numbers, which are numbers based on 16 digits instead of 10 digits in our normal counting system. The hexadecimal system is more efficient for computers because more values can be expressed using only 2 digits instead of 3.

FIGURE 9.63

The Color palette for the Web Safe color mode

Because of the difference between system color sets on Mac and Windows systems, some Web-page colors viewed on one system look dramatically different from the same Web page viewed on a different system. To fix this problem, a 216-color palette that includes colors that are common between Windows and Mac systems has been defined as a Web Safe palette. Using these colors ensures that the colors are consistent between different systems.

NOTE   Although systems that display only 256 colors are rare with the modern monitors and video cards, Web-safe colors are important for ensuring that specific colors such as logos are consistent across all systems.

HTML code refers to Web colors using the hexadecimal (base-16) numbering system. The results are two-digit numbers instead of three, but the value is still the same. The hexadecimal equivalents to the RGB numbers are displayed in the Color Picker dialog box.

HSB color mode

The HSB color mode defines colors using the common physical properties of hue, saturation, and brightness. This color mode is useful if you need to change the brightness or a color without changing its hue. Hue is measured as a position on a circular color wheel, which ranges from 0 to 360 degrees. Red is found at 0 (and 360) degrees, yellow at 60 degrees, green at 120 degrees, cyan at 180 degrees, blue at 240 degrees, and magenta at 300 degrees. Figure 9.64 shows the Color palette with the HSB color mode selected.

Understanding Hexadecimal Numbers

Understanding the hexadecimal numbering system isn't difficult. Our current numbering system is *base 10,* meaning that the numbers range from 0 to 9 before another digit is added. But the hexadecimal numbering system is *base 16,* meaning that the numbers range from 0 to 15 before adding another digit.

The characters used to represent the numbers 10 through 15 in the hexadecimal system are the letters A through F. So, counting in hexadecimal would be 00, 01, 02, 03, 04, 05, 06, 07, 08, 09, 0A, 0B, 0C, 0D, 0E, 0F, followed by 10.

For Web pages, the three hexadecimal values for red, green, and blue are combined into a single number that begins with a number sign such as #FF9910. If you know a few hexadecimal values, you'll be able to approximate color values listed in HTML code. Full color is denoted as FF, no color is 00, half color is 80, so #20FF31 is a green tint and #0C8091 is a darker-cyan color.

The advantage that hexadecimal numbers have for Web pages is that an RGB color is represented by seven digits. If the base-10 numbering system was used, then 10 digits would be needed. Although saving three digits for each color doesn't seem like much, if you multiply that times the total number of pixels included in an image, the result makes a huge difference in the file size.

Web-safe colors are specified in hexadecimal by matching triplet pairs of 0, 3, 6, 9, A, C, and F. So, 0033FF is safe and 01d3FF is not. In code, three-letter shorthand is legal: 03F is understood to be 0033FF.

FIGURE 9.64

The HSB color mode displays its values as percentages.

Colors found in between are a mixture of the primary colors. For example, orange is represented by 48 degrees between red and yellow. Colors on the opposite side of the color wheel are inverted pairs—red and cyan, yellow and blue, and green and magenta.

The Saturation value determines the purity of the color. This value can range from 0 to 100 percent. Reducing a color Saturation value is analogous to mixing the color with white. Colors with a 0 percent Saturation value are displayed as pure white, regardless of the Hue value.

Brightness is the opposite of saturation. It ranges from 0 to 100 percent and measures the amount of black that is mixed with the color. Reducing the brightness makes the color darker. HSB colors with a Brightness value of 0 are pure black.

CMYK color mode

The CMYK color mode is based on cyan, magenta, and yellow inks that are mixed to create colors. The *K* stands for black. This color mode is used for designs that you print. Figure 9.65 shows the Color palette with the CMYK color mode selected.

> **NOTE** The letter *B* typically represents the color blue, so *K* represents black. Although you can create black by mixing full equal portions of cyan, magenta, and yellow inks, the actual result from mixing these inks is a muddy brown, so true black is printed using black ink.

FIGURE 9.65

When the CMYK color mode is selected, the out-of-gamut warning icon appears for all colors that are out of the CMYK gamut.

You specify CMYK colors by providing a percentage between 0 and 100 percent for each color. Digital printers typically print CMYK documents using a four-color process where the sheets are run once for each color.

Grayscale color mode

The Grayscale color mode converts all colors to grayscale values. This color mode is used for black and white images. Grayscale values are represented by a single brightness value that ranges from 0 to 100 percent with 0 percent being white and 100 percent being black. When colors are converted to grayscale, the color's luminosity value determines its grayscale value. Figure 9.66 shows the Color palette with the Grayscale color mode selected.

FIGURE 9.66

The Grayscale color mode includes a single value for brightness only.

> **NOTE** Photoshop and InDesign actually includes an additional color mode called the Lab color mode. The *L* stands for lightness, the *a* is for the green-red color wheel axis, and the *b* is for the blue-yellow color wheel axis. This color mode makes it intuitive to work with the luminance of an image.

Understanding Spot versus Process Colors

For colors saved to the Swatches palette, you can select the Color Type as a spot color or as a process color. These types correspond to different types of ink that are used to print the colors. Spot colors are printed using premixed inks, and process colors are printed in separate passes using CMYK values.

Spot colors require a separate printing plate for each spot color that is used in a document, but process colors can represent a wide range of colors using only four printing plates. So a document that has only one or two spot colors may be less expensive than a document with all process colors. Another advantage of spot colors is that they're used to print colors that are out-of-gamut for the CMYK color method.

Spot colors in Illustrator and InDesign are identified in the Swatches palette by a small black dot that appears in the lower-right corner of the swatch. You can switch between spot and process colors in the Color palette by clicking the spot or process color icons.

Using the Color palette

Colors may be applied to an object's fill or stroke using the Fill and Stroke boxes in the Toolbox. Fill and Stroke boxes also are found in the Color palette (refer to Figure 9.67) for convenience, which lets you choose specific colors using color values or select a color by simply clicking the color bar.

NOTE   To see the Fill and Stroke boxes and the color values for the selected color mode in the Color palette, select the Show Options palette menu command.

When the mouse is moved over the top of the color bar, the cursor changes to an eyedropper. Clicking the color bar changes the color for either the Fill or Stroke box, whichever is active.

TIP   If you drag one of the color value sliders, except for Black, with the Shift key held down, all color values scale along with the selected color. This works for all color modes except for the HSV and Grayscale.

Beneath the Fill and Stroke boxes in the Color palette are two icons that appear as you drag about the color bar. The top icon is the Web Safe color warning. This icon looks like a simple cube and informs you that the current color is not a Web Safe color. The color swatch next to the icon displays the nearest Web Safe color, and clicking it changes the current color to the nearest Web Safe color.

Beneath the Web Safe color icon, another icon may appear that looks like a yellow triangle with an exclamation point inside it. This icon appears when the current color is out-of-gamut and is not available in the CMYK color mode. The color swatch next to it is the nearest color available in the CMYK color mode, which means it may be printed. A similar color swatch appears next to the Out of Gamut warning icon.

Understanding Gamut

Color models are based on theoretical values, but in real life all the colors that are defined mathematically aren't always possible. The actual range of colors possible for a certain color space or device is called its *gamut*. Any color that falls outside of its gamut is called *out-of-gamut* and may cause a problem for the device.

FIGURE 9.67

The Web Safe color warning icon and the Out of Gamut color warning icon both appear within the Color palette.

Out of Web Color Warning

Out of Gamut Warning

The Color palette menu in Illustrator also includes two commands (Inverse and Complementary) for quickly locating the inverse or complementary color to the current color. An *inverse color* is opposite the current color in the color wheel for the current color model; a *complementary color* offers a decent amount of contrast to the original color.

Using the Color Picker

If you double-click the Fill box in the Toolbox in Illustrator and Photoshop, a Color Picker, shown in Figure 9.68, appears. Using the Color Picker, you may select any color by manipulating the color values or by selecting a color from the color spectrum. Flash requires only a single click to access the Color Selector.

The color values for several color modes are displayed in the Color Picker. Toward the top of the Color Picker dialog box, the Web Safe and Out-of-Gamut icons appear just like the Color palette along with color swatches that you can click to reset the color. The Only Web Colors option in the lower-left corner limits the colors in the color spectrum so only Web Safe colors are displayed. Figure 9.69 shows the Color Picker with this option enabled.

FIGURE 9.68

The Color Picker lets you select color, and it shows the color values.

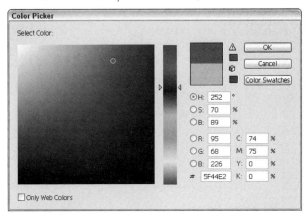

FIGURE 9.69

With the Only Web Colors option enabled, the total number of colors is severely limited.

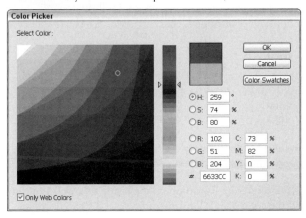

The Color Swatches button (called Color Libraries in Photoshop) opens a dialog box of distinct named colors that coordinate to the color swatches available in the Swatches palette. In Photoshop, you can choose from a specific color book at the top of the dialog box. These color books include several Pantone specific color libraries like the one shown in Figure 9.70.

FIGURE 9.70

The Color Swatches (Libraries) button in the Color Picker opens a specific list of color swatches or libraries.

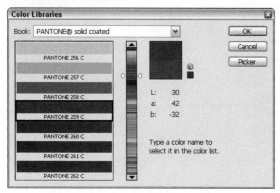

Using the Eyedropper tool

In addition to using the Color Picker, you can select colors from within the image using the Eyedropper tool. The Eyedropper tool works differently in Photoshop and Illustrator. The tool in Photoshop, Flash, Fireworks, and Dreamweaver is used to get only color. But in Illustrator and InDesign, the Eyedropper tool can retrieve appearance attributes, character style, and paragraph style.

Using Photoshop's Eyedropper tool

Dragging over an image with the Eyedropper tool changes the Foreground color. In the Options bar, you can use the color of the point directly under the tool or to sample a 3×3 or a 5×5 grid around the cursor. Holding down the Option/Alt key while dragging in the image with the Eyedropper tool changes the Background color.

 **TIP**   The Eyedropper tool may be selected temporarily while using one of the painting tools by holding down the Option/Alt key.

The Color Sampler tool is available as a flyout under the Eyedropper tool. Using this tool, you can click four different points in the image and the color values for those points are displayed in the Info palette. Only four color sample points may be placed in an image, but you can drag these points to new locations as needed or clear them all using the Clear button in the Options bar.

Using Illustrator's Eyedropper tool

You can use Illustrator's Eyedropper tool to gather property values from one object and apply them to another object. The specific properties that are gathered by the Eyedropper tool is set using the Eyedropper Options dialog box, shown in Figure 9.71, which is opened by double-clicking the Eyedropper tool.

FIGURE 9.71

The Eyedropper Options dialog box

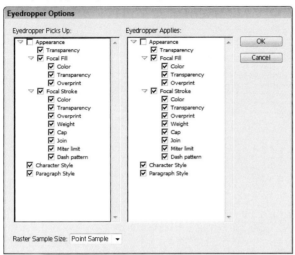

The attributes that are picked up by the Eyedropper tool are immediately applied to the selected object. These attributes may include Appearance attributes such as Transparency, Fill Color, Stroke Color, Stroke Weight, Cap and Join Type, and even Character and Paragraph Style. If you hold down the Shift key, then only the color attribute is gathered and holding down the Alt (Option) key toggles between the applied version of the eyedropper. You also can gather color from the computer's desktop using the Eyedropper tool by clicking and holding in the Illustrator document window and then dragging around the desktop.

The Eyedropper Options dialog box also lets you sample raster images using a point sample, a 3×3-pixel sample or a 5×5-pixel sample.

Using InDesign's Eyedropper tool

The Eyedropper tool in InDesign works the same as the one in Illustrator. It is used to both gather and apply selected attributes. Double-clicking the Eyedropper tool opens a dialog box of options, shown in Figure 9.72, that may be gathered using the Eyedropper tool.

Clicking an object gathers all the attributes for that object, and the cursor changes so the Eyedropper is pointing in the opposite direction and appears to be filled. Clicking another object applies the attributes. You can click multiple objects while the Eyedropper is filled. To fill the Eyedropper with new attributes, hold down the Option/Alt key while clicking another object.

FIGURE 9.72

The Eyedropper Options dialog box in InDesign

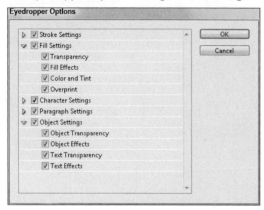

Using Live Color

Choosing the right colors for a design often can make or break a design. Illustrator's Live Color interface includes a set of controls that alter all the colors in a document. It also is used to give you color hints and lets you experiment with different color groups.

The Live Color dialog box, shown in Figure 9.73, shows all the colors used in the current selection and lets you edit or reduce these colors. The Live Color dialog box is opened using the Edit ⇨ Edit Colors ⇨ Recolor Artwork menu. All the selected colors can be saved as a color group that can be reused on other documents. All the available color groups on shown in the right side of the dialog box.

You also can select to change specific colors by clicking the color in the New column or by clicking one of the random color shift buttons. If you click the arrow between the Current Colors column and the New column, you can preserve an existing color from being changed. The Preset drop-down list lets you choose to use a specific color library or reduce the total number of colors to a specified number.

At the top of the Live Color dialog box, the Edit button switches the dialog box to a separate panel that shows all the selected colors in a color wheel, as shown in Figure 9.74. This panel lets you see how the colors in the current group are related. You can change any of the colors by dragging the color indicator around the color wheel. If you click the Link button, all colors move together when one is moved.

FIGURE 9.73

The Live Color dialog box lets you experiment with different color groups.

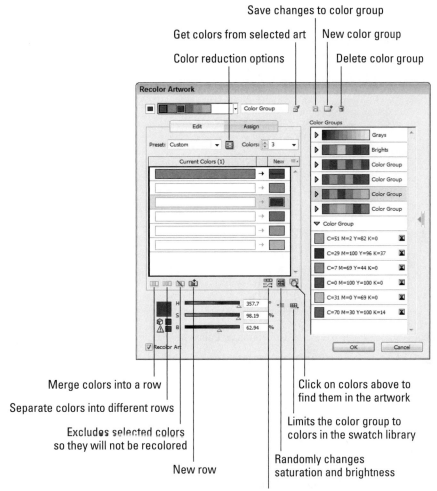

Save changes to color group

Get colors from selected art

New color group

Color reduction options

Delete color group

Merge colors into a row

Separate colors into different rows

Excludes selected colors
so they will not be recolored

New row

Randomly change color order

Click on colors above to
find them in the artwork

Limits the color group to
colors in the swatch library

Randomly changes
saturation and brightness

FIGURE 9.74

The Edit panel of the Live Color dialog box lets you switch among several color harmony settings.

Color Harmony List

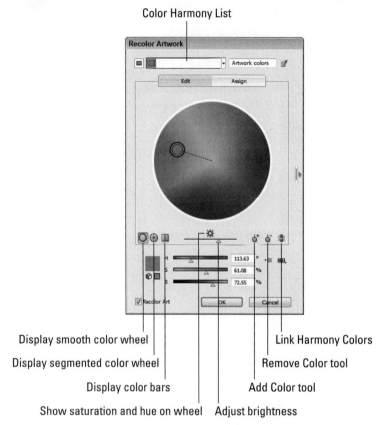

Display smooth color wheel

Display segmented color wheel

Display color bars

Show saturation and hue on wheel   Adjust brightness

Link Harmony Colors

Remove Color tool

Add Color tool

The Color Harmony list includes several design options based on the first color swatch. The available design schemes include the likes of Complementary, Split Complementary, Analogous, Monochromatic, Shades, Triad, Compound, Tetrad, High Contrast, and Pentagram. If you need some inspiration in your color design, these options are a great place to start.

Using the Color Guide palette

Another helpful tool in Illustrator is the Color Guide palette, shown in Figure 9.75. As you use colors in your document, the Color Guide automatically suggests harmonious colors that match the current colors in the document. From the palette menu, you can save the colors as swatches, access the Variation Options dialog box, or switch between Tints/Shades, Warm/Cool, and Vivid/Muted color schemes. The Variation Options offer controls for changing the number of steps and a slider for altering the amount of variation in the suggested colors. You can also select the same Harmony Rules that are listed in the Live Color interface from the drop-down list at the top of the palette.

FIGURE 9.75

The Color Guide palette suggests harmonious colors that match the current document colors.

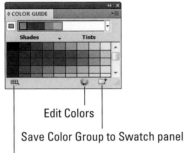

Edit Colors

Save Color Group to Swatch panel

Limit Color Group to colors in the Swatch panel

Managing color profiles and settings

Adobe understands all the issues surrounding color and has endowed the print-oriented CS4 applications including Photoshop, Illustrator, InDesign, Acrobat, and Bridge with color-management methods including a Color Settings dialog box accessed under the Edit menu.

This dialog box, shown for Photoshop in Figure 9.76, lets you select from several different color setting profiles. Using the same profile, settings, and color management policies for all applications produces consistent color output regardless of the application or system. Some of these color setting profiles include North America General Purpose Defaults, U.S. Prepress Defaults, Web Graphics Defaults, as well as profiles for Europe and Japan.

The Color Settings dialog box also lets you define a custom color setting. Custom settings may be saved and loaded for use across applications. Adobe Bridge can synchronize the color management settings for the print-oriented CS4 applications.

CROSS-REF The Color Management features found in the various CS4 applications are covered in Chapter 5.

FIGURE 9.76

The Color Settings dialog box lets you select a default color profile.

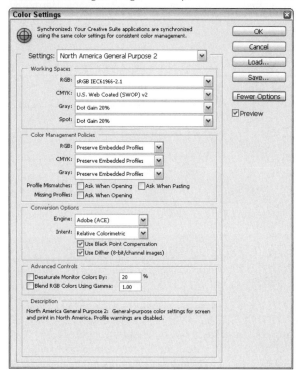

Working with Gradients

When a light source shines on an object, the point closest to the light is usually the brightest and the light intensity gradually decreases the further you get away from the light. This decrease in light intensity over distance is called *attenuation,* and it's common for most light sources.

Simple light attenuation may be simulated in Illustrator, InDesign, Photoshop, and Flash using gradients. Gradients let you specify two or more colors, and the gradient interpolates between these two colors by gradually changing between the specified colors.

Using the Gradient palette

In addition to color, gradients may be applied as an object fill by clicking the Gradient button in the Toolbox or by clicking the gradient in the Gradient palette. The Gradient palette, shown in Figure 9.77, includes controls for specifying gradient colors and behavior.

FIGURE 9.77

The Gradient palette lets you create custom gradients.

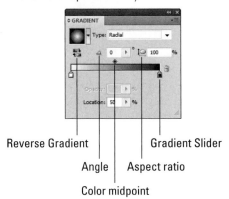

Reverse Gradient

Angle   Aspect ratio

Color midpoint

Gradient Slider

You can expand the Gradient palette in Illustrator and InDesign to show some additional controls including a Type drop-down list, which includes two gradient Types: Linear and Radial. Photoshop goes even further offering Linear, Radial, Angle, Reflected, and Diamond gradient options.

Linear gradients run in a straight line from the color specified at one end of the gradient to the color specified at the other end. For Linear gradients, you can specify an Angle value, which determines the direction that the gradient runs.

Radial gradients place the gradient color specified at one end of the Gradient palette at a specified point, and the changing colors are displayed as concentric circles around this designated point. Figure 9.78 shows examples of linear and radial gradients.

The color bar at the bottom of the Gradient palette lets you specify gradient colors and the midpoints between those colors. The color stop icons appear below the gradient bar; the midpoint markers appear as diamond icons above the gradient bar. To change the position of either of these icons, drag them to the left or right. The position of the icon is displayed in the Location field as a percentage of the entire gradient.

To change the color of a color stop, select the color stop and choose a new color from the Color palette. When a color stop is selected, the small arrow above it turns black.

FIGURE 9.78

Linear and radial gradients are uniquely different from each other.

Linear gradient

Radial gradient

> **NOTE** You can select a color swatch to use in the gradient color stop by holding down the Option/Alt key while clicking a color swatch, or you can drag swatch colors to the gradient color stops. But if you select a gradient color stop and click a color swatch, the color in the swatch is selected and the gradient goes away.

To add new color stops to a gradient, click below the gradient bar where you want to position the new color stop, drag a color swatch from the Swatches palette to the gradient bar, or hold down the Option/Alt key and drag an existing color stop to the side. A new midpoint icon is added for each new color stop that is added.

Using the Gradient tool

Although the Angle may be specified for Linear gradients in the Gradient palette, the Gradient tool (found in the Toolbox) is useful for interactively specifying the gradient angle. With the gradient tool selected, click a selected object where you want to position the leftmost gradient color and drag to where you want to place the rightmost gradient color. This lets you control precisely how the gradient runs across an object.

If the line that is dragged with the gradient tool lies at an angle, the Angle value is set accordingly. Holding down the Shift key while dragging constrains the angle to 45-degree increments.

The Gradient tool also may be used to cause a single gradient to span multiple objects. To do this, select all the objects, apply a gradient fill to them, and then drag with the Gradient tool across the selected objects.

The Gradient panel includes values for specifying the gradient's angle and aspect ratio. With the Gradient slider marker, you can set the gradient's location and opacity. If you double-click on the slider marker, then you can set the color for the slider. If you click below the color bar, then you can add a new slider.

STEPS: Creating and Applying a Custom Gradient

1. **Create a new Illustrator document.** With Illustrator open, choose File ⇨ New to create a new document. Select the Star tool, and drag in the art board to create a star object.

2. **Apply a radial gradient.** With the star selected, click the Gradient button at the bottom of the Toolbox. Then in the Gradient palette, select the Radial type. The star is filled with a radial gradient, as shown in Figure 9.79.

FIGURE 9.79

Selecting the Radial type applies a radial gradient to the object using its center as an endpoint for the gradient.

3. **Change the gradient colors.** With the Swatches palette and the Gradient palette opened at the same time, drag a bright yellow color swatch from the Swatches palette to the first color stop at the left end of the gradient bar in the Gradient palette. Then drag a red color swatch from the Swatches palette to the last color stop at the right end of the gradient bar in the Gradient palette. The colors are immediately applied to the star, as shown in Figure 9.80.

FIGURE 9.80

Dragging colors from the Swatches palette to the gradient bar color stops changes the colors applied to the gradient.

4. Add a new gradient color stop. Click under the middle of the gradient bar to create a new color stop. This new color stop uses the intermediate color from the gradient bar. Drag a black color swatch from the Swatches palette to the new color stop in the Gradient palette. The new color stop changes the color applied to the star dramatically, as shown in Figure 9.81.

FIGURE 9.81

Clicking under the gradient bar adds a new color stop to the gradient bar.

5. Reduce the black color stop spread. To reduce the spreading color of the black color stop, select the midpoint icons above the gradient bar on either side of the black color stop and drag them toward the black color stop. This limits the spread of the black color within the gradient, as shown in Figure 9.82.

FIGURE 9.82

Dragging the midpoint icons changes how far a gradient color stop can spread its color.

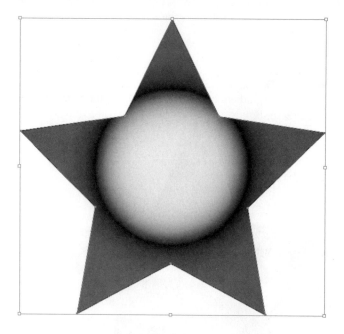

Creating gradient meshes in Illustrator

You can change vector objects within Illustrator to mesh objects using the Mesh tool or the Object ➪ Create Gradient Mesh menu command. Mesh objects are divided into rows and columns with editable points located at each intersection. A gradient color stop also may be positioned at each intersecting point. Choosing Object ➪ Create Gradient Mesh opens a dialog box, shown in Figure 9.83, where you can specify the number of rows and columns to divide the object into.

FIGURE 9.83

The Create Gradient Mesh dialog box

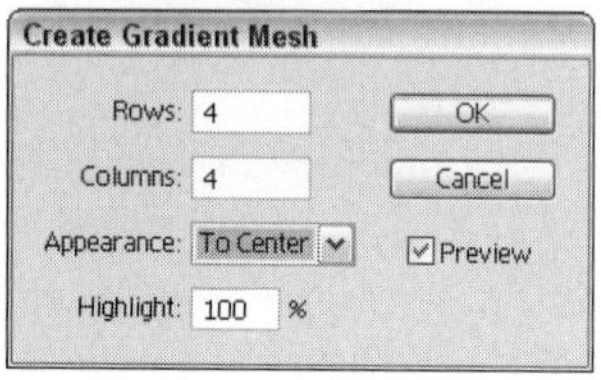

The Appearance drop-down list includes Flat, To Center, and To Edge options. The Flat option colors the entire object with a single fill color. The To Center option adds a white highlight at the center of the object that gradually changes to the fill color at the edges. The To Edge places a white highlight at the object's edges that gradually changes to the object's fill color at its center. The Highlight percentage sets how white the highlight color is.

CAUTION Mesh objects in Illustrator take up lots of system resources and can greatly slow down your system if they're overly complex. It's best to keep mesh objects simple if you experience performance problems.

Figure 9.84 shows three simple rectangles that have been converted to meshes by choosing Object ⇨ Create Gradient Mesh. The top mesh object uses the Flat appearance option, the middle one uses the To Center appearance option, and the bottom one uses the To Edges appearance option.

The Mesh tool is used to place the intersecting mesh points within an object. After clicking to place an intersecting point on an object, you can choose a color from the Color palette to apply as a gradient color for the new intersecting point. Clicking the object again with the Mesh tool creates another new intersecting mesh point. Holding down the Shift key while clicking an object creates an intersecting mesh point without changing its fill color.

FIGURE 9.84

The Gradient Mesh feature creates some interesting objects.

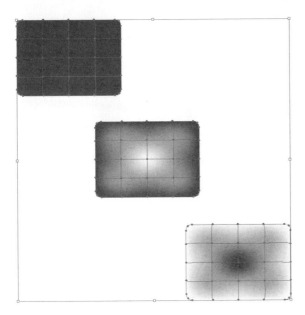

Objects that have a gradient fill applied to them may be expanded to a gradient mesh object with the Object ➪ Expand menu command. This opens a dialog box where you can select to expand the gradient to a Gradient Mesh object. Mesh object points may be selected and moved using the Direct Selection tool. You can change mesh point colors by dragging a color to either mesh points or mesh areas or apply a color using the Eyedropper tool. Dropping a color onto a mesh point changes only the node color and the gradient changes between nodes, but dropping a color on the mesh area has the effect of changing all four mesh points that define the mesh area.

Editing Objects

After you create objects, you have several ways to edit them. An object's position and orientation may be altered using the transformation tools, its properties may be changed using the various palettes such as Illustrator's Appearance palette, and filters and effects may be applied to change the object in many different ways.

 Transformations are covered in Chapter 12. Applying filters and effects is covered in Chapter 13.

In addition to these editing methods, there are several other ways to edit objects including joining, slicing, and cutting paths; blending objects; distorting objects; and using the Pathfinder features.

Editing paths in Illustrator

Paths are created by dragging with tools such as the Pen, Paintbrush, Pencil, and Line Segment tools, but several additional tools let you edit paths.

Using the Smooth and Path Erase tools

Drawing freehand paths with the Pencil tool often results in jagged lines, but these lines are easily smoothed over with the Smooth tool. The Smooth tool is a flyout under the Pencil tool. Dragging over a freehand line with the Smooth tool gradually removes all the sharp changes in the line and smoothes it. Double-clicking the Smooth tool opens a dialog box where you can set the Fidelity and Smoothness values for the tool. The Path Erase tool, a flyout under the Pencil tool, may be used to delete a portion of the selected path. By dragging over the selected path with the Path Erase tool, the section that is dragged over is deleted.

Figure 9.85 shows a rough line drawn with the Pencil tool. The second line has been smoothed with the Smooth tool, and the portions of the last line were erased using the Erase tool.

 You can select the Smooth tool by holding down the Option/Alt key when the Paintbrush or Pencil tool is selected.

FIGURE 9.85

You use the Smooth and Erase tools to edit existing paths.

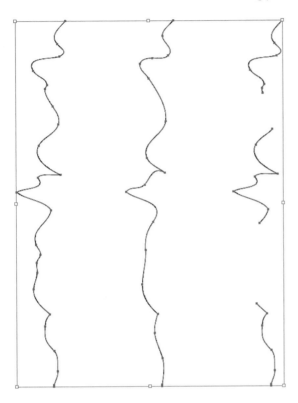

Using the Reshape tool

The Reshape tool (located as a flyout under the Scale tool) lets you select an anchor point, several anchor points, or a line segment as part of a path and drag it while maintaining the overall shape of the path. This causes the entire path to move along with the selected portion. By comparison, anchor points and line segments selected with the Direct Selection tool are moved independent of the entire path; the Scale tool moves all points equally in the scaled direction.

To select anchor points or line segments with the Reshape tool, simply click or drag over the portions of the path that you want to select. The relative distance between the selected points won't change as you drag the path; adjacent anchor points move in proportion to the distance from the selected points.

Figure 9.86 shows three duplicate paths. The left line was drawn with the Pencil tool. The middle path is a duplicate that was scaled horizontally, and the right path is a duplicate that was modified using the Reshape tool. Notice how the scaled path is distorted, while the reshaped path maintains its path details.

305

FIGURE 9.86

The Reshape tool can bend a path while maintaining its details.

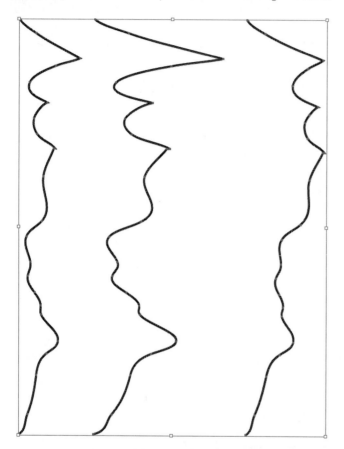

Other methods to editing paths

The following is a list of other ways to edit paths:

- **Splitting paths:** You can use the Scissors tool to cut a path in two. You don't need to select the path to split it. The location where you click with the Scissors tool determines where the path is split.

- **Joining and averaging paths:** If the endpoints of two different paths are selected with the Direct Selection tool, you can make a straight line connect these two endpoints by choosing Object ⇨ Path ⇨ Join (⌘/Ctrl+J). The Object ⇨ Path ⇨ Average (Alt+Ctrl+J in Windows; Option+⌘+J on the Mac) menu command also is used to connect the endpoints of two paths, but instead of a straight line, this command opens a simple dialog box where you can select to move the endpoints to an average Horizontal, Vertical, or Both position. After two paths are joined or averaged, they become a single closed shape.

■ **Converting strokes to filled objects:** You can convert strokes into filled objects by choosing Object ➪ Path ➪ Outline Stroke.

■ **Offsetting paths:** Choosing Object ➪ Path ➪ Offset Path opens a dialog box, shown in Figure 9.87, where you can specify an offset distance and a join type. The join types are the same as those in the Strokes palette, namely Miter (with a Miter Limit value), Round, and Bevel. This command may be used on open or closed paths. A positive Offset value offsets each point of the path outward; a negative Offset value offsets the path points for a closed shape inward.

 The Control panel includes many ways to edit paths including converting points, aligning and distributing points, cutting and closing paths, and deleting points.

FIGURE 9.87

The Offset Path dialog box

Simplifying and cleaning up paths

Cleaning up a document reduces the file size. Choosing Object ➪ Path ➪ Simplify opens a dialog box, shown in Figure 9.88, where you can specify settings that reduce the path's complexity by eliminating unneeded anchor points. The Curve Precision value sets the amount that the path may change during the simplification process. A value of 100% requires that the original path be fully maintained.

FIGURE 9.88

The Simplify dialog box lets you define how radically a path is simplified.

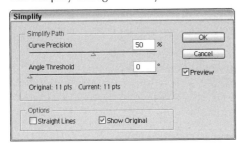

The Angle Threshold value determines the corner smoothness. If the angle of a corner point is less than the Angle Threshold value, the corner isn't smoothed.

 **TIP** When you enable the Preview option, the total number of points in the original and simplified curves is displayed.

The Straight Lines option simplifies the curve using only straight lines; the Show Original option displays the original line in the art board.

Choosing Object ➪ Path ➪ Clean Up opens a dialog box, shown in Figure 9.89, where you can select to eliminate stray points, unpainted objects, and empty text paths. Stray points can appear by clicking once with the Pen tool, which typically happens when you click to select an object when the Pen tool is selected instead of the Selection tool. Unpainted objects are objects with None set for both the fill and stroke. Empty text paths are created by clicking the art board with the Type tool and then not typing.

FIGURE 9.89

The Clean Up dialog box lets you select which cleanup objects to delete.

Splitting objects into grids

With a closed object selected, you can choose Object ➪ Path ➪ Split into Grids, which opens a dialog box, shown in Figure 9.90, where you can specify the number of rows and columns of a grid. You also can specify the height, width, gutter, and total dimensions of the grid cells. The Add Guides option creates guides for the top and bottom of each row and column, letting you change all the cells in a single row or column quickly.

FIGURE 9.90

The Split into Grid dialog box divides a closed path into grid cells.

Cutting objects

Sometimes shape editing calls for removing or separating a portion of an object. You can split an object in several ways:

NOTE   You use the Slice tool to separate images and objects into slices. Each slice can hold vector or raster sections. By slicing documents, you can move them to the Web as separate files that work together.

- **Using the Knife tool:** The Knife tool (located as a flyout tool under the Scissors tool) is a freehand tool that cuts through a selected object. Objects split where you drag the tool. Holding down the Option/Alt key drags a straight line.

- **Cutting holes in shapes:** You can use a closed shape as a cookie cutter to punch out the selected shape from all the objects beneath it. To do this, position the cutting object on top of the object that you want to cut, and choose Object ➪ Path ➪ Divide Object Below.

Creating compound paths and shapes in Illustrator

Compound objects are created when two or more selected paths or shapes are combined to create a single object. Compound objects are different from grouping objects. Objects within a group may have different attributes, but all the paths or shapes in a compound object share the same appearance attributes. Even though compound objects are combined to make a single object, the individual items still may be selected using the Direct Selection or Group Selection tools, just like groups. Compound objects may be restored to their original components using the Release menu command.

Creating compound paths

You can combine two or more paths into a compound path by choosing Object ➪ Compound Path ➪ Make (⌘/Ctrl+8). When paths are combined to create a compound path, the paths create a single path and a hole is left in the fill where the two paths were overlapped. Whenever paths are combined to create a compound path, the appearance attributes of the bottommost object are applied to the resulting path.

Using Pathfinder features

In addition to compound paths, Illustrator can create compound shapes using the Pathfinder palette, shown in Figure 9.91. Open this palette by choosing Window ➪ Pathfinder (Shift+F9). Selected objects are made into a compound shape using the Make Compound Shape palette menu command. This eliminates all the interior paths and combines all the shapes into a single compound shape.

In addition to the palette menu command, you also can use the icon buttons found in the Pathfinder palette to add to the shape area, subtract from the shape area, intersect shape areas, or exclude overlapping shape areas. The Subtract button removes from the first object all shape areas that overlap the first object. The Intersect button leaves only those areas that are common to all selected shapes. The Exclude button removes all areas of the objects that overlap another shape.

FIGURE 9.91

The Pathfinder palette includes shape modes.

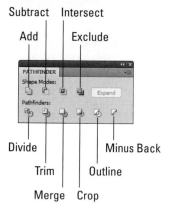

After a compound shape is created, you can change the shape mode for any of the objects that make up the compound shape by selecting it with the Direct Selection tool and choosing a new button in the Pathfinder palette.

Whenever objects are combined to create a compound shape, the appearance attributes of the top-most object are applied to the compound object.

 **Compound shapes use the appearance attributes of the topmost shape. Compound paths use the appearance attributes of the bottommost path.**

Using InDesign's Pathfinder tools

In addition to Illustrator, InDesign also has a robust set of pathfinder features that make it possible to create any type of shape. It is found in the Window ➪ Object & Layout ➪ Pathfinder menu. The top section of InDesign's Pathfinder palette, shown in Figure 9.92, includes the standard path-finder features that work the same as Illustrator's, but the lower section includes options for con-verting shapes. Using the Convert Shape features, you can change a frame into a Rectangle, Rounded Rectangle, Beveled Rectangle, Inverse Rounded Rectangle, Ellipse, Triangle, Polygon, Line, or Horizontal or Vertical Line. Additional options are Open a Path, Close a Path, or Reverse a Path.

FIGURE 9.92

InDesign's Pathfinder palette includes pathfinder and Convert Shape options.

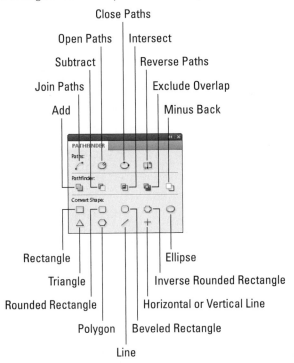

Blending objects in Illustrator

The Blend tool (W) may be used to morph the shape, path, color, or style of one object to another. To use this tool, click an object and then on a second object to blend to. Several intermediate objects appear between the two objects. Figure 9.93 shows a blend that moves between different shapes, strokes, and fills.

Blend objects are selected as a single object, but you may select individual objects that make up a blend object by using the Direct Selection tool. Changing a selected shape or color of either of the objects that make up the blend also updates the intermediate objects.

FIGURE 9.93

Blends can interpolate shapes, strokes, fills, and styles.

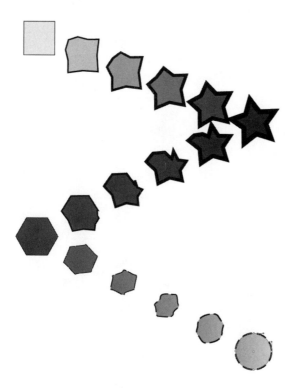

Double-clicking the Blend tool opens the Blend Options dialog box, shown in Figure 9.94, where you can select a Spacing option of Smooth Color, Specified Steps, or Specified Distance. When the Smooth Color option is selected, Illustrator determines the number of steps needed to make a smooth color transition between the two blend objects. For the Specified Steps and Specified Distance options, you can enter the number of steps or the distance between steps.

FIGURE 9.94

The Blend Options dialog box lets you define the number of steps between each blend object.

The Blend Options dialog box also lets you set the Orientation to be either Align to Page or Align to Path. The Align to Page option orients all the blend objects relative to the art board; the Align to Path option orients the blend objects relative to the blend's spine path.

When a blend is made between two objects, a straight path connects the two objects. With the Direct Selection tool, you can select this path and add anchor points to it with the Add Anchor Point tool or by choosing Object ➪ Path ➪ Add Anchor Points. Dragging these new anchor points gives you control over how the path moves. As the path is altered, all the intermediate objects that are part of the blend follow the path.

In addition to the Blend tool, you also can blend two selected objects by choosing Object ➪ Blend ➪ Make (Alt+Ctrl+B in Windows; Option+⌘+B on the Mac). Blended objects also may be undone by choosing Object ➪ Blend ➪ Release (Alt+Shift+Ctrl+B in Windows; Option+Shift+⌘+B on the Mac). Choosing Object ➪ Blend ➪ Expand separates all the intermediate objects from the blend object and makes them independent, editable objects.

The line connecting two blend objects is called the *spine*. You may choose Object ➪ Blend ➪ Reverse Spine or choose Object ➪ Blend ➪ Reverse Front to Back to change the direction and stacking order of the blend objects. If a separate path is selected along with the blend, choosing Object ➪ Blend ➪ Replace Spine causes the blend to use the new selected path instead of the straight-line spine.

Creating a clipping mask in Illustrator

A clipping mask is a closed object positioned over the top of objects that are to be clipped. With all these objects selected, choosing Object ➪ Clipping Mask ➪ Make (⌘/Ctrl+7) causes the top object to hide all the objects underneath. The clipping mask may be undone by choosing Object ➪ Clipping Mask ➪ Release (Alt+Ctrl+7 in Windows; Option+⌘+7 on the Mac).

When a file is placed in Illustrator, a Mask button appears on the Option bar that lets you use the placed file as a clipping mask. The Options bar also lets you access the mask, the content or both. Also, when aligning to a clipping mask, the alignment uses the clip instead of the extents of the content. This makes it easier to align clipping masks to other objects in the document. Clip masks also hide clipped content and can be accessed in Isolation mode.

Distorting objects in Illustrator

There are several different ways to distort objects with the Liquify tools and with Envelope Distort commands.

Using the Liquify tools

Illustrator includes several tools that you may use to distort selected objects. You use these tools by dragging over the selected objects with the selected tool. The longer you drag with the selected tool, the greater the effect. Figure 9.95 shows a simple circle that has been distorted using each of these Liquify tools. These tools collectively are called the Liquify tools and include the following:

- **Warp tool (Shift+R):** Stretches object paths by pushing or pulling them.
- **Twirl tool:** Causes paths to be twirled.
- **Pucker tool:** Sucks paths toward the cursor.
- **Bloat tool:** Pushes path edges away from the cursor.
- **Scallop tool:** Adds arcs and barbs to a path edge.
- **Crystallize tool:** Adds spikes to path edges.
- **Wrinkle tool:** Wrinkles the edge paths with details.

CROSS-REF Most of the available Liquify tools also may be applied as filters and effects, which are covered in Chapter 13.

FIGURE 9.95

The Liquify tools provide several unique ways to distort objects.

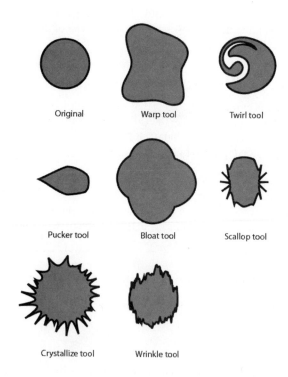

Original

Warp tool

Twirl tool

Pucker tool

Bloat tool

Scallop tool

Crystallize tool

Wrinkle tool

Double-clicking a Liquify tool opens a dialog box of options, like the Pucker Tool Options dialog box, shown in Figure 9.96. Using this dialog box, you can set the Width, Height, Angle, and Intensity of the tool's brush. You also can set the individual settings for the selected tool. The Show Brush Size option changes the cursor to an outline of the brush.

FIGURE 9.96

The settings for the various Liquify tools

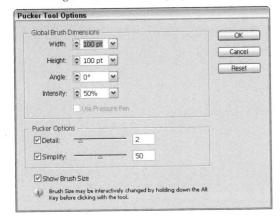

Using the Envelope Distort command in Illustrator

Envelopes are preset or selected shapes into which an object is distorted to fit inside. Choosing Object ⇨ Envelope Distort ⇨ Make with Warp (Alt+Shift+Ctrl+W in Windows; Option+Shift+⌘+W on the Mac) opens a dialog box of preset envelope shapes, shown in Figure 9.97, including Arc, Arc Lower, Arc Upper, Arch, Bulge, Shell Lower, Shell Upper, Flag, Wave, Fish, Rise, Fisheye, Inflate, Squeeze, and Twist.

FIGURE 9.97

The Warp Options dialog box

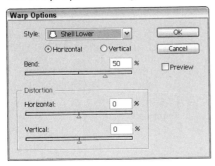

Most of these preset envelope shapes are applied horizontally or vertically by a certain Bend amount. You also can specify the Horizontal and Vertical Distortion amounts.

You apply the envelope as an editable mesh by moving its points with the Direct Selection tool. To apply a mesh to the selected object with a specified number of rows and columns, choose Object ⇨ Envelope Distort ⇨ Make with Mesh (Alt+Ctrl+M in Windows; Option+⌘+M on the Mac). This opens a dialog box where you can enter the number of mesh rows and columns.

Choosing Object ⇨ Envelope Distort ⇨ Make with Top Object (Alt+Ctrl+C in Windows; Option+⌘+C on the Mac) causes the top selected object to act as the distortion envelope. Any selected distortion envelopes are released by choosing Object ⇨ Envelope Distort ⇨ Release.

Choosing Object ⇨ Envelope Distort ⇨ Envelope Options opens a dialog box of options. Using these options, you can specify whether raster objects are anti-aliased and whether to preserve clipping masks or transparency. You also can set the *fidelity,* which determines how well the selected object fits within its envelope, as well as whether an object's appearance, linear gradients, and/or pattern fills are distorted along with the object.

Editing Images

Just as when editing objects, several tools and commands are useful when editing images.

Cropping images in Photoshop

Image sizes are set when a document is first created or loaded into Photoshop, but you can cut out a portion of the image using the Crop tool or the Crop and Trim commands found in the Image menu.

- **Using the Crop tool:** With the Crop tool (C), you can drag on the portion of an image that you want to keep. This selected area is marked with a bounding box that is moved, scaled, and rotated by dragging on the handles at their edges and corners. When the crop area is correctly positioned and oriented, double-click with the Crop tool within the selected area, click the Commit button on the Options bar or press the Return/Enter key, and the image is cropped to the selected area.

- **Cropping and trimming an image:** You also may crop an image using a selection made with one of the default selection tools with the Image ⇨ Crop menu command. Choosing Image ⇨ Trim opens a dialog box of trimming options, shown in Figure 9.98. This command is useful for editing scanned images or images taken with a digital camera that include a border of color that you want to trim.

> **TIP** A quick and easy way to crop and trim is with the Crop and Straighten Photos script located in the File ⇨ Automate menu. This script is especially handy when working with a scanner.

FIGURE 9.98

The Trim dialog box lets you trim unneeded edges from the image.

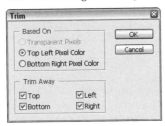

The Transparent Pixels option trims all the transparent pixels along the image edges. The Top Left Pixel Color and Bottom Right Pixel Color options trim all pixels that match the color of the top-left or bottom-right pixels. You also can select to trim just along the top, bottom, left, or right of an image.

Summary

■ You can create and use objects in all the various CS4 applications. To create objects, tools and menu commands are used.

■ Tools that create objects include the Pen, Type, Line Segment, and Shape tools. You create freehand path objects with the Paintbrush and Pencil tools. The Paintbrush, Pencil, and Paint Bucket tools apply paint to the canvas in Photoshop.

■ Most of the CS4 applications include tools to select objects and images. These tools include Shape tools like Photoshop's Marquee tools and Freehand tools like the Lasso tool. Objects and images with similar areas are selected using the Magic Wand tool.

■ Fills and strokes offer a way to add color to objects. Pixel selections also may be filled and stroked. Objects also may be filled with gradients and patterns as well as colors. Live Paint offers options for automatically filling discreet faces.

■ Color is applied using the Color palette, the Color Picker, and color swatches. Illustrator can also applied colors using the Color Guide, Live Color, and Live Paint.

■ The CS4 applications deal with several different color models, including RGB, HSV, CMYK, Grayscale, Lab, and Web Safe RGB colors. The Live Color dialog box lets you use preset color schemes.

■ Illustrator, InDesign, Photoshop, and Flash can apply linear and radial gradients as fills and may be used to create custom patterns.

■ Often-used items are saved in libraries. Libraries include symbols, styles, swatches, and brushes.

■ Each of the CS4 applications includes various tools and commands for editing objects and images, including tools and commands to combine objects and split and distort objects.

Chapter 10

Using Patterns, Symbols, and Styles

Patterns are designs that repeat themselves over and over. They are commonly used in the place of a solid fill within objects. Using the various features for working with patterns, you can position and orient patterns within an object.

Symbols are simple design elements that are stored in libraries. They have the advantage of being easily reused without requiring extra memory. Styles are collections of design properties that are stored where they can be applied easily from a library to an object.

Working with Patterns

In addition to colors and gradients, Photoshop and Illustrator can use patterns to fill objects or paint onto images. Patterns are used differently in both of these applications.

Using patterns in Illustrator

Patterns may be selected from the Swatches palette and applied as an object fill. Any artwork may be used as a new pattern by simply dragging the artwork to the Swatches palette or by selecting the artwork and choosing Edit ⇨ Define Pattern. This opens a dialog box, shown in Figure 10.1, where you can name the pattern.

FIGURE 10.1

Choosing Edit ⇨ Define Pattern creates a new swatch.

To add some spacing behind the pattern, drag a rectangle with its fill and stroke colors set to None, arrange this object as the backmost object, and include it as part of the pattern.

If the pattern fills an object that is larger than the pattern, then the pattern is tiled to fill the entire shape.

STEPS: Creating a Custom Pattern in Illustrator

1. **Create a new Illustrator document.** With Illustrator open, choose File ⇨ New to create a new document.

2. **Create a background area.** Select the Rectangle tool, and drag in the art board to create a rectangle object that is the size of the pattern that you want to create. With the background object selected, set its Fill and Stroke to None.

3. **Add shapes to the pattern area.** Select the Ellipse tool, and drag several small circles within the background square with the Shift key held down to make them perfect circles. Set each circle to have a different fill color, as shown in Figure 10.2.

FIGURE 10.2

Patterns may be created using the Illustrator tools.

4. **Resize the background square.** After creating all the pattern objects, select the background square object and resize it to fit all the objects within it.

5. **Define the pattern.** Drag over all the objects including the background square and all the colored circles, and choose Edit ➪ Define Pattern. In the New Swatch dialog box, name the new swatch and click OK. The new pattern is added to the Swatches palette.

6. **Test the pattern.** Select the Rectangle tool, and drag in the art board to create a rectangle that is larger than the pattern. Then click the pattern swatch in the Swatches palette, and the new pattern is applied to rectangle, as shown in Figure 10.3.

FIGURE 10.3

Apply new patterns to an object to see how the pattern tiles.

CROSS-REF A pattern also can be scaled, moved in relation to its container, and rotated. This is covered in Chapter 12.

Using patterns in Photoshop

Patterns show up on the Options bar when the Paint Bucket, Pattern Stamp, Healing Brush, and Patch tools are selected. By clicking the Pattern pop-up, you can access several default patterns, shown in Figure 10.4. The pop-up palette also includes a palette menu that you can use to create new patterns, load and save pattern sets, and access different pattern sets.

FIGURE 10.4

The Pattern pop-up palette displays the current library of loaded patterns.

New patterns are created by selecting a portion of an image with the Rectangular Marquee tool and choosing Edit ➪ Define Pattern. This opens a dialog box where you can name the pattern. To apply a pattern to a selected area use the Edit ➪ Fill menu command and select the Pattern option in the Fill dialog box or use the Pattern Overlay layer style.

CROSS-REF　Patterns also may be created in Photoshop by choosing Filter ➪ Pattern Maker. This opens a window where you can select and preview patterns. This window and the other filters are covered in Chapter 13.

Using Symbols, Graphic Styles, and Swatches

Most of the CS4 applications make use of libraries. Open your favorite Creative Suite application, and you'll find libraries of symbols, styles, swatches, and brushes. Libraries are used to store any feature that has lots of settings, allowing you to recall the settings at an instant without having to enter all the settings again. Across the various CS4 applications, creating and using library items are fairly consistent whether you're dealing with brushes, styles, symbols, or swatches.

Many of the CS4 applications include many default libraries that you can open and use. For example, Illustrator's Window menu includes submenus of brushes, styles, swatches, and symbol libraries, and Photoshop includes default libraries of swatches, styles, and brushes that may be selected from the various palette menus.

Working with symbols in Illustrator

Symbols in Illustrator and Flash are a special type of object with a key advantage—reuse. If you add a symbol to a document and then reuse it elsewhere in the same document, a new copy isn't required, because the symbol references the first object. This makes symbols very convenient to work with because adding hundreds of symbols to a single document doesn't dramatically increase the overall file size or the size of the compiled SWF file.

CROSS-REF　Reference symbols are particularly useful for files viewed on the Web, such as SWF files. This file type is discussed in Chapter 23.

Accessing symbol libraries

Symbols are stored in libraries, and Illustrator includes several default symbol libraries that you may access by choosing Window ➪ Symbol Libraries or the Open Symbol Library palette menu command off the Symbols palette. Symbol libraries appear in their own custom palette when opened. Selecting the Persistent palette menu option causes the palette to open automatically when Illustrator starts. The icon in the lower-left corner of the various Illustrator library palettes lets you access the various libraries without having to select from the palette menu. The library palettes also include left and right arrows that cycle through the available libraries.

In addition to the symbol libraries, the Symbols palette, shown in Figure 10.5, includes several default symbols. All symbols that are included in the current document are displayed in the Symbols palette. These symbols are associated with the current document and are saved as part of the document.

TIP To remove all symbols that aren't used in the current document from the Symbols palette, choose the Select All Unused palette menu command and then choose the Delete Symbol palette menu command.

FIGURE 10.5

The Symbols palette holds symbol instances used in the document.

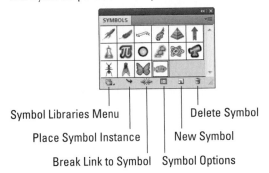

Symbol Libraries Menu

Place Symbol Instance

Break Link to Symbol   Symbol Options

Delete Symbol

New Symbol

You add symbols to the Symbols palette by selecting an object and using the Add to Symbols palette menu command or by dragging the symbol to the Symbols palette. Also, any symbols selected from a symbol library are automatically added to the Symbols palette. You delete symbols from the Symbols palette with the Delete Symbol palette menu command or the trashcan icon at the bottom of the palette. You can save all symbols in the Symbols palette to create a new symbol library using the Save Symbol Library palette menu command.

Inserting, editing, and creating symbols

From a symbol library or the Symbols palette, you can add a symbol to the current document by dragging it from the library to the art board or by selecting the symbol and choosing the Place

Symbol Instance palette menu command. Any symbols that are duplicated using the Option/Alt drag or the copy and paste methods are still symbol instances.

You can edit a symbol instance by using the transform tools or by changing its color and style while still maintaining its symbol status. If more drastic editing is required, you can unlink a symbol using the Break Link to Symbol palette menu command. This command causes the symbol to be expanded.

To rename the new symbol, double-click it in the Symbols palette. A Symbol Options dialog box appears, shown in Figure 10.6; here, you can type a new name for the symbol. You also can specify the new symbol as a Graphic or a Movie Clip. The Flash Registration icon lets you specify where the symbol is positioned in Flash.

FIGURE 10.6

The Symbol Options dialog box lets you rename symbols.

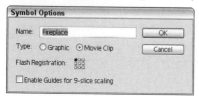

Using the Symbolism tools

You may use Illustrator's Symbolism tools to create a large number of symbols very quickly. The various tools let you alter specific object properties such as size, rotation, color, and style while creating a set of symbols.

The Symbolism tools include the following:

- **Symbol Sprayer:** Creates a set of symbols by dragging in the art board.
- **Symbol Shifter:** Moves symbols within a set relative to one another and to adjust the stacking order.
- **Symbol Scruncher:** Changes the density of symbols within a set by pushing them closer together or pushing them farther apart.
- **Symbol Sizer:** Increases or decreases the size of symbols within a set.
- **Symbol Spinner:** Rotates the symbols within a set.

- **Symbol Stainer:** Changes the colors of symbols within a set by adjusting their hue.
- **Symbol Screener:** Adjusts the transparency of symbols within a set.
- **Symbol Styler:** Applies a selected graphic style to symbols within a set.

With any of these tools selected, you can double-click the tools to open the Symbolism Tools Options dialog box, shown in Figure 10.7. Using this dialog box, you can set the diameter, intensity, and symbol set density. The Options dialog box also shows any shortcut keys available for the various tools, such as holding down the Option/Alt key to reduce the size, coloring, transparency, and style that is applied.

FIGURE 10.7

The Symbolism Tools Options dialog box

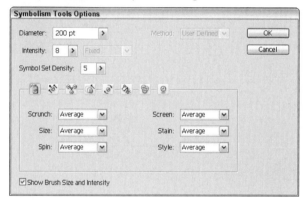

Figure 10.8 shows a simple example of the Symbol Sprayer tool created by selecting the fire symbol (found in the Nature library) and dragging with the Symbol Sprayer. After this set of symbols is created, you can use the other Symbolism tools to change the position, size, rotation, color, transparency, and style of the symbols in the set.

If a symbol is selected within the document, you can choose a new symbol within the Symbols panel and use the Replace Symbol menu to replace the existing symbol with a new one. This lets you quickly replace a whole set of symbols with a new design.

FIGURE 10.8

The Symbol Sprayer draws a path of symbol objects.

Selecting a symbol and selecting the Edit Symbol menu command opens the symbol in Isolation mode, as shown in Figure 10.9, where you can concentrate on the symbol design without the distractions of the other elements. The document border turns red when in Isolation mode. Clicking the arrow at the left end of the title bar exits Isolation mode and returns the original view.

FIGURE 10.9

Isolation mode lets you focus on one element at a time.

Exit Isolation Mode

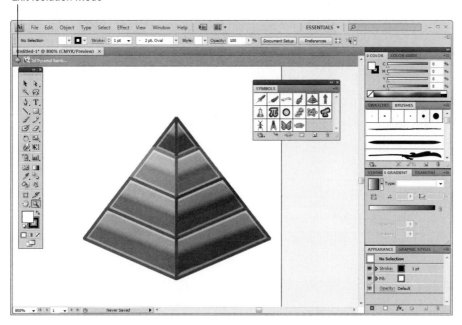

Working with object styles in InDesign

Symbols are easy to grasp. They are simply small nuggets of graphics. Graphic styles are bit trick-
ier. They are a set of styles applied to a standard element. For example, a frame in InDesign can
have a two-pixel black line around its outside or it can have a blue dashed line that is five pixels
thick. These attributes define a specific style. A graphical style is a way to save these style elements
in a library for easy recall.

The concept of graphic styles applies to objects in Illustrator and Photoshop, but it applies equally
well in InDesign. InDesign already has features for handling paragraph and character styles, but it
also can handle graphical styles. Object styles (as they are called in InDesign) are kept in the
Object Styles palette, shown in Figure 10.10.

You can add new object styles by selecting an object and choosing the New Object Style palette
menu command or by clicking the Create New Style button at the bottom of the palette. This
opens the Object Style Options dialog box, shown in Figure 10.11. Using this dialog box, you can
select and alter any of the object attributes that are associated with the object including Fill, Stroke,
transparency, corner effects, drop shadows, text wrap, and so on.

FIGURE 10.10

The Object Styles palette holds graphical attributes for InDesign objects.

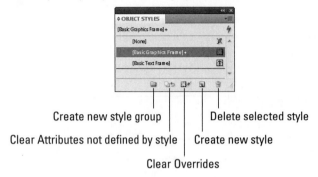

Create new style group

Clear Attributes not defined by style

Clear Overrides

Delete selected style

Create new style

FIGURE 10.11

The Object Style Options dialog box includes settings for defining the object style.

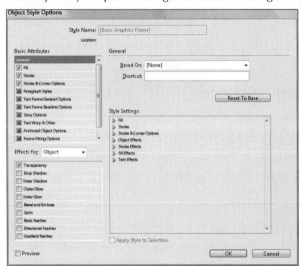

Defined object styles can be applied to an object by dragging the style from the Object Styles pal-ette and dropping it on the object; an even easier method is to select objects and click the style name in the Object Styles palette. You can also drag the default icons for graphic and text frames to any object style to control the attributes of all new objects.

Working with graphic styles in Illustrator and Photoshop

If you've tinkered with the appearance attributes applied to an object until it is perfect, you can save all these settings so they may be easily reapplied to other objects using styles. A *graphic style* is a collection of appearance settings stored within a library for easy recall. The Graphic Styles palette, shown in Figure 10.12, holds a library of default styles. These styles are applied to objects by simply dragging the style icon from the Graphic Styles palette and dropping it on an object.

FIGURE 10.12

The Graphic Styles palette includes appearance attributes.

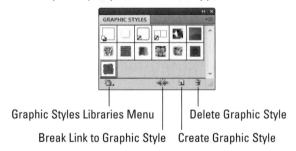

Graphic Styles Libraries Menu   Delete Graphic Style

Break Link to Graphic Style   Create Graphic Style

Illustrator includes, by default, several additional libraries of styles that you can access by choosing Window ⇨ Graphic Style Libraries or by selecting the Open Graphic Style Library palette menu command in the Graphic Style palette. You may save the styles contained within the Graphic Styles palette as a new library using the Save Graphic Style Library palette menu command.

Photoshop also includes several default style libraries that are accessed from the Styles palette menu. To apply a style to the current layer, simply click the style in the Styles palette or drag it to the canvas. Opening a style library presents a dialog box where you can select to replace the current styles in the Styles palette with the new library or append them to the end of the palette.

Creating new styles

You add new styles to the Graphic Styles palette by selecting an object with a style that you want to add to the palette and choosing the New Graphic Style palette menu command or by clicking the small New Graphic Style button at the bottom of the palette.

You can add custom styles to the Graphic Styles palette by dragging the Appearance icon at the top-left of the Appearance palette for the selected object to the Graphic Styles palette. Double-clicking the style icon opens a dialog box where you can rename the style.

Working with swatches

If you've mixed and selected specific colors that you want to keep, you could write down the values for that color or you could add the color to the Swatches palette. Colors in the Swatches may be selected and applied to the Fill and Stroke boxes.

> **NOTE**   **Swatches palettes are found in most of the various CS4 applications. Swatches in Photoshop are mainly used to hold colors, but Illustrator uses the Swatches palette to hold colors, color groups, gradients, and patterns. InDesign also uses the Swatches palette to save mixed inks and mixed ink groups.**

Using the Swatches palette

To add the current Fill or Stroke color to the Swatches palette, shown in Figure 10.13, simply drag the color from the Fill or Stroke box in the toolbar to the Swatches palette or select the New Swatch palette menu command. If the New Swatch menu command is used, the New Swatch dialog box opens; here, you can name the new color swatch, specify the color type, and choose the color mode. The New Swatch dialog box also includes the values to specify a color depending on the selected color mode.

FIGURE 10.13

The Swatches palette holds colors, but in Illustrator it also may hold gradients and patterns.

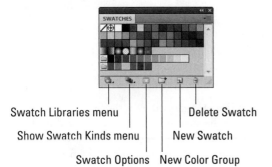

Swatch Libraries menu   Delete Swatch

Show Swatch Kinds menu   New Swatch

Swatch Options   New Color Group

Creating Custom Swatch libraries

Several default Swatch libraries are available by choosing Window ➪ Swatch Libraries; new swatch libraries may be created and saved. To create a new swatch library, choose the Save Swatch Library palette menu command. This opens a file dialog box where you can name the swatch library file. Swatch libraries use the AI file format just like standard Illustrator documents.

> **NOTE**   **Although the discussion of palettes in this section focuses on colors, you also can add and store gradients and patterns within swatch libraries. You use the buttons at the bottom of the Swatches palette in Illustrator to show only a single category of swatches.**

You also can drag colors from the various swatch library palettes and drop them on the Swatches palette. Colors in the Swatches palette may be saved as a new swatch library using the Save Swatch Library palette menu command.

Sharing swatches between CS4 applications

If you've spent some time establishing a set of color swatches for your design, you'll be happy to know that you can save color palettes in a format that you can open in the other CS4 applications. This unique format is the ASE format, and you can select to save the current swatch palette in this format using the Save Swatches for Exchange palette menu command. You can find the Save Swatches for Exchange menu command in the Swatch palette in Photoshop, Illustrator, and InDesign.

 **Kuler support is included the various CS applications. You can use Kuler to create a color scheme and then add the colors to the Swatches panel.**

Using the Library palette

To keep content organized, InDesign allows you to create libraries of content. To create a new library, which appears as a palette, simply select the File ➪ New ➪ Library menu command. This causes an empty library palette to appear. You can add items, including text frames and graphics, to the palette by dragging and dropping them on the empty palette, or you can add the selected item with the Create Library Item palette menu command. Figure 10.14 shows a new Library palette with several items added to it.

FIGURE 10.14

The InDesign Library palette can hold graphics, graphic frames, guides, and text frames that you can reuse as needed.

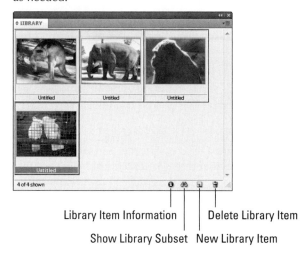

Library Item Information   Delete Library Item

Show Library Subset   New Library Item

You can reopen saved library palettes using the File ➪ Open menu command. Library palettes are saved using the INDL file extension. You can place library items on the page by dragging them from the Library palette and dropping them on the current page or by using the Place Item palette menu command. If any item is selected in the Library palette, you can select the Item Information palette menu command to access a dialog box, shown in Figure 10.15, which includes information about the item and a field for entering a description.

FIGURE 10.15

The Item Information dialog box includes information about the selected item and lets you enter a description.

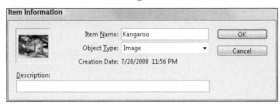

The Show Subset palette menu command opens a dialog box, shown in Figure 10.16, which allows you to search for specific items using keywords. The palette menu also includes options to sort items by Name, Oldest, Newest, and Type.

FIGURE 10.16

The Show Subset dialog box lets you search for specific items in the Library palette.

Exporting snippets

Snippets are XML-based content from InDesign that is saved as a separate file. You save snippets into a library or open them into another document. To export the selected items, simply select the item to export and choose the File ➪ Export menu command. In the file dialog box that appears, select the InDesign Snippet as the Save as Type. You also can create snippets by dragging items into the Bridge window or into any OS window. If you drag to a Bridge window, you'll see a preview of the snippet's contents. The file with the INDS file extension can then be loaded within other InDesign documents.

 A snippet can be any part of a layout including guides, but you cannot drag guides to make a snippet; you must export guides to create a snippet.

To place a snippet, use the File ⇨ Place menu command or drag the snippet onto the layout.

CROSS-REF Transformations are covered in Chapter 12. Applying filters and effects is covered in Chapter 13.

Using Photoshop's Preset Manager

Photoshop includes a clever way to manage all the various presets and libraries using a special dialog box called the Preset Manager, shown in Figure 10.17. This dialog box may be opened from most of the palette menus that include presets or libraries or by choosing Edit ⇨ Preset Manager.

FIGURE 10.17

The Preset Manager dialog box in Photoshop

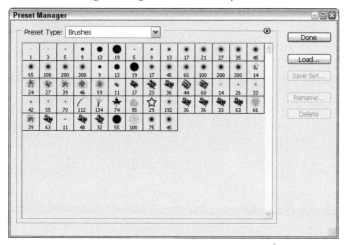

At the top of the dialog box is a drop-down list of the various preset types, including brushes, swatches, gradients, styles, patterns, contours, custom shapes, and tools. When a preset type is selected, its library of items is displayed. Using the palette menu, you can change how the items are displayed or choose one of the default libraries to open. The dialog box also includes buttons to load, save, rename, and delete the current sets.

Using Transparency

Another common property that may be applied to objects is transparency. When an object has some transparency applied to it, all objects underneath it are visible. For example, placing transparent text on top of an image lets the overlapped image show through the text.

Applying transparency to objects and images

Transparency is applied to the selected object in Illustrator using the Opacity setting in the Transparency panel, shown in Figure 10.18. Open this panel by choosing Window ➪ Transparency. By default, the Transparency palette includes only a drop-down list of blending modes and an Opacity value. Changing the Opacity value changes the transparency of the selected object using the selected blending mode. Transparency in Photoshop is applied to layers using the Opacity setting in the Layers panel. Opacity settings can be changed in InDesign using the Effects panel. Transparency is also available in Flash, but it is called Alpha.

CROSS-REF Layers are covered in detail in Chapter 14 and the InDesign Effects panel is covered in Chapter 13.

FIGURE 10.18

The Transparency palette lets you set an object's opacity.

Changing the Opacity value in the Transparency palette applies transparency to the selected object's fill and stroke. This value is then listed at the bottom of the Appearance panel, but you can apply different transparency values to the fill and stroke by selecting each in the Appearance palette prior to changing the Opacity value in the Transparency palette. The Opacity value for the fill or stroke is listed under each in the Appearance palette.

Selecting the Show Thumbnails palette menu command expands the palette to reveal a thumbnail of the selected object. The Show Options palette menu command reveals some additional options at the bottom of the palette.

Using blending modes

When you apply transparency to an object, the colors of the object positioned underneath the object blend together. Choosing a blending mode defines how the blend color and the base color are blended together. The *blend color* is the color of the overlaid object; the *base color* is the color of the underlying object.

The blending modes alter the color of the selected object in the following ways:

- **Normal:** Uses the blend color.
- **Darken:** Uses either the base or blend color depending on which is darker. This is the opposite of the Lighten mode.
- **Multiply:** Multiplies the base and blend colors resulting in a darker color. Any color multiplied by white doesn't change the color, and multiplying any color with black produces black. This is the opposite of the Screen mode.
- **Color Burn:** Darkens the base color. This is the opposite of the Color Dodge mode.
- **Lighten:** Uses either the base or blend color depending on which is lighter. This is the opposite of the Darken mode.
- **Screen:** Multiplies the inverse of both the base and blend colors resulting in a lighter color. Any color screened with black doesn't change the color, and screening any color with white produces white. This is the opposite of the Multiply mode.
- **Color Dodge:** Lightens the base color. This is the opposite of the Color Burn mode.
- **Overlay:** Mixes the base color with the blend color to lighten the highlights and darken the shadows.
- **Soft Light:** Lightens the light areas of the blend color and darkens the dark areas.
- **Hard Light:** Screens the light areas of the blend color and multiplies the dark areas of the base color.
- **Difference:** Subtracts the lighter of the base or blend colors from the other.
- **Exclusion:** Removes all the light value of the base or blend colors from the other.
- **Hue:** Colors the object using the luminance and saturation values of the base color and the hue of the blend color.
- **Saturation:** Colors the object using the luminance and hue values of the base color and the saturation of the blend color.
- **Color:** Uses the luminance of the base color and the hue and saturation of the blend color. This is the opposite of the Luminosity mode.
- **Luminosity:** Uses the hue and saturation values of the base color and the luminance of the blend color. This is the opposite of the Color mode.

 Photoshop includes several additional blend modes not listed here.

Figure 10.19 shows examples of all the blending modes.

FIGURE 10.19

Side-by-side comparisons of all the different blending modes are helpful in understanding how they work.

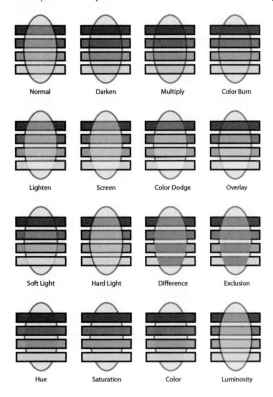

Creating an opacity mask

An *opacity mask* in Illustrator is used to define how much transparency is applied to the objects on the linked layer. The white areas on the opacity mask have no transparency applied, but black areas are fully transparent. Gray areas are partially transparent.

To make an opacity mask, select two objects and choose the Make Opacity Mask palette menu command. The top object is used as the opacity mask, and the bottom objects are objects that are affected by the opacity mask.

In the thumbnail section of the Transparency palette, the objects that are affected by the opacity mask are displayed to the left, and the opacity mask is displayed to the right. The Clip option causes the opacity mask to act also as a clipping mask, and the Invert Mask option inverts the opacity mask, making the transparent areas opaque and vice versa. Figure 10.20 shows an example of an opacity mask. The snapshots in the Transparency palette show the objects used to determine the transparency of the objects below.

FIGURE 10.20

The colors in the opacity mask determine which objects are visible below.

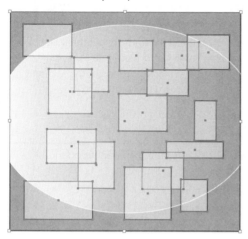

STEPS: Creating an Opacity Mask

1. **Create a new Illustrator document.** With Illustrator open, choose File ➪ New to create a new document.

2. **Create an object to mask.** Drag a symbol object on the art board from the Symbols palette, and resize it to fit the art board. The resized object is shown in Figure 10.21.

FIGURE 10.21

This symbol is fully opaque with no transparency applied.

3. **Draw a mask object.** Select the Rectangle tool, and drag it over the top of the symbol. With the fill box selected, choose the Gradient button in the Toolbox to apply a linear gradient to the rectangle. Make sure the rectangle is positioned above the symbol.

4. **Select all objects, and create an opacity mask.** Drag over both objects with the Selection tool to select them. Open the Transparency palette, and choose the Make Opacity Mask palette menu command. The symbol object and the gradient rectangle both show up as thumbnails in the Transparency palette; the black portions of the gradient mark where the underlying symbol is transparent, as shown in Figure 10.22.

FIGURE 10.22

Using the opacity mask, the house gradually changes from transparent to opaque.

Summary

- Patterns provide a alternative to fill objects with solid colors and gradients.
- Often-used items are saved in libraries. Libraries include symbols, styles, swatches, and brushes.
- Symbols provide an efficient way to work with many duplicate objects.
- Transparency is another common property that allows objects underneath overlapped objects to be partially visible.

Chapter 11

Acquiring and Correcting Images

In addition to objects, images are another important design element. Although all applications handle images, Photoshop is the main tool for working with images. The first task is to load digital images. Photoshop includes lots of features not only to scan and acquire digital photos but also to correct them.

After you load images within Photoshop, you can edit them using Photoshop's vast array of features. You can then easily transport these images to the other CS4 applications using the Clipboard, exported files, or Adobe Bridge.

Scanning Images in Photoshop

One method for loading images into Photoshop is with a scanner. Several different manufacturers make scanners that employ several different drivers. Scanners almost always come with a CD-ROM of compatible drivers that you can install to interface with Photoshop or with their own proprietary software.

If your scanner includes Photoshop compatible drivers, then the scanner's name appears in the File ➪ Import menu. If the scanner's driver doesn't include a Photoshop driver, check the manufacturer's Web site for an updated driver.

If the scanner manufacturer doesn't have a Photoshop driver available, you can take advantage of a TWAIN compatible interface. The TWAIN compatible device is listed in the File ➪ Import menu.

A third driver option is to scan images using the WIA (Windows Image Acquisition) Support driver. You select this option using the File ⇨ Import ⇨ WIA Support menu. This menu opens the WIA Support dialog box, shown in Figure 11.1, where you can specify a Destination Folder and options to open the image after the scan has completed.

 **NOTE** WIA Support is available only for Windows XP computers. Macintosh computers use the Image Capture features to access scanning devices.

FIGURE 11.1

The WIA Support dialog box lets you access a scanner's software.

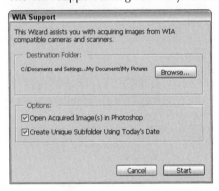

Clicking the Start button opens a dialog box, shown in Figure 11.2, where you can choose the Scanner, Video Camera, and/or Digital Camera to access. Selecting a device and clicking OK opens the device's software. The Properties button opens a dialog box of properties that let you define how the device can be used to scan directly into Photoshop.

FIGURE 11.2

The Select Device dialog box lets choose which scanning device to use.

STEPS: Setting up Photoshop Scanning

1. **Open Photoshop, and select WIA Support.** With Photoshop open, choose File ➪ Import ➪ WIA Support to access the WIA Support dialog box.

2. **Set a Destination Folder.** Click Browse, and select a destination folder where the scanned images are saved. Enable the Open Acquired Images in Photoshop option to view the images in Photoshop after they are scanned. Then click Start.

3. **Access the Scanner's Properties.** In the Select Device dialog box, choose the installed scanner and click Properties. This opens a dialog box of properties for the selected device.

4. **Set the Scan button to open Photoshop.** In the device Properties dialog box, shown in Figure 11.3, click the Events tab and select the Scan Button event. In the Actions section, choose the Start this Program option and choose Photoshop as the program to open. Then click OK.

FIGURE 11.3

You can set Photoshop to open when you push the scan button on the scanner device.

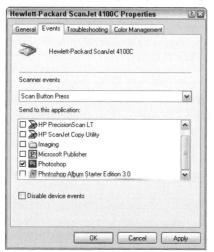

After clicking OK in the Select Device dialog box, a Scan dialog box appears, shown in Figure 11.4. Options to scan the image include scanning as a Color picture, a Grayscale picture, or a Black and white picture or text. The Adjust the quality of the scanned picture link opens another dialog box where you can adjust the Brightness, Contrast, and Resolution of the scanned image. The Preview button shows the scanned image in the preview pane, where you can set its cropping using the corner handles.

FIGURE 11.4

You can scan images as Color, Grayscale, or Black and white.

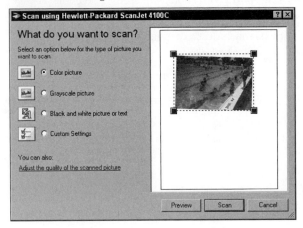

Acquiring Digital Camera Images

Digital cameras work the same as scanners. Images from a digital camera can be accessed using the File ⇨ Import menu command using the TWAIN driver, the WIA Support driver, or Mac's Image Capture feature.

CROSS-REF Adobe Bridge also can be used to download images from a digital camera with its File ⇨ Get Photos from Camera command. This command opens the Photo Downloader dialog box, which includes features to rename the downloaded files and convert the files to the DNG format. You can learn more about using Adobe Bridge in Chapter 6.

Using camera raw

Most digital cameras have a varied assortment of configuration settings for controlling everything from brightness and aperture to contrast and digital noise. These settings are crucial for getting just the right picture, but they also include many of the same settings found in Photoshop. If you capture an image with the incorrect brightness setting while hanging halfway over a fence at the zoo, you don't need to throw away the image; you can simply download the raw camera data, which is the actual digital data captured by the camera's optical sensor. Then you can reclaim much of the image data in Photoshop at your leisure without having to revisit the zoo to take another shot.

CAUTION Not all cameras can record raw camera data. Check the Adobe Web site for a list of compatible cameras.

Raw camera data can be imported into Photoshop using the File ⇨ Open menu command. The file extension for this data may be different depending on the camera, but Photoshop can recognize a huge variety of raw formats. When you open a raw camera file, the Camera Raw plug-in opens.

CROSS-REF You can open the Camera Raw plug-in from within Photoshop or within Adobe Bridge. More details on this plug-in are covered in Chapter 6.

Understanding Digital Negative specification

Working with raw camera data makes lots of sense, but there is a problem with the current raw camera formats. Each camera manufacturer uses a different format to output its raw camera data, which makes it difficult to standardize when you load the data in a program like Photoshop.

Although CS4 supports a majority of the available raw camera formats, there are some less popular camera makers that aren't supported. To address this issue, Adobe has defined and made publicly available the Adobe Digital Negative (DNG) format. One advantage of this new format is that it also includes support for metadata that describes the images.

As of this printing, many camera manufacturers have announced support for this new raw camera format. Adobe also has made a conversion utility available that converts many of the existing raw camera data formats to the DNG format. For more information on this format, see Adobe's Web site.

Correcting red eye

Attentive camera subjects looking directly at the camera typically have red eyes when the digital camera's flash lights their eyes. This can quickly be fixed using the Red Eye tool, which is located as a flyout under the Healing Brush in Photoshop. To use the tool, simply drag it over an eye with this problem. Figure 11.5 shows an example where this tool was used. This toddler's left eye (the eye on ther right in the photo) has been corrected using this tool. When this tool is selected, the Options bar includes settings for controlling Pupil Size and Darken Pupil.

NOTE The Camera Raw dialog box available in Photoshop and Bridge also includes a red-eye correction tool.

FIGURE 11.5

The Red Eye tool can quickly fix images with red eyes.

Using the Lens Correction filter

Another common problem with images taken with a digital camera are lens flaws such as barrel and pincushion distortion. These are especially visible when the image includes many parallel straight lines.

Lens flaws can be remedied in Photoshop using the Lens Correction filter located in Filter ⇨ Distort ⇨ Lens Correction. This filter opens the Lens Correction dialog box, shown in Figure 11.6.

FIGURE 11.6

The Lens Correction filter can fix many lens flaws added by the digital camera.

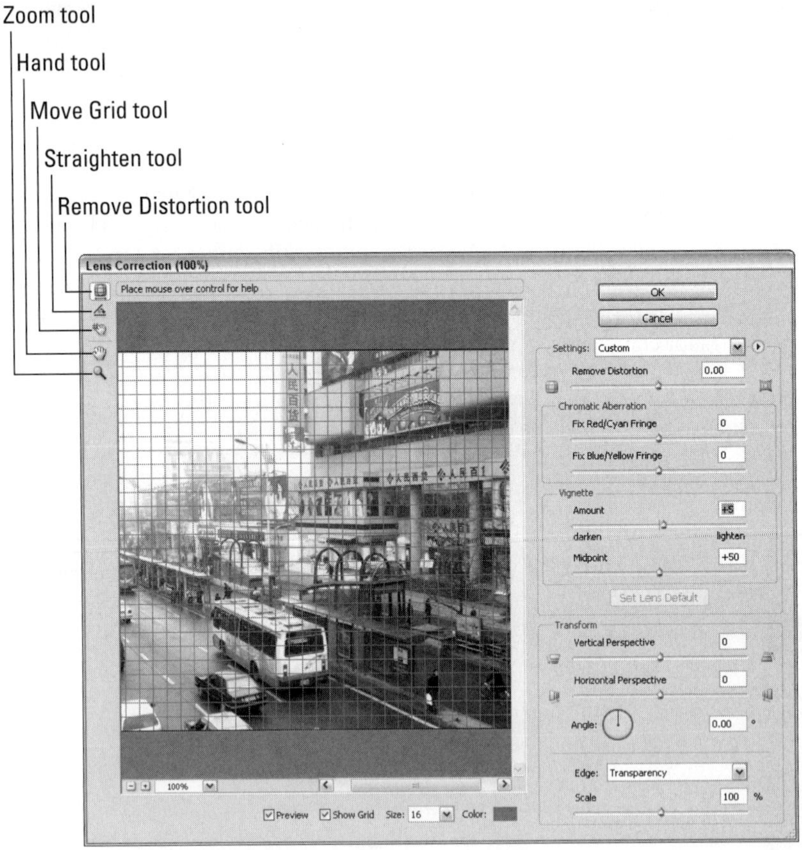

Zoom tool

Hand tool

Move Grid tool

Straighten tool

Remove Distortion tool

The upper-left corner of the Lens Correction dialog box includes several tools. The Remove Distortion tool alternates the image between a pincushion and barrel settings. Dragging with the Straighten tool causes the image to reorient about the dragged line. This provides a way to recreate the horizontal and vertical axis for the image. Over the top of the image is a grid that can be turned on and off. The Move Grid tool is used to move and reposition this grid.

CROSS-REF For additional coverage on Photoshop filters, see Chapter 13.

To the right of the preview pane are several sliders that can be used to further modify the image. The Remove Distortion slider associates a value to the distortion. The Chromatic Aberration values are used to change the colors located at the fringe of the lens. You can adjust for Red/Cyan and Blue/Yellow colored fringes. The Vignette value alters the brightness of the image about the lens center. The Vertical and Horizontal Perspective settings tilt the image to or away from the image center. You also can change the image's orientation Angle and Scale. The Edge setting determines how the edge is colored when the image's perspective, angle, or scale is changed. The options include Edge Extension, Transparency, and Background.

CROSS-REF The Camera Raw dialog box also includes a Lens Correction tool and several other handy tools for making adjustments. This dialog box is covered in Chapter 6.

Correcting Images

After digital images are loaded into Photoshop, you have lots of control in adjusting the images. This is the power of Photoshop—to correct images.

CROSS-REF Many image adjustments also can be applied to a specific layer using Adjustment Layers, but not all. Adjustment Layers are covered in Chapter 25.

Using Levels

One of the first corrections you'll want to make to acquired digital images is to adjust the image's levels. This can be done in the Levels dialog box, shown in Figure 11.7, which is opened for the current image using the Image ⇨ Adjustment ⇨ Levels menu command. The Levels dialog box shows a histogram for the image, which is a graph showing the number of pixels for each color intensity level.

At the top of the Levels dialog box is the Channels drop-down list, where you can view the levels for All RGB Channels, or just the Red, Green, or Blue channels. Level settings can be saved and restored using the Load and Save buttons.

FIGURE 11.7

The Levels dialog box shows the tonal range for the image.

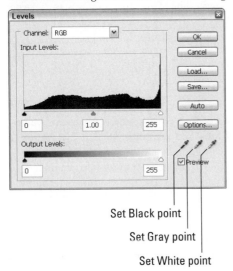

Set Black point

Set Gray point

Set White point

The Input Level values are associated with the black and white color values in the shadows and highlights. The middle value represents the gamma setting for the image. The tonal range can be adjusted manually by changing the Input Level values, by dragging the markers under the level graph or by clicking Auto to automatically set the range. Dragging the middle gray marker under the levels graph alters the image's midtones. The Options button opens the Auto Color Correction Options dialog box, shown in Figure 11.8. Using these settings, you can set how the Auto button corrects the image.

FIGURE 11.8

The Auto Color Correction Options dialog box lets you set how the Auto button works.

You also can correct colorcast in the Levels dialog box by double-clicking the Set Black, Gray, or White Point icons. You can then select the color in the Color Picker for the selected point and click in the image where that color point is located.

Using Curves

In addition to the Levels dialog box, the Curves dialog box, shown in Figure 11.9, also can be used to alter the tonal range of an image, but with more precision. The Curves dialog box shows the intensity for the entire image range from black's 0 value to white's 255 value.

Most of the settings in this dialog box are identical to those in the Levels dialog box, including viewing individual channels, loading and saving curves, the Auto and Options buttons, and setting black, gray, and white points.

FIGURE 11.9

The Curves dialog box offers a more precise way to change the tonal range of an image.

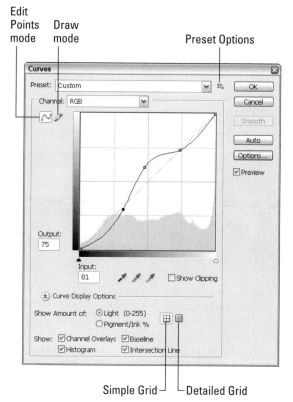

Edit Points mode

Draw mode

Preset Options

Simple Grid — └─Detailed Grid

The Curves dialog box can add up to 14 additional points to the curve, each of which you can move as needed by dragging with the cursor. You can remove points by dragging them off the curve or by selecting them and pressing the Delete key. You also can draw a curve using the Draw Curve tool. The Smooth button becomes enabled when a curve is drawn.

If you've configured the Curves dialog box with some unique settings, you can save these settings as a preset that can be recalled and applied to other images.

Using Auto adjustments

Within the Image ➪ Adjustment menu are options for Auto Color, Auto Contrast, and Auto Levels. These commands correspond to the algorithms found in the Auto Color Correction Options dialog box and selecting these menu commands is the same as selecting each in the Options dialog box and clicking Auto.

STEPS: Adjusting Shadows and Highlights

1. **Open Photoshop, and select an image.** With Photoshop open, load an image that needs to have its shadows and highlights set. Figure 11.10 shows the image before any adjustments have been made.

FIGURE 11.10

This image needs to have its tonal range reset.

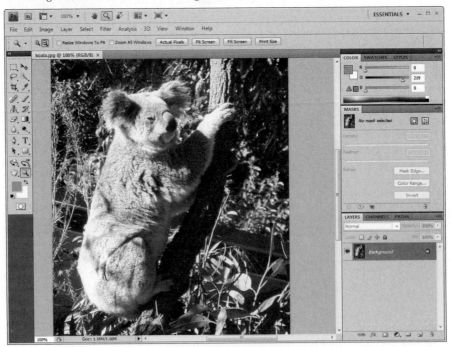

2. **Open the Levels dialog box.** With the image selected, choose the Image ⇨ Adjustment ⇨ Levels menu command. The image shows lots of pixels in the lower third of the levels graph.

3. **Adjust the highlights.** Drag the midtones marker in the middle of the graph to the right until the midtones are darkened slightly, as shown in Figure 11.11.

FIGURE 11.11

Dragging the right marker resets the highlights.

Using Photoshop's Adjustments Panel

In addition to the adjustments available in the Image menu in Photoshop, you can use the Adjustments panel, shown in Figure 11.12. This panel lets you choose from a wide assortment of adjustments including Brightness/Contrast, Levels, Curves, Exposure, Vibrance, Hue/Saturation, Color Balance, Photo Filter, Channel Mixer, Invert, Posterize, Threshold, Gradient Map, and Selective Color.

FIGURE 11.12

The Adjustments panel lets you choose from multiple different image adjustments.

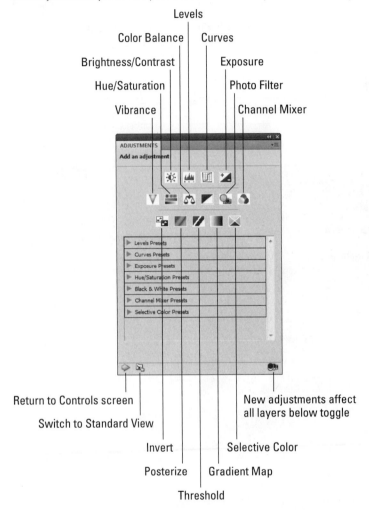

The Adjustments panel includes a wide variety of categorized presets. Selecting these presets automatically applies the applicable adjustment and displays the adjustment's settings. A preview of the adjustment is displayed on the current image.

You can move back and forth between the Adjustment selection screen and the adjustment settings using the arrow keys in the lower-left corner of the panel. The coolest part of these adjustments is that each applied adjustment is placed on a separate layer, which makes it non-destructive. You can remove the adjustment at any time if you need to return to the unadjusted image. Figure 11.13 shows an image with several adjustments added.

FIGURE 11.13

Each applied adjustment appears as a separate layer.

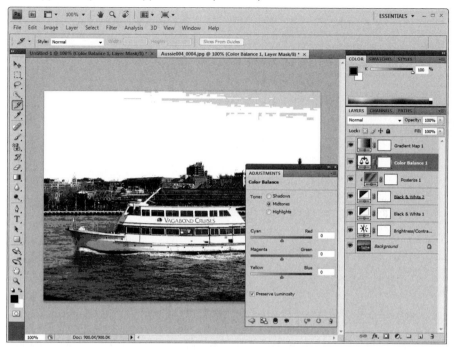

Editing 32-bit high Dynamic Range Images

Even if you adjust the tonal range of an image, our eyes can detect a greater range than a computer monitor represents. Think of how your eyes react when you walk out in the bright sun. The range that makes everything seem to glow can't be represented using any of the existing image formats, but another format has been developed that captures this extended range and it actually allows the color range to change as needed. This new format is called High Dynamic Range (HDR) images.

HDR images are represented using 32-bit numbers instead of the standard 8-bit or 16-bit image formats. The extra numeric values are used to represent the luminance associated with each pixel in the image. HDR images are created by merging in multiple photographs of different exposures.

To merge several images of the same scene taken with different exposure settings into a single HDR file, use the File ⇨ Automate ⇨ Merge to HDR menu command. This opens the Merge to HDR dialog box, shown in Figure 11.14, where you can select individual files using the Browse button, select a folder, and choose to merge the existing open files. After clicking OK, the files are merged and you can save the file.

FIGURE 11.14

The Merge to HDR dialog box can combine multiple images into a single HDR image.

Photoshop's File ⇨ New command can create a new 32-bit image. Once a new HDR image is created, you can use all of Photoshop's existing tools to paint directly on the HDR image. Photoshop's HDR Color Picker, shown in Figure 11.15, also includes the ability to select brightness values that are greater than 1.0. As you edit an HDR image, there is a slider that you can use to preview the HDR image at different exposure settings.

Retouching images in Photoshop

Photoshop includes many tools to retouch an image. Most of these tools redistribute pixels by moving or copying pixels to other places within the same image. The tools used to retouch images include the Clone Stamp tool, the Pattern Stamp tool, the Healing Brush tool, the Spot Healing tool, the Patch tool, and the Color Replacement tool.

FIGURE 11.15

The HDR Color Picker can set Intensity values to greater than 1.0.

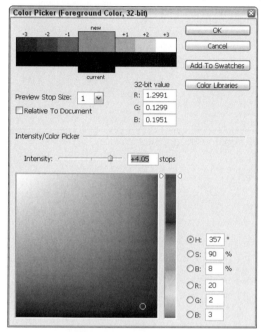

Using the Stamp tools

Two tools are available in Photoshop: the Clone Stamp tool and the Pattern Stamp tool.

The Clone Stamp tool allows you to paint pixels copied from a selected area to another area in the image. With the Clone Stamp tool selected, you can choose a brush tip and blending mode to use in the Options bar. Then hold down the Option/Alt key and click in the image to mark the area that you want to clone pixels from and paint in the area where you want the cloned pixels to appear.

If the Aligned option is selected, the pixels relative to the marked area are copied for every painted stroke. If the Aligned option is disabled, every new stroke starts painting from the marked area.

When the Clone Stamp tool is selected, you can use the Clone Source palette, shown in Figure 11.16, to select up to five different clone source locations. For each clone source, you can set the Offset, Width and Height, and Rotation values. You also have an option to display an Overlay, which helps to show how the cloned areas look when painted.

NOTE If you're using Photoshop CS4 Extended, then you can use the Clone Stamp tool across video and animation frames. The Frame Offset value is the current frame being painted.

FIGURE 11.16

The Clone Source palette lets you specify up to five different positions from which to clone.

Lock Options

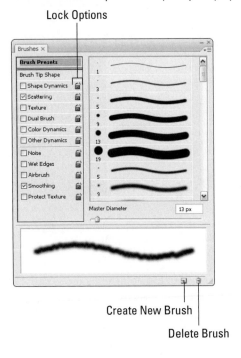

Create New Brush

Delete Brush

The Clone Stamp includes a preview that shows the area from which the clone will be painted. This is a great check to make sure that the correct area is being copied, as shown in Figure 11.17.

FIGURE 11.17

The Clone Stamp brush shows a preview of the cloned area.

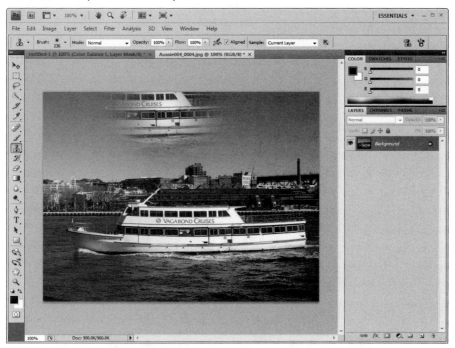

The Pattern Stamp tool works just like the Clone Stamp tool, except it lets you paint with the pattern selected in the Options bar.

Using the Healing Brush and Patch tools

The Healing Brush tool, like the Clone Stamp tool, lets you select an area of pixels where the painted pixels are taken from using the Option/Alt key. But the Healing Brush tool matches the surrounding pixels where they're painted, making the pixels blend in with the image. This tool is great for removing small imperfections from a scanned image or a digital photo.

The Patch tool also can copy an area of pixels to another area in the image, and the moved pixels are blended into their new area matching the surrounding pixels. With the Patch tool, you can drag to select a freehand area like the Lasso tool. You can add to the selection by dragging with the Shift key held down or remove from the selection by dragging with the Option/Alt key held down. Holding down the Shift+Option/Alt keys while dragging over the selection keeps only the intersected selection. You also can change the selection area using the Add, Subtract, and Intersection buttons on the Options bar.

After a selection is made, you can choose the Source option in the Options bar and drag from within the selection. This projects the area under the cursor to the selected area, and if you release the mouse, the displayed pixels are copied to the selected area.

If the Destination option in the Options bar is enabled, then you can drag the selected area to the pixels that you want to cover. Each time the mouse is released, the dragged area is copied over the area that it's on top of. Dragging and releasing the mouse lets you replace many areas quickly.

Using the Spot Healing Brush

One drawback to the Healing Brush is that you need to take time to select an area where the painted pixels are taken, but the Spot Healing Brush doesn't require this step. The Spot Healing Brush is specifically made to replace spots in the image by sampling pixels around the area. It provides a quick clean way to remove spots from images without the fuss. Figure 11.18 shows an original image and the same image fixed with the Spot Healing Brush. Notice how the bright reflection off the glass has been removed without drastically altering the image.

FIGURE 11.18

The Spot Healing Brush can quickly remove spots from an image by sampling the pixels surrounding the area.

Using the Color Replacement tool

The Color Replacement tool, located as a flyout under the Brush tool, may be used to replace a selected color with the foreground color. The Mode options let you choose to replace pixels based on Hue, Saturation, Color, or Luminosity. The Sampling options let you replace the pixels continuously, just once, or using the background swatch color to replace the background color with the foreground color.

The Limits options include Discontiguous, which replaces any colors that you paint over; Contiguous, which paints only connected areas of color; and Find Edges, which also replaces only connected areas of color but keeps the edges sharp.

Using the Eraser tools

Photoshop includes three different eraser tools used to remove pixels. The Erase tool removes pixels revealing the background color underneath. If there is no background layer, then the Eraser tool erases to transparency. The Mode options let you choose a smooth-edged brush, a hard-edged pencil, or a square block, which is useful to get the sharp corner areas. You also can set the opacity and flow to use as you erase. The Erase to History option removes all changes applied to an image, leaving the base saved image when enabled.

The Background Eraser tool is used to replace the background of an image with transparency. When you drag with this tool, the color that is immediately under the center of the tool is sampled and removed from the areas where you paint, but the other colors and the edges of the images are retained.

The Magic Eraser tool works like the Magic Wand tool, letting you click a background color that you want to erase. All connected pixels (if the Contiguous option is enabled) are erased, or all similar pixels in the entire image are deleted (if the Contiguous option is disabled).

Distorting images

Another useful way to edit images is to distort the pixels using the various distorting tools. These tools include Smudge, Blur, Sharpen, Dodge, Burn, and Sponge.

CROSS-REF The effects of these pixel distortion tools also may be accomplished using the various Filters, which are covered in Chapter 12.

- **Smudge tool:** This tool is used to smear the color of several pixels together like wiping wet paint across the canvas. This tool lets you choose from several different modes and a Strength value. The Finger Painting option uses the foreground color as you begin to smear the pixels.

- **Blur and Sharpen tools:** These tools are the opposite of each other. The Blur tool softens hard edges and reduces details, and the Sharpen tool makes edges harder and more pronounced.

- **Dodge and Burn tools:** These tools are used, respectively, to lighten and darken the pixels of an image. For each tool, you can set the Range to lighten or darken the highlights, the midtones, or the shadows.

- **Sponge tool:** This tool increases or decreases the saturation of pixels in the image. For this tool, you can select a brush tip, a Flow amount, and a Mode to be either Saturate or Desaturate.

- **History Brush and Art History tools:** As you make changes to an image, you may want to return to the original image, but only in one section. The History Brush lets you paint over pixels and replace the painted area with the pixel from the saved image file. The History palette keeps a list of commands applied to the current image. From this palette you can choose a specific state and snapshot to restore as you paint.

  The Art History brush, like the History Brush tool, replaces the painted pixels with pixels from the original saved image file, but it paints them using a specialized Style simulating various famous artistic painting methods. These styles include Tight Short, Tight Medium, Tight Long, Loose Medium, Loose Long, Dab, Tight Curl, Tight Curl Long, Loose Curl, and Loose Curl Long.

Summary

- Photoshop allows you to acquire images from scanners and digital cameras and includes tools to clean up problems such as red eye and lens flaws.

- Many of Photoshop's key features let you correct and adjust images. You can make tonal adjustments with the Levels and Curves dialog boxes.

- In addition to acquiring loaded images, Photoshop also can create custom images using the Painting tools and a robust set of paintbrushes.

- You also can obtain images by rasterizing vector objects from Illustrator, but the reverse also is possible with Illustrator's Live Trace feature.

- Photoshop includes several tools for selecting pixels including the Marquee tools and freehand tools like the Lasso tool. The Quick Select tool makes choosing odd-shaped selections easy. Pixels with similar colors are selected using the Magic Wand tool.

- However you decide to obtain Photoshop images, you have many tools to edit them, including features such as Crop and tools such as the Stamp and Healing Brush tools.

Chapter 12

Transforming Objects and Images

After you select objects, you can easily move them by clicking and dragging them to a new location. You also can move selected images using Photoshop's Move tool, but there is much more to transforming than just dragging an object or image to a new location.

The CS4 applications include many different ways to transform objects and images. You also can use the bounding box that surrounds a selection to rotate and scale an object. Understanding the visual cursor cues allows you to transform objects without bothering with tools or menus.

Within the Photoshop, Illustrator, InDesign, and Flash toolboxes are several tools that are used to transform objects, such as the Rotate tool, the Scale tool, the Reflect tool, the Shear tool, and the Free Transform tool. If you choose Object ⇨ Transform or go to the Transform palette in Illustrator and InDesign, you can find even more features that enable you to transform objects in multiple ways with a single action.

In addition to covering altering a selection's position and orientation, this chapter also discusses stacking order, alignment, and distribution, all of which are nothing more than special transformation cases.

IN THIS CHAPTER

Transforming objects, fills, and images

Arranging stacking order

Aligning and distributing objects and images

Transforming Objects in Illustrator

Objects are found in most of the CS4 applications. The various transformation methods let you place those objects into the precise location needed to create an appealing design. Acrobat and Dreamweaver are the oddballs among the group. In Acrobat, you can rotate pages and you can move objects, but you have no options for transforming objects on a PDF page. Dreamweaver allows only the placement of layers, and transformations of these layers are limited. The remaining CS4 applications offer you tools and methods for transforming objects.

A selected object or group is identified by a bounding box that surrounds the object. The color of this bounding box is the layer color. If multiple objects are selected, the bounding box encompasses all the selected objects, as shown in Figure 12.1.

CROSS-REF   Selecting objects is covered in Chapter 9.

FIGURE 12.1

Selected objects are surrounded by a bounding box, which is the same color as the layer where the object appears.

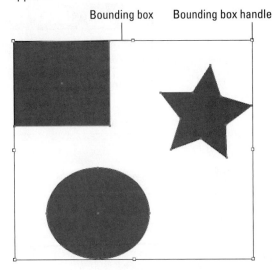

You can move and scale even the simplest objects in most of the CS4 applications using the bounding box. Clicking inside the bounding box and dragging moves the selected object. Dragging on one of the handles that surrounds the object scales its size. But these actions are common features, and the bounding-box features covered next enable a wider range of transformations.

Using the bounding box

Perhaps the easiest and certainly the quickest way to transform objects is to use the selection's bounding box. You can use bounding-box transformations in Illustrator, Photoshop, InDesign, Flash, and Dreamweaver (except for rotate).

For all these applications, the bounding box is always rectangular and includes transformation handles at each corner and along each edge. By dragging these handles, you can scale or rotate an object using the Selection tool. Dreamweaver lets you scale objects, but doesn't let you move or rotate objects.

> **NOTE** In Illustrator, you can hide the bounding box by choosing View ⇨ Show/Hide Bounding Box (Shift+Ctrl+B in Windows; Shift+⌘+B on the Mac), or in Photoshop, by disabling the Show Transform Controls option in the Control panel when the Move tool is selected or by selecting the Edit ⇨ Free Transform (Ctrl[cmd]+T) command. If the bounding box isn't visible when an object is selected, check these options.

Moving objects

To move selected objects, you simply need to click the object's path or fill and drag it to its new position. If you drag an object with the Option/Alt key held down, then a duplicate copy of the original object is moved and the original copy stays in its place. Holding down the Shift key while dragging an object constrains it to move along regular 45-degree angles. The Preferences dialog box includes a setting for the Custom Constrain Angle if you want to constrain the angle with the Shift key to something besides 45 degrees.

In addition to dragging with the mouse, you also can move objects using the arrow keys. The distance that the object moves when pressing each arrow key is determined by the Keyboard Increment value set in the General panel of the Preferences dialog box, shown in Figure 12.2. The default is set to 1 point. Holding down the Shift key while pressing an arrow key moves the selected object ten times the increment value.

Snapping Objects

You can control where an object moves in Illustrator by choosing View ⇨ Snap to Grid (Shift+Ctrl+" in Windows; Shift+⌘+" on the Mac) and View ⇨ Snap to Point (Alt+Ctrl+" in Windows; Option+⌘+" on the Mac).

If the Snap to Grid option is enabled, the corner points of objects that are moved snap to align with the grid intersection points. This enables you to precisely position objects relative to one another. Make grids visible by choosing View ⇨ Show/Hide Grids. Set the grid size using the Guides & Grids panel in the Preferences dialog box.

The Snap to Point option aligns the point under the cursor when the selected object is clicked to the anchor point of another object or to a guideline. The cursor turns white when it's over a point to which it can snap.

Photoshop, InDesign, and Flash also include snapping options. In Photoshop, you can select to snap to Guides, Grids, Slices, or Document Bounds using the View ⇨ Snap To menu command. Snapping functionality may be turned on and off using the View ⇨ Snap (Shift+⌘/Ctrl+;) menu command. InDesign includes commands in the View menu to Snap to Guides (Shift+⌘/Ctrl+;) and Snap to Document Grid (Shift+⌘/Ctrl+').

 In InDesign, you can use the Ctrl/⌘+Shift+arrow to move the selected object ¹⁄₁₀th of the designated keyboard increment.

CROSS-REF For more information on adjusting preferences, see Chapter 3.

FIGURE 12.2

The Keyboard Increment value in the General panel of the Preferences dialog box determines the amount an object moves when you press the arrow keys.

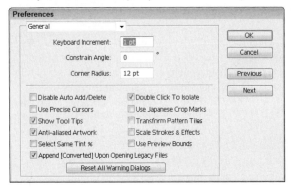

Rotating objects

When you move the Selection tool cursor near one of the bounding-box handles, the cursor changes. When the cursor looks like two small arrows and a curved line, you can drag the object to rotate it about its center point. Figure 12.3 shows three selected objects in Illustrator being rotated by dragging on the bounding box when the rotation cursor is visible.

Rotating an object also rotates its bounding box. If you want to reset the bounding box in Illustrator, you can choose Object ⇨ Transform ⇨ Reset Bounding Box.

When objects are selected in Photoshop, a Reference Point is positioned within the center of the object. If the object is moved or scaled, the reference point remains in the center, but if you click and drag, you can reposition the reference point. This reference point is used to define the center about which the object is rotated. It can be positioned anywhere within the canvas.

NOTE When an object is selected within InDesign, its bounding box doesn't enable rotation. InDesign objects can be rotated using the Object ⇨ Transform ⇨ Rotate menu command, the Free Transform tool, or the Rotation tool, but not using its bounding box. Flash lets you shear an object by dragging the corner of its bounding box. You can also bend object edges in Flash by dragging them away from the object.

FIGURE 12.3

When the rotation cursor displays, you can rotate the selected object about its center point.

Rotation cursor

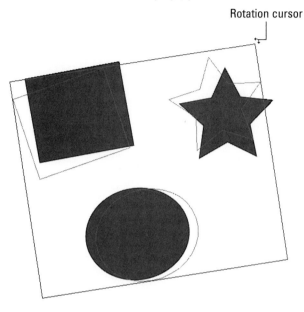

Scaling and reflecting objects

Positioning the cursor directly over one of the bounding-box handles changes it to a double-headed arrow, and dragging the object with this cursor scales the object, as shown in Figure 12.4. If you drag a corner, the object scales horizontally and vertically; if you drag one of the segment midpoint handles, the object scales in a single dimension.

Holding down the Shift key while dragging one of the corner handles constrains the scaling to be uniform so that no distortion is introduced. Holding down the Option/Alt key while dragging, scales the object about the center of the bounding box. Figure 12.5 shows an object that has been scaled with the Shift and Option/Alt keys held down. Notice how all objects have been scaled equally from the center outward.

FIGURE 12.4

Dragging a selected object when the scale cursor is displayed scales the object.

Scale cursor

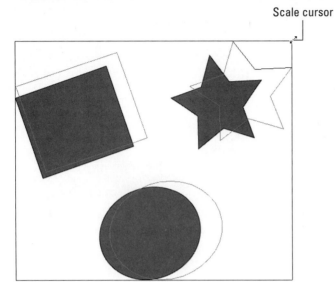

FIGURE 12.5

Scaling objects with the Shift key held down maintains the proportions of the object; with the Option/Alt key held down, it scales the objects about the selection center.

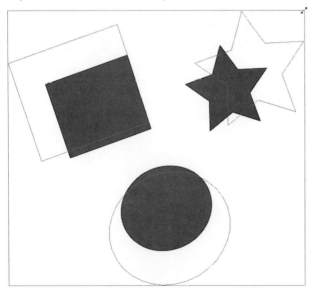

If you drag one of the handles through the object to its opposite side, the object is reflected about the bounding-box sides through which it was dragged.

Using the transform tools

The third section of tools in both the Illustrator Toolbox and the InDesign Toolbox includes several tools that you can use to transform objects. These tools include the Rotate, Scale, Reflect, Shear, and Free Transform tools, as shown in Figure 12.6. In InDesign, the Reflect and Rotate buttons are in the Control panel.

 **The Shear tool is located as a flyout under the Scale tool and the Reflect tool is a flyout under the Rotate tool in Illustrator. InDesign doesn't include a Reflect tool.**

FIGURE 12.6

Transform tools are found in the Toolbox in Illustrator and in InDesign.

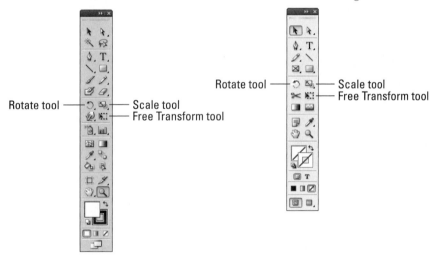

Double-clicking any of these tools opens a dialog box where you may enter precise values.

Using the Rotate tool

When the Rotate tool is selected, the rotation center for the selected object, called the reference point, is positioned in the center of the object as indicated by a small circle icon with four small lines extending from it, as shown in Figure 12.7. Dragging in the art board rotates the selected object, but if you click in the art board with the Rotate tool, you can position the rotation center. Any dragging then rotates about the new rotation center. Holding down the Shift key rotates the selected object using 45-degree increments.

FIGURE 12.7

The rotation reference point marks the center about which the rotation takes place.

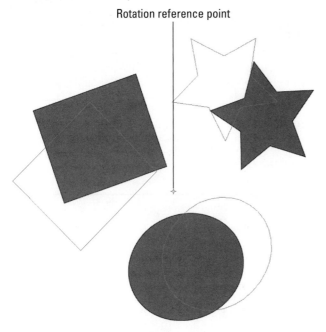

Rotation reference point

If you double-click the Rotate tool or choose Object ➪ Transform ➪ Rotate command in Illustrator or InDesign, a simple dialog box opens, shown in Figure 12.8. Here, you can enter a precise angle value. The Copy button rotates a duplicate copy of the object and leaves the original object in its place.

FIGURE 12.8

The Rotate dialog box

Using the Scale tool

The Scale tool works like the Rotate tool in that the scale point is positioned initially in the center of the selected object, but by clicking the art board, you can place it in a different location. Dragging up and down scales the selected object in the vertical direction; dragging left and right scales the selected object in the horizontal direction about the scale point. Holding down the Shift key while dragging at a 45-degree angle constrains the scaling, making it uniform or equal both horizontally and vertically.

Double-clicking the Scale tool or choosing Object ⇨ Transform ⇨ Scale opens a dialog box, shown in Figure 12.9, where you can choose to scale the selected object uniformly or non-uniformly using precise values. The Copy button scales a duplicate copy using the scale values and leaving the original object in place. You also can enable the Scale Strokes & Effects option, which scales, along with the object, any strokes and effects that were added to the object. If disabled, the strokes and effects maintain their original size and only the path is scaled.

FIGURE 12.9

The Scale dialog box lets you scale an object in a uniform or non-uniform manner.

Using the Reflect tool

The Reflect tool allows you to flip the selected object about an axis. To select the axis about which to flip the selected object, click once to place one point of the axis line and click a second time to define the second point of the axis line. When you click a second time, the selected object is reflected about this line. Figure 12.10 shows several selected objects that have been reflected about an imaginary axis created by clicking two times in the art board.

If you hold down the Option/Alt key while clicking the second point, a copy of the original object is reflected. If you drag after clicking the second point, you can control the position of the reflected object; holding down the Shift key constrains the axis to 45-degree increments.

FIGURE 12.10

FIGURE 12.10

The Reflect tool mirrors the selected object on the opposite side of a designated axis.

Reflect axis

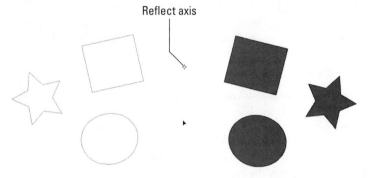

> **NOTE** The Reflect tool is available in Illustrator as a flyout under the Rotate tool, but you can flip and reflect objects in InDesign using the Control panel buttons and in Photoshop using menu commands.

The Reflect dialog box, shown in Figure 12.11, opened by double-clicking the Reflect tool or by choosing Object ➪ Transform ➪ Reflect, lets you reflect the selected object horizontally, vertically, or about a specified angle. The dialog box also includes a Copy button.

FIGURE 12.11

The Reflect dialog box lets you reflect the selected object horizontally, vertically, or about a designated angle.

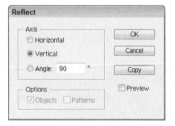

Using the Shear tool

The Shear tool is a flyout under the Scale tool in Illustrator and InDesign. It lets you distort the selected object by moving the opposite bounding-box edges in opposite directions. Dragging up and down shears the object vertically; dragging left and right shears the object horizontally. Clicking twice in the art board lets you place a shear axis, just like with the Reflect tool. If the shear axis is located below an object, the entire object slants in the same direction with portions farther from the shear axis being sheared to a greater extent. Holding down the Shift key maintains the height or width of the object as it's sheared. Figure 12.12 shows several objects that have been sheared to the right. The square background was added to make the shear effect more obvious.

FIGURE 12.12

Placing the shear axis below the object causes the entire object to be sheared in one direction.

The Shear dialog box, shown in Figure 12.13, lets you specify a shear angle and the shear axis as horizontal, vertical, or a specified angle.

FIGURE 12.13

The Shear dialog box lets you specify the amount of shear with the shear angle and the axis about which the shear takes place.

Using the Free Transform tool

The Free Transform tool enables you to perform all the transformations with a single tool. In many ways, it works just like the bounding box, but it has some additional features built in. Moving, rotating, scaling, and reflecting work just like with the bounding box, but you also can shear an object by holding down Ctrl+Alt (⌘+Option on the Mac) while dragging sideways on one of the side handles.

NOTE In Photoshop, you can enable free transformation of paths using the Edit ⇨ Free Transform Path (⌘/Ctrl+T) menu command. Dragging with the Ctrl[cmd]+ Alt[option] key causes a shear and Ctrl[cmd] dragging transforms a shape by pulling the edge.

Another unique feature of the Free Transform tool is that you can distort the selected object by moving a single bounding box corner without moving any of the other corner points. To do this, start dragging a corner handle and then press the ⌘/Ctrl key to move only the selected point. Figure 12.14 shows the selected objects in the process of being distorted in this way by dragging the upper-right corner handle.

FIGURE 12.14

You can distort the bounding box by moving a single corner handle by holding down the ⌘/Ctrl key and dragging with the Free Transform tool.

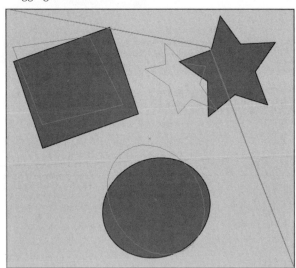

You also can use the Free Transform tool to alter perspective by moving two corner points at the same time. You can accomplish this by dragging a corner point and then holding down Shift+Ctrl+Alt (Shift+⌘+Option on the Mac) at the same time. Figure 12.15 shows an object whose perspective has been altered using the Free Transform tool.

FIGURE 12.15

Dragging a bounding box corner handle with the Free Transform tool while holding down Shift+Ctrl+Alt (Shift+⌘+Option on the Mac) alters an object's perspective.

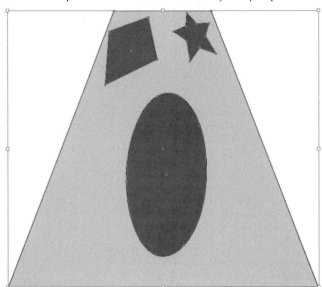

> **NOTE** The Free Transform tool has no dialog box that opens when you double-click the tool.

STEPS: Transforming in Illustrator

1. **Create a symbol.** Create a sample object in Illustrator, or drag an object from the Symbols palette. The symbol for these steps comes from the Logos Symbol Library accessed by choosing Window ➪ Symbol Libraries ➪ Logo Elements.

2. **Select the object.** With the Selection tool, click the symbol to select it. A bounding box surrounds the selected object.

3. **Create several duplicate copies.** Click the symbol, and begin to drag it downward. Then press and hold down the Shift and Option/Alt keys to create an aligned duplicate underneath the original. Repeat this step until six planets are aligned, as shown in Figure 12.16.

4. **Use the Rotate tool.** Select the second planet, and double-click the Rotate tool. In the Rotate dialog box, set the Angle value to 60 and click OK. The second planet is rotated so its rings are almost vertical.

FIGURE 12.16

Dragging an object with the Option/Alt key held down moves a duplicate copy and keeps the original.

5. **Use the Scale tool.** Select the third planet, and double-click the Scale tool. In the Scale dialog box, select the Non-Uniform option and set the Horizontal value to 60% and the Vertical value to 120%. Then click OK.

6. **Use the Reflect tool.** Select the fourth planet, and click the Scale tool. Click to the right of the planet, and click again directly below the first click to form a vertical axis. Drag with the Option/Alt key held down to create a reflected duplicate of the planet to the right.

7. **Use the Shear tool.** Select the fifth planet, and double-click the Shear tool. In the Shear dialog box, enter **45** for the Shear Angle and choose the Horizontal axis. Then click OK. The planet is elongated by fitting it into a stretched bounding box.

8. **Use the Free Transform tool.** Select the sixth planet, and choose the Free Transform tool. Drag the upper-right corner while holding down the Option/Alt key to scale the object about its center. Figure 12.17 shows all the resulting transformed planets.

FIGURE 12.17

Each of these planets was transformed using a different transform tool.

Using the Transform menu

The Object ⇨ Transform menu in Illustrator and InDesign includes several commands to open the dialog boxes for the various transform tools. You may access these same dialog boxes by double-clicking the respective tool in the Toolbox, but the Transform menu in Illustrator also includes some additional commands such as Transform Again, Transform Each, and Reset Bounding Box. In Illustrator, choosing Object ⇨ Transform ⇨ Move (Shift+Ctrl+M in Windows; Shift+⌘+M on the Mac) opens the Move dialog box, shown in Figure 12.18, where you can enter precise values to move an object. You also can move objects by selecting an Angle and Distance values.

FIGURE 12.18

The Move dialog box lets you specify an object's horizontal and vertical position values or move an object a given distance along a specified angle.

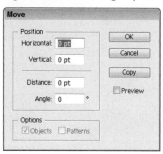

Photoshop also includes several menu commands for transforming paths. These are located in the Edit ➪ Transform Path menu and include commands such as Again, Scale, Rotate, Skew, Distort, Perspective, and several Rotate and Flip options. None of these menu commands opens a dialog box, but each allows the path's bounding box to be transformed in a certain way. If the active layer includes pixels or text, they also can be transformed by choosing Edit ➪ Transform.

Using Transform Again

Choosing Object ➪ Transform ➪ Transform Again (⌘/Ctrl+D) in Illustrator repeats the last transformation again. This enables you to quickly create multiple aligned copies of an object.

For example, if you select and move an object downward with the Shift and Option/Alt keys held down, the result is a duplicate copy of the object that is positioned directly under the first. After this is done, you can use the Transform Again menu command to quickly create a whole column of objects.

A similar command is found in Photoshop, Edit ➪ Transform ➪ Again (Shift+Ctrl+T in Windows; Shift+⌘+T on the Mac). This command repeats the last applied transformation, which may include multiple transformations, to the selected object.

STEPS: Creating an Array of Objects in Illustrator

1. **Create an object to duplicate.** Create or select an object that you want to duplicate many times in a repeating pattern. A simple symbol like this planet may be used.

2. **Select the object.** With the Selection tool, click the symbol to select it. A bounding box surrounds the selected object.

3. **Create a single duplicate copy.** Click the symbol, and begin to drag the symbol downward. Then press and hold the Shift and Option/Alt keys to create an aligned duplicate underneath the original.

4. **Use the Transform Again command.** Choose Object ⇨ Transform Again (⌘/Ctrl+D) to repeat the transformation. This creates a third planet object that is moved the same distance as the first duplicate. Hold down the ⌘/Ctrl key, and press the D key six more times to create a column of planets that are equally spaced, as shown in Figure 12.19.

FIGURE 12.19

You can choose Object ⇨ Transform ⇨ Transform Each to quickly and precisely repeat a transformation operation several times.

5. **Select the column of planets.** With the Selection tool, drag over the entire column of planets to select them all.

6. **Create a duplicate column.** Begin to drag the selected planets to the right, and then press and hold down the Shift and Option/Alt keys to constrain the movements of the planets to the horizon, and the Option/Alt key creates a duplicate column of planets.

7. **Use the Transform Again command.** Choose Object ➪ Transform Again (⌘/Ctrl+D) and press the ⌘/Ctrl+D keyboard shortcut four more times. The resulting array of planets, shown in Figure 12.20, was created fairly quickly.

FIGURE 12.20

By duplicating and transforming objects and then using the Transform Again menu command, you can quickly and easily create an array of objects.

> **TIP** Another technique to accomplish this same task in InDesign is to use the Edit ➪ Step and Repeat. This feature creates rows and columns of duplicated objects. To use it, simply select the object to duplicate and choose the command, and then specify the repeat count and the offsets and click OK.

Using Transform Again in InDesign

The Transform Again feature also is found in InDesign. Every transformation applied to an object is remembered and can be reapplied to another selection using the Object ➪ Transform Again menu command. Transformations that are remembered include moving, scaling, rotating, resizing, reflecting, shearing, and fitting.

The Transform Again menu in InDesign includes four options:

- **Transform Again:** This option applies the last single transformation to the selected object, not to the individual objects within the selection.

- **Transform Again Individually:** This option applies the last single transformation to all selected objects separately instead of as a group.

- **Transform Sequence Again:** This option applies the last sequence of transformations to the selected object.

- **Transform Sequence Again Individually:** This option applies the last sequence of transformations to all selected objects separately instead of as a group.

Using the Transform Each dialog box

In Illustrator, choosing Object ⇨ Transform ⇨ Transform Each (Alt+Shit+Ctrl+D in Windows; Option+Shift+⌘+D on the Mac) opens the Transform Each dialog box, shown in Figure 12.21. This dialog box combines several transformations into a single location and includes Scale, Move, and Rotate values. It also includes options to Reflect an object about the X or Y axis.

FIGURE 12.21

The Transform Each dialog box combines the transformation values of several different transformations into a single dialog box.

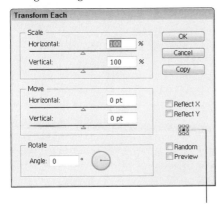

Reference point selector

The small icon underneath the Reflect options lets you select the point about which the selected object is transformed. The selected transformation point is marked black. You can click any of these points to specify the transformation point, which could be the object center, any object corner, or any object side.

The Random option chooses a random value between the default value and the specified value and applies the transformation using these random values. To see some of the random possibilities, enable and disable the Preview option multiple times to see some of the random transformations. Figure 12.22 shows many random stars created using the Random option in the Transform Each dialog box.

FIGURE 12.22

Enabling the Random option in the Transform Each dialog box produced a varied assortment of stars.

STEPS: Creating a Flower in Illustrator

1. **Create a simple path.** Click the Paintbrush tool, and drag in the art board to create a simple, mostly vertical line. In the Stroke palette, set the Weight to 3 pt, select the Round Cap button, and set the color to a dark red, as shown in Figure 12.23.

You can place the path near the middle of the document to create a simple path with the Paintbrush tool.

2. **Open the Transform Each dialog box.** Choose Object ➪ Transform ➪ Transform Each (Alt+Shift+Ctrl+D in Windows; Option+Shift+⌘+D on the Mac) to open the Transform Each dialog box. Set the Horizontal and Vertical Scale values to 100% and the Move values to 0. Then set the Rotate value to 360 degrees, select the center point as the reference point, and enable the Random option. Then click Copy to close the dialog box and create a copy that is randomly rotated about its center point. Figure 12.24 shows the Transform Each dialog box after the values have been set.

The Transform Each dialog box with the Random option enabled randomly rotates the selected object.

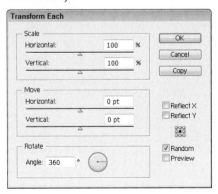

3. **Create duplicate objects.** With the duplicate selected, reopen the Transform Each dialog box using the Alt+Shift+Ctrl+D (Option+Shift+⌘+D) keyboard shortcut, and click Copy again or simply press Command/Ctrl+D. Repeat this step until enough copies are created to fill in the flower.

4. **Add a flower center.** Create a simple circle with the Ellipse tool, and set its fill color to a bright yellow. Then drag the circle to the center of the flower. The resulting flower is shown in Figure 12.25.

FIGURE 12.25
_____

Using the random option in the Transform Each dialog box and the Copy button, you can create a flower.

Rotating and flipping InDesign objects

You can quickly rotate and/or flip selected objects in InDesign using the commands in the Object ➪ Transform menu and the buttons in the Control panel. The menu commands found there include Rotate 180 Degrees, Rotate 90 Degrees Clockwise, Rotate 90 Degrees Counterclockwise, Flip Horizontal, Flip Vertical, and Flip Both. There is even a simple graphic that shows whether the object is flipped or mirrored.

InDesign also includes a feature to rotate the spread view about 90-degree increments.

Rotating and flipping in Photoshop

Photoshop includes some menu commands found in the Edit ⇨ Transform Path menu to rotate and/or flip the selected object. The options include Rotate 180 Degrees, Rotate 90 Degrees CS, Rotate 90 Degrees CCW, Flip Horizontal, and Flip Vertical. The commands apply to text and pixels also.

Photoshop also includes commands to rotate and flip the entire Canvas. These commands are useful if you need to transform all objects. The commands are located in the Image ⇨ Rotate Canvas menu and include 180 Degrees, 90 Degrees CW, 90 Degrees CCW, Arbitrary (which lets you select an Angle value), Flip Canvas Horizontal, and Flip Canvas Vertical.

Using the Transform palette

In addition to the bounding box, tools, and menus, several of the CS4 applications include a Transform palette including Illustrator, InDesign, and Flash.

Using the Transform palette in Illustrator and InDesign

Illustrator's Transform palette, shown in Figure 12.26 and which you can open by choosing Window ⇨ Transform, displays information about the object's position and size. By changing these values, you can transform the selected object. The Transform palette in InDesign looks and acts the same.

FIGURE 12.26

The Transform palette displays information about the position and dimensions of the selected object.

Constrain Height and Width

Reference point

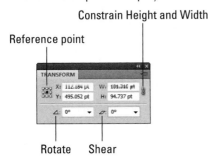

Rotate   Shear

The X and Y values denote the horizontal and vertical positions of the reference point selected using the icon at the left of the Transform palette relative to the art board's lower-left corner. For example, if the object's center point is selected and the object is positioned on the page 100 points above the bottom of the art board and 50 points from the left edge, then the X and Y values in the

Transform palette would be 100 pt and 50 pt. Changing the X and Y values in the Transform palette moves the selected object. The X and Y values are measured from the upper-left corner in Photoshop, InDesign, Flash, and Dreamweaver, but Illustrator measures X and Y values from the lower-left corner. InDesign also has several different measurement options that deal with the spine positions and spreads.

> **NOTE**   All the same values found in the Transform palette also are displayed in the Control panel panel in InDesign and in the Properties panel in Flash.

The W and H values denote the object's Width and Height. Clicking the link icon to the right of these values links the values together, so that changing one automatically changes the other. Changing the W and H values in the Transform palette scales the selected object. If the link icon is enabled, changing the values causes the selected object to be scaled uniformly. The Width and Height values are located in the Control panel.

At the bottom of the Transform palette are Rotate and Shear values. Changing these values causes the selected object to be rotated or sheared the given amount. InDesign's Transform palette also includes values for the Scale X and Scale Y Percentage values. These values can be linked to stay equal.

Illustrator's Transform palette also may be used to reflect the selected object using the Flip Horizontal or Flip Vertical palette menu commands. The palette menu also includes an option to Scale Strokes & Effects and options to Transform the object only, the pattern only, or both.

The palette menu options for the Transform palette in InDesign are different than the options in Illustrator. Within InDesign, you can select options to Scale Text Attributes, Transform Group Content, and Reset Scaling to 100%. You also have options to Rotate and Flip the selected object.

At the bottom of InDesign's Transform palette menu are several toggle options that can be enabled including Transform Content, Dimensions Include Stroke Weight, Transformations are Totals, Show Content Offset, and Scale Strokes. The Transform Content option causes the content within the selected frame to be transformed along with the frame when enabled. The Dimensions Include Stroke Weight option changes the Width and Height displayed values to include the stroke weight.

The Transformations are Totals option causes the displayed transformation values to be absolute relative to the document. For example, if a selected image inside a rotated frame also is rotated even further, enabling the Transformation are Totals option displays the image's angle relative to the bottom of the document page, and disabling the Transformations are Total option displays a rotation value that includes the rotation values of both the image and its frame.

The Show Content Offset option is used when content is selected within the frame. It displays the amount that the content is offset from the frame's reference point. When an offset value is displayed, two small plus signs appear next to the X and Y values, as shown in Figure 12.27.

FIGURE 12.27

Two small plus signs appear in InDesign's Transform palette when the Show Content Offset option is enabled.

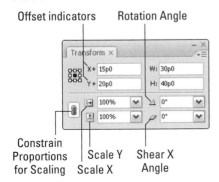

Offset indicators   Rotation Angle

Constrain
Proportions   Scale Y   Shear X
for Scaling   Scale X   Angle

Transforming Patterns and Fills

When an object is filled with a solid color, rotating the object has no affect on the fill color. However, if an object is filled with a gradient or a pattern, rotating an object may or may not impact the filled gradient or pattern depending on the setting in the Transform palette.

Transforming patterns in Illustrator

Using Illustrator's Transform palette menu, you can select to apply a transformation to the object only, the pattern only, or to both. When the Pattern Only option is selected, a small warning icon appears in the lower-left corner of the Transform palette, as shown in Figure 12.28, to remind you that any transformations are applied only to the pattern.

NOTE   Selecting the Pattern Only option in the Transform palette applies only to transformations that are done using the Transform palette. Transformations completed using the transform tools or by choosing Object ➪ Transform are determined by the respective transformation dialog boxes.

FIGURE 12.28

A small warning icon appears in the lower-left corner of the Transform palette when the Pattern Only option is selected.

Rotate Pattern Only warning icon

To transform a pattern or gradient using one of the transform tools or the Object ⇨ Transform menu, you need to enable the Patterns option in the dialog box for the selected transformation. Each transform dialog box includes options for selecting objects and patterns. Enabling the Patterns option applies the transformation to the pattern.

STEPS: Rotating a Pattern in Illustrator

1. **Create a filled object.** Select the Ellipse tool, and drag in the art board to create a simple ellipse object. In the Swatches palette, select a striped pattern as the fill. The stripes run horizontally across the ellipse object, as shown in Figure 12.29.

FIGURE 12.29

An ellipse object filled with a striped pattern that runs horizontally across the object

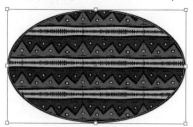

2. **Select and duplicate the object.** With the Selection tool, click the ellipse object to select it. Then drag it downward with the Option/Alt key held down to create a duplicate copy.

3. **Create a single duplicate copy.** Then choose Object ⇨ Transform ⇨ Transform Again to duplicate another ellipse for a total of three.

4. **Enable the Transform Pattern Only option.** Choose Window ⇨ Transform to open the Transform palette. In the palette menu, select the Transform Pattern Only option. A warning icon appears in the bottom-left corner of the Transform palette.

5. **Rotate the pattern.** Select the second ellipse object, and type **45** in the Rotate field of the Transform palette. The pattern within the ellipse is rotated.

6. **Enable the Transform Both option.** In the Transform palette menu, select the Transform Both option.

7. **Rotate the pattern.** Select the third ellipse object, and type **90** in the Rotate field of the Transform palette. The pattern and the ellipse are both rotated. Figure 12.30 shows the resulting rotations.

> **TIP** An easy way to transform an object's fill pattern is to hold down the Tilde "~" key while using the Selection, Scale, Reflect, and Shear tools.

FIGURE 12.30

Using the options available in the Transform palette, you can rotate just the object, just the pattern, or both.

Transforming patterns in Photoshop

When a path or shape is created in Photoshop, it is automatically filled with the Foreground color. This color of the selected object may be changed to a pattern or a fill using the Layer ⇨ New Fill Layer ⇨ Pattern menu command. Applying this menu command opens a dialog box, shown in Figure 12.31, where you can select a pattern from the available presets and set the Scale of the pattern. The Snap to Origin button realigns the pattern so the upper-left corner of the pattern corresponds to the upper-left corner of the object.

After a pattern or a gradient is applied to a path or shape, a fill thumbnail appears in the Layers palette next to the Vector Mask. Double-clicking this fill thumbnail in the Layers palette opens the Pattern Fill dialog box again where you can change the Scale value.

FIGURE 12.31

The Pattern Fill dialog box lets you scale the pattern used to fill an object. A similar scale setting also is available for Gradients.

CROSS-REF **More on working with layers is covered in Chapter 25.**

A pixel selection also may be filled with a pattern using the Layer ⇨ New Fill Layer ⇨ Pattern menu command. This menu command creates a new layer and opens a dialog box where you can name the layer, choose a layer color, and set the blending mode and Opacity value. The Pattern Fill dialog box opens, letting you select a pattern and set a scale value.

Another way to apply a pattern to a layer is with the Pattern Overlay layer effect. To apply a layer effect, select a layer in the Layers palette and choose the Layer ⇨ Layer Style ⇨ Pattern Overlay menu command. Layer effects may be applied to any layer, and all pixels or objects on that layer are covered with the selected pattern. Using the Layer Style dialog box, shown in Figure 12.32, you can set the pattern's blending mode, Opacity, and Scale.

FIGURE 12.32

The Layer Style dialog box lets you overlay an object with a pattern. The pattern also may be scaled.

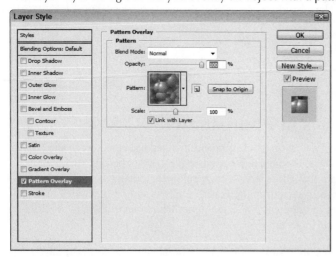

NOTE Although patterns may be scaled and repositioned in Photoshop, you cannot rotate a pattern after it is applied. Gradients, however, include both Angle and Scale controls that allow you to rotate and scale applied gradients.

Transforming content in InDesign

InDesign is unique in how it handles content positioned within objects because all content in InDesign are placed within containers such as a frame or a drawn object. Images and drawings are added to a document using the File ⇨ Place menu command. InDesign lets you change, move, rotate, and scale a container and its content together or independently.

With a frame that holds some content selected, the Control panel lists the position and dimensions of the selected frame, as well as its Scale, Rotate, and Shear values. From the Object ⇨ Select menu, you can select to work with the Container or with the Content. You also have options to select the previous or next object in a group. If you select the content, then the values in the Control panel are updated, a new bounding box appears that shows the dimensions of the content, and all transform tools may be used to transform the content independent of the container.

When a filled container is selected, the Object ⇨ Fitting menu includes several options for synching the size of the content with the container. These options include the following:

- **Fit Content to Frame:** Scales the placed image to fit the frame.
- **Fit Frame to Content:** Scales the frame to fit the placed image.
- **Fill Frame Proportionally:** Proportionally scales the frame to fill the image.
- **Fit Content Proportionally:** Proportionally scales the placed image to fit within the frame.
- **Center Content:** Moves the placed image so its center matches the frame without scaling the image.

The keyboard shortcuts are Fit Content to Frame (Option/Alt+⌘/Ctrl+E), Fit Frame to Content (Option/Alt+⌘/Ctrl+C), Fill Frame Proportionally (Shift+Option/Alt+⌘/Ctrl+C), Center Content (Shift+⌘/Ctrl+E), and Fit Content Proportionally (Option/Alt+Shift+⌘/Ctrl+E). Figure 12.33 shows each of these options applied to an image placed in a frame.

NOTE When working with placed graphics in InDesign, you can double click the graphic to toggle between the Selection and Direct Selection tools and quickly access either the frame or the contents of the frame.

FIGURE 12.33

InDesign includes several methods for automatically scaling content and frames.

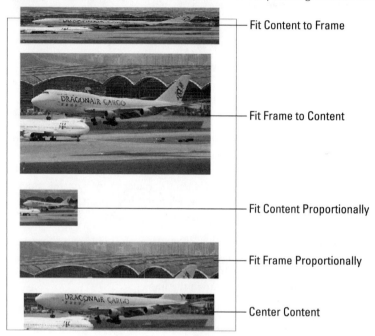

— Fit Content to Frame

— Fit Frame to Content

— Fit Content Proportionally

— Fit Frame Proportionally

— Center Content

Transforming Images in Photoshop

Images in Illustrator and InDesign are contained within objects and may not be selected or edited using pixel selections. But in Photoshop, pixel selections are very common, and they have several tricky aspects when dealing with transformations. One of the key differences between transforming objects and transforming images is that image selections are usually not rectangular, depending on the selection tool that was used. But if the Move tool is selected, a rectangular bounding box is placed about the selection. Using the bounding box, you can move, rotate, and scale the selected pixels in a manner that is the same as that used for objects.

Another key aspect of transforming images is that every time you apply a transformation to a pixel selection, you potentially alter the selection. Applying multiple successive transformations to a pixel selection distorts the pixels. To limit this effect, Photoshop keeps track of all the transformations that are made to a pixel selection at one time. Then when a different tool is selected, a confirmation dialog box, shown in Figure 12.34, appears asking if you want to apply the transformation with buttons for Apply, Cancel, and Don't Apply. By waiting until all the desired transformations are completed before applying them, the number of actual transformations is minimized and the fidelity of the pixel selection is maximized.

FIGURE 12.34

This confirmation dialog appears after several transformation operations have been combined within Photoshop.

Transforming a selection

When a selection is made, marching ants surround the selection and show the selected area. If you choose the Select ⇨ Transform Selection menu command, then a bounding box surrounds the selection. Using this bounding box, the options in the Options bar, or the Edit ⇨ Transform menu commands, you can transform the selection without altering the pixels within the selection.

Moving pixels

When an area of pixels is selected with one of the Marquee tools, dragging the selection with the Marquee tool has no impact on the pixels; instead, it moves only the selection. To move the selected pixels, you need to select the Move tool. With the Move tool selected, you can click within the selection and drag it to move the actual pixels. Figure 12.35 shows an image where a pixel selection has been moved using the Move tool.

FIGURE 12.35

Moving a pixel selection with the Move tool can abruptly alter the continuity of an image.

Holding down the Option/Alt key while dragging a pixel selection creates a duplicate copy of the pixels and leaves the original pixels in place. Holding down the Shift key while dragging a pixel selection constrains the movement to regular 45-degree angles.

Using Free Transform

Photoshop's Edit ⇨ Free Transform (⌘/Ctrl+T) menu command places a bounding box around the selection or encloses all objects on the current layer within a bounding box if there is no selection.

This bounding box works just like the bounding boxes used to transform objects. Clicking within the bounding box and dragging moves the selection. Dragging one of the corner or side handles scales the selection; moving the cursor near one of the handles until it changes to a rotation icon allows you to rotate the selection. You also can reflect an object by dragging it through its opposite side.

Holding down the Shift key while dragging a corner handle causes uniform scaling; holding down the Shift key while moving constrains the movements to 45-degree angles; and holding down the Shift key while rotating constrains the rotations to 15-degree increments. To scale opposite handles relative to the reference point, hold down the Option/Alt key while dragging. To move a corner handle independent of the other corner handles, hold down the ⌘/Ctrl key while dragging. To shear the selection, hold down the Shift+Ctrl keys (Shift+⌘ on the Mac) while dragging a side handle. Finally, to alter perspective, drag with the Shift+Alt+Ctrl keys (Shift+Option+⌘ on the Mac) held down.

With the Free Transform command selected, the values for the various transformations appear on the Options bar, as shown in Figure 12.36. The Reference Point icon lets you select the position about which the transformations take place. The X and Y values denote the position of the reference point relative to the upper-left corner of the image. The W and H values denote the Width and Height of the selection's bounding box. The final three values are the rotation, horizontal, and vertical shear values.

NOTE The link icon between the W and H values links the W and H values together so that altering one automatically alters the other. This causes all scaling to be uniform.

FIGURE 12.36

When the Free Transform command is selected, various transformation values appear in the Options bar.

Using the Transform menu

In Photoshop, choosing Edit ⇨ Transform ⇨ Again (Shift+Ctrl+T in Windows; Shift+⌘+T on the Mac) causes the last transformation to be repeated.

If remembering all the various keyboard keys to use for the various transformations is tricky, you can select the specific type of transformation that you want to apply to the object from the Edit ⇨ Transform menu. The options include Scale, Rotate, Skew, Distort, and Perspective.

The Edit ➪ Transform menu also includes commands to rotate 180 degrees, rotate 90 degrees clockwise, rotate 90 degrees counterclockwise, flip horizontal, and flip vertical. The rotations and flipping takes place about the designated reference point.

Controlling perspective

Photoshop includes a transform feature for changing the perspective of an image selection. With a selection made, choose Edit ➪ Transform ➪ Perspective and the selection is surrounded with a handled box. Clicking and dragging any of the corner or edge handles changes the perspective for the selection. Figure 12.37 shows an example where a portion of an image has been altered in its perspective.

CROSS-REF Photoshop includes a valuable feature for setting and painting in perspective view called Vanishing Point. This feature is covered in Chapter 13.

FIGURE 12.37

Choose Edit ➪ Transform ➪ Perspective to change the perspective of the selected area.

You also can set perspective using the Crop tool by enabling the Perspective option in the Control panel. This tool changes the perspective when the image is cropped.

Using Image Warp

In addition to the Free Transform mode, Photoshop includes another unique transformation method called Warp mode. Warp mode covers the current selection with a grid that you can modify by dragging its control points.

To access Warp mode, choose Edit ➪ Transform ➪ Warp. This makes the Warp commands available in the Control panel at the top of the interface. The warp settings on the Control panel include a drop-down list of warp presets including Arc, Arc Lower, Arc Upper, Arch, Bulge, Shell Lower, Shell Upper, Flag, Wave, Fish, Rise, Fisheye, Inflate, Squeeze, and Twist. When a warp preset is selected, settings for controlling the amount of bend and vertical and horizontal distortion display to the left of the drop-down list in the Control panel. This panel also contains a button for controlling the warp orientation.

CROSS-REF If the warp presets look familiar, then you probably remember seeing them in Illustrator's Effects menu or in Photoshop's Type Warp presets. You can see examples of each in Chapter 13.

At the right end of the Control panel are buttons for switching between Warp and Free Transform modes and for canceling or committing the transform. Figure 12.38 shows an image warped with the Squeeze preset.

FIGURE 12.38

Using the Transform Warp Mode, you can bend twist and distort image selections.

Arranging Stacking Order

The order in which objects are displayed or printed is determined by the stacking order in Illustrator and InDesign. This order places the object at the bottom of the stacking order on the document first and then stacks each additional object in order on the document up to the top object based on their layers. If an object that is higher in the stacking order is placed on top of an existing object, and if the top object doesn't include any transparency, the lower object is obscured.

When objects are created, each new object is placed higher in the stacking order than those already created.

Controlling stacking order using layers

The easiest way to control stacking order is using layers. Layers at the top of the Layers palette have a higher stacking order and appear on top of all layers below it. By placing objects on a new higher layer, you may be assured that it appears above the objects on a lower layer.

 **Layers and the Layers palette are covered in more detail in Chapter 25.**

Layers provide a way to control stacking order, but within a single layer, objects may be stacked on top of one another. If you expand a layer in Illustrator by clicking the arrow button to the left of the layer name, all objects within the layer are visible, as shown in Figure 12.39. The expanded objects in the Layers palette are listed in their stacking order with the top objects toward the top of the Layers palette.

FIGURE 12.39

You can make all the objects contained on a single layer visible by expanding the layer.

If you select a layer in the Layers palette and drop it above another object, the stacking order is changed.

You also can reverse the order of several objects or layers using the Reverse Order palette menu command in the Layers palette. To use this command, select several adjacent objects or layers by selecting a layer, holding down the Shift key, clicking the last sequential layer, and then selecting the Reverse Order palette menu command.

Illustrator also includes the Object ➪ Arrange ➪ Send to Current Layer menu command, which moves the selected object to the current layer.

Changing stacking order with the Arrange menu

You also can control an object's position in the stacking order within a layer using the Object ➪ Arrange menu, found in Illustrator and InDesign.

The Object ➪ Arrange menu includes the following commands:

- Bring to Front (Shift+Ctrl+] in Windows; Shift+⌘+] on the Mac)
- Bring Forward (Ctrl+] in Windows; ⌘+] on the Mac)
- Send Backward (Ctrl+[in Windows; ⌘+[on the Mac)
- Send to Back (Shift+Ctrl+[in Windows; Shift+⌘+[on the Mac)

The Bring to Front and Send to Back menu commands move the selected object to the very top or very bottom of the stacking order, and the Bring Forward and Send Backward menu commands move the selected object forward or backward one place in the stacking order. With these commands, you can quickly arrange the objects within a layer.

Changing stacking order with the Clipboard

Another way to change the stacking order of objects in Illustrator is to copy and paste them using the Edit ➪ Paste in Front (⌘/Ctrl+F) and the Edit ➪ Paste in Back (⌘/Ctrl+B) menu commands. These commands paste the object in front of or behind the selected object.

If no object is selected or if the Edit ➪ Paste (⌘/Ctrl+V) menu command is used, the object is pasted at the top of the stacking order for the selected layer.

Changing stacking order within a group

Objects within a group also have a stacking order, but only within Illustrator. You can alter a group's stacking order by expanding the group in the Layers palette and dragging the one object above another, or by selecting an object within the group with the Group Selection tool and using the Object ➪ Arrange menu commands to alter its order.

Stacking order in Photoshop and Flash

The concept of objects in Photoshop is much more limited that Illustrator and InDesign, but you can work with objects in Photoshop. However, the stacking order of Photoshop objects is controlled by their layers, except for the Background layer, which always appears at the bottom of the layer's stack.

Flash allows groups and symbols to have a stacking order that can be manipulated, but objects within a layer don't have a stacking order.

Changing Z-Index in Dreamweaver

Most objects on a Web page cannot be stacked on top of one another. The exception to this rule is Dreamweaver layers, which are called AP DIVs. The stacking order for Dreamweaver layers is determined by a Z-Index value, which is set in the Properties palette for the selected layer. Layers with a higher Z-Index value appear in front of layers with a lower value.

Aligning and Distributing Objects

To create aesthetic designs, there are times when you'll want to precisely orient two or more objects together. You can do this by recording the position values of the various objects and then changing those values for one of the objects to align it with the other one, but these can be time consuming if you have lots of objects to align. Instead of a manual process, all the CS4 applications include palettes and controls that make aligning and distributing objects easy.

Commands to align and distribute objects are contained on the Control panel in Photoshop, Illustrator, and InDesign and in the Align palette (shown in Figure 12.40) for Illustrator, InDesign, and Flash. Dreamweaver offers align commands in a menu. You can access this palette by choosing Window ➪ Align (Shift+F7). The panel includes several icon buttons that align or distribute the selected objects to an edge or center.

Illustrator offers a command to align and distribute individual points. To use this feature, select several points with the Direct Selection tool, and the align and distribute buttons appear on the Control panel. You can also align points to the artboard of to a crop area.

FIGURE 12.40

The Align palette includes several rows of buttons used to align and distribute multiple objects.

Before you use an align or distribute icon button, you must select more than one object with the Selection tool. When you select one of the align or distribute icons, you can move all the selected objects to match the edge or center of the selection boundary box. However, if you click one of the objects after making the selection, that object becomes the Key Object and you must complete all alignment using the Key Object's center and edges.

If you select the wrong object as the Key Object, you can use the Cancel Key Object palette menu command to cancel the existing key object and select a new key object or you can just click the preferred key object with the Key Object tool to set it when the Align to Key Object option in the Options bar is selected. The Key Object is displayed with a bold border.

> **NOTE** The Align and Distribute buttons have no affect on objects that have been locked, except in InDesign where a locked object can be selected and used as a key object.

Aligning objects

To use the Align palette, select two or more objects that you want to align; then click the align icon in the Align palette for the alignment that you want. The align options include Align Left Edges, Align Vertical Centers, Align Right Edges, Align Top Edges, Align Horizontal Center, and Align Bottom Edges.

If you enable the Use Preview Bounds option in the Align palette menu, you can align the objects by their edges using the stroke width. If the Use Preview Bounds option is disabled, the objects are aligned by the path edge, denoted by the bounding box.

To align objects to the artboard edges, enable the Align to Artboard option in the Align palette menu. This option works for aligning objects to the center of the art board as well as the artboard edges.

Distributing objects

Distributing objects is different from aligning objects in that the distribution icons in the Align palette position the selected objects so that the distance between the selected edges or centers of the selected objects is equal. For example, if three objects are selected and the Distribute Vertical Centers button is clicked, then the middle object is moved so that the distance between the center of the bottom object and the middle object is equal to the distance between the center of the top object and the middle object.

The Distribution icons available in the Align palette include Distribute Top Edges, Distribute Vertical Centers, Distribute Bottom Edges, Distribute Left Edges, Distribute Horizontal Centers, and Distribute Right Edges. These options are also available in the Options bar at the top of the window.

Distributing spacing

If the Show Options palette menu command is selected, the Distribute Spacing buttons for Distribute Vertical Space and Distribute Horizontal Space appear. Using these buttons and the spacing value, you can space all the selected objects from the Key Object by the specified space amount.

The drop-down field at the bottom of the Align palette also includes an Auto option that automatically spaces the objects using an average of their current position. The Auto option also doesn't require that a Key Object be selected.

STEPS: Aligning Objects in InDesign

1. **Open an InDesign document.** Choose File ⇨ Open, and open an InDesign file that includes several misaligned objects like the images shown in Figure 12.41.

FIGURE 12.41

You can easily align randomly placed objects using the Align palette.

2. **Select all the objects to align.** With the Selection tool, drag over the top of all the objects that you want to align or hold down the Shift key and click each one individually.

3. **Aligning objects with the Align palette.** With the objects selected, choose Window ⇨ Object & Layout ⇨ Align (Shift+F7) to open the Align palette. Click the Align Bottom Edges button in the Align palette. The bottom edges of all the image objects are aligned, as shown in Figure 12.42.

FIGURE 12.42

The Align palette enables you to align all these image objects using the Align Bottom Edges button in the Align palette.

4. **Distribute the image objects.** The alignment of the image objects looks good, but the spacing between the objects is still a problem. To fix this, use one of the Distribution buttons in the Align palette. With the image objects still selected, click the Distribute Right Edges button in the Align palette. This action evenly spaces the image objects, as shown in Figure 12.43.

5. **Move the final objects.** As a final step, you'll want to drag the image objects upward slightly with the Selection tool. With all the objects selected and aligned, they move together, maintaining their alignment and spacing.

FIGURE 12.43

After distributing the image objects using their right edges, they line up perfectly spaced.

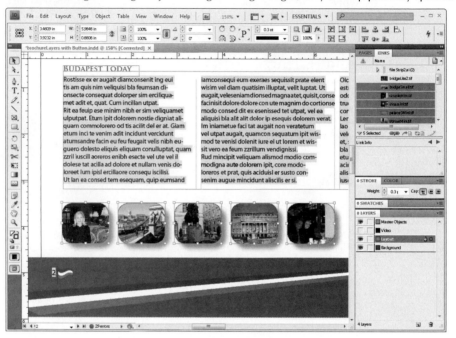

Aligning and Distributing Image Layers in Photoshop

Photoshop includes align buttons on the Control panel when the Move tool is selected. Using these buttons, you can align the current layer with the current selection. When three or more layers are selected, the distribution buttons become active on the Options bar.

Image selections may be aligned and distributed to a selected layer using the Move tool in Photoshop. With a selection made, click the Move tool. Several align and distribute icon buttons appear on the Options bar, as shown in Figure 12.44.

FIGURE 12.44

When you select the Move tool, several align and distribute buttons appear on the Options bar.

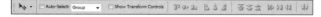

Aligning image layers

To align a selection to a layer, make an image selection, choose a layer in the Layers palette, and then click one of the align icon buttons in the Options bar. For example, if you have a rocket ship image selected and you want to center it with a layer that holds a starry background, you can select the rocket image on one layer and then choose the layer that holds the starry background and click both align center buttons. This moves the starry background layer so it is centered on the rocket image. If multiple layers are linked together, each of the linked layers is aligned with the selection.

The align icon buttons include the following: Align Top Edges, Align Vertical Centers, Align Bottom Edges, Align Left Edges, Align Horizontal Center, and Align Right Edges.

CROSS-REF More on aligning and distributing layers is covered in Chapter 25.

Distributing image layers

If three or more layers are selected, the distribute icon buttons become active and may be used to distribute the layer objects. The distribute icon buttons include Distribute Top Edges, Distribute Vertical Centers, Distribute Bottom Edges, Distribute Left Edges, Distribute Horizontal Centers, and Distribute Right Edges.

Using Smart Guides

Guides are helpful as you begin to move objects and image selections about a document, but Photoshop includes another incredibly useful feature—Smart Guides. You can enable Smart Guides by choosing View ➪ Show ➪ Smart Guides. When enabled, guides appear to align the moved object or selection to the edge and center of surrounding objects. Figure 12.45 shows an arrow symbol being moved. Smart Guides magically appear to align the top of the arrow to the top of the rounded rectangle and another Smart Guide appears to align the right edge of the arrow to the right edge of the text. Smart Guides also are found in Illustrator.

Smart Guides in Illustrator are enabled from the View menu. These guides have been improved in a couple of ways. They are aware of centers and the bounding box of the selection rather than just the cursor position.

InDesign also includes Smart Guides. The Smart Guides in InDesign can detect alignment, spacing, and even rotation. The guides are also aware of how far you zoom in on a document, so as you get closer to objects, the guides are more detailed.

Smart Guides make aligning objects in Photoshop easy.

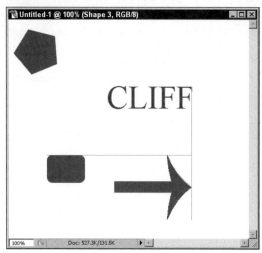

Summary

- The CS4 applications include many different ways to transform objects including the bounding box, transform tools, a Transform menu, and a Transform palette.

- The common transformation tools include Move, Rotate, Scale, Reflect, Shear, and Free Transform.

- The Transform Each dialog box in Illustrator lets you combine several transformations into a single operation.

- In addition to objects, patterns and gradients also may be transformed.

- Images may be transformed in many of the same ways as objects using the Photoshop tools.

- Stacking order determines which objects appear in front of other objects and is altered using layers and the commands in the Arrange menu.

- Aligning and distributing objects is accomplished using the Align palette or the Control panel in Photoshop, Illustrator, and InDesign.

Chapter 13

Applying Effects to Objects and Images

When Adobe first introduced the concept of filters in Photoshop, it was a risky move. To allow other developers to access the inner workings of the Photoshop graphics engine and develop their own filters to alter images was brilliant or a huge mistake. History has now validated that the move was, indeed, brilliant.

Filters are found mainly in Photoshop, but Illustrator has taken the concept one step further with the introduction of effects. Effects are essentially filters applied in memory, allowing them to be edited or even removed at any time from the Appearance palette without affecting the rest of the attributes. This same benefit can be realized in Photoshop using Smart Filters. Both Photoshop and Illustrator include filters and effects.

The variety of filters and effects found in both Photoshop and Illustrator are quite diverse, covering everything from unique brush strokes and object distortion to color adjustment and even 3-D effects.

Many filters in Photoshop are moving into complex interfaces like the Filter Gallery that lets you explore, preview, and apply many filters at once. Other common filter interfaces include the Extract, Liquify, and Pattern Maker interfaces.

Using Photoshop Filters

All the filters that may be applied to an image are contained within the Filter menu. Filters are applied to a selection or to the active layer if there is no selection. The top menu command in the Filter menu always lists the last filter command used. It includes a keyboard shortcut of ⌘/Ctrl+F, allowing it to be accessed quickly.

> **NOTE** Some filters may be applied only to images with the RGB color mode selected, and some filters may be applied only to an 8-bit image. Filters that cannot be applied to the current image are disabled. In Photoshop, choosing Image ➪ Mode lets you change these properties for the current image.

Accessing the Filter Gallery

The Filter Gallery lets you apply multiple filters at once or a single filter multiple times. To open the Filter Gallery, choose Filter ➪ Filter Gallery. The Filter Gallery, shown in Figure 13.1, includes a preview pane that shows the results of the applied filters.

> **NOTE** All the filters listed in the Filter Gallery also include their own menu commands in the Filter menu. Selecting a filter menu command for a filter that is part of the Filter Gallery opens the Filter Gallery with the selected filter highlighted.

FIGURE 13.1

The Filter Gallery includes most of the Photoshop filters and lets you apply many filters at once.

Show/Hide Filters

New Layer Effect

Delete Effect Layer

The Filter Gallery interface is divided into three different panes. The left pane is the preview pane that displays the current layer or selection. The middle pane includes thumbnails of all the available filters. Clicking a filter highlights it in gray and selects the filter. The right pane includes all the settings for the selected filter.

 Although the Filter Gallery includes many filters, it doesn't include all filters available in Photoshop.

Using the Preview pane

Moving the mouse over the Preview pane changes the cursor to a hand. Dragging with this hand cursor pans the preview image within the pane. The buttons and pop-up menu at the bottom of the Preview pane are used to zoom in, zoom out, and select a specific zoom percentage. The pop-up menu also includes an Actual Pixels option, which displays the image at its actual size of 100%; a Fit in View option, which zooms the image so the entire image is visible in the Preview pane; and a Fit on Screen option, which maximizes the Filter Gallery to fill the entire screen.

Clicking the Show/Hide button in the top-left corner of the Settings pane hides the filter thumbnails and uses that space to increase the size of the Preview pane, as shown in Figure 13.2.

FIGURE 13.2

Clicking the Show/Hide button increases the size of the Preview pane by hiding all the filter thumbnails.

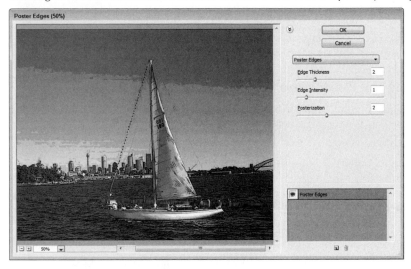

Using the Filter pane

The Filter pane is organized into several different categories of filters including Artistic, Brush Strokes, Distort, Sketch, Stylize, and Texture. Similar categories are found in the Filter menu. The category that includes the current selected filter is highlighted in bold.

Clicking the small arrow to the left of the filter category name expands the category to reveal all the filters within that category. Clicking on filter thumbnail selects the filter and displays all its settings in the Settings pane. The selected filter's name is displayed at the top of the interface along with the zoom percentage, and the background of its thumbnail is highlighted dark gray.

Using the Settings pane

The Settings pane includes a drop-down list of all the filters. Filters may be selected from this list when the filter thumbnails are hidden. Below this list, the settings for the current selected filter are displayed. Changing any of these settings alters the effects of the filter, and the Preview pane shows the changes.

At the bottom of the Settings pane is a list of filters applied to the preview listed in the order in which they are applied to the image. If you click a new filter, it replaces the currently selected filter. To apply an additional filter to the image, click the New Effect Layer button at the bottom of the Settings pane. This freezes the current selection and adds a new filter layer to the interface. The name of this filter layer is that of the filter that was applied.

If you click the Visibility icon to the left of the filter layer name to toggle it off, the Preview pane is updated to show the image without the filter. Selecting the filter layer and clicking the Delete Effect Layer button at the bottom of the Settings pane deletes filter layers.

If multiple filter layers exist in the Filter Galley, you can rearrange them by dragging one layer above or below another. Changing the order in which filters are applied can drastically change the resulting image.

When you're satisfied with the resulting preview, click OK to apply the listed filter layers to the image. Click Cancel to exit the Filter Gallery without applying any filters.

STEPS: Using the Photoshop Filter Gallery

1. **Open an image in Photoshop.** Within Photoshop, choose File ➪ Open to open an image to which you want to apply some filters. To apply the filter to the entire image, do not select any portion.

2. **Open the Filter Gallery.** Choose Filter ➪ Filter Gallery to open the Filter Gallery interface. The image shows up in the Preview pane. Click and drag the image in the Preview pane until an interesting portion of this image is visible.

3. **Select a filter.** Click the Artistic category, and select the Poster Edges filter. In the Settings pane, set the Edge Thickness to 2, the Edge Intensity to 1, and the Posterization to 2. Figure 13.3 shows the image with this single filter applied in the Filter Gallery.

4. **Add another filter.** Click the New Effect Layer button at the bottom of the Settings pane to add another filter to the image. Click the Texture category, and select the Texturizer filter. In the Settings pane, select the Canvas option from the Texture drop-down list. Set the Scaling value to 100%, the Relief value to 4, and the Light option to Top. Figure 13.4 shows the resulting image in the Preview pane.

FIGURE 13.3

The Preview pane in the Filter Gallery shows a preview of the applied filter with its modified properties.

FIGURE 13.4

The Preview pane shows the resulting image after two filters are applied.

5. **Apply the selected filters.** Click OK to apply the two selected filters to the image. Figure 13.5 shows the resulting image with the filters applied.

FIGURE 13.5

Several filters may be applied to an image at one time using the Filter Gallery interface.

Using other filters

In addition to the filters included in the Filter Gallery interface, Photoshop has several other filters that are applied using the Filter menu.

Most of these filters have their own dialog boxes of settings that appear when the filter's menu command is selected. Some of the filters don't have any dialog boxes that open. The menu commands that have an ellipsis (. . .) following their menu command open a dialog box.

Most filter dialog boxes include a Preview option and a Preview pane, like the Gaussian Blur dialog box, shown in Figure 13.6. The Preview pane gives you an idea of what the filter effect is before it's applied to the entire image. By clicking and dragging the image in the Preview pane, you can reposition the portion of the image that is displayed in the Preview pane. The plus and minus buttons underneath the Preview pane let you zoom in and out of the image. Enabling the Preview option applies the current filter settings to the entire image.

 Applying some filters, even in Preview mode, can take some time depending on the calculations involved in the filter and the size of the image.

FIGURE 13.6

The Gaussian Blur dialog box, like most filter dialog boxes, includes a Preview pane.

Blurring an image

The Filter ⇨ Blur menu includes several different filters used to blur an image or a selection by averaging local groups of pixels.

The first three Blur filters—Average, Blur, and Blur More—are applied without a dialog box. Average takes the average of all the selected colors and applies that average color to the entire selection. The Average filter is useful when used with the Magic Wand tool to create a single area with a single color.

The Blur filter removes any noise along hard edges by averaging the colors along these hard edges, resulting in a smoother overall image. The Blur More filter does the same but to a greater extent.

The Box Blur filter blurs the selected area by taking the average color value of pixels within a square area. The Radius value determines the size of the box.

The Gaussian Blur filter opens a dialog box where you can specify the amount of blur to add to the image. The Radius value determines the size of the groups of pixels that are averaged.

The Lens Blur filter opens a dialog box, shown in Figure 13.7, that lets you simulate a depth-of-field effect where the camera is focused on a particular point in the scene and all objects farther or nearer than that point are blurred in relationship to their distance from the focal point.

FIGURE 13.7

The Lens Blur dialog box includes a Preview pane.

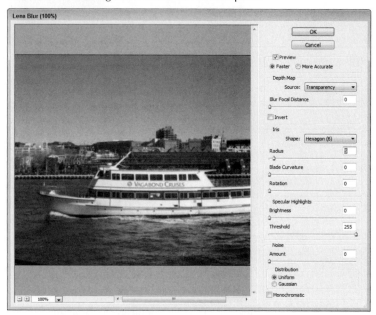

The Source field lets you base the focal point on the image's Transparency value or an included Depth Mask. The Iris Shape field lets you choose the shape of the defined averaged areas where the blur is applied as well as its Blade Curvature and Rotation. You also can specify values for Specular Highlights and Noise.

The Motion and Radial Blur filters let you control the direction of the blur lines. The Motion Blur filter specifies an Angle and a Distance value to blur the image linearly, as shown in Figure 13.8. The Radial Blur filter blurs the image in concentric circles about a point that you can select in the Radial Blur dialog box, also shown in Figure 13.8.

The Shape Blur filter blurs the image using a selected shape. The Shape Blur dialog box, shown in Figure 13.9, includes several default options, but you can load new shapes using the pop-up menu. The Radius setting determines the size of the shape that blurs the image. Notice in the figure how the circular shape causes details in the image to be blurred in circular patterns.

FIGURE 13.8

The Motion Blur and Radial Blur dialog boxes let you blur the image using linear or radial lines.

FIGURE 13.9

The Shape Blur dialog box blurs areas using a selected shape.

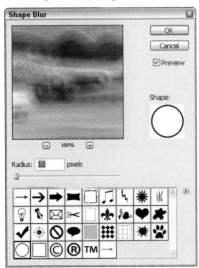

The Smart Blur filter is unique in that it lets you blur areas of similar colored pixels based on the Threshold value. The Mode may be set to Normal, Edge Only, or Overlay Edge. The Edge Only and Overlay Edge options color the edges white based on the Threshold value. Figure 13.10 shows the Smart Blur dialog box. In the Preview pane, similar areas have been blended together.

FIGURE 13.10

The Smart Blur dialog box blurs local areas of similar pixels.

You can use the Surface Blur filter to blur the image while preserving its edges. This has the effect of softening the entire image while maintaining the image details. The larger the Radius setting, the more that the pixels bleed into one another and the Threshold value sets the limit for edges that are blurred. Figure 13.11 shows the Surface Blur dialog box.

FIGURE 13.11

The Surface Blur dialog box blurs the image while preserving its edges.

STEPS: Blurring an Image's Background

1. **Open an image in Photoshop.** Within Photoshop, choose File ⇨ Open and select an image that includes a background that you want to blur.

2. **Select the background.** Click the Quick Selection tool, and click on the airplane and drag to the edge of the airplane to roughly select the background. After making an initial selection, hold down the Alt/Option key and deselect any portions of the airplane that were accidentally selected. Figure 13.12 shows the selected background area.

FIGURE 13.12

You can select the background and then apply the Lens Blur filter to make the background blurry.

3. **Apply the Lens Blur filter.** Choose Filter ⇨ Blur ⇨ Lens Blur. In the Lens Blur dialog box that opens, set the Radius value to 5 and zoom in on the Preview pane to see the applied blur, as shown in Figure 13.13. Then click OK.

FIGURE 13.13

The Lens Blur dialog box lets you control how blurry the background becomes.

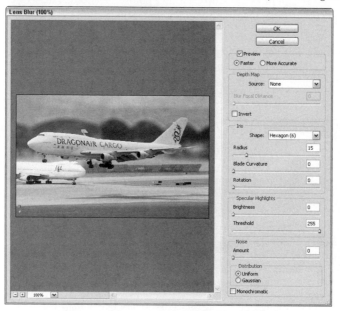

Distorting an image

The Filter Gallery interface includes three filters in its Distort category, but the Filter ➪ Distort menu includes many more filters, including Displace, Lens Correction, Pinch, Polar Coordinates, Ripple, Shear, Spherize, Twirl, Wave, and Zig Zag.

The Displace filter distorts the image based on a loaded displacement map. The displacement map defines how the pixels move, with black areas marking a negative displacement and white areas marking a positive displacement. Figure 13.14 shows a patterned image with the Displace filter applied using the simple displacement map.

NOTE Displacement maps must be saved using the PSD file format. Some sample displacement maps are found in the `plug-ins\displacement` maps directory.

CROSS-REF The Lens Correction filter, found in the Filter ➪ Distort ➪ Lens Correction menu, is covered in Chapter 11.

The remaining Distort filters all open a dialog box where you can enter the amount of distortion to apply. Most of these dialog boxes, like the Twirl dialog box shown in Figure 13.15, include a graphical representation of what the distortion looks like. In some cases, such as for the Shear filter, the graphical representation may be manipulated to define the distortion.

FIGURE 13.14

The Displace filter distorts images based on an externally loaded displacement map.

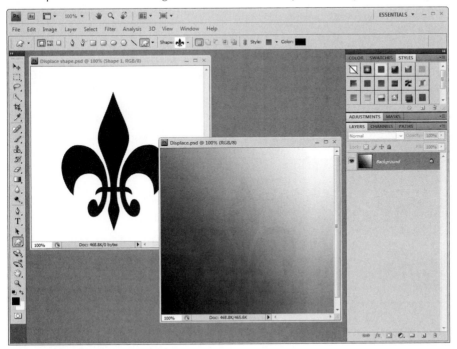

FIGURE 13.15

The Twirl dialog box includes a Preview pane and also a graphical representation of the distortion that is applied.

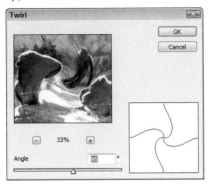

Of all the Distort filters, the Wave filter dialog box, shown in Figure 13.16, includes many unique settings for distorting the image such as selecting the Wave Type as Sine, Triangle, or Square, as well as a Randomize button.

FIGURE 13.16

The Wave dialog box includes many settings for precisely controlling the distortion of an image.

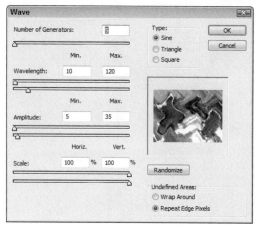

Adding noise to an image

When noise is added to an image, it randomly alters the colors of many of the surrounding pixels, making the image grainy. But it also can be used to blend areas that have been retouched, making them appear more realistic. The Filter ⇨ Noise menu includes several noise filters used to add and remove noise to an image or a selection.

The Add Noise filter opens a dialog box, shown in Figure 13.17, where you can specify the amount of noise to add to the image. The Uniform option randomly adds noise about the selected value, and the Gaussian option adds noise using a bell-shaped average curve. The Monochromatic option causes the noise to be black and white.

The Despeckle filter doesn't open a dialog box, but it removes noise from the image. It also detects edges to maintain the details of the image. The Median filter also removes noise from the image by replacing the brightest and darkest pixels with a median-colored pixel.

Most scratches and dust irregularities are small enough that they may be removed using the Dust & Scratches filter. This filter looks for small abrupt changes that are as small as the designated Radius value and with a given threshold. This filter applies a general blurring of the entire image. Figure 13.18 shows the dialog box for this filter.

FIGURE 13.17

The Add Noise dialog box determines the amount of noise that you add to an image.

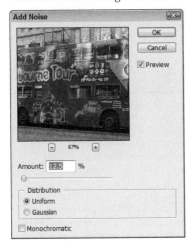

FIGURE 13.18

The Dust & Scratches dialog box eliminates irregular high-contrast dots and lines from an image.

Removing noise and JPEG artifacts

Adding noise to an image can soften an image by including a grainy feel, but having too much grain can affect image clarity. Some cameras can add film grain to an image and digital cameras add digital noise. Saving images to the JPEG format also can add unwanted noise and can reduce the image to the point that ugly artifacts and distortions appear. Photoshop includes a filter that can help remove noise from an image. It also is found in the Filter ➪ Noise menu and is called Reduce Noise.

The Reduce Noise dialog box, shown in Figure 13.19, includes a preview pane along with several settings. You can save and recall settings using the Settings dialog box. You also can switch the dialog box between Basic and Advanced displays. The Basic display includes settings for Strength, Preserve Details, Reduce Color Noise, and Sharpen Details. You also have an option to Remove JPEG Artifact:

You can use the Reduce Noise dialog box to remove noise and artifacts from images.

- **Strength:** Removes luminance noise in all channels that cause the image to appear grainy.
- **Preserve Details:** Controls how aggressively the image edges and details are affected.
- **Reduce Color Noise:** Removes any random color pixels that exist in the image caused by noise.
- **Sharpen Details:** Increases the sharpness lost by noise reduction.
- **Remove JPEG Artifacts option:** Enables the filter to deal with the blocky artifacts caused by saving the image to the JPEG format. These artifacts appear because of the compression algorithm used by the JPEG format.

If you determine that the luminance noise exists in only a single channel, you can switch to the Advanced display to make a Per Channel pane available. This pane displays the Red, Green, and Blue channels and lets you set the Strength and Preserve Details for only the selected channel.

Using the Pixelate filters

The Filter ➭ Pixelate filters are used to emphasize the pixel nature of an image by grouping several pixels together. The filters in this category include Color Halftone, Crystallize, Facet, Fragment, Mezzotint, Mosaic, and Pointillize. The Facet and Fragment filters apply the filter directly without opening a dialog box.

The shapes of the grouped pixels in each of these filters are slightly different, each creating a unique stylized look. For example, the Color Halftone filter changes each pixel group into a circle based on its brightness, the Crystallize filter changes groups of pixels into an irregular polygon shape, the Mosaic filter changes each grouping into a square, and the Pointillize filter groups pixels into solid dots. Figure 13.20 shows examples of several of these filters.

FIGURE 13.20

The Pixelate filters are used to alter an image by expanding the shape of specific pixel groups.

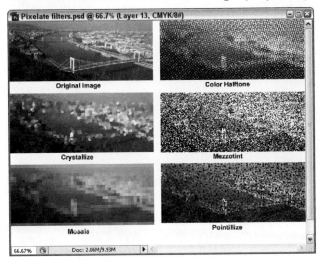

Using the Render filters

The process of rendering involves additional computations that alter the image in new and interesting ways. Using the filters in the Render category enables you to create clouds, fibers, and lighting effects like lens flares.

The Render filters include two filters for creating clouds—Clouds and Difference Clouds. The Clouds filter replaces the current image or selection with a random distribution of pixels using the Foreground and Background colors.

TIP   Holding down the Option/Alt key while choosing Filter ➭ Render ➭ Clouds results in a cloud pattern that has a much higher contrast.

417

The Difference Clouds filter is similar, but instead of replacing the image, it blends the clouds with the image or the selection using a Difference blending mode, which inverts the colors of the image. Figure 13.21 shows an image where the Clouds filter has been applied to the left half, and the Difference Clouds filter has been applied to the right half.

CROSS-REF You can learn more about the various blending modes in Chapter 9.

FIGURE 13.21

The Clouds filter has been applied to the selection on the left of this image, and the Difference Clouds filter has been applied to the right half of the image.

The Render ⇨ Fibers filter replaces the current selection or image with threads of fibers created using the Foreground and Background colors. The Variance value controls how long fibers of a single color are, and the Strength value defines how stringy the fibers are. The Randomize button mixes these two values; this filter is excellent for creating textures that are used as hair. Figure 13.22 shows the Fibers dialog box.

Lens flares are lighting anomalies that appear when you point a camera at a bright light. The Lens Flare filter opens a dialog box, shown in Figure 13.23, where you can click in the Preview pane to position the lens flare. You also can set the brightness of the lens flare and choose one of four lens types.

FIGURE 13.22

The Fibers dialog box creates long strands of fiber.

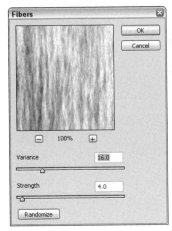

FIGURE 13.23

The Lens Flare dialog box lets you position the flare by dragging within the Preview pane.

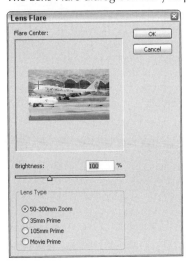

Each of the various lens types creates a different pattern of streaks, rings, and glows. You can see results of each lens type in Figure 13.24.

FIGURE 13.24

Each of the lens types creates a unique lens flare.

Using the Lighting Effects filter

Of the various filters in the Render category, the Lighting Effects filter offers the most functionality. This filter may be applied only to RGB images using the Filter ➪ Render ➪ Lighting Effects menu command.

CAUTION The Lighting Effects filter requires a substantial amount of memory, and if your system doesn't have enough memory available, a warning dialog box appears. You can make more memory available using the Edit ➪ Purge menu command to free memory used by the Undo, Clipboard, and Histories features.

When the Lighting Effects filter is applied, the Lighting Effects dialog box, shown in Figure 13.25, is displayed. Using this dialog box, you can add multiple lights to shine upon the image shown in the Preview pane.

FIGURE 13.25

The Lighting Effects dialog box lets you position multiple lights around the image and change their settings.

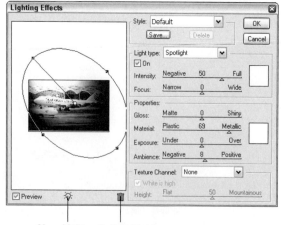

New Light   Delete Light

To add a light to the image, click the Light icon at the bottom of the Preview pane and drag it into the Preview pane, or hold down the Option/Alt key and drag from an existing light to duplicate the light. All lights appear in the Preview pane as white dots. These lights may be repositioned by dragging the white dots to a new location.

When a light is selected in the Preview pane, an ellipse that represents the light's range is displayed. By dragging on its handles, you can change the light's range. Holding down the Shift key while dragging these handles constrains the ellipse to change only a single dimension.

Lights are deleted by dragging their white dots to the Trash Can icon beneath the Preview pane.

The Light Type field lets you select from three different light types: Directional, Omni, and Spotlight. A Directional light shines light rays from a distant source, and all its rays are parallel much like the Sun. An ellipse represents a Spotlight and controls the Spotlight's angle and direction. A Spotlight decreases in intensity the further from its source it gets. An Omni light, represented by a circle, casts light equally in all directions, much like a light bulb.

Each light is enabled or disabled using the On option. Each light type also has an Intensity value, which may be positive or negative. A negative light value actually pulls light away from the image. Each light also can have a color, which is specified by the color swatch to the right of the Intensity setting. Click the color swatch to open a Color Picker where you can change the light's color.

When the Spotlight type is selected, one end of the ellipse acts as the source and is the brightest point (or the darkest if the Intensity value is negative). The Focus value sets how much of the ellipse is filled with light.

The Properties values determine how the light interacts with the image surface. The Gloss value determines how shiny the surface is and how much the light reflects. The Material setting controls whether the light color (Plastic) or the image color (Metallic) gets reflected. The Exposure setting is a multiplier for the light, and the Ambience setting controls the background lighting in the image. The color swatch to the right of the Properties is for the ambient light color.

The Texture Channel field lets you select a channel and use it to emboss the image by raising the channel relative to the remaining pixels.

With all these controls, it may be difficult to configure an effective lighting setup. Photoshop includes several default Style settings from which you can select. These presets include a variety of settings, and you can save your own presets using the Save button at the top of the dialog box.

STEPS: Applying Lighting Effects

1. **Open an image in Photoshop.** Within Photoshop, choose File ➪ Open and open an image that includes a background to which you want to apply lighting effects.

2. **Open the Lighting Effects dialog box.** Choose Filter ➪ Render ➪ Lighting Effects to open the Lighting Effects dialog box.

3. **Select a lighting style.** From the Style drop-down list at the top of the dialog box, select the Five Lights Down style. This adds several lights to the Preview pane, as shown in Figure 13.26.

FIGURE 13.26

Selecting a lighting style automatically configures the Lighting Effects dialog box.

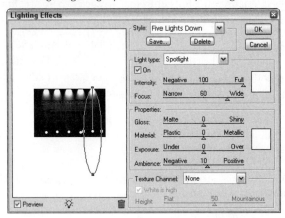

4. **Configure the lights.** Click one of the white dots to select a light in the Preview pane. Notice that the Intensity value is already at maximum, but the lighting is still too dark. Drag the Ambience slider up to 25 to increase the overall light for the scene. Then click OK to apply the lighting to the image. Figure 13.27 shows the resulting image.

FIGURE 13.27

Applying a lighting effect to this image changes the image from a daytime image to a nighttime image.

Sharpening an image

The Sharpen filters are used to enhance the details of blurry images by increasing the contrast of edges. Choose Filter ➪ Sharpen ➪ Sharpen to apply a general sharpening over the entire image without a dialog box. The Sharpen More filter increases the sharpening effect, and the Sharpen Edges focuses specifically on the image edges.

The Unsharp Mask filter opens a dialog box, shown in Figure 13.28, that lets you adjust the amount of sharpness that is applied. This filter works by increasing the pixel contrast for areas where adjacent pixels have a value that is greater than the specified Threshold. The Radius value determines the size of the area where the pixel values are compared, and the Amount setting controls how much the contrast of adjacent pixels within the Threshold is increased.

Be warned that over sharpening an image adds halos to the image edges. Images that include particularly bright colors may be oversaturated if you set the Amount setting too high. Figure 13.29 shows an image with the Unsharp Mask filter applied to different sections. The left end of the palace image has a large Radius value and a low Threshold causing the contrast to be increased for the entire section. The right end of the image has been sharpened with high Amount and Radius settings and a low Threshold setting, causing the section to be over-saturated. The middle section is unchanged.

FIGURE 13.28

The Unsharp Mask dialog box lets you control the amount of sharpening applied to an image.

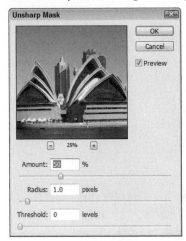

FIGURE 13.29

The Unsharp Mask filter has been applied to this image using different settings.

Using the Stylize filters

The Stylize filters apply a variety of unique effects that give an image a specific style. The filters in this category include the Diffuse, Emboss, Extrude, Find Edges, Glowing Edges, Solarize, Tiles, Trace Contour, and Wind.

The Diffuse filter moves pixels around to make the image appear unfocused. The options include Normal, Darken Only, Lighten Only, and Anisotropic. The Emboss filter colors the entire image gray and raises the image along its edges to form a relief. The Emboss dialog box lets you choose Angle, Height, and Amount values.

The Extrude filter divides the image into squares and then colors each square to look like it is rising from the surface of the image. In the Extrude dialog box, you can select to use blocks or pyramids, set the size of the squares, and set the depth that they rise to.

The Find Edges and Solarize filters are applied without a dialog box. The Find Edges filter identifies all the edges in the image and displays them as dark borders on a white background. The Solarize filter combines the image with the image's negative to produce a darkened image with inverted colors.

The Tiles filter divides the entire image into square tiles and offsets each one slightly. In the Tiles dialog box, you can select the number of tiles and a maximum offset. The Trace Contour filter outlines the edges of the image, based on brightness, and displays them on a white background. The Wind filter spreads the edges of an image in different intensities as if something were dragged over the image when it was wet. Figure 13.30 shows a sampling of the Stylize filters applied to an image.

FIGURE 13.30

The Stylize filters may be used to create a number of unique effects.

Diffuse Emboss Extrude

Find Edges Glowing Edges Solarize

Tiles Trace Contour Wind

Using the other filters

At the bottom of the Filter menu are two miscellaneous filter categories—Video and Other. The Video filters include De-Interlace, which is used to remove interlaced lines from images captured from a video source, and NTSC Colors, which limits the color palette to those used for broadcast television.

The Other category includes the Custom filter. This filter opens a dialog box, shown in Figure 13.31, that includes an array of value fields. Each text field represents the brightness value of the pixels that surround the pixel represented by the center text field. These brightness values can range from –999 to +999. The Scale value is used to divide the sum of all brightness values and the Offset value is added to the brightness values after scaling. By entering custom values into these text fields, you can create your own custom filter. These custom filters may be saved and reloaded as needed. The custom filters are saved with an ACF extension.

FIGURE 13.31

The Custom dialog box lets you create your own original filters.

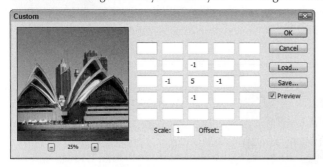

The Other category also includes a High Pass filter, which highlights all the sharp color changing edges. The Minimum and Maximum filters look at a grouping of pixels defined by the Radius value and remove the brightest (or darkest) pixel from the group.

The Other category also includes the Offset filter. This filter offsets all the pixels in an image, making the image edges appear within the image interior. This filter often is used to mask the image edges to make an image tileable.

STEPS: Creating a Custom Filter

1. **Open an image in Photoshop.** Within Photoshop, choose File ➪ Open and open an image.
2. **Open the Custom dialog box.** Choose the Filter ➪ Other ➪ Custom menu command to open the Custom dialog box.

3. **Enter filter values.** Enter a value of **5** in each cell in the top and bottom rows of the Custom dialog box. Then set the Scale value to **50**, as shown in Figure 13.32.

FIGURE 13.32

Entering values in these positions causes the image to blur.

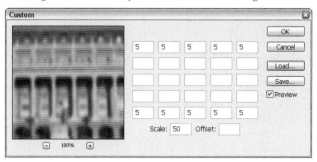

4. **Save the custom filter.** Click the Save button, and save the custom filter with the name **Double exposure**. The resulting image is shown in Figure 13.33.

FIGURE 13.33

This double-exposure image has a custom filter applied to it.

Using third-party filters

At the bottom of the Filter menu is a separator line. All third-party filters installed appear below this line. Photoshop, by default, includes one third-party filter category. The Digimarc filters enable you to embed a digital watermark into an image to secure copyright information.

Using the Filter interfaces

At the top of the Filter menu, along with the Filter Gallery, are several additional interfaces that let you interactively filter an image or a selection. These interfaces include the Liquify interface and the Vanishing Point filter.

Using the Liquify interface

The Liquify interface may be used to stretch and distort images and image selections as if they were placed on putty. To open the Liquify interface, shown in Figure 13.34, choose Filter ⇨ Liquify (Shift+Ctrl+X in Windows; Shift+⌘+X on the Mac).

FIGURE 13.34

The Liquify interface lets you distort images by pushing and pulling pixel areas.

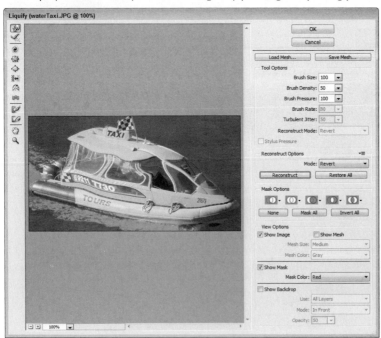

Moving the cursor over the Preview pane where the image is displayed reveals the outline of a brush. The brush options include Size, Density, Pressure, Rate, and Turbulence Jitter. Each of these options is set using the controls listed to the right.

The various liquify tools are displayed in a toolbar to the left of the Preview pane and include the following:

- **Forward Warp tool:** This tool is used to push pixels in a forward direction as you drag the mouse. Holding down the Shift key while dragging moves the mouse in a straight line.

- **Reconstruct tool:** This tool is used to remove any liquify effects from the image and restore the brushed area to its original look.

- **Twirl Clockwise tool:** This tool is used to rotate the pixels about the center of the mouse in a clockwise direction. Holding down the Option/Alt key while dragging rotates the pixels in the counterclockwise direction.

- **Pucker tool:** This tool is used to move the pixels toward the center of the brush.

- **Bloat tool:** This tool is used to move the pixels away from the center of the brush.

- **Push Left tool:** This tool is used to move the pixels to the left when you drag upward. Dragging the mouse downward moves the pixels to the right. Rotating the mouse in a clockwise direction increases the areas. Rotating in a counterclockwise direction reduces the area. Holding down the Option/Alt key forces the mouse to drag straight up or down.

- **Mirror tool:** This tool is used to copy the pixels being dragged over to the opposite side of the brush. Holding down the Option/Alt key while dragging flips the effect to the other side.

- **Turbulence tool:** This tool is used to randomly move pixels underneath the brush area.

- **Freeze Mask tool:** This tool is used to paint a mask layer onto the Preview pane.

- **Thaw Mask tool:** This tool is used to erase a mask layer onto the Preview pane.

- **Hand tool:** This tool is used to drag the Preview pane to reposition the visible portion of the image. Double-click to fit in window.

- **Zoom tool:** This tool is used to zoom in on the image in the Preview pane. Holding down the Option/Alt key lets you zoom out. You also can zoom in on the image using the small plus and minus icon buttons in the lower-left corner. Double-click to see 100%.

Dragging with any of the Liquify tools in the Preview pane distorts the image. These distortions may be undone using the Reconstruct tool. The Reconstruct tool has several modes including Revert, Rigid, Stiff, Smooth, and Loose. Each of these modes reconstructs the image in a different manner. Pressing the Restore All button returns the image to its original state.

At any time during the modifications, you can use a mask to lock an area from any changes. The Mask Options dialog box includes buttons to replace, add, subtract, intersect, or invert the current mask selection, transparency, or layer mask.

The View Options let you toggle on and off the image, the distortion mesh, the mask, and the backdrop. The *backdrop* is the faded version of the original image.

STEPS: Using the Liquify Interface

1. **Open an image in Photoshop.** Within Photoshop, choose File ⇨ New and create a new image.

2. **Set the Foreground color.** Click the Fill box in the Toolbox, and select a dark red color from the Color palette.

3. **Apply the Fiber filter.** Choose Filter ⇨ Render ⇨ Fibers to apply the Fibers filter to the blank canvas. In the Fibers dialog box, set the Variance to 16 and the Strength to 4. Then click OK. The fibers appear running vertical on the canvas, as shown in Figure 13.35.

FIGURE 13.35

The Fibers filter is useful for creating strands of fiber.

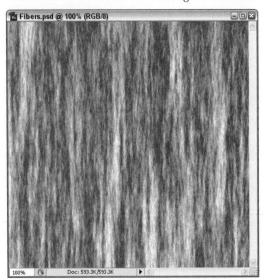

---

4. **Rotate the canvas.** Choose Image ⇨ Rotate Canvas ⇨ 90 degrees CW to rotate the canvas so the fibers run horizontally, as shown in Figure 13.36.

5. **Use the Liquify interface.** Choose Filter ⇨ Liquify to open the Liquify interface.

6. **Drag with the Liquify tools.** Select the Forward Warp tool, and drag up and down throughout the image to create some ripples. Select the Bloat tool, and drag small lines up and down to expand areas of the image. Finally, select the Turbulence tool, and drag throughout the image to add some turbulence to the image. Figure 13.37 shows the final distorted image.

FIGURE 13.36

Rotating the canvas makes the fibers run horizontally.

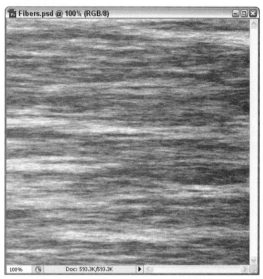

FIGURE 13.37

The Liquify interface allows you to add variety to the current image.

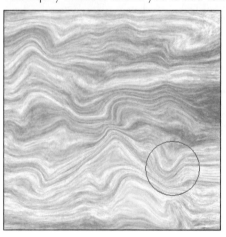

Controlling Vanishing Point

Painting walls in Photoshop is easy enough when the wall is a solid color, but if you're trying to add a patterned texture to the wall, it can be difficult to match the perspective view as you apply the paint. A work-around is to apply a Perspective transformation to the texture before applying the transformation, but you need to match the area exactly or apply it to a different layer that you can clean up later.

Photoshop CS4 has a unique way of handling this complex problem. The Vanishing Point interface, under the Filter menu, has a dialog box that opens with the current image in its preview pane (Alt+Ctrl+V in Windows; Option+⌘+V on the Mac). The interface then expects you to click four points that mark the corners of the plane. From these selected points, Photoshop can create a perspective plane that aligns to the perspective view, as shown in Figure 13.38.

FIGURE 13.38

The Vanishing Point interface lets you define perspective planes by clicking the plane's four corner points.

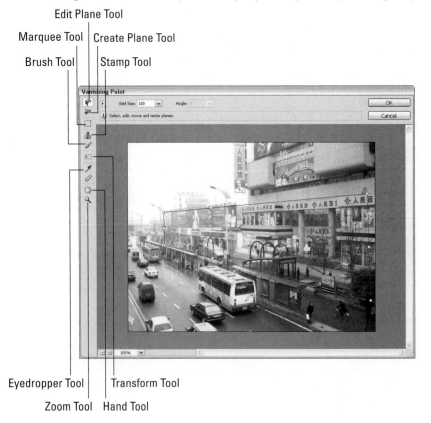

Edit Plane Tool
Marquee Tool | Create Plane Tool
Brush Tool | Stamp Tool

Eyedropper Tool | Transform Tool
Zoom Tool | Hand Tool

After you define a perspective plane, you can use the tools located in the upper-left corner of the Vanishing Point interface to edit the perspective plane, paint, or transform selections. When a tool is selected, its settings appear in the Control panel at the top of the interface. Each of these tools works the same and has the same keyboard shortcuts as the original interface.

STEPS: Using the Vanishing Point Interface

1. **Open an image in Photoshop.** Within Photoshop, choose File⇨Open and open an image that includes a well-defined perspective plane.

2. **Open the Vanishing Point filter.** With the image selected, choose Filter⇨Vanishing Point.

3. **Click each of the corners of the perspective plane.** When the Vanishing Point interface is first opened, the Create Plane Tool is selected. Click each of the four corners that make up the perspective plane. The plane is highlighted with a grid as shown in Figure 13.39.

FIGURE 13.39

The perspective plane is highlighted with a grid.

4. **Select a paint area.** To control where the paint is applied, click the Marquee tool in the upper-left corner of the interface and drag over the left portion of the perspective plane where the gray wall is.

5. **Use the Stamp tool.** Select the Stamp tool, and hold down the Alt/Option key while clicking the lower portion of the rock texture under the Panda sign. Then paint a new rock face in to the left of the Panda sign. Continue to reset the Stamp tool's origin, and repaint the rest of the left gray wall. Figure 13.40 shows the new perspective painted rock wall.

 Another way to accomplish this is to simply turn off the align option. With the align option off, the stamp tool keeps going back to the same location automatically.

 The stamp tool in the Vanishing Point interface shows a preview of the stamp data, which is very helpful.

FIGURE 13.40

With the Vanishing Point interface, the Stamp tool copies image portions while maintaining the perspective view.

The preceding tutorial is a simple example of a single plane vanishing point image, but the Vanishing Point dialog box can deal with multiple grids, enough to recreate a cube. If you hold down the Ctrl/Command key and pull on an edge, a linked grid is created that is positioned at 90 degrees from the original grid. If you click and drag an edge handle with the Alt/Option key held down, you break the 90 degree lock on the linked grids and allow the grids to swing into new positions.

Any new artwork that is pasted into the Vanishing Point dialog box is automatically wrapped around all of the defined grids. Furthermore, if you are using Photoshop CS4 Extended, then you can export the 3D grids and textures to the DXF and 3DS formats for use in a 3D modeling package.

Blending filters

Filters are applied with an Opacity value of 100%, making the filter take over the image completely. But you can make the applied filter effect transparent and even specify a blending mode by choosing Edit ➪ Fade (Shift+Ctrl+F in Windows; Shift+⌘+F on the Mac).

This command opens the Fade dialog box, shown in Figure 13.41, where you can specify an Opacity value and select a blending mode.

CROSS-REF For more details on the various blending modes, see Chapter 9.

FIGURE 13.41

The Fade dialog box lets you blend the last applied filter by setting an Opacity value and selecting a blending mode.

Using Photoshop effects in Illustrator

Most of the default filters found in Photoshop also are available in Illustrator under the Effect menu. These effects are located at the bottom of the Effect menu underneath the Illustrator default filters.

NOTE These same Photoshop filters also are found in Illustrator in the Effect menu, allowing them to be applied as effects.

CAUTION Most Photoshop filters work only in RGB mode, not in CMYK mode.

Using Smart Filters

Smart Filters are any filters that are applied to a Smart Object. The key benefit of Smart Filters is that you can change the settings, hide and even remove them in a nondestructive way. This shields the image from any permanent changes and lets you experiment with the filters without having to worry about messing up the image.

435

To apply a Smart Filter, simply select a Smart Object layer in the Layers palette and apply a filter. Any of the Photoshop filters can be used except for the Liquify, Lens Blur, and Vanishing Point filters. Once applied, the Smart Filter appears directly below the Smart Object layer in the Layers palette, as shown in Figure 13.42.

 Creating a Smart Object allows Shadow/Highlights and Variations to be applied as smart filters using the Image ⇨ Adjustments menu.

FIGURE 13.42

Smart Filters appear below the Smart Object layer in the Layers palette.

Using Filters in Flash

Flash includes a set of filters, but filters in Flash can be applied only to text, buttons, and movie clips. To apply a filter, open the Filters panel and click the plus icon to select a filter. The available filters include Drop Shadow, Blur, Glow, Bevel, Gradient Glow, Gradient Bevel, and Adjust Color. Flash can also use filters imported from Fireworks. Filters also can be copied and pasted between objects.

In addition to object filters, Flash includes a category of Timeline effects that can be applied to motion sequences. These effects include the ability to make objects expand, transform, explode, and transition over time.

Using Illustrator Effects

The drawback to using effects is that they take up valuable memory, and applying too many of them can significantly slow down the system. If you have lots of RAM, this shouldn't be a problem.

 If memory becomes an issue, the Appearance panel lets you turn on and off individual effects to help control processing load.

At the top of the Effect menu are two commands for instantly repeating the last applied effect and for recalling the dialog box used in the last applied effect.

 Effects also can be applied using a button located at the bottom of the Appearance panel.

All applied effects show up in the Appearance palette, as shown in Figure 13.43, where they may be selected, edited, and removed at any time.

FIGURE 13.43

The Appearance palette lists all effects applied to the current selection.

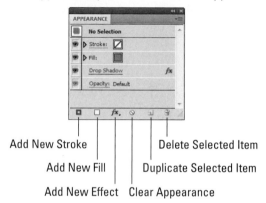

Add New Stroke

Add New Fill

Add New Effect   Clear Appearance

Delete Selected Item

Duplicate Selected Item

After an effect is applied to an object, the same effect is applied by default to all new objects that are created. To make new objects appear without these effects, click the New Art Has Basic Appearance button at the bottom of the Appearance palette.

Effects can be removed from the selected object by selecting an effect in the Appearance palette and choosing the Remove Item palette menu command or by clicking the Delete Selected Item button at the bottom of the Appearance palette. To remove all effects, click the Reduce to Basic Appearance button. This command causes all effects to be removed, but it doesn't change the stroke or fill settings. Clicking the Clear Appearance button removes all effects and sets the stroke and fill colors to None.

Using the Visibility toggle, you can turn each appearance item on or off.

If multiple items are selected, then you can edit the attributes for each of the selected items all at once. This is a very powerful feature when combined with the select shared appearance attribute that is used in the Select Similar Object button in the Options bar.

Rasterizing effects

Many effects convert the object to a raster image before the effect is applied. Actually, the conversion doesn't happen until the file is outputted or rasterized with the Rasterize command, but the object still maintains its vector outline. Choose Effect ➪ Document Raster Effects Settings to open the dialog box shown in Figure 13.44. Here, you can set the global rasterization settings for all objects that are converted to raster images. The effects that require rasterization include all the SVG filters, and several of the Stylize effects.

CROSS-REF SVG filters and the Document Raster Effects Settings dialog box are covered in more detail in Chapter 23.

FIGURE 13.44

The Document Raster Effects Settings dialog box lets you specify the settings to use when an object is rasterized.

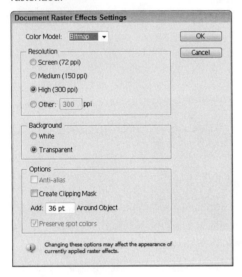

The Effect menu also includes a Rasterize menu command that opens up a dialog box with the same settings as the Document Raster Effects Settings dialog box. The settings in this dialog box are object-specific.

Using the Convert to Shapes effects

The Convert to Shapes effects let you change the shape of an object into a Rectangle, a Rounded Rectangle, or an Ellipse. Each effect opens a dialog box, like the one shown in Figure 13.45, where you can specify the dimensions of the new shape.

FIGURE 13.45

The Shape Options dialog box lets you convert shapes and bitmaps into a rectangle, a rounded rectangle, or an ellipse.

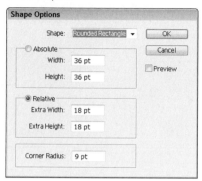

The Crop Marks effect adds crop marks to the current document based on the current selection.

 **Crop marks created with the Crop Marks filter conform to neither the artboard crop set nor to those created with the Crop Area tool.**

Using the Distort & Transform effects

The Distort effects let you distort object paths in a number of different ways, including Free Distort, Pucker & Bloat, Roughen, Tweak, Twist, and Zig Zag. Each of these effects opens a dialog box where you can control the settings for the distortion.

These effects may be applied only to object paths, not to raster images, symbols, or text objects.

The Free Distort effect lets you distort a path by dragging the corner points of its bounding box. Figure 13.46 shows this dialog box.

FIGURE 13.46

The Free Distort dialog box lets you distort an object path by dragging the corners of its bounding box.

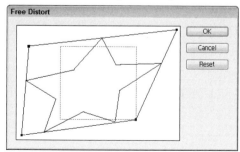

The Pucker & Bloat effect is used to push the center of each segment toward the object center (Pucker) or away from the object center (Bloat).

The Roughen effect may be used to add small random changes to the path as if someone scribbled with a pen. The Tweak effect also applies randomness to a path by bending each segment inward or outward. The Twist effect lets you specify an Angle value that defines how much the path is twisted about its center. The Zig Zag effect causes the path to be angled back and forth in a regular pattern.

Figure 13.47 shows each of the Distort effects applied to a simple rectangle.

FIGURE 13.47

The Distort effects offer several unique ways to alter Illustrator paths.

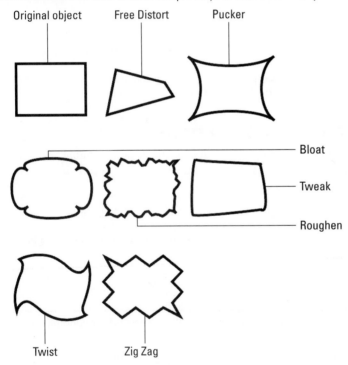

Using the Stylize effects

There are several Illustrator Stylize effects including—Add Arrowheads, Drop Shadow, and Round Corners.

The Add Arrowheads effect may be applied only to an open path. The Add Arrowheads dialog box, shown in Figure 13.48, lets you select from a library of arrowheads for the start and end of the path.

FIGURE 13.48

The Add Arrowheads dialog box lets you select the arrow type to use for the Start and End of a path.

The Drop Shadow effect adds a simple drop shadow to the selected object using the Drop Shadow dialog box, shown in Figure 13.49. For the drop shadow, you can select a blending mode, an opacity, offset distances, a blur amount, and a color.

FIGURE 13.49

The Drop Shadow dialog box lets you control the look and position of the drop shadow.

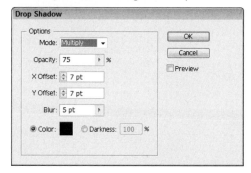

The Feather effect opens a simple dialog box where you can enter a Feather Radius amount. The Inner and Outer Glow effects open a dialog box like the one in Figure 13.50, where you can select a blending mode, a glow color, an opacity, and blur values, as well as whether the glow emanates from the center or from the edges of the object.

The Round Corner effect opens a simple dialog box where you can specify a radius to use to round the corners of the selected path.

FIGURE 13.50

The Inner Glow dialog box lets you add a glow to the stroke of an object.

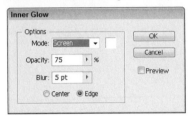

The Scribble effect opens a dialog box, shown in Figure 13.51, where you can make a path look like it was drawn using scribbled strokes. Although the resulting line looks like it was drawn free-hand, the object is still a path and maintains it vector properties.

FIGURE 13.51

The Scribble Options dialog box lets you specify the options to create a rough scribbled look.

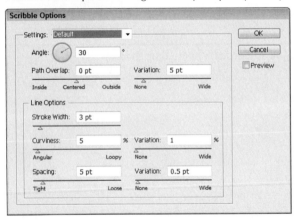

At the top of the Scribble Options dialog box is a drop-down list of presets. These presets lets you choose from several different setting configurations including Childlike, Dense, Loose, Moire, Sharp, Sketch, Snarl, Swash, Tight, and Zig Zag.

The Angle setting defines the angle at which the strokes are aligned, and the Path Overlap defines how often a drawn path crosses itself. Most settings include a Variation setting that is used to specify how random the attribute is. You also can define the Stroke Width, Curviness, and Spacing of the scribble marks.

Figure 13.52 shows examples of the Inner and Outer Glow effects and the Scribble effect.

FIGURE 13.52

The Stylize effects offer some unique features that would be difficult or impossible to create manually.

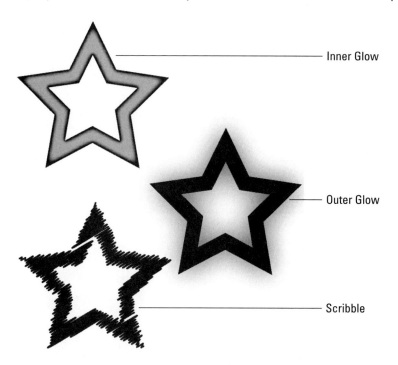

Inner Glow

Outer Glow

Scribble

Using the Warp effects

All the effects in the final category of the Effect menu open the same Warp Options dialog box, shown in Figure 13.53. Using this dialog box, you can deform the selected object into several different shapes including an Arc, Arc Lower, Arc Upper, Arch, Bulge, Shell Lower, Shell Upper, Flag, Wave, Fish, Rise, Fisheye, Inflate, Squeeze, and Twist.

The shape applied may be selected from the Style drop-down list at the top of the dialog box. For each shape, you can specify a Bend value, as well as Horizontal and Vertical Distortion values. The Bend value determines how closely the object matches the designated shape and the Distortion values skew the shape either vertically or horizontally.

Figure 13.54 shows each of the Warp styles found in the Effect ➪ Warp menu applied to a simple rectangle.

FIGURE 13.53

The Warp Options dialog box lets you choose the shape style to make the shape conform toward.

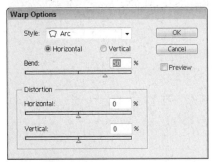

FIGURE 13.54

The Warp effects cause the selected object to warp to conform to the chosen shape.

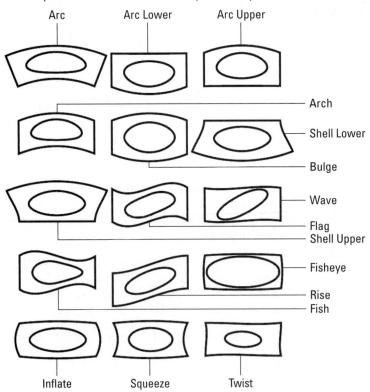

Using Photoshop's Layer Effects and Styles

Although effects are typically found in Illustrator, Photoshop has a similar feature that may be applied to a layer called Layer Effects. A pop-up menu of Layer Effects is found at the bottom of the Layers palette.

CROSS-REF   Layers and the Layers palette are covered in detail in Chapter 25.

Not only can you apply these Layer Effects to a layer, but you also can store them as Styles in the Styles palette, shown in Figure 13.55. From the Styles palette, you can apply the Layer Effects to any image or selection.

FIGURE 13.55

The Styles palette holds all styles, which include Layer Effects.

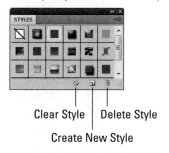

Clear Style | Delete Style

Create New Style

All the Layer Effects found in the Layers palette open the same dialog box, shown in Figure 13.56. This Layer Style dialog box includes a panel for each of the Layer Effects including Blending Options, Drop Shadow, Inner Shadow, Outer Glow, Inner Glow, Bevel and Emboss, Satin, Color Overlay, Gradient Overlay, Pattern Overlay, and Stroke.

Each Layer Effect may be turned on or off using the check box to the left of the effect name. To the right of the dialog box is a sample thumbnail of the defined style and a New Style button. Clicking the New Style button opens a dialog box where you can name the new style. Clicking OK adds the defined style to the Styles palette.

Each Layer Effect applied to a layer is listed in the Layers palette. Double-clicking the effect in the Layers palette opens the Layer Style dialog box where you can edit the effects settings.

FIGURE 13.56

The Layer Style dialog box includes a separate panel for each Layer Effect.

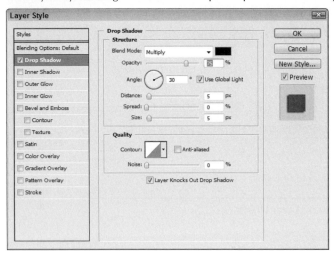

Applying Effects in InDesign

InDesign includes an interface that lets you apply several of the more popular effects to InDesign objects. This interface is available from the Object ➪ Effects menu. The available effects include Transparency, Drop Shadow, Inner Shadow, Outer Glow, Inner Glow, Bevel and Emboss, Satin, Basic Feather, Directional Feather, and Gradient Feather. All of these effects are applied using the same Effects dialog box, shown in Figure 13.57.

FIGURE 13.57

The Effects dialog box in InDesign lets you add drop shadows and many other effects to any object.

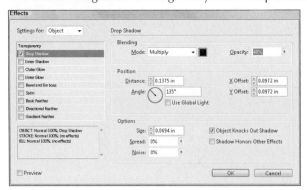

The effects selected from the Effects dialog box are applied to the selected object, which could be the object, the stroke, fill, or even text. InDesign CS4 keeps track of all the effects applied to the current selection in the Effects palette, shown in Figure 13.58. The Effects palette also lets you set the Opacity and select a blending mode independent of the Effects dialog box. You can also isolate the blending to a particular group or knockout objects inside a group.

FIGURE 13.58

The Effects palette shows all the effects applied to each of the object's elements.

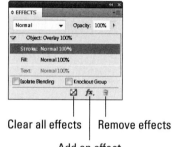

Clear all effects | Remove effects

Add an effect

In the Settings for option list at the top of the Effects dialog box, you can choose to apply the effect to the current Object, the Fill, Stroke, or Text. A single object can have several effects applied at the same time.

Adding drop shadows

Choosing Object ➪ Effects ➪ Drop Shadow opens a dialog box, similar to the one for Illustrator's Drop Shadow effect, where you can set the properties of the drop shadow including a blending mode, an opacity, an X and Y offset, a blur, and a color or you can use the drop shadow button on the Control panel. The bottom of the dialog box includes several swatches from which you can select.

 For drop shadows, the default blending mode, Multiply, creates the most realistic shadow and is probably the most reliable blending mode for printing.

Feathering objects

Choosing Object ➪ Effects ➪ Basic Feather, Directional Feather, or Gradient Feather to access a set of controls in the Effects dialog box where you can set the Feather Width, Choke, and Noise values and choose whether the corners stay sharp, rounded, or diffused. A Directional Feather includes an Angle setting and separate feather width values for Top, Bottom, Left, and Right. The Gradient Feather lets you control the feathering based on a defined gradient and includes Linear and Radial gradients.

Creating corner effects

In addition to the Effects dialog box, you also can alter the container frame by choosing Object ➪ Corner Effects. This opens a simple dialog box where you can choose from the available effects. The options include None, Fancy, Bevel, Inset, Inverse Rounded, and Rounded. You also can set the size of the effect.

 **Corner effects can be applied without the dialog box using the Pathfinder panel.**

Figure 13.59 shows each of the corner effects available in InDesign.

Effects can be part of a defined Object Style allowing the effect to be added easily to other objects.

FIGURE 13.59

Using corner effects adds some flair to the rectangular frames.

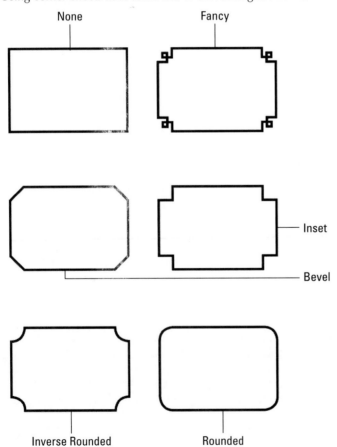

Summary

- Most Photoshop filters are applied using the Filter Gallery interface. This interface includes a wide assortment of filters and allows you to preview and apply multiple filters at once.

- The Filter menu in Photoshop also includes many other filters that aren't part of the Filter Gallery. These filters are selected from the Filter menu.

- Photoshop includes several additional filter interfaces for working with images, including the Liquify and Vanishing Point interfaces.

- Most of the Photoshop filters also may be applied to objects within Illustrator as effects.

- In addition to the Photoshop filters, Illustrator also includes some effects that may be used only on vector objects.

- Effects used in Illustrator show up in the Appearance palette and may be edited or removed at any time.

- Layer Effects in Photoshop appear in the Layers palette and may be used to create a new style.

- InDesign includes an Effects palette for applying transparency and effects to the object, stroke, fill, or text.

Chapter 14

Working with 3D Objects

IN THIS CHAPTER

Using 3D in Photoshop

Painting 3D objects

Creating 3D objects in Illustrator

Adobe products have always focused on 2D graphics. Using special techniques, you could make 2D graphics have a 3D look, but the end result always could be printed. While the Adobe products have continued to introduce new features and more efficient workflows, a host of 3D programs have continued along the same vein.

Today several robust 3D packages are available such as Autodesk's 3ds Max and Maya, and the ability to produce 3D objects is becoming much easier. 3D objects are common in many avenues of graphical design. The ability to work with these assets defines an efficient workflow.

This chapter takes a closer look at working with 3D objects in CS4. Photoshop CS4 Extended includes a host of features for incorporating and working with 3D objects. Illustrator also includes the ability to work with basic 3D objects.

Working with 3D Objects in Photoshop

The 3D features available in Photoshop CS4 Extended include the ability to load, move, rotate, and scale 3D models. You also can paint on the surface of the 3D objects.

Loading and Exporting 3D Objects

The first step in working with 3D objects is to load the 3D objects into Photoshop. 3D objects are saved using a 3D file format that keeps track of all the vertices, edges, and faces that make up the object. These formats also keep track of other information including the object's texture, any scene lights, and animations.

A large number of 3D file formats are available and Photoshop supports several of them. The supported file formats include the following:

- **U3d:** This format is produced by Acrobat 3D Version 8.
- **3ds:** This format is created by Autodesk's 3ds Max product.
- **obj:** This format was initially created by Wavefront, but is a common format used by many different 3D packages.
- **kmz:** This format is exported by Google Earth and holds geographical data used for maps and earth features.
- **Collada:** This format is a fairly new non-proprietary format with broad industry support.

3D models saved using one of these formats are loaded into Photoshop using the File ➪ Open command. Before loading the 3D model, Photoshop lets you specify the dimensions of the layer. The 3D model is added to a 3D layer in the Layers palette as a Smart Object. 3D objects also can be added to a document using the File ➪ Place menu. Figure 14.1 shows a simple 3D table loaded into Photoshop.

3D models can be loaded into an existing document using the 3D ➪ New Layer from 3D File menu. This opens a file dialog box, but it limits the file formats to the available 3D formats.

3D layers also can be exported from Photoshop to the U3d, OBJ, KMZ, and Collada formats using the 3D ➪ Export 3D Layer menu command.

Transforming 3D Objects

Several tools in the Toolbox allow you to move, rotate, and scale loaded 3D objects. Once these tools are selected, you can drag in the scene to transform the 3D object or the view. These tools are available as flyouts under the 3D Rotate tool (N) and include:

- **3D Rotate tool:** Rotates the 3D object about its center.
- **3D Roll tool:** Spins the 3D object about its center point.
- **3D Pan tool:** Moves the 3D object to either side.
- **3D Slide tool:** Moves the 3D object toward or away from the current view.
- **3D Scale tool:** Resizes the 3D object.

FIGURE 14.1

3D models are added to a 3D layer in Photoshop.

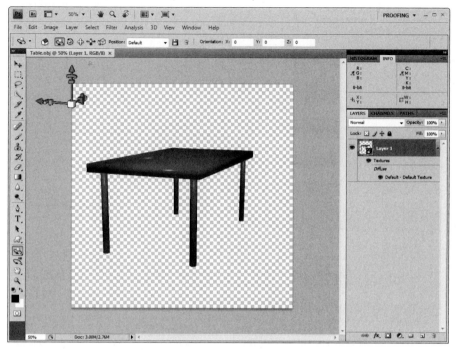

The Toolbox includes several tools that change the view of the 3D object. Changing the view keeps the 3D objects in their current orientation but changes the camera view that is used to view the 3D scene. This is most noticeable when several objects are next to one another. The tools under the 3D Orbit tool (K) flyout include:

- **3D Orbit tool:** Rotates the camera view about the object's center.
- **3D Roll View tool:** Spins the camera view about the object's center point.
- **3D Pan View tool:** Moves the camera view to the left or right.
- **3D Walk View tool:** Moves the camera toward or away from the center.
- **3D Zoom tool:** Zooms into and out of the 3D scene.

When the 3D layer is selected and any of the tools in the preceding list are selected, a transformation widget is displayed in the upper-left corner of the document. Using this widget you can move, rotate, or scale the 3D object. As you move the mouse over the top of the transformation widget, different parts of the widget are highlighted yellow, as shown in Figure 14.2. Dragging when the different parts are highlighted yellow transforms the 3D object in different ways:

FIGURE 14.2
_____

The transformation widget lets you move, scale, and rotate the 3D object.

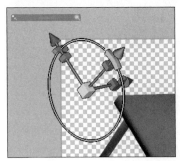

- **Conic arrows:** Dragging when one of the conic arrows is highlighted yellow moves the 3D object along the highlighted axis.

- **Arched section:** Dragging when one of the arched sections is highlighted yellow rotates the 3D object about the perpendicular axis. A ring appears about the rotation axis when highlighted.

- **Rectangular block:** Dragging when one of the rectangular blocks is highlighted yellow scales the 3D object along a single axis.

- **Centered square block:** Dragging the centered square block from which all axes extend causes the entire 3D object to be uniformly scaled.

- **Square plane:** Positioning the mouse between two axes causes a square plane to appear. Dragging when this square plane is highlighted allows the 3D object to be moved within the defined plane.

After the 3D model is transformed, you can save the view and recall these views using the controls on the Options bar. The drop-down list in the Options bar includes standard views for Default, Left, Right, Top, Bottom, Back, and Front. The Return button takes you to the initial camera position if the camera movement gets lost. Figure 14.3 shows the 3D table object after it has been rotated to its side.

FIGURE 14.3

3D objects can be rotated using the 3D tools.

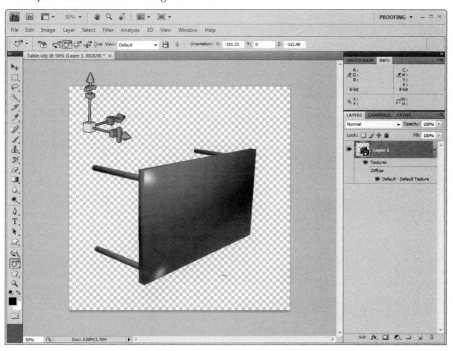

Creating 3D Objects in Photoshop

Within the 3D menu are several menu options for making 2D drawings into 3D objects. These features include the following:

- **New 3D Postcard from Layer:** Any layer can be placed on a 3D plane that can be rotated using the 3D tools. This menu converts any standard layer to a 3D layer as if it were place on a postcard. Figure 14.4 shows a kangaroo image that has been placed on a 3D postcard and rotated.

FIGURE 14.4

Standard layers can be made into 3D postcards.

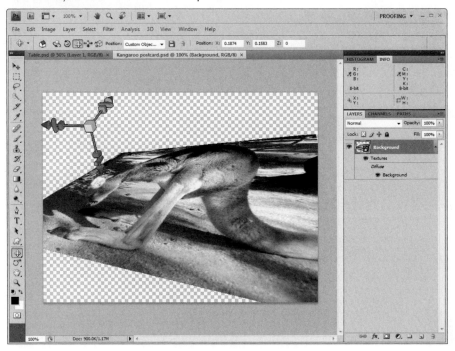

- **New Shape from Layer:** This menu option includes a number of standard 3D primitive objects that are placed in a 3D layer. The available shapes include Cone, Cube, Cylinder, Donut, Hat, Pyramid, Ring, Soda Can, Sphere, Spherical Panorama, and Wine Bottle. Figure 14.5 shows the Wine Bottle 3D shape added on top of the table object.

- **New Mesh from Grayscale:** Uses the grayscale values in a standard layer to create a 3D depth map. These depth maps can be Planar, Two-Sided Planar, Cylindrical, or Spherical.

- **New Volume from Layers:** This menu requires that you select at least two layers. Each layer defines a different cross-sectional area. Once selected, a dialog box appears where you can specify the depth of the volume for each cross-section. For Figure 14.6 several cross-sections of a tree were created on four different layers. All four layers were then selected and the 3D⇨ New Volume from Layers menu was selected. In the Convert to Volume dialog box, a value of 1 was entered for the Z value, which defines the thickness of each layer cross-section.

FIGURE 14.5

3D shapes can be added to a document.

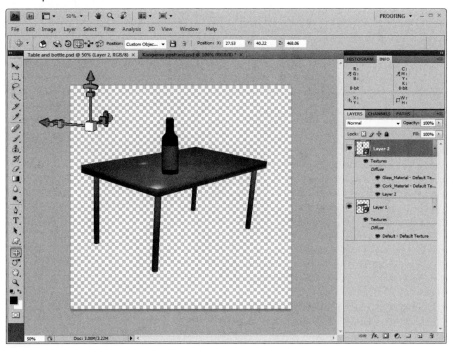

Painting 3D Objects

3D objects are interesting, but sometimes they can be boring. Adding textures to the surface of a 3D objects adds a level of visual quality to the object. Photoshop is often used to create the textures that are applied to 3D objects, but using the 3D texturing and painting features in Photoshop is a much more efficient workflow.

When a 3D object is loaded into Photoshop, its textures are listed in the 3D layer in the Layers palette. These textures can be turned on and off using the Visibility icon. Better yet, if you click the texture name, you can open the texture in another window for editing.

FIGURE 14.6

Several layers can be used as cross-sections for a 3D volume.

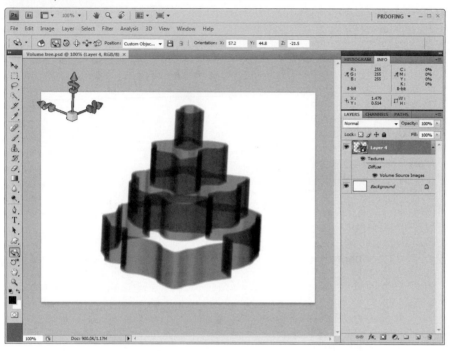

3D objects can have several different textures. The default texture that holds the surface colors is called the Diffuse texture, but other textures are available. For example, the Bump texture holds the height of each surface point and is used to add bumps and relief to the model. The textures supported by Photoshop CS4 Extended include:

- **Diffuse:** The Diffuse texture holds the surface color information.
- **Bump:** The Bump texture holds the height information at each surface point.
- **Glossiness:** The Glossiness texture defines how bright and sharp the highlights are at each surface point.
- **Opacity:** The Opacity texture defines the places on the object where the surface is transparent or semi-transparent.
- **Shininess:** The Shininess texture shows those places where the highlights are the strongest and where the object reflects its surroundings.

■ **Self-Illumination:** The Self-Illumination texture defines areas where the surface tends to glow like a light-bulb.

■ **Reflectivity:** The Reflectivity texture defines the areas where the surface is highly reflective.

Typically the Diffuse texture shows colors, but other textures such as Bump and Opacity use a grayscale map to define how the Opacity is applied. White areas show where the surface is completely opaque and black areas show where the surface is fully transparent. Gray areas are semi-transparent. Figure 14.7 shows a 3D hat object with and without textures applied.

FIGURE 14.7

Textures can do a lot to enhance a 3D model.

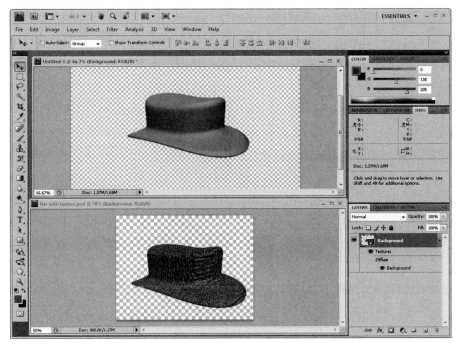

Rendering 3D Objects

Once the 3D models are placed, you can define the visual style of the rendered objects using the 3D ➪ Render Settings menu. This opens the 3D Render Settings dialog box, shown in Figure 14.8.

Using this dialog box you can display and configure the object's face, edges, and points. For volume objects, you can configure the volume style. A stereo rendering option enables the image to appear 3D when you use red/blue stereo glasses.

The Render Settings dialog box lets you define the final look of the 3D layer.

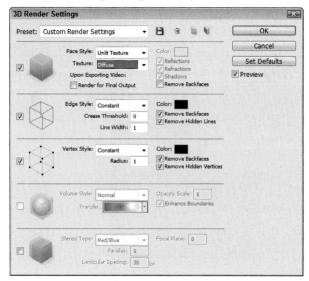

For the Face rendering option, several face styles are available including Solid, Ray Traced, Unit Texture, Flat, Constant, Bounding Box, Normals, Depth Map, and Paint Mask. You also can specify a color to be used if no diffuse texture is present. You also can enable reflections, refractions, and shadows.

At the top of the Render Settings dialog box is a list of available presets. You also can define and save your own presets.

After the settings are configured, you can have Photoshop render the final result with all shadows and lighting effects with 3D⇨Render for Final Output. Figure 14.9 shows the resulting render of a 3D ring with the Ray Traced render option.

FIGURE 14.9

After setting the render settings, you can render the final output to see all shadows and reflectivity.

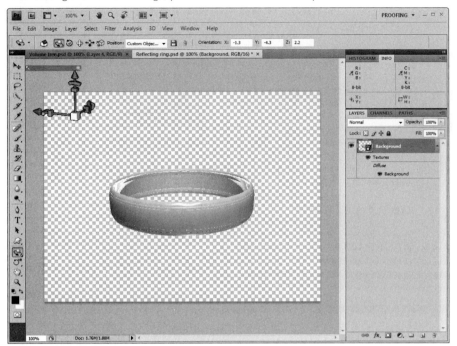

Using 3D and video layers

Photoshop CS4 Extended not only loads video and animation files; it also edits and paints on the frames of these files. Video and animation files that are loaded into Photoshop appear in the Layers palette as a special video layer, which is marked with a filmstrip-like icon in the lower-right corner of the thumbnail. The layer gives you access to the video's frames using the Animation palette.

The video formats supported by Photoshop CS4 Extended include MPEG, MOV, AVI, and image sequence formats including BMP, DICOM, JPEG, OpenEXR, PNG, PSD, Targa, and TIFF.

The Animation palette can display the video sequence in Timeline mode or in Frame mode. Timeline mode, shown in Figure 14.10, shows the duration of the sequence and all the animation properties. Frame mode displays a thumbnail of the animation at each frame.

Using the Animation palette menu, you can navigate and manipulate the timeline frames, copy and paste keyframes, and set the keyframe interpolation. Additional options let you change the frame rate and the sequence duration.

FIGURE 14.10

Photoshop CS4 Extended also allows video and animation files to be loaded and edited in Photoshop.

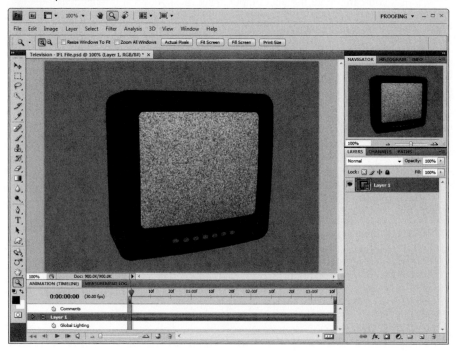

Creating 3D Objects in Illustrator

The 3D category of effects lets you convert simple 2D paths into simple 3D objects. The 3D menu includes three different effects—Extrude & Bevel, Revolve, and Rotate. For example, a simple square path can be made into a cube with the Extrude effect, and a half circle path may be revolved to create a sphere. 3D objects in Illustrator created with these effects include shading using controllable lights.

Extruding objects

Extruding a 3D path is simply the process of adding depth to the path. This is accomplished using the 3D Extrude & Bevel Options dialog box, shown in Figure 14.11.

The Position field at the top of the dialog box lets you select one of the default preset positions. Selecting a position preset automatically updates the X-axis, Y-axis, Z-axis, and Perspective values. If any of these values are changed, then the Custom Rotation preset is used. The default position presets include positions such as Front, Left, Top, Off-Axis Front, Off-Axis Top, Isometric Left, and so on. Isometric views are views where the Perspective value equals 0 and all parallel lines remain parallel.

FIGURE 14.11

The 3D Extrude & Bevel Options dialog box lets you specify the direction and distance to extrude the selected path.

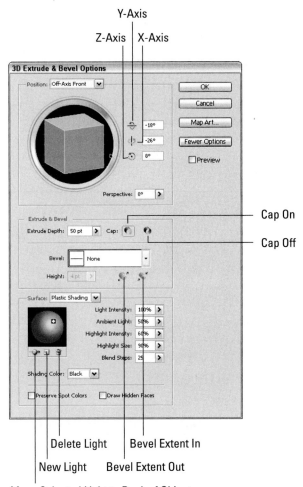

Y-Axis

Z-Axis | X-Axis

Cap On

Cap Off

Delete Light   Bevel Extent In

New Light   Bevel Extent Out

Move Selected Light to Back of Object

> **TIP** You can drag in the Preview pane, and the X-Axis, Y-Axis, and Z-Axis values are automatically updated. Dragging a cube face spins the object about all three axes, but clicking an edge spins the object about only a single axis.

The Extrude Depth value determines how far the path is moved to create depth. The Cap On and Cap Off buttons determine whether the extruded object is hollow or capped on either end.

The Bevel pop-up menu lets you choose the type of bevel to apply to the object. Each bevel type shows a profile curve. This curve matches the extruded portion of the object, and the Height value sets the maximum distance from the edge of the path. The bevel profile curve may be applied outward or inward using the Bevel Extent In and Bevel Extent Out buttons.

The Surface options define how the extruded object is shaded. The options include Wireframe, No Shading, Diffuse Shading, and Plastic Shading. If you click the More Options button, several lighting controls appear. Figure 14.12 shows several extrude, bevel, and shading options applied to an object.

The Wireframe option only draws the lines used to make up the 3D object. The No Shading option colors each face of the object using the selected fill and stroke colors. Neither the Wireframe nor the No Shading options have any lighting settings.

FIGURE 14.12

The Extrude & Bevel dialog box includes several options for creating extruded 3D objects.

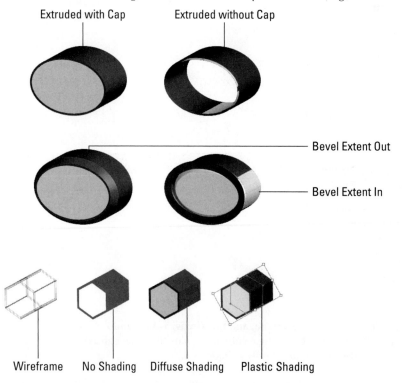

The Diffuse Shading option colors each face a different shade depending on how the light is cast upon the object. For this option, you can specify the Light Intensity, the Ambient Light percentage, the number of Blend Steps to use, and the Shading Color.

The Plastic Shading option colors the object as if the light were shining on an object with the surface made of plastic. Plastic objects are highly reflective and include specular highlights. For this option, you also have settings for the Highlight Intensity and Size.

When either the Diffuse or Plastic Shading options are selected, you can position the precise location of the lights used to illuminate the object by dragging in the Lighting Preview pane. Using the buttons underneath the pane, you can move the selected light to the back of the object so it shines from behind, create new lights, or delete a selected light. Lights are represented by the small white dots, and a single object can have many lights.

The Light Intensity value determines the strength of the light, which is at 100 percent at the center of its highlight. The Ambient Light value determines how much background light is used to light the object. The Blend Steps value defines the number of different colors that are used to blend colors from the highlight to the shadows. The Shading Color is the color reflected off the object away from the highlight.

Mapping artwork

Within the Extrude & Bevel dialog box, the Map Art button opens another dialog box, shown in Figure 14.13, where you can select a Symbol to map onto the various surfaces of the extruded object.

FIGURE 14.13

The Map Art dialog box lets you add symbols to the surfaces of the selected extruded object.

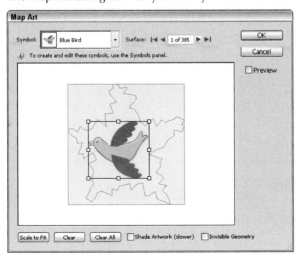

The Symbol pop-up menu lets you choose a Symbol from the active Symbol palette to apply to the selected surface. The Surface control includes arrows, which let you cycle through all the various surfaces that make up the extruded object. When a surface is selected, it is highlighted red in the art board.

CROSS-REF   **Symbols and the Symbol palette are covered in Chapter 9.**

The Scale to Fit button causes the selected symbol to be scaled to fit within the selected surface. The Clear button removes the mapped symbol from the selected surface, and the Clear All button removes all mapped symbols from the entire object. The Shade Artwork option includes the mapped artwork as part of the shading calculations and the Invisible Geometry option may be selected to hide the geometry and show only the mapped artwork. Using the Invisible Geometry option is helpful to warp artwork along a 3D surface.

Revolving objects

The Effect ⇨ 3D ⇨ Revolve menu command opens a dialog box, shown in Figure 14.14, which is very similar to the Extrude & Bevel dialog box.

FIGURE 14.14

The 3D Revolve Options dialog box is similar to the dialog box for the Extrude & Bevel effect.

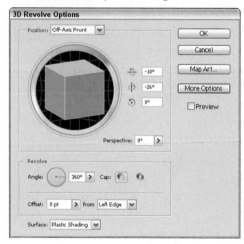

Using the Revolve effect, you can revolve a path about an axis to create a 3D object like the glass shown in Figure 14.15. The 3D Revolve Options dialog box lets you specify how much of an Angle to revolve about and whether the open ends are capped or not.

FIGURE 14.15

Revolving an open path about its left edge creates a 3D revolved object.

The Offset lets you specify the location of the center axis about which the selected path is revolved. The Surface options are the same as those for the Extrude & Bevel effect.

Rotating objects

The final effect in the 3D category is the Rotate effect. This effect lets you rotate and shade 2D and 3D objects and paths. The 3D Rotate Options dialog box includes the same position and shading controls as the other 3D effects.

Summary

- You can repurpose documents created in InDesign for use on the Web by exporting for Dreamweaver. This process bundles all the necessary files into a folder that Dreamweaver can use.

- A site project includes many Web pages. You can create site projects using Dreamweaver's Site Wizard.

- Dreamweaver is a robust editor for creating and designing Web pages. These Web pages can include a myriad of objects. You edit object properties using the Properties palette.

- Cascading Style Sheets are an efficient way to apply text styles to a section of text within a Web page and to multiple pages throughout the site.

- Dreamweaver includes templates for creating Web pages for mobile devices and features for editing and viewing mobile Web pages using Device Central.

Part IV

Working with Type

Part III covered many different types of edits you can apply to objects and images. In Part IV we deviate from the graphics and concentrate on type. We begin with Chapter 15 where we talk about fonts and overcoming font problems. In Chapter 16 we move on to using type styles, particularly in Adobe InDesign.

In Chapter 17 we discuss text frames and how the common metaphor for type handling is used consistently among several CS applications. This part concludes with Chapter 18 where we talk about using special type characters.

Chapter 15

Working with Fonts

Understanding how to manage and utilize fonts for CS applications is essential for creating an efficient workflow environment. This can be a daunting task, however, because it typically requires keeping track of hundreds or even thousands of fonts, which come in a variety of formats such as Type 1 or OpenType. In addition, fonts may have varying degrees of functionality depending on the kind of computer and software you use.

IN THIS CHAPTER

Understanding fonts

Managing fonts

Creating type outlines and special effects

Understanding Fonts

Typesetting on desktop computers has been around for more than 20 years. During this evolutionary era of digital page layout and design, there have been phenomenal changes in the tools and methods we use to produce our work. As rapid advances have been made in software development, so also has font technology evolved. And just as software packages are available that aren't suitable for current operating systems and design needs, there are also different font formats that aren't suitable for layout and imaging.

Fonts have been developed over the years using different technologies and categorized as different formats. Some font formats are obsolete today and won't work properly in some of the CS applications and with newer printing devices. Knowing what fonts are acceptable for use with the CS programs will help you prevent problems associated with printing and font embedding.

Font formats

With literally thousands upon thousands of fonts to choose from, it's important to know the different formats and which ones are best suited for your individual working environment. Ideally, you should have a thorough knowledge of all the fonts currently installed on your system.

The various font types are covered in the following sections.

- **Type 1:** The most popular PostScript font today. These fonts are single-byte fonts handled well by all PostScript printers. Type 1 fonts use a specialized subset of the PostScript language that has been optimized for performance. Type 1 fonts are reliable, and present the fewest problems when embedding and printing to PostScript devices.

  Type 1 fonts were designed to be used with the Compact Font Format (CFF). CFF was designed for font embedding and substitution with Acrobat PDFs. As is the case with all PostScript fonts, you must install two files to view and print fonts properly. Screen fonts display a font on your monitor; printer fonts carry the PostScript code necessary to download to your printer. Each font in your layout needs an accompanying printer font. For example, if you use Adobe Garamond Bold, you need an Adobe Garamond Bold printer font. If you attempt to bold a font by using the "B" in a type formatting palette, the font may display properly on the monitor and may even print properly on your laser printer. But if you don't have the matching printer font, it typically does not print properly when printing to commercial devices.

NOTE When preparing files for output for commercial printing, Acrobat PDFs offer you an advantage, because the fonts used in a design piece can be embedded in the PDF file. (Be sure the font licensing agreement doesn't prohibit embedding.) This way, the fonts do not need to be supplied separately to your commercial printer.

- **Type 3:** Type 3 fonts are PostScript fonts that have often been used with type design and stylizing applications. These fonts can have special design attributes applied to them such as shading, patterns, exploding 3-D displays, and so on. Type 3 fonts can't be used with Adobe Type Manager (ATM), and they often present problems when printing to PostScript devices.

- **Type 4:** Type 4 was designed to create font characters from printer font cartridges for permanent storage on a printer's hard drive (usually attached by a SCSI port to the printer). PostScript Level 2 provided the same capability for Type 1 fonts and eventually made these font types obsolete.

- **Type 5:** This font type is similar to the Type 4 fonts but used the printer's ROM instead of the hard drive. PostScript Level 2 made this format obsolete.

- **Type 32:** Type 32 fonts are used for downloading bitmap fonts to a PostScript interpreter's font cache. By downloading directly to the printer cache, space is saved in the printer's memory.

- **Type 42:** Type 42 fonts are generated from the printer driver for TrueType fonts. A PostScript wrapper is created for the font, making the rasterization and interpretation more efficient and accurate. Type 42 fonts work well when printing to PostScript printers.

- **OpenType:** OpenType is a new standard for digital type fonts, developed jointly by Adobe and Microsoft. OpenType supersedes Microsoft's TrueType Open extensions to the TrueType format. OpenType fonts can contain either PostScript or TrueType outlines in a common wrapper. An OpenType font is a single file, which can be used on both Mac and Windows platforms without conversion. OpenType fonts have many advantages over previous font formats because they contain more glyphs, support more languages (OpenType uses the Unicode standard for character encoding), and support rich typographic features such as small caps, old style figures, and ligatures—all in a single font.

Beginning with Adobe InDesign and Adobe Photoshop 6.0, applications started supporting OpenType layout features. OpenType layout allows you to access features such as old style figures or true small caps by simply applying formatting to text. In most applications that don't actively support such features, OpenType fonts work just like other fonts, although the OpenType layout features are not accessible.

- **Compact Font Format:** Compact Font Format (CFF) is similar to the Type 1 format but offers much more compact encoding and optimization. It was designed to support Type 2 fonts but can be used with other types. CFF can be embedded in PDFs for all levels of PDF compatibility. Fonts supporting this format are converted by Acrobat Distiller during distillation to CFF/Type 2 fonts and embedded in the PDF. When viewed on-screen or printed, they're converted back to Type 1.

- **CID-keyed fonts:** This format was developed to take advantage of large character sets, particularly the Asian CJK (Chinese, Japanese, and Korean) fonts. The format is an extension of the Type 1 format and supports PostScript printing. Kerning and spacing for these character sets are better handled in the OpenType format.

- **TrueType:** TrueType is a standard for digital type fonts that was developed by Apple Computer and subsequently licensed to Microsoft Corporation. Each company has made independent extensions to TrueType, which is used in both Windows and Mac operating systems. Like Type 1, the TrueType format is available for development of new fonts.

Advantages of OpenType fonts

You can copy an OpenType font from Mac to Windows and vice versa. The OpenType format is supported for font embedding in Acrobat PDFs. Fonts produced with this technology are as reliable as you find with Type 1 and Type 42 fonts. In addition, OpenType offers a means for flagging the fonts for embedding permissions.

The OpenType format is an extension of the TrueType SFNT format that also can support Adobe PostScript font data and new typographic features. OpenType fonts containing PostScript data, such as those in the Adobe Type Library, have a filename extension of .otf, while TrueType-based OpenType fonts have a .ttf extension.

OpenType fonts can include an expanded character set and layout features, providing broader linguistic support and more precise typographic control. Feature-rich Adobe OpenType fonts can be identified by the word "Pro" in their name. OpenType fonts can be installed and used alongside PostScript Type 1 and TrueType fonts.

CROSS-REF See Chapter 18 for more information on working with expanded character sets.

Creative Suite 1 came with 83 OpenType fonts that are installed as part of the Illustrator CS application. If you upgraded the Creative Suite you have these fonts available. In addition, the Creative

Suite 2 included more than 180 bundled fonts—most of which are OpenType fonts. The CS3 applications came with more than 30 OpenType fonts. In CS4 the fonts are installed in your application folders. OpenType fonts offer you an extended set of characters where you find more *ligatures* (character combinations) and special characters and symbols. Whereas PostScript fonts offer you a maximum of 256 glyphs (individual characters), OpenType fonts can contain more than 65,000 glyphs. Look for the OpenType "Pro" fonts and you'll find extended character sets.

As a standard of practice, you would be wise to replace your TrueType and PostScript fonts with OpenType fonts. This is likely to be an expensive proposition, but if you gradually begin to convert your font library and acquire new fonts in OpenType format, you'll benefit by having access to more characters, enhanced typographic features, and increased printing reliability.

Font licenses

Fonts generally carry licensing restrictions, and you need to be sure to honor them. This can be a confusing issue, however, because different font manufacturers impose different restrictions, and many licensing agreements are difficult to interpret. In order to provide font files to your service center or printer, developers often require you to get permission to distribute the font. Many developers prohibit such distribution altogether. In addition, some developers prohibit font embedding as you might do in programs like Acrobat. It's important to be aware of these limitations.

One possible way around font licensing issues is by converting any type not within your service provider's library to outlines in your documents before submitting them. In this way, the type becomes a graphic, and you don't need to copy your font files. This eliminates the transfer of the font's computer code, which is protected by copyright law. As a matter of practice, you should avoid converting large bodies of type to outlines, but in an emergency situation, it may mean the difference between getting the job out on time or not at all.

Managing Fonts

Font management has become more complicated for Mac OS X users. Prior to OS X, you could manage fonts easily using one of several different utilities, as well as by installing fonts in a single, logical location on your hard drive. With the introduction of Mac OS X, fonts are stored in several areas on your hard drive and, if not installed in the right folders, become inaccessible to your programs. In order to avoid complicated font installation procedures and ensure that fonts are accessible by CS applications, we highly recommend using a professional font-management utility. You'll find that this is a better solution than installing fonts in folders and letting your operating system handle the font management.

Installing fonts in Mac OS X

Mac OS X allows you to create accounts for multiple users, and you can choose to install fonts at the system level so all users of the computer have access to the same fonts, or you can store the fonts in individual users' Home folders to make them accessible only to a specific user.

Fonts for the Mac are installed in these locations:

- **Fonts accessible to all users of the computer:** Store them on the hard drive in `Library/Fonts`. To install fonts in the system `Library` folder, open your hard drive and open the `Library` folder at the root level. Inside the `Library` folder, you'll find a `Fonts` folder. You can copy TrueType, PostScript, and OpenType fonts to this location.

- **User-specific fonts:** Store them in `~/Library/Fonts`. (The tilde represents a user's Home folder.) Fonts stored here are available only to the owner of the active Home folder, which means different users may have access to different fonts. In case of font conflicts, fonts in this location take precedence over those in other folders.

- **System fonts:** The Mac OS X System folder also contains a `Library` folder. Once again, a `Font` folder resides inside the `Library` folder. As a default, Apple fonts required by the operating system are placed in this location. It's possible to add fonts here, but as a general rule, don't.

- **Mac OS 9:** For Classic applications, fonts are installed in the `System Folder/Fonts` location. Notice that the folder is titled `System Folder`, not `System`. Because all the CS applications run in native mode on OS X, you don't need to bother loading fonts here.

By default, system fonts are installed in one of the above four font locations. In addition, some fonts required by applications are also installed in these locations. Many CS4 applications contain font folders inside the application's folders where fonts are installed. However, for creative professionals who use fonts for design purposes where operating systems do not require the fonts, you should build a separate folder on your hard drive and copy all your fonts to the folder. Use a font management utility such as FontAgent Pro to load and unload fonts as needed for any given project.

Installing fonts in Windows

For Windows, like the Mac, you're best served by using a font utility.

STEPS: Installing Fonts

1. **Open the Settings menu from the Start menu.**

2. **From the Settings menu, select Control Panel and double-click on Fonts in the submenu.** The Fonts folder opens.

3. **From the File menu, select Install New Font, as shown in Figure 15.1.** A navigation dialog box opens where you can search your hard drive and locate a font to install.

4. **Select the fonts you want to install and click OK.**

FIGURE 15.1

Open the Fonts dialog box and choose File ⇨ Install New Font to install TrueType fonts in Windows.

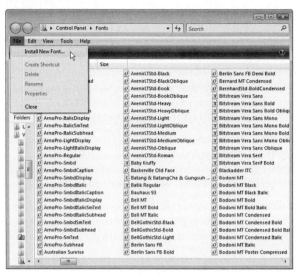

Fonts are also located in the `Windows/Fonts` folder. On your boot drive (usually drive `C:`), open the folder and copy PostScript and OpenType fonts to this folder.

Organizing your fonts

Fonts play a crucial role in any designer's work. Thus, it's important to take some time to learn how to best organize your fonts to ensure maximum productivity. The amount of time you invest up front in organizing your fonts will more than pay off down the road, especially if you face an eleventh-hour deadline and can't afford for anything to go wrong at the last minute.

Check your computer's fonts on a regular basis to be sure they are organized properly. Whenever you add, move or delete fonts, there is a chance that something can go awry. Or, if you install a new operating system or font-management utility, you may need to reorganize your fonts, throw out obsolete formats, or replace existing formats to become more compatible with your current operating system and programs. If you continue to use old fonts that aren't optimized for current technology, you'll eventually experience problems.

On the other hand, if you use high-quality fonts designed to work with current software and output devices, you avoid annoying imaging problems. One of the more common font errors is the inability of the printing device to recognize the font information in the file. The printing device then automatically substitutes a default font for the one you specified, with the end result looking nothing like what you intended. Thus, choosing fonts that have a high degree of printing reliability may mean the difference between getting the job out on time and missing a critical deadline.

Using font-management tools

Font-management tools greatly facilitate font accessibility and usage. They also help prevent the installation of duplicate fonts, especially on the Mac. Mac OS X users have a utility that ships with the operating system called Font Book. Font Book 2.1 is installed with OS X . This is a good, basic utility that allows you to enable and disable fonts. It doesn't offer the convenience of auto-activation, however. You can also use third-party tools such as Suitcase or FontAgent Pro.

Using Font Book (Macintosh)

Like the other font management utilities, Font Book offers you an option for detecting corrupt fonts. If you use Font Book and you suspect a font may be corrupted, use the validation features in Font Book to be certain your font is usable.

Open Font Book, select a font appearing in the Font list, and select Validate Font from the pull-down menu in the top left corner of the Font Book dialog box. The Font Validation dialog box opens as shown in Figure 15.2. The dialog box displays the selected font with icons representing the validation results. A checkmark icon informs you the font passed validation.

FIGURE 15.2

Select Validate Font from the Font Book pull-down menu and the validation results are reported for the selected font.

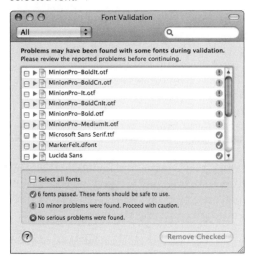

Another nice feature in Font Book is the ability to easily size fonts for previews. Suitcase and FontAgent Pro offer you the option to preview different sizes, but Font Book provides you a slider to size up and down the font preview. Rather than select fixed sizes or type a point size in a text box like you do in Suitcase, just drag the slider up or down to size the font and see the results dynamically in the preview area, as shown in Figure 15.3.

FIGURE 15.3

Drag the slider on the far right of the window to size the preview up or down.

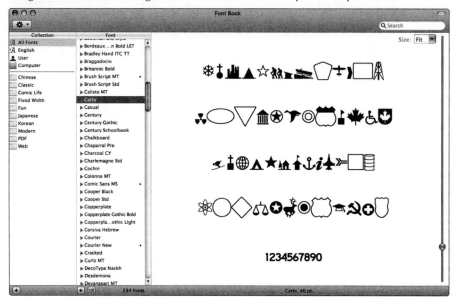

Using FontAgent Pro

Perhaps the most aggravating nightmare for creative professionals on Macintosh OS X is related to reliable font activation. You may have copied fonts to all of the system font locations (see the section "Installing Fonts on the Macintosh") and find one of the CS4 programs informing you a font is missing. You then uninstall the font from system font folders, attempt to load the font in another font management utility, and an alert dialog box opens informing you the font is already loaded by the system. Your aggravation continues as you poke around your hard drive trying to find a way to load the offending font and make it available to the CS4 programs.

If you're a designer who has experienced problems with alert dialog boxes informing you that a font is not available, we have a solution for you. FontAgent Pro from Insider Software (www. insidersoftware.com) solves annoying font-management problems. This $99 (as of this writing) utility is our personal choice for reliable font management on the Macintosh.

When you install FontAgent Pro (FAP), the first thing you encounter in the install wizard is a dialog box prompting you to import your fonts into a user-defined font folder FAP manages. During the import process, FAP isolates corrupt and duplicate fonts and stores them in folders apart from your font library where the reliable fonts are stored. Fonts are organized in folders and subfolders for each font family. With this feature in FAP, you don't need to use Font Book's validation options.

One very nice feature is that FAP automatically splits font suitcases into one font style per set. This means you can activate only those fonts used in a design without loading the entire font family. When it comes time to send your files off to a service bureau or print shop, only the used fonts are packaged with the application document and file links.

CROSS-REF For information on packaging documents for service providers, see Chapter 40.

Auto-loading fonts

FontAgent Pro isn't stingy in supporting application programs with auto-loading features. Unlike other utilities that support only Illustrator CS4 and InDesign CS4 and that auto-load a font when the program launches an application document, FAP automatically loads a font from any application document you open. This could be your mail client, MS Office programs, text editors, or any document having a font not activated at the time of launch.

FontAgent Pro features

FontAgent Pro offers you an intuitive workspace where you can view and activate fonts, create new libraries and sets, share fonts in workgroups, and change the font display in the FAP window from lists to WYSIWYG (What You See Is What You Get) views. The FontAgent Pro screen is shown in Figure 15.4.

FIGURE 15.4

FontAgent Pro offers an intuitive workspace where you can easily manage your fonts.

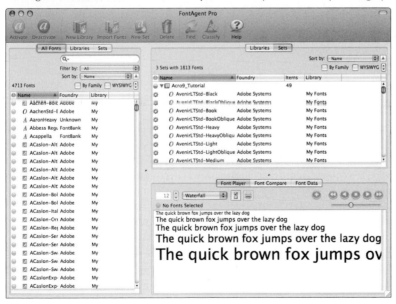

In addition to reliable font management, FAP also offers you some very nice options for viewing fonts in WYSIWYG style. From tools in the Font Player pane, you can view a selected font character set and a sample sentence in the view window. Click the Display Paragraph tool and the display changes to paragraphs of text set in Greek type. Moving to the right side of the Font Player pane, you have buttons that offer you a slide show. Select a root folder containing sub folders of font families and click the "Auto play fonts forward" (or backward) button and the window shows you a slide show of the fonts displayed in WYSIWYG views in the Font Player display window. This option lets you quickly view all font families within a given face. Another nice feature with Font Agent Pro is that you have options for identifying and finding fonts as well as purchasing fonts online.

Try before you buy

Obviously, there are many more features available than in this short description of FontAgent Pro. To test the product, visit the Insider Software Web site (`www.insidersoftware.com`) and download the free trial version. Insider Software offers you a 30-day free trial option where you can freely try all features and access the free user guide available as a PDF document. If font activation is a problem for you on Mac OS X, we guarantee this product is likely to solve all your font-management nightmares.

Creating Type Outlines and Special Effects

Creating outlines from type has long been a common practice by graphic artists and imaging technicians. If a stubborn font problem is encountered, a workaround solution is to convert the text to outlines so the type is transformed into an object. This way, the font information doesn't need to be downloaded to the output device in order for the document to be imaged properly. When word got out that converting text to outlines eliminated font-imaging problems, many designers decided to convert text to outlines as a matter of practice.

One disadvantage in converting text to outlines is that the resulting file size can become quite large and thus take an inordinate amount of time to print. In some cases, the document is rendered unprintable. So, before you convert text to outlines, be certain that you use this option as a last resort.

Another disadvantage in converting text to outlines is that, unless you save a back-up copy of your document, you lose the ability to access and edit your file utilizing the original font information. Say, for example, you create a half a dozen logotype variations for a client using different fonts. You then convert the type to outlines in order to apply special effects, and resave the document. You won't be able to go back into the Character palette to see which fonts you used, nor will you be able to edit any text if there are copy changes. The caveat here is always to save a separate copy of the document that contains the original font information when you choose to convert text to outlines. Fortunately, when using the CS applications, you can use Version Cue to save a different version of the same document or save an Alternate version. When you want to return to the document containing the original font information, promote that version to the top level in Version Cue or select the Alternate in the Bridge.

CROSS-REF For information on using Version Cue and promoting versions, see Chapter 7. For information on using Alternates, see Chapters 6 and 7.

So, you may need to convert text to outlines either as a workaround for stubborn font printing issues, or when you want to apply certain type effects. The Create Outlines command is available in Illustrator, Photoshop, and InDesign.

Converting type to outlines in Illustrator

To convert type to outlines in Illustrator, select the type with either of the selection tools in the Tools palette. (Note that you cannot use the Type tool here as you can in InDesign.) Next, Choose Type ➪ Create Outlines or press Shift+⌘+O or Shift+Ctrl+O. As you can see in Figure 15.5, after creating outlines each character becomes a compound path, editable with either the Selection tool or the Direct Selection tool. To edit or move individual characters with the Selection tool, just double-click to enter a group.

FIGURE 15.5

Type shown before and after converting to outlines. Each character becomes a compound path, which you can edit with the selection tools.

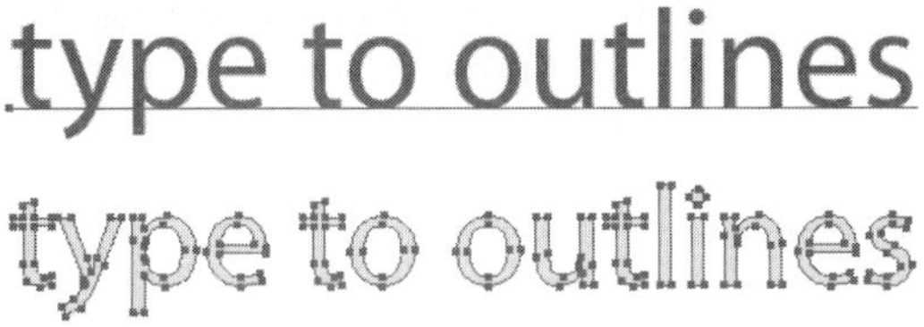

Creating type effects in Illustrator

The options are almost limitless when it comes to creating eye-catching type effects with Illustrator. You can apply custom gradients, transparency, meshes, shadows, lighting and shading, distortion, stylization, 3D effects, and more. Figure 15.6 shows an example of the 3D type effects you can achieve quickly in Illustrator. For a more in-depth look at the ways you can use Illustrator to enhance your type, see the *Illustrator CS4 Bible* by Ted Alspach (published by Wiley).

FIGURE 15.6

In Illustrator, this 3D effect was easily created using regular type (top) and then applying a stroke, gradient, extrude effect, warp effect, and drop shadow.

Creating type masks in Illustrator

Other interesting effects can be achieved by using type as a mask. Note that when creating type masks in Illustrator, you can create a mask without converting the type to outlines.

Position the type in front of the artwork that will be masked. Select both the type and the item to be masked by drawing a marquee around the objects or by Shift-clicking if necessary (two objects must be selected for this command to work). Then choose Object ➪ Clipping Mask ➪ Make, or press ⌘+7 or Ctrl+7. Areas of the background artwork that are outside the type mask disappear, and your type now appears filled with the portion of the artwork directly behind it, as shown in Figure 15.7. (The top portion of the figure shows the text added on top of a background. The bottom half of the figure shows the result after a mask was applied.) You can move the background image or the type around to experiment with different mask positions.

Converting raster type to vector type

You may have a need to re-create logos for clients where original artwork for the company logo is not available in digital form. If your client faxes you a copy of the company logo and you need to size it up for use in a large tradeshow display, a scan of the logo is likely to lose image quality. If you convert a logo to a vector object, you can then freely size the object without being concerned about losing image quality.

FIGURE 15.7

You can create type masks in Illustrator without converting the text to outlines.

With Illustrator CS4, you can easily convert raster data to vector objects using Live Trace. The results of the Live Trace object will be as good as the scan you use, so be certain to obtain good-quality originals and scan at high resolutions. To see how easy it is to convert a scanned logo from a Photoshop image to a vector object in Illustrator using Live Trace, follow the steps below.

STEPS: Converting Raster Data to Vector Objects

1. **Scan the logo.** Scan a logo at a high resolution and save the file as a TIFF file from Adobe Photoshop.

2. **Create a new document in Adobe Illustrator.** Choose File ➪ New and supply the desired dimensions in the New Document dialog box. Click the Color mode you want to use and click OK to create a new blank document.

3. **Open Adobe Bridge.** Choose File ➪ Browse in Bridge to open the Bridge window. The Illustrator document window remains open in the background. Locate the file you saved from Photoshop in the Bridge window and drag the file to the Illustrator artboard. Alternately, after opening Illustrator, you can choose File ➪ Open With ➪ Adobe Illustrator or File ➪ Place, and select the file to import. (Note that you can also place the file directly when in the Bridge window.) The image appears in Illustrator as an image, as shown in Figure 15.8. Make certain the image is selected before proceeding to the next step.

CROSS-REF For more information about using Adobe Bridge to manage files, see Chapter 6.

FIGURE 15.8

Drag and drop, open, or place the image in Illustrator.

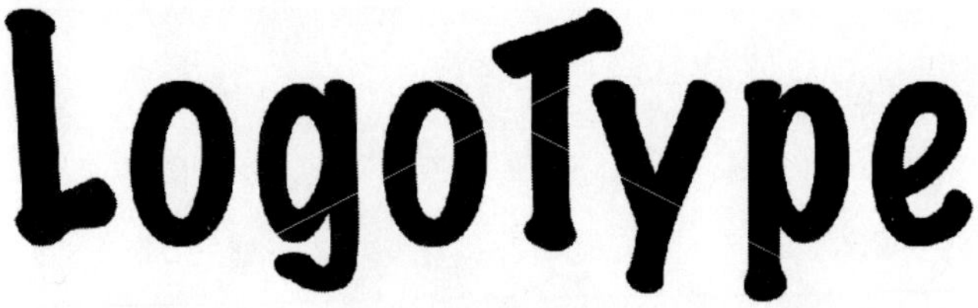

LogoType

4. **Adjust the trace settings.** Choose Object ➪ Live Trace ➪ Tracing Options. The Tracing Options dialog box appears, as shown in Figure 15.9. Set the Mode and Threshold options. If tracing a black-and-white logo, use the Black and White mode. Leave the remaining settings as you see in Figure 15.9.

CAUTION If you trace logos with gradients, be certain to set the maximum number of 256 for the Threshold. If scanning color logos with gradients, set the Max Colors setting to 256. If you don't set these values high, Live Trace may clip or posterize the image.

FIGURE 15.9

Open the Tracing Options dialog box and make settings choices for the type of image you intend to trace.

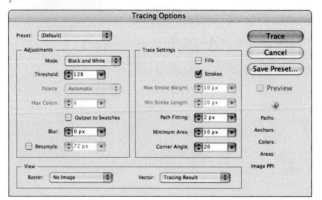

CROSS-REF For more information on using Live Trace, see Part III.

5. **Trace the object.** Choose Object ➪ Live Trace ➪ Make and Expand (or Make and Convert to Live Paint). If you have potential problems with overlapping colors, use the Make and Convert to Live Paint option. Otherwise, use Make and Expand. Either choice expands the trace so the individual characters can be masked, edited, or used with a variety of effects. In Figure 15.10, the image is traced.

FIGURE 15.10

Live Trace renders the image as a vector object.

6. **Apply effects.** You may need to expand the object. Select Object ➪ Expand and expand the strokes and fills. Use the Direct Selection tool and delete a background if one appears. Apply effects to create the look you want by selecting options from the Effect menu. In Figure 15.11, the type is masked, stroked, filled with a Graphic Style, warped, and has a drop shadow applied.

FIGURE 15.11

After converting to a vector object, you can mask the type and apply many different effects.

Converting type to outlines in Photoshop

If it's a matter of printing a font, Photoshop files can always be rasterized in order to convert the type object to pixels. When type is rasterized in Photoshop it loses all the type attributes and prints like any Photoshop image.

In Photoshop CS4, you can also convert type to outlines. If you want to mask type originally created in Photoshop in Illustrator, you can convert the type to outlines in Photoshop and then import the Photoshop file into Illustrator, where you can apply the mask. Of course, if your mask object is in Photoshop, you can also mask type in Photoshop. With the new Photoshop CS4 features, you have a choice for where you want to apply type masks.

Photoshop type converted to outlines is recognized only in Illustrator. If you import a Photoshop file with outline type in InDesign, the text is not recognized as a vector object. To experiment a little with type converted as outlines in Photoshop, follow these steps.

STEPS: Converting Type to Outlines in Photoshop

1. **Add type to a document in Photoshop.** Create a new file in Photoshop. Select the Horizontal Type tool and add some type to the document. Type is added on a new layer.

2. **Convert the type to outlines.** Open a context menu on the layer containing type and select Convert to Shape as shown in Figure 15.12. The Photoshop type is converted to outline type and remains a vector graphic.

FIGURE 15.12

Open a context menu and select Convert to Shape.

3. **Copy the type in Photoshop.** Select the Path Selection tool in the Toolbox and drag a marquee around the type to select it. Choose Edit ➪ Copy. When you select the type, you can see the paths around the type as shown in Figure 15.13.

4. **Paste the type in Illustrator.** Create a new document in Illustrator. Choose Edit ➪ Paste. A dialog box opens and prompts you to paste as a Compound Shape (fully editable) or Compound Path (faster). Choose Compound Shape (fully editable) and click OK.

5. **Apply effects to the type.** You can size the type and apply effects from the Effect menu or from palettes such as the Graphic Styles palette. In Figure 15.14, the type was sized and a neon effect was added using a Neon Effects Graphic Style.

FIGURE 15.13

Select the type using the Path Selection tool.

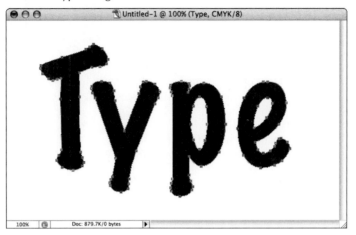

FIGURE 15.14

After pasting the Photoshop type in Illustrator, you can size the type and add effects.

You can create many effects for type masks in Photoshop as well as stylize type with shadows, embossing, filters, and brightness enhancements after rasterizing type. Photoshop's array of editing tools allows you to apply effects to type in the same way you apply them to images. When you create type in Photoshop, type is added to a separate layer and remains as a vector object until you either flatten the layers or rasterize a layer by choosing Layer ➪ Rasterize ➪ Type.

If you import Photoshop files in InDesign, text is rasterized. If you save a Photoshop file with a text layer as PDF, you can keep your type in vector form by saving the Photoshop document with layers. Formats that can preserve layers include the native PSD, Photoshop PDF, and TIFF. Saving with layers keeps type as text and it remains editable. If you flatten the layers, the text is rasterized and you lose the ability to edit your text.

If you open a Photoshop PDF file in Acrobat with layers and vector data preserved, the text is searchable and editable. If you open the same file in Illustrator, Illustrator automatically converts the type to outlines. The same file saved as a native Photoshop (PSD) file opened in Illustrator preserves all type editing.

The type effects you can create in Photoshop are mind-boggling. For comprehensive coverage, see the *Photoshop CS4 Bible* by Stacy Cates and Simon Abrams (Wiley).

CROSS-REF   **For more information on creating type effects in Photoshop, see Part III.**

Converting type to outlines in InDesign

InDesign offers you the option for converting type to outlines as inline objects. With this feature, you can create many type effects directly in InDesign without having to create them in Illustrator and import them. After outlines have been created in InDesign, you have similar options as Illustrator for shaping text objects with the selection tools, as well as creating type masks.

To convert type to outlines in InDesign, select the characters you want to convert to outlines by highlighting them with the Type tool or by selecting the text frame with a selection tool. With the Type tool, you can select one character or a range of characters. If you want to convert your entire page to outlines as a workaround for font downloading problems or licensing issues, select all by choosing either of the selection tools in the Tools palette and then pressing ⌘/Ctrl+A. Next, choose Type ➪ Create Outlines or press ⌘+Shift+O or Ctrl+Shift+O. Alternately, you can press Command/CTRL+Shift+Option/Alt+O to copy and convert type in one set of keystrokes.

TIP   **There's an even more powerful and flexible technique in both Adobe Illustrator and Adobe InDesign to convert type to paths when you encounter output problems or undesired flattening effects. Create a Transparency Flattener Preset that includes Convert text to outlines, then use some transparency on the InDesign spreads or in the Illustrator file. When the file is output, printed to PostScript, or exported/printed to a PDF/X 1.3 file all text will automatically be converted to outlines in the print stream. This way your original file remains editable text for future work, but you don't have any font problems in your output stream.**

Creating type effects in InDesign

Many type effects can be achieved in InDesign without converting the type to outlines. As demonstrated in Figure 15.15, you can create sophisticated type treatments with strokes, fills, gradients, and drop shadows and still be able to edit the text. This is a difficult or impossible feat in some other page-layout programs.

FIGURE 15.15

InDesign allows you to create sophisticated type effects without converting the type to outlines. The text remains fully editable.

Creating type masks in InDesign

Type masks are created a little differently than they are in Illustrator. Instead of placing type over artwork to be masked, the type is essentially turned into a graphics frame. You can then paste or import an image into the frame.

After you've converted your type to outlines, simply select it and choose File ⇨ Place, or press ⌘/Ctrl+D, and navigate to the image you want to import. When selecting the type, you can use either the Selection tool or the Direct Selection tool. In Figure 15.16, type is converted to outlines and the text is selected with the Selection tool.

FIGURE 15.16

After converting type to outlines, select the type with either the Selection tool or the Direct Selection tool.

When the Place dialog box appears, be certain to select the check box for Replace Selected Item, as shown in Figure 15.17. If you don't check the box, the cursor is loaded with the graphic and InDesign expects you to place the file somewhere on the document page. Alternately you can use the Place command and when the cursor is loaded with the object to place; just click on the object on the page to replace it. When you select Replace Selected Item, the file is placed within the outlined type, resulting in a mask. If you want to place an item in a multi-page document, be certain to select the Show Import Options check box as shown in Figure 15.17. You might use this option if you have a selected item on a master page and want to scroll pages in your document to choose what page to replace the graphic.

FIGURE 15.17

Be certain to select the check boxes for Replace Selected Item and Show Import Options in the Place dialog box.

When selecting Show Import Options, another dialog box appears. The type of dialog box and the options available are dependent on the file type you place. In Figure 15.18, the Place PDF dialog box opens because the file type being placed is a PDF. In the Preview window, you can navigate pages and see page thumbnails before committing to place the document.

InDesign provides options for selecting layers when you place Photoshop and PDF files. Click the Layers tab in the Place PDF dialog box and the Layers pane opens with choices for selecting layers on a given page to place. You toggle layers on and off like you do in any of the CS4 programs. Click the right-pointing arrow to open the nested layers and click the eye icon to toggle layers on and off. The Layers pane in the dialog box displays a preview of the selected layers, as you can see in Figure 15.19.

FIGURE 15.18

Be certain to Show Import Options when placing multiple-page PDF documents and layered files.

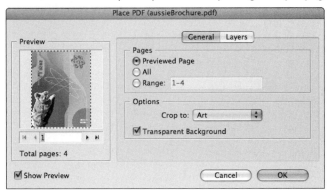

FIGURE 15.19

When you place layered Photoshop, Illustrator, InDesign, and layered PDF files, you can click the Layers tab and toggle layer views.

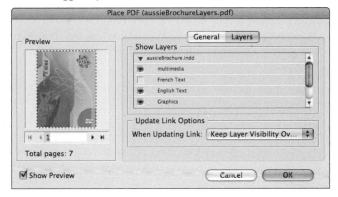

CROSS-REF For more information on working with layers in the CS applications, see Chapter 14.

Click OK in the Place PDF dialog box and the layer view you see in the preview is placed inside the type, as shown in Figure 15.20. If you need to move the image within the mask, select the Direct Selection tool. When the cursor approaches the text, the cursor changes to a Hand tool, thus informing you that the image can be moved within the mask.

FIGURE 15.20

When the Replace Selected Item check box is selected, the image is placed within the selected object.

TIP   When you drag with the Hand tool, click and pause a moment. When you drag the cursor after pausing, you can see the entire image previewed as you move around the document window.

Summary

- The three main font formats in use today are PostScript Type 1, TrueType, and OpenType.

- OpenType fonts have two advantages: they work in cross-platform environments (Mac and Windows), and they support expanded character sets.

- Font-management utilities such as FontAgent Pro help streamline your font-management tasks.

- Converting all type to outlines in your documents is a way to circumvent font downloading problems, but this approach should be used as a last option.

- Special type effects are easy to achieve in Illustrator, Photoshop, or InDesign. Illustrator offers a sophisticated array of transformation tools, including extrusion (3-D) and lighting effects for type objects. Photoshop CS4 enables you to create type outlines. InDesign allows certain type effects to be applied without first converting the type to outlines.

- Photoshop provides virtually unlimited options for creating type effects. If you want your text to remain editable, however, be sure to keep the type in vector form by preserving layers when saving your file.

Chapter 16

Working with Styles

Adding type to a page is one of the more common tasks performed by creative professionals. Long gone are the days when we ordered type from a professional typesetter. Today's graphic artists are both artists and typographers. Fortunately, the typographic tools in the CS4 applications make your job easier when setting type.

For anyone who has set type for manuals, books, and other long documents, style sheets should be familiar tools. It's hard to imagine working with large bodies of text without using style sheets. Without them, your labors would be tenfold. You would have to manually set the styles for each body of text throughout a document, and any style changes would require the same laborious process.

Illustrator supports character and paragraph styles that make layouts much more flexible. Photoshop supports text styles for applying effects to type. In InDesign, you'll find impressive style sheet capabilities such as nested styles and style sheets for tables. In Dreamweaver, you have abundant opportunities for adding styles to Web page designs.

CROSS-REF For information on working with styles in Dreamweaver, see Chapter 27. For more information on cell and table styles in InDesign, see Creating Cell and Table Styles later in this chapter.

This chapter takes you through setting type in CS4 applications and creating character, paragraph, and graphic styles and styles for formatting cells, tables, and objects in InDesign.

IN THIS CHAPTER

Formatting type

Working with character style sheets

Working with paragraph style sheets

Combining styles to create nested style sheets

Using styles with tables

Working with graphic and object styles

Setting Type

If you have type created in programs like Microsoft Word, you can import text into both Illustrator and InDesign, as described in Chapter 17. If you don't use a word-processing program to set type, you can add type in Illustrator, Photoshop, or InDesign with the Type tool. In Illustrator, setting type adds some flexibility when setting type on irregular shapes and paths. Each program has its own strength in regard to typesetting, and it's worth your time to look at both programs so you know which one is best for a particular job.

Setting type in Illustrator

Illustrator has two kinds of type functions, both created with the Type tool. You create *point type* by clicking the cursor in the document window and type. The primary limitation of point type is that the type doesn't wrap or conform to a specific area. If you keep typing, the characters eventually go off the page, unless you add a carriage return at the end of each line.

The other kind of type in Illustrator is *area type.* Area type conforms to a specific boundary, and the type wraps to the outside boundary. The type boundary is created by clicking and dragging open a rectangle with the Type tool or by clicking the cursor on the edge of an object with the Type tool or Area Type tool. Doing so binds the type to the shape of the object. The object can be a simple geometric shape, a polygon, or an irregular shape.

You also have tools for creating vertical type. Click the Type tool, and keep the mouse button depressed to expand the toolbar. There are two vertical type tools—one for vertical type (used for both point and area type) and one specifically for area type. The results of creating type with the type tools are shown in Figure 16.1.

Creating point type

To create point type, simply click the Type tool in the Illustrator Toolbox and click the cursor at the location where you want to begin typing. A blinking cursor appears.

After typing a line of text, you can use the Character panel or keyboard shortcuts to change type appearances. Choose Window ➪ Type ➪ Character or press ⌘/Ctrl+T to open the Character panel. The default view of the Character panel is collapsed. To expand the view and show more options, click the down-pointing arrow to open the panel menu and select Show Options. In Figure 16.2, the panel view is shown with the options expanded.

FIGURE 16.1

Type created in Illustrator can appear as (1) vertical point type, (2) point type, (3) area type, (4) type on a path, or (5) vertical area type.

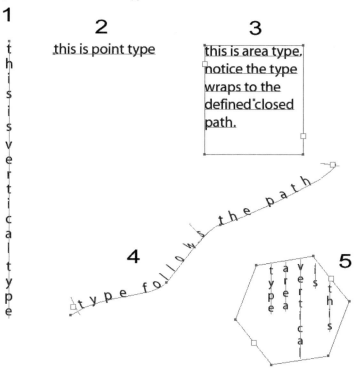

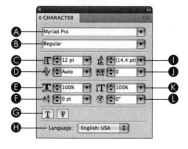

FIGURE 16.2

The Character panel

The type control available in the Character panel includes the following:

A   Type selection is made from the pull-down menu.

B   Type style is selected from options in the pull-down menu.

C   Type point size can be selected from fixed sixes in the pull-down menu or by typing values in the field box. The values range from 0.1 points to 1,296 points.

D   Kerning type is handled by selecting from fixed sizes or by typing values in the field box.

E   Horizontal scaling is defined from fixed values or by typing values in the field box.

F   Baseline shifts move the baseline of the type up when positive values are entered and down when negative values are entered.

G   Underline and strikethrough. Select type, and click either the underline option or the strikethrough option or both to apply the respective type effects.

H   Language selection is made from the pull-down menu. This item is important for hyphenation and spell checking. If None is selected, the spell checking is skipped. This is a selection you might make for ignoring spell checking items such as catalog part numbers.

I   Leading is controlled by selecting from fixed values or by typing values to $^1/_{100}$th of a point.

J   Tracking amounts are specified in whole numbers ranging from $-1,000$ to 10,000 points.

K   Vertical scaling of type can be adjusted in increments ranging from 1 percent to 10,000 percent.

L   Characters can be rotated in increments up to $^1/_{100}$ degree.

In addition to using the Character panel, you can perform several adjustments using keyboard shortcuts. To modify the type, use the following key combinations:

■   **Alt+right arrow (Option+right arrow on the Mac):** Increases tracking. Select type characters for the characters of which you want to change tracking amounts.

■   **Alt+left arrow (Option+left arrow on the Mac):** Decreases tracking. Select type characters for the characters of which you want to change tracking amounts.

■   **Alt+up arrow (Option+up arrow on the Mac):** Decreases leading. Affects only selected characters.

■   **Alt+down arrow (Option+down arrow on the Mac):** Increases leading. Affects only selected characters.

■   **Alt+ Shift+up arrow (Option+Shift+up arrow on the Mac):** Increases baseline shift. Affects only selected characters.

■   **Alt+Shift+down arrow (Option+Shift+down arrow on the Mac):** Decreases baseline shift. Affects only selected characters.

- **Alt+Ctrl+left arrow (Option+⌘+left arrow on the Mac):** Decreases tracking on all selected characters. Clicking in a line of type decreases tracking between characters at the cursor position.

- **Alt+Ctrl+right arrow (Option+⌘+right arrow on the Mac):** Expands kerning. Clicking in a line of type expands kerning between characters at the cursor position.

Other options available in the Character panel are selected from the panel menu. Click the right-pointing arrow in the upper-right corner of the panel, and the panel menu opens as shown in Figure 16.3. The menu options include the following:

FIGURE 16.3

The right-pointing arrow opens the panel menu.

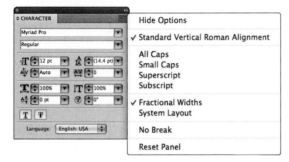

- **Standard Vertical Roman Alignment:** The direction of half-width characters such as Roman text or numbers changes in vertical alignment. When this option is checked, you can rotate selected individual characters within a block of text without affecting the rotation of the unselected characters.

- **All Caps:** Sets all selected characters to caps, as shown in Figure 16.4.

- **Small Caps:** Sets all selected characters to small caps, as shown in Figure 16.4.

- **Superscript:** Selected characters appear as superscript above the baseline, as shown in Figure 16.4.

- **Subscript:** Selected characters are subscripted below the baseline, as shown in Figure 16.4.

- **Fractional Widths:** As a default, leave this item checked because the type is displayed in the best appearance. The spacing between characters varies. If disabled, the characters are monospaced.

- **System Layout:** Characters are previewed using the operating system's default text handling. This option is particularly helpful when designing user-interface designs where you might create dialog boxes, panels, and menus.

■ **No Break:** Should be applied manually to selected type that you don't want to break across lines. This is appropriate for technical names or other words that should not be split across lines.

■ **Reset Palette:** Restores the default character settings in the panel.

FIGURE 16.4

Type styles: All caps, small caps, superscript, and subscript

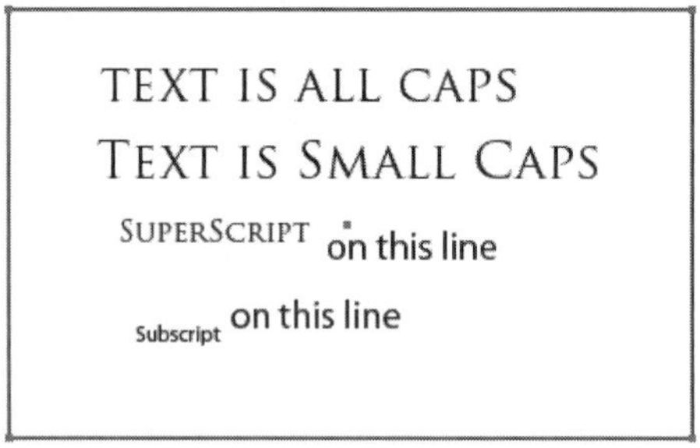

TEXT IS ALL CAPS
TEXT IS SMALL CAPS
SUPERSCRIPT on this line

Subscript on this line

Creating area type

The Character panel by default is nested together with two other panels. The Paragraph panel is used for paragraph formatting, and it makes sense to describe the options when discussing area type. The OpenType panel offers options for a number of different settings you can make when using OpenType fonts.

CROSS-REF   For more information on OpenType fonts, see Chapter 16.

Area type is created using the Type tool. Instead of clicking the cursor where point type is created, click the cursor and drag open a rectangle. By default, when you release the mouse button, a blinking I-beam cursor appears in the top-left corner of the rectangle. Area type also can be created within closed paths. Any object you draw in Illustrator can define the boundaries for area type. When adding area type to a closed path, simply click the cursor on the edge of the object and the blinking I-beam informs you the object is ready to accept type. In Figure 16.5, you can see results of area type applied to different shapes.

In the Paragraph panel, you'll find options for paragraph formatting. Some of the options, such as paragraph alignment, also can apply to point type. However, indents and paragraph spacing, although available with point type, are more likely to be applied to area type.

When you create area type and want to change paragraph formatting, click the Paragraph tab to show the options. If the panel is not in view, choose Window ➪ Type ➪ Paragraph, and the panel shown in Figure 16.6 opens.

FIGURE 16.5

Area type added to different shapes

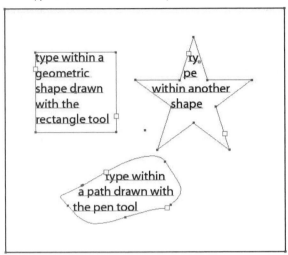

FIGURE 16.6

The paragraph panel has options for paragraph formatting.

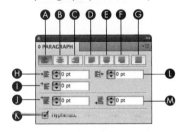

As shown in Figure 16.6, the panel contains many options. These include the following:

A **Align Left:** Text alignment for the paragraph is aligned left.

B **Align Center:** Paragraph text is aligned centered.

C **Align Right:** Paragraph text is aligned right.

D **Justify with Last Line Aligned Left:** The paragraph is fully justified with the last line aligned left.

E **Justify with Last Line Aligned Center:** The paragraph is fully justified with the last line aligned center.

F   **Justify with Last Line Aligned Right:** The paragraph is fully justified with the last line aligned right.

G   **Justify All Lines:** All text is justified, even the last line. If you have only two words appearing in the last line of text, one word is aligned left and the other word is aligned right.

H   **Left Indent:** Text is indented from the left edge of the text block.

I   **First Line Left Indent:** The first line of text in the paragraph is indented left, and the other lines are aligned left without indentation.

J   **Space Before Paragraph:** This option adds space above the paragraph in amounts specified in the field box.

K   **Hyphenation:** When the check box is checked, hyphenation is applied to the paragraph.

L   **Right Indent:** Text is indented from the right edge of the text block.

M   **Space After Paragraph:** This option adds space after a paragraph in amounts specified in the field box. Use the space after and space before paragraphs instead of using carriage returns.

The seven views of type formatted using the different paragraph formats are shown in Figure 16.7. From the Paragraph panel fly out menu, the Adobe Every-line Composer was selected to compose the type in Figure 16.7.

FIGURE 16.7

The seven different paragraph formats

Align left   Align center   Align right

Justify last line left   Justify last line center   Justify last line right

Justify all items

500

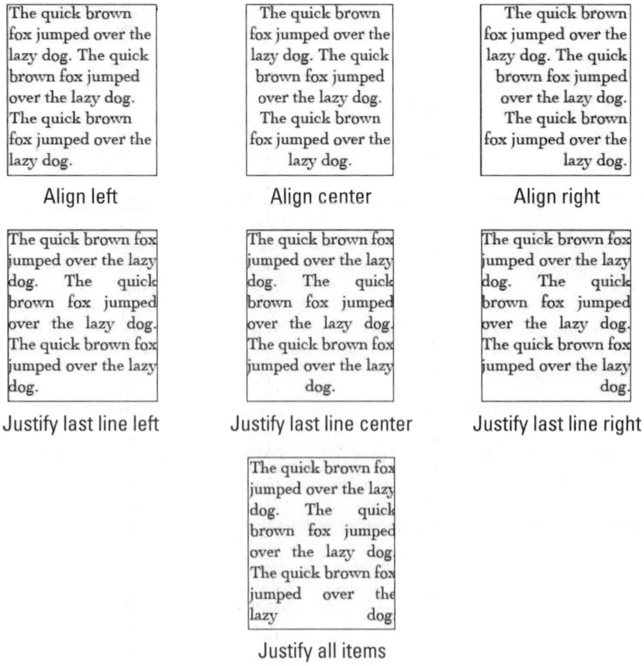

Using OpenType

As detailed in Chapter 16, OpenType fonts offer you many more glyphs than TrueType or PostScript fonts. With more glyphs available in an OpenType Pro font, you have alternate choices for the way you want to display characters. Because the number of characters can vary between OpenType fonts, be aware that all options are not available with every font. As you open the Character panel and view the tabs, the final tab is the OpenType tab. Click this tab, and the options shown in Figure 16.8 appear.

FIGURE 16.8

The OpenType tab has options for OpenType fonts panel in Adobe Illustrator.

The panel displays two pull-down menus and a line of buttons. To have the menu commands and buttons active, you need to have an OpenType font selected. Not all options are available for all OpenType fonts. Depending on the number of characters and styles contained within an OpenType font, the options vary. From the Figure pull-down menu, the options include the following:

**NOTE** If using Asian OpenType fonts (Chinese, Japanese, and Korean), you may have more options available in the OpenType panel.

- **Default Figure:** Choose this option to use the default style for numbers appearing in the selected font.

- **Tabular Lining:** Only when the OpenType characters are available, the full-height figures line up in a monospaced appearance and do not cross the baseline. You might use this option when setting type in tables and charts.

- **Proportional Lining:** Proportional spacing is used with numbers for aligning the numerals to the baseline.

- **Proportional Oldstyle:** When characters are available, use this option when you want a classic type appearance. It creates a more sophisticated look when using lowercase characters.

- **Tabular Oldstyle:** Applies to varying height characters with fixed, equal widths. This option might be used when you want a classic appearance of old-style figures, but you want the characters to align in columns.

Another set of menu commands appears in the Position pull-down menu. The Position options offer choices for the placement of characters respective to the baseline. These options are particularly helpful when working with numbers and fractions. Again, these are available only if they are offered in the current OpenType font for a given selection of type. The menu choices include the following:

- **Default Position:** Keeps the default position of characters for the selected font.

- **Superscript/Superior:** Raises characters above the baseline.

- **Subscript/Inferior:** Lowers characters below the baseline.

- **Numerator:** Applies to numerals designed as fractions. The fractional characters only are raised to appear as numerators.

- **Denominator:** Applies to numerals designed as fractions. The fractional characters only are lowered to appear as denominators.

Figure 16.9 displays the various options choices when using the Cronos Pro OpenType font and applying the different position options to alpha and numeric characters.

FIGURE 16.9

The five different OpenType options for Position are applied to the OpenType font Cronos Pro.

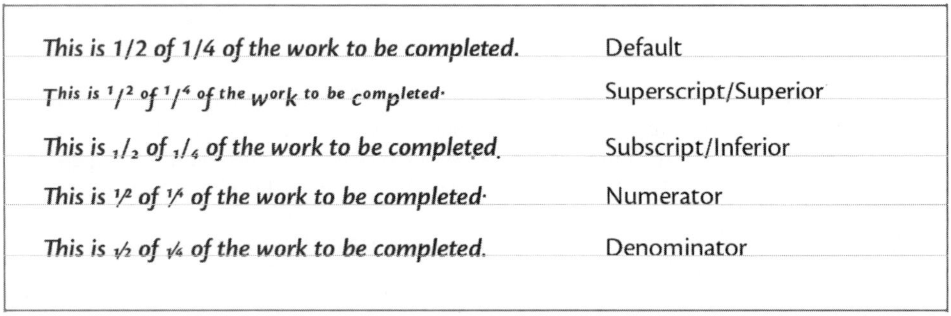

This is 1/2 of 1/4 of the work to be completed.	Default
This is ¹/² of ¹/⁴ of the work to be completed.	Superscript/Superior
This is ₁/₂ of ₁/₄ of the work to be completed.	Subscript/Inferior
This is ½ of ¼ of the work to be completed.	Numerator
This is ½ of ¼ of the work to be completed.	Denominator

Combining point type and area type

Many different types of documents can be opened and edited in Illustrator. Often, the objects appear to be translated without problems, but you may find that much of the original paragraph formatting is lost. Files you may want to convert to Illustrator documents—CAD drawings, page layouts from other programs, charts, graphs, and so on—typically open in Illustrator with broken type blocks. To convert the point type segmented throughout a document, look over the following steps to see how you can fix such problems.

STEPS: Converting Point Type to Area Type

1. **Open an EPS file in Illustrator.** For this example, we use a QuarkXPress document saved from XPress using the Save Page as EPS menu command. Notice that in Figure 16.10, when all the type is selected in Illustrator, you see point type on each line of text and broken along the lines of type. This copy would be difficult to edit in its present form.

FIGURE 16.10

After selecting type, you can see where the type blocks are broken by observing the handles (small squares) on the baselines.

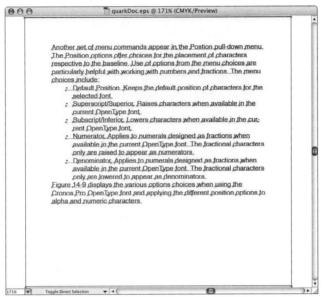

2. **Cut the text from the art board.** Choose Edit ⇨ Select All or press ⌘/Ctrl+A to select all the type. Be certain to have either the Selection tool or the Direct Selection tool selected in the Toolbox before selecting the type. If the Type tool is selected and the cursor is blinking in a line of type, only that segment of type is selected. After selecting all the related type objects, choose Edit ⇨ Cut to cut the text to the Clipboard.

3. **Paste the type.** Select the Type tool, and drag open a rectangle to define the boundaries for the area type. Choose Edit ⇨ Paste. The type is pasted from the blinking cursor and fills the area type boundary. When the type is pasted, all paragraph formatting is lost, as shown in Figure 16.11. However, the type is one contiguous body of text.

4. **Format the type.** Add carriage returns and tabs where needed to create the paragraph format you want to apply to the body of text. Use the Paragraph panel to set type formats such as space before and after, as well as any alignment considerations you need, as shown in Figure 16.12.

FIGURE 16.11

Although the paragraph formatting is lost, the text is pasted as one contiguous body of type.

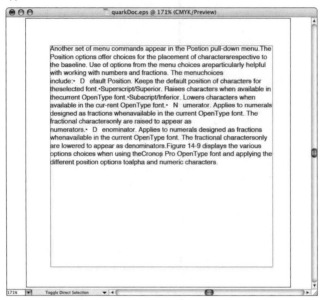

FIGURE 16.12

As a contiguous body of text, you can use the Paragraph panel to format the type.

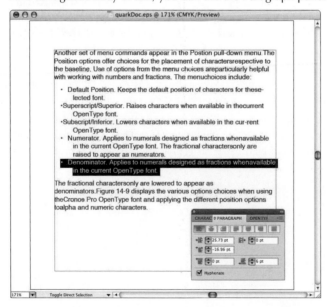

For more-precise placement and sizing of the text block, you can use guides and create text frames according to guide positions. If you have legacy Illustrator files that were designed with point type where it makes more sense to use area type and paragraph formatting, you can cut the point type and paste it back into a type frame.

Updating type

The new additions to the type features in Illustrator required recoding the Illustrator type engine. The results of the update create some problems when opening legacy files in Illustrator CS2 and CS3. Any Illustrator document created from version 10 and prior uses a different type engine than Illustrator CS2 through CS4. In addition new type enhancements in Illustrator CS4 are significant and will often trigger many warnings when opening legacy files. When you open a legacy file in Illustrator CS4, you first see an alert dialog box, as shown in Figure 16.13.

FIGURE 16.13

Opening legacy files in Illustrator CS4 prompts you to preserve the type appearance in the document or update the text.

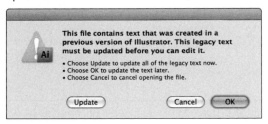

If you click Update, the text is updated to conform to the new type engine. The text is editable, but you may experience shifts in type appearance and position. If you click OK, the text is not updated, and the type appearance and position remain intact. The type is not editable, however. The type blocks appear within rectangular bounding boxes, as shown in Figure 16.14.

You can elect to update text on a block-by-block basis. If you click OK and don't update the type when opening a legacy file, you can individually update text blocks by clicking with the Type tool on a given body of text or by double-clicking the type with the Selection tool. Illustrator then prompts you in another alert dialog box, offering you a few choices. In Figure 16.15, you can see the choices appearing for Copy Text Object and Update.

When you select Copy Text Object, a duplicate of the text block is placed behind the converted text. After copying the text, the foreground text is selected when you click with the Type tool. The other option for Updating the text accomplishes the same result as when you first open a legacy document and click Update, as shown in Figure 16.15.

If you open legacy files without updating the text, text blocks appear within bounding boxes when the text is selected.

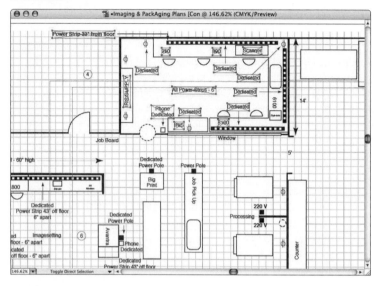

Clicking any legacy text block with the Type tool opens a dialog box where you can decide how the type is updated.

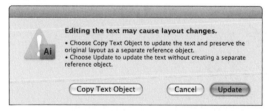

If you want to update multiple items, options are available in a menu command. Choose Type ➪ Legacy Text, and a submenu offers options for handling legacy text. Note that the menu is grayed out unless you open a legacy file and do not update the text. If you click Update when opening a file, the Legacy submenu options are grayed out as they are when opening files originally authored in Illustrator CS4.

In the Legacy submenu, the options include the following:

■ **Update All Legacy Text:** If you open a legacy file and choose to not update the text, you can later select this option to update all the text in the file. This gives the same result as if you had opened a legacy file and clicked Update.

- **Update Selected Legacy Text:** You can select individual text blocks to update by using the Selection tool and pressing the Shift key as you continue clicking additional text blocks. With a group of objects selected, choose this menu item and the selected text is updated.

- **Show/Hide Copies:** When clicking Copy Text Object, as shown in Figure 16.15, copies of the original text are placed behind the updated text. If you click Hide Copies, the copied text is hidden. Conversely, when clicking Show Copies, all hidden text is shown. If you have a converted unedited text block in front of the original text, you won't see the copies hidden or shown. To see the original text, hide the foreground text by selecting it and choose Object ⇨ Hide ⇨ Selection (⌘/Ctrl+3).

- **Delete Copies:** Selecting this menu command deletes all copies.

- **Select Copies:** This menu command selects all copies.

It's best to keep copies of your artwork until your text conversions are made successfully. When updating text, you may encounter problems such as the following:

- **Character position and attribute changes:** Updating text may shift characters and change attributes such as leading, tracking, and kerning.

- **Word shifts:** Words may shift to the next line. The text within a bounding box may scroll past the bottom of the text frame thereby hiding one or more lines of text. Hyphenation may be altered.

- **Word overflows:** In linked text frames, words may overflow to the next thread.

As a matter of practice, you should carefully check the type conversions on legacy files. Before deleting copies, be certain that the text attributes and word flow follow your design intent.

Setting type in Photoshop

Setting type in Photoshop is a task you optimally perform only on small bodies of text and when creating headlines and stylizing type. We say *optimally* because Photoshop is not as well suited for setting type as are Illustrator and InDesign. Therefore, we won't spend much time talking about typesetting in Photoshop.

You create type in Photoshop by clicking the Type tool in the Toolbox and then clicking the cursor in the document window. A blinking I-beam appears, and you are now ready to type. The default type tool is Horizontal Type. If you click and hold down the mouse button in the Toolbox, you also can choose the Vertical Type tool, the Horizontal Type Mask tool, or the Vertical Type Mask tool. The latter two are used to create type masks that essentially are selections that can be filled, painted, or used to capture underlying pixels.

Type in Photoshop changed from raster-based to vector-based back in version 6. When you set type in Photoshop, it appears on a separate layer and remains fully editable as long as the Photoshop image is not flattened or the layer is not rasterized. If you want to preserve the type on a layer and keep it editable, you need to save the file with layers intact. Saving as a PDF (with layers) preserves the type on the layers and keeps it in vector form.

If you prepare files for PDF viewing, leave the type on a layer and save as Photoshop PDF. When the PDF is opened in Acrobat, all the type is searchable with Acrobat Search.

For typesetting in Photoshop, you have attribute choices you can make in the Options bar as well as two panels where character and paragraph options choices are made.

Using the Options bar

When you click the Type tool in the Photoshop Toolbox, the Options bar displays options for setting type. As shown in Figure 16.16, the choices extend from character attributes to paragraph options. The individual settings include the following:

FIGURE 16.16

The Type tool changes its options to reflect attribute choices for setting type.

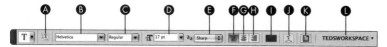

A **Change Text Orientation:** Click the icon to change from horizontal to vertical and vice versa. If a block of text has been created on a layer, you can change type orientation by simply selecting the layer and applying the change.

B **Font Family:** The pull-down menu lists all fonts available to your system. Photoshop reads installed fonts when you launch the program. Therefore, if you load a new font with a font-management tool, you need to quit Photoshop and relaunch it before the font is recognized in the menu.

C **Font Style:** You have choices for font style from pull-down menu commands. Choose from options such as Regular, Bold, Italic, and Bold Italic when the styles are available for a given font.

D **Font Size:** From the pull-down menu, you have choices for fixed point sizes, or you can enter a value in the field box. Sizes range from 0.01 to 1,296 points. Because the type is vector art, however, you can use the transformation tools to create any type size you want.

CROSS-REF For more information on transforming objects, see Chapter 12.

E **Anti-Aliasing Method:** Anti-aliasing creates an illusion of smoothing objects. When you anti-alias objects, small partially transparent pixels are added to objects, giving the appearance of smoother edges. Photoshop offers you several choices for anti-aliasing, including the following:

- **None:** Applies no anti-aliasing.
- **Sharp:** Adds a slight amount of anti-aliasing, keeping the type sharp in contrast.

- **Crisp:** Similar to Sharp but adds a little more anti-aliasing, making the appearance slightly less sharp.

- **Strong:** Creates a slightly bold appearance to the type. If you anti-alias type and it appears to lose the normal type weight, add Strong to thicken the characters.

- **Smooth:** Adds more anti-aliasing. A good choice for type that may appear with strong jagged edges.

F   **Align Left:** Aligns text left.

G   **Align Center:** Aligns text centered.

H   **Align Right:** Aligns text right.

I   **Text Color:** Click the color swatch, and the Photoshop Color Picker opens. You can make choices for the type color from the Color Picker, from the Color and Swatches panels, or from the Foreground Color tool in the Photoshop Toolbox.

J   **Create Warped Text:** Photoshop offers you many options for applying effects to type from the Create Warped Text tool. Select the type you want to use to apply a new style, and the Warp Text dialog box opens as shown in Figure 16.17. When warping text, you can apply changes by either selecting the text with the Type tool or selecting the layer containing the text.

FIGURE 16.17

Selecting the type of warp effect you want

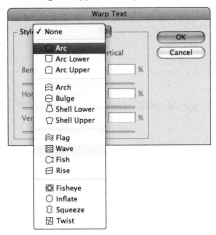

K   **Toggle the Character and Paragraph Panels:** This toggles the Character and Paragraph panels open and closed.

Using the Character panel

Some character attributes are the same in the Character panel as you find in the Options bar. Choices for font family, font style, and anti-aliasing methods are duplicated in the Character panel. The panel also contains other options. When you open it, you'll notice the panel appears similar to the Character panel found in Illustrator. To open the panel, choose Window ➪ Character or click the Toggle the Character and Paragraph Panels icon in the Options bar. The panel shown in Figure 16.18 opens.

FIGURE 16.18

The Photoshop Character panel

As you can see, the options are almost identical to those found in Illustrator. Notice that the horizontal and vertical scaling is flopped in the Photoshop Character panel, but the six attribute choices below the pull-down menus for font and style are identical to Illustrator.

Photoshop does offer additional choices that appear at the bottom of the panel. From the row of icons, reading left to right, you have the following choices:

- **Faux Bold:** Enables you to bold a font that does not have a bold equivalent with the chosen typeface

- **Faux Italic:** Enables you to italicize a font that does not have an italic equivalent

- **All Caps**

- **Small Caps**

- **Superscript**

- **Subscript**

- **Underline**

- **Strikethrough**

From the lower-left pull-down menu, you can choose from installed languages. The pull-down menu in the lower right is where anti-aliasing choices are made.

Using the Paragraph panel

When creating type in Photoshop, you press the Num Pad Enter key to complete the typesetting and signal Photoshop that you've ended your type edits. If you press the Return/Enter key, Photoshop adds a carriage return to the body of type. The ability to add carriage returns means Photoshop supports paragraph type. The attributes you can assign to paragraphs are, in part, located in the Options bar, where you can choose from three justification methods. The remaining choices are located in the Paragraph panel. When the Character panel is open, click the Paragraph tab to open the panel shown in Figure 16.19.

FIGURE 16.19

The Paragraph panel offers options for paragraph formatting.

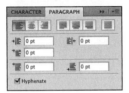

As you can see in Figure 16.19, the Paragraph panel options in Photoshop are identical to those in Illustrator. As is the case with changing character attributes, you can select the text with the Type tool or simply click the layer in the Layers panel. Changes you make in the Paragraph panel are applied to the text regardless of which selection you make.

Line Illustrator and InDesign Photoshop offers two composers that are selectable in the paragraph panel. Open the fly-away menu and choose one of the following:

- **Adobe Single-line Composer.** The single-line composer offers a traditional approach to composing type one line at a time. This option is helpful when you want manual control over line breaks.

- **Adobe Every-line Composer.** The Every-line composer considers a range of lines and applies line breaks to the range resulting in a more attractive type appearance.

As a matter of default, you might choose the Adobe Every-line Composer option when setting type in Illustrator, Photoshop, and InDesign. When you need manual control over line breaks and want to apply soft and hard breaks manually, choose the Adobe Single-line Composer option from the fly-away menu in the Paragraph panels in all these applications.

Setting type in InDesign

In many design workflows, you're likely to be handed copy that has been composed in a word processing program. If you work with copywriters or obtain copy from clients, the files are usually Microsoft Word documents. And unless the author used style sheets you can import, you'll need to reformat the text in InDesign.

CROSS-REF   **For more information on importing Microsoft Word documents, see Chapter 19.**

For some creative professionals, using word-processing programs may not be as appealing as setting type in InDesign. Certainly, for single-page ads and smaller pieces, you may use InDesign for both creating copy and performing the layout tasks. Fortunately, InDesign does have some impressive tools if you decide to use the program for creating copy.

Using the Story Editor

InDesign's Story Editor is like having your own word processor built into the program. In order to use the Story Editor, you need to have a text frame selected on a document page. If no text frame exists, the Story Editor is not accessible.

To open the Story Editor, select a text frame or several text frames and then choose Edit ➪ Edit in Story Editor (⌘/Ctrl+Y) as shown in Figure 16.20. If you select noncontiguous text frames, each body of text opens in separate Story Editor windows.

FIGURE 16.20

Noncontiguous text frames open in different Story Editor windows.

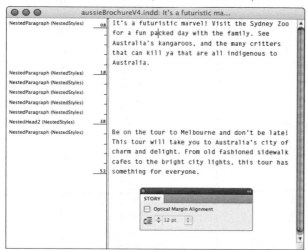

The Story Editor opens and appears in front of the document window. The Story Editor is dynamic in many ways. As you type in the Story Editor, the text is updated on the corresponding text frame. As its own document window, the Story Editor does not prevent you from using other tools and menus in InDesign that are needed for setting type. Panels used for styles and text formatting are accessible to you while working in the Story Editor. In Figure 16.20, the Story Editor is open where text is added in the editor and displayed on the document page. The Paragraph Styles panel is used to select styles and apply them in the Story Editor.

In Figure 16.20, notice the appearance of the vertical ruler. InDesign offers you a vertical depth ruler to measure the depth of text. Another feature in InDesign is support for viewing overset text with markers. When you set type and your type frame is not large enough to display the type, the text is overset and hidden from view. You need to open the text frame to reveal the hidden text. In the Story Editor, the hidden text is marked with an Overset, as you see in Figure 16.21.

FIGURE 16.21

Overset text is marked with a line. The text falling below the line is hidden from view when you return to the Layout mode.

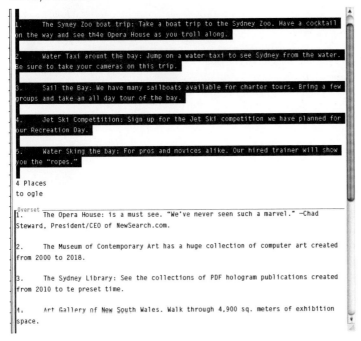

While working in the Story Editor, you can make choices from the Type menu and panels where type attributes are selected, or you can make similar choices from a context menu. To open a context menu in the Story Editor, press the Control key and click (Mac) or right-click (Windows) and the context menu shown in Figure 16.22 opens.

When you want to return to the InDesign document window, click the close box in the Story Editor window, select Edit in Layout from the context menu, or choose Edit ➪ Edit in Layout. Alternately, you can press Command/CTRL+Y to toggle back and forth between the Story Editor and the layout. You can also use some of the n-up layouts in the Application bar to split your workspace to show both the layout and story editor simultaneously.

FIGURE 16.22

Context menus offer choices similar to the menu commands and panel options.

Using the Character panel

The Character panel in InDesign offers the same options as Illustrator, with the exception of the Skew option in place of the Rotate option. Below the Horizontal Scale setting, you see the Skew option (shown as a slanted *T*), as shown in Figure 16.23.

FIGURE 16.23

The InDesign Character panel offers almost identical options to those in the Illustrator Character panel.

From the panel menu, you can see some other options choices available only in InDesign. The underline and strikethrough options are listed in the panel, but each contains a companion Options menu where you can change attributes for underlines and strikethroughs, such as line weight, spacing, color, gaps, and so on. Select Underline Options, and the dialog box opens, as shown in Figure 16.24. Most items in the dialog box should be self-explanatory. A little more confusing are the Offset options. Increasing the Offset pushes an underline down while decreasing the Offset pushes the line up. This may be counterintuitive and not logical to you. Try to remember that increase in this instance is down while decrease is up.

FIGURE 16.24

InDesign offers many options for setting underline attributes.

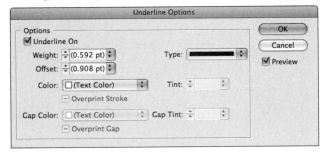

The options for strikethrough are similar to the options for underlining. Click the Strikethrough Options menu command, and a similar dialog box opens. Again, the options should be self-explanatory.

Another distinction you'll find between the Character panels in Illustrator and InDesign are the options selections for OpenType fonts. In Illustrator, buttons appear in the bottom of the OpenType panel, and in InDesign you can see the submenu items in Figure 16.25 offering the same options.

Another feature in InDesign is an option for selecting Stylistic Sets, as you see in Figure 16.25. OpenType fonts contain many alternate characters such as ligatures, fractions, swashes, ornaments, ordinals, titling, stylistic alternates, and so on. The OpenType panel lets you set up rules for using glyphs such as using ligatures, titling characters, and fractions for a given body of text. By using Stylistic Sets, you can apply alternates to a selected block of text without having to change each character individually.

FIGURE 16.25

OpenType options in a submenu of the Character panel

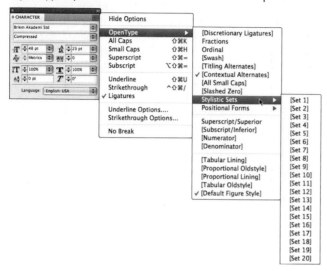

Using the Control panel

Setting type in InDesign does not require you to access Character and Paragraph panels to change attributes. The Control panel that appears by default at the top of the screen when you launch InDesign is one of the most frequently used tools favored by design professionals. Depending on the tool you select in the InDesign Toolbox, the panel changes to reflect options choices for the selected tool. In Figure 16.26, formatting options are shown for characters (top), paragraphs (middle), and objects (bottom).

FIGURE 16.26

When the Type tool is selected, you can toggle between formatting options for characters (middle) and paragraphs. When other tools are selected, options for transforming objects are displayed (bottom).

NOTE When using wide monitors looking at paragraph Controls InDesign CS3 and higher also shows some character controls at the same time.

With the Type tool selected, you can toggle between character and paragraph options in the Control panel. Simply click either the letter *A* or the paragraph symbol on the far left side of the panel. From there, you can make attribute choices by changing field box values and using pull-down menus. When using tools other than the Type tool, the panel displays options for applying attributes to objects, as shown in the last panel in Figure 16.26.

The Control panel is a handy place to select either character or paragraph styles. In addition, when selecting objects you have options for showing graphic styles. From the flyout menu, all the style sheets contained in your document are listed. When you add a new style, it's added to the appropriate menu.

CROSS-REF For information on creating style sheets, see the sections "Creating Character Styles," "Creating Paragraph Styles," and "Creating Cell and Table Styles."

Another menu is found when you click the right-pointing arrow. Depending on the panel shown, you'll see different menu items with additional choices for setting type or for working with objects. Many of the options choices you see in pull-down menus are the same options found in the panels. You can choose among top-level menus, panels, or the Control panel to apply the same edits. Additionally you can use the panel menu on the Control panel to customize which information is displayed in this panel. InDesign offers you this flexibility so you can make choices quickly and easily.

Using placeholder text

One nice distinction between InDesign and the other CS applications is the ability to use dummy copy when preparing templates, creating styles, or creating comps for a new design project. Rather than search your hard drive for the *Lorem Ipsum* Greek text file you've probably used since the early days of PageMaker, you can now use InDesign's built-in support for filling text frames with placeholder text.

To use placeholder text, click in any text frame or any object where you want to convert the object to a text frame. When you see the I-beam cursor blink, choose Type ➪ Fill with Placeholder Text. Greek text is added from the point of the blinking cursor to the end of the text thread, as shown in Figure 16.27.

FIGURE 16.27

Filling a frame with Greek text

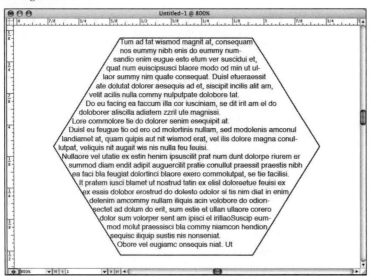

If you create comps and layouts where Greek type is used frequently, you may want to create a keyboard shortcut to access the menu command. Look over the steps that follow to see how you can assign a keyboard shortcut to access the Fill with Placeholder Text menu command.

STEPS: Using Placeholder Text

1. **Assign a keyboard shortcut to the Fill with Placeholder Text menu command.** Choose Edit ➪ Keyboard Shortcuts. The Keyboard Shortcuts dialog box opens. Select Type Menu from the Product Area pull-down menu, and click Fill with Placeholder Text. With the menu command selected, press the shortcut keys you want to use to assign to the menu command. A good choice is to use Alt/Option+F12. This keyboard shortcut is easily accessible and doesn't conflict with any existing InDesign keyboard shortcuts.

    Click the Assign button, and InDesign informs you that you can't edit the default set. Click Yes in the dialog box to create a new set, and the New Set dialog box opens. Type a name for your personal custom set, and click OK. Click OK again to exit the Keyboard Shortcuts dialog box. The new shortcut is added to your new set. In Figure 16.28, we added the new keyboard shortcut to a set we named MyShortcuts.

2. **Create an object.** From the InDesign Toolbox, click the Rectangle tool, the Ellipse tool, or the Polygon tool, and draw an object on the document page. For this example, we created an ellipse using the Ellipse tool.

FIGURE 16.28

Assigning menu commands

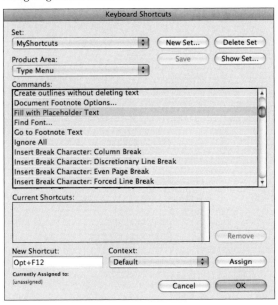

3. **Convert the object to a text frame.** When you draw an object in InDesign, the object appears as an Unassigned object. You can convert the object to a text object or a graphic object via a menu command. For a quick and easy method, select the Type tool and position the cursor within the object. When the cursor shape changes to the Type tool, displayed with a marquee oval around the *T* character, click the mouse button. The I-beam cursor starts to blink, signifying that the object is ready to accept type.

4. **Set the font attributes.** From the Control panel, select a font, point size, and other attributes that you want displayed on the type. The type attributes you assign before filling the object with text are used when filling with placeholder text.

5. **Use your keyboard shortcut to fill with placeholder text.** Press the keyboard shortcut you assigned to the Fill with Placeholder Text command. The object is filled with text using the font attributes you selected in the Control panel. Figure 16.29 shows the results of filling an object with placeholder text.

FIGURE 16.29

Use your new keyboard shortcut to fill the object text.

Using the Paragraph panel

The Paragraph panel in InDesign offers some of the same options as found in Illustrator, with the exception of two icons used for defining drop caps in paragraphs two alignment features, a last line indent and snap to baseline adjustments. The last two icons, shown in Figure 16.30 as A and B at the bottom of the panel, contain an option for defining the height of a drop cap (A). Setting the value to 2, for example, creates a drop cap whose height is equivalent to the first two lines of the paragraph. On the lower-right side of the panel, you can specify the number of sequential characters you want to appear as drop caps (B).

You find more distinction between the Illustrator Paragraph panel and the InDesign Paragraph panel when opening the panel menus. InDesign offers some advanced formatting features not found in the other CS4 programs and some that are not found in any other layout and design program. When you open the panel menu, the options shown in Figure 16.30 appear. The menu commands include the following:

FIGURE 16.30

The last two field boxes offer options for choosing the number of lines a drop cap is applied to (A) and the number of characters to be used as drop caps (B).

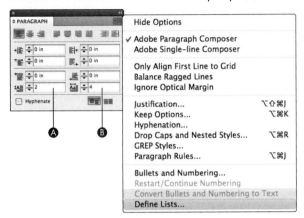

- **Adobe Paragraph Composer:** (Known as the Adobe Every-line Composer in Illustrator and Photoshop). Break points are created to help prevent unattractive line breaks in paragraphs. Traditional methods for creating break points handled only one line at a time. The Adobe Paragraph Composer composes the breaks by taking into consideration all the lines in the paragraph. This results in a more attractive paragraph (available in InDesign, Illustrator, and Photoshop).

- **Adobe Single-Line Composer:** This option uses the more traditional method of creating break points, taking into consideration only single lines of text (available in InDesign, Illustrator, and Photoshop).

- **Only Align First Line to Grid:** When aligning text to a grid, only the first line of text is aligned to the grid.

- **Balance Ragged Lines:** This option is helpful for headlines and pull quotes and when centering paragraphs. Multiple lines of type appear more balanced, as widow-type oversets at the end of the text block are eliminated. You must use Adobe Paragraph Composer and the paragraph composer to see any results with this menu command.

- **Ignore Optical Margin:** This option overrides the Optical Margin option shown in Figures 16.32 and 16.33. In Figure 16.32 we set the optical margin in the Story Editor. In Figure 16.33 you see the text without the optical margin setting on the top and with the optical margin setting enabled on the bottom.

- **Justification:** This option opens the Justification dialog box where paragraph justification options are set.

- **Keep Options:** This option opens a dialog box where you can assign attributes to lines in paragraphs that you want to stay together when the paragraph flows to other frames and pages.

- **Hyphenation:** This offers similar options for controlling hyphenation as you find in Illustrator with two more options added to InDesign for hyphenating across columns and hyphenating last words.

- **Drop Caps and Nested Styles:** One of the truly amazing features available for typesetting is the ability to create nested styles. You have controls for drop cap positions relative to optical margins and collisions between descenders and lines beneath the drop cap and looping options for nested styles. When you are selecting the command, the Drop Caps and Nested Styles dialog box opens.

CROSS-REF For more information on nested styles, see the section "Creating Nested Styles."

- **GREP Styles:** GREP styles allow a designer to automatically and dynamically apply character styles to the content of a paragraph using GREP patterns. We could automatically style something like a Social Security number that appears anywhere in a paragraph with this feature.

- **Paragraph Rules:** The attributes for rules assigned to paragraphs are handled in the Paragraph Rules dialog box. Select this menu command to open the dialog box.

- **Bullets and Numbering:** Bullets and Numbering opens the Bullets and Numbering dialog box shown in Figure 16.31. You have choices for selecting from preset characters to use as bullet markers (or number styles), or click Add to display any character set loaded in your active system fonts. Attribute choices enable you to choose font, point size, style, color, indentation, and tab positions.

- **Restart/Continue Numbering:** Select Numbers from the List Type pull-down menu and you find options for restarting numbered lists. You might use this command when you have a second list following a first list where you want the numbers in the second list to begin at 1. You also can open the dialog box from a context menu when the cursor is placed in a paragraph containing bullets and/or numbered lists.

- **Convert Bullets and Numbering to Text:** To convert bullets and numbering to text, select a block of bulleted or numbered text and select this menu command. This command converts InDesign's automated bullets and numbers into selectable and editable content. Once this conversion takes place the automatic qualities are removed. The bullets and numbers are not cleared; they become part of the text flow. If a paragraph style was used you'll see that manual overrides have been applied.

FIGURE 16.31

Select Bullets and Numbering from the Paragraph panel flyout menu, and the Bullets and Numbering panel opens.

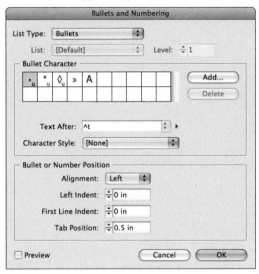

Paragraph formatting also can be applied in the Control panel and via menu commands. One particular option not found in either the Control or Paragraph panels is setting paragraphs for Optical Margin Alignment. When you choose Window ➪ Type & Tables ➪ Story, the Story panel opens, as shown in Figure 16.32. The panel contains options for applying optical margin text and adjusting the type point size.

FIGURE 16.32

The Story panel contains an option for selecting Optical Margin Alignment.

When you select the Optical Margin Alignment check box, paragraph alignment displays a different appearance. With traditional computer typesetting methods, paragraphs can appear misaligned, especially when punctuation marks and/or wide characters are used. In Figure 16.33, you can see where Optical Margin Alignment was applied to the bottom text block compared to the default margin alignment on the first text block. Because the punctuation hangs outside the text frame on the second block of text, the characters appear more aligned.

FIGURE 16.33

Optical Margin Alignment corrects misaligned characters.

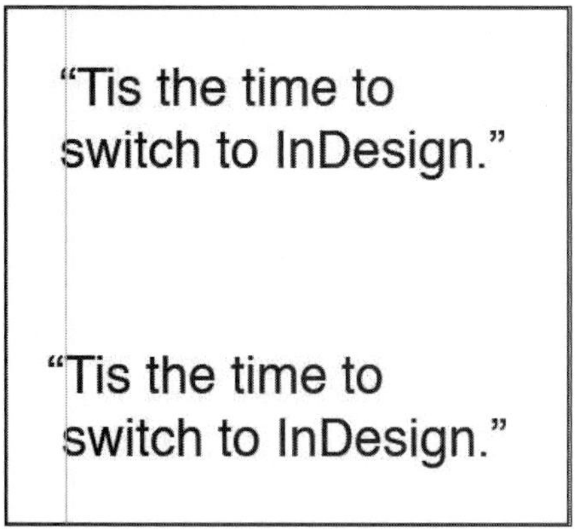

"Tis the time to
switch to InDesign."

"Tis the time to
switch to InDesign."

InDesign has so many different options for setting character and paragraph attributes that a complete coverage would take the space occupied by all the chapters in this book. We've highlighted some of the main features here and discussed the options found in the menus and panels. For a comprehensive view of setting type in InDesign, see the *InDesign CS4 Bible* by Galen Gruman (Wiley, 2008).

Creating type on paths

Once the job of Illustrator, applying type to paths also is available in Photoshop and InDesign. Applying type to paths opens up worlds of possibilities for each application. With the capability for adding type to paths in Photoshop, you can use familiar methods for stylizing type with shadows, embossing, filter effects, and so on, and you don't need to rely on rasterizing type in Photoshop that was originally created in Illustrator. In addition, in InDesign CS4 you can apply transparency effects to Photoshop .psd files imported in an InDesign layout.

Adding type to paths is a simple process in any of the CS4 programs where this feature is available. Basically, you create a path either with the Pen tool or use segments from paths created with other tools used for drawing objects. In Photoshop, select the Type tool, click a path, and begin typing. In Illustrator and InDesign, use the Type on a Path tool. Access the Type on a Path tool by pressing the mouse button down on the Type tool and selecting it from the pop-up menu.

To add type to freeform paths, click the mouse button on the path and begin typing. For closed paths in either Illustrator or InDesign, the type is added to the outside edge of the path by default. The respective program knows the distinction between adding type to a path and creating type inside a closed path. This is determined with the proper selection of the Type tool. When the Type on a Path tool is selected, the type conforms only to the path and not to the inside of a closed path.

In Photoshop, the task is a little different. When you have a closed path, placing the cursor on the path and clicking the mouse button enables you to type on the path. If you move the cursor inside the path, the cursor shape changes to the oval marquee around the letter *T*, signifying that type is to be added inside the path. The shape of the cursor informs you where the type will be placed.

In Figure 16.34, you can see type added to a path in Photoshop. When adding type to a path, be certain to check the paragraph attributes for alignment. If your type doesn't show up on the path, you may need to adjust the alignment from center-aligned to left-aligned or reduce the type size. After adding the type, you can change the alignment and other text attributes.

Both Illustrator and InDesign permit adjustments to type on paths in the same manner. When you add type to an open path, the type is added in a straightforward fashion. However, if you start with a closed object and then delete one side, type may be added to the shape flopped or upside-down. In each program, you can move type along a path or flop it by moving the centerline appearing within the type. In InDesign, the line is much less visible than in Illustrator, but it does exist. In Figures 16.35 and 16.36, you can see type added to a semicircle that began as an elliptical shape. The type is flopped. To move the type up where the type reads from left to right, drag the line at the center point upward.

FIGURE 16.34

In Photoshop, create a path with the Pen tool and select the Type on a Path tool.

FIGURE 16.35

To align type on a path in Illustrator, drag the centerline left/right or upward.

Drag this line up/down or left/right to reposition type

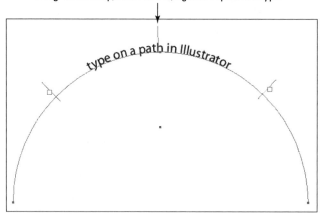

FIGURE 16.36

The same centerline appears in InDesign, but the line is less visible.

Drag this line upward to flop type

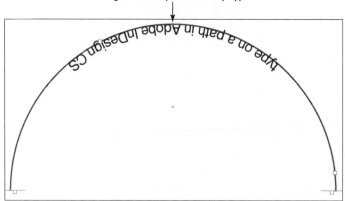

Additional editing options are available in both Illustrator and InDesign in a separate dialog box specifically handling type on a path effects. Select type on a path in either program and select Type ⇨ Type on a Path to open a submenu. In Illustrator choose Type on a Path Options from the submenu, and in InDesign choose Options. The Type on a Path Options dialog box opens as shown in Figure 16.37.

In the Type on a Path Options dialog box, you can make various choices for type effects and base-line alignments.

The Type on a Path Options dialog box shown from Adobe Illustrator.

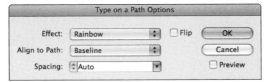

Creating Character Styles

In both InDesign and Illustrator, you have the ability to create style sheets at the character level. Using character styles allows you to specify formatting attributes for a selected range of text within your documents. For example, you may want to use different character formatting for Web-site URLs and e-mail addresses that appear in your copy. Instead of changing type in the Character panel, or using tedious find-and-replace commands to alter attributes of single characters or a string of words within a document, you can apply global changes to characters quickly and easily by changing formatting options in the Character Styles panel. All text to which you've applied the specific style is changed automatically. Using both character and paragraph styles saves time and ensures that your documents have a consistent look.

Using character styles in Illustrator

In Illustrator, you can set up character styles from scratch or by designating preformatted text as the basis of the new style. You also can copy an existing style and make formatting variations in order to create a new style.

Creating new character styles

To create a new character style, open the Character Styles panel by choosing Window ➪ Type ➪ Character Styles. The panel lists all the styles that have been created for the document. If no custom styles have been created, the only style that appears is the default, Normal Character Style, as shown in Figure 16.38.

To create a new style from scratch, click the Create New Style button in the lower-right portion of the panel. A new style with a default name automatically appears in the panel. An alternative way to create a new style is to select New Character Style from the panel menu. At this point, you're prompted to give the style a custom name. Either way, when the new style name appears in the list, double-click it to edit its attributes with the Character Style Options box, shown in Figure 16.39.

CAUTION Double-clicking a style in the Character Styles panel applies the style to any text you currently have selected in your document. If no text is selected, the style is applied to any new text you type. To keep either of these events from happening, press Shift+Ctrl (Shift+⌘ on the Mac) when you double-click the style name.

FIGURE 16.38

The Character Styles panel

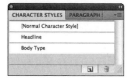

FIGURE 16.39

The Character Style Options dialog box

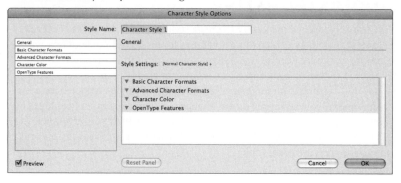

When the Character Style Options dialog box opens, you see the name of the selected style at the top and five options to the left. The options include the following:

- **General:** This is the pane displayed when you first open the Character Style Options dialog box. It's a summary of the remaining four settings, the style settings. You can view attributes of the separate style settings by toggling the gray arrows in the right side of the pane.

- **Basic Character Formats:** In this menu, you can specify font family, font style, size, leading, kerning, tracking, case, position (superscript or subscript), and whether or not you want Standard Vertical Roman Alignment.

- **Advanced Character Formats:** Here you can specify horizontal and vertical scale, baseline shift, character rotation, and desired language.

- **Character Color:** Choose your desired fill, stroke, and overprint options here.

- **OpenType Features:** This panel allows you to set OpenType options just like those found in the OpenType panel (see the section "Using OpenType").

After you've set up your attributes the way you want them, simply click OK.

You can easily create copies of existing character styles by either dragging the style onto the Create New Style button, or by choosing Duplicate Character Style from the Character Styles panel menu.

To delete styles, simply drag the style name to the trash icon, or select the style and choose Delete Character Style from the panel menu. You also can import styles from other Illustrator documents by using the Load Styles command.

TIP You can easily create a new style sheet based on the formatting of existing text. This is handy if you're experimenting with different design options because it eliminates the need to manually type all the formatting details in the Character Style Options menus ahead of time. Simply select the text whose attributes you want to use, and click the Create New Style button.

Applying character styles

To apply character styles in Illustrator, first select the characters with the Type tool or a selection tool. If you're typing new characters, place the cursor where you want the style to begin. Then simply click the style name in the Character Styles panel. To designate a style to be used for any new type in the document, be sure to deselect all type objects first; then click the style name.

Using styles in Photoshop

Photoshop doesn't have character or paragraph style panels. Logically, you wouldn't use Photoshop for setting large bodies of type. However, Photoshop is often used when stylizing type where you may apply various effects and filters. The edits you make to type in Photoshop can be captured as graphic styles. To see how graphic styles and tool presets are used with Photoshop, see the section "Working with graphic styles in Photoshop."

Using character styles in InDesign

The process of setting up and using character styles in InDesign is very similar to Illustrator. InDesign does offer a few additional options for refining your typesetting capabilities, however.

Creating new character styles

Open the Character Styles panel by choosing Type ➪ Character Styles or Window ➪ Type & Tables ➪ Character Styles. As in Illustrator, the panel lists all the styles that have been created for the document. If no custom styles have been created, all you'll see is the default: None.

Creating a new style is the same procedure as in Illustrator: Click the Create New Style button in the lower-right portion of the panel, or open the panel flyout menu and select New Character Style. You can then specify attributes with the Character Style Options or New Character Style box. The options here are pretty much like Illustrator's, with a few minor differences. As shown in Figure 16.40, with InDesign you have the added ability to base styles on existing styles and create shortcuts. You also have advanced options for underlining, strikethroughs, and ligatures, as well as a no-break option and a skew option in place of Illustrator's rotation option. You also can apply a style to a selection using the Apply Style to Selection option in the New Character Style window. This option is handy when you create a new style and text is selected in the layout. You can apply the new style to the selected text without leaving the New Character Style dialog box.

FIGURE 16.40

InDesign offers more character style options than Illustrator.

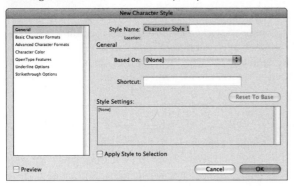

Notice in Figure 16.41 the Character Styles panel also has a folder icon. Click this icon and a new styles group is created. You can nest styles in groups of folders in InDesign.

Duplicating, editing, and deleting Character Styles is the same as in Illustrator. InDesign can import character styles from other InDesign documents using the Load Character Styles command. A distinction between defining and applying styles between Illustrator and InDesign is InDesign's support for defining type attributes without adding a typeface to the style. For example, you can define a style for italicized text and apply the style to text having different faces with the result being just the italics applied to the type without changing typefaces.

Applying character styles

You can use four ways to apply a character style to selected text in InDesign. You first select text and then click the style name in the Character Styles panel, choose the style name from the pull-down menu in the Control panel, choose Edit ➪ Quick Apply (Ctrl+Enter, Windows; Ctrl+Return, Mac), or use the keyboard shortcut you've assigned to the style.

Creating Paragraph Styles

Paragraph styles are especially helpful for managing large amounts of text in both InDesign and Illustrator. The one limitation you have with respect to both character and paragraph styles among the CS4 applications is that styles created in either Illustrator or InDesign cannot be imported across programs. You can import styles from application documents using the same application. For example, you can load character styles in Illustrator from another Illustrator document. However, you cannot load character styles in Illustrator from an InDesign document or vice versa. The same applies to paragraph styles. Furthermore, when you import Illustrator files containing style sheets in InDesign, or copy and paste text between programs, the style-sheet information is lost.

Using paragraph styles in Illustrator

Just like with Character Styles, you can set up paragraph styles from scratch or by designating pre-formatted text as the basis of the new style. You also can copy an existing style and make formatting variations in order to create a new style.

Creating new paragraph styles

Open the Paragraph Styles panel, shown in Figure 16.41, by choosing Window ➪ Type ➪ Paragraph Styles. You can change the display size of the panel items by choosing either Small List View or Large List View in the panel menu.

FIGURE 16.41

The Paragraph Styles panel

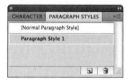

By default, every paragraph is assigned the Normal Paragraph Style if no paragraph style exists. Otherwise, the default is the default paragraph style in the document. To create a new paragraph style, click the Create New Style button in the lower-right portion of the panel. A new style with a default name automatically appears in the panel. Or create a new style by selecting New Paragraph Style from the panel menu. At this point, you'll be prompted to give the style a custom name. Either way, when the new style name appears in the list, double-click it to edit its attributes with the Paragraph Style Options box, shown in Figure 16.42.

FIGURE 16.42

The Paragraph Style Options dialog box

When the Paragraph Style Options dialog box opens, you see the name of the selected style at the top and ten options to the left. These include the following:

- **General:** This pane is displayed when you first open the Paragraph Style Options box. It's a summary of the remaining nine settings, the style settings. You can view attributes of the separate style settings by toggling the gray arrows in the right side of the pane.

- **Basic Character Formats:** Specify font family, font style, size, leading, kerning, tracking, case, position (superscript or subscript), and whether or not you want Standard Vertical Roman Alignment.

- **Advanced Character Formats:** Specify horizontal and vertical scale, baseline shift, character rotation, and desired language.

- **Indents and Spacing:** Specify alignment, left indent, first-line indent, right indent, space before, and space after.

- **Tabs:** Specify tab settings.

- **Composition:** Specify the Adobe Composer and hanging punctuation.

- **Hyphenation:** Specify hyphenation preferences.

- **Justification:** Specify justification preferences.

- **Character Color:** Choose desired color and stroke options.

- **OpenType Features:** This panel allows you to set OpenType options just like those found in the OpenType panel (see the "Using OpenType" section earlier in this chapter).

After you've set up your paragraph attributes the way you want them, click OK.

You can easily create copies of existing paragraph styles by either dragging the style onto the Create New Style button, or by choosing Duplicate Paragraph Style from the Paragraph Styles panel menu. To delete styles, simply drag the style name to the trash icon, or select Delete Paragraph Style from the panel menu. You also can import styles from other Illustrator documents by using the Load Paragraph Styles command in the panel menu.

Applying paragraph styles

To apply paragraph styles in Illustrator, insert the cursor in a single paragraph or select a range of paragraphs. Simply click the style name in the Paragraph Styles panel. To designate a style to be used for all new paragraphs in the document, be sure to deselect all type and objects first; then click the style name in the panel.

About overrides

If you see a plus sign next to a paragraph style in the Paragraph Styles panel, it means the selected text has overrides. *Overrides* are formatting attributes that don't match the defined style. To clear overrides, simply reapply the same style or use the Clear Overrides command in the Character Styles panel menu. Illustrator preserves overrides when you apply a different style to text with overrides, and to clear them you need to Option/Alt-click the style name when you apply the style.

Using paragraph styles in InDesign

Just like with character styles, the process for setting up and using paragraph styles in InDesign is very similar to Illustrator. InDesign offers additional options here as well.

Creating new paragraph styles

Open the Paragraph Styles panel by choosing Type ⇨ Paragraph Styles or Window ⇨ Type & Tables ⇨ Paragraph Styles. As in Illustrator, the panel lists all the styles that have been created for the document. If no custom styles have been created, all you see is the default: Basic Paragraph.

Creating a new style is the same procedure as in Illustrator: Click the Create New Style button in the lower-right corner of the panel, or select New Paragraph Style from the panel menu. Additionally you can create a style group by clicking the folder in the Paragraph Styles panel. Drag and drop new styles in the folder you add to the Paragraph Styles panel.

You specify attributes with the Paragraph Style Options or New Paragraph Style box. The options here are similar to Illustrator, but greatly expanded to include: the addition of keyboard shortcuts, basing styles on other styles, paragraph rules, keeping lines together, drop caps, nested styles, next style, Apply Style to Selection, ligature options, more OpenType options, skewing instead of character rotation, and underline and strikethrough options. As shown in Figure 16.43, the many options for paragraph-style formatting are selected in the left pane where individual options appear on the right side of the dialog box.

FIGURE 16.43

InDesign offers advanced features for creating paragraph styles.

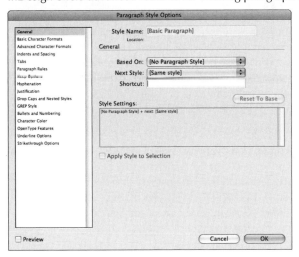

Duplicating, editing, and deleting Paragraph Styles in InDesign is the same as in Illustrator. You can import Paragraph Styles from other InDesign documents using the Load Paragraph Styles command. One additional feature you have with InDesign is synchronizing all style systems via a Book to make many documents have exactly the same styles. This feature is particularly helpful in workflow environments where you can create layout templates with paragraph and character styles, and workgroup members can work on different chapters/sections of a document that is eventually converted to a book. For working on independent documents you might use a template where all members of your workgroup can load styles from a master template and set type according to the styles defined for a particular project.

Applying paragraph styles

There are four ways to apply a paragraph style to selected text in InDesign. You can select the text and click the style name in the Paragraph Styles panel, choose the style name from the pull-down menu in the Control panel, use the Quick Apply method by selecting Edit ⇨ Quick Apply, or use the keyboard shortcut you've assigned to the style.

NOTE   When you apply a paragraph style to text, it doesn't automatically remove any existing character formatting in the paragraph. A plus sign (+) appears next to the paragraph style in the Paragraph Styles panel if there is any formatting applied that doesn't match the current style. Even if you click No Paragraph Style, the formatting remains intact. If you want to remove all formatting, including the existing character styles, you must press Alt or Option and then click No Paragraph Style in the panel or use the Clear Overrides buttons at the bottom edge of the styles panels.

Creating Nested Styles

Nested styles enable you to apply complex formatting to text using one or more character styles. You may decide, for example, that multiple paragraphs in your layout need to include a custom drop cap, a special style treatment for the first sentence, and a third style for the remainder of the body copy. In this instance, you would create two separate character styles, capture them as a nested style, and apply the nested style to other paragraphs in your composition. Each time the nested style is applied to a new paragraph, the drop cap, first sentence characters, and remaining body copy styles are applied automatically.

The easiest way to create a nested style is to first create the individual character styles required. These individual styles need to be listed in the Character Styles panel. For the body copy, create a paragraph style and add it to the Paragraph Styles panel. Drag the paragraph style name to the Create New Style icon to create a duplicate style. Notice in Figure 16.44 the style named *Body* is selected. Drag the style name to the Create New Style icon, as shown in the figure. The duplicated style appears in the panel with the word *copy* after the style name.

You can double-click the paragraph style copy to open the Paragraph Styles panel. However if text is selected, you'll first apply that style to a paragraph. A better option is to right click (Control + click on a Mac with a mouse with one button) to open a context menu and select Edit <style

name>. In the Paragraph Style Options dialog box, scroll down the list and select Drop Caps and Nested Styles in the left pane, as shown in Figure 16.45. The options change to settings used for creating nested styles. To make this process a little more comprehensible, work through the following steps to see how a nested style is created and then applied to a body of text.

FIGURE 16.44

You can duplicate the style by dragging it to the Create New Style icon.

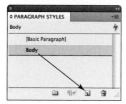

FIGURE 16.45

Select Drop Caps and Nested Styles on the left to access the attribute choices for creating nested styles.

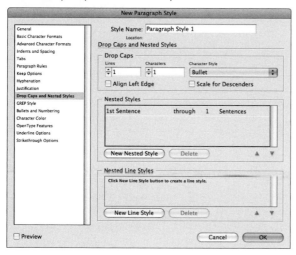

STEPS: Creating and Applying Nested Styles

1. **Create a text passage in InDesign.** Import text from a text file, or use placeholder text containing several paragraphs.

2. **Set type attributes for the body copy.** Select all the placed text, and choose a font style and point size that represents the main body copy you intend to use.

3. **Define a new paragraph style.** Click the cursor anywhere in the placed text after setting the font attributes, and select New Paragraph Style from the Paragraph Styles panel menu. Provide a name for the style. In our example, we use *Body* for the style name. After creating the style, select all the text by placing the cursor anywhere in the text body and press ⌘/Ctrl+A to select all. Click the Body style name in the Paragraph Styles panel to apply the style to the selected text.

4. **Select the first two words in the first paragraph, and change the font attributes.** Change the selected text point size to a larger point size than the body copy. Add points to the type in the Control panel, and change the font. Open the Color panel, and assign a new color to the character.

5. **Create a character style for the first two words.** Select the first two words you changed in Step 4, and select New Character Style from the Character Styles panel menu, shown in Figure 16.46. Name the style *1st two Words*.

FIGURE 16.46

Create a character style for the first two words.

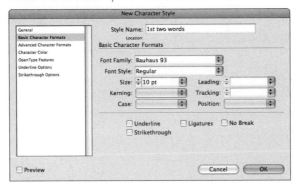

6. **Create another style for the first sentence.** Select the first character in the third word through the last character in the first sentence. Change type attributes to a different font style from the style used for the body copy. Open the Character Styles panel menu, and select New Character Style. Be certain the cursor appears within the sentence where you just changed the font attributes before opening the New Character Style dialog box. Provide a name for the style, such as *1st Sentence*, and click OK.

7. **Duplicate the Body text paragraph style.** Select Body in the Paragraph Styles panel, and drag it to the Create New Paragraph Style icon. InDesign automatically names the new style *Body copy*.

8. **Create a nested style.** Right-click (Control + click on the Mac) on the Body copy style you created in the Paragraph Styles panel and select Edit Body to open the Paragraph Style Options dialog box. Click Drop Caps and Nested Styles in the left pane.

Click New Nested Style. In the Nested Styles window, the highlighted item appears as None. When you click the item, a pull-down menu shows all the character styles you created in the Character Styles panel. Select *1st Two Words* from the menu items. Select Words on the right side of the new nested style entry in the Nested Styles window, as shown in Figure 16.47. Select the default number 1 and type 2 in the field box.

Create a new nested style, and choose the style from the first pull-down menu. In the new entry added to the Nested Styles list, select Words from the last pull-down menu and change 1 to 2 for assigning the style to two words.

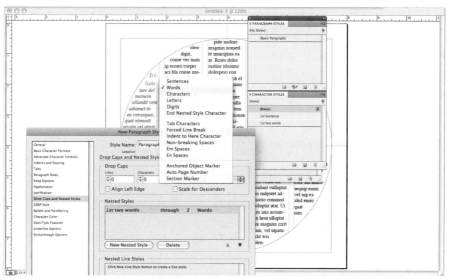

9. **Add a second character style to the nested style.** Click New Nested Style. From the Character Style pull-down menu on the left, select *1st Sentence* (the second character style you created) as shown in Figure 16.48. Select Sentence in the last pull-down menu. Click OK when you're finished defining the style. Be certain to leave the value in the field box at the default 1 for one sentence.

10. **Apply the nested style to the copy.** Click the cursor in the text passage, and press ⌘/Ctrl+A to select all the text. Click the new nested style in the Paragraph Styles panel to apply it to all the selected paragraphs.

11. **Deselect the text.** Click the cursor anywhere on the page, and the text is deselected. The final styling appears as shown in Figure 16.49.

FIGURE 16.48

Add a second character style to the nested style.

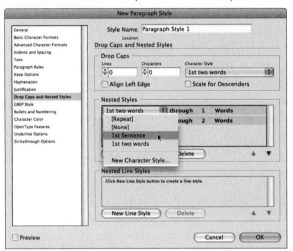

FIGURE 16.49

Deselect the text, and examine the copy. All the paragraphs should appear with the assigned character styles.

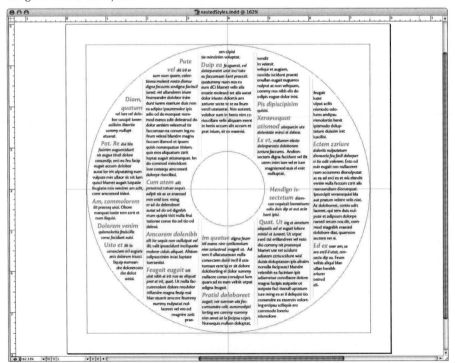

 When working with selected text, press the Esc key to toggle out of the text mode and deselect all.

Making changes to type attributes where nested styles have been assigned is easy. As is the case with paragraph styles, the nested style is based on the various character styles. You can revisit the Character Styles panel and make changes to type attributes. The type changes are dynamically updated in the nested style, which directly changes the type where the nested style was applied.

What Happens When You Forget to Add a Character Style?

The steps used to create a nested style assume you had all the proper character styles defined. If you forgot to create a character style, you needed to bail out of the Drop Caps and Nested Styles dialog box, create the character style you need to add to the nested style, and reopen the Drop Caps and Nested Styles dialog box. All this you had to do prior to InDesign CS4. Now in InDesign CS4, when in the Drop Caps and Nested Styles dialog box you can add a new character style without leaving the dialog box. Just open the Character Style pull-down menu and choose New Character Style. The new style dynamically appears in the list of available styles in the Drop Caps and Nested Styles dialog box.

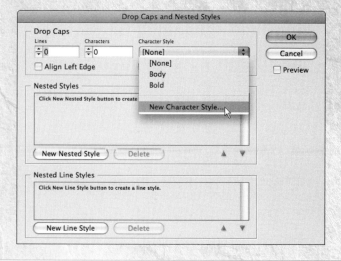

Creating Cell and Table Styles

One of the best features added to InDesign CS4 was the ability to use style sheets with tables. If you've spent hours formatting tables in InDesign and then had to repeat all the steps to produce an attractive table, you'll very much appreciate having cell and table styles to speed up your work.

Creating a table style

Before you begin using the cell styles in InDesign, your best workflow is to first format a table and create a table style. You create tables in InDesign using Character and Paragraph Styles with the Character and Paragraph Styles panels. All the text formatting for type should have at least one occurrence of a paragraph style and that style should be applied to all type having identical appearances in your table. In addition, add a table header and or footer using menu commands in the Table menu.

When your first table is formatted as you like including fills, strokes, text formatting from Paragraph Styles, header row, and so forth, select the table and open the Table Styles panel. Click the Create new style icon in the panel or open the flyout menu and choose New Table Style. The New Table Style dialog box opens as shown in Figure 16.50.

FIGURE 16.50

Open the New Table Styles dialog box from the Table Styles panel.

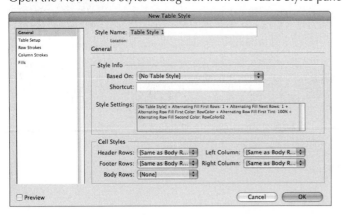

Type a name for your new style in the Style Name text box. Along the left side of the dialog box, you see options for the Table Setup, Row Strokes, Column Strokes, and Fills. If you formatted your table using stokes and fills you needn't bother adjusting the settings in the different panes in the New Table Style dialog box. If you want to change the cell attributes when formatting new tables, you can make these adjustments in the various panels.

At the bottom of the New Table Styles dialog box shown in Figure 16.50, you find options for selecting cell styles. As yet, we haven't created any cell styles, so you should leave the settings at the default and click OK in the New Table Style dialog box.

At this point, you created a table style ready for use when adding a new table having similar attributes to your layout. The next step in the process is to create cell styles.

NOTE **InDesign CS4 has a new feature where you can create a new style on the fly in any style selection. This feature permits you to create new cell styles in the New Table Style dialog box just like the options you have with nested styles as shown earlier in the sidebar figure.**

Creating cell styles

To repeat what we said at the beginning of this section on Creating a Table Style, you need to format text using styles from the Paragraph Styles panel. You first add the various character styles for formatting type, then proceed to creating paragraph styles using the character styles. When all the text is properly formatted for cells using paragraph styles, select the type in a cell and open the Cell Styles panel. To create a new cell style, choose New Cell Style from the flyout menu. The Cell Style Options dialog box opens as shown in Figure 16.51.

FIGURE 16.51

Open the Cell Style Options dialog box from the Cell Styles panel.

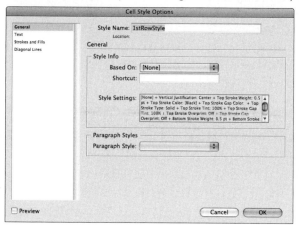

Name the style by typing a new name in the Style Name text box. At the bottom of the General pane shown in Figure 16.51, you see a drop-down menu where choices can be made from the paragraph styles you created in the Paragraph Styles panel. Be sure to select the proper style for the cell you are formatting.

As with the New Table Style dialog box, you have options for formatting Strokes and Fills by click-ing the respective label in the left pane. Additionally you have options for formatting text and diag-onal lines. If your cell is properly formatted, simply click OK to create the new style. If you want to make changes for other new tables you add to your layout, use the various panes in the panel to make the desired changes.

Applying table styles

In Figure 16.52 you see a table that has been formatted for a layout at the top of the figure. Below the formatted table is an unformatted table. The top table has been selected and a new table style created in the Table Styles palette.

When you select the unformatted table and apply the table style, the table takes on some of the attributes of your formatted table such as row and column fills and strokes, as you can see in Figure 16.53. However, InDesign doesn't know what the type formatting should be for the cells in the table. This is where your cell styles help you finish the formatting.

FIGURE 16.52

The top table is formatted for the layout and the bottom table is an unformatted table.

FIGURE 16.53

When a table style is applied to a new table, only partial table attributes are applied.

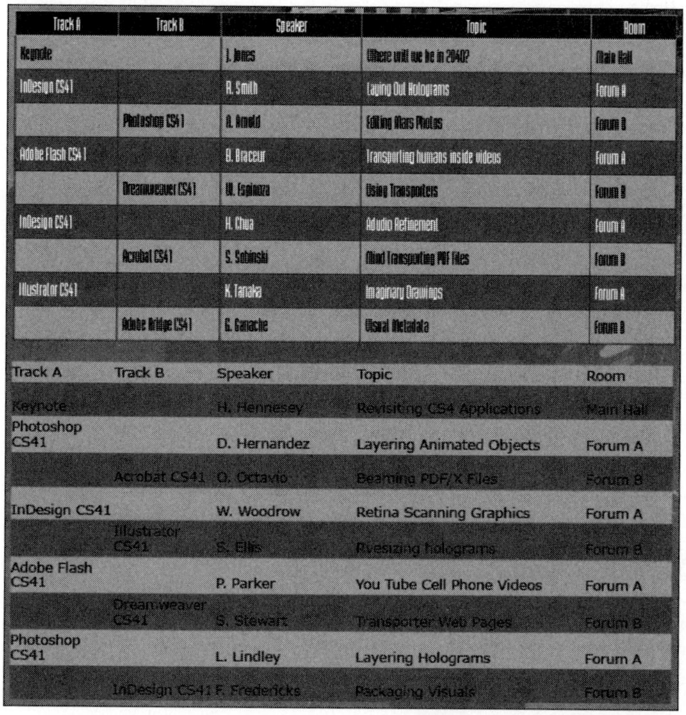

Track A	Track B	Speaker	Topic	Room
Keynote		J. Jones	Where will we be in 2040?	Main Hall
InDesign CS41		A. Smith	Laying Out Holograms	Forum A
	Photoshop CS41	A. Arnold	Editing Mars Photos	Forum B
Adobe Flash CS41		B. Braceur	Transporting humans inside videos	Forum A
	Dreamweaver CS41	W. Espinoza	Using Transporters	Forum B
InDesign CS41		H. Chua	Audio Refinement	Forum A
	Acrobat CS41	S. Sobinski	Mind Transporting PDF Files	Forum B
Illustrator CS41		K. Tanaka	Imaginary Drawings	Forum A
	Adobe Bridge CS41	G. Ganache	Visual Metadata	Forum B

Track A	Track B	Speaker	Topic	Room
Keynote		H. Hennesey	Revisiting CS4 Applications	Main Hall
Photoshop CS41		D. Hernandez	Layering Animated Objects	Forum A
	Acrobat CS41	O. Octavio	Beaming PDF/X Files	Forum B
InDesign CS41		W. Woodrow	Retina Scanning Graphics	Forum A
	Illustrator CS41	S. Ellis	Rvesizing holograms	Forum B
Adobe Flash CS41		P. Parker	You Tube Cell Phone Videos	Forum A
	Dreamweaver CS41	S. Stewart	Transporter Web Pages	Forum B
Photoshop CS41		L. Lindley	Layering Holograms	Forum A
	InDesign CS41	F. Fredericks	Packaging Visuals	Forum B

To apply all the cell styles to your table for the text formatting, you use the Table Styles panel. Right-click (Control + click on the Mac) the table style name in the Table Styles panel or double-click the Table Style name you created for your table style, or open a context menu and select Edit <style name>. The Table Style Options dialog box opens. This dialog box is identical to the New Table Styles dialog box.

At the bottom of the Table Style Options dialog box you make selections for the cell styles you created in the Cell Styles panel. Notice in Figure 16.54 we created cell styles for header rows and body rows. The pull-down menus reflect the cell style names used when we created the cell styles.

Click OK and your cell styles are applied to the cells in the table. If you need to convert the first row to a header, select the first row and choose Table ➪ Convert Rows ➪ To Header or use the Table ➪ Table Options ➪ Headers and Footers command to open the Headers and Footers pane in the table Options dialog box.

Assuming you followed the recommended procedure described here, an unformatted table should appear with the same formatting attributes as the table used to create the table style. In Figure 16.55 you can see the second table after we added the cell styles in the Table Style Options dialog box.

FIGURE 16.54

Cell styles are selected in the Table Style Options dialog box.

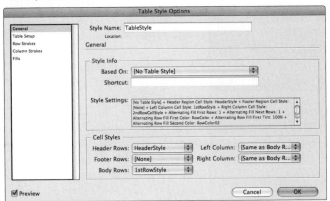

FIGURE 16.55

An unformatted table after applying the table and cell styles appears identical to the formatted table.

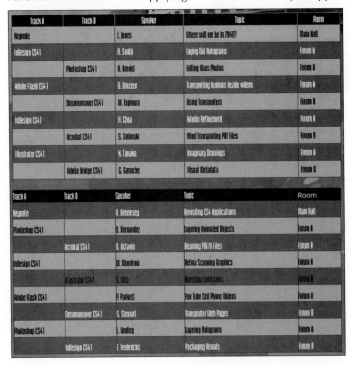

Using Graphic and Object Styles

Graphic styles are used when you want to apply effects to type and objects. Instead of using the character and paragraph panels, Illustrator, Photoshop, and InDesign offer you a styles panel where effects applied to type can be captured as a style. When you add additional type to a document, you can click a graphic style in Photoshop and Illustrator or object style in InDesign and all the effects associated with that style are applied to the selected type.

Graphic styles are not restricted to text. You can use graphic styles with objects as well as with type. Just to stay consistent with the content in this chapter, we'll confine the discussion on graphic styles to applying them to type.

Using graphic styles in Illustrator

Illustrator provides you with a number of different graphic styles libraries you can load in the Graphic Styles panel. Choose Window ➪ Graphic Styles or press Shift+F5 to open the panel. From the panel menu, you have several menu commands used when creating and working with graphic styles. Select Open Graphic Style Library, and a submenu displays preset styles you can load in the panel as shown in Figure 16.56.

FIGURE 16.56

Choose Window ➪ Graphic Styles to open the Graphic Styles panel, or press Shift+F5. Open the panel menu, and select Open Graphic Style library to view the preset styles available to you in Illustrator.

In addition to applying preset styles, you can create custom styles and add them to your Graphic Styles panel. Graphic styles are created much like character and paragraph styles. You first edit text or an object and then capture the edits as a new graphic style. To see how easily you can create graphic styles, follow the steps below.

STEPS: Creating Graphic Styles in Illustrator

1. **Create text.** Type a single character on a page. Use 72 points or more for the point size. You can create more than one text character; but if you decide to apply effects that take some time to render, everything will move faster when using a single character.

2. **Fill and stroke the character.** Use the Swatches or Color panel and the Stroke panel, and select colors to add for the fill and stroke. Set the stroke value between 3 to 5 points.

3. **Apply a second stroke.** Open the Appearance panel, and from the panel menu select Add New Stroke, or click the Add New Stroke tool at the bottom of the panel. While the new stroke is selected in the Appearance panel, you can change attributes for color and stroke value right in the Appearance pane as shown in Figure 16.57. In our example, we use a 4-point stroke for the first stroke and 1.5 for the second stroke. Click a contrasting color in the Swatches color panel to change the color of the stroke.

FIGURE 16.57

Open the Appearance panel, and select Add New Stroke from the panel menu.

> **TIP**   When you want to add multiple strokes to a path, always use the Appearance panel. You might want to illustrate a map with road paths where a white path appears above a larger black path to give the appearance of parallel lines. Rather than creating two strokes where the narrower white stroke appears above a larger black stoke, just use the appearance panel to add a second stroke. Your illustration will have fewer objects, and it is much easier to edit the stroke sizes and colors using the Appearance panel.

4. **Apply an effect.** Select Type or Character in the Appearance panel, and open the 3D Extrude & Bevel Options dialog box by choosing Effect ⇨ 3D ⇨ Extrude and Bevel. Edit the Extrude Depth to a value lower than the default 50 points. Select the Preview check box, and you can see your results in the document window as you make changes to the extrude and bevel attributes, as shown in Figure 16.58. Click OK when the extrusion appears as you like.

CAUTION   Be certain that you select the top-level name (default is Type) or character in the Appearance panel before applying other effects. If you select one of the strokes or a fill in the panel, a new effect is applied only to the item selected.

FIGURE 16.58

Open the 3D Extrude & Bevel Options dialog box, and select the Preview check box to preview the changes in the document window.

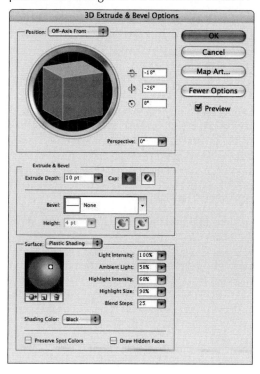

5. **Apply a drop shadow.** Drop shadows can be applied directly in the Appearance panel. Open the Effects pull-down menu and choose Stylize ⇨ Drop Shadow.

TIP   When you want to make changes to effects such as Extrude and Bevel, open the Appearance panel and double-click 3D Extrude & Bevel. The 3D Extrude and Bevel Options dialog box opens where you can change the settings. If you attempt to use the 3D Extrude & Bevel menu command to edit a previous 3D effect, you'll be applying another extrusion to an object that already has one 3D effect applied to it.

The Appearance panel lists all the effects applied to an object.

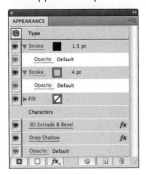

6. **Create a new graphic style.** Place the Appearance panel adjacent to the Graphic Styles panel. Drag the item listed as *Type: Graphic Style* in the Appearance panel to the Graphic Styles panel as shown in Figure 16.60. The effects applied to the type are added as a new graphic style.

Drag the *Type: Graphic Style 1* item in the Appearance panel to the Graphic Styles panel to create a new graphic style.

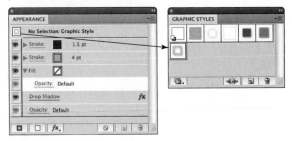

7. **Name the style.** Double-click the new style in the Graphic Styles panel. The Graphic Styles Options dialog box appears. Type a name for the style, and click OK.

8. **Apply the style to new type.** Type a text in the document window and select it. Click the new style you added to the Graphic Styles panel. All the attributes assigned to the style are applied to your new type as shown in Figure 16.61.

FIGURE 16.61

The style is applied to new type.

Using graphic styles in Photoshop

Photoshop doesn't support character and paragraph styles, but you do have many options for creating and applying graphic styles to objects in Photoshop.

To open the Styles panel, choose Window ➪ Styles. From the panel menu shown in Figure 16.62, you can see a selection of preset styles available for loading. The items denoted as Abstract Styles through Web Styles offer you style libraries that can be loaded in the panel. When you select a style library, a dialog box appears offering choices for appending the selected library to the current library or replacing the open library with the selected library.

In addition to the preset library styles, Photoshop offers you an option for creating your own custom style by selecting the New Style menu command. You can define style attributes for vector and raster artwork.

You apply styles from the library style options to selected layers or objects in Photoshop. Create any type characters in Photoshop, and click a style in the Styles panel. In addition, you can create type and vector objects in Illustrator, copy the artwork, and paste the artwork as a Smart Object in Photoshop.

When you choose Edit ➪ Paste in Photoshop, a dialog box appears offering you an option to paste the object as a Smart Object. This means you can apply all the type and object effects available in Illustrator such as using Live Trace, 3D Effects, and all other effects that you can apply to vector objects. Copy the object, paste it into Photoshop, and apply a style. In Figure 16.63, type was created in Illustrator. The Roughen effect was applied by choosing Effect ➪ Distort & Transform ➪ Roughen. The type was copied to the Clipboard and pasted as a Smart Object in Photoshop. In Photoshop, the Type Effects library was loaded in the Styles panel. With the new type layer selected, Brushed Metal was selected in the Style panel.

FIGURE 16.62

The Styles panel offers options for selecting style libraries that you can load in the Styles panel.

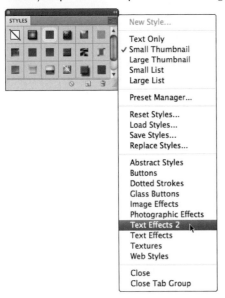

FIGURE 16.63

The Brushed Metal style was used in Photoshop to create the final effect.

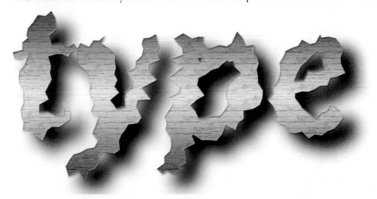

Objects created as 3D renditions in Illustrator lose the 3D views when applying styles in Photoshop unless pasted as a Smart object. When a 3D object is not pasted as a smart object and you apply a style in Photoshop, the object appears as a 2D object. In Figure 16.64, a simple object was drawn in Illustrator, and the object was revolved in the 3D Revolve Options dialog box. When pasted in Photoshop where a style was applied to the object, the end result produced a 2D object, as you see on the right side of the figure.

FIGURE 16.64

Illustrator 3D objects lose the 3D view when styles are applied in Photoshop.

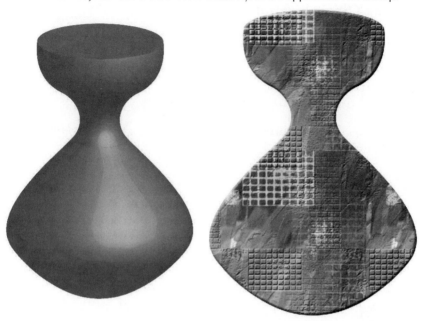

Using object styles in InDesign

InDesign provides you with an Object Styles panel. Object styles offer the same kind of options in InDesign for stylizing type and objects as you have available in Illustrator and Photoshop. InDesign goes much farther with object styles than you have available with graphic styles in Illustrator and Photoshop as you can see by the options shown in Figure 16.66.

To open the Object Styles panel, choose Window ➪ Object Styles. The panel opens and appears similar to other style panels you have available in InDesign. From a panel menu, you have some similar menu commands that provide, among other choices, an option to Load Object Styles. Object styles can be imported from other InDesign documents. Unfortunately, exchanging object styles with graphic styles from Illustrator and Photoshop is not available InDesign due to the vast differences between the styles panels in the programs.

Object styles can be used with text frames and the object styles can apply paragraph styles to the contents of frames. You have options for separate stroke, fill, and text transparencies. If you want to apply type attributes such as font style, color, character and paragraph formatting, and so on, you need to create a paragraph style for those attributes. You can then add additional effects in the Object Styles panel.

To understand how object styles are used in InDesign, follow these steps.

STEPS: Creating Object Styles in InDesign

1. **Add type to a document page.** Type a word on a new blank document.

2. **Set the type attributes.** Select a font, and set the point size. Add color from the Swatches or Color panels. Use a gradient color if you like.

3. **Create a paragraph style.** Open the Paragraph Styles panel menu, and select New Paragraph Style. Type a name for the new style in the New Paragraph Styles dialog box.

CROSS-REF   For information on creating paragraph styles in InDesign, see the section "Using paragraph styles in InDesign."

4. **Apply effects to the text frame.** You can add fill and stroke colors to the text frame; add corner effects to the frame corners; add transparency, drop shadows, and feather edges; set text wrap attributes and story options; and set anchored objects attributes.

5. **Create a new Object Style.** Choose Window ⇨ Object Styles to open the Object Styles panel. From the panel menu, shown in Figure 16.65, select New Object Style. This opens the Object Style Options dialog box. Type a name for the style in the Style Name text box. In our example, we use *TypeGradient* for the style name, as shown in Figure 16.66.

FIGURE 16.65

Select new Object Style from the Object Styles panel menu.

FIGURE 16.66

Open the New Object Style dialog box, and type a name for your new style.

The list of check boxes on the left side of the dialog box enables you to select the settings that you want to apply to the object style. You can remove check marks for those items that you want eliminated from your style. When using fills and strokes, you can click the Fill and Stroke tool in the dialog box to apply either when a Fill or Stroke is selected in the left pane. For example, you can add a stroke color when Fill is selected in the left pane by clicking the Stroke tool in the right pane and selecting a color from the scrollable color list.

6. **Apply additional settings.** Click each of the items in the left pane to open attribute choices in the right pane for each respective item. The most important item to select is Paragraph Styles. Be certain to select Paragraph Styles and select the style you added for your type effect.

7. **Apply the Style.** Click OK when you finish adding all the settings in the Object Styles Options dialog box. When you return to the document window, add a new line of type and click the text frame. Click the style name in the Object Styles panel to apply the style to the new text frame. In Figure 16.67, we added a drop shadow, added a stroke to the frame, and applied corner effects to the frame corners. The type is filled with a gradient defined in the Paragraph Style Options dialog box.

FIGURE 16.67

Create text, and click the style name in the Object Styles panel.

If you want to reuse styles, save your InDesign document. Open a new document, and select Load Object Styles from the Object Styles panel menu. The Open a File dialog box appears. Locate the file containing the style you want to load, and select it in the Open a File dialog box. Notice in Figure 16.68 that you can see a document thumbnail of a page containing the style. Click OK, and the Load Styles dialog box appears.

NOTE Loading Object Styles also loads paragraph and character styles in the Paragraph and Character Styles panels.

FIGURE 16.68

Select a file to load, and click OK to open the Load Styles dialog box.

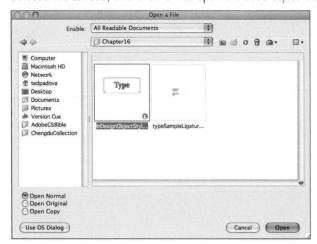

The Load Styles dialog box offers you options for selecting which styles you want to load in your new document as shown in Figure 16.69. The first two styles are defaults. These styles are added to each new document you create in InDesign. Deselect the styles, and select the custom styles you want to load. Notice that the Load Styles dialog box offers you a description for a selected style in the dialog box and the style you are about to import. Click OK, and the style is added to the Object Styles panel in your new document.

FIGURE 16.69

Select the styles you want to load, and click OK to add the styles to your new document.

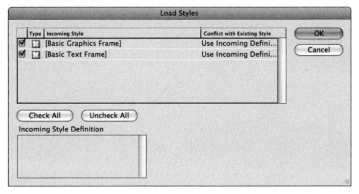

Summary

- Illustrator text is created as either point type or area type. When formatting paragraphs and working with larger bodies of text, click and drag the cursor to create area type.

- Legacy Illustrator files need to be updated to edit type in Illustrator CS4. You can update type when opening a legacy file in Illustrator CS4 or at a later time after a document has been opened without updating the type.

- OpenType fonts offer you many more sophisticated typesetting features as compared to PostScript and TrueType fonts.

- Both Illustrator and InDesign offer options for creating character and paragraph style sheets. Style sheets are used to apply type formatting when repeating format designs throughout a layout.

- InDesign provides an impressive typesetting feature in the form of nested style sheets. Nested styles are used when several different character styles are applied to a paragraph and you want to duplicate the paragraph formatting throughout a passage of text.

- Illustrator, Photoshop, and InDesign have styles panels you can use to create styles when applying graphic effects to text and objects. The styles are not transportable among the programs, but you can import styles in new documents for styles created in the respective program.

Chapter 17

Working with Text Frames

P hotoshop, Illustrator, and InDesign allow you to create type within bounding boxes. In Photoshop, you can create multiple paragraphs within a bounding box and choose justification options, but you have no ability to link multiple blocks of text (known as text threading). When you set type in a bounding box in Illustrator, the box is called area type; in InDesign, it is referred to as a text frame. To make our discussion easier in this chapter, type bounding boxes in both InDesign and Illustrator are referred to as text frames.

Both Illustrator and InDesign offer advanced options for handling text blocks, including the ability to thread text, apply attributes to text frames, and wrap text around objects. Text frames can assume many different shapes and can appear as graphic objects or flow around objects and images. In both Illustrator and InDesign, text frames give you great flexibility when working with type.

IN THIS CHAPTER

Adding text frames to documents

Managing text frames

Using master frames

Wrapping type around objects

Creating Text Frames

Text frames are created in the same manner in both Illustrator and InDesign. Simply click the Type tool, and drag to create a rectangle. A blinking cursor tells you the program is ready to accept type within the frame you created.

To resize a text frame, click and drag any one of the handles on the bounding box and reshape as desired. Any text within the frame conforms to the new size. If you start typing in a text frame and you want to quickly reshape the frame, press the ⌘/Ctrl key and you temporarily gain access to the frame handles. Drag the handles to reshape the frame; when you release the keyboard modifier, the Type tool is left uninterrupted, and you're ready to continue typing.

 **InDesign CS4 and Illustrator CS4 have a new pop-up measurement readout that shows you the width and height of a frame as you draw text frames and objects.**

Working with text threads

You can add text to a frame either by typing it in directly from the keyboard or by importing it from another document. If the text oversets the frame (that is, the bounding box is not large enough to hold all the text), you will see a tiny red plus sign (+) in a box at the bottom-right corner of the text frame. If you don't want the text to carry over to a new text frame, you need to make the type size smaller or the text frame larger, until the plus sign disappears. However, if you want to create a text thread (that is, carry the text over to a new frame), click the plus sign with the Selection tool. This action "loads" the cursor with all the overset text. Click and drag open a new text frame, and the overset text automatically flows into the new frame.

 **You can resize text frames to fit the content in InDesign by double-clicking on the control handles.**

In Illustrator, when you select threaded text frames, you see a visible link between them, as shown in Figure 17.1. You can hide the text threads by choosing View ➪ Hide Text Threads.

FIGURE 17.1

Visible text threads in Illustrator

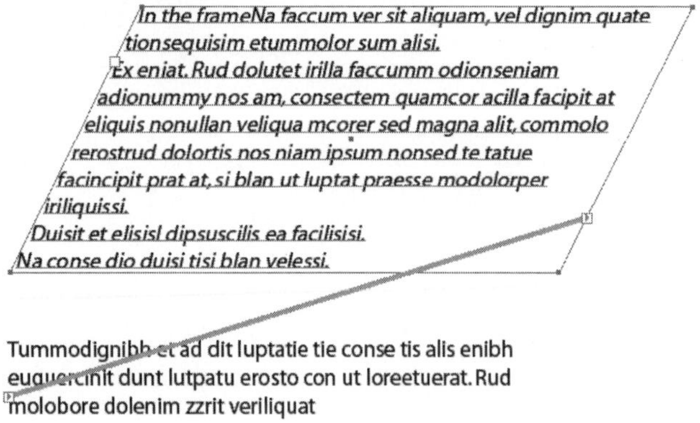

In the frameNa faccum ver sit aliquam, vel dignim quate tionsequisim etummolor sum alisi.
Ex eniat. Rud dolutet irilla faccumm odionseniam adionummy nos am, consectem quamcor acilla facipit at eliquis nonullan veliqua mcorer sed magna alit, commolo rerostrud dolortis nos niam ipsum nonsed te tatue facincipit prat at, si blan ut luptat praesse modolorper iriliquissi.
Duisit et elisisl dipsuscilis ea facilisisi.
Na conse dio duisi tisi blan velessi.

Tummodignibb et ad dit luptatie tie conse tis alis enibh euguercinit dunt lutpatu erosto con ut loreetuerat. Rud molobore dolenim zzrit veriliquat

InDesign's default setting hides the text threads. There is no visible indication that the text blocks are linked. If you want to view the text threads, choose View ➪ Show Text Threads and the text threads appear as shown in Figure 17.2.

FIGURE 17.2

InDesign's default setting keeps text threads hidden.

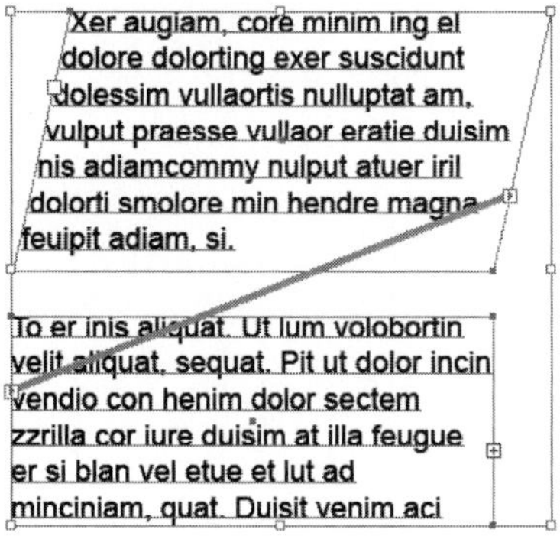

Xer augiam, core minim ing el
dolore dolorting exer suscidunt
dolessim vullaortis nulluptat am,
vulput praesse vullaor eratie duisim
nis adiamcommy nulput atuer iril
dolorti smolore min hendre magna
feuipit adiam, si.

To er inis aliquat. Ut lum volobortin
velit aliquat, sequat. Pit ut dolor incin
vendio con henim dolor sectem
zzrilla cor iure duisim at illa feugue
er si blan vel etue et lut ad
minciniam, quat. Duisit venim aci

Adding new frames to a text thread

Text frames in both Illustrator and InDesign have *in ports* and *out ports* that enable linking to other text frames for continuation of a thread. The in port is a small square located in the top-left area of the text frame, and the out port is located at the bottom-right. An empty port indicates that no text precedes or follows the text frame. A port containing a right arrow indicates that text is threaded from one frame to another. An out port with a plus (+) symbol indicates that more text is contained within the frame but has not yet been threaded and remains hidden. In Figure 17.3, you can see a thread where the symbols are placed.

To flow overset text to a new text frame, simply click the plus sign on the out port with the Selection tool. Click a blank area of the document, or drag open a rectangle, and the overset text flows to the new frame.

If you need to add a new text frame between frames in an existing thread, use the Selection tool to click the out port preceding the frame where you want to add the new frame. Clicking the out port loads the cursor with text following the selected frame. Click and drag open a new text frame, and the text is then threaded through it. Note that you can also click the in port and thread the text backwards.

To make this process a little clearer, look at Figure 17.4. At the top, you see two linked text frames with overset text as indicated by the plus sign (+) in the out port of the second text frame. To eliminate this overset, we want to create a new text frame in the second column and thread the text through it. To do this, we click the out port at the bottom-right of the text frame in column one. The cursor changes to indicate that it is loaded with all the text following that frame. Then we click and drag to create a new text frame in column two. As you can see in the bottom example in Figure 17.4, the text thread now runs through the newly created text frame and is no longer overset in the third frame.

FIGURE 17.3

An empty port (1) indicates no text precedes the text in the frame. A port with a right arrow (2) indicates the thread flows from one frame to another. A plus (+) symbol in an out port (3) indicates that overset text in the frame has not yet flowed to another frame.

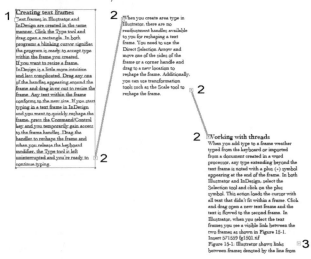

FIGURE 17.4

The top example shows an existing text thread with overset text in InDesign. The bottom example shows a new text frame added in the middle of the existing thread. The text now runs through the new frame, eliminating the overset text.

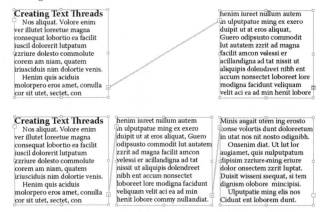

Unthreading text frames

Illustrator and InDesign differ a little when unthreading frames. In Illustrator, you can break a thread between two objects, release an object from a text thread, or cut the threads without changing the placement of the text. In InDesign, you have only two options: You can unthread frames that result in breaking the thread to all subsequent frames, or you can cut a frame from a thread. The methods for handling each of the three options in Illustrator and the two options in InDesign include the following:

- **Breaking a thread in Illustrator:** Using the Selection tool, double-click an out port to break the thread to the next frame; double-click an in port to break the thread to a previous frame; or single-click an in or out port, move the cursor to another in or out port, and click the cursor.

- **Releasing an object from a text thread in Illustrator:** Click the object you want to release from the thread with the Selection tool. Choose Type ⇨ Threaded Text ⇨ Release Selection. This action removes the selected frame(s) from the thread but preserves threading through other frames.

- **Cutting threads in Illustrator:** Select a linked text object with the Selection tool, and choose Type ⇨ Threaded Text ⇨ Remove Threading. This removes all threading but leaves the text in the individual frames.

- **Breaking frames in InDesign:** To unthread or break frames in InDesign, start by clicking an in or out port with the selection tool. The cursor loads with text. Move the cursor over an in or out port in another frame, and double-click the mouse button. Note that when the cursor is loaded and positioned over an in or out port, the cursor shape changes to a broken-chain-link symbol informing you that the thread will be broken. Likewise you can just double-click an in/out port to break the thread.

- **Cutting frames in InDesign:** To cut a frame in InDesign, start by selecting one or more frames in a thread with the Selection tool. For multiple frame selection where you want to cut several frames, use Shift+click. Choose Edit ⇨ Cut. The frames are cut from the thread, but text is not lost—it flows from the frame preceding the cut frame(s) to the next frame in the thread order. You can then paste the frames to retain the text.

NOTE You have some sample scripts installed in the InDesign folder on your hard drive that handle splitting frames and stories. Open the Window ⇨ Automation ⇨ Scripts panel and select from sample scripts for splitting selected frames and stories. For splitting frames use the BreakFrame script, and for splitting stories use the SplitStory script.

Setting Text Frame Attributes

Text frame attributes include options for creating columns, creating offsets, setting type, adjusting baselines, and so on. The ability to change text frame attributes is a timesaver because it allows you to make text formatting and/or layout changes quickly and easily. For example, if you need to change the type style and column width of multiple text frames, you can make these changes simply by selecting the text frames and applying the desired attributes. In both Illustrator and InDesign, dialog boxes offer options for setting attributes of text frames. In InDesign, using Object Styles makes this much more powerful.

CROSS-REF   **For information about Object Styles in InDesign, see Chapter 16.**

Creating columns and insets

When you create layouts in InDesign, you can specify the number of columns applied to pages. You can create threaded text frames within individual columns and flow the text through multi-columned pages. Likewise, in Illustrator, you can create several text frames and link the frames to create a single thread. As an alternative to creating multiple frames, you can create single text frames and divide the single frames into multiple columns. You can create multi-column text frames in either Illustrator or InDesign.

In Illustrator, create an area type frame by selecting the Type tool and dragging open a rectangle. From the Type menu, select Area Type Options, and the Area Type Options dialog box opens, shown in Figure 17.5.

FIGURE 17.5

You can apply Area Type attributes in Illustrator.

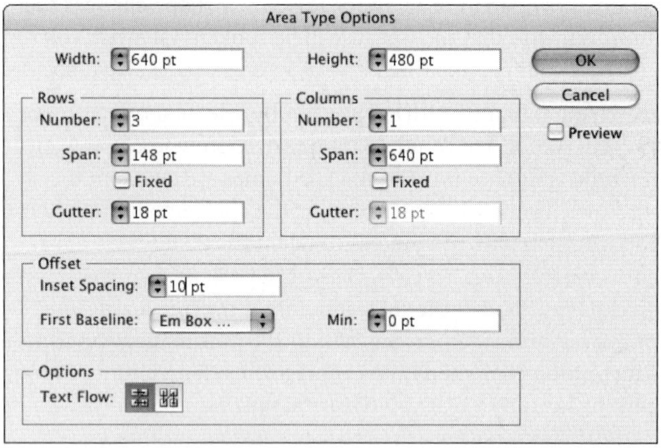

In Illustrator's Area Type Options dialog box, you can specify overall width and height, define rows, columns, and offset values, and select a text flow method. When experimenting with different attributes, place a check mark in the Preview box to dynamically preview the results.

InDesign has a similar dialog box for setting text frame attributes. In InDesign, choose Object ⇨ Text Frame Options, and the Text Frame Options dialog box opens. Notice that there are two panes in the Text Frame Options dialog box. The dialog opens with the General pane selected, as shown in Figure 17.6.

FIGURE 17.6

By default, the General tab is active when you open the dialog box.

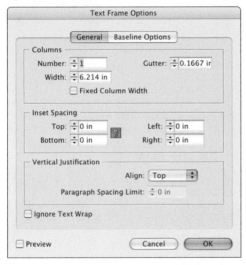

The Text Frame Options dialog box offers you a Preview check box. This InDesign feature enables you to preview settings made in the Text Frame Options dialog box dynamically in the page layout as you make settings adjustments.

InDesign CS4 provides you additional settings for baseline adjustments. You can set up baselines for frames instead of the entire document. Click the Baseline Options tab in the Text Frame Options dialog box, and the options choices for baseline settings appear, as shown in Figure 17.7. The choices for using a custom baseline include defining a start point (offsetting from the layout grid); setting the baseline relative to the page, page margin, frame or inset; increment values (normally this setting is equal to the body text leading); and displaying a user-defined color for the grid lines. Custom baseline grids are particularly helpful when using rotated text layouts.

FIGURE 17.7

_____

To apply baseline settings on a frame, select the Use Custom Baseline Grid check box and make settings choices for the offset, relative to, and a gridline color.

The following steps show how you might apply options for text frame attributes using the Text Frame Options dialog box in InDesign.

STEPS: Setting Text Frame Options in InDesign

1. **Create a new document.** Open InDesign, and choose File ➪ New Document. In the New Document dialog box, set the page size to 6 inches by 6 inches and uncheck Facing Pages.

2. **Create a frame object.** Drag guidelines from the ruler wells to the 3-inch vertical and horizontal ruler marks. The guidelines intersect at the center point of the document. Select the Ellipse Frame tool, and position the cursor at the center point. Hold the Option/Alt key, and press Shift to drag from center and constrain the angle to create a perfect circle. Click and drag from the center out toward the outside guidelines to create a circle. The default margin guides appear at 0.5 inches around the inside of the document page, as shown in Figure 17.8.

3. **Convert the object to a text frame.** Select the object, and choose Object ➪ Content ➪ Text or click inside the object with the Type tool. The object becomes a text frame.

FIGURE 17.8

Create an ellipse by dragging from the center with the Alt/Option key depressed.

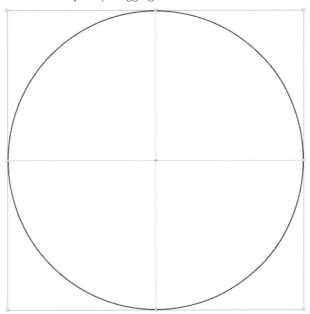

4. **Set the text frame options.** Select the text frame, and choose Object ⇨ Text Frame Options. The Text Frame Options dialog box opens. In the Columns section, set Number to **5** and Gutter to **0p6** points. If your unit of measure is currently set to inches and you want to specify point measurements instead, you can apply point units to the field boxes using 0p*n*—where 0 is picas, *p* stands for points, and *n* is the number of points. In the example shown in Figure 17.9, 0p6 is used in the Gutter field box. When you tab out of the field box, the value is translated to the defined unit of measure. In this example, 6 points translates to 0.833 inches. In the Inset Spacing section, type **0p8** for the Inset. This insets the text 8 points from the outer edge of the frame.

5. **View the text frame edges.** By default, you may not be able to see the column and inset spacing guidelines. If the guidelines are not shown, choose View ⇨ Show Frame Edges. When the guidelines are visible, you should see an object similar to Figure 17.10.

FIGURE 17.9

The Text Frame Options dialog box

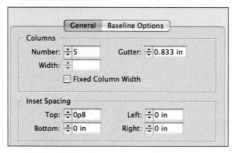

FIGURE 17.10

To view a text frame's guidelines for columns and inset spacing in InDesign, select Show Frame Edges from the View menu.

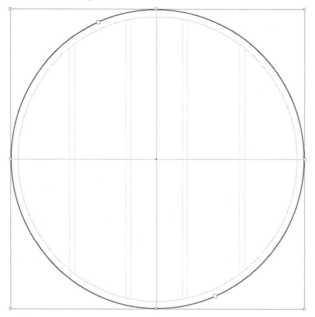

6. **Set the text attributes.** Click the Type tool and from the Control palette, select the font and point size for your type. In Figure 17.11, Kabel Book was selected from the Font drop-down list and the type size was set to 8 points.

7. **Fill with placeholder text.** If you created a keyboard shortcut for filling with placeholder text as discussed in Chapter 16, press Shift+F12. If you didn't create a keyboard shortcut, choose Type ➪ Fill with Placeholder Text. The final result should appear similar to Figure 17.11.

FIGURE 17.11

After setting font attributes, fill the columns with text.

Setting text attributes

You can set text attributes via the Control palette for options such as typeface, font size, leading, kerning, and tracking. In addition, you have a couple of text formatting options in the Text Frame Options dialog box. They include First Baseline positioning and Vertical Justification options.

In the Text Frame Options dialog box (refer to Figure 17.7), the First Baseline pane allows you to choose a first baseline offset method from a pull-down menu and also lets you specify a minimum value for first baseline offset. The following explains these items in more detail:

- **Ascent:** With this setting, the first baseline is calculated so that the top edges of characters with ascenders (such as *d* and *b*) fall just below the top inset of the text frame.

- **Cap Height:** With this option, the top edges of uppercase letters touch the top inset of the text frame.

- **Leading:** This setting uses the text's leading value as the distance between the baseline of the first line of text and the top inset of the frame.

- **x Height:** This option calculates the first baseline whereby the top of the *x* character falls just below the top inset of the text frame.

- **Fixed:** This option allows you to specify the distance between the baseline of the first line of text and the top inset of the frame.

- **Minimum:** The field box to the right of the Offset pull-down menu is where you can specify a minimum value for the first baseline offset.

Vertical Justification in the General pane allows you to specify how text is aligned vertically within a text frame. When you choose Top, Center, or Bottom from the Align menu, the text retains its specified paragraph leading and paragraph spacing values. When you choose Justify as the vertical alignment option, the lines are spaced evenly to fill the frame, regardless of the specified leading and paragraph spacing values. Figure 17.12 shows examples of the four vertical justification options available in InDesign.

FIGURE 17.12

Four vertical justification options for text are available in InDesign. Shown clockwise from top, they are Top, Center, Justify, and Bottom.

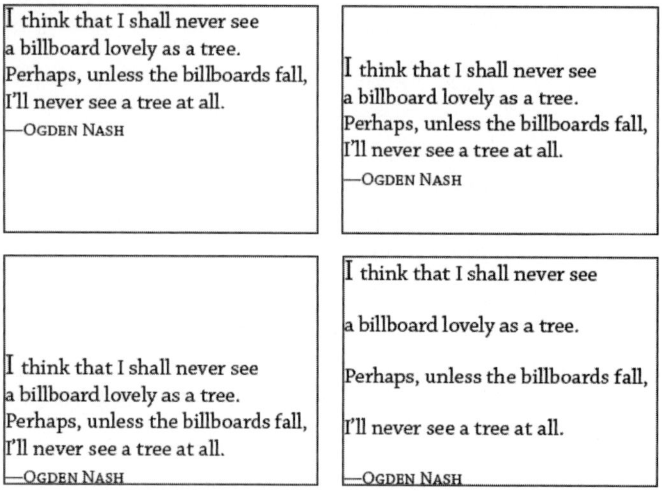

Creating Text Frames on Master Pages

One big advantage of using layout programs is the ability to use *master pages*. Elements placed on the master page automatically appear on all subsequent pages where the master page is applied. The use of master pages eliminates repetitive keystrokes, ensures greater design consistency, speeds up the editing process, and conserves memory because objects are applied on a single page and referenced on all other pages. Master pages are available only in InDesign.

Illustrator CS4 now offers multiple artboards where you can create multi-page documents. For more information on creating multiple pages in Illustrator, see Chapter 24.

You can add a text frame on a master page and define the type attributes for the frame. On all subsequent pages where a given master page is applied, the text frame is positioned and ready for use. When you create a new document check the Master Text Frame checkbox in the New Document dialog box to add master frames to new documents. You can either type text in a master frame or import text from another document. The text automatically picks up the attributes you established on the master page.

CROSS-REF For a more comprehensive view on creating master pages, see Chapter 24.

Creating manual text frames

You create text frames on master pages in the same way you create them on regular pages. Use either the Type tool or convert objects to text frames. To set text attributes, styles, and other options, click the cursor inside the frame or select the frame with the Selection Tool. While selected, set the attributes using the various palettes and menu options used for type, such as the Control palette, the Character palette, and the Paragraph palette. In Figure 17.13, you can see a master page containing two separate text frames, and several objects. You set text attributes for the separate frames by clicking in each frame and then setting options.

FIGURE 17.13

On a master page, add the objects and text frames.

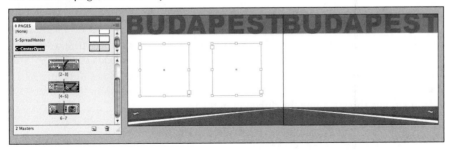

When you have one or more frames created on a master page and you apply the master page to document pages, you can type in the frames or import text. Selecting the Type tool and clicking on a frame, however, does not access the frame. Neither the Type tool nor the Selection tools alone can activate a text frame from a master page. You need to use ⌘/Ctrl+Shift + click a frame. It doesn't matter what tool you select in the Toolbox; pressing the ⌘/Ctrl key temporarily activates the Selection tool. Add the Shift key and click, and the I-beam cursor starts blinking in the text frame. At this point, you can type text or import text into the frame. In Figure 17.14, you can see two text frames with different text attributes. Both text frames were created on a master page.

TIP If you want to place a file in a frame, choose File ⇨ Place and click the loaded cursor on a master frame. The file places inside the frame.

FIGURE 17.14

Assigning different type attributes to different frames on a master page

All the options you have for creating text threads, autoflowing text, and assigning attributes are available to you when creating frames on master pages. If you create frame threads on master pages, you can flow text through the frames, as shown in Figure 17.15. The frames in Figure 17.15 were drawn on the master page, and text was placed on a document page based on the master page. Notice that the frame threads show the direction of the text flow.

Creating master text frames

When you want to flow text through a document using InDesign's text autoflow feature, you can use autoflow features with or without frames on master pages. InDesign permits you to add Master Text Frames at the time you create a new document by checking the Master Text Frame check box in the New Document dialog box. If, after creating a layout you want to add a master frame, you can do so on a master page. If you created a Master Text Frame in a new document, when using the master page you can change attributes of text frames easily by adjusting the single master page items and the text flows on all documents according to the adjustments made on the master pages. To understand quite simply how to work with master text frames, follow these steps where we begin by creating a master text frame on a master page.

FIGURE 17.15

Frame threads on master pages can be applied to document pages keeping the thread order.

STEPS: Autoflowing Text in Master Frames

1. **Create a new document.** Open InDesign, and choose File ➪ New ➪ Document. In the New Document dialog box, check the box for Master Text Frame, as shown in Figure 17.16. Set attributes for the number of columns and margin distances.

> **NOTE** If you don't see the Bleed and Slug area in the New Document dialog box, click More Options.

2. **Import text.** Choose File ➪ Place. The Place dialog box opens. Locate a text file you want to import, select the file, and then click Open. You also can double-click the file to be placed, but be certain not to triple-click the mouse button. The third click adds the text to the page.

FIGURE 17.16

To add a master frame to the master page, select the Master Text Frame check box.

3. **Autoflow the text.** When you double-click a filename or select a file in the Place dialog box and click Open, the cursor is loaded with text from the selected file. To place the text, you simply click the cursor to place text in an existing frame or click and drag the cursor to place text within a new frame. However, when placing text within a master frame, where you want to flow the text through many pages in your document, press the Shift key, and you see the cursor change shape. Click the mouse button with the Shift key depressed, and the text flows through the master text frame. If more text is placed than can fit within the current frame, InDesign adds new pages with new master frames and threads the text. More new pages are created with frames until the end of the passage of text is reached. In Figure 17.17, we added text to a master frame in a one-page document, and InDesign created an additional nine pages to accommodate the text file.

FIGURE 17.17

InDesign automatically adds new pages to accommodate text placement when using autoflow.

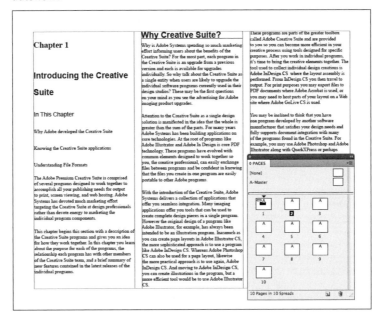

Modifying master text frames

When you create a master text frame, you can return to it and modify its attributes. Changes made on the master frame are reflected on all pages where the frame is used.

To modify a master frame, double-click the master page in the Pages palette where the frame is positioned. Select the frame with a Selection tool, and either open a context menu and select Text Frame Options or select the Object menu and select Text Frame Options. The Text Frame Options dialog box opens. You can make changes to the number of columns, gutter spacing, inset spacing, baseline shifts, and vertical justification the same as when you make changes to frames drawn manually on individual pages. Likewise, you also can apply attribute choices for text styles and transformations to the master frames and Object Styles.

After making adjustments on the master frame, all text within a master frame thread is readjusted to the changes made to the frame on the master page. In Figure 17.18, text was placed on a page in a single column. The text was placed within a frame created from a master frame on the master page. By adjusting the Text Frame Options and changing the frame from one column to three columns, all the text in the document using the master frame adjusts automatically, as shown in Figure 17.19.

NOTE When changing master text frame attributes, you can create overset text. InDesign CS4 has new controls for whether, how, and where new pages will be added and removed from a layout as overset text is generated.

FIGURE 17.18

Text placed in a master frame where the frame attributes are set to one column

Chapter 1

Introducing the Creative Suite

In This Chapter

Why Adobe developed the Creative Suite

Knowing the Creative Suite applications

Understanding File Formats

Understanding File Types

The Adobe Premium Creative Suite is comprised of several programs designed to work together to accomplish all your publishing needs for output to print, screen viewing, and web hosting. Adobe Systems has devoted much marketing effort targeting the Creative Suite at design professionals rather than devote energy to marketing the individual program components.

This chapter begins this section with a description of the Creative Suite programs and gives you an idea for how they work together. In this chapter you learn about the purpose for each of the programs, the relationship each program has with other members of the Creative Suite team, and a brief summary of new features contained in the latest releases of the individual programs.

Why Creative Suite?

Why is Adobe Systems spending so much marketing effort informing users about the benefits of the Creative Suite? For the most part, each program in the Creative Suite is an upgrade from a previous version and each is available for upgrades individually. So why talk about the Creative Suite as a single entity when users are likely to upgrade the individual software programs currently used in their design studios? These may be the first questions on your mind as you see the advertising for Adobe imaging product upgrades.

Attention to the Creative Suite as a single design solution is manifested in the idea that the whole is greater than the sum of the parts. For many years Adobe Systems has been building applications on core technologies. At the root of programs like Adobe Illustrator and Adobe In Design is core PDF technology. These programs have evolved with common elements designed to work together so you, the creative professional, can easily exchange files between programs and be confident in knowing that the files you create in one program are easily portable to other Adobe programs.

With the introduction of the Creative Suite, Adobe Systems delivers a collection of applications that offer you seamless integration. Many imaging applications offer you tools that can be used to create complete design pieces in a single program. However the original design of a program like Adobe Illustrator, for example, has always been intended to be an illustration program. Inasmuch as you can create page layouts in Adobe Illustrator CS, the more sophisticated approach is to use a program like Adobe InDesign CS. Whereas Adobe Photoshop CS can also be used for a page layout, likewise the more practical approach is to use again, Adobe InDesign CS. And moving to Adobe InDesign CS, you can create illustrations in the program, but a more efficient tool would be to use Adobe Illustrator CS.

These programs are parts of the greater toolbox called Adobe Creative Suite and are provided to you so you can become more efficient in your creative process using tools designed for specific purposes. After you work in individual programs, it's time to bring the creative elements together. The tool used to collect individual design creations is Adobe InDesign CS where the layout assembly is performed. From InDesign CS you then travel to output. For print purposes you may export files to PDF documents where Adobe Acrobat is used, or you may need to host parts of your layout on a Web site where Adobe GoLive CS is used.

You may be inclined to think that you have one program developed by another software manufacturer that satisfies your design needs and fully supports document integration with many of the programs found in the Creative Suite. For example, you may use Adobe Photoshop and Adobe Illustrator along with QuarkXPress or perhaps you use Adobe Photoshop and create layouts in Macromedia FreeHand. If any of these situations apply why would you abandon what you use now in favor of one of the tools Adobe Systems provides? There are several reasons you might consider if this question comes to mind:

- **Native file support:** One of the strongest arguments for using Adobe Photoshop CS, Adobe Illustrator CS, Adobe InDesign CS, and Adobe GoLive CS together is the fact that native file formats are easily transported between the CS programs. You no longer need to make decisions for saving Photoshop files as TIFF, EPS, GIF, PNG, or JPEG. A native Photoshop PSD or Illustrator .ai file can be imported into Adobe InDesign CS complete with layers and transparency. Native Illustrator and Photoshop files can also be imported directly in Adobe GoLive CS. The native file format import feature alone can save you space on your hard drive since only a single file needs to be saved. Additionally, you save time in importing the correct file since only a single file is saved from the host application and used in your page layout or web design. Native Illustrator CS files can also be opened directly in any Adobe Acrobat viewer and PDF documents can be opened in Illustrator and

FIGURE 17.19

By changing the master text frame attributes from one column to three columns, all text using the frame is adjusted automatically.

Chapter 1

Introducing the Creative Suite

In This Chapter

Why Adobe developed the Creative Suite

Knowing the Creative Suite applications

Understanding File Formats

Understanding File Types

The Adobe Premium Creative Suite is comprised of several programs designed to work together to accomplish all your publishing needs for output to print, screen viewing, and web hosting. Adobe Systems has devoted much marketing effort targeting the Creative Suite at design professionals rather than devote energy to marketing the individual program components.

This chapter begins this section with a description of the Creative Suite programs and gives you an idea for how they work together. In this chapter you learn about the purpose for each of the programs, the relationship each program has with other members of the Creative Suite team, and a brief summary of new features contained in the latest releases of the individual programs.

Why Creative Suite?

Why is Adobe Systems spending so much marketing effort informing users about the benefits of the Creative Suite? For the most part, each program in the Creative Suite is an upgrade from a previous version and each is available for upgrades individually. So why talk about the Creative Suite as a single entity when users are likely to upgrade the individual software programs currently used in their design studios? These may be the first questions on your mind as you see the advertising for Adobe imaging product upgrades.

Attention to the Creative Suite as a single design solution is manifested in the idea that the whole is greater than the sum of the parts. For many years Adobe Systems has been building applications on core technologies. At the root of programs like Adobe Illustrator and Adobe InDesign is core PDF technology. These programs have evolved with common elements designed to work together so you, the creative professional, can easily exchange files between programs and be confident in knowing that the files you create in one program are easily portable to other Adobe programs.

With the introduction of the Creative Suite, Adobe Systems delivers a collection of applications that offer you seamless integration. Many imaging applications offer you tools that can be used to create complete design pieces in a single program. However the original design of a program like Adobe Illustrator, for example, has always been intended to be an illustration program. Inasmuch as you can create page layouts in Adobe Illustrator CS, the more sophisticated approach is to use a program like Adobe InDesign CS. Whereas Adobe Photoshop CS can also be used for a page layout, likewise the more practical approach is to use again, Adobe InDesign CS. And moving to Adobe InDesign CS, you can create illustrations in the program, but a more efficient tool would be to use Adobe Illustrator CS.

These programs are parts of the greater toolbox called Adobe Creative Suite and are provided to you so you can become more efficient in your creative process using tools designed for specific purposes. After you work in individual programs, it's time to bring the creative elements together. The tool used to collect individual design creations is Adobe InDesign CS where the layout assembly is performed. From InDesign CS you then travel to output. For print purposes you may export files to PDF documents where Adobe Acrobat is used, or you may need to host parts of your layout on a Web site where Adobe GoLive CS is used.

You may be inclined to think that you have one program developed by another software manufacturer that satisfies your design needs and fully supports document integration with many of the programs found in the Creative Suite. For example, you may use Adobe Photoshop and Adobe Illustrator along with QuarkXPress or perhaps you use Adobe Photoshop and create layouts in Macromedia FreeHand. If any of these situations apply, why would you abandon what you use now in favor of one of the tools Adobe Systems provides? There are several reasons you might consider if this question comes to mind:

• **Native file support:** One of the strongest arguments for using Adobe Photoshop CS, Adobe Illustrator CS, and Adobe InDesign CS, and Adobe GoLive CS together is the fact that native file formats are easily transported between the CS programs. You no longer need to make decisions for saving Photoshop files as TIFF, EPS, GIF, PNG, or JPEG. A native Photoshop PSD or Illustrator .ai file can be imported into Adobe InDesign CS complete with layers and transparency. Native Illustrator and Photoshop files can also be imported directly in Adobe GoLive CS. The native file format import feature alone can save you space on your hard drive since only a single file needs to be saved. Additionally, you save time in importing the correct file since only a single file is saved from the host application and used in your page layout or web design. Native Illustrator CS files can also be opened directly in any Adobe Acrobat viewer and PDF documents can be opened in Illustrator and imported in InDesign and GoLive.

Cross-reference
For information on importing native file formats across programs, look over chapters contained in Part 3.

• **Consistent user interface:** Programs used by creative professionals today are sophisticated and complicated. One of the major problems facing many designers is the long learning curve necessary to become productive in a computer program. When you use several programs from several different computer software manufacturers, your learning curve rises. Application software companies develop software according to standards each company sets forth in the design of the user interface. One company may make extensive use of context sensitive menus while another company may avoid them. One company may use palettes and panes liberally while another company relies on menu commands and dialog boxes. Add to these differences the extended use of keyboard shortcuts and the differences between programs requires you to spend much time learning shortcuts not to mention the confusion of remembering one key sequence in one program invokes a different command than the same key sequence in another program.

In workflow environments, consistency is crucial. Time is money and the more time needed to train staff cuts into your productivity and your profits. By using tools all developed from a single software manufacturer you find much more consistency in the design of the user interface and the keyboard shortcuts that access menus, tools, and commands. Adobe has taken the user interface design one step farther in offering you customizable keyboard shortcuts and custom workspaces in several CS programs.

Creating Text Wraps

Wrapping text around graphic elements in your design layouts can add greater visual appeal to your document. If you must manually set type around objects to create a text wrap, your job could become tedious and time-consuming. Fortunately, both Illustrator and InDesign offer you many different options for wrapping text around objects and images.

Wrapping text in Illustrator

You can wrap text around any placed object, type objects, imported images, and objects you draw in Illustrator. If you save files as bitmaps from Photoshop with transparency, Illustrator can wrap text while ignoring transparent pixels. In Figure 17.20, you can see a text wrap around a Photoshop bitmap image with transparency.

Illustrator can wrap type around objects as well as images with transparency, clipping paths, and transparent layers.

Wrapping graphic objects

To understand how to wrap text around graphic objects, look over the following steps.

STEPS: Applying Text Wraps to Objects in Illustrator

1. **Create area type on a new document page.** Create a text block by selecting the Type tool and dragging open a rectangle where you want the text to appear. You can import text or type text in the text block.

TIP If you want to use Greek text in Illustrator, open InDesign and use the Fill with Placeholder Text command to add Greek text to a text frame. Click the cursor inside the frame and choose Edit ⇨ Select All or press ⌘/Ctrl+A. Copy and paste the text in Illustrator.

2. **Place a graphic you want to use for the text wrap.** You can place an object created in another program or use objects created in Illustrator. If you don't have an object handy, use the Symbols palette and drag an object to the document window. Use the transformation tools to size the object as desired. In Figure 17.21, an object from the Symbols palette was sized and placed on top of the text. Be certain that the object to be wrapped is on the same layer as the text and that it appears in front of the text.

Objects to be wrapped need to be placed on the same layer as the text and appear in front of the text used for the wrap.

3. **Assign a text wrap to the object.** Objects are assigned attributes for a text wrap. Select the object with one of the selection tools, and choose Object ➪ Text Wrap ➪ Make Text Wrap.

4. **Open the Text Wrap Options dialog box.** Choose Object ➪ Text Wrap ➪ Text Wrap Options. The Text Wrap Options dialog box opens, as shown in Figure 17.22. Click the Preview check box, and the text wraps in the document window, showing you the results of the wrap and offset. To adjust the offset amount, change the value in the Offset field box. Click OK when the wrap appears the way you want.

FIGURE 17.22

Select the Preview check box in the Text Wrap Options dialog box, and the background document window displays the results of the text wrap. To change the distance between the object and the text, edit the value in the Offset field box.

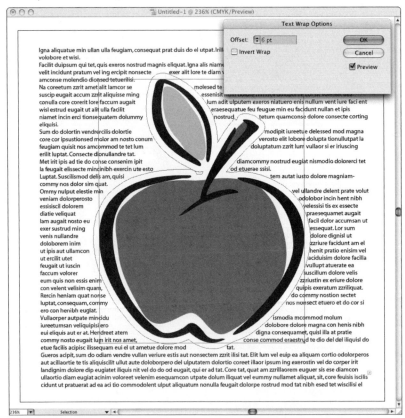

In the Text Wrap Options dialog box, an option appears for inversing a wrap. Check the box, and click Preview to see the results of an inverse wrap. This option is used for containing text within objects, as shown in Figure 17.23.

FIGURE 17.23

Select the Invert Wrap check box to contain text within an object.

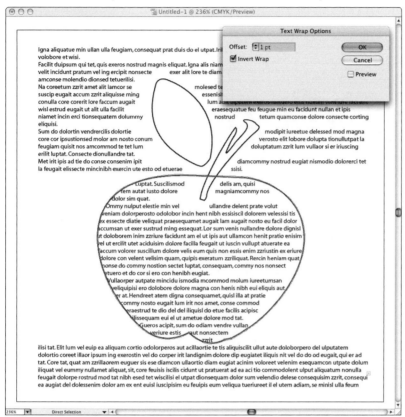

Wrapping text objects

You also can wrap text around type objects. You can use the text frame as the object, or you can create outlines and wrap text around the outlined type. Follow the same procedures for applying text wraps to graphic objects. In Figure 17.24, you can see the effects of wrapping text around a text frame (top) and text converted to outlines (bottom).

FIGURE 17.24

Text frames and type converted to outlines can be assigned text wrap attributes.

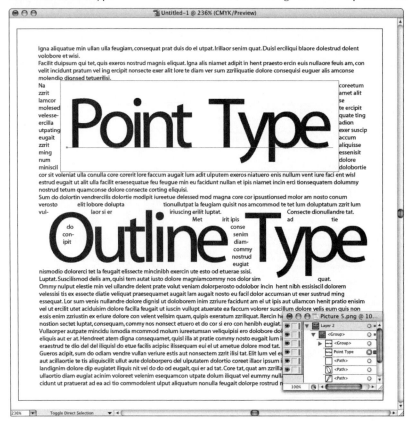

Wrapping images

Images from Photoshop can be assigned text wraps. Follow the same steps as mentioned previously for applying text wraps to graphic objects. Be certain that the placed Photoshop file is contained in the same group as the text that wraps the object. If a Photoshop file contains a mask or transparency, be certain to create a clipping path and save the file with the path in either Photoshop native format or EPS. In Figure 17.25, a clipping path is added to the image. Notice that the transparency is not enough to create the wrap around the object in Illustrator to properly designate the path. The clipping path is needed to mask the object so the text wrap falls around the image.

FIGURE 17.25

Create and save a clipping path in a Photoshop file when you want to mask an image. Save the document in Photoshop native format (PSD) or as an EPS.

Notice that the text neatly wraps the image, as shown in Figure 17.26, at the offset distance defined in the Text Wrap Options dialog box.

FIGURE 17.26

Text wraps around the clipping path assigned in a Photoshop document.

Wrapping text in InDesign

InDesign offers significantly better options for wrapping text that you find in Illustrator that include additional options for setting the text-wrap and path attributes. You can adjust clipping paths and path tolerances in InDesign, as well as set the same options found in Illustrator's Text Wrap Options dialog box.

Importing text wraps into InDesign

If you have an Illustrator document that needs to be imported into InDesign, you can create text wraps and complete the layout in Illustrator. When the file is imported into InDesign, the text wraps and layout appearance are preserved in InDesign when you place the file. In Figure 17.27, you can see the results of importing a native Illustrator document with a text wrap into InDesign.

InDesign offers you options for adjusting the clipping path on placed objects and also on objects placed in Illustrator and imported into InDesign. The path defined in Photoshop is the default path used in Illustrator and ultimately appears in the InDesign view.

FIGURE 17.27

Text wraps created in Illustrator are preserved when placed in InDesign. Save the Illustrator files in native Illustrator Document (AI) format and import directly by choosing File ➪ Place in InDesign.

You may have situations where artifacts appear around the edges of an image to which you have assigned a clipping path. If you need to adjust the tolerance so more of the path edge is cut off or the edge is pushed out to show more image and less mask, you can make the adjustments in InDesign. With the placed object selected, choose Object ➪ Clipping Path. The Clipping Path dialog box opens, and here you can make adjustments to a path.

From the Type drop-down list, select Detect Edges. The Threshold and Tolerance sliders enable you to adjust the path. In Figure 17.28, you can see the results of changing the Tolerance and Threshold on the same image used in Figure 17.26.

FIGURE 17.28

Open the Clipping Path dialog box to adjust the path edge. This dialog box lets you clip more of the image or reduce the mask to show more of the image.

Using InDesign text-wrap options

InDesign offers you a more elaborate set of options for wrapping text than you find in Illustrator. InDesign's Text Wrap palette lets you specify wrap options for a selected object in the foreground, as well as specify how the text behind the object is wrapped. Shown in Figure 17.29, the Text Wrap panel is opened by choosing Window ➪ Text Wrap. As you learn from viewing the Text Wrap palette, you have many different options for controlling the text-wrap attributes. InDesign enables you to apply text wraps on Master Pages that affect frames on document pages without having to create overrides on the separate document pages.

FIGURE 17.29

Choose Window ⇨ Type and Tables ⇨ Text Wrap to open the Text Wrap palette.

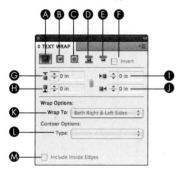

In the Text Wrap palette, you see five icons across the top of the palette, some field boxes, and drop-down lists, all used to adjust text-wrap options. The items include the following:

A **No Text Wrap icon:** The first icon in the top row turns off text wrap.

B **Wrap Around Bounding Box icon:** The second icon sets the text wrap around the bounding box of all objects. The bounding box represents the periphery of the farthest elements to the edge of the object.

C **Wrap Around Object Shape icon:** This icon wraps the shape of objects and can include images with clipping paths. When this icon is selected, the drop-down lists for the Contour Options become active.

D **Jump Object icon:** Selecting this icon stops the wrap at the top of the image and starts it again at the bottom of the image. In essence, the wrap jumps over the object/image.

E **Jump to Next Column icon:** When you want the text to stop at the top of the image and not continue below the image, select this icon and text jumps to the next column. In essence, the wrap offset is used for the top of the image only, without regard to the sides or bottom of the image.

F **Invert check box:** This option is the same as you find in Illustrator. It is used to invert the text wrap and wrap text inside objects.

G **Top Offset field:** This option controls the offset distance on the top edge of the object/ image. Edit the field box or click the up/down arrows to adjust the offset distance. Note: When contour options are selected (see below), Top Offset is the only available field and applies to the entire contour, not just the top of the object.

H **Bottom Offset field:** This option acts the same as Top Offset but controls the bottom off-set distance.

I   **Left Offset field:** This choice offers the same offset options controlling the left side of the object/image.

J   **Right Offset field:** This option controls the offset for the right side of the object/image.

K   **Wrap to drop-down menu:** This choice includes options for the sides of the object to wrap to.

L   **Contour Options drop-down list:** From the Contour Options Type drop-down list, you have options that are used when you select the Wrap Around Object Shape icon. The options in the menu include the following:

- **Bounding Box:** Choose this option when you want to place the wrap around the frame where the outside edges appear.

- **Detect Edges:** InDesign can automatically detect edges in objects and images with paths. To enable auto-detection of edges, use this option.

- **Alpha Channel:** Use this option when a Photoshop image contains an Alpha Channel or transparency and you want the image masked. InDesign interprets layered Photoshop files with transparency the same as when creating a clipping path. All the transparency is masked when you select this option.

- **Photoshop Path:** This option is the same as Alpha Channel, except you need a path created in the image. InDesign clips the image to the path saved in Photoshop.

- **Graphic Frame:** The frame holding an object or image can be larger or smaller than the imported item. When you select this option, the wrap forms around the frame, ignoring the frame contents.

- **Same As Clipping:** This option is the same as Photoshop Path when a clipping path has been saved. You can import native PSD files as well as EPS files saved with clipping paths.

M   **Include Inside Edges check box:** If you have an object with a cutout inside the object and want text to wrap around the outside and fill the inside cutout, select this option.

As is the case with Illustrator, you can adjust the text-frame options and change frames from single to multiple columns. In multiple-column frames, text wraps apply to all columns interacting with the object, as shown in Figure 17.30. If you create multiple frames on a page and either link the frames or keep them isolated as independent frames, the text wraps likewise occur for all text interacting with the object/image.

FIGURE 17.30

FIGURE 17.30

Text wraps are applied to multiple-column frames and linked frames.

Summary

- Text is typed or imported into text frames in Illustrator and InDesign.

- When text is extended from one frame to another, the text follows a thread. Text frames in threads can be linked, unthreaded, or cut from frames. New frames can be added between existing threaded frames.

- Text frames in Illustrator and InDesign can be assigned different properties. You can specify number of columns, inset spacing, column gutter widths, and font attributes as well as paragraph and object styles.

- Text can be wrapped around graphic objects, text objects, and images in both Illustrator and InDesign.

- Text wraps can be applied to paths, transparencies, and clipping paths of Photoshop images placed in InDesign.

Chapter 18

Working with Special Characters

Both Illustrator and InDesign allow you to handle typography like a master, especially when working in conjunction with the OpenType fonts that offer you thousands of character selections. InDesign, in particular, with its abundant set of menu commands and palette options, is the most powerful typesetting tool developed to date for desktop computers. With it, you have the ability to set high-quality type that rivals the output from professional typesetting machines used before the computer revolution.

Older PostScript fonts give you a maximum of 256 different characters, or glyphs. With the OpenType fonts, however, you get as many as 65,000 glyphs per font. These additional characters offer you many more options for pairing characters in ligatures, customizing fractions, accessing foreign language characters, and working with a wide variety of symbols and special characters that can be used as type or graphic elements.

IN THIS CHAPTER

Understanding glyphs

Accessing special characters

Working with inline graphics

Working with Glyphs Palettes

Both Illustrator and InDesign have a Glyphs palette that shows you, at a glance, the different characters available in any given font. It's much like the old Keycaps control panel available in earlier Mac operating systems. In addition to viewing glyphs in a scrollable palette, you can also create custom glyph sets in InDesign and you can view different special characters by selecting menu options in the palettes in both InDesign and Illustrator.

In Illustrator, choose Type ➪ Glyphs to open the Glyphs palette shown in Figure 18.1. The palette contains several menus, scrollbars to view any hidden characters, font selection menus, and zoom tools.

FIGURE 18.1

The Glyphs palette displays all characters in a given font.

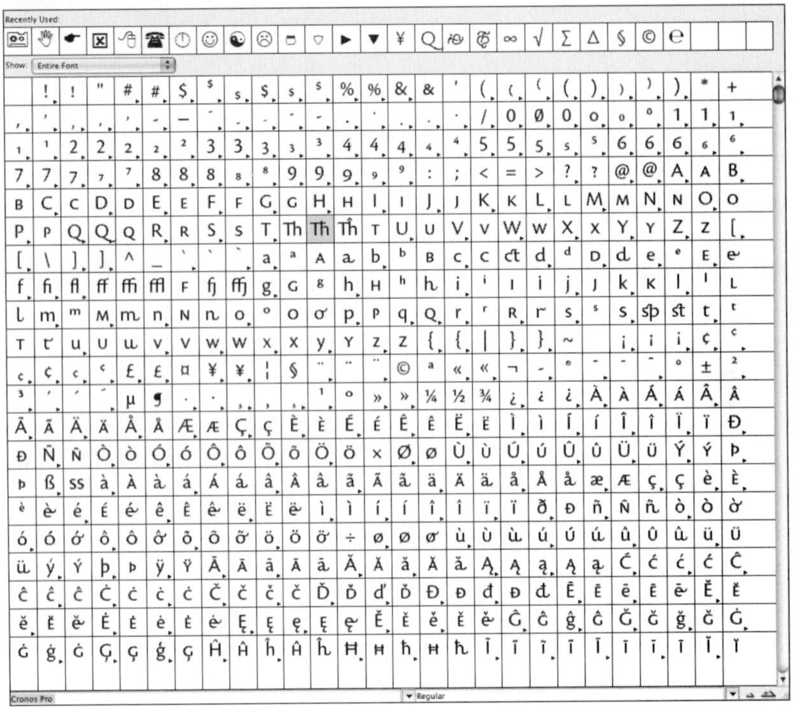

The default selection in the Show menu at the top is Entire Font. All characters in a given font are displayed in the scrollable palette. The Show menu lets you focus the information shown in the palette to show either all glyphs or only alternates of a selected glyph in your layout. Note in Figure 18.1 that when you press the mouse button on a particular character with a flag in the lower-right corner, a pop-up bar shows alternate characters. When you select the menu command, the alternate characters are displayed in the palette. Other options you have from the menu choices include many of the same options found in the Character palette.

NOTE   The Show pull-down menu offers different options depending on the type of font selected. More options are available with OpenType fonts than you find with TrueType fonts, and more options are available with OpenType Pro fonts than you find with OpenType fonts.

CROSS-REF   For more information on using the Character palette, see Chapter 16.

To use glyphs, and particularly to use alternate characters in Illustrator, you can easily access the palette and select characters for insertion in text as you type. For character insertions you might use in both Illustrator and InDesign, follow these steps.

STEPS: Inserting Special Characters in Text Using the Glyphs Palette

1. **Begin by typing a body of text.** Add some area type to a page in Illustrator. Select an OpenType Pro font you want to use by choosing Type ⇨ Font. Next, drag open a rectangle with the Type tool, and begin to type.

2. **Open the Glyphs palette.** Choose Type ⇨ Glyphs to open the Glyphs palette.

3. **Locate the character you want to insert.** The Glyphs palette opens with the current selected font displayed in the palette. Scroll the palette and find a character to insert. In our example, we use a ligature for combining the *f, f* and *l* characters into a single character.

4. **Insert the character.** When you find the character in the Glyphs palette, double-click on the character. The character is inserted at the cursor location. In Figure 18.2, the inserted character is highlighted.

FIGURE 18.2

Double-clicking on a character inserts it at the cursor.

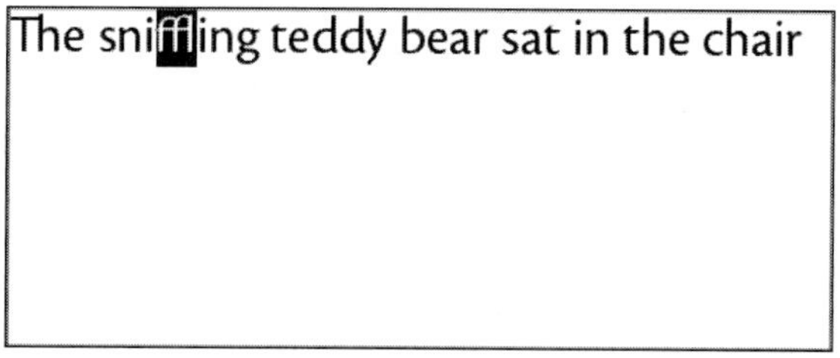

The sniffling teddy bear sat in the chair

In addition to the different displays in the palette for showing characters via the Show menu, you can make font selections from the pull-down menu at the bottom of the palette. If you're searching for a special character or want to view a specific font, use the menu to select fonts without disturbing your text editing. You can select a font family from the pull-down menu at the bottom left side of the palette; you select the font style from the second pull-down menu at the bottom of the palette. In Figure 18.1, the selected font family is Myriad Pro and the selected style is Regular.

To the right of the Style pull-down menu, zoom buttons offer different zoom views. Click on the smaller mountain symbols to zoom out, and click on the larger symbol to zoom in on the characters in the palette.

In InDesign, you have a few more style combinations that you can view in the Show menu, but the main distinction between Illustrator and InDesign exists with the flyout menu commands accessible via the arrow at the top right of the Glyphs palette. In Illustrator, the only option available here is resetting the palette to the default view. But in InDesign there are options for working with glyph sets. Click on the right-pointing arrow to open the flyout menu, and the options shown in Figure 18.3 appear.

FIGURE 18.3

InDesign supports several menu commands unavailable in Illustrator.

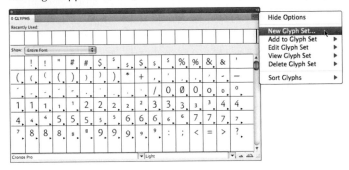

In addition to flyout menu command differences, InDesign also offers you a display of recently used glyphs at the top of the panel, and additional information about a font when the cursor appears over a character such as Unicode values. These options are also available with Illustrator.

The menu commands available from the flyout menu enable you to create and edit custom glyph sets. This feature can be a time-saver when you need to access special characters or alternatives while typesetting in InDesign. To understand how custom sets are created and used, follow these steps.

STEPS: Working with Custom Glyph Sets in InDesign

1. **Open the Glyphs palette in InDesign.** Choose Type ⇨ Glyphs to open the Glyphs palette.

2. **Create a new glyph set.** You can use the Glyphs palette with or without a document open in the InDesign application window. You can temporarily ignore the current font selected. When you create a new set and add characters to your custom set, you can add characters from different fonts. From the flyout menu, select New Glyph Set.

3. **Name the new glyph set.** The New Glyph Set dialog box opens. Type a name in the field box for the name you want to use for your custom set. In our example, we use myGlyphs for the set name. You can view your new glyph set by choosing it from the Show menu or via View Glyph Set in the flyout menu. Currently the palette includes no characters.

4. **Select a font family and font style.** Be sure the Show option is set to Entire Font. At this point, you can view all your installed fonts and available styles by making selections in the pull-down menus at the bottom of the Glyphs palette. Select a font family and the font style you want to view.

5. **Add a character to the custom glyph set.** When you find a character you want to add to the set, click on it to highlight it. Open the flyout menu, and choose Add to Glyph Set (alternately open a context menu and make a menu selection). A submenu opens where you should see your new custom set listed. If you create several sets, select the one you want to edit. In our case, we select myGlyphs from the submenu.

6. **Add additional characters to the custom glyph set.** Continue selecting and adding characters to the glyph set with the Add to Glyph Set command in the flyout menu. When you want to use the custom set, select it from the Show menu at the top of the Glyphs palette or by choosing View Glyph Set in the flyout menu. The characters you added to the set appear in the Glyphs palette, as shown in Figure 18.4. When you want to access a character from the set while you are typing in InDesign, simply open the set and double-click the desired character. It is automatically inserted at the cursor location.

FIGURE 18.4

You can add a custom glyph set to the Glyphs palette.

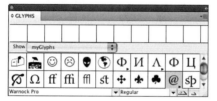

7. **Delete a character from your custom glyph set.** If you want to delete a character from your glyph set, select the set in the Show menu. In the flyout menu, select Edit Glyph Set. The Edit Glyph Set dialog box opens, as shown in Figure 18.5. Select the character you want to delete, and click Delete from Set. In addition to deleting characters, the Edit Glyph Set dialog box also enables you to change the font and style of individual characters included in the set.

FIGURE 18.5

To delete a character, click Delete from Set.

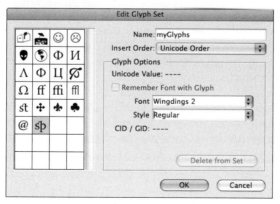

Using Special Typographic Characters

A number of advanced typographic features are available to you in InDesign. By using simple menu commands, you can easily achieve special effects that are popular with layout artists and typographers. In the Type menu, you will find several options for handling special characters. Three of these options provide an even wider selection of options in submenus. They include Insert Special Character, Insert White Space, and Insert Break Character.

Inserting special characters

When you choose Type ⇨ Insert Special Character ⇨ Markers, a submenu opens where a number of options provide you with features for handling special characters, as shown in Figure 18.6.

FIGURE 18.6

You find numerous special typographic features via the Type menu.

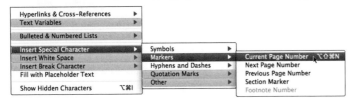

> **TIP**   You also can make the same menu command choices for special character options by using a context menu. Create a text box, and Ctrl+click (Macintosh) or right-click (Windows) to open a context menu on the text frame. Select Insert Special Character ⇨ Markers, and the same menu choices appear.

The submenu items available from the Markers submenu include the following:

- **Auto Page Number:** The keyboard shortcut for automatic page numbering is Alt+Shift+Ctrl+N (Windows) or Option+Shift+⌘+N (Mac). If you don't want to memorize the keyboard shortcut, you can use a menu command. To use the Current Page Number command, open a master page, draw a text frame, and select a font and font style. With the cursor blinking in the text frame, select the menu command. Automatic numbering is then applied to all pages associated with the master page. Although you often apply Auto Page Number to master pages, you aren't required to use it on master pages exclusively. You can also use it on regular document pages to number them individually.

- **Next Page Number:** The Next Page Number and Previous Page Number (see Previous Page Number below) commands are helpful when you have blocks of text that start on one page and then continue on another page in your document (also known as "story jumps"). Where the text ends on one page, for example, you would want to inform the reader that it continues on another page with a "Continued on page X" notation (also known as a "jump line") To do this, create a separate text frame that overlaps the text frame of the story you are jumping. Be sure to group these two text frames together so if you move the story, the jump line stays with it. Type **Continued on page** (note a space is added preceding the text), and then choose Type ➪ Insert Special Character ➪ Next Page Number. InDesign automatically inserts the "continued to" page number.

- **Previous Page Number:** This option works like Next Page Number, but instead of using a "continued to" page number, you use a "continued from" page number. Again, create a separate text frame that overlaps the text frame of the jumped part of the story. Type **Continued from page** (note a space is added after the text), and then choose Type ➪ Insert Special Character ➪ Previous Page Number. InDesign automatically inserts the "continued from" page number. Again, you should group the text frames so the page reference stays with the story if you decide to move it.

- **Section Marker:** You can divide documents into sections using the Layout ➪ Numbering and Section Options menu command. This marker inserts the section marker text from Numbering and Section Options.

In earlier versions of InDesign, other special characters were included in the Insert Special Character submenu. This menu has been divided into several submenus, such as the Markers submenu mentioned above. The Symbols submenu contains additional special characters that include the following:

- **Bullet Character:** The ability to insert special symbols with a menu command is particularly helpful to people who work in cross-platform environments and don't know the key combinations for certain characters. The bullet character inserts a bullet at the cursor insertion point.

- **Copyright Symbol (©):** Inserts the copyright symbol.

- **Ellipsis (. . .):** Inserts an ellipsis.

- **Paragraph Symbol (¶):** Inserts a paragraph symbol.

- **Registered Trademark Symbol (®):** Inserts a registered trademark symbol.

- **Section Symbol (§):** Inserts a symbol representing a new section.

- **Trademark Symbol (™):** Inserts a trademark symbol.

The Hyphens and Dashes submenu contains the following:

- **Em Dash (—):** Inserts an em dash.

- **En Dash (–):** Inserts an en dash.

- **Discretionary Hyphen:** Add a hyphen as desired by using this option if a word needs to break a line.

- **Nonbreaking Hyphen:** Select this option when you don't want a hyphenated word to break to the next line. Nonbreaking hyphens only prevent a line break at that hyphen. The compound text around the hyphen can break.

The Quotations submenu contains the following:

- **Double Left Quotation Mark** ("): Inserts a double left quotation mark.

- **Double Right Quotation Mark** ("): Inserts a double right quotation mark.

- **Single Left Quotation Mark** ('): Inserts a single left quotation mark.

- **Single Right Quotation Mark** ('): Inserts a single right quotation mark.

- **Straight Double Quotation Marks** ("): Inserts straight double quotes instead of smart quotes.

- **Straight Single Quotation Mark** ('): Inserts a single quote mark instead of a smart quote mark.

The last submenu for Insert Special Characters is the Other submenu. This menu contains the following options:

- **Tab:** Has the same effect as pressing the Tab key.

- **Right Indent Tab:** Adds a tab indented from the right side of the text line.

- **Indent to Here:** Indents to the cursor position.

- **End Nested Style Here:** Ends a nested style at the cursor position.

- **Non-joiner:** Used for setting zero width non-joiner text.

Inserting white space characters

The next set of typographic controls you find in the Type menu are the spacing options. When you choose Type ⇨ Insert White Space, a submenu offers commands for adding space between characters and words. The commands include the following:

- **Em Space:** Em spaces are equal in horizontal width to the vertical point size for a font. For example, in 18-point type, the em space is 18 points wide.

- **En Space:** En spaces are exactly one-half the width of an em space.

- **Nonbreaking Space:** This option adds space equal to that produced when you press the spacebar, but prevents the line from being broken at that point.

- **Nonbreaking Space (Fixed Width):** This is a fixed width space that prevents the line of type from being broken at a space character.

- **Hair Space:** This option adds the smallest space between characters. It's $\frac{1}{24}$ the width of an em space.

- **Sixth Space:** One-sixth the width of an em space.

- **Thin Space:** One-eighth the width of an em space.

- **Quarter Space:** One-fourth the width of an em space.

- **Third Space:** One-third the width of an em space.

- **Punctuation Space:** The same amount of space used for other punctuation marks such as commas, periods, colons, and exclamation marks.

- **Figure Space:** The same space used for a numeric character in a font. This option is helpful when aligning numbers in columns.

- **Flush Space:** You apply this option to fully justified paragraphs. A variable amount of space is added to the last line in a paragraph and justifies the last line of text.

Inserting break characters

Rounding out the options for using special typographic characters, you'll find a selection in the Type menu that controls line breaks. Choose Type ⇨ Insert Break Character and the submenu items include the following:

- **Column Break:** When inserting a column break, text following the break flows to the next column in a multiple-column text frame. If text is set to a single-column frame, the text flows to the next frame in the thread.

- **Frame Break:** Flows text to the next frame in the text thread. If text is set to multiple columns and you insert a frame break in column 1, the text is flowed to the next frame thread, ignoring columns 2 and 3.

- **Page Break:** Flows text to the next page when text is threaded across pages.

- **Odd Page Break:** Flows text to the next odd-numbered page when following a thread.

- **Even Page Break:** Flows text to the next even-numbered page when following a thread.

- **Paragraph Return:** Inserts a paragraph return (same as pressing Enter/Return).

- **Forced Line Break:** Forces a line break (same as pressing Shift+Enter/Return).

- **Discretionary Line Break:** Prevents problems with hyphenated words appearing in the middle of a line of type after text reflows.

Inserting Inline Graphics

You can automatically thread text to separate text frames. Graphics placed in your layout in image frames do not follow the threading behavior of the text. This is a problem if you reformat your text and you need the graphics to stay connected to specific parts of the copy. Normally, you would have to move the graphic elements separately each time your text reflowed. However, if you use inline graphics, the graphic is interpreted similarly to the way text is interpreted and maintains its respective position within a given line of text.

Creating an inline graphic is easy. You simply select an object or image, cut it from a page, and paste the graphic back into a text frame with the cursor blinking at the spot where you want the object to appear. To see an example of this process, look over the following steps.

STEPS: Creating an Inline Graphic

1. **Place type within a frame.** Either place a body of text from a file or type a few lines of text.

2. **Cut a graphic from the document page.** Use an object imported from Illustrator, use the Glyphs palette, select a character and convert the character to outlines, or draw an object in InDesign. Select the object, and choose Edit ⇨ Cut.

3. **Identify the insertion point in the text.** Place the cursor at the point where you want to insert the inline graphic in the text frame. Use the Type tool, and wait for the blinking I-beam cursor to appear.

4. **Paste the graphic.** Choose Edit ⇨ Paste. The graphic is now part of the text block and follows the same scrolling behavior as the line of text where it resides. Figure 18.7 shows the results of pasting a graphic in a line of text.

FIGURE 18.7

To place a graphic as an inline object, cut the object and click in a text block. Choose Edit ⇨ Paste, and the object is pasted at the cursor position.

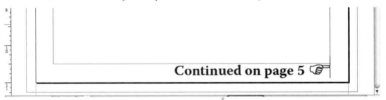

Continued on page 5 ☞

Summary

- OpenType fonts support more than 65,000 glyphs in a given font. Opening the Glyphs palette in Illustrator or InDesign displays examples of all the glyphs contained within a selected font.

- InDesign allows you to create custom glyph sets where you can access frequently used characters in a single palette.

- InDesign has numerous options for accessing special typographic characters and functions. These include symbols, punctuation, white space options, line breaks, automatic page numbering, tab settings, and more.

- Inline graphics are inserted in text frames and scroll with the text as it is flowed through a frame or frame thread.

Part V

Using Creative Suite and Microsoft Office

In this part we talk about the Microsoft Office programs and how to work between those programs and the Creative Suite applications. We begin in Chapter 19 by showing how to import Microsoft Word files in several Adobe Creative Suite programs.

If you need to edit some legacy files, you need to know how to get the content from several CS applications back to Microsoft Word, which is what we cover in Chapter 20.

Tables are a great asset to many layouts. Working effectively with tables is covered in Chapter 21 where we talk about using table styles in InDesign and connecting tables to Microsoft Excel files.

Chapter 22 shows how to prepare Microsoft Office documents for professional printing.

Chapter 19

Importing Microsoft Word Documents

Whether it is copy for an InDesign layout, product descriptions for a Dreamweaver Web page, or a marketing line you want to manipulate in Illustrator, the standard workflow for most text starts in a word processor like Microsoft Word and then the text is imported into one of the CS4 applications. Although the CS4 applications handle type very well, many copywriters are more comfortable with word processors; so importing design text is common.

This chapter covers the crucial workflow step of importing text from a word processor like Word to the CS4 applications. Although several different word processors are available, Microsoft Word is the most popular word processor available today, and it is used for all the examples in this chapter.

You have essentially two methods for importing text from Microsoft Word. One method uses the Clipboard and the Cut, Copy, and Paste features. The other method exports (or saves the Word document) in a format that you can easily import into the CS4 applications. Both Illustrator and InDesign open or place Word documents saved in the Word (DOC) format, and Dreamweaver can import Word documents directly. After you import the text, you can easily move the text among any of the CS4 applications using the PDF format.

Importing a Word document into InDesign or Illustrator not only moves text but also can import the text styles.

Using the Clipboard

In Microsoft Word, you copy selected text to the Clipboard by choosing Edit ➪ Cut (⌘/Ctrl+X) or Edit ➪ Copy (⌘/Ctrl+C). You can then paste the text into the various CS4 applications by choosing Edit ➪ Paste (⌘/Ctrl+V). Text pasted into Illustrator and InDesign appears within a newly created text object, like that shown in Figure 19.1.

FIGURE 19.1

Text pasted into InDesign from Microsoft Word

Chapter 19

Importing Microsoft Word Documents

Whether it is copy for an InDesign layout, product descriptions for a Dreamweaver Web page, or a marketing line you want to manipulate in Illustrator, the standard workflow for most text starts in a word processor like Microsoft Word and then the text is imported into one of the CS3CS4 applications. Although the CS3CS4 applications handle type very well, many copywriters are more comfortable with word processors, so importing design text is common.

This chapter covers the crucial workflow step of importing text from a word processor like Word to the CS3CS4 applications. Although several different word processors are available, Microsoft Word is the most popular word processor available today, and it is used for all the examples in this chapter.

You have essentially two methods for importing text from Microsoft Word. One method uses the Clipboard and the Cut, Copy, and Paste features. The other method exports (or saves the Word document) in a format that you can easily import into the CS3CS4 applications. Both Illustrator and InDesign open or place Word documents saved in the Word (DOC) format, and Dreamweaver can import Word documents directly. After you import the text, you can easily move the text among any of the CS3CS4 applications using the PDF format. Importing a Word document into InDesign or Illustrator not only moves text but also can import the text styles.

Using the Clipboard

In Microsoft Word, you copy selected text to the Clipboard by choosing Edit@@>Cut (@@cmd/Ctrl+X) or Edit@@>Copy (@@cmd/Ctrl+C). You can then paste the text into the various CS3CS4 applications by choosing Edit@@>Paste (@@cmd/Ctrl+V). Text pasted into Illustrator and InDesign appears within a newly created text object, like that shown in Figure 20.19.1.

FIGURE 20.19.1

Text pasted into InDesign from Microsoft Word

In addition to the standard Edit@@>Paste menu command, Illustrator also includes Paste in Front (@@cmd/Ctrl+F) and Paste in Back (@@cmd/Ctrl+B) commands. These commands place the pasted text on top of (or behind) the currently selected object.

InDesign includes Paste without Formatting (Shift+Ctrl+V on Windows; Shift+@@cmd+V on the Mac), Paste Into (Alt+Ctrl+V on Windows; Option+@@cmd+V on the Mac), and Paste in Place (Alt+Shift+Ctrl+V on Windows; Option+Shift+@@cmd+V on the Mac) commands. The Paste without Formatting command strips all formatting out of the pasted text. You use the Paste Into command to mask an image by pasting into a converted outline. You cannot use this command on imported text. The Paste in Place command places the clipboard text in a text frame in the center of the document. The Paste in Place command is useful for moving positioned objects between InDesign pages, but Word has no positional information that it shares with InDesign, so the text is positioned in the document center.

Text pasted into Illustrator and InDesign appears within a newly created text object unless you previously selected some text using the Type tool. If you selected text, the pasted text replaces the selected text.

In addition to transporting text using the Clipboard, text that you select in Word and drag and drop in an Illustrator or InDesign document moves the text into the target application.

Maintaining formatting

Although text pasted into Illustrator maintains formatting, text pasted into InDesign gives you the options to paste All Information or Text Only. This is set in a Preference setting found in the Clipboard Handling panel of the Preferences dialog box. The InDesign Preferences dialog box is opened by choosing InDesign/Edit@@>Preferences@@>Clipboard Handling, as shown in Figure 20.19.2.

Note

When the Text Only option is enabled in the Clipboard Handling panel of the Preferences dialog box, the Paste without Formatting command is not available.

In addition to the standard Edit ⇨ Paste menu command, Illustrator also includes Paste in Front (⌘/Ctrl+F) and Paste in Back (⌘/Ctrl+B) commands. These commands place the pasted text on top of (or behind) the currently selected object.

InDesign includes Paste without Formatting (Shift+Ctrl+V on Windows; Shift+⌘+V on the Mac), and Paste in Place (Alt+Shift+Ctrl+V on Windows; Option+Shift+⌘+V on the Mac) commands. The Paste without Formatting command strips all formatting out of the pasted text. You use the Paste Into command to mask an image by pasting into a converted outline—like pasting into a shape. You cannot use this command on imported text. The Paste in Place command places the clipboard text in a text frame in the center of the document. The Paste in Place command is useful for moving positioned objects between InDesign pages, but Word has no positional information that it shares with InDesign, so the text is positioned in the document center.

Text pasted into Illustrator and InDesign appears within a newly created text object unless you previously selected some text using the Type tool. If you selected text, the pasted text replaces the selected text.

In addition to transporting text using the Clipboard, text that you select in Word and drag and drop in an Illustrator or InDesign document moves the text into the target application.

Maintaining formatting

Although text pasted into Illustrator maintains formatting, text pasted into InDesign gives you the options to paste All Information or Text Only. This is set in a Preference setting found in the Clipboard Handling panel of the Preferences dialog box. The InDesign Preferences dialog box is opened by choosing Edit ⇨ Preferences ⇨ Clipboard Handling (Windows) or InDesign/Edit ⇨ Preferences ⇨ Clipboard Handling (Mac), as shown in Figure 19.2.

NOTE By default, InDesign's preferences are set to paste Text Only without preserving formatting. Open the Clipboard Handling Preferences and click the All Information (Index Markers, Swatches, Styles, etc.) radio button to preserve formatting.

Text pasted into Dreamweaver from Microsoft Word also maintains formatting, but you can use the Paste Special option to access a dialog box that gives you options to paste the Text Only, Text with structure, Text with structure plus basic formatting, and Text with structure plus full formatting.

FIGURE 19.2

The InDesign Preferences dialog box lets you choose how text is pasted into the application.

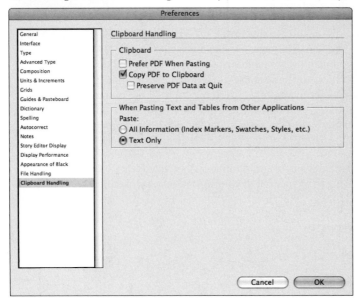

Missing fonts

If the text that you paste into Illustrator or InDesign from Microsoft Word is missing a font, a warning dialog box, like the one in Figure 19.3, appears listing the offending font. In addition to the warning dialog box, both applications list the missing font in brackets in the Control palette, and highlight the text that uses this font in pink, as shown in Figure 19.4.

FIGURE 19.3

The Missing Fonts dialog box

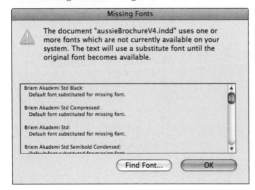

FIGURE 19.4

Pink highlighting identifies missing fonts.

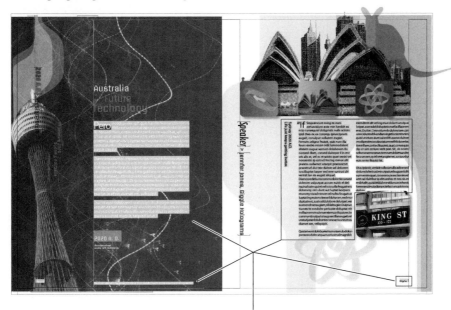

Pink highlighted text

If you choose Type ⇨ Font, you'll find a Missing category that lists all missing font faces and styles.

You can choose to have Illustrator highlight all Substituted Fonts and all Substituted Glyphs using the Document Setup dialog box, shown in Figure 19.5. You open this dialog box by choosing File ⇨ Document Setup. The Highlight Substituted Fonts and Highlight Substituted Glyphs options cause all text that uses a missing font or a missing glyph to be highlighted in pink.

CROSS-REF For more information on glyphs, see Chapter 18. Installing and locating missing fonts is covered in Chapter 16.

FIGURE 19.5

Illustrator's Document Setup dialog box

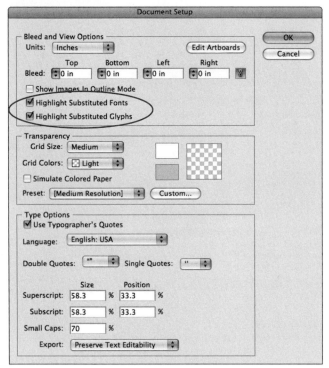

Exporting Text from Word

Part IV covers in-depth working with text in the CS4 applications, but if you already have the text available in a Word documents, the easy workflow path is to export it from Word and import it into the CS4 applications.

Word doesn't include a File ➪ Export menu command, but you use the File ➪ Save As menu command to save the file into one of several different formats, including Rich Text Format (RTF) and Plain Text (TXT). In addition to these formats that are imported into most CS4 applications, Illustrator can open and place native Word (DOC) files and InDesign can place native Word files.

CAUTION Although Word includes a File ➪ Save as Web Page menu command, Word adds some markup to the Web page content that might confuse Dreamweaver and some Web browsers. The best approach is to import the Web-page text into Dreamweaver using the Rich Text Format or the Plain Text format and let Dreamweaver add the Web-page markup.

The difference between the Rich Text Format and Plain Text is that the former maintains any formatting within the text and the latter strips out all formatting.

Importing Text

Importing text into the various CS4 applications happens by opening a file saved from within Word into a CS4 application. The two most useful CS4 applications for doing this are Illustrator and InDesign, but Dreamweaver can import Word text also on Windows only. All three of these CS4 applications can use native Word documents (DOC), as well as files saved using the Plain Text (TXT) format. Illustrator and InDesign also can open Rich Text Format (RTF) files. Illustrator can open these files using the File ➪ Open menu command, InDesign can import these files using the File ➪ Place menu command, and Dreamweaver uses the File ➪ Import command for Word files and the File ➪ Open command for Plain Text files. The Dreamweaver import options are covered at the end of this chapter.

CROSS-REF Working with fonts and text is covered in Part IV.

Opening Word documents in Illustrator

You open Word documents natively within Illustrator by choosing File ➪ Open (⌘/Ctrl+O). In the file dialog box that appears, select the Microsoft Word (DOC) file type. This format includes support for files created using all versions of Word since Word 97 including Word 2007. All formatting in the Word document is maintained as the file is imported into Illustrator.

After you select and open a file, another dialog box of options opens, as shown in Figure 19.6. This dialog box lets you specify whether to import the Table of Contents Text, Footnotes/Endnotes, and Index Text. You also can select Remove Text Formatting.

FIGURE 19.6

The Microsoft Word Options dialog box

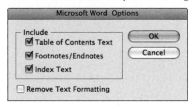

If the fonts used in the Word document are not available to Illustrator, a Font Problems dialog box opens, shown in Figure 19.7, listing the fonts in question.

FIGURE 19.7

The Font Problems dialog box

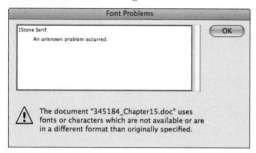

Opening and placing text documents in Illustrator

Text files saved using the Rich Text Format (RTF) and Plain Text (TXT) formats also are opened in Illustrator with the File ⇨ Open menu command. Rich Text Format files use the same Options dialog box as the Word (DOC) files, but Plain Text files present a different dialog box of Options, as shown in Figure 19.8.

NOTE Although it may seem unlikely that you'd want to open a Word document within Illustrator, there are several unique workflows where opening a text file in Illustrator is helpful. For example, using Illustrator's dynamic data features along with some actions, you can automatically turn a client list into a set of personalized greeting cards.

FIGURE 19.8

The Text Import Options dialog box

The Text Import Options dialog box lets you specify the encoding platform as Windows or Mac and which Character Set to use. The dialog box also has options to select how to handle extra carriage returns and to replace a specified number of spaces with a tab.

If you want to import a Word document into an existing Illustrator document, choose File ➪ Place. This command opens the Word or text document into the current Illustrator document.

Placing Word documents into InDesign

Although Illustrator can both open and place Word, RTF and TXT files, InDesign can only place these text formats. The File ➪ Place (⌘/Ctrl+D) menu command in InDesign opens a file dialog box where you select Microsoft Word and Excel files that you want to open and place into the current document. After you select a file and click Place, the mouse cursor changes to indicate that it is holding the imported text. To place the imported text, you need to click the location in the document where you want to place the upper-left corner of the imported text.

CROSS-REF Importing Excel data as tables is covered in Chapter 21.

The Place dialog box, shown in Figure 19.9, includes a Show Import Options check box and a Replace Selected Item check box. Holding down the Shift key while clicking the Open button forces the Options dialog box to appear. If you disable the Show Import Options check box, then the document is imported using the same settings used the last time the Import Options dialog box was set.

FIGURE 19.9

The Place dialog box

The Microsoft Word Import Options dialog box, shown in Figure 19.10, includes the same features as mentioned previously for Illustrator including the ability to specify the inclusion of table of contents text, footnotes and endnotes, and index text. It also offers the Use Typographer's Quotes check box.

This Word Import Options dialog box includes several options for handling formatting. You can select to Remove Styles and Formatting from Text and Tables or preserve the same. If you select to remove styles and formatting, the Preserve Local Overrides options become available along with options to Convert Tables to Unformatted Tables or Unformatted Tabbed Text. If you select to preserve styles and formatting, several additional options become available including handling Manual Page Breaks. The options include Preserve Page Breaks, Convert to Column Breaks, or No Breaks. You also can select to Import Inline Graphics, Import any Unused Styles, and Convert Bullets & Numbers to Text. The dialog box also shows the number of Style Name Conflicts that exist between the current InDesign file and the imported Word document. For Paragraph and Character Style Conflicts, you can choose to automatically import styles with options to Use the InDesign Style Definition, Redefine the InDesign Style, or Auto Rename; or you could Customize the Style Import by defining a style mapping between the two documents. Defined options can be saved as a preset for easy recall. For RTF files, the same options are available.

Plain Text files open the Text Import Options dialog box, shown in Figure 19.11. This dialog box lets you select a character set, platform, and dictionary. It also offers options for handling extra carriage returns, replacing spaces with tabs, and using typographer's quotes.

FIGURE 19.10

The Microsoft Word Import Options dialog box

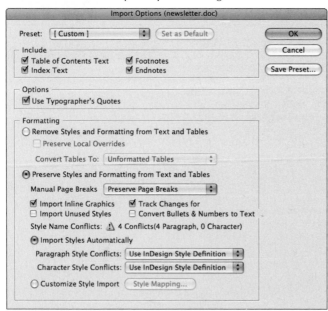

FIGURE 19.11

The Text Import Options dialog box

Text Import Options (newsletter.txt)

Character Set: Macintosh Roman
Platform: Mac (Intel-based)
Set Dictionary to: English: USA

OK
Cancel

Extra Carriage Returns
☐ Remove at End of Every Line
☐ Remove Between Paragraphs

Formatting
☐ Replace 3 or More Spaces with a Tab
☑ Use Typographer's Quotes

Mapping Word styles to InDesign styles

If you select the Custom Style Import option in the Microsoft Word Import Options dialog box (or when importing RTF files), the Style Mapping button becomes active. Clicking this button opens the Style Mapping dialog box shown in Figure 19.12. The Style Mapping dialog box includes two lists of styles, one for Word styles and one for InDesign styles. For each imported Word style, you can select an InDesign style to map the Word style to.

FIGURE 19.12

The Style Mapping dialog box

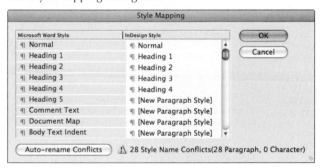

Microsoft Word Style	InDesign Style
¶ Normal	¶ Normal
¶ Heading 1	¶ Heading 1
¶ Heading 2	¶ Heading 2
¶ Heading 3	¶ Heading 3
¶ Heading 4	¶ Heading 4
¶ Heading 5	¶ [New Paragraph Style]
¶ Comment Text	¶ [New Paragraph Style]
¶ Document Map	¶ [New Paragraph Style]
¶ Body Text Indent	¶ [New Paragraph Style]

Auto-rename Conflicts ⚠ 28 Style Name Conflicts(28 Paragraph, 0 Character)

At the bottom of the Style Mapping dialog box is a count of the style name conflicts. Clicking the Auto-rename Conflicts automatically maps all the conflicted style names with the Auto Rename option. Once imported, the auto rename styles are appended with "wrd_1" on the end of the style, making them easy to identify and rename in the Paragraph Styles palette.

After all the work to map styles has been completed, you can use the Save Preset button on the Microsoft Word Import Options dialog box to save the import options including the style mapping to a file that can be recalled for another file using the drop-down list at the top of the dialog box.

Importing Word documents in Photoshop

Of all the Creative Suite applications, Photoshop is one of the more popular. Many designers are so comfortable with Photoshop that they choose to create layouts including the extensive use of text in Photoshop rather than InDesign or Illustrator. For these designers, this section covers importing Microsoft Word into Photoshop.

If you copy and paste text from Word into Photoshop, it appears as a graphic image with all its formatting in place. This is fine, but it requires that you make all the edits in Word, which leaves you with only Word's design features.

A better way to handle the import process is to create a text layer in Photoshop by dragging a bounding box with the Type tool before pasting the Word text. With the text bounding box selected, the pasted text appears as editable text in the text bounding box. The drawback to this approach is that all the formatting is stripped from the Word text, but you can still use Photoshop's type formatting tools. Figure 19.13 shows some text that has been imported into a Photoshop text object from Word.

FIGURE 19.13

You can edit text from Word in a text object in Photoshop.

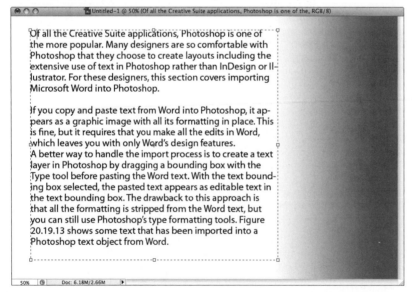

TIP If you hold down the Option/Alt key while dragging with the Type tool, a dialog box is drawn from the center and opens a dialog box. If you press Option/Alt and click, the draw is from the click point (down and to the right) and a dialog box opens.

You also can import Word text into a Point text object. You create Point text objects by simply clicking in the document rather than dragging an area. Be warned that importing text into a Point text object won't limit the text within an area but places an entire line of text (up to a paragraph return) on a single line. All paragraph returns in the pasted text wrap the text to a new line.

CROSS-REF More details on creating text layers and Point text objects are in Part IV.

Formatting imported text in Photoshop

When you import text into a Photoshop text layer, you use the Type tool to select and edit the text. Clicking once on the text object text with the Type tool selects the text layer. When the text layer is selected, you can drag with the mouse over the text to select words or characters. The selected text is highlighted. Clicking twice selects a word, clicking three times selects an entire line of text, clicking four times selects an entire paragraph, and clicking five times selects all the text in the text layer.

Pressing the Delete key deletes any selected text, and typing new text replaces the selected text with the newly typed text. Any characters that you add to the text use the same formatting as the existing text area.

Selected text is formatted using the Character panel, which is opened by choosing Window ➪ Character (or press Ctrl/⌘+T). With this palette, you can change the text font, style, size, leading, kerning, scale, color, and anti-aliasing.

Paragraph formatting such as text alignment, indentation, and paragraph spacing is set for the selected paragraph in the Paragraph palette, which is accessed by choosing Window ➪ Paragraph.

Pasting Word text in Acrobat

Acrobat is typically used to turn Word documents into PDF files by choosing File ➪ Create PDF. If you've converted a Word document to a PDF file and then found some minimal edits that need to be made, you can use the TouchUp Text tool to edit the PDF document. If major text edits are required, you should make the edits within Word and then regenerate the PDF document.

CAUTION You can edit text within a PDF file with the TouchUp Text tool only if the font you used to create the PDF file is installed on your system or embedded within the PDF document.

When using the TouchUp Text tool, you can copy and paste text from within Word. To do this, choose Tools ➪ Advanced Editing ➪ TouchUp Text Tool to select the TouchUp Text tool. Then select the text that you want to edit and press Delete to delete the selected text, type new text to replace the selected text, or choose Edit ➪ Paste (⌘/Ctrl+V) to paste text copied from Word.

You also can use the TouchUp Text tool to add new portions of text to the existing PDF document. With the TouchUp Text tool selected, hold down the Option/Ctrl key and click the position where you want to place the new text. A dialog box appears, shown in Figure 19.14, letting you select a font face to use for the new text. Clicking OK creates a text object with "New Text" selected in it.

FIGURE 19.14

The New Text Font dialog box lets you select a font face.

With the new text object selected, you can type new text to replace this text or paste text from Word by choosing Edit ⇨ Paste. Text pasted from Word loses its formatting. The pasted text also loses all its line returns, but you can easily place these back in with the TouchUp Text tool. The line returns are easy to identify because they're replaced with a character (often just a simple square). Selecting each square character with the TouchUp Text tool and pressing the Enter key reformats the pasted text.

If you need to move the newly created text object, you can select the TouchUp Object tool by choosing Tools ⇨ Advanced Editing. This tool lets you select and move text objects by clicking and dragging with the mouse.

This process requires some additional work, and it's not a chore we recommend undertaking. If some major edits are to be made in a document, you can export from PDF in a variety of formats and lay out a new piece in Adobe InDesign.

Importing Styles

When importing text files into InDesign, both paragraph and character styles are imported as determined by the import settings. All imported styles from Microsoft Word appear in the Paragraph and Character Styles palettes using the same style name. The imported styles also are identified by a small disk icon to the right of the style's name, as shown in Figure 19.15. Both types of styles are also supported when opening a Word file in Illustrator, except that the small disk icon isn't shown in the Illustrator palettes.

FIGURE 19.15

Placing a Word document within InDesign can import the Word styles into the Paragraph Styles palette.

CROSS-REF   **Using text styles in Illustrator and InDesign is covered in Chapter 16.**

You can prevent the styles from being imported by enabling the Remove Styles and Formatting from Text and Tables option in the Microsoft Word Import Options dialog box. If the Preserve Styles and Formatting from Text and Tables option is enabled, styles also are imported when text is pasted from Word using the designated settings. The Import Options settings take precedence over the application preferences set in the Type panel of the Preferences dialog box.

NOTE   **If the imported style has the same name as an existing InDesign style and if the Style Conflicts option in the Word Import Options dialog box is set to Use InDesign Style Definition, then the style is not imported from Word, and the text is formatted using the InDesign style. Or, you can set the Style Conflict options to redefine the InDesign Style or Auto Rename the imported style.**

CROSS-REF   **You can load styles in the Character and Paragraph panels too. For more information on loading styles see Chapter 16.**

Editing imported styles

In the Paragraph Styles palette, right click on a style to select it. Then choose Edit from the pop-up menu. This action opens the Paragraph Style Options dialog box, shown in Figure 19.16. Using these options, you set the paragraph formatting style options.

TIP   **If you click a style, then the selected style is automatically applied to the selected text frame, but right-clicking a style lets you open the Style Options dialog box.**

FIGURE 19.16

FIGURE 19.16

The Paragraph Style Options dialog box

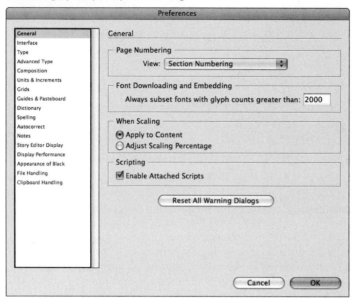

Deleting imported styles

The Paragraph Styles panel menu includes several useful commands. When a layout is complete, use the Select All Unused menu command to instantly select all the styles that aren't referenced in the document. These styles, whether native or imported, are then deleted with the Delete Style palette menu command. Deleting unused styles is an easy way to clean up a document, especially if text has been imported from Word.

Working with Imported Text

As a final working example of the process of importing and using Microsoft Word documents, we'll walk you through the steps involved. These steps are similar for both Illustrator and InDesign, with only slight differences between the two.

STEPS: Importing Microsoft Word Text into InDesign

1. **Open the DOC document in Word.** Figure 19.17 shows a Word document that includes all the text for a poem. Using the features of Word, the document has been spell-checked and grammar-checked, and all edits are ready to be moved to InDesign.

FIGURE 19.17

Open a Word document.

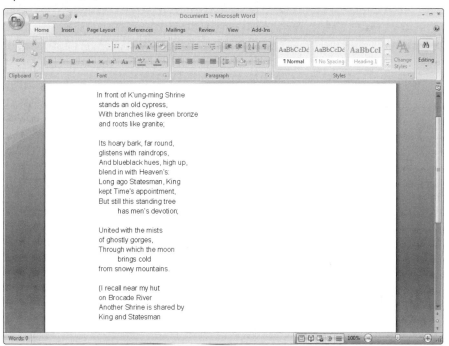

2. **Save the Word document.** Choose File ⇨ Save As in Word, and save the file using the default DOC file format. This format includes all the referenced styles. After you save the file, close the Word file by choosing File ⇨ Close.

CAUTION If you forget to close the Word document within Windows, InDesign opens an alert dialog box stating "This file is already in use by another application," when you try to place the Word document in InDesign. The same alert doesn't seem to happen on Macintosh systems.

3. **Open the current InDesign file.** If you already have a start on the layout, open the existing file in InDesign by choosing File ⇨ Open.

4. **Place the text file in InDesign.** Choose File ⇨ Place (⌘/Ctrl+D) to open the Place dialog box. Make sure Show Import Options is enabled; then select the Word document, and click the Open button.

5. **Set the import options.** In the Microsoft Word Import Options dialog box, shown in Figure 19.18, you can disable the Table of Contents Text, Footnotes and Endnotes, and Index Text options because none of these elements is included in the original document. Also, make sure the Preserve Styles and Formatting from Text and Tables option is enabled. Notice how 28 paragraph style conflicts have been identified in the Import Options dialog box. Select the Import Styles Automatically option, and set the Paragraph Style Conflicts setting to Auto Rename. Click OK to proceed.

FIGURE 19.18

The Import Options dialog box displays the number of style conflicts.

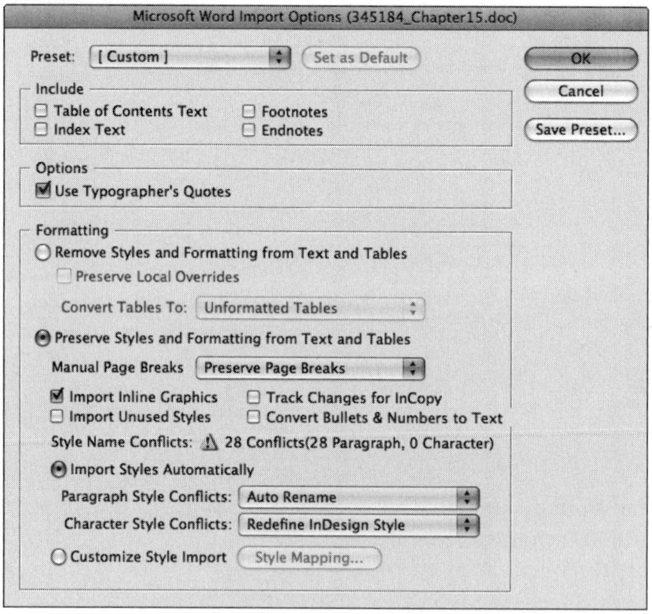

6. **Locate the missing fonts.** When the import options are set, the import process proceeds and a Missing Fonts dialog box appears. The dialog box lists all the fonts used in the Word document that aren't available to InDesign. Click the Find Font button to open the Find Font dialog box, shown in Figure 19.19. Using this dialog box, locate and change the missing fonts. The Find Next button locates the first instance of text in the InDesign document that uses the specified font. If you enable the Redefine Style When Changing All option, then all paragraph and character styles font family settings are updated also. Click Done when you're finished.

FIGURE 19.19

The Find Font dialog box

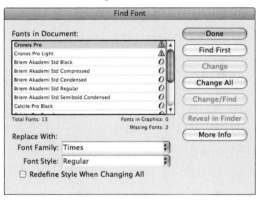

7. **Place the text into the InDesign document.** The cursor holds the imported text. Click at the location in the InDesign document where you want to place the imported text. The Word styles are imported into InDesign and appear in the Paragraph Styles panel. The result is shown in Figure 19.20.

FIGURE 19.20

Imported text and styles used within InDesign

Moving Word Content to Dreamweaver

Text for Web pages can start out in Word, but if you don't follow the right path, it could end up being a real mess. Although Microsoft Word can save text files as an HTML document, Word files saved using the HTML format include many unnecessary markup tags recognized only by Word. However, Dreamweaver also includes a command for cleaning up Word documents saved as HTML pages.

Using the Clipboard for Web page text

The best way to move text from Word to Dreamweaver is to use the Clipboard. Simply copy the selected text to the Clipboard in Word by choosing Edit ➪ Copy, and choose Edit ➪ Paste in Dreamweaver to paste it in its desired location. For most cases, this is sufficient, but be aware that the text will flow around the existing Web page elements such as images. By default, the pasted text tries to maintain its formatting using the HTML markup, but this is usually limited.

Using the Paste Special command

If you need more control over the pasted text, you can choose Edit ➪ Paste Special in Dreamweaver. This opens the Paste Special dialog box shown in Figure 19.21. This dialog box gives you the options to paste the clipboard text as Text only, Text with structure, Text with structure plus basic formatting, and Text with structure plus full formatting. You also have options to Retain line breaks and to Clean up Word paragraph spacing. If the Text with structure option is selected, only the paragraphs, lists, and tables are retained, the structure with basic formatting retains formatting such as bold and italics, and the full formatting option retains all HTML formatting and CSS styles. The Clean up Word paragraph spacing option deletes the extra spaces between paragraphs.

FIGURE 19.21

The Paste Special dialog box in Dreamweaver

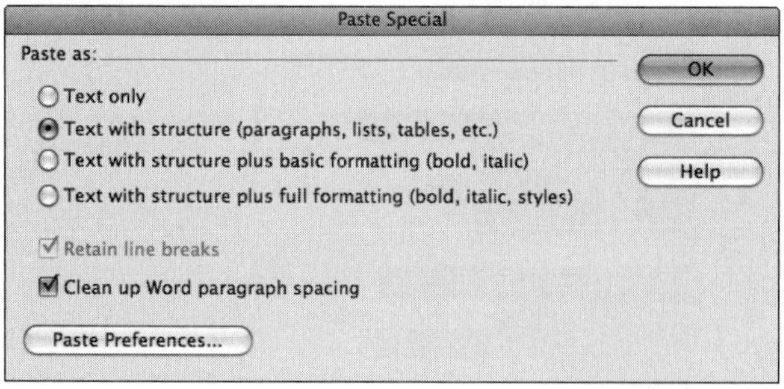

If you click the Paste Preferences button, then the Copy/Paste panel of the Preferences dialog box appears. In this dialog box, you can globally set the paste settings that are used for the Paste command.

The Paste Special menu is available only in Dreamweaver's Design view and not in the Code view.

Dropping text files

Text files dropped in Dreamweaver make the Insert Document dialog box appear. This dialog box lets you insert the text in the dropped document as text only, with structure, or with structure and formatting. There is also an option to create a link to the dropped document. After clicking OK, the text or link is added to the Web page at the position where the cursor is located.

Opening text files

Dreamweaver also can import text files by choosing File ⇨ Open. By changing the Files of Type setting in the Open Document dialog box, you can choose to open HTML files, XML files, and TXT files. HTML and TXT files open directly within the Dreamweaver Code view, shown in Figure 19.22. From this viewer, you can copy and paste text into the open Dreamweaver pages, but all formatting is lost when you do this.

FIGURE 19.22

Text files can be opened in the code editor.

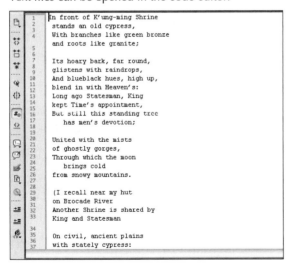

Importing Word files

Even though Dreamweaver can open text files directly, Word files saved with the .doc extension are imported into a Dreamweaver document using File ➪ Import ➪ Word Document. This import feature is available only in Windows. Dreamweaver also can import Excel documents. Within the Import Word Document dialog box are options to import Text Only, Text with Structure, Text with Structure and basic or full formatting. There is also an option to clean up Word paragraph spacing that works the same as described previously.

Cleaning up Word HTML

Although Word files can be saved as HTML files, Word adds in specific markup that it uses to display the file. These markup tags can cause problems when the page is loaded into Dreamweaver, but Dreamweaver includes a command for eliminating this problem markup. After an HTML-saved Word document is loaded into Dreamweaver, select the Command ➪ Clean Up Word HTML command. This opens the Clean Up Word HTML dialog box, shown in Figure 19.23.

FIGURE 19.23

The Clean Up Word HTML dialog box lets you choose which custom markup tags to remove.

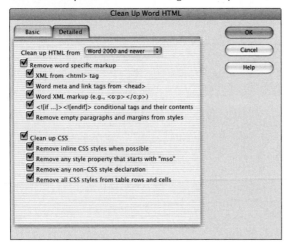

Using this dialog box, select which options to remove. You can choose the version of Word that was used to generate the HTML file. It is a good idea to enable all the options to ensure that the Word markup doesn't interfere with the current Web page. The Detailed panel breaks down the markup into more specific options.

Summary

- A word processor like Microsoft Word makes a good workflow piece for creating importable text.

- Text in Word may be easily copied and pasted into all of the CS4 applications.

- Illustrator can open and InDesign can place existing Word documents using Word's native DOC file format. The Rich Text Format (RTF) and Plain Text (TXT) file formats also are supported.

- Text styles defined in Microsoft Word also are imported and show up in the Paragraph Styles panel in InDesign.

- Dreamweaver also includes methods for opening Word, text, and HTML files.

Chapter 20

Exporting Text to Microsoft Word

Although CS4 includes many programs that can work with type or text (which you can learn about in Part IV), a word processor is not included as part of the suite. Text for design purposes is very different from text produced with a word processor, but there are times in your design workflow when you want to export text from CS4 applications into a word processor.

Writing copy is often much easier in a word processor because its features focus on manipulating text rather than design. For example, Microsoft Word includes a grammar checker that benefits longer sections of text. You can take advantage of this feature by exporting text to a word processor, checking its grammar, and then importing it again.

Of the available word processors, Microsoft Word is the most popular. Most word processors available today have similar features, so we focus only on Word in this chapter. We also cover the text-export features found in the CS4 applications that enable you to move text to Microsoft Word and the other Office applications.

IN THIS CHAPTER

Exporting text using the Clipboard

Exporting text using export commands

Exporting Acrobat comments to Word

Updating text in layouts

Exporting Text

The chapters in Part IV focused on creating text within the Creative Suite applications, and the last chapter covered importing text. This chapter completes the topic by discussing how to export text from the various CS4 applications to Microsoft Word.

> **CROSS-REF** Part IV covers creating text within the CS4 applications. Importing text from Word is covered in Chapter 19.

Before we discuss the techniques used in exporting text, we need to discuss the purpose behind exporting text. The first question to ask yourself is this: With all the power found in Creative Suite, why would you want to export text to an application like Microsoft Word? The answer lies in Word's ability to do what it does best—create text documents.

Recognizing the advantages of Word

Many of the features found in Word are out of place in the Creative Suite applications. Here is a list of some of the Microsoft Word features of which you can take advantage when working with large portions of text:

- **Outline mode:** Word can view documents in several different modes including Normal, Web Layout, Print Layout, and Outline. The layout modes are a far cry from the features found in Illustrator, Photoshop, and InDesign, but the Outline mode is very helpful for organizing a table of contents or a large structured list of items. In Word's Outline mode, you can quickly promote and demote headings and rearrange entire structures by dragging.

- **Headers, footers, and footnotes:** Word's ability to automatically create and adjust headers, footers, and footnotes is much easier to use than anything you find in Creative Suite (although anchored text in InDesign works better for inline graphics and sidebars). InDesign's text variables might also be used to create headers and footers. There are even specific variables for output.

- **AutoCorrect:** Word's AutoCorrect feature is very helpful as you type long sections of text. This feature can automatically capitalize the first letter of a sentence, and that makes it worth the trouble to export the text into Word. With some fine-tuning, the AutoCorrect feature saves many keystrokes, allowing you to finish a document in less time.

- **Interactive spelling and grammar check:** Word underlines all misspelled words in red and all grammatical errors in green as you type. This immediate feedback lets you fix the problems as you type, which offers a benefit over the spell-check features found in the CS4 applications.

 **InDesign is perhaps the most powerful CS4 app for working with large sections of text. It even includes AutoCorrect and spell checker features that rival Word's.**

This short list isn't exhaustive, nor does it do justice to the plethora of features found in Word, but it gives you a brief idea of the types of features that you can take advantage of by exporting text to Word.

Identifying exporting methods

All the CS4 applications deal with text, and all can export text to Word. There are essentially three different methods for exporting text from the various CS4 applications, and each of these methods has its advantages and disadvantages:

- **Copy and paste to the Clipboard:** Most CS4 applications can take advantage of this feature. By selecting text objects or portions of text, you can cut (⌘/Ctrl+X) or copy (⌘/Ctrl+C) them to the system Clipboard and then paste (⌘/Ctrl+V) them into the Word document.

- **Using an export command:** Several applications include a File ⇨ Export command that you can use to export the text from the source application to RTF and in a few cases directly to Word format.

- **Save to an importable file:** The final method is to save the text using a text-file format (such as TXT or RTF) that you can import into Word.

Selecting text

Before exporting any text to Word, you need to locate and select the text that you want to move. For most CS4 applications, you select text using the Type tool. To select text, just click the Type tool and drag over the text that you want to select. The selected text is highlighted.

Illustrator and InDesign use text objects. If a text object is selected with the Selection tool, the borders that make up the text object are highlighted using its layer color and all text contained within the text object is selected. If multiple text objects are selected, all text contained within the selected text objects is selected. Use the Type tool and not the Selection Tool to select text.

Exporting formatting

Through the exporting process, the text formatting is often lost. Some techniques maintain formatting and others do not. Copy and pasting via the Clipboard typically discards formatting. Exporting text using the TXT file format also discards formatting. If you need to keep the formatting intact, look to export the text using the Rich Text Format (RTF), which maintains the formatting during export.

> **TIP**   If you lose your formatting during an export, keep track of the changes that you make to the text in Word and manually enter those changes into the formatted text in the CS4 application.

When exporting text from Illustrator, the export command offers you the chance to specify the Platform (Windows, Mac-PowerPC, or Mac-Intel) and Encoding (Default and Unicode). If the text includes foreign language characters, then choose the Unicode option. This lets you maintain your fonts as you export them, regardless of the system to which you export them.

> **CROSS-REF**   You can learn more about the OpenType font standard in Chapter 16.

Using the Clipboard

The easiest way to export smaller pieces of text from the CS4 applications is to use the Clipboard. Although the Clipboard can handle large sections of text, it relies on the amount of available memory.

The Office Clipboard (Windows only) can copy many pieces of text to the Clipboard at a time (up to 24 by default). You can then select these different pieces from the Office Clipboard and paste them into the current Word document. You can make the Office Clipboard, shown at the right in Figure 20.1, appear by choosing Edit ➪ Office Clipboard or by pressing ⌘/Ctrl+C twice. After you select text, simply click on it to paste it into the current document. Right-click on the text to reveal a pop-up menu with a Delete option.

FIGURE 20.1

Items on the Office Clipboard are placed within Word simply by clicking on them.

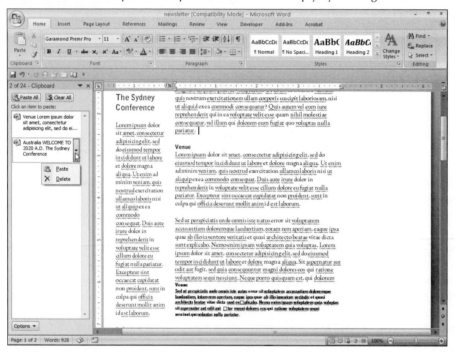

Moving Illustrator, Photoshop, Flash, and Dreamweaver text into Word

To select text in Illustrator, either select the text object with the Selection tool or drag over a portion of text with the Type tool. Selected text within Illustrator is then copied to the Clipboard by choosing Edit ⇨ Cut (⌘/Ctrl+X) or Edit ⇨ Copy (⌘/Ctrl+X). This moves the selected text to the Clipboard. From the Clipboard, text is pasted into Word by choosing Edit ⇨ Paste (⌘/Ctrl+V).

CAUTION You can paste text that you cut or copy from an Illustrator document into Word as only unformatted text. Text you copy from InDesign and Acrobat maintains its formatting.

Word also includes a Paste Special menu command that opens the dialog box shown in Figure 20.2. This dialog box identifies the source application and allows you to paste the Clipboard contents as unformatted text, several image formats, or unformatted Unicode text. Text that you save on the Clipboard cannot be saved as an image using the Paste Special command.

NOTE In Word 2007, you may need to open the Word Options dialog box and add Paste Special to your Quick Access toolbar in order to find the Paste Special command.

CAUTION Be aware that any text you export to Word loses its positional constraints, such as wrapping around images or type on a path.

FIGURE 20.2

The Paste Special dialog box identifies the source application and offers several paste choices based on that application.

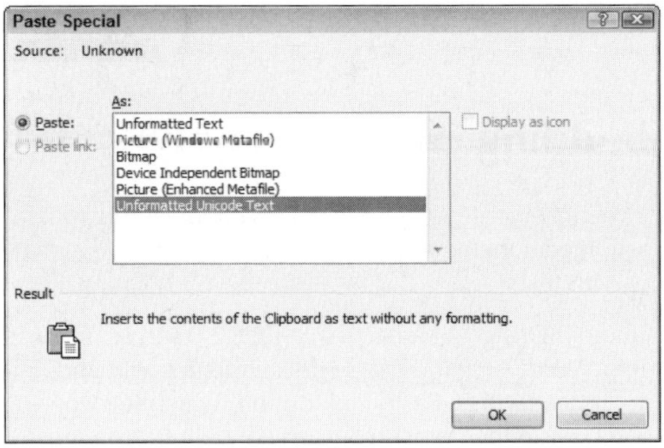

You move text in Photoshop and Flash to Word using the same Clipboard technique discussed for Illustrator in this section. The only exception is that you must select the text using Photoshop's Type tool. Selecting text in Dreamweaver is easy, you simply drag over the text to select. This text can be either in the Code or the Design views. Text copied and pasted from Dreamweaver to Word looses its formatting.

Moving InDesign text to Word

You move formatted text in InDesign to Microsoft Word using the Copy and Paste features. The standard Copy and Paste features retain the formatting created in InDesign.

CAUTION   In order to copy text in InDesign to the Clipboard, you need to select the Type tool and drag over the text. You can't just select the text object as you can in Illustrator.

Within Word, you also can choose Paste Special from the Quick Access toolbar (Windows). This action opens the Paste Special dialog box, shown in Figure 20.2, which includes the same options as those for Illustrator, except that it can handle RTF text.

Moving Acrobat text to Word

You select text in Acrobat using the Select Text tool. You can then cut or copy the selected text to the Clipboard by choosing Edit ➪ Cut (⌘/Ctrl+X) or Edit ➪ Copy (⌘/Ctrl+C). Acrobat also offers an option to copy an entire file to the Clipboard, Edit ➪ Copy File to Clipboard (Windows). On the Mac, view the pages as Continuous and click the Select tool in some text on a page. Press Command+A to select all and choose Edit ➪ Copy.

The Edit ➪ Paste Special command in Word opens the same dialog box as the one shown in Figure 20.2, including the option to paste as formatted text.

Object Linking and Embedding (Windows only)

Another exporting option is to create a link between the content created in a CS4 application and Microsoft Word using a technology known as Object Linking and Embedding (OLE). However, object linking works only with image content, not with text.

CS applications—including Photoshop, Illustrator, and InDesign—can act as an OLE 2.0 server. This allows you to copy and paste a piece of content into Word using the Paste Special menu command. This action causes the Paste Special dialog box to appear with a Paste Link option, which lets you paste an object as a recognized CS4 object. After you paste the object, you can double-click on the object in the Word document to load it within the native CS4 application for more editing. Changes made to the object are automatically forwarded back to the object in the Word document, thereby keeping the two in sync. You can force the documents to update by choosing File ➪ Update.

Using Export Menu Commands

When it comes to moving entire documents, the Clipboard isn't the best choice. Instead, you should rely on the export menu commands, typically found in the File menu. These export commands let you save CS4 documents to a format that is easily imported into Word.

 **Be aware that text in Photoshop is exported via the Clipboard only.**

Exporting Illustrator text

You export text from Illustrator by choosing File ⇨ Export and using the TXT format, but be aware that you lose all formatting applied to the text in Illustrator. All text included in an Illustrator document is exported to a single text file by choosing File ⇨ Export. If you select a text object, multiple text objects, or text within a text object, only the selected text exports.

The File ⇨ Export menu command opens an Export dialog box, like the one shown in Figure 20.3. The Save as Type pull-down menu includes many different file formats that you can use to export the existing document, but only the TXT format makes the text editable within Word.

FIGURE 20.3

The Export dialog box

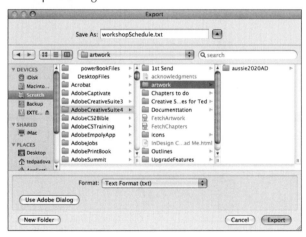

After clicking Export (Mac) or Save (Windows), another dialog box, shown in Figure 20.4, opens. This dialog box lets you specify the Platform as PC or Mac, as well as the Encoding standard to use. The Encoding options are Default Platform and Unicode. If the text you're exporting includes any foreign text or any special glyphs, use the Unicode Encoding option.

 The File ⇨ Export command exports all visible text objects, even if the text within those text areas isn't visible. However, hidden text objects in the document are not exported.

FIGURE 20.4

The Text Export Options dialog box

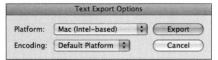

If you export text using the Default Encoding and not Unicode, you can open the file in Word without having to make any choices for conversion options.

CAUTION Illustrator includes tight integration with Microsoft Office using the File ⇨ Save for Microsoft Office menu command. Be aware that this command saves the Illustrator document as a PNG image file that you can import into Word, but you can't edit any of the text.

Exporting text from InDesign

InDesign includes an Export command under the File menu that exports formatted text to a number of different formats. To export text, you must first select the text within a text object using the Type tool to select a portion of a story. If the text tool is not in a story the entire story is exported, and the Rich Text Format and Text Only options are available as file types in the Export dialog box.

Choosing File ⇨ Export in InDesign gives you the options to export the current file using the following formats: Adobe InDesign Tagged Text, Adobe PDF, EPS, InDesign Interchange, JPEG, Rich Text Format (RTF), SVG, SVG Compressed, Text Only, and XML. Note that only the RTF format and the Text Only format are used to import text into Word.

If you export text from InDesign using a format other than RTF or Text Only, the file includes lots of additional mark-up information that you probably don't want to see.

Exporting text from Acrobat

Choosing File ⇨ Save As from within Acrobat lets you save the current PDF file using a number of different formats, many of which are suitable for moving text to Word including Word's default format (DOC). The Rich Text Format (RTF) and Text Only (TXT) formats are options also.

NOTE By default, any images contained within a PDF file that you save as a Word document are saved using the JPEG format. However, you can select the PNG format in the Settings dialog box if you prefer.

In Acrobat's file dialog box, you can click the Settings button, which opens the Save As Settings dialog box. The Save As DOC Settings dialog box is shown in Figure 20.5. The Settings dialog box for RTF is the same as that for the DOC format.

The Save As DOC Settings dialog box

In the Save As DOC Settings dialog box, you can choose to include comments and/or images. You also can downsample the image resolutions, which is a good idea if you're exporting to Word to check just the text. You also may want to keep the text files small by specifying Grayscale as the Colorspace. PDF files that were saved in Acrobat using the RTF format that are subsequently imported into Word are easy to identify because each piece of content is separated from the others by a section break.

Occasionally, you may have PDF documents that need to be reworked, but you don't have the original InDesign documents. In this case, open a PDF in Acrobat and choose the File ➪ Export command. From the Export submenu, you have a number of export options, as shown in Figure 20.6. The Save As and Export commands offer essentially the same options when exporting PDF content to Word.

For exporting text to Word, choose Word Document. A Save As dialog box opens. In this dialog box, notice the Settings button. Click Settings, and you can make some choices for the export attributes.

Batch-converting files in Acrobat

You also can use Acrobat Pro to convert a large number of Acrobat files to Word or RTF files using the Batch Sequences dialog box. You can access this dialog box (which is available only within Acrobat Professional) by choosing Advanced ⇨ Batch Processing.

The Batch Sequences dialog box, shown in the figure, includes a predefined batch command called Save All as RTF. Selecting this command and clicking Run Sequence executes the command, allowing you to select the files you want to convert. The Batch Sequence dialog box includes a number of predefined commands, but you also can create a new sequence of commands or edit an existing one.

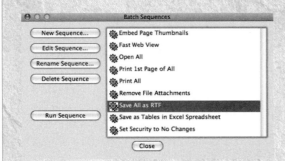

Clicking New Sequence or Edit Sequence lets you create a different set of commands for execution. For more information on using the Batch Sequence commands, see Chapter 15.

FIGURE 20.6

To export content from Acrobat, choose File ⇨ Export and select a file format from the Export submenu.

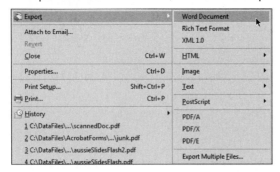

For Word exports, you can choose to retain the text flow or retain the page layout. If you want to import the text into InDesign, choose Retain Flowing Text. Acrobat provides options for exporting images from another Export submenu command. If you don't want the images exported in the Word document, be sure to uncheck the Include Images box. Click OK to return to the Save As dialog box. Click Save, and your file is exported to Word format and can be imported nicely in Adobe InDesign.

> **TIP** If you do lots of conversions from PDF to InDesign, look into purchasing a third-party utility for converting PDFs to InDesign format. The folks at Recosoft (`www.recosoft.com`) developed an excellent tool called PDF2ID for converting PDFs to InDesign files. This product works superbly for converting complex documents containing tables, graphic elements, images, capturing styles, and more.

If you want the images contained in the PDF file to be included in a new layout, choose File ➪ Export ➪ Image and choose from several image formats. If your file was originally prepared for print, it most likely has TIFF images included in the file. Choose TIFF from the Images submenu, and again a Save As dialog box opens. Click the Settings button, and you can choose from options for resolution and color management.

> **TIP** You can easily determine the file format for images by opening the Print Production toolbar in Acrobat. (Open a context menu on the Acrobat Toolbar Well and choose Print Production to access this toolbar.) Click the Output Preview tool to open the Output Preview dialog box. Click Object Inspector, and click the cursor on an image. The Output Preview dialog box shows you all the file attributes (such as file type, resolution, and colorspace) you need to know to determine if it's worthwhile to export the images.

Exporting comments from Acrobat (Windows only)

In addition to moving text to Word, Acrobat also offers an option to export all comments in the Acrobat document to Word. Choosing Comments ➪ Export Comments to Word from within Acrobat causes an information dialog box to appear. This information dialog box explains the procedure for importing comments from a PDF file. Within the Export Comments menu also are options to export comments to AutoCAD and to a Datafile.

> **NOTE** Exporting comments to Word is available only in Acrobat running on Windows with Office 2002 or greater installed. Comment exports to Word are not available on the Mac.

Before you can export comments to Word, you must be certain to use the proper comment tools. The Text Edit tools are designed to mark text for insertions, deletions, underlines, strikethroughs, and so on that are exported to Word. If you know that you're going to export your comments to Word, be certain to inform all users in your workflow to use these tools. Inasmuch as Mac users can't export comments to Word, the Text Edit tools are available in Acrobat on the Mac and comments you make with these tools can be exported to Word from Acrobat running on Windows.

> **CROSS-REF** For more information on using commenting tools, including the Text Edit tools, see Chapter 25.

Using this menu command opens Word and presents the Import Comments from Adobe Acrobat dialog box, shown in Figure 20.7. Selecting a source PDF file and a destination DOC file and clicking Continue moves all the comments from the Acrobat file to the Word file. This dialog box also gives you options to export All Comments, All Comments with Checkmarks, or Text Edits Only. The Text Edits Only option includes only the text that has been edited with the Commenting toolbar. You also can select to turn on Word's Track Changes feature. Remember to save any comments added to the PDF file, or they won't be exported. Click Continue in the Import Comments from Adobe Acrobat dialog box, and another dialog box opens reporting the successful integration of the Acrobat comments in the original Word file.

> **NOTE** The Exporting Comments to Word command also can be initiated from within Word using the Adobe Comments ⇨ Import Comments from Acrobat menu command. This command uses the same dialog boxes as the command in Acrobat.

FIGURE 20.7

The Import Comments from Adobe Acrobat dialog box

After you move the comments to Word, you can use the Acrobat Comments menu to review the changes, accept or delete all changes, and enable the Reviewing toolbar.

Dynamic Text Editing

Exporting text from one of the CS4 programs is typically an exercise where you need to get copy back to Microsoft Word, create changes in the copy, and import the text back to your original design. The most likely candidates for this activity are Illustrator and InDesign. Unless you want to burden yourself with clumsy typesetting tools and extraordinary file sizes, you'll stay away from Photoshop.

Reintroducing type in an existing design can mean quite a bit of work. If the edits are extensive, you may need to delete long passages of text and then reformat pages in InDesign after importing the edited text. For Illustrator files, you have to deal only with single pages, but the complexity of the design could be quite complicated and take some time to rework the text.

Ideally, you're best bet is to recompose a layout when you need to make major edits. However, in some circumstances, you may have moderate to light modifications to make in layouts. If you exported documents to PDF and need to make text changes, you need to return to the original authoring program, make your edits, and re-create the PDF document. In some workflows, this is a simple task, especially if all the native files are easily accessible. However, if you have only a PDF document and don't have access to the native application document, you may want to use another method by editing text and let the text edits dynamically change the PDF file.

Dynamic text editing is handled in Adobe Illustrator when text is targeted for editing from within Acrobat. You start in Acrobat and select the body of text you want to edit with the TouchUp Object tool. Click on the text line to be edited or marquee a paragraph, multiple paragraphs, or an entire page. When the text is selected, open a context menu and choose Edit Object. Alternately, you can press Option/Alt and double-click on the selected objects. This action launches Illustrator CS4 and opens the selected text in a document window. Unfortunately, the text is broken up in Illustrator, and all paragraph formatting including word wrap is lost. To reform the paragraphs, select all the text and click the Type tool in the document page at the same location where the first character in the first line of text was. Then cut the text with the Edit ➪ Cut menu command. When the I-beam cursor starts blinking, choose Edit ➪ Paste. The text may need a little tweaking, but the paragraph formatting including word wrap is regained.

To update a PDF document after making such edits in Illustrator, choose File ➪ Save. Be certain you don't use Save As and write the file using a new filename. The current document has a link to the PDF file. When you choose Save and return to Acrobat, the text is dynamically updated.

CAUTION Be certain you have all the type fonts used in the original document loaded on your system before attempting to edit text externally in Illustrator. Also, check your work very carefully. Some edits may not be accurate, especially when you attempt to edit text with transparency and other forms of stylized fonts.

This process seems a little complicated, but after you've made a few text edits, you won't find it difficult to repeat. To illustrate the process further, look over the following steps where text is edited in Illustrator and dynamically updated in Acrobat.

STEPS: Dynamically Updating Text in PDF Documents

1. **Open a PDF document in Acrobat.** In Figure 20.8, a document is opened in Acrobat. The text in the column on the right needs to be edited. You could try to edit the text in Acrobat, but with text in a column the results can often be unsatisfactory. A document like this needs to have the text edited in an external editor.

Open a document in Acrobat where you want to edit text.

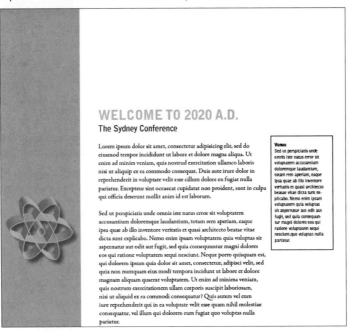

WELCOME TO 2020 A.D.
The Sydney Conference

Lorem ipsum dolor sit amet, consectetur adipisicing elit, sed do eiusmod tempor incididunt ut labore et dolore magna aliqua. Ut enim ad minim veniam, quis nostrud exercitation ullamco laboris nisi ut aliquip ex ea commodo consequat. Duis aute irure dolor in reprehenderit in voluptate velit esse cillum dolore eu fugiat nulla pariatur. Excepteur sint occaecat cupidatat non proident, sunt in culpa qui officia deserunt mollit anim id est laborum.

Sed ut perspiciatis unde omnis iste natus error sit voluptatem accusantium doloremque laudantium, totam rem aperiam, eaque ipsa quae ab illo inventore veritatis et quasi architecto beatae vitae dicta sunt explicabo. Nemo enim ipsam voluptatem quia voluptas sit aspernatur aut odit aut fugit, sed quia consequuntur magni dolores eos qui ratione voluptatem sequi nesciunt. Neque porro quisquam est, qui dolorem ipsum quia dolor sit amet, consectetur, adipisci velit, sed quia non numquam eius modi tempora incidunt ut labore et dolore magnam aliquam quaerat voluptatem. Ut enim ad minima veniam, quis nostrum exercitationem ullam corporis suscipit laboriosam, nisi ut aliquid ex ea commodi consequatur? Quis autem vel eum iure reprehenderit qui in ea voluptate velit esse quam nihil molestiae consequatur, vel illum qui dolorem eum fugiat quo voluptas nulla pariatur.

Venue
Sed ut perspiciatis unde omnis iste natus error sit voluptatem accusantium doloremque laudantium, totam rem aperiam, eaque ipsa quae ab illo inventore veritatis et quasi architecto beatae vitae dicta sunt ex-plicabo. Nemo enim ipsam voluptatem quia voluptas sit aspernatur aut odit aut fugit, sed quia consequun-tur magni dolores eos qui ratione voluptatem sequi nesciunt.quo voluptas nulla pariatur.

2. **Select the text needing editing.** Selecting the text you want to edit can at times be a challenge. You can edit the entire page, but often you'll find it best to select just the text you want to edit. In this example, it makes sense to select the text column. To select the text shown in Figure 20.9, marquee through the text with the TouchUp Object tool. If you select other objects not needed for the edits, press the Shift key and click on selected objects to deselect them.

3. **Open the text in Illustrator.** From a context menu, open the selected text. Choose Edit Objects from the menu commands as shown in Figure 20.9. Alternately, you can press Option/Alt and double-click the selected text. (Be certain the TouchUp Object tool is used with either the context menu or the double mouse click.) Acrobat initiates the Illustrator CS4 launch, and the selected text is opened in a new document window.

NOTE Depending on how your text was formatted, you may see some warning dialog boxes open, informing you that tags must be eliminated and the appearance of the page may appear different. Click Yes in the dialog boxes, and the file eventually opens in Illustrator.

FIGURE 20.9

Select the text objects you want to edit, and choose Edit Objects from a context menu.

Cut
Copy
Delete

Select All
Select None

Place Image...
Set Clip

Flip Horizontal
Flip Vertical
Rotate Clockwise
Rotate Counterclockwise
Rotate Selection

Create Artifact...

Find...

Edit Objects...
Properties...

4. **Select all the text.** Press ⌘/Ctrl+A to select all. Notice the selected objects in Figure 20.10. The selected text is broken, and Illustrator interprets each line of text as a separate paragraph.

FIGURE 20.10

Select all objects, and you can easily see where text is broken up.

Venue
Sed ut perspiciatis unde
omnis iste natus error sit
voluptatem accusantium
doloremque laudantium,
totam rem aperiam, eaque
ipsa quae ab illo inventore
veritatis et quasi architecto
beatae vitae dicta sunt ex-
plicabo. Nemo enim ipsam
voluptatem quia voluptas
sit aspernatur aut odit aut
fugit, sed quia consequun-
tur magni dolores eos qui
ratione voluptatem sequi
nesciunt.quo voluptas nulla
pariatur.

5. **Draw guidelines.** Drag guides from the ruler wells to the left, right, top, and bottom of the visible text. You want to create a rectangle around the text without encroaching on the territory occupied by the text.

6. **Cut the text.** Drag the Selection tool through the text to select it, and press ⌘/Ctrl+X to cut it to the clipboard.

7. Select the Text tool, and draw an area text box by dragging at the guideline intersection points. The area text box should be a rectangle around the text box.

CROSS-REF Chapter 17 includes details on creating Area text frames in Illustrator.

8. **Paste the text.** The text should paste nicely within the area text box frame.

9. **Save your edits.** Be certain to choose File ➪ Save and not Save As. When you save the file, you update the temporary document, which is a link to the Acrobat PDF. Close Illustrator and your Acrobat view should show the updated file, as shown in Figure 20.11.

FIGURE 20.11

After saving, maximize Acrobat or bring it into view, and the edited elements are dynamically updated in the open PDF file.

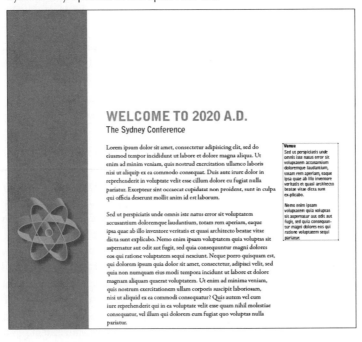

Summary

- Many Creative Suite applications can export text to Microsoft Word using several different methods. Some applications can export only the plain text, and others can export text with formatting intact.

- One common method for exporting text to Word is to use the Clipboard. Illustrator and Photoshop can export text to Word using the Clipboard without formatting, but Acrobat and InDesign can export text to Word using Rich Text Format (RTF) with formatting intact.

- Using export commands enables you to move text from Illustrator to Word without formatting, from InDesign to Word with formatting, and from Acrobat natively to the Word (DOC) format.

- You can export comments in Acrobat to Word directly using the File ⇨ Export Comments to Word menu command (Windows only).

- You can dynamically update text in Acrobat by selecting objects with the TouchUp Object tool and selecting Edit Objects from a context menu.

- Text object editing is handled in Illustrator CS4. When editing objects such as type from a PDF file, be certain to save the edits to dynamically update the PDF file.

Chapter 21

Working with Tables

IN THIS CHAPTER

Importing tables created in Microsoft Word and Excel

Creating and using InDesign tables

One common way to present data is in tabular format. Tables orient data into rows and columns. The intersection of each row and column is called a cell. Cells can hold text, images, or even another table. The format applied to a table is typically consistent across all the cells that make up the table.

Tables created in external applications such as Microsoft Word or Excel may be imported into CS applications such as InDesign, Illustrator, and Dreamweaver. The Clipboard is often used to move tables between applications.

In addition to importing tables, InDesign supports tables and table styles for easy creation and duplication of tables. InDesign includes table features for adding rows and columns, merging cells and creating a table from tab-delimited text. Individual cells are formatted in a number of ways, including alignment, cell strokes and fills, and evenly distributed cells. In addition, you can create dynamic links between Excel spreadsheets and InDesign tables so that changes in a spreadsheet are dynamically updated in InDesign files.

Dreamweaver also can create tables based on HTML. Although most of the table-formatting options in Dreamweaver are the same as the options for tables in InDesign, there are some differences between the two.

In this chapter, we talk about tables as they relate to Illustrator, Photoshop, and InDesign. For information related to Dreamweaver tables, see Chapter 27.

Importing Tables

InDesign, Illustrator, and Dreamweaver can create tables natively in the authoring applications. You can import tables in these programs as well as Photoshop from Microsoft Word and Microsoft Excel files.

CROSS-REF For information related to tables in Dreamweaver, see Chapter 27.

Importing Microsoft Word tables

Microsoft Word has a fairly robust table-creation feature allowing you to create tables by selecting the number of rows and columns, creating rows and columns, and converting text to a table. Tables created in Word are moved into the CS applications either by copying the table onto the Clipboard and pasting it into the target application or by using import commands such as File ➪ Place.

Before a table is copied to the Clipboard, the cells that you want to move must be selected. Selecting table cells in Word is as easy as dragging over the cells with the mouse. All selected cells are highlighted, as shown in Figure 21.1.

NOTE The entire table is selected by clicking on the Table Move icon located in the upper-left corner of the table in Print Layout viewing mode in Word 2007 for Windows. On the Mac, change your view to Page Layout mode. This selects the entire table and all its contents.

After the cells are selected, choose Edit ➪ Cut (⌘/Ctrl+X) or Edit ➪ Copy (⌘/Ctrl+C) to copy the selected table cells to the Clipboard. From the Clipboard, choose Edit ➪ Paste (⌘/Ctrl+V) to paste the table into the CS application.

Using Word tables in Illustrator

Importing Microsoft Word tables in Illustrator can be handled in three ways:

- **Open a Word file in Illustrator.** Choose File ➪ Open (or File ➪ Place), and you can open a Word document directly in Adobe Illustrator. When you choose to use this option, the Microsoft Word Options dialog box opens, as shown in Figure 21.2.

  You choose what elements to convert when opening the file by checking the boxes in the Microsoft Word Options dialog box. Be certain to leave the defaults as shown in Figure 21.2 if you want to retain paragraph/text formatting.

  When you click OK in the Microsoft Word Options dialog box, the text appears in Illustrator with the formatting intact. However, any strokes and cell fills are lost when importing Word tables using this option, as shown in Figure 21.3.

FIGURE 21.1

FIGURE 21.1

Table cells are highlighted when selected. Clicking the Table Move icon selects the entire table.

Table Move icon

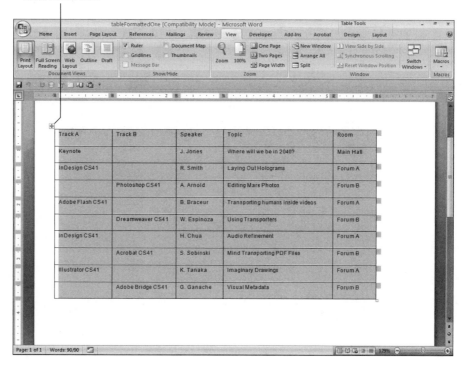

FIGURE 21.2

Choose File ⇨ Open, and open an MS Word file to see the Microsoft Word Options dialog box.

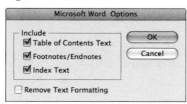

Paragraph and text formatting are retained when you open a Word file in Illustrator, but the strokes and cell fills are lost.

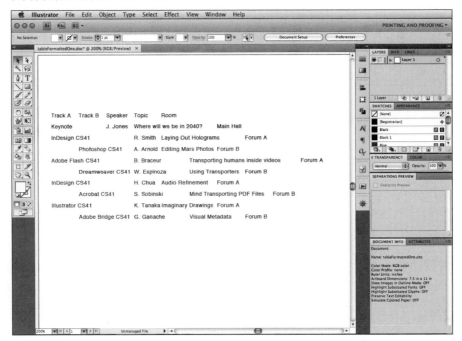

Opening a Word file produces the same result as choosing File ➪ Place. The same Microsoft Word Options dialog box opens and the paragraph/text formatting is retained.

- **Copy/Paste a Word table.** Select a table in Microsoft Word and copy it, then open Illustrator. Choose Edit ➪ Paste, and the table with strokes and cell fills is pasted into Illustrator, as shown in Figure 21.4. This option provides you with the best visual appearance of a pasted table, but editing the table cells is very difficult. The table is pasted as a grouped object with the text broken up in each cell. Even when using the Object ➪ Expand command, you can't quite get the data to easily reformat and edit.

- **Paste text into an Area Text Frame.** When you choose Edit ➪ Paste, a table is pasted as an object. If you click the Type tool in Illustrator and create an Area Text Frame, then choose Edit ➪ Paste, the text is pasted with formatting the same as when opening or placing a Word file. Text is easily edited by setting tabs in the Tabs panel, as shown in Figure 21.5.

FIGURE 21.4

Visual appearances of pasted tables are best with this option, but editing the table data is extremely difficult.

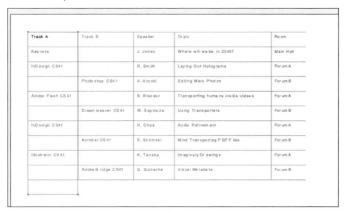

FIGURE 21.5

Draw an Area Text Frame, and choose Edit ⇨ Paste to paste a Word table with formatting intact.

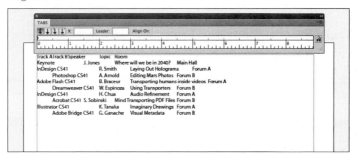

Of the three options available when importing Word tables in Illustrator, using the Open or File ⇨ Place command and using the Edit ⇨ Paste command when pasting into an Area Text Frame work best. You have to draw table strokes and create cell fills, but formatting the text with the Tabs panel makes the job much easier than trying to reformat a pasted table as an object in Illustrator.

Although Illustrator thinks of tables as text surrounded by line objects, there is one feature in Illustrator that understands table data very well—the Graph Data window. Table data may be pasted directly into the Graph Data window, but to create a graph you need to use data that would logically form a graph. If you try to create a graph with text as shown in Figure 21.6, Illustrator cannot create the graph.

FIGURE 21.6

Table data pasted into the Graph Data window must contain numeric values. Illustrator cannot create a text-only graph.

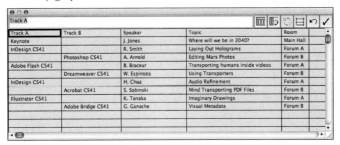

Track A	Track B	Speaker	Topic	Room
Keynote		J. Jones	Where will we be in 2040?	Main Hall
InDesign CS41		R. Smith	Laying Out Holograms	Forum A
	Photoshop CS41	A. Arnold	Editing Mars Photos	Forum B
Adobe Flash CS41		B. Braceur	Transporting humans inside videos	Forum A
	Dreamweaver CS41	W. Espinoza	Using Transporters	Forum B
InDesign CS41		H. Chua	Audio Refinement	Forum A
	Acrobat CS41	S. Sobinski	Mind Transporting PDF Files	Forum B
Illustrator CS41		K. Tanaka	Imaginary Drawings	Forum A
	Adobe Bridge CS41	G. Ganache	Visual Metadata	Forum B

Using Word tables in Photoshop

Suppose you want to create some large over-sized prints containing table data and Photoshop is your tool of choice. Generally for graphic design pieces, Photoshop is not the best application for large amounts of text. However, if you create some large posters for announcing conference sessions, events, or other similar types of designs, you might want to use Photoshop.

Creating tables in Photoshop is much more difficult than creating a table in another application and importing it into a Photoshop file. In Figure 21.7, you see a simple table added to a Photoshop file. The table data were first created in MS Word and then imported into the Photoshop design.

You have only one option to choose if you want to preserve formatting from a Word table when pasting into Photoshop. You must select the table in Word as described in "Using Word tables in Illustrator" and paste the table into Photoshop by choosing Edit ➪ Paste. In addition, you don't want to create a text frame in Photoshop. If you paste data into a text frame when the Type tool is active, the text is imported without formatting, as shown in Figure 21.8.

When you paste text into Photoshop, the text remains a vector object and can be scaled using the Transformation tools without loss of resolution.

CROSS-REF   For more information on using the Transformation tools, see Chapter 12.

FIGURE 21.7

A table imported from MS Word into a Photoshop design

Track A	Track B	Speaker	Topic	Room
Keynote		J. Jones	Where will we be in 2040?	Main Hall
InDesign CS41		R. Smith	Laying Out Holograms	Forum A
	Photoshop CS41	A. Arnold	Editing Mars Photos	Forum B
Adobe Flash CS41		B. Braceur	Transporting humans inside videos	Forum A
	Dreamweaver CS41	W. Espinoza	Using Transporters	Forum B
InDesign CS41		H. Chua	Audio Refinement	Forum A
	Acrobat CS41	S. Sobinski	Mind Transporting PDF Files	Forum B
Illustrator CS41		K. Tanaka	Imaginary Drawings	Forum A
	Adobe Bridge CS41	G. Ganache	Visual Metadata	Forum B

FIGURE 21.8

If you paste text in Photoshop with the Type tool active and an I-beam cursor visible, the text is pasted without formatting.

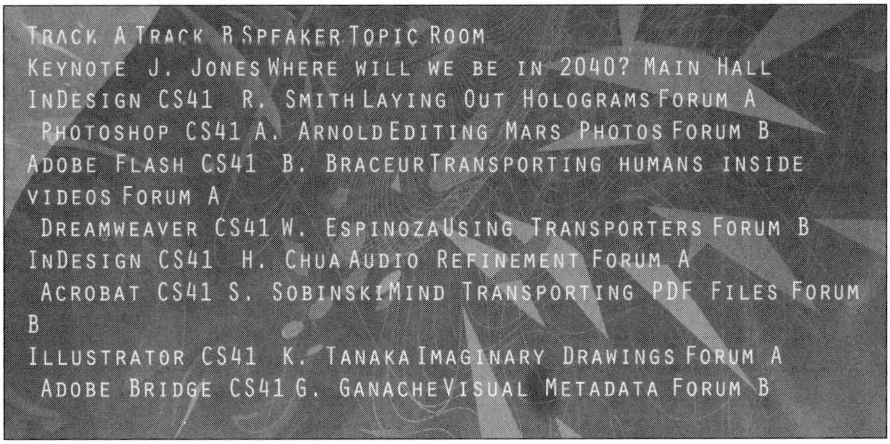

```
TRACK A TRACK B SPEAKER TOPIC ROOM
KEYNOTE J. JONES WHERE WILL WE BE IN 2040? MAIN HALL
INDESIGN CS41  R. SMITH LAYING OUT HOLOGRAMS FORUM A
 PHOTOSHOP CS41 A. ARNOLD EDITING MARS PHOTOS FORUM B
ADOBE FLASH CS41  B. BRACEUR TRANSPORTING HUMANS INSIDE
VIDEOS FORUM A
 DREAMWEAVER CS41 W. ESPINOZA USING TRANSPORTERS FORUM B
INDESIGN CS41  H. CHUA AUDIO REFINEMENT FORUM A
 ACROBAT CS41 S. SOBINSKI MIND TRANSPORTING PDF FILES FORUM
B
ILLUSTRATOR CS41  K. TANAKA IMAGINARY DRAWINGS FORUM A
 ADOBE BRIDGE CS41 G. GANACHE VISUAL METADATA FORUM B
```

Using Word tables in InDesign

Table cells that are copied in Word and pasted into InDesign can be recognized in InDesign as tables and are edited using InDesign's table features. All table and character formatting in Word is also pasted into InDesign.

Another way to import Word files containing tables into InDesign is by choosing File ➪ Place. Microsoft Word is one of the importable file formats that InDesign supports. If you check the Show Import Options box in the Place dialog box (or if you hold down the Shift key while clicking the Open button), the Microsoft Word Import Options dialog box appears, as shown in Figure 21.9.

FIGURE 21.9

The Microsoft Word Import Options dialog box includes options for handling text formatting.

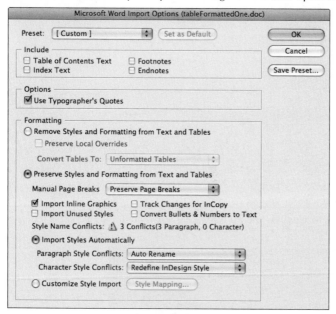

Tables imported in this manner from Word appear in InDesign as editable tables, but if you want to remove the table formatting, you can select the Remove Styles and Formatting from Text and Tables option in the Microsoft Word Import Options dialog box. This makes the Convert Tables To drop-down list become active with options to convert as Unformatted Tables and Unformatted Tabbed Text.

TIP If you have any trouble with the imported tables, try to import the table as Unformatted Tabbed Text and use InDesign's Table ⇨ Convert Text to Table menu command to create the table.

Importing Microsoft Excel tables

Although tables in Word are useful, the real king of tables among the Microsoft Office products is Excel. Excel tables include formulas that compute the value of a cell based on other cells. This is a powerful concept that saves countless hours of manual calculations. However, after an Excel table is imported into a CS application, all of its formulas and automatic calculations are lost.

Using the Clipboard

You can copy Excel spreadsheets to the Clipboard and paste them into Photoshop, Illustrator, and InDesign by choosing Edit ⇨ Paste (⌘/Ctrl+V). When table cells are selected in Excel and copied to the Clipboard, a moving dashed line (known as marching ants) surround the copied cells. This is done to maintain the formulas within Excel.

Excel tables that are copied into InDesign are converted to InDesign tables, allowing them to be edited using the InDesign table features. Using InDesign, you can create dynamic links to Excel spreadsheets so when a spreadsheet is updated in Excel, the updates are dynamically updated in the InDesign file.

The data found in Excel tables, like Word tables, also can be copied and pasted into the Graph Data window for graphing in Illustrator.

TIP Remember that Excel tables, like Word tables, that are copied and pasted into Illustrator must first be ungrouped before the table text may be edited within Illustrator.

Excel tables by default do not include cell borders. To have borders appear when a table is copied and pasted into a CS application, you need to make the cell borders visible in Excel. This is done in Excel by opening the Format Cells dialog box (Format ⇨ Cells). In the Format Cells dialog box, select the Border tab, shown in Figure 21.10, and click on the Outline and Inside buttons to add cell borders. This causes the Excel table cells to have borders when they're copied and pasted.

FIGURE 21.10

The Border tab of the Format Cells dialog box in Microsoft Excel is used to add visible cell borders to tables being copied and pasted into the various CS applications.

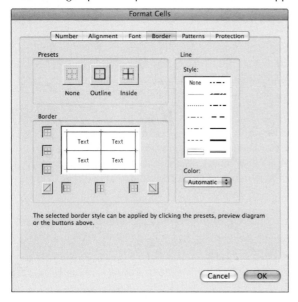

Pasting Excel tables in Photoshop

The same conditions apply to Excel tables as you find with pasting tables from Word. If you copy cells in Excel and choose Edit ⇨ Paste, you paste the table with all the appearances defined in Excel, as shown in Figure 21.11.

FIGURE 21.11

Pasted tables from Excel spreadsheets in a Photoshop layout retain the data formatting.

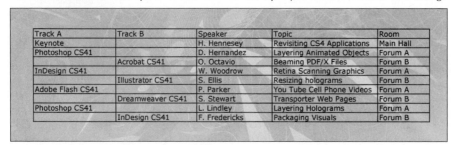

Track A	Track B	Speaker	Topic	Room
Keynote		H. Hennesey	Revisiting CS4 Applications	Main Hall
Photoshop CS41		D. Hernandez	Layering Animated Objects	Forum A
	Acrobat CS41	O. Octavio	Beaming PDF/X Files	Forum B
InDesign CS41		W. Woodrow	Retina Scanning Graphics	Forum A
	Illustrator CS41	S. Ellis	Resizing holograms	Forum B
Adobe Flash CS41		P. Parker	You Tube Cell Phone Videos	Forum A
	Dreamweaver CS41	S. Stewart	Transporter Web Pages	Forum B
Photoshop CS41		L. Lindley	Layering Holograms	Forum A
	InDesign CS41	F. Fredericks	Packaging Visuals	Forum B

You'll find one distinction between pasted Word files and pasted Excel files in Photoshop. When you paste Word files, the data remain as vector objects and the text can be edited. When you paste Excel files in Photoshop, the data are rasterized and you lose all editing capabilities.

TIP If you want Excel tables passed as vector objects in Photoshop, open the Excel file in Word, copy the table from Word, and then paste in Photoshop.

Pasting Excel files in Illustrator

Pasted Excel files in Illustrator follow similar principles as when pasting Word files. If you paste an Excel table in Illustrator, you retain the table appearance, but you lose the editing capabilities. If you create an Area Text Frame and choose Edit ➪ Paste, the formatted data are pasted in Excel, but you lose the table formatting such as borders and fills, as shown in Figure 21.12.

FIGURE 21.12

Pasted tables from Excel spreadsheets in Illustrator show the difference between pasting a table and pasting the data within an Area Text Frame.

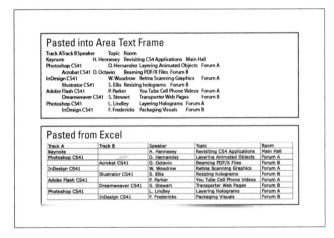

Placing Excel tables in InDesign

In addition to the Copy and Paste features, you also can place Excel documents within an InDesign document by choosing File ➪ Place (⌘/Ctrl+D). This works the same as placing Word tables, as discussed in "Using Word files in InDesign" earlier in this chapter. Note that the Microsoft Excel Import Options dialog box, shown in Figure 21.13, is unique to the Word import options.

FIGURE 21.13

When you place a Microsoft Excel document within an InDesign document, this dialog box of options appears letting you select which sheet and view to open and letting you specify how to format the tables.

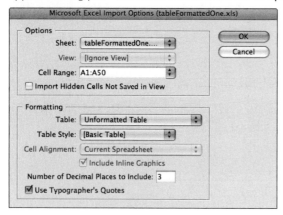

Excel documents are divided into sheets, which are selected using tabs at the bottom of the Excel window. Large sheets of data also can be made up of customized views. As you import data into InDesign, you can select which sheets and views to import. The Cell Range drop-down list displays the row and column numbers referenced in Excel; hidden cells also can be imported.

The formatting options include a formatted table, unformatted table, and unformatted tabbed text. Although the Formatted Table option works most of the time, if you encounter any trouble, select to format the table as Unformatted Tabbed Text and let InDesign's Table ➪ Convert Text to Table menu command create the table.

The Cell Alignment options include Left, Center, Right, and Current Spreadsheet alignment.

NOTE   After clicking OK to place an Excel spreadsheet, an Information dialog box appears if the Formatted Table option was selected. This dialog box instructs you that you can speed up the import process by choosing to import the table as an unformatted table.

Creating links to Excel spreadsheets

Adobe InDesign is the only program discussed in this chapter that permits you to create a link from the application document to the original Excel spreadsheet. By default, linking to spreadsheets is disabled. You need to adjust some preferences settings in order to link to spreadsheet files in InDesign.

To create links to spreadsheet files, open the InDesign Preferences by pressing Ctrl/⌘+K. Click File Handling in the left pane, and check Create Links When Placing Text and Spreadsheet Files, as shown in Figure 21.14.

FIGURE 21.14

Open the File handling Preferences, and check Create Links When Placing Text and Spreadsheet Files.

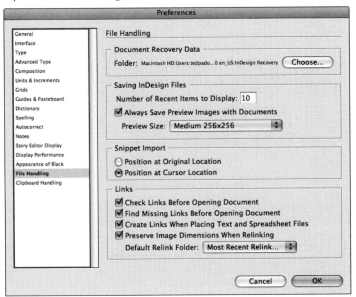

When you edit a spreadsheet file and open InDesign, you are prompted to update file links. Click OK, and any edits made in the spreadsheet document are updated in InDesign.

Working with Tables in InDesign

Although several applications can import and use tables imported from external files such as Microsoft Word and Microsoft Excel documents, only InDesign and Dreamweaver deal natively with tables. And of these two applications, Dreamweaver tables are hindered by the restrictions that HTML requires.

CROSS-REF For more information on Dreamweaver tables, see Chapter 27.

Tables in InDesign, however, are very robust and offer a host of formatting and editing options. Tables are part of a story and can flow through the threaded frames of a story in an InDesign document.

Creating tables

Tables in InDesign are a specialized form of text object. To create a table, you must first create a text object using the Type tool or position the cursor within an existing text object at the place where the new table is located.

Choose Table ⇨ Insert Table (Alt+Shift+Ctrl+T in Windows; Option+Shift+⌘+T on the Mac) to open the Insert Table dialog box, shown in Figure 21.15. This dialog box lets you specify the number of body rows and columns to include in the new table. You also can select the number of header and footer rows, and you can select a Table Style to apply to the new table. Table Styles work just like Paragraph and Character Styles and are defined and reused between tables.

 Table and Cell Styles are new to InDesign CS.

FIGURE 21.15

When you create a new table, the Insert Table dialog box specifies the number of rows and columns to include in the table.

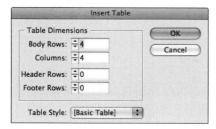

The new table fills the width of the text frame that contains it with the specified number of columns. The cell height is determined initially by the size of the text contained in the text object. After the table is created, the container text frame has no control over the table's height and width. You alter the cell size by dragging on the cell borders using the Type tool. The cursor changes to show the directions that the cell can move.

CAUTION Be aware that tables can be set to a width that exceeds the width of the text frame. This can cause problems for your layout if you're not careful.

NOTE Tables cannot be added to type positioned along a path.

Populating tables

After a table is created, you can populate it with data using the Type tool. Just click in a cell, and type the data. Add graphics to a cell by choosing File ⇨ Place (⌘/Ctrl+D). You also can copy and paste text into the various table cells using the Type tool.

Tables also can be populated by copying and pasting data from other tables created in InDesign or imported from Excel or Word into the new table. Be aware that if you copy and paste data into a single cell, then the entire copied selection of data is nested within the single table cell. If you select a two or more cells before pasting, then the copied data is pasted within the new table aligning the upper left copied cell data with the upper left selected cell.

You can copy and paste tab-delimited text or data from an Excel file into an InDesign table without nesting the content inside a cell.

Moving between cells

Tab and Shift+Tab move the cursor between adjacent cells. Tab moves to the next cell, and Shift+Tab moves to the previous one. If the next cell already has some data, that data is selected. Pressing the Tab key when the cursor is positioned in the last cell adds a new row to the table.

The arrow keys also can be used to move between cells, but they move directly between rows and columns. For example, if you press the up arrow when the cursor is positioned in the top cell of a row, then the bottom cell of the same column is selected. The Escape key toggles the selection of the cell content on and off. You also can extend the selection between cells by holding down the Shift key while moving to a different cell.

If you're dealing with a particularly long table, choose Table ➪ Go to Row to jump to a specific Header, Body Row, or Footer using the dialog box, shown in Figure 21.16. This causes the entire row to be selected.

FIGURE 21.16

The Go to Row dialog box jumps to a specified table row.

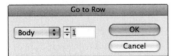

Converting text into a table

Normal text is converted into a table using common delimiters such as tabs, commas, and paragraph returns. Before converting text to a table, make sure that you separate the text for each cell with a common separator and that you separate the end of each row with a different separator. For example, separate each text cell using a comma and each row using a paragraph return.

Select the text that you want to convert into a table with the Type tool, and choose Table ➪ Convert Text to Table. A dialog box opens, shown in Figure 21.17, letting you select the separators used for the columns and rows.

FIGURE 21.17

The Convert Text to Table dialog box lets you select the separator to use to delineate rows and columns. The options include Tab, Comma, Paragraph, and Other.

InDesign also includes a command to do the opposite—convert tables into text. During this process, you select the separators that are placed in the text for separating rows and columns. The menu command (Table ⇨ Convert Table to Text) is available only when the Type tool's cursor is placed within a table cell.

Threading a table between frames

Longer tables are formatted to run between several different text frames. If the size of the table exceeds the text frame, the frame's out port has a red plus sign in it, as shown in Figure 21.18. If you create a new text frame, you can click on the out port for the first frame and then on the in port (or just on the frame) for the second frame to connect (or thread) the two frames. This causes the table data not visible in the first frame to be displayed in the second frame; if new rows or columns are added to the first frame's table, the table data is pushed down to the second frame.

 Frame threading and in and out ports are covered in Chapter 17.

Using headers and footers

Tables that span several frames and/or pages benefit from using headers and footers. Headers and footers are specified when a table is created, but you can convert the topmost row (or a number of rows) to a header and the bottom-most row (or a number of rows) to a footer (or any header or footer to a body row) by choosing Table ⇨ Convert Rows ⇨ To Header, To Footer, or To Body.

Headers and Footers have an option to appear in every text Column, once per frame, or once per page. This makes tables that span multiple frames or pages easier to understand.

FIGURE 21.18

Connecting a frame's out port to another frame's in port threads the two frames together. Content in the first frame that isn't visible appears in the second frame.

Frame out port

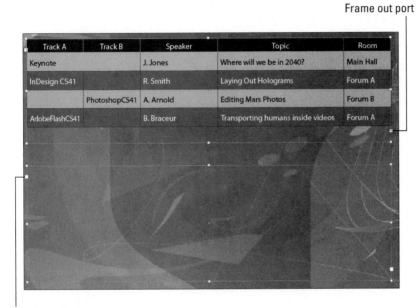

New frame in port

Editing tables

After an InDesign table is created, you have complete control over the size and number of cells. New rows and columns may be added or deleted and individual cells merged or split.

Selecting cells

You can easily select table cells using the Type tool. A single click on an empty cell positions the cursor within the cell, and a double click on a populated cell selects text in a cell. Dragging a marquee over several cells selects multiple cells at once.

TIP Double-clicking the contents of a table cell selects it contents, but if you press the Escape key, the selection toggles between the cell contents and the cell. If you watch the Control panel, you can see different settings selected.

Moving the cursor over the top or left edge causes the cursor to change to an arrow. If you click when this arrow cursor is visible, then the entire column or row is selected. If you position the cursor in the upper-left corner, it changes into a diagonally pointing arrow. Clicking selects the entire table.

You also select table elements—including Cell (⌘/Ctrl+/), Row (⌘/Ctrl+3), Column (Option/Alt+⌘/Ctrl+3), and Table (Option/Alt+⌘/Ctrl+A)—by choosing Table ➪ Select. You also can use the Table ➪ Select menu to select header, footer, and body rows.

Inserting rows and columns

It is unnerving to find that you need a new row or column in the middle of a table that has already been formatted correctly. Luckily, InDesign offers an easy way to do this. Hold down the Option/Alt key while dragging to resize a row or a column and a new row or column is created.

 To create a new row by dragging with the Option/Alt key held down, you must drag a distance at least equal to the height of the table's text.

You add multiple rows and/or columns to a table by choosing Table ➪ Insert ➪ Row (⌘/Ctrl+9) or Table ➪ Insert ➪ Column (Alt+Ctrl+9 in Windows; Option+⌘+9 on the Mac). These menu commands, which are available only if the cursor is positioned within a table's cell, cause a dialog box, like the one shown in Figure 21.19, to appear.

FIGURE 21.19

The Insert Rows dialog box positions the new rows above or below the current selection.

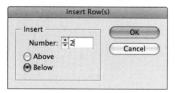

The total number of rows and columns that make up a table are listed in the Table Options dialog box and in the Table palette. Entering a new value for either the Row or Table field adds or deletes rows or columns from the current table.

Deleting rows and columns

You can delete rows and columns by choosing Table ➪ Delete ➪ Row (⌘/Ctrl+Backspace) or Table ➪ Delete ➪ Column (Shift+Backspace). The Table ➪ Delete menu also includes a command to delete the entire table. Deleting a row or a column also deletes all the content contained within its cells.

 When you select a single cell, a row, or a column, pressing the Delete key only clears the contents of the selected cells; it doesn't remove the cells.

Rows and columns also are deleted by dragging the bottom edge upward or the right edge leftward with the Option/Alt key held down.

Merging cells

Often, the first row or column of cells is used as a header to describe the data that follows. Because this single header applies to all cells, you can merge all the cells in the header to make a single cell that extends the entire width of the rows or columns. To merge several cells, just select them and choose Table ⇨ Merge Cells. This keeps the common dimension of the cells and extends the other dimension the extent of all the selected cells. Merged cells do not need to be a header or footer row. You can unmerge merged cells by choosing Table ⇨ Unmerge Cells. Figure 21.20 shows a sample table that has had a number of cells merged. Notice the title at the top of the table; all the cells in the first row have been merged, and the title has been centered in the first row.

FIGURE 21.20

Merged cells make more room for text such as titles to be displayed.

Merged cells

2020 AD Conference Schedule - Day One				
Track A	Track B	Speaker	Topic	Room
Keynote		J. Jones	Where will we be in 2040?	Main Hall
InDesign CS41		R. Smith	Laying Out Holograms	Forum A
	PhotoshopCS41	A. Arnold	Editing Mars Photos	Forum B
AdobeFlashCS41		B. Braceur	Transporting humans inside videos	Forum A

Splitting cells

You can split selected cells into two by choosing Table ⇨ Split Cell Horizontally or Table ⇨ Split Cell Vertically. These commands add another table border and split each selected cell into two equal cells.

NOTE Splitting a row creates a new row that is the same height of the original row. Splitting a row vertically results in twice as many cells in a row.

Formatting tables

Text and images contained within a table are formatted just as normal using the Control palette, but tables and table cells have several unique formatting options. You can set these options in the Table Options dialog box, shown in Figure 21.21; choose Table ⇨ Table Options ⇨ Table Setup (Alt+Shift+Ctrl+B in Windows; Option+Shift+⌘+B on the Mac).

The Table Setup panel of the Table Options dialog box lists the total number of body rows, columns, header rows, and footer rows. Increasing or decreasing these values adds or deletes from the table. The Table Setup panel also includes controls for defining the table border and the spacing before and after the table. The Headers and Footers panel is used to specify the number of header and footer rows and where they're repeated for tables that span several frames or pages.

FIGURE 21.21

The Table Options dialog box is divided into several different panels for controlling the table settings, the row and column strokes, the background fills, and the headers and footers.

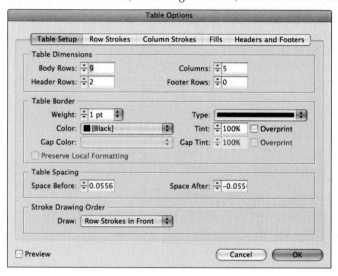

Alternating strokes

The strokes used to create the rows and column borders are changed using the Row and Column Strokes panels in the Table Options dialog box, shown in Figure 21.22. Access this panel by clicking on the Row Strokes tab (or Column Row tab) or by choosing Table ⇨ Table Options ⇨ Alternating Row Strokes.

Using the First and Next fields, you can establish any type of pattern. The Weight, Type, Color, and Tint settings let you control the look of the row borders. The Preserve Local Formatting check box keeps any cell formatting applied to a single cell when enabled. Using the Preview option lets you make changes and view the results without closing the dialog box.

Alternating fills

The Fills panel of the Table Options dialog box changes the background cell color for the specified alternating pattern. The options include Every Other Row/Column, Every Second Row/Column, Every Third Row/Column, and Custom Row/Column.

FIGURE 21.22

The Row Strokes panel defines the look of the row borders. The Column Strokes panel is similar but applies to columns.

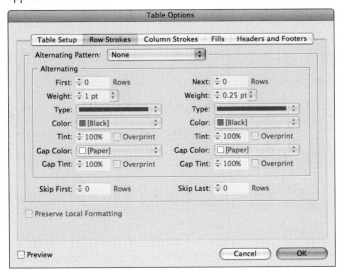

Using Table Styles

Table styles hold all the formatting properties for a table in a panel where they can be reapplied to other tables quickly and easily. All defined styles are listed in the Table Styles panel. New table styles are created by clicking the Create New Style button located at the bottom of the panel.

Double-clicking on a style opens the Table Style Options dialog box. When double-clicking a style you can inadvertently apply a style; therefore a better option is to open a context menu and choose Edit <style name>, and the Table Style Options dialog box opens as shown in Figure 21.23. Within this dialog box, you can rename the style and select one of the option panels listed to the left. The panels include General, Table Setup, Row Stroke, Column Stroke, and Fills. Each of these panels holds settings for defining how the table is constructed, how it looks, and all the properties that affect the entire table.

Styles are applied to new tables by selecting the table and choosing one of the styles from the Table Styles palette. If you want to change the table independent of the style without affecting the style, you can use the Break Link to Style palette menu command.

CROSS-REF Table Styles was perhaps one of the best new features added to InDesign CS3. We cover cell and table styles thoroughly in Chapter 16.

FIGURE 21.23

The Table Style Options dialog box includes settings for defining the look of the entire table.

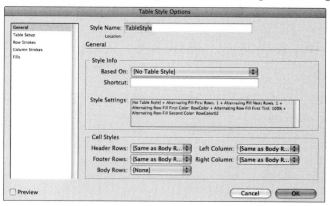

Formatting cells

You control cell formatting in the Cell Options dialog box, shown in Figure 21.24. Open this dialog box for the current cell by choosing Table ➪ Cell Options ➪ Text (Alt+Ctrl+B in Windows; Option+⌘+B on the Mac).

FIGURE 21.24

The Cell Options dialog box is divided into several different panels for controlling the cell's alignment, strokes and fills, and cell dimensions, as well as for adding diagonal lines.

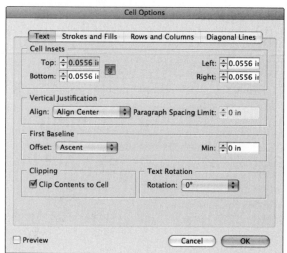

Changing row and column dimensions

You change row and column size by positioning the mouse cursor over a cell border and dragging to increase or decrease the row or column size. The mouse cursor changes to show the direction that the border can move, as shown in Figure 21.25. If the text entered into a cell exceeds the width of the column, the text is displayed as a red dot to indicate that the text exceeds the cell size.

FIGURE 21.25

The cursor changes to show the directions that the cursor can move to resize the selected row. Overset text is marked with a red dot indicating that the text doesn't fit in the cell.

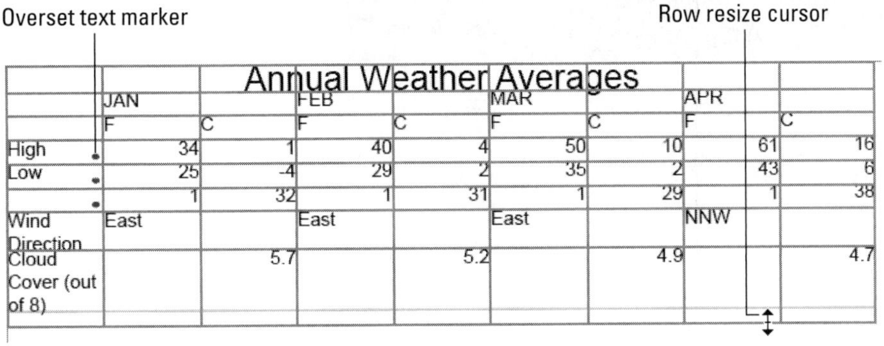

Overset text marker — Row resize cursor

Annual Weather Averages							
JAN		FEB		MAR		APR	
F	C	F	C	F	C	F	C
High	34	1	40	4	50	10	61	16
Low	25	-4	29	2	35	2	43	6
	1	32	1	31	1	29	1	38
Wind Direction	East		East		East		NNW	
Cloud Cover (out of 8)		5.7		5.2		4.9		4.7

Holding down the Shift key while dragging an internal row or column border changes the adjacent row or column at the expense of the other. Dragging the bottom or rightmost border with the Shift key held down proportionally sizes all the rows or columns at once.

Initially, the row height is set based on the text size, and increasing the text size increases the row height. This is based on Row Height set to the At Least option. It also can be set to use the Exactly option, which makes the cell size consistent regardless of the text size. These controls are found in the Rows and Columns panel of the Cell Options dialog box.

Evenly distributing rows and columns

To make several rows and columns have the same dimensions, select the rows or columns that you want to distribute and choose Table ➪ Distribute Rows Evenly or Table ➪ Distribute Columns Evenly.

Aligning cell content

The Cell Inset value is the amount of space between the cell text and the cell border. A Cell Inset value of 0.0 causes the text to print on top of the cell border. The Vertical Justification options include Top, Center, Bottom, and Justify; the First Baseline options include Ascent, Cap Height, Leading, x Height, and Fixed.

The Text Rotation values include 0, 90, 180, and 270 degrees. This allows the text to be rotated and displayed vertically. Figure 21.26 shows a sample table where the text for the months has been rotated 90 degrees.

FIGURE 21.26

This sample table shows some text that has been rotated 90 degrees.

2020 AD Conference Schedule - Day One				
Track A	Track B	Speaker	Topic	Room
Keynote		J. Jones	Where will we be in 2040?	Main Hall
InDesign CS41		R. Smith	Laying Out Holograms	Forum A
	PhotoshopCS41	A. Arnold	Editing Mars Photos	Forum B
AdobeFlashCS41		B. Braceur	Transporting humans inside videos	Forum A
	DreamweaverCS41	W. Espinoza	Using Transporters	Forum B

Altering cell strokes and fills

The Strokes and Fills panel of the Cell Options dialog box includes settings for defining the border stroke and fill for the selected cell. This is useful if you want to highlight a specific table value. The Diagonal Lines panel includes options to place a diagonal line through the selected cell.

Using Cell Styles

In addition to Table Styles, there is a palette for defining and applying Cell Styles. Cell Styles work similar to table styles, except they set the style and properties to a single or multiple cells instead of the entire table.

CROSS-REF **For more information on Cell Styles, see Chapter 16.**

Using the Story Editor

InDesign CS4 now permits you to edit tables in the Story Editor. To open a table in the Story Editor, select a table and choose Edit in Story Editor. The Story Editor displays the text for all cells in a table as shown in Figure 21.27.

FIGURE 21.27

FIGURE 21.27

Select a table and choose Edit ⇨ Open in Story Editor to open a table in the Story Editor.

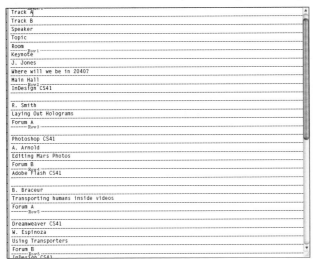

While in the Story Editor you can add notes to the table cells. Open a context menu on a line of text and choose New Note. The cursor appears blinking within two icons. Type text and you add the note text in the Story Editor as shown in Figure 21.28. When you return to the layout the notes are not visible in the table. You need to reopen the Story Editor to view the note comments.

FIGURE 21.28

Open the Story Editor and choose New Note from a context menu. Type text and the text is added as a note comment.

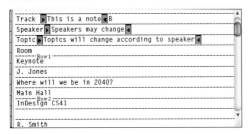

667

Exporting tagged tables from InDesign

Tables created in InDesign can be tagged and exported using the XML format. Keep in mind that the table as well as the individual cells all need to be tagged in order to be exported. To see the applied tags, choose View ➪ Structure ➪ Show Structure to open the Structure pane. Tags can be applied from the Tags palette, which is opened by choosing Window ➪ Tags. Once tagged, the table can be exported by choosing File ➪ Export and selecting the XML file type.

Summary

- Tables created in Microsoft Word may be imported into InDesign, Illustrator, and Photoshop using the Clipboard.
- Tables copied from Word or Excel may be pasted into Illustrator's Graph Data window.
- Tables created in Microsoft Word and Excel may be imported directly into InDesign.
- InDesign can create, edit, and format tables.

Chapter 22

Microsoft Office and Professional Printing

IN THIS CHAPTER

Special printing considerations for Microsoft Word documents

Using PowerPoint presentations

Working with Excel documents

A s a professional designer, you wouldn't dream of using Microsoft Office documents for professional output and commercial printing. If all your work is limited to the design pieces you create without using Office documents collected from colleagues or clients, this chapter won't mean much to you. However, if you do receive documents from clients that you need to output to print or to host on Web sites, you'll want to look over some of the more common issues discussed in this chapter that you can potentially face when serving your customers who supply you with Microsoft Office files.

At times, you may need to output an Office file "as is" without reworking the documents by importing text from Word or charts and tables from Excel into InDesign. As stand-alone applications, Microsoft Office programs fall short of features needed for professional output. A book you create in Word can't be printed directly to most high-end devices due to a lack of print controls for screening, printer's marks, and other features needed to print to commercial printing equipment. Excel charts can't be color-separated from Excel. And PowerPoint's Print dialog box lacks attribute settings to successfully print slides to commercial printing devices.

As a design professional or printing technician, you can be certain that on occasion you'll be called upon to take your clients' Office files and prepare them for output to commercial printing devices. In this chapter, you learn how to prepare Office documents for printing on professional equipment.

Printing Microsoft Word Documents

If Word documents are designed to be taken from your clients without modifying them, you can choose one of two options to prepare the documents for professional output—either import the Word document in InDesign and then print from InDesign or print the Word file via Acrobat. Assuming you have a file like a book, manual, story, or other long publication primarily comprised of text, the labor involved in importing the file in InDesign and formatting pages with proper page breaks is going to take you much more time than if you find a way to print the existing document without reformatting it. The problem you encounter when printing Word files to high-end imaging devices is that the Microsoft Word Print dialog box doesn't give you options for selecting commercial print controls. Options such as printer's marks and setting halftone frequency are not available in the Word Print dialog box.

CROSS-REF   For more information on controlling halftone frequency, see Chapter 40.

In order to print a Word file utilizing commercial print options, you need to get the Word document into a program capable of printing with these options or convert the file to Adobe PDF where the PDF can be printed from Acrobat. The method requiring the least amount of effort is converting the file to PDF.

Converting standard page sizes to PDF

For Word documents using standard page sizes, you can simply convert the Word file to PDF without fussing around with special page handling options. Conversion to PDF from all Microsoft Office programs is best achieved with the PDFMaker macro if you're a Windows user. Beginning with Acrobat 9 Pro on the Macintosh the PDF Maker is no longer supported. Mac users need to print to PDF to covert Word files to PDF documents.

When you install Acrobat on Windows, Acrobat tools are added to the Word toolbar. You'll find the PDFMaker tools and an Acrobat menu in Word if you're using MS Word 2003. If using Word 2007 on Windows, you can find the Acrobat tab in the Office Ribbon. On Windows, click Acrobat, and the Ribbon expands to the view you see in Figure 22.1.

FIGURE 22.1

In MS Word 2007 for Windows, click the Acrobat tab in the Ribbon to view options you have for converting Word documents to PDF.

Conversion to PDF from Word 2007 for Windows is easy. Click the Create PDF tool in the Acrobat tab in the Ribbon, and the Save Adobe PDF File As dialog box opens. Before converting to PDF, you can set some conversion options by clicking the Options button in the Save Adobe PDF File As dialog box. Choosing this action opens the Acrobat PDFMaker dialog box shown in Figure 22.2.

FIGURE 22.2

Click Options in the Save Adobe PDF File As dialog box to open the Acrobat PDFMaker dialog box.

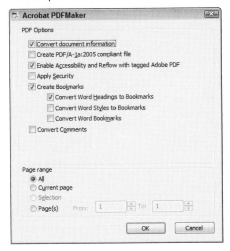

When converting a Word document to be viewed as a PDF document, you may want to check the Create Bookmarks box and choose options for which styles to convert to Adobe PDF bookmarks. If you are preparing a file for print, you needn't bother with creating bookmarks.

Make your choices in the Acrobat PDFMaker dialog box, and click OK; then click Save when you return to the Save Adobe PDF File As dialog box. Your file is converted to PDF seamlessly and opens in Acrobat by default.

To convert to Adobe PDF on the Mac, choose File ➪ Print. In the Print dialog box, choose Adobe PDF 9.0 as your Printer as shown in Figure 22.3. Click the Print button and the Save dialog box opens. Locate the folder on your hard drive, and click the Save button to save the Word file as a PDF document.

FIGURE 22.3

In Microsoft Word for Macintosh, choose File ➪ Print and print the document to the Adobe PDF Printer.

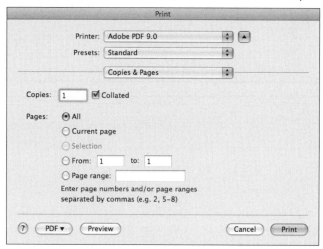

Converting Word files with custom page sizes

PDF conversion from Microsoft Word using the PDFMaker tool (Windows) or printing to a PDF file (Macintosh) for standard page sizes is straightforward and requires little preparation. For documents that use custom page sizes, you need to prepare your printer driver and create any custom page sizes that are not part of the default set of page sizes.

Creating custom page sizes can be performed on both Mac OS X and Windows. The results are the same, but the means for achieving the results vary a little.

Creating custom page sizes on the Mac

Custom page sizes on the Mac are handled a little different when using Mac OS X Leopard than when using Mac OS X Tiger and below. There have been a few minor changes to dialog boxes when using Page Setup; however, if you haven't upgraded to Mac OS X Leopard, you can follow the steps below and poke around a little in the dialog boxes to figure it out. On Mac OS X Leopard, do the following to create a custom page size in MS Word.

STEPS: Creating Custom Page Sizes in Word on Mac OS X Leopard

1. **Open the Page Setup dialog box.** While in Word, you need to have a document open to access the Page Setup dialog box. You can open a blank document and create a new custom page size or use an existing document to create the custom page size. If using an existing document, the Word file will reform to the new page size after you create it. To begin, open the Page Setup dialog box by choosing File ⇨ Page Setup. In the Page Setup dialog box, open the Paper Size pull-down menu and select Manage Custom Sizes, as shown in Figure 22.4.

FIGURE 22.4

Choose Paper Size ⇨ Manage Custom Sizes to open the Custom Page Sizes dialog box where new custom page sizes are created.

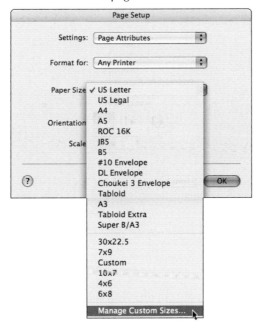

2. **Set the page size attributes.** Type the width and height for your new custom page size in the Width and Height text boxes. Below the Printer Margins pull-down menu, edit the margins in the four text boxes.

3. **Add the new size to the list of available sizes.** Click the plus (+) symbol on the left side of the dialog box. The attributes defined in the text boxes are added as a new custom page size.

4. **Name the new custom page size.** When you click the plus (+) symbol your new custom page is added with an *Untitled* label. Double-click Untitled and type a name for your new page size. Use a descriptive name for the page such as simply using the page dimensions as a name. In Figure 22.5, you can see several custom page sizes all labeled with the page dimensions.

FIGURE 22.5

Click the plus (+) symbol to add a new page size. When the size appears in the custom page sizes list, it is labeled as *Untitled*. Double-click the text and type a name for the new custom page size.

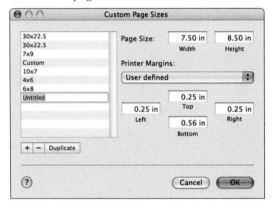

5. **Select the page size.** Click OK after defining a new custom page size. You are returned to the Page Setup dialog box. Open the Paper Size pull-down menu and select your new custom page size. The size is dynamically added to the menu after creating it in the Custom Page Sizes dialog box. If you have a document open in MS Word, the file reforms to the new page size and margins. You are now ready to create a PDF document suitable for commercial printing.

CAUTION   If the Word file you use to convert to PDF contains any graphic images, you'll need to lay out the final document in InDesign. Your clients are likely to use graphic formats not suitable for commercial printing. Steps noted here are designed to assist you when needing to print text-only documents.

In some CS4 applications, when you create custom page sizes, it's important to remember to return to the Page Setup dialog box after creating a new custom page size. In programs like Adobe InDesign, custom pages are set up in the InDesign Print dialog box. When you first create the page size, you haven't set the document to the new size. Choose File ➪ Page Setup and select the new page size from the Paper Size pull-down menu. A readout below the page name in the pull-down menu shows the size that appears, as you can see in Figure 22.6. This readout helps you identify page sizes in the event that the name you gave the new custom page is obscure.

FIGURE 22.6

Return to the Page Setup dialog box and select a new page size.

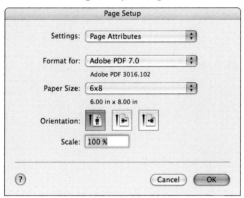

If you're using Microsoft Word, your document conforms to the page size. You may need to read-just margins and examine a file if you're changing page sizes in documents that you have created at another page size. After examining the file for correct page setup, print to PDF, and the new PDF document is created with the page margins adhering to the page size you selected in the Page Setup dialog box.

Creating custom page sizes on Windows

Windows users follow a similar path as Mac users when creating custom page sizes. On Windows, your first task is to go to the Desktop and open the Start menu. Choose Settings ➪ Printers and Faxes ➪ a *PostScript printer*. You can choose to select either a target printer or the Adobe PDF printer that is installed when you install Acrobat. If selecting a target printer, be certain to select a PostScript printer.

There are several settings you need to make on Windows to create a custom page size for your printer. To understand the process more clearly, Windows users should look over the following steps.

STEPS: Creating Custom Page Sizes in Windows

1. **Open the Adobe PDF Properties.** From the Start menu, select Settings ➪ Printers and Faxes. In the Printers and Faxes dialog box, you should see icons for all printing devices installed on your computer. Among the printer drivers, you'll find the Adobe PDF printer driver. Select this driver, and either select File ➪ Properties in the Printers and Faxes window or right-click the Adobe PDF driver to open a context menu and select Properties as shown in Figure 22.7.

FIGURE 22.7

Open a context menu on the Adobe PDF Printer, and select Properties.

2. The Adobe PDF Properties dialog box opens, as shown in Figure 22.8, with the General tab selected by default.

FIGURE 22.8

The General tab of the Adobe PDF Properties dialog box

3. **Open the Printing Preferences.** In the Adobe PDF Properties dialog box, shown in Figure 8.9, click the Printing Preferences button. The Adobe Printing Preferences dialog box opens. In this dialog box, click Adobe PDF Settings, as shown in Figure 22.9.

FIGURE 22.9

The Adobe PDF Printing Preferences dialog box

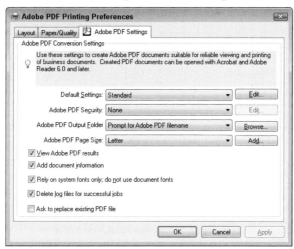

4. **Add a new custom page size.** Click the Add button to open the Add Custom Paper Size dialog box, as shown in Figure 22.10.

FIGURE 22.10

The Add Custom Paper Size dialog box

5. **Edit the Custom Page Size.** Type the width and height values in the Width and Height text boxes, and select the unit of measure from the Unit section of the dialog box. Type a name for the custom paper size in the Paper Name text box. Use a name that defines the page size, as shown in Figure 22.10.

677

6. **Save the new custom page size.** Click the Add/Modify button in the Add Custom Paper Size dialog box, and you return to the Adobe PDF Printing Preferences dialog box. Click OK, and your new custom page size is available each time you use the Adobe PDF printer driver.

7. **Set up a Word document with a custom page size.** Open Microsoft Word, and open a file or create a new document.

   By default Word 2007 doesn't have a Microsoft Menu ⇨ Page Setup command. You may need to open the Microsoft menu and choose Word Options. In the Word Options dialog box, click Customize and select Page Setup in the left column. Click the Add button to move the Page Setup command to the Quick Access toolbar. Click OK, and click the Page Setup button in the Quick Access toolbar. In the Page Setup dialog box, choose the custom page size you want from the Page Size pull-down menu, as shown in Figure 22.11.

FIGURE 22.11

In Microsoft Word, open the Page Setup dialog box and choose the new paper size in the Paper size pull-down menu.

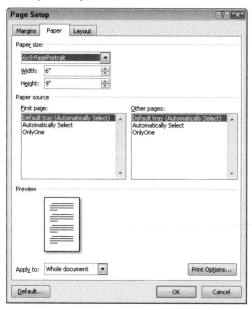

8. **Convert to Adobe PDF.** Click the Convert to Adobe PDF tool in the Word Toolbar Well. If you enabled the View Adobe PDF result option in the Acrobat PDFMaker Settings tab, the resulting PDF opens in Acrobat.

Creating custom page sizes is particularly important for programs like Photoshop, Illustrator, and the Microsoft Office applications where you want to print oversized color documents for trade-show panels, display prints, and similar output. When converting files to PDF, always be certain you have the proper page size defined for the Adobe PDF Printer before attempting to convert to PDF. Acrobat supports a page size of up to 200 inches by 200 inches.

Cropping pages in Acrobat

If you print a lot of Word files with different sizes or you don't want to set up custom pages in Word or any other program, you have an alternative in Acrobat for printing files with trim marks. If a page size large enough to accommodate trim marks using your printer's PPD is not available to you, you can use Acrobat to create a size large enough to print the marks on your output device.

To understand how to apply trim marks and create larger page sizes to accommodate the marks in Acrobat, follow these steps.

STEPS: Applying Trim and Crops in Acrobat

1. **Convert a Word file to PDF.** Use a standard letter-size page and convert to PDF using the PDFMaker (Windows) or print to PDF (Mac). Note that the steps here can be applied to any document converted to PDF. If your client sends you files from other programs, you can print using the same steps.

2. **Open the file in Acrobat.** After conversion to PDF, launch Acrobat and open the file or open the Bridge and locate the PDF document. Double-click the PDF in the Bridge to open the file in Acrobat.

3. **Adjust the Page Setup.** Before opening the Print dialog box, be certain to double-check the Page Setup for page size and orientation. Acrobat has a nasty habit of always defaulting to U.S. letter-size pages with Portrait orientation rather than defaulting to the document's page size and orientation. If printing a landscape page, be certain to make the proper selection in the Page Setup dialog box.

4. **Open the Print Production tools.** Open a context menu on the Acrobat Professional Toolbar Well by right-clicking (Windows) or Control + click (Macintosh with a one-button mouse) and select Print Production from the menu commands. Alternately, you can select View ➪ Toolbars ➪ Print Production. Accessing either menu command opens the Print Production toolbar. The two tools you use to add marks and increase the page size to accommodate the marks are the Add Printer Marks and Crop Pages tools shown highlighted respectively in Figure 22.12.

FIGURE 22.12

Open the Print Production toolbar from a context menu on the Toolbar Well or select View ➪ Toolbars ➪ Print Production.

5. **Add printer marks.** Click the Add Printer Marks tool in the Print Production toolbar. The Add Printer Marks dialog box appears.

6. **Set the printer marks attributes.** If you want all printer marks options provided in Acrobat, select the All Marks check box. If you want selective marks, select the check boxes for the marks you want to appear on the printed page. If you have a multi-page document, be certain to select the check box for All under the Page Range category, as shown in Figure 22.13.

FIGURE 22.13

Select the check boxes for the marks you want to appear in the printed document, and select the All option in the Page Range section when printing multiple pages.

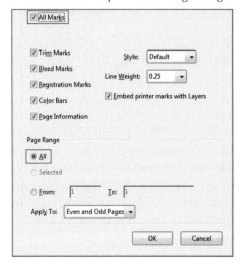

7. **Apply the marks.** Click OK in the Add Printer Marks dialog box. The marks are applied to the page. A warning dialog box opens informing you that you may need to expand the crop box using the Crop dialog box. Click OK in the warning dialog box to proceed.

8. **Open the Crop Box.** If you applied crops to a page size equal to the page size you have selected in the Page Setup dialog box, you won't see the crop marks on the page in the Document pane. The marks are there, but you need to expand the page size in order to see the marks. To add more page area to accommodate the marks, you begin by opening the Crop Box. Click the Crop Pages tool in the Print Production toolbar and the Crop Pages dialog box opens.

9. **Define a custom size.** Select the Custom radio button and add the width and height dimensions to accommodate the trim marks. Add one-half inch to the existing page size in the Width and Height text boxes.

10. **Select the page range.** If you want all pages to print with marks, select All in the Page Range area of the Crop Pages dialog box. Custom page ranges can be selected by selecting the From radio button and typing the page ranges in the two adjacent text boxes.

11. **Preview the results.** Observe the thumbnail preview and note the new page size reported below the page preview. Adjustments in our example are shown in Figure 22.14 for a custom page cropped to 8 inches x 10 inches. (Note that in Figure 22.11 we started with a page size that was 7 × 9 inches, hence after adding .5 inches to each side we end up with a page size of 8 × 10 inches.)

FIGURE 22.14

Add a custom page size, check the page range, and view the preview in the Crop Pages dialog box.

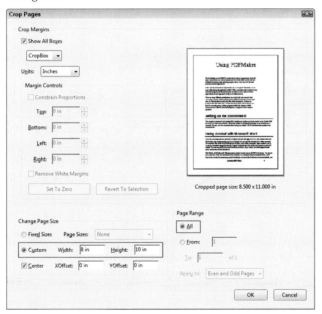

12. **Apply the crop settings.** Click OK to return to the Document pane.

13. **Observe the results.** When you return to the Document pane view the current page to be certain all printer marks appear on the page as shown in Figure 22.15. The file is now ready to print.

14. **Adjust the Page Setup.** Before opening the Print dialog box, be certain to double-check the Page Setup for page size and orientation. If printing a landscape page, be certain to make the proper selection in the Page Setup dialog box.

FIGURE 22.15

FIGURE 22.15

Printer's marks are displayed on a new page sized in Acrobat large enough to accommodate the marks.

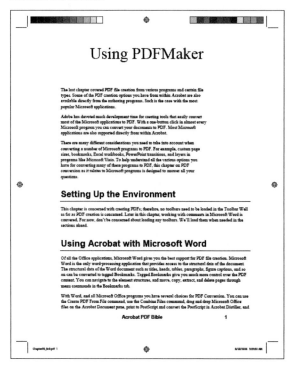

TIP If you want to create client proofs for custom page sizes on your desktop color printer, you can use the same steps outlined here. Crop marks can be added to a PDF file created from any authoring program. Add the printer marks and crop the pages. Print the file to your desktop printer and trim the pages to the crop marks for a client proof. If creating standard U.S. letter or larger pages with bleeds, you can print to oversized paper (like tabloid) and trim to the bleed edges.

These steps work well for preparing a file for print on a desktop printer and when sending a file to a print shop. If your work is finished as a designer, you don't need to bother with any further editing. If you're a technician at a print shop, then you have one other issue to deal with before a file is printed to plate or to press. You need to be concerned about the color. Office applications default colors to RGB. The blacks in a Word file are specified in RGB color. For professional printing you need to convert all RGB blacks to K (or black). In Acrobat Pro 9 and above you have some new tools for color conversion found in the Print Production tools. We explain more in the chapter where we talk about professional printing.

CROSS-REF For more information on printing PDF files to commercial printing devices and converting color, see Chapter 40.

Printing from PowerPoint

In design workflows, it's very common to receive PowerPoint files from clients who want to print to large-format color printers for display posters and trade-show panels. PowerPoint is a primary application used for graphics representations by business workers for everything from slide presentations to large prints. When you need to print slides to desktop color printers, you don't need any CS application interventions. However, when you want to output a PowerPoint slide to large-format devices and commercial printing equipment, you need to get the PowerPoint slides to CS applications to access features such as oversized printing, printing with crop marks, setting half-tone frequencies, and so on.

To export a PowerPoint file for oversized printing, you use the Print dialog box and set the page size to your output size in the printer Properties dialog box. To begin setting up an oversized print, choose File ➪ Print. The Print dialog box opens, shown in Figure 22.16. From the Name pull-down menu, select Adobe PDF for your printer. If you have large-format inkjet printers on your network, be certain to not use the device printer driver. In many cases, the page sizes for custom pages don't work. Your best solution is to use the Adobe PDF Printer.

FIGURE 22.16

In the Print dialog box, you make choices for the printer driver by selecting options from the Name (Windows) pull-down menu.

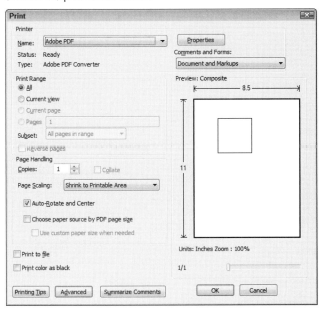

To adjust the page properties, click Properties, and the Adobe PDF Document Properties dialog box opens, as shown in Figure 22.17. From the Adobe PDF Page Size drop-down list, select a fixed page size as close to your final output size as possible. If you try to set up a custom page size, PowerPoint may produce some unexpected results and the actual output size may be clipped.

Select a fixed page size from the Adobe PDF Page Size drop-down menu.

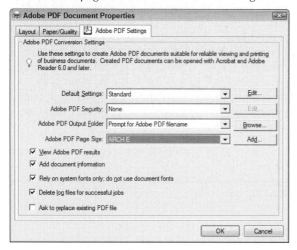

Click OK after making adjustments, and you're returned to the Print dialog box. Select the Scale to Fit Paper check box and click OK. The Save dialog box opens, prompting you to name the resultant PDF document and target a location on your hard drive. Click Save and the PowerPoint slide is exported to PDF.

If you don't find an exact fit for a page size in the Adobe PDF Document Properties dialog box, you can open the PDF document in Photoshop and size to final dimensions. When you open a PDF document in Photoshop, where the PDF was created from any other source but Photoshop, the Import PDF dialog box opens, as shown in Figure 22.18.

In this dialog box, you can specify the resolution of the file to *rasterize* it. If you need a file sized 300 percent, be certain to select a resolution that accommodates a 300 percent size at the target resolution for the printing device. For example, suppose you have an 8-x-10-inch document that needs to be sized 400 percent to produce a final image size of 32 inches x 40 inches. If the required resolution for the printing device is 150 dpi, you need to set the resolution in Photoshop's import dialog box to 600 ppi (pixels per inch). As you decrease the resolution, the physical size proportionately changes.

FIGURE 22.18

Opening PDF files in Photoshop created from any program but Photoshop opens the Import PDF dialog box.

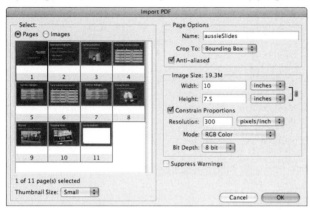

> **NOTE** Rasterizing data in Photoshop is the process of converting objects, such as drawing objects and text to pixels. As objects, the elements contain no resolution and always print at the resolution of the printing device. Raster images that are pixel based have fixed resolutions. Through the process of rasterizing vector objects and text, you can determine the resolution you want the final file to be.

To understand more about opening PowerPoint files converted to PDF and rasterizing the file in Adobe Photoshop CS4, follow these steps.

STEPS: Rasterizing PDFs in Adobe Photoshop

1. **Open a PDF in Photoshop.** Open the Bridge and locate the PDF file you want to open in Photoshop. If you need to convert a PowerPoint document to PDF, follow the directions outlined at the beginning of this section. From the Bridge menu, open a context menu on a document thumbnail and select Open With. From the submenu, select Photoshop CS4. Alternately, you can select File ➪ Open With in the Bridge menu as shown in Figure 22.19, drag a PDF document on your desktop to the Photoshop application icon or an application icon alias, or from within Photoshop chose File ➪ Open.

> **CROSS-REF** For more information about opening files from Adobe Bridge, see Chapter 6.

2. **Select a page to open.** The Import PDF dialog box offers all the options you need to rasterize a PDF in Photoshop in a single dialog box. You have an option for selecting any page in a multi-page PDF document to rasterize. From the Thumbnail Size pull-down menu, select Large if you need to see a larger thumbnail view. Click a page thumbnail to select it to open in Photoshop and click OK. (Refer to Figure 22.18.)

FIGURE 22.19

From the Bridge menu, choose Open With ⇨ Adobe Photoshop CS4.

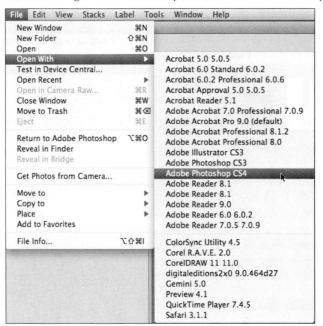

> **TIP**
>
> If you want to rasterize multiple pages, you can Shift+click or ⌘+click to select a contiguous or noncontiguous range of pages, respectively. When you click OK, all pages are opened in Photoshop as separate documents. The document titles are named according to the filename or name you add to the Name field in the Import PDF dialog box. Each page is identified with a number corresponding to the original page number in the PDF document. For example, if you add the name Slide in the Name field and select pages 3, 5, and 9 in a PDF document, the document names Photoshop adds to the resultant open files are Slide-3, Slide-5, and Slide-9.

3. **Select the resolution to rasterize the file.** Type in the field box the resolution you want for the final file size while considering how much you need to increase or decrease the file dimensions. Where you see Bounding Box selected in the Crop To pull-down menu, be certain to leave the menu choice at the default. A Bounding Box selection opens the file at full size without cropping the page(s).

> **CAUTION**
>
> If the resolution for images imported into PowerPoint is not sufficiently sized for a larger output size than the image resolution can support, the final file may show significant image degradation. For example, if you import a Photoshop image in PowerPoint at 72 ppi to fit on a 10x7½-inch slide and output the slide for a 40x30-inch print (a 400 percent increase in size), the Photoshop image is reduced to an effective resolution of 18 ppi (25 percent of the original size). If you open the PDF file in Photoshop and add resolution to the file, the resolution is interpolated and will noticeably degrade the image.

4. **Select the color mode.** If using the final image for Web use, leave the default selection as sRGB. If using the file for print, select RGB for the color mode. Be aware that if you intend to print the file on large format color printers, the preferred color mode is RGB. Do not use CMYK.

5. **Set the Bit depth and anti-aliasing.** Under most circumstances, 8-bit images are fine. You typically won't achieve any better options when rasterizing PowerPoint slides, especially when the slides contain photos. However, if rasterizing vector art, select 16-bit from the Bit Depth pull-down menu. You can make some adjustments in Photoshop in 16-bit mode that won't destroy some precious data. Be certain also to select the Anti-aliased check box especially when you have type on the slides. Anti-aliased type rasterized at the recommended device resolution will print much better.

6. **Open the slide in Photoshop.** Click OK, and the slide is rasterized and opens in Photoshop. If you add 300 ppi or more to the resolution, you may need to wait a few minutes for Photoshop to complete its work and open the file.

7. **Change the image size to the desired output size.** Choose Image ⇨ Image Size to open the Image Size dialog box shown in Figure 22.20. Be certain the Resample Image check box is deselected so you don't lose image data when resizing. Type the output resolution in the Resolution text box, and the Width and Height dimensions adjust automatically. Click OK to change to the new image size and resolution.

FIGURE 22.20

Be certain the Resample Image check box is deselected when you change resolution.

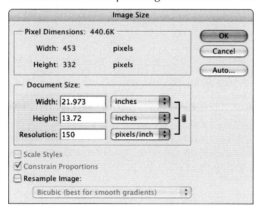

8. **Add a new layer to the Photoshop file.** If you submit files to imaging centers for output to large format devices, the files are typically not printed from a Print dialog box and, as such, won't be printed with trim marks. Quite often, large-format color prints in TIFF format are submitted direct to the device RIP (Raster Image Processor) for output while bypassing printing from an application program. If you have any white space on the

image, particularly at any corner, it will be difficult to accurately cut the print to final size. To be certain your file is trimmed properly at a service center, add your own trim marks in Photoshop. To begin, create a new layer in Photoshop by clicking the New Layer tool in Photoshop's Layers palette. Drag the new layer down in the Layers palette so the new layer is behind the image layer.

9. **Change the canvas size.** Choose Image ⮞ Canvas Size. The Canvas Size dialog box opens. Be certain the unit of measure is in inches and click the center square to apply resizing from the center. Click the cursor in the Width field and press the up arrow on your keyboard. The width dimensions are sized up approximately 30 pixels. Click the cursor in the Height text box and press the up-arrow key to size the height up the same value.

10. **Add a trim color.** Click the empty layer (first layer in the Layers palette, as shown in Figure 22.21), and fill the layer with Black. (Press D to return to the default colors of black foreground and white background. Press Option/Alt+Delete/Backspace to fill with the foreground black color.) If the edges or your image area is black, use another color for the trim color. Any contrasting color will work, but don't select white.

FIGURE 22.21

Add a new layer below the content layer and fill it with black after resizing the canvas.

CAUTION   If you have transparency inside the image area, you need to add a white layer between the content layer and the new layer you fill with black.

11. **Flatten and save.** Flatten the layers in the Layers palette and choose File ⮞ Save As. Select Tiff for your output format and save the file. The final file is ready for output to a service center. In Figure 22.22, you can see a PowerPoint file rasterized in Photoshop with the trim line added to the file.

CROSS-REF   For more information on using Layers in Photoshop, see Chapter 25.

FIGURE 22.22

Flatten layers and save in the format used by your service center.

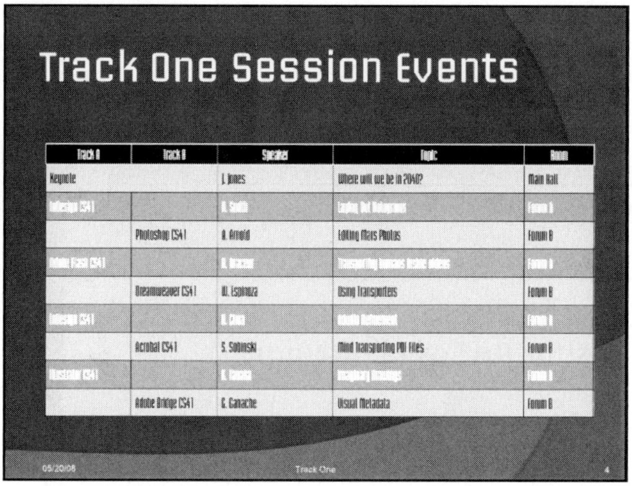

Preparing Excel Files

With Microsoft Excel, you find the same lack of support for commercial printing devices as you have with Word and PowerPoint. No support for color separations, printer's marks, or specification of halftone frequency is available in the Microsoft Excel Print dialog box. The process for conversion to PDF is the same in Excel as in Word. Use the PDFMaker in Excel on Windows or the Adobe PDF Printer in the Print dialog box on the Macintosh, and the Excel worksheet is exported to PDF.

TIP If you want to use more sophisticated typesetting features when formatting tables, import the Excel files in InDesign. InDesign offers you much more advanced type features in a layout view that provides a print preview while laying out the table.

If an Excel chart is something you want to introduce in a design for print, you can import the PDF file in InDesign. If you need to rework the file and make edits to type, you can convert to PDF and use Acrobat's Copy Table command to copy text in a table, then paste the text in InDesign. You can also copy a chart from Excel, paste it into Illustrator, and after saving the Illustrator file, place it into an InDesign layout.

CROSS-REF For more information on working with type from Microsoft Excel, see Chapter 30.

If you have charts you want to edit and prepare them for output to commercial printing devices, you copy a chapter in Excel and paste it into Illustrator. This method is shortest and requires the least amount of work to prepare a file for printing.

You can also convert to PDF and open the PDF document in Adobe Illustrator. If you use this option you most likely need to change fonts and re-form paragraphs for editing. Illustrator will open the PDF document generated from Excel and almost every other program with broken lines of text. In Figure 22.23 you can see how Illustrator sees type after opening a PDF file created in a program other than Illustrator. When selecting the type, you can see that each line is broken into separate characters—indicated by the multiple anchor points on each line of type.

FIGURE 22.23

Illustrator doesn't maintain paragraph formatting when opening PDFs generated from any program but Illustrator.

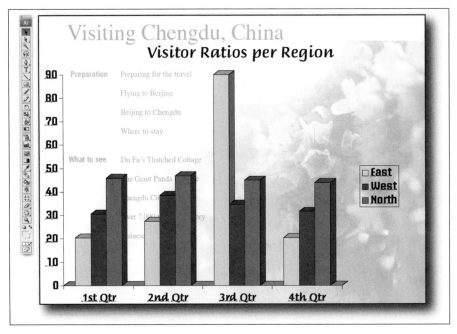

If you need to re-form a paragraph in Illustrator, select all the text and copy it to the clipboard. Select the Horizontal Type tool and drag a marquee around the area approximately at the same boundaries as the original text occupied. Choose Edit ⇨ Paste, and the text is pasted as a single paragraph, as shown in Figure 22.24. You may need to do some formatting, but formatting text in Illustrator in paragraphs enables you to better control the text placement.

FIGURE 22.24

To re-form text into paragraphs, cut the text and paste it back into Illustrator as area type.

CROSS-REF For more information on working with type in Illustrator and creating area type, see Chapter 21.

Summary

- Microsoft Word documents that you want to print to commercial printing should be converted to PDF and edited to support professional printing standards.

- You can create PDF documents from Word files with nonstandard page sizes by adding custom page sizes to your printer driver.

- You can add printer marks to a PDF document in Acrobat and increase the page size to accommodate the marks.

- You can export PowerPoint files to PDFs tor print large display prints. To crop and size files, open the PDFs exported from PowerPoint in Photoshop.

- When you open PDF files in Photoshop that were not originally created in Photoshop, all vector objects and type are rasterized.

- You can export Excel files as PDFs and edit them in Illustrator.

- To reform text blocks to regain paragraph formatting in Illustrator, select text with the Direct Selection tool, cut the text, and paste it back into the document.

Part VI

Integrating Creative Suite Documents

Adobe Flash has become an important tool throughout the CS applications. In Chapter 23 we give you a short course on creating some simple Adobe Flash files. We talk about integrating Flash movie files in other CS applications in several chapters throughout the book.

In Chapter 24 we talk about designing layouts, primarily in Adobe InDesign. Chapter 25 covers working with layers in many Creative Suite programs. After you have a handle on using layers, Chapter 26 moves on to modifying layouts.

We conclude this part in Chapter 27 where we cover Adobe Dreamweaver and creating Web pages.

Chapter 23

Creating Adobe Flash Files

The Web's popularity has seen the appearance of several new technologies that add interactivity and portability within Web pages. Of these, Flash (SWF) files are vector-based image formats used for creating files a fraction of the size of their raster-based counterparts and making them useful for creating Web graphics and, specifically, Web animations. You also can use these formats to scale images to any size without sacrificing image quality.

You can create Flash (SWF) files using both Flash and from within Illustrator and use them in Dreamweaver and Acrobat. You create SWF animation in Illustrator by placing the graphics for each frame of the animation on a separate layer, which you then convert to animation frames.

You also can use InDesign to create SWF files. InDesign CS4 allows exporting documents directly to SWF or exporting to the XFL format that can be imported by Flash.

NOTE Another related technology is Adobe's Scalable Vector Graphics (SVG). These files are also vector-based and saved as XML files. However, Adobe has announced that it will drop support for SVG from its upcoming developments.

IN THIS CHAPTER

Creating content with Flash

Creating SWF files in Illustrator

Using SWF files in Dreamweaver

Using SWF files in Acrobat

Creating Flash Content

Creative Suite 4 Design Premium includes the best package that can generate Flash files—the Flash CS4 program itself. Flash is a valuable addition to CS4 and provides a powerful tool for creating amazing Web site graphics and animations.

Although Flash files can include bitmap images, it really is designed to use vector-based objects like those found in Illustrator. These objects have some distinct advantages when used in Web pages. First, the graphics are resolution-independent, which allows them to be mathematically perfect regardless of their size. And second, vector-based objects are a fraction of the size of their pixel-based siblings. This means that visually rich graphics can be downloaded at a much quicker rate than other graphics.

Learning the Flash interface

Flash animations are created on the section in the middle of the interface called the stage, shown in Figure 23.1. Keyframes are added to the layers in the Timeline palette at the top of the interface, and all object properties are set in the Properties palette at the bottom of the interface. Tools for selecting and drawing objects are found in the Toolbox, located on the left side of the interface.

FIGURE 23.1

The Flash interface allows objects to be created, edited, and animated.

Toolbar   Canvas

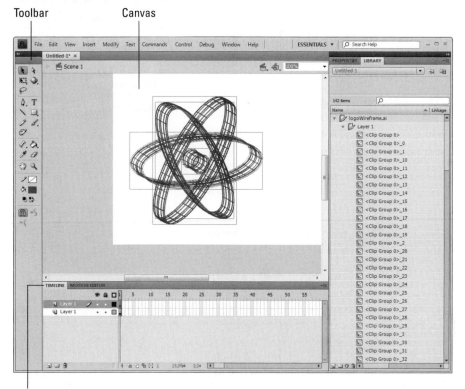

Timeline

In addition to these main windows, Flash also includes a large set of palettes that work in the same way as the other CS apps. You can open palettes using the Window menu, and palettes can be stacked and docked as needed.

CROSS-REF Working with CS palettes is covered in Chapter 4.

Importing content into Flash

Flash allows a large assortment of content including images, sounds, and video to be imported into either the Flash stage or into its Library palette using the File ➪ Import menu. Objects loaded to the stage appear in the stage window, where they can be selected and moved. Objects loaded in the Library can be accessed by any Flash project. Flash can import Illustrator and Photoshop layers. During the importing process, Flash checks and warns of any incompatibilities. It also gives you the option to load the layers as a movie or as a bitmap, as shown in Figure 23.2.

FIGURE 23.2

While importing, Flash checks the file content for compatibility.

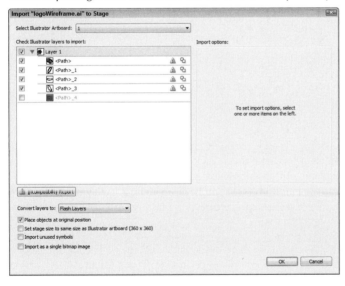

Using Flash Libraries

Objects that are imported into a Library appear in the Library palette, as shown in Figure 23.3. From the Library palette, objects can be dragged and dropped on the stage. Libraries stay with the current Flash file, but you can open a Library with a new Flash file using the File ➪ Import ➪ Open External Library menu command.

FIGURE 23.3

The Library palette holds and organizes Flash content.

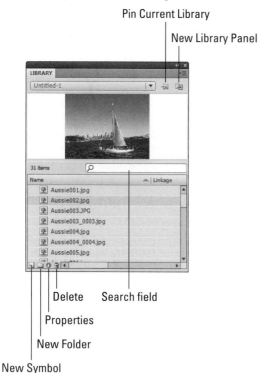

Pin Current Library

New Library Panel

Delete   Search field

Properties

New Folder

New Symbol

Multiple Library panels can be opened at the same time. Click the New Library Panel icon to create a new panel. In addition to imported content, Libraries also can contain symbols. Symbols in Illustrator are collections of small pieces of artwork that can be easily reused, but symbols in Flash are simply artwork saved in the Library. Symbols can be drawn in Flash or imported from another application.

An instance is a copy of a symbol that is used elsewhere in the same document. The advantage of using instances is that they are included in memory only once and referenced for any other appearances of the instance. This can help keep the file size down. To create a new symbol instance, click the New Symbol icon button at the bottom of the palette.

The Library palette also can include folders to organize groups of content together. New folders are created using the New Folder button at the bottom of the palette. Items can be dragged and dropped into the folders.

Library content can be edited using the Edit palette menu command. The Edit With command lets you open the current item for editing in a designated application.

Drawing content in Flash

Within the Flash toolbox, shown in Figure 23.4, you find several tools for creating content within Flash. Many of these are similar to the tools found in Illustrator. The drawing tools found in the Flash toolbar include the following:

NOTE Several of the Flash drawing tools have multiple keyboard shortcuts. One shortcut is from the original Flash product, and the new shortcut synchs the tools with the other CS apps. Note that the Rectangle tool shortcuts are not the same as the other CS4 apps.

FIGURE 23.4

The Toolbox includes many tools that are similar to other CS tools.

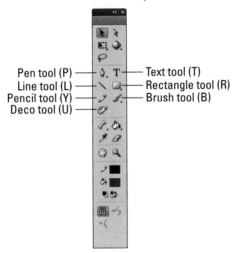

Pen tool (P)
Line tool (L)
Pencil tool (Y)
Deco tool (U)
Text tool (T)
Rectangle tool (R)
Brush tool (B)

■ **Pen tool:** This tool is used to draw smooth curves by placing control points and manipulating handles. Tools found under the flyout include the same options as found in Illustrator: the Add Anchor Point, Remove Anchor Point, and Convert Anchor Point tools. When a Pen object is selected, you can change its Stroke width, line style, color, fill, cap, join, and meter settings.

TIP A nifty preference setting in the Drawing panel of the Preferences dialog box called Show Path Preview shows the path as you move to the next point. This option is handy when you're starting to learn to control the Pen tool.

■ **Type tool:** This tool creates text. The properties for text include font, size, color, style, auto kerning, anti-aliasing, and hyperlinking.

■ **Line tool:** This tool draws straight lines and has similar properties to the Pen tool.

- **Rectangle tool:** Drag with this tool to create rectangular shapes. Flyouts under this tool include the Oval, Rectangle Primitive, Oval Primitive, and Polystar tools. The Rectangle Primitive object creates rectangles with rounded corners, and the Oval Primitive tool includes Start and End Angle values and an Inner Radius value for creating C-shaped objects. The Polystar tool creates polygons and star objects where you can specify the number of sides and/or points.

- **Pencil tool:** This tool allows freehand drawing on the stage using a consistent width pencil.

- **Brush tool:** This tool allows you to paint with a freehand brush. In the Toolbox are options to change the Brush shape, size, and mode. Available modes include Paint Normal, Paint Fills, Paint Behind, Paint Selection, and Paint Inside.

- **Deco tool:** This tool allows drawing effects including Vine Fill, shown in Figure 23.5, which fills the background with a connected set of vines; Grid Fill, which creates a defined grid of regularly spaced lines; and the Symmetry Brush, which draws duplicate objects simultaneously with the current path about an axis or radially.

FIGURE 23.5

Drawing with the Deco tool creates several unique patterns.

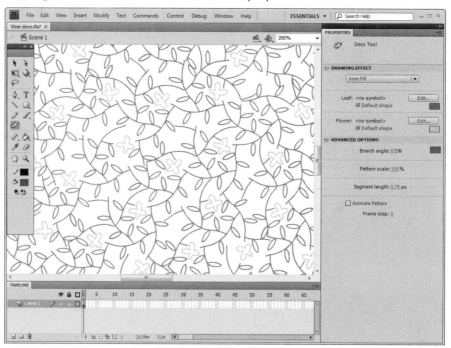

Working with shapes

Shapes drawn in Flash are unique when compared to Illustrator, Photoshop, and InDesign. One of the key differences is that when two objects on a layer are overlapped, path operations are performed immediately. For example, if you draw a simple closed circle and then overlap it with another circle, the two paths are immediately joined and the whole shape moves together, but Illustrator keeps these paths separate until you use the join command.

Another interesting difference is that when two strokes overlap, they cut the existing stroke, but when two strokes that are the same fill color intersect, the strokes are all joined together. So, if a red circle is intersected by a drawing vertical line, the red circle is cut into two halves. If the circle is intersected with another red line, then the red line joins the red circle and they all move as one object.

All Flash edges are fluid and can be bent by dragging the edge away from the shape. If you move the cursor over a shape edge, it switches to an arc shape, as shown in Figure 23.6. If you drag when this arc cursor is present, you can pull and bend the shape edge away from the other edge without moving the edge's corners.

FIGURE 23.6

Edges easily can be bent into an arc by dragging on them.

If you create some artwork that you don't want to be combined with other edges, you can do this in several ways. One way is to simply group the pieces you don't want combined. Grouped objects aren't joined to other paths. Another method is to place the artwork on another layer, or you can save the artwork as a symbol to keep it safe from combining and slicing with other strokes.

Working with Flash layers

Flash doesn't include a Layers palette, like the other CS apps. Instead, layers are listed in order in the Timeline palette, as shown in Figure 23.7. Top layers appear at the top of the Timeline palette, and objects on the top layers obscure any objects that are overlapped on layers underneath.

FIGURE 23.7

The Timeline palette lists all the file layers.

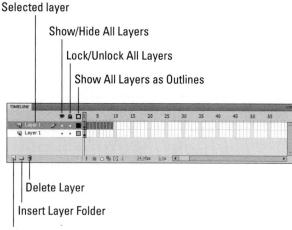

Selected layer

Show/Hide All Layers

Lock/Unlock All Layers

Show All Layers as Outlines

Delete Layer

Insert Layer Folder

Insert Layer

If you drag and drop the layers in the Timeline palette, you can reorder the layer order. When a layer is selected, all objects contained on that layer are highlighted. Any new objects that are created are automatically added to the current layer. The current layer is marked by a pencil icon to the right of the layer name.

You see three columns to the right of the layer name. The first column is used to hide/show layers. When layers are hidden, a red X icon appears in the row for the hidden layers. The second column is used to lock layers. Objects on locked layers cannot be selected or moved. The third column allows layer objects to be viewed as outlines. The third column also shows the layer color. Clicking this icon opens the Layer Properties dialog box, shown in Figure 23.8.

FIGURE 23.8

The Layer Properties dialog box lets you change the layer's name and color.

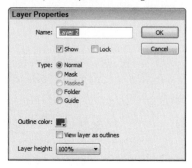

To create a new layer, click the Insert Layer icon at the bottom left of the Timeline palette. Layers can be grouped together in Layer Folders. To create a new layer folder, click the Insert Layer Folder icon.

Animating objects in Flash

Although drawing in Flash is accomplished with tools that are similar to the other CS applications, the animation features found in Flash are a distinguishing feature. Any object that may be selected can be animated using the Timeline palette found at the bottom of the interface.

Animating objects in Flash is accomplished by setting keyframes in the Timeline. These keyframes mark the position and properties of objects during different frames of the animation. After two or more keyframes are set, Flash computes all the intermediate positions and properties for the tweened object by interpolating between the two keyframes when a tween command is used. Keyframes are marked on the Timeline as small solid dots, as shown in Figure 23.9.

FIGURE 23.9

Keyframes are shown as small dots on the layer row.

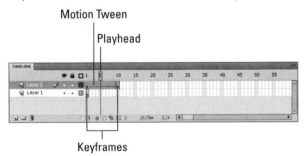

The available frames for the animation are numbered sequentially at the top of the Timeline palette. The current frame shown on the stage is indicated by the red rectangle called the Playhead. You can drag the Playhead back and forth to move through the frames, or you can manually control the playback using the controls found in the Controller panel.

Creating keyframes

When an object is in the correct position for the animation, a keyframe is created by selecting the object, dragging the Playhead to the right frame, and choosing the Insert ➪ Timeline ➪ Keyframe menu command, or by right-clicking in the Timeline and selecting Insert Keyframe from the pop-up menu. When a new keyframe is created, a solid circle appears in the Timeline for that frame.

Creating a motion tween

Keyframes aren't enough by themselves to create motion; they only mark the position and/or properties of an object for a given frame. To have Flash compute the intermediate steps between two keyframes, you need to drag over the range of frames between and including the two keyframes and select the Insert ➪ Timeline ➪ Create Motion Tween or select the same command from the right-click pop-up menu. This adds an arrow between the two keyframes and shades the frames light blue to indicate the tween is a motion tween.

The preceding paragraph describes the manual process for creating a motion tween, but a new method is now available that is much simpler. For this new process, you select the object that you want to animate, right-click, and select the Create Motion Tween option. This converts the art to a symbol and inserts a tween and a keyframe positioned one second from the current position. The playhead is then moved forward one second. The only remaining step for the user is to move the object to a new position. This creates a tween path that can be reformed. All in all, what used to be about five to ten precise steps are now just two easy steps.

 Because selecting keyframes can be tricky, it is easier to select the first keyframe and add the tween. The tween always is identified with the first keyframe.

Creating a shape tween

Another way to animate an object is to change its shape. You do this by altering the object's properties for two different keyframes. Then you select the frame range between the two keyframes and choose the Insert ➪ Timeline ➪ Create Shape Tween. Shape tweens also have an arrow, but are shaded light green instead of blue.

NOTE When a tween is broken because it is incomplete or has only one key, it is shown as a dashed line. Broken tweens can be fixed by creating a new end key. Light gray ranges indicate that the object has no tween and that it doesn't change over the marked range.

Enabling onion skinning

Onion skinning is a feature that displays an object's position and size in the frames before and after the current frame. The onion skinned object can be set to be displayed as an outline. This feature gives you a good idea of how the object is moving in the scene and helps as you try to synch an object's motion.

The settings for enabling and configuring onion skinning are found at the bottom of the Timeline palette, as shown in Figure 23.10. When enabled, two bracket markers appear around the Playhead. Dragging these markers out increases the number of frames that are onion skinned.

Changing the frame rate

The frame rate determines how long each frame is displayed before the next frame appears. Frame rate is the number of frames that are displayed per second. Common frame rates include 24 frames per second (fps) for film, 30 fps for television, and 12 fps for Web animations. The current frame rate setting is displayed at the bottom of the Timeline palette.

FIGURE 23.10

The onion skin controls are located at the bottom of the Timeline palette.

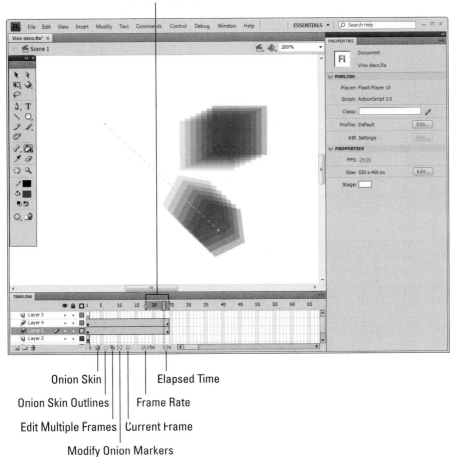

Onion Skin Markers

Onion Skin

Onion Skin Outlines

Edit Multiple Frames

Modify Onion Markers

Elapsed Time

Frame Rate

Current Frame

You can change the current frame rate using the Document Properties dialog box, shown in Figure 23.11. This dialog box is opened with the Modify ➪ Document menu. It also includes settings for entering the document title, a description, and the dimensions of the document. You also can set the background color and ruler units.

FIGURE 23.11

The Document Properties dialog box includes a frame rate setting.

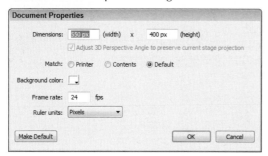

Creating an SWF file in Flash

After the animated sequence is completed, you can save the file using the File ⇨ Save As menu command, but this saves the file using the .FLA extension, which can be reopened only within Flash. To produce an SWF file that can be used on the Web, you need to use the File ⇨ Publish menu command. This command gives you the option to save the Flash file as an SWF file. You can have Flash create an HTML file that also references the SWF file.

To control the publishing process, the Publish Settings dialog box is accessible using the File ⇨ Publish Settings menu. The Publish Settings dialog box lets you specify the Formats that are supported, including SWF, HTML, GIF, JPEG, and QuickTime. The Flash panel of the Publish Settings dialog box, shown in Figure 23.12, lets you set which version of Flash Player to use. It also gives you the option to set a password on the Flash file.

STEPS: Creating a Flash Animation

1. **Open Flash, and load content.** With Flash open, choose File ⇨ Import to Stage to load the Aussie 2020 logo. Select and move the logo to the upper-left corner of the stage.

2. **Create a rectangle object.** Create a new layer in the Timeline panel, click the Rectangle tool, and drag in the stage to create a rectangle shape. Then move this rectangle to the lower-left corner of the stage. Change the fill color to blue.

FIGURE 23.12

The Publish Settings dialog box lets you set the publishing options.

Duplicate Profile

Create New Profile | Rename Profile

Import/Export Profile | Delete Profile

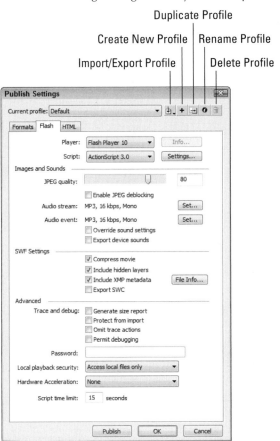

3. **Create some text.** Create another new layer in the Timeline panel, click the Text tool, and type **China Air**. Then, in the Properties palette, change the font to Tunga, the style to bold, the size to 25, and the color to red. Move the text to the top of the stage to the right, as shown in Figure 23.13.

FIGURE 23.13

The animation objects are in place and ready to be animated.

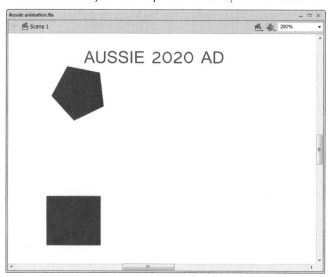

4. **Create motion tweens.** Select the rectangle shape, and choose the Create Motion Tween menu from the right-click menu. Then move the rectangle to the upper right. Then repeat this step for the other two elements.

5. **Enable onion skinning, and view the resulting animation.** Click the Onion Skin button at the bottom of the Timeline palette, and drag the Onion Marker at the top of the palette so all frames are included. Then drag the Playhead back and forth to check the resulting animation on the stage, as shown in Figure 23.14.

6. **Publish the resulting animation.** When the final animation looks fine, save the file as an .FLA file so you can work on it again in the future. Then select File ➪ Publish Settings to open the Publish Settings dialog box. In the Formats tab, enable the Flash and HTML check boxes. In the HTML tab, disable the Loop option, and click the Publish button. The files are saved to the hard drive where the HTML file can be loaded into a Web browser to see the resulting animation.

 An important final step is to test the movie by opening it in a Web browser.

FIGURE 23.14

FIGURE 23.14

Check the resulting animation.

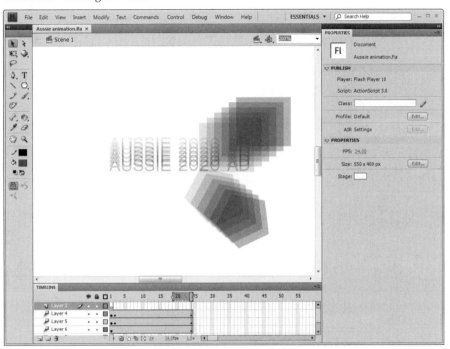

Exporting SWF Files from InDesign

The common approach to repurposing designs that are created for print and layouts is to use InDesign to export the documents for use in Dreamweaver. This is a valid workflow and is demonstrated in Chapter 27. However, designs often fall apart when converted to HTML because HTML lays out elements in a linear left-to-right, top-to-bottom flow. These issues can be addressed with CSS, but another alternative exists.

Designs also can be exported from InDesign to the Flash SWF format. Because Flash is vector-based and viewed in a Player within Web browsers, it doesn't have to follow the linear constraints imposed by HTML. The end result is a site that is closer to the original design. The drawback is that visitors need to have a Flash-enabled browser to view the design. This is a minimal problem because Flash-enabled browsers are common.

To export an InDesign document to the SWF file format, select the File⇨Export menu from within InDesign. Within the Export dialog box are options to export to various formats including SWF and XFL. The XFL format can be imported into Flash. The SWF format can be opened immediately in a Flash-enabled Web browser without being opened in Flash.

The Export SWF dialog box, shown in Figure 23.15, appears as you export the design. Using this dialog box, you can set the size of the exported document with a Scale value. You can set it to fit within a given set of dimensions, and you can set to export a specific set of pages. The Generate HTML File option creates a small HTML file that opens and displays the SWF file.

FIGURE 23.15

The Export SWF dialog box includes options for setting the scale of the exported document.

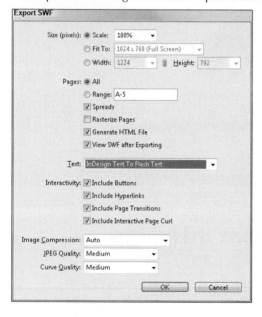

The Export SWF dialog box includes options for how to handle text. The options include converting the text to Flash text, converting the text to vector paths, and converting the text to raster images. All interactive elements created in InDesign; including buttons, hyperlinks, page transitions, and interactive page curl effects; can be exported. You also can set the image compression values.

Figure 23.16 shows the exported SWF file within a Web browser. The design is intact and much closer to the original design than its HTML equivalent.

FIGURE 23.16

Exported InDesign documents can be viewed in a Web browser.

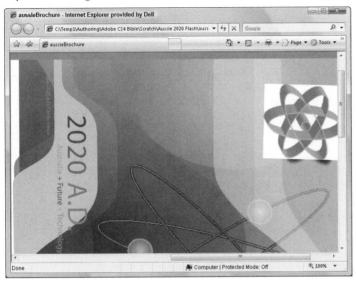

Creating SWF Files in Illustrator

Although you typically create SWF files using the Adobe Flash program, Flash isn't the only application that works with vector-based images. Adobe Illustrator also creates vector-based designs, so converting a native Illustrator graphic to the SWF format is a simple conversion. You can save any Illustrator graphic as an SWF file for use on the Web. You also can use Illustrator to create SWF animations by placing each frame of the animation in a separate layer.

Saving SWF files

You have two different paths for exporting Illustrator graphics to the SWF file format. You can choose File ➪ Export or File ➪ Save for Web from within Illustrator, or you can simply import or copy and paste the Illustrator files directly into Flash. The Save for Web dialog box lets you preview and change options before saving the file, but working directly in Flash gives you many more features for updating the SWF file.

 **Keep in mind that SWF files require that you install the Flash Player browser plug-in to view files on the Web.**

Exporting SWF files

Choose File ⇨ Export to open the Export dialog box. Within this dialog box, you can select Flash (SWF) as the Save as Type. Click Save, and the SWF Options dialog box appears, as shown in Figure 23.17. You have these options in this dialog box:

FIGURE 23.17

The SWF Options dialog box

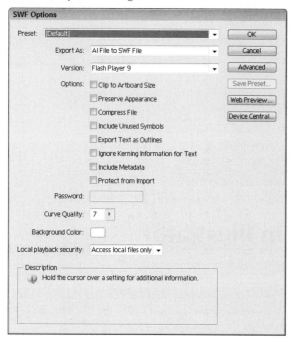

- **Export As:** You have four options—AI File to SWF File, AI Layers to SWF Frames, AI Layers to SWF Files, and AI Layers to SWF Symbols. You also can choose which version of Flash to export to. The AI File to SWF File option exports the Illustrator document to a single frame. The other two options convert the artwork contained on each layer to either an SWF frame or to a separate SWF file.

- **Clip to Artboard Size:** This option sets the size of the exported file to match the entire art board document.

- **Preserve Appearance:** This option flattens all objects before exporting.

- **Compress File:** This option compresses the exported file to reduce its size, making it quicker to download.

 **Flash Players prior to version 6 cannot load compressed files.**

- **Export Symbols in the Panel:** To keep all defined movie and graphic symbols as part of the file, enable this option.

- **Export Text as Outlines:** This option converts all text to object paths as part of the export. This helps maintain the look of the text in all browsers without relying on fonts.

- **Ignore Kerning Information for Text:** This option removes all kerning from text objects to keep them clean and to guarantee their appearance.

- **Include Metadata:** The metadata added in the File Info dialog box is included with the file.

- **Protect from Import:** This option prevents the SWF file from being downloaded and edited, thereby protecting your design. You also can specify a Password required to view the file.

- **Curve Quality:** This option sets the accuracy of the Bézier curves for the artwork. Lower Curve Quality values reduce the file size by decreasing the number of points as well as the curve's quality. Higher values maintain the curve quality but increase the overall file size.

 **Most standard curves are adequately maintained with a Curve Quality setting of 7.**

- **Background Color:** A color swatch lets you set the background color for the exported file.

If you click the Web Preview button, the file is loaded within the default Web browser or you can click the Device Central to view the file in a number of different mobile devices.

The Advanced button opens a panel of additional controls, as shown in Figure 23.18, for defining the quality settings of the exported file include the following:

- **Image Format:** This option can be set to Lossless, which keeps all the image data, resulting in large file sizes, or Lossy, which compresses the images using a JPEG format that throws away image data depending on the JPEG Quality setting. If you select Lossy, you can specify the amount quality as Low, Medium, High, or Maximum (or using a numeric value from 1 to 10). The Low setting results in the smallest file sizes at the expense of image quality, and the High setting yields a large file size but maintains the image quality.

- **JPEG Quality:** If the Lossy (JPEG) option is selected, you can alter the quality settings. Lower-quality images result in smaller file sizes.

- **Method:** You also can select to use the Baseline (Standard) or Baseline Optimized compression method. The Baseline Optimized method provides an additional level of compression. When the Export As setting is set to AI File to SWF File, you can choose between the Preserve Appearance and the Preserve Editability Where Possible options. The Preserve Appearance option flattens all layers to a single layer. The Preserve Editability Where Possible option maintains all layers during exporting.

- **Resolution:** This option lets you specify the resolution value for the SWF artwork. For SWF files that are viewed online, a setting of 72 ppi is sufficient, but if you plan to print your artwork, select a higher ppi setting. Higher resolution settings result in larger file sizes.

FIGURE 23.18

The Advanced panel of the SWF Options dialog box offers more settings.

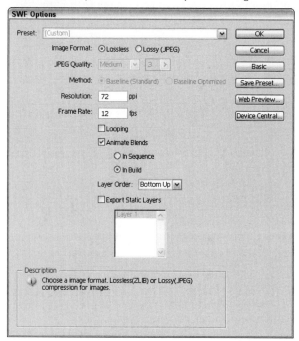

The Animation controls become available when the Export As option is set to All Layers to SWF Frames. The animation controls include the following:

- **Frame Rate:** This setting is the rate at which the animation frames play. Most animations on the Web are fine at 12 frames per second (fps), but if your animation includes lots of fast-changing details, you may want to increase this value to 24 fps.

- **Looping:** This setting lets the animation play continuously. If disabled, the animation plays through only once.

- **Animate Blends:** This setting allows blended objects to be animated using two different options. The In Sequence option places each object of the blend on a separate frame. The In Build option keeps the existing objects and adds a new blend to each frame, so that the final frame includes all objects that make up the blend.

- **Layer Order:** This setting sets the order in which the layers are drawn when the SWF is rendered. The options include Bottom Up and Top Down. The Bottom Up option displays the background before the higher layer content. This makes it easy to reverse an animation.

 Setting the Layer Order is critical for Flash exported SWFs because it is common to place an ActionScript either at the top or bottom of the SWF and you want this to load before anything else.

■ **Export Static Layers:** Selecting this option lets you choose a single layer or several layers to export, along with every layer that is used as a background. It also is used to control which layers are not exported with an animation of blends.

Using the Save for Web window

Another way to save Illustrator artwork using the SWF format is with the Save for Web window. Open this interface by choosing File ⇨ Save for Web & Devices (Alt+Shift+Ctrl+S in Windows; Option+Shift+⌘+S). The Save for Web window displays a preview of the artwork to be exported, as shown in Figure 23.19.

TIP The preview pane in the Save for Web window is convenient for viewing the changes to the artwork as a result of lowering the Curve Quality setting.

FIGURE 23.19

You can save Illustrator artwork to the SWF format using the Save for Web window.

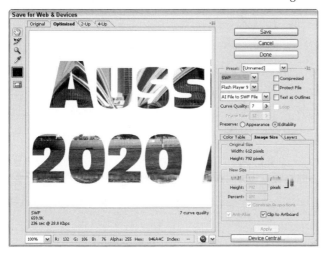

To save the artwork to the SWF format, you must select SWF from the format drop-down list located to the right. All the settings for this format type appear, including many of the same settings mentioned for the File ⇨ Export process.

NOTE When using the Save for Web window, all image files (including the SWF file) are exported to a separate images folder when you select to save both the HTML and Image files.

With the SWF format selected, the drop-down list under the Format list includes only options to save the AI file to an SWF file or to save the AI layers to SWF frames. In the Save for Web window, you cannot choose to save each layer as a different SWF file. The window also doesn't include options for setting how you save raster images, nor does it include an option to generate HTML. However, when the file dialog box appears, you can save the images only, the HTML only, or both. The Clip to Artboard option is found within the Image Size panel.

NOTE Although the Save for Web window doesn't include any options for setting how raster images are saved, any raster images included within the artwork are saved using the last used settings specified in the Export SWF Options dialog box.

The Save for Web window does offer an option to export the layers as CSS Layers. The Export As CSS Layers option is found in the Layers panel, as shown in Figure 23.20. After the Export As CSS Layers options is enabled, you can select each layer and set it as Visible, Hidden, or Do Not Export. Layers set to Visible or Hidden are included within the HTML file where JavaScript controls which layers are visible and which are hidden.

FIGURE 23.20

The Layers panel in the Save for Web window

Illustrator and SWF differences

Several objects behave differently between Illustrator and Flash, which could affect the file when it's exported:

- **Gradients and meshes:** Gradients and mesh objects that use eight stops or more convert to a raster image during export. Gradients with less than eight stops export as gradients. To keep file sizes low, only use gradients with fewer than eight stops for artwork exported to the SWF format.

- **Patterns:** All patterns are rasterized and tiled when exported to the SWF format.

- **Text and strokes:** Text and strokes that are filled with a pattern are converted to paths and then filled with a rasterized pattern during export.

■ **Text kerning, leading, and tracking:** These are not supported in exported SWF files. Instead, the text is exported as a separate text object positioned to simulate the kerning, leading, and tracking. To maintain text as a single object, enable the Convert Text to Outlines option during exporting.

Creating SWF animations with layers

You can create simple animations in Illustrator using layers. By placing each frame of an animation on a separate layer, you can then cycle through the layers to create an animated sequence. The Layers palette includes a feature that automatically creates a layer for each object in the current file and places each object in its own layer.

Before using this feature, you must create and position each object that appears in the animation. If the animation features a single moving object, you must duplicate that object for each frame of the animation. Here's an easy way to do this: Create the object, choose Edit ➪ Copy (⌘/Ctrl+C), and then choose Edit ➪ Paste in Front (⌘/Ctrl+F). After pasting a copy of the object, move it to its correct position.

> **TIP** You also can duplicate the selected object by pressing and holding Option/Alt while dragging the object to a new location. Another easy way to create multiple copies along a path is to use Illustrator's Blend feature.

After you copy and position all the objects, you can select the Release to Layers (Sequence) palette menu command from the Layers palette, as shown in Figure 23.21. This command creates a new layer for each object, placing each in its own layer.

FIGURE 23.21

Each frame of the animation is placed on a separate layer.

You may now export the file to the SWF format by choosing File ➪ Export. If you select the AI Layers to SWF Frames option in the Adobe Flash (SWF) Format Options dialog box, the animation sequence exports to the SWF file.

The Layers palette also includes a Release to Layers (Build) menu command. This command is similar in that it also creates a new layer for each object, but each new object is cumulatively added to the existing objects. For example, if the original layer includes five objects, the first layer includes a single object, the second layer two objects, and the fifth layer all objects.

Using symbols

If a simple animation sequence requires a separate object for every frame of an animation, file sizes could potentially grow progressively larger as an animation sequence gets longer. However, a solution that keeps file sizes small is to use symbols.

When you use a symbol in an SWF file, the symbol is included only once and simply referenced every other time it is used within the file. So a simple animation that includes a symbol moving across the screen would require that you duplicate the symbol multiple times and place a copy of the symbol on a separate layer for each frame of the animation, but the SWF file would include the symbol only once.

You can either use a symbol from Illustrator's Symbols palette or create your own symbol:

■ **Using the Symbols palette:** Illustrator includes many symbols in the Symbols palette, shown in Figure 23.22. You can access additional symbols using the symbol libraries, which you open by choosing Window ⟿ Symbol Libraries. To use a symbol contained in the Symbols palette or in a symbol library, simply drag it onto the art board.

FIGURE 23.22

The Symbols palette holds all the symbols you need in Illustrator.

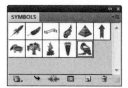

■ **Creating your symbols:** Draw and select the artwork that you want to use as a symbol, and then select the New Symbol panel menu command (F8) or drag the artwork to the Symbols palette. If you double-click a symbol in the Symbols palette, a dialog box appears where you can rename the symbol.

NEW FEATURE Illustrator CS4 has borrowed a keyboard shortcut from Flash. The F8 key is used to create a symbol.

STEPS: Creating a Simple Animation Sequence and Exporting It as an SWF File

1. **Open a new file in Illustrator.** Within Illustrator, choose File ⇨ New to create a new document.

2. **Add a symbol to the document.** Choose Window ⇨ Symbol Library ⇨ 3D Symbols to open a symbol library of 3D objects. Drag a 3D atomic symbol to the art board. The symbol displays, as shown in Figure 23.23.

FIGURE 23.23

Adding symbols to a document

3. **Duplicate and position the symbol.** Hold down the Option/Alt key, and drag the atomic symbol to the right. Repeat this action four times until several atomic symbols surround the original, as shown in Figure 23.24.

FIGURE 23.24

Creating duplicate copies of the object

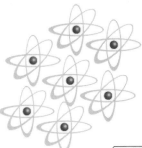

4. **Release objects to layers.** Choose Window➪Layers to open the Layers palette. Then choose the Release to Layers (Sequence) palette menu command. This creates five new sublayers under Layer 1, as shown in Figure 23.25. Each sublayer includes a single symbol object.

FIGURE 23.25

New sublayers are created for each separate layer object.

5. **Export to SWF.** Choose File➪Export. This opens a file dialog box. In the Save as Type drop-down list, select Adobe Flash (*.SWF). Then type a name in the File Name field, and click Save.

6. **Set export options.** Clicking Save opens the Adobe Flash (SWF) Format Options dialog box, shown in Figure 23.26. Within this dialog box, set the Export As option to AI Layers to SWF File. This makes each layer a separate SWF frame. Also enable the Protect from Import option. Then open the Advanced panel, and enable the Clip to Artboard Size and Looping options. Finally, set the Image Format to Lossless with a Resolution of 72 ppi. Then click OK.

7. **View the animated SWF file.** Locate the saved `Atomic Symbol animation.html` file in the Finder (Mac) or in Explorer (Windows), and double-click it. This launches the default Web browser for your system and displays the animated SWF file.

NOTE To import the SWF file in an Acrobat PDF document, use the Movie tool and double-click in the Document pane. The Add Movie dialog box opens. Click the Choose button in the Add Movie dialog box, and locate the SWF file. Click the filename, and click Select. The SWF document is added as a movie clip.

FIGURE 23.26

Selecting the AI Layers to SWF File option

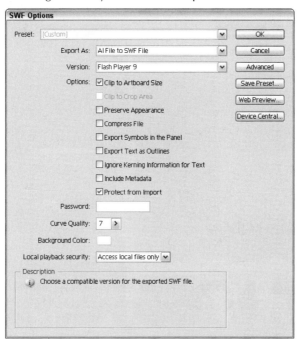

Using SWF Files in Dreamweaver

After you create an SWF file, you can use it to enhance a Web page in Dreamweaver. You add SWF files to a Web page as objects by dragging them from the Layout tab of the Insert toolbar or by using the Insert ⇨ Media ⇨ Flash menu command.

Adding SWF objects to a Web page in Dreamweaver

After you have an SWF file saved on your hard drive, you can add it to a Dreamweaver Web page by dragging the respective SWF object icon from the Insert panel and dropping it on a Web page at the position where you want the SWF file to appear. You also can insert SWF files using the Insert ⇨ Media ⇨ Flash menu command.

Dropping an SWF object onto a Web page displays an object icon. These object icons are place-holders for the file, and you can resize them by dragging their borders. The properties for the selected object also display in the Properties palette. Figure 23.27 shows a blank Web page with an SWF object dropped onto it.

FIGURE 23.27

The SWF object appears as an icon on the Web page.

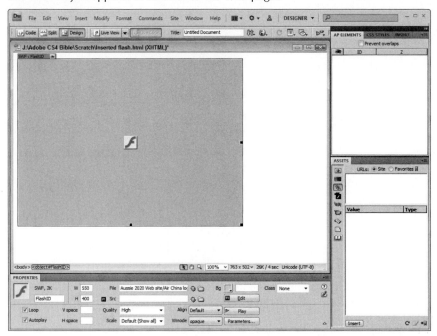

After you select the command to load a Flash object, a file dialog box appears where you can specify the object. The filename then appears in the Properties palette, and the file loads into the Web page within the Design view. The size of the loaded SWF file is set automatically when the object is loaded.

When the SWF object is selected in the Web page, the Properties palette includes several unique settings:

■ **Edit:** The Edit button opens the designated file within Flash where it can be modified as needed.

NOTE When you click the Edit button, you must navigate to the original .FLA file to edit the file in Flash. After this file is located, you can get roundtrip editing, but you need to use the Done Editing button in Flash to generate a replacement SWF when you're finished.

■ **Loop:** This causes the animation sequence to repeat after it's finished.

■ **Autoplay:** This causes any animation associated with the SWF file to begin as soon as the Web page is loaded in a browser.

■ **Quality:** You can set this to High, Auto High, Auto Low, and Low. These settings correspond to the appearance of the animation versus the playback speed. The Low setting sacrifices the quality of the animation frames in order to play back the animation at the target frame rate. The Auto High and Auto Low settings work to maintain image appearance and playback speed, respectively, while improving the other when it can.

- **Scale:** This setting determines how to handle the display of SWF files where the size specified on the Web page is different from the size of the actual SWF file. The Default setting maintains the aspect ratio of the original file within the designated Web page area. This causes borders to appear on two sides of the SWF object. The No Border option also maintains the aspect ratio of the SWF file but crops the file so no borders appear. The Exact Fit option stretches the SWF file to fit within the given area. This may distort the SWF file.

- **Play:** This button plays the animated file. It changes to a Stop button when enabled.

- **Parameters:** This option opens a dialog box where the defined parameters for the Flash file are displayed.

STEPS: Adding an SWF File to a Web Page

1. **Open a Web page in Dreamweaver.** Within Dreamweaver, choose File ⇨ Open to open a Web page where you want to add the SWF file, or locate and double-click the Web page.

2. **Insert the SWF objects to the Web page.** With the Web page open, select the Insert ⇨ Media ⇨ Flash menu command. In the file dialog box that appears, locate and load the Flash SWF file. The object appears as an icon, as shown in Figure 23.28.

FIGURE 23.28

Objects initially dragged from the Toolbox display as icons.

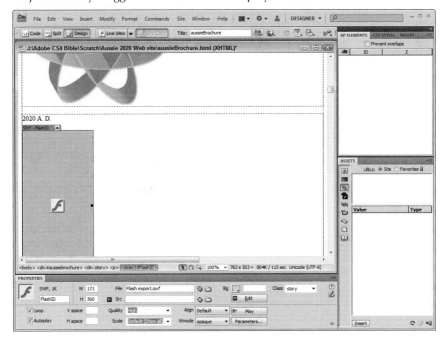

3. **Preview the SWF file.** With the Flash object selected, click the Play button in the Properties panel to preview the animation. Figure 23.29 shows the Web page with the file loaded.

4. **Set the SWF properties.** With the SWF object selected, enable the Autoplay and Loop options and set the Quality setting to Auto Low. This ensures that the playback speed stays constant.

FIGURE 23.29

Selected SWF files load into the Web page.

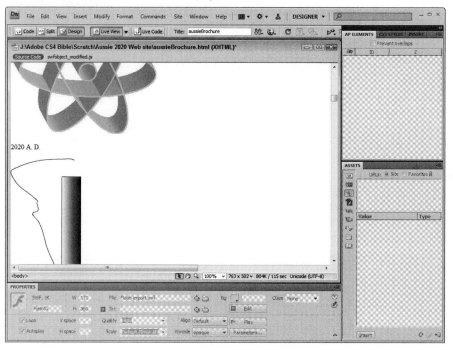

Using SWF Files in Acrobat

Acrobat offers you two interesting ways to import SWF files in PDF documents. One method is to convert animated Web pages containing SWF files to PDF documents. The other use for SWF with PDFs is to import the motion graphics directly in a PDF file as a movie-file import. Depending on your source files and the content you want to create in Acrobat, you'll find benefits using both of these methods.

Converting Web pages to PDF

You can convert Web pages to PDF using the File➪Create PDF➪From Web Page menu command in Acrobat on either the Mac or Windows. Windows users have an extra benefit when using Microsoft Internet Explorer, because a task button appears in the Explorer window that enables you to convert Web pages in view to PDF. When you create PDF documents from Web pages, all the page content is converted and the page is viewed in Acrobat viewers much like you see when the page is viewed in a Web browser, including Flash animations.

Acrobat 6 and greater viewers support two different media compatibilities. You can import a variety of media files using either the Acrobat 5 compatibility or Acrobat 6 compatibility. A few differences between the two compatibility levels are that you can embed Acrobat 6–compatible media in the PDF document and more media formats are supported. When you convert Web pages or import SWF files, the files are imported as Acrobat 6–compatible media and either embedded or linked to a PDF file. You have no option for importing SWF files as Acrobat 5–compatible media.

To convert a Web page to a PDF document, choose File➪Create PDF➪From Web Page (Shift+Ctrl+O in Windows; Shift+⌘+O on the Mac). This opens the Create PDF from Web Page dialog box, shown in Figure 23.30. Note that Windows users can use the PDF Maker task button installed in Microsoft Internet Explorer. By default, this task button is installed in Explorer at the time of your CS Premium or Acrobat 8 installation.

FIGURE 23.30

The Create PDF from Web Page dialog box

The Create PDF from Web Page dialog box has the following options:

- **URL:** To select a Web site, type the URL in the URL field box or click the Browse button to select a Web site stored locally on your hard drive or network server.

- **Settings section:** You have the following options:

    - **Get only/Get entire site:** You can select linked pages according to the number of levels contained on a Web site, or you can convert the entire site to PDF. Note that if you convert more than one level or use the Get Entire Site option, you can convert an extraordinary number of pages. When converting Web sites you aren't familiar with, be certain to gradually convert pages rather than the entire site to avoid creating PDFs of extraordinary size.

■ **Stay on same path/Stay on same server:** These options prevent linked Web pages from other sites and servers being converted to PDF, thereby keeping your resultant PDF smaller in size with less clutter. Obviously, if you need linked pages to be converted to PDF, you'll want to reach out to other servers and levels. You can always return to the PDF file and append more pages if needed.

Any SWF files included in the converted Web pages are added to the final PDF document. You can embed the SWF files in the PDF document or link the files to the PDF. Either way, you can select, copy, and paste them between PDF files.

NOTE You can embed or link multimedia files, including SWF, to a PDF file. By default, the media is embedded in the PDF during HTML-to-PDF conversion. If you want to link the files, click Settings in the Create PDF from Web Page dialog box. In the Web Capture dialog box, scroll the list and select HTML. Click the Settings button, and the HTML Conversion Settings dialog box opens. From the Multimedia pull-down menu, select Reference Multimedia Content by URL. The file is then linked to the PDF.

If you want to convert a Web site containing an animated page using an SWF file, convert the file and use either the Movie tool or the Select Object tool in Acrobat to select the movie frame. Copy the file by choosing Edit ➪ Copy and paste the file into another PDF document. These steps might be helpful when working in a workflow where you want to use animated graphics from your client's Web site and don't have immediate access to the Web site source files or a password to retrieve files from the client's Web site. In such a case, simply convert Web pages to PDF and copy and paste the movie frames as needed.

NOTE SWF files can be viewed in PDF documents, but SVG files are not supported in Acrobat. As of this writing, you cannot convert SVG files to PDF nor import them in existing PDFs.

Importing SWF files in PDF documents

You use the Movie tool to import SWF files into Acrobat PDFs. If you convert Web pages to PDF, you need to copy and paste SWF files using the Video tool or the Select Object tool to select the movie frame and copy the file. However, you cannot export the frame back to an SWF file for use in HTML documents or for viewing in standalone SWF viewers. If you create an SWF file in either Flash or Illustrator, you can import the SWF file directly into a PDF document.

To import an SWF file, click the Movie tool in the Advanced Editing toolbar. You can either drag open a rectangle frame or double-click the Video tool in the Document pane. Either action opens the Add Video dialog box. In the Add Video dialog box, click the Browse button and locate a SWF file to add to the document. Then click OK, and the SWF appears in the PDF.

 **InDesign also supports SWF placement within its documents.**

You have the following options in this dialog box:

- **Adobe Compatibility options:** The first two items let you choose either Acrobat 5 or Acrobat 6 compatibility. If you select Acrobat 5 (and Earlier) Compatible Media, Acrobat won't recognize the SWF files on your computer as you try to import them into the open PDF document. You need to select Acrobat 6 (and Later) Compatible Media and click the Choose/Browse button to open the Select Movie File dialog box where movie files are identified for importing. You select the file and click the Select button; the file is imported into the PDF document. After importing the movie file (including SWF files), you're returned to the Add Movie dialog box.

- **Snap to content proportions:** This keeps the movie frame proportional as you size it, thereby preventing distortion when playing the movie.

- **Embed content in document:** This offers an option to either embed the content (when the check box is enabled) or create a link to the file (when the check box is disabled). If you uncheck this box, the movie file needs to travel along with the PDF document as you send the file to other users.

- **Poster Settings:** These settings have to do with the visual contained within the movie frame known as the movie poster. You can choose to use no poster, create a poster from the first frame in the movie, or create a poster from a file. When creating posters from files, you click the Choose/Browse button to navigate your hard drive to locate the image you want to use as the poster. Any file compatible with Create PDF from File can be used as a poster image. Select the file you want to use, and it's converted to PDF and placed as the contents for the movie frame. As the movie plays, the poster disappears; it returns after the movie stops playing.

After using the Movie tool and importing an SWF file or other type of movie file, you can adjust various properties for the movie and the playback in Acrobat. To open the Properties dialog box, select either the Movie tool or the Select Object tool and open a context menu on the movie frame, or double-click with either tool on the movie. Select Properties from the menu options, and the Multimedia Properties dialog box opens, as shown in Figure 23.31.

The default pane that appears when opening the Multimedia Properties dialog box is the Settings pane. To edit various options for the movie play, click the Edit Rendition button. The Rendition Settings dialog box, shown in Figure 23.32, opens. In this dialog box, you have a considerable number of choices to describe attributes for playing media files.

FIGURE 23.31

The Multimedia Properties dialog box

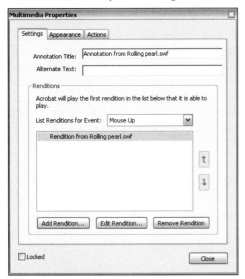

FIGURE 23.32

The Rendition Settings dialog box

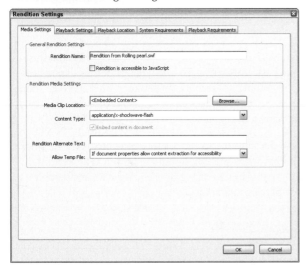

Of particular importance to many users are the settings found in the Playback Settings pane. Click Playback Settings at the top of the Rendition Settings dialog box, and the pane shown in Figure 23.33 opens.

FIGURE 23.33

The Playback Settings pane

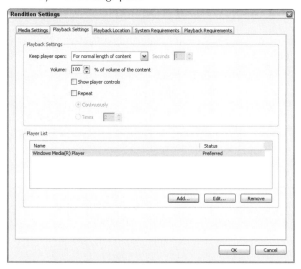

If you want to show player controls where a media clip can be stopped, paused, restarted, and so on, check the box for Show player controls. After exiting the Renditions Settings dialog box, you'll see a player control appear at the bottom of the movie frame.

The rendition settings offer you much more than controlling the media play with player controls. You can create several renditions in the same PDF document and identify what rendition is played according to download speeds for different users. For example, users who have modem connections at 28.8 baud can receive and view a small media file, while users with DSL and cable-modem connections can view media clips of larger sizes. You can create renditions that play according to user download speeds, where Acrobat analyzes a user's connection and delivers the media defined for the respective speed. Other options in the rendition settings offer choices for where media is played within the document, embedding or linking options, associating JavaScripts with media plays, timing movie plays for a given length of time, foreign-language selections, showing subtitles, and much more.

CROSS-REF For a detailed review of multimedia and PDF files, refer to the *Adobe Acrobat 9 PDF Bible* (published by Wiley).

Keep in mind that the SWF files you create in Illustrator are ultimately media clips. They're handled in Acrobat and assigned properties, as any movie file would be.

Summary

- Flash is the primary tool for creating SWF files.

- Flash includes some powerful drawing and animation tools.

- You can use Illustrator to export graphics to SWF files or copy and paste artwork directly from Illustrator and Photoshop into Flash.

- You create SWF animation sequences in Illustrator by placing the objects for each frame on a separate layer. These layers convert to frames during export.

- You can separate several objects included on a single layer in layers using the Layers palette's Release to Layers command.

- You place SWF objects within Web pages using Dreamweaver.

- You convert Web pages containing SWF files into PDF documents using Acrobat's File ➪ Create PDF ➪ From Web Page menu command.

- You import SWF files into PDF documents using the Movie tool. As movie clips, you can assign SWF files a number of different play options and rendition settings.

Chapter 24

Designing Layouts

Imagine the process of creating a sidewalk. The first step is to create the forms that define the edges of the sidewalk. If you create these before you mix the cement, the cement easily flows into the right location and the job is completed rather quickly. However, if the forms are not straight or secure, the cement flows outside the bounds and finished work won't be smooth and straight. Similarly, if you complete the layout design beforehand, the text and images flow easily into the document in the correct positions.

This chapter covers the basics of creating a useful layout in InDesign. The initial settings for a layout document are set when you create a new document. You can use the Pages palette to add and delete pages, rearrange pages, and create spreads and Master pages. Master pages provide a convenient way to update similar content on many pages at once. Several other useful layout objects include rulers, grids, guides, and frames. Using these objects, you can quickly lay out all the objects that are included in a page before the content is ready. The content can then be easily placed within these frames when it's ready.

Establishing an InDesign Layout

You establish layouts in InDesign when you create a new document. The New Document dialog box that opens when you create a new document. It includes settings for defining the number of pages, the page size, the orientation, the margins and columns, and the bleed and slug areas. You can save these settings and reuse them to create other new documents.

Creating new documents

You initially specify basic layout design in InDesign when you first create a new document. Choose File ⇨ New ⇨ Document (⌘/Ctrl+N), and the New Document dialog box opens, shown in Figure 24.1. The settings specified in this dialog box determine the initial document layout.

FIGURE 24.1

The New Document dialog box includes settings for initial layout.

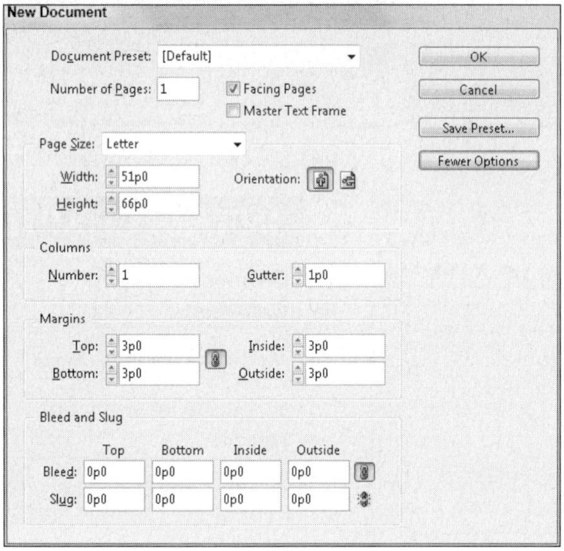

Pages versus Spreads

The seemingly simple Facing Pages option in the New Document dialog box defines the differences between pages and spreads. If the Facing Pages option is disabled, each page is separate from the others and displays on its own art board. If you enable the Facing Pages option, then adjacent pages are combined together to create a spread.

To understand a spread, open a book or a magazine and notice how two pages are viewed at once with one page on each side. Together these pages make up a spread. Spreads in InDesign are displayed together on a single art board.

When you create a spread, you always place odd-numbered pages on the right (the *recto*) and even-numbered pages on the left (the *verso*). The first page (numbered page 1 by default) appears by itself. Each successive even-and-odd-page pair is a spread.

Using the New Document dialog box, you can specify the total number of pages that make up the layout. The Facing Pages option causes left and right pages to face one another. If this option is disabled, each page stands alone. The Master Text Frame option causes a text frame to be added to the Master.

The following options on the New Document dialog box control the page layout of your new document:

- **Page Size options:** The Page Size drop-down list includes several common paper-size options including Letter, Legal, Tabloid, Letter – Half, Legal – Half, A4, A3, A5, B5, Compact Disc, and Custom. Selecting any of these sizes automatically adjusts the Width and Height settings. The Custom option lets you manually set the Width and Height values.

TIP You can add your own options to the Page Size menu by editing the `New Doc Sizes.txt` file located in `InDesign's Presets` folder. Just follow the same format used by the other entries in this text file.

The Orientation icon buttons include Portrait and Landscape options. A Portrait orientation has a height greater than its width, and a Landscape orientation has a larger width than height. Clicking the unselected icon button swaps the Width and Height values. Figure 24.2 shows two new Letter-sized documents. The right one has a Portrait orientation, and the left one has a Landscape orientation.

NOTE Within the New Document dialog box, you can enter "8i" to specify 8 inches regardless of the unit of measurement that you're using.

FIGURE 24.2

You orient new documents with a Portrait (right) or a Landscape setting (left).

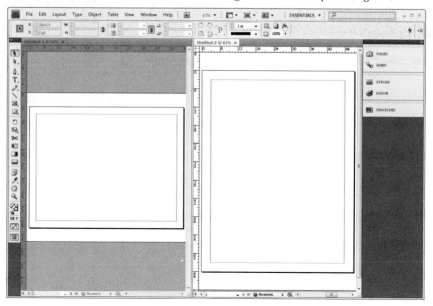

■ **Column options:** The Columns section of the New Document dialog box lets you specify the number of layout columns used in the default master page. The gutter is the space between each column. Figure 24.3 shows two new layouts. The left layout has two columns, and the right layout has three columns.

Columns split the page into several different areas.

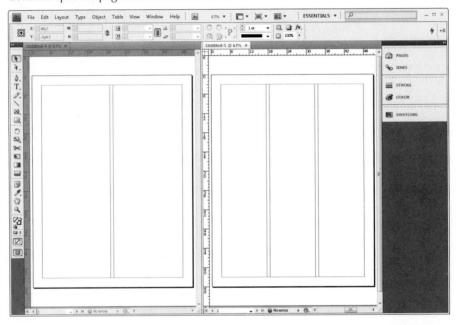

■ **Margins options:** *Margins* are the space between the edge of the paper and the page content. Guides, which appear where you specify margins, denote this space. You have four margin values correlating to each edge of the page—Top, Bottom, Left, and Right. If you select the Facing Pages option, the Left and Right margins become the Inside and Outside margins. Between the margin values is an icon button with an image of a link on it. Clicking this button sets all settings to equal values.

■ **Bleed and Slug:** Clicking More Options expands the dialog box to reveal Bleed and Slug settings. The Bleed and Slug areas of a page extend beyond the edges of the page. They contain information and guides to help the printer. The *Bleed* includes guides on how far to extend a color or image beyond the edge of the page in order to ensure that the color or image runs all the way to the paper edge after trimming. The *Slug* area displays printer instructions and other information that isn't intended to be part of the printed page. Bleed and Slug values include settings for each margin and an icon button to make all values equal.

When you create a new page, several guides denote the various page-layout settings. These guides are color-coordinated, with the margins represented by pink-colored guides, the columns and gutters represented by purple guides, the Bleed areas represented by red guides, and the Slug area represented by light-blue guides. The page edges are displayed as black guides. Figure 24.4 shows the various guides.

FIGURE 24.4

The layout of each new document is denoted with color-coded guides.

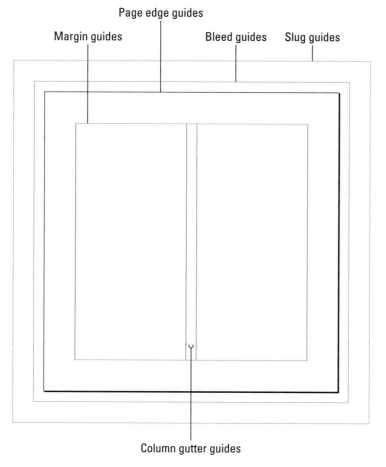

Creating a document preset

If you find yourself changing the default layout options every time you create a new document, you may benefit from a document preset. When you make the setting changes, click Save Preset and a simple dialog box appears where you can name the new preset.

After it's saved, the new preset is available for selection from the Document Preset list at the top of the dialog box. Selecting the preset name changes all the settings automatically. Saved presets also are available by choosing File ⇨ Document Presets.

> **TIP** Holding down the Shift key while selecting a preset from the File ⇨ Document Presets menu command creates a new document without opening the New Document dialog box.

Choosing File ⇨ Document Presets ⇨ Define opens the Document Presets dialog box, shown in Figure 24.5, where you can manage all the various presets. Selecting a preset from the list of presets displays all the settings associated with this preset in the lower text pane. Clicking Edit opens the settings within a dialog box that is identical to the New Document dialog box, where you can edit the settings. The New button lets you create a new document preset, and the Delete button deletes the selected preset.

FIGURE 24.5

You can create and manage document presets here.

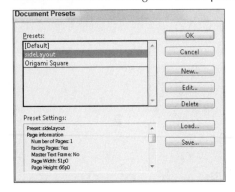

You can save and load document presets from the hard drive. These presets are saved using the DCST extension. These presets can be shared among team members to insure a consistent layout among several different design teams in an organization.

Changing the Default Layout Settings

When you first create a new document, the default layout settings are used. You can alter these default settings by changing the settings in the Document Setup dialog box (choose File ⇨ Document Setup) and/or the Margins and Columns dialog box (choose Layout ⇨ Margins and Columns) when you have no documents open.

If you don't have any other documents opened when you make changes to these dialog boxes, and you create a new document, the default layout updates.

Changing document settings

If you discover that you need to change one of the layout settings for the entire document, you can revisit most of the same settings in the New Document dialog box by opening the Document Setup dialog box. Choosing File ⇨ Document Setup (Alt+Ctrl+P on Windows; Option+⌘+P on the Mac) opens, shown in Figure 24.6, which includes settings for the Number of Pages, Page Size and Orientation, and Bleed and Slug.

FIGURE 24.6

The Document Setup dialog box resets most of the New Document dialog box options.

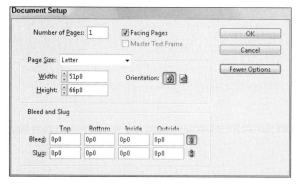

You use the Margins and Columns dialog box to change the margins and columns settings, shown in Figure 24.7. You open this dialog box by choosing Layout ⇨ Margins and Columns. However, any changes entered into this dialog box affect only the current page or spread, but you also can use it on a master page.

FIGURE 24.7

The Margins and Columns dialog box changes only the current page or spread.

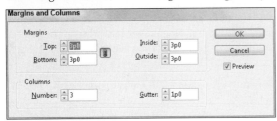

To change the margin and column settings for all pages in the document, select all pages in the Pages palette before opening the Margins and Columns dialog box. An easier method is to make the change on the master page.

Exporting InDesign CS4 documents to earlier versions

Layouts created with CS4 can be exported using the InDesign Interchange (INX) format and opened within CS3, but you'll need to download the latest updater from the Adobe Web site at www.adobe.com. This backward compatibility enables you to work with people who haven't upgraded to the latest software version. To export a document, choose File ➪ Export and select the InDesign Interchange option in the Save as Type field. Some new CS4 features included in an exported file may not be visible when the file is opened in the earlier versions.

Converting Quark and PageMaker files

If you have some existing layouts created in either Quark or PageMaker, you'll be happy to know that these layouts can be opened and converted to InDesign files. Choose File ➪ Open, and InDesign can open files created in PageMaker 6.0, 6.5, and 7.0, and QuarkXPress 3.3 to 4.1.

 Files created using QuarkXPress 5.0 and 6.0 can be opened in InDesign by first saving them using the QuarkXPress 4.0 format and then opening them in InDesign.

When a Quark or PageMaker file is opened in InDesign, the layout elements are converted to native InDesign elements. Note that although most elements are comparable between the different systems, there are some differences that may cause problems. For example, the color profiles in Quark aren't used in InDesign and are ignored during the conversion. It is also common for kerning, tracking, and line ends to change.

Working with Pages and Spreads

After establishing a layout, you use the Pages palette to work with the different pages and/or spreads. Using this palette, you can select, target, rearrange, delete, or add pages and/or spreads. The Pages palette also provides access to Master pages.

Using the Pages palette

The Pages palette, shown in Figure 24.8, provides a high-level view of all the pages in the current document. It displays each page and spread as an icon. You use it to quickly select, add, and delete pages as well as to apply a Master document to specific pages. You can open the Pages palette by choosing Window ➪ Pages (or by pressing F12).

FIGURE 24.8

The Pages palette shows icons for all pages, spreads, and Masters in the current document.

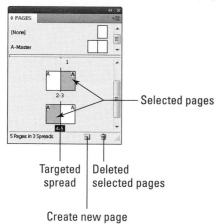

Selected pages

Targeted spread | Deleted selected pages

Create new page

You can change the size and position of icons in the Pages palette using the Palette Options palette menu command. This dialog box, shown in Figure 24.9, lets you set an icon size for Pages and Masters to be Small, Medium, Large, or Extra Large. You also can select to display the icons Vertically or Horizontally and enable or disable the thumbnails. If the Show Thumbnails option is selected, then a small representation of the current page is displayed. The final option lets you place the Pages or the Masters at the top of the palette.

There are also some settings for controlling how the page icons are displayed including whether to show if there's transparency on the spread, if the spread view is rotated, and whether there are page transitions set for exporting to PDF and/or SWF.

FIGURE 24.9

The Palette Options dialog box changes the icon size and placement within the Pages palette.

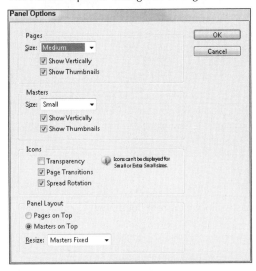

Selecting and targeting pages and spreads

You can easily select and target pages and spreads by using the following actions in the Pages palette:

- **Click:** This selects the page or spread icon.
- **Double-click:** This *targets* the page or spread or moves it to the center of the interface.
- **Holding down the Shift key while clicking on the page icons:** This selects multiple pages or spreads.

The Pages palette icons are highlighted for all selected pages. When you apply certain actions, such as applying a Master or adding page numbers, they affect all selected pages.

Targeted pages are the pages that are currently active, and they're the pages that receive any newly created objects or any object that is pasted from the Clipboard. You also can identify the targeted page because it is the page whose ruler is not dimmed. Dimmed rulers are easiest to see in the vertical ruler. You can target only one page or spread at a time. The targeted page in the Pages palette has its page numbers highlighted.

 **You also can select and target pages using the Page Number drop-down list located at the bottom-left corner of the interface.**

The Layout menu includes several commands for select pages and spreads:

- **Layout ⇨ First Page** selects the first page.
- **Layout ⇨ Last Page** selects the last page.
- **Layout ⇨ Previous Page/Next Page** moves between adjacent pages.
- **Layout ⇨ Previous Spread/Next Spread** moves between adjacent spreads.
- **Layout ⇨ Go Back/Go Forward** moves you back and forth through pages.

Inserting, deleting, and rearranging pages

You add pages to a new document using the Insert Pages palette menu command, which opens the Insert Pages dialog box, shown in Figure 24.10. This dialog box lets you add a specified number of pages to the current document. The Insert options include After Page Number, Before Page Number, At Start of Document, and At End of Document. You also can select a Master page to use.

NOTE   You can add pages to the current document by entering a high value in the Number of Pages field for the Document Setup dialog box. The new pages are added onto the end of the current pages.

FIGURE 24.10

The Insert Pages dialog box places new pages exactly where you want them.

You can add pages to the current document by clicking on the Create New Page icon button at the bottom of the Pages palette.

In addition to inserting pages, the palette menu includes several other menu commands that are applied to the selected pages. The Duplicate Page (or Duplicate Spread, if a spread is selected) palette menu command creates a duplicate of the selected page (or spread). This duplicate also includes a duplicate of the page contents.

The Delete Page (or Spread) palette menu command removes the selected pages from the current document. If these pages contain any content, a warning dialog box appears, asking if you're sure about the deletion. You also can delete selected pages by clicking on the Delete Selected Pages icon button at the bottom of the Pages palette.

In addition to the palette menu, the Pages palette also is used to rearrange pages and spreads. By selecting and dragging the page icons in the Pages palette, you can rearrange the page order.

Creating and Using Master Pages

A Master is a page that holds all the elements that are common for several pages. It can include items such as page numbers, headers and footers, logos, and so on. All the items placed on the Master show up on the pages that the Master is applied to.

Each new document includes a single Master called the A-Master. This Master is selected from the top of the Pages palette, shown in Figure 24.11. You create and apply new Master pages to selected pages, so a document may have several Master pages applied to different pages. Each page may only have a single Master applied to it.

 **TIP** You also can select Master pages using the drop-down list located at the bottom left of the document window. This drop-down list includes all pages and named Masters.

FIGURE 24.11

The top of the Pages palette holds the Master pages unless you change the preferences as mentioned above.

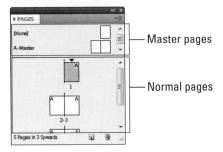

Master pages

Normal pages

Creating a Master

To create a new Master page, select the New Master panel menu command in the Pages panel. This opens the dialog box shown in Figure 24.12, which allows you to give the Master document a Prefix and a Name and to select another Master to base it on. You also can select the number of pages in the Master spread.

TIP By basing all newly created Masters on a single main Master page, you can make changes to the main Master page, and all other Masters based on this main Master inherit the changes also.

New Masters also are created by dragging a page or spread from the Pages palette to the Masters section at the top of the Pages palette. If the dragged page contains any objects, those objects become part of the Master page. If the dragged page has a Master applied to it, the new Master is based on the applied Master.

FIGURE 24.12

You name a new Master document with the New Master dialog box.

You can change the Master options by selecting the Master and choosing the Master Options palette menu command. This opens the Master Options dialog box again.

You can delete Master pages, like normal pages, by dragging them to the trash icon button at the bottom of the Pages palette or by selecting the Delete Master Spread palette menu command. Selected pages are deleted by selecting Delete Master Page option from the palette menu, dragging the Master page to the Delete Selected Pages icon at the bottom of the palette, or clicking the Delete Selected Pages icon.

Applying Masters

The Pages palette makes it easy to apply Masters to different pages and spreads. Simply drag the Master that you want to apply and drop it on the icon in the Pages palette of the page or spread that you want to apply it to. Masters should be applied only to spreads with the same number of pages. The Pages palette displays the prefix for the Master applied to it in the upper outside corner of the page, as shown in Figure 24.13. This figure also shows the Pages palette with the Show Thumbnails options enabled.

FIGURE 24.13

The letter on the page icon shows which Master has been applied to it.

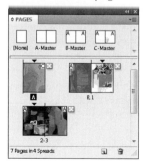

If you select multiple pages and Option/Alt+click on a Master page, that Master page is applied to all the selected pages. You also can select the Apply Master to Pages palette menu command. This action opens a simple dialog box where you can select a Master and type in the page numbers of the pages that you want to apply the Master to. To include multiple contiguous pages, use a dash symbol (for example, 4-7).

Overriding, detaching, deleting, and hiding Master objects

If a page or a spread is selected, you typically can't edit the objects that are part of the Master. However, if you override the Master object, you can change any and all attributes of the object with no restriction, such as its stroke, fill, and transformations. If some attributes on the overridden object are not changed, then changes to the Master item will still ripple down to the unchanged object. If you need to change the Master object even more, you can detach it from the Master page. Detaching an object from its master cuts all ties between the two objects.

Overriding all Master objects on the selected page is accomplished using the Override All Master Page Items (Alt+Shift+Ctrl+L on Windows, Option+Shift+⌘+L on the Mac) palette menu command. This command lets you edit all Master objects for the selected page without changing the Master.

If you want to edit only a single Master object on the selected page or spread, you can hold down the Shift+⌘/Ctrl keys while clicking on the item to change only the single Master item for the selected page without altering the other Master objects.

All Master page objects are detached using the Detach All Objects from Master palette menu command.

NOTE Be careful when detaching pages from a master. The process works in levels. The first level is override, applied singly or to all master page objects in a spread. At this point individual changes can be applied to objects, but any unchanged qualities are still controlled by the master page object. Overrides can be removed later if desired. The second level is to detach an overridden object. When you detach an overridden object from the master, it severs all ties to the master object. You cannot detach without first overriding. You cannot detach all unless something has been overridden, and then only the overridden objects are detached; non-overridden objects are left alone.

All page objects that are provided by a Master may be hidden or shown by choosing the Show/Hide Master Items menu from the panel menu. Master page objects are displayed with a dotted line on the document page. Master page items can be locked so they cannot be overridden. To lock a master page item, simply select the item and make sure that the Allow Master Item Overrides on Selection option in the Pages palette menu is disabled.

Using Layers

Document pages as well as Master pages have layers. Layers are used to organize page objects and to control which objects appear above other objects. Objects placed on a higher layer appear on top of objects placed on a lower layer. Both document pages and master pages share the same layers, layer stacking order and interaction. Master objects on a specific layer actually lie beneath all objects on the same layer on a document page.

CROSS-REF **More details on working with layers can be found in Chapter 25.**

Creating new layers

All layers are displayed in the Layers palette, shown in Figure 24.14. Each layer has a name and a color associated with it. All objects are highlighted with their layer color when selected. The layer highlight color is also shown when no object is selected and View ➪ Show Frame Edges is turned on. Using the columns in the Layers palette to the left of the layer name, you can make a layer Visible or Locked.

FIGURE 24.14

The Layers palette lists all the available layers.

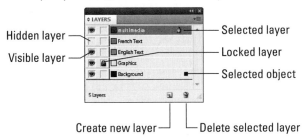

All new documents include a single layer named Layer 1. New layers are created using the New Layer palette menu command or by clicking the Create New Layer button at the bottom of the Layers palette. The New Layer menu command opens a dialog box, shown in Figure 24.15, where you can enter a name, choose a color, and select other options.

FIGURE 24.15

The New Layer dialog box lets you name the new layer, choose its color, and set other options such as visibility and locking.

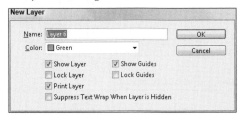

Positioning Master objects on top of document objects

By default, all Master page objects appear behind the document objects, but you can force objects on a Master page to appear on top of the document objects by assigning a higher layer to the Master objects.

If you've already created an object on a Master page that has a lower layer number than the document object that you want to place it on top of, you can create a higher layer in the Layer palette by selecting the New Layer palette menu command or by clicking on the Create New Layer button at the bottom of the Layers palette. Then select the objects that you want to move to the new layer and drag the small square icon to the right of the layer name to the new layer. The frame edge of the object changes colors to match the new layer.

NOTE You also can move objects between layers by choosing Edit ⇨ Cut, Edit ⇨ Copy, or Edit ⇨ Paste in Place, but if you enable the Paste Remembers Layers option in the Layer palette menu, pasting an object on a new layer won't change its layer.

Adding Page Numbering

Page numbering automatically updates as you rearrange, add, or delete pages from the current document. Auto page numbers may be added to a Master page or to a normal page.

Adding auto page numbering

To add auto numbering to a page, select the page or Master and drag with the Type tool to create a text object. Then type any text that you want to appear before the page number. Choose Type ⇨ Insert Special Character ⇨ Markers ⇨ Current Page Number (Alt+Shift+Ctrl+N in Windows, Option+Shift+⌘+N on the Mac). The text objects are formatted using the standard formatting features found in the Character and Paragraph palettes.

CROSS-REF For more information on formatting text, see Part IV.

By default, auto numbering calls the first page "page 1," the second page "page 2," and so on, but you can change the number formatting to Roman numerals or letters and also start with a number other than 1 using the New Section dialog box, shown in Figure 24.16. Open this dialog box by choosing Layout ➪ Numbering & Section Options. This dialog box also includes the ability to configure the numbering of chapters.

FIGURE 24.16

Use the New Section dialog box to add sections.

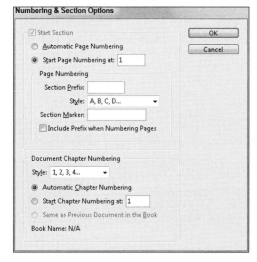

Defining sections

To define a section, choose the first page for the section in the Pages palette; then open the Numbering & Section Options dialog box, and choose the numbering options. Enabling the Start Section option creates a new section. You also can specify a Section Prefix and a Section Marker. The Section Prefix displays along with the page number when you enable the Include Prefix When Numbering Pages option. You can add the Section Marker to the numbering text object by choosing Type ➪ Insert Special Character ➪ Markers ➪ Section Marker.

NOTE You also can use the specified numbering style in the table of contents and the index pages using section markers. The Layout ➪ Numbering & Section Options let you choose the type of number and or keyword to use.

When the dialog box is closed, the Pages palette displays the page numbers using the selected numbering style and a small down-arrow icon appears above the first page of each section in the Pages panel. Double-clicking on the section arrow icon in the Pages palette, choosing the Numbering & Section options from the pop-up menu, or by selecting this command from the palette menu, opens the Numbering & Sections dialog box. You can add several sections to the current document.

 **You can set InDesign to display absolute page numbers or section page numbers in the Pages palette using the Page Numbering option in the General panel of the Preferences dialog box.**

Enhancing Layouts

After you create a layout, you can enhance various elements that you want to appear consistently throughout the document. For example, you can quickly add a sidebar element to designated pages by creating a guide that identifies the placement of the element. Using rulers, grids, and guides provides an effective way to enhance a layout.

Using rulers

Rulers are positioned on the left side and above the pasteboard and are consistent to the page regardless of the amount of zooming. If you right-click on the ruler, you can change its measurement units using the pop-up menu shown in Figure 24.17. The options include Points, Picas, Inches, Inches Decimal, Millimeters, Centimeters, Ciceros, Agates, and Custom.

TIP   **If the rulers aren't visible, you can make them appear by choosing View ⇨ Show/Hide Rulers (⌘/Ctrl+R).**

FIGURE 24.17

Right-clicking on a ruler presents a pop-up menu of measurement units.

Using grids

InDesign has two different types of grids that can overlay the document. The Baseline Grid, shown in Figure 24.18, includes horizontal lines used to mark text baselines. It's confined to the page.

The Document Grid type, shown in Figure 24.19, is made up of small grid squares and overlays the entire art board.

Both of these grids are made visible by choosing View ➡ Grids & Guides ➡ Show/Hide Baseline Grid (Alt+Ctrl+' in Windows, Option+⌘+' on the Mac) or View ➡ Grids & Guides ➡ Show/Hide Document Grid (Ctrl+' in Windows, ⌘+' on the Mac). You also can cause objects to snap to the Document Grid lines by enabling the View ➡ Grids & Guides ➡ Snap to Document Grid (Shift+Ctrl+' in Windows, Shift+⌘+' on the Mac) menu command. You configure both the Baseline Grid and the Document Grid using the Preferences ➡ Grids panel.

FIGURE 24.18

The Baseline Grid is displayed within the current page only.

FIGURE 24.19

Items snap in place when you overlay a Document Grid if snapping is enabled.

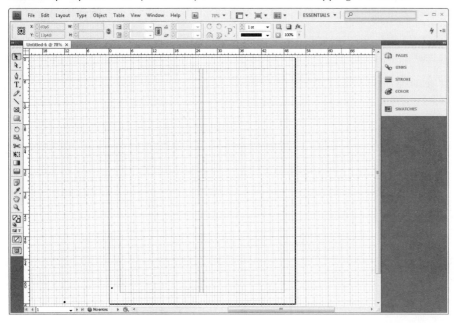

Using guides

Guides are simply lines that extend from the ruler, providing a visual boundary for page objects. InDesign uses two different types of guides. Page guides are seen only within the page, and Spread guides run across the entire spread including the art board.

You create a Page guide by clicking on a ruler and dragging onto the page. Holding down the ⌘/ Ctrl key while dragging from the ruler onto a page creates a Spread guide. Holding down the Shift key when creating a guide makes the guide snap to the ruler's tick marks. Double-clicking the ruler creates a guide at the clicked position or you can double-click with the Shift key held down to create and snap a new guide to the closest ruler tick mark. Figure 24.20 shows each of these guide types. Choosing Layout ➪ Ruler Guides opens a simple dialog box where you can set the View Threshold and Color for these guides.

You create a series of consistent guides using the Create Guides dialog box, shown in Figure 24.21, which you access by choosing Layout ➪ Create Guides. This dialog box lets you specify the number of rows and columns and the gutter between each.

You can select and move guides after they're created. To lock all guides so they can't be moved accidentally, choose View ➪ Lock Guides (Option/Alt+;). All guides are hidden by choosing View ➪ Show/Hide Guides (⌘/Ctrl+;).

FIGURE 24.20

Guides are useful for positioning objects.

Page guide   Spread guide

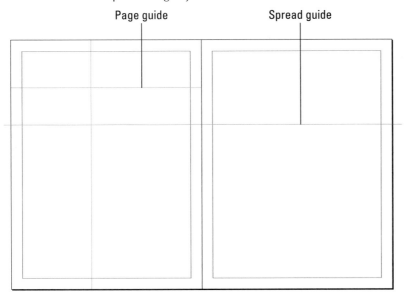

FIGURE 24.21

The Create Guides dialog box creates a series of evenly spaced guides.

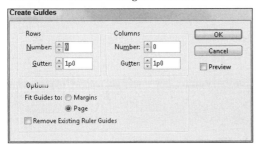

Guides are actual objects in InDesign and belong to a specific layer. As such, they are hidden and/or locked along with its respective layer. Guides can also be selected, distributed, copied, and pasted.

 **Guides can be selected and exported as a snippet to be used elsewhere.**

751

Using frames

With grids and guides in place, another helpful object is a layout frame. You create frames, which act as placeholders for graphics or text, using any path or object in the Toolbox including Rectangles, Ellipses, Polygons, objects drawn with the Pen tool, or any freehand drawn shape.

To create a frame, select a drawing tool in the Toolbox, such as the Rectangle Frame tool (F) and drag in the page to create a frame. With the frame selected, you can specify what type of content the frame holds by choosing Object ➪ Content ➪ Graphic, Object ➪ Content ➪ Text, or Object ➪ Content ➪ Unassigned.

NOTE   You also can create text-assigned frames with the Type tool.

Graphic frames have an X through their center, and text-assigned frames have ports that thread multiple frames, as shown in Figure 24.22.

FIGURE 24.22

Frames create placeholders for different content types.

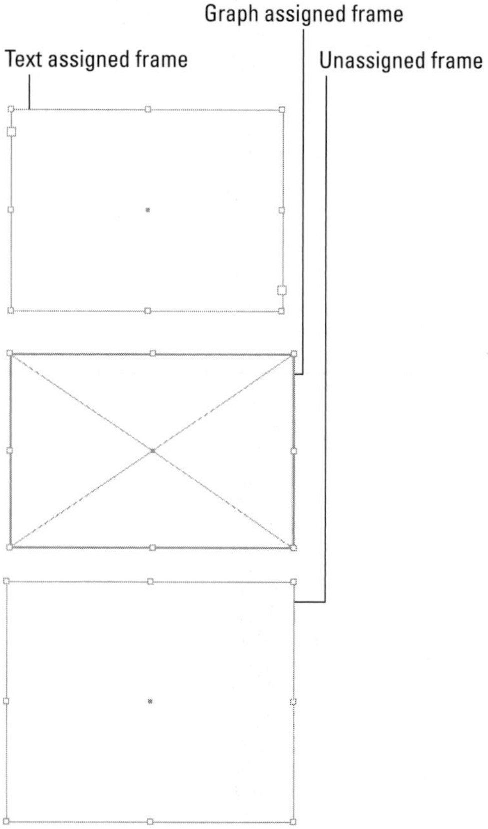

Graph assigned frame

Text assigned frame   Unassigned frame

Importing Images and Objects

As you create a layout with frames, it's often helpful to import a stub image, which acts as a place-holder for final artwork, with the correct dimensions from Photoshop and Illustrator. After importing stub images, you can create the artwork using either Photoshop or Illustrator, and if you establish links between the two packages, the artwork can be updated dynamically.

 **Stub objects are frequently called FPO objects, which stands for For Placement Only.**

The File ➪ Place menu command lets you select multiple files to place simultaneously. To place multiple files, simply select several files in the Place dialog box by holding down the Ctrl/cmd key while clicking the file to place. If the Show Import Options option is enabled, then the respective dialog box is opened for each file.

Importing Photoshop artwork

You can import Photoshop artwork into a selected frame by choosing File ➪ Place (⌘/Ctrl+D). If you enable the Show Import Options, the Image Import Options dialog box, shown in Figure 24.23, appears after you select the image file in the file dialog box. The settings found in the Image Import Options dialog box are different depending on the type of image format that was selected.

CROSS-REF **Chapter 2 includes a good example of placing an imported file into InDesign.**

FIGURE 24.23

The Image Import Options dialog box includes panels for selecting the Alpha Channel and Color Management profiles.

The Apply Photoshop Clipping Path and the Alpha Channel drop-down list options are enabled if the imported object includes a clipping path and/or an Alpha Channel. For imported images that include an Alpha Channel, you can select the Transparency or Graduated Transparency option. PSD files also give you the option to control which layers are visible. If the file includes some Layer Comps, you can choose which ones to import.

Placed files also can benefit from the Proportional Placing features. When a graphic file is ready to place, you can click-drag and InDesign constrains the dimensions of the frame you create to match the proportions of the file being placed.

 **InDesign offers the option of importing an image with Graduated Transparency— a feature that isn't offered in QuarkXPress.**

Importing Illustrator artwork and PDF files

Artwork created in Illustrator and PDF files that are placed within a selected frame in InDesign open the Place PDF dialog box if Show Import Options is enabled. This dialog box, shown in Figure 24.24, includes two separate panels: General and Layers. The General panel includes settings that let you select to place the Previewed Page, All pages, or a Range of pages from the PDF file; it also includes options to set a cropping option and to make the background transparent. The Layers panel lets you see all the layers that are in the imported artwork. For each layer, you can select to Use PDF's Layer Visibility or to Keep Layer Visibility Overrides. If the imported Illustrator file includes bleed values, InDesign recognizes and uses these values.

FIGURE 24.24

You import Illustrator's AI and PDF files into InDesign with the Place PDF dialog box options.

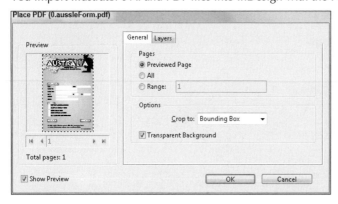

Importing Adobe Flash files

Flash files are placed within an InDesign document using the File ➪ Place command. If you select the Files of Type drop-down list to Media Files in the Place dialog box, then Flash SWF files are listed. These files may be selected and placed, but there are no Import Options for Flash files.

 **Placing SWF files in InDesign is tricky. There are a number of Flash features that InDesign cannot handle.**

Dynamically updating content

You may open and edit artwork created using Photoshop and/or Illustrator in their original application by right-clicking the image and choosing Graphics ➪ Edit Original. This causes the image to open within the original application. Any saved edits you make to the image in the original application are automatically updated within InDesign. You also can use the Open With command to open the selected item in several applications.

 **Holding down the Option/Alt key while double-clicking on a placed source file opens the file in its native application.**

Importing existing InDesign pages

The File ➪ Place menu command can also be used to import existing InDesign documents and pages into the current document. The options dialog box lets you choose to import a specific page, a range of pages, or all pages from the imported document. Like other placed objects, the imported pages are listed in the Links palette.

Assembling a Layout

This chapter concludes with an example that takes you through the steps to create a sample layout and to add auto page numbering to a Master page in InDesign.

STEPS: Creating an InDesign Layout

1. **Create a new document.** Within InDesign, choose File ➪ New ➪ Document (⌘/Ctrl+N). In the New Document dialog box, set the Number of Pages to 6 and enable the Facing Pages option. Select the Letter Page Size, which sets the Width to 8.5 in. and the Height to 11 in. with a Portrait orientation. In the Margins section, set the Top margin to 0.5 in. and click the Make All Settings the Same button (located in between the margin values, it looks like a link button). In the Columns section, set the number of Columns to 1 with a Gutter of 0.1667 in.

2. **Set the Bleed and Slug settings.** If the Bleed and Slug section isn't visible, click More Options. Set the Bleed values to 0., and click the Make All Settings the Same button. Set all Slug values to 0. Figure 24.25 shows the New Document dialog box with the appropriate settings. Click OK to create the new document.

3. **Edit the Master spread.** In the Pages panel, select and target the A-Master spread by double-clicking its title. The spread icons are highlighted in the Pages panel, and the spread is centered in the interface. Select the Master Options for "A-Master" command from the Pages panel menu. This opens the Master Options dialog box for the A-Master spread. Change the Prefix to S and the Name to SpreadMaster. Click OK to close the dialog box.

4. **Create a New Master spread.** In the Pages palette, select the New Master palette menu command. The New Master dialog box opens, shown in Figure 24.26. Enter a Prefix value of C, enter a Name of CenterOpen, and set the spread to Based on the S-SpreadMaster Master. Click OK to close the dialog box.

5. **Apply the Master spreads to the pages.** In the Pages palette, drag the Master page named None to the first page. Then drag the C-CenterOpen Master to the spread in pages 2 and 3. The remaining spreads already have the S-SpreadMaster Master applied to them.

FIGURE 24.25

The New Document dialog box includes many initial settings for creating a layout document.

FIGURE 24.26

The New Master dialog box lets you name the Master spread and give it a prefix.

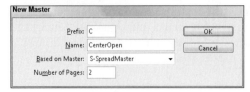

6. **Adding content to the Master spreads.** Double-click the S-SpreadMaster to select and target it. Create some objects, and position them within the Master spread. Figure 24.27 shows the Master spread with several content items added to it.

FIGURE 24.27

Content added to the Master spread appears on every page that the Master is applied to.

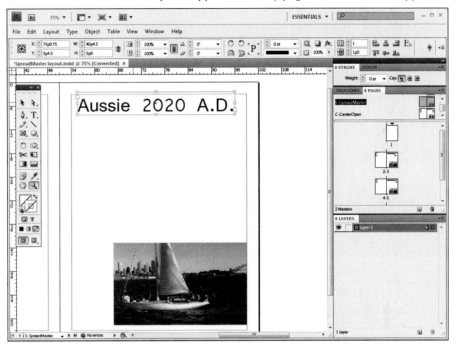

7. **Add Auto Page Numbering.** With the Type tool, drag to create a small text object in the upper-left and upper-right corners of the Master spread. With the text object selected, choose Type ➪ Insert Special Character ➪ Markers ➪ Current Page Number. A letter *S* appears in each text object, which is the prefix for the Master spread. Click on several of the pages in the Pages palette, and see the numbering updated.

8. **Place artwork on the secondary Master.** Double-click the title for the C-CenterOpen Master in the Pages palette. This selects and targets the second Master spread. With the Secondary Master spread selected and targeted, choose File ➪ Place. In the file dialog box that opens, select the artwork pieces that you want to place within the Secondary Master spread and click OK. The artwork is added to the spread. Select the artwork, and position it. Figure 24.28 shows the Secondary Master spread with some artwork added to it. Using two Master pages gives the design flexibility and power.

FIGURE 24.28

The Secondary Master can include different content from the original Master.

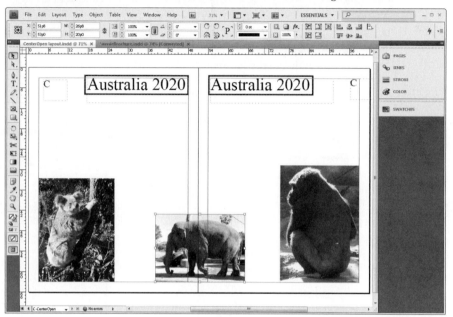

Summary

- You create Layout documents using File ➪ New ➪ Document to open a dialog box of settings including the number of pages, the page size and orientation, the margins, and the columns.

- You use document presets to save layout settings for reuse.

- You change layout settings for an existing document via the Document Setup and the Margins and Columns dialog box.

- Icons of all pages and spreads are viewed from within the Pages palette.

- The Pages palette helps you create Master pages, which hold objects that appear on all pages to which you apply the Master.

- The Layers palette is used to place objects on different layers.

- You enable Auto page numbering by adding the Auto Page Number object to a text object. When placed on a Master page, all pages based on the Master page show the page number. The document also may be divided into sections, each with a different numbering scheme.

- Rulers, grids, guides, and frames are useful in establishing layouts.

- You can import artwork created in Photoshop, Illustrator, and Acrobat into InDesign.

Chapter 25

Working with Layers

T he real benefit of layers is their ability to organize a project into several easy-to-select sections. Previously, this was done with groups, but groups can be tricky to work with, requiring the Group Selection tool to work within a group. Layers are a much more convenient way to organize all the images and objects in a document.

Another benefit of layers is that you can quickly turn them on and off. If a project is sluggish because of its size and content, you could place these slow-to-refresh items on a layer and make them invisible so they don't slow down the rest of the project.

Layers also may be locked. You may want to lock parts of your completed project, so you don't accidentally select and move them.

You also can create several design ideas and keep them on several layers. Then you can quickly switch between the various designs using layers. This is a concept mastered by Photoshop with the Layer Comps feature.

Layers are available in Photoshop, Illustrator, InDesign, Flash, Dreamweaver, Fireworks, and Acrobat, but the ways layers are used in each of these applications are very different. Layers in each of these applications include some basic concepts that are common for all applications:

- **InDesign:** Layers in InDesign use the most basic layer features, but even InDesign includes some specialized layer features.

- **Illustrator:** Illustrator expands on the layer basics with many additional layer features, including support for sublayers, template layers, releasing items to layers, and clipping and opacity masks.

- **Photoshop:** Photoshop takes layer functionality to a whole new level with support for layer sets, linked layers, transparency, adjustment and fill layers, layer effects, masks, and layer comps.

IN THIS CHAPTER

Using the Layers palette

Using layers in InDesign

Using layers in Illustrator

Using layers in Photoshop

Using layers in Flash

Using layers in Dreamweaver

Viewing layers in Acrobat

■ **Acrobat:** In Acrobat 6, you find support for Adobe PDF Layers. PDF documents containing layers must be authored in applications supporting layers and having the ability to export to the PDF 1.5 format. If you view a layered PDF document in earlier versions of Acrobat, the layers are flattened and viewed as a single layer document.

In this chapter, we present these layer basics first, starting with InDesign. We then move on to the specific layer features for each individual application. Finally, we show you how layered files exported to the PDF format can access layers in Acrobat.

Using the Layers Palette

Within Photoshop, Illustrator, and InDesign, layers for the current file and all the layer features are contained in the Layers palette, shown in Figure 25.1. Open this palette by choosing Window ⇨ Layers.

All layers for the current InDesign document display in the Layers palette.

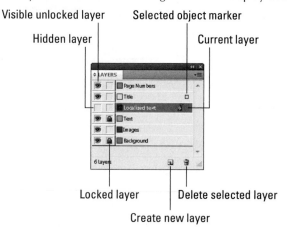

All new projects created in Illustrator and InDesign include a default layer named Layer 1; a new layer added to the document is named Layer 2 by default. Double-clicking a layer opens a dialog box where you can rename the layer and set the layer's properties.

Within the Layers palette are several visual icons that determine whether the selected layer is visible, locked, selected, or targeted. The eye icon in the first column to the left of the layer name determines layer visibility. The lock icon in the second column to the left of the layer name is used to show whether a layer is locked.

Actually, in Illustrator, it's a lock icon; in Photoshop, it's a lock icon at the top of the Layers palette; and in InDesign, it's a no-write icon. There are subtle differences among the different CS4 applications.

Other icons appear to the right of the layer name and are used to denote the targeted layer and any selected objects on that layer. The targeted layer is highlighted.

Creating layers

To create a new layer, select the New Layer palette menu command or click the Create New Layer button at the bottom of the Layers palette. If you select the menu command, the Layer Options dialog box appears, as shown in Figure 25.2. Here, you can name the new layer, select a layer color, and specify several layer properties. Clicking the Create New Layer button creates a new layer using default values without opening the Layer Options dialog box. To force the Layer Options dialog box to appear when you click Create New Layer, hold down the Option/Alt key when clicking.

FIGURE 25.2

The Layer Options dialog box

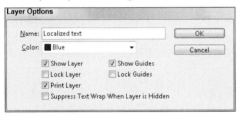

The layer properties that appear in the Layer Options dialog box set options such as whether the layer is visible or locked. You can open the Layer Options dialog box for any existing layer by double-clicking the layer.

Other than layer name and color, the specific layer properties found in the Layer Options dialog box are unique for each CS4 application. For example, InDesign includes options to show guides, lock guides, and suppress text wrap when the layer is hidden; Illustrator includes options to make the layer a template, print, preview, and dim images to a percentage; and Photoshop includes options to use the previous layer to create a clipping mask, select a blending mode, and set an opacity.

If you double-click a layer name or if you select a layer and choose the Layer Options palette menu command, the Layer Options dialog box reappears, letting you change the layer properties. Double-clicking the layer name in Photoshop selects the name and lets you rename it within the Layers palette.

In InDesign and Illustrator, new layers always appear at the top of the Layers palette, but if you hold down the ⌘/Ctrl key while clicking the Create New Layer button, the new layer appears directly above the selected layer; if you hold down the Ctrl[cmd]+Alt[option] keys, then the new layer is created below the selected layer; and if you hold down the Alt[option] key while clicking the Create New Layer button, the New Layer dialog box opens. In Photoshop, you can make the new layer appear directly below the current layer by holding down the Ctrl [cmd] key and holding down the Alt [option] key. This opens the New Layer dialog box.

Selecting and targeting layers

Clicking a layer name targets a layer. To select multiple layers, hold down the ⌘/Ctrl key while clicking each layer that you want to select, or hold down the Shift key and click the first and last layers to select all layers between these two layers.

The targeted layer in InDesign is marked with a Pen icon to the right of the layer name. Targeted layers in Illustrator are marked with a small triangle in the upper-right corner; the targeted layer in Photoshop is the selected layer. All new objects that you add to the project, including all newly created objects and any imported, pasted, or placed files, are placed on the active layer.

Hiding and locking layers

The first column in the Layers palette holds the Visibility icon. If the eye icon is present, the layer is visible, but if the eye icon isn't present, the layer is hidden. You can toggle the eye icon by clicking it. Hidden layers are not printed either, although you can print hidden layers in Illustrator and InDesign if you select the Print option in the Layers Options dialog box.

The second column is the Lock icon. If the lock icon is present, the layer is locked and cannot be selected or edited, but if the lock icon isn't present, the layer is editable. You also can toggle the lock icon by clicking it.

NOTE Within InDesign, the lock icon looks like a pencil icon with a red line through it; in Illustrator, the lock icon looks like a lock. Photoshop uses the second column for other purposes and allows layers to be locked using the Lock properties at the top of the palette. Photoshop includes the option to lock specific attributes; the lock icon is displayed to the right of the layer name.

To hide or lock multiple layers at once, choose the Hide Others or Lock Others palette menu commands, and all layers that aren't selected are hidden or locked or you can hold down the Alt[option] key while clicking several different layers. If at least one layer is hidden or locked, these menu commands change to Show All Layers or Unlock All Layers.

Using Isolation mode

As a document becomes more and more crowded, it can be tough to work on a specific object, group, symbol, or Live Paint group without affecting the rest of the objects. The answer is to use

Illustrator's Isolation mode. Isolation mode is activated when you click the Isolate Selected Group button located on the Option bar. You can also enter isolation mode by double-clicking a group with the Selection tool or selecting the Enter Isolation Mode palette menu command in the Layers palette.

When isolation mode is active, the selected object is displayed in full color and all other objects are dimmed and temporarily locked and a special border surrounds the document screen. You can exit isolation mode with the Exit Isolation Mode button displayed at the top of the window or by double-clicking outside of the isolated group. The current layer and sublayer are also displayed along the top edge of the document interface to remind you where these objects fit into the document.

Rearranging layers

The order in which the layers are listed in the Layers palette determines the stacking order of objects on the page, with the layer listed at the top of the Layers palette appearing in front of all other objects in the document.

You can rearrange layers by selecting and dragging one layer above or below another. A dark black line appears between the two layers where the dragged layer is positioned if dropped.

Copying objects between layers

The Selection tool may be used to select any object on any layer that is not locked. A small square icon appears to the right of the layer name of each layer that includes a selected object in Illustrator and InDesign.

The bounding box of the selected object is colored using the layer color.

TIP To select all objects on a single layer in InDesign and Illustrator, hold down the Option/Alt key while clicking the layer name in the Layers palette. If the layer doesn't contain any objects, then you can't select it with the Option/Alt key held down.

To move a selected object to another layer, click and drag the small square icon to the layer to which you want to move the object. If you hold down the Option/Alt key while dragging the small square icon, a copy of the selected object moves to the selected layer. If you hold down Ctrl (Windows) or ⌘ (Mac) while dragging the small square icon, the selected object may be moved onto a hidden or locked layer. If you hold down Ctrl+Alt (Windows) or ⌘+Option (Mac) while dragging the small square icon, the selected object may be duplicated onto a hidden or locked layer.

You can choose Edit ➪ Cut, Edit ➪ Copy, or Edit ➪ Paste to move objects between layers and between documents. If you enable the Paste Remembers Layers option (available only in Illustrator and InDesign) in the palette menu, then the pasted objects are pasted in the same layers from which you copied them. If you paste the copied objects into a document without the same layer names, the layer names for the selected objects are added to the new document and the copied objects are pasted on these new layers.

Duplicating layers

You can use the Duplicate palette menu command to duplicate a layer and all the objects on that layer. The duplicated layer appears directly above the original layer. You also can duplicate a layer by dragging it to the Create New Layer button at the bottom of the palette. The duplicated layer appears with the same layer name with the word *copy* after it, so duplicating a layer named "Sword" results in a layer named "Sword copy." Duplicating this layer again results in a layer named "Sword copy 2."

Deleting layers

You can use the Delete palette menu command to delete the selected layers, or you can click the Delete Selected Layers button at the bottom of the Layers palette. If the layer contains any objects, a warning dialog box appears confirming that you want to delete the objects on the layer.

To delete any empty layers in the current document, select the Delete Unused Layers palette menu command. This removes any layers that don't contain any objects.

Merging layers

You use the Merge Layers palette menu command to combine all objects on the selected layers. The objects all appear on the targeted layer, and the other selected layers are deleted. Selecting all layers and choosing this command offers a way to flatten all layers to a single layer.

STEPS: Creating a Layered Document

1. **Create a new document.** Within Photoshop, Illustrator, or InDesign, choose File ➪ New to create a new document.

2. **Open the Layers palette.** Choose Window ➪ Layers to open the Layers palette. The default layer is listed as Layer 1.

3. **Add content to the layer.** Using the tools in the Toolbox, add some content to the existing layer.

4. **Create a new layer.** Before you begin to add a new type of content, click the Create New Layer button at the bottom of the Layers palette to create a new layer. In the New Layer dialog box that appears, name the layer appropriately.

5. **Hide and lock the first layer.** To hide the content on the first layer so it isn't accidentally edited, click the eye icon to the left of the first layer's name. This icon hides the layer. If you need to see the content in the first layer, but you don't want it edited, click the eye icon again to make the layer visible; then click the lock icon in the second column to lock the layer.

6. **Rearrange the layers.** The new layer appears in front of the first layer. To change this order, click and the drag the first layer above the new layer in the Layers palette. Placing the first layer above the other layer makes its content come to the front of the stacking order.

STEPS: Dividing an Existing Document into Layers

1. **Open a document in InDesign.** Within InDesign, select a document that you want to divide into layers for better organization.

2. **Open the Layers palette.** Choose Window ➪ Layers to open the Layers palette.

3. **Create new layers.** Click the Create New Layer button at the bottom of the Layers palette several times to create some new layers.

4. **Rename the layers.** Double-click each of the new layers, and in the Layer Options dialog box that appears, type a new descriptive name for the layer such as Background, images, text, guides, and so on.

5. **Move objects to their correct layer.** Move through each page in the document, and select the objects on that page. Then drag the square selected icon in the Layers palette to the correct layer for that object. After an object is moved to its correct layer, its bounding box changes to the same color as its layer. Continue this step for all objects in the document. Figure 25.3 shows the layers created for this document.

FIGURE 25.3

After creating and naming the necessary layers, objects are easily placed on the correct layer.

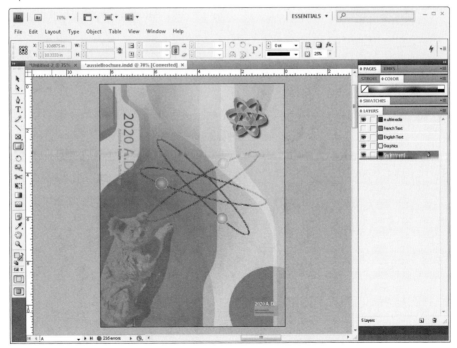

Using Layers in InDesign

In addition to the basic features found in the Layers palette, InDesign also includes a couple of layer features that are unique to the application, including the ability to condense the layers list in the Layers palette, show and lock layer guides, suppress text wrap, and features for dealing with objects on Master pages. InDesign also has a feature that lets you designate a layer as non-printing by disabling the Print Layer option in the Layer Options dialog box.

Condensing the Layers palette

Within InDesign and Illustrator, the Layers palette may be condensed using the Small Palette Rows palette menu option. Figure 25.4 shows the Layers palette in InDesign with the Small Palette Rows option enabled.

FIGURE 25.4

The Small Palette Rows option condenses layer sizes.

Using guides

Guides in InDesign are especially useful for aligning and positioning elements; each layer may have its own set of guides. Guides are created for the selected layer by clicking the Horizontal or Vertical rulers and dragging into the page. If the rulers aren't visible, you can choose View ➪ Grids & Guides ➪ Show Rulers to make them visible.

Guides appear as straight lines in the document, and the selected guide has the same color as the selected layer.

The View ➪ Grids & Guides ➪ Show/Hide Guides menu command and the View ➪ Lock Guides menu command are used to show, hide, and lock all guides in the current document. But you also can select to show, hide, and lock guides on a specific layer using the Show Guides and Lock Guides options in the Layer Options dialog box. Double-clicking a layer in the Layers palette opens this dialog box.

Suppressing text wrap on hidden layers

In an InDesign document, it's often helpful to separate text and graphics onto separate layers. By doing so, you can make the graphics hidden when you're proofreading the text, and you can hide the text when you're working on the graphics.

If the text object is set to wrap around a graphic, making either layer hidden affects the text wrapping. You can control whether the text is wrapped when the graphic layer is hidden using the Suppress Text Wrap When Hidden option in the Layer Options dialog box.

Figure 25.5 shows two similar documents that have separated the graphics and text onto two different layers. Although the text is set to wrap around the center graphic, the document on the left has the Suppress Text Wrap When Hidden option disabled in the Layer Options dialog box, so the text wrap is still visible; the document on the right has enabled this option, causing the text wrap to be suppressed.

FIGURE 25.5

The Suppress Text Wrap When Hidden option controls whether the text wraps when the graphic layer is hidden.

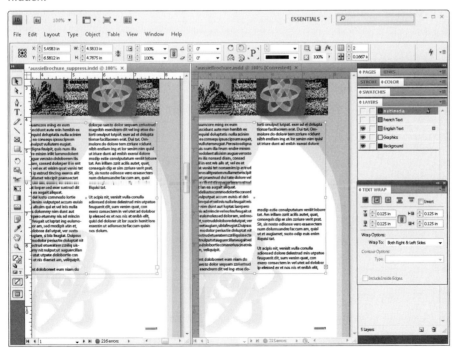

Reordering Master objects above layers

By default, Master objects placed on the same layer as page objects appear behind those page objects. To make the Master object, such as auto page numbers, appear in front of the page objects, place the Master objects on a layer that is above the page object's layer.

STEPS: Making Page Numbers Appear in Front of Other Elements

1. **Open a document in InDesign.** Within InDesign, open a document that includes Master pages and auto page numbers.

2. **Add an element to the Master page.** In the Layers palette, select the Background layer. Then in the Pages palette, double-click the master page you want to change to select them. Then click the Rectangle tool, and drag a rectangle over the top of the page number in the upper-right corner of the Master page. Change the rectangle's Fill color to blue and its Stroke color to black with a Weight of 2 pt, as shown in Figure 25.6.

FIGURE 25.6

Adding an object onto the current layer places the object on top of the other Master objects that are in the same layer.

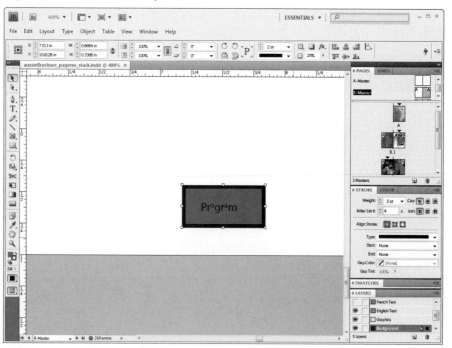

3. **Create a new layer for the Master page numbers.** In the Layers palette, click the Create New Layer button at the bottom of the Layers palette. A new layer is added at the top of the Layers palette. Then double-click the new layer, name the layer Master Page Numbers, and click OK.

4. **Move the Master Page Number element to the new layer.** Click the Visibility icon for the background layer to temporarily hide the background layer so you can see the page number element hidden behind the rectangle. Then select the page number element. In the Layers palette, drag the small rectangle to the right of the Master Objects layer to the Master Page Numbers layer to move the selected object to the new layer that is higher than the layer with the rectangle on it.

5. **Make all layers visible.** As a final step, click the eye icon for the background layer to show all layers. The results are shown in Figure 25.7, where the page number is positioned in front of the red rectangle.

FIGURE 25.7

Moving the Master elements to a layer positioned above the layer with the obscuring object makes the Master elements visible.

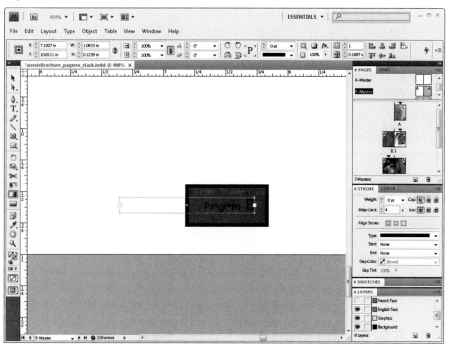

Importing layered files

When layered files such as Photoshop, Illustrator, PDF, and TIFF images are placed within InDesign by choosing File ⇨ Place, InDesign displays a flattened representation of the current state of the placed file as defined in the Object Layer Options dialog box for PSD, Illustrator, and layered PDF files. This flattening affects only the display within InDesign and does not affect the original image file or its layers. If you access the Import Options dialog box, you can control the layer visibility of the placed file.

If you need to edit the original file, you can select the file in the Links palette and choose the Edit Original palette menu command. This opens the image file in the application that was used to originally create the image, or if you double-click the file in the document with the Option/Alt key held down, the file is opened in its native app. Holding down the Option/Alt key and double-clicking the linked file in the Links palette goes to the link in the InDesign document.

 **CROSS-REF** To learn more about working with the Links palette, see Chapter 24.

Applying transparency and blending modes to a layer

You use blending modes in Illustrator to define how the colors of two overlapping transparent objects are blended. Although InDesign doesn't include a way to apply transparency or blending mode to an InDesign document layer, you can quickly select all objects on a selected layer by holding down the Option/Alt key while clicking the layer in the Layers palette. With all objects on a layer selected, you can set the layer's Opacity value and blending mode using the Effects palette to set the opacity of all the individual selected objects, shown in Figure 25.8.

 **NOTE** Within InDesign, the layer is used to select all the objects on the layer, but the transparency is actually applied to every object individually.

 **NOTE** Illustrator allows you to apply an Opacity value and blending mode to an entire layer.

FIGURE 25.8

The Effects palette in InDesign

 **CROSS-REF** Details on using transparency and the blending modes are found in Chapter 9.

Using Layers in Illustrator

Layers in Illustrator have much more functionality than those found in InDesign, but the Layers palette still includes all the basic layer features already covered. One of the key benefits is that the Illustrator's Layers palette lets you drill down within layers to view and select the each individual item included in a layer.

The Layer options within Illustrator also are unique, offering options to specify whether the layer objects are shown in Preview or Outline mode.

Layers in Illustrator are capable of holding appearance attributes. You can select and move these attributes between different layers. You also can apply graphic styles directly to a targeted layer from the Graphic Styles palette. Illustrator's Layers palette also includes a simple way to create clipping masks.

CROSS-REF   Using Graphic Styles and attributes is covered in Chapter 8.

Figure 25.9 shows the Layers palette in Illustrator. It includes additional palette buttons for creating sublayers and clipping masks.

FIGURE 25.9

The Layers palette in Illustrator offers some additional features.

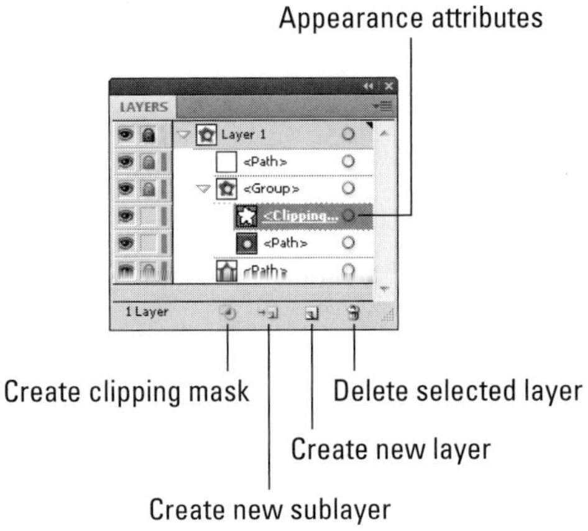

Appearance attributes

Create clipping mask

Delete selected layer

Create new layer

Create new sublayer

Changing the Layers palette view

Illustrator offers several different ways to view the Layers palette, as specified in the Layers Palette Options dialog box, shown in Figure 25.10. This dialog box is accessed using the Palette Options palette menu command.

FIGURE 25.10

The Layers Palette Options dialog box

The Show Layers Only option hides all sublayers and displays only the top-level layer names.

The Row Size section lets you choose the size of the layer rows in the Layers palette from Small, Medium, Large, or Other, where you can set the row size in pixels. The Small option displays the layers without any thumbnails, similar to the Layers palette in InDesign when the Small Palette Rows option is enabled. The Medium option displays smaller thumbnails (refer to Figure 25.9); the Large option is shown in Figure 25.11.

FIGURE 25.11

The Large option increases the size of the layer thumbnails.

The Thumbnails section lets you display the thumbnails for layers, the top level only, groups, and/ or objects. Selecting the Top Level Only option shows thumbnails only for the top level and hides the thumbnails for all sublayers.

Using sublayers

All layers that contain objects have a small arrow to the left of the layer name. Clicking this arrow changes the arrow's direction and expands the layer to reveal all the layer's sublayers or objects. Clicking an expanded arrow icon collapses the layer again. If you hold down the Option/Alt key while clicking an arrow, all sublayers expand.

You can create new sublayers in Illustrator just as new layers by selecting the New Sublayer palette menu command or by clicking the Create New Sublayer button at the bottom of the Layers palette. Selecting this command or holding down the Option/Alt key while clicking the Create New Sublayer button causes the Layer Options dialog box to appear.

NOTE If you select the Top Layer Only option in the Palette Options dialog box, then thumbnails don't display for any sublayers.

Because layers and/or sublayers are rearranged by dragging them in the Layers palette, if you drop a layer when a layer name is highlighted, the dropped layer becomes a sublayer under the selected layer.

With all the layers and sublayers, it can become difficult to find objects in the Layers palette. To locate an object's layer using the object, just select the object in the art board and choose the Locate Object palette menu command; the object's sublayer is revealed and selected in the Layers palette.

Object groups created by choosing Object ➪ Group show up in the Layers palette as a sublayer identified with the word *Group* listed in brackets. Expanding the Group sublayer reveals all the objects that are part of the group. If you create a group from several objects on different layers, all the objects move to the same layer as the topmost object.

CROSS-REF Chapter 12 describes the concept of stacking order.

Printing and previewing layers

The Layer Options dialog box, shown in Figure 25.12, for layers in Illustrator includes Print and Preview options. These options determine whether the designated layer is printed and whether the layer is displayed in Preview or Outline mode.

FIGURE 25.12

The Layer Options dialog box in Illustrator

Holding down the ⌘/Ctrl key while clicking the Visibility icon toggles the selected layer between Preview and Outline mode. This changes the Visibility icon, as shown in Figure 25.13. Using the Outline Others palette menu command or holding down Ctrl+Alt (Windows) or ⌘+Option (Mac) while clicking the Visibility icon changes all layers to Outline mode except for the selected one.

FIGURE 25.13

The eye icon shows which layers are in Outline mode.

The Layer Options dialog box also includes an option to dim images by a specific percentage. This is helpful if you're tracing images, as shown in Figure 25.14.

FIGURE 25.14

The Dim Images By option makes tracing images easy.

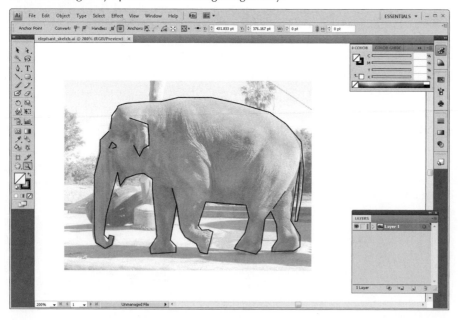

Disabling the Print option prevents the layer from printing when you choose File ➪ Print, even if the layer objects are visible. If you disable the Preview option, the layer objects are viewed in Outline mode. This is a useful option if you have a complex object that takes a long time to redraw.

Creating a template layer

The Layer Options dialog box also includes an option to make a layer into a template layer. You also can make a layer a template by selecting the Template palette menu command. The Visibility icon for templates changes as shown in Figure 25.15.

FIGURE 25.15

Template layers don't print or export with the rest of the layers.

Normal layer

Template layer

Template layers are unique because you cannot print or export them. You also can hide them by choosing View ➪ Show/Hide Template (Shift+Ctrl+W in Windows; Shift+⌘+W on the Mac).

When you choose File ➪ Place, the Place dialog box includes a Template option. If this option is selected, the placed image is put on a new template layer. This new layer is positioned directly below the selected layer. By default, this template layer is locked and the layer dims to 50 percent.

You may change template layers back to normal layers by disabling the Template option in the Layer Options dialog box.

STEPS: Tracing Layers in Illustrator

1. **Open a new document in Illustrator.** Within Illustrator, open a new document by choosing File ➪ New.

2. **Open an image to trace from.** Choose File ➪ Place. In the file dialog box that opens, select an image that you want to trace from and enable the Template option, as shown in Figure 25.16. Then click the Place button. The image is placed on a new template layer, and the Dim Layer to 50% option is enabled in the Layer Options dialog box.

FIGURE 25.16

The Place dialog box includes a Template option.

3. **Trace the image.** Select a layer above the template layer, and trace over the image with the Paintbrush tool, as shown in Figure 25.17.

4. **Hide the template layer.** After the sketch is complete, you can hide the template layer by clicking the Visibility icon.

CROSS-REF Another approach is to use Illustrator's Live Trace feature, which is covered in Chapter 9.

FIGURE 25.17

A dimmed image lets you easily trace an image.

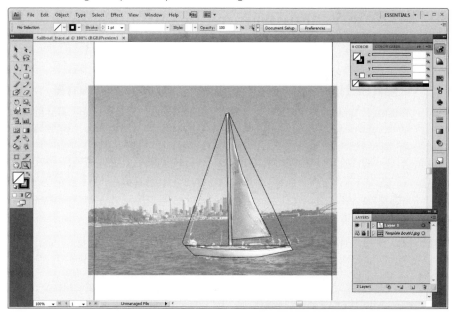

Releasing items to layers in Illustrator

If a single layer has many different objects, you can use the Release to Layers palette menu commands to move (or copy) each successive object to its own layer.

CROSS-REF Illustrator's Release to Layers menu commands are useful in building animation sequences that you can then export to the SWF format. More information on this format and using the Release to Layers commands to create animations is covered in Chapter 30.

There are actually two different Release to Layers menu commands. The Release to Layers (Sequence) palette menu command moves each object to its own layer, but the Release to Layers (Build) menu command copies and accumulates the objects to new layers where the first object gets copied to a new layer, the second object along with the first gets copied to the second layer, and so on until the final layer has all objects.

When objects within a layer are released to layers, the objects are added to layers starting with the object farthest back in the stacking order and moving forward, so the frontmost object is placed on the highest layer.

With several layers selected, you can select to reverse their order in the Layers palette by using the Reverse Order palette menu command.

Collecting layers and flattening artwork

Illustrator includes palette menu commands for merging, collecting, and flattening layers. Merging layers places all objects from several layers into the topmost layer. Collecting layers is similar to merging layers, but instead it collects the objects on several layers and moves them to a new layer while making the layers sublayers under the new layer. The Collect in New Layer palette menu command moves all objects on the selected layers to a new layer and deletes the old layers.

Illustrator also includes a Merge Selected menu command that merges the objects on all selected layers into the targeted layer.

The Layers palette only lets you select multiple layers within the same hierarchical level, so you cannot merge or collect layers at different levels within one another.

To merge all layers together, you could select all layers and use the Merge Selected palette menu command, or you could use the Flatten Artwork palette menu command. This merges all layers into one layer that includes all the objects in the file.

CAUTION The Flatten Artwork palette menu command cannot include layers that are hidden or locked. If you try to use the Flatten Artwork palette menu command with a hidden layer, a warning dialog box appears, asking if you want to discard the hidden art. Clicking the Yes button throws away all objects on the hidden layer and combines the rest of the objects into a single layer.

Importing Photoshop layers and comps into Illustrator and InDesign

When you choose File ➪ Open or File ➪ Place to open or place a layered Photoshop image into the current document, the Photoshop Import Options dialog box appears, shown in Figure 25.18. The Photoshop Import Options dialog box gives you the option to convert the Photoshop layers to objects or flatten the Photoshop layers.

NOTE The Photoshop Import Options dialog box also gives you the option to import image maps and/or slices if they exist in the Photoshop image.

If you select to convert the layers to objects, Illustrator imports the Photoshop layers, as best it can, into the current selected layer. It also does its best to make any text in the Photoshop file editable. However, if the Photoshop layer includes features not supported in Illustrator such as Layer Effects, Adjustment or Fill layers are merged during the conversion process.

FIGURE 25.18

When you place layered Photoshop images in Illustrator, you can convert the layers to objects or flatten all the layers.

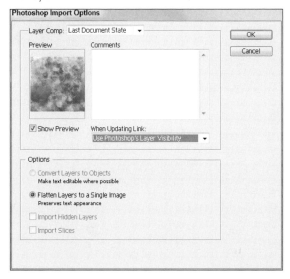

You also can select to import any hidden layers included in the Photoshop image, but if the hidden layer includes a feature that isn't supported, the layer is simply ignored.

If the layered Photoshop image includes any layer comps, then you can select which comp to import after viewing them in the Preview pane. If the layer comp has any comments, they are shown in the Comments field. The When Updating Link option includes two options—Keep Layer Visibility Overrides and Use Photoshop's Layer Visibility. This setting determines how the visibility of the file is determined for images that are linked into Illustrator or InDesign.

Exporting CSS layers

When exporting Illustrator artwork to a Web-based format using the File ➪ Save for Web & Devices menu command, you can choose to export the layers as Cascading Style Sheet (CSS) layers. These layers are recognized within Dreamweaver and may be used to add animated effects on a Web page.

To export layers as CSS layers, select the Layers panel in the lower-right corner of the Save for Web & Devices dialog box, as shown in Figure 25.19, and enable the Export As CSS Layers option. The Layers panel also lets you select a specific layer and designate it as Visible, Hidden, or Do Not Export. If the Preview Only Selected Layer option is selected, only the layer selected in the Layer panel is visible in the Original panel.

FIGURE 25.19

The Layers panel in the Save for Web & Devices dialog box

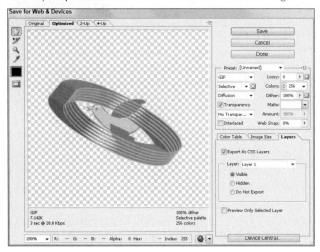

When you save the document, each layer is saved within a folder named images using the format designated in the Save for Web & Devices dialog box. The first layer is given the specified filename, and each additional layer has a sequential number following it. For example, if you save an Illustrator document with three layers as a GIF image with the name myFile, the first layer is named myFile.gif, the second layer becomes myFile-01.gif, and the third layer becomes myFile-02.gif.

If you select to have the Save for Web & Devices dialog box create an HTML page for you, then opening the HTML page in Dreamweaver displays all layers as CSS layers in their same positions that were found in the Illustrator artwork, as shown in Figure 25.20. The layers are separate files given a name based on the original filename within Dreamweaver.

 **NOTE** CSS Layers are specified in the HTML page, so if you don't select to create an HTML page along with the graphics, the exported image won't include any layers.

FIGURE 25.20

Opening the separated layers as images within a Web page (top) keeps all layer objects separate, but opening the HTML page places all layers in their original positions (bottom).

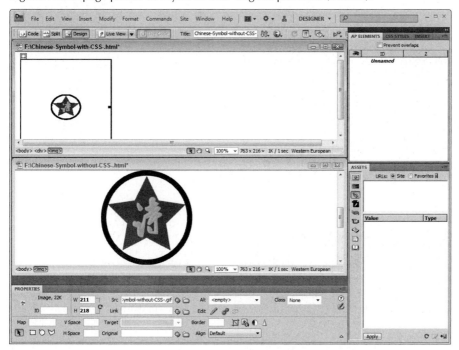

Applying appearance attributes to layers in Illustrator

The column of circles to the right in the Layers palette allows appearance attributes to be set for all objects on the targeted layer or sublayer.

Clicking the circle once targets that layer to receive any appearance changes, such as fill or stroke color, an effect, or a style from the Graphic Styles palette. When a layer is targeted, an additional circle surrounds the existing circle, as shown in Figure 25.21. You can target multiple layers at the same time by holding down the Shift key while clicking the circle icon for several layers.

With a layer (or several layers) targeted, change an attribute setting such as the fill color, a stroke setting, or a style in the Graphic Styles palette, or apply an effect from the Effect menu, and all the objects on the targeted layers are changed. Individual objects may have a different value that affects how they look.

FIGURE 25.21

The circle target is circled again when a layer is targeted.

Appearance targeted

Additional appearance exists

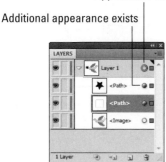

NOTE If you move an object out of a layer that has certain appearance attributes applied, the moved object no longer has those attributes. Attributes that you assign to a layer stay with that layer, not with the objects.

When a layer includes any appearance attributes other than standard fill and stroke attributes, the appearance attribute circle in the Layers palette appears shaded solid.

You can move appearance attributes between layers by dragging the appearance attributes circle from one layer to another. Holding down the Option/Alt key while dragging an appearance attribute copies the attribute to the other layer. Dragging the appearance attribute circle to the Delete Selection icon button at the bottom of the Layers palette deletes the attributes from the layer, except for the fill and stroke colors, which remain.

 More on using effects and styles is covered in Chapter 12.

STEPS: Tracing Layers in Illustrator

1. **Open a new document in Illustrator.** Within Illustrator, open a new document by choosing File ➪ New. In the New Document dialog box, click OK.

2. **Create a circle.** Select the Ellipse tool, and drag in the center of the art board with the Option/Alt and Shift keys held down to create a perfect circle in the center of the art board. Set the Fill color to white and the Stroke color to black with a Stroke Width of 2.

3. **Scale down the circle.** Choose Object ➪ Transform ➪ Scale. In the Scale dialog box, set the Uniform Scale value to 80% and click the Copy button.

4. **Duplicate the scaling command.** With the inner circle selected, choose Object ➪ Transform ➪ Transform Again or use the ⌘/Ctrl+D keyboard shortcut to apply

this transformation eight more times. This creates nine centered circles in the center of the art board on a single layer, as shown in Figure 25.22.

FIGURE 25.22

After scaling a duplicate object, you may use the Transform Again menu command to quickly create many additional copies.

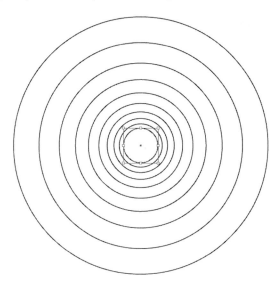

5. **Release the objects to separate layers.** With the layer that holds all these objects selected in the Layers palette, choose the Release to Layers (Sequence) palette menu command. This moves each object to its own layer. Although each object was selectable as a sublayer previously, releasing the objects to layers makes them easier to reference and work with.

6. **Apply a fill color to every other circle.** Within the Layers palette, hold down the Shift key and select the appearance attribute-targeting circle for every odd number layer starting with Layer 3. Then select a red color swatch from the Swatches palette or use the Appearance panel to change the fill color. Every other circle is filled with this color, as shown in Figure 25.23.

7. **Change the stroke weight for all layers.** In the Layers palette, click the appearance attribute target for the top layer named Layer 1 to select all objects. Then set the Weight value in the Strokes palette to 4 pt. This adds a darker ring to each object, as shown in Figure 25.24.

FIGURE 25.23

Using the target circle in the Layers palette, you can selectively choose exactly which layers get a certain appearance attribute.

FIGURE 25.24

With all the sublayers conveniently located under a parent layer, you can easily target all layers.

8. **Apply an effect.** With the top layer still targeted, choose Effect ⇨ Distort & Transform ⇨ Pucker & Bloat. In the Pucker & Bloat dialog box that appears, set the Pucker/Bloat value to 50% and click OK. The result is shown in Figure 25.25. Notice how the appearance attribute target is now shaded for the top layer, indicating that an appearance attribute other than a fill and stroke has been applied. You also can apply the effect using the button at the bottom of the Appearance panel.

FIGURE 25.25

Even effects may be targeted and applied to specific layers.

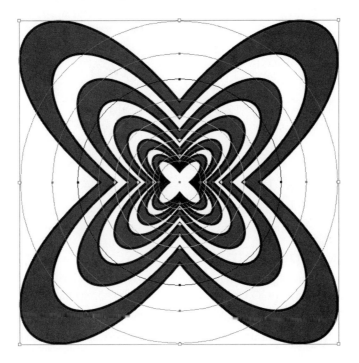

9. **Increase the Bloat effect.** Just for fun, try reapplying the Bloat effect with a value of 200% by double-clicking the effect in the Appearance palette. This pushes the edges of the circles through each other to create an interesting pattern, shown in Figure 25.26.

FIGURE 25.26

Manipulating the effect settings lets you create many unique shapes.

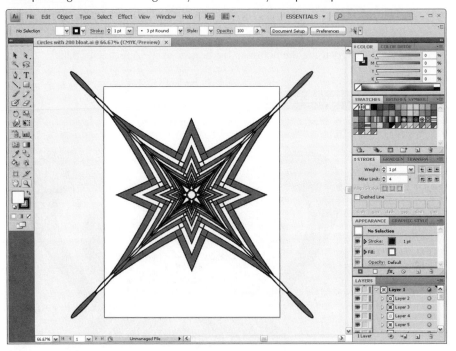

Creating clipping masks

Illustrator includes an Object ⇨ Clipping Mask ⇨ Make menu command for creating clipping masks. You can specify that an Opacity Mask is used as a clipping mask, but you also can create clipping masks using a layer or sublayer.

CROSS-REF   Standard Illustrator clipping masks and opacity masks are covered in Chapter 9.

When creating a clipping mask using a layer or sublayer, the topmost object in the layer becomes the clipping mask and it masks all objects in the layer underneath it. To create a clipping mask from a layer, select the layer and choose the Make Clipping Mask palette menu command, or click the Make/Release Clipping Mask button at the bottom of the Layers palette. Figure 25.27 shows a sample clipping mask applied to a placed image.

 You can use vector objects as clipping masks only in Illustrator. If you want to use a raster image as a clipping mask, use Photoshop.

FIGURE 25.27

By placing an object above the placed image, you can use the Make Clipping Mask palette menu command in the Layers palette.

The object used as the clipping mask loses its appearance attributes, and its stroke is changed to none. If you want to use the stroke or effect outline as part of the clipping mask, choose Object ➪ Expand Appearance before making a clipping mask.

You can identify clipping masks in the Layers palette because they're separated from the objects that they mask by a dotted line. If you need to reposition the clipping mask or any of the objects that it masks, simply click the target circle in the Layers palette and then click and drag the object or the mask to its new location. You also can choose Select ➪ Object ➪ Clipping Mask to select the clipping mask.

If you select a layer with a clipping mask, the palette menu changes to Release Clipping Mask, allowing you to remove a clipping mask.

STEPS: Creating a Clipping Mask

1. **Open a document in Illustrator.** Within Illustrator, choose File ⇨ Place and open an image to which you want to apply a clipping mask. Figure 25.28 shows an image placed within an Illustrator document.

FIGURE 25.28

The File ⇨ Place menu command places an image within an Illustrator document.

2. **Add some text to the image.** Select the Type tool and drag a text area on top of the image. Then type **Aussie 2020 AD**. In the Character palette, change the Font to Antique Olive Compact and the Size to 120 pt. The text, shown in Figure 25.29, covers most of the image.

3. **Create a clipping mask.** In the Layers palette, click the top layer and all other objects that you want to be affected by the mask, and select the Make Clipping Mask palette menu command. The area beneath the text object is clipped, as shown in Figure 25.30.

FIGURE 25.29

Use the Type tool to add text to an Illustrator document.

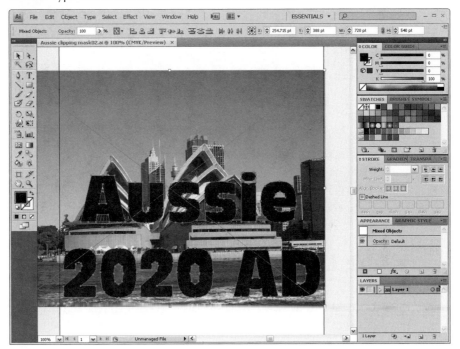

FIGURE 25.30

When all letters are combined into a single compound path, the object is used as a clipping path to the image underneath.

Using Layers in Photoshop

Layers in Photoshop are more advanced than any other CS4 applications, enabling many additional features including layer sets, linked layers, specialized type and shape layers, property-specific locking, an opacity setting, layer effects, adjustment and fill layers, layer masking, and layer comps. Figure 25.31 shows the Layers palette found in Photoshop.

Like Illustrator, Photoshop also includes a Layers Palette Options dialog box, shown in Figure 25.32, which lets you change the size of the thumbnails viewed in the Layers palette. You also can choose to have the layer thumbnail show the Layer Bounds or the Entire Document. You also have an option to Use Default Masks on Adjustments.

FIGURE 25.31

The Layers palette in Photoshop

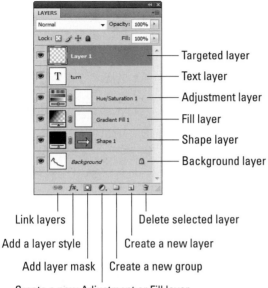

Targeted layer
Text layer
Adjustment layer
Fill layer
Shape layer
Background layer

Link layers
Add a layer style
Add layer mask
Create a new Adjustment or Fill layer
Delete selected layer
Create a new layer
Create a new group

FIGURE 25.32

The Layers Palette Options dialog box

Working with a background layer

When you create a new document in Photoshop, Photoshop creates a single layer named Background. You set the color of this background layer using the New dialog box. The choices are White, Background Color, or Transparent. If you select either the White or Background Color option, a background layer appears in the Layers palette. If Transparent is selected, then a gray and white checkerboard pattern appears denoting the transparent area and instead of a background layer, you get a layer named "Layer 1."

The background layer by default is locked and cannot be moved, but you can paint and draw on the background layer. You also cannot change its opacity or blending mode. It's always the lowest layer. By choosing Layer ➪ New ➪ Layer from Background or by choosing Layer ➪ New ➪ Background from Layer, you can convert a background layer to a normal layer or a normal layer to a background layer.

The lock status in Photoshop is different from that found in Illustrator and InDesign. In Illustrator and InDesign, you cannot add anything to a locked layer, but the background layer in Photoshop only has its position locked.

When you choose Layer ➪ New ➪ Layer from Background, the New Layer dialog box appears, shown in Figure 25.33. Here, you can set the layer's options, including the layer name, the layer color, the blending mode, and the opacity.

TIP Double-clicking the background layer opens the New Layer dialog box, allowing you to turn the background layer into a normal layer.

FIGURE 25.33

The New Layer dialog box displays the layer options.

Selecting and controlling multiple layers

Photoshop allows you to select multiple layers. To select multiple layers, simply hold down the Ctrl (or ⌘) key and click the layers to select in the Layers palette. To select multiple contiguous layers, click the first and last layers with the Shift key held down and all layers in between the first and last selected layers are selected.

You also can select all layers using the Select ⇨ All Layers menu command or just layers that are similar to the current layer with the Select ⇨ Similar Layers menu command. The Select ⇨ Deselect Layers menu command deselects all layers making the background layer the current layer.

 **Many common tools won't work with multiple layers selected, including the various paint tools.**

Auto Selecting layers with the Move tool

Photoshop allows you to select different layers with the Move tool. If the Auto Select Layer option in the Control panel is enabled, then clicking the document selects the topmost layer under the cursor. You also can select the Auto Select Group option to click and select a layer group. Another way to select layers is to right-click (Ctrl-click on the Mac) the document with the Move tool and all layers underneath the cursor's position are shown in a pop-up menu where they can be selected.

Aligning and distributing image layers

When two or more layers are selected, the layers can be aligned and distributed using the Layer ⇨ Align to Selection and the Layer ⇨ Distribute menu commands. The various align and distribute commands let you align and distribute layers to their left, right, top, and bottom edges, and to their horizontal and vertical centers. These commands also are available as icons in the Control panel when two or more layers are selected.

Selecting one of the distribute menu options moves the middle layers so that the space between the middle layer and the layers at either end are equal. For example, if you have five images that are horizontally aligned, you can equally space them by choosing to distribute them using their vertical centers.

Creating layer groups

Photoshop lets you create new layers just like the other applications, but you also can create layer groups. A layer group is a folder that includes several layers, and like Illustrator's sublayers, it provides a way to bundle several layers together, as shown in Figure 25.34. Layer sets may be nested up to five levels deep and can contain any type of layer.

FIGURE 25.34

Layer sets are used to collect several layers together.

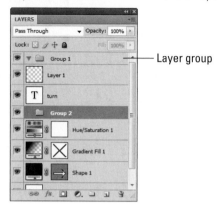 ——— Layer group

To create a layer group, select the New Group palette menu command or click the Create a New Group button at the bottom of the Layers palette. You also can create a new layer group from the selected layers using the New Group from Layers palette menu command or simply press ⌘/Ctrl+G. A layer group appears as a folder icon in the Layers palette. Using the palette menu command or holding down the Option/Alt key while clicking the Create a New Set button opens the New Layer Group dialog box, shown in Figure 25.35, where you can name the layer set, select a color, a blending mode, and an opacity.

 **Holding down the ⌘/Ctrl key while creating a new layer or a new group adds the layer below the current selected layer.**

FIGURE 25.35

The New Group dialog box lets you set the attributes for the layer group.

To add layers to a layer group, drag them in the Layers palette and drop them when the layer group is selected, or select the layer group folder before creating a new layer.

Selected layer groups can be deleted using the Delete Group palette menu command. This opens a dialog box that gives you the choice to delete the Group Only, the Group and Contents, or Cancel.

Linking layers

In addition to selecting multiple layers, you also can move the contents of multiple layers together by linking the layers together. To link a layer, select the layers that you want to link and choose the Link Layer palette menu command or click the small link icon at the bottom of the Layers palette. Linked layers have a bounding box in the canvas that surrounds all objects in both layers. A small link icon appears to the right of the layer name for all linked layers when one of the linked layers is selected.

Clicking the link icon a second time unlinks the layer, or you can choose the Unlink Layers palette menu command. Figure 25.36 shows both linked layers. To quickly select all linked layers, simply select one of the linked layers and choose Layer ➪ Select Linked Layers.

Merging and flattening layers

When multiple Photoshop layers are selected at the same time, the palette menu includes some additional menu commands for working with them.

FIGURE 25.36

The link icon to the right of the layer name marks whether a layer is linked or unlinked.

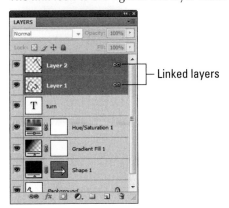

— Linked layers

The Merge Layers (⌘/Ctrl+E) palette menu command merges all selected layers into the topmost layer. Merging layers decreases the size of your file. To reduce the file size even more, you can select the Merge Visible palette menu command. This causes all visible layers to be combined into the topmost layer. It is different from flattening an image in that it retains all hidden layers separately, where the Flatten Image command gives you the option of discarding hidden layers.

STEPS: Distributing Images

1. **Open a new document in Photoshop.** Within Photoshop, open a new document by choosing File ➪ New. In the New dialog box, click OK.

2. **Open several images.** Choose File ➪ Open, and open several images within Photoshop.

3. **Copy and paste the images.** Select the first layer, and select an image. Choose Select ➪ All to select the entire image, and then copy and paste the selected image into the new document. Repeat this until every open image is pasted onto a different layer, as shown in Figure 25.37.

 Pasting into a document creates a new layer automatically.

TIP These steps are accomplished quickly using keyboard shortcuts with ⌘/Ctrl+A to select the entire image, ⌘/Ctrl+C to copy the selected image to the Clipboard, and ⌘/Ctrl+V to paste the image into the new document.

FIGURE 25.37

Placing each image on a separate layer makes aligning and distributing the images easy.

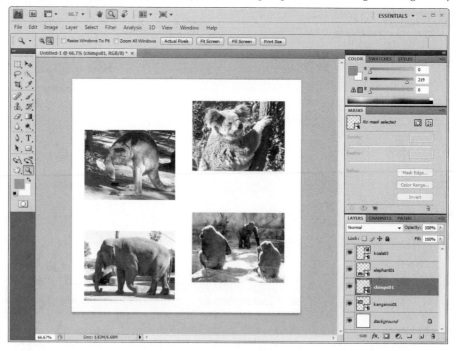

4. **Position the aligning image.** With the Move tool selected, move one of the images to its correct position.

5. **Align the images.** With the aligning image's layer selected, hold down the Ctrl (⌘) key and select the other layers or choose the Select ⇨ All Layers menu command. Then choose Layer ⇨ Align ⇨ Left Edges. All the images are moved to align with the selected layer, as shown in Figure 25.38.

FIGURE 25.38

All the layers are aligned with the selected layer by using the Layer ⇨ Align menu command.

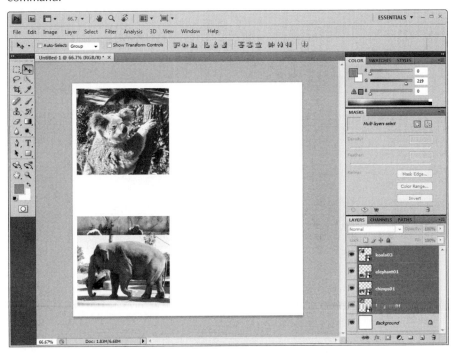

6. **Position the two end images.** Before distributing the images, select the images that are to appear on either end of the row of images and place them in their correct positions.

7. **Distribute the images.** With the layers all still selected, choose Layer ⇨ Distribute ⇨ Vertical Centers. This evenly spaces the aligned images, as shown in Figure 25.39.

FIGURE 25.39

When you distribute images, it equalizes the space between the layers.

Locking transparency, pixels, and position

You can lock each layer in Photoshop in a number of different ways using the Lock icon buttons at the top of the Layers palette, as shown in Figure 25.40. The Lock transparent pixels button prevents you from being able to paint on transparent areas. The Lock image pixels button won't let you paint on the image with any of the paint tools. The Lock position button prevents the selection from being moved. The Lock all button prevents any edits to the layer objects.

If the Lock Image Pixels button is enabled, the Lock Transparent Pixels button becomes disabled. If the Lock All button is enabled, all other locks are disabled.

When the Lock All button is selected, a black lock icon appears to the right of the layer name; when any of the other locks are selected, a white lock appears to the right of the layer name.

If the selected layer is part of a layer group, then you can choose the Lock All Layers in Group palette menu command to lock the entire group. This command is used to open a dialog box, shown in Figure 25.41, where you select which locks to apply to the group layers.

FIGURE 25.40

The Lock icon buttons are used to lock transparency, pixels, position, or all of these.

Lock transparent pixels

Lock image pixels

Lock position

Lock all

FIGURE 25.41

The Lock All Layers in Group dialog box

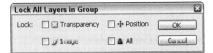

Working with type and shape layers

Type and shape layers cannot be edited with any of the painting tools or filters because they hold vector-based data, but you can use the Layer ⇨ Rasterize menu commands to convert these layers to pixel-based data. The options in the Rasterize menu include Type, Shape, Fill Content, Vector Mask, Layer, Linked Layer, and All Layers.

Creating a type layer

When the Type tool is used to add type to an image, a type layer is added to the Layers palette. Type layers are identified by a capital *T* in the thumbnail, as shown in Figure 25.42. Type layers automatically have both the Lock Transparent Pixels and Lock Image Pixels options disabled.

CROSS-REF Working with type is covered in detail in Part IV.

FIGURE 25.42

Type layers have a capital *T* in their thumbnail in the Layers palette.

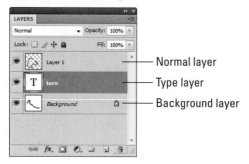

— Normal layer
— Type layer
— Background layer

The key benefit of a type layer is that you can select the text with the Type tool and edit, delete, and add new text even after it has been manipulated. When a type layer is selected in the Layers palette, several menu commands are available in the Layer ⇨ Type menu.

TIP If you double-click the type layer thumbnail, all the text is instantly selected.

Changing type orientation and anti-aliasing

By default, text entered into a text layer appears horizontally from left to right, but you can change the text orientation so it runs vertically from top to bottom using the Layer ⇨ Type ⇨ Vertical menu command. You can use the Layer ⇨ Type ⇨ Horizontal menu command to reorient vertical text horizontally again.

Figure 25.43 shows two type layers—one with a horizontal orientation and one with a vertical orientation.

The Layer ⇨ Type menu also includes several anti-alias options that are applied to the type layer. The options include None, Sharp, Crisp, Strong, and Smooth.

Converting between paragraph and point text

If you click the canvas with the Type tool, you create point text. Point text doesn't have a bounding box—the cursor just appears and lets you type without constraining the text flow to a certain area. Point text is typically used for headings or single lines of text.

FIGURE 25.43

Type layers may be orientated horizontally or vertically.

If you click and drag the canvas with the Type tool, you create Paragraph text. Paragraph text confines the text to the bounding box, so that any text that extends beyond the edge of the bounding box gets wrapped to the next line. This is useful for longer paragraphs of text, because the text is automatically wrapped to fit the designated area.

The Layer ⇨ Type menu includes commands to switch between these two types. When a layer containing point text is selected, the Convert to Paragraph Text menu command is available, and vice versa.

CAUTION When you convert paragraph text to point text, all characters that overflow outside the bounding box are deleted. To avoid this, resize the bounding box before performing the conversion.

Warping text

When type layers are rasterized, you can distort and manipulate them using all the standard Photoshop tools, but doing so makes them uneditable as text objects. However, there are several distortions that you can do to text while keeping it editable, such as transforming and warping the text.

To warp a selected type layer, choose Layer ➪ Type ➪ Warp Text or Edit ➪ Transform ➪ Warp. This opens a dialog box, shown in Figure 25.44, where you can select from several different warp types: Arc, Arc Lower, Arc Upper, Arch, Bulge, Shell Lower, Shell Upper, Flag, Wave, Fish, Rise, Fisheye, Inflate, Squeeze, and Twist.

CROSS-REF These warp types are the same as those available within Illustrator and are covered in Chapter 13.

FIGURE 25.44

The Warp Text dialog box allows you to warp text objects in Photoshop the same way as text in Illustrator.

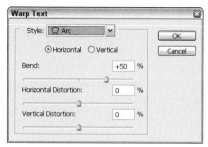

Creating a shape layer

In addition to type layers created with the Type tool, Photoshop's Toolbox includes the Pen tool and several shape tools for creating rectangles, rounded rectangles, ellipses, polygons, straight lines, and custom shapes. When these tools are selected, the Options bar includes three different modes for applying these shapes as Shape Layers, Paths, and Fill Pixels.

The Shape Layers mode creates a shape layer in the Layers palette, as shown in Figure 25.45, the Paths mode creates a temporary work path that appears in the Paths palette, and the Fill Pixels mode lets you create a raster-based shape when a normal layer is selected.

CROSS-REF The Paths and Fill Pixels modes, along with the Pen and Shape tools, are covered in more detail in Chapter 12.

Shape layers are displayed in the Layers palette with two thumbnails. The first thumbnail is the fill applied to the shape, and the second thumbnail shows the shape as a layer mask called a vector mask. When the Vector Mask thumbnail is selected, you can move the shape. The link icon between the fill and layer mask thumbnails binds the layer mask to the layer. If you click the link icon to unlink the layer mask, you can no longer reposition the layer mask.

CROSS-REF Layer masks are covered in more detail later in this chapter.

FIGURE 25.45

Shape layers show up in the Layers palette with two thumbnails—one for the fill and one for the layer mask.

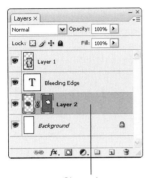

Shape layer

STEPS: Creating a Simple Logo

1. **Open a new document in Photoshop.** Within Photoshop, create a new document by choosing File ➪ New. In the New dialog box, click OK.

2. **Create a type layer.** Select the Type tool, click and drag in the center of the canvas, and type the text within the bounding box. The type layer appears in the Layers palette.

3. **Change the text style and size.** Choose Window ➪ Character to open the Character palette. Select the Type tool, drag over the text in the text layer to select it, and then change the font to Croobie (or some other stylized font) and the size to 36 pt. In the Paragraph palette, select the Center Text button. The text should now look like Figure 25.46.

FIGURE 25.46

You can use the Type tool to select type and the Character and Paragraph palettes to change the text settings.

4. **Warp the text.** With the type layer selected, choose Layer ⇨ Type ⇨ Warp Text. In the Warp Text dialog box, select the Arc style and set the Bend value to 50%. Then click OK to apply the warp, as shown in Figure 25.47.

FIGURE 25.47

Using the Warp Text dialog box, you can distort text in a number of different ways.

5. **Add a background rectangle.** Click the Rectangle tool, and select the Shape Layer button in the Options box. Change the foreground color to red, and drag to create a rectangle that covers the text. This adds a shape layer to the Shapes palette. With the shape layer selected, choose Layer ⇨ Arrange ⇨ Send to Back. This moves the shape layer below the type layer and moves the red rectangle behind the text, as shown in Figure 25.48.

FIGURE 25.48

You can use the Rectangle tool to add shapes that you may move behind the text.

6. **Rasterize the shape layer.** To add some details to the background rectangle with a filter, you'll need to rasterize the rectangle. With the shape layer selected, choose Layer⇨Rasterize⇨ Shape. This converts the shape layer to a normal layer named Shape 1.

7. **Apply a filter to the background.** With the rectangle layer still selected, choose Filter⇨Distort⇨Ripple. This opens the Ripple dialog box. Set the amount to 150% and the size to Large; then click OK to ripple the edges of the background rectangle, as shown in Figure 25.49.

FIGURE 25.49

To add some details to the edges of the rectangle layer, the Ripple filter adds just what is needed.

Setting layer opacity and selecting a blending mode

Although you can set the opacity and blending mode when a layer is first created in the New Layer dialog box, the options may be changed at any time using the controls at the top of the Layers palette. The Opacity value and blending mode are applied to the entire layer.

 You cannot change the opacity or blending mode for the Background layer or for any locked layer.

To change the blending options, select a different blending mode from the list at the top of the Layers palette, or choose Layer⇨Layer Style⇨Blending Options, or double-click one of the normal layers. This command opens the Blending Options panel of the Layer Style dialog box, shown in Figure 25.50.

CROSS-REF More on transparency and blending modes is covered in Chapter 9.

FIGURE 25.50

The Layer Style dialog box lets you set the blend mode for the layer.

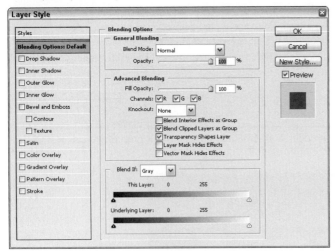

Creating a knockout

A knockout layer is used to remove, or knock out, a layer underneath it to reveal the Background layer or the bottom layer in a layer set. To create a knockout layer, simply place the knockout layer above the layer that you want to remove pixels from and choose one of the Knockout options in the Blending Options panel of the Layer Style dialog box.

The Knockout options include None, Shallow, and Deep. The Shallow option knocks out all layers to the bottom of the layer set that contains the knockout layer, but the Deep option knocks out all layers between the Knockout layer and the Background layer. If no Background layer exists, the knocked out area is made transparent.

You can control the amount of knockout using the Fill Opacity value. A Fill Opacity value of 0 knocks out all the in-between layers to reveal only the background, and a Fill Opacity of 100 doesn't knock out any of the in-between layers. Figure 25.51 shows an arrow shape used as a Knockout layer, revealing a pattern in the Background layer.

Setting fill opacity

Directly beneath the Layer Opacity value is another value marked as Fill. This value is the Fill Opacity value. It is used to set the opacity for the layer pixels or shapes without affecting the opacity of any pixels added as layer effects, such as drop shadows or glows.

FIGURE 25.51

The arrow shape in the top layer is used as a knockout for the gradient layer, allowing the pattern on the Background layer to show through.

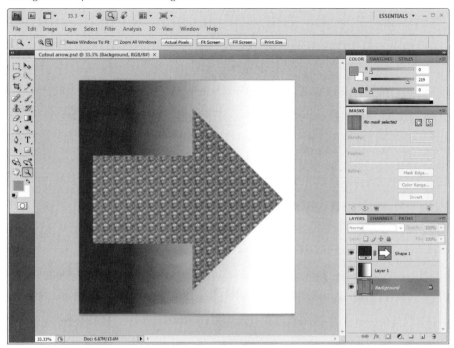

Using advanced blending options

In the Advanced Blending section of the Blending Options panel of the Layer Style dialog box are several additional options besides Fill Opacity and Knockout. The Channels check boxes let you apply the selected blending mode and options to specific channels only. Deselecting a channel causes it *not* to be included in the blending process. The availability of the channels depends on the color mode for the given image:

- **The Blend Interior Effects as Group option** treats any effects applied to the interior of the current layer as part of the layer and blends them with the layer pixels. Interior effects include Inner Glow, Satin, Color, and Gradient Overlay but not Inner Shadow.

- **The Select Blend Clipped Layers as Group option** applies the blending mode to all layers that are part of a clipping mask. If this option is deselected, then each clipping mask retains its original blending mode and options. This option is enabled by default.

- **The Transparency Shapes Layers option** prevents knockouts and layer effects from interfering with the layer's pixels. This option also is selected by default.

- **The Select Layer Mask Hides Effects and Select Vector Mask Hides Effects options** are used to confine layer effects to the area defined by the Layer or Vector Mask.

You can use the sliders at the bottom of the Blending Options panel of the Layer Style dialog box to target only a certain range of pixels for blending. The Blend If field lets you choose which color channel to blend. Select Gray for all channels. The This Layer slider lets you specify the bright- and dark-colored pixels to blend for the current layer, and the Underlying Layer slider lets you specify the pixels to blend for a layer under the current one.

 **If you hold down the Option/Alt key while dragging the slider arrows, you can split the arrows in half to define a specific range of pixels.**

Figure 25.52 shows a simple layer (top left) created with a stylized brush. The pixel-blending slider to the right has been moved to include all the bright pixels in the blending process, and the lower image shows the same document with all the dark pixels blended.

FIGURE 25.52

By manipulating the sliders in the Blending Options dialog box, you can select exactly which pixels are included in the blending operation.

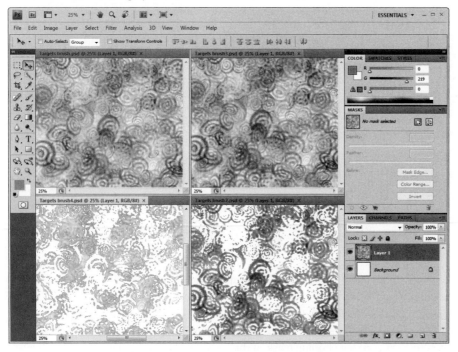

STEPS: Creating a Knockout Border

1. **Open a document in Photoshop.** Within Photoshop, open a new image by choosing File ⇨ Open.

2. **Convert the image to a Background layer.** Select the Background layer, and choose the Delete Layer palette menu command to remove the existing background. Then, with the image layer selected, choose Layer ➪ New ➪ Background From Layer. This converts the image layer to the Background layer.

3. **Create a new border layer.** Click the Create a New Layer button at the bottom of the Layers palette. The new layer appears in the Layers palette. Change the Fill color to red, click the Paintbrush tool, and select the Scattered Maple Leaves brush tip from the Brushes palette. Then drag over the entire layer to create a layer to use as a border, as shown in Figure 25.53.

FIGURE 25.53

This layer, created with the scattered leaves, is used as a border for the image.

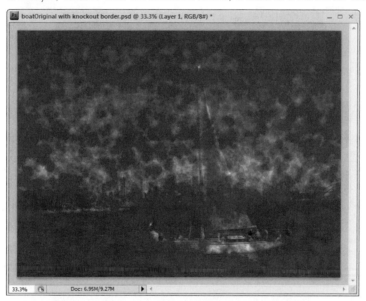

4. **Create a shape layer.** Select the Rectangle tool, and make sure the Shape Layer mode is selected in the Options bar. Then set the fill color to white and drag in the canvas to create a rectangle that leaves a border around the image, as shown in Figure 25.54. This creates a new shape layer in the Layers palette.

5. **Make the shape layer a knockout.** Double-click the shape layer mask thumbnail to open the Blending Options panel of the Layer Style dialog box. Select the Deep option in the Knockout field and set the Fill Opacity value to 0%. Then click OK. Figure 25.55 shows the resulting image.

FIGURE 25.54

Shape layers are useful for selecting areas to be knocked out.

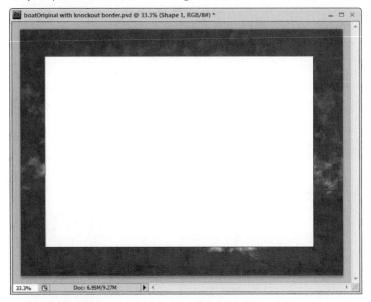

FIGURE 25.55

By knocking out the area defined in the shape layer, the image has a nice border.

Using layer effects

You can add layer effects to the current layer by enabling an effect in the Layer Style dialog box. This dialog box is opened by selecting the Blending Options palette menu command, by selecting one of the Layer Effects from the Add a Layer Style button at the bottom of the Layers palette, or by double-clicking the layer thumbnail. Figure 25.56 shows the Layer Style dialog box for the Drop Shadow effect.

 Layer effects may not be added to the Background layer or to a locked layer.

FIGURE 25.56

Each of the layer effects has its own panel in the Layer Style dialog box.

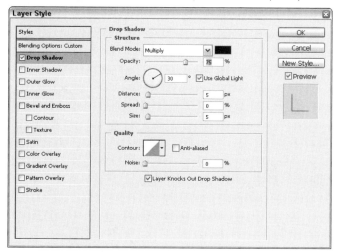

The available default Layer Effects include Drop Shadow, Inner Shadow, Outer Glow, Inner Glow, Bevel and Emboss, Satin, Color Overlay, Gradient Overlay, Pattern Overlay, and Stroke. Figure 25.57 shows each of these layer effects. Selecting any of these Layer Effects from the Add a Layer Style button opens the Layer Style dialog box and displays the settings for the selected effect.

CROSS-REF Each of these layer effects is covered in Chapter 13.

When a Layer Effect has been applied to a layer, the Layer Effect icon appears to the right of the layer title. Clicking the arrow that appears next to this icon expands and displays the list of effects. Double-clicking any of these listed effects opens the Layer Style dialog box again; here, you can edit the effect's settings.

FIGURE 25.57

Photoshop's Layer Effects adds and controls effects.

To remove a layer effect, simply drag the effect to the Delete Selected button at the bottom of the Layers palette.

Adjusting global lighting

Several of the layer effects depend on a lighting effect to determine where the shadows are cast, including the Drop Shadow, Inner Shadow, and Bevel and Emboss layer effects. Although each of these effects has a setting that controls the light's Angle and Altitude, you can select the Use Global Light option. When this option is selected, the light settings are controlled using the Global Light settings.

To Access the Global Light settings, choose Layer ➪ Layer Style ➪ Global Light. This opens a dialog box, shown in Figure 25.58, where you can set the Angle and Altitude values. You also can drag the crosshairs within the light circle to reposition these values. Using the Global Light dialog box, you can ensure that all shadows within the document are consistent.

FIGURE 25.58

FIGURE 25.58

The Global Light dialog box

Scaling effects

Layer effects may be saved as styles and reapplied to other layers, but an effect that looks great on one layer may be too small or too big when applied to another layer. Instead of reconfiguring the settings for the effect, you can simply change its scale by choosing Layer ➪ Layer Style ➪ Scale Effect.

CROSS-REF To learn more about working with styles and effects, see Chapter 9.

This command opens a simple dialog box with a slider for determining the scale of the effects applied to the current layer.

Turning effects into layers

You can separate effects from a layer by choosing Layer ➪ Layer Style ➪ Create Layers. This makes the layer effect an independent layer that you can manipulate and edit. Double-clicking the new layer still opens the effect's settings in the Layer Style dialog box.

STEPS: Adding Layer Effects

1. **Open a document in Photoshop.** Within Photoshop, open an image file by choosing File ➪ Open.

2. **Add a type layer.** Click the Type tool, and click in the lower center of the image. Choose Window ➪ Character to open the Character palette. Select the Rockwell Extra Bold font with a bold face, and set the size to 140 points with a color of white. Then type **AUSSIE 2020 AD**, as shown in Figure 25.59.

3. **Add an Inner Glow layer effect.** With the type layer selected, click the Add a Layer Style button at the bottom of the Layers palette and select the Inner Glow effect. In the Layer Style dialog box, set the blend mode to normal, the color to black, and the size to 25 pixels. Click OK. The text should now look blurred, and the layer effect is added beneath the type layer in the Layers palette, as shown in Figure 25.60.

FIGURE 25.59

Text helps identify the location, but the type is harsh against the image.

FIGURE 25.60

Using the Inner Glow layer effect, the text is made to look somewhat blurred.

4. **Add an Outer Glow layer effect.** With the type layer still selected, click the Add a Layer Style button at the bottom of the Layers palette and select the Outer Glow effect. In the Layer Style dialog box, click the color swatch to open the Color Picker; then click the Eyedropper tool, and click in the image to select a light color from the image. Set the size to 25 pixels, and click OK. The layer effects offset the text so it isn't so harsh, as shown in Figure 25.61.

FIGURE 25.61

The Outer Glow layer effect smoothes the transition into the image using a color from the image.

Using adjustment and fill layers

Within Photoshop, the Image ➪ Adjustment menu lets you adjust image properties such as contrast, color balance, and saturation, but applying the menu commands found in the Image ➪ Adjustment menu permanently changes the image.

You also can use the Adjustment and Mask panels to apply adjustments in a non-destructive way.

Using the Layers palette, you can apply an Adjustment layer to the image that holds the adjustment changes in a separate layer, so you can edit or even remove the adjustment changes at any time without affecting the image.

Fill layers are similar to adjustment layers. They're used to fill the canvas with a solid color, a gradient, or a pattern, but fill layers don't change the layers underneath them.

 **NOTE**   Another benefit of working with fill layers is that they do not increase the file size significantly, but adding a layer with a solid color can increase the file size significantly.

To add an adjustment layer, select one of the commands from the Layer⇨New Adjustment Layer menu or from the pop-up menu at the bottom of the Layers palette. The available adjustment layers include Brightness/Contrast, Levels, Curves, Exposure, Vibrance, Hue/Saturation, Color Balance, Black & White, Photo Filter, Channel Mixer, Invert, Posterize, Threshold, Gradient Map, and Selective Color. Figure 25.62 shows the Layers palette with an adjustment and a fill layer.

CROSS-REF You can learn more about these adjustment options in Chapter 9.

FIGURE 25.62

Adjustment and fill layers keep adjustments and fills separate from other layers.

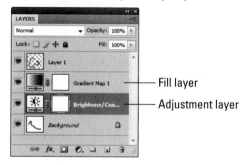

— Fill layer
— Adjustment layer

To add a fill layer, select one of the commands from the Layer⇨New Fill Layer menu or from the pop-up menu available at the bottom of the Layers palette. The available fill layers include Solid Color, Gradient, and Pattern.

Selecting any of these layers opens the appropriate dialog box for the layer type that was selected. Figure 25.63 shows the New Layer dialog box for the Color Fill layer.

FIGURE 25.63

Creating a new fill layer opens the New Layer dialog box.

Masking with layers

Masks are used in Photoshop to hide areas of a layer. Photoshop creates masks out of pixel selections or shapes. When a mask is applied to a layer, it appears as an additional thumbnail in the Layers palette positioned to the right of the main thumbnail. The mask thumbnail shows all hidden areas as black, all visible areas as white, and all semitransparent areas as gray.

Creating a layer mask

To apply a mask to a layer, select the layer and choose Layer ➪ Add Layer Mask ➪ Reveal All to add a mask that displays the entire layer underneath, or click the Add Layer Mask button at the bottom of the Layers palette. You also can choose Layer ➪ Add Layer Mask ➪ Hide All, or click the Add Layer Mask button at the bottom of the Layers palette with the Option/Alt key held down to create a layer mask that hides the image underneath.

If a pixel selection exists, that selection may be used as the basis for the mask. To make the interior of the selection a mask, choose Layer ➪ Add Layer Mask ➪ Hide Selection. To make all but the interior selection a mask, choose Layer ➪ Add Layer Mask ➪ Reveal Selection. The Add Layer Mask button at the bottom of the Layers palette also may be used with a selection.

The link icon that appears between the thumbnails in the Layers palette is used to make the layer move with its mask. Clicking the link icon unlinks the two and allows the mask to move independently of the layer.

Editing a layer mask

To edit a mask, click its thumbnail in the Layers palette and use the paint tools to color the canvas using black, white, and grayscale colors. A mask thumbnail appears to the right in the Layers palette, as shown in Figure 25.64, when a mask is selected and the foreground and background colors change to black and white. Masks use shades of gray to depict the varying opacity in the layer, but this gray is visible in the final image.

FIGURE 25.64

The mask is displayed in the second column for any layer that has a mask.

 — Mask layer

To see the mask in black and white while editing it, hold down the Option/Alt key while clicking the mask thumbnail in the Layers palette. To get back to the normal editing mode, click the layer thumbnail.

If you click the Layer Mask thumbnail with the Shift key held down, or if you choose Layer ⇨ Disable Layer Mask, the layer mask is disabled and a red X appears through the thumbnail. Clicking the mask thumbnail again makes the mask active again.

Creating vector masks

Vector objects such as paths, shapes, and text also may be used as masks. One benefit of vector masks is that you can move and edit them after they've been applied. This is true for all masks, not just vector masks. To create a vector mask, choose Layer ⇨ Add Vector Mask ⇨ Reveal All or choose Layer ⇨ Add Vector Mask ⇨ Hide All, just like the layer mask.

To use a vector object as a mask, select the layer that you want to mask and then select the Paths option (located between the Shapes and the Fill Pixels buttons) in the Options bar. This allows you to create a path without creating a new layer. Then choose Layer ⇨ Add Vector Mask ⇨ Current Path.

Vector masks may be converted to a normal layer mask by choosing Layer ⇨ Rasterize ⇨ Vector Mask. However, layer masks cannot be converted to vector masks.

Removing masks

To remove a layer mask, simply drag its thumbnail down to the Delete Selected button at the bottom of the Layers palette, or select the mask that you want to remove and choose Layer ⇨ Delete Layer/ Vector Mask. When a mask is removed, a warning dialog box appears, giving you the option to apply, cancel, or discard the mask. If you choose to apply the mask, the layer assumes the results of the mask. Figure 25.65 shows the results of painting on a layer mask to reveal the image underneath.

FIGURE 25.65

Painting on a layer mask with a spatter brush creates the effect of looking through a foggy window.

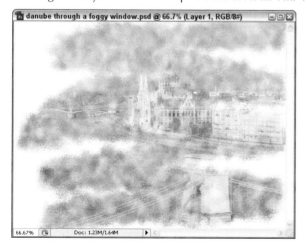

Using Smart Objects

Beside layer groups, Photoshop offers another way to combine several layers together. Smart Objects are a special object type that embeds the content of several layers into a single container. Smart Objects can include both raster and vector data and can be edited in a separate application while maintaining its ties to Photoshop. For example, an Illustrator file can be placed within a Photoshop file to make it a Smart Object.

To create a Smart Object, select several layers and choose the Convert to Smart Object palette menu command. This creates a new layer that is identified as a Smart Object by the small icon in the lower-right corner of the thumbnail, as shown in Figure 25.66.

Smart Objects are identified by a small icon in the lower right of the thumbnail.

Smart Object

You also can create a Smart Objects by placing Illustrator, PSD, or Camera RAW files in the current document using the File ➪ Place menu command or by copying and pasting Illustrator objects. When pasting an Illustrator object with the Edit ➪ Paste command, a simple dialog box, shown in Figure 25.67, appears with the options to paste the object as a Smart Object, as Pixels, as a Path, or as a Shape Layer. Smart Object layers can be copied to a new layer using the Layer ➪ Smart Objects ➪ Layer via Copy menu command.

FIGURE 25.67

Smart Objects also are created by pasting Illustrator objects into the Photoshop document.

Double-clicking a Smart Object layer or selecting the Edit Object palette menu command opens the Smart Object as a separate document in the original creator software, which may be Illustrator, Photoshop, or the Camera Raw dialog. When the command is first selected, a warning dialog box appears explaining that if you simply save the file being edited, then the changes are automatically updated in the Photoshop document.

Smart Objects can be exported independently of the document that contains them. To export a Smart Object layer, select the layer in the Layers palette and choose the Layer ➪ Smart Objects ➪ Export Contents menu command. This opens a file dialog box where the Smart Object can be saved using the format of its original software (AI for Illustrator, or PSB for Photoshop).

To update an existing Smart Object with new content, choose the Layer ➪ Smart Objects ➪ Replace Content menu command. A file dialog box opens where you can choose a new file to replace the current one. The new content assumes the size and position of the current Smart Object layer.

Using layer comps

Layer compositions (or *comps,* for short) offer a way to display multiple renditions of a Photoshop file. Stored in the Layers Comps palette, shown in Figure 25.68, layer comps record a snapshot of the Layers palette by keeping track of each layer's Visibility, Position, and Appearance.

To create a new layer comp, click the Create New Layer Comp button at the bottom of the Layer Comp palette. This opens a dialog box, shown in Figure 25.69, where you can name the new layer comp, specify which properties to record, and add a comment.

If changes are made to a layer comp, you may update the comp by clicking the Update Layer Comp button at the bottom of the Layer Comp palette.

FIGURE 25.68

The Layer Comps palette holds snapshots of the visible layers.

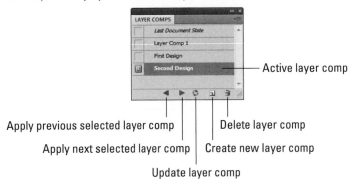

Apply previous selected layer comp

Apply next selected layer comp

Update layer comp

Active layer comp

Delete layer comp

Create new layer comp

FIGURE 25.69

The New Layer Comp dialog box lets you name the layer comp and select which layer attributes to record.

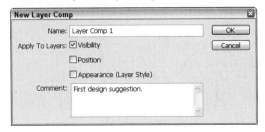

The Apply Previous and Apply Next Layer Comp buttons at the bottom of the Layer Comps palette let you quickly cycle through the various layer comps.

To delete a layer comp, select it and click the Delete Layer Comp button at the bottom of the Layer Comps palette.

 **NOTE** Deleting a layer comp deletes the memory of the layer configuration, but it doesn't delete the related layers in the file.

STEPS: Creating Several Layer Comps

1. **Open a document in Photoshop.** Within Photoshop, open a new document, such as the image with text and layer effects applied, by choosing File ➪ Open.

2. **Apply multiple layer effects.** Select the type layer, and apply each of the available layer effects to the type layer. Figure 25.70 shows the image with the Pattern Overlay and Stroke layer effects applied.

Layer effects are displayed in the Layers palette where you can quickly hide or show them.

3. **Creating new layer comps.** Experiment with the applied layer effects by enabling and disabling certain combinations. When you come across a design that is appealing, choose Window ⇨ Layer Comps to open the Layer Comps palette, and click the Create New Layer Comp button at the bottom of the palette. In the New Layer Comp dialog box that appears, name the layer comp appropriately, select the Visibility and Appearance options, and click OK. Figure 25.71 shows the Layer Comps palette with several options.

The Layer Comp palette lets you quickly cycle through a number of different design ideas.

4. **Preview the layer comps.** When you've finished creating a number of layer comps, click the Apply Next Selected Layer Comp several times to cycle through the available layer comps.

Placing layer comps in Illustrator and InDesign

When Photoshop files that include layer comps are placed within Illustrator or InDesign, the Options dialog box, shown in Figure 25.72, includes a drop-down list of the available layer comps. Using the Preview pane and comments, you can select the exact layer comp that you want to open and place in the current document.

FIGURE 25.72

When Photoshop files containing comps are placed in Illustrator, you can choose which comp to open.

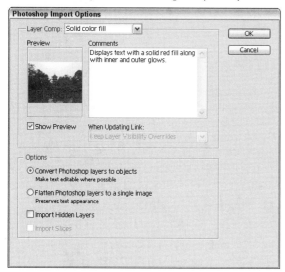

Using Layers in Flash

Layers in Flash are integrated into the Timeline panel, so don't look for a layers palette because there isn't one. At the base of the Timeline panel are buttons for creating new layers, creating layer folders, and deleting layers.

Flash allows you to select more than one layer at a time, but only one layer is active at a time. The active layer is the one with the pencil icon next to it, and it is the layer where all new objects are added. Just like layers in Photoshop, Illustrator, and InDesign, Flash layers include icons for turning off the visibility of the layer and for locking the layer.

Flash also has several different special layers including layers that hold sound files, ActionScript layers, frame label, and comment layers. There are also guide layers that work like the guides in Illustrator and InDesign and mask layers for hiding objects.

Flash also has an option, next to the Lock column, to view the layer as outlines. This works like Illustrator and can quickly make all objects react quickly to work on the timing of the animation.

Layers can be reorganized by dragging and dropping them into a different order. Objects on layers at the top of the Timeline panel are stacked on top of objects on layers that are below them in the Timeline panel.

Using Layers in Dreamweaver

Layers in Dreamweaver in some ways are similar to layers used in the other CS4 applications, but Dreamweaver layers actually represent layers that are defined as part of the CSS specification, which makes them behave differently in many ways. CSS stands for Cascading Style Sheets, which is a specification for handling and defining styles for Web pages.

CSS layers work like the layers in the other CS4 applications in that they allow you to stack content on top of each other, but there are some differences that you need to be aware of, including the following:

- CSS layers are always rectangular.
- CSS layers are positioned relative to the Web page's upper-left corner or relative to the upper-left corner of other layers.
- CSS layers may inherit attributes from a CSS.
- CSS layers are contained within the HTML code inside a <DIV> tag.
- CSS layers are not supported on all browsers and may not appear correctly if a user has disabled CSS features for his browser.
- CSS layers may be connected to execute actions when certain mouse events occur.
- CSS layers may be used to create simple animations by changing layers positioned in the same place.

Another huge difference is that CSS layers in Dreamweaver aren't called layers. They are called AP Elements. The AP stands for absolute position, and these objects are created using an <AP Div> tag.

Adding layers to a Web page

You add AP Divs to a Web page using the Insert ➪ Layout Objects ➪ AP Div menu, or you can create one by drawing in the Web page after clicking the Draw AP Div button in the Layout tab.

When an AP Div is created, its name appears in the AP Elements palette, as shown in Figure 25.73. Any layers that are imported from one of the other CS4 apps that support layers appear in the AP Elements palette as Unnamed. You can rename an AP element by simply double-clicking its name in the AP Elements palette. The AP Elements palette is opened by choosing Window ➪ AP Elements. The default names for new layers are simply apDiv1, apDiv2, and so on. A layer's name is known within the HTML code as its ID, and this ID is used in JavaScript to refer to the layer for interactive effects.

FIGURE 25.73

The AP Elements palette lets you sort layers by clicking the column headings.

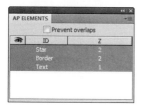

When an AP element is created, its dimensions appear in the CS Styles palette and also in the Properties panel, and each layer is given a number based on the order in which the layers were created. This number, called the Z-order value, is displayed in the right column of the AP Elements palette. These Z-order numbers also are used in the Timeline Editor to animate the layers.

AP elements are selected by clicking their edge or by clicking the position marker in the upper-left corner, by clicking the borders when the cursor changes to a hand icon, or by clicking its name in the AP Elements palette. When the hand icon appears when you click a layer's border, you can move the layer by dragging it to a new position. Dragging the layer handles lets you resize the layer.

TIP When a layer is selected, you can move it by pressing the arrow keys. Holding down the Shift key while using the arrow keys lets you move a layer 10 times the normal nudge value or 10 pixels by default; holding down the ⌘/Ctrl key while using the arrow keys lets you resize the selected element.

To delete a layer, just select the AP Element in the Design view and press the Delete button.

Using the AP Elements palette

The AP Elements palette includes some of the same layer features found in the other CS4 applications, including the eye icon. Clicking the first column of the AP Elements palette, you can change the visibility of the selected layer.

To the right of the element's name is another column that lists the Z-Index value, which is also called the Z-order value. Clicking the Name or Z-Index column head lets you sort the layers by their name or Z-Index value.

NOTE When an AP element is selected, it's automatically brought to the front of the stacking order so the layer is visible. But when the layer is unselected, it returns to its correct position in the stacking order.

Editing layer attributes

When an AP element is selected, its attributes display in the Properties palette, shown in Figure 25.74.

The Properties palette changes depending on the selected object.

The Properties palette includes the element's Name in an editable field, its positions and/or dimensions, a Z-Index value, and a Visibility menu. The layer's position values may be specified using the Top and Left position values along with the Width and Height values.

The Z-Index value determines the stacking order of the layers with the higher values appearing on top of the lower values, so a layer with a Z-Index of 10 appears in front of a layer with a Z-Index of 2.

The Properties panel also lets you select a background color for the layer or load an image to be displayed within the layer. To change the background color, click on the color swatch and a pop-up color picker appears with Web-safe color swatches.

The Image option lets you browse for an image. If the image is larger than the available size, only the portion of the image that fits in the layer is displayed. If the image is smaller than the layer, the image is placed in the upper-left corner of the layer.

STEPS: Creating Layers in Dreamweaver

1. **Open a Web page in Dreamweaver.** Within Dreamweaver, open a new Web page with the File ➪ New Page menu command.

2. **Click the Draw AP Div icon.** In the Layout tab, click the Draw AP Div icon and drag in the blank Web page at the position where the new AP element is located. The element appears as a rectangle at the position where you drag, and the layer name appears in the AP Elements palette, as shown in Figure 25.75.

FIGURE 25.75

AP Div elements are added to the Web page by clicking the Draw AP Div icon and dragging in the Web page.

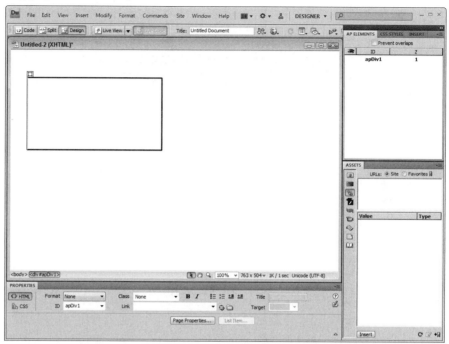

3. **Resizing and positioning the layer.** Drag the mouse over the element's edge, and click when the mouse icon changes to a hand icon. Resize the layer by dragging its corner handles, and drag the layer edges to reposition the layer.

4. **Change the layer's background color.** In the Properties palette, select the BG Color icon, where you can select a new background color.

5. **Add an image to the layer.** Click the Browse for File button in the Properties panel to load a background image. The loaded image is positioned within the AP Div element, as shown in Figure 25.76.

FIGURE 25.76

Content such as this image may be added to an AP Div element by browsing for the image in the Properties panel.

6. **Add text to the layer.** Click in the AP Div to have the text cursor appear. Enter the text, and use the Properties panel to change the text color, size, and position, as shown in Figure 25.77.

FIGURE 25.77

Clicking in the AP Div positions the text cursor within the layer. You can then enter text directly in the element.

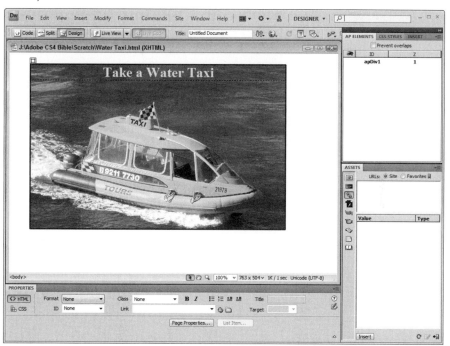

Summary

- Layers provide a way to organize objects into easy-to-select groups. These layers include properties such as visibility and locking that are enabled with a single click in the Layers palette.

- The Layers palette is used to create new layers, change the layer properties, move objects between layers, and manage layers.

- Layers may be used in all the CS4 applications, but the features available in each application are slightly different.

- Layers in Illustrator include the ability to work with sublayers, release layers, add styles to layers, and create clipping masks.

- Layers in Photoshop include layer sets, linked layers, transparency and blending modes, multiple locking attributes, adjustment and fill layers, type and shape layers, layer effects, and masks.

- The Layer Comps palette in Photoshop lets you take snapshots of different layer configurations and recall these snapshots quickly.

- Layers in Dreamweaver enable you to place Web page content on top of other layers. The Dreamweaver layers follow the CSS specification.

- Dreamweaver layers may be animated using the Timelines panel.

- The visibility of Individual layers in Acrobat may be toggled on and off for a PDF file that includes layers within Acrobat using the Layers tab.

Chapter 26

Modifying Layouts

A fter you create a layout, you may need to modify it. For example, embedding all the images you use in your layout in an InDesign document may result in a large, difficult-to-handle file size. However, you can place links to the larger original artwork elements within InDesign to make your file more manageable and embed smaller elements. You also can anchor graphics to a section of text so the graphic moves as the text moves.

This chapter shows you how to access links via the Links palette to see what links you need to relink, move, update, or embed, as well how to update edited image files.

Using Placed Artwork

When you place images in an InDesign document, the image file isn't copied into InDesign. Instead, a lower-resolution version of the image displays allowing you to position the image in the layout while maintaining a link to the original image. Using links to the original image helps keep the size of the InDesign document manageable. When you print, package, preflight, or export the document, all the links are followed and the original images are used. The original images also are used when the High Quality Display option is selected.

NOTE This chapter mainly focuses on the features found in InDesign, but Illustrator includes a similar manner of using linked artwork.

You place images using the File ➪ Place (⌘/Ctrl+D) menu command. All images that you import into InDesign show up in the Links palette listing the image filename and the page it appears.

Using the Links palette

The Links palette, shown in Figure 26.1, lists all placed files in an InDesign document. It also lists the file's location in the document. You open the Links palette by choosing Window➪Links (Shift+Ctrl+D in Windows; Shift+⌘+D on the Mac). The listed files can include images, placed InDesign files, and if you create links when placing, it also can list .DOC, .RTF, .TXT, and .XLS files. A preview of the linked file is displayed as an icon in the Links panel.

The Links palette lists all the placed files.

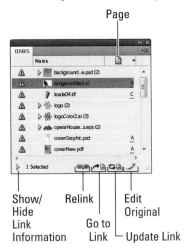

Page

Show/
Hide
Link
Information

Relink

Go to
Link

Edit
Original

Update Link

Depending on the state of the linked file, one of the following icons may appear to the right of the file name:

- **Missing file:** A red stop sign icon indicates that the placed file is missing. This means that the defined link is broken and that the file has been moved or renamed or is on a network or CD-ROM that can no longer be found.

- **Modified link:** A yellow triangle icon denotes that a more up-to-date version of the placed file is available and that you need to update the link.

- **Embedded link:** A gray square icon marks any embedded linked files within the current document.

- **Layer Visibility Override:** This icon shows up when the Layer Visibility Override toggle is enabled for the linked file. This uses the layer visibility settings for the InDesign document instead of the native application.

You can sort the placed files listed within the Links palette by Name, Page, Type, or Status using the commands found in the palette menu. You also can change the column arrangement using the Panel Options dialog box.

If you want to pull all of the linked files from their various places on your hard drive to a single folder, you can use the Copy Links to command in the Links palette menu. This is a handy command if you want to bundle the entire document with all its linked files together into a single folder.

Editing and locating original artwork

All placed files in the Links palette have links that point to the original file location. If you double-click on a placed file in the layout with the Option/Alt key held down, the original file opens within the application originally used to create it. You also can open a file in its original application by selecting the Edit Original palette menu command in the Links palette or by selecting an item in the Links palette and clicking the Edit Original button at the bottom of the palette. Another option is to open the selected object with another application using the Edit With option.

The Links palette also is helpful in locating files placed within InDesign. Selecting a placed file in the Links palette and choosing the Go to Link palette menu command displays the page upon which the placed file is located and selects the placed content. You also can jump to the linked content by clicking the page number shown to the right of the object in the Links panel. Alternatively, you can retrieve information by clicking the Go to Link button at the bottom of the Links palette. If a placed object is selected, then its corresponding link is highlighted in the Links palette.

Viewing link information and relinking

If you click the Show/Hide Link Information button in the Links panel, the lower panel reveals the Link Information for the selected link. This panel, shown in Figure 26.2, shows information about the linked file including its name, the last date it was modified, size, color space, file type, and so on. It also lists the link to the original object with a Relink button.

Clicking Relink in the Link Information dialog box opens a file dialog box that points to the selected placed file. If the linked file displays the Missing Image icon, you can use this button to locate the original file and reestablish the link.

If you do not select objects in the Links palette, selecting the Relink palette menu option or clicking the Relink button at the bottom of the palette causes InDesign to scan for any missing placed files. When a missing placed file is found, a file dialog box opens, allowing you to locate the missing file. When the file is found or when you click the Skip button, the list is scanned again until all the missing files have been relinked.

Clicking Relink in the Link Information dialog box opens a file dialog box that points to the selected placed file. If the linked file displays the Missing Image icon, you can use this button to locate the original file and reestablish the link.

FIGURE 26.2

The Link Information panel

If you do not select objects in the Links palette, selecting the Relink palette menu option or clicking the Relink button at the bottom of the palette causes InDesign to scan for any missing placed files. When a missing placed file is found, a file dialog box opens, allowing you to locate the missing file. When the file is found or when you click the Skip button, the list is scanned again until all the missing files have been relinked.

Any out-of-date placed files may be manually updated using the Update Link palette menu command or by selecting the file link in the Links palette and clicking on the Update Links button at the bottom of the palette. The same tip for scanning the files in the Links palette can be used to update links. If no objects are selected, you can click the Update Link palette and InDesign will scan and present a dialog box for each file that needs to be updated.

STEPS: Relinking Placed Image Files

1. **Open an InDesign document.** Choose File ➪ Open, and locate an InDesign document that includes placed images.

2. **Open the Links palette.** Choose Window ➪ Links to make the Links palette appear, as shown in Figure 26.3. If the links are broken for any of the placed images, the Missing Image icon appears next to the image file name in the Links palette.

FIGURE 26.3

Files you need to relink are marked with a question mark and moved to the top of the palette when sorting by Status.

3. **Relink missing files.** From the palette menu, select the Relink palette menu command. InDesign scans the Links palette and presents a file dialog box, for each image file that is missing. The Links palette displays all missing files at the top of the Links palette for easy reference. Locate the missing file, and click the Open button. Repeat this step for all missing files.

Embedding linked images

To ensure that images don't end up missing, you can embed them within the InDesign document using the Embed File palette menu command from the Links palette. This action places a small gray square icon next to the image's name in the Links palette and disables the link to the original file. Any future changes made to the original image file do not update in InDesign. In addition, the InDesign file size increases to accommodate the embedded file.

 **Embedding images increases the file size of the InDesign document and should be used judiciously.**

You unembed embedded files using the Unembed File palette menu command or by relinking the file to its original.

Setting the display quality

For placed images, you can set the display quality of raster images, vector images, and images that include transparency. The three display options available for placed images include Fast, Typical, and High Quality. Figure 26.4 shows an example of each of these options.

837

Display-quality options are Fast (left), Typical (middle), and High Quality (right).

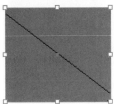  

Switching object display quality

You set the Display Performance level for the selected object by choosing Object ➪ Display Performance. The options include each of the levels along with Use View Setting. If you select the Use View Setting option, the level set in the View menu determines the Display Performance level.

Switching document display quality

In addition to changing the display quality for the selected object, you can also change it for the entire document. For the current view, you can select each of the following settings by choosing View ➪ Display Performance:

- **Fast:** Alt+Ctrl+Shift+Z in Windows; Option+⌘+Shift+Z on the Mac.
- **Typical:** Alt+Ctrl+Z in Windows; Option+⌘+Z on the Mac.
- **High Quality:** Alt+Ctrl+H in Windows; Option+⌘+H on the Mac.

Changing display quality preferences

The Preserve Object-Level Display Settings option causes the various display quality settings for all placed images to be remembered after the document is saved, closed, and reopened. This setting is off by default, which causes all objects to use the display settings specified in the View menu to be used when the document is opened again.

The display quality settings are configurable using the InDesign/Edit ➪ Preferences ➪ Display Performance menu command. The Display Performance panel of the Preferences dialog box, shown in Figure 26.5, lets you adjust the view settings for each of these levels. You also can enable anti-aliasing. Greeking displays text and images as a gray-shaded bar instead of individual letters. Using the Greek Type Below setting, you enable all type below a given point size to be displayed as a shaded bar. You can use the Scrolling slider to adjust the Hand tool to Greek type and images, to Greek just the images, or to have no Greeking. This applies only when the Hand tool is used to scroll.

 The Text Greeking preference isn't an absolute point size.

The Display Performance panel of the Preferences dialog box

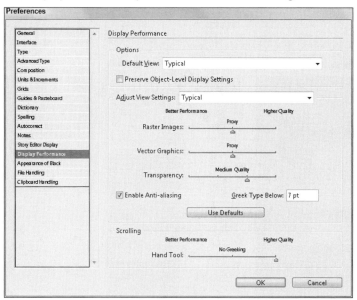

Anchoring objects

Anchored objects, which can include text frames, placed graphics, or even groups, are attached to a section of text. When the text frame moves, the anchored object moves with it. This is convenient for sidebars or inline graphics that highlight some text.

Anchored graphics

To create an anchored graphic, you need to select a text position with the Type tool, then choose File ➪ Place to place the graphic object or you can click the text and choose the Object ➪ Anchored Object ➪ Insert menu command. It is important to have the text position selected before you insert the anchored object or InDesign gets confused on where to place the anchored object. If a section of text is selected, then the anchored object replaces the selected text. The anchored graphic appears as a frame within the text frame, as shown in Figure 26.6.

> **TIP** An existing placed graphic can be anchored by cutting the graphic by choosing Edit ➪ Cut and pasting it by choosing Edit ➪ Paste after selecting the text to anchor it to with the Type tool.

FIGURE 26.6

Anchored graphics are created by placing an image when a text position is selected with the Type tool.

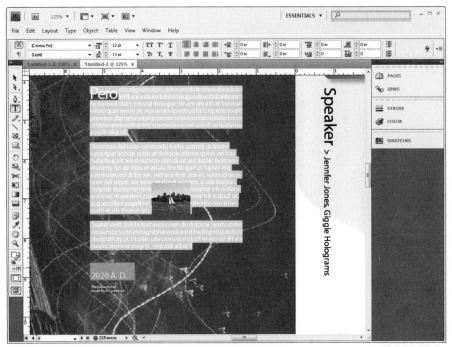

With the anchored graphic selected, choose Object ➪ Anchored Object ➪ Options to open the Anchored Object Options dialog box. The dialog box includes two Position settings—Inline or Above Line and Custom. These options are shown side by side in Figure 26.7.

Inline anchored objects can only be moved up or down within the text object, but custom anchored objects can be positioned anywhere in the layout. For the Inline position, you can set the Y Offset and the Above Line position lets you set the Alignment to Left, Center, Right, Towards Spine, Away from Spine, or according to the Text Alignment. You also can set the Space Before and After the anchored object. The selected anchored object can be moved manually by dragging on the object if the Prevent Manual Positioning option isn't selected.

If you want even more control over the position of the anchored object, you can select the Custom Position setting, which gives you many more options. Custom anchored objects can be positioned with referenced points on either side of the spine by enabling the Relative to Spine option. There are also settings for specifying the reference point for the Anchored Object and the Anchored Position. The X position can be relative and offset from the Anchor Marker, Column Edge, Text Frame, Page Margin, or Page Edge, and the Y position can be positioned relative and offset from the Baseline, Cap Height, Top of Leading, Column Edge, Text Frame, Page Margin, or Page Edge. There is also an option to Keep within Top/Bottom Column Boundaries to insure that the column layout is maintained.

FIGURE 26.7

The Anchored Object Options dialog box includes different settings for setting the object's position.

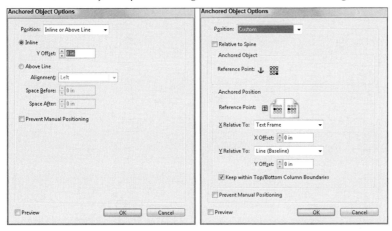

Anchored text frames

In addition to graphics, you also can anchor text frames or any other frame type. Anchored text frames are created in the same way that graphic anchors are created by selecting a text location with the Type tool and choosing Object ➪ Anchored Object ➪ Insert. This command opens the same Insert Anchored Object dialog box shown in Figure 26.8 with several more settings available.

The Insert Anchored Object dialog box lets you select the object type using the Content setting, which can be Text, Graphic, or Unassigned. You also can select an Object and Paragraph Style and the object Height and Width.

To break the link between an anchored object and its text object, select the anchored object and choose Object ➪ Anchored Object ➪ Release.

FIGURE 26.8

The Insert Anchored Object dialog box creates text or graphic anchored objects.

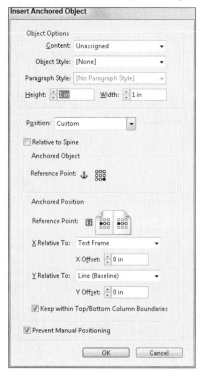

STEPS: Anchoring Graphics to Text

1. **Open a layout file in InDesign.** For this layout, you anchor an image of a koala to the third page.

2. **Select the anchoring text.** Click the Type tool from the Toolbox, and place the text cursor at the start of the second paragraph on the third page, which is the anchor text for the graphic.

 **Don't select any text in the text frame or the placed graphic replaces the selected text.**

3. **Create an Anchored Object.** With a text position selected within the anchor text frame, choose File ⇨ Place. Locate and open the `koala_small.tif` file. The image gets embedded within a new frame in the text frame, as shown in Figure 26.9.

The placed graphic is embedded within the text frame.

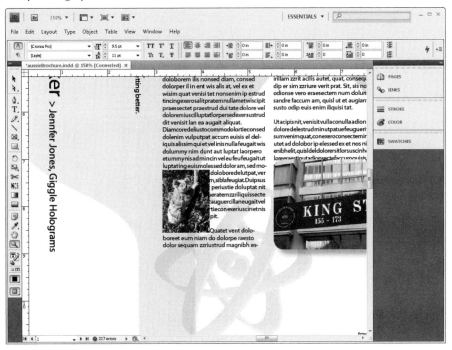

4. **Set the options for the Anchored Object.** With the Selection tool, click the anchored graphic and choose Object ⇨ Anchored Object ⇨ Options. In the Anchored Object Options dialog box, select the Custom option from the Position drop-down list. For the Anchored Object's Reference Point, select the lower-right corner; for the Anchored Position's Reference Point, select the point on the left side. Then set the X and Y Relative options to Text Frame with an X Offset of 0.25. Click OK. Figure 26.10 shows the resulting anchored graphic. This graphic moves with the text frame when the text frame is repositioned.

FIGURE 26.10

The anchored graphic is positioned relative to the text frame.

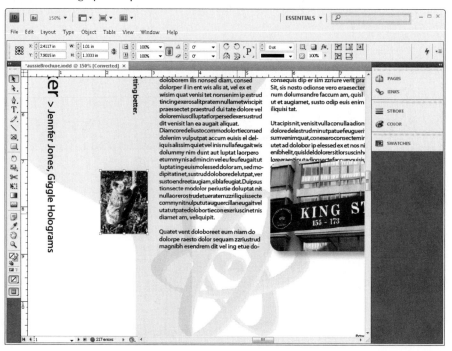

5. **Reposition the Text Frame.** With the Selection tool, select and drag the text frame to the right. Notice how the anchored graphic moves along with the text frame.

Summary

- Image files placed within an InDesign document appear in the Links palette.

- The Links palette may be used to relink missing image files, to update changed image files, and to locate placed images within the layout.

- InDesign's Anchoring feature lets you bind images to text fields.

Chapter 27

Creating Web Pages

D ocument repurposing deals with reusing designs for different media. In today's business climate, designs created for print are frequently reused to produce Web sites, CD-ROMs, PDF files, and video products. Repurposing designs can save lots of time and presents a consistent look across several products.

This chapter presents one repurposing example among many. Documents created for print in InDesign may be exported for use in Dreamweaver to create Web sites. You also can use Device Central to test how various pages look in different mobile devices.

After you've completed the design for your Web site, the final step in the repurposing workflow is uploading Web content to an online server. But you must first obtain some server space from a hosting company and enter the server information within Dreamweaver. You can then upload, download, or synchronize with the server. In addition, you can use Dreamweaver to export the site to a local Web folder that an external FTP client can use to upload the files.

PDF files offer another common way to present designs on the Web. PDF files may include links to other Web resources and, if hosted using Adobe's Policy Server, can be made secure.

Exporting InDesign Documents to Dreamweaver

One common design-repurposing path is to move layouts created in InDesign to the Web. To facilitate this process, InDesign includes an export feature that enables you to quickly move a print design to Dreamweaver and the Web. Choose File ➪ Export for Dreamweaver, and select a location to save the HTML file. This compiles all graphics and text in the current document and places them in a neat little folder where you can open and manipulate them in Dreamweaver.

The exporting process converts all the InDesign text content into a single XHTML page. The formatting for this text is converted to a Cascading Style Sheet (CSS). All other images and objects are converted to either the JPEG or GIF formats or packaged in their native format for more controlled optimization later in Dreamweaver.

NOTE If any linked image files are missing from the InDesign document, a warning dialog box appears, informing you that if you continue, the missing images are packaged with low-resolution versions of themselves.

Exporting an InDesign document

To export an InDesign document for use in Dreamweaver, open the document in InDesign and choose File ➪ Cross-Media Export ➪ XHTML/Dreamweaver. This opens a file dialog box where you can give the package a name and specify a location. After clicking Save, the XHTML Export Options dialog box appears, as shown in Figure 27.1.

FIGURE 27.1

The XHTML Export Options dialog box lets you specify how documents get moved to Dreamweaver.

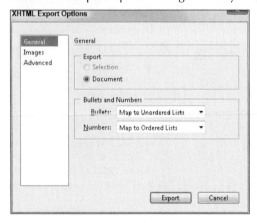

The General panel of the XHTML Export Options dialog box includes a setting for exporting just the selection or the entire Document. It also includes options for handling bulleted and numbered lists. Because both of these are different in InDesign from how they are treated in HTML, you have options to use Unordered Lists, standard text, or Ordered Lists.

CAUTION When exporting an InDesign document to HTML, be aware that manual formatting like bold and italic is not preserved, but paragraph and character styling are preserved.

The Images panel of the XHTML Export Options dialog box, shown in Figure 27.2, lets you specify to copy images to the exported folder as Optimized images, as Originals, or as Links to the Server Path. All images contained within the InDesign document are copied to a separate `Images` folder located within the export folder. Selecting the Original option moves a copy of the original images to the `Images` folder. Formatted images are images that have been cropped or scaled within InDesign. These images have `_fmt` added to their filenames, and optimized images have `.opt` added to their filenames.

If you choose the Links to the Server Path, then only the text that defines the links to the location of the images on the server is exported. This keeps all the images from having to be exported, but it requires that the images be manually placed on the server.

FIGURE 27.2

The Images panel of the XHTML Export Options dialog box lets you specify how images get converted.

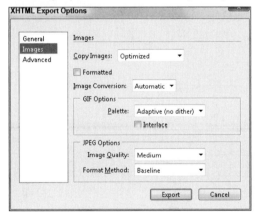

The Advanced panel of the XHTML Export Options dialog box, shown in Figure 27.3, lets you add links to an external CSS or JavaScript files.

FIGURE 27.3

The Advanced panel of the XHTML Export Options dialog box lets you create a link to an external CSS or JavaScript file.

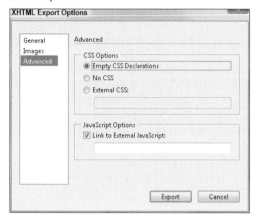

Export incompatibilities

Web pages conform to the Hypertext Markup Language (HTML), which has its own methods for displaying and formatting content. Although HTML can be used to create some interesting layouts, its feature set is fairly simplistic when compared to InDesign, and several specific InDesign elements aren't exported. The following is a short list of InDesign elements that are not exported as they are in InDesign:

NOTE   If you need to preserve the layout and all the content of an InDesign document, try exporting it and using it on the Web as a PDF document.

- Drawn objects and shapes created with the Rectangle, Polygon, Pen, and Pencil tools are not exported.
- Video files are not exported with the exception of Flash (SWF) files.
- Hyperlinks and bookmarks are not exported, but hyperlinks within the text are recreated as anchor links in HTML.
- Outlined text isn't exported.
- Master page objects such as page numbers aren't exported.

Preparing an InDesign document for export to Dreamweaver

If you use grouping within an InDesign document, you can control how the content is exported to an XHTML file. Groups in InDesign are exported as DIV tag objects, which keeps the objects together as part of a Dreamweaver page. If you want a section of text and its associated graphics to stay together on the Web page, use groups in InDesign to accomplish this.

Defined paragraph and character styles are also exported as DIV and SPANS objects in Dreamweaver. These HTML types are fairly basic, but they can represent text styles like bold and italics and text weight and size.

Opening an exported InDesign document in Dreamweaver

To view an exported InDesign document in Dreamweaver, simply open the HTML file; and all the image links are loaded automatically. Figure 27.4 shows an exported InDesign layout page opened in Dreamweaver. Once loaded, you can manipulate the content as desired.

FIGURE 27.4

Opening the exported HTML file lets you view the document in Dreamweaver.

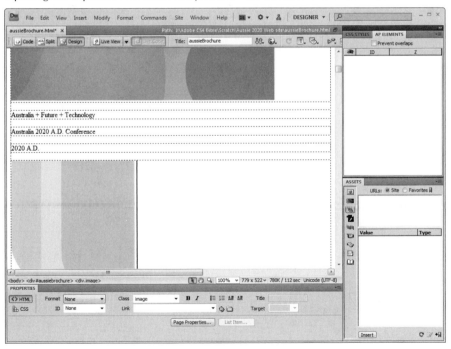

Copying and pasting content

Another way to move content between InDesign and Dreamweaver is to select and copy the various content objects to the Clipboard and paste them into Dreamweaver. Copying and pasting works well for text selected with the Text tool in InDesign, but images cannot be copied and pasted between the two, because InDesign deals with image links. However, embedded images can be copied and pasted. The same behavior works for images and text that is dragged and dropped between the two packages.

Although linked images cannot be copied and pasted between InDesign and Dreamweaver, images in Photoshop can be copied and pasted (or dragged and dropped) into Dreamweaver. When a Photoshop image is pasted into Dreamweaver, the Image Preview dialog box, shown in Figure 27.5, automatically opens. Using this dialog box, you can quickly specify the conversion options for the image. If you have a specific file size that you want to convert the image to, click the Optimize to Size Wizard button and the optimization settings are changed so the targeted file size is matched.

FIGURE 27.5

The Image Preview dialog box opens when a Photoshop image is dropped in Dreamweaver.

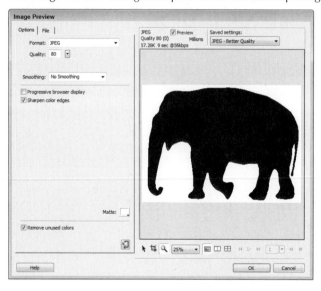

When a graphic is pasted into Dreamweaver, you also can double-click the graphic to load the image in Photoshop for more editing.

Setting Up a Site Window with the Site Wizard

Often, starting from a blank Web page to create a Web site is easier than some other creation methods. Exporting an existing layout has some benefit, but you also can create Web pages by reusing the existing content and laying out the pages using blank pages.

Each of the applications included in the Creative Suite has its own purpose, and the purpose of Dreamweaver is to create Web pages and manage Web sites. Web pages are much different from the layout designs found in any of the other CS4 applications, because they're constrained to conform to Hypertext Markup Language (HTML).

HTML is the language that Web browsers read that defines the placement of text and images on a Web page. HTML is very linear in its layout approach, with objects positioned on top of one another from the upper-left corner of the page to the bottom of the page following the left edge of the page.

Web sites are a collection of Web pages that you publish to the Web. The typical workflow for Web sites is to design the site first and then to flesh out the individual Web pages.

Using the New dialog box

When Dreamweaver launches, a Welcome dialog box appears, as shown in Figure 27.6. This dialog box provides quick links to the new features of Dreamweaver CS4, tutorials, and resources. It also includes icons for creating a New Document, opening an existing one, or creating one from a sample. You can deselect the Don't Show Again option to make this dialog box go away.

FIGURE 27.6

The Dreamweaver Welcome dialog box provides all the links you need to get started.

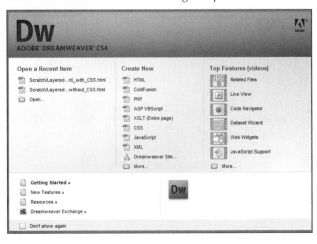

Clicking the New Document icon in the Welcome dialog box or choosing File ➪ New makes the New dialog box appear, as shown in Figure 27.7. This dialog box includes templates for several different types of Web sites and pages. If you want to add new templates to the New dialog box using Adobe Exchange, click the Get More Content link at the bottom of the dialog box. This connects you to an Adobe Web site where you can download more templates and samples.

The New dialog box lets you choose from a number of different types of templates.

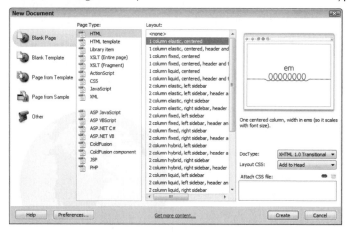

Creating a new site

The New Document dialog box opened with the File ➪ New command creates single pages that can be combined into an existing site, but to create a new site, you need to use the commands in the Site menu.

To create a new Web site, select the Site ➪ New Site menu. This opens the Site Definition dialog box, shown in Figure 27.8. This dialog box has Basic and Advanced tabs. The Basic tab runs a Site Definition wizard that steps you through the process of defining a site; the Advanced tab includes all the various settings for manually defining a site.

Adding pages to a site

You can add Web pages that you created before creating the site using several different methods. With the Files palette open, as shown in Figure 27.9, select File ➪ New File from the palette menu to create and add a new blank page to the site. You also can drag and drop a file into the Files palette or copy and paste files in the site window. This window also lets you rename and delete pages as needed. From the site window, you can open Web pages by double-clicking them in the Files section.

FIGURE 27.8

FIGURE 27.8

The Site Definition dialog box lets you create and define the settings for a new site.

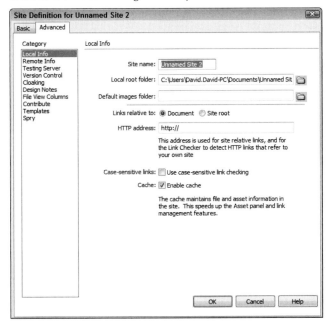

FIGURE 27.9

All site pages are listed in the Files palette.

Updating pages

When you add pages to a site, Dreamweaver includes a command to automatically check the new page links to see if they are correct using the File ➪ Check Links palette menu. If a problem occurs, a report of the broken links is displayed, as shown in Figure 27.10. The broken links are listed in the Link Checker panel of the Results palette. If the Results palette isn't open, you can access it using the Window ➪ Results menu.

One of the most common errors are links that point to pages that don't exist. To fix bad links, locate the link on the page and change its link. To update the site file view after the incorrect links have been fixed, simply choose View ➪ Refresh or Refresh Files from the right-click pop-up menu.

FIGURE 27.10

Pages with incorrect links are listed in the Check Links report.

Creating Web Pages in Dreamweaver

Text on a single Web page isn't placed within a text frame like InDesign; it pushes surrounding objects to fit all the text in the designated size. Images, likewise, aren't cropped or sized; they appear at their actual resolution where they rest between sections and paragraphs of text on the page.

These rules are understood by Dreamweaver, but be aware that if objects don't seem to stay where you put them, HTML and the Web browser, not Dreamweaver, is to blame.

Building Web pages and using views

The first place to start building Web pages is with the files you exported from InDesign, or you can drag and drop content directly on a blank Web page.

Each Web page displays in its own window, as shown in Figure 27.11. Dreamweaver lets you have multiple files open at the same time, and each file's name is listed along the top edge of the window. You have several ways to view each page using the tabs at the top of the window:

**NOTE** When an open file hasn't been saved, an asterisk appears next to its name.

FIGURE 27.11

Each Web page displays in its own window.

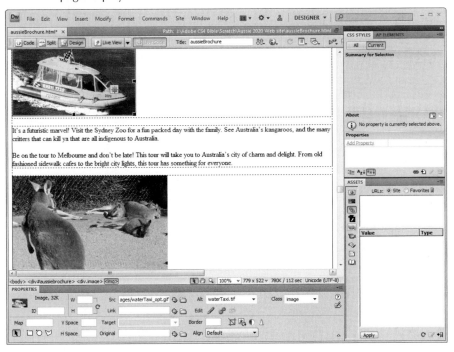

- **Code:** This window displays the HTML code that generates the Web page.
- **Split:** This window divides the Web page into two panels—one displaying Code view and the other displaying Design view, as shown in Figure 27.12.
- **Design:** The default view, which displays laid-out Web-page objects, allows you to easily select and reposition objects.

FIGURE 27.12

The Split view displays both Code and Design views.

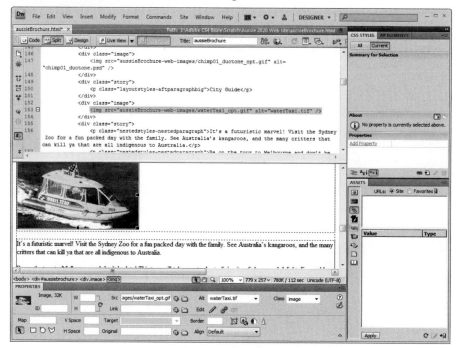

Using the Web page tools

The Insert palette, shown in Figure 27.13, includes several different tools that you can add to a Web page. Using these several tools, you can add and define the various Web page objects. The Insert palette is divided into several different groups:

- **Common:** This panel includes the most commonly used Web page elements, such as Hyperlinks, Tables, Images, and Media.

- **Layout:** This panel includes objects designed to help lay out the Web page, such as Frames, DIV tags, and table definitions.

- **Forms:** This panel includes objects found on form pages, such as buttons, labels, pop-ups, and text fields.

- **Data:** This panel includes objects and features for working with data, such as importing data, creating and managing records, and defining dynamic data.

- **Spry:** This panel includes a set of pre-built JavaScript templates for doing data validation, menu bars, and tabbed panels.

- **Incontext Editing:** This panel includes options for creating repeating and editable regions and for managing CSS classes.

- **Text:** This panel includes icons for formatting a text selection, including bold, italics, size, headings, ordered lists, and unordered lists.

- **Favorites:** This panel can be customized to hold any of your favorite tool icons.

FIGURE 27.13

The Insert bar holds all the various Web page objects.

After you locate the correct object in the Insert palette, you can add it to a Web page window by dragging it from the Toolbox and dropping it on the Web page or by double-clicking an object to add it at the cursor's location.

Changing object properties

You select objects on a Web page in the Layout Editor by clicking them with the Selection tool. A border around the object appears, and the properties for the selected object appear in the Properties palette. Figure 27.14 shows the Properties palette when an image is selected in the Web page. The exact properties displayed in the Properties palette depend on the object selected.

FIGURE 27.14

Properties for the selected Web page object are displayed in the Properties palette.

Adding Web page text

Text can be easily added to a Web page by simply typing on the page. The text is added at the position of the cursor. Dreamweaver also includes basic formatting options on the Insert Toolbox under the Text tab at the top of the interface and in the Text menu. Formatting options include text alignment, font size, text style (strong, emphasis, and teletype), and text color. You also have options to create numbered and unnumbered lists. These text-formatting options are implemented in HTML and create markup tags for the text.

When text is added to a Web page, it flows around the other objects on the page, including headings and images depending on the settings for the objects. You can overlay text on top of other items using layers. Text also can be imported from other applications such as Microsoft Word using the Clipboard.

Linking Web pages

You can add links, which open another Web page within a browser, to text or images within a Web page. To create a link, select the text you want for a link and click the Hyperlink icon in the Insert palette. The Hyperlink dialog box, shown in Figure 27.15, appears. In the Hyperlink dialog box, you can click the Browse button and select the Web page or image to which you want to link. The Web page name appears in the Link field. You also can specify the following: a Target that defines whether the link is opened in a new window, a Title that appears when the mouse cursor moves over the link, and an Access Key and Tab Index.

FIGURE 27.15

At the top of the Inspector palette, you specify the Web page or object to which you want to link.

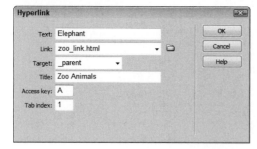

Graphics also can act as hyperlinks using the Link property. Two helpful icons lie to the right of the Link property. The Point to File icon lets you click and drag to the file name that you want to link to. Whichever file in the Files palette that you drop the mouse on is added to the Link value. The next icon is the Browse File icon, which lets you locate the linked file from a file dialog box.

The Point to File icons are available for other properties, including the image SRC and Low SRC values.

After you create links between Web pages, the File ➪ Check Links menu lets you test the links.

Working with Basic Objects and images

The Common category of the Toolbox includes many of the core objects that you can use to create Web pages, including images, tables, multimedia objects, and so on.

To load an image onto a Web page, simply locate the cursor where you want the image located and click the Image icon in the Insert palette. The Image icon includes several options including Image, Image Placeholder, Rollover Image, Fireworks HTML, Navigation Bar, and several hotspot shapes. If the Image option is selected, the Select Image Source dialog box, shown in Figure 27.16, opens. Use the Browse button found in the Properties palette. Other Properties palette properties include the image's size, alignment, and Alt Text, which is the text that appears when the cursor is placed over the image. Images also can be links to other Web pages.

FIGURE 27.16

The Select Image Source dialog box lets you load images into the current Web page.

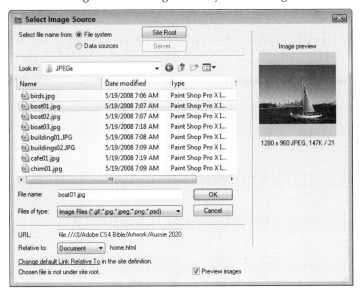

STEPS: Building a Web page

1. **Open an existing site, and add a Web page to the site.** Choose the Site ⇨ Manage Sites menu command, and select a site to open from the list. Then click the Edit button. The Site Definition dialog box opens. Click the OK button to view the Site Management window. Right-click the site window, and choose New File from the pop-up menu. A new page is added to the site window titled `untiltled.html`, as shown in Figure 27.17. Double-click the blank Web page to open it for editing.

> On a Mac, the New File command is accessed using the panel menu.

FIGURE 27.17

A blank HTML page is added to the site window.

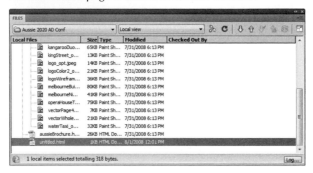

2. **Add and format a heading.** At the top of the new blank Web page, type a heading for the Web page. Then select the Text tab in the Insert Toolbox. Select Format ⇨ Align ⇨ Center to center the text, and choose Format ⇨ Paragraph Format ⇨ Heading 1 to resize the heading.

3. **Add some more text.** At the end of the heading text, press Enter to move the cursor to the next line. Then type the main text of the Web page, as shown in Figure 27.18. Typing text here is similar to using a word processor.

4. **Add an image icon to the Web page.** From the Insert panel, select the Common category and locate the Image object. Then click the image icon to open the Select Image Source dialog box. Locate an image to load, and click OK. The resulting Web page is shown in Figure 27.19.

5. **Correct the image alignment.** To make the text wrap around the new image, select the image object and change the Alignment value to Left in the Properties palette. This allows the text to wrap around the image.

6. **Add some white space to the image.** To set the image off from the text, with the image selected and change the HSpace and VSpace values to 10 in the Properties palette. This adds 10-pixel-wide margins around the image, as shown in Figure 27.20.

The new Web page with an added heading and text

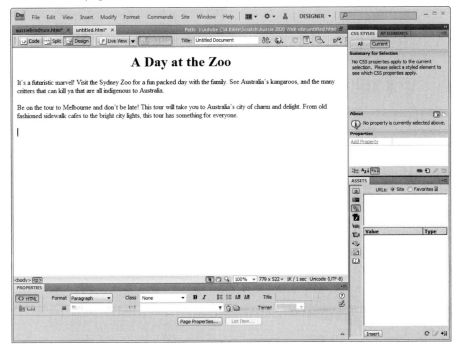

FIGURE 27.19

The new Web page with an added image

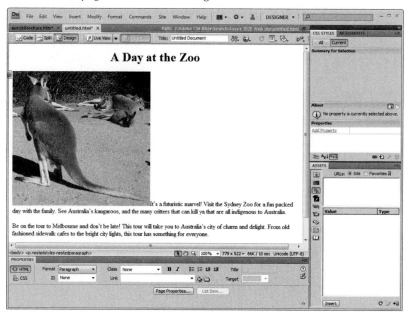

FIGURE 27.20

HTML text can wrap around image objects.

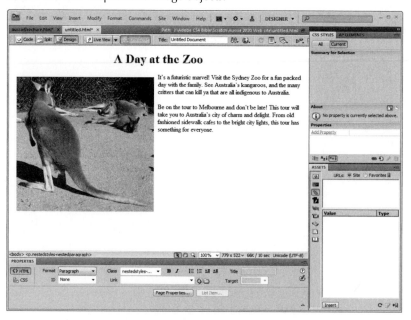

Cascading Style Sheets

All text within a Web page can have formatting applied to it using standard HTML tags such as
<B> for bold text or <H1> for a heading level 1. These standard formatting options don't deal with
CSS and are saved as part of the HTML code. But another method for formatting text is available
using Cascading Style Sheets.

CSS allows formatting styles to be defined, named, and saved. These formatting styles are saved in
a style sheet and may be applied to several sections of text within the Web page by referencing the
defined name. If you need to change the style of text in the Web page, you can make the change to
the style sheet and all text sections using that style are automatically updated.

A single Web page may have several style sheets applied to it. For example, a single Web page may
have an internal style sheet defined within its header that affects only the text within that Web
page, but Web pages also may reference an external style sheet that governs the text styles for all
the Web pages within a site. When this happens, the style that you apply to a specific text section
is cascaded down according to a defined precedence.

To understand the style precedence, you need to realize that the closer the style definition is to the
content, the more likely it will be applied. For example, an external style is more remote than an
internal style, so the internal style takes precedence and is applied.

 **An external style sheet makes the text styles for a whole Web site consistent, con-
trolled, and easy to update.**

Using the CSS Editor

You create Cascading Style Sheets (CSS) within Dreamweaver using the CSS Styles palette. You can
open this editor by choosing the Window ➪ CSS Styles. Figure 27.21 shows the CSS Styles palette.
In the lower-left corner of the CSS Editor are two icons that show information about the selected
tag and also show the cascading rules.

Double-clicking a named style sheet tag in the CSS Styles palette opens it so you can see the individual styles that make up the current style sheet for editing, as shown in Figure 27.22. The Rule
Definition dialog box shows all the properties for the selected tag.

Defining styles

You may define styles for standard HTML elements, such as h1, h2, body, p, and so on. You also
can define styles using a .class definition and styles that are applied to all objects that have specific IDs. Using these tabbed panels, you may set many different properties, including Font, Text,
Block, Margin, and so on.

FIGURE 27.21

You use the CSS Editor to create style sheets and define styles.

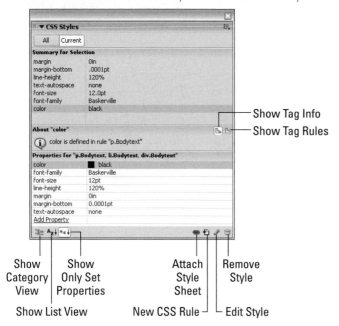

Show Tag Info
Show Tag Rules

Show Category View
Show Only Set Properties
Attach Style Sheet
Remove Style

Show List View
New CSS Rule
Edit Style

FIGURE 27.22

You can use the CSS Editor to view style examples.

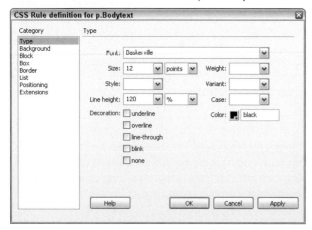

Applying styles

Element styles (h1, p, a, and so on) are applied automatically whenever you use the HTML element. To apply class styles, you can select the text and select the type of style to use the CSS Styles palette menu, or select the style from the Properties panel, or use the Text ⇨ CSS menu. You can apply class styles to an inline section of text, an entire block of text, a spanned section, or a selected element.

You apply ID styles by adding `ID="id_name"` to the HTML tag for the text item to which you want to apply the style. This is done in Code view.

Creating an external style sheet

When you define and apply styles to text, they're automatically added to the Web page. An external style sheet is saved as a separate file. The benefit of an external style sheet is that all your defined styles for an entire Web site with multiple pages can be derived from a single source, and global style changes to the entire site can be made easily in a single location.

To create an external style sheet, you first need to create a reference to the external style sheet by clicking the Attach Style Sheet menu command from the palette menu. This opens a panel where you can click the Create button to locate an existing style sheet, or browse to one using the Browse button.

If the defined styles in a Web page are ones you want to use across your site, you can use the Move CSS Rules palette menu command to save the style definitions to an external file.

Designing for Mobile Devices

Web browsers on personal computers have made great strides in becoming standardized, but many mobile devices including cell phones, PDAs, and even portable game devices can connect to the Internet and view Web pages. Such devices struggle with the following limitations that make displaying Web pages on these devices difficult:

- They have small, limited viewing displays, which make Web pages designed for standard Web browsers incompatible.

- The bandwidth for many mobile devices is much lower than their computer counterparts, resulting in much slower connection speeds.

- No standard language definition exists for viewing or for displaying content on mobile Web devices.

The available language definitions for mobile devices include the following:

- **XHTML Basic/XHTML Mobile:** Defined and endorsed by the governing W3C organization, the XHTML Basic language definition is the standard for many mobile devices.

- **i-mode HTML:** This language definition is the standard for Japanese and European mobile device markets.

- **WML:** Wireless Markup Language is the standard used on WAP-enabled mobile phones and is endorsed by the OMA organization.

- **MMS:** Multimedia Messaging Service defines a mobile messaging standard, but it also can handle multimedia objects such as audio and images.

Despite all these problems, the good news is that Dreamweaver supports all these various language definitions and can be used to create Web pages that users can view on a majority of mobile devices.

Creating new Dreamweaver documents for Mobile Devices

Templates for each of these mobile device standards can be selected from the New dialog box by choosing File ➪ New and selecting one of the mobile options found in the Other category.

When you select any of the mobile templates from the New dialog box, Design view is automatically set to Mobile view. You can manually set this view by choosing View ➪ Style Rendering. Mobile view reduces the width of the layout space and changes the rendering portion.

Previewing mobile pages in Device Central

After you create or design a Web page for a mobile device, you'll want to view it using that device. This may present some difficulty because you probably don't own one of every type of mobile device. The solution to this problem is emulation. Mobile device manufacturers have created simple XML-based definitions that emulate the actual device using a computer program. After a Web page is designed for a mobile device, you can use Device Central to see how it actually looks when viewed on a range of devices. Device Central, shown in Figure 27.23, is accessed using File ➪ Preview in Browser ➪ Device Central.

 **Device Central is accessible from the other CS4 apps, including Adobe Bridge.**

Device Central includes a fairly diverse set of currently available devices, but new devices are being added to the list all the time. Using the Devices ➪ Check for Device Updates menu command, you can update Device Central with new device information.

FIGURE 27.23

Device Central uses multiple emulators to show how Web pages look on various devices.

 Most emulators use the arrow keys to navigate the Web page simulating the device's buttons.

In addition to changing the view mode, Dreamweaver automatically disables the features that aren't available with the selected mobile language definition. For example, if the XHTML Basic mobile template is selected, the Type Size options are disabled.

TIP Although the tools and objects in the Toolbox aren't disabled when a new mobile template is opened, you can customize the Toolbox to match the selected mobile template by clicking the Palette Options button at the bottom of the Toolbox, selecting the Customize pop-up menu option, and choosing the mobile template definition that matches the current Web page.

Converting existing documents to XHTML Mobile

The New dialog box works well, but many times you'll have an existing Web site that you simply need to convert to a specific mobile standard. To convert an existing Web page to a mobile standard, choose File ➪ Convert ➪ To XHTML Mobile 1.0.

Preparing to Publish a Web Site

One of the key advantages of Dreamweaver is that it's a complete Web-authoring and Web-publishing solution: It's used to design and create Web sites and also to publish those sites to a Web server. The first step in publishing Web sites is to configure Dreamweaver so that it can access the Internet and locate the Web servers. Dreamweaver provides a wizard to help define the site. This wizard walks you through locating a working copy of the site on your local hard drive and configuring a shared copy of these files on the Web server.

Setting up Internet access

The steps to defining a site in Dreamweaver so that it can publish to a Web site are simple, but much of the information required to configure the system comes from the Internet Service Provider (ISP) that you're using to host your site. Each ISP has different required settings, but you must follow some general guidelines.

Before you can upload any files to a Web server, you need to get your computer connected to the Internet. This requires that you have the TCP/IP protocol on your system.

NOTE   Internet connections use the TCP/IP network protocols. Before you can connect to the Internet, you need to set up this networking protocol for your system.

FTP versus HTTP

Two different protocols are commonly used to transfer files on the Internet—File Transfer Protocol (FTP) and Hypertext Transfer Protocol (HTTP). FTP sites are structured like a file system with subfolders within subfolders. Understanding this directory structure helps you place files in the correct location. Web browsers use HTTP to retrieve Web pages. HTTP uses a Uniform Resource Locator (URL) to specify the location of files. The URLs are the Web addresses that request Web pages and resources.

Another key difference between the FTP and HTTP protocols is that FTP is a connection-oriented protocol and HTTP is a connectionless protocol. When you establish a connection to an FTP server, the connection usually remains open until you send a command to disconnect it. When you make a request using HTTP, the request is fulfilled and the connection is immediately released. By not holding the connection open, many HTTP requests are handled simultaneously. This can make uploading a large number of files much slower on HTTP than on FTP, because connections need to be reestablished for every file.

Another difference is the port numbers that the two protocols typically use. The Web server uses port numbers to identify the different protocols. The default port number for HTTP requests is typically 80, and the default port number for FTP requests is typically 21, but check with your ISP to confirm these port numbers.

If you're having trouble with any of the information required to connect to your Web server such as the Web address, contact your ISP. Your ISP can provide you with this information.

 **If you're having trouble connecting to a server, the server may be offline.**

Specifying a publish server

After you connect to the Internet, you can browse Web pages and get e-mail using your system. You also can repurpose your designs and publish them to a Web server using Dreamweaver. The first step in this process is to tell Dreamweaver where your files are saved locally and where the Web server is located on the Internet.

You can open the Site Definition dialog box by clicking the Create New Dreamweaver Site link on the Welcome Screen dialog box or by using the Site⇨New Site menu. It can be accessed by using the Basic panel, which uses a wizard to collect the needed information, or by using the Advanced panel, shown in Figure 27.24. The general information includes a Local Root folder and an HTTP address. With this information, Dreamweaver can establish a local site that you can work on.

FIGURE 27.24

The Advanced panel of the Site Definition dialog box

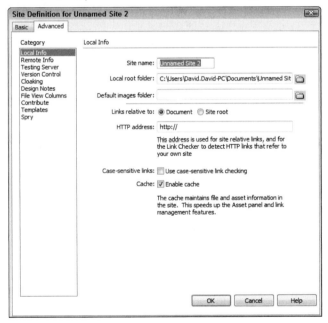

During the site definition process, the wizard asks several questions. One of the first questions is whether you want to work with server technology such as ColdFusion, ASP.NET, ASP, JSP, or PHP. These technologies require additional installations in order to be used on the site. If you plan on using any of these, be sure to inform the wizard that you want to work with these technologies.

The wizard also gives you the option to edit local files and then upload them to the server or to edit the files directly on the server. Enabling the option to edit files directly on the server allows pages in the site to be broken as they are being editing and removes the safeguards of testing the Web pages before they are published. However, it is convenient for making quick changes. It really depends on the type of workflow you want to establish.

The Site Definition wizard offers several connection options to the remote Web server including FTP, Local/Network, WebDAV, RDS, and Visual SourceSafe. Again, the method you choose depends on your workflow and on which connection method your ISP supports.

Finally, the wizard lets you decide whether to enable a check-in/check-out process. This process sets up a system called version control that locks any file that is checked out so other workers cannot make changes to it at the same time that someone else is working on the file. It also requires files to be checked back in when the changes are saved. This can be a lifesaver if you have many people working on the site at a single time. Dreamweaver includes support for Subversion, a popular version control system.

The Advanced panel of the Site Definition dialog box includes many additional configuration settings.

After a site is created, it is found in the Files palette along with all the files that are part of the site, as shown in Figure 27.25. Open this palette by choosing Window ⇨ Files.

FIGURE 27.25

The Files palette holds all the site's various files.

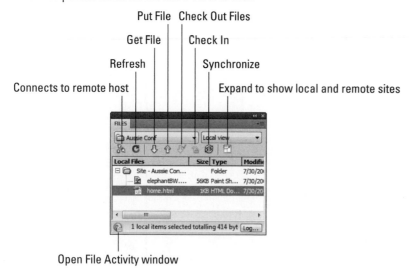

Managing sites

As multiple sites are added to your system, the Manage Sites dialog box, shown in Figure 27.26, becomes helpful. Using this dialog box, you can add new sites, edit existing sites, duplicate and remove sites, and export and import sites.

FIGURE 27.26

The Manage Sites dialog box has all the site settings.

If you select to edit an existing site, the Site Definition dialog box opens again where you can use the Advanced panel to change any of the site configuration settings.

Testing Your Site

Prior to pushing your changes to a live server, you should always check your site for problems. Dreamweaver includes several helpful utilities that make it possible to check all your links automatically.

Checking links

From the main menu, you can choose the Site ➪ Check Links Sitewide menu command. This command follows every link on every page of the entire site looking for links that are dead or links that are connected to a page that doesn't exist. After the check is completed, Dreamweaver supplies a report that shows you what it found.

Cleaning up HTML

Another good habit is to use Dreamweaver's Clean Up HTML/XHTML utility before publishing any Web page changes. This utility is found in the Command ➪ Clean Up HTML menu command. It opens the dialog box shown in Figure 27.27.

The Clean Up HTML/XHTML dialog box offers several useful options.

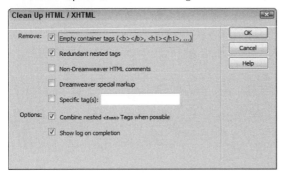

When some Web pages are imported or generated by an external program such as Microsoft Word, the resulting HTML code often has lots of extra characters that are proprietary to the application that generated the HTML. This extra code can cause problems for some Web browsers, but more than likely, they'll just add extra size that is unnecessary to the site files. By removing this unnecessary information, the files are smaller and quicker to download. Also, problems are less likely to occur when you remove the extra code.

Validating code

Markup and scripting code is very picky about requiring correct syntax to be used. If you enter code directly in Code View, then typos can cause trouble that may be tough to figure out. To handle and eliminate these problems, you can use Dreamweaver's Validator to validate the code syntax.

To validate the code for the current page, select the File ➪ Validate ➪ Markup menu. The results of the code validation are displayed in the Results panel, as shown in Figure 27.28. The File ➪ Validate menu also includes an option to validate XML files.

 **Web page files need to be saved before they can be validated.**

Any coding errors reported by the Validator are listed in the Results panel.

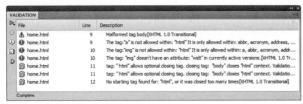

The Validator panel in the Preferences dialog box includes multiple different markup specifications that you can have Validator check the code against. This list includes HTML, XHTML, Internet Explorer and Netscape extensions, ColdFusion, wireless markup language, and JavaScript.

Checking for Browser Compatibility

Even if you're code is correct, the displayed page may still not display correctly if the markup code is incompatible with the selected browser. You can check for potential problems using the File ⇨ Check Page ⇨ Browser Compatibility. The results of this check are also displayed in the Results panel.

Publishing a Web Site Using Dreamweaver

After you configure your system to connect to a Web server, the steps involved in publishing a site are rather simple. Dreamweaver provides two methods for actually uploading the Web site files to the Web server. One method connects directly to the server using the Files palette, and the other uses the FTP Browser.

Connecting to a server

Before you can view a Web site on the Internet, you must transfer all the files that make up the site to the Web server. The Web server then presents the files to the user's browser upon request. You accomplish the process of moving these files using the Files panel. Start by clicking the Connect to Remote Host button to establish a connection between your local root files and the Web server. Then select the files to push to the Web server, and click the Put Files button. This copies the selected file to the Web server.

The dialog box also contains a button to Get Files, which copies the selected content off the Web server and places a copy in the local root folder.

The Synchronize button causes all files that don't have the same date and time stamp to be copied to the Web server, or vice versa. This provides an easy way to quickly update the site. Clicking the Expand to Show Remote and Local Sites button opens two side-by-side panes, as shown in Figure 27.29. This view is convenient and even lets you drag the files back and forth between the two panes.

FIGURE 27.29

The Expand button lets you see the remote and local sites side by side.

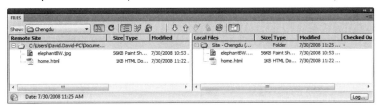

If Dreamweaver has any trouble connecting to the server, a warning dialog box appears with information on the problems that were encountered.

Uploading, downloading, and synchronizing files

After connecting, you can upload, download, or synchronize files, depending on your situation. You upload and download files using the Get File and Put File buttons. You synchronize files using the Synchronize button. These commands also are available in the Site menu. When you click the Synchronize button, Dreamweaver compares the time and date stamp for the local file with the one on the server. If a newer file exists on either side, then the file is downloaded or uploaded to synchronize the date and time stamps between the two files. Files that have the same date and time stamp can be ignored because they are already synchronized. With both boxes, if you select a file in the Site column, information about the file is displayed. Icons to the right of the site filenames indicate whether a file is to be skipped, uploaded, downloaded, or deleted.

NOTE When you upload files to the Web server using the Files palette, Dreamweaver copies to the server the last modification date and time for each file, not the date and time when the files were uploaded. Because of this, the local files may be synchronized with the files on the Web server.

Importing a Web site

From the Manage Sites dialog box, you have an option to Import a Web site. Dreamweaver looks for files that have the .ste extension. The .ste file is an XML file that carries all the site definition data such as the site settings and a list of the all the files that make up the site and where they are located. Using this file, Dreamweaver can upload the site files to a local server or migrate the site from an older version of Dreamweaver.

Exporting a Web Site

If you have difficulty connecting or uploading files to a Web server using Dreamweaver, you can always export the files to a local directory and then upload the directory using an external file-transfer program.

To export a site, open the Manage Sites dialog box and click the Export button. This command opens a file dialog box where you can give the site definition data a filename and a location for exporting. The site definition file is exported using the Site Definition File format, .ste and all the site files are copied to the designated folder.

Summary

- You can repurpose documents created in InDesign for use on the Web by exporting for Dreamweaver. This process bundles all the necessary files into a folder that Dreamweaver can use.

- A site project includes many Web pages. You can create site projects using Dreamweaver's Site Wizard.

- Dreamweaver is a robust editor for creating and designing Web pages. These Web pages can include a myriad of objects. You edit object properties using the Properties palette.

- Cascading Style Sheets are an efficient way to apply text styles to a section of text within a Web page and to multiple pages throughout the site.

- Dreamweaver includes templates for creating Web pages for mobile devices and features for editing and viewing mobile Web pages using Device Central.

- To upload a Web site, you must configure Dreamweaver by entering the server information in the Site Definition wizard, which includes settings for uploading, exporting, and cleaning up files.

- After you configure and connect to the Web server, you can see the files on the Web server in the site window.

- Check your site links and clean up the HTML code before publishing.

- You can use the Files panel to upload, download, or synchronize files between the local file system and the Web server.

- Using the site map view, you can see all the files that make up the site and their relationships.

Part VII

Preparing Documents for Deployment

This part focuses on preparing files for distribution. We begin this part in Chapter 28 by talking about document security and protecting your files against editing. For files that you want to distribute for screen viewing, we cover adding interactivity to make your files more dynamic for your clients in Chapter 29.

You also can realize dynamic interactivity when creating forms. In Chapter 30 we talk about some of the new simple means for creating forms using Acrobat 9 and distributing forms for data collection. This chapter also covers aggregating form data.

When making a presentation to a client for a new ad campaign, you'll want to work with some of the great features for creating slide presentations and easily convert presentations to dynamic Adobe Flash content. We cover all the presentation opportunities you have in the CS applications in Chapter 31.

In Chapter 32 we talk about redacting documents to remove sensitive information and data when revising designs for client approval.

Chapter 28

Understanding Digital Rights Management

igital Rights Management (DRM) is a term used to describe protecting intellectual property against unauthorized viewing, editing, reproduction, and/or distribution. When using a creative-design workflow, you may want to restrict document viewing to selected individuals; or you may want to share design concepts with clients so they can view your designs, although you don't want the documents printed or edited.

Most of the CS programs offer you a vehicle for protecting documents via export to PDF. Document security is applied to PDF files and not directly in the CS application documents. Therefore, you first need to know how to generate a PDF from the other CS applications and then apply security either at the time of PDF creation or from within Acrobat. In this chapter, you learn how to export CS application documents to PDF and secure the files against unauthorized viewing, editing, and printing.

Understanding Document Security

Securing documents created with CS applications means you ultimately get a document to PDF and apply Acrobat security either at the time of exporting a file to PDF or later, after you open a PDF in Acrobat. In either case, Acrobat security is used.

Methods of security available in Acrobat include two primary types of encryption. You can secure a file against opening and editing by applying Acrobat security at different levels of encryption, or you can secure files using certificates acquired from users when they create digital IDs. The first method should be thought of as security you might apply globally to PDFs either from within the CS programs at the time of exporting to PDF or later in Acrobat. Security added at the time of export to PDF is generally when you want the public to have a password to open your PDFs or you want to restrict editing features. These are referred to as *unknown users*.

The second method of security is restrictions you want to apply for a selected group of people in your workgroup (coworkers, colleagues, or individuals with whom you have direct communication) or among your client base. These are referred to as *known users*. This method requires the use of digital IDs and Trusted Certificates.

Permissions

Permissions relate to the access you grant end users. You may restrict printing a document and, as such, you grant permission for users to view and possibly edit a file but prevent users from printing. When using the second method of security for known users, you can grant different permissions for different users all in the same document. This form of security uses digital ID identities and is discussed later.

Understanding levels of encryption

Depending on the version of Acrobat compatibility you use (for example, Acrobat 4-, 5-, or 6-compatible files), the level of encryption changes according to each compatible file format. Acrobat 4 compatibility uses 40-bit encryption, Acrobat 5 and 6 use 128-bit RC4 encryption, Acrobat 7 and 8 use 128-bit AES (Advanced Encryption Standard) encryption, and Acrobat 9 uses 256-bit AES encryption. The level of encryption is not as important for you to understand as just realizing that, with each level of encryption, Acrobat offers you additional permissions. For example, with Acrobat 4 compatibility, you can grant permissions to print a document or prevent a user from printing a document. With Acrobat 5, 6, 7, 8, and 9 compatibility, where you use 128-bit or greater encryption, you can add to the printing permissions a restriction to print files only as low-resolution prints. This feature and others are added to encryption methods above 40-bit encryption.

> **CAUTION**   Be aware that anyone using an earlier version of Acrobat cannot open a document with advanced encryption. For example, users of Acrobat 6 cannot open files secured with Acrobat 9-compatibility encryption.

Working with signature handlers

When you use digital IDs to encrypt files for restricting permissions, Acrobat offers you a choice for using Acrobat Certificate Authority or a signature handler you acquire from a third-party supplier. Acrobat warns you that files secured with Acrobat Certificate Authority carry no guarantee that the security cannot be compromised. For more critical Digital Rights Management, warning dialog boxes point you in the direction of third-party vendors offering signature handlers.

In normal production workflows, you're not concerned with sophisticated signature handlers from third-party vendors. When sending clients drafts of your artwork, the turnaround time is relatively short and the likelihood of a client exerting the energy and taking the time to break password security is incredibly far-fetched. Some algorithms running on powerful computers can take years to break a password.

As a matter of practice, use a minimum of 10 to 12 characters when supplying passwords to protect a file. The more characters you use, the more difficulty a software routine has in trying to break the code.

If you work with sensitive material that requires sophisticated security measures offered by third-party vendors, you can find a list of vendors offering various solutions on Adobe's Web site (`www.adobe.com/security`).

Securing Documents

If you create an illustration or a layout, or you have some photos that you need to secure, you can save or export your files as PDF documents and add security at the time you create the PDF. You also can add security in Acrobat for all PDFs created without setting permissions at the time of PDF creation. Regardless of where you add permissions, the options available to you for securing PDFs are the same in all the CS4 programs.

NOTE Because all the print-oriented CS4 applications including Photoshop, Illustrator, InDesign, and Fireworks use the same Adobe PDF settings used by Acrobat and Acrobat Distiller, security is equally available to all these programs. However, PDF Export in from Dreamweaver is locked to the operating system dialog and the Acrobat settings dialog box is not available.

Adding security in Acrobat

For documents converted to PDF to which you want to add security later, you add permissions in Acrobat. The options you choose are contained in the Password Security–Settings dialog box. To open the dialog box with a document currently open in the Document pane, choose Advanced ➪ Security ➪ Password Encrypt or just click on the Secure button in the Acrobat main toolbar and select the Password Encrypt option from the pop-up menu. When this command is selected, a warning dialog box appears asking if you want to change the security of the current document. If you click Yes, then the Security ➪ Password Encrypt dialog box opens, as shown in Figure 28.1. By default, the security is turned off if you added no security when you exported the PDF or distilled it in Acrobat Distiller.

FIGURE 28.1

The Password Security–Settings dialog box

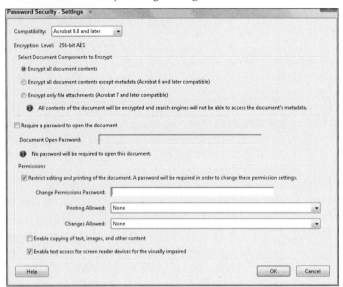

> **NOTE** The same options for adding security exist in the PDFMaker for Microsoft Office files and in the Acrobat Distiller for PostScript files. For more information on using Distiller and applying security during distillation, refer to the *Adobe Acrobat 9 PDF Bible* (published by Wiley).

The security you add in this dialog box restricts a user from opening or changing a file's content. Users must know the password you assigned in this dialog box to open a file and/or make changes. Realize that you can restrict a file from opening unless a password is supplied or you can omit a password for opening a file but limit permissions for printing and editing. You can add two passwords—one for opening a file and another for restricting editing or printing features. You have these options in the Password Security–Settings dialog box:

- **Compatibility:** The options from this pull-down menu include Acrobat 3, Acrobat 5, Acrobat 6, Acrobat 7, Acrobat 8, and Acrobat 9 compatibility. If you select Acrobat 9 compatibility and save the PDF document, users need an Acrobat viewer of version 9 or greater to open the file. The same holds true when saving with Acrobat 5 compatibility for users who have Acrobat viewers lower than version 5.

- **Encryption Level:** Below the Compatibility pull-down menu Acrobat informs you what level of encryption is applied to the document based on the compatibility choice made in the pull-down menu. If you select Acrobat 3 from the Compatibility pull-down menu, the encryption level is 40-bit encryption. Acrobat 5 and Acrobat 6 compatibility are encrypted at 128-bit RCA encryption. Acrobat 7 and 8 are 128-bit AES, and Acrobat 9 is 256-bit AES. All the higher encryption levels offer you more options for restricting printing and editing.

- **Encrypt all document contents:** This option applies encryption to all document contents including text, images, and media content.

- **Encrypt all document contents except metadata (Acrobat 6 and later compatible):** Use this option to apply encryption to all document contents except document metadata. As the item name implies, this level of security is compatible with Acrobat 6 and above. This is a good selection if you want to have the metadata in your secure documents available for a search engine.

- **Encrypt only file attachments (Acrobat 7 and higher compatible):** Use this option to encrypt file attachments but not the PDF document. This option is compatible only with Acrobat 7 and above.

CROSS-REF For information regarding using file attachments and securing PDFs, see the section "Securing Files with Attachments" later in this chapter.

- **Require a password to open the document:** Enable this option if you want a user to supply a password to open the PDF document. Once enabled, the field box for Document Open Password becomes active and you can add a password. Before you exit the dialog box, Acrobat prompts you in another dialog box to confirm the password.

- **Use a password to restrict printing and editing of the document and its security settings:** You can add a password for opening the PDF document and also restrict permissions from the items active in the Permissions area of the dialog box. You also can eliminate the option for using a password to open the PDF document and make permissions choices for printing and editing. Either way, you check this box to make choices in the Permissions options.

- **Permissions Password:** Fill in the field box with a password. If you apply permissions options for opening the PDF and restricting permissions, the passwords must be different. Acrobat opens a dialog box and informs you to make different password choices if you attempt to use the same password for opening the file and setting permissions.

- **Printing Allowed:** If you use Acrobat 3 compatibility, the options are available to either enable printing or disallow printing. The choices are None and High Resolution. Although the choice reads High Resolution, the result simply enables users to print your file. With Acrobat 5 and 6 compatibility, you have a third choice for enabling printing at a lower resolution (150 dpi). If you select Low Resolution (150 dpi) from the menu options, users are restricted to printing the file at the lower resolution. This choice is typically something you might use for files intended for digital prepress and high-end printing or to protect your content from being printed and then re-scanned.

- **Changes Allowed:** From this pull-down menu, you make choices for the kinds of changes you allow users to perform on the document. Acrobat 3 compatibility offers you four choices; Acrobat 5, 6, and 7 compatibility offer six choices, including these:

  - **None:** This option prevents a user from performing any kind of editing and content extraction.

  - **Inserting, Deleting, and Rotating Pages:** This option is not available when using Acrobat 3 compatibility. Users are permitted to insert, delete, and rotate pages. If you create PDFs for eBooks, allowing users to rotate pages can be helpful when they view PDFs on tablets and portable devices.

883

      ■ **Page layout, filling in forms, and signing existing signature fields (Acrobat 3 only):** Select this option to enable users to extract pages, insert pages, and also perform actions on form fields.

      ■ **Filling in form fields and signing existing signature fields:** If you create Acrobat Forms and want users to digitally sign documents, enable this check box. Forms are useless to users without the ability to fill in the form fields.

      ■ **Commenting, filling in form fields, and signing existing signature fields:** You might use this option in a review process where you want to have users comment on a design but you don't want them to make changes in your file. You can secure the document against editing, but allow commenting and form field filling in and signing. When you enable form filling in with this option or the Filling in form fields and signing existing signature fields option, users are restricted against changing your form design and cannot make edits other than filling in the fields. A good example of using this option is when you want customers to fill out a form that includes comments that describe their selections.

      ■ **Any Except Extracting Pages:** All the permissions are available to users except extracting pages from the document and creating separate PDFs from selected pages.

  ■ **Enable copying of text, images, and other content and access for the visually impaired:** If you restrict permissions for any of the previous pull-down menu options, users aren't allowed to copy data. You can add permission for content copying by enabling this check box. This option is available to users of all Acrobat viewers version 3 and greater.

  ■ **Enable text access for screen reader devices for the visually impaired:** This option is available for all versions except Acrobat 3 compatibility. As a matter of practice, selecting this check box is always a good idea because you can restrict all editing features while permitting users with screen-reading devices the ability to read your files. If the check box is not selected, screen readers cannot read the PDF document and all the options for using the View ⇨ Read Out Loud menu command are grayed out. Furthermore, users can index your files with Acrobat Professional by using Acrobat Catalog when this check box is selected, regardless of the other items you prevent users from accessing.

After making decisions for the permissions you want to restrict, you need to save the file. Choose either File ⇨ Save or File ⇨ Save As after making choices in the Password Security–Settings dialog box.

Setting permissions in the Password Security–Settings dialog box works fine for a single PDF document you want to secure, but it's a bit tedious when you want to secure a number of files. For automating the task where a common password is used in all files that need to be secured, you can use the Acrobat Batch Processing command. For a firsthand view of creating a batch sequence and applying steps in the sequence to a collection of PDF documents, follow these steps.

STEPS: Creating and Running Batch Sequences

1. **Open Batch Sequences.** Choose Advanced ⇨ Document Processing ⇨ Batch Processing. The Batch Sequences dialog box opens, shown in Figure 28.2.

 You can create and run batch sequences only in Acrobat Professional.

FIGURE 28.2

The Batch Sequences dialog box creates a new sequence.

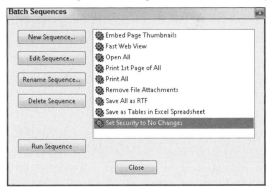

---

2. **Create a new sequence.** Click New Sequence in the Batch Sequences dialog box. The Name Sequence dialog box opens. Type a name for your sequence, and click OK to open the Batch Edit Sequence–*[name of your sequence]* dialog box shown in Figure 28.3. Note that the name for the dialog box in the figure is Batch Edit Sequence–Add Security. We created a new sequence and named the sequence *Add Security*; thus the name is reflected in the dialog box name. For purposes of clarity, this dialog box is henceforth referred to as the Batch Edit Sequence dialog box.

3. **Add Security to the sequence.** Click Select Commands in the Batch Edit Sequence dialog box. The Edit Sequence dialog box opens, shown in Figure 28.4. In the left pane, scroll down the window until you see Security appear at the end of the Document options. Select Security in the left pane, and click Add to move Security to the right pane.

4. **Edit the security permissions.** To set the security permissions, open the Password Security–Settings dialog box. Click on Security in the right pane, and click Edit or double-click on Security in the right pane to open the Document Security dialog box. From the pull-down menu, select Password Security and click the Change Settings button to open the Password Security–Settings dialog box, shown in Figure 28.5.

FIGURE 28.3

The Batch Edit Sequence dialog box

FIGURE 28.4

The Edit Sequence dialog box

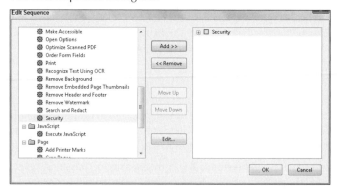

FIGURE 28.5

The Password Security–Settings dialog box

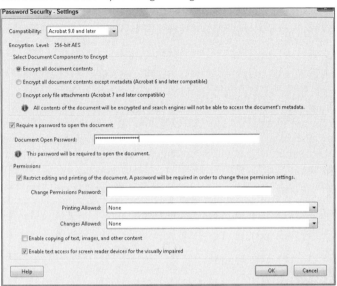

Edit the security items you want to use, and be certain to use passwords of ten or more characters. Click OK, and a warning dialog box opens. Click OK again, and the Confirm Permissions Password dialog box opens. Retype your password using the same letter case, and click OK. You're returned to the Document Security dialog box. Click Close, and you're returned to the Edit Sequence dialog box. Click OK, and you arrive at the Batch Edit Sequence dialog box. Click OK again, and you see your new sequence added to the Batch Sequences dialog box.

Note that the number of dialog boxes is extraordinary. Just keep in mind that after editing the security options, you return to the Batch Sequences by clicking OK through all the dialog boxes. When the sequence is added to the Batch Sequences dialog box, you're ready to run the sequence. You can run a sequence immediately after creating it or at a later time in another Acrobat editing session. After the new sequence is added to the batch Sequences dialog box, the sequence remains there until you physically remove it. If you want to dismiss the dialog box without running a sequence, click Close.

Sequences are designed for you to apply the same settings to a collection of PDF documents. When you set the attributes for the command you want to use and the sequence has been created, you run the sequence by selecting a file, a number of files, or a folder. To run a sequence for applying security to a collection of files, follow these steps.

STEPS: Running a Sequence

1. **Edit a sequence.** Select the new sequence you created in the Batch Sequence dialog box, and click Edit Sequence. The attributes for the security permissions have been defined, but now you need to inform Acrobat where the edited files are to be saved and the file-naming convention you want to use. Note that these options can be assigned at the time you create a sequence, but it's a good idea to visit the Batch Edit Sequence dialog box whenever you run a sequence to be certain you know where your files are saved and the names given to the new files.

2. **Running a command.** In the Batch Edit Sequence dialog box, shown in Figure 28.6, open the pull-down menu for item 2. You have several options from which to choose for when a command is run. The default is Ask When Sequence is Run. When selected, this option instructs Acrobat to prompt you for which files to run a sequence. Other choices enable you to identify a specific folder location, specific files, or currently opened files. The default is set to run a sequence by asking in a navigation dialog box that opens and permits you to search through your hard drive to find files you want to add to the sequence. Unless you want to run the sequence on a specific folder, leave the setting at the default.

FIGURE 28.6

The Batch Edit Sequence–Add Security dialog box

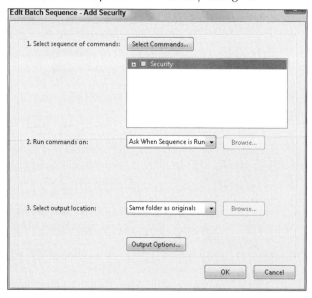

3. **Select an output location.** From the pull-down menu for item 3, you determine where the edited files are saved. The default is set to save files in the same folder as the original files. You also have choices for saving to a specific folder (prompting you for a folder location) or not saving changes. If you save files to the same folder, be careful about overwriting existing files. If you leave the default at Same Folder as Originals, edit the filenames in the Output Options so new files are saved with new names as opposed to overwriting files. If you make mistakes when assigning attributes in your batch sequence, you can always return to the original files.

4. **Set output options.** Click Output Options and the Output Options dialog box, shown in Figure 28.7, opens. In this dialog box, you assign filenames. You can choose to use the default name for saving files with the same name that ultimately overwrites your existing files, or you can add to an existing name either a prefix or a suffix. If you click Add to Original Base Name(s), the field boxes for Insert Before and Insert After become active. Enter a prefix or suffix extension by typing characters in the field boxes. If you leave the default at Same As Original(s) and check the box for Do Not Overwrite Existing Files, Acrobat automatically adds to the filenames to prevent the new files from overwriting the old files. Make your choices in this dialog box, and click OK to return to the Batch Edit Sequence dialog box. Click OK, and you return to the original Batch Sequences dialog box.

FIGURE 28.7

The Output Options dialog box

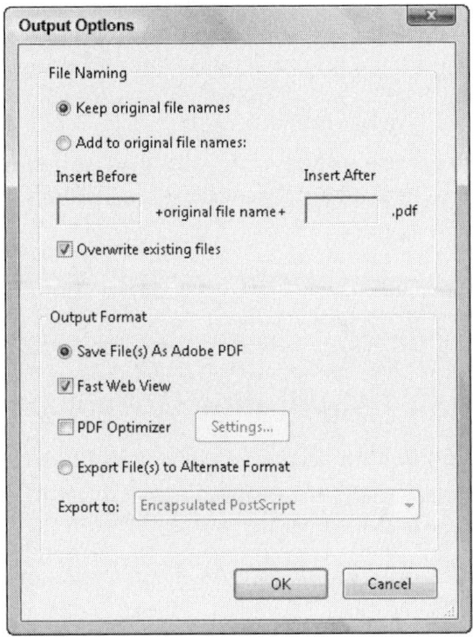

5. **Run a sequence.** In the Batch Sequence dialog box, click on your new sequence and click Run Sequence. If you elected to be prompted for files to select, the Select Files to Process dialog box opens. Navigate your hard drive, and open the folder where the files you want to process are located. To select files individually, ⌘/Ctrl+click to select files in a noncontiguous order. For a contiguous selection, select a file and press the Shift key to select the last file in a list. All files between the two you clicked are selected.

Click the Select button, and Acrobat adds security to all the files you selected for processing. After completing the task, be certain to verify files and note the password used to protect the files.

Adding security in other CS programs

The common denominator for securing all CS applications documents is Adobe PDF. You have two choices for securing documents. You can export the file and essentially turn it into a PDF document whereby security is applied, or you can attach a native file to a PDF whereby Acrobat security is also applied. Either way, you eventually work with a PDF document.

CAUTION Be aware that PDF support is much stronger for the print-oriented apps like Photoshop, Illustrator, and InDesign. PDF support is not included for Dreamweaver and Flash, but it is available for Fireworks.

CROSS-REF For information on securing PDFs with file attachments, see the section "Securing Files with Attachments" at the end of this chapter.

When using Photoshop and Illustrator, you create a PDF file by choosing File ➪ Save As and writing the file to the PDF format. When using InDesign, you create PDF documents by choosing File ➪ Export.

NOTE In all applications, you address the Adobe PDF Settings that include applying security. All the options are the same for all CS programs, regardless of whether you use Save As or Export.

To understand how security settings are applied to any CS application document, look over the following steps.

STEPS: Adding Security to CS4 Application Documents

1. **Launch the Bridge, and double-click an image to open it in Photoshop.** You can use any CS4 program and follow the same steps. In this example, Photoshop is used to secure image files.

2. **Open the Save As dialog box.** Choose File ➪ Save As. The Save As dialog box appears. Select Photoshop PDF from the Format menu, and click Save. The Save Adobe PDF dialog box appears.

3. **Apply security settings.** Select an Adobe PDF Preset from the pull-down menu at the top of the dialog box. Select a compatibility option from the Compatibility pull-down menu. Click Security in the left pane. Select the options you want to use for your security settings such as using an open password and/or adding editing privileges. Add a password, and click Save PDF. In Figure 28.8, a password is used for opening the document.

FIGURE 28.8

Apply security settings in the Save Adobe PDF dialog box.

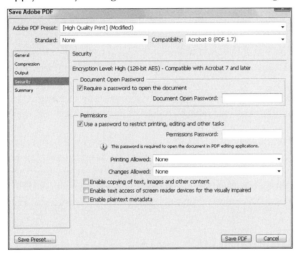

4. **Confirm your password.** A second dialog box appears, prompting you to confirm the password. Type the same password used in the first dialog box, and click OK. The file is saved with the settings applied for security. Note that passwords are case sensitive. Be certain to record passwords used for your files, including case sensitivity.

NOTE There are more options available to you for securing documents using the Adobe Policy Server and CDS partners. The scope of document security in Acrobat is enormous and is beyond the scope of this book. For an exhaustive authoritative description on Acrobat security, see the *Adobe Acrobat 9 PDF Bible* (Wiley Publishing).

Securing Files with Attachments

If your workflow requires you to exchange original documents that need to be secured, obviously converting to PDF isn't a solution. The CS programs don't offer you options for securing files unless you convert to PDF. However, you can use PDF to protect native documents against unauthorized opening and viewing, and you can attach any file to a PDF. If the need arises for protecting word-processing files, spreadsheets, financial documents, layouts, images, and so on, you can use PDF as the container for native files and password-protect the contents.

 **You can attach all files to PDF documents with the exception of ZIP and EXE files on Windows. These file types are prohibited to prevent the spread of viruses.**

By using file attachments in Acrobat, you use the PDF as a wrapper and secure the PDF document with open permissions. If a user doesn't have a password to open the PDF document, the attached file is inaccessible. If your clients use the Adobe Reader software, you can secure PDFs with file attachments and exchange the PDFs with Adobe Reader users who can extract and open the attachments.

There are restrictions when using file attachments compared to using PDF security. For example, if you want to secure an InDesign file against unauthorized viewing, you can embed the InDesign document in a PDF and use an open password to protect the file. However, you can't restrict editing and printing the InDesign file. When using file attachments, you prevent users from viewing the documents or grant all permissions: There are no other options for securing native documents.

Acrobat is a handy tool for exchanging files that need to be protected against unauthorized viewing, and you can easily secure any kind of document by attaching the file to a PDF. For users to extract a file from a secured PDF, they need to have the open password and the original application that created the file attachment. For example, embedding a Microsoft Word file in a PDF document requires you to have MS Word installed on your computer in order to extract the file.

Creating security policies

Acrobat provides you with a feature designed for creating secure PDF eEnvelopes know as Security Envelope. eEnvelopes are PDF document templates used for attaching any file and securing the PDF document. Before you can use Security Envelope, you need to create a security policy.

Security policies are like style sheets used to apply security to PDF documents. With all the attributes from which to choose for applying security to a PDF document, you need to spend some time opening the Password Security–Settings dialog box, selecting options for securing a file, and applying a security password. To simplify the process, you can capture all the settings used for securing a file and save the settings as a new policy. When you want to use the same policy to secure additional files, you select the policy without having to revisit the Password Security–Settings dialog box and adjust all the options choices.

You can use security policies with digital IDs and when you apply Acrobat Security. Creating and using digital IDs is complex and a lengthy subject. If you want to learn how to create and use digital IDs, see the Acrobat Help file or the lengthy description covering the subject in the *Adobe Acrobat 9 PDF Bible* (Wiley Publishing). To create a security policy using Acrobat Security, follow these steps.

STEPS: Creating a Security Policy

1. **Launch Acrobat 9 Pro.** Double-click the Acrobat program icon or an alias of the program on your desktop to launch Adobe Acrobat.

2. **Open the Managing Security Policies window.** Click the Secure task button, and from the pull-down menu shown in Figure 28.9, click Manage Security Policies. The Managing Security Policies window opens.

FIGURE 28.9

Open the Secure task button pull-down menu, and select Manage Security Policies.

3. **Open the New Security Policy wizard.** Click New in the top-left corner of the Managing Security Policies window. The New Security Policy wizard opens. Creating security policies is handled in a wizard that walks you through each step in the process.

4. **Select the type of security to use in the new policy.** You have three options in the first pane in the New Security Policy wizard. Leave the default selection for Use Passwords selected, and click Next. The other options offer you choices when creating digital IDs and using the Adobe Policy Server. (See the Acrobat Help document to learn more about the other options.)

5. **Add a policy name and description.** The next pane in the New Security Policy wizard provides options for adding a name and description. You can choose to discard the settings after using the policy, but if you want to reuse the same security settings when you create additional eEnvelopes, be certain the Save these settings as a policy radio button is selected. In the Policy name text box, type a name for your new policy. Below the policy name, type a description for the policy. Be certain to add descriptive information that adequately identifies your policy similar to what you see in Figure 28.10. Select the Save passwords with the policy check box. Saving the password enables you to use the same password each time the policy is used. If you leave the check box deselected, you can change the password each time the policy is applied. Click Next after setting the attributes in the General settings pane.

FIGURE 28.10

Add a name and description in the General Settings pane.

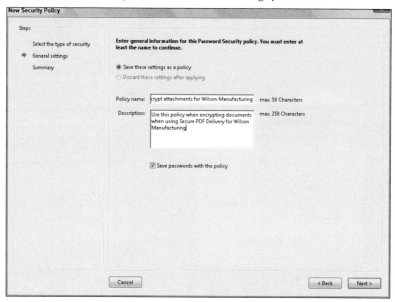

6. **Make security settings choices for the policy.** The Document restrictions pane offers you security settings options identical to the options described in the section "Securing Documents" earlier in this chapter. Make choices for the compatibility level, the document components you want to encrypt, passwords to open and/or change the document, and the permissions you want to grant. Note that using restrictions in the Permissions section of the pane shown in Figure 28.11 applies only to PDF documents. If you want to use the policy strictly to grant permissions for accessing a file attachment, don't select both options choices in the Permissions section. Click Next when you finish adding the options choices.

7. **Confirm the password.** After clicking Next, a dialog box appears prompting you to confirm the password(s) used in the Document restrictions pane. Type the password(s) exactly the same as applied in the Document restrictions pane including case sensitivity. Be certain to record the passwords used for the policy.

8. **Review the Summary.** The next pane provides you a summary view for the settings you made for your policy (see Figure 28.12). Be certain to review the information, and be certain that what you see is an accurate description for the policy you want to create. If all information is correct, click Finish to complete creating the new policy. If you need to revisit a pane, click Back to make adjustments in the previous panes.

FIGURE 28.11

Make security choices for the new policy.

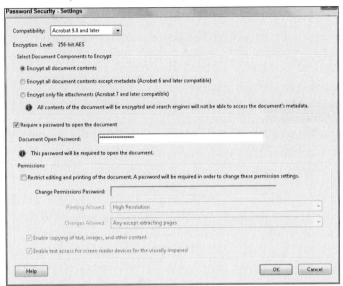

FIGURE 28.12

Review the Summary, and click Finish if the settings accurately describe the policy choices you made.

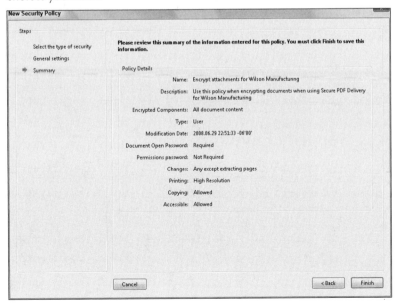

9. **Close the Managing Security Policies window.** After you finish creating a new policy, you are returned to the Managing Security Policies window where your new policy appears listed and available for use. This window is like a character or paragraph styles palette where you select a style to apply to a selection. When applying a security policy in Acrobat, you use one of the policies listed in the Managing Security Policies window. As you can see in Figure 28.13, several policies can be added to the list, and the name and description for your policy appears when you select it in the list window.

FIGURE 28.13

The Managing Security Policies window lists all the policies you create with policy name and description.

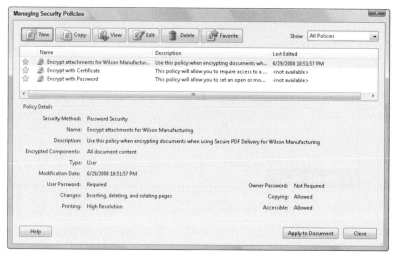

After you create a policy, you use your policy when using Security Envelope to secure eEnvelopes with file attachments. Security policies also can be used with other forms of encryption such as securing individual documents, using digital IDs, and creating certified documents.

Using Security Envelope

Security Envelope is an easy method for securing PDF documents containing file attachments. When you need to send native files to your clients or others in your workflow, you can create an eEnvelope and attach any kind of document to the envelope. You need to have at least one security policy in order to proceed, so be certain to follow the steps outlined in the section "Creating security policies."

Follow these steps to create a secure PDF eEnvelope using Security Envelope.

STEPS: Using Security Envelope

1. **Launch Acrobat.** If Acrobat is not open, double-click the program icon or an alias of the program on your desktop. When Acrobat opens, you don't need to open a file in the Document pane. Create Security Envelope can be used without open files in Acrobat.

2. **Open the Create Secure Envelope wizard.** Click the Secure task button, and select Create Security Envelope, as shown in Figure 28.14. The Create Secure eEnvelope wizard opens when you create an eEnvelope.

FIGURE 28.14

Open the Secure task button pull-down menu, and select Create Security Envelope.

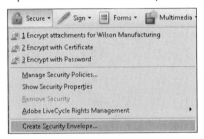

3. **Select a file to attach to the eEnvelope.** The first pane in the Create Secure Envelope wizard provides an option for selecting the file you want to attach to your envelope. Any file on your hard drive can be used except a ZIP or EXE file on Windows. Click the Add file to send button below the list window. The Choose the files to enclose dialog box opens. Navigate your hard drive, and select the file(s) you want to attach to the envelope. Note that you can Shift+click (⌘/Ctrl+click) to select multiple files. You can add a file and click the Add files to enclose button again when adding files from different folders. After adding files, click Next to advance to the next pane.

4. **Choose the envelope template.** The second pane offers some predesigned templates from which you can choose or an option for using your own design. If you choose a custom template, the file needs to be a PDF document. Select a template from the list shown in Figure 28.15, or click Browse to locate your own custom design. In this example, template2.pdf is used. This template adds a date stamp from your system clock. After selecting a template, click Next to advance to the next pane.

FIGURE 28.15

Select a template, or click Browse to locate a custom design of your choice.

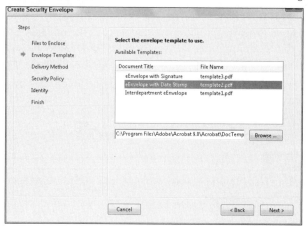

5. **Choose a delivery method.** The Delivery method pane offers two options. Select the Complete the eEnvelope manually option or the Email the completed eEnvelope option. If you choose the first option, you create the envelope and can save it to your hard drive for sending at a later time. If you select the second option, you save the envelope to your hard drive and the saved file is added to a new message window as an e-mail attachment in your default e-mail program. Make a choice from the options, and click Next. In this example, the envelope is completed manually for e-mailing at a later time.

6. **Choose a Security Policy.** Select the check box for Show all policies, and the list window displays the policies available to you, as shown in Figure 28.16. You can select one of the policies you previously created or click the New Policy button, and the Managing Security Policies window opens where you create a new policy as was described in the "Creating security policies" section earlier in this chapter. Select a policy or create a new one, and click Next to advance to the next pane.

7. **Review the summary.** The last pane provides a summary of the options selected for your eEnvelope. Review the summary, and click Finish to create the eEnvelope.

8. **Secure the file.** The eEnvelope opens in Acrobat with the Attachments pane open showing you the file attachments added to the envelope. Note in Figure 28.17 the document is time and date stamped. The file is not secure until you save it. Choose File ➪ Save, and the Save As dialog box appears where you can choose the folder to save the document and provide a name for the envelope. If you complete the eEnvelope manually, you can save the file and e-mail it at a later time.

FIGURE 28.16

Choose a security policy, and click Next to move to the last pane.

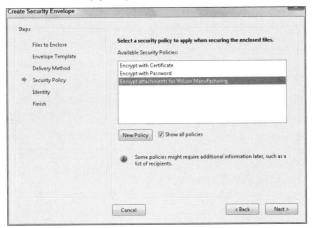

FIGURE 28.17

The eEnvelope is created from the template, and the Attachments pane displays the file attachments added to the envelope.

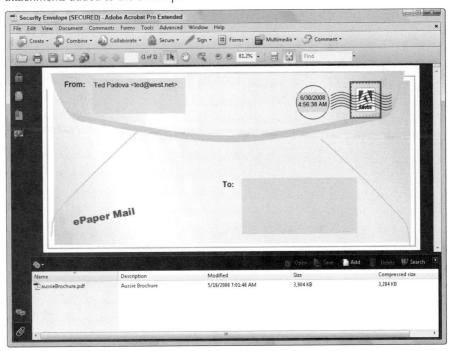

Summary

- Different levels of security can prevent users of Acrobat viewers earlier than version 6 from opening files. It's important to know your user audience and which version of Acrobat viewers they use before securing files.

- You can apply security to PDF documents that restrict open permissions and different levels of editing.

- You can secure files from any CS4 application when you convert them to PDF. The print-oriented CS4 applications use the same Adobe PDF settings to convert document files to PDF.

- PDF documents can contain file attachments from any document type except ZIP and EXE files on Windows. You can secure the PDF against unauthorized opening to prevent anyone from viewing the file attachments.

- Security policies are like style sheets. You can create a policy setting all the permissions attributes and reuse the policy each time you want to encrypt a file with the same permissions.

- You use Security Envelope to create eEnvelopes where you can create PDFs from templates, attach documents to the template, and secure the file with security policy permissions.

Chapter 29

Adding Interactivity to Documents

With increasing demand for more dynamic messaging, the world of advertising and graphic design has changed greatly in recent years from the delivery of static printed matter to more interactive content. With the advent of the Web and its fruition in the mid-1990s, the vehicle for communication has set standards for creative professionals to meet demands for more interesting delivery of information in the form of multimedia and interactive tools that enable readers to explore information according to personal interests. Today's reader audience is becoming more familiar with information that stimulates the senses and provides for quick access to the interests of individual readers.

With the Creative Suite applications, you have many tools for creating dynamic content in the form of integrating video, sound, and interactive buttons that provide readers methods for exploring information in exciting ways. In one way or another, each CS4 program provides you with opportunities to add dynamic content and/or interactive elements to your documents.

Creating Hyperlinks

Hyperlinks are nothing new to computer programs and computer systems. In the late 1980s, Apple Computer introduced a program called HyperCard that might be thought of as the foundation for interactive document viewing that we now see on the Web. HyperCard was designed to provide users a tool whereby they could create links and buttons to branch out to other HyperCard pages containing information according to user interest. The premise was that we investigate and explore information in a nonlinear form according to our areas of interest. Unlike newspaper and magazine articles designed for linear viewing starting at the beginning and reading through to the end, hypertext reading enables you to navigate to a page and then branch to another page you choose from a selection of hypertext references (buttons).

Hyperlinks obviously are tools you use when viewing electronic documents and therefore require you to move away from print and look at other alternatives for deploying your creative work, such as CD/DVD-ROM, the Internet, or locally on your own computer. The CS4 programs provide you with tools to create hypertext references and enable you to explore new markets for eMagazines, eBooks, and a variety of other eContent.

When creating electronic brochures, magazines, and other content designed for interactive viewing, you have choices for creating interactive elements in the CS programs or in Adobe Acrobat. The final packaging of your content is likely to be either PDF documents or Web pages. In some cases, you may create interactive PDFs that are deployed as Web-hosted documents.

NOTE When it comes to creating hyperlinks, Dreamweaver is clearly the best tool for the job, but this chapter extends hyperlinks to other CS4 programs including Acrobat and InDesign. Making hyperlinks in Flash is also a simple matter.

At the creation stage of your workflow, you choose either of the following paths:

- Add hyperlinks in a program like Adobe InDesign.
- Create an InDesign document without hyperlinks, convert to PDF, and then create the hyperlinks in Acrobat.

If you decide to create the links in Adobe InDesign, you can export the InDesign document to PDF, and the resultant PDF recognizes the hyperlinks you added in InDesign. Where you create the links is a matter of personal choice. In some cases, you may find it easier to create links in InDesign, and at other times, you may find it easier to create links in Acrobat. Therefore, it's helpful if you know a little bit about the methods in each program so you can recognize benefits and limitations of using one program or another.

TIP Regardless of what program you work with, the process for creating links is the same. You always navigate to the destination view and then assign the link properties. In InDesign, you create a destination view, such as Page 3 at 200 percent. You then create a hyperlink where you select the destination view in the hyperlink properties. In Acrobat, you create a link or button, navigate to the destination view, and then assign the link/button properties to the view. This is a consistent method regardless of whether you link to page views or layer views or you open secondary document views.

Creating links and buttons in InDesign

The most common hyperlinks are used for page and document navigation. You create a button or link with an action that opens a page view in the existing document or opens another document. InDesign supports creating these views. However, before you decide to create links in InDesign, you should be aware of the benefits and limitations of InDesign links. The primary benefit and limitation are:

■ **Benefit:** If you intend to export to PDF, you can create interactive links in InDesign that are included in the exported document. This option eliminates a need to know more about creating links and buttons in Acrobat. When you need frequent revisions on an InDesign document, creating links in InDesign can be beneficial.

■ **Disadvantage:** If you intend to export your InDesign file to PDF, links that you create in InDesign are converted to *Destinations* in Adobe Acrobat. Destinations are similar to bookmarks where destination views are captured. You click the link button, and the action takes you to the destination. Destinations have one disadvantage over bookmarks and links in Acrobat because they carry with them lots of unnecessary overhead, resulting in larger files sizes. Therefore, when files need to be smaller for Web hosting, creating links in Acrobat keeps the files smaller.

Hyperlinks and destinations are managed in the Hyperlinks palette, shown in Figure 29.1. Choose Window ➪ Interactive ➪ Hyperlinks to open the palette. As you create hyperlinks, the hyperlink names are added to the palette. Several options exist for hyperlinks. You can create a link to a Page, a Text Anchor, to a URL, to an Email address, to a File, or to a Shared Destination. As the links are added, their titles are added to the Hyperlink list. You also can use the Hyperlink palette to create Cross-References to link to other paragraphs or text anchors in the current document.

FIGURE 29.1

The Hyperlinks palette lists all hyperlinks for a document.

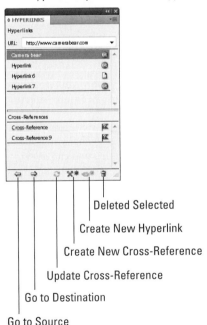

Deleted Selected
Create New Hyperlink
Create New Cross-Reference
Update Cross-Reference
Go to Destination
Go to Source

The tools at the bottom of the palette are used for navigating links. Click the left arrow takes you to the link source and the right arrow jumps to the link destination. The Update Cross-Reference button updates any changed cross-reference links. The Create New Cross-Reference and Create New Hyperlink buttons are used to create new entries in the list. The Trash icon is used to delete the selected cross-references or hyperlinks listed in the palette. The palette menu icon opens a palette fly-out menu where options appear for selecting hyperlink attributes such as editing names, destinations, sorting the link names, resetting links, and updating them.

Specifying a hyperlink destination

Before creating a hyperlink, it's easiest if you first to create a destination. This is the target location for the hyperlink. To create a new destination, select the New Hyperlink Destination palette menu command. This opens the dialog box shown in Figure 29.2 and presents three different destination types: Page, Text Anchor, and URL.

FIGURE 29.2

The New Hyperlink Destination dialog box helps you create destinations.

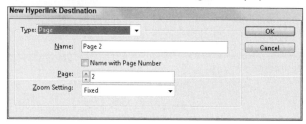

NOTE If you link to a text anchor, you must first select text on a page before you create the hyperlink destination. Creating page and URL destinations doesn't require selecting any content.

A Page destination lets you create a hyperlink that jumps to a specified page, like what you'd link from in a table of contents or an index. The Name field lets you enter a name that you can select when you create the hyperlink, or you can enable the Name with Page Number option to automatically set the name to the selected page number. The Zoom Setting option lets you specify the zoom level when the page is displayed. The options include Fixed, Fit View, Fit in Window, Fit Width, Fit Height, Fit Visible, and Inherit Zoom.

The Text Anchor option makes the selected text an anchor that the hyperlink jumps to. For this anchor, you may give it a name that is used to select the anchor in the Create Hyperlink dialog box. The URL option lets you name and specify the Web address of a site on the Web.

Creating a new hyperlink

After you create and name a destination, you can select an item in the current document for use as a new hyperlink. You then create the hyperlink using the New Hyperlink palette menu command or by clicking the Create New Hyperlink button at the bottom of the Hyperlinks palette.

This opens the New Hyperlink dialog box, shown in Figure 29.3, where you can give the hyperlink a name, specify a destination, and determine its appearance. In the Destination section, select a document from the open documents, or browse to another local document using the Browse option. The Type list includes the Page, Text Anchor, URL, and All Types options, and the Name drop-down list lets you choose from the named destinations already created. A None option is available if you have not yet created or named the destination.

FIGURE 29.3

The New Hyperlink dialog box lets you specify link properties.

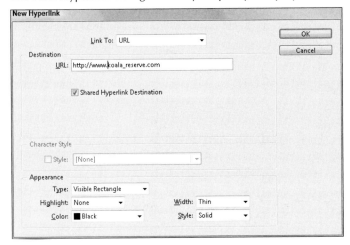

The Appearance section lets you define how the hyperlink looks. The Type could be Visible Rectangle or Invisible Rectangle; the Highlight could be None, Invert, Outline, or Inset; the Color could be one of many default named colors; the Width could be Thin, Medium, or Thick; and the Style could be Solid or Dashed. The Highlight appearance shows up only when the document is exported to PDF.

After the Create Hyperlink dialog box is closed, the new hyperlink appears in the Hyperlinks palette, and the hyperlink content in the document is highlighted using the designated appearance settings. An icon denoting the type of hyperlink appears to the right of the hyperlink name in the Hyperlinks palette. Choose View ➪ Show/Hide Hyperlinks to hide all the hyperlinks. To edit an existing hyperlink, double-click it in the Hyperlinks palette or select the Hyperlink Options menu command.

Testing hyperlinks

To test a hyperlink, simply select it in the Hyperlinks palette and choose the Go to Destination palette menu command. To see the hyperlink's source, select the Go to Source menu command. These commands also are available as icon buttons at the bottom of the Hyperlinks palette. If the destination is a URL, a Web browser opens and tries to load the requested URL.

Creating buttons

You can create buttons in InDesign to jump to a page or perform a certain action like playing a movie or sound. When you export an InDesign document containing buttons to Acrobat, the defined button and its function remain active.

To create buttons in InDesign, begin by designing the button object. You create simple buttons in InDesign using any designed object. Drag the tool in the layout where you want to locate the button, or click in the document to open a simple dialog box where you enter the button's width and height. Holding down the Shift key while dragging constrains the button to a square shape. Holding down the Option/Alt key while dragging lets you drag from the button's center. If you hold down the spacebar while dragging, you can move the button's location. Buttons are identifiable by a button icon and name that displays in the corner of the button.

Once you have a good design, open the Buttons panel, shown in Figure 29.4, using the Window ⇨ Interactive menu. With the button object selected, click the Convert Object to a Button link at the bottom of the panel. This creates and names a button.

Regular shape objects created with the Rectangle or another tool can be selected and converted to buttons by choosing Object ⇨ Interactive ⇨ Convert to Button. Button objects also may be converted to normal objects by choosing Object ⇨ Interactive ⇨ Convert from Button.

Setting button options and behavior

Once a button is defined, you can create alternate states for the Rollover and Click states. The Actions section of the Buttons palette lets you define what happens when you interact with a button. The Event options are different ways to interact with a button. You also can select an Event such as On Release, OnClick, OnRollOver, OnRollOff, OnFocus, and OnBlur. The OnRelease and OnClick events occur when the mouse button is pressed and released. The OnRollOver and OnRollOff events occur when the mouse moves over and away from the button's bounding box. The On Focus and On Blur events occur when the button has or loses focus. A button has focus when it's been selected with the mouse or Tab key.

FIGURE 29.4

InDesign's Button panel includes all the features for creating and defining buttons.

Add new action
for selected action

Delete selected action

Convert object to a button

Delete optional state and its contents

For the selected event, you can tie it to an Action such as Close, Exit, Go to First, Next, Last, Previous Page, Go to URL, Play a Movie, Open a File, Play a Sound, or Zoom. The Action options are all the actions that may be set when the designated event happens. The available behaviors include the following:

- **Close:** Closes the current PDF document.
- **Exit:** Causes the application to exit.
- **Go to Anchor:** Jumps to a specified hyperlink anchor or bookmark.
- **Go to First Page:** Jumps to the first page in the document.
- **Go to Last Page:** Jumps to the last page in the document.
- **Go to Next Page:** Jumps to the next page in the document.
- **Go to Next View:** Jumps to the next page in the view history. This behavior becomes active only after the Go to Previous View behavior is used.

- **Go to Previous Page:** Jumps to the previous page in the document.
- **Go to Previous View:** Jumps to the last viewed page in the view history.
- **Go to URL:** Opens a Web browser with the designated URL address loaded.
- **Movie:** Lets you play, pause, stop, and resume a movie.
- **Open File:** Opens another selected PDF file or opens another file type in its default application.
- **Show/Hide Fields:** Show or hide a specified form field.
- **Sound:** Lets you play, pause, stop, and resume a sound.
- **View Zoom:** Lets you designate how the current page zooms. The options include Full Screen, Zoom In, Zoom Out, Fit in Window, Actual Size, Fit Width, Fit Visible, Reflow, Single Page, Continuous, Continuous-Facing, Rotate Clockwise, and Rotate Counterclockwise.

If you place a button on the master page, then it automatically appears on all the pages in the spread. The document can be exported using PDF, which retains the page transitions. The flyout menu even includes a library of sample buttons, shown in Figure 29.5.

FIGURE 29.5

InDesign includes a library of sample buttons.

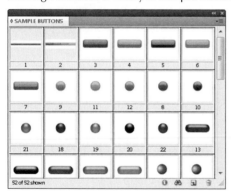

Various settings appear under the Behavior field depending on the behavior that you select. For example, selecting the Go to Anchor behavior displays settings for choosing the document from the active documents, a Browse button for locating a local document, and a field for selecting an anchor by name. The Go to URL behavior lets you type a URL. The Movie and Sound behaviors display a field where you can select a movie or sound added to the document, as well as an option to Play, Pause, Stop, or Resume. The Open File behavior lets you browse and select a file to open. All the go to page options, plus the Go to Anchor and the View Zoom behaviors, offer a list of zoom options to use when the user jumps to the page. The Show/Hide Fields behavior presents a list of fields in the current document along with check boxes to mark which ones are visible.

Setting button states

Although you can create various button states for rollovers using behaviors, button states are more easily defined using the various states. Each button maintains three different states—Normal, Rollover, and Click:

- **Normal:** The button's default state.
- **Rollover:** Occurs when the mouse cursor moves over the top of the button.
- **Click:** Occurs when a user clicks the button.

You can use the States settings in the Buttons palette to change the button's look for each of these states.

Creating links and buttons in Acrobat

If your InDesign document or any other CS4 application document is designed for deployment in PDF, then you can create the interactivity for the document in either InDesign or in Acrobat. InDesign's button system is intuitive and easy to use. InDesign also includes a Buttons Library that works in a manner similar to Acrobat. Acrobat also provides many options for adding hypertext and interactivity in a document, so you'll want to work in either.

Creating icon appearances

For a moment, let's deviate from Acrobat and look at how you might go about creating icons that can be used for button faces in Acrobat. In order to use a button face, simply create a shape in InDesign and make it into a button. You can then use the Buttons panel to add in the interactive values.

To create button icons, you can use Illustrator, InDesign, or Photoshop. In Illustrator CS4, you can create multipage PDF files, and Illustrator provides you with all the tools needed to create some nifty buttons. To create such a file, follow these steps.

STEPS: Creating Link Button Faces in Adobe Illustrator

1. **Create a new document in Adobe Illustrator.** Choose File ⇨ New in Illustrator. In the New Document dialog box, create an Artboard Setup of 2 inches by 2 inches. Select the RGB color option, as you see in Figure 29.6.

> **NOTE** If your unit of measure is not set to inches, press Command/Ctrl+K to open the
> Preferences dialog box. Select Units and Display Performance from the pull-down
> menu. Select Inches from the General pull-down menu, and click OK. When you return to the
> document window, your unit of measure displays inches.

2. **Draw ruler guides.** Press Command/Ctrl+R to show rulers. Drag a guideline to the vertical and horizontal centers (the 1-inch mark on the rulers). The guidelines display four quadrants that eventually become your four pages.

FIGURE 29.6

Create a new custom page 2 inches square, and set the color mode to RGB.

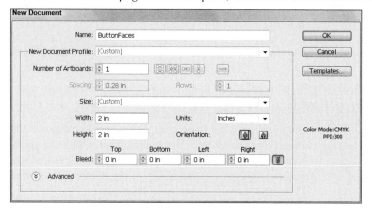

3. **Create an icon.** Choose Type ⇨ Glyphs to open the Glyphs palette. Select a font from the pull-down menu at the bottom of the palette. Locate a symbol in the palette you want to use. With the Type tool, click the document page and double-click the character in the Glyphs palette. The symbol is added as type to the document page, as shown in Figure 29.7.

> **CROSS-REF** For more information regarding working with the Glyphs palette, see Chapter 17.

4. **Define the type attributes.** Set the type character to a size within one-eighth inch of the first quadrant. Open the Control palette, and stroke and/or fill as you like.

5. **Create the rollover icon.** Duplicate the icon by pressing Option/Alt, and drag it to the second quadrant. Use a different color for the rollover appearance. Repeat Steps 3 through 5 to create icons symbolizing moving in an opposite direction. The final image should look like something similar to the preview shown in Figure 29.8.

FIGURE 29.7

Click the document page, and double-click the character you want to use in the Glyphs palette.

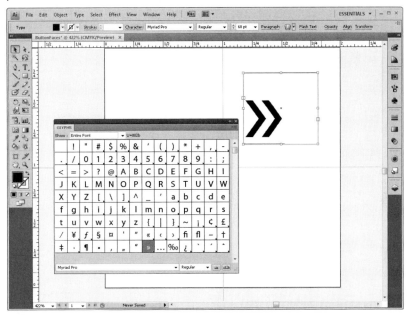

FIGURE 29.8

Select Tile Imageable Areas from the Tiling pull-down menu.

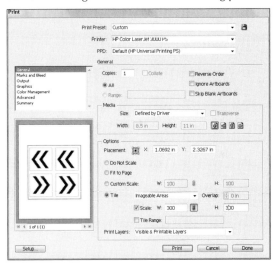

6. **Set the tile attributes.** Illustrator does not support multiple pages, but you can print tiles (divisions of a page) as separate PDF files. To set up the tiling of a document, choose File ⇨ Print. In the General pane, select Custom from the Media pull-down menu. Type **1** in the Width and Height text boxes, as shown in Figure 29.9. Note the values here have to be smaller than the art board size you created in Step 1 in order to tile the document.

FIGURE 29.9

For a 2-inch-square art board, add 1 inch for the width and height for the Media size.

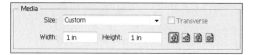

7. **Set the tile marks.** Click Setup in the left pane of the Print dialog box. Open the Tiling pull-down menu, and select Tile Imageable Areas. Note the preview in the Print dialog box. You should see the page tiles represented by dashed lines (refer to Figure 29.9). Click the Print button. Figure 29.10 shows the resulting printed page.

NOTE If you select the View ⇨ Show Page Tiling menu, then non-printing numbers appear in each of the four quadrants. These numbers show the printing order.

CROSS-REF For more information on tiling pages in Illustrator, see Chapter 39.

Why Use Type Characters for Button Faces?

We could have created hand-drawn or scanned illustrations and saved the file in PDF. However, using type characters gives you a benefit that illustrated artwork doesn't. The type characters' attributes can be changed in Acrobat. You can change the color of your icons in Acrobat even if you don't have the embedded font installed in your system.

Open a PDF document in Acrobat. Select the TouchUp Text tool, and drag across the type character. From a context menu, select Properties. The TouchUp Properties dialog box opens, as shown in the following figure. Click the Fill (or Stroke) swatch to open the pop-up color swatch palette. Select a color, or click Other Color to select a custom color from your system palette. Click Close, and the highlighted text changes color as defined in the swatch palette.

FIGURE 29.10

The final document page shows the tile marks and nonprinting page numbers.

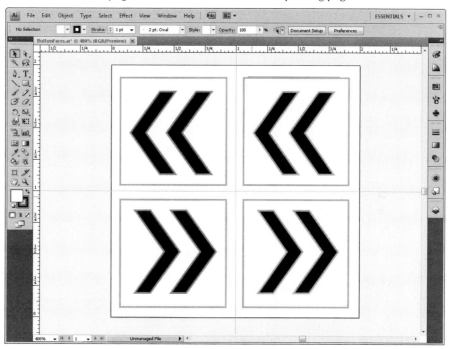

Adding links in Acrobat

Acrobat Professional has two tools you can use for creating links to document views and to link to secondary documents. The Link and Button tools can be used to link to the same destinations. Where links and buttons differ is with appearances and the ability to replicate across multiple pages. Only the Button tool offers you icon representations for image appearances and the ability to duplicate the buttons across all pages in a document. As an example, you might use a button as a navigation instrument to help users move forward and backward between pages while viewing PDFs in Full Screen mode. While in Full Screen view, the navigation tools are hidden. If you followed the steps for Creating Link Button faces in Adobe Illustrator, you can use the PDF file to follow the following steps.

STEPS: Adding Linked Buttons in Acrobat

1. **Open a PDF document in Acrobat.** Create a design in InDesign, and convert it to PDF. Try to use a design of multiple pages.

2. **Open the Advanced Editing toolbar.** Choose Tools ⇨ Advanced Editing ⇨ Show Advanced Editing Toolbar. The Advanced Editing toolbar opens as a floating toolbar in the Acrobat window, as shown in Figure 29.11.

FIGURE 29.11

The Button tool is located on the Advanced Editing toolbar.

3. **Create a button.** The first tool in the Advanced Editing toolbar is the Button tool. Select the tool, and drag a rectangle on the first page in the document. You can draw the rectangle anywhere on the page and move it after setting the button properties.

4. **Name the button field.** After creating a rectangle on the document page, the Button Properties dialog box opens with the General pane in view, as shown in Figure 29.12. Type a name in the Name text box. In this example, *goNext* is the name used for the button field.

FIGURE 29.12

Type a name for the button field.

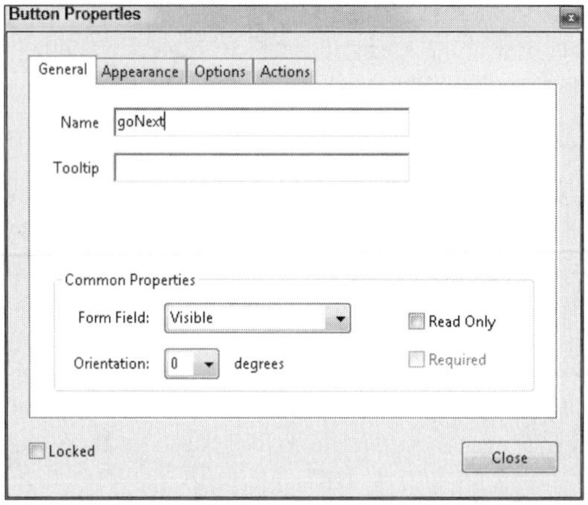

Button Properties
General	Appearance	Options	Actions
Name	goNext
Tooltip	
Common Properties
Form Field: Visible	☐ Read Only
Orientation: 0 degrees	☐ Required
☐ Locked	Close

5. **Set the button appearance.** Click the Appearance tab to open the Appearance pane shown in Figure 29.13. Click the Border Color and Fill Color to open pop-up palettes, and select No Color from the palette options.

FIGURE 29.13

Set the appearance to no border color and no fill color.

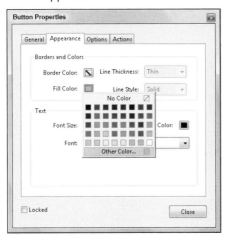

6. **Add a button face.** Click the Options tab to open the Options pane. From the Layout pull-down menu, select Icon only. Select Push from the Behavior pull-down menu. Click Up in the State window, and click Choose Icon. A Select Icon dialog box appears. Click Browse, and navigate your hard drive to locate a file to use as your button image. The file should be a PDF document. If using a multipage PDF document, you can scroll pages in the Select Icon dialog box by moving the scroll bar at the right side of the dialog box, shown in Figure 29.14.

FIGURE 29.14

Scroll pages by dragging the scroll bar on the right side of the dialog box.

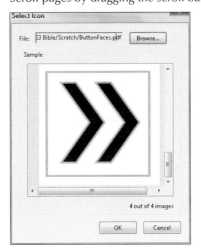

7. **Add a rollover effect.** Click OK in the Select Icon dialog box, and you return to the Button Properties. Select Rollover in the State window, shown in Figure 29.15, and click Choose Icon. Select the icon you want to use for the rollover appearance in the Select Icon dialog box, and click OK to return again to the Button Properties.

FIGURE 29.15

Select Rollover, and click Choose Icon again to select an icon for the rollover appearance.

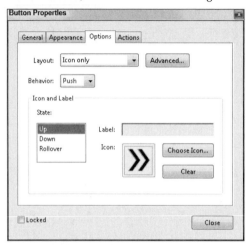

Creating URL Links in PDF Files

When you assign actions to buttons, links, and a number of other items such as bookmarks, page actions, document actions, and so on, you can select from a number of different action types. Among the action types is Open a Web Link. If you create a button or link, you can use the Open a Web Link action and type a URL in the Edit URL dialog box that appears when you click Add in the Actions tab.

Each link or button added to a PDF document increases file size. If you duplicate buttons across all pages, the buttons can add significantly to the file size. Rather than create URL links from links or buttons in Acrobat, you can type URL text in InDesign before PDF creation. If you want to add a URL link on all pages in the document, create the URL on a master page and be certain to use the complete URL address such as http://www.mycompany.com. For information related to working with master pages in InDesign, see Chapter 24.

When you open PDFs in Acrobat or Adobe Reader 8, you don't need to create links or buttons for URL links. Acrobat and Adobe Reader 8 are intelligent enough to recognize URL links described in text on pages.

8. **Assign an Action.** Click the Actions tab to open the Actions pane. From the Select Action pull-down menu, select Execute Menu Item. The Execute Menu Item action enables you to use all the menu commands in Acrobat as the button action. For example, if you want to open a file, you would use the Execute Menu Item and choose File ➪ Open for the menu item to execute.

9. **Define the Action.** With the Execute a Menu Item option selected, click Add in the Actions pane. Clicking this button makes the Menu Item selection dialog box appears. Select the menu item in the dialog box you want to use. In this example, choose View ➪ Go To ➪ Next Page. Click OK, and you should see the Execute Menu Item added to the Actions window as a Mouse Up action, as shown in Figure 29.16.

FIGURE 29.16

Actions added in the Button Properties are shown in the Actions window.

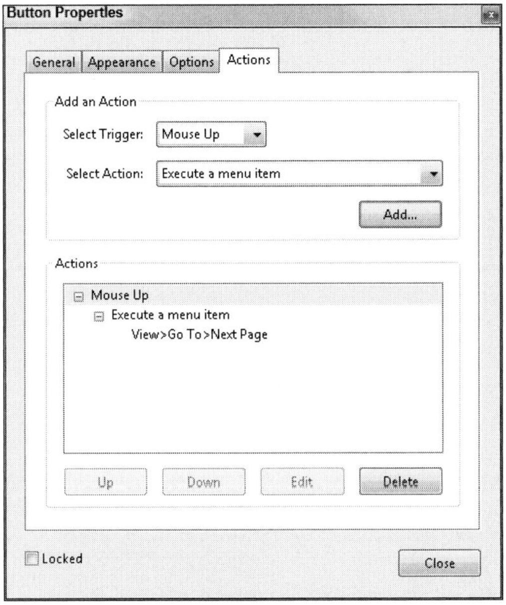

The advantage of using buttons in Acrobat instead of links has to do with the options you have for quick and easy duplication of buttons across all pages in a document. To duplicate buttons, follow these steps.

STEPS: Duplicating Button Links

1. **Duplicate a button on a page.** To follow these steps, first complete all previous steps in the section "Adding Hypertext Links in Acrobat." Click the Select Object tool in the Acrobat Toolbar Well (selection arrow). Move the button rectangle on the page to the lower-right corner of the document page. Press Option/Ctrl, and then press Shift and drag the rectangle to the left corner of the page. The button is duplicated.

2. **Name the new button.** You should still have the Button Properties dialog box open. If not, double-click the new button using the Select Object tool. Click General, and type a new name for this button. In this example, *goPrev* is used for the second button name.

3. **Change icon appearances.** Click Options. Select Up in the State window, and click Choose Icon. Select the icon you want to use for the button to navigate backward in the document. Click OK, and you return to the Button Properties. Click Rollover, and click Choose Icon. Select the rollover icon, and click OK. If using a multipage PDF document, you don't need to search for the document in the Select Icon dialog box. The last file you visited becomes the new default and remains the default until you select another file.

4. **Edit the Action.** Click Actions. When you copied the button, all the button attributes were also copied. The last action assigned to the button was Execute Menu Item. Select Execute Menu Item in the Actions list window, and click Edit. Visit the View menu, and choose View ➪ Go To ➪ Previous Page. Click OK to return to the Button Properties, and click Close to dismiss the dialog box.

5. **Duplicate the buttons across all pages.** Draw a marquee through both buttons with the Select Object tool. Open a context menu, and select Duplicate from the menu commands, as shown in Figure 29.17.

FIGURE 29.17

Open a context menu on the selected buttons, and choose Duplicate.

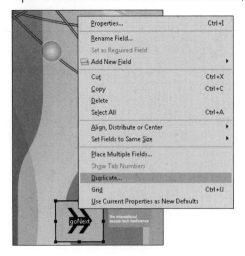

6. **Specify the page range.** The Duplicate Field dialog box opens after selecting the Duplicate command. Select All in the Duplicate Field dialog box, shown in Figure 29.18, to duplicate the button across all pages. Click OK, and the button is duplicated.

FIGURE 29.18

Select All, and click OK to duplicate the buttons across all pages.

7. **Remove nonfunctional buttons.** The first page *goPrev* button doesn't have a page to open, and the last page *goNext* button doesn't have a page to open. Click each of these buttons with the Select Object tool, and press Delete/Backspace or Num Pad Del to remove the buttons. To test the actions, click the Hand tool in the Toolbar Well and click the buttons to navigate pages. As you move the cursor over a button, you should see the button appearances change with the rollover effects.

Working with Animation

All CS4 programs work with animations in one way or another. You can create animations in some programs while other programs offer options for viewing animations. Of all the CS4 programs, Flash includes the strongest feature set for creating, but simple animation effects can be created and viewed in the programs.

Animation and Adobe Illustrator

Adobe Illustrator supports exporting files as Adobe Flash files (SWF). You can create layers in Illustrator and export the layered Illustrator document as SWF.

 **CROSS-REF** For a complete description on exporting to SWF format from Adobe Illustrator and creating simple animations using Flash, see Chapter 23.

Animation and Adobe Photoshop

The Animation palette in Photoshop is used to create animation sequences from layered Photoshop files. You create the animation in the Animation palette and export the Photoshop file as an animated GIF or SWF file that can be viewed in Dreamweaver and used in Web page designs. Photoshop CS4 Extended also includes the ability to render video in a number of different formats.

The first step in creating an animation is to create a layered Photoshop file, as you see in Figure 29.19. Each layer should contain an image that is transformed in one way or another different from the previous layer. For example, if you want to rotate an object so the animation displays a revolving icon, you rotate each layer using the transformation tools in Photoshop so each image appears with a different rotation. When the animation is played, the different layer views appear at short intervals to create the illusion of a moving object.

FIGURE 29.19

Create a layered Photoshop file with all layers containing different transformations.

CROSS-REF   For more information about transforming images and objects, see Chapter 13.

Choose Window ⇨ Animation to open the Animation palette. The palette, shown in Figure 29.20, is used to identify the frames and set the frame attributes. From a fly-out palette menu, you can create new frames, copy/paste frames, select frames, reverse frames, and more.

FIGURE 29.20

Choose Window ⇨ Animation to open the Animation pane.

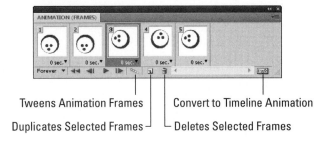

Tweens Animation Frames

Duplicates Selected Frames

Convert to Timeline Animation

Deletes Selected Frames

The palette has tools to set the frame intervals and preview the animation. The frames are created by selecting New Frame from the fly-out menu or by clicking the Duplicate Selected Frames button in the palette window. When a new frame is added, select the layer view you want for that frame by clicking the respective layer in the Layers palette. Continue adding frames and changing layer views to create the animation. After previewing the animation by clicking the right-pointing arrow in the Animation palette, choose File ⇨ Save for Web & Devices. Be certain GIF is the format appearing in the Save For Web dialog box, and click Save. The Save Optimized As dialog box opens. If you want to open the animation in a Web browser, select HTML and Images from the Format pull-down menu, as shown in Figure 29.21.

FIGURE 29.21

Select HTML and Images to save the animated GIF and the HTML code that creates the animation in a Web browser.

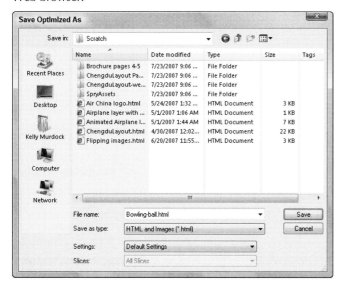

TIP If you use another form of animation other than rotating objects such as fading an object from 0 to 100% opacity or vice versa, you can create a quick transition between the layers using the Tween animation frames tool in the Animation palette. Just create two layers containing an image with different opacities and display the two layers as separate frames in the Animation palette. Click the Tween animation frames tool (to the left of the Duplicates selected frames tool). The Tween dialog box opens, where you can select parameter attributes and the number of frames to create for the transition.

The HTML export from Photoshop can be opened directly in Dreamweaver, or you can copy the code and paste it into the source code of a Dreamweaver project. If you click the Preview tab in Dreamweaver, shown in Figure 29.22, the animation plays exactly as you previewed in Photoshop.

FIGURE 29.22

Open the HTML file, and the first frame appears in a Dreamweaver window. Click Preview to play the animation.

Animation in InDesign and Acrobat

Animation files are placed in InDesign and viewed in Acrobat. You can choose to import an animation file such as SWF in InDesign or in Acrobat. Animation files are handled like other multimedia files where compatibility options and play buttons can be assigned.

CROSS-REF For information regarding compatibility options in Acrobat, see the section "Using Multimedia in Designs."

Acrobat has an added benefit with the ability to capture Web pages containing animation and video. You might have a client who has a Web site containing animation files and needs to repurpose documents or convert Web pages to PDF documents that you intend to integrate in a PDF collection of files to be published on CD/DVD-ROM. Once converted to PDF, the animation files can be copied and pasted into other PDF files.

NOTE You can capture Flash animation from Web sites in Acrobat, but animated GIF files are not converted with the animation effect. Captured Web pages containing animated GIF files capture the first image in the animation sequence.

There are a number of benefits in converting Web pages to PDF. You can create a Web site for a client, convert HTML files to PDF, and secure the PDF documents against any unauthorized copying or editing; you can convert pages from several sources and search the PDFs locally on your hard drive using Acrobat Search; and you can integrate captured Web pages in designs for display ads or brochures, and more. To understand how Acrobat is used to capture Web pages, follow these steps.

STEPS: Converting Web Pages to PDF

1. **Open a URL in Acrobat.** Launch Acrobat. From the Create PDF task button pull-down menu, select From Web Page. The Create PDF from Web Page dialog box shown in Figure 29.23 opens.

FIGURE 29.23

Open the Create PDF task button pull-down menu, and select From Web Page to open the Create PDF from Web Page dialog box.

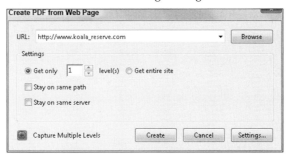

2. **Adjust download settings.** Add the URL for the Web site you intend to capture. Type **1** in the Get only text box to capture one level of Web pages. Select the Stay on same path and Stay on same server check boxes to be certain you are capturing Web pages from the specified URL.

3. **Adjust Web Capture Settings.** Click Settings in the Create PDF from Web Page dialog box to open the Web Capture Settings dialog box shown in Figure 29.24. Select HTML, and click Settings to open the HTML Conversion Settings dialog box.

4. **Embed the media in the Web page.** From the Multimedia pull-down menu, select Embed multimedia content when possible, as shown in Figure 29.25. Media can be either a link to a Web page or embedded in the resultant PDF document. When you embed the media, it is available locally on your hard drive and can be played when you are offline.

If you capture a Web page containing an animation or video clip, you can select the clip with the Select Object tool and copy it. The clip then can be pasted in another PDF document.

 You can paste copied media from Acrobat only into PDF documents. You cannot paste the media in an InDesign file.

FIGURE 29.24

Select HTML, and click Settings to adjust the conversion settings.

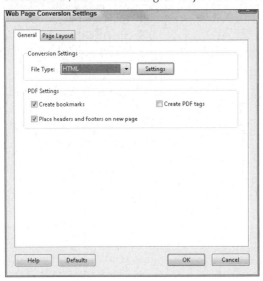

FIGURE 29.25

Select Embed multimedia content when possible from the Multimedia pull-down menu.

Using Multimedia in Designs

Of course, none of the CS4 programs are dedicated video editors, so if you need to create video clips, you need to work with iMovie on the Macintosh or MovieMaker on Windows for low-end video-editing programs. If you do serious video editing, you need to use more professional editing tools such as Adobe Premiere Pro CS4 or Apple's Final Cut Pro. Photoshop CS4 Extended includes the ability to work with video.

Regardless of what application is used to create media, you can import the media in InDesign, Acrobat, and Dreamweaver. The CS4 programs supporting media imports offer you options for creating buttons and links to control the media visibility.

Importing multimedia in InDesign

Both movies and sound files can be imported into InDesign layouts. Although InDesign supports the placing of these files in a document, they cannot actually be played until the document is exported in PDF.

The movie formats supported by InDesign include QuickTime, AVI, MPEG, and SWF movies, and WAV, AIF, and AU sound files.

NOTE The MPEG and SWF movie formats are playable only in Acrobat version 6 or greater or Adobe Reader version 6 or greater. QuickTime and AVI movie formats are playable only in Acrobat version 5 or later.

You add movie and sound files to the current document by choosing File ⇨ Place. The placed media file appears within a frame. Selecting the object and choosing Object ⇨ Interactive ⇨ Movie Options or Object ⇨ Interactive ⇨ Sound Options opens a dialog box where the settings for the movie or sound file are specified. If you create an empty frame, you may access either Options dialog box and select a file at a later time.

Setting movie options

The Movie Options dialog box, shown in Figure 29.26, includes Name and Description fields. The Name appears in the object's frame; the Description appears in Acrobat when the mouse cursor is moved over the top of the object.

The Movie Options dialog box lets you either choose a file or specify a URL. Although you cannot embed movies within the InDesign document, you can embed the movie in the PDF. If you select the Embed Movie in PDF option, the movie file embeds within the PDF file when it's exported. If you deselect this option, you must move the movie file along with the exported PDF file that references it. The Specify URL option lets you type the address to a media file on the Web. If a connection to the Internet is established when the media file is viewed, the movie file is downloaded into the PDF document. The Verify URL and Movie Size button checks the URL to make sure it's valid and points to a movie file.

FIGURE 29.26

The Movie Options dialog box defines which movie file plays and when it plays.

A Poster is an image that fills the movie frame. This image appears when the movie isn't being played. There are several Poster options you can add to movie frames:

- **None:** Hides the movie file when it isn't being played.

- **Standard:** Displays the image contained in the `Default Poster` image file. This generic image displays to the right in Figure 29.25.

- **Default Poster:** Presents the poster image that is bundled with the movie file. If the movie doesn't include a poster image, the first frame of the movie is used.

- **Choose Image as Poster:** Lets you browse and load an image and display it as the movie poster.

- **Choose Movie Frame as Poster:** Lets you view the movie using the pane to the right, where you may select a single frame of the movie to use as a poster.

The Mode options define how many times the movie file plays. The options include Play Once Then Stop, Play Once Stay Open, and Repeat Play. The Play on Page Turn option causes the movie to start playing when the page that includes the movie is displayed. The Show Controller During Play option shows controls along with the movie file. These controls let the viewer play, pause, and stop the movie file. The Floating Window option displays the movie within a floating window. The size and position of the floating window are set using the fields at the bottom of the dialog box.

Setting sound options

The Sound Options dialog box, shown in Figure 29.27, includes Name and Description fields. The Name is the name that appears in the object's frame; the Description appears in Acrobat when the mouse cursor is moved over the top of the object.

FIGURE 29.27

The Sound Options dialog box

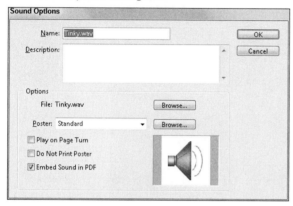

The Sound Options dialog box, like the Movie Options dialog box, also lets you Browse for a new sound file. The Poster options are limited to None, Standard, and Choose Image as Poster. The Play on Page Turn option causes the sound file to play when the page that contains it is displayed. The Do Not Print Poster option ensures that the sound frame isn't printed with the rest of the document when the document is printed. The Embed Sound in PDF option causes the sound file to be embedded within the PDF, which frees you from the concern of copying the sound file along with the exported PDF, but it increases the PDF file size. Note that InDesign adds no more compression to media files to reduce their sizes.

Importing multimedia in Acrobat

If your ultimate display for designs containing multimedia is Acrobat PDF, you have much better solutions in Acrobat for assigning button behaviors and file linking. Acrobat provides you with a rich set of features that are expanded to almost limitless options when you consider the flexibility you have with writing JavaScripts. As an example of an impressive electronic brochure design containing interactive buttons and imported multimedia, take a look at Figure 29.28.

FIGURE 29.28

An electronic brochure created by Robert Connolly of BC Pictures in Toronto, Canada, contains interactive buttons and multimedia.

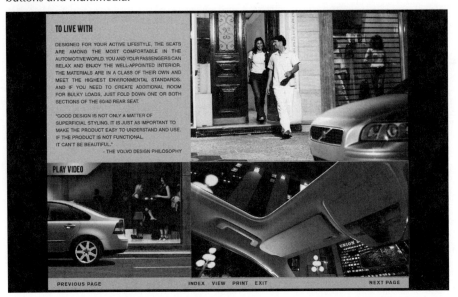

The Volvo brochure created by Robert Connolly of BC Pictures in Toronto, Canada (www.bc pictures.com) has interactive links at the bottom of the page. The design was originally created in InDesign, and the interactive elements were added in Acrobat. The brochure opens in Full Screen mode in Adobe Acrobat or Adobe Reader. Therefore, the navigational buttons provide the reader options for moving about the brochure.

The photo in the lower-left corner contains a button that opens an embedded movie clip as a floating window. The movie frame in the lower-right corner of the page is a QuickTimeVR movie where the reader can click and move the cursor around the movie frame to view a 360-degree view of the auto interior.

On the opening page of the electronic brochure, a pop-up menu, shown in Figure 29.29, contains links to pages throughout the brochure. This menu is created with JavaScript in Acrobat. With the extensive list of links, the pop-up menu conveniently economizes space by serving as an alternative to a list of links on the page. When the menu is collapsed, the reader sees the nicely constructed design and photo images.

Using Preview and Trim settings

To import a movie in Acrobat, you use the Video tool. Double-click the Video tool, and the Insert Video dialog box appears, as shown in Figure 29.30. After selecting a video file, a preview of the file is displayed in the Insert Video dialog box. Using this preview, you can view the loaded video and select an image from the video to use as a poster image.

FIGURE 29.29

Robert Connolly created interactive links via a pop-up menu designed with Acrobat's implementation of JavaScript.

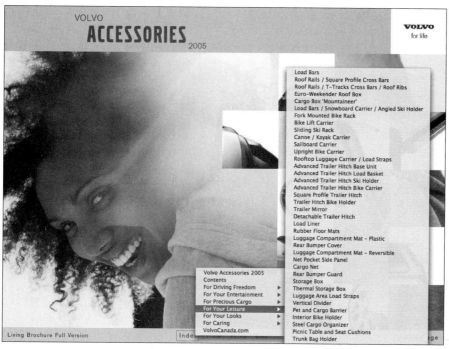

Using Compatibility settings

All loaded videos are automatically converted to the Flash format, which provides broad support across all Adobe products. However, if you want to use an older video format, you can click the Create Legacy Multimedia Content button, which opens the Add Movie dialog box, shown in Figure 29.31.

The first two radio buttons offer options for choosing the compatibility setting:

- **Acrobat 6 (and later) Compatible Media:** Acrobat 6-compatible media permits you to embed media clips in the PDF file. If you choose Acrobat 6-compatible media, you have a choice for embedding the media or linking to it. Users of Acrobat 6 and above can see the media. Users of Acrobat and Adobe Reader below version 6 won't see the media.

- **Acrobat 5 (and earlier) Compatible Media:** Selecting this option allows the user to see the media as a link to the PDF file. If you use this option, users of Acrobat/Reader prior to version 6 can see the media. The PDF and the movie file need to be copied to a CD/DVD or a Web site together for the media to play in Acrobat/Reader.

FIGURE 29.30

The Insert Video dialog box lets you load and preview a video file.

 **Mac users need to upgrade to Acrobat to a version higher than version 7.03 to play Acrobat 6-compatible media on Mac OS X Tiger.**

The poster options provide you the same settings as when importing media in InDesign.

Creating renditions

One of the advantages of setting media attributes in Acrobat versus InDesign is the ability to add renditions. You can add a media clip to a PDF document and specify settings for the media such as playback attributes, playback location, showing or hiding player controls, and system requirements such as download speeds. You then can create a different rendition in the same PDF document for different media attributes. For example, you may have one media setting for users with broadband Internet feeds to download movies at 384 Kbps (kilobytes per second). You then can open the media properties, create a second rendition, and in the Rendition Settings dialog box specify a different download speed, as shown in Figure 29.32.

FIGURE 29.31

Double-click the Video tool to open the Add Movie dialog box where you make choices for media compatibility and browsing for the media location.

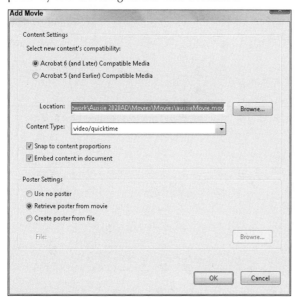

FIGURE 29.32

Renditions enable you to set different media settings to movie clips in the same PDF document.

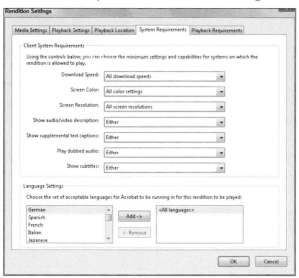

Creating play buttons

You create buttons to play media the same way buttons are created as links to views. In the Actions tab, you have options for selecting Acrobat 5- or Acrobat 6-compatible media. When you select the action and click Add in the Actions dialog box, the Multimedia Properties dialog box opens as shown in Figure 29.33. From the pull-down menu, select the play options. You can create buttons to play, stop, resume, play from beginning, and add a custom JavaScript when selecting Acrobat 6-compatible media.

FIGURE 29.33

Select Play Media (Acrobat compatibility), and click Add. The Multimedia Properties dialog box opens where play actions are assigned.

In Figure 29.34, a PDF file contains buttons assigned with different play actions.

 **NOTE** Users of Mac OS X Tiger need to upgrade Acrobat/Adobe Reader above version 7.03 in order to see Acrobat-compatible media.

Several buttons are used in a document to control the media play actions.

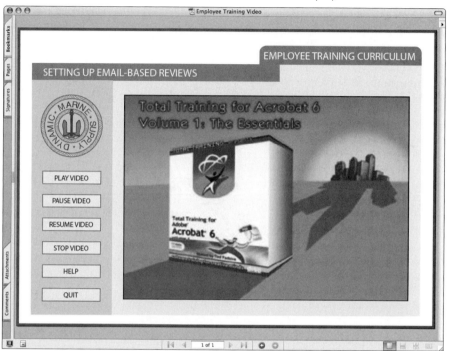

Hyperlinks and Publications

Buttons and links are items you add to InDesign or PDF pages. In order to invoke an action, you need to have the button or link appear on a page when you want to initiate the action. If you have the same action assigned to a button such as opening another PDF document, it makes more sense to add the action to a bookmark. Bookmarks are visible from all pages, and they add significantly less overhead to a PDF file than when creating multiple buttons or links on pages.

If you create long documents such as manuals, books, guides, and so on, your document viewing and searching information is much faster if you break up the documents to multiple PDFs and use bookmarks to open and close files. You can organize and add interactive links to many files and create an illusion for the end user that browsing multiple files actually appears as a single file. The user is not likely to know the difference between scrolling pages in one document and opening and closing files from many documents.

Bookmarks in InDesign

Bookmarks in many ways are very similar to hyperlinks. They also mark text or images that link to places with the PDF file for quick navigation. Bookmarks are available in PDF files and appear in the left Bookmark pane, but they aren't recognized when the layout is converted to a Web page. Bookmarks are also available in InDesign and can be used for navigation in the InDesign document.

NOTE When InDesign creates a table of contents, all entries in the table of contents are automatically added to the document as bookmarks if you enable the Bookmark option when you export to the PDF format.

You create and manage bookmarks using the Bookmarks palette, shown in Figure 29.35, which is accessed by choosing Window ➪ Interactive ➪ Bookmarks.

FIGURE 29.35

The Bookmarks palette manages all bookmarks for the document.

You add new bookmarks to the document by selecting the bookmark item and choosing the New Bookmark palette menu command or by clicking the Create New Bookmark button at the bottom of the Bookmark palette. If no bookmarks are selected in the palette, the new bookmark is added to the bottom of the list of bookmarks. But if a bookmark is selected, the new bookmark is added as a child bookmark under the selected bookmark.

After creation, a bookmark's name appears as highlighted text, which you can edit. The bookmark's name appears in Acrobat's Bookmark pane. If some selected text is the bookmark, the selected text appears as the bookmark's name unless you change it.

The order of bookmarks within the Bookmarks palette also determines the order in which the bookmarks appear in Acrobat's bookmark pane. You can rearrange the listed bookmarks by dragging the bookmarks within the Bookmarks palette. As you're dragging a bookmark, a line appears defining where the bookmark appears when you release the mouse. If you drop a bookmark on top of an existing bookmark, the bookmark becomes a child to the highlighted bookmark.

Bookmarks in Acrobat

The most common bookmark used in Acrobat is a bookmark to a page in the existing document. Bookmarks in Acrobat are easy to create. You first navigate to the page and view you want and press ⌘/Ctrl+B. Alternately, you can open the Bookmarks pane and select New Bookmark from the fly-out menu in the pane. When a bookmark is created, it is temporarily named Untitled. Type a name for the bookmark while Untitled is selected, and you can rename the bookmark.

If you have title headings on pages such as Chapter 1, Section 1, Part 1, and so on, you can use the Select tool and drag across the title on the pane or a section heading. When you press ⌘/Ctrl+B, the bookmark is created and linked to the existing view, and the bookmark name appearing in the Bookmark is derived from the selected text.

Opening files using bookmarks

The real power in using bookmarks is when you add different action types to the bookmark properties. In particular, writing JavaScripts provides a limitless number of opportunities to create dynamic interactive PDF documents.

When assigning properties to bookmarks, you can create the bookmark from any given page. Bookmarks and their associated actions are accessible from any page in a PDF document. If you are organizing long publications broken into sections, bookmarks provide the ideal avenue for opening and closing the various sections. Using buttons or links requires you to add a button or link to every page so a reader can quickly explore a different section. Adding these elements increases the file size considerably. Adding bookmarks to do the job results in file size increases that are hardly noticeable.

To organize a collection of PDF documents, follow these steps.

STEPS: Navigating Files with Bookmarks

1. **Organize a collection of related documents.** If you intend to distribute documents, you must be certain that the file paths for all linked files remain identical within folders and nested folders. To simplify your file organization, create a folder in Adobe Bridge and add the folder as a Favorite. You can drag files to this folder from the content area. If you want to copy files, press Option/Alt and drag to your Favorite folder.

CROSS-REF For more information on creating Favorites and organizing files in Adobe Bridge, see Chapter 6.

2. **Create a blank document.** Acrobat does not have a command for you to create a new document; however, you can use one short line of JavaScript code to create a blank page that opens in the Document pane. Press ⌘/Ctrl+J to open the JavaScript Debugger. Click the Trash icon to clear any default code and messages in the window. Type the following code in the Console window:

```
app.newDoc();
```

The line of code is case sensitive, so be certain to type it as shown in Figure 29.36. Press the Num Pad Enter key, and a new blank document opens in the Document pane. Click the Close button in the Debugger to dismiss the window.

FIGURE 29.36

Type the code in the Console window, and press the Num Pad Enter key to create a new blank document.

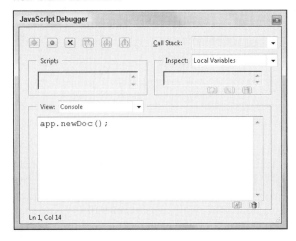

3. **Create a new bookmark.** Press ⌘/Ctrl+B. The Bookmarks pane opens, and a new bookmark is created. The word *untitled* appears as the name, and the text is highlighted.

4. **Type a name for the bookmark.** Type a name, and the highlighted bookmark name is replaced with the text you type. Press the Num Pad Enter key to register the name.

5. **Open the Bookmark Properties dialog box.** Place the cursor on the bookmark name, and open a context menu. Select Properties from the menu choices, and the Bookmark Properties dialog box opens.

6. **Open the Actions tab.** By default, the Appearance tab is selected. Click the Actions tab in the Bookmark Properties dialog box. The Actions tab opens.

7. **Delete the existing action.** When you created the bookmark, the action was automatically set as a link to the view of the blank page in the Document pane. Delete this action by selecting the first line of text in the Actions window and clicking Delete. The Actions window should now appear empty.

8. **Add an Action to open a file.** Open the Select Action pull-down menu. Select Open a File from the menu options. Click Add.

9. **Select a file to open.** The Select File dialog box opens. Search your drive for the folder you created in Adobe Bridge, and select the file you want to use for a contents page or opening file. Click OK in the Select File to Open dialog box.

10. **Select a window preference.** The Specify Window Preference dialog box opens. You have three choices as shown in Figure 29.37. Select Existing Window from the available choices. When you select Existing Window, the document containing this action closes as the target file opens. Click OK, and you are returned to the Actions pane.

FIGURE 29.37

Select Existing window in the Specify Open Preference dialog box.

11. **Create another bookmark.** Follow Steps 3 through 10 to add new bookmarks for additional files to open. Be certain to set the same window preference for all actions. Your bookmarks should appear listed in the bookmarks pane as shown in Figure 29.38.

 **You can leave the Actions pane open while creating new bookmarks.**

FIGURE 29.38

Bookmarks are listed in the order they were created in the Bookmarks pane.

12. **Specify initial view options.** Choose File ➪ Document Properties. Click the Initial View tab. From the Show pull-down menu, select Bookmarks Panel and Page. Select Single Page from the Page Layout pull-down menu and Fit Page from the Magnification menu. Select Document Title from the Show pull-down menu. The settings should look like Figure 29.39.

FIGURE 29.39

Adjust settings for the initial view that will appear each time the document opens.

13. **Add metadata.** Click the Description tab. Add data common to all your files if any exist for the Author, Subject, and Keywords fields. Note that the Title field should be different for each file.

CROSS-REF For more information about adding Initial Views and Document Descriptions, see Chapter 34.

14. **Save the file.** Choose File ➪ Save, and save the file as a temporary working document. You may want to use a name for the file like `temp.pdf` to distinguish it from your other files.

15. **Import bookmarks.** You can import a file in your temp document, or you can import the temp document into other files. In order to preserve the Initial View and the metadata, you should import each file in your template. To import a PDF in the open document, click the Pages tab in the Navigation pane. Open a context menu on the first page, and select Insert Pages. The Select File to Insert dialog box opens. Select a file to insert, and click Select.

16. **Select the location for the inserted pages.** The Insert Pages dialog box opens. Select After from the Location pull-down menu to insert pages after the selected page. Click OK to insert the pages, as shown in Figure 29.40.

Select After from the Location pull-down menu, and click OK.

17. **Delete the blank page.** The template page is contained in the document. Open a context menu on the Blank page and select Delete. Click OK in the alert dialog box.

18. **Delete the dead bookmark.** If you added bookmarks to open every file contained in your folder, the file you inserted in the open document does not need a bookmark. Select the respective bookmark in the Bookmarks pane, and open a context menu. Select Delete from the menu.

19. **Edit the Title field and any unique metadata.** Open the Document Description (⌘/Ctrl+D), and click Description. Edit the fields where data need to be added to uniquely describe this file.

20. **Save the file.** Choose File ⇨ Save As. Be certain to provide a unique name or overwrite the file you inserted to preserve the template file.

21. **Finish the project.** Open the template file, and insert the next file to modify. Follow Steps 15 through 20 for each file contained in your collection. When one of the files opens, the Bookmarks pane is opened. Clicking a bookmark from any page closes the open file and opens the target file. The reader can browse your collection freely without opening several documents in the Document pane, thereby eliminating confusion when navigating documents.

Creating On Demand Documents

The power of interactivity is best exemplified in PDF documents with JavaScript routines. JavaScript provides you with a limitless opportunity to create new design looks, add more sophisticated dynamic linking, and explore a world of features not available with tools and menu commands in the other CS4 programs. As Emeril says, "It's time to kick it up a notch."

To illustrate an example for where you might use JavaScript and PDF documents, let's assume you have a document used to record ongoing progress on a campaign or design assignment. The document might be a PDF form used to fill in form data on a series of designs as they are completed by members of your workgroup. Contained within the form is the respective design piece itself. Therefore, you start with two documents. One document is a form template, and the other is a design piece.

Your task is to merge the two documents for the purpose of record keeping and for your client to sign off on the final designs. Because one file contains form fields in a PDF, you can't copy and paste one document on the same page as the other in Adobe InDesign. You need some way to merge the two files together to create a single page document with the form fields.

To begin, you'll need two files that, when merged together, appear as a single page layout. You might initially lay out a document in InDesign, convert to PDF, and add form fields like you see in Figure 29.41. In Adobe Acrobat, the bottom half of this design is where the merged file will eventually appear.

CROSS-REF Working with PDF forms and adding form fields in Acrobat is not difficult, but there is much to it. For a more comprehensive view of creating Acrobat PDF forms, see the *Adobe Acrobat 9 PDF Bible* (Wiley Publishing).

To understand how to merge data in PDF documents, follow these steps.

STEPS: Dynamically Creating Content Using JavaScript

1. **Add a bookmark.** You should have two PDF documents that you want to merge together. If you're not familiar with creating a PDF form, you can use any layout where two halves of a layout are converted to PDF. One layout is used as a template. Open the file in Acrobat, and press ⌘/Ctrl+B to create a bookmark. Name the bookmark by typing a name immediately after the bookmark is created. In this example, we use *merge* as the bookmark name.

2. **Add an Execute a menu item action.** Open a context menu on the bookmark name, and select Properties. Click Actions. Select the existing page view action, and click Delete to remove it from the Actions list. Open the Select Action pull-down menu, and select Execute a menu item. Click Add, open the Document menu, and select Insert Pages. Click OK, but leave the Bookmark Properties dialog box open.

CROSS-REF For more information on creating an Execute a menu item action, see "Adding links in Acrobat" earlier in this chapter.

When the user clicks the bookmark, the Insert Pages dialog box opens. This enables the user to locate and select the file to merge with the template.

FIGURE 29.41

Create a layout in InDesign, and convert to PDF. Add form fields in Adobe Acrobat.

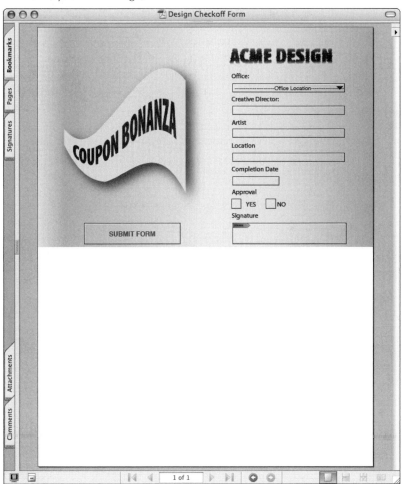

3. **Add a JavaScript.** After a page is inserted, you need to move ahead to the inserted page to follow the remaining steps. You could use another Execute a menu item action, or you can add a JavaScript to accomplish the same task. Add a JavaScript here to do the job. Select Run a JavaScript from the Select Action pull-down menu and click Add, and the Create and Edit JavaScripts window opens. Type the following code in the window, and be certain to use the exact same letter case:

```
this.pageNum++;
```

4. **Add another Execute a menu item action.** Click OK in the Create and Edit JavaScripts window, and you return to the Bookmark Properties dialog box. Select Execute a menu item from the Select Action pull-down menu, and choose Advanced ➪ Forms ➪ Page Templates. You are converting the inserted page as a PDF page template. In Acrobat, you can spawn a page from a template. The spawned page can be inserted in the PDF, or it can overlay an existing page. In order to spawn a page, you first need to create a page template. When you click OK, three actions now appear in the Actions tab in the Bookmark properties dialog box, as shown in Figure 29.42.

FIGURE 29.42

Click OK in the Execute a menu item dialog box, and you can see three actions nested in the Actions list.

5. **Add another JavaScript.** Your final action is a script that you write to spawn a page from the page template, delete the page after spawning it, and delete the bookmark so a user doesn't inadvertently click it again to create another template. Select Run a JavaScript from the Select Action pull-down menu, and click Add. In the Create and Edit JavaScripts window, type the following code exactly as shown here and in Figure 29.43:

```
this.pageNum--;

if(this.templates.length)
{
        var a = this.templates[this.templates.length-1];
        if(a != null)
```

```
        {
            a.spawn ({
                    nPage:this.pageNum,
                    bRename:true,
                    bOverlay:true,
            })

            this.deletePages(this.pageNum+1);

            bookmarkRoot.remove();

    }
```

FIGURE 29.43

Type the code that spawns a page from the template and deletes the page and bookmark.

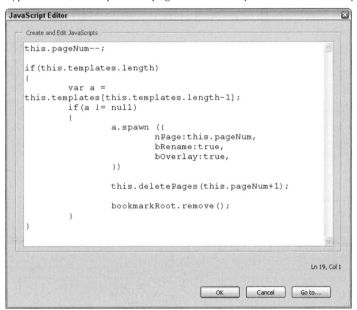

6. **Save the file.** Click OK in the Create and Edit JavaScripts window, and click Close in the Bookmark Properties dialog box. Choose File ➪ Save As, and save the file with a new name.

CROSS-REF Before saving the document, open the Initial View document properties and select Bookmarks and Page for the opening view. When a user opens the file, the bookmark is in view in the Bookmarks pane. See the section "Opening files using bookmarks."

Understanding the code

The code written in Step 5 of the "Dynamically Creating Content Using JavaScripts" series of steps performs several actions. The actions specified in the script include:

- **this,pageNum--;:** The first line of code moves the user to the first page in the file and makes that page the active page.

- **if(this,templates.length) through the 5th line of code (if (a != null)):** This sets up a condition where the user can type any name for the page template name. As page templates are created, they need to be named. Rather than have the user try to remember a name, this code accepts any name for the page template.

- **a.spawn ({ through line 10 (bOverlay:true,):** This spawns the page from the template. The bOverlay:true statement takes the page template data and overlays it on the existing page.

- **this.deletePages(this.pageNum+1):** This deletes page 2 in the template. Because the user is currently on page 1, the pageNum+1 portion of the statement targets the next page for deletion.

- **bookmarkRoot.remove();:** This deletes the bookmark from the document.

Running the scripts

After you add the Execute a menu item and JavaScripts actions, test the sequence of actions to be certain they work properly. Be certain you save the file before attempting to run any actions. You can always revert to the last-saved version by choosing File ⇨ Revert. If your JavaScript contains an error, revert to the saved version, make an edit, and run the action. If it works properly, revert again, make the same edit, and save the file.

To test your series of actions, follow these steps.

STEPS: Executing Menu Items and JavaScripts

1. **Click the bookmark.** To invoke the actions, click the bookmark with the Hand tool.

2. **Insert a page.** The first item you see after clicking the bookmark is the Select File to Insert dialog box, shown in Figure 29.44. Select a file to be merged with the open template document, and click Select. The Insert Pages dialog box opens next. Be certain that the Location pull-down menu shows After, and click OK.

3. **Add a template.** The next dialog box appearing is the Page Templates dialog box, as shown in Figure 29.45. Type a name for the template. The name can be any text you want to add in the Name text box. In this example, we use *xyz*. Click Add, and an alert dialog box opens as shown in Figure 29.46. Click Yes to continue.

FIGURE 29.44

Select a file to insert, and click Select.

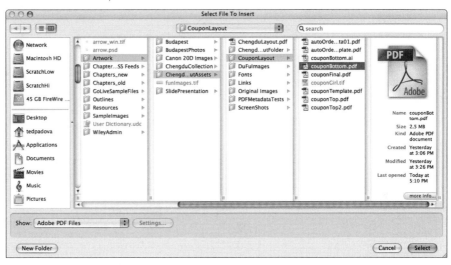

FIGURE 29.45

Type a name for the template and click Add, and an alert dialog box opens.

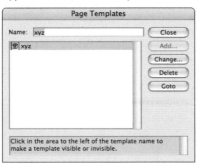

4. **Close the Page Templates dialog box.** After a template name is added, the name appears in the Page Templates window, as shown in Figure 29.47. Click Close to continue.

Click Yes in the alert dialog box, and the template name is added in the Page Templates dialog box.

5. **Save the file.** The remaining part of the JavaScript finishes up the job. The inserted page data are overlaid on the first page, the second page is deleted, and the bookmark is deleted. If you have form fields in the document, fill in the fields. The final document is shown in Figure 29.48. Choose File ➪ Save As to save the document with a new filename.

Spawning pages in Acrobat is a powerful tool that enables you to create pages on demand according to user needs. You might have a law firm as a client that needs to have comments added on separate pages in an arbitration agreement. Rather than adding blank pages throughout the document, you let the client create pages as needed for commenting on arbitration issues. You might have an accounting firm that needs calculation fields added to various pages in a tax organizer for auditing purposes, or you might have needs in your own design studio to merge layouts with form templates for tracking jobs. The more you become familiar with this powerful feature in Acrobat, the more you'll find solutions for your clients and your in-house needs.

CROSS-REF For more information on spawning pages from templates and writing JavaScripts, see the Acrobat JavaScript Scripting Reference. You can download it free from Adobe's Web site at `http://partners.adobe.com/public/developer/acrobat/sdk/index_doc.html#js`.

FIGURE 29.47

The final document shows the inserted page data merged with the template.

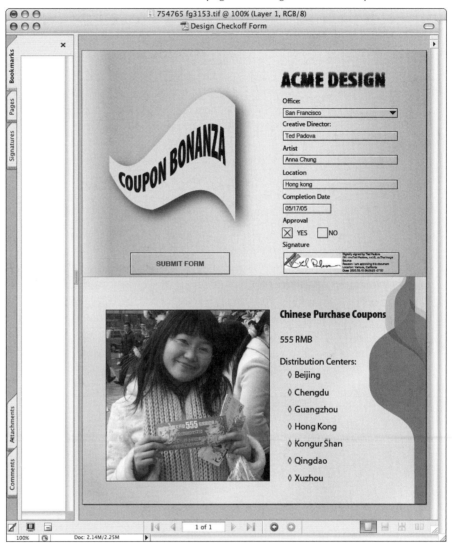

Summary

- You can add various interactive elements including hyperlinks, bookmarks, buttons, and media files to InDesign documents and Acrobat PDF files.

- Hyperlinks can link to pages or text anchors within the document or to a URL in InDesign. You can link to page views, open files, and link to URLs in Acrobat. For URLs contained in text in a PDF file, Acrobat 8 and Adobe Reader 8 do not require adding links.

- Bookmarks in an InDesign document may link to pages, text anchors, or URLs. These bookmarks show up in the Bookmarks tab within Acrobat if the Bookmark option is enabled.

- During the PDF export process from InDesign, you can include or exclude interactive elements.

- In Acrobat, you can link to views as well as add actions to bookmark properties for executing menu commands and running JavaScripts.

- You can endow buttons with events and behaviors that define a resulting action. This action occurs when a user performs an event such as a mouse-click or a mouse-rollover.

- You can add media files, including movies and sounds, to an InDesign document and select options for playing them.

- You can add media files, including movies and sounds, in Acrobat as Acrobat 5- or later-compatible media. Acrobat 6 and later-compatible media enables you to embed media files in the PDF.

- You can add different renditions for media clips in Acrobat. You can assign renditions according to end-user download speeds.

- You can create PDF documents that meet user needs for modifying files on demand using page templates and JavaScripts.

Chapter 30

Working with PDF Forms

A crobat PDF forms and HTML forms are the most popular types of electronic forms in existence today. We're all familiar with HTML forms and most of us have filled out these kinds of forms when making online purchases. PDF forms are standardized in many industries such as government, education, and large business organizations. And most of us are also familiar with PDF forms like those used by the U.S. Internal Revenue Service for income tax preparation.

As a designer, you may be called upon to create PDF forms where your clients want to host the forms on Web sites, distribute forms on CD-ROMs, or use forms for electronic file exchanges.

With the marvelous design tools you have available in the Creative Suite and the use of Adobe Acrobat (Pro, Pro Extended, or Acrobat Standard edition), you have great opportunities to create attractive and powerful dynamic PDF forms.

What Are Acrobat Forms?

Forms in Acrobat are PDF files with data fields that appear as placeholders for user-supplied data. In Acrobat, you can use text string fields, numeric fields, check boxes, radio buttons, data fields, calculation fields, signature fields, and a variety of custom fields created with JavaScripts. The advantage of using forms in Acrobat is that doing so enables you to maintain design integrity for the appearance of a form while providing powerful control over data management. Rather than using a database manager, which may limit your ability to control fonts and graphics, Acrobat PDFs preserve all the design attributes of a document while behaving like a data manager.

Forms are created in Acrobat or Adobe LiveCycle Designer. Adobe LiveCycle Designer is a separate executable application available to Windows users and installed on your hard drive with your Acrobat Pro installation. Unfortunately, this program is not available to Macintosh users.

As we discuss in Chapter 36, you can add certain usage rights to PDF files for Adobe Reader users. With Acrobat 8 or 9, forms can be completed and saved with Acrobat and Adobe Reader. When opening PDFs in Adobe Reader that have not been enabled with Reader Extensions, you cannot save, import, or export data. In developing PDF workflows for a company or organization, all users expected to design forms in Acrobat can use any one of the Acrobat commercial products.

CROSS-REF Creating Acrobat PDF forms is relatively easy when using auto field detection and working with some simple office forms. However, PDF forms can be quite complex, and your opportunities for assigning field properties, adding scripts, performing calculations, adding dynamic features, and doing more are almost limitless. We can only hope to offer a brief introduction to creating Acrobat PDF forms in this book. For a comprehensive view for working with Acrobat PDF forms and Adobe LiveCycle Designer forms, see *PDF Forms Using Acrobat and LiveCycle Designer Bible* (Wiley Publishing, Padova/Okamoto, 2009).

The non-PDF form

The one thing to keep in mind regarding Acrobat and forms is that a form in the context of PDF is not a paper form scanned as an image and saved as PDF. Tons of these so-called *forms* are around offices and on the Internet. These documents may have originated as forms, but by the time you understand all of Acrobat's available features, you'll see that these scanned documents can hardly be called forms. Simply put, they're scanned images saved to PDF. The power of Acrobat gives you the tools to create *smart forms*. These forms can be dynamic, intuitive, and interactive, and they can save both you and the end user much time in providing and gathering information.

Development of a PDF form

PDF forms created in Acrobat usually start out as a document converted to PDF from an authoring program. Programs like Microsoft Office, Adobe InDesign, and Adobe Illustrator create the layout and background for a PDF form. After the design is created in an authoring program and converted to PDF, you use tools in Acrobat to add form fields and form attributes.

You also can scan paper forms and convert them to fillable PDF forms. Scanning paper forms, of course, doesn't require you to use any of the other CS applications. The forms are scanned directly in Acrobat where form fields are added.

Whereas many PDF forms in businesses are first created in Microsoft Word, you have many more design tools available to you for creating attractive forms using Adobe InDesign or Adobe Illustrator. These two Creative Suite tools together with Acrobat offer you all that you need to create impressive dynamic PDF forms.

If you create a design and then add form fields in Acrobat, and then later decide to change your design, you can edit the design back in your original authoring application. Simply save the design, and open the form you created in Acrobat. Select Document ⇨ Replace Pages, and select the modified PDF document. Replace the page, and your modified design appears without disturbing any form fields added to the original design.

Working in the Forms Editing Environment

As we mentioned at the beginning of this chapter, you use a design application to create a form layout, convert to PDF, and then add the form fields and form features in Acrobat.

Acrobat 9 has a new forms editing environment called Form Editing Mode that adds form fields to your PDF forms. When you first open a form design, you are in Preview mode. To enter Form Editing Mode, choose Forms ⇨ Add or Edit Fields. The new Acrobat 9 Form Editing Mode opens, as shown in Figure 30.1.

FIGURE 30.1

Acrobat 9 introduces Form Editing Mode, where you add fields to a PDF form.

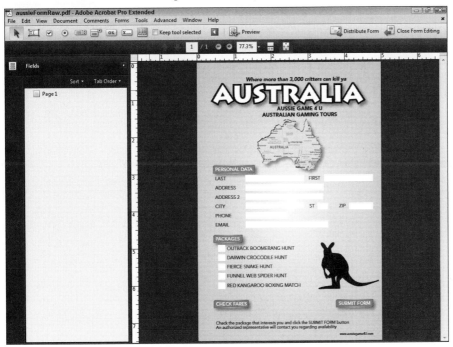

If you've created forms in Acrobat 8 or earlier, you'll immediately notice that Acrobat 9 contains no Forms toolbar in the normal Viewer mode. All form tools are now accessible only in Form Editing Mode. Additionally, the Fields panel you see on the left side of the Form Editing Mode interface appears only when in this mode. If you open the Advanced Editing toolbar in Viewer mode, you'll find the Button tool. This is the only form tool accessible in Viewer mode.

Editing field properties can be accomplished in either mode. By default, the Select Object tool is active when you are in Form Editing Mode and remains the selected tool until you click a Form tool. You cannot access the Hand tool while in Form Editing Mode unless you click the Preview button or use a key modifier. Press the Spacebar to access the Hand tool. While in Viewer mode, you can double-click a field object with the Select Object tool and open the Properties window.

For the occasional user of Acrobat, and well suited for the Creative Suite users, you'll find that creating forms in Acrobat is much easier in Acrobat 9 than in earlier versions. A few menu commands help you create forms in Acrobat without having to be a sophisticated forms designer. Acrobat provides all the tools necessary for creating sophisticated PDF forms, but you can choose simplicity if your forms authoring demands don't require scripting or adding dynamic elements.

Automating PDF Form Creation

One of the marvelous tools in Acrobat is the ability to use an auto field detection feature, in which Acrobat searches through a form and automatically adds fields on a new form design. A simple menu command can save you much time in creating a PDF form. The auto creation of form fields isn't perfect, and sometimes you may need to spend quite a bit of editing time perfecting your form. However, if you design forms knowing how to optimize auto recognition of form fields, you can save yourself much time.

To illustrate, see Figure 30.2. This document is a simple form that originated in Adobe InDesign.

To populate this form using the auto field creation feature in Acrobat 9, open the Forms menu and select Add or Edit Fields. This command takes you into Form Editing Mode. An Acrobat dialog box asks if you want Acrobat to detect form fields. Click Yes, and Acrobat automatically recognizes form fields..

In an instant, Acrobat adds form fields to the document. Notice that the field positions in Figure 30.2 appear with underlines. This type of design works best. If you use rectangular boxes or other graphic elements, auto field detection has a harder time populating the form.

After detecting fields, the form appears as shown in Figure 30.3. The Welcome to Form Editing Mode dialog box opens where information is displayed related to creating form fields in Acrobat.

Using the Form Wizard

Another menu command available in Acrobat for creating forms is the Forms ⇨ Start Forms Wizard command. When you choose this command, the Create or Edit Form wizard opens. The options for Macs and Windows are different, as shown in Figure 30.4.

FIGURE 30.2

A simple form created in Adobe InDesign and converted to PDF

These options are available in the Create or Edit Form wizard:

- **An existing electronic document (Windows)/Start with a PDF document (Macintosh).** In Windows, you can start with a document that can be converted to PDF on the fly using the same options you have with File ⇨ Create PDF ⇨ From File. For example, a Microsoft Word document can be opened, converted to PDF, opened in Form Editing Mode, and have the form detected for form fields in one single step. On the Macintosh, you're limited to working only with existing PDF files.

- **A paper form.** Choose this option on either platform, and a paper form can be scanned directly in Acrobat. The scan is recognized for text, opens in Form Editing Mode, and has fields automatically detected.

- **No existing form (Windows only).** Choose this option and click Next, and Adobe LiveCycle Designer launches using either Acrobat Pro or Acrobat Pro Extended.

FIGURE 30.3

After you open a form in Form Editing Mode and allow Acrobat to detect form fields, fields are added and a Welcome dialog box opens, providing you information related to creating PDF forms.

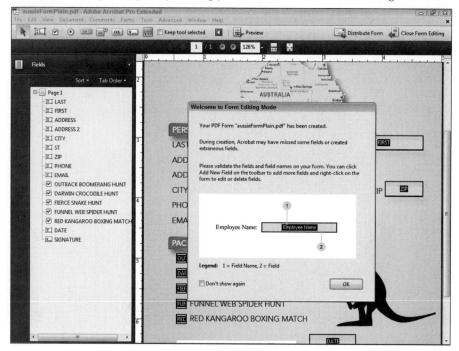

FIGURE 30.4

Choose Forms ➪ Start Forms Wizard to open the Create or Edit Form wizard. The options are different in Windows (left) and Mac (right).

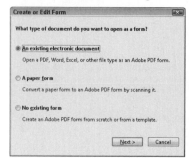
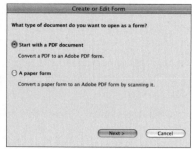

Authoring form designs

What kinds of authoring application files can be used with auto field detection? Look at this brief list of many different original document formats converted to PDF that work well with this command:

- **Microsoft Office:** All Microsoft Office files work well with auto field detection. Use the PDFMaker from the Office applications (Windows) or use the Print command on the Macintosh to print to a PDF file to convert to PDF. (For more on PDFMaker and Microsoft Office applications, see Chapter 22.)

- **Adobe Creative Suite:** Files created in Adobe InDesign and Adobe Illustrator work well with auto field detection. Native Adobe Illustrator and Illustrator PDFs are both supported.

- **Adobe Photoshop and scanned forms:** Adobe Photoshop files and scanned forms are also supported. After conversion to PDF, you need to run OCR Text Recognition in Acrobat. Select Document ⇨ OCR Text Recognition ⇨ Recognize Text Using OCR. When you complete the text recognition, select Forms ⇨ Add or Edit Fields and click Yes when prompted to detect form fields.

- **RTF:** From a text editor, save files as RTF (Rich Text Format). Use the Create PDF ⇨ From File command in Acrobat to convert to PDF, and then select Forms ⇨ Add or Edit Fields and click Yes when prompted to detect form fields.

- **Web Pages and Adobe Dreamweaver:** There's no need to use auto field detection with HTML documents and Web pages. When you use Create PDF ⇨ From Web Page or the PDFMaker in Microsoft Internet Explorer on Windows, form fields on Web pages are converted at the time you create the PDF file. (Note that most fields containing JavaScripts won't work in Acrobat. The Acrobat implementation of JavaScript is much different than JavaScript used in Web pages.)

If you have other application program files such as Lotus Notes, Corel Draw, WordPerfect, e-mail messages, and so on, most of these file types also can be used with auto field detection as long as clearly defined form field locations appear on the document.

Preparing files for auto field detection

Using auto field detection does a very good job of recognizing form fields on simple forms. However, when forms become more complex and when you create forms with graphics, gradients, and complex design elements, auto field detection falls apart and won't create fields on most graphically intense form designs. As an example, look at Figure 30.5. When we chose Forms ⇨ Add or Edit Fields in Acrobat, no fields were recognized on the form.

FIGURE 30.5

Using auto field detection on this graphically intense form produced no fields.

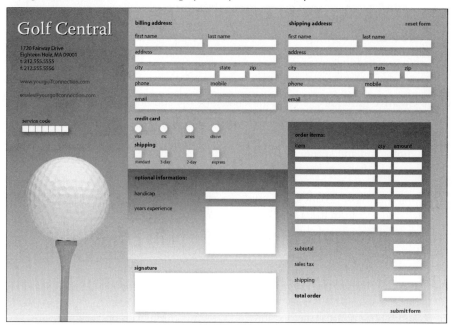

If you use programs like Adobe Illustrator or Adobe InDesign to create forms with complex graphic elements, you can prepare your files for using auto field detection by adding an extra layer that you use just for the auto field detection command. Using programs like Illustrator or InDesign provide you the benefit for using layers in your design. You can easily create a background with all the graphic elements, a text layer containing all the text in the form, a layer for fields used in the final design, and a separate layer for temporary fields designed for auto field detection in Acrobat. An example of such a form we created in Adobe Illustrator is shown in Figure 30.6. Notice that the Temp Fields and Text layers are the only visible layers in Figure 30.6.

If you create a similar form in a program like Adobe Illustrator or Adobe InDesign, save your file to PDF as a PDF version 1.5 or greater document (Acrobat 6 and above compatibility) and check options for creating Adobe PDF Layers. You must save the file as a layered file that appears with Layers in Acrobat. In Acrobat, you can view just the Text and Temp Fields layers (while in Viewer mode only), all layers, or any combination of layers. Acrobat won't complain, and auto field detection creates form fields from the Temp Fields layer whether or not it is visible. After using auto field detection, our file appeared with the form fields as you see in Figure 30.7.

FIGURE 30.6

Creating a temporary layer designed for use with auto field detection is used to auto populate the form.

A little polish is needed on the form for sizing some field boxes and adding the radio button and check box fields, but the little time it took to create the temporary layer in the authoring application was a fraction of the time you would need to spend in Acrobat to manually create all the text fields. By using an authoring application supporting layers, you can easily create a PDF file that is auto field detection friendly. Planning ahead when designing forms in authoring programs can save you much time when using auto field detection.

> **TIP** When designing forms in authoring programs, use geometric shapes such as squares or rectangles for check boxes. Don't use text characters such as those you find in fonts like Carta and Wingdings. auto field detection can detect box shapes and convert them to check box fields, but it cannot detect text characters.

To finish up our form design in Acrobat, we flatten the layers. Be certain to turn off all layers you want discarded; when you select Flatten Layers from the Layers panel Options menu, the hidden layers are discarded and the PDF is flattened. All field objects remain undisturbed regardless of what layer views you have on or off.

FIGURE 30.7

Running Form Field Recognition with a design having a temporary layer used for optimizing the auto recognition of fields produces good results

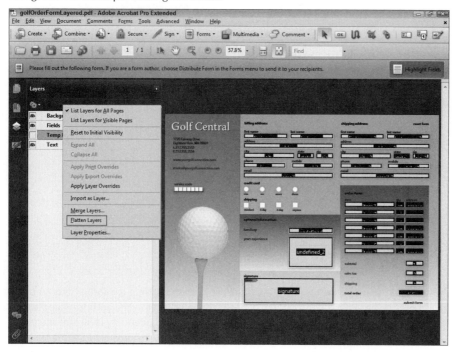

Understanding Form Fields

Forms contain different types of data fields that hold data, act as buttons that invoke actions, and execute scripts to produce a series of actions. Form fields can assume different appearances and possess the capability to include graphic icons and images to represent hot links that invoke actions. Acrobat forms are more than a static data filing system—they can be as vivid and dynamic as your imagination.

Form data fields are created with the form tools in Form Editing Mode in Acrobat 9. In order to use the form tools, you first need to Form Editing Modechoose Forms ➪ Add or Edit Fields to enter Form Editing Mode. In Form Editing Mode, you can view all Form tools by opening the Add New Field pull-down menu and choosing Show Tools on Toolbar, as shown in Figure 30.8.

FIGURE 30.8

To display the form tools in Form Editing Mode across the top of the toolbar, choose Show Tools on Toolbar from the Add New Field pull-down menu.

After you make this choice, the tools appear neatly in a horizontal row across the Form Edit tool-bar, as shown in Figure 30.9. The eight form field types available in Acrobat are drawn with the tools shown in Figure 30.9. From left to right following the Selection Arrow, they are the Text Field tool, Check Box tool, Radio Button tool, List Box tool, Combo Box tool, Button tool, Digital Signature tool, and Barcode tool.

FIGURE 30.9

Eight separate form field tools are used to create fields on a PDF form.

Here's an overview of the field types:

- **Text field:** Text fields are boxes in which text is typed by the end user to fill out the form. Text fields can contain alphabetical characters, numbers, or a combination of both.

- **Check box:** Check boxes typically appear in groups to offer the user a selection of choices. Yes and no items or a group of check boxes might be created for multiple-choice selections.

- **Radio button:** Radio buttons perform the same function in PDF forms as radio buttons in dialog boxes. Usually you have two or more choices for a category. Forms are usually designed so that when one radio button in a group is turned on, the other buttons in the group are turned off.

- **Combo box:** When you view an Acrobat form, you may see a down-pointing arrow similar to the arrows appearing in panel menus. Such an arrow in a PDF form indicates the presence of a combo box. When you click the arrow, a pull-down menu opens with a list of choices. Users are limited to selecting a single choice from combo boxes. Additionally, if designed as such, users can input their own choices.

- **List box:** A list box displays a box with scroll bars, much like windows you see in application software documents. As you scroll through a list box, you make a choice of one or more of the alternatives available by selecting items in the list.

- **Button:** A button is usually used to invoke an action or hyperlink. A button face can be text or a graphic element created in another program that you could apply as an appearance to the button. You also can use different appearance settings in the button properties for adding stroke and fill colors. Buttons also are used to import images.

- **Digital signature:** Digital signatures can be applied to fields, PDF pages, and PDF documents. A digital signature can be used to lock out fields on a form.

- **Barcode:** The Barcode tool was not a completely new feature in Acrobat 7. Acrobat 7 supported a plug-in to create 2D and 3D barcodes; the plug-in was shipped long after the initial release of Acrobat 7.0. Later with Acrobat 8.0 and 9.0, the Barcode tool appears in the Forms toolbar in Form Editing Mode. This tool provides options for adding barcodes to a PDF form.

Although not form fields per se, these additional tools also appear in the Forms toolbar in Form Editing Mode:

- **Preview/Edit Layout:** When you open the Form Editing Mode, your default view is the Edit Layout view where fields are added to a form. Click the Preview button, and you remain in Form Editing Mode, but you can edit text fields by filling them in. The button name changes to Edit Layout. Click Edit Layout, and you return to the Edit Layout mode.

- **Distribute Form:** This tool is used to start an ad hoc data collection workflow. You can send the form by e-mail or post the form on Acrobat.com or a Web page.

- **Close Form Editing:** Click the button, and you return to Viewer mode.

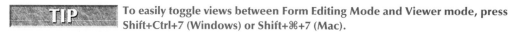 **To easily toggle views between Form Editing Mode and Viewer mode, press Shift+Ctrl+7 (Windows) or Shift+⌘+7 (Mac).**

All these form field types and tools are available to you in Form Editing Mode when you create or edit a PDF form in Acrobat. On the right of the Keep tool selected check box on the toolbar, the left-pointing arrow collapses the toolbar and makes available the tools from the Add New Field pull-down menu.

Assigning Form Field Properties

The process of adding form fields to a form is the same for all fields. You click a form tool either from the Add New Field pull-down menu or the tool in the expanded toolbar in Form Editing Mode. This action loads the cursor with the selected tool. Move the cursor to a location on a form and click the mouse button to drop the field object on the page. Alternately, you can click and drag the cursor to shape the field object rectangle to a custom size.

Using the mini Properties window

When you click a form tool and then click a page to drop the field object on your form, a mini Properties window opens, as shown in Figure 30.10. In this window, you can name a field and click the blue text (Show All Properties) to open the field object's Properties window. In the Properties window, you specify additional attributes for a field object.

FIGURE 30.10

When you click a loaded cursor on a form, the mini Properties window opens.

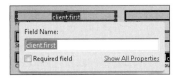

Another choice you have for all field types is the Required field check box. Click this check box if you want to be certain that a form filler completes filling in a field before submitting the form to you.

Using the Properties window

Other than changing a field name and a few other options you have when creating radio button fields, the mini Properties window is an abbreviated form of assigning properties to field objects. You have a much more elaborate set of options when you open a field object's Properties window.

You can open the Properties window by clicking Show All Properties when you first drop a field object on a page, or when double-clicking a field object with the Select Object tool in either Form Editing Mode or Viewer mode. Additionally, you can open a context menu on a field object with the Select Object tool and choose Properties at the top of the menu. Any of these options opens the Properties window, shown in Figure 30.11, where several tabs offer you options for setting a field's properties.

 If you don't click a form tool while in Form Editing Mode, the default active tool is the Select Object tool.

FIGURE 30.11

Double-click a field object with the Select Object tool in either Form Edit more or Viewer mode to open the field Properties window.

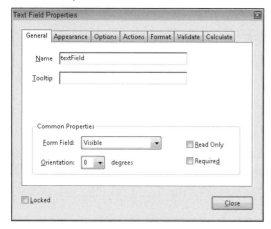

General properties

The General properties tab is the default tab where general properties are assigned. These properties are common to all field types. The properties include:

- **Name:** By default, Acrobat adds a name in the Name field. As a matter of practice, you should type a descriptive name in the Name text box. Don't use names with spaces, and try to use parent/child names for fields in common groups. A parent/child name might appear as item.1, item.2, item.3, and so on; or you might have client.first, client.last, client.address, and so on.

- **Tooltip:** Type a name, and when the cursor is placed over the field in Preview mode, the text appears as a tooltip below the Hand tool cursor.

- **Form field:** From the pull-down menu, make choices for visibility and printing. By default, the field is visible and prints when the file is printed.

- **Orientation:** A field and a field's contents can be rotated in 90-degree rotations. By default, fields are at a 0 (zero)-degree rotation. Select from 90, 180, and 270 to rotate fields in fixed rotations.

- **Read Only:** When a field is marked as Read Only, the field is not editable. The user is locked out of the field. A Read Only field might be something you use to show fixed price costs where you don't want users changing a fixed purchase price on an order form. Another example is a value that is pre-populated from a database or with fields that show results of other calculated data.

- **Required:** If a field needs to be filled in before the data is submitted, select the Required box. (Note that you can click the Required field check box when you first create a field object on a form.)

- **Locked:** Locking a field prevents the field from being moved. You can still type data in the field or make a choice from options for other fields. This item is used to fix fields in position as you edit a form.

Appearance properties

The Appearance tab relates to form field appearances. The rectangles you draw can be assigned border colors and content fills. The text added to a field box or default text you use for a field can be assigned different fonts, font sizes, and font colors. These options exist in the Appearance properties for all field types except barcode fields. (Barcode fields don't have an Appearance tab.) Figure 30.12 shows the Appearance properties for a selected text field.

FIGURE 30.12

Click the Appearance tab for any field properties, and make choices for the appearance of fields and text.

The Appearance options include the following:

- **Border Color:** The keyline created for a field is made visible with a rectangular border assigned by clicking the Border Color swatch and choosing a color.

- **Fill Color:** The field box can be assigned a background color. If you want the field box displayed in a color, enable this option, click the color swatch next to it, and choose a color the same way you do for the borders. When the check box is disabled, the background appears transparent.

- **Line Thickness:** Select the pull-down menu, and choose from Thin, Medium, or Thick. The pull-down menu is grayed out unless you first select a Border Color.

- **Line Style:** You can choose from five style types from the pull-down menu. The Solid option shows the border as a keyline at the width specified in the Width setting. Dashed shows a dashed line; Beveled appears as a box with a beveled edge; Inset makes the field look recessed; and Underline eliminates the keyline and shows an underline for the text across the width of the field box.

- **Font Size:** Depending on the size of the form fields you create, you may need to choose a different point size for the text. The default is Auto, which automatically adjusts point sizes according to the height of the field box. Choices are available for manually setting the point size for text ranges between 2 and 300 points.

- **Text Color:** If you identify a color for text by selecting the swatch adjacent to Text Color, the field contents supplied by the end user change to the selected color.

- **Font:** From the pull-down menu, select a font for the field data. All the fonts installed in your system are accessible from the pull-down menu. When designing forms for screen displays, try to use sans serif fonts for better screen views. The first 14 fonts are installed with Acrobat. You can use these fonts to be certain all users have the same fonts.

The Appearance settings are identical for all field types except Digital Signature fields, Radio Button fields, Check Box fields, and Barcode fields. The Radio Button and Check Box fields use fixed fonts for displaying characters in the field box. You choose what characters to use in the Options tab. When creating Radio Button and Check Box fields, you don't have a choice for Font in the Appearance properties. By default, the Adobe Pi font is used.

Options properties

The Options tab provides selections for specific attributes according to the type of fields you add to a page. Options are available for all fields except the Digital Signatures field. Options tab attributes for the other six field types include options for text, radio buttons, combo and list boxes, and buttons.

Text options

When you use the Text Field tool to create a field and you click on the Options tab, the Properties window appears, as shown in Figure 30.13.Each of the following attribute settings is optional when creating text fields:

- **Alignment:** The Alignment pull-down menu has two functions. First, any text entered in the Default field is aligned according to the option you specify from the pull-down menu choices. Alignment choices include Left, Center, and Right. Second, regardless of whether text is used in the Default field, when the end user fills out the form, the cursor is positioned at the alignment selected from the pull-down menu choices. Therefore, if you select Center from the Alignment options, the text entered when filling out the form is centered within the field box.

- **Default Value:** The Default Value field can be left blank, or you can enter text that appears in the field when viewing the form. The Default item has nothing to do with the name of the field. This option is used to provide helpful information when the user fills out the form data. If no text is entered in the Default field, when you return to the form, the field appears empty. If you enter text in the Default field, the text you enter appears inside the field box and can be deleted, edited, or replaced.

- **Multi-line:** If your text field contains more than one line of text, select the Multi-line option. When you press the Return key after entering a line of text, the cursor jumps to the second line where additional text is added to the same field. Multi-line text fields might be used, for example, as an address field to accommodate a second address line.

- **Scrolling long text:** If Multi-line is selected and text entries exceed the height of the field, you may want to add scroll bars to the field. Enable the check box to permit users to scroll lines of text. If the check box is disabled, users won't be able to scroll, but as text is added, automatic scrolling accommodates the amount of text typed in the field.

- **Allow Rich Text Formatting:** When you check this box, users can style text with bold, italic, and bold italic font styles. You may want to enable the check box if you want users to emphasize a field's contents.

- **Limit of [ ] characters:** The box for this option provides for user character limits for a given field. If you want the user to add a state value of two characters, for example, check the box and type **2** in the field box. If the user attempts to go beyond the limit, a system warning beep alerts the user that no more text can be added to the field.

- **Password:** When this option is enabled, all the text entered in the field appears as a series of asterisks when the user fills in the form. The field is not secure in the sense that you must have a given password to complete the form; it merely protects the data entry from being seen by an onlooker.

- **Field is used for file selection:** This option permits you to specify a file path as part of the field's value. The file is submitted along with the form data. Be certain to enable the Scrolling long text option described earlier in this list to enable this option.

- **Check spelling:** Spell checking is available for comments and form fields. When the check box is enabled, the field is included in a spell check. This can be helpful so the spell checker doesn't get caught up with stopping at proper names, unique identifiers, and abbreviations that may be included in those fields.

- **Comb of [ ] characters:** When you create a text field box and enable this check box, Acrobat automatically creates a text field box with subdivision lines according to the value you supply in the Characters field box. Be certain to disable all other check boxes. You can set the alignment of the characters by making a choice from the alignment pull-down menu, but all other check boxes need to be disabled to access the Comb of check box.

NOTE   Comb fields are limited to single characters. If you need to create comb fields where two characters are contained in each subdivision, you need to create separate field boxes for each pair of characters.

FIGURE 30.13

The Options settings in the Text Field Properties dialog box

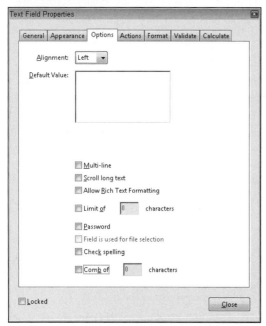

Check box and radio button options

Check boxes and radio buttons have similar Options choices. When you select either field and click the Options tab, the settings common to both field types include the following:

- **Button/Check Box Style:** If a radio button is selected, the title is Button Style. If the field is a check box, the title is listed as Check Box Style, as shown in Figure 30.14. From the pull-down menu, you select the style you want to use for the check mark inside the radio button or check box field.

- **Export Value:** When creating either a check box or radio button, use the same field name for all fields in a common group where you want one check box enabled while all the other check boxes or radio buttons are disabled. To distinguish the fields from each other, add an export value that differs in each field box. You can use export values such as Yes and No or other text, or number values such as 1, 2, 3, 4, and so on.

The creation of radio buttons and check boxes on Acrobat forms has been confusing to many users, and users often inappropriately create workarounds for check boxes and radio buttons to toggle them on and off. To help eliminate confusion, notice that the

Options properties in Figure 30.13 includes a help message informing you to name fields the same name but use different export values. (See the nearby sidebar "Creating Mutually Exclusive Fields" for more information.)

FIGURE 30.14

You can choose various options for radio buttons and check boxes, including those for the style of the check marks or radio buttons.

- **Button/Check box is checked by default:** If you want a default value to be applied for either field type (for example, Yes), enter the export value and select the box to make the value the default.

One distinction appears in the Options dialog box between radio buttons and check boxes. The second check box in the radio button properties is unique to radio buttons:

- **Buttons with the same name and value are selected in unison (applies to radio buttons only):** For data export purposes, you'll want to add a different export value for each radio button and check box. If you don't need to export data to a database with unique export values for each radio button, you can add radio buttons to a page with the same export values, and by default, when a user clicks one radio button all other radio buttons are disabled.

The Button/Check Box Style selection from the pull-down menu in both field types provides identical appearances. The styles are shown in Figure 30.15.

FIGURE 30.15

Six icon options are available for check boxes and radio buttons.

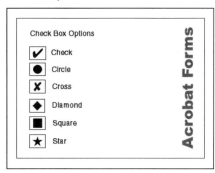

Combo box and list box options

Combo boxes enable you to create form fields with a list of selections appearing in a pull-down window. The user completing a form makes a selection from the menu items. If all items are not visible, the menu contains scroll bars made visible after selecting the down-pointing arrow to open the menu. A list box is designed as a scrollable window with an elevator bar and arrows as you see in authoring application documents. When you create a ist box you define the choices in the List Box Properties window as shown in Figure 30.16.

Creating Mutually Exclusive Fields

Creating mutually exclusive fields where one radio button or check box is turned on within a group and all others within the same group are turned off has been a problem for PDF form authors for some time. In Acrobat 9, Adobe made creating mutually exclusive radio button fields easier and more intuitive.

When you add a Radio Button field in Form Editing Mode, the mini Properties window offers you options for creating mutually exclusive fields. The Button Value for each field in the same group must appear different. You can type any text in the Button Value text box. However, the Radio Group Name must be the same name for every field in the same group. When you are ready to add another field to a group, just click Add another button to group in the mini Properties window, and a new radio button field is added to the form using the same Radio Group name.

FIGURE 30.16

Different views for Combo Boxes and List Boxes

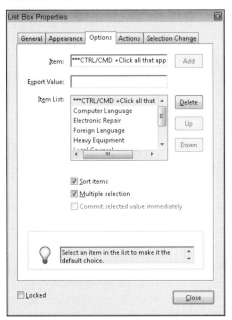

The two field types differ in several ways. First, combo boxes require less space for the form field. The combo box menu drops down from a narrow field height where the menu options are shown. List boxes require more height to make them functional to the point where at least two or three options are in view before the user attempts to scroll the window. Second, you can select only one menu option from a combo box. List boxes enable users to select multiple items. Finally, combo boxes can be designed for users to add text for a custom choice by editing any of the menu items. List boxes provide no option for users to type text in the field box, and the menu items are not editable.

The data exported with the file include the selected item from the combo boxes and all selected items for list boxes. The item choices and menu designs for the field types are created in the Options tab for the respective field type. Attributes for list boxes also are available for combo boxes. The options include the following:

- **Item:** You enter the name of an entry you want to appear in the scrollable list in this field.
- **Export Value:** When the data are exported, the name you enter in this field box is the exported value. If the field is left blank, the exported value is the name used in the item description typed in the Item field. If you want different export values than the name descriptions, type a value in this field box. As an example, suppose you create a consumer satisfaction survey form. In that form, the user can choose from list items such as Very Satisfied, Satisfied, and Unsatisfied, and you specify the export values for these items to be 1, 2, and 3, respectively. When the data are analyzed, the frequency of the

three items is tabulated and defined in a legend as 1=Very Satisfied, 2=Satisfied, and 3=Unsatisfied.

- **Add:** After you enter the Item and Export Values, click the Add button to place the item in the Item List. After adding an item, you can return to the Item field and type a new item in the field box and, in turn, a new export value.

- **Item List:** As you add items, the items appear in a scrollable list window. To edit a name in the list window, delete the item, type a new name in the Item text box, and then click the Add button to add the newly edited item back in the list.

- **Delete:** If an item has been added to the list and you want to delete it, first select the item in the list. Click the Delete button to remove it from the list.

- **Up/Down:** Items are placed in the list according to the order in which they are entered. The order displayed in the list is shown in the combo box or list box when you return to the document page. If you want to reorganize items, select the item in the list and click the Up or Down button to move one level up or down, respectively. To enable the Up and Down buttons, the Sort Items option must be disabled.

- **Sort items:** When checked, the list is alphabetically sorted in ascending order. As new items are added to the list, the new fields are dynamically sorted while the option is enabled.

- **Multiple selection (List box only):** Any number of options can be selected by using modifier keys and clicking the list items. Use Shift-click for contiguous selections and Ctrl/⌘-click for noncontiguous selections. This option applies only to list boxes.

- **Commit selected value immediately:** The choice made in the field box is saved immediately. If the check box is disabled, the choice is saved after the user exits the field by tabbing out or clicking the mouse cursor on another field or outside the field.

With the exception of the multiple selection item, the preceding options also are available for combo boxes. In addition to these options, combo boxes offer two more items:

- **Allow user to enter custom text:** The items listed in the Options tab are fixed in the combo box on the Acrobat form by default. If this check box is enabled, the user can create a custom value. Acrobat makes no provision for some items to be edited and others to be locked out from editing.

- **Check spelling:** Spell checking is performed when a user types in a custom value. As text is typed, the spelling is checked.

Button options

Buttons differ from all other fields when it comes to appearance. You can create and use custom icons for button displays from PDF documents or file types compatible with Convert to PDF from File. Rather than entering data or toggling a data field, buttons typically execute an action. You might use a button to clear a form, export data, import data from a data file, or use buttons as navigation links. When you add a button to a page, the Options tab attributes change to those shown in Figure 30.17.

FIGURE 30.17

The Options tab for the Button field properties includes options for button face displays and several different mouse behaviors.

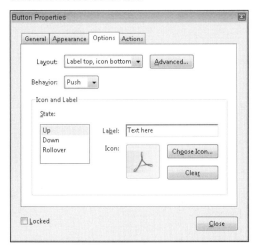

When you create a button, you make choices from the Options tab for the highlight view of the button, the behavior of the mouse cursor, and the text and icon views. The Options attributes for buttons are as follows:

- **Layout:** Several views are available for displaying a button with or without a label, which you add in the Label field described later in this list. The choices from the pull-down menu for Layout offer options for displaying a button icon with text appearing at the top, bottom, left, or right side of the icon, or over the icon. Figure 30.18 shows the different Layout options.

- **Behavior:** The Behavior options affect the appearance of the button when the button is clicked. The None option specifies no highlight when the button is clicked. Invert momentarily inverts the colors of the button when clicked. Outline displays a keyline border around the button, and Push makes the button appear to move in on Mouse Down and out on Mouse Up.

- **Icon and Label State:** Three choices are available in the list when you select Push in the Behavior pull-down menu. Up is the appearance of the button before the mouse enters the button area and triggers the rollover appearance. Down displays the highlight action when the mouse button is pressed. Rollover changes the icon when a second icon has been added to the rollover option. When the user moves the mouse cursor over the button without clicking, the image changes to the second icon you choose—much like a rollover effect you see on Web pages.

FIGURE 30.18

The Layout options include Label only; Icon only; Icon top, label bottom; Label top, icon bottom; Icon left, label right; Label left, icon right; and Label over icon.

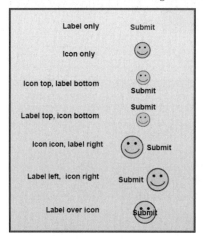

- **Label:** If you've selected a layout type that includes a label, type text in the field box for the label you want to use. Labels are shown when one of the options for the layout includes a label view with or without the icon.

- **Choose Icon:** When you use an icon for a button display, click Choose Icon to open the Select Icon dialog box. In the Select Icon dialog box, use a Browse button to open a navigation dialog box where you locate a file to select for the button face. The file can be a PDF document or a file compatible with converting to PDF from within Acrobat. The size of the file can be as small as the actual icon size or a letter-size page or larger. Acrobat automatically scales the image to fit within the form field rectangle drawn with the Button tool. When you select an icon, it is displayed as a thumbnail in the Select Icon dialog box.

TIP   An icon library can be created easily from drawings using a font such as Zapf Dingbats or Wingdings or patterns and drawings from Adobe Illustrator. Create or place images on several pages in a layout application. Distill the file to save as a multiple-page PDF document. When you select an icon to use for a button face, the Select Icon dialog box enables you to scroll pages in the document. You view each icon in the Sample window as a thumbnail of the currently selected page. When the desired icon is in view, click OK. The respective page is used as the icon.

- **Clear:** You can eliminate a selected icon by clicking the Clear button. Clear eliminates the icon without affecting any text you added in the Layout field box.

- **Advanced:** Notice the Advanced button at the top of the Options tab. Clicking the Advanced button opens the Icon Placement dialog box where you select attributes related to scaling an icon. You can choose from icon scaling for Always, Never, Icon is Too Big, and Icon is Too Small to fit in the form field. The Scale option offers choices between

Proportional and Non-proportional scaling. Click Fit to bounds to ensure the icon placement fits to the bounds of the field rectangle. Sliders provide a visual scaling reference for
positioning the icon within a field rectangle.

Barcode options

Barcode fields have unique options designed to work with barcode scanners. You have options
from pull-down menus and pop-up dialog boxes opened from buttons, as shown in Figure 30.19.
In order to make choices for the items in the Options pane in the Barcode Field Properties dialog
box, you need to know what parameters are used by your barcode scanner, fax server, or document scanner. Setting the options requires reviewing the documentation supplied by the hardware
used to scan barcodes.

FIGURE 30.19

The Options tab for the Barcodes requires setting options conforming to the tools you use to scan barcodes.

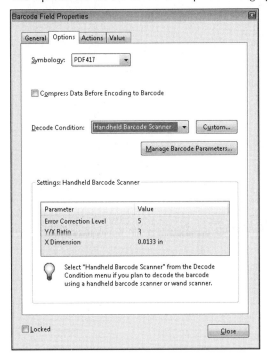

Actions properties

The Actions tab enables you to set an action for any one of the eight field types; the attribute
choices are identical for all fields. The same action items available for links, Bookmarks, and page
actions also are available to form fields. Click the Actions tab, and the pane changes, as shown in
Figure 30.20.

FIGURE 30.20

Actions are available for all field types.

From the Select Trigger pull-down menu, you make choices for different mouse behaviors that are assigned to invoke the action. From the menu options, you have choices for the following:

- **Mouse Up:** When the user releases the mouse button, the action is invoked.

- **Mouse Down:** When the user presses the mouse button, the action is invoked.

- **Mouse Enter:** When the user moves the mouse cursor over the field, the action is invoked.

- **Mouse Exit:** When the user moves the mouse cursor away from the field, the action is invoked.

- **On Focus:** This option specifies moving into the field boundaries through mouse movement or by tabbing to the field. As the cursor enters the field, the action is invoked.

- **On Blur:** This option specifies moving away from the field boundaries through mouse movement or by tabbing to the field. As the cursor exits the field, the action is invoked.

Actions assigned to the cursor movements are similar to those in the context of creating links. You first select the trigger, and then select an action type from the Select Action pull-down menu. Click the Add button to add the action to the Actions list.

The action is assigned to the mouse cursor option when you click Add. The default is Mouse Up. When Mouse Up is selected, the action is invoked when the mouse button is released.

CAUTION Trigger choices other than Mouse Up may sometimes complicate filling in form fields for end users. Just about any program dealing with link buttons has adopted the Mouse Up response to invoke an action. Many users often click down, think about what they are doing, and then move the mouse away without releasing the button. This behavior enables the user to change his/her mind at the last minute. Deviating from the adopted standard might be annoying for a user.

When you click the Add button, a dialog box specific to the action type you are adding opens. The actions listed in this dialog box are the same as those in the Link Properties dialog box and can be viewed by opening the pull-down menu. A few of the more important action types used with form fields include importing form data, resetting a form, submitting a form, and showing and hiding a field.

Importing form data

You can export the raw data from a PDF file as a Form Data File (FDF) or XML file that can later be imported into other PDF forms. To import data, you use a menu command from the list of action types (Import Form Data) or create a JavaScript. Rather than retyping the data in each form, you can import the same field data into new forms where the field names match exactly. Therefore, if a form contains field names such as First, Last, Address, City, State, and so on, all common field names from the exported data can be imported into the current form. Those field names without exact matches are ignored by Acrobat.

NOTE In earlier versions of Acrobat, you also had an option to Execute a menu item that appears in the Select Action pull-down menu. From the menu items, you could select Import (or Export) Data. In Acrobat 8 and 9, the Execute a menu item options have been greatly reduced, and you can no longer manage data using this action type.

The Import Data to Form command enables you to develop forms for an office environment or Web server where the same data can be included easily in several documents. When designing forms, using the same field names for all common data is essential. If you import data and some fields remain blank, recheck your field names. You can edit any part of a form design or action to correct errors.

Resetting a form

This action is handy for forms that need to be cleared of data and resubmitted. When the Reset a form action is invoked, data fields specified for clearing data when the field was added are cleared. When you select Reset a form and click the Add button, the Reset a Form dialog box opens. You make choices in this dialog box for what fields you want to clear. Click the Select All button, and all data fields are cleared when a user clicks on the button you assign with a Reset a form action. When you use this action, you should associate it with Mouse Up to prevent accidental cursor movements that might clear the data and require the user to begin over again. Reset a form also can be used with a Page Action command. If you want a form to be reset every time the file is opened, the latter may be a better choice than creating a button.

TIP When you design a form and view the form in either Form Edit Preview mode or Viewer mode, you can select Forms ⇨ Clear Form to reset a form. Using this command is handy if you have not yet added a Reset button to your form.

Submitting a form

Form data can be e-mailed or submitted to Web servers. You can design forms so users of the Adobe Reader software can submit data via e-mail or to Web servers. When using the Submit a form action, you have access to options for the type of data format you want to submit.

Format properties

The General, Appearance, and Actions tabs are available for all field types. Option attributes are available for all field types except digital signatures. The options vary significantly depending on which field type is used. Table 30.1 gives you a quick glance at the tab differences according to field type.

As shown in Table 30.1, the Format, Validate, and Calculate tab options are available only for Combo Box and Text field types. To access the Format tab, select either of these field types. The Format options are the same for both field types.

When you click the Format tab, you'll find a pull-down menu for selecting a format category. To define a format, open the Select format category and choose from the menu choices the format you want to assign to the Text or Combo Box field. As each item is selected, various options pertaining to the selected category appear directly below the pull-down menu. When you select Number from the menu choices, the Number Options appear as shown in Figure 30.21.

FIGURE 30.21

When you choose either Combo Box or Text as the field type, you can select data format options from the Format tab.

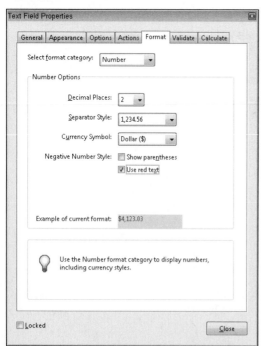

TABLE 30.1

Tab Options for Field Types in the Field Properties Window

Field Type	Appearance	Options	Actions	Format	Validate	Calculate	Selection Change	Signed	Value
Button	X	X	X						
Check Box	X	X	X						
Combo Box	X	X	X	X	X	X			
List Box	X	X	X				X		
Radio Button	X	X	X						
Text	X	X	X	X	X	X			
Signature	X		X					X	
Barcode	X	X	X						X

The Select format category menu options include the following:

- **None:** No options are available when None is selected. Select this item if no formatting is needed for the field. An example of where None applies would be a text field where you want text data such as name, address, and so on.

- **Number:** When you select Number, the Number Options choices appear below the Select format category pull-down menu. The options for displaying numeric fields include defining the number of decimal places, indicating how the digits are separated (for example, by commas or by decimal points), and specifying any currency symbols. The Negative Number Style check boxes enable you to display negative numbers with parentheses and/or red text.

- **Percentage:** The number of decimal places you want to display for percentages is available when you select Percentage from the pull-down menu. The options are listed for number of decimal places and the separator style.

- **Date:** The date choices offer different selections for month, day, year, and time formats.

- **Time:** If you want to eliminate the date and identify only time, the Time category enables you to do so, offering choices to express time in standard and 24-hour units and a custom setting where custom formats are user-prescribed in a field box.

- **Special:** The Special category offers formatting selections for Social Security number, Zip code, extended Zip code, phone number, and an arbitrary mask. When you select Arbitrary Mask, a field box is added where you define the mask. The acceptable values for setting up an arbitrary mask include these:

  - **A:** Add *A* to the arbitrary mask field box, and only the alphabetical characters A – Z and a – z are acceptable for user input.

  - **X:** When you add *X* to the arbitrary mask field box, most printable characters from an alphanumeric character set are acceptable. ANSI values between 32 – 166 and 128 – 255 are permitted. (To learn more about what ANSI character values 32 – 166 and 128 – 255 are translated to, search the Internet for ANSI character tables. You can capture Web pages and use the tables as reference guides.)

  - **O:** The letter *O* accepts all alphanumeric characters (A – Z, a – z, and 0 – 9).

  - **9:** If you want the user to be limited to filling in numbers only, enter *9* in the Arbitrary Mask field box.

- **Custom:** Custom formatting is available by using a JavaScript. To edit the JavaScript code, click the Edit button and create a custom format script. The JavaScript Editor dialog box opens where you type the code. As an example of using a custom JavaScript, assume that you want to add leading zeros to field numbers. You might create a JavaScript with the following code:

```
event.value = "000" + event.value;
```

The preceding code adds three leading zeros to all values supplied by the end user who completes the form field. If you want to add different characters as a suffix or prefix, enter the values you want within the quotation marks. To add a suffix, use this:

```
event.value = event.value + "000";
```

Validate properties

Validate helps ensure that proper information is added on the form. If a value must be within a certain minimum and maximum range, select the radio button for validating the data within the accepted values, as shown in Figure 30.22. The field boxes are used to enter the minimum and maximum values. If the user attempts to enter a value outside the specified range, a warning dialog box opens, informing the user that the values entered on the form are unacceptable.

FIGURE 30.22

Validate is used with Combo Box and Text field types to ensure acceptable responses from user-supplied values.

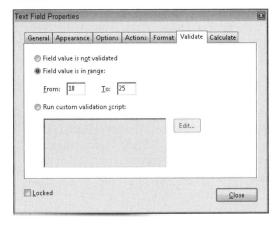

Selecting the Run custom validation script radio button and clicking the Edit button enables you to add a JavaScript. Scripts that you may want to include in this window would be those for validating comparative data fields. A password, for example, may need to be validated. If the response does not meet the condition, the user is denied access to supplying information in the field.

Calculate properties

The Calculate tab (supported in Text and Combo Box fields) in the Field Properties window enables you to calculate two or more data fields. You can choose from preset calculation formulas or add a custom JavaScript for calculating fields, as shown in Figure 30.23.

FIGURE 30.23

The Calculate tab offers options for calculating fields for summing data, multiplying data, and finding the average, minimum, and maximum values for selected fields. In addition, you can add custom calculations by writing JavaScripts.

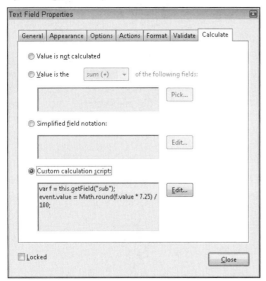

The preset calculation formulas are limited to addition, multiplication, averaging, assessing the minimum in a range of fields, and assessing the maximum in a range of fields. For all other calculations, you need to select the Simplified field notation or Custom calculation script radio button and click the Edit button. In the JavaScript Editor, you write JavaScripts to perform other calculations not available from the preset formulas. Simplified field notation is written in the JavaScript editor and follows syntax similar to writing formulas in spreadsheets. JavaScripts, also written in the JavaScript Editor, require you to know JavaScript as it is supported in Acrobat.

Selection Change properties

The Selection Change tab, shown in Figure 30.24, is available for List Box fields only. If a list box item is selected and then a new item from the list is selected, JavaScript code can be programmed to execute an action when the change is made. As with the other dialog boxes, clicking the Edit button opens the JavaScript Editor dialog box where you create the JavaScript code.

Many uses exist for the Selection Change option. You might want to create a form for consumer responses for a given product—something such as an automobile. Depending on information preceding the list box selection, some options may not be available. For example, a user specifies "four-door automobile" as one of the form choices, and then from a list, that user selects "convertible." If the manufacturer does not offer a convertible for four-door automobiles, then using a JavaScript in the Selection Change tab, the user is informed that this selection cannot be made based on previous information supplied in the form. The displayed warning could include information on alternative selections that the user could make.

FIGURE 30.24

The Selection Change tab is available only for List Box fields. When using a Selection Change option, you need to program JavaScript code to reflect the action when a change in selection occurs.

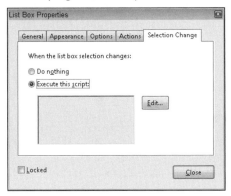

Digital Signature fields properties

The Digital Signature tool enables you to create a field used for electronically signing a document with a digital signature. The Signed tab offers options for behavior with digital signatures as follows:

- **Nothing happens when signed:** As the item description suggests, the field is signed but no action takes place upon signing.

- **Mark as read-only:** When signed, the selected fields are changed to read-only fields, locking them against further edits. You can mark all fields by selecting the radio button and choosing All fields from the pull-down menu. Choose All fields except these to isolate a few fields not marked for read-only, or select Just these fields to mark a few fields for read-only.

- **This script executes when the field is signed:** Select the radio button, and click the Edit button to open the JavaScript Editor. Write a script in the JavaScript Editor that executes when the field is signed.

Digital signatures can be used to lock data fields. You also can use them to indicate approval from users or PDF authors, or you may want to display a message after a user signs a form. In Figure 30.25, a JavaScript was added to the Digital Signature Signed Properties.

The script in this example instructs a user to print the form and hand-deliver it to the accounting department. A dialog box opens after the user signs the form.

Barcode properties

The unique property settings in the Barcode field are located in the Value tab. Options in this tab are available only with Barcode fields, as shown in Figure 30.26. You have options for Encoding from a pull-down menu offering a choice between XML and Tab Delimited data.

FIGURE 30.25

For custom actions when a user signs a form, use a JavaScript.

FIGURE 30.26

The Value tab appears only in Barcode fields.

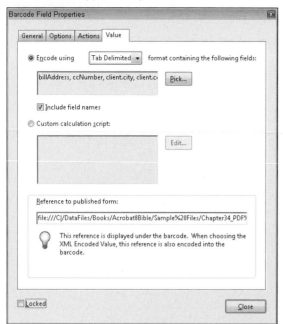

> **NOTE** When creating barcodes, always add all the fields to a page and populate the fields with data then create the barcode as the last step. A barcode needs to calculate sizes to accommodate the field data.

Click the Pick button and the Field Selection dialog box opens as shown in Figure 30.27. You use this dialog box to determine what field data are added to the barcode. Uncheck those items you don't want added, such as buttons that invoke actions, temporary calculation fields, and so on. The Include field names text box offers an option to include field names along with the data in the barcode.

FIGURE 30.27

Click Pick, and check the items you want to appear as data in the barcode.

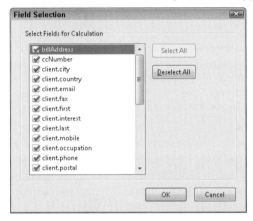

An additional box appears for adding a Custom calculation script. Click the radio button, and click Edit to open the JavaScript Editor.

Organizing and Managing Fields

For purposes of explanation, we use the term *managing fields* to mean dealing with field duplication, deleting fields, and modifying field attributes. After you create a field on a PDF page, you may want to alter its size, position, or attributes. Editing form fields in Acrobat is made possible by using one of several menu commands or returning to the respective Field Properties window.

Organizing fields

To edit a form field's properties, use the Select Object tool in either Form Edit Mode or Viewer mode and double-click the field rectangle. The Properties window opens after you double-click with the tool. You also can use a context-sensitive menu opened from using either tool and clicking the form field to be edited. At the top of the context-sensitive menu, select the Properties command. Also, you can select Forms ⇨ Show Field Properties in Form Editing Mode only. Using any one of the menu commands opens the Properties dialog box.

To select multiple fields of different types, you must use the Select Object tool. Ctrl/Shift-click each field you want to select. You can drag through fields to select them, but you can do so only with the Select Object tool.

When you select multiple fields and choose Properties from the context-sensitive menu, options in the General tab, the Appearance tab, and the Actions tab are available for editing. Specific options for each different field type require that you select only common field types. For example, you can edit the appearance settings for a group of fields where the field types are different. However, to edit something like radio button field options for check mark style, you need to select only radio button fields in order to gain access to the Options tab.

> **TIP** If the fields you want to select are located next to each other or you want to select many fields, use the Select Object tool and drag a marquee through the fields to be selected. When you release the mouse button, the fields inside the marquee and any fields inter-sected by the marquee are selected. The marquee does not need to completely surround fields for selection—it must just include a part of the field box within the marquee.

Duplicating fields

You can duplicate a field by selecting it and holding down the Ctrl/Option key while clicking and dragging the field box. Fields also can be copied and pasted on a PDF page, between PDF pages, and between PDF documents in both Form Editing Mode and Viewer mode. Select a field or multi-ple fields, and then choose Edit ⇨ Copy. Move to another page or open another PDF document, and choose Edit ⇨ Paste. The field names and attributes are pasted together on a new page.

> **TIP** To ensure that field names are an exact match between forms, create one form with all the fields used on other forms. Copy the fields from the original form, and paste the fields in other forms requiring the same fields. By pasting the fields, you ensure that all field names are identical between forms and can easily swap data between them. If you have JavaScripts at the document level, then use the Document ⇨ Replace Pages command when you want to populate a form having a similar design to an original form.

Moving fields

You can relocate fields on the PDF page by selecting the Select Object tool in the Advanced Editing toolbar, and then clicking and dragging the field to a new location. To constrain the angle of move-ment, select a field with the Select Object tool, press the Shift key, and drag the field to a new loca-tion. For precise movement, use the arrow keys to move a field box left, right, up, or down.

Deleting fields

You delete fields from PDF documents in three ways. You can select the field and press the Backspace key (Windows) or Delete key (Macintosh). You also can select the field and choose Edit ⇨ Delete, or you can open a context menu and choose Delete. In all cases, Acrobat removes the field without warning. If you inadvertently delete a field, you can Undo the operation by choosing Edit ⇨ Undo.

Aligning fields

Even when you view the grids on the PDF page (View ⇨ Grid or ⌘/Ctrl+U) and align to the grid (View ⇨ Snap to Grid or ⌘/Ctrl+Shift+U), aligning fields can sometimes be challenging. Acrobat simplifies field alignment by offering menu commands for aligning the field rectangles at the left, right, top, and bottom sides, as well as for specifying horizontal and vertical alignment on the PDF page. To align fields, select two or more fields and then open a context menu and select Align, Distribute, or Center, as shown in Figure 30.28. The alignment options for Left, Right, Top, Bottom, Horizontally, and Vertically appear in a submenu.

FIGURE 30.28

Open a context menu using the Select Object tool on one field in a group of selected fields, and choose Align from the menu.

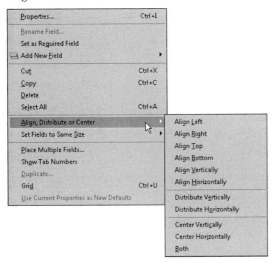

Acrobat aligns fields according to the first field selected (the anchor field appearing with handles around the field object). In other words, the first field's vertical position is used to align all subsequently selected fields to the same vertical position. The same holds true for left, right, and top alignment positions. When you use the horizontal and vertical alignments, the first field selected determines the center alignment position for all subsequently selected fields. All fields are center aligned either vertically or horizontally to the anchor field.

TIP Fields are aligned to an anchor field when multiple fields are selected and you use the align center, distribute, and size commands. The anchor field appears with handles on the corners and the midpoint on each side while the remaining selected field highlights are blue. If you want to change the anchor (the field to be used for alignment, sizing, and so on), select all fields, press the Shift key and click the field you want to be the anchor. The selected field appears with handles.

You can distribute fields on a PDF page by selecting multiple fields and choosing Distribute from a context-sensitive menu. Select either Horizontally or Vertically for the distribution type. The first and last fields in the group determine the beginning and ending of the field distribution. All fields within the two extremes are distributed equidistant between the first and last fields.

Center alignment is another menu command available from a context menu. When you choose Center ⇨ Vertically or Horizontally from a context menu, the selected field aligns to the horizontal or vertical center of the page. Choose Center ⇨ Both to align a field to the center of a page. If multiple fields are selected, the alignment options take into account the relative positions of the field boxes and center the selected fields as a group while preserving their relative positions.

Sizing fields

Field rectangles can be sized to a common physical size. Once again, the anchor field determines the size attributes for the remaining fields selected. To size fields, select multiple field boxes, and then open a context menu and choose Set Fields to Same Size ⇨ Height, Width, or Both. Size changes are made horizontally, vertically, or both horizontally and vertically, depending on which menu option you choose. To size field boxes individually in small increments, hold down the Option/Alt key and move the arrow keys. The left and right arrow keys size field boxes horizontally, whereas the up and down arrow keys size field boxes vertically.

Creating multiple copies of fields

To create a table array, select fields either in a single row or single column and open a context menu. From the menu options, select Place Multiple Fields. The Create Multiple Copies of Fields dialog box opens, as shown in Figure 30.29. In the Create Multiple Copies of Fields dialog box, enter a value in the field box for Copy selected fields down (for creating rows of fields) or Copy selected fields across (to create columns of fields). In Figure 30.29, we created three fields and wanted our duplicated fields to be added below the top row. Notice that when you make selections in the Create Multiple Copies of Fields dialog box with the Preview check box enabled, you see a dynamic preview in the document for how the fields appear when duplicated.

 You also can create a table array by first creating a single field and selecting options for both Copy Selected Fields down and Copy Selected Fields across.

If you want to add both rows and columns, you can supply values in both field boxes for the desired number of columns and rows. The Change Width and Change Height field boxes enable you to adjust the field distance respective to each other—editing the values does not change the physical sizes of the fields. Click the Up/Down buttons for moving all fields vertically or the Left/Right buttons to move fields horizontally. When the preview box is enabled, you see a preview of the duplicated rows and columns before you accept the attribute choices by clicking OK.

If, after you click OK, you need to polish the position of the new fields, you can move the top and bottom fields (for aligning single columns), and then open a context menu and choose Distribute ⇨ Vertically or Horizontally—depending on whether you're adjusting a row or column.

To create a table array, select a row or column of fields and open a context menu. Select Place Multiple Fields, and make selections in the Create Multiple Copies of Fields dialog box for the number of rows or columns to be duplicated.

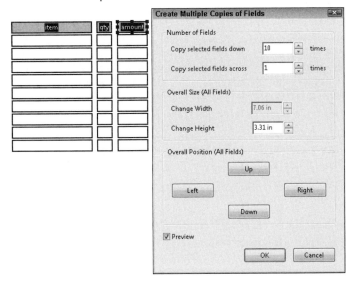

When using the Distribute command, you can distribute only single rows or columns. If you attempt to select all fields in a table and distribute several rows or columns at once, the results render an offset distribution that most likely creates an unusable alignment.

Duplicating fields

Using the Place Multiple Fields menu command from a context menu enables you to create table arrays or individual columns or rows only on a single page. If you want to duplicate fields either on a page or through a number of pages, another menu command exists for field duplication.

You can use the Duplicate command to duplicate fields; however, the duplicate command is used to duplicate fields across multiple pages such as duplicating a navigation button. To duplicate a field on a page, use the copy/paste commands or press the Option/Control key while dragging a field.

Setting attribute defaults

If you spend time formatting attributes for field appearances, options, and actions, you may want to assign a default attribute set for all subsequent fields created with the same form tool. After creating a field with the attributes you want, open a context menu and select Use Current Properties as New Defaults. When you choose the menu command, the properties options used for the field selected become a new default for that field type. As you change form tools and create different fields, you can assign different defaults to different field types.

Setting field tab orders

You have two options for setting the tab order on a form. This is one item you should address before saving your final edited form. You should be able to press the Tab key to enter the first field on a page and tab through the remaining fields in a logical order to make it easy for the end user to fill in your form. Before deploying your form, be sure to check the tab order.

The first option you have for setting Tab order is in the Pages panel. Enter Viewer mode, and open the Pages panel. Open a context menu on the page where you want to set tab order. Select Page Properties from the menu options, and the Page Properties dialog box opens, as shown in Figure 30.30. By default, the Tab Order pane opens with options for setting tab order by making radio button selections.

FIGURE 30.30

To set tab order, open the Pages panel and open a context menu on the page where you want to edit the tab order. Select Page Properties from the menu choices, and click Tab Order in the Pages Properties dialog box.

You have these options for setting tab order:

- **Use Row Order:** This option tabs through rows from left to right. If you want to change the direction for tabbing through fields, choose File ⇨ Properties. Click Advanced in the left pane, and select Right Edge from the Binding pull-down menu. When you select Use Row Order and the document binding is set to Right Edge, the tab order moves from right to left.

- **Use Column Order:** This option tabs through columns from left to right, or right to left if you change the binding as described in the preceding bullet.

- **Use Document Structure:** When selecting this option, you first need to use a PDF document with structure and tags. The tab order is determined by the structure tree created by the original authoring application when the file was exported to PDF.

■ **Unspecified:** All documents you created in earlier versions of Acrobat that you open in Acrobat 6 through 9 have the Unspecified option selected. Unless you physically change the tab order to one of the preceding options, the tab order remains true to the order set in Acrobat 5 or earlier.

The order in which you create fields and add them to a page is recorded. If you happen to create a row of fields, and then change your mind and want to add a new field in the middle of the row, Acrobat tabs to the last field in the row from the last field created. Changing the tab orders in the Page Properties won't help you fix the problem when the fields need to be reordered.

Fortunately, you do have more options for setting tab orders. The second method, and perhaps your best choice for arranging fields in proper tab order, is in Form Editing Mode.

In Acrobat 9, you can drag and drop fields in the Fields panel to change the tab order. Click a field in the Fields panel in Form Editing Mode, and drag the field up or down in the Fields panel to change the tab order.

If you want to see a visual order of your fields on a form, open a context menu on any field and choose Show Tab Numbers. Each field displays the tab order number in the top-left corner of the field box as shown in Figure 30.31.

FIGURE 30.31

Numbers on each field show the current tab order.

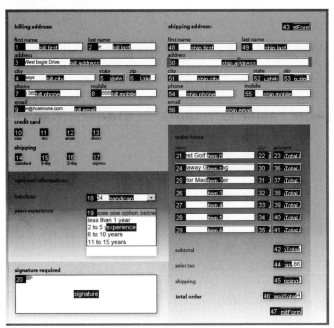

Distributing Forms

Independent graphic designers and small ad agencies have had a problem distributing forms to servers with previous versions of Acrobat. Unless you had an IT department and people capable of programming servers, you were left out of the data collection phase of working with PDF forms using servers and had to rely on e-mail exchanges.

Along with the introduction of Acrobat 9 and later with the Creative Suite 4, Adobe introduces a service called Acrobat.com. Along with Acrobat 9 and Acrobat.com, anyone can distribute forms to the Adobe server to collect form data without having to worry about any programming issues.

Using the services of Acrobat.com, you can use the service to e-mail forms, or submit forms to the server.

CROSS-REF   For more information on using Acrobat.com, see Chapter 33.

E-mailing forms using Acrobat.com

Choose Forms ⇨ Distribute Form, and the Distribute Form dialog box opens, as shown in Figure 30.32. The pull-down menu at the top of the dialog box contains a choice to manually collect responses in your e-mail inbox. Choose this item, and click Next to begin stepping through the wizard.

FIGURE 30.32

Select Forms ⇨ Distribute Form to open the Distribute Form wizard.

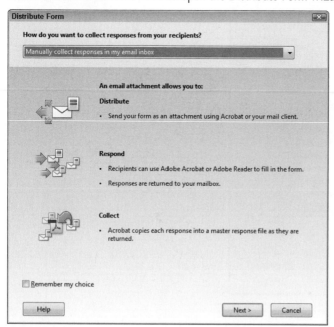

TIP Note that when you choose a distribution host such as e-mail, the Distribute Form wizard displays information on what will occur when you proceed to distribute the form according to the selection made in the pull-down menu. As you change distribution methods, the wizard window updates information informing you of the distribution process details for each choice made from the pull-down menu.

Choosing to manually distribute forms on Acrobat.com sends your form as an e-mail attachment using Acrobat for your mail client. Your e-mail client is not used when you make this choice, and responses are returned to your mailbox. Acrobat copies each response to a dataset file in the form of a PDF Portfolio hosted on Acrobat.com.

The next pane in the Distribute Form window provides you with two choices, as shown in Figure 30.33. You can choose to Send it automatically using Acrobat or Save a local copy and manually send it later. If you choose to send the file using Acrobat, Acrobat serves as your email client.

FIGURE 30.33

Choose an option for handing your e-mail responses.

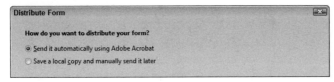

If you elect to use Acrobat.com and click the next button, the Acrobat log-on pane opens for you to log in with your Adobe ID and password, as shown in Figure 30.34. Supply the necessary information and click Sign-in. You file is then uploaded to Acrobat.com.

CROSS-REF For more information on creating an Adobe ID and signing into Acrobat.com, see Chapter 33.

After you log in, an automated e-mail message opens in the Distribute Form wizard, as shown in Figure 30.35. Here you add recipient names and either send an automated message or edit the Subject and/or Message text boxes. Click Send, and your file is uploaded to your Acrobat.com workspace and a URL link is placed in the e-mail message that is sent to your recipient list. This e-mail uses Acrobat as your mail client.

NOTE Don't open your e-mail client and look for a file attachment on a new e-mail message. Using the steps outlined here, Acrobat is serving as your mail client and no intervention is made from your local e-mail client.

FIGURE 30.34

Choose to have Acrobat.com manage your e-mail responses, and you need to log into your Acrobat.com workspace.

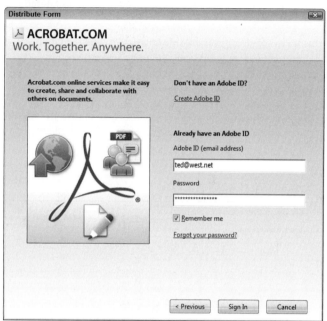

Several things happen when you use Acrobat.com to manage e-mail responses. First, a Submit button is added to the Document Message bar when the form filler opens your form in an Acrobat viewer. Form fillers can click this button to submit responses to you. Second, the file is enabled with Adobe Reader usage rights without warning or notification. Your forms can be filled in by Adobe Reader users. Last, a dataset file is created in your Acrobat.com workspace. As form fillers submit forms, the data are collected on Acrobat.com in a master response file.

When the upload is completed, the Forms Tracker opens immediately in Acrobat with a current status report on your uploaded form, as shown in Figure 30.36. Using the Forms Tracker, you can view responses, open the original form stored locally on your hard drive, add new recipients for completing the form, stop form data collection to terminate the form distribution, send e-mail reminders, and generally keep updated information about the form distribution process.

At any time during your form distribution process, you can monitor the updates for responses by choosing Forms ➪ Track Forms. Acrobat opens the same Forms Tracker and reports any new activity.

Because the dataset file is hosted on Acrobat.com, you can organize, view, export, and manage data through your Acrobat.com environment.

FIGURE 30.35

Add recipient names, and click send to upload your form to Acrobat.com and send a message to your recipients with a URL link where they can download the file.

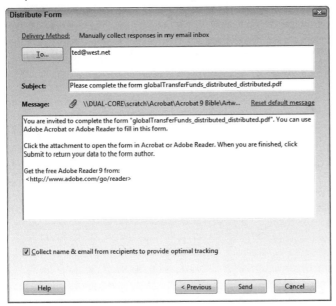

FIGURE 30.36

After sending an e-mail invitation to recipients, the Forms Tracker opens.

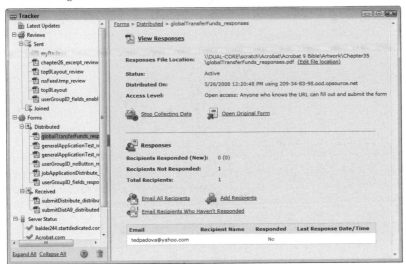

Submitting forms to Acrobat.com

We need to roll back momentarily to the Forms ⇨ Distribute Forms command that opens the Distribute Forms wizard. When you open the wizard, don't choose the option for distributing forms via e-mail; instead, choose Automatically download & organize responses with Acrobat.com. The Distribute Form wizard opens, as shown in Figure 30.37. At first glance, the Distribute Form wizard selections for using Acrobat.com appear identical as when choosing to distribute forms via e-mail. Upon closer look, however, you see that the descriptions for handling distribution, responses, and data collection do vary some.

FIGURE 30.37

The Distribute Form wizard as it appears after choosing Automatically download & organize responses with Acrobat.com

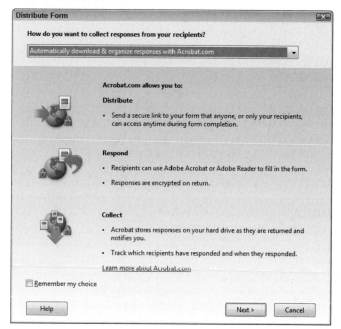

These are some of the differences between Acrobat.com and e-mailing forms:

- **Distribute:** The message you send to recipients contains a secure link to your form that recipients can access. You can allow anyone who visits your Acrobat.com Library to download the form, or you can restrict access to only those whom you've invited to complete the form.

- **Respond:** In addition to enabling the form with Adobe Reader usage rights, responses are encrypted when returned to you.

■ **Collect:** Acrobat stores responses on your hard drive as the forms are returned to you. All the forms processing actions can be monitored in the Forms Tracker.

When you click the Next button, Acrobat verifies your login ID and brings you to the mail message pane in the Distribute Form wizard. In Figure 30.38, you see a screen very similar to Figure 30.32. However, notice at the bottom of the window that you have the additional choice for determining the level of access. The Access level pull-down menu is not available when you e-mail forms and let Acrobat.com manage the data.

FIGURE 30.38

When submitting forms to Acrobat.com, you can limit access to only the participants you've invited to fill in the form.

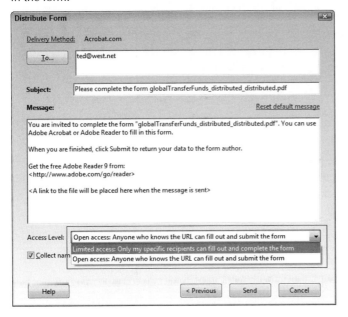

After you distribute a form, you can view and analyze returned form data on Acrobat.com in a number of ways. You can filter fields, sort data, and perform a number of analysis functions. When new responses are received from e-mail distributions or distributing via Acrobat.com, a pop-up window opens when you log into Acrobat.com, as shown in Figure 30.39. Click Get Started, and you can perform a number of viewing and analysis tasks.

FIGURE 30.39

When responses are received, a pop-up window displays your options for analyzing data.

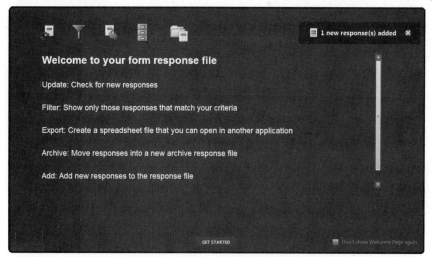

Summary

- Acrobat forms are not scanned documents converted to PDF. They are dynamic and can include interactive elements, data fields, buttons, and JavaScripts.

- Data fields are created from many different field types including text, buttons, combo boxes, list boxes, signatures, check boxes, radio buttons, and barcodes.

- You set all data field attributes in the Field Properties window. Properties can be described for fields by selecting the tabs labeled Appearance, Options, Actions, Calculations, or other tabs associated with specific field types.

- Acrobat 9 has a new interface called Form Editing Mode where filed objects are added to forms.

- In Acrobat 9, you edit forms in Form Editing Mode and fill in or check form functionality in Preview or Viewer mode.

- You can edit fields with a context-sensitive menu. Acrobat has several editing commands used for aligning fields, distributing fields, and centering fields on a PDF page.

- Field duplication is handled in a context menu. You can duplicate fields on a page to create tables with the Place Multiple Fields command, or you can duplicate fields across multiple pages with the Duplicate command.

- Button fields can be created to submit form data from any Acrobat viewer. For Adobe Reader users to submit a PDF with data back to the PDF author, the form must be enabled with Adobe Reader usage rights.

- Forms can be deployed via e-mail and hosted on Acrobat.com.

Chapter 31

Creating Slide Presentations

Slide presentations may be something you want to use in client meetings when proposing new concepts or campaigns, or your clients may ask you to create presentations they want to use at trade shows, meetings, and conferences. Whether for your own needs or your clients' needs, at one time or another design professionals periodically find a need to create slide presentations. If creating slide presentations is not something you usually do, the last thing you'll want to do is try to learn a new program to quickly assemble a presentation for yourself or your client.

Dedicated slide-creation programs like Microsoft PowerPoint and Apple's Keynote are designed specifically for creating presentations. However, if you're not up to speed with these programs and need to design a presentation quickly, you'll find working in programs you know to be much less frustrating. In this chapter, you learn how to use the CS4 programs for creating slide presentations and converting presentations from the dedicated slide-presentation applications to file formats usable with the CS4 programs.

IN THIS CHAPTER

Converting slide presentation files

Authoring presentations in CS programs

Using layers with presentations

Creating transitions

Using full-screen views

Converting Presentation Documents to PDF

Because slide presentations may exist in a variety of different formats, you may need to convert an existing file that was created by your client to something workable with the CS4 programs. The most popular presentation documents you'll find are Microsoft PowerPoint files—but you're not necessarily limited to PowerPoint. You may find old layouts in QuarkXPress, Adobe PageMaker, or other application documents that were once used for presentations and now need to be updated or refined for current presentations.

In addition to converting existing documents to a format workable with the CS4 programs, you may need to integrate current files created in Illustrator, Photoshop, InDesign, Adobe Flash, and/or Dreamweaver with older presentation documents. Assuming you're not up to speed in a program designed to create presentations, you need to convert files to a format usable as a display tool for presentations. Fortunately, you can convert all files from any authoring program to PDF, and you can use Adobe Acrobat or Adobe Reader as a presentation tool.

Acrobat is not a mere substitute for presentation programs. Acrobat can stand alone as a sophisticated presentation tool where you can add transitions, create links to documents, show multimedia film clips, display presentations in self-running modes for kiosks, add animation, and take advantage of all the other features one would expect from a presentation program. If you've begun to master the CS4 programs, you'll find creating PDF files for presentations a better solution in your workflow if you aren't familiar with creating slides in a presentation program.

Unfortunately, one of the best tools for converting PowerPoint slides is available only on Windows. If you happen to be a Windows user or a Mac Intel user with Windows installed on your computer, you can take advantage of Adobe Presenter that's installed with the Acrobat Professional Extended version of Acrobat 9.0 (Windows only). With Adobe Presenter, you can export an animation from a PowerPoint file that results in an Adobe Flash movie file inside a PDF document.

Converting PowerPoint slides to PDF

The de facto standard presentation program on Windows is Microsoft PowerPoint. Microsoft Office users are so familiar with PowerPoint that they tend to create documents ranging from slide presentations to large-format display prints. If you work with corporate clients who supply files to you, you'll definitely see many PowerPoint files.

You can convert PowerPoint slides to PDF and add slide pages to an InDesign document for further development of a presentation, or convert PowerPoint slides to PDF while preserving animation effects created in PowerPoint. Any Acrobat viewer can see the animation exported with the PowerPoint slides.

NOTE Knowing you can view the files you convert to PDF in any Acrobat viewer is an important issue. You may author files in Acrobat Professional, yet you may deliver PDF documents to coworkers or clients who use either Acrobat Standard or Adobe Reader. File conversions from PowerPoint can be viewed in any Acrobat viewer, complete with transition effects.

To convert PowerPoint slides to PDF, you can use the Convert to PDF from File command in Acrobat or the PDFMaker in PowerPoint (Windows). On the Mac you print to PDF from PowerPoint. You must have PowerPoint installed on your computer to convert to PDF. Therefore, if you receive PowerPoint files from your clients, be certain you own a copy of Microsoft Office, have your clients send you a PostScript file, or have them convert the PowerPoint PPT files to PDF.

The PDFMaker macro is installed automatically in Microsoft Office applications (Word, Excel, and PowerPoint) when you first install Microsoft Office and then install either Adobe Acrobat or the CS applications that include the Acrobat installation. The order of installation is not critical when installing Acrobat 7, 8, or 9. MS Office can be installed before or after Acrobat. Acrobat's self-healing features can detect MS Office files and automatically install the PDF Maker.

Converting to PDF on the Mac

Converting PowerPoint slides to PDF on the Mac has been challenging with each release of Acrobat. The PDFMaker in PowerPoint failed in earlier versions of Acrobat more often than it worked. If you use Print to PDF, you find problems converting the proper page sizes where pages are clipped and problems with page orientation where pages are rotated. You can convert PowerPoint slides on the Mac, but the process is not intuitive and you can experience some problems.

Ideally, if you have access to a Windows machine, your best opportunity for PowerPoint conversion to PDF is in Windows using the PDFMaker. If you don't have access to a Windows machine and you need to convert PowerPoint files to PDF, use the following steps to do the job.

Steps: Converting PowerPoint to PDF on the Mac

1. **Set up a custom page.** In PowerPoint, choose File ➪ Page Setup. When the Page Setup dialog box appears, click Options and a second Page Setup dialog box opens. In the second dialog box, open the Page Size pull-down menu and select Manage Custom Sizes. The Custom Page Sizes dialog box opens, as shown in Figure 31.1. In the Width and Height text boxes, add 8 inches for the Width and 10.19 inches for the Height. This is where things may begin to get confusing. You would think that a landscape page would have the width and height set to 10.19 x 8. However, pages get clipped when you set the width and height at 10.19 x 8.

FIGURE 31.1

In the Custom Page Sizes dialog box, set the width to 8 inches and the height to 10.19 inches.

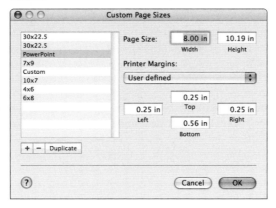

2. **Name the custom page size.** Click the plus (+) symbol to add the page to the list of custom pages. Double-click on the default untitled name, and type PowerPoint. Click OK in the Manage Page Sizes dialog box. Click OK in the Page Setup dialog boxes, and your new custom page size is ready to use.

3. **Select the custom page size.** PowerPoint has a terrible time remembering the last settings made to Page Setup. Each time you covert to PDF, be certain to revisit the Page Setup dialog box. Choose File ⇨ Page Setup. Click Options in the Page Setup dialog box, and a second Page Setup dialog box opens. From the Paper Size pull-down menu, select the PowerPoint page size you created, as shown in Figure 31.2.

Select your new custom page size in the Page Setup dialog box.

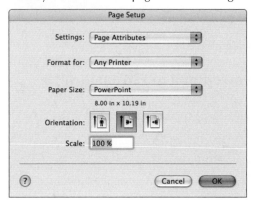

4. **Select the orientation.** The default orientation is landscape. If you print the PowerPoint slides to PostScript and distill the PostScript file, the PDF opens with all the pages rotated 90 degrees. If you export to PDF using Leopard's PDF export features, the PDF pages open in the proper page orientation. Changing the orientation to Portrait produces unsatisfactory results using either PDF conversion tool. Leave the landscape orientation at the landscape default, and click OK.

5. **Convert to PDF.** Choose File ⇨ Print. In the Print dialog box, select Adobe PDF 9.0 from the Printer pull-down menu, as shown in Figure 31.3. The Save dialog box opens. Select a target location on your hard drive, and click Save. The PowerPoint file is saved as a PDF document.

If you select Save PDF as PostScript and distill the resultant PostScript file in Acrobat Distiller, the pages are rotated. When you use the PDF printer driver and Save as PDF, the pages in the PDF appear with the proper orientation.

NOTE Using either Save as PDF or distilling a PostScript file loses all animation in the PDF file. The only way to preserve animated effects added in PowerPoint is to use Adobe Presenter in Acrobat Pro Extended.

FIGURE 31.3

Select a PostScript printer or the Adobe PDF printer. Select Save as PDF, and save the file as a PDF document.

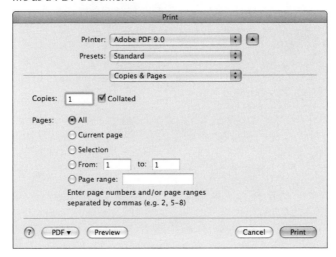

Using PDFMaker on Windows

On Windows the PDFMaker is your tool of choice, and converting PowerPoint slides to PDF with this tool is both consistent and reliable. Additionally, you have the advantage of editing Conversion Settings by clicking tools in the PowerPoint Ribbon (in Office 2007 applications). Conversion Settings offer you choices for how the PDF is created in terms of file compression, preserving various settings made in PowerPoint including transitions, converting multimedia, adding bookmarks, and a host of options you have available by editing the Adobe PDF settings. To open the Adobe PDF Maker dialog box where Conversion Settings are adjusted, click on the Adobe PDF tab in PowerPoint Ribbon, as shown in Figure 31.4. Select Preferences in the Acrobat tab, and the Acrobat PDFMaker dialog box opens, as shown in Figure 31.5.

In the Adobe PDFMaker dialog box, shown in Figure 31.5, select the check boxes for the items you want to enable or disable. To edit the Adobe PDF Settings that are employed with Acrobat Distiller, click the Advanced Settings button. The same options you have available when adjusting the Distiller Adobe PDF Settings are available to you when you click on the Advanced Settings button. In most cases, you won't need to create custom PDF settings. Therefore, just select the conversion settings you want to use from choices in the Conversion Settings pull-down menu. By default, you should see Standard appear in the menu. Using the Standard settings generally does the job for creating slide presentations shown on-screen but not printed on commercial printing devices.

FIGURE 31.4

Click Preferences in the Acrobat tab in Microsoft PowerPoint.

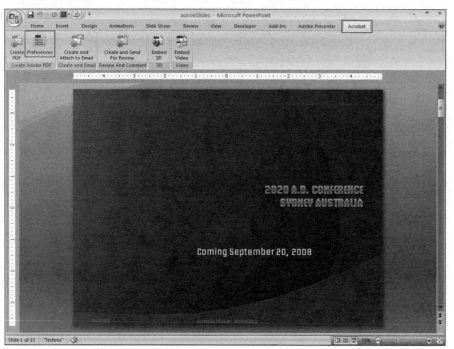

CROSS-REF Understanding the Adobe PDF Settings (called *job options* in earlier versions of Acrobat) is an elaborate and complicated process. For almost all the PDF creation you perform with the CS programs, you won't need to adjust conversion settings and won't find a need to create custom Adobe PDF Settings. If you do find that you need to understand more and want to create your own custom settings files, see the *Adobe Acrobat 9 PDF Bible* (published by Wiley).

Leave the default check boxes selected in the Adobe PDFMaker dialog box, and click OK to return to the PowerPoint application window. To create the PDF file, click the Create PDF tool in the Ribbon (refer to Figure 31.4). When you click this tool, the Save Adobe PDF File As dialog box opens, where you can click the Options button to open a different Adobe PDFMaker dialog box. Many of the adjustments you have in the dialog box shown in Figure 31.5 also are included in the dialog box that opens when you click the Options button. You can use this dialog box to double-check your settings when converting PowerPoint files to Adobe PDF documents.

Using Adobe Presenter (Windows only)

Adobe Presenter is installed with Acrobat Professional Extended on Windows only. When it comes to presentations and showing slides from a computer monitor, Presenter is the tool that creates the most impressive-looking slides from Microsoft PowerPoint. You must have PowerPoint installed on Windows before you can use Adobe Presenter.

FIGURE 31.5

The Adobe PDFMaker dialog box offers options for creating a PDF.

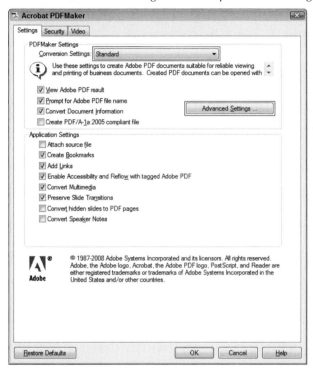

In the PowerPoint Ribbon, click the Adobe Presenter tab to view the options available with Presenter, and the Ribbon changes to the view shown in Figure 31.6.

FIGURE 31.6

Click the Adobe Presenter tab in the PowerPoint Ribbon to display the Adobe Presenter tools.

A number of different options are available with Presenter to make your slide creations much easier. You can add video and sound, import webcam snapshots, insert Adobe Flash files, create quiz questions, set attributes for slide displays, and more.

Adobe Presenter also captures all the animation effects you add to a PowerPoint presentation. Keep in mind that you must add the animations—such as text flying in or out of a slide, fading text and objects, transitions, and so on—to slides using tools in PowerPoint. After the animations have been added to the slide presentation using PowerPoint tools and menu commands, you can export the presentation using Adobe Presenter, which retains the PowerPoint effects in the resultant PDF document.

To export a PowerPoint presentation using Adobe Presenter, click the Publish tool in the Adobe Presenter tab in PowerPoint. The Adobe Presenter – Publish Presentation window opens, as shown in Figure 31.7.

FIGURE 31.7

Click Publish in the Adobe Presenter tab in the PowerPoint Ribbon to open the Adobe Presenter – Publish Presentation window.

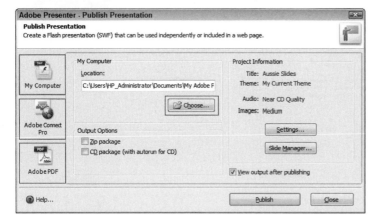

Your first choice is to determine which output purpose you want to use. If you click My Computer, you publish a presentation for Web viewing. If you choose Adobe Connect Pro, you publish the presentation for sharing the file on Acrobat.com. If you choose Adobe PDF, you create a PDF document locally on your computer.

Click Adobe PDF to produce a PDF document, and click the Choose button to target a location on your computer where you want to save the file. After you determine the target folder for the saved file, click the Publish button and the presentation is converted to PDF.

By default, your presentation opens in Acrobat. In Figure 31.8, you can see a presentation converted to PDF using Adobe Presenter. Notice that the total number of pages for the document is only one page. Our example presentation has eleven slides, but you see only one page in the PDF file because the presentation was converted to an Adobe Flash file. All the slides are there in a Flash interface. You have complete navigation control using Flash skins to play, pause, and jump around slides.

FIGURE 31.8

The resultant PDF document contains an Adobe Flash file.

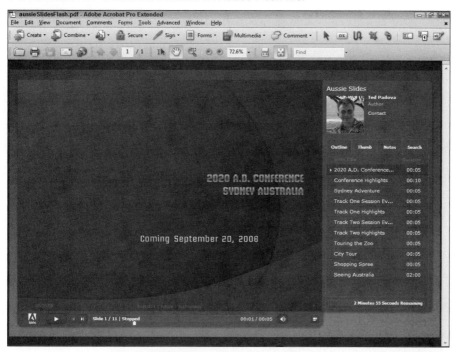

All the transition effects and animations you add in PowerPoint are captured and displayed the same in the Flash file as when viewing a slide show in Microsoft PowerPoint. The Adobe Flash interface also offers some other options, such as a speaker profile, a time code, and more controls for viewing the slides.

Creating Presentations in CS programs

If your comfort zone is strictly limited to the CS applications, you may not want to learn either PowerPoint or Keynote. If so, then you can use some of the CS programs as presentation-authoring tools. All the CS programs except Adobe Acrobat can be used as the authoring tool, while Acrobat is used as the display tool for showing presentations. In practicality, using Adobe Dreamweaver is more cumbersome (unless, of course, the presentation format will be HTML), while the most likely candidate to help you create a presentation project is Adobe InDesign.

Using InDesign as a presentation-authoring tool

Creating slides in InDesign has its advantages and disadvantages. In terms of disadvantages, InDesign does not offer you dynamic outlining where you add text in an outline format that is automatically applied to individual slides. The actual creation of text on slides is much faster in a dedicated slide-creation tool. Additionally, you have no options for printing notes or handouts, adding animation to text and objects, editing charts and graphs, and a few other specific slide-creation features.

On the advantage side of using InDesign, you have much more design freedom than using dedicated slide-creation programs, including the ability to import native CS application documents; the ability to import files saved from a wider range of formats; better typographic control; more-sophisticated editing of graphic elements such as applying drop shadows, adding transparency, and feathering objects, creating layers, using style sheets and graphic styles, and all the options InDesign offers you for creating sophisticated layouts. As an example, in Figure 31.9, you can see a native Photoshop image in the lower-left corner of the slide breaking the page edge in the PDF document. This type of effect can be created only using Adobe InDesign.

FIGURE 31.9

Using InDesign to create slides allows you to create unique design effects.

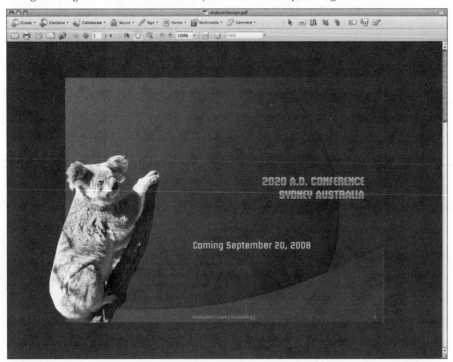

Creating bookmarks

As a final editing task, you may want to add bookmarks to your presentation. Bookmarks can help you easily return to areas of discussion when answering questions or adding information on topics as you make a presentation. You have a choice for adding bookmarks directly in InDesign and having those bookmarks exported in the PDF document or creating bookmarks in Acrobat. In some workflows, you may find a benefit in creating bookmarks in InDesign if a layout specialist is unfamiliar with Acrobat and doesn't have the full version installed on a computer.

To create bookmarks in InDesign, choose Window ➪ Interactive ➪ Bookmarks to open the Bookmarks palette. Creating bookmarks is easy in both InDesign and Acrobat. Find text on a page you want to use as a bookmark title and select the text. Click on the right-pointing arrow in the palette to open the flyout menu, and select New Bookmark, as shown in Figure 31.10. In Acrobat, the menu command to create a new bookmark is found in the Bookmark pane Options menu.

FIGURE 31.10

To capture the page view, select New Bookmark.

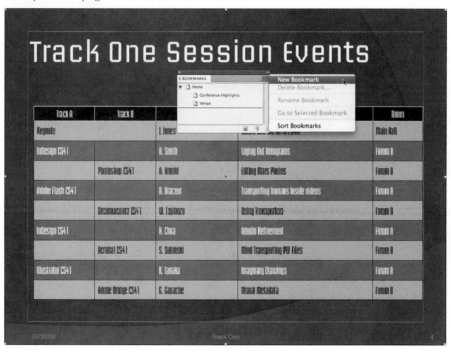

If you want to create a bookmark without capturing highlighted text as the bookmark name, don't select any text, but select New Bookmark from the flyout palette. InDesign automatically names the bookmark simply as Bookmark. To edit the name, select Rename Bookmark in the palette menu. A dialog box opens where you edit the name.

Creating Bookmarks: Acrobat or InDesign?

There's a big difference between bookmarks created in InDesign and bookmarks created in Acrobat. When you create bookmarks in Acrobat, the bookmark captures the view of the bookmarked page. When zooming in 400 percent and creating a bookmark, you capture the page and the zoom view. Therefore, if you are in a 100 percent view and click on a bookmark that was bookmarked at a 400 percent view, Acrobat takes you to the page bookmarked and zooms in to a 400 percent view. When you create a bookmark in InDesign, the zoom is derived from the current view. Therefore, if you zoom to 400 percent to view pages, and then click a bookmark, the bookmarked page opens at 400 percent even though the bookmark may have been created at 100 percent view. If you zoom out to a Fit Page view in the same document and continue clicking on bookmarks, the bookmark zooms inherit the current view (for example, Fit Page). Note that if the bookmarks are created in InDesign and the file is exported to PDF, viewing the bookmarked pages in Acrobat treats the zoom levels with the same inherited page views.

At first blush, you may think it more of an advantage to create bookmarks in InDesign so that all page links go to inherited zoom levels. However, there's a price to pay for having the feature. When you create bookmarks in InDesign, you add more overhead to your file because InDesign creates not only bookmarks but also Destinations. In Acrobat, Destinations are similar to bookmarks where you can click on Destinations to navigate views. However, adding Destinations to a PDF file significantly adds to the file size. For small to moderate-size presentations that are viewed from files stored on your hard drive, it shouldn't be an issue. However if you post files on the Web or use very large PDF documents, you'll want to avoid using Destinations. The added file sizes can slow down performance in Acrobat and add to the download time with Web-hosted documents.

After creating bookmarks, scroll the Bookmark palette and review the bookmark names. To check the bookmark links, double-click on a name and InDesign opens the page associated with the bookmark. Note that InDesign requires you to double-click a bookmark name to view the destination, while Acrobat requires only a single mouse click.

CROSS-REF For more information about creating bookmarks and interactive links in InDesign, see Chapter 29.

Exporting to PDF

After you've created your slides, added bookmarks, and reviewed the document, you need to export the file as a PDF for a more-suitable file format for viewing slides. Don't attempt to use InDesign as a slide viewer, especially when you need to exchange files with clients or across platforms. Obviously, one advantage to creating PDF documents is that any user can display the slide presentation with the free Adobe Reader software. If you distribute InDesign files, every user who wants to view the presentation needs a licensed copy of InDesign.

To export the file to PDF, choose File ➪ Export, type a filename in the Save As field box, and navigate your hard drive for a destination. Be certain Adobe PDF is selected in the Format pull-down menu, and click Save.

The next dialog box that opens is the Export Adobe PDF dialog box, shown in Figure 31.11. Here, you make choices for the PDF attributes. First, select the preset you want to use from the Preset pull-down menu.

FIGURE 31.11

Choose a preset, and make attribute choices.

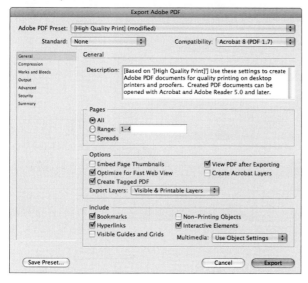

If you create bookmarks and video files, check the box for Bookmarks and Interactive Elements that you may have included in the InDesign file. When you're finished with the attribute choices, click Export and the file is exported to PDF. If you selected View PDF after Exporting, the file opens in your default Acrobat viewer. In Figure 31.12, you can see a PDF exported from InDesign with bookmarks.

Creating notes and handouts

All the InDesign editing features you learned in Parts III, IV, and V are available to you when creating slide presentations just like other kinds of layouts. Using master pages, character and paragraph styles, tables, and so on is helpful in creating any kind of layout. Creating notes and handouts, however, is another matter. If you want to create note pages with slides on each page as you can with the slide-presentation programs, you need to export slide pages from InDesign and import them back into a template designed for creating note pages. Assuming you have a PDF document you want to use as a slide presentation, the following steps demonstrate how you can use InDesign to create note handouts.

FIGURE 31.12

The exported bookmarks should be visible in the open Bookmarks panel.

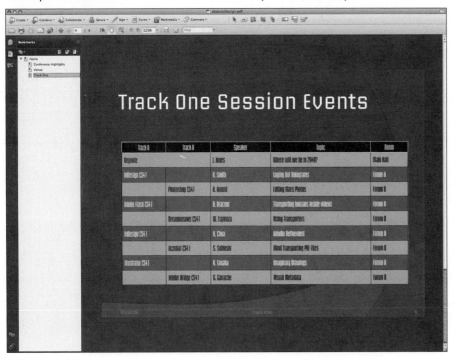

STEPS: Creating Note Handouts in InDesign

1. **Create a new document in Adobe InDesign.** Launch Adobe InDesign, and choose File ➪ New to create a new document. Set the page attributes to a letter-page size (8½ x 11 inches) and a portrait orientation. Set the margin distance to 0.5 inches for all sides, and click OK in the New Document dialog box.

NOTE If you know ahead of time the number of slides in the presentation, enter the value in the Number of Pages field box. If you don't remember the exact number of pages in your PDF document, enter an approximate value and you can add or delete pages when working in the InDesign document.

2. **Create a master page.** Open the Pages Panel and double-click the default A-Master master page. On the master page, draw lines for note comments, and add any graphic objects, an auto page number, a title, and other items you want to display on each note page.

CROSS-REF For information on working with master pages and adding auto page numbers, see Chapter 24.

3. **Add a graphic frame placeholder to the master page.** Select the Rectangle Frame tool in the InDesign toolbox, and click the cursor anywhere on the document page. The Rectangle dialog box opens. Enter the width and height you used in your slide presentation, and click OK. Drag the frame rectangle so the top-left corner resets at the top and left guidelines. Press ⌘/Ctrl+Shift to constrain the frame size, and drag the lower-right corner to rest on the right guideline, as shown in Figure 31.13.

TIP   You can use a note template for not only slides created in InDesign, but also slides you may have created in PowerPoint or Keynote. After they're exported to PDF, you have the same opportunities to design note handouts in InDesign. If you want more freedom for the way your handouts are designed, import them into an InDesign layout. If you use the standard 10x7½-inch slide format, enter those values in the Rectangle dialog box that opens when clicking on the Rectangle Frame tool.

FIGURE 31.13

Set up the master page with the text and graphics.

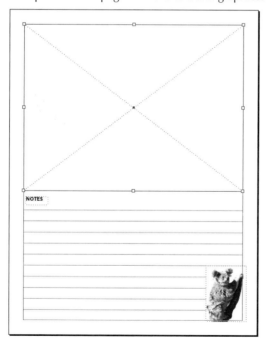

CROSS-REF   For more information on sizing frame rectangles, see Part III.

4. **Select the PDF file to import.** Navigate to the first page in your InDesign file, and select File ➪ Place. In the Place dialog box, navigate your hard drive and locate the PDF document to be imported. At the bottom of the Place dialog box, check the box for Show Import Options, as shown in Figure 31.14. When the Show Import Options check box is checked, the Place PDF dialog box opens, where you have options for selecting pages in the PDF document to be placed in the InDesign file.

FIGURE 31.14

When Show Import Options is checked in the Place dialog box, the Place PDF dialog box opens.

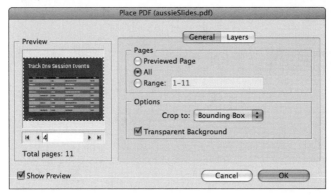

5. **Select All pages.** Click Open in the Place dialog box, and the Place PDF dialog box opens, as shown in Figure 31.14. Select All in the dialog box to place all pages.

6. **Place the first page in the rectangle frame.** Click OK in the Place PDF dialog box, and the cursor loads the graphic. Be certain to move anywhere atop the rectangle frame location on page 1, and click the cursor. The first page in the PDF file is placed inside the rectangle frame, as shown in Figure 31.15.

7. **Size the graphic to the frame size.** Select the frame and press ⌘+Option+E (Ctrl+Alt+E on Windows) and the graphic image is proportionally sized to fit inside the rectangle frame. The cursor remains loaded and you can continue clicking on subsequent pages to place the remaining PDF pages. Continue to place pages from the PDF to the remaining pages in the InDesign document. Alternately, you can use frame fitting options on the frame on the master page.

8. **Export to PDF.** If you want to send your file off to a copy shop for printing or host the note handouts on a Web site for attendees to download, convert the file to PDF. The copy shop won't need links, fonts, or a copy of InDesign CS to print the file, and those downloading your file from a Web site can use the free Adobe Reader software to view the document.

FIGURE 31.15

The first page in the PDF document is placed in the frame.

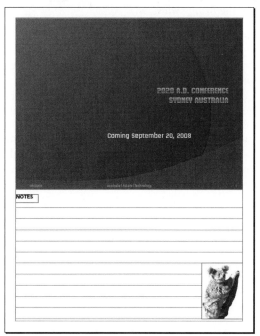

You also have another alternative that works very well. When you create an InDesign file you can place the file in a Master Frame just like using PDF files. When InDesign files are placed, you have all the editing options available to you for changing text and objects.

If you want to make edits in your note handouts, you can easily return to the master page and edit any text or images, or modify the rectangle frame.

Using Photoshop as an authoring tool

Obviously, using Photoshop to create slides is not the most practical solution. Having only one page to edit in a file at one time is certain to slow your progress, not to mention that it results in much larger files than you have using any other application. However, Photoshop does have one nice feature for creating slide presentations when creating a presentation from a collection of photos or design comps you want to display as slides: You can easily create a self-running slideshow complete with transitions and add sound to the presentation if desired.

To create a slide presentation in Photoshop, start by opening the Bridge. Select the thumbnails of the images you want to convert to PDF in the Bridge content area, or press ⌘/Ctrl+A to select all images in a folder. Select Tools ➪ Photoshop ➪ PDF Presentation.

> **TIP**   **If you have a digital camera and want to select files from your digital camera, you can open the Bridge and navigate to a camera attached to a USB or FireWire port on your computer (if such ports exist on your camera). Thumbnail images of the photos on your camera's memory card display in the Bridge window.**

The PDF Presentation dialog box shown in Figure 31.16 appears.

You have several options for setting attributes of the resultant PDF file. If you click the check box for Add Open Files, any files open in Photoshop are added to the file exported to PDF. In the Save As area under Output Options, click the radio button for Presentation. From the Transition pull-down menu, you can choose from a variety of different transitions applied to slide wipes.

When you click Save, the image files selected in the Bridge convert to PDF and combine together in a single PDF document. The file opens in Acrobat in Full Screen mode complete with transitions as slide pages scroll automatically at the interval specified in the PDF Presentation dialog box. By default, the transition interval is 5 seconds. To bail out of Full Screen mode, press Esc or press ⌘/Ctrl+L.

FIGURE 31.16

The PDF Presentation dialog box can be opened from the Bridge or from Photoshop.

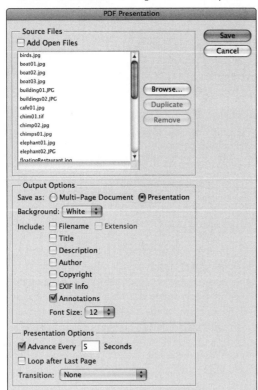

Using Illustrator as an authoring tool

The last tool you should use to create a slide presentation among the CS programs is Illustrator. However, we know there are creative professionals who rely on Illustrator for everything from single-page illustrations to multipage catalogs. We don't recommend it, but we do know some artists who feel so comfortable with Illustrator that they wouldn't take a second look at a layout program no matter what it had to offer.

The good news is that Illustrator CS4 now supports multipage documents. It took only 14 versions of Illustrator for Adobe to finally acquiesce to users' demands to include support for multipage documents. The time is now, and it's finally arrived.

If you're a die-hard Illustrator designer who wants to create some down-and-dirty slide presentations, try using the new multipage document options in Illustrator by following these steps.

STEPS: Using Illustrator as a Presentation Design Tool

1. **Determine the layout.** Choose File ➪ New in Illustrator to open the New Document dialog box. Choose an artboard size by typing values in the Width and Height text boxes for custom sizes. Type the number of artboards you want to appear in your file. In our example, we chose a landscape page size of 10 inches by 7.5 inches and typed 6 for the number of artboards, as shown in Figure 31.17.

FIGURE 31.17

Set up a new document with the page size and number of artboards you want for your presentation.

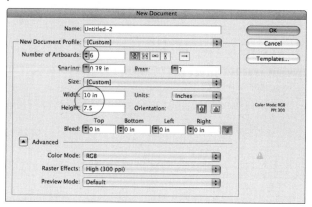

2. **Create your layouts.** Each artboard is a separate work area, but you can create artwork in each artboard using copy/paste commands, use the same color palette, and access all Illustrator tools, palettes, and menu commands. In Figure 31.18, we created a six-page layout for slides in Illustrator.

FIGURE 31.18

Six artboards are used to create a slide presentation in Illustrator.

3. **Create a PDF file.** Choose File ➪ Save As, and choose Adobe PDF in the Save As dialog box as shown in Figure 31.19. When you click Save, the second Save As dialog box offers you an option for choosing the page range. If you want all artboards to be saved as separate pages in the resultant PDF document, leave the default All radio button enabled and click Save. Presto! Your slide show is now an Acrobat PDF file with multiple pages.

FIGURE 31.19

Choose a page range, and click Save.

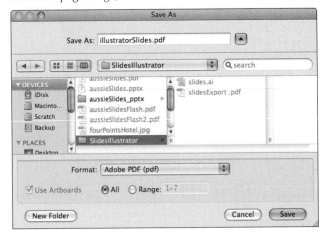

Using Layers with Presentations

Layers offer you another dimension when creating slide presentations. Text can pop up as you cover topics in a presentation when you use layers and toggle on and off layer views. You can also use layers when you need to toggle back and forth between two slide views. Think of a slide where you want to use text and images, then move to a video, return to the text, and move to another video. Layers can handle some of these switching-back-and-forth routines as opposed to creating different slides. In many cases, changing layer views results in faster screen refreshes than changing slide pages.

To create presentations using layers, the authoring program you use needs to support two essential ingredients:

- Support for creating Layers
- Writing to the PDF 1.5 format or later and exporting Adobe PDF Layers

Although Photoshop and Dreamweaver support layers, they don't export Adobe PDF Layers. InDesign and Illustrator both export layers that you can view in Acrobat with layers intact.

For an example of using layers and changing layer visibility in the Acrobat PDF, look at Figure 31.20. The default layer view is shown when the user opens the PDF document. You can see the Layers panel showing the Content and Background layers in view while the Video layer is hidden. A button labeled Play Video has a link action that changes layer visibility to hide the Content layer and show the Video layer. In addition, the button action plays a video that was originally imported in InDesign before exporting to PDF.

The button and button actions to show and hide layer visibility were added in Acrobat. When the user clicks the button on the default layer, the visibility changes to show the hidden layer. Notice as you look at Figure 31.21 that the background data assigned to the Background layer does not change. The elements assigned to the background are the banners at the top and bottom of the page and the filmstrip off the left side of the page. When you're creating layers, you can place text and images on layers common to different layer views and keep these layers visible. This eliminates a need to show/hide data that remains constant while other data is hidden and shown with different layer visibility. The result is faster screen refreshes, because some data remains in view.

CROSS-REF For more information on creating layers in CS programs and exporting Adobe PDF Layers, see Chapter 25. For information on creating buttons and interactive actions, see Chapter 29.

TIP When you create buttons in Adobe InDesign, the buttons are assigned to individual layers. When you hide a layer in Acrobat, the button field object also is hidden. This makes showing and hiding field objects much easier. In Acrobat, all field objects you create using form tools are visible on all layers. This requires you to create separate actions to show/hide button fields when one button appears directly on top of another button, as is the case in the document shown in Figures 31.19 and 31.20.

FIGURE 31.20

The default layer appears when the document is opened in an Acrobat viewer.

FIGURE 31.21

Clicking the button on the default layer changes the layer visibility.

Adding Page Transitions

Page transitions are available in both Edit mode and Full Screen mode in Acrobat 8. A *page transition* is an effect such as a fade-out and fade-in applied to pages as they're turned. You can set page transitions for all pages in a file or among selected pages in the Pages panel. You might add page transitions to PDF documents for trade-show displays where you want to show slides in self-running kiosks.

To set transitions on all pages in a document, or a specified range of pages while remaining in Edit mode (as opposed to Full Screen mode), click the Pages panel icon, and from either the Options menu in the Pages panel or a context menu, select Set Transitions. If you want to set transitions for pages in a noncontiguous order, open the Pages panel and ⌘/Ctrl+click on the individual pages where you want page transitions. The Set Transitions dialog box opens, shown in Figure 31.22.

FIGURE 31.22

In this dialog box, select a page transition from the Transition menu.

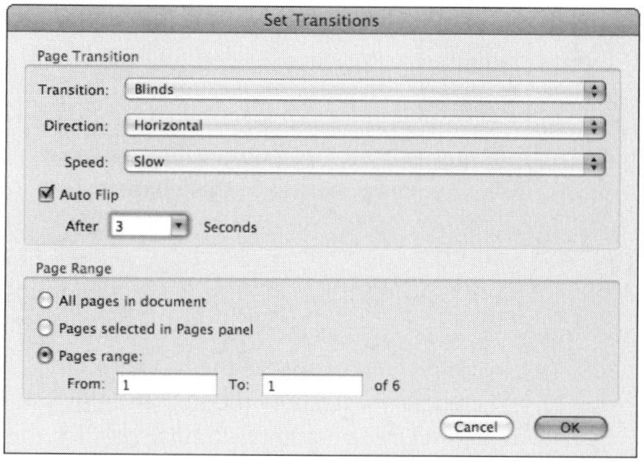

From the Transition pull-down menu, you select the transition you want to apply to the selected pages, either from pages you selected in the Pages panel or a range of pages you specify in the Pages Range field boxes. Acrobat offers you a total of 50 different choices for different effects. One choice is to set no transition, with the remaining 49 choices being different effects.

If you check the Auto Flip check box, pages scroll at an interval automatically according to the number of seconds you select from the pull-down menu below the Auto Flip check box. Choices for the interval range from 1 to 32,767 seconds. You can select fixed interval options or type a value within the acceptable range. If you want to manually scroll pages, leave the check box disabled.

If you don't select pages in the Pages panel, you make choices for applying transitions to all pages or specify a page range in a contiguous order by clicking on the Pages range and typing in the page From and To field boxes. When you select pages in the Pages panel, the Pages Selected in the Pages panel check box becomes active by default and the transitions are applied to the selected pages.

After setting the effects and page range, click OK and transitions apply to the pages when you scroll pages in Edit mode.

TIP During your design phase and before you convert files to PDF, you can preview a slide show in Adobe Bridge. To preview a collection of CS4 files, open a folder in the Bridge window containing your native documents. Choose View ➪ Slide Show, or press ⌘/Ctrl+L. The Bridge window changes to a full screen view like you see in Acrobat. While in slide view, press H to access settings you can use when viewing the slides.

CROSS-REF For more information on viewing documents in slide view in Adobe Bridge, see Chapter 6.

Using Full Screen Views

The Full Screen view shows PDF pages without the presence of the Acrobat tools, title bar, menu, or palettes. Not only do Full Screen views offer you a different appearance for displaying PDF pages, but the mode is also necessary if you want to view certain effects. PowerPoint presentations with animation, for example, can only display effects created in the original PowerPoint file while viewing a PDF in Full Screen mode.

CROSS-REF For more information on creating PDF documents from PowerPoint files, see the "Converting Presentation Documents to PDF" section, earlier in this chapter.

Viewing slides in Acrobat

If you converted PowerPoint slides containing animation effects, such as motion objects and transitions, the animation is not viewable in Edit mode. You need to change the viewing mode to Full Screen mode. Press ⌘/Ctrl+L or choose Window ➪ Full Screen View to show the PDF in Full Screen mode. Press the Page Down key, press the down-arrow key, press Enter/Return, or click the mouse button to scroll pages. As you scroll pages, any animations associated with graphics or text are visible as long as you remain in Full Screen mode.

If you prepare presentations for clients and want to make it easier for them to launch Full Screen mode, you can save the PDF file so the document always opens in Full Screen view. Choose File ➪ Document Properties while the slide presentation is open and active in the Document pane. The Document Properties dialog box opens, as shown in Figure 31.23.

In the Document Properties dialog box, click on Initial View in the left pane and check the box for Open in Full Screen. Click OK, and save the file. The next time you open the PDF file either by double-clicking the document icon or by choosing File ⇨ Open inside Acrobat, the file opens in Full Screen mode.

Setting Full Screen preferences

If you want to set up a kiosk or workstation for viewing documents in Full Screen mode, start by making some choices in the Full Screen preferences. In the preference settings, you can control some of the viewing options. Choose Edit ⇨ Preferences on Windows or Acrobat ⇨ Preferences on the Mac. In the left pane, select Full Screen; the preference choices appear, as shown in Figure 31.24.

FIGURE 31.23

You activate Full Screen mode in the Document Properties dialog box.

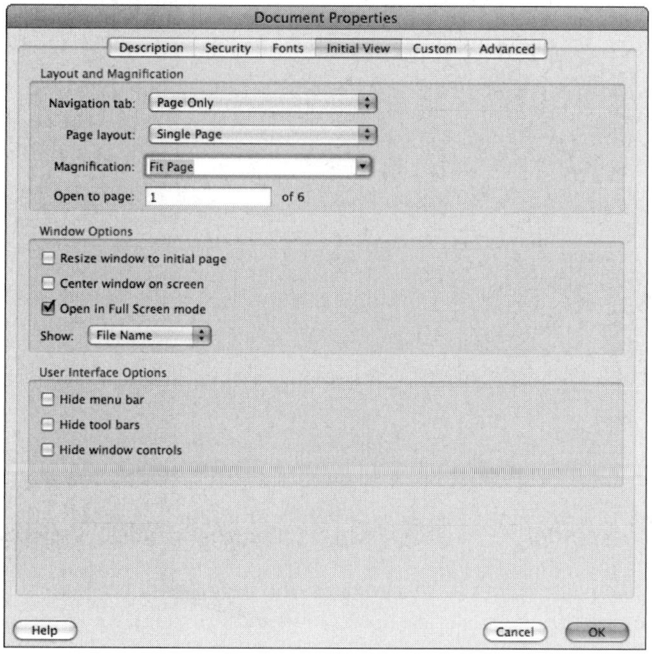

FIGURE 31.24

To open Full Screen preferences, press ⌘/Ctrl+K and click Full Screen in the left pane.

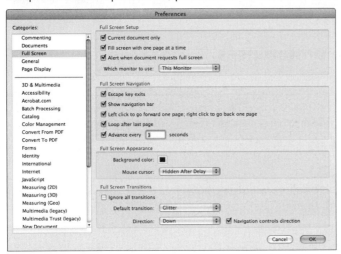

The preference choices include the following:

- **Current document only:** This option applies transitions to only the open document.

- **Full screen with one page at a time:** This option sets the page view to the maximum screen coverage by a single page.

- **Alert when document requests full screen:** When enabled, a warning dialog box opens asking you to confirm opening in full screen mode.

- **Escape key exits:** If you want to exit Full Screen view, you can strike the Esc key when you enable this check box. Be certain to leave the check box at the default switch. If you disable the check box, remember to use ⌘/Ctrl+L to exit Full Screen view.

- **Show navigation bar:** This option enables the viewer to use buttons for advancing and retracing pages.

- **Left-click to go forward one page; right-click to go back one page:** With this option, you can navigate pages with mouse clicks. For both Windows and Mac users who use a two-button mouse, clicking on the left or right button navigates pages in the respective direction.

- **Loop after last page:** Using this option and the preceding setting for auto-advancing, you can set up a kiosk and have the slide presentation continue with auto repetition. After the last page, the presentation starts again.

- **Advance every:** Enter a value in the text box to set the time interval for advancing to the next slide.

- **Background color:** Click on the color swatch, and the preset color palette opens; here, you can make choices for the background color. The background color appears outside the slide pages on all pages that don't fit precisely within the monitor frame. If you want to use a custom color, click on Other Color at the bottom of the palette and select a custom color from your system palette.

- **Mouse cursor:** You have three choices from the pull-down menu for the mouse-cursor display while viewing slides in Full Screen mode. You can choose from Always Visible, Always Hidden, or Hidden After Delay. The Hidden After Delay menu choice shows the cursor position when you scroll pages and then hides it after a short delay.

- **Ignore all transitions:** If you set transitions while in Edit mode and want to eliminate the transition effects while in Full Screen view, enable this option.

- **Default transition:** From the pull-down menu, you have choices for one of the same 49 different transition effects. If you apply a transition in the Full Screen preferences, then all pages use the same transition. Selecting Random from the menu choices offers you effects that change randomly as you move through slide pages. If you want to use specific transitions that change for selected pages, set the transitions from the Document ⇨ Pages ⇨ Page Transitions menu command before opening the Preferences dialog box. Disable Ignore All Transitions, and the effects you choose for page transitions applied to selected pages in the Pages Panel are used when you enter Full Screen mode.

- **Direction:** This option specifies the direction (Horizontal/Vertical or Up/Down, depending on the transition type).

Scrolling pages

To advance through slides when in Full Screen mode, you can use the preference setting and scroll pages with mouse clicks. If you disable the preference choice for left-click to go forward one page; right-click to go back one page, you scroll pages with keystrokes. Strike the Page Down or Page Up keys (or press the Spacebar or Enter/Return key) to move forward and press Shift+Enter/Return to move backward through slides. Additionally, you can use the up- or left-arrow keys to move backward and the down- or right-arrow keys to move forward. Use the Home key to move to the first page and the End key to move to the last page. If you want to move to a specific page without leaving Full Screen mode, press Shift+⌘/Ctrl+N and the Go to Page dialog box opens. Enter the page number to open in the field box, and click OK.

Creating interactivity in Full Screen mode

You may have a slide presentation that doesn't require access to Acrobat menus and tools, but you want to show cross-document links. Perhaps you design a presentation about a company's financial status, economic growth, or projected growth, and your client wants to show a financial spreadsheet, another PDF document, or a scanned image of a memo or report. The slideshow created in PowerPoint with the motion objects and viewing in Full Screen mode is what you want, but you also want the flexibility for opening other files without leaving the Full Screen mode.

Creating links and buttons for cross-document linking

If you want to open a secondary document while in Full Screen mode, you can create links or form-field buttons to secondary files. When you click on the link, the link action is invoked. If opening a secondary file, the file link opens in Full Screen mode. After viewing the file, press ⌘/Ctrl+W to close the file and you're returned to the last slide view also in Full Screen mode.

To set up a file link, create a link or form-field button and create a link to open a file. Acrobat offers you options for opening a linked document in the existing window or a new window. You can create the kind of file linking and views to make things easy on your clients, and they won't need to struggle finding files located on a hard drive or launching external applications. All the file linking and activation can be created with buttons in Acrobat.

CROSS-REF For information on creating interactive links and buttons, see Chapter 29.

You can also create URL links to display a Web site while in Full Screen mode by using the Open a Web Link action. Click on the link, and your Web browser opens at the specified URL. When you quit the Web browser, you're returned to the slide presentation in Full Screen mode. If you use PowerPoint effects, the effects aren't disturbed.

CROSS-REF To learn more about setting link actions to URLs, see Chapter 29.

TIP In Acrobat 7 and above, you do not need to create links to URLs using links or buttons. If you design your documents with URLs in text using the full URL address such as http://www.company.com (or www.company.com) before PDF creation, Acrobat 7 and above recognize the text as a link to a URL. Position the cursor over the text in Acrobat, and click. Your default Web browser is launched and opens the URL Web page.

Using interactive devices

Another interactivity tool that you can use with Full Screen view is a remote-control device. For about $50 to $75, you can purchase a handheld remote control. The control comes in two parts. The control device has two buttons used for moving forward and backward in the slide presentation. The companion unit is plugged into a USB port on a laptop or desktop computer. You open the slide presentation in Full Screen view and click the left or right button to navigate slides while you walk across a stage. Some devices also have a button for cursor control. You can remotely move the cursor on a slide and click on a button that opens a secondary file, Web link, or other action associated with the button or link.

When using remote devices, be certain to set your Full Screen preferences to left-click to go forward one page; right-click to go back one page.

Summary

- You convert PowerPoint slides to PDF with the PDFMaker macro.

- To create note handouts from PowerPoint, use the Print dialog box and print the file to the Adobe PDF Printer after making the attribute choices in the Print dialog box for the type of handouts you want to create.

- You can export Apple Keynote slides to PDF and PowerPoint formats. Keynote offers Macintosh users a robust slide-creation program with easy, intuitive palettes and tools.

- You can use layout programs such as InDesign to create slide presentations. For creating handout notes, set up a master page with objects and elements to be added to each page. Import the PDF slide presentation and convert to PDF.

- Adobe Illustrator can be used to create multipage PDF documents. New in Illustrator CS4 is support for multipage documents using multiple artboards.

- Layered PDFs add additional viewing options in slide presentations. To create layered PDFs, use programs, such as InDesign CS4 and Illustrator CS4, that support layers and that export to the PDF 1.5 format (Acrobat 6, 7, or 8 compatibility).

- Page transitions are applied to pages individually using the Document ➪ Pages ➪ Set Page Transitions command in Acrobat. To apply different transitions to different pages, select pages in the Pages panel and adjust the transitions in the Set Transitions dialog box.

- When using Full Screen mode, open the Preferences dialog box and select Full Screen.

- Full Screen views support file linking with link and button actions, Microsoft PowerPoint animation, and transitions applied to pages with either the Full Screen preferences or the Set Page Transitions command.

Chapter 32

Redacting Documents

Q uite simply, redaction is the deletion of information from a document. You may want to use redaction to remove sensitive information for security purposes, to protect rights and privacy information, to eliminate classified information, to delete names of minors in legal documents, or to delete any other information you don't want viewed by others.

Redaction is much different from blotting out or hiding text, graphics, handwriting, or any other kind of marks. If you use tools like some of the comment tools in Acrobat to create markups that blot out some text and graphics in a document, the items are not permanently deleted. The document appears fine onscreen where you can't see items marked for deletion on a document page, but the PDF document still contains the original items. If the file is distributed, other users can access marked text and other data.

To understand why redaction tools are needed to permanently delete content from a PDF document, see the following steps.

IN THIS CHAPTER

Understanding redaction

Using the redaction tools

STEPS: Understanding the need for redaction

1. **Open a PDF document in Acrobat.** Convert any InDesign CS file or an MS Office document to PDF, and open it in Acrobat.

2. **Open the Comment & Markup tools.** Open a context menu on the Toolbar Well, and select Comment and Markup. The Comment & Markup tools open in a floating toolbar.

3. **Mark out some text.** Select the Rectangle tool in the Comment & Markup toolbar. Draw a rectangle around some text. Alternately, you can use the Highlight tool so select text and hide it with a dark highlight color.

4. **Open the Rectangle Properties dialog box.** Right-click (Windows) or Control+click (Macintosh) to open a context menu on the rectangle. Select Properties from the context menu.

5. **Edit the properties.** Click the Color swatch for both Color and Fill Color. From the color choices select Black, as shown in Figure 32.1. Click the Make Properties Default check box. The next time you draw a rectangle, the rectangle will have the same style and fill color.

FIGURE 32.1

Set the Rectangle comment properties to black color and black fill.

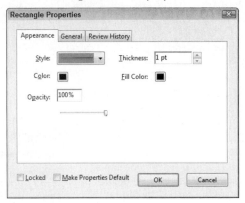

6. **Draw additional rectangles.** Using the rectangle comment tool, draw some additional rectangles to block out more text. Figure 32.2 shows a text document with several markings where I don't want the text to be seen. Onscreen this is fine, but the text is not deleted and can be extracted by other users.

7. **Copy the text.** Click the Select tool, and drag through the text to select it. Select Edit ➪ Copy to copy the text, as shown in Figure 32.3. Note that you also can use the Search pane to search for text that you marked. You'll notice that the search results report all the hidden text.

8. **Paste the text into a word processor.** In my example, I opened Microsoft Word and selected Edit ➪ Paste. As you can see in Figure 32.4, I was able to copy the text beneath all my comment markups.

As shown in Figure 32.4, this form of redacting a document doesn't delete the marked text. You need another method to mark and eliminate data from PDFs. This is where the Redaction tools in Acrobat 9 come into play.

FIGURE 32.2

Text onscreen is blocked out, but the text still can be extracted.

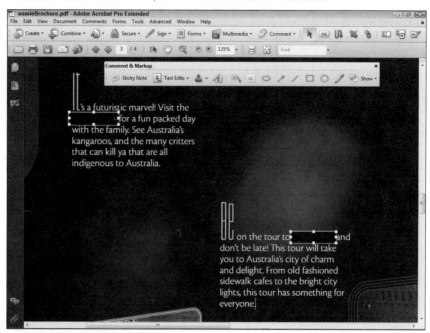

FIGURE 32.3

Drag through all the text with the Select tool, and choose Edit ⇨ Copy.

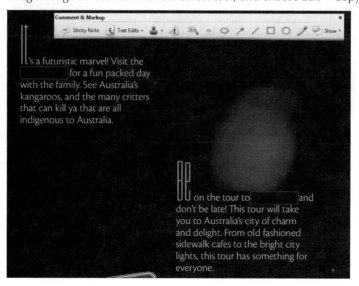

FIGURE 32.4

When you paste all the text into a Word processor, the marked out text appears in the new document window.

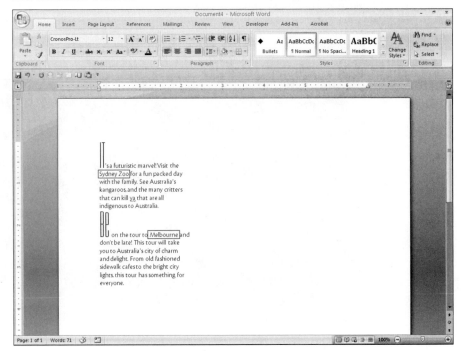

Using the Redaction Tools

Redaction is permanently deleting text, graphics, signatures, handwriting, and any other data you desire to remove from a document. In addition to marking and deleting text and other data that you can see, a good redaction tool also provides you a means for deleting certain metadata and hidden information in a file so that all the content you decide you want to eliminate cannot be retrieved by anyone viewing your PDF files.

Acrobat 9 offers a few solutions for marking content for deletion, applying the redactions, eliminating metadata, and eliminating any hidden text. You first start a redaction session using the Redaction tools. When you open the Redaction toolbar by either selecting View ➪ Toolbars ➪ Redaction, choosing Advanced ➪ Redaction ➪ Show Redaction Toolbar, or selecting the toolbar in the More Tools window, the tools contained in the toolbar appear as you see in Figure 32.5.

FIGURE 32.5

The Redaction toolbar contains four tools.

The tools on the Redaction toolbar are as follows:

- **Mark for Redaction.** Use this tool to mark text and other data that you want to delete from a document. Marking the content does not yet delete it from the file.

- **Apply Redactions.** When you are ready to permanently delete content that you marked for deletion, click the Apply Redactions tool.

- **Redaction Properties.** Use this tool to set the redaction marking properties. You can mark content using the Mark for Redaction tool, and the markings can be adjusted for color and other attributes in the Redaction Properties dialog box. Click the tool, and the Redaction Properties dialog box shown in Figure 32.6 opens.

FIGURE 32.6

Click the Redaction Properties tool, and the Redaction Properties dialog box opens.

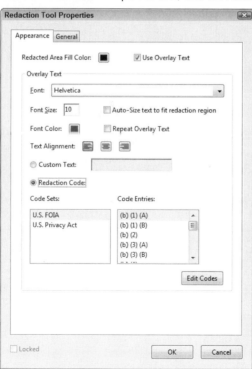

As you can see in the Redaction Properties dialog box, you can select a color for your redaction marks, use text as an overlay, specify the font for the overlay text, set a number of different font attributes for the overlay text, and select from some redaction code standards. When you change the properties in this dialog box, the properties remain in effect for all redaction marks you make on a document until you again adjust settings in the Redaction Properties dialog box.

■ **Search and Redact.** This tool is a powerful addition to the Redaction tools. Click the Search and Redact tool, and the Search window opens as shown in Figure 32.7. Type a word or phrase in the first field text box, and choose a location. Your options include searching the open document or a folder location on your hard drive or network server. You can mark content for redaction in a collection of PDF documents contained in a common folder. Select the All PDF Documents in radio button. From the pull-down menu below the radio button, select Browse for Location. The Browse For Folder dialog box opens, and you select a folder containing files you want to redact.

FIGURE 32.7

Click the Search and Redact button, and the Search window opens. Type a word or phrase, and select either the open document or a folder of PDFs to mark for redaction.

Click the Search and Redact button in the Search window, and the Search window reports results of your search, as shown in Figure 32.8. As yet, no items have been marked for redaction. In the results list, you see the reported results appearing next to check marks. If you want all items in the list to be redacted, click the Check All button. If you want to individually mark the results items, scroll the list checking the boxes adjacent to the items you want to redact.

FIGURE 32.8

Click Check All or individually check the items you want to redact in the open PDF or from a collection of PDF files.

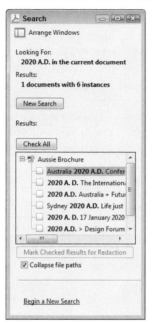

Redacting PDF Files

The tool set and options for redaction are very straightforward and intuitive. In the first section of this chapter, you looked at marking files to hide content that didn't remove the items you marked. Let's compare that first effort with a true redaction that Acrobat 9 provides you by following some steps.

STEPS: Redacting a PDF document

1. **Open a file from which you want to eliminate some content by using the Redaction tools.**

2. **Click the Mark for Redaction tool.**

   When you first click the Mark for Redaction tool, the Using Redaction Tools help dialog box opens, as shown in Figure 32.9. This dialog box provides you some instructions on redacting documents. If you don't want the dialog box to open in future redaction sessions, click the Don't show again check box.

Using Redactions

The Redaction Tool Properties window contains choices for using Redaction Codes. These codes comply with U.S. codes for legal and rights and privacy issues and are designed for use by the U.S. legal system. Graphic designers who have clients in the courts may use the codes when the time arises; however, the most frequent uses designers may have for redactions is when providing clients with design concepts.

If you have certain layouts that require revisions, such as an annual county fair poster, a conference program schedule, an annual sale, and so on, you might use redactions on the previous year's artwork to eliminate dates, venues, graphics, and other items that may change for the next event. You can delete old text and replace it with new text for developing a new concept for your client's approval.

FIGURE 32.9

When you first click the Mark for Redaction tool, the Using Redaction Tools help dialog box opens.

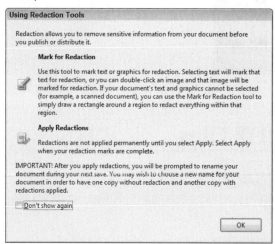

3. **Mark a graphic for redaction.** If you have a graphic in the file either as a vector object or an image file, you can remove it just like removing text. In my example, the logo is a vector graphic object. Clicking the Mark for Redaction tool changes the cursor to a crosshair when positioned over a graphic or an I-beam cursor when positioned over text. Draw a marquee around the object, as shown in Figure 32.10, or drag the I-beam cursor through text you want to redact.

 If you want to quickly mark a graphic object for redaction, select the Mark for Redaction tool and double-click the graphic.

FIGURE 32.10

Draw a marquee around a graphic or select text to mark for redaction.

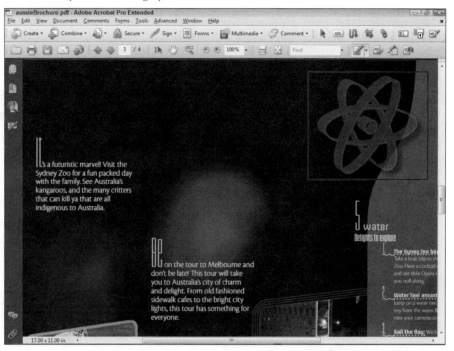

4. **Mark text for redaction.** Drag the I-beam cursor through the first occurrence of text you want to redact. In our example, we dragged through a country name we want to remove from the file.

5. **Click the Search and Redact tool.** The Search window opens. Type any other occurrence of the text you want to redact. In our example, we typed the same name as the first text marked for redaction. Click the Search and Redact button, and the first occurrence of the word to be redacted is highlighted.

6. **Check all occurrences for redaction.** In the Search window, click the Check All button and all occurrences of the search results are now marked for redaction.

7. **Mark the search results for redaction.** After clicking the Check All button, the Mark Checked Results for Redaction button appears in the Search window. Click this button, and all occurrences of the search results are now marked for redaction, as shown in Figure 32.11.

8. **Continue marking all the content you want to eliminate in your document.** If you have other text or graphics you want to redact, follow Steps 3 through 7 for each redaction.

9. **Apply redactions.** Click the Apply Redactions tool. A warning dialog box opens. Click Yes, and the redactions are applied.

FIGURE 32.11

After clicking Check All or individually checking the items you want to redact in the open PDF or from a collection of PDF files, click the Mark Checked Results for Redaction button.

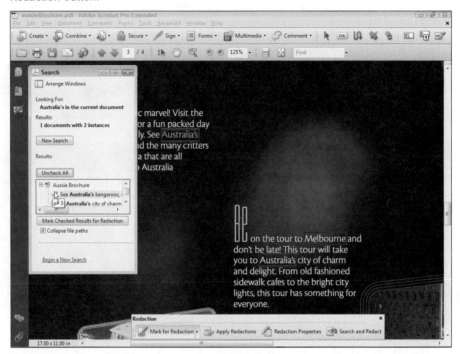

10. **Redact additional content.** After Acrobat redacts the items you marked, a dialog box opens confirming your action and prompts you to examine the document for additional content. Click Yes in the dialog box shown in Figure 32.12.

11. **Examine the document.** When you click Yes in the confirmation dialog box, the Examine Document panel opens in the Navigation pane. A number of different items can appear in your file that don't appear on the document pages. You may have metadata, hidden text, file attachments, hidden layers, bookmarks, and other items that use the same text you want to delete. To be certain that all information is deleted from the document, the Examine Document panel provides a list of found items matching the items you deleted. Click the Remove button at the bottom of the panel, as shown in Figure 32.13, and all the selected items are removed.

12. **Verify that the redactions were made.** If you used objects with fills to redact the document, these objects are selectable and you can delete them. Select Tools⇨Advanced Editing⇨Touchup Object Tool to select the Touchup Object tool. Move the tool to one of your marks and click. Press the Delete (Del) key on your keyboard, and the redaction frame is deleted. You can easily see that the redaction process did indeed remove the underlying content.

FIGURE 32.12

Click Yes to open the Examine Document dialog box.

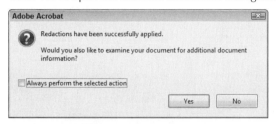

FIGURE 32.13

Click the Remove button in the Examine Document panel to eliminate any other occurrences of the text and graphics you want to delete.

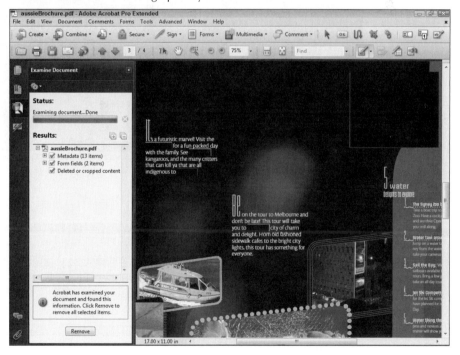

You should see that the text beneath the redaction frames truly has been deleted from your document. When you use the select tool and drag through the text, you'll notice that no selection appears where you redacted text (and/or objects), as shown in Figure 32.14. Alternately, you can verify redactions by opening the Search window and invoking a search for the words you redacted. You should see no results reported for all text that was redacted.

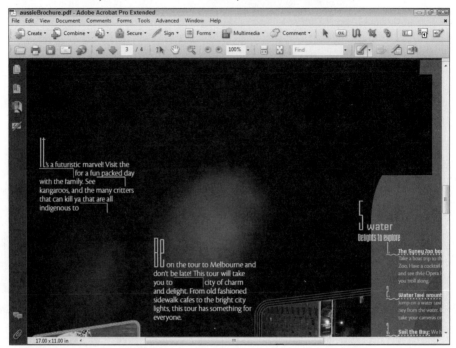

FIGURE 32.14

After removing redaction marks and selecting all the text, the redacted file shows you that all the text/objects have been successfully deleted from the file.

Summary

- Redaction involves permanently removing data from a file.

- Only Acrobat 9 Professional and Professional Extended contain tools for redacting content, searching and redacting, applying redactions, and examining documents for content not visible on pages.

- Using tools other than the Redaction tools won't delete data from PDF files.

- Redaction marks can be modified for color changes, the use of text, and formatted text used to replace deleted data.

Part VIII

Deploying Documents

This part has to do with distributing files for screen views. We begin in Chapter 33 by introducing the new Acrobat.com online share space you have available when upgrading to Acrobat 9. The free Acrobat.com service is an online library for your documents to be shared and exchanged with your clients.

Chapter 34 covers many things you can do to optimize your files for screen viewing. In Chapter 35 you learn about preparing files to share with others. Chapter 36 shows how to set up shared reviews so you can interact with clients to refine layouts and ad campaigns.

More dynamic real time conferencing comes to you in the Creative Suite 4 applications. In Chapter 37 we talk about how you can use Adobe ConnectNow to host live review sessions and campaign pitches to your clients.

As a new revenue source you can add Yahoo! ads to PDF documents for your own design firm and for your clients. Chapter 38 covers adding Yahoo! ads.

Chapter 33

Using Acrobat.com

A crobat.com is an Adobe service and not really part of any application. The service was first introduced along with the release of Acrobat 9, which has a variety of menu commands to access services found on Acrobat.com. In addition, all the Creative Suite 4 applications have menu commands that enable you to get to Acrobat.com for Web conferencing.

Any user of any application can make use of the Acrobat.com services. You don't have to be a user of any particular Adobe software application to use Acrobat.com. You can use these free services to share files, distribute forms, host and participate in Web conferences, and use the Adobe Buzzword service for an online word processor.

Because you don't have to be an Adobe software user to access Acrobat.com, interacting with clients and refining concepts and ad campaigns is much easier for designers using Creative Suite applications.

In this chapter, we cover getting started using Acrobat.com and in Chapters 30, 35, 36, and 37, we talk about specific services you might use with forms, file sharing, review sessions, and Web conferencing. Consider this chapter your gateway to the Acrobat.com service center where you can explore the many options that this service affords.

IN THIS CHAPTER

Setting up your Acrobat.com login

Exploring the Acrobat.com services

Getting started on Acrobat.com

Obtaining an Adobe ID

Regardless of the type of activity you want to use on Acrobat.com, you need to create an Adobe ID. Creating an Adobe ID is merely registering your login name and password with Adobe. No personal information is obtained when you create an Adobe ID, and you can use your ID for a number of services at Adobe, such as purchasing products at the Adobe Store and registering for PDF Ads Powered by Yahoo!.

CROSS-REF For more information on PDF Ads Powered by Yahoo!, see Chapter 38.

If you don't have an Adobe ID, you can obtain one in several ways. When you log onto Acrobat. com (www.acrobat.com), the welcome screen provides you several choices for activities you can do there. Click any of the icons, and you are prompted to sign in with your Adobe ID, as shown in Figure 33.1.

FIGURE 33.1

Click any of the icons on the welcome page at www.acrobat.com, and you are prompted to sign in.

If you don't have an Adobe ID, click the Sign Up! text in the lower-left corner of the pop-up window. The Sign Up! pop-up window opens, and you are prompted to supply information for your Adobe ID account, as shown in Figure 33.2.

Fill in the text boxes for e-mail, password, and name; select your country from the pull-down menu; and check the box for agreeing to the terms of the service. When you click Begin, you'll be notified that an e-mail message is sent to your e-mail account. When the message arrives in your e-mail inbox, you'll find a URL link in the message. Click the link, and you've completed your Adobe ID registration.

The next time you log onto Acrobat.com, use your e-mail address for the Adobe ID and type your password, and you can enter your library on Acrobat.com.

FIGURE 33.2

The sign-up screen for Acrobat.com

You also may create an Adobe ID by choosing Share My Screen in any of the Creative Suite applications or from a number of different menu commands in the File ⇨ Collaborate submenu in Acrobat 9. Regardless of how you get to Acrobat.com, the first step you need to perform is creating an Adobe ID.

Knowing the Acrobat.com Services

When you arrive at Acrobat.com, you find five icons on the welcome page. Clicking any of the icons shown in Figure 33.3 first prompts you for your Adobe ID login and then takes you to the respective service. The services include:

FIGURE 33.3

The welcome page of Acrobat.com displays five icons representing access to various services.

- **Adobe Buzzword:** Adobe Buzzword is an Adobe Flash-based word processor. You can write documents online, and the files are stored in your Acrobat.com library. You don't need to be concerned about saving files on a flash drive and copying to a laptop when you're on the road. You can access your Buzzword documents wherever you have an Internet connection. Buzzword documents can be shared, reviewed, and co-authored with other Acrobat.com/Buzzword users. The documents can be exported in a number of useful file formats including Word, RTF, and text files.

- **Acrobat ConnectNow:** This version of Acrobat Connect is a free service for Web conferencing where you can have up to three people in a meeting room complete with VOIP and screen sharing.

CROSS-REF   For more information on Web conferencing, see Chapter 37.

- **Create PDF:** This option enables you to convert up to five native files to PDF. The service is intended for Adobe Reader users who do not have PDF creation opportunities in the free Reader software.

- **Share:** You use Share for sharing files with colleagues, coworkers, and clients.

CROSS-REF   For more information on sharing files on Acrobat.com, see Chapter 35.

- **My Files:** Click My Files, and you are taken to your Acrobat.com online library. Here you find all the files you've shared, forms you've distributed, Buzzword documents you created, and files others have shared with you, and you have access to all the other services provided by Acrobat.com.

Logging onto Acrobat.com

You can always open your Web browser and navigate to www.acrobat.com to access your Acrobat.com library. If you happen to be working in Acrobat or Adobe Reader, you can choose File ➪ Collaborate ➪ Go to Acrobat.com. When you choose the menu command, you are prompted in Acrobat to supply your Adobe ID, as shown in Figure 33.4.

Type your login e-mail address and password, and click Sign In. Your default Web browser launches and takes you to Acrobat.com. If you regularly visit Acrobat.com, you can set up your Acrobat preferences to remember your login information so you don't need to type your Adobe ID and password each time you log on.

To set your preferences in Acrobat for remembering your Adobe ID and password, open the Preferences dialog box by pressing Ctrl/⌘+K. In the left pane, click Acrobat.com, and the right pane changes to display the options you have from within Acrobat for handling your Acrobat.com login, as shown in Figure 33.5.

FIGURE 33.4

FIGURE 33.4

When you choose Go to Acrobat.com from within Acrobat, the Acrobat.com login dialog box opens.

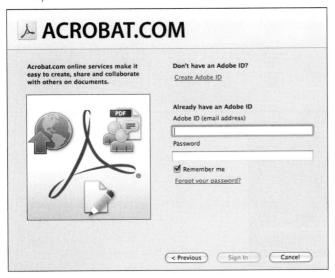

FIGURE 33.5

Open the Acrobat preferences, and click Acrobat.com in the left pane to display options for Acrobat.com login in the right pane.

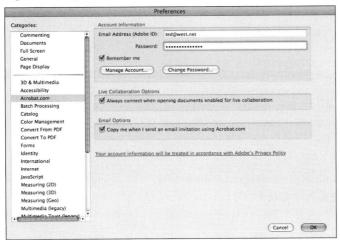

Type your login Adobe ID, and check the Remember Me box. When this box is checked, you can type your password in the Password text box. Click OK, and each time you log onto Acrobat.com, your Adobe ID and password are automatically handled by Acrobat.

From any other CS application, you can access Acrobat.com and Web conferencing by choosing File ➪ Share My Screen. When you make this choice in any of the CS programs, the Adobe ConnectNow login dialog box opens, as shown in Figure 33.6.

FIGURE 33.6

Choose File ➪ Share My Screen to open the Adobe ID login dialog box.

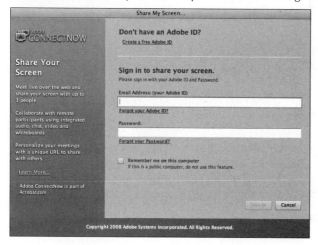

Choosing Share My Screen takes you to a ConnectNow meeting room that is part of Acrobat.com. You won't see your library by choosing this menu command.

Logging onto Acrobat.com via your Web browser or by choosing Go to Acrobat.com from the File ➪ Collaborate menu in Acrobat or Adobe Reader takes you to the welcome page. To view your library of files, click the My Files icon; all the files in your library are shown in the Acrobat.com user interface, as shown in Figure 33.7.

After you're logged into Acrobat.com, you have options for browsing files, creating PDFs online, sharing files, analyzing data from collected forms that were distributed, uploading and downloading files, accessing Adobe Buzzword, accessing Acrobat ConnectNow, maintaining a contacts list, and sending e-mails to invite people to view your files.

CROSS-REF For information on analyzing form data, see Chapter 30. For information on sharing files, see Chapter 35. For information on conducting review sessions, see Chapter 36. For information on Web conferencing, see Chapter 37.

FIGURE 33.7

Click My Files on the Acrobat.com welcome page, and you are taken to your library on Acrobat.com.

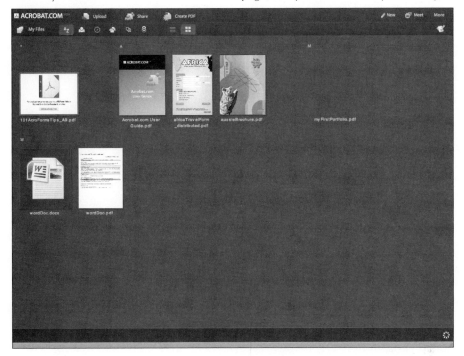

Summary

- Acrobat.com is a separate service provided by Adobe systems and doesn't require purchase of any Adobe product. The services on Acrobat.com are free.

- Before you can log onto Acrobat.com, you must first create an Adobe ID.

- Accessing Acrobat.com can be accomplished by typing www.acrobat.com in your Web browser's Location bar or by choosing from a variety of menu commands in Acrobat or Adobe Reader.

- Accessing Acrobat ConnectNow for Web conferencing can be handled via the File ➪ Share My Screen found in all CS applications except Acrobat.

- When you log onto Acrobat.com, you arrive at your library where you can see files you've uploaded and files sent to you by other users.

Chapter 34

Preparing Documents for Distribution

Electronic documents are often created for one purpose and eventually modified to suit another purpose. You may initially create a design piece for print where images are optimized for high-resolution output and later want to modify the design piece for screen viewing, where image-resolution requirements are significantly less than for print. Taking a document designed for one purpose and modifying it for another purpose is known as document repurposing.

To prepare files for distribution electronically, via the Web, or on CD-ROM/DVDs, you may need to resample files for image resolutions appropriate for viewing, set viewing attributes suited for on-screen viewing, and create search indexes for easy access to selected files. In this chapter, we discuss preparing files for a variety of output purposes and how to optimize files for viewing.

IN THIS CHAPTER

Optimizing documents for various output solutions

Setting initial views

Creating search indexes

Searching index files

Repurposing Documents

One of the more common needs for repurposing documents is taking a file originally designed for print and modifying it for downloading from a Web site. For high-resolution output, image files can be 300 ppi (pixels per inch) or more. For Web viewing and viewing documents on your computer monitor, you need file sizes of 72 ppi when viewing in a 100 percent view. Files with lower resolutions are smaller; when you are downloading documents from a Web server, smaller file sizes mean shorter download times.

Native files created in Illustrator, Photoshop and InDesign require much more work to modify documents originally designed for print to a file suited for Web hosting. Furthermore, you must convert files hosted on the Web to either PDF or HTML to make them easily accessible to other users.

Fortunately, if files are converted to PDF for any kind of output, you can easily repurpose a file for other types of output. There is one caveat in this notion: You can repurpose files for downward optimization only. In other words, you can take a document with high-resolution images designed for print and downsize the images to make it suitable for Web viewing, but you cannot upsize a Web-designed document and make it suitable for print.

The ideal file format for documents you want to repurpose is PDF. You can convert a page layout in InDesign to PDF while keeping all images at high resolution and send off the document to a commercial printer for high-end prepress and printing. You can then take the same PDF and *down-sample* images (reduce the file sizes) for a piece to be hosted on a Web site or electronically exchanged with other users. When you're using PDFs for your output needs, you have several ways to repurpose files through Acrobat menus and commands.

Reducing file size

Reduce File Size is a menu command found in the Document menu in both Acrobat Standard and Acrobat Professional. Choose Document ➪ Reduce File Size, and the Reduce File Size dialog box opens, shown in Figure 34.1.

FIGURE 34.1

The Reduce File Size dialog box

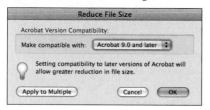

From the pull-down menu in the Reduce File Size dialog box, you have six options for Acrobat PDF compatibility. The more recent the Acrobat compatibility, the more file-size reduction you can expect. Therefore, using Acrobat 8 or 9 compatibility reduces a PDF document size more than using either Acrobat 4 or Acrobat 5 compatibility.

The Reduce File Size command offers you a simple tool for reducing file size and offers no options choices for how much image sampling you can apply to the file-size reduction. If you're using Acrobat Standard, the Reduce File Size command is the only tool you have available in Acrobat to reduce file sizes. For Acrobat Pro and Pro Extended users you have another option using the PDF Optimizer. (See "Using PDF Optimizer" later in this chapter.)

After choosing Acrobat compatibility, click OK and the Save As dialog box opens. Find a folder location on your hard drive, supply a filename, and click Save. Acrobat uses an internal algorithm to downsample images and adds compression, thereby reducing file size.

If you want to examine file size after exercising the command and saving a new file, choose File ⇨ Document Properties or press ⌘/Ctrl+D. The Document Properties dialog box, shown in Figure 34.2, appears. Click the Description tab, and you can see the file size noted at the bottom of the dialog box.

FIGURE 34.2

The Document Properties dialog box

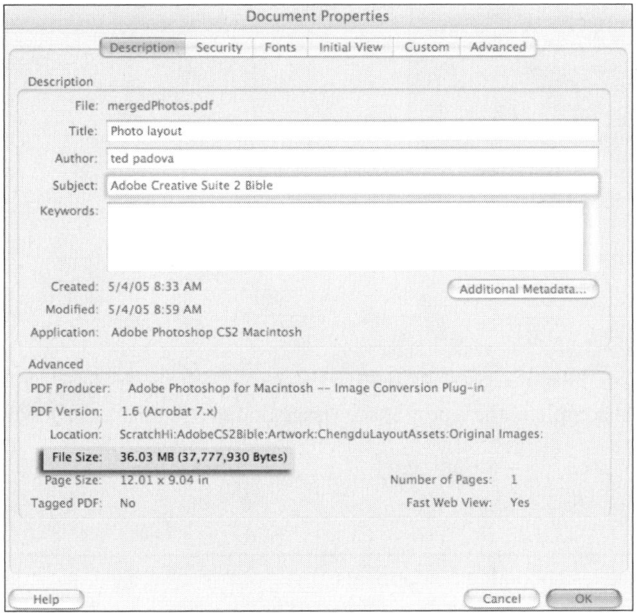

Using PDF Optimizer

A much more sophisticated approach to optimizing files and reducing their size is to use the PDF Optimizer, found only in Acrobat Pro and Pro Extended. The PDF Optimizer reduces file sizes through downsampling images according to user-specified amounts and a variety of other settings that offer options for eliminating unnecessary data. With the Reduce File Size command in the last section, you don't have user-definable settings to determine how file reduction affects data. With PDF Optimizer, you can choose different settings to determine what data is affected during optimization. The PDF Optimizer also offers you an option for analyzing a file so you can see what part of the PDF document occupies higher percentages of memory.

Auditing space usage

You analyze a document and use the PDF Optimizer (shown in Figure 34.3) by choosing Advanced ⇨ PDF Optimizer. The first step in optimizing files with the PDF Optimizer is to analyze a file so you can see what content occupies the larger amounts of memory.

FIGURE 34.3

The PDF Optimizer dialog box

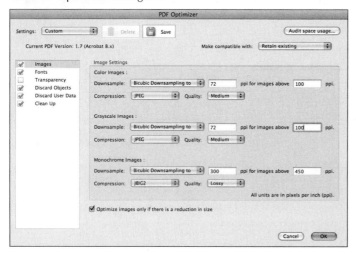

Click Audit space usage. Depending on the size and complexity of the document, the analysis can take a little time. When the analysis is complete, the Audit Space Usage dialog box appears, shown in Figure 34.4.

FIGURE 34.4

After the analysis is completed, the Audit Space Usage dialog box appears.

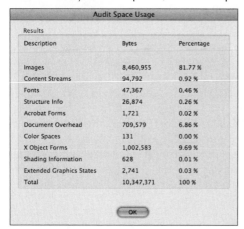

In the example shown in Figure 34.4, notice that over 80 percent of the document space is used for images. The analysis informs you that because images occupy such a large percentage of the space, you should be able to resample images at lower resolutions to reduce file size.

Optimizing files

The file analyzed in Figure 34.4 was originally created for professional printing, and the images are all sampled at 300 ppi. To repurpose the document and reduce the file size for Web hosting, the images need to be resampled at 72 ppi. Using the PDF Optimizer, you can specify image-size reductions as well as perform cleanup of content that occupies space for unnecessary items like comments, bookmarks, destinations, or other items that add to overhead in the file.

Image settings

To reduce file size with the PDF Optimizer, use the first set of options that opens in the Images tab, as shown in Figure 34.3. You can make choices for downsampling color, grayscale, and bit-map images by typing values in the field boxes for the sampling amounts desired. In our example, we edited the field boxes for color and grayscale images and chose 72 ppi as the amount of down-sampling. To the right of the downsampling amount, another field box is used to identify images that are downsampled. In this box, we added 100 ppi, which instructs Acrobat to look for any image above 100 ppi and downsample the file to the amount supplied in the first field box—in this example, to 72 ppi. Other options in the PDF Optimizer dialog box include the following:

- **Downsample pull-down menu:** Offers choices for Retain Existing, JPEG, and Zip. Retain Existing retains the compression used when you convert the original document to PDF. JPEG is a lossy compression scheme while Zip is lossless.

- **Compression:** When JPEG is selected, different Quality options are available to control the amount of compression for the JPEG format.

- **Quality:** Five options offer choices for image quality when using JPEG compression. Use Medium for repurposing files for Web hosting.

- **Monochrome images:** Monochrome images are 1-bit line art images (black and white). Monochrome images are best sampled no lower than 300 ppi for better quality displays. Use Bicubic Downsampling to for the Downsample option and CCITT4 for the best quality.

Fonts settings

When you click the Fonts tab in the PDF Optimizer, only fonts available for unembedding are listed. On the left side of the dialog box, fonts are listed that can be unembedded. If no fonts appear in the list, you can move on to the next tab. If fonts are listed in the left window, select the fonts to unembed and click the Move button adjacent to the right chevron.

On the right side of the dialog box are fonts listed for unembedding. If you want to keep the font embedded, select it in the right window and click the Move button adjacent to left chevron. To select multiple fonts in either window, Shift-click to select a list in a contiguous group, or ⌘/Ctrl-click to select fonts in a noncontiguous group.

Transparency settings

You can flatten transparency and save the file with the flattening adjustments made in this pane. This item is more applicable for files going to print rather than repurposing for Web hosting.

 For more information on transparency flattening, see Chapter 40.

Discard Objects settings

Items such as JavaScript, embedded thumbnails, hidden layers, and so on, are contained in this pane. Be careful to not select items that may render the PDF document nonfunctional. If there are JavaScript that execute actions, be certain to preserve the fields and scripts.

Discard User Data

Items such as comments, metadata, file attachments, hidden layers, and so on are discarded when you check the respective check boxes.

Clean Up settings

Click the Clean Up tab and you find a list of items checked by default that you can safely use without affecting the functionality of your document. You can enable all other items that appear unchecked, but you should have an idea of what will happen to the PDF, in terms of functionality, if you optimize the file with any additional items checked. If you check one or more of the items and return to the PDF Optimizer, the new checked items in the Clean Up section of the PDF Optimizer or any other pane become a new set of default settings. To restore the PDF Optimizer to original defaults, click Settings pull-down menu and change from Custom shown in Figure 34.5 to Standard.

FIGURE 34.5

By default, a partial list of Clean Up settings is checked.

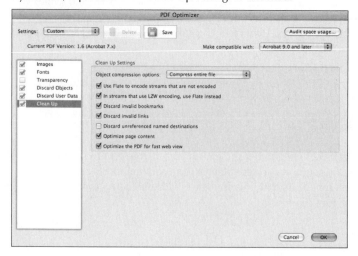

After you make your preferred settings in the PDF Optimizer, click OK and wait for the processing to finish. As a comparison between using Reduce File Size and the PDF Optimizer, using the same file with an original file size of 3.06MB, we reduced the file size with the Reduce File Size command and produced a PDF that was resampled to 454KB. The same file processed with PDF Optimizer was reduced to 285KB. The increased file reduction from PDF Optimizer was due to eliminating some document overhead and structural information.

Notice the Save button in the PDF Optimizer. Click this button and all settings you make to change the Standard options to a new Custom set can be saved. After saving the settings, the new set appears in the Settings pull-down menu. This option is particularly helpful when adjusting transparency and preparing files for print.

Setting Document Open Preferences

When users acquire your PDF documents from media disks, from Web downloads, from network servers, or from documents you send via e-mail, one double-click on the file opens the PDF in a user's default Acrobat viewer. The initial view of the PDF in the Document pane is the opening view. Depending on which user preferences are set up on a given computer, the initial view conforms to the preference settings, unless you specifically assign open view preferences and save them within a document.

To understand document viewing preferences, choose Acrobat ➪ Preferences (Mac) or Edit ➪ Preferences (Windows) or press ⌘/Ctrl+K to open the Preferences dialog box. Click Page Display in the left pane, and the options choices for initial views appear in the right pane. From the pull-down menu options at the top of the dialog box, you have choices for Default page layout where you can choose which additional panes you want to display when the file is opened—items such as Page Only, Bookmarks and Page, Layers and Page, and so on are available. The Default zoom pull-down menu offers choices for several zoom magnifications as you can see in Figure 34.6.

The preferences choices made here affect all PDF documents that you open in Acrobat on your computer where no initial view has been saved inside a PDF file. For example, you can view a PDF document at a 100% view as long as Default was selected for the initial view when the file was last saved. Typically, all PDF documents exported from the CS applications save PDFs with default selections unless you specifically assign an initial view when creating the PDF.

Setting initial views

If you distribute a collection of PDF documents and use interactive buttons to open and close files for users to browse different documents, you may want to embed initial views in all your PDF documents. Because the Default view depends on settings assigned by each user, your files could conceivably be shown at different sizes depending on how a given user sets the Page Display preferences.

You can keep the viewing of your files consistent by embedding initial views in files. To set a view and save that opening view as part of the PDF, choose File ➪ Document Properties or ⌘/Ctrl+D. In the Document Properties dialog box, click Initial View at the top of the dialog box, and the choices available for setting initial views appear as shown in Figure 34.7.

FIGURE 34.6

Choices for various viewing options when you first open a PDF

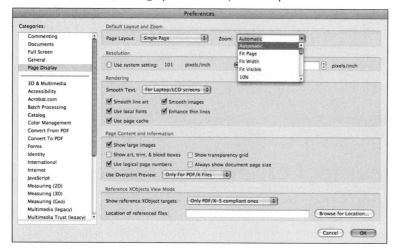

FIGURE 34.7

Setting initial views as part of the PDF document

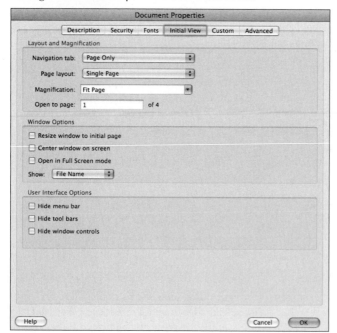

In this dialog box, you make choices for the opening view and viewing magnification. When no settings have been saved with a file, the individual user preferences prevail. Acrobat provides you with many different choices for controlling the initial view of a PDF when opened in any Acrobat viewer. Settings you make here can be saved with your document. When you establish settings other than defaults, the settings saved with the file override the end user's default settings. The options available to you for controlling the initial view include the following:

- **Layout and Magnification:** The default opening page is the first page of a PDF document. You can change the opening page to another page, and you can control the page-layout views and magnification by selecting choices from the Document Options section. The choices include:

  - **Navigation tab:** Four choices are available from the pull-down menu. Select Page Only to open the page with the Navigation Pane collapsed. Use Bookmarks Panel and Page to open the Bookmarks tab when the file opens. Use Pages Panel and Page to open the Pages tab where the thumbnails of pages are viewed. Use Attachments panel and Page to show file attachments in the Attachments pane. Use Layers Panel and Page to open the Layers tab when the file opens.

  - **Page Layout:** The default for Page Layout is noted in the pull-down menu as Default. When you save a PDF file with the Default selection, the PDF opens according to the default setting a user has set for page viewing on the user's computer. To override the user's default, you can set a page layout in the opening view from one of seven choices. Choose Single Page to open the PDF in a single-page layout. Choose Single Page Continuous to open in a single page continuous page view. Choose Two-Up Facing to open with facing pages, Two-Up Continuous for facing pages in a continuous view, Two-Up (Cover) to show facing pages with a cover page, or use Two-Up Continuous (Cover Page) to open with a cover page and continuous facing pages.

  - **Magnification:** Choose from preset magnification views from the pull-down menu. If you want the PDF document to open in a fit-in-window view, select Fit Page. Choose from other magnification options in the pull-down menu or edit the field box for a custom zoom level.

  - **Open to page:** You can change the opening page to another page by entering a number in the field for Page Number. You might use this setting if you wanted a user to see a contents page instead of a title page. If Last-viewed page is selected you need to open the Startup preferences and change the "Reopen Documents to Last Viewed Page" option. Select Digital Editions only from the menu choices and you can select a page to open in the Document Properties. If you select the All Files option in the Startup Preferences, options for opening to specific pages is grayed out.

- **Window Options:** The default window for Acrobat is a full screen where the viewing area is maximized to occupy your monitor surface area. You can change the window view to size down the window to the initial page size, center a smaller window on-screen, and open a file in Full Screen mode. If you enable all three check boxes, the Full Screen mode prevails.

- **Show:** From the pull-down menu choose either File Name or Document Title. If File Name is selected, the title bar at the top of the Acrobat window shows the filename. If Document Title is used, the information you supply in the Document Properties dialog box for Document Title is shown in the title bar.

- **User Interface Options:** The Interface Options in the Initial View Document Properties dialog box have to do with user-interface items in Acrobat viewers such as menu bars, toolbars, and scrollbars. You can elect to hide these items when the PDF document opens in any Acrobat viewer; however, in Acrobat 9 only two of the three check boxes can be enabled at one time. You can hide any one or a combination of the three items listed under the User Interface Options as long as you don't choose all three options. When the Hide menu bar and Hide tool bars options are chosen, the PDF is viewed as shown in Figure 34.8. If you elect to save files without the menu bar and toolbars in view, it's a good idea to create navigational buttons so users can move around in your document.

FIGURE 34.8

Here, toolbars and the menu bar are hidden.

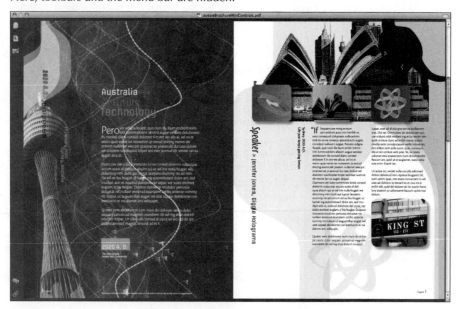

At the user level, individual users can hide the Navigation pane by opening a context menu in the pane and choosing Hide Navigation Panel Buttons. As a PDF author, however, you cannot force this view when the window controls for the menu bar and the toolbars are hidden. In Figure 34.9, the Navigation pane is in view on the left and hidden on the right.

FIGURE 34.9

From a context menu, choose Hide Navigation Panel Buttons and the Navigation pane is hidden (right).

Navigation pane

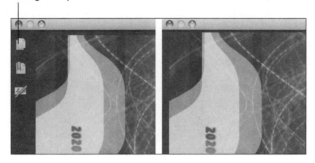

CAUTION If you elect to eliminate the toolbars and menu bar from view and later want to go back and edit your file, you need to use shortcut keys to get the menu bars and toolbars back. Be certain to remember the F8 and F9 keys (Windows) —F8 shows/hides the toolbars and F9 shows/hides the menu bar. On the Mac, F8 shows/hides the toolbars and Shift+⌘+M shows/hides the menu bar.

Saving the initial view

When you decide which view attributes you want assigned to your document, you can choose between one of two save options. The first option updates the file. Click the Save tool in the Acrobat File toolbar or choose File ➪ Save. Any edits you make in the Initial View properties activates the Save command. The Save command is inactive and grayed out by default until you make any changes to your file or reset any kind of preferences that can be saved with the document.

The second method for updating your file uses the Save As command. When you choose File ➪ Save As, the Save As dialog box opens. The default filename is the same name as the file you opened. If you elect to save the file to the same folder where it resides, Acrobat prompts you with a warning dialog box asking whether you want to overwrite the file. Click Replace and the file is rewritten. There are many times during your Acrobat sessions that using Save As will be a benefit. As you work on documents, they retain more information than necessary to view and print the file. By using Save As and overwriting the file, you optimize it for a smaller file size. In some cases, the differences between Save and Save As can be extraordinary in terms of the file sizes. As a matter of habit, try to use the Save As command after eight to ten different saves and completely rewrite the file. If you need a backup copy of a document, you can also use Save As and supply a new name in the Save As dialog box. When you click Save, a copy of your PDF is written to disk with the new name.

Using Acrobat Catalog

Regardless of whether you create PDF documents for clients for wide distribution or you use PDF documents to catalog your own files in your studio, searching through archives is a task you frequently repeat. Acrobat 9 does offer you the capability of searching collections of PDFs on CD/DVDs, on network servers, and on local hard drives without the use of a search-index file. However, the internal search capabilities in Acrobat 9 is slower and more limiting compared to searching an index. As a matter of common practice, you'll want to create a search-index file when archiving or distributing large quantities of documents.

To search an index file, you must have one present on your computer, network server, or some media-storage device. Index files are files containing all the words among PDF documents that were catalogued with Catalog. You create index files by launching Catalog from within Acrobat. Note that in earlier versions of Acrobat, Catalog was a separate executable program. In Acrobat 6 through 9, Catalog is a plug-in and requires you to first launch Acrobat before you can access Catalog.

> **NOTE** Catalog is available only in Acrobat Pro and Pro Extended. All Acrobat viewers, including Adobe Reader, can use search indexes. A search index is not usable in Acrobat when hosted on Web sites.

To launch Catalog from within Acrobat Professional, choose Advanced ➪ Document Processing ➪ Full Text Index with Catalog. Catalog is robust and provides many options for creating and modifying indexes. After a search index is created, any user can access the search index from any Acrobat viewer to find words using search criteria in the search pane.

Creating a new index file

After your files are saved in final form, it's time to create the search index. Choose Advanced ➪ Document Processing ➪ Full Text Index with Catalog to open the Catalog dialog box, shown in Figure 34.10. In the dialog box, you make choices for creating a new index file or opening an existing index file. Click New Index to create a new index file.

The New Index Definition dialog box, shown in Figure 34.11, opens where you set specific attributes for your index and determine what folder(s) are to be indexed.

- **Index title:** The title that you place in this field is a title for the index, but not necessarily the name of the file you ultimately save. The name you enter here does not need to conform to any naming conventions because in most cases it won't be the saved filename. When you open an index file, you search your hard drive, server, or external media for a filename that ends with a PDX extension. When you visit the Search Pane and select the menu option for Select Index, the Index Selection dialog box (Figure 34.12) opens. The Index Selection dialog box lists indexes by their Index Title names. These names are derived from what you type in the Index Title field in Catalog.

FIGURE 34.10

You create an index file by using the Catalog dialog box.

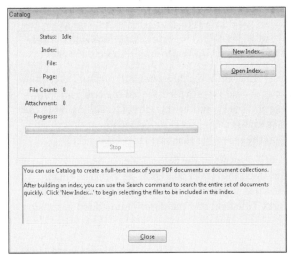

FIGURE 34.11

Set attributes for index files in the New Index Definition dialog box.

NOTE   **When you get ready to build a file, Acrobat prompts you for the index filename. By default, the text you type in the Index Title field is listed in the File Name field in the Save Index File dialog box. This dialog box opens when you click the Build button in the Catalog dialog box (see the section "Building the index" later in this chapter). In most cases where you supply a name as a description in the Index Title, you'll want to change the filename to a name consistent with standard DOS conventions (that is, an eight-character maximum with a three-character maximum extension). Make this change when you're prompted to save the file.**

■ **Index description:** You can supply as many as 256 characters in the Index Description field. Descriptive names and keywords should be provided so that the end user knows what each index contains. Index descriptions should be thought of as adding more information to the items mentioned earlier in this chapter regarding document descriptions. Index descriptions can help users find the index file that addresses their needs.

When an index is loaded, the index title appears in the Select Indexes dialog box. To get more information about an index file, click Info (refer to Figure 34.12). The Index Information dialog box opens, as shown in Figure 34.13. The Index Information dialog box shows you the title from the Index Title field and the description added in Catalog in the Index Description field.

FIGURE 34.12

The Index selection dialog box lists all loaded indexes.

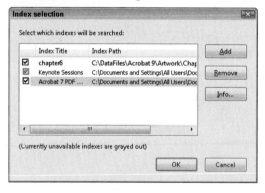

■ **Include these directories:** If you add nothing in this field, Catalog won't build an index because it won't know where to look for the PDF files to be included in the index. Adding the directory path(s) is essential before you begin to build the index. Notice the first Add button on the right side of the dialog box in Figure 34.14. After you click Add, a navigation dialog box opens, enabling you to identify the directory where the PDFs to be indexed are located. Many directories can be added to the Include These Directories list. These directories can be in different locations on your hard drive. When you select a given directory, all subfolders are also indexed for all directory locations unless you choose to exclude certain folders. When the directories have been identified, the directory path and folder name appear in the Include These Directories field.

FIGURE 34.13

The Index information dialog box

- **Exclude these subdirectories:** If you have files in a subdirectory within the directory you're indexing and want to exclude the subdirectory, you can do so in the Exclude These Subdirectories field. The folder names and directory paths of excluded directories appear in the Exclude These Subdirectories field, as shown in Figure 34.11.
- **Remove:** If you decide to remove a directory from either the Include These Directories or Exclude These Subdirectories lists, select an item in the list and click Remove. You can add or delete directories in either list prior to building an index or when modifying an index.

Saving index definitions

Two buttons appear at the top-right corner of the Catalog dialog box for saving a definition. If you begin to develop an index file and supply the index title and a description and want to come back to Catalog later, you can save what you type in the Index Definition dialog box using the Save As button. The Save button does not appear active until you've saved a file with the Save As option or you're working on a file that has been built. Saving the file only saves the definition for the index. It doesn't create an index file. The Save As option enables you to prepare files for indexing and interrupt your session if you need to return later. For example, suppose you add an index title and you write an index description. If you need to quit Acrobat at this point, click Save As and save the definition to disk. You can then return later and resume creating the index by adding the directories and building the index.

After you've saved a file, you can update the file with the Save button. After a definition is saved, when you return to Catalog, you can click Open in the Catalog dialog box and resume editing the definition file. When all the options for your search index have been determined, you click Build to actually create the index file.

Using Save As or Save is not required to create an index file. If you set all your attributes for the index and click Build, Catalog prompts you in the Save Index File dialog box to supply a name for the index and save the definition. Essentially, Catalog is invoking the Save As command for you.

If, at any time, you click Cancel in the lower-right corner of the Index Definition dialog box, all edits are lost for the current session. If you add definition items without saving, you'll need to start over when you open the Index Definition dialog box again. If you start to work on a saved file and click Cancel without saving new edits, your file reverts to the previously saved version.

Options

To the right of the Index Description field in the New Index Definition dialog box (refer to Figure 34.11) is a button labeled Options. Click this button and the Options dialog box appears, allowing you to choose from a number of different attributes for your index file, as shown in Figure 34.14. Some of these options are similar to Preference settings for Catalog made in the Preferences dialog box. Any edits you make here supersede preference settings. The options in this box include the following:

CROSS-REF For information on setting catalog preferences, see the section "Setting preferences."

FIGURE 34.14

The Options dialog box assigns attributes to the index file.

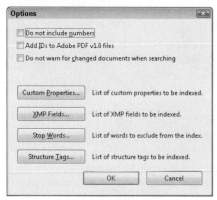

- **Do not include numbers:** By selecting this option, you can reduce the file size, especially if data containing many numbers is part of the PDF file(s) to be indexed. Keep in mind, though, that if numbers are excluded, Search won't find numeric values.

- **Add IDs to Acrobat 1.0 PDF files:** Because Acrobat is now in version 9.0, it may be rare to find old PDF 1.0 files that you need to updated with IDs for Acrobat 1.0 files. If you do have legacy files saved as PDF 1.0 format, it's best to batch-process the older PDFs by saving them out of Acrobat 6.0. As software changes, many previous formats may not be supported with recent updates. To avoid this, update older documents to newer file formats.

  If you have legacy files that haven't been updated and you want to include them in your search index, check the box. If you're not certain whether the PDFs were created with Acrobat 1.0 compatibility, check it anyway just to be safe.

- **Do not warn for changed documents when searching:** If you create an index file, then return to the index in Catalog and perform some maintenance functions, save the index, and start searching the index, Acrobat notifies you in a dialog box that changes have been made and asks whether you want to proceed. To sidestep the opening of the warning dialog box, check the Do not warn for changed documents when searching option.

- **Custom Properties:** This button opens a dialog box (Figure 34.15) which helps you customize Acrobat with the Acrobat Software Development Kit (SDK). This item is intended for programmers who want to add special features to Acrobat. To add a Custom Property to be indexed, you should have knowledge in programming and the PDF format.

FIGURE 34.15

You can add custom data fields to Acrobat.

You add Custom Properties to the field box and select the type of property from the pull-down menu. You type the property values in the field box, identify the type, and click Add. The property is then listed in the window below the Custom Property field box. The types available from the pull-down menu include:

- **String:** This is any text string. If numbers are included with this option, they are treated as text.

- **Integer:** The integer field can accept values between 0 and 65,535.

- **Date:** This is a date value.

Support for programmers writing extensions, plug-ins, and working with the SDK is provided by Adobe Systems. For developers who want to use the support program, you need to become a member of the Adobe Solutions Network (ASN) Developer Program. For more information about ASN and SDK, log on to the Adobe Web site at http://adobe.com/go/acrobat_developer.

- **XMP Fields:** Click XMP Fields and another dialog box opens where you add to a list of XMP fields. The dialog box is virtually identical to the Stop Words dialog box shown in Figure 34.16. Type a name in the field box and click Add. All new XMP fields are added to the list window.

■ **Stop Words:** To optimize an index file that produces faster search results, you can add stop words. You may have words, such as *the, a, an, of,* and so on that you would typically not use in a search. You can exclude such words by typing the word in the Word field box and clicking Add in the Stop Words dialog box. Click Stop Words in the Options dialog box to open the Stop Words dialog box (Figure 34.16). To eliminate a word after it has been added, select the word and click Remove. Keep in mind that every time you *add* a word, you're actually adding it to a list of words to be excluded.

FIGURE 34.16

You can eliminate words from an index file.

 You can create an elaborate list of stop words and may want to apply the list to several index files, but Acrobat (as of this writing) does not include an ability to import or swap a list of words to be excluded from an index file. For a workaround, you can open any existing Index Definition field and change all attributes except the stop words. Add a new index title, a new index description, and select a new directory for indexing. Save the definition to a new filename and click the Build button. A new index is built using stop words created in another index. In workgroups, you can save an index definition file (using Save As and renaming the file) without adding directories and use it as a template so all index files have consistent settings for the stop words.

■ **Tags:** If you have a Tagged PDF, you can search document tags when the tags are included in the search index. Click Tags in the Options dialog box to open the Tags dialog box (Figure 34.17). Tagged PDFs with a tagged root and elements can have any item in the tagged logical tree marked for searching. To observe the tags in a PDF file, open the Tags palette and expand the tree. All the tags nest like a bookmark list. To mark tags for searching, type the tag name in the Tags dialog box and click Add. You remove tags from the list window by selecting a tag and clicking Remove.

NOTE For more information on creating tagged PDF documents and the use of tags, see the *Adobe Acrobat 9 PDF Bible* (Wiley Publishing).

FIGURE 34.17

You can mark tags for searches in index files.

Building the index

After you set all the attributes for the index definition, you're ready to create the index file. Clicking the Build button in the New Index Definition dialog box (refer to Figure 34.11) creates indexes. When you click this button, Catalog opens the Save Index File dialog box, where you supply a filename and target a destination on your hard drive. The default file extension is PDX. Don't modify the file extension name. Acrobat recognizes these files when loading search indexes.

The location where you instruct Catalog to save your index file can be any location on your hard drive regardless of where the files being indexed reside. You can save the index file inside or outside the folder that Catalog created during the indexing. Therefore, you have an index file and a folder containing index resources. The relationship between the index file and resource folder locations is critical to the usability of the index. If you move the index file to a different location without moving the supporting folder, the index is rendered unusable. To avoid problems, create a folder either when you're in the Save Index File dialog box or before you open Catalog and save your index file to your new folder. Make the name descriptive and keep the index file together in this folder. When you want to move the index to another directory, to another computer, or to an external media cartridge or CD/DVD-ROM, copy the folder containing the index and supporting files.

Click Save in the Save Index File dialog box and Catalog closes the Index Definition dialog box, returns you to the Catalog dialog box, and begins to process all the files in the target folder(s). Depending on how many files are indexed, the time to complete the build may be considerable. Don't interrupt the processing if you want to complete the index generation. When Catalog finishes, the progress bar stops and the last line of text in the Catalog dialog box reads "Index build successful." If the build is not successful, you can scroll the window in the Catalog dialog box and view errors reported in the list.

Stopping builds

If you want to interrupt a build, you can click the Stop button while a build is in progress. When building an index, Catalog opens a file where all the words and markers to the PDF pages are written. When you click the Stop button, Catalog saves the open file to disk and closes it with the indexed items up to the point you stopped the build. Therefore, the index is usable after stopping a build and you can search for words in the partial index. When you want to resume, you can open the file in Catalog and click Rebuild in Catalog.

Building existing indexes

When files are deleted from indexed folders and new files are added to the indexed folders, you'll want to maintain the index file and update to reflect any changes. You can open an index file and click Build for a quick update. New files are scanned and added to the index, but the deleted files are marked for deletion without actually deleting the data. To delete data no longer valid, you need to use the Purge button. Purging can take a considerable amount of time even on small index files. Therefore, your routine maintenance might be to consistently build a file and only periodically purge data.

Building index files from secure documents

In all earlier versions of Acrobat, you could not create index files from secure PDFs encrypted with either Acrobat Standard Security or Acrobat Self-Sign Security. In versions 8.0 and 9.0 of Acrobat, you have complete access to secure files with Catalog. Any form of encrypted file using the Acrobat-supported security features can be included in your index files. Creating an index does not compromise your security and won't affect the permissions you set forth when the files were saved.

If you have legacy files that have been secured, you can index them like other files saved in earlier PDF format compatibilities. You can only use these files, or any other files you create with Acrobat Professional, with Acrobat viewers 6.0 and later.

CROSS-REF For more information on encryption and security, see Chapter 28.

Rebuilding an index

Rebuilding index files completely re-creates a new index. You can open an Acrobat 6.0–compatible index file and click Rebuild. The file rewrites the file you opened much like you would use a Save As menu command to rewrite a PDF document. If a substantial number of PDF documents have been deleted and new files added to the indexed folders, rebuilding the index could take less time than purging data.

Purging data

As indexes are maintained and rebuilt, you'll need to perform periodic maintenance and purge old data. A purge does not delete the index file, nor does it completely rewrite the file; it simply recovers the space used in the index for outdated information. Purging is particularly useful when you remove PDF files from a folder and the search items are no longer needed. If you've built a file several times, each build marks words for deletion. A purge eliminates the marked data and reduces the file size. With a significant number of words marked for deletion, a purge improves a search's speed. This operation might be scheduled routinely in environments where many changes occur within the indexed folders.

 **TIP** When changing options for eliminating words and numbers from indexes or adding tags and custom properties in the Options dialog box, first open the `index.pdx` file in Catalog and purge the data. Set your new criteria in the Options dialog box and rebuild the index. Any items purged will now be eliminated from the index.

Setting preferences

Preference settings are contained in the Preferences dialog box. Choose Edit ➪ Preferences (Win) or Acrobat ➪ Preferences (Mac), and click the Catalog item in the left pane, as shown in Figure 34.18. Notice that the Index Defaults items use the same settings as found in the Options dialog box from the New Index Selection dialog box. The top three options under Indexing in Catalog Preferences are obtained only here in these preference settings.

FIGURE 34.18

Open the Preferences dialog box and click Catalog.

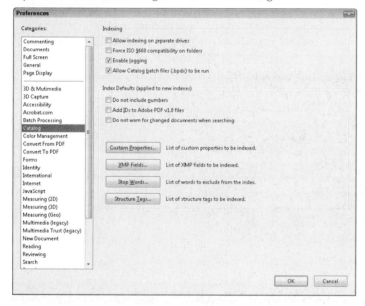

- **Indexing:** The three options found in the Indexing section of the Catalog preferences include:

  - **Allow indexing on separate drives:** When creating index files where you want to include folders on network servers and/or computers on your network, select this item. The indexing option only includes indexing files on local drives. Unfortunately, you can't index files on Web servers and use indexes from within Web browsers.

  - **Force ISO 9660 compatibility on folders:** This setting tells Catalog to look for any folders that aren't compliant with standard DOS conventions (eight-character maximum with three-character-maximum extensions) for folder/directory names. If Catalog encounters an unacceptable folder name, it stops the process and reports an error in the Catalog dialog box. Folder names and directory paths are listed for all incompatible names. You can review the list and manually rename folders. After changing folder names, try to create the index again.

1069

▦ **Enable logging:** A log file, created during an index build, describes the processing for each indexed file. You can open the file, which is ASCII text, in any text editor or word processor. Any errors are noted in the log file, along with all documents and directory paths. If you don't want to generate a log file at the time of indexing, deselect the check box, but realize that you're prevented from analyzing problems.

▦ **Allow Catalog batch files (.bpdf) files to be run:** Permits you to run catalog files in a batch sequence.

■ **Index Defaults:** These options are identical to the options you have available in the New Index Definition Options dialog box (refer to Figure 34.14). These default/options settings exist in two locations for different reasons:

▦ When you set the options in the Preferences dialog box, the options are used for all index files you create. When you elect to use the options from the New Index Selection Options dialog box, the settings are specific to the index file you create. When you create a new index file, the options return to defaults.

▦ If you set a preference in the Catalog Preferences and disable the option in the New Index Selection Options dialog box, the latter supersedes the former. That is to say, the New Index Selection Options dialog box settings always prevail.

Using Index Files

As stated earlier, the main reason you create index files is for speed. When you search hundreds or thousands of pages, the amount of time to return found instances for searched words is a matter of seconds compared to using the Search tool in the Search pane.

Loading index files

To search using an index file, you need to first load the index in the Search pane. Click the Search tool or press ⌘/Ctrl+Shift+F to open the Search pane and click Use Advanced Search Options. From the Look In pull-down menu, choose the Select Index menu option, as shown in Figure 34.19.

The Index Selection dialog box opens after making the menu selection. Click the Add button and the Open Index File dialog box opens, as shown in Figure 34.20. In this dialog box, navigate your hard drive to find the folder where your index file is located. Click the index filename, and click Open.

After selecting the index to load, you're returned to the Index Selection dialog box. A list of all loaded indexes appears in the dialog box. To the left of each filename is a check box. When a check mark is in view, the index file is active and can be searched. Disabled check boxes have the index file loaded, but the file remains inactive. Search will not return results from the inactive index files. If an index file is grayed out, as shown in Figure 34.20, the file path has been disrupted and Acrobat can't find the index file or the support files associated with the index. If you see a filename grayed out, select the file in the list and click Remove. Click Add and relocate the index. If the support files aren't found, an error is reported in a dialog box, indicating the index file could not be opened.

FIGURE 34.19

Your first step in using indexes is to load the index file(s).

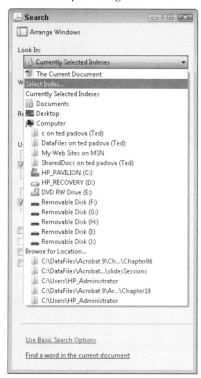

If you can't open a file, you need to return to the Catalog dialog box by choosing Advanced ⇨ Document Processing ⇨ Full Text Index with Catalog and clicking Open. Find the index file that you want to make active and rebuild the index. After rebuilding, you need to return to the Index Selection dialog box and reload it.

NOTE If you load an index file from a CD-ROM and the CD is not inserted in your CD-ROM drive, the index-file name is grayed out in the Index Selection dialog box. After inserting the CD-ROM containing the index, the index-file name becomes active. If you know index files are loaded from CDs, don't delete them from the Index Selection dialog box. Doing so requires you to reload the index file each time you insert a CD.

Disabling indexes

If you want to eliminate an index from searches, you can deactivate the index by disabling its check box. In a later Acrobat session, you can go back and enable indexes listed in the Index Selection dialog box (open the Search pane as described in the previous section and choose Select Index from the Look In pull-down menu to open the Index Selection dialog box). You should always use this method rather than deleting an index if you intend to use it again in a later Acrobat session. However, at times, you may want to delete an index file. If you no longer intend to use the index, or you relocate your index to another drive or server, you may want to completely remove the old index. If this is the case, select the index file you want to delete and click Remove. You can enable or disable indexes before you click Remove. In either case, the index file is removed without warning.

FIGURE 34.20

Select an index to load and click Open.

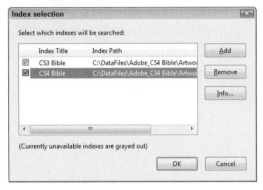

If you inadvertently delete an index, you can always reload the index by clicking Add. Placing index files in a directory where you can easily access them is a good idea. To avoid confusion, try to keep indexes in a common directory or a directory together with the indexed PDF files. Acrobat doesn't care where the index file is located on your hard drive or server—it just needs to know where the file is located and the file needs to keep the relative path with the support files. If you move the index file to a different directory, be certain to reestablish the connection in the Index Selection dialog box.

Index information

When a number of index files are installed on a computer or server, the names for the files may not be descriptive enough to determine which index you want to search. If more-detailed information is desired, the information provided by the Index Information dialog box may help identify the index needed for a given search. To open the Index selection dialog box click Select Index in the Look In pull-down menu. Click Info in the Index selection dialog box to display the index information.

NOTE   Index information may be particularly helpful in office environments where several people in different departments create PDFs and indexes are all placed on a common server. What may be intuitive to the author of an index file in terms of index name may not be as intuitive to other users. Index information offers the capability of adding more-descriptive information that can be understood by many users.

Fortunately, you can explore more-descriptive information about an index file by clicking Info in the Index Selection dialog box. When you click Info, the Index Information dialog box opens, displaying information about the index file, as shown in Figure 34.21. Some of the information displayed requires user entry at the time the index is built. Catalog automatically creates other information in the dialog box when the index is built. The Index information dialog box provides a description of the following:

FIGURE 34.21

The Index information dialog box

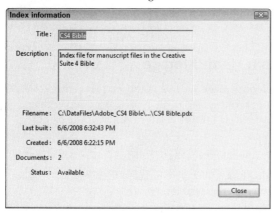

- **Title:** The user supplies title information at the time the index is created. Titles usually consist of several words describing the index contents. Titles can be searched so the title keywords should reflect the index content.

- **Description:** Description can be a few words or several sentences containing information about the index. (In Figure 34.23, the description was supplied in Catalog when the index was created.)

- **Filename:** The directory path for the index file's location on a drive or server displays with the last item appearing as the index filename.

- **Last built:** If the index file is updated, the date of the last build is supplied here. If no updates have occurred, the date is the same as the date of creation.

- **Created:** This date reflects the time and date the index file was originally created and is, therefore, a fixed date.

- **Documents:** Indexes are created from one or more PDF documents. The total number of PDF files from which the index file was created appears here.

- **Status:** If the index file has been identified and added to the list in the Index Selection dialog box, it will be Available. Unavailable indexes appear grayed out in the list and are described as Unavailable.

Searching an index

After your index file is prepared and loaded in the Index Selection dialog box, it's ready for use. You search index files in the Advanced Search pane. From the Look In pull-down menu, select Currently Selected Indexes.

All the options discussed earlier for advanced searches are available to you. Select from the Return Results Containing pull-down menu, enter your search criteria, and select the options you want. Click Search and you'll find the search results reported much faster than using other search methods.

Index files can be created from PDF collections contained on external media where the index file can remain on your computer without the need for copying the PDF documents to your hard drive. When you insert a media disc like a CD-ROM, your search index is ready to use to search the media. To understand a little more about creating search indexes and using them with external media, follow these steps.

STEPS: Creating Index Files from Media Storage

1. **Set preferences.** Choose Edit ➪ Preferences. Click Catalog in the left pane. Check Allow Indexing on Separate Drives. In order to create an index file from a device other than your local hard drive(s), this preference setting must be enabled. Click OK to exit the Preferences dialog box.

2. **Open Catalog.** Choose Advanced ➪ Document Processing ➪ Full Text Index with Catalog.

3. **Open the New Index Definition dialog box.** Click New Index in the Catalog dialog box and the New Index Definition dialog box opens in the foreground.

4. **Add an Index title.** Click in the first field box and type a title for your index file. The example in Figure 34.24 uses "Aussie 2020 AD Conference" for the title.

5. **Add an Index Description.** Type a description for the index. You can use any text you want to help remind you later what this index file is used for. An example description appears in Figure 34.22.

6. **Change Options.** Click Options to open the Options dialog box where you can make options choices. Check Do Not Warn for Changed Documents When Searching. Click OK.

7. **Add a folder to the Include These Directories list.** Click the first Add button adjacent to the list for Include These Directories. The Browse for Folder dialog box opens. If you have a folder you want to catalog, select the folder in the Browse for Folder dialog box. If you have a CD where your files are stored, click the CD drive where the CD containing the files is located. Click OK in the Browse for Folder dialog box.

8. **Build the index.** Click the Build button in the Catalog dialog box. Acrobat prompts you with the Save Index File dialog box for the location to save your index file. Select the location on your hard drive where you want to save your file. Type a name in the File Name field. Use a short name for the file. The extension defaults to PDX. Leave the default extension and click Save.

   Acrobat Professional reads all the files on the CD-ROM and writes the Index file. Let your computer continue writing the index until it finishes the build.

9. **Examine the build results.** When Acrobat completes the build, the Catalog dialog box reports the results of the build. The last line in the results list reports the index build as successful.

10. **Quit Catalog.** Click Close to quit Catalog.

FIGURE 34.22

Add an index title and an index description.

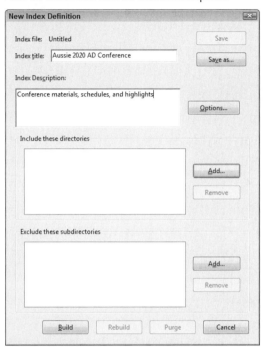

11. **Load the index file.** Click the Search button in the Acrobat File toolbar or press ⌘/ Ctrl+Shift+F and select Use Advanced Search Options. Open the Look In pull-down menu and click Select Index. The Index Selection dialog box opens. Deselect any active index files by clicking on the check boxes to remove the check mark adjacent to the index names in the list. Click Add and select your new index in the Open Index File dialog box. Click OK to return to the Index Selection dialog box. Verify that your new index is listed and the check box is enabled.

12. **Review the index information.** Select the index file in the Index Selection dialog box. Click Info to open the Index Information dialog box. Review the contents and notice the description appears as you added it in the Index Description dialog box. Click Close to return to the Index Selection dialog box. Click OK in the Index Selection dialog box to return to the Acrobat Document pane.

13. **Search the new index file.** The index file is loaded and active. Be certain the menu option for Currently Selected Indexes is active in the Look In pull-down menu. Enter **Search word AND second search word** in the first field box. We used Conference AND Zoo in our example. Select Boolean Query from the Return Results Containing pull-down menu. Click Include Bookmarks and Include Attachments at the bottom of the Search pane, as shown in Figure 34.23.

FIGURE 34.23

Type the words that you want to search for.

14. **Invoke the Search.** Click Search at the bottom of the Search pane. The results are reported in the list within the Search pane. Click any text highlighted in blue to open the file and page where the results are found.

Practice searching your new index file using different options and search criteria. To compare the difference between using a search index file and using the advanced search options, you can choose the Browse for Location menu item and search the CD-ROM for the same criteria. Go back and forth to see the differences between searching folders and searching an index file. It should be obvious that when using an index file your search results are reported much faster.

Searching external devices

A computer network server, another computer on your network, a CD-ROM, a DVD-ROM, an external hard drive, or a removable media cartridge is considered external to your local computer hard drive(s). Any of these devices can be indexed and the index file can be located on any of the devices you index. If you want to save an index file on a device different from where the PDF collection is stored, be certain to open the Preferences dialog box for the Catalog Preferences and enable the check box for Allow Indexing on Separate Drives. This preference setting enables you to index across media devices.

NOTE When you want to write index files to read only media such as CD-ROMs and DVDs, you need to create the index file from PDFs stored on your hard drive. After the index file is created, copy the index file, the supporting files, and the PDFs to your media and burn the disk.

When you want to search an index, you can activate the index in the Index Selection dialog box and invoke a search, whether your external media is mounted and accessible or not. The search index returns results from the index PDX file and the IDX files without looking at the PDFs that were indexed. You can examine the results of the search in the Search pane and find the files where the search criteria match the PDF documents in the index collection.

If you want to open the link to the PDF document where a result is reported, you need to have the media mounted and accessible. If a network server or other computer contains the related files, the server/computer must be shared with appropriate permissions and visible on your desktop. If you use external media-storage devices, the media must be mounted and visible on your desktop in order to view the PDFs linked to the search results. If you attempt to view a document when the device is not mounted, Acrobat opens an error dialog box.

If you see an error dialog box, click OK in the dialog box and insert your media, connect an external hard drive, or access a computer or network server. Wait until the media is mounted, and click a search result. Acrobat opens the linked page and you're ready to continue your search.

A search-index file created on one computer can be moved or copied to another computer. To copy an index file to another computer, be certain you copy the index file (PDX) and all supporting files in the folder created by Catalog.

You can load the index file and external media on another computer and perform the same searches as were performed where the index file was created. When you're distributing CD-ROMs and DVDs, you can copy these index files to your media and all users can access the index files. If you access an index file on a network server and the PDF collection is stored on an external device such as a CD-ROM, you cannot open files from another computer unless the CD-ROM is mounted. You may see your network server, but the associated devices with the server need to be individually mounted in order to open PDF files remotely.

Embedding indexes

If you work with large files, where only one file or a few files are copied to a CD or hosted on a network server, having an index file embedded in a PDF file is more practical. Acrobat 8 Professional and Acrobat 9 Pro offer you an option for creating and embedding index files using one simple menu command.

Open a file that you want to use with an embedded index, and choose Advanced ⇨ Document Processing ⇨ Manage Embedded Index. The Manage Embedded Index dialog box shown in Figure 34.24 opens. If an index file is already embedded in the PDF document, the Embed Index button is grayed out.

Choose Advanced ➪ Document Processing ➪ Manage Embedded Index to open the Manage Embedded Index dialog box.

If the Embed Index button is not grayed out, click the button and Acrobat completely automates creating and embedding an index. The file is saved with the embedded index, and when you copy the file to a CD or another computer, any user with an Acrobat viewer can search using the embedded index file. No special search options need to be selected when searching an embedded index. Just open the Search pane and click the radio button for In the Current Document. Acrobat automatically uses the embedded index.

Summary

- You can reduce file sizes with the Reduce File Size menu command.

- You use the PDF Optimizer, available with Acrobat Professional, to reduce file sizes and eliminate unnecessary data in PDF files. PDF Optimizer can often reduce file sizes more than when using the Reduce File Size command.

- Selecting options in the Clean Up tab in the PDF Optimizer other than the default options can interfere with the PDF functionality.

- Users determine initial views when setting preferences for all files saved with default views. When you save initial views in PDF files, they override user preferences.

- Search index files are created in Catalog. Searching index files returns results much faster than Acrobat built-in search tools.

- You can search document descriptions with advanced searches and via index file searches.

- Index files can be built, rebuilt, and purged with Catalog. Old index files created with PDF formats earlier than version 6.0 need to be rebuilt with Catalog.

- Tags and XML data can be searched with advanced searches and from index searches.

- You can copy index files to other computers, network servers, and external media-storage units.

- Index files can be embedded in PDFs using Acrobat 9 Pro and Pro Extended.

Chapter 35

Sharing Files

In Chapter 33, we introduced you to Acrobat.com. As we mentioned in Chapter 33, Acrobat.com is a service provided by Adobe Systems during the Acrobat 9.0 release and just prior to the introduction of the Creative Suite 3.3.

Using your Acrobat.com account, you can share files with clients and colleagues without having to worry about configuring your own local server for permissions access.

To share a single file with other users, you can easily use methods you're familiar with such as e-mailing a document. However, if you have several files and files of different types, you may want to create a PDF Portfolio in Acrobat 9 and share the portfolio with other users via Acrobat.com or via e-mail.

In this chapter, we talk about creating PDF Portfolios, sharing files via e-mail, and sharing files via Acrobat.com using some sharing methods you find in Acrobat 9.0.

Creating PDF Portfolios

In Acrobat 8, Adobe introduced a new method for assembling different files in what was called a PDF Package. PDF Packages were designed to support needs by designers and knowledge workers to collect a variety of file types and assemble them neatly in a single package that could be distributed to others via e-mail or Web hosting.

In Acrobat 9, you find all the features we had available with PDF Packages introduced in Acrobat 8 and additional features that have greatly improved the collection of various documents into a single file. For the creative people, the thing you'll like most about PDF portfolios is that the focus of the new feature is on design. Whereas PDF Packages limited your options for customizing the appearance of a package, PDF Portfolios offer you an almost limitless number of ways to enhance the visual appearance of your portfolio presentation.

Assembling a portfolio

You may have a number of clients who want to share files with you when you begin a design piece. Perhaps an Excel spreadsheet, some Word files, a PowerPoint presentation, and related documents might be sent to you in native formats for you to create a concept for a new design. You also might want to share files with your clients such as proofs for an advertising campaign that may include print material, Web hosted material, and perhaps a video file.

Both you and your client can assemble files in a PDF Portfolio, submit the portfolio to Acrobat. com, and enjoy an easy sharing experience. As a PDF author, you'll want to know a few things about assembling a PDF Portfolio.

To begin the process of creating a PDF portfolio, do the following:

Steps: Adding files to a PDF Portfolio

1. **Create a new PDF Portfolio.** Several menu commands are available for creating PDF Portfolios. Choose File ⇨ Create PDF Portfolio. Alternately, you can choose File ⇨ Create PDF ⇨ Assemble PDF Portfolio, Create (task button pull-down menu) ⇨ Assemble PDF Portfolio, or use the Combine Files wizard.

2. **Add files to the new portfolio.** You have several choices for adding files to PDF Portfolios in the new PDF Portfolio interface shown in Figure 35.1. You can drag files from your desktop or a folder on your hard drive, click the Add button in the PDF Portfolio interface, or add a folder of files by clicking the Add Existing Folder button. If you click a button to add files/folders, the Add Files dialog box opens, as shown in Figure 35.2.

3. **Select files to add to the portfolio.** If you decide to use the Add Files button, choose the files you want to add by selecting them in the Add Files dialog box shown in Figure 35.2.

4. **Click Open.** Regardless of the method you use to add files to your new portfolio, the files appear with thumbnail previews as shown in Figure 35.3. In this figure, several different file types are added to a new PDF Portfolio.

Designing a portfolio layout

If you follow steps as outlined in the section "Assembling a portfolio," you can save your portfolio and distribute it to recipients. However, you may want to add some design to the presentation of your portfolio for a more appealing view. PDF Portfolios offer you a variety of design controls to create the look that you want displayed to end users.

When files are added to a portfolio, the Edit PDF Portfolio panel on the right side of the portfolio interface opens. From the list of categories, click Choose a Layout. In the Choose a Layout panel, you have several options to decide what layout view you want to use to display your files.

FIGURE 35.1

Drag and drop files in the PDF Portfolio Document pane, or click Add Files or Add Existing Folder.

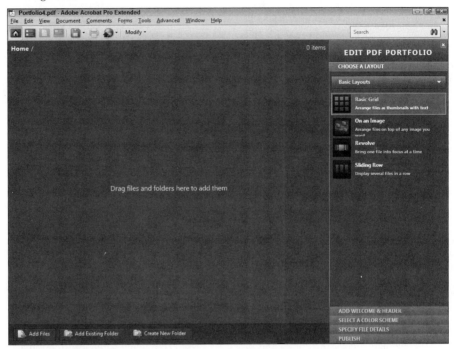

FIGURE 35.2

Select files in the Add Files dialog box.

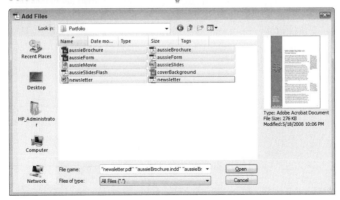

FIGURE 35.3

After adding files, the files appear with thumbnail images.

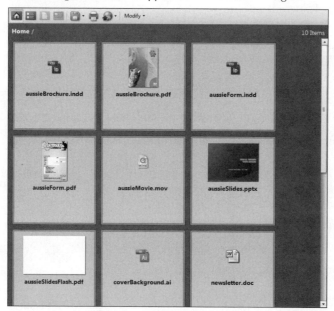

You can edit a description for each file regardless of the layout view you decide to use. Below the file name, click the cursor and type a description to detail some information about the file. In Figure 35.4, we chose the Sliding Row layout and added a brief description for the files.

Adding a Welcome page

Click the Add Welcome & Header item in the Edit PDF Portfolio, as shown in Figure 35.5, and you can add a Welcome page. The Welcome page can be text only, image only, text on top of an image, or an Adobe Flash file. Select the item you want to use for a Welcome page, and the left pane changes where you can add text, an image, or both text and image, or you can drag and drop an Adobe Flash file to the pane.

Welcome pages are optional. If you have something like an animation of your company logo or summary of your company, you can add a Flash file to the Welcome page. Keep in mind that end users can dismiss the Welcome page and not show it again when reopening your portfolio. Therefore, be certain to add only nonessential information to a Welcome page that doesn't require a viewer to look over the page for any pertinent information.

Customizing the appearance of a portfolio

More options are available for customizing the appearance by changing colors for text and cards. Click the Select a Color Scheme option, and you can choose from preset colors or add custom colors to change the appearance and make the color scheme consistent with your corporate colors.

FIGURE 35.4

Choose a layout, and type a description below the filenames appearing in the cards.

FIGURE 35.5

Click Add Welcome & Header, and choose an option for a Welcome page.

In addition to customizing the colors you have a few other panels in the Edit PDF Portfolio panel. Use the Specify File Details panel to add and sort columns when viewing files in the Detail View and use the Publish panel to save a file, e-mail it, or upload the file to Acrobat.com.

Securing portfolios

From the Modify pull-down menu, choose Secure Portfolio. The Document Properties window opens with the Security tab selected, as shown in Figure 35.6. From the Security Method pull-down menu, choose a security method. You have the same security options that are available with PDF files.

FIGURE 35.6

Choose Modify ➪ Secure Portfolio to open the Security properties.

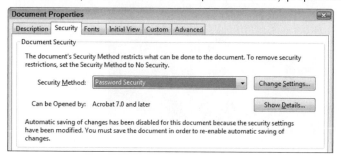

When you secure a document and prevent editing, all files in the portfolio are secured as well as the layout and design of the portfolio itself.

 For more information on securing files, see Chapter 28.

Sharing Files via E-mail

No doubt you are familiar with e-mailing file attachments. In addition to adding a file attachment to a new e-mail message, you have some commands within Acrobat and within a PDF Portfolio to use for e-mailing documents. Depending on the option you choose, either your e-mail client application is used or Acrobat can serve as your e-mail client.

You have several choices for e-mailing files from within Acrobat. If you have a single PDF file, you can open the file and click the E-mail tool in the File toolbar shown in Figure 35.7. When you click the E-mail tool, your default e-mail client opens and the file shown in the Document pane is automatically added as a file attachment, as shown in Figure 35.8.

FIGURE 35.7

Open a PDF file in Acrobat, and click the E-mail tool.

E-mail tool

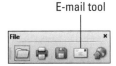

If you want to e-mail a PDF Portfolio, you can open the Share pull-down menu in the PDF Portfolio toolbar and choose Email, as shown in Figure 35.8. You also can choose File ➪ Attach Portfolio to Email, or as a third option, you can choose Modify ➪ Edit Portfolio to open the Edit PDF Portfolio panel and click Publish. From the options in the Publish panel, choose Email.

FIGURE 35.8

In a PDF Portfolio, choose Email from the Share pull-down menu for an easy way of e-mailing your portfolio.

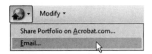

Any of the options you use to e-mail a PDF Portfolio opens a new message in your default e-mail client with the file added as an attachment. Simply add your recipient(s) and a subject line, and type a message, as shown in Figure 35.9. Click Send, and the file is e-mailed.

NOTE   Not all e-mail clients automatically open when you use an Email option in Acrobat. For some e-mail clients, you may need to open the program in order to see the new e-mail message.

Using Acrobat as your e-mail client

Another option you have for e-mailing files is to use Acrobat.com and let Acrobat serve as your e-mail client. Rather than a file attachment added to an e-mail message, you use the Share Documents on Acrobat.com wizard and Acrobat sends an e-mail to your list of recipients. In the e-mail message is a file link where recipients can download the file. This option is particularly helpful when recipients have an e-mail server capped at a certain file size that may be much less than the size of a file you want to e-mail to your colleagues and clients.

To e-mail a file to recipients using Acrobat.com, follow these steps:

STEPS: Submitting Files via Acrobat.com

1. **Open a PDF document or a PDF Portfolio.** You use the same steps regardless of whether you choose to e-mail a file or a PDF Portfolio.

2. Choose File ➪ Collaborate ➪ Share Files on Acrobat.com.

3. **Log onto Acrobat.com.** The Acrobat.com login dialog box opens, as shown in Figure 35.10. Log on with your Adobe ID and password.

FIGURE 35.9

Choose an Email option, and the open portfolio (or file) is added to a new message window in your default e-mail client.

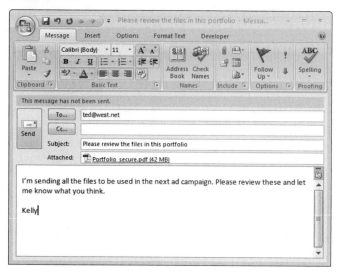

CROSS-REF If you don't have an Adobe ID, see Chapter 33 for information about creating an Adobe ID and logging onto Acrobat.com

4. **Click OK in the Acrobat.com login dialog box.** When you click OK, the Share Documents on Acrobat.com wizard opens. The first pane in the wizard shows you the file you are about to upload to Acrobat.com. You can change the file or add additional files by clicking the Browse button. When you have the appropriately identified file listed, click Next and you arrive at the second pane in the wizard.

5. **Add recipient(s), and choose an access level.** Type names of your recipients in the To text box, and open the Access Level pull-down menu, as shown in Figure 35.11. Choose either Limited access or Open access from the menu choices. Limited Access is used when you want only those you've invited to download your file. Open access permits anyone whom you've invited to visit your Acrobat.com library to download the file.

6. **Send the e-mail.** Click Send, and Acrobat now becomes your e-mail client and performs several steps. Your file is uploaded to your Acrobat.com library, and e-mail messages are sent to your list of recipients. Within the e-mail message, Acrobat adds a URL link where the recipients can locate the file you're sharing with them from your Acrobat.com library.

FIGURE 35.10

Log onto Acrobat.com using your Adobe ID and password.

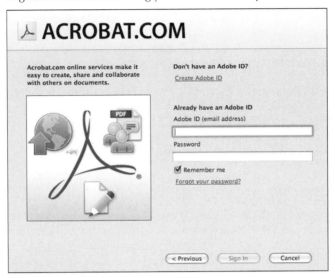

FIGURE 35.11

Type the recipient e-mail addresses, and choose an access level. Click Send to have Acrobat upload the file to your Acrobat.com library and send the e-mail messages.

Sharing Files via Acrobat.com

You can control the sharing of files from within Acrobat or from within your Acrobat.com library. As a Creative Suite user, you have Adobe Acrobat as part of the suite applications and you can use all the menu commands within Acrobat to initiate file sharing. In Addition, Adobe Reader 9 and above users also can initiate file sharing from within Adobe Reader. But you may have clients who aren't using Adobe Reader 9 or don't even have Adobe Reader installed on their computer.

As an added benefit for sharing files, anyone can use the free Acrobat.com service provided by Adobe to share files. Therefore, when clients need to send you files, you can instruct them to easily upload files to Acrobat.com and send you a URL link for where you can download the files. In addition, you may have several files you want to share with recipients, and working in your Acrobat.com workspace may be easier than launching wizards in Acrobat.

Uploading a file

To access Acrobat.com, use the File ⇨ Collaborate ⇨ Go to Acrobat.com menu command. Alternately, you can open a Web browser and type www.acrobat.com in the Location bar. When you arrive at your Acrobat.com workspace, you again log in using your Adobe ID, and you find options to upload and share files. If you upload several files, you can set sharing options after you've completed the uploads.

When a file has been uploaded to your Acrobat.com library, click the down arrow to open a pull-down menu and choose Share, as shown in Figure 35.12. This action opens the share options on Acrobat.com.

FIGURE 35.12

Open a menu on a file, and choose Share to open the share options choices on Acrobat.com.

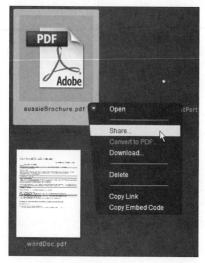

Sharing a file

In the Acrobat.com interface, you have some choices for uploading files and sharing files. When you click the Share tab, the interface changes, as shown in Figure 35.13. You have a number of choices to make once you arrive at the screen shown in Figure 35.13 detailed in these steps.

FIGURE 35.13

Click the Share tab to display options for sharing files.

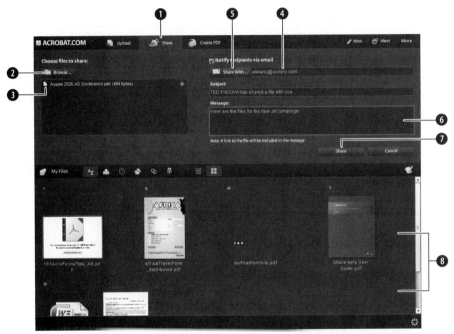

STEPS: Choosing Options for File Sharing

1. Click the Share tab to display options for sharing files.

2. Click the Browse button to locate a file on your hard drive that you want to upload to Acrobat.com.

3. ReviewThe file(s) you've chosen in the file list.

4. Type the names of recipients in the text box.

5. **Click the Share With button.** Your Contacts list opens. You can add and remove names and e-mail addresses from the Contacts list you maintain on Acrobat.com. When the Contacts list is open, check the boxes adjacent to contact names that you want to include in the file sharing.

6. Type a message that will be received by recipients in an e-mail message.

7. **Click the Share button, and a message is sent to your list of recipients.** In the message box, a URL link is automatically added by Acrobat.com for the recipients to click. After a recipient clicks the link, the user's default Web browser opens and the file is downloaded from Acrobat.com.

8. **Below the Share options, review your library of files on Acrobat.com.**

Acrobat.com serves as your e-mail client to send the e-mail messages.

Summary

- PDF Portfolios are a new feature in Acrobat 9 that offer more custom design features than were available with PDF Packages in Acrobat 8.

- Files of different types can be added to PDF Portfolios.

- PDF files and Portfolios can be e-mailed via e-mail attachments by choosing options in Acrobat to e-mail files.

- Files can be shared on Acrobat.com with open access and limited access.

Chapter 36

Creating Review Sessions

Reviewing documents, marking up comps for corrections, and adding comments are standard practices for creative professionals. In electronic review sessions, your client needs to have the same software applications as you have if you exchange native files. For most of your clients, however, it's unlikely that the people you serve use any of the Creative Suite programs. What you need is a file format that can be read by anyone, and a program that permits your clients to engage in electronic reviews and markup documents for corrections and comments. Furthermore, your clients need to use a program they don't have to purchase.

That's a tall order, but don't worry. You have all you need with the Creative Suite. Using Adobe Acrobat 9 Pro or Adobe Acrobat 9 Pro Extended (Windows only), you can add special rights to PDF files that permit users of the free Adobe Reader software to add comments and markups on your files and save their edits. You need Acrobat that comes as an part of the Creative Suite software, and your clients only need Adobe Reader / or above that can be freely downloaded from Adobe's Web site.

Comment review sessions are handled several ways in Acrobat. You can create an Attach for Email Review, or create a shared review either via e-mail, using Acrobat.com, or via your own Web server. E-mail reviews and shared review sessions are the easiest methods available to you for creating reviews and are the primary subject of this chapter.

IN THIS CHAPTER

Understanding enabling features for Adobe Reader users

Using Comment and Markup tools

Working with e-mail–based reviews

Setting up shared reviews

Understanding Reader Usage Rights

Adobe Acrobat permits you to add special usage rights to PDF files so Adobe Reader users can take more advantage of participating in comment reviews and working with Acrobat PDF forms. In Acrobat Standard 9.0, as well as the Acrobat Pro products, you can add special rights for form filler to save form data and add digital signatures to forms. Using Acrobat Pro and Pro Extended, you can add rights for Adobe Reader users to comment and mark up PDF documents. PDF documents without special usage rights cannot be saved from within Adobe Reader, and the comment and markup tools are not available to Reader users.

Acrobat 7 Professional introduced the ability to add usage rights to PDFs for saving comment notes and markups from within Adobe Reader. In Acrobat 8 Professional, usage rights were extended to Reader users for saving form data and adding digital signatures from within Adobe Reader. In Acrobat 9, Acrobat Standard was added to the list of Acrobat products that could enable PDFs with usage rights, but just for form saves and digital signatures.

You can add usage rights in the Acrobat Pro products for either or both comment and review and form saves and digital signatures via menu commands such as selecting Comments ➪ Enable for Commenting and Analysis in Adobe Reader or selecting Advanced ➪ Extend Features in Adobe Reader. The first option adds usage rights only for saving comments and markups. The second enabling feature adds usage rights for both comment saves and saving form data and adding digital signatures.

If you plan to engage in either an Attach for Email Review or Send for Shared Review Session, a wizard automatically adds usage rights for saving comments and markups in Adobe Reader when you activate the review.

CROSS-REF For more information on adding usage rights to PDFs for saving form data, see Chapter 30.

Understanding the Comment and Markup Tools

Acrobat provides you an extensive set of comment and markup tools. To view the Comment & Markup toolbar where all the comment and markup tools are contained, select Tools ➪ Comment & Markup ➪ Show Comment and Markup Toolbar. The Comment & Markup toolbar opens. When all the tools are loaded in the Comment & Markup toolbar the tools appear as shown in Figure 36.1.

FIGURE 36.1

Select Tools ➪ Comment & Markup ➪ Show Comment and Markup.

NOTE Alternately, you can open the Comment & Markup toolbar by opening a context menu (Ctrl-click on the Macintosh; right-click in Windows) on the Acrobat Toolbar Well and selecting More Tools. You also can use the Comments>Show/Hide Comment & Markup Toolbar command. When the More Tools window opens, check the box adjacent to Comment & Markup Toolbar.

These tools are available to you for commenting and marking up documents:

- **Sticky Note tool:** This tool adds a note comment similar to a Post-It note.

- **Text Edits:** Click the down-pointing arrow to open a menu where tools exist for highlighting text, underscores, cross-outs, and similar markups. Using these tools permits you to export the markups on a PDF document to the original MS Word file that was converted to PDF. Unfortunately, exporting comments to Word is available only to Windows users. You can use the tools on either platform to display the markups in the PDF file.

- **Stamp tool:** Some predefined stamps are available to you with your Acrobat installation for common office stamps such as *Approved, Sign Here, Accepted, Rejected, Revised,* and so on. In addition, you can create custom stamps and add them to the menu.

- **Highlight tool:** Use this tool to mark through text like you might highlight text on paper with a yellow marker.

- **Underline tool:** This tool lets you add underlines to text.

- **Crossout tool:** This tool crosses out text.

- **Attach a File tool:** Use this tool to attach a file (any file type) to a PDF document. This tool is especially helpful if you want to secure a PDF document with password security. All the file attachments such as InDesign files, Illustrator files, Microsoft Office files, and so on are protected if a user doesn't have a password to open the PDF document and extract the attachment.

- **Record an Audio Comment:** With a microphone attached to your computer, you can record sounds to use for commenting on a file.

- **Paste a Copied Image as a Stamp tool:** Content copied to the clipboard can be pasted as a Stamp comment.

- **Callout tool:** Use this tool to create a callout box with a line pointing to the area where you make the comment.

- **Text Box tool:** Use this tool to add a text box where you can add a long passage of text for a comment.

- **Cloud tool:** Use this tool to mark a graphic or text passage with a freeform line made up of a series of arcs.

- **Arrow tool:** Use this tool to point to a graphic or text where you want to make a comment.

- **Line tool:** Use this tool to underscore or create a diagram where you want to add comments.

- **Rectangle tool:** Use this tool to draw rectangles around a graphic or body of text.

- **Oval tool:** This tool is used in a similar manner as the Rectangle tool but for drawing ovals and circles.

- **Polygon Line tool:** Use this tool to draw a polygon shape where you want to leave the polygon open ended.

- **Polygon tool:** Use this tool to draw polygons such as pentagons, octagons, and so on.

- **Pencil tool:** Use this tool to draw freeform line shapes.

- **Pencil Eraser tool:** Use this tool to remove parts of a pencil drawing.

- **Show Pull-Down Menu:** A number of menu commands for handling comments are contained in the pull-down menu.

All the tools in the Comment & Markup toolbar with the exception of the Text Box tool, Attach a File tool, Record an Audio Comment tool, and Pencil Eraser tool have associated comment notes. A comment note is the same type of note you create with the Sticky Note tool. Just double-click a markup made with any of the remaining tools in the Comment & Markup toolbar, and a comment note opens where you can add a description for the comment you make for a particular markup.

You can change the colors and various styles of comments and markups by opening the Properties dialog box. Control (Mac) or right (Windows) + click to open a context menu and choose Properties.

Creating an Attach for Email Review

The abundant number of comment tools, properties, and menu commands are nothing more than overkill if all you want to do is add some comments on PDF pages for your own use. Acrobat is designed with much more sophistication when it comes to commenting, and the tools provided to you are intended to help you share comments in workgroups.

Comment and review among workgroups is handled in two ways. You can set up an Attach for Email Review and exchange comments with your coworkers and colleagues where PDFs and data are exchanged through e-mail, or you can set up a Send for Shared Review where comments are uploaded and downloaded by participants to your Acrobat.com account or via e-mail exchanges.

Adobe's Acrobat team wanted to make it almost seamless for any user not only to start a review session but also to participate in a review session. With the ability to enable documents with usage rights for Adobe Reader users, anyone with the free Adobe Reader software can participate in a review.

Initiating an Attach for Email Review

An Attach for Email Review is a method for you, the PDF author, to share a document that needs input from other members of a workgroup (in an e-mail exchange), such as a proposal or draft document, and ask them to make comments for feedback. As comments are submitted, you can track comments from others and make decisions about how the comments are treated. Decisions such as accepting or rejecting comments are part of this process. The comment exchanges between you and your workgroup members are handled through e-mail exchanges. When using this kind of review, the review initiator is the only person who sees comments from all the reviewers.

When you send a file for review, the PDF contains information about you, the author/initiator, who's invited to the review, and where the original is located on your system. When a recipient receives the e-mail inviting him or her to review your document, the attachment to the e-mail is a PDF that the recipients use to make comments. The recipients open the PDF e-mail attachment in Acrobat or Adobe Reader and make comments. When a reviewer finishes commenting, the reviewer sends the data back to the PDF author. The data sent from the reviewers can either be a data file such as FDF (Form Data File) data or XML data or both the data and the PDF document. If you start with a large PDF file, the comment exchanges using FDF/XML data require much less data transfers because the comment data are typically much smaller than the original PDF files.

When reviews are initiated, you *must* send the PDF file to all reviewers. You can then make a decision in the Reviewing Preferences for whether the PDF or an FDF file is returned to you. In the Preferences dialog box (⌘/Ctrl+K), click Reviewing in the left pane and type a value in the Send comments as FDF for files greater than text box. The default is 5MB. Therefore, FDF data are returned for all files greater than 5MB. You can raise or lower the number by typing a new value in the text box. This setting is applied only to comments returned to you. If you have a PDF greater than 5MB—or any file size for that matter—you must first send the PDF document to the recipients.

When comments are returned to you either in PDF or FDF form, double-click the file attachment in your e-mail application. Double-clicking either file type appends comments from recipients to the original PDF you used when you invited recipients to participate in a review.

> **NOTE** Before initiating a review, be certain to add your e-mail address in the Identity preferences. If you don't add the Identity preferences, Acrobat prompts you in a dialog box and opens the Identity preferences for you. You can't proceed until you fill in the preferences text boxes. Open the Preferences dialog box (⌘/Ctrl+K), and select Identity in the left pane. Add your personal identity information including your e-mail address in the right pane. The e-mail address supplied in the Identity preferences is used when e-mailing PDFs from within Acrobat.

To understand how to start an e-mail–based review, follow these steps.

STEPS: Initiating an E-mail–based Review

1. **Open a document in Acrobat Professional.** Opening a document is optional because you can begin a review without a document open in the Document pane. In this example, we start with a document open in Acrobat Pro 9.0. If you don't have a document open you can select a document to share in a review by clicking the Browse button in the Getting Started wizard that opens when you make the menu choice for initiating a review.

2. **Initiate the review.** If you want to make a comment on your document, you can do so, but be certain to save all your updates. After saving the file, select Attach for Email Review from the Comment task button pull-down menu. The Getting Started wizard opens, as shown in Figure 36.2. This is the first of three panes appearing in the wizard when you initiate a review.

   By default, a document active in the Document pane are specified in the field box in the first pane. If you change your mind or you start a review without a document open in Acrobat, click the Browse button and browse your hard drive to locate a file.

> **NOTE** You can access the same menu command by choosing Comments ➪ Attach for Email Review.

FIGURE 36.2

To start a review session, open the PDF to be used for the review and choose Attach for Email Review from the Comment task button pull-down menu or the Comments menu.

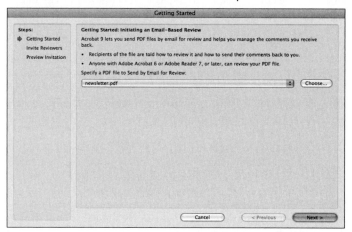

3. Invite reviewers. After identifying the file to send out for review, click the Next button to open the Invite Reviewers pane, as shown in Figure 36.3. The Address Book window contains a list of recipients for your review. Type the e-mail addresses for the people you want to participate in the review, or click Address Book to launch your e-mail address book to select reviewers to invite.

FIGURE 36.3

Add e-mail addresses for the review participants.

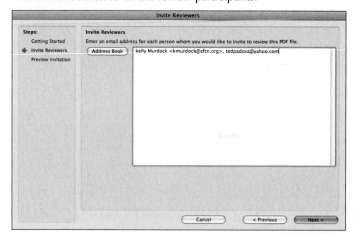

4. **Send the invitation.** Click Next, and click Send Invitation in the Preview Invitation pane, as shown in Figure 36.4. Acrobat alerts you with a dialog box informing you that a new e-mail message has been sent to your e-mail client, as shown in Figure 36.5. When you send the invitation, your PDF document is automatically enabled for Adobe Reader users to participate in the review, add comments, and save their edits.

5. **Initiate a send in your e-mail program.** Click OK in the information dialog box. If your e-mail program does not immediately send the invitation to reviewers, open your default e-mail program and click the Send (or Send/Receive) button to commence the e-mail initiation. In Figure 36.6, an invitation is displayed in Apple Mail showing the recipients in the To field, the Subject of the e-mail, and a file attachment. The message is derived from the Send by Email for Review dialog box. Note that you can still edit the message before initiating a send. Click the Send (or Send/Receive) button, and the e-mail and attachment are sent to the reviewers.

FIGURE 36.4

Click Send Invitation in the Preview Invitation page.

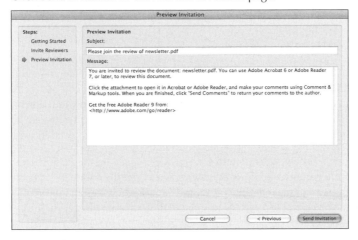

FIGURE 36.5

A dialog box informs you that a new message has been delivered to your e-mail application.

If your default e-mail program does not send the message automatically, open the program and click the Send (or Send/Receive) button.

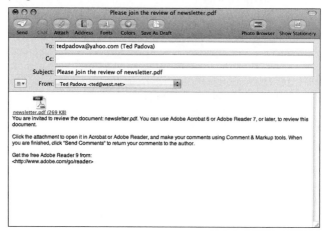

Participating in a review

Participants in a review include you—the PDF author and review initiator—and the people you select as reviewers. In your role, you field all comments from reviewers. If you use the Attach for Email Review to send comments back to users, Acrobat permits you to reply to users' comments. A review session is designed for a single set of responses between you and the recipients; however, you can exchange comments back and forth in comment threads between you and individual reviewers.

Before you begin a review, be certain to save any edits made on the PDF. If you insert pages, delete pages, or perform a number of other edits without saving, the comments retrieved from others will appear out of place and make it difficult to understand where comments are made from the reviewers. Also, be certain to keep the original PDF in the same folder. If you decide to move the PDF to another folder, be certain to keep track of the location where the PDF resides. As you update comments, Acrobat needs to keep track of the directory path where the original PDF can be found. If Acrobat can't find the PDF, you are prompted to search for it.

During a review period, you and your recipients use tools in Acrobat/Reader designed for use with e-mail reviews. When starting an e-mail review, the first time you access the Attach for Email Review menu command, the PDF is sent to recipients. All subsequent comment exchanges between you and reviewers are handled with other tools. Be certain to not return to the Attach for Email Review command if you decide to respond to user comments. Doing so sends another PDF to a recipient.

Recipient participation

A recipient receiving your e-mail with the PDF attachment can open the attachment directly within the e-mail message. Double-clicking the e-mail file attachment launches Acrobat or Adobe Reader and loads the PDF in the Document pane.

Reviewers make comments with any of the comment tools discussed earlier in this chapter in the section "Understanding the Comment and Markup Tools." After a reviewer completes a review session, the reviewer clicks the Send Comments button in the Comment & Markup toolbar, as shown in Figure 36.7.

When working on a PDF in review, the Send Comments tool is added to the Comment & Markup toolbar to the right of the Show tool.

When the reviewer sends a response to the PDF author, the PDF author's e-mail address is automatically supplied in the To field in the e-mail program. The reviewer clicks Send, and either a PDF or FDF is sent back to the PDF author. Again, the file type is determined in the Reviewing Preferences.

Author participation

As comments are submitted from reviewers, you'll want to track reviews and decide to mark them for a status such as accepted, rejected, and so on. If you want to reply to the recipients, you can elect to send a reply to recipient comments; however, in many cases, you'll want to make corrections and start a new review session. If you send a reply, each comment is treated as a separate thread in Acrobat. Rather than your having to select different tools to make responses scattered around a document page, Acrobat keeps each thread nestled together to make following a thread easier. Replies are contained in Note pop-up windows. If you want to reply to a comment, open a context menu on the note pop-up and select Reply or select Reply from the Options pull-down menu on a comment note. Additionally you can click the Reply tool in the Comments panel.

 You can open a context menu on a comment in the Comments panel and select Reply to reply to a comment.

Updating comments

You send a file to recipients for review. The reviewers then send comments back to you. Your original document needs updating to reflect the new additions added by other reviewers. When you receive an e-mail attachment, the comment data are submitted back to you. Only a single PDF resides on your computer. If you want to merge the data sent by other reviewers with your existing PDF document, double-click the file attachment sent back to you. Acrobat updates the original PDF document with the new comments.

Asking new reviewers to participate

You may begin a review and later decide you want to add new users to participate in the review. You can add new reviewers to a review at any time. To add a reviewer, open the Tracker from the Comments menu, the Review & Comment task button, or the Options pull-down in the Comments panel. The Tracker opens in a separate window. Click Add Reviewers in the Tracker to add additional reviewers. The same wizard opens where you can add recipients' e-mail addresses and any additional message in the Invitation Message window, and click OK.

Using the Tracker

The Tracker is a separate window that opens on top of the Acrobat window where you find menu commands to help manage e-mail–based, browser-based, and shared reviews as well as distributed forms. To open the Tracker, select Track Reviews from the Comment task button, or choose Comments ⇨ Track Reviews, or from the Options pull-down menu in the Comments panel, select Track Reviews. All three menu items open the Review Tracker shown in Figure 36.8.

FIGURE 36.8

The Tracker window provides information and tools for working with documents in review.

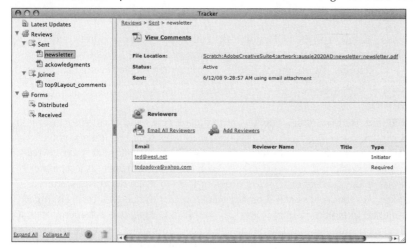

Viewing documents in the Tracker

The left pane in the Tracker lists all documents you have in review under the Reviews category. From the list, select a filename. The right pane changes to reflect information related to the selected review.

Two categories appear in the left pane in Figure 36.8. All reviews we initiated are listed in the Sent list. Expand the list to see reviews by filename. The Joined list contains all reviews sent to me by another review initiator.

From a context menu opened on a document listed in the Sent list shown in Figure 36.9, you have the following commands:

- **Open:** This command opens the selected file the same as clicking the Open tool.

- **Remove Review From Tracker:** This command removes the selected file from the review category and is the same as clicking the Remove tool.

- **Email All Reviewers:** Select this option, and your default e-mail application is opened with the To field populated with all review participants. This command is a review reminder for participants to receive an e-mail from you to remind them to send back comments.

- **Add Reviewers:** This command also launches your default e-mail application with an automated message to invite other reviewers. The selected PDF file used for initiating the original review is added as a file attachment.

- **Create PDF From Tracker Details:** Click this item, and you can create a PDF document summarizing the details for your reviews.

- **Create New Folder:** You can create a folder in the tracker Sent list and organize your reviews in folders.

- **Send To Folder:** As you add new folders, open the submenu and select the folder to send a particular review to the given folder.

FIGURE 36.9

Open a context menu on a file listed in the left pane of the Tracker for more options.

On Windows, a collapsed list is marked with a plus (+) symbol. On the Macintosh, a collapsed list is marked with a right-pointing arrowhead. Click this symbol, and the list is expanded. If a list is already expanded, a minus symbol (Windows) or down arrow (Macintosh) appears. Click this symbol, and the list is collapsed.

Forms Tracker

The Forms Tracker lists all forms you have distributed and received.

CROSS-REF For more information on the Forms Tracker, see Chapter 30.

RSS (Subscriptions)

Click the RSS button, and you open the Subscriptions pane in the Tracker. RSS (Really Simple Syndication) is a lightweight XML format designed for sharing headlines and other Web content. The Tracker allows you to manage subscriptions using RSS feeds. By default the RSS button is not shown in the Tracker. You need to open Acrobat's Preferences (Ctrl/⌘ + K) and click Tracker in the left pane. Check Enable RSS Feeds in Tracker and click OK. The RSS button then appears in the Tracker.

You might want to list RSS feeds that provide you with technical support for solving problems with a program like Adobe Acrobat. You can subscribe to an RSS feed and receive up-to-date information from the service.

This is a valuable tool at your hands in the Tracker. When you subscribe to a service, you can create a PDF file of all the threads shown in an RSS feed.

Working with Shared Reviews

Working with shared reviews just got easier in Acrobat 9. From the beginning of when browser-based reviews where introduced in Acrobat 5, Adobe has been trying to simplify review sessions for people to comment on documents in real-time where all participants can see each other's comments. We've seen simplicity added in each release of Acrobat, and now in Acrobat 9 things have gotten much better.

The bottleneck for many users, especially independent graphic designers and small ad agencies, has been lack of access to sophisticated IT departments. Unless you had the programming skills to set up a server and configure it for shared reviews and file exchanges, you were left out of server-based reviews.

Now with Acrobat 9 and Acrobat.com, you can easily engage in shared reviews without the complex task of having to configure a server.

You have several choices to make when working in Shared Reviews. You can share reviews locally on your computer and on network servers, or you can share reviews on a Web server. In regard to Web servers, you have several types of Web servers from which to choose. Depending on the choice you make, the process can be very simple or quite complicated.

These are among the choices you have for setting up a shared review:

- **Acrobat.com:** You can set up review sessions on Acrobat.com, and you don't need to worry about any special configurations of a server to collect comments and integrate the comments from multiple users.

- **Network Folder:** You can configure a network folder locally on your intranet to set up a shared review among a workgroup.

- **SharePoint Workspace:** For Windows SharePoint workspaces, users must have read and write access to engage in reviews. This option requires some help from your IT department to configure the server and set up the permissions for the participants.

- **Web Server:** Again, this option requires some help from your IT department to configure a Web server with a shared folder and configure the participants for read/write services.

One of the best new additions to Acrobat 9 is the introduction of Acrobat.com. This choice takes the configuration steps out of the process for initiating and engaging in shared reviews. For individual graphic designers and small design firms without intranets and sophisticated IT departments, using Acrobat.com is something you'll learn to love.

For the purposes of this chapter, we cover only two of the options you have for conducting shared reviews: setting up network folders and using Acrobat.com. If you work in an enterprise where you want to share reviews on Web servers, look to the Acrobat help document and online information you can find at http://www.adobe.com/devnet/acrobat/pdfs/online_collaboration.pdf and http://www.adobe.com/devnet/acrobat/online_review_admin.html.

Using network folders

Setting up a network folder for shared reviews is intended for workgroups having internal local area networks. You begin setting up a network folder the same way as when using Acrobat.com for shared reviews. From a menu command, a wizard opens that walks you through the steps to configure a folder on a network server.

To see how easy it is to set up a network folder for shared reviews, do the following.

STEPS: Starting a Shared Review using a Network Folder

1. **Open the Comment task button pull-down menu, and select Send For Shared Review.** The Send for Shared Review wizard opens as shown in Figure 36.10.

2. **Choose a location for collecting reviewer's comments.** Open the pull-down menu at the top of the Send for Shared Review wizard, and choose Automatically collect comments on my own internal server.

3. **Select a host.** Click Next in the Send for Shared Review wizard, and the second pane in the wizard opens, as shown in Figure 36.11. For setting up a network folder, click the first radio button for Network folder.

FIGURE 36.10

Open the pull-down menu choose the method for collecting reviews.

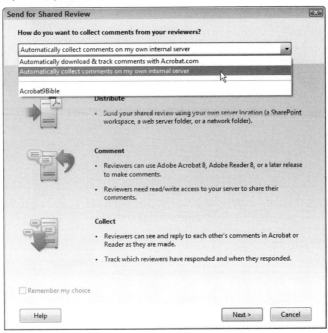

4. **Target a location to host your review.** Click the Browse button, and the Browse for Folder dialog box opens, as shown in Figure 36.12. Choose a directory path, and if you need a new folder created, click the Make New Folder button. Name a new folder, and click OK. Click OK in the Browse for Folder dialog box, and you return to the second pane in the Send for Shared Review wizard.

5. **Review the configuration summary.** Click Next, and the third pane in the Send for Shared Review wizard opens. This pane summarizes your choice for the location where the comments will be collected as shown in Figure 36.13. Review the summary, and click Next.

6. **Determine how you want to distribute the PDF document for review.** You have two choices when you arrive at the last pane in the Send for Review wizard. Choose either Acrobat.com or Save a local copy and manually send the file later to recipients. If you choose the second option, you have to manually send the document to reviewers. The space on the network server will collect comments from all the reviewers. When you finish the setup, the PDF document appears in the Document pane with a message informing you that the file has been saved to your local hard drive and you can send the file to recipients at anytime, as shown in Figure 36.14.

FIGURE 36.11

Click the Network folder radio button, and click the Browse button to identify a folder where the review data are collected.

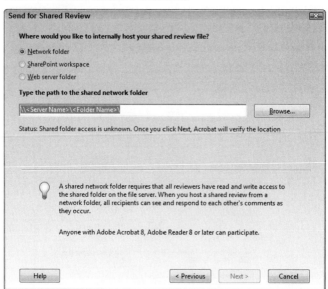

FIGURE 36.12

Use this dialog box to choose a location in which to save the review.

FIGURE 36.13

Review the summary, and click Next to complete the network folder setup.

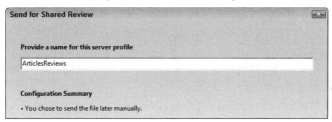

In the Document Message bar in Figure 36.14, you find some new tools for commenting. The Check for New Comments button checks the network folder for new comments added by recipients and populates your PDF document with new comments. The Publish Comments button uploads any new comments you add to the PDF file as XML data collected at the network folder.

From the pull-down menu adjacent to the Publish Comments button, you have a few choices for opening the Tracker and working offline. If you work in an area where you don't have access to your server, choose Work Offline and you can make comments while on the road. When you return to your office and connect to the network folder, your offline comments can be published.

FIGURE 36.14

The last step in preparing a document for review

Setting up shared reviews on Acrobat.com

Perhaps the easiest way to initiate and participate in shared reviews is via Acrobat.com. As we said earlier, you don't have to worry about any configurations as long as you have set up your Adobe ID and can log onto Acrobat.com. This option provides you a seamless, hassle-free approach to engaging in shared reviews.

 For setting up an Adobe ID and logging onto Acrobat.com, see Chapter 33.

To learn how easily you can initiate and participate in shared reviews on Acrobat.com, do the following.

STEPS: Starting a Shared Review using Acrobat.com

1. **Open the Comment task button pull-down menu, and select Send For Shared Review.** The Send for Shared Review wizard opens the same as shown in Figure 36.10.

2. **Choose Acrobat.com for your host.** When you open the Send for Shared Review wizard, choose Automatically download & track comments with Acrobat.com.

3. **Log onto Acrobat.com with your Adobe ID.** Click Next, and the Send for Shared Review Adobe ID login pane opens, as shown in Figure 36.15. Type your ID and Password, and click Sign In to log onto Acrobat.com.

FIGURE 36.15

Logging onto Acrobat.com

4. **Identify recipients.** The next item you see is an e-mail message box in the Send for Shared Review wizard, as shown in Figure 36.16. Type the names of recipients in the To text box. If you want to edit the Subject and/or message, you can edit the respective items in the wizard. Click Send, and several things happen to your PDF document:

- The file you send to Acrobat.com is enabled with Adobe Reader usage rights so Adobe Reader users can participate in the review.

- The e-mail message is sent to your list of recipients when you click the Send button

- The file is automatically uploaded to Acrobat.com. You don't need to do anything else other than identify your recipients and click the Send button. What could be easier?

- You have an option for choosing an access level —either Open so anyone visiting your Acrobat.com library can download the file or Closed so only those you invite to share the file with can download it.

Amazingly, the four preceding steps are all you have to do to initiate a shared review using Acrobat.com. Creating, publishing, and downloading comments are handled just like using network folders described in the section "Using network folders" earlier in this chapter.

Acrobat confirms your upload with the message box shown in Figure 36.17 when you click the Send button in the e-mail message. As with network folder reviews, you have a Check for New Comments button and a Publish Comments button to download recipient comments and upload your own comments.

FIGURE 36.16

Type recipient names in the To text box, and click Send to initiate the review.

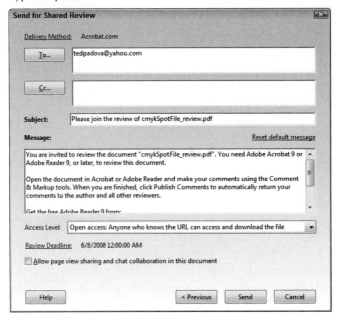

FIGURE 36.17

The buttons for checking for new comments and publishing comments available with network folders are identical when engaging in reviews on Acrobat.com.

When you check for comments on Acrobat.com by clicking the Check for New Comments button in the Document Message bar, new comments added in the review are reported in a message box, as shown in Figure 36.18. To accept the comment, click the Click here to accept link, and the comments are downloaded and populated to your PDF document on your computer.

In Windows, you can easily monitor new comment additions on Acrobat.com in the Windows Status bar shown in Figure 36.19. A mouse-over on the Tracker icon in the Status bar reports any activity or no activity with shared reviews. Right-click the Tracker icon and choose Open Tracker from a context menu, and the Tracker opens.

FIGURE 36.18

When new comments are downloaded from Acrobat.com, a message box reports the number of comments added to your PDF file.

FIGURE 36.19

You can open the Tracker for reviews and when distributing forms from a context menu opened on the Tracker icon in the Windows Status bar.

Additional items available in the Tracker when working with shared reviews include changing the deadline for a review and ending a review. In Figure 36.20, the text for these items will open windows for informing recipients that a review deadline has been extended or the review has ended.

FIGURE 36.20

You can extend a review or end a review using the Tracker.

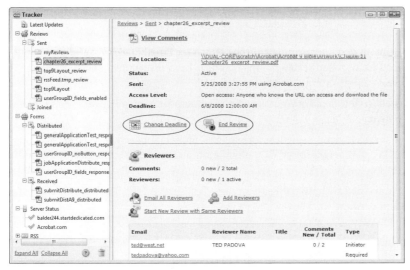

Working offline

Acrobat also offers you an opportunity to work offline when sharing comments on any kind of server. You may be temporarily away from an Internet connection or network connection and want to organize comments and later submit them. To work offline, open the pull-down menu on the Server status button in the top-right corner of the Document Message bar, as shown in Figure 36.21. Select Work Offline, and you can add comments while disconnected from the server.

NOTE   If you open a document that is in a shared review and you don't select Work Offline and you are disconnected from the Internet, Acrobat automatically puts you in an offline state. The Document Message Bar changes to reflect your offline status.

FIGURE 36.21

Select Work Offline from the Server status pull-down menu to add comments to the PDF file while working offline.

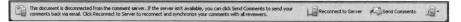

When you want to (or are able to) go back online, click Reconnect to Server. Your server connection is completed, and you can upload and download comments.

Summary

- You can initiate e-mail and shared reviews in Acrobat and participate in reviews in any Acrobat viewer. For Adobe Reader participation, documents need to be saved from Acrobat Pro or Pro Extended with Reader usage rights or by using a wizard that enables files.

- The Tracker lists all documents initiated from Attach for Email Reviews, Send for Shared Review, Upload for Browser Review, forms that have been distributed, and RSS Subscriptions.

- Send for Shared Review enables you to send files to Acrobat.com, a network server, or your own company server.

- You can host shared reviews using network folders, SharePoint servers, Web servers, and Acrobat.com. When it comes to server configuration, Acrobat.com is the easiest method for sharing reviews on servers.

- When files are enabled with Adobe Reader usage rights, the Adobe Reader users can participate in ad-hoc review workflows.

Chapter 37

Using Adobe ConnectNow for Web Conferencing

During the release of Acrobat 8 and subsequently the release of the Creative Suite 3, Adobe introduced Acrobat Connect and Acrobat Connect Professional. Acrobat Connect and Connect Pro were paid subscriptions for hosting Web conferences in meeting rooms. With Acrobat Connect, you could host meetings for 15 or more participants; with Connect Pro, you could host meetings with up to 2,500 participants.

When Acrobat 9 was introduced, Adobe introduced Adobe ConnectNow, which is part of Acrobat.com and designed as a free Web conferencing service to conduct meetings for a maximum of three people. You still have options for using Acrobat Connect and Connect Pro, but these services are still paid subscriptions.

Adobe ConnectNow is just the ticket for independent graphic designers and small ad agencies. Using Acrobat.com to enter your Adobe ConnectNow meeting room, you can host meetings in real-time for engaging in meetings with clients, no matter where they are on the planet. And to top it off, Adobe ConnectNow is free!

In this chapter, we talk about using Adobe ConnectNow for hosting and participating in online meetings.

IN THIS CHAPTER

Learning about real-time conferencing

Using Web conferencing tools

Understanding Real-Time Conferencing

Before we get into using Adobe ConnectNow for Web conferencing, we want to point out one of the outstanding features you find with the design of this Acrobat.com service. In Acrobat 8, we had Acrobat Connect to allow users to host a meeting. You can step through PowerPoint presentations and Adobe

InDesign files in online meetings to describe an advertising campaign such as the introduction of a new product, a new marketing program, an event, or some similar type of discussion.

Using Acrobat 8 and the PDF documents you created using Acrobat 8 worked well for an Acrobat Connect meeting. The only pauses you experienced were momentary delays when a new page came into view.

In Acrobat 9 and with many CS4 applications, we have a quantum leap in the delivery of files. The user audience palette has changed over the past several years, and people are asking for more dynamic presentations such as those you create with Adobe Presenter (as covered in Chapter 31), adding Adobe Flash to your documents (as covered in Chapter 23), and presenting documents in the form of PDF Portfolios (as covered in Chapter 35).

If you viewed media-rich PDF files in a Web conferencing application like Acrobat Connect, as it was introduced with Acrobat 8, then the meeting participants had to wait for video, manipulation of 3D objects, and Adobe Flash animations. These files came across the Internet very choppy and sluggish and were painfully slow even with the fastest Internet connections.

In Acrobat 9 using Acrobat.com (and particularly when hosting meetings in Adobe ConnectNow), Adobe introduces real-time collaboration. When you choose File ➪ Collaborate ➪ Send & Collaborate Live from within Acrobat 9, a recipient is invited to a real-time collaboration session. Instead of viewing your screen on a remote system and waiting for the video to play from the host machine, each participant downloads the same video file. When the host triggers something like a play button, the play is sent to other users as an *event*. Instead of the video streaming to other users from the host's computer, only the events are passed to the participants. Each user then watches a video locally, but the events are controlled by the host. This is real-time collaboration and a huge development edge provided by Adobe.

As you conduct meetings in Adobe ConnectNow, you can upload files that contain rich media to your meeting room, and your participants can download these files for uninterrupted viewing.

 **Although we're covering the features in the CS4 applications, the introduction of Acrobat.com services for CS4 users first appeared with the CS3.3 upgrade.**

Hosting a Web Conference

To take advantage of using Adobe ConnectNow, you first need to acquire an Adobe ID and log onto Acrobat.com. If you don't have an Adobe ID, you need to follow the steps for acquiring an ID, which are outlined in Chapter 33.

After you have your Adobe ID, you can access Adobe ConnectNow from any CS4 application. From within Acrobat 9, choose File ➪ Collaborate ➪ Share My Screen. From the other CS applications, choose File ➪ Share My Screen. When you select the menu command, your default Web browser opens the Adobe ConnectNow workspace on Acrobat.com and you log on using your Adobe ID.

Inviting participants

Your first view in Adobe ConnectNow displays your meeting room and a dialog box with a URL, as shown in Figure 37.1. Your participants use this URL to log onto your meeting room. On your clients' end, the only application they need is a Web browser; they don't even need an Adobe ID to be a meeting participant.

FIGURE 37.1

Choose File ⇨ Share My Screen in one of the CS4 applications, and the first item you see is an information dialog box with the URL for your meeting room.

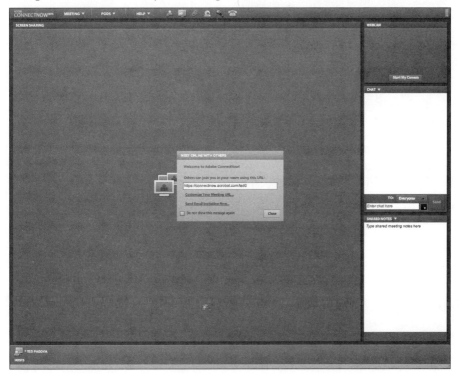

> **NOTE** You can also log onto Adobe ConnectNow by opening Acrobat.com in your Web browser and clicking the Adobe ConnectNow button on the welcome page.

As shown in Figure 37.1, two links appear in the Meet Online With Others dialog box. Click Customize Your Meeting URL, and your Web browser opens the screen shown in Figure 37.2. You can make changes for your login information and take a snapshot from your webcam or upload an image to be displayed on your meeting room Web page. After making edits, click OK to return to the initial login page.

FIGURE 37.2

Click Customize Your Meeting URL, and a window opens in your Web browser where you can change your login attributes and upload a photo.

Click Send Email Invitation Now, and your default e-mail client opens with the meeting URL added in the message box, as shown in Figure 37.3. You can copy the URL from the initial screen when you first log on and send the e-mail later, or you can use this link to send an e-mail right away when you're ready to start a meeting. The location of your meeting room is always at the same URL, so you can keep a copy of the URL and send e-mails in advance when you want to schedule meetings.

FIGURE 37.3

Click Send Email Invitation Now to open your default e-mail client with a new message window containing your meeting URL.

Adjusting settings

At the top of your screen in your meeting room, you find a toolbar with tools available for making settings adjustments and displaying various views as shown in Figure 37.4. The tools include the following:

FIGURE 37.4

Across the top of your screen, some tools are available to customize settings and views.

A   **Meeting:** The first item in the toolbar across the top of the screen is the Meeting pull-down menu with the options shown in Figure 37.5.

FIGURE 37.5

Click Meeting to open the Meeting menu.

These commands are available:

- **Invite Participants:** Click this command, and you can add additional participants to your meeting. You can have a maximum of three participants in a meeting.

- **Share My Computer Screen:** Your screen is invisible to other viewers until you either select Share My Computer Screen when you first arrive as Adobe ConnectNow, choose this menu item, or click the Share My Computer Screen tool in the toolbar. You can prepare your files and the choose this menu command or click the Share My Computer Screen tool when you're ready for the participants to see your screen.

- **Upload a file:** Click this command, and a Browse dialog box opens where you can locate a file on your hard drive and upload it to your meeting room. The file limit size for any file you upload is 10MB.

- **Share My Webcam:** Click this command, and you can share a webcam.

1115

■ **Preferences:** Click Preferences, and the Preferences screen opens, as shown in Figure 37.6. In the Preferences window, you can determine whether participants require approval to enter your room or allow anyone having the URL to enter your room. In terms of permissions for attendees, you can choose to allow attendees to share their screens, share files, share a webcam, type notes on chat and draw on a white board, or limit the attendee participation to viewing your presentation only with questions they can type in a Chat Pod.

FIGURE 37.6

Choose Meeting ⇨ Preferences to open the Preferences window.

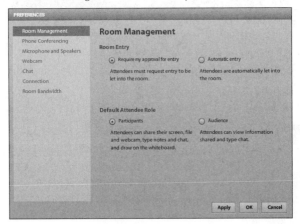

■ **End Meeting:** When you're finished with a meeting, choose Meeting ⇨ End Meeting.

B **Pods:** Pods are those items you see loaded when you log onto your meeting room. The large pod occupying most of your screen is the Screen Sharing pod where you display files you are discussing. On the right, as shown earlier in Figure 37.1, you see the Webcam, Chat, and Shared Notes pods. Open the Pods pull-down menu, and you find a few other pods, as shown in Figure 37.7.

FIGURE 37.7

Open the Pods pull-down menu to display the Pods options.

The Files pod is a window that displays file uploads you and the attendees have made during a session. The Whiteboard is a drawing board where you can draw notes and markups using the elaborate set of tools shown in Figure 37.8.

FIGURE 37.8

The Whiteboard pod is used for notes and markups.

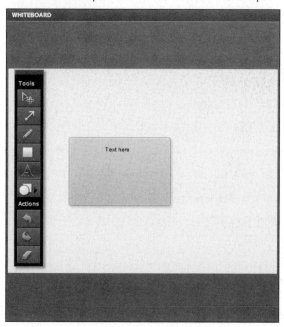

C **Help:** The Help menu provides some links to Web pages where you can customize settings and obtain help information on Adobe ConnectNow.

D **Invite Participants:** This tool is used the same as choosing Meeting ⇨ Invite Participants.

E **Share My Computer Screen:** This tool is used the same as choosing Meeting ⇨ Share My Computer Screen. Note that when you share your screen, you see your screen change to displaying your desktop or application window and the interface from Acrobat.com disappears while a single panel remains in the foreground. Attendees see the screen displayed on your computer.

F **Upload a File:** This tool is used the same as choosing Meeting ⇨ Upload a File. A file is uploaded into the File Share Pod and becomes available for attendees to download the file.

G **Share My Webcam:** This tool is used the same as choosing Meeting ⇨ Share My Webcam.

H **Share My Microphone:** Click the tool, and the Adobe Flash Player Settings dialog box opens, as shown in Figure 37.9. To share your microphone (and also when you choose Share My Webcam), click Allow so participants can hear you when speaking into a microphone connected to your computer.

FIGURE 37.9

Click Share My Microphone, and select Allow in the Adobe Flash Player Settings dialog box.

I **Set up your phone conferencing information:** You can set up a phone conversation between you and your participants. Click this tool to set up the phone number.

Hosting a Session

When you want to host a session, you log onto your Adobe ConnectNow workspace using your Adobe ID and login information and arrive at the screen shown earlier in Figure 37.1. You send the URL for your meeting room to participants via an e-mail message.

When a user logs onto your meeting room, and assuming you want to verify participants as they enter your room, the pop-up window shown in Figure 37.10 opens. To accept a visitor, click Accept.

FIGURE 37.10

Click Accept to accept a new visitor to your meeting room.

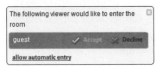

When your participants are in attendance, click the Share My Screen button appearing in your Screen Sharing pod, and the Start Screen Sharing dialog box shown in Figure 37.11 opens. Click the Share button to confirm sharing your screen, and you arrive at another information screen, as shown in Figure 37.12. This screen is informational, and you can eliminate displaying it in subsequent sessions by clicking the check box for Do not show this message again.

At this point, whatever you display on your monitor is shown on your participants' screens. Your view when you share a screen appears as shown in Figure 37.13. The pods on the right are loaded by default. You can use the Chat pod to type messages and see responses from participants.

FIGURE 37.11

Click Share to begin sharing your screen.

FIGURE 37.12

Read the information, and click OK to begin sharing your screen.

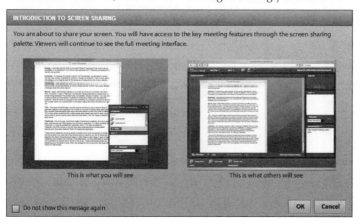

If you want to eliminate the view of the pods, click the close box (X) in the top-right corner of the Pods panel. Clicking the close box simply minimizes the view, and you can return to the Pods view by clicking the ConnectNow icon in the Status bar (Windows) or Dock (Mac).

Participants see the view shown in Figure 37.14. They can click the full screen button to open the window up to a full screen view, select tool options in the top-level toolbar, type text in the Chat pod, and share notes in the Shared Notes pod.

At times, you may want to give control over your computer to a participant to navigate documents or promote a user to share his screen. Click a user in the Attendees pod, and from the Role pop-up menu, you can promote a user to a host level. At the bottom of the menu, you can select Give this user control of my computer, as shown in Figure 37.15 and the participant can navigate documents on your computer.

All the options described in Adjusting settings are available where you can upload files, have participants upload files, use audio via a microphone, share webcams, use a white board, load additional pods, and promote users to host levels.

FIGURE 37.13

When you share your screen, several pods appear by default.

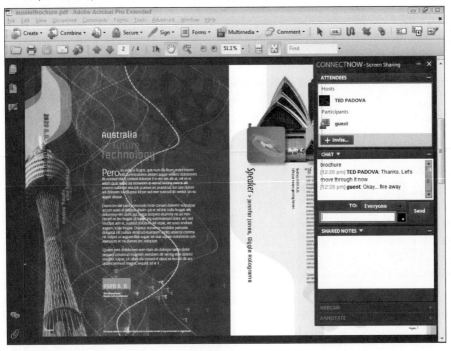

FIGURE 37.14

The view as participants see your screen.

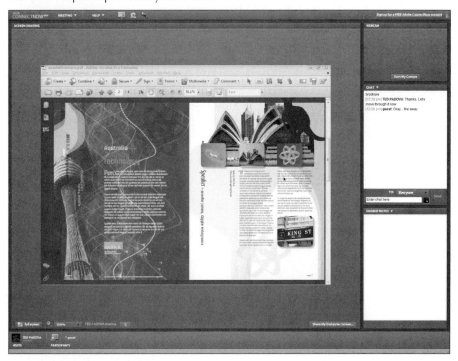

FIGURE 37.15

Click a name in the Attendee pod, and a pop-up menu provides options for changing the role of the participant.

Summary

- Using Adobe ConnectNow, you can host online meetings free for a maximum of three participants.

- As a host, you are required to log on to Adobe ConnectNow with your Adobe ID.

- Participants don't need an Adobe ID to participate in a meeting.

- You can share your screen with participants, ask participants to share their screens with you, and allow participants to take control over your screen.

- A number of tools and Pods are installed with ConnectNow that provide many options for sharing files, using audio and video, opening pods, finding helpful information, and more.

Chapter 38

Enabling PDFs with Yahoo! Ads

A dvertising on Web sites is becoming commonplace for many businesses. We see Google Ads and Yahoo! ads on many different commercial Web sites and individual blogger sites.

It stands to reason that the natural evolution of advertising ultimately gets into individual graphic design pieces such as brochures, pamphlets, and many different files you create for your clients.

As an extension of Web page advertising, Adobe has introduced PDF Ads powered by Yahoo!, where advertising similar to what we see on Web pages can be included directly in PDF documents. The inclusion of ads in PDF documents is not a feature available in Acrobat. Yahoo!-enabled PDFs are derived from a service provided by Adobe Systems.

In this chapter, you learn how to add Yahoo! ads to PDF documents using the Adobe service Ads for Adobe PDF Powered by Yahoo!.

IN THIS CHAPTER

Adding Yahoo! ads to PDF documents

Adding Ads from Yahoo! to PDF Files

Depending on the design piece you create for a client, you may be able to entice your clients into exploring advertising within design pieces your clients host on their Web servers. A brochure for a resort, a product brochure for a reseller, a company newsletter, and other types of design pieces might be good candidates for including advertising in the files that a client hosts on a local Web server.

Ads for Adobe PDF is a means for your clients or you to monetize your documents through a free service provided by Adobe. You don't need to worry about protecting files because you'll want to encourage wide distribution. As a matter of fact, the more people who view your files, the better chance you have of earning more money.

Understanding how Yahoo!-enabled PDFs work

Ads for Adobe PDF is a free service available from Adobe. To use the service you need to do the following:

- **Apply to the program.** Submit the application form found on the Adobe Labs Web site. Log onto `http://labs.adobe.com/technologies/adsforpdf/`. The Adobe Labs Ads for Adobe PDF Web page opens in your Web browser, as shown in Figure 38.1. On the Adobe Labs Web site, you can review the information related to Ads for PDF, some sample screen shots of Yahoo!-enabled PDFs, and the process for getting started.

- **Subscribe to the service.** If you are designing a piece for your client and your client is going to earn the income from ad clicks, you need to have your client apply for a subscription. If you are enabling PDFs for your own personal use, you need to apply directly to the service. Click the How do I get started button on the Adobe Labs Web site, and the application form shown in Figure 38.2 opens. Fill out this form (or have your client fill out the form), and click the Submit button.

NOTE Participation in the program requires review and acceptance by Adobe. If you are accepted into the program, you'll receive an e-mail containing instructions on how to create your account.

- **Submit your PDF documents to Adobe.** When you are accepted into the program, you'll receive a URL where you submit files to the service.

- **Upload your file(s) to the Adobe service via the service Web site URL.** The Adobe service analyzes your files to enable Yahoo! ads to be matched and displayed in the PDF document, as shown in Figure 38.3. After a file has been ad-enabled, you receive an e-mail message from Adobe with a URL link on where to download your file.

- **Click the URL link e-mailed to you, download the ad-enabled PDF document, and distribute it on your Web site or via e-mail.**

FIGURE 38.1

Your first step is to log onto the Adobe Labs Web site.

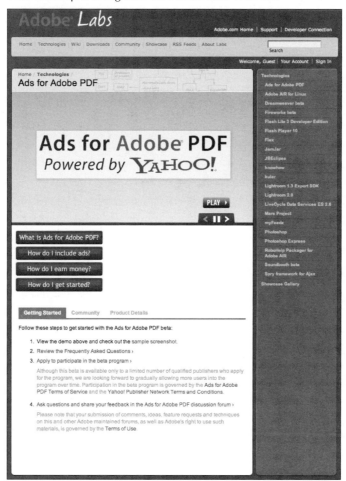

FIGURE 38.2

Submit the application form.

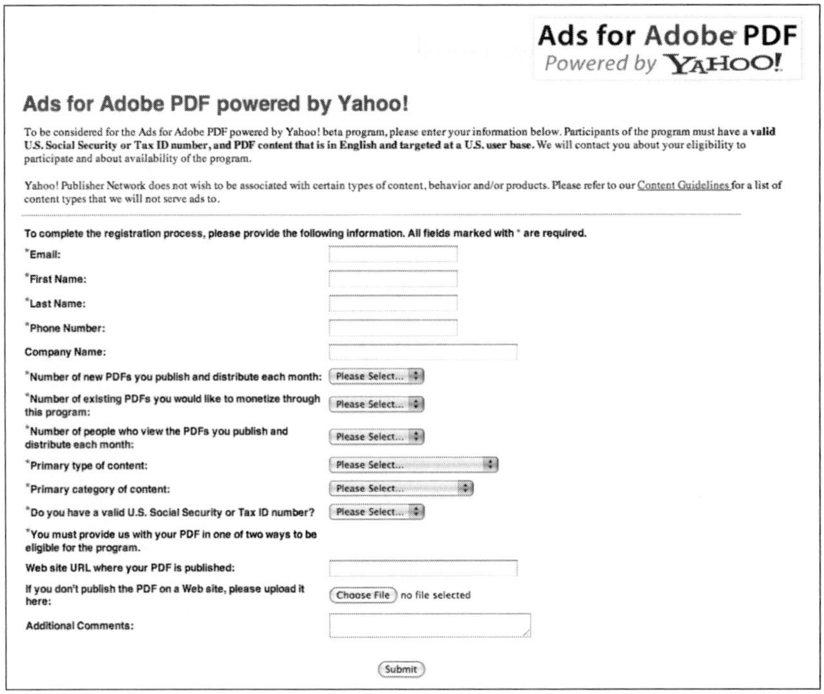

Each time a reader of your PDF clicks an ad, you earn money.

Currently, one set of ads shows up for an entire PDF and on all pages. However, by the time you have this book in your hands, Adobe will have upgraded the service to provide you with options for displaying page-specific ads.

What makes this next upgrade attractive is that ads are added to each page in your document relative to the content on the respective page. For example, if you design a product brochure for a manufacturer of golf accessories, you might have golf clubs shown on some brochure pages, and the ads on these pages might show resellers of those products. On another page where you talk about the golf grip, you might find ads related to golf gloves. Move on to another page where you talk about driving long distances, and you might find ads related to long-distance golf balls. In short, each page displays ads according to the content displayed on the page.

Adobe also built in a way for you to be selective about the kind of ads you want shown in your documents. If you're designing a brochure for Toyota, you won't want ads popping up from competitors such as Ford and Chevrolet. You have choices for blocking out competitor ads and selecting the kinds of ads you want to include in your files. All the questions you may have about Ads for Adobe PDF are answered on the Adobe Labs Web site.

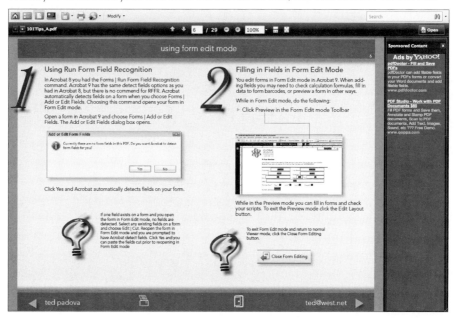

When you download your files from the Adobe service, the files contain Yahoo! ads.

Editing PDF documents with ads

When Adobe creates the sidebar that supports the Yahoo! ads, the ad metadata are digitally signed to prevent tampering. This prevents another user from cracking the metadata and redirecting revenue elsewhere.

Any content changes are viewed as tampering, and the signature is corrupted. Therefore, if you try to edit a file by changing anything on the document pages, inserting new pages, deleting pages, or replacing pages, the ads are invalidated. You need to resubmit an edited file to the Adobe service to have the document re-enabled with ads.

When you prepare PDF files for distribution, be aware that you need to make all edits on your files before submitting them to Adobe for enabling the files with Yahoo! ads. If you want to distribute files on CD-ROM or the Web, and you want links to open and close files or use URL links, you must add these link actions before the files are edited by Adobe. Adding link actions on files with ads disturbs the metadata signature and breaks the ad links.

If you have product brochures of substantial size you may need to break up the PDF documents into smaller files and use a contents page to link to the various sections of the brochure. As of this writing, PDFs with Yahoo! ads are limited to files of 10MB or less.

Summary

- Yahoo! Ads for PDF is a free service offered by Adobe Systems.

- To participate in the program, you must submit an application to Adobe.

- After acceptance into the program, you can submit PDF files to be ad-enabled.

- Yahoo!-enabled PDF documents cannot be edited without breaking the signature and disabling the ads.

- PDF documents can be ad-enabled for all PDFs of 10MB and less.

Part IX

Printing and Digital Prepress

In this part we talk about printing and preparing files for commercial printing. In Chapter 39 we discuss printing to desktop printers for the purpose of creating client proofs. Chapter 40, the final chapter in this book, covers printing files in commercial print shops. This chapter talks about printing separations, preflighting files, and preparing files for output on a variety of commercial printing devices.

Chapter 39

Choosing Print Setups

Files created for print fall into two categories—designs for composite prints and designs for color separations or commercial printing. When you design documents for composite printing, your output device might be a laser printer, a desktop inkjet printer, a large-format inkjet printer, a color copier, a film recorder, or a high-end commercial color printer. Files designed for commercial printing are typically color-separated and printed to film, direct to plate, or direct to press.

This chapter is concerned with setting print attributes for composite color that may print to your office desktop printers as well as advanced settings for commercial devices designed for printing prepress.

IN THIS CHAPTER

Choosing printers

Working with print setups

Selecting Desktop Printers

The first step in printing files is to select the target printer and the print attributes associated with the printer, such as paper size, paper feed, paper tray, and so on. If you work as an independent designer in a small shop, you may have only one printer on your network. After you assign your printer as the default printing device, you don't need to worry about printer selection. However, if you work in production workflows in larger shops, you may have a variety of printers attached to your network. In these environments, it's essential you make the proper printer selection before sending off a job for print. Selecting printers varies between Mac OS and Windows.

Printer selection on the Mac

One of the clear disadvantages of using the CS programs when you print a document is the inconsistency between what you see in an application document window versus what prints. The programs vary in what dialog boxes you access, whether you have access to a printing device PPD

(PostScript Printer Description), how to set up custom pages, and what print attributes to use. To fully comprehend printer selection, we need to look at the CS programs individually.

InDesign

In InDesign on Mac OS, you make printer selections in the Print dialog box. Notice that you don't have a command under the File menu for Page Setup. If you choose File⇨Document Setup, the Document Setup dialog box opens; here, the options choices are restricted to page sizes and defining bleeds and slugs. No options for printer choices or print attributes are made in the Document Setup dialog box.

To make a printer choice, choose File⇨Print. In the Print dialog box, shown in Figure 39.1, you choose your target printer from the Printer pull-down menu. You select a printer from the menu choices and then make various print-attribute choices by clicking the items listed in the left pane and respective choices on the right side of the dialog box.

FIGURE 39.1

The InDesign Print dialog box on a Mac

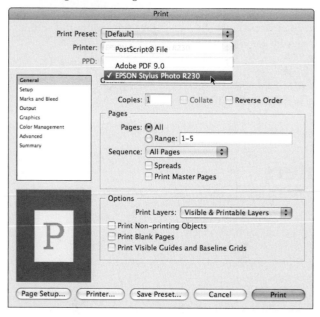

Notice that you have a choice for accessing the Page Setup dialog box in the Print dialog box. Click Page Setup, and a warning dialog box opens, as shown in Figure 39.2. The warning informs you that settings can be made in InDesign's Print dialog box without opening the Page Setup dialog box. Be certain to use the InDesign option rather than the Page Setup dialog box. Conflicts can persist if you make choices in the Page Setup dialog box.

FIGURE 39.2

Clicking Page Setup opens a warning dialog box.

Illustrator

Also in the Print dialog box is a Printer pull-down menu where you select your target printer in Illustrator. Like InDesign, Illustrator has a Document Setup dialog box where no print options are selected.

To select a target printer in Illustrator, choose File ⇨ Print. The Print dialog box opens, shown in Figure 39.3. From the Printer pull-down menu, select the printer you want to use.

 **Adobe PDF is a printer option in all applications because it's installed with Adobe Acrobat. For device output, you typically should use the Adobe PDF printer.**

FIGURE 39.3

Select a printer from the Printer menu in the Print dialog box.

Photoshop, Dreamweaver, and Acrobat

Photoshop, Dreamweaver, and Acrobat all make use of a Page Setup dialog box. Rather than use the Print dialog box to access a printer, your first choice in these programs is the Page Setup dialog box, shown in Figure 39.4. From the Format For pull-down menu, select the printer you want to use.

NOTE Dreamweaver doesn't have a Print command for use in printing a Web page preview. The Print Code command in Dreamweaver is used to print the HTML code of a Web page. If you want to print a Web page design, select Preview in Browser and choose the Web Browser from the submenu. Use your chosen browser to print the Web page.

FIGURE 39.4

Photoshop, Dreamweaver, and Acrobat use the Page Setup dialog box.

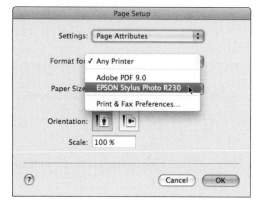

If you need to define custom page sizes for your output, set up the custom page by selecting Custom Paper Size in the Settings pull-down menu. After you create a custom page size, return to the Page Setup dialog box and select the new page size before moving to the Print dialog box.

CROSS-REF For more information on creating custom page sizes, see Chapter 22.

Printer selection on Windows

Similar to printer selections on the Mac, Windows users access printers in the Page Setup or Print dialog boxes. Also like the Mac CS applications, some programs don't have a Page Setup dialog box, while others require you to first visit a Page Setup dialog box when selecting a printer and paper size.

InDesign and Illustrator

When using InDesign and Illustrator on Windows, you make your printer selections in the Print dialog boxes. The Document Setup dialog boxes offer the same options as you find in the Mac counterparts. In InDesign, choose File ⇨ Print, and make a printer selection from the Printer drop-down list, shown in Figure 39.5.

FIGURE 39.5

InDesign on Windows

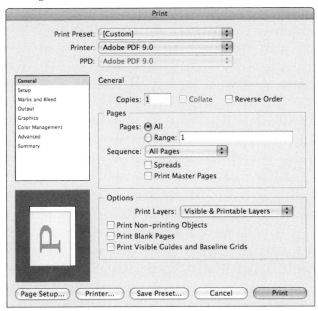

Likewise, in Illustrator choose File ➪ Print, and select your target printer from the Printer drop-down list. Notice that the print options available in the InDesign and Illustrator Print dialog boxes match the options found on the Mac.

Photoshop Dreamweaver and Acrobat

Photoshop, Dreamweaver, and Acrobat all use different dialog boxes for printer selection than the dialog box you use for printing. In Photoshop and Dreamweaver, you use the Page Setup dialog box; in Acrobat, you use the Print Setup dialog box. Most of the CS applications also let you choose a printer from the Print dialog box, as you can see in Figure 39.6. For adjusting settings for the print driver such as paper size, orientation, defining custom pages, and so on, you need to use the Page Setup dialog box and adjust the properties for the printer.

Acrobat

Acrobat handles printer selection in either the Print dialog box or by using the File ➪ Print Setup menu command. After selecting Print Setup, the Print Setup dialog box opens as shown in Figure 39.7.

FIGURE 39.6

Select your target printer from the Name pull-down menu in Acrobat.

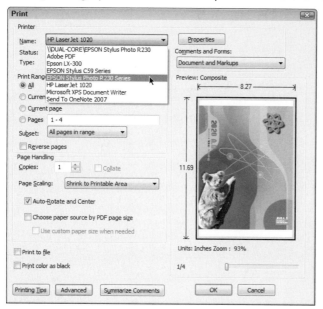

FIGURE 39.7

In Acrobat, select a printer in the Print Setup dialog box.

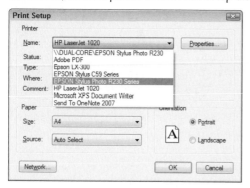

From the Name drop-down list, you make a choice for your target printer. After selecting the target printer, click the Properties button to open the printer properties for the selected printer. In Figure 39.8, you can see the Properties dialog box for an HP LaserJet 1020.

FIGURE 39.8

Click Properties in a Page Setup or Print Setup dialog box to open the printer driver properties.

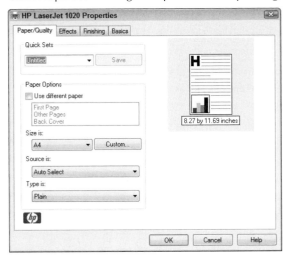

After making a printer selection and adjusting properties, you then make choices for print attributes in the Print dialog boxes. If paper selection is handled in Page Setup or Print Setup dialog boxes, be certain to make the proper paper choice before opening the Print dialog box.

Setting Print Options

If your task is to print composite color to desktop or large-format commercial printers, you don't need to manage many of the print attributes in the print dialog boxes. Items such as emulsion, screening, separations, and so on are used for prepress and commercial printing. In some circumstances, you must use an option designed for commercial printing when printing composite color. For example, when printing on Mylar on your desktop color printer, you must print emulsion down so the image is reversed on the back of the *substrate* (printing material). Special conditions like this require you to know all the print features in the Print dialog boxes.

Although you may not use all the options available to you when printing CS application documents, an elaborate description is offered here for both composite and commercial printing. Use this information in conjunction with the material in Chapter 40 when printing to commercial printing devices. Because each program has some different attribute settings, look over the settings descriptions according to the program you use for final output.

Setting print options in Illustrator

In Illustrator, choose File ➪ Print to open the Print dialog box, where you select your printing device. As a matter of rule, you first want to select the printing device. Items such as page sizes and PPDs (PostScript Printer Description files) are accessed after making the printer choice. A PPD contains information related to your printer when printing to PostScript devices. Such information relates to a series of fixed page sizes, color handling, screening, and similar characteristics. When you open the Print dialog box, a list of categories appears in the left pane. Clicking an item in the left pane changes options on the right side of the dialog box.

> **TIP**   PPD files are text documents. If you need to install a PPD from a Mac to a Windows machine or vice versa, you can copy the file to either platform. As text-only documents, they're completely cross-platform compliant.

General settings

The default series of settings are the General print options shown in Figure 39.5. When you select General in the left pane, the options choices include the following:

- **Print Preset:** At the bottom of the dialog box, notice the Save Preset button. You can change options in all the settings related to selections in the left pane and, as a last option setting, click Save Preset. Illustrator opens a dialog box where you supply a name for the preset, and the new preset appears in the Print Preset drop-down list. When you want to use the same print options, choose the preset name from the drop-down list, and all the settings associated with the preset are applied. The file prints according to the preset options.

- **Printer:** As discussed in the previous "Printer selection on Windows" and "Printer selection on the Mac" sections, you select the target printer from the drop-down list. You also have a selection for Adobe PostScript File. Use this option if you want to create a PostScript file that ultimately downloads to a printing device. You might use a PostScript file if you have a printer driver and a PPD for a commercial printing device at your service center, but you don't have the printer online at your studio. You can create a PostScript file that your service center can download to its printer using all the attribute choices made from the PPD file.

- **PPD:** You select PostScript Printer Description file from the PPD drop-down list shown in Figure 39.9. Desktop color printers do not use PPDs. Unless your printer is a PostScript printer, you won't have an option for PPD selection. If you're using a PostScript printer, choose the associated PPD for your printer.

- **Copies:** If you're printing more than one copy, change the value in the field box to the desired number of copies. By default, 1 appears in the field box. Below Copies, you find options for printing All pages or a page range.

- **Reverse Order:** These items work when you print Illustrator documents as tiled pages or print multiple artboards.

- **Ignore Artboards:** If you have data on multiple artboards and check this box, the bounding box for the data is used as the defined print area.

- **Skip Blank Artboards:** Any artboards containing no data are skipped to avoid printing blank pages.

- **Media:** If you're using a PostScript printer, the PPD contains all the page sizes supported by the printer and generally supports a custom page size. If the PPD supports custom pages, select Custom from the Size drop-down list and enter values in the Width and Height field boxes. If you use a non-PostScript printer, the Printer driver contains the fixed page sizes and you lose options for creating custom pages.

- **Transverse:** If a PPD supports transversing media, the check box is active. Transverse rotates pages 90 degrees and is typically used on roll-fed machines to conserve paper. For example, you can rotate a portrait letter page 11 inches high so the page height is 8.5 inches high. The print is still a portrait view, but the image is rotated 90 degrees so the roll of paper uses 8.5 inches instead of 11 inches.

- **Orientation:** Click one of the four icons below the Transverse check box for Portrait, Landscape, Portrait Rotated, or Landscape Rotated.

- **Options:** Placement, scaling, and tiling options are found in this section of the General print properties. Do Not Scale is the default and prints the document at 100 percent. Fit to Page reduces or enlarges the illustration to the page size you print. The Custom Scale option allows you to type scaling values in the Width and Height boxes. The chain link between Width and Height is activated by default, ensuring proportional scaling. If you click the chain link, you can distort the drawing by typing values independently for width and height, without regard to proportional sizing.

  From the Print Layers drop-down list, Visible & Printable limits output to visible layers but not layers designated as non-printing. Visible Layers is all layers currently visible including layers set as non-printing. All Layers will output all layers regardless of their non-print status and visibility—this option prints everything.

  The Tile options are helpful when you print composite color on small desktop devices where you design a piece for a large display print. If you need to proof the artwork on your printer before sending it off to an imaging center, use the Tiling options for Tile Full Pages or Tile Imageable Areas. The artwork prints on several pages in sections, which you can piece together to see the full print.

Marks and bleeds

Printer's marks are essential when printing files to commercial equipment especially when printing color separations. Items such as color names, registration marks, and crop marks are needed when preparing printing plates and trimming paper. On composite color prints, you may print an image on a larger-size paper to accommodate a bleed and, therefore, need to add crop marks so you know where to trim the paper. Click Marks and Bleed, and the options for adding printer's marks appear in the Print dialog box, as shown in Figure 39.9.

- **All Printer's Marks:** When you check All Printer's Marks, the marks for Trim, Registration, Color Bars, and Page Information appear in the output and are visible in the thumbnail proof (refer to Figure 39.9). If you want some of the available printer's marks to print, individually check those items.

- **Printer Mark Type:** The choices are Roman or Japanese. Select the type of mark from the drop-down list. To see the differences between the two marks, toggle the view by selecting from the two options in the drop-down list.

- **Trim Mark Weight:** You have choices for the stroke weight of the trim marks at 0.125, 0.25, and 0.5 stroke weights. Select the desired weight from the drop-down list.

- **Offset:** Specifying an offset amount offsets the bleed and trim marks from the artwork. (Available only for Roman printer marks).

- **Bleeds:** You can specify the bleed amount uniformly on all sides or in individual distances by typing values in the Bleeds field boxes. Click the chain-link icon to toggle between uniform distances and non-uniform distances.

FIGURE 39.9

The Marks and Bleed options for adding printer's marks

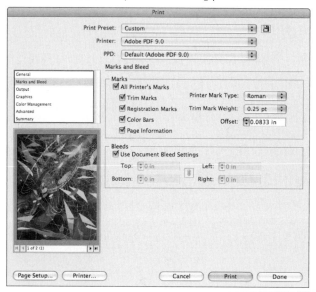

> **TIP** The chain link icon you see in the Bleeds section in Figure 39.9 appears in many dialog boxes in the CS applications, particularly in Adobe InDesign. When the icon is highlighted, a value in any one of the four text boxes is linked to the remaining text boxes. Therefore, if you type 18 pt in one box, all other text boxes automatically add the same value. If you click the link icon to deselect it, values are uniquely added to each box individually.

Output

Output settings offer options for printing composite or separations, controlling emulsion, and screening and setting halftone frequencies. For composite color, you probably won't need separations or screening. For some composite color printers, several options are grayed out, as shown in Figure 39.10.

FIGURE 39.10

Click Output to open options for color and screening.

- **Mode:** Three choices appear for Composite, Separations (Host-Based), and In-RIP Separations. Host-based separations separate the file before it is delivered to the PostScript RIP (Raster Image Processor). In-RIP separations deliver the composite file to a PostScript 3 RIP, where the RIP separates the file.

- **Emulsion:** The choices are for Up (Right Reading) or Down (Wrong Reading). Typically, composite prints are printed positive emulsion up, while film separations are printed negative emulsion down. On occasion, you may need to print emulsion down for such items as iron transfers, Mylar, LexJet, and so on.

- **Image.** The choices are for Positive or Negative image. If printing a composite image, the menu item is grayed out and defaults to Positive.

- **Printer Resolution:** For imagesetting and platesetting equipment at commercial print shops, you find resolution and halftone settings in the Printer Resolution drop-down list. These options are related to the PPD used for PostScript printers but are not accessible for non-PostScript printers such as desktop color printers. For printing composite color, you won't need to access any resolution/screening options.

- **Convert All Spot Colors to Process:** If your file contains spot color and you need four-color process printing, click the check box for converting spot color to process color. Note that the option is used for spot color only and does not apply to RGB color. Also note that the conversion takes place at the printing device RIP and does not change the color in the file.

- **Overprint Black:** For files where you have black type against color backgrounds, you may want to globally overprint the black.

- **Document Ink Options:** A list of all used colors appears at the bottom of the Output settings. You can change Frequency, Angle, and/or Dot Shape by clicking in the respective column according to color and editing the value and you can click on the eye icon to turn off printing for colors you don't want to print. After clicking, a field box appears where you can type new values.

Graphics

The Graphics settings offer some options that help improve the ability to print complex Illustrator files on PostScript printers. For composite color printing on non-PostScript printers, the options are grayed out. Click Graphics in the left pane, and the options shown in Figure 39.11 are available.

FIGURE 39.11

Click Graphics to open options for simplifying printing.

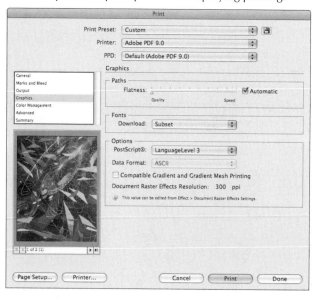

- **Paths:** Move the slider to the right to increase the flatness. Flatness breaks up complex paths to more simplified paths that make the entire drawing easier to print. If you increase the amount of flatness to the maximum, you can run the risk of distorting shapes where circles appear as polygons. In Figure 39.12, you can see how the flatness amount is measured. The original circle with an exaggerated flatness setting appears as a polygon. The flatness amount is measured by the distance between the original circle and a midpoint on a chord created with the flatness adjustment.

FIGURE 39.12

If you greatly increase flatness, circular shapes become polygons.

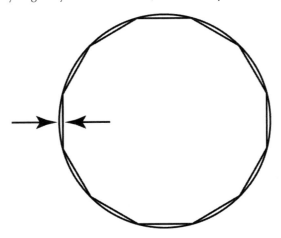

- **Fonts:** For PostScript printing, you can download fonts to the printer's RIP at the time a file is printed. Select None to download no fonts. Select Subset to download only font characters within font sets that are contained in the file. Select Complete to download the entire font character set.

- **PostScript:** Select a Language level for the PostScript printer used. In some cases, the drop-down list is grayed out, and Illustrator makes an automatic selection between PostScript Level 2 and PostScript 3, depending on the printer used.

- **Data Format:** When printing a PostScript file, you have choices for selecting Binary or ASCII encoding. For almost all purposes, use binary encoding and the file sizes become much smaller than selecting ASCII. For other printer selections, Illustrator makes the choice for you for ASCII or Binary and grays out the drop-down list preventing you from changing the option.

- **Compatible Gradient and Gradient Mesh Printing:** Unless you experience problems printing gradients or gradient meshes on a PostScript RIP, don't select this check box. This option resolves problems when these gradients don't print.

- **Document Raster Effects Resolution:** This item is informational in the Print dialog box. It reports the current setting for document raster effects resolution. If you print to imaging equipment capable of printing at high resolutions such as 1200, 2400, or 3600 dpi, and so on, you should change the value from the default to a higher resolution such as 300 ppi. To make the settings adjustments, you need to close the Print dialog box and choose Effect ➪ Document Raster Effects Settings. The Document Raster Effects Settings dialog box appears, as shown in Figure 39.13. Select Other, and type a Resolution in the Other text box. Click Use Document Raster Effects Resolution, and click OK, and you return to the Print dialog box.

FIGURE 39.13

Choose Effect⇨Document Raster Effects Settings to adjust document raster effects resolution.

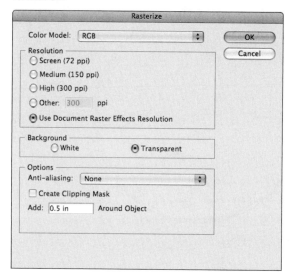

Color management

For color-managed workflows, you can use ICC profiles and select your profiles from the Printer Profile drop-down list, as shown in Figure 39.14. Select a Rendering Intent from the drop-down list options for Perceptual, Saturation, Relative Colorimetric, or Absolute Colorimetric. The choices you make in the Color Management settings should be consistent with the color-managed workflow in your environment.

CROSS-REF For more information on ICC profiles, managing color, and understanding the print space intent, see Chapter 5.

Advanced

Advanced options include the following:

- **Print as Bitmap:** For a quick proof print, you might use this option where all the vector art in your illustration is printed as a bitmapped image. Selecting this option prints the file as a rasterized bitmap but does not rasterize the file.

- **Overprints:** Select from options for overprinting items identified in your drawing for overprints. The options are Simulate, Preserve, or Discard. If you want to simulate an overprint on text comps, select the Simulate option. If you want to preserve overprints you identified in Illustrator, select Preserve from the drop-down menu. If you want to discard all overprints, select Discard and all overprints you assigned in Illustrator are ignored.

FIGURE 39.14

Click Color Management to display the Color Management options.

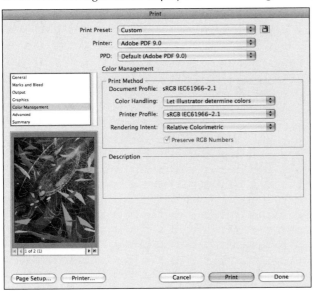

■ **Preset:** Select Low, Medium, or High for resolution related to transparency flattening and bitmap conversion. If you click Custom, the Custom Transparency Flattener Options dialog box opens as shown in Figure 39.15. In this dialog box, select the amount of transparency flattening you want by moving the slider for the Raster/Vector Balance and adjust resolution for line art and text conversion to bitmaps as well as gradients and gradient meshes. If you want to convert text and/or strokes to outlines at the time of printing, select those options. Clip Complex Regions also simplifies printing; if you have difficulty printing a file, enable this check box.

Summary

Click Summary, and the summary options appear in the Print dialog box, as shown in Figure 39.16. The Options list displays a list of the settings you made from all the other categories. If your document contains items that won't print correctly or if you made options choices that prevent printing with optimum results, the Warnings box lists potential problems you may encounter. Read the warnings, and return to your document or to the other categories and make corrections as needed.

FIGURE 39.15

Click Advanced to move to the Advanced options. Click Custom to adjust transparency flattening.

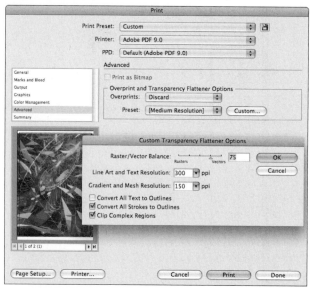

FIGURE 39.16

Summary summarizes the choices made in the Print dialog box.

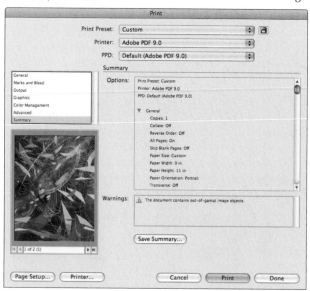

Printing Illustrator files to non-PostScript printers

Depending on your printer and the complexity of your design, you may find rasterizing your Illustrator file in Adobe Photoshop to be the only way you can print the document. Some desktop printers do well with printing directly from Illustrator, while some printers may have some difficulties for properly printing a file. In addition, some older PostScript printers may likewise have problems printing your Illustrator artwork. If you experience such problems, open the Illustrator file in Photoshop. The Import PDF dialog box opens regardless of whether you saved the file as an AI file or a PDF file. You make choices for cropping, image resolution, color mode, and bit depth. Under most circumstances, you want to be certain to select the Anti-aliased check box. Click OK, and the file is rasterized and opens in Photoshop.

As a Photoshop file, you can print directly from Photoshop or save the file in a format that can be downloaded directly to printers supporting direct file downloads. For example, many large-format inkjet printers support downloading TIFF files. In such cases, you would save the file from Photoshop in TIFF format.

Using device print settings

Color printers have unique attributes that you select from the device printer driver. On the Mac, when you choose File ➪ Print and make your choices for the print options you want to use, your next series of options is selected in another Print dialog box. Click Printer in the Print dialog box, and a warning dialog box opens, as shown in Figure 39.17.

FIGURE 39.17

A warning to make print options choices in the Print dialog box

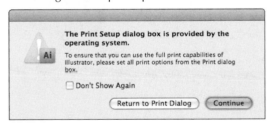

The Print Setup dialog box is provided by the operating system.

To ensure that you can use the full print capabilities of Illustrator, please set all print options from the Print dialog box.

☐ Don't Show Again

[Return to Print Dialog]   (Continue)

NOTE Device print settings are accessible from all the CS programs. When printing to devices where special paper handling is needed, as well as options for resolution output and color-mode selections, use the device print settings.

Click Continue to pass through the warning dialog box. Another Print dialog box opens offering a range of print options as well as specific settings for your color printer. From the drop-down list below the Presets drop-down list, select Print Settings. In this Print dialog box, you make choices for the media type, inks, and various settings for the print mode. In Figure 39.18, the options for a low-end Epson color printer are shown.

FIGURE 39.18

Specific print options for desktop color printers

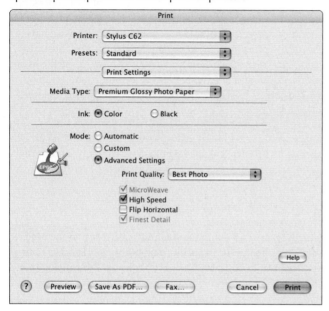

On Windows, you make the same kinds of choices from the Page Setup dialog box. Click Printer in the Page Setup dialog box to open the Print dialog box. Select your printer from the Name drop-down list, and click the Properties button. Advanced print settings are made in subsequent dialog boxes, and other options are similar to those found on the Mac.

Because the range of printers is so great, discussing all the options for all printers isn't possible. For specific information related to the options choices you need to make for media type, inks, color profiles, and mode settings, consult your printer's user manual.

Setting print options in Photoshop

Printing from Photoshop is usually performed when you print composite color. For prepress and color separations, Photoshop files most often find their way into Illustrator or InDesign documents. You can print to commercial equipment from Photoshop, but most imaging technicians generally import the Photoshop files into a layout program for printing.

If you're printing composite color, you first visit the Page Setup dialog box and set the page size for the output on your printer. When you create a custom page size in the Page Setup dialog box, be certain that you return to the Page Setup dialog box and select the new custom page.

 You can open the Page Setup dialog box from within the Print dialog box.

After selecting the Page Setup, choose File ↪ Print. You'll notice that Photoshop CS4 no longer provides two Print dialog boxes (Print and Print with Preview) as was the case in earlier CS versions of Photoshop. All the print options including a thumbnail preview are contained in the Print dialog box shown in Figure 39.19.

FIGURE 39.19

Choosing Print shows a thumbnail of your artwork.

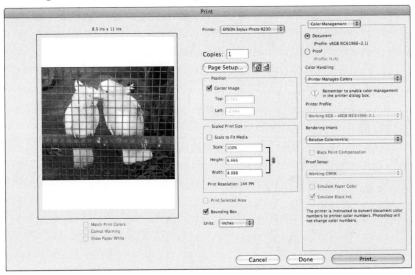

In the Print dialog box that opens, the following options appear:

■ **Match Print Colors (below the image preview):** This option is used with Proof Setup to match colors when printing a hard proof. (Available when you let Photoshop manage the color).

■ **Gamut Warning:** This option shows the range of colors that are outside the printable color region. (Available when you let Photoshop manage the color).

■ **Show Paper White:** This option simulates the white point of the target media and device, it will show a duller set of colors and gray paper when proofing to a Japan Web paper simulation. (Available when you let Photoshop manage the color).

■ **Printer:** From the drop-down menu, choose your printer.

■ **Copies:** In the text box, type the number of copies you want to print.

■ **Page Setup:** Click the Page Setup button to open the Page Setup dialog box.

■ **Position:** If you uncheck Center Image, you can move the artwork around the page where a dynamic preview displays in the thumbnail. You can type coordinate values in the field boxes or click and drag the image in the preview box.

- **Scaled Print Size:** Use the field boxes to scale the image up or down. Be aware that, when scaling images up, you need to consider the relationship between scaling size and resolution. As a 150 ppi (pixels per inch) image is scaled up 200 percent (or twice the size) the resolution drops to 75 ppi (or one-half the resolution). You can scale by editing the Scale field box, by checking the box to scale the image to fit the media, by typing values for the height and width, or by dragging handles at one of the four corners of the bounding box.

- **Print Selected Area:** This option prints a selection in the image.

- **Bounding Box:** You may have white space at one or more sides of your image or around the entire image. When you check the box for Show Bounding Box, a rectangle is displayed at the image size including the white space.

- **Output/Color Management:** Open the pull-down menu where you see Color Management, and select Output for the output options. Check the boxes for the types of printer marks and emulsion control, as shown in Figure 39.20.

FIGURE 39.20

When you choose Output from the top level pull-down menu on the right side of the Print dialog box, the options change from Color Management to Output options.

- **Functions:** The Functions area of the Print dialog box includes the following options:
  - **Interpolation:** This option prints with interpolation to upsample/downsample images not meeting the resolution requirements of the output device.
  - **Include Vector Data:** This option prints placed vector objects, type, and vector data created in Photoshop as vector items without rasterizing them.
  - **Send 16-bit Data:** For 16-bit images, this option sends the 16-bit data.
  - **Background:** By default, the background or area outside the image area is white. You can change the color by clicking Background and selecting a new color in the Color Picker dialog box that opens after clicking the Background button.

■ **Border:** Border prints a border around the bounding box. You specify point size for the border in the Border dialog box that opens after clicking the Border button.

■ **Bleed:** If you want a bleed, click the Bleed button and a dialog box opens enabling you to specify the bleed amount.

CROSS-REF For the Color Management items in the Print dialog box, see Chapter 40.

Managing color at print time

The Color Handling pull-down menu in the Photoshop Print dialog box contains four options for managing color:

■ Printer Manages Color

■ Photoshop Manages Color

■ Separations

■ No Color Management

If you choose the first option and let your printer manage color, you need to be certain that color management is turned on in the Print driver. The dialog box that opens after you click Print in Photoshop is where you make selections for the print driver to manage color.

If you choose the second option and let Photoshop manage color, you need to address two more settings. The first is to select a Printer Profile from the drop-down menu for the paper and printer you use. After clicking Print, you need to turn color management off. Leaving color management on in the print driver "double profiles" your output, which will be much less than a true color representation of your image.

Choosing Separations is available only with CMYK image files. It is used for printing separate color and spot plates on a press.

Choosing the last option for No Color Management is used only when you convert color in Photoshop to an output profile. In this case, you don't select a color profile in the Print dialog box and you turn all color management off in the Print driver.

Photoshop is the only program in the CS applications that provides you with these options and the ability to use developer-supplied printer profiles when using desktop inkjet printers. The other CS applications merely support choosing the application to manage color on PostScript-only printing devices.

Using the printer to manage color

When you choose to let your printer manage color, color profiling is handled automatically by the printer. This option works only in Photoshop. All other CS applications depend on using a PostScript printer only. Do not use this option in Illustrator, InDesign, or Acrobat unless your output device is a PostScript color printer.

To print a file from Photoshop (or any CS application) on a Macintosh while letting the printer determine the color, choose File ⇨ Print. From the Color Handling pull-down menu in the Print dialog box, choose Printer Manages Color. Click Print, and the operating system Print dialog box opens. From the second pull-down menu, choose Print Settings, as shown in Figure 39.21.

FIGURE 39.21

Choose Print Settings.

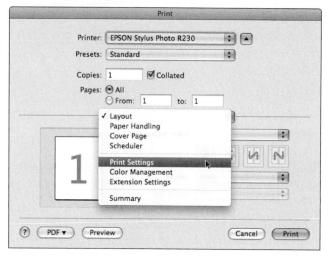

Make a choice for the paper from the Media Type pull-down menu, and choose Color Management from the pull-down menu above the Page Setup item, as shown in Figure 39.22.

When you open the Color Management panel, shown in Figure 39.23, in the Print dialog box, you need to be certain that Color Controls is selected. This choice is a default, but if you change it in a previous print session, be sure you make this choice. Essentially, we are telling the printer to manage the color. In order to do so, the Color Controls need to be enabled. Click Print, and your file is printed using the printer's built-in color profiling system.

In Windows, choose Printer Manages Color in the Photoshop Print dialog box and click Print. The next Print dialog box opens and lists your available printers. Choose your target printer, and click Preferences. Depending on the type of printer you use, you'll find options for color controls. The Epson R230 printer we use in this example has an Advanced button in the Printing Preferences dialog box. Click Advanced, and choose Color Controls in this dialog box, as shown in Figure 39.24.

FIGURE 39.22

Make a choice for the media type, and choose Color Management.

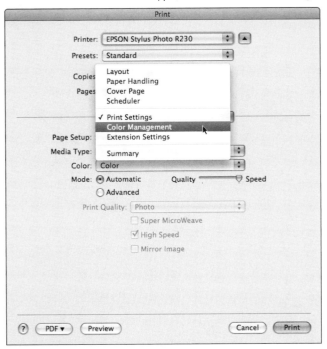

FIGURE 39.23

When the printer manages color, be certain to enable Color Controls.

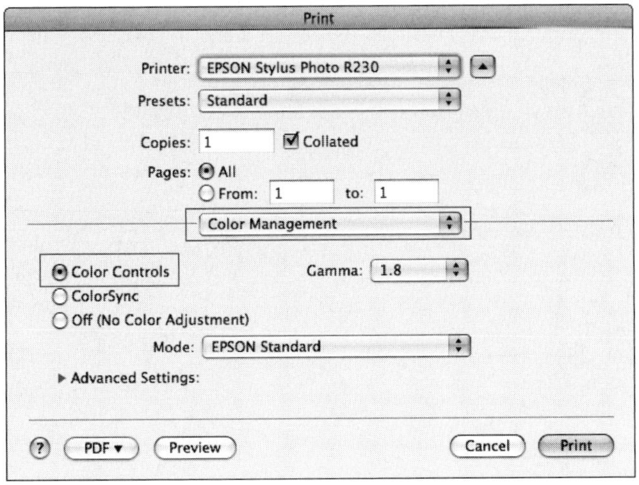

FIGURE 39.24

Click Color Controls in the Printing Preferences dialog box.

Click OK in the Printing Preferences dialog box, and click Print to print your file using the printer to manage color.

Using Photoshop to manage color

You use Photoshop to manage color when you have color profiles installed on your computer. Some low-end color printers rely on canned profiles that are part of the printer driver, and you won't find the profiles individually installed on your computer. Move up to a little more expensive model of printer, and you often find separate individual profiles installed on your computer.

All other CS applications like Illustrator, InDesign, or Acrobat also provide the option of letting the application determine color. If you use low-end printing devices that do not install profiles, you must make a choice for the color profile in the application using a generic sRGB profile such as the choice made in Acrobat in Figure 39.25 when printing to a device that doesn't have a corresponding color profile available.

FIGURE 39.25

In CS applications other than Photoshop, choose sRGB for the color profile when your printer doesn't install individual color profiles.

If you have a color profile installed with your printer installation and you're using Photoshop to print while making the choice to let Photoshop determine color, open the Printer Profile pull-down menu and choose the profile for the paper you're using, as shown in Figure 39.26.

FIGURE 39.26

Choose Photoshop Manages Colors when you have printer profiles available, and choose the profile suited for your paper type from the Printer Profile pull-down menu.

The next step in your print process is critically important. Because you are letting Photoshop manage the color, you need to turn off color management used by your printer. When you open the Color Management (on a Macintosh) or Printing Preferences (in Windows), as shown in Figures 39.23 and 39.24 respectively, you need to turn off the color management.

Follow the steps described in "Using the printer to manage color" to get to the color controls. When you arrive at there, turn them off as shown in Figure 39.27 for the Macintosh and Figure 39.28 for Windows.

FIGURE 39.27

Turn color controls off on the Macintosh.

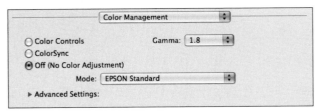

When you click the Print button, Photoshop uses your selected profile to manage the color.

Printing with no color management

You may print with no color management when you convert images to a target profile. In Photoshop, choose Edit ⇨ Convert to Profile. Choose a target profile, and when you print your file, turn off all color management (refer to Figures 39.27 and 39.28).

FIGURE 39.28

Turn color controls off in Windows.

Setting print options in InDesign

When you print from InDesign, all the print controls are contained in the Print dialog box. Unlike Photoshop, the page setup and paper size selections are made in the same dialog box where you set all the other print attributes. Select File ➪ Print and the default General print options open, as shown in Figure 39.29.

FIGURE 39.29

All the print options, including page size and page setup, are contained in the Print dialog box.

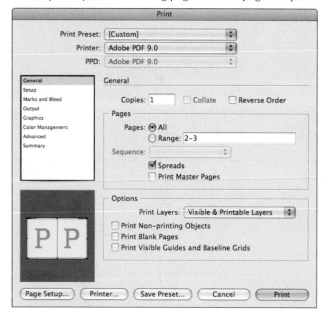

General print options

Items such as printer selection, page range, and collating are the same in InDesign as you find in the other CS applications. As you look over the settings below, realize that the items noted here are those items *not* found in either the Illustrator or Photoshop Print dialog boxes:

- **Spreads:** Printer spreads can be output from InDesign. The Spreads option prints two across the spine. InDesign can have up to ten pages in a spread. When you set up the page size for printing spreads, be certain to add the width dimension to accommodate all pages. Two letter portrait pages, for example, would be set up for 17 by 11 (2 times 8.5 inches by 11 inches high).

- **Print Master Pages:** Check this box to print the master pages.

- **Print Layers.** Choose from All Layers, Visible Layers, or Visible and Printable Layers.

- **Print Non-Printing Objects:** You can identify some objects and layers for nonprinting. When this option is selected, all objects targeted for nonprinting are printed.

- **Print Blank Pages:** Just as the name suggests, any blank pages contained in the file are printed.

- **Print Visible Guides and Baseline Grids:** Something that can help you in the design of a piece is to print the pages with guides and baseline grids. You can see the guide and grid lines on the printed pages and carefully look them over for alignment and formatting.

Setup print options

Click Setup in the left pane to show options for selecting paper size, scaling, and tiling as shown in Figure 39.30:

FIGURE 39.30

Click Setup to open options settings for selecting paper size and scaling choices.

- **Setup:** The Setup options include choices for selecting paper sizes. In InDesign you have choices for choosing fixed paper sizes from the Paper Size pull-down menu or by adding a Custom paper size and typing values in the Width and Height field boxes. The fixed sizes are derived from the PPD selected in the PPD pull-down menu. Custom sizes can be added in InDesign without going to a Page Setup dialog box and defining a custom page size. As you tab out of the Width and Height fields, the thumbnail preview shows you how the page sizes appear on selected or custom page sizes.

  The document setup should be the final trim size of the document, the media size (set in this dialog) controls how the document prints on the output device; scaling and position options also control how the document is output to the media.

- **Offset:** For roll-fed imaging equipment, the offset value offsets the printed image from the paper edge.

- **Gap:** Also on roll-fed machines, the gap is the distance between printed pages.

- **Orientation and Transverse:** The same options are available in InDesign that you find in Illustrator.

- **Options:** Options settings include scaling output, page position in one of four locations, printing thumbnail images of a layout, tiling large pages that can't fit on a single paper size, and setting the overlap gap for tiled pages.

Note that the thumbnail preview in the lower left corner of the Print dialog box shows a proxy view of the page setup.

Marks and bleeds

Marks and bleeds are similar to options you find in Illustrator and Photoshop. The items in the Marks area of the Marks and Bleed section of the Print dialog box shown in Figure 39.31 are self-descriptive. InDesign has an additional item not found in either Illustrator or Photoshop in the Bleed and Slug area of the dialog box. Check Include Slug Area to print any content you add in the slug area such as job numbers, dates, and other information you want included in a slug.

Output

Output options include specific settings for printing composites or separations. Color control and ink management are included in the options shown in Figure 39.32:

- **Color:** Choices are Composite Leave Unchanged, Composite Gray, Composite RGB, Composite CMYK, Separations, and In-RIP Separations. Choices made for the kind of composite print you want can affect the color, so be certain to choose the setting appropriate for your desired output. The Color choices defined include the following:

  - **Composite Leave Unchanged:** This option is intended for use where you print to color printers that are Pantone-certified and can simulate spot-color inks. Very few printers are capable of rendering accurate spot colors, so this option is one you won't use unless working with a printer that can accurately reproduce spot colors.

FIGURE 39.31

Options for setting marks, bleeds, and slugs

FIGURE 39.32

Option settings that control inks and emulsion

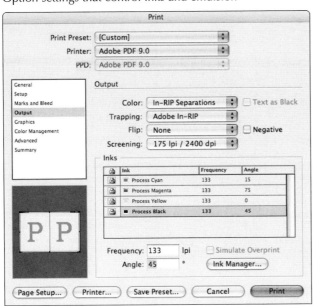

■ **Composite Gray:** When printing to grayscale printers, use this option. All colors are printed with varying levels of gray.

■ **Composite RGB:** Use this option when outputting for screen or when printing to ink-jet color printers that prefer printing from RGB mode. Most inkjets typically use CMYK color inks, but large-format inkjets like the Colorspan DisplayMakers prefer printing RGB files.

■ **Composite CMYK:** For most composite color prints, you're likely to use this option. When your inkjet printer prefers printing CMYK color, select this option from the drop-down list.

■ **Separations:** Use separations when printing to RIPs using PostScript Level 2 and below or when printing to PostScript RIPs not supporting In-RIP separations. Also, if you aren't certain of the RIP PostScript level or whether In-RIP separations are supported and you're preparing PostScript files for your service center, use Separations.

■ **In-RIP Separations:** A composite image is sent to the printer's RIP where the RIP separates the file. Many PostScript 3 RIPs support In-RIP separations, but not all PostScript 3 RIPs. If preparing files for imaging centers, be certain to inquire about their capabilities for printing before sending PostScript files.

■ **Text as Black:** Check this box to print text as pure black color as opposed to printing a mix of RGB or CMYK color to produce black.

■ **Trapping:** The drop-down list commands are made available only when Separations or In-RIP Separations are selected. Options include one of three choices. You can turn trapping off, use InDesign built-in trapping, or use In-RIP trapping. InDesign has a sophisticated built-in trapping technology, and the Adobe In-RIP Trapping engine is even more powerful. If you don't have more-powerful dedicated trapping software, either option provides you with some impressive results. Note that In-RIP Trapping is available only on PostScript 3 RIPs that support In-RIP Trapping.

■ **Flip:** Flipping a page is available for separations as well as composite printing. If you print to Mylar, LexJet, and other substrates necessitating printing documents flipped, InDesign CS offers new options over previous versions of the program and can accommodate separation and composite printing when page flipping is needed. For printing to imagesetters and platesetters, reading and emulsion are typically handled at the writing engine or the RIP. Therefore, you most often print files emulsion up and without flipping a page.

■ **Screening:** Derived from the selected PPD, you make fixed halftone screen selections from the drop-down list. To add a custom frequency not available from the drop-down list, you can manually adjust the inks for frequency and angle below the Inks table.

■ **Frequency:** You can adjust the halftone frequency manually by selecting inks in the Inks table and typing values in the Frequency field box.

■ **Angle:** The default angles for process color includes Cyan at 15°, Magenta at 75°, Yellow at 0°, and Black at 45°—the same angle used for black. If you introduce spot colors, be certain that the color angles are set apart from the other color angles. For example, on a two-color job containing Black and a spot color, change the spot color to either the Cyan or Magenta angle of 15° or 75°. If you have process color and a spot color, set the spot color angle 22° apart from the other process colors—something like 22° or 37°.

Graphics

The Graphics pane includes options for how image files are printed, font handling, and PostScript level. These options are generally used for proofing when printing for high-end prepress and commercial printing. The options shown in Figure 39.33 include the following:

The Graphics pane has options for image and font handling as well as PostScript level.

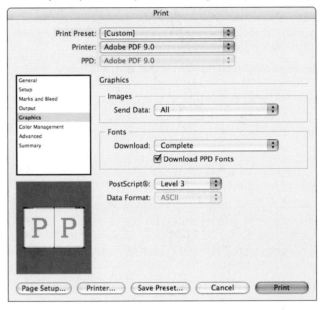

- **Images:** From the drop-down list, you have choices for what data is sent to your printer:
  - **All:** Sends all the image data to the printer and is the choice you want to use for composite color printing.
  - **Optimized Subsampling:** Sends enough data to the printer for an optimized print but downsamples images if the resolution is more than needed to output a satisfactory print.
  - **Proxy:** Sends a 72-ppi image to the printer, resulting in a faster print for proofing purposes.
  - **None:** Sends no image data for a quick print where you can examine type and layout without printing the images.
- **Fonts:** From the drop-down list, you have three choices:
  - **None:** Downloads no fonts. Use this option only when you know that all the fonts in your document reside in your printer's memory or on a hard drive attached to your printer.

- ☐ **Complete:** Downloads all fonts to your printer's memory.

- ☐ **Subset:** Sends only the characters in a font to your printer's memory.

- **Download PPD Fonts:** Fonts listed in your printer's PPD are downloaded to your printer's memory. The PPD fonts are generally the fonts contained in your printer's memory. Most laser printers have the fonts Courier, Helvetica, Times, and Symbol burned into the ROM chips in the printer. The PPD for the printers lists these fonts where the printer retrieves them when files containing the fonts are printed.

- **PostScript:** Choices are PostScript Level 2 or PostScript 3. Choose the PostScript level according to your printer if printing to a PostScript printer. If printing composite color to non-PostScript printers, don't worry about changing the default. PostScript-level choices won't have an effect on printing to non-PostScript devices.

- **Data Format:** Generally, the choice is made for you. By default, Binary is selected and you'll see ASCII grayed out.

Color management

Click the Color Management item in the left pane, and the Color Management options open, as shown in Figure 39.34.

FIGURE 39.34

Options settings for managing color

■ **Print:** Choose either Document, which uses the document's color space, or Proof, which uses the color space provided by the printer.

■ **Options:** From the Color handling drop-down menu, either choose your PostScript printer or let InDesign determine the color handling. If using a color profile calibrated for your printer, choose Let InDesign Determine Colors. From the Printer Profile drop-down list, select a color space that InDesign uses to map the color from the document's color space to the printer's color space. If you select PostScript Color Management, you use a profile based on the CRD (color rendering dictionary) available for PostScript 3 devices that have built-in color management. Choosing the option for InDesign to handle color lets you select a profile you calibrated for your printer.

■ **Output Color:** Check Preserve RGB Numbers to preserve the color profile in the file. If the box remains unchecked, the printer's color profile is used.

■ **Simulate Paper Color:** This option is available if you print a Proof. Select the check box, and the colors appear as when printed on specific papers, such as printing to newsprint or uncoated stock.

Advanced

Click Advanced in the left page to open options for the Advanced settings, as shown in Figure 39.35. Options such as OPI (Open Prepress Interface) management and transparency flattening are contained in this pane. You have these options:

Options settings for OPI management and transparency flattening

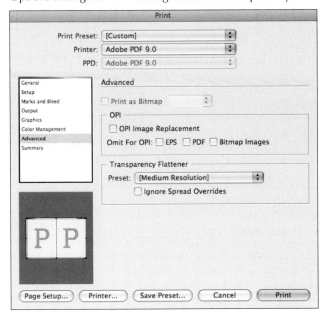

- **Print as Bitmap:** Check this box, and select a resolution to print a raster image. This setting is something you might use if you're having a problem printing fonts and vector art on a desktop printer. The option is not used when printing on commercial printing devices.

- **OPI Image Replacement:** This option and the check boxes for EPS, PDF, and bitmap images relate to replacing FPO (for-position-only) low-resolution images with high-resolution images during layout. When computers were less powerful and had less memory, OPI was used when service centers archived high-resolution images and designers used low-resolution images to create layouts. Today, with powerful computers that have plentiful RAM and hard-drive space, most people use high-resolution images for layout. For composite color printing, you're likely to never use the OPI settings.

- **Transparency Flattener:** On most PostScript RIPs, you need to flatten transparency to successfully print your document. Any use of the Transparency palette, applying drop shadows to objects in InDesign, applying a feather, using blending modes, or using transparency in imported images requires you to flatten the transparency. From the presets, use these settings in these situations:

  - **Low Resolution** for quick proof prints on desktop printers

  - **Medium Resolution** for desktop proofs on desktop color printers and copy machines, on-demand printers, and so on

  - **High Resolution** for all files printed as separations and on high-end commercial PostScript devices

- **Ignore Spread Overrides:** You can flatten transparency on spreads by viewing a spread in the Document window and choosing Spread Flattening on the Pages menu. You can override spread-specific flattener settings by selecting this check box at the time of printing or export.

Summary

As in other CS applications, a Summary dialog box lists all the settings made through the panes in the Print dialog box. If you want to save the summary to a text file that you can send to a service center, or that you can retain for future use, click Save Summary in the Summary pane to save a file defining all the print attributes select for a given print job.

Setting print options in Acrobat

Acrobat contains all the print controls needed for high-end prepress as well as all the settings you need for printing composite color. Additionally, you can use Acrobat to print files originating in the other CS applications after converting documents to PDF. Using Acrobat as your printing tool simplifies the printing process because you need to learn only those print options from a single set of dialog boxes.

CROSS-REF For a description of all the print tools in Acrobat 8, see Chapter 40.

The first place to start when printing files from Acrobat is to visit the Page Setup dialog box. After selecting the proper page size and orientation or defining a custom page size, choose File ➪ Print to open the Print dialog box shown in Figure 39.36.

FIGURE 39.36

The Print dialog box in Acrobat

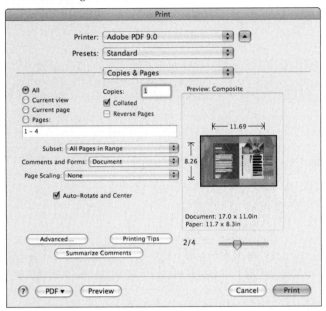

There are two sets of Print dialog boxes in Acrobat. The default opening view is the Print dialog box. The second Print dialog box is the Advanced Print Setup dialog box that opens after you click the Advanced button; this is the place where options typically used for commercial printing are found. The Print dialog box includes the following options:

- **Copies/Collated:** Use the field box to enter the number of copies you want to print. The Collated check box collates pages when printing multiple copies.

- **All:** This option prints all pages in the document.

- **Current View:** This option enables you to print a portion of a page. Zoom in to the document page and select Current View to print the page as you see it displayed on your monitor.

- **Current Page:** Navigate to the page you want to print, and select Current Page. The result is a print of the page currently viewed in the Document pane.

- **Reverse Pages:** Click this radio button to print from back to front.

- **Pages:** Click Pages, and select the range of pages you want to print.

- **Subset:** Subset contains several options in the drop-down list. Choose to print all pages in a range, odd pages only, or even pages only. Click the Reverse Pages check box to print pages in back-to-front order.

- **Comments and Forms:** From the drop-down list, you have choices for printing the document as you might print any file. Acrobat offers additional options not available in other CS applications, such as comment notes, stamps, and form fields. The Document and Comments option prints the document and the contents of the comment notes. When you select the item, the comments on the first page, if they exist, display in the Preview area. The Form Fields Only option prints only the form fields from an Acrobat form.

- **Page Scaling:** Page Scaling offers options for None, Fit to Printable Area, Shrink to Printable Area, Tile Large Pages, Tile All Pages, Multiple Pages per Sheet, and Booklet Printing. Select the option you want from the drop-down list choices.

  In Acrobat 9, you'll find some new additions to this menu. Choose Tile Large Pages or Tile All Pages, and you can tile large prints that you create for oversized inkjet printers. Choose the Multiple pages per sheet option, and you can define the number of pages you want to print on a single sheet of paper.

- **Auto-Rotate and Center:** When enabled, pages are auto-rotated and centered.

- **Summarize Comments:** Prints a comment summary for PDFs containing Comments & Markups.

- **Preview:** A document preview shows the current page as a thumbnail in the preview box. By default, the opening page previews. If you navigate to another page, the respective page displays in the preview box. Because Acrobat accommodates pages of different sizes in the same document, you can easily check a page to see if it prints properly on the current page setup. If you select the Reverse Pages check box, the Preview shows the pages in reverse order.

For composite color printing where you don't need bleeds and printer's marks, the options in the Print dialog box are all you need to send your PDF documents to your printer. When high-end commercial prepress and printing are needed, the Advanced Print Setup dialog box is where you need to make options choices. Click the Advanced button in the Print dialog box, and the Advanced Print Setup dialog box opens, shown in Figure 39.37.

On the left side of the Advanced Print Setup dialog box, you make choices for options associated with output, marks and bleeds, PostScript options and color management. The first item available for selection is Print As Image. For composite color printing when you have difficulty printing a document to your desktop printer, use this option as a last resort. When you check the box, all vector objects and type convert to bitmaps. The results are often less than optimal but can mean the difference between printing the page or not. If you experience PostScript errors when printing a file, check the Print as Image check box.

The drop-down menu adjacent to the Print As Image check box provides a list of preset values for output resolution. If you want to supply a custom resolution, type a value in the text box. You can greatly improve the appearance of files printed with the Print As Image option by raising the resolution to 300 dpi or more.

FIGURE 39.37

The Advanced Print Setup dialog box has commercial printing options.

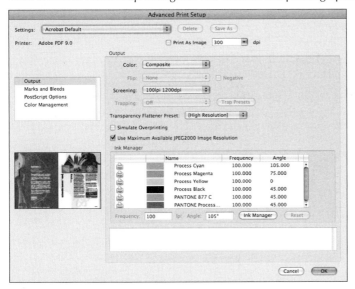

Output

Output options offer choices for handling color and screening. In the Output pane, you find settings for the following:

- **Color:** The same options for composite and separations are available in Acrobat as you find in InDesign and Illustrator. See "Setting print options in Illustrator" and "Setting print options in InDesign" earlier in this chapter.

- **Flip/Negative:** Flip is available only when printing color separations. If you need Emulsion down on a Composite print, you need to import the PDF in InDesign and flip the page. Check the box for Negative if you want to print the file as a negative.

- **Screening:** Fixed values are derived from the PPD for PostScript printers. You select custom frequencies and screen angles in the Ink Manager at the bottom of the Output pane.

- **Trapping Off:** Turns off trapping.

- **Trap Presets:** Opens the trap presets dialog box where you can define traps.

- **Transparency Flattener Preset:** Choose from High, Medium, and Low Resolution options for flattening transparency. Any custom flattener presets created in Acrobat are also available here.

- **Simulate Overprinting:** This option, also available for composite, prints a proof showing the effects of overprints assigned in the document. This feature emulates the overprinting previews of high-end color proofers that display overprints in composite proofs.

CROSS-REF **For more on flattening transparency, see Chapter 38.**

- **Simulate Overprinting:** This option, also available for composite, prints a proof showing the effects of overprints assigned in the document. This feature emulates the overprinting previews of high-end color proofers that display overprints in composite proofs.

- **Use Maximum Available JPEG2000 Image Resolution:** When enabled, the maximum usable resolution contained in JPEG2000 images is used.

- **Ink Manager:** If your file contains spot colors or RGB colors, you can convert spot or RGB to CMYK color by clicking the Ink Manager button to open the Ink Manager dialog box. To edit the frequency and angle for each plate, double-click a color and the Edit Frequency and Angle dialog box opens. Supply the desired frequency and angle for each color by successively opening the dialog box for each color.

Marks and bleeds

Click the Marks and Bleeds option in the left pane, and the marks and bleeds options appear, shown in Figure 39.38. Acrobat behaves a little differently from the other CS applications because you don't have a document setup to define page size as in the other applications. You need to be certain that the Page Setup page size is large enough to accommodate printer's marks. However, you need to define the bleeds in the document you convert to PDF. If bleeds were not included (say, from an InDesign file), the PDF won't set a bleed outside the printer's marks. Be certain you include bleed amounts in your Illustrator and InDesign files before exporting to PDF.

FIGURE 39.38

Click Marks and Bleeds to apply printer's marks.

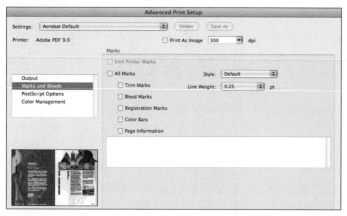

Check All Marks, or individually click the check boxes below the Marks Style drop-down list. From the drop-down list options, you can choose a number of different styles that support U.S.A. and Eastern marks and bleed styles.

PostScript options

The PostScript Options section includes a variety of settings used for preserving embedded half-tone frequencies, transfer functions, handling color, and some other miscellaneous settings. Click PostScript Options to open the options choices for the PostScript settings, as shown in Figure 39.39. You have these options:

FIGURE 39.39

The PostScript Options pane has various settings for PostScript printing.

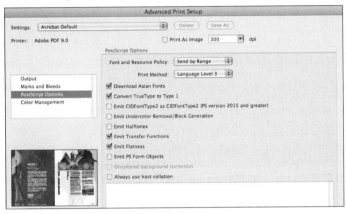

- **Font and Resource Policy:** Three options are available from the drop-down list:
  - **Send at Start:** Sends all fonts to the printer as the print job starts.
  - **Send by Range:** Sends fonts encountered on the pages while new pages print and where the fonts stay in memory until the job finishes printing.
  - **Send for Each Page:** Conserves memory where the fonts are flushed after each page prints. This option takes more time to print but can overcome problems when you experience difficulty in printing a job.
- **Print Method:** Choose from PostScript Level 2 or PostScript 3 depending on the level of PostScript used by the RIP.
- **Download Asian Fonts:** Check the box if Asian characters are in the document and not available at the RIP.
- **Convert TrueType to Type 1:** This option converts TrueType fonts to Type 1 fonts.
- **Emit CIDFontType2 as CIDFontType2 (PS version 2015 and greater):** This option sends older CID Type 2 fonts as a newer PostScript version.
- **Emit Undercolor Removal/Black Generation:** GCR/UCR removal is necessary only if the original file contains embedded settings. Deselect the box to remove any embedded settings that you might have inadvertently added and saved in Photoshop. If you want to apply any embedded settings, checking the box to emit the settings applies them as they were embedded in the authoring program.

- **Emit Halftones:** If the PostScript file contained embedded halftones, you can preserve them here, and the frequency assigned in the Output options is used to print the file. Check the box to apply the frequency embedded in a file. You preserve halftones when you want an embedded halftone frequency in an image to print at a different frequency than the rest of the job.

- **Emit Transfer Functions:** Deselect the box to eliminate any transfer functions that might have been embedded in Photoshop images. If you know you want images to print with embedded transfer functions that you may have applied according to instructions provided from a publication house, check the box to preserve the transfer functions.

- **Emit Flatness:** This option applies flatness settings for vector data saved with EPS files.

- **Emit PS Form Objects:** PostScript XObjects store common information in a document—things like backgrounds, headers, and footers. When PostScript XObjects are used, the printing is faster, but it requires more memory. To speed up the printing, check the box to emit PostScript XObjects.

- **Discolored Background Correction:** Enable this option only when printing composite proofs where backgrounds print darker or with a discolored appearance like a yellow tint.

- **Always use host collation:** If you select this option, you need to select Collated in the Print dialog box. Check this box if the target printing device supports a collated option, and override the Collated function in the Print dialog box if it fails to collate on a given printer.

Color Management

Click Color Management in the left pane, and the Color Management options open, as shown in Figure 39.40.

FIGURE 39.40

Click Color Management to open the color management options in the right pane.

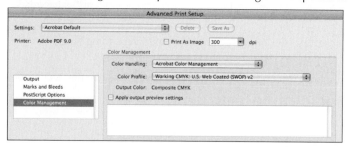

For color handling, choose Acrobat Color Management. Your choices for profile support for non-Postscript printers are limited to a sRGB or a CMYK profile. If you use a PostScript device, you can choose to let the printer determine color and choose a profile suited for your paper.

The Apply output preview settings are available for composite printing only. If you want to apply settings made in the Proof Setup for a simulated print, enable the check box.

Printing PDF files to PostScript devices

For composite printing to desktop PostScript devices, you can successfully print using the Print and Advanced Print Setup dialog boxes. However, for commercial printing to imagesetters, plate-setters, and direct-to-press equipment, printing direct from Acrobat can produce some unexpected results. A better option is to generate a PostScript file and download the PostScript file to your printer. When printing directly to high-end devices, you can experience problems with color handling, black type printing with tints, and PostScript errors that prevent the job from being printed.

For commercial output, choose File ⇨ Save As and select PostScript as the output format. Click the Settings button where options choices identical to the Advanced Print Setup dialog box are contained. Make your options choices, and save the file as PostScript. The resultant PostScript file is then downloaded to your printer. This method generally produces more-reliable output.

 **For more information on saving files as PostScript for printing purposes, see Chapter 40.**

Summary

- Some CS applications require you to use the Page Setup dialog box before opening the Print dialog box.

- Print options for screening, color handling, separations, printer's marks, and so on are found in advanced print options dialog boxes generally available through the Print dialog box.

- Desktop color printers often have special print options where choices for paper types and color handling are accessed via the printer's print driver.

- InDesign and Acrobat are the most commonly used applications for commercial printing to imagesetters, platesetters, and on-demand devices. Photoshop is the most common application used when printing to large format inkjet printers.

Chapter 40

Commercial Printing

A s a production artist, you participate in workflows with production workers and technicians at prepress houses and print shops. Your role extends beyond the creative work you do to include proper file preparation, proofing your work, checking files for potential problems, and delivering a product that has an excellent chance for successful output. The Creative Suite applications offer you many tools for diagnosing documents and reporting potential imaging problems to you. In addition, some CS applications offer you options for creating file formats optimized for high-end prepress and printing.

This chapter begins with soft-proofing color and separations on your monitor before you send files to an imaging center, and continues with the file checking process known as *preflighting*. The last part of the chapter covers packaging jobs for imaging centers. Consider the contents of this chapter as the most important aspects of your production workflow when you create documents designed for commercial printing.

Soft-Proofing Documents in the CS Programs

Soft-proofing a document is the process of viewing the file on your monitor and checking various conditions for potential printing problems. You can check issues such as overprints, proper color assignment, transparency flattening, and font problems using some of the CS applications. Illustrator, InDesign, and Acrobat Pro all provide a wealth of tools for soft proofing color.

 For more information on packaging documents, see the section "Packaging Documents for Commercial Printing" at the end of this chapter.

Soft-proofing files in InDesign

In InDesign, you can check files for transparency flattening and color separations. Open the Window menu, select Output and you see submenu menu commands for Flattener Preview and Separations Preview. Select one of the menu commands, and the respective palette opens as a floating palette.

Transparency flattening

As described in Chapter 39, transparency flattener previews show you the results of applying flattening amounts. To open the Transparency Flattener, choose Window ➪ Output ➪ Flattener Preview. The Flattener Preview palette opens, as shown in Figure 40.1.

FIGURE 40.1

The Flattener Preview palette

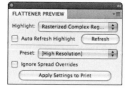

The Flattener Preview palette offers you various options for previewing the results of flattening transparency. You navigate to pages and see results on the page in the Document window as you apply settings and refresh the screen to update different settings options. The following options are available from the Highlight pull-down menu in the palette:

■ **Rasterize Complex Regions:** From the drop-down list, the first choice is this option. From the Flattener Preview palette menu, which opens when you click the right-pointing arrow, you can show Transparency Flattener Presets in a dialog box. The dialog box contains buttons for creating new presets or editing presets you load or create.

■ **Transparent Objects:** When you select this option from the drop-down list, transparent objects are highlighted on the page, including alpha channels in Photoshop images, objects with blending modes, and objects with opacity attributes such as drop shadows applied in InDesign.

■ **All Affected Objects:** Next in the drop-down list is this setting, which highlights overlapping objects where at least one of the objects contains transparency. All the highlighted objects are flattened according to the amount specified in the Transparency Flattener Preset Options dialog box.

■ **Affected Graphics:** This setting highlights placed objects where transparency effects are involved.

- **Outline Strokes:** Following along in the drop-down list, this option highlights all strokes that have been marked for outlines.

- **Outline Text:** This option highlights all text converted to outlines when involved with transparency.

- **Raster-fill Text and Strokes:** You can rasterize object fills and strokes during transparency flattening. This option previews the results of rasterizing.

- **All Rasterized Regions:** Objects and intersections throughout the document are highlighted to show the results of rasterization. Photoshop files are also previewed for the results of rasterization, as are all effects that involve transparency, such as drop shadows and feathering.

- **Auto Refresh Highlight:** When you select this check box, the highlighted preview refreshes as you toggle menu commands and adjust settings.

- **Refresh:** If you want to manually refresh the preview, uncheck the Auto Refresh Highlight check box and click the Refresh button to update the preview.

- **Preset:** InDesign is installed with three presets for transparency adjustments. You can add custom presets and the new presets are added to the drop-down list. Select from the menu the preset you want to use. When you create or edit a preset, the Transparency Flattener Preset Options dialog box opens; here, you control the amount of transparency by moving the Raster/Vector Balance slider. The slider position in the Transparency Flattener Preset Options dialog box determines the amount of rasterizing complex regions.

- **Ignore Spread Overrides:** For individual spreads where you want to ignore spread-specific flattener presets, select the check box. If a spread has a custom flattener assigned to it via the Pages panel this checkbox overrides the custom settings and applies the flattener selected in the Flattener Preview panel.

- **Apply Settings to Print:** When the preview results look appropriate for your output, click the Apply Settings to Print button to apply the transparency flattening settings to your document.

The Transparency Flattener Presets dialog box provides options for managing presets. You open the dialog box shown in Figure 40.2 by selecting Transparency Flattener Presets from the fly-out menu in the Flattener Preview palette. Options for managing presets include the following:

- **New:** This option opens the Transparency Flattener Preset Options dialog box where you assign attributes for new presets. These new presets are saved and listed in the Presets list in the Transparency Flattener Presets dialog box. You can save presets and share them with colleagues so all designers use the same transparency flattening for all files for a given ad campaign.

- **Edit:** You can return to a given preset and edit it in the Transparency Flattener Presets dialog box (Figure 40.3). Select the preset to edit, and click Edit. Note that you cannot edit or delete the default presets installed with InDesign.

- **Delete:** Click a preset you want to remove, and click Delete.

- **Load:** You load saved presets back into the Transparency Flattener Presets dialog box. Specific Flattener Presets can be part of a Printer Preset for a specific printing device and used at print time.

- **Save:** Click Save to open the Save Transparency Flattener Presets dialog box where you can type a name for the preset and save the settings to a folder on your hard drive.

You can define options for a transparency flattener preset in the Transparency Flattener Preset Options dialog box. When you click either the New button or the Edit button, the dialog box shown in Figure 40.3 opens. Make your adjustments in this dialog box, and the collective settings are captured to the preset you create or edit.

FIGURE 40.2

The Transparency Flattener Presets dialog box manages presets.

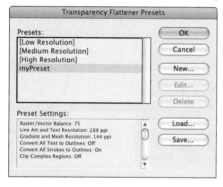

FIGURE 40.3

The Transparency Flattener Preset Options dialog box

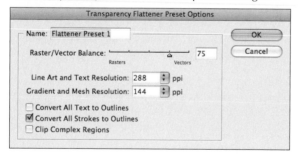

The options choices you have for defining attributes for a preset include the following:

- **Name:** Type a name in the field box, and the name is reflected in the Transparency Flattener Presets dialog box. Try to use descriptive names so you can easily recall a particular preset used for a given job.

- **Raster/Vector Balance:** Move the slider to apply varying amounts of flattening. As you move the slider and target a particular amount, you can return to the Flattener Preview palette and preview the transparency settings.

- **Line Art and Text Resolution:** You adjust resolution for rasterizing line art and text in the field box or by clicking on the up and down arrows to change the value. Line art resolutions would be set to match device resolutions—something like specifying 1200 ppi for image and platesetters.

- **Gradient and Mesh Resolution:** A separate field box is used for rasterizing gradients and meshes. Mesh resolutions would be close to halftone frequency values such as 1.5 to two times the halftone frequency.

- **Convert All Text to Outlines:** When checking the box, you can preview the results in the Flatten Transparency dialog box by selecting Outline Text from the drop-down list.

- **Convert All Strokes to Outlines:** The same applies to this option as the Convert All Text to Outlines. Use the Raster-Fill and Strokes Menu command in the Flattener Preview palette to preview the flattening.

- **Clip Complex Regions:** Once again, the same applies to this option. Use the Flattener Transparency dialog box, and choose Rasterize Complex Regions to preview the results. Clipping complex regions can be helpful when printing complex vector art.

Previewing separations

InDesign offers a method to preview separations and color modes before you send a file off to the printer. If you inadvertently specify spot colors where you intend to print a process color job, the Separations Preview palette immediately shows you all process and spot color in a document to help you avoid costly errors. To open the Separations Preview palette, shown in Figure 40.4, choose Window ⇨ Output ⇨ Separations Preview.

Once you open the Separations panel, you still must turn Separations on. This puts the document into Overprint Preview to more accurately proof the document and uses more CPU power to show high-resolution graphics—that's why you have to turn it on.

FIGURE 40.4

The Separations Preview palette displays all color plates.

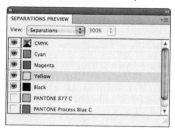

While the Separation Preview palette is open and Separations are turned on, you can move the cursor around the document page, and ink percentages are reported in the palette for the cursor position. Select Separations from the View pull-down menu and you can toggle each color on and off by clicking on the eye icon. Clicking the ink color in the palette turns off all colors but the selected color. Single inks or combinations of inks can be displayed in the palette and reflected in the Document window.

From the View drop-down list, you have a menu command to display ink limits. Select the menu command, and the Separation Preview palette changes to the view shown in Figure 40.5. You can alter the ink coverage warning by selecting from fixed values in the drop-down list or typing values in the field box. Ink limit is designed to show where the limit has been exceeded in a document. Ink limits do not change or restrict ink output to match a press or the limit value. If the limits have been exceeded, they must be corrected in InDesign or the native editing application for a linked file.

FIGURE 40.5

To alter ink coverage warnings, select Ink Limit and a fixed ink-limit value.

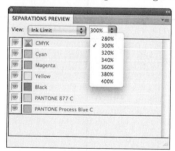

From the palette menu, you can access the Ink Manager where you assign neutral densities that influence trapping amounts and apply spot color to process conversions. Open the palette menu by clicking the right-pointing arrow and selecting Ink Manager. The Ink Manager dialog box opens, shown in Figure 40.6.

FIGURE 40.6

The Ink Manager dialog box

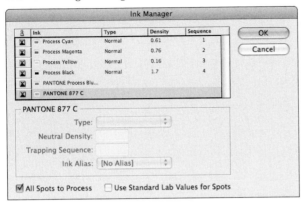

You make settings changes in this dialog box according to recommendations from your commercial printer. You can define the neutral densities, which are established as the default values upon InDesign's installation, according to the language version you use during your installation. As you use printers from other parts of the world, you might find changes in standards for neutral densities. Neutral densities are important because the trapping engine uses the values to determine precise placement of traps. You don't want to mess around with the values, until you receive precise guidelines for adjustments from your printer.

The check box for All Spots to Process is the item in this dialog box you're likely to use often. If you specify spot-color inks during a design stage, you can convert the output of spot colors to process values with this option.

In the Separations Preview palette menu, you have a menu option for displaying spot colors as black. Select Show Single Plates in Black, and when previewing the spot colors in the file without the CMYK colors previewed, each spot color displays in the Document window as black. Note that you need to turn off all the process colors to see the spot colors appear as black. When you deselect the menu command, all spot colors display in their color values when you view plates and all plates.

Soft-proofing files in Illustrator

Many of the transparency flattening preview options found in Illustrator are the same as the ones in InDesign. Open the Window menu and select Flattener Preview to open the Flattener Preview dialog box, as shown in Figure 40.7.

FIGURE 40.7

The Flattener Preview palette has options similar to InDesign.

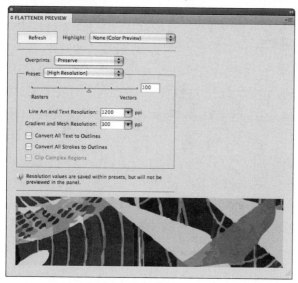

Transparency flattening in Illustrator

The options choices for highlighting transparency settings that differ between Illustrator and InDesign include:

- **Affected linked EPS Files:** The preview shows all EPS files linked to the current document as they related to affected transparency.

- **Expanded Patterns:** The highlights show all patterns that will expand because they involve transparency.

From the Overprints drop-down list, you have additional options that you don't find in InDesign. The default choice is to preserve all overprints. You have other options to eliminate all overprints or to simulate overprints:

- **Discard:** Obviously, this discards all overprints. You might use this option when you send files to print shops that perform all the trapping on your files.

- **Simulate:** This option maintains the appearance of overprinting in composite proofs. Use this when you print to composite color printers that can display the overprints.

The Presets drop-down list offers you choices for different presets installed as defaults in Illustrator and a list of all presets you save by selecting Save Transparency Flattener Preset from the palette menu. Illustrator handles saving presets differently than InDesign. When you select the menu command, you get a dialog box prompting you to name the preset. You can return to the Presets drop-down list, and the saved preset is listed.

Editing a preset works a bit differently in Illustrator than it does in InDesign. To change options on a preset you saved, select the preset in the Presets drop-down list. Make your new options choices, open the palette menu, and select Redefine Preset. The new attributes are assigned to the saved preset.

Managing presets

If you need to delete a preset, you won't find an option in the Flattener Preview dialog box. Instead, you must open the Edit menu and select Transparency Flattener Presets. The transparency Flattener Presets dialog box opens. Refer to Figure 40.2 to see the dialog box with similar options choices as you have in InDesign. Notice that you can edit a preset in this dialog box as well as when redefining a preset, as mentioned earlier in the "Transparency flattening" section.

Separations Preview

From the Window menu choose Separations Preview, and the Separations Preview panel opens. You can check separations in Illustrator CS4 very similar to the way you preview separations in InDesign.

Proofing and printing in Acrobat Pro

Acrobat PDF is the best form of document format for submitting files to print shops. The ability to embed graphic images and type fonts is one of the advantages you have with PDF files. In addition to being a desirable format for delivering documents for press, Acrobat Pro also offers an abundance of soft-proofing and preflighting tools.

There are two sources for accessing features related to soft-proofing and preparing files for print in Acrobat Pro. You can set up Preferences view Overprinting in the Page Display Preferences and you can access the Print Production tools from the Advanced menu.

The other options for proofing and preparing files exist in a set of tools in the Print Production toolbar, which neatly houses the tools that creative and service professionals use to prepare files for digital prepress and printing.

Soft-proofing menu commands

Overprint previews are set in the Page Display Preferences. Press Ctrl/⌘+K to open the Preferences dialog box, and click Page Display in the left pane. In the right pane, you can choose to always preview overprints for different file types. For example, a PDF/X file can be selected to always show the overprints.

Select Advanced ⇨ Print Production ⇨ Preflight to access the preflight tools. Other commands for soft-proofing color and resolving potential printing problems are contained in the Print Production submenu and the Print Production toolbar.

Overprint preview

You often use overprints to *trap* colors in files intended for printing separations. Trapping a color creates a color overlap that prevents gaps from appearing between colors when paper moves on a press during the printing process. You might assign an overprint to text to avoid any trapping problems where black text prints on top of a background color. In other cases, a designer might unintentionally assign an overprint to a color during the creative process. As a measure of checking overprints for those colors that you properly assign and to review a document for potential problems, you can use Acrobat's Overprint Preview to display on your monitor all the overprints created in a file. To view overprints in a PDF document, open the Page Display Preferences and choose Always from the Use Overprint Preview pull-down menu. This preference choice offers options to view overprints from PDF/X only files, for all files, or for not viewing the overprints for all files.

 Overprint Preview is available in Acrobat Standard and Acrobat Pro as well as Adobe Reader 9. The remaining preflighting and soft-proofing tools are available only in Acrobat Pro and Acrobat Pro Extended.

To understand what happens with overprints and knockouts, look at Figure 40.8. The composite image is created for printing two colors. These colors are printed on separate plates for two different inks. When the file is separated, the type is *knocked out* of the background, leaving holes in the background, as shown in Figure 40.9. Because the two colors butt up against each other, any slight movement of the paper creates a gap where one ink color ends and the other begins. To prevent the problem, a slight bit of overprinting is added to the type. In an exaggerated view, in Figure 40.10, you can see the stroke around the type characters. The stroke is assigned an overprint so its color, which is the foreground color, prints on top of the background color without a knockout.

Designers can apply overprints in programs like Illustrator and InDesign. If a designer inadvertently makes a mistake and selects the fill color to overprint, the color of the foreground image results in a different color created by the mix of the two colors. In Figure 40.11, you view a file in Acrobat without an overprint preview. The figure shows the document as it should print. When you change the overprint preferences to show all overprints, the overprints shown in Figure 40.12 appear. As you can see, the assigned overprints in the file were a mistake. Using Acrobat's Overprint Preview preference option, you can check for any overprint errors in illustrations.

 Both InDesign and Illustrator provide you with overprint previews. If you use these design applications, you can check for overprint problems before converting files to PDF.

FIGURE 40.8

Separate plates print a composite image.

FIGURE 40.9

The background appears with the foreground type knocked out.

FIGURE 40.10

The overprint area of the type color prints on top of the background color.

FIGURE 40.11

The file as the designer intended it to print

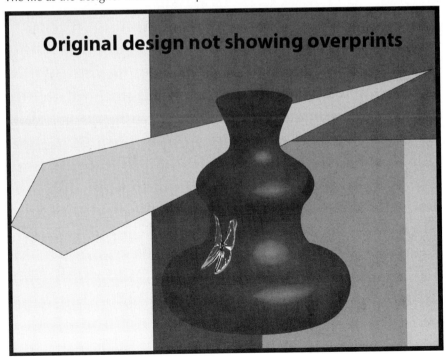

FIGURE 40.12

Viewing all colors in an overprint shows erroneous overprint assignments.

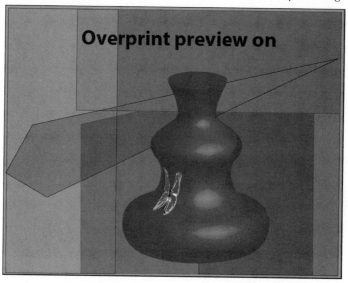

> **TIP**
>
> To carefully examine overprints assigned to type characters, click the Loupe tool in the Zoom toolbar. Move the cursor around the document to preview overprints on small type.

Output Preview

Output Preview provides options for previewing color handled in the Output Preview dialog box. Choose Advanced ⇨ Print Production ⇨ Output Preview, and the Output Preview dialog box shown in Figure 40.13 appears. You have three categories to preview and a number of different options choices for what you want to see within each category.

Separations preview

In the Output Preview window in Figure 40.13, select Separations and you preview separations like the separations preview you use in InDesign. Notice in Acrobat you need to use the check-boxes to toggle visibility of plates whereas InDesign allows you to click the plate names to toggle the visibility.

If you intend to print a file in four-color process, the Separation Preview dialog box identifies any potential problems if you have spot colors in the file. Likewise, if a spot-color job contains colors that you don't intend to print, they also appear.

You can selectively view individual colors by deselecting the check boxes adjacent to each color name, view selected colors only, and view spot colors converted to CMYK. Click Ink Manager, and you can convert spot color to process color (see Figure 40.19 later in this chapter).

FIGURE 40.13

Output Preview shows you all the colors contained in a file—both process and spot.

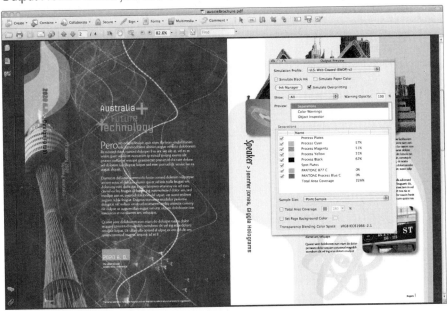

You evaluate color values by moving the cursor around the document with the Separation Preview dialog box open. Notice the percentage values on the far right side of Figure 40.13. These values represent the percent of ink at the cursor position.

From the Show pull-down menu, you have several options for what you want to examine in the preview. Choose from the menu options to preview images, spot color, grays, smooth shading, and so on, and the preview dynamically shows the data you choose to view.

Select the Simulate Ink Black check box to see how the blacks actually print on press.

If you select the check box for Simulate Paper White in the Output Preview dialog box, the preview shows you a particular shade of gray as simulated for the paper color by the color profile you choose. You may find that the preview looks too gray or has too much black. This preview may not be the profile used, but rather the brightness adjustment on your monitor. If your monitor is calibrated properly and the profile accurately displays the paper color, the preview should show you an accurate representation of the document as it is printed on paper.

At the bottom of the dialog box, you find an option for checking Total Area Coverage. To change the threshold for where the warning is given check this box.

Color Warnings

Click Color Warnings in the Preview box, and the Output Preview dialog box changes as shown in Figure 40.14. Select the check boxes for Show Overprinting and Rich Black, and the preview displays warnings for overprints and rich black printing in the colors appearing in the color swatches adjacent to the check boxes. If you want to display warnings in different colors, click a swatch and choose a preset color from the drop-down color palette or click Other Color to open your system color palette. In the system color palette, you can choose any color appearing in the palette to display the out-of-gamut color warnings.

FIGURE 40.14

Click Color Warnings to display previews for out-of-gamut color warnings.

Soft-proofing tools

Proofing and editing tools are accessible from the Advanced ⇨ Print Production submenu or from the Print Production toolbar.

To open the Print Production toolbar shown in Figure 40.15, open a context menu on the Toolbar Well and select Print Production from the menu commands. The toolbar opens as a floating toolbar in the Acrobat window. If you want to dock the toolbar in the Toolbar Well, open a context menu again and select Dock Toolbars or drag the toolbar to the Toolbar Well.

FIGURE 40.15

Open the Print Production toolbar from a context menu opened from the Toolbar Well.

The Print Production tools include:

A **Trap Presets:** You can trap PDF files for commercial printing by applying trap presets from a selection installed as defaults or from custom trap presets you create in Acrobat. Before you trap a file, you may need to fix hairline rules. Make adjustments as needed; then click the Trap Presets tool to open the Trap Presets dialog box shown in Figure 40.16.

CROSS-REF For more on fixing hairlines, see the section "Fix Hairlines" later in this chapter.

FIGURE 40.16

Click the Trap Presets tool in the Print Production toolbar to open the Trap Presets dialog box.

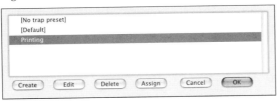

The first dialog box that opens enables you to select an existing preset or create a new one. Click Create, and the New Trap Preset dialog box opens as shown in Figure 40.17. In order to make adjustments in the dialog box, you should be familiar with trapping and the acceptable amounts to apply for trap widths, miter adjustments, and attributes assigned to images and thresholds. If you know how to trap a file, you'll know which settings to apply. If you don't know anything about trapping, it's best to leave the job to your commercial printer.

FIGURE 40.17

Set the attributes for the trap preset in the New Trap Preset dialog box.

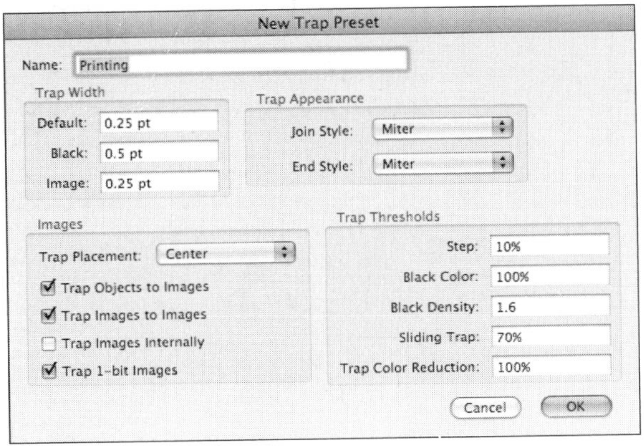

Click OK after typing a name for the new preset and making the adjustments. You are then returned to the Trap Presets dialog box where your new preset is listed in the window. Click Assign, and the trap values are applied to the document.

B **Output Preview:** This tool opens the same Output Preview dialog box as when you choose Advanced ⇨ Output Preview.

C **Preflight:** You can also access preflight from the Advanced ⇨ Print Production submenu. Clicking the tool or choosing the menu command opens the Preflight dialog box.

CROSS-REF For information related to Output Preview, see the section "Output Preview" earlier in this chapter. For information related to using the Preflight dialog box, see the section "Preflighting PDF Files."

D **Convert Colors:** The Convert Colors dialog box in Acrobat 9 has many changes compared to earlier versions of Acrobat. Click the Convert Colors tool in the Print Production toolbar, and the Convert Colors dialog box, shown in Figure 40.18, opens. In the dialog box, you can convert color for individual items such as images, text, line art, any object, and smooth shades from the current colorspace to a new target colorspace.

You also can map spot colors from one spot value to another. This is very helpful if you have two spot names such as Pantone 185 CV and Pantone 185 CVC that are intended to be printed on the same plate. At the bottom of the dialog box, you have a check box available to Preserve Black Inks. This option is helpful if you have RGB black that you want to change to K-black for print production.

FIGURE 40.18

Click Convert Colors to open the Convert Colors dialog box.

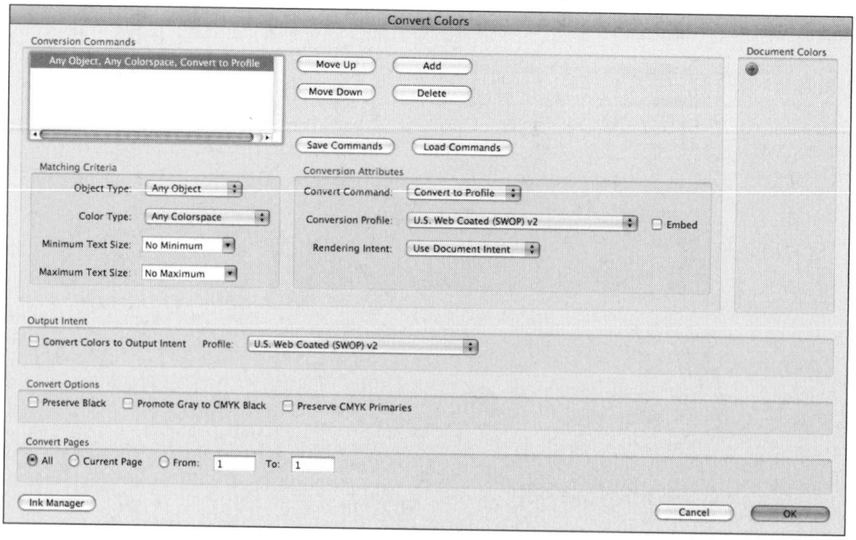

E **Ink Manager:** The Ink Manager dialog box enables you to change ink values and convert colors. Changes you apply to the options choices aren't saved with the PDF file. If you convert spot colors to CMYK, for example, and save the document, the colors are unaffected when you reopen the file. The changes applied in the Ink Manager take effect only when you print a PDF document. To open the Ink Manager, click the Ink Manager tool in the Print Production toolbar. The Ink Manager dialog box, shown in Figure 40.19, opens.

FIGURE 40.19

Click Ink Manager to open the Ink Manager dialog box.

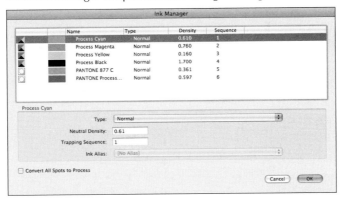

Select from the pull-down menu options for aliasing the type of color (Normal, Opaque, Transparent, and OpaqueIgnore). You change density values and the trapping sequence by editing the field box. To alias spot colors, select a spot color and alias the color to the same angle and density as a process color.

F **Add Printer Marks:** Use this tool to add printer marks to a page.

CROSS-REF For more information on adding printer marks and cropping pages, see Chapter 24.

G **Crop Pages:** If you add printer marks to a page, you need to resize the page in order to see and print the marks. The Crop tool opens a dialog box where you can size a page large enough to view and print printer marks.

CROSS-REF For information on adding printer marks in Acrobat or for cropping pages in Acrobat, see Chapter 22.

H **Fix Hairlines:** You might see hairlines print fine on desktop printers while they appear almost invisible when printed on commercial high-resolution printing devices. If the hairlines are too small, they won't appear on the final color separation. This is particularly true if you need to trap areas around hairlines. To add larger point sizes to hairlines, click the Fix Hairlines tool in the Print Production toolbar. You can replace narrow hairlines with larger strokes, as shown in Figure 40.20.

FIGURE 40.20

Click the Fix Hairlines tool to open the Fix Hairlines dialog box.

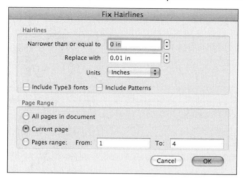

I **Transparency Flattening:** You have as many similar options for flattening transparency in Acrobat as you have in Adobe InDesign. Acrobat's Flattener Preview is a little more elaborate, as you can see in Figure 40.21, compared to InDesign's Flattener Preview, shown earlier in Figure 40.1.

FIGURE 40.21

Click the Transparency Flattening tool to open the Flattener Preview dialog box.

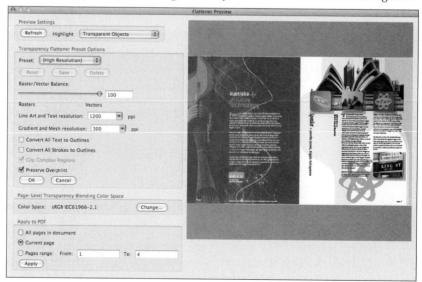

Whereas InDesign shows you previews on the document page, Acrobat's previews are shown in the Flattener Preview dialog box. As you determine the adjustments needed to flatten transparency, click Apply. In Acrobat Pro, you can apply transparency flattening and save the results when you choose File ➪ Save.

Some unique features you find in Acrobat's Flattener Preview dialog box not found in Illustrator and InDesign are the Preserve Overprint check box, OK, and Apply buttons. Clicking OK closes the dialog box. Clicking Apply applies the settings to the range of pages in the document you specify in the Pages range text boxes.

J   PDF Optimizer: Click the tool, and you open the PDF Optimizer dialog box. The same dialog box opens when you choose Advanced ➪ PDF Optimizer.

CROSS-REF **For a more detailed description of the choices in the Flattener Preview dialog box, see the section "Transparency flattening." For information related to using the PDF Optimizer, see Chapter 34.**

K   JDF Job Definitions: You use a Job Definition File (JDF) in production workflows to include information necessary for a production process and information related to the PDF creation. You assign the information in a JDF file through a collection of dialog boxes that begin with your clicking the JDF Job Definitions tool at the far-right side of the Print Production toolbar. Click the tool, and the JDF Job Definitions dialog box, shown in Figure 40.22, opens.

FIGURE 40.22

Click the JDF Job Definitions tool to open the JDF Job Definitions dialog box.

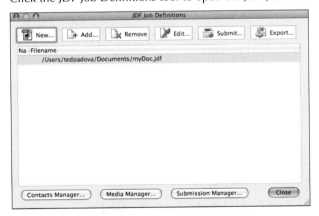

Click the New button to open the Edit JDF Job Definition dialog box, shown in Figure 40.23. You find options for adding information such as job identifying information, profile compliance, description, and printing and postprocessing information. The entire process for creating and using JDF files is extensive and beyond the scope of a thorough discussion in this chapter. For more information about JDF, see the Help document installed with Acrobat.

FIGURE 40.23

Click New in the JDF Job Definitions dialog box to add a new definition.

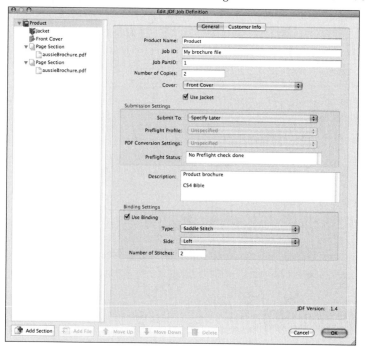

Preflighting Files

Preflighting is a term that creative professionals and service technicians use to describe the process of analyzing a file for suitability for printing. A preflight assessment might examine a file for the proper color mode of images, for image compression, for accessibility of embedded fonts, for accessibility of fonts to the operating system, or for any number of other conditions that might interfere with successfully printing a job.

The two applications you use for preflighting are InDesign and Acrobat. Acrobat has a much more elaborate set of preflight options, so we'll focus on using Acrobat in this chapter. If you submit native InDesign files to service centers, you can use the InDesign preflight options for checking your files and links to be certain the files will print properly at an imaging center.

Preflighting in InDesign

To access InDesign's preflight options, choose Window ⇨ Output ⇨ Preflight. The Preflight panel opens, as shown in Figure 40.24. In this panel, you find a list of any preflight profiles you've created and a check box to turn on the Preflight option in InDesign. When it's on and you select a profile, your document is checked against the conditions specified in a given profile. To create a new profile, open the flyout menu and choose Define Profiles.

FIGURE 40.24

To open the Preflight panel, choose Window ➪ Output ➪ Preflight.

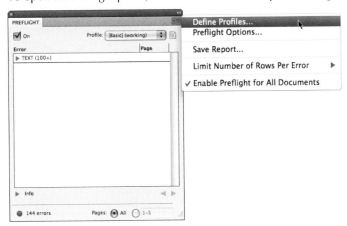

When you choose Define Profiles, the Preflight Profiles window opens, as shown in Figure 40.25. Here you can click the +/- buttons to add or delete profiles or open the pull-down menu to the right of the minus (-) icon to load and export profiles.

FIGURE 40.25

Open the fly-away menu in the Preflight panel and choose Define Profiles to open the Preflight Profiles dialog box.

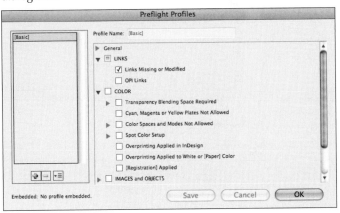

When you create a new profile, you click the Plus (+) icon and name a profile. Then scroll the list and check the boxes for the items you want included in your profile. As a graphic designer, you might receive a profile from a print service as a file attachment or a file download from a Web site. In this case, you would open the pull-down menu adjacent to the minus (-) icon, and choose Load Profile. All the work for setting up the profile is performed by your service center, and you only have to check your file against the profile before submitting files.

Preflighting a file in Acrobat

Acrobat requires you to have a file open in the Document pane in order to run a preflight check. To preflight a document, be certain that a file is open and click the Preflight tool in the Print Production toolbar, or choose Advanced ⇨ Preflight. The Preflight dialog box, shown in Figure 40.26, opens. The Preflight window contains a number of preset profiles in a scrollable list. The profiles contain descriptions. When you select a preflight rule you can read the description information by clicking the right-pointing arrow to expand the profile view. Each profile has an icon to the left of the profile name that indicates what a given profile does such as: analyze or fix, analyze only, and so on.

FIGURE 40.26

Click the Preflight tool in the Print Production toolbar, or choose Advanced ⇨ Preflight to open the Preflight window.

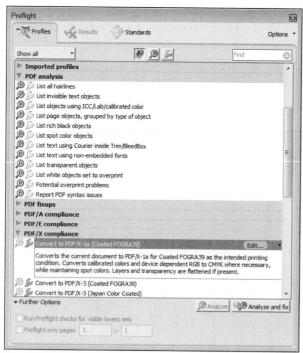

If a profile contains the conditions you want to check, select a profile and click Analyze or Analyze and fix. If a profile has been created that lets you perform just an analysis, you can click Analyze. Many profiles, however, are intended to analyze and fix a file to make it compliant with the profile conditions. When you analyze a file, a report is generated. When you choose Analyze and fix, Acrobat may take a little time to fix all the problems with the file. Eventually, the Preflight window shows you a list of the fixes and an option to click a button to examine a report, as shown in Figure 40.27.

FIGURE 40.27

After choosing Analyze and fix, the Preflight window lists the fixes applied to the file.

Producing a PDF/X-compliant file

For commercial printing, you'll want to create PDF/X-compliant files. If a file is not converted to PDF/X during the PDF creation process, you can postprocess the file in Acrobat to check the file for PDF/X compliance. To produce a PDF/X file, choose a PDF/X option and click Analyze and fix. Acrobat prompts you to save the file. Choose a new file name, and click Save.

Understanding PDF/X

PDF/X has gained acceptance among commercial printing companies for creating files suitable for printing. PDF is a reliable format for any kind of electronic file exchanges. However, files developed for Acrobat viewers, Acrobat PDF forms, Web-hosted documents, and so on carry lots of overhead not necessary for printing on commercial printing devices. The PDF/X compliance standard was developed to streamline documents by eliminating unnecessary data and optimizing files for print. Tailoring a PDF document for print by creating a PDF/X-compliant file does not necessarily reduce file size. In many cases, file sizes grow from a standard PDF to a PDF/X file.

The PDF/X options available to you in Acrobat Distiller and the CS programs produce either a PDF/X-1a:2002, PDF/X-1a:2003, PDF/X-3:2002, or PDF/X-3:2003-compliant file. With the CS4 applications you also get the PDF/X-4 specification that supports RGB workflows. These file types are different versions of the PDF/X format. PDF/X-1a is designed to work well with both process and spot color, but no support is provided for color management or profile embedding. PDF/X-3 supports process and spot color and does support color-managed workflows and ICC (International Color Consortium) profile embedding.

The two distinctions between the versions for PDF/X-1a:2002, and PDF/X-1a:2003 have to do with versions of the same subset. With PDF/X-1a:2002, you have compatibility with Acrobat 4. With PDF/X-1a:2003, you have compatibility with Acrobat 5. The same applies to the version 2002 and version 2003 of the PDF/X-3 subset.

When you export as PDF/X or create a PDF using Acrobat Distiller, you are checking the file for PDF/X compliance. If the file does not meet the PDF/X standard you select (that is, PDF/X-1a or PDF/X-3), a PDF is not created. If a file meets PDF/X compliance, you have much greater assurance that your PDF document will print on almost any kind of commercial printing device.

In versions 3 and 4 of the CS programs, Illustrator and InDesign export to PDF/X. Other PDF producers such as PDFMaker (on Windows), which you use with Microsoft Office applications, Microsoft Project, Microsoft Visio, and AutoDesk AutoCAD do not support PDF/X. If you want to print any of these files on commercial printing devices, print PostScript files and distill them with Acrobat Distiller using a PDF/X setting.

One thing to keep in mind is to always check with service providers before creating PDF/X files. You'll need some information particularly on how to handle transparency flattening from your provider or they may not be able to print your files. Ideally, your provider should offer you a preset to use to create PDF/X files in Acrobat Pro.

Creating new Preflight profiles

Like InDesign, Acrobat provides you options for creating new profiles. Acrobat has more than 400 conditions that you can add to a profile. To create a new profile, choose Create New Preflight Profile from the Options pull-down menu. The Preflight Edit Profile dialog box opens where new profiles are created.

Because most preflight analyses for output to commercial print shops are included in the preset profiles, you're not likely to do much custom profile editing. Refer to the Acrobat documentation if you want to look more closely at creating new profiles.

Creating a preflight droplet

Just like the InDesign profiles, you can import profiles created by your service center to check files for given output devices. When you receive or download a preflight file, you can add the profile to your list of profiles in the Preflight window. Once added, you can create a droplet.

A *droplet* is like a small executable application. You can keep droplets in folders or on your desktop, and when you want to preflight a file, just drag the file on top of the droplet.

To create a droplet from an existing profile, select the profile in the Preflight window and open the Options pull-down menu. From the menu choices, select Create Preflight Droplet. The Preflight: Droplet Setup dialog box opens, as shown in Figure 40.28. You have options for where to save successful preflights and where to save files that don't meet the conditions of the profile. Make your choices, and click Save. The droplet is saved to your target location and ready to use when you're ready to check or check and fix a file.

FIGURE 40.28

Choose Create Preflight Droplet from the Options pull-down menu to open the Preflight: Droplet Setup dialog box.

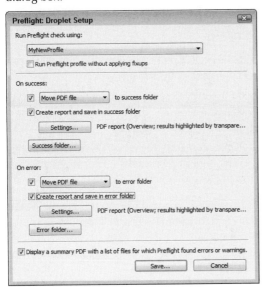

Packaging Documents for Commercial Printing

Packaging a file for printing involves collecting all the assets required for printing and gathering them on a disk, CD-ROM, or a compressed archive you intend to e-mail or send via FTP to your service center. With Photoshop documents, you don't need to package for printing; all assets are contained within the Photoshop document. Flatten a copy of the image and send the file off to your printer. With Illustrator and InDesign, you have issues needing attention, such as font usage and links. When you package these files, you must include all links and fonts with the active file to send to your printer.

With fonts, you're faced with some potential problems related to font licensing. Many font-manufacturer licensing restrictions prevent you from legally distributing fonts to your service provider. If your provider does not have a given font, the provider must purchase the font or you need to search for a different provider.

The complex issues related to packaging native files together with legal restrictions is reason enough to search for a better solution rather than send your native files to service providers. Fortunately, the CS applications offer you a much better alternative. Quite simply, your package utility is Acrobat PDF. When you send PDF documents to your printer, you have advantages such as:

- **Font embedding:** Not all fonts are licensed for font embedding in PDF documents. However, the more popular Adobe fonts, OpenType fonts, and many TrueType fonts carry no licensing restrictions for embedding the fonts in PDF documents. When the fonts are embedded, you don't have to worry about whether your service provider has the fonts contained in your document.

- **Image embedding:** All images are embedded in PDF documents. You don't need to worry about missing links when sending PDF files to your printer.

- **Smaller file sizes:** PDF documents occupy the least amount of space on your hard drive and are most often smaller than compressed native files. The results of smaller file sizes provide you with faster electronic transfer times via e-mail and FTP.

- **Optimized file types for printing:** With PDF documents, you can create PDF/X files that are optimized for commercial printing. Developing PDF/X-compliant files provides a much more reliable format for correctly imaging your documents.

Because PDF is the best file format for sending files to prepress and commercial printing, we'll skip the packaging features for bundling native documents and focus on creating PDF documents optimized for professional printing.

PDF creation in Illustrator

If you intend to print Illustrator files rather than introduce them into an InDesign layout, you can save directly to PDF from Illustrator. Choose File ➪ Save As, and select Adobe PDF as the file format. After you name the file and click Save in the Save As dialog box, the Save Adobe PDF dialog box opens, as shown in Figure 40.29.

FIGURE 40.29

To print commercially, select a PDF/X subset from the Standard pull-down menu.

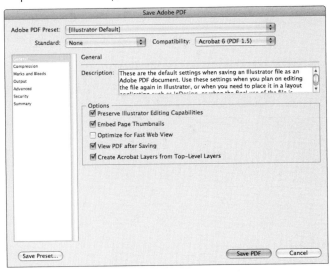

From the Standard pull-down menu, select one of the PDF/X options. Review the categories in the left pane. Add marks and bleeds, color settings, transparency flattening, and adjust the settings needed for your output.

All other choices are made for you when you select a PDF/X option. Look at the Summary item in the left pane. If you see a warning icon, click Summary and review the summary information. In some cases, you need to return to the document and fix any problems before saving as a PDF/X file. Click Save PDF. If the file meets PDF/X compliance, the file is saved to PDF.

PDF creation in InDesign

In InDesign, you might use the preflight check built into the program before exporting to PDF. InDesign enables you to completely package the file for press via an export to PDF. After preflighting, choose File ➪ Export. Provide a name for your file, and be certain that you select the PDF in the Format drop-down list. Click Save, and the Export PDF dialog box opens, as shown in Figure 40.30, to offer you the very similar options that you find with PDF exports from Adobe Illustrator.

Select a PDF/X Adobe PDF Preset, and adjust the options you need to print the file, such as printing spreads, adding marks and bleeds, and so on. As with Adobe Illustrator, be certain to check the Summary and correct any errors before exporting. Click Export, and the InDesign file is exported as PDF/X.

FIGURE 40.30

The Export Adobe PDF dialog box in Adobe InDesign

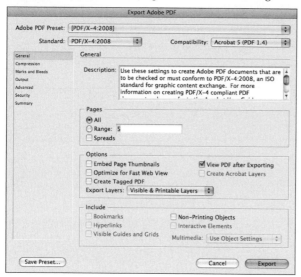

Summary

- InDesign, Illustrator, and Acrobat provide tools for flattening transparency.

- InDesign, Illustrator, and Acrobat offer you tools for preflighting documents against potential printing problems and for soft-proofing files for proper color assignment.

- Acrobat offers the most sophisticated tools for preflighting and soft-proofing color. You can create or acquire preflight profiles suited to specific output equipment.

- For packaging files for prepress and printing, Acrobat PDF format offers many benefits, including font embedding, image embedding, and smaller file sizes.

- PDF/X is a subset of the PDF format and is the most desirable format for commercial prepress and printing.

Index

Numbers